ECONOMICS

Yun Fei Wang

Allen

No: 0409758

ECONOMICS

TENTH EDITION

LIPSEY & CHRYSTAL

OXFORD

UNIVERSITY PRESS

OXFORD
UNIVERSITY PRESS

Great Clarendon Street, Oxford OX2 6DP

Oxford University Press is a department of the University of Oxford.
It furthers the University's objective of excellence in research, scholarship,
and education by publishing worldwide in

Oxford New York

Athens Auckland Bangkok Bogotá Buenos Aires Calcutta
Cape Town Chennai Dar es Salaam Delhi Florence Hong Kong Istanbul
Karachi Kuala Lumpur Madrid Melbourne Mexico City Mumbai
Nairobi Paris São Paulo Singapore Taipei Tokyo Toronto Warsaw

with associated companies in Berlin Ibadan

Oxford is a registered trade mark of Oxford University Press
in the UK and in certain other countries

Published in the United States
by Oxford University Press Inc., New York

Tenth edition published 2004
Reprinted 2004

ISBN 019925 784 1

10 9 8 7 6 5 4 3 2

Typeset by Graphicraft Limited, Hong Kong
Printed by Ashford Colour Press Limited, Gosport, Hampshire

CONTENTS

Part Six **Macroeconomic Policy in a Monetary Economy**

Part Seven **Global Economic Issues**

DETAILED CONTENTS

MICROECONOMICS

PART ONE AN INTRODUCTION TO THE MARKET ECONOMY

PART FOUR **THE GOVERNMENT IN THE ECONOMY**

MACROECONOMICS

PART FIVE **MACROECONOMICS: GROWTH AND CYCLES**

WHY STUDY ECONOMICS?

Some of you may already be excited by the prospect of studying economics, but others may answer the question posed in the heading with 'It was part of my course of study, so I had no choice.' To both the reluctant conscripts and the willing volunteers, we offer hope and encouragement. Economics covers topics that are highly relevant both to decision-making in most jobs that you are likely to do in life, and to understanding many of the most pressing issues facing today's world—free markets versus government intervention, resource exhaustion, pollution and environmental degradation, government taxes and spending, employment and unemployment, inflation, the EU, the euro, changing living standards in advanced nations, growth and stagnation among the world's poorer nations. Thus, economics is both a preparation for taking day-to-day decisions in a firm or other organization, and a training in the analysis of many of the 'big issues' of our time.

One of the most important events in the first three quarters of the twentieth century was the rise of communism. One of the most important events in the last quarter of that century was the fall of communism. By the dawn of the 21st century, the century-long battle between free markets and government planning as alternatives for organizing economic activity had been settled with a degree of decisiveness that is rare for great social issues. Understanding why market-oriented, capitalist economies perform so much better than fully planned or highly government-controlled economies is a core issue in economics. Economic theories are expressly designed to help us understand the successes (and, where they occur, the failures) of free-market societies.

The triumph of market-oriented economies suggests that income- and wealth-creating activities are usually best accomplished through the efforts of private citizens buying and selling in largely unregulated markets. But this is not the end of the story, for at least three fundamental reasons.

First, although market economies certainly work better than fully planned economies, they do not work perfectly. One of today's great social issues is the reallocation of the responsibilities of government, leaving it to do what it can do best and allowing free markets to do what they can do best. We ask: 'What are the important roles that governments can play in improving the functioning of a basically market-oriented economy?'

Second, market economies produce severe cycles as well as long-term growth. Long-term growth has immeasurably improved the lives of ordinary working persons, who suffered the horrors and degradations described by Charles Dickens in the 19th century but today enjoy living standards higher than those of 99.9 per cent of all the people of all classes who ever lived on the Earth. Yet capitalist growth is uneven growth. Severe business cycles operate around the rising trend of economic growth. In recessions, unemployment is high and living standards typically stand still or even fall. Although each cycle tends to leave living standards higher than all previous cycles, the ups and downs of uneven market-driven growth can be upsetting to those affected by it.

Third, capitalist growth is unequal growth. Although it is desirable to create income and wealth, we also care about how these are distributed among the population. Poverty for a minority in the midst of plenty for the majority has always been a problem in wealthy countries—just as poverty for the majority has always been a problem for poor countries. We ask: 'What is the place of government in pursuing social policies that alleviate the poverty and suffering of those who do not share in the income and employment that well-functioning market economies create for the majority?'

Economists have been in the forefront of analysing, explaining, and, where appropriate, offering solutions to all of the issues mentioned above—and many more. They have succeeded in these tasks mainly because economics has a core of useful theory that explains how markets work and evaluates their performance. Although some economic analysis is extremely abstract, and sometimes even economists wonder about its value, the basic core of economic theory that is the secret of the subject's success can be understood by anyone who is willing to make the effort. This basic theory has an excellent record in illuminating issues in ways that lead both to deeper understanding and to useful policy recommendations.

When you start reading this book, you are setting out on the study of a subject that, as the above discussion suggests, is highly relevant to understanding and improving the world in which we live. Approached in the right way, your study will be an adventure. The basic theory must be mastered. Whether or not you find this effort fun in itself, you will find, surprisingly early in your studies, that theories can be used to understand many practical issues. The world is complex, and fully understanding its economic aspects requires much more economic theory than can be packed into one elementary textbook. But mastery of the subject to the level of this one book will contribute greatly to your understanding of many important issues and many of the policies directed at dealing with them.

Good luck, and good studying!

RICHARD LIPSEY and ALEC CHRYSTAL

Vancouver, BC, and London, England
April 2003

HOW TO USE THIS BOOK

It may help you to know some of this book's devices that are designed to make learning easier.

Format

Figures, tags, and captions

Each figure caption begins with a tag line in bold type that states its main message. The full formal analysis related to each figure is given in a caption attached to that figure. This has the advantages of keeping the reasoning physically attached to its associated figure and allowing that reasoning to be studied at the point that seems best to you. The text is made self-sufficient by providing an intuitive explanation of the formal reasoning given in each figure caption. This means that the text can be read on its own, without the figure captions—say, on first reading or for revision. *The basic analytical reasoning that is the core of economics is, however, given in the captions, all of which you must study carefully at some time.*

Summaries

Every chapter ends with a set of summary points grouped under the chapter's main headings. These points provide a useful review as well as a warning that some of the chapter needs to be re-read when the reasoning behind one or more of the summary points cannot be reconstructed.

Topics for review

Every chapter also ends with a series of topics for review. These can be treated in the same way as the summaries: as checks on what has just been learned, and as signals during revision.

Learning exercises

Chapters 1–30 each have a set of learning exercises. These are mainly numerical and are designed to help students understand the theory by working out a specific example of the analysis involved. Teachers will be sent answers to these learning exercises on request.

Exam questions

These are questions for discussion or for essay topics, and are in the format of questions that are used in essay style exams. They could be used for classroom discussions or for revision in preparation for exams.

Boxes

Boxes are set off from the body of the chapter by a different type and a colour surround. Boxes cover many different types of material, such as empirical illustrations, more detailed elaboration of various points made in the text, points of historical interest, and occasional formal proofs, all of which may be of interest to some, but not all, readers. The main unifying point about all the boxes is that they contain material that can be omitted without loss of continuity. Thus, all can be skipped, although we trust that you will find many of them interesting as well as useful.

Mathematical appendices

The text is written entirely using words, numerical examples and diagrammatic analysis. The mathematical appendices are there for those who would like a more formal presentation of results in the text. These can be skipped by students who do not wish to take economics any further; but those who do wish to study economics to a more advanced level will find it beneficial to read this material at some stage.

Glossary

The first time a technical term is used extensively in the text, it is printed in bold type so that it can be easily recognized as such. The definitions of all such terms are gathered together in a Glossary at the end of the book.

Companion Web site

This text is accompanied by a range of high quality downloadable supplements. These have been carefully designed to complement the main text, explaining and developing key ideas and principles.

• An Instructor's Manual discusses the main themes in each chapter and provides solutions to the end-of-chapter questions in the book, following each of these with a brief explanation

• A set of approximately one hundred Overhead Transparency Masters presents the most important figures from the book in an enlarged format suitable for projection in class or the lecture theatre. These will help lecturers to illustrate concepts in diagrammatic form during teaching

• A multiple choice test-bank with 25 multiple choice questions per chapter

All of these products are available free of charge from Oxford University Press to tutors who adopt the main text.

More information on the text and ancillaries is available through the Internet on the web page www.oup.co.uk/best.textbooks/economics. Updates to this will cover some of the main policy topics in the book plus links to official sources such as the UK Treasury, the Bank of England, the International Monetary Fund, and the European Central Bank. You can access further information about other Oxford University Press textbooks and products from this site: www.oup.com.

Approaches to studying economics

You need to study a book on economics in a different way from how you would study a book on, say, history or English literature. Economic theory has a logical structure that builds on itself from stage to stage. Thus, if you understand some concept or theory only imperfectly, you will run into increasing difficulty when, in subsequent chapters, this concept or theory is taken for granted and built upon. Because of its logical structure, quite long chains of reasoning are encountered—if A then B; if B then C; if C then D; and if D then E. Each step in the argument may seem simple enough, but the cumulative effect of several steps, one on top of the other, may be bewildering on first encounter. Thus, when, having followed the argument step by step, you encounter the statement 'it is now obvious that if A then E', it may not seem at all obvious to you. This is a problem that everyone encounters with chains of reasoning. The only way to deal with it is to follow the argument through several times. Eventually, as the reasoning becomes familiar, it will become obvious that *if A then E*.

Economics has its own technical language or jargon. At first you may feel that you are merely being asked to put complicated names to commonsense ideas. To some extent this is true. It is a necessary step, however, because loose thinking about vaguely formed ideas is a quick route to error in economics. Furthermore, when you begin to put several ideas together to see what follows from them, jargon—a clearly defined term to refer to each idea—becomes a necessary part of your equipment.

A book on economics is to be worked at, and understood, step by step. It is usually a good idea to read a chapter quickly in order to see the general run of the argument, and at this stage you might omit the captions to the figures. You will then need to re-read the chapter carefully, making sure that the argument is understood step by step. On this reading, you *must* study the captions to all the figures carefully. If you do not understand the captions, you have not understood economics. You should not be discouraged if, occasionally at this stage, you find yourself spending quite a bit of time on only a few pages.

A pencil and paper are valuable adjuncts to your reading. Difficult arguments should be followed by building up your own diagram while the argument unfolds, rather than relying on the printed diagram, which is, perforce, complete from the beginning. Numerical examples can be invented to illustrate general propositions.

In short, the technical vocabulary aside, you must seek to understand economics, not to memorize it. Theories, principles, and concepts are always turning up in slightly unfamiliar guises. If you have understood your economics, this poses no problem; if you have merely memorized it, this spells disaster.

Write to us

Economics is a subject in which one never stops learning. We are grateful to many users—students and teachers—who have taken the trouble to write to us pointing out possible errors, making comments, and offering suggestions. We hope that readers will continue to teach us with as many further comments and criticisms as they have in the past. We try to acknowledge every such letter.

OUTLINES FOR SHORT OR MODULAR COURSES

This book provides a comprehensive coverage of basic economics suitable for a full one-year course. We have, however, designed the text to be flexible enough to cover shorter courses. To illustrate, we give our suggestions for the chapter content of several shorter courses.

A short Introduction to Economics course (twenty weeks)
Chapters 1, 3–4, 6 or 7, 8–12, 15–16, 19–20, 21–28, 31, 32, 35

A short course for Business students (twenty weeks)
Chapters 1, 3–4, 6 or 7, 8–12, 15–16, 19–20, 20–25, (21, 26–28 optional), 35

An Introduction to Microeconomics course (one semester)
Chapters 1, 3–5, 6 or 7, 8–12, 15–16, 19–20

An Introduction to Macroeconomics course (one semester)
Chapters 20, 22–28, 31, 32, 35 (alternatively, for a course with a growth emphasis include chapters 21 and 34; for a course with an international emphasis the key chapters are 29 and 30, plus 33 and 34)

ACKNOWLEDGEMENTS

Finally we wish to say a word of thanks to those people who have made this book possible. Joanna Lipsey and Robyn Wills have shown unlimited patience in providing the many and varied secretarial duties associated with the production of the book. Lizzie Gillett and Safia Reddy provided important help in preparation of many graphs and tables. Sue Hughes has been helpfully creative in her editing of the manuscript. At the OUP we are particularly grateful for the constant aid and encouragement provided by Tim Page. The usual disclaimer of course holds here: for all remaining shortcomings and mistakes, the authors may blame each other, but the reader should blame us both.

R.G.L.
K.A.C.

Chapter 1

ECONOMIC ISSUES AND CONCEPTS

Economics studies how basic resources are transformed by producers into all the many goods and services that modern consumers want. In this chapter you will learn:

- That a modern market economy uses price signals to solve the complex problems involved in using resources to produce the goods and services that people want

- How economics studies the choice between competing demands for scarce resources

- How production, employment and consumption decisions interact

- That the market economy generally delivers outcomes desired by consumers

- That governments step in when markets fail to produce results that are regarded as successful

A modern economy makes available millions of goods and services for people to choose from. It provides jobs for most people who want to work. It allows us to travel and communicate easily with anybody anywhere in the world. Yet nobody has sat down and planned how all this will work. It has evolved as a response to economic forces interacting with individuals and institutions. It is the wonder of how this all works that is the subject of this book.

If you want a pint of milk, you go to the shop and buy it. The shop owner is just one part of a complex supply chain that makes this milk available when you want it. When the shop owner needs more milk, he orders it from the distributor, who in turn gets it from the bottling plant, which in its turn gets it from the dairy farmer. The dairy farmer buys cattle feed and electric milking machines, and gets power to run all his equipment by putting a plug into a wall socket where the electricity is supplied as he needs it. The milking machines are made from parts manufactured in several different parts of the world, and these in their turn are made from materials mined and refined in a dozen or more different countries.

As it is with the milk you drink, so it is with everything else that you buy. When you go to the appropriate shop, what you want is normally in stock. Those who make these products find that all the required components and materials are available when needed—even though these things typically come from many different parts of the world and are made by people who have no direct dealings with each other. The economy is so good at delivering what we want when we want it that we tend to notice only when it goes wrong.

The complexity of the modern economy

The sales and purchases in which you are involved are only a small part of the fantastically complex set of transactions that take place every day in a modern society. Shipments arrive daily at our sea and airports. These include raw materials such as iron ore and logs, parts such as transistors and circuit boards, tools such as screwdrivers and digging equipment, perishables such as fresh flowers and fruits, and all kinds of manufactured goods such as washing machines and TV sets. Rail and road shippers receive and dispatch these goods to thousands of different destinations.

Some go directly to consumers. Others are used by local firms to manufacture their products—of which some will be sold domestically and some exported.

Most people who want to work can find work. By working, they earn incomes, which they then spend on what they, and others like them, produce. Other people own firms that employ workers to assist in the making and selling of their products. They earn their incomes as profits from their enterprises.

Self-organization

Economics as a subject began when thoughtful observers asked themselves how such a complex set of dealings is organized. Who co-ordinates the whole set of efforts? Who makes sure that all the activities fit together, providing jobs to produce the things that people want and delivering those things to where they are wanted?

The answer is: no one!

The great insight of the early economists was that an economy based on free-market transactions is self-organizing.

By following their own self-interest, doing what seems best and most profitable for themselves, and responding to the incentives of prices set on open markets, people produce a spontaneous social order. In that order, literally thousands of millions of transactions and activities fit together to produce the things that people want within the constraints set by the resources that are available to the nation.

The great Scottish economist and political philosopher Adam Smith, who was the first to develop this insight fully, put it this way:

It is not from the benevolence of the butcher, the brewer, or the baker, that we expect our dinner, but from their regard to their own interest. We address ourselves, not to their humanity but to their self-love, and never talk to them of our own necessities but of their advantages. Nobody but a beggar chuses to depend chiefly upon the benevolence of his fellow-citizens.

Smith is not saying that benevolence is unimportant. Indeed, he praises it in many passages. He is however saying that the massive number of economic interactions that characterize a modern economy cannot all be motivated by benevolence. Although benevolence does motivate some of our actions, often the very dramatic ones, the majority of our everyday actions are motivated by self-interest. Self-interest, not benevolence, is therefore the foundation of economic order.

Efficient organization

Another great insight, which was hinted at by Smith and fully developed over the following century and a half, was that this spontaneously generated social order is relatively efficient. Loosely speaking (we will be more precise later), efficiency means that the resources available to a nation are organized to produce the maximum possible total output.

Smith said that market society produces ordered behaviour that makes it appear as if people are guided by a hidden hand. He did not literally mean that a supernatural presence guides economic affairs. Instead, he referred to the amazing emergence of order out of so many independent decisions. The key to the explanation is that all individuals respond to the same set of prices, which are determined in markets that respond to overall conditions of national

scarcities or plenty. Much of the first half of this book is devoted to a detailed elaboration of how this market order is generated.

A planned alternative

A century after Adam Smith, another great economist and political philosopher, Karl Marx, argued that, although this market system would produce high total output, it would distribute that output in such a way that, over time, the rich would get richer and the poor poorer. He went on to argue that, when societies became rich enough, they should dispense with the spontaneous social order. They should then replace it by a consciously created system, called a command economy, or communism, in which the government plans all of the economic transactions and, in so doing, creates a more equal and just distribution of the total output.

Beginning with the USSR in the 1920s, many nations listened to Marx and established systems in which conscious government central planning largely replaced the spontaneous order of the free market. For much of the twentieth century two systems, the centrally planned and the market, competed with each other for the favour of undecided governments. Then, within the last two decades of the century, governments of one communist country after another abandoned their central planning apparatus. More and more economic transactions and activities were then left to the market. Seldom has a great social issue been settled with such conclusiveness.

Adam Smith was right and Karl Marx was wrong.

Box 1.1 explains some of the reasons for the failure of centrally planned economies. Marx was right about many things, including the importance of technological change in raising living standards over the centuries. Where he was wrong, however, was in believing that the market could be replaced by central planning as a way of organizing all of a nation's economic activities.

In contrast to the failures of command economies, the performance of the free-market price system is impressive. One theme of this book is market success—how the price system works to co-ordinate with relative efficiency the decentralized decisions made by private consumers and producers. However, this does not mean that doing things better implies doing things perfectly. Another theme of this book is market failure—how and why the unaided price system sometimes fails to produce efficient results and fails to take account of social values that cannot be expressed through the marketplace.

In short, today, as in the time of Smith, economists seek to understand the self-organizing forces of market economies, how well they function, and how governments may intervene to improve (but not to replace) specific aspects of their workings.

Box 1.1 **The failure of central planning**

The abandonment of communism by many countries at the end of the 1980s signalled to the world what many economists had long argued: the superiority of a market-oriented price system over central planning as a method of organizing economic activity. The failure of central planning had many causes, but four were particularly significant.

The failure of co-ordination

In centrally planned economies a body of planners tries to co-ordinate all the economic decisions about production, investment, trade, and consumption made by the producers and consumers throughout the country. This proved impossible to do with any reasonable degree of efficiency. Bottlenecks in production, shortages of some goods, and gluts of others plagued the Soviet economy for decades. For example, in 1989 much of a bumper harvest rotted on the farm because of shortages of storage and transportation facilities; and for years there was an ample supply of black-and-white television sets but severe shortages of toilet paper and soap.

Failure of quality control

Central planners can monitor the number of units produced by any factory, rewarding those who overfulfil their production targets and punishing those who fall short. It is much harder, however, for them to monitor quality. A constant Soviet problem was the production of poor-quality products. Factory managers were concerned with meeting their quotas by whatever means were available, and once the goods passed out of their factory what happened to them was someone else's headache. The quality problem was so serious that in the 1990s very few Eastern European-manufactured products were able to stand up to the newly permitted competition with superior goods produced in the advanced market societies.

In market economies poor quality is punished by low sales, and retailers soon give a signal to factory managers by shifting their purchases to other suppliers. The incentives that obviously flow from such private sector purchasing discretion are generally absent from command economies, where purchases and sales are planned centrally.

Misplaced incentives

In market economies relative wages and salaries provide incentives for labour to move from place to place, and the possibility of losing one's job provides an incentive to work diligently. This is a harsh mechanism, which punishes shirkers with loss of income (although social programmes provide floors to the amount of economic punishment that can be suffered). In planned economies workers usually have complete job security. Industrial unemployment is rare, and even when it does occur new jobs are usually found for those in need of them. Although the high level of security is attractive to many, it proved impossible to provide sufficient incentives to work reasonably hard and efficiently under such conditions. In the words of Oxford historian Timothy Garton Ash, who wrote eyewitness chronicles of the developments in Eastern Europe from 1980 to 1990, the social contract between the workers and the government in the Eastern countries was 'We pretend to work, and you pretend to pay us.'

Environmental degradation

Fulfilling production plans became the all-embracing incentive in planned economies, to the exclusion of most other considerations, including the environment. As a result, environmental degradation occurred in all the countries of Eastern Europe on a scale unknown in advanced Western nations. A particularly disturbing example occurred in central Asia, where high quotas for cotton output led to indiscriminate use of pesticides and irrigation. Birth defects were found there in nearly one child in three. This is but one example of a general phenomenon that included toxic chemical dumps and atomic waste scattered throughout the land.

The failure to protect the environment stemmed from a combination of pressure to fulfil plans and lack of a political marketplace. The democratic process allows citizens to express views on the use of scarce resources for environmental protection. Imperfect though the system may be in democratic economies, their record of environmental protection has been vastly better than that of command economies

Main characteristics of market economies

What then are the main characteristics of market economies that produce this spontaneous self-organization?

• Individuals pursue their own self-interest, buying and selling what seems best for themselves and their families.

• People respond to incentives. Other things being equal, sellers seek high prices while buyers seek low prices.

• Prices are set in open markets in which potential sellers compete to sell their wares to would-be buyers.

• People earn their incomes by selling their services to those who wish to use them—by selling things they have produced by their labour, or the services of property that they own.

• All of these activities are governed by a legal framework largely created by the state.

Resources and scarcity

All of the issues discussed so far would not matter much if we lived in an economy of plenty where there was enough of everything for everybody. However, instead we live in a world of scarcity. Most of us want better food, clothing, housing, schooling, holidays, hospital care, and entertainment. But there is not enough to go around. Even the richest economy can produce only a small fraction of the goods and services that people would like to have if these things were free. This gives rise to the basic economic problem of choice under conditions of scarcity. If we cannot have everything we want, we must choose what we will and will not have. To go further, we need to clarify a few terms that you will need throughout your study of economics.

Kinds of resources

An economy's resources fall into four main categories:

- All those gifts of nature, such as land, forests, minerals, etc., commonly called natural resources and called by economists **land**, for short.

- All human resources, mental and physical, both inherited and acquired, which economists call **labour**.

- All those man-made aids to further production, such as tools, machinery, and factories, which are used up in the process of making other goods and services rather than being consumed for their own sake. Economists call these **capital**.

- Those people who take risks by introducing new products and new ways of making old products. They develop new businesses and forms of employment and are called **entrepreneurs** or **innovators**. The resource they provide is **entrepreneurship**.

Traditionally these resources have been called **factors of production**, but we shall more frequently refer to them just as different types of input into the production process. Part III of this book focuses explicitly on **resource allocation**, that is, the determinants of which activities resources get drawn into—for example whether people work in agriculture, manufacturing or services.

Ownership of resources

Private property is a key institution of a market economy. Individuals own the majority of the nation's resources. They also own the goods that they produce and the things that they buy. Some assets are owned by the state—roads, schools, public buildings, etc.—but most are, and must be, in private hands. People cannot make contracts to buy and sell what is not theirs. So without private ownership, the market economy cannot function.

Kinds of production

The resources of the economy are used in a production process to make **goods**, which are tangible, in that they have a physical existence, such as cars and shoes. They also produce **services**, which are intangible, such as haircuts, education and telephone calls. Throughout this book we shall use the term 'goods' to cover both goods and services, unless we explicitly make a distinction between the two.

The nation's total output of all goods and services over one year is called its **gross domestic product or GDP** for short. The act of making goods and services is called **production**, and the act of using up these goods and services to satisfy wants is called **consumption**. Anyone who makes goods or provides services is called a **producer**, and anyone who consumes them to satisfy his or her wants is called a **consumer**.

Choice and opportunity cost

You might want a mobile phone so that you can call your friends. Your parents might want a car to get them to work or to visit your grandparents at the weekend. In general, people value specific goods and services because these help them to satisfy their needs. Goods and services are thus regarded as means to an end, the satisfaction of wants. Because no economy can produce enough goods and services to satisfy all of its citizens' wants, choices must be made.

Most of us have only a specific amount of income that we can spend. If we want to have more of one thing, then we must have less of something else. For example, suppose a friend of yours is considering whether to go out and have a few drinks with friends. The cost of these extra drinks could be measured as the money cost of so much per pint of beer or glass of juice. A more revealing way of looking at the cost, however, is in terms of what other consumption your friend must forgo in order to obtain the drinks. Suppose that he or she decides to give up going to the cinema and use the money instead to buy the drinks. If the price of one drink is, say one third of the price of a cinema seat, then the cost of three drinks is one cinema visit; put the other way around, the cost of one more cinema trip is three drinks.

Now think of the same problem at the level of a whole society. If the government decides to build more roads, and finds the required money by building fewer schools, then the cost of the new roads can be expressed as so many schools per hundred miles of road.

Opportunity cost is a measure of costs expressed as alternatives given up, rather than in terms of money. If some course of action is adopted, there are typically many alternatives that might be sacrificed. For example, once the government has decided on its total spending for any given year, it must then decide how to allocate that spending between various competing parts of the public sector, such as health, education, and the police. So it could be, for example, that if the government decides that it wants to hire 1,000 extra police it will have to reduce spending on education and 900 fewer teachers can be afforded. So the opportunity cost of 1,000 police would be 900 teachers.

Of course it would not necessarily have to be the education budget that was cut. It could have been the health budget or the defence budget or some other part of the public sector. Indeed, it might be a little bit cut off all the other spending components. The point is that, for any given aggregate resource constraint, if you want more of one thing you have to give up something else. The something else given up is the opportunity cost of what more is obtained.

The concept of opportunity cost highlights the choices that must be made by measuring the cost of anything that is chosen in terms of the alternative that could have been chosen instead.

The production-possibility boundary

We are now going to illustrate on a diagram some of the issues surrounding economic choices. As you will soon see, diagrams or figures pervade elementary economics books. If you find them difficult to follow, you should study the section on graphs in Chapter 2, pages 21–27, in some detail.

All the things that governments provide, such as schools, national defence and roads, are produced in the public sector. Everything else, including all of the goods and services that consumers buy, is produced in the private sector. How should the nation's productive resources be divided between these two sectors? To illustrate this choice, we put all the goods and services that governments provide into one group, called 'public sector goods'. The rest are provided by non-government organizations and we call these 'private sector goods'. The balance between public and private provision is determined through the political process by government tax and spending policies. Higher public provision requires higher taxes, and higher taxes reduce private consumption.

The choices that each country must make are illustrated in Figure 1.1. The horizontal axis measures the quantity of public sector goods while the vertical axis measures the quantity of private sector goods. The [blue] curve on the figure shows all those combinations of public and private goods that can be produced if all the nation's resources are fully employed. It is called a **production-possibility boundary**. Points outside the boundary show combinations that cannot be obtained because there are not enough resources to produce them. Points on the boundary are just obtainable: they are the combinations that can just be produced using all the available supplies of resources.

Choice, scarcity, and opportunity cost illustrated

A single production-possibility boundary illustrates three concepts that we have already discussed: scarcity, choice, and opportunity cost. Scarcity is shown by the unattainable combinations beyond the boundary. There are some things we just cannot have. Choice arises because of the need to select one of the attainable points on or inside the boundary. No economy can be at more than one point at one time. Any combination of public sector and private sector goods that is within the [blue] shaded area is achiev-

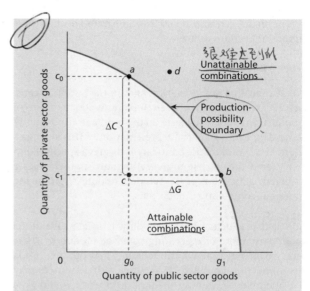

Figure 1.1 A production-possibility boundary
The negatively sloped boundary shows the combinations that are just attainable when all of the society's resources are efficiently employed. The quantity of public sector goods produced is measured along the horizontal axis, the quantity of private sector goods along the vertical axis. Any point on the diagram indicates some amount of each kind of good produced. The production-possibility boundary separates the blue-shaded attainable combinations, such as a, b, and c, from unattainable combinations, such as d. It is negatively sloped because in a fully employed economy more of one good can be produced only if resources are freed by producing less of other goods. Moving from point a (whose coordinates are c_0 and g_0) to point b (whose coordinates are c_1 and g_1) implies producing an additional amount of public sector goods, indicated by ΔG in the figure, at an opportunity cost of a reduction in private sector goods by the amount indicated by ΔC. Points a and b represent efficient uses of society's resources. Point c represents either an inefficient use of resources or a failure to use all the resources that are available.

able and anything outside is not. *Opportunity cost* is shown by the negative slope of the boundary. As the economy moves along that boundary, more of one type of good is being obtained at the cost of less of the other type.

Increasing opportunity cost The production-possibility boundary of Figure 1.1 is drawn with a slope that gets steeper as one moves along it from left to right. The increasing slope indicates increasing opportunity cost as more and more private goods have to be given up for each additional unit of public goods. Start, for example, at the vertical axis, where all production is of private sector goods. A small increase in the production of public goods moves the economy along a fairly flat part of the curve, indicating a small reduction in the production of private sector goods. But the loss of private goods gets greater (for each additional unit of public goods) as we move further along the boundary.

The figure can also be used to illustrate another three important economic issues.

Three key issues

What should be produced How should the nation's scarce resources be allocated between the various possible kinds of production? Where to locate on the production-possibility boundary is the graphical representation of this key question. Each point on the boundary indicates a specific combination of the possible outputs. Alternative points indicate different allocations of the nation's resources, producing different combinations of outputs.

Efficient production If an economy is located inside its boundary, more of everything could be produced. There are two main reasons why an economy may produce inside its production boundary. First, some of its resources may be unemployed. Putting them back to work would raise the production of some goods without having to lower the production of anything else. Second, although its resources are fully employed, some of them may be inefficiently employed. If they could be used more efficiently, the production of some goods could be increased without having to produce less of anything else. We will have much more to say about inefficient uses of resources in later chapters.

These two possibilities help to reveal the source of opportunity cost.

If all of the nation's resources are fully employed, and none is employed inefficiently, then more of one good can be produced only by taking resources away from the production of another good.

The lost production of the other good is the opportunity cost of the first.

Economic growth There is one other way an economy can get more of everything without having less of anything. If the economy's capacity to produce goods is increasing through time, the production-possibility boundary will be moving outwards over time, as illustrated in Figure 1.2. More of all goods can then be produced. This is what economic growth has accomplished from one decade to the next for the last several hundred years—and sporadically before then, back to the beginning of history. We will study this growth later in the book. In the meantime, we merely note that in the long term growth is driven by technological change. Over the years we learn to make existing products better and more cheaply, and also to make many new products that satisfy old needs in new ways and to create altogether new needs.

Box 1.2 deals with some of the sometimes confusing terminology that surrounds the concept of the production-possibility boundary.

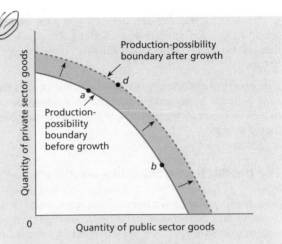

Figure 1.2 The effect of economic growth on the production-possibility boundary

Economic growth shifts the production-possibility boundary outward, allowing more of all commodities to be produced. Before growth in productive capacity, points *a* and *b* were on the production-possibility boundary and point *d* was an unattainable combination. After growth point *d* becomes attainable, as do all points within the dark blue band.

 Box 1.2 The terminology of production possibilities

We have used the term 'production-possibility boundary'. 'Boundary' emphasizes that the points on the line are maximum points. It is always possible to produce at points inside the line by not employing some factors of production, or by using them inefficiently. Two other terms, 'frontier' and 'curve', are often used instead of 'boundary'.

The words 'production-possibility' emphasize the alternative possibilities available to a society. However, the term 'transformation' is often used instead. The idea behind the term 'transformation' is that society can, in effect, 'transform' one product into another by moving resources from the production of one product into the production of the other. Speaking of transforming one product into another involves the idea of opportunity cost. Of course, one good is not literally transformed into another; but, by moving resources from producing one type of good to producing another, quantities of the first type of good are sacrificed to gain quantities of the second type.

You can make up six terms by combining the following words:

Production-possibility *or* Transformation	with	Curve *or* Boundary *or* Frontier

All six terms mean the same thing. All six are commonly used.

Who makes the choices and how

Economic choices have to be made, but who makes them and how are they made?

The flow of <u>income</u> and <u>expenditure</u>

Figure 1.3 shows the main players in the economy and the flows of income and expenditure that they generate. Individuals own resources used in production, including their own labour. They sell the services of these resources to producers and receive payments in return. These are their incomes. Producers use the inputs that they buy to make goods and services for consumption. They sell these to individuals, receiving payments in return. These are the incomes of producers. These basic flows of income and expenditure pass through markets. Individuals sell the services of the resources they own in the labour and capital markets. Producers sell their outputs of goods and services in the consumption goods markets. The prices that are set in these markets determine the incomes that are earned and the purchasing power of those incomes. People who get high prices for their services earn high incomes; those who get low prices earn low incomes. The **distribution of income** indicates how the nation's total income is distributed among its citizens. This is determined largely by the price that each type of resource input can command

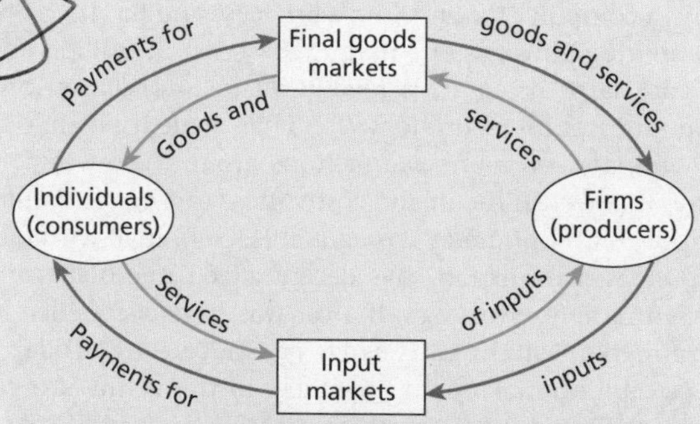

Figure 1.3 The circular flow of income and expenditure
The green line shows the flows of goods and services while the blue line shows the payments made to purchase these. Inputs flow from individuals who own the resources (including their own labour) which they sell to firms that use them as inputs to make goods and services. These then flow through final goods markets to those who consume them. Money payments flow from firms to individuals in the form of wages to workers or profits to shareholders. This becomes the income of individuals. When they spend this income buying goods and services, money flows through goods markets back to producers.

and by how equally the endowments of these resources are distributed. Labour is equally endowed to individuals, for example, because each individual only has one body. However, talents are not equally endowed, and neither is ownership of land and other property.

Maximizing decisions In this story of what drives economic outcomes the basic decision-makers are individuals and firms. Later we shall discuss also the role of the government. The most important characteristic of how individuals and firms take their decisions is that everyone tries to do as well as possible for themselves. In the jargon of economics, we are all *maximizers*. When individuals decide how much of their labour services to sell to producers and how many products to buy from them, they make choices designed to maximize their well-being. When managers of firms decide how many inputs to buy from individuals and other firms, and how many of their own products to make and sell to them, they seek to maximize their profits.

Marginal decisions Most of the economic choices that individuals and firms make are made *at the margin*. When you enter a shop to buy a newspaper and a pint of milk, you are deciding to buy one more newspaper and one more pint of milk. You do not have to decide which product to spend your entire income on, and neither do you have to decide what to spend your income on next week and next year. You can, and do, decide to spread your expenditure among many products and to make these decisions incrementally (more or less) one at a time. Today you could buy two newspapers and a half-pint of milk. Tomorrow you might buy one newspaper, six eggs, and two pints of milk. These are marginal decisions—decisions to buy a bit more or a bit less. These decisions are made sequentially, not all at once.

Maximizing individuals and firms are constantly taking marginal decisions about whether to buy or produce a bit more or a bit less of the things that they consume or make.

Production choices

Managers of businesses decide what to produce and how to produce it. Some products, like haircuts, are quite simple to produce. But some other production processes are very complex. A typical car manufacturer assembles a product out of thousands of individual components. It makes some of these components itself. Most are subcontracted to other parts manufacturers, and many of the major parts manufacturers subcontract some of their work out to smaller suppliers. This kind of production displays two characteristics noted two centuries ago by Adam Smith, and one that is more recent. These are specialization, the division of labour, and globalization.

Specialization 特殊化·专业化·

In ancient hunter–gatherer societies, and in modern subsistence economies, most people make most of the things they need for themselves. However, from the time people first engaged in settled agriculture and some of them began to live in towns, individuals have specialized in doing particular jobs. Farmers, carpenters, soldiers, and priests are some of the earliest specialized occupations. The allocation of different jobs to different people is known as **specialization of labour**, or **the division of labour**. There are two fundamental reasons why specialization is extraordinarily efficient compared with self-sufficiency.

First, individual abilities differ, and specialization allows each person to do what he or she can do relatively well while leaving everything else to be done by others. Even when people's abilities are unaffected by the act of specializing, production is greater with specialization than with self-sufficiency. This is one of the most fundamental principles in economics. It is called the principle of **comparative advantage**. An example is given in Box 1.3 and a much fuller discussion is found in Chapter 33.

The second reason is that people's abilities change when they specialize. A person who concentrates on one activity becomes better at it than could a jack-of-all-trades. This is called **learning by doing**. Learning by doing is very important in many jobs today where complex tasks are required.

The division of labour 区分.

Throughout most of history, each worker who was specialized in making some product made the whole of that product. Over the last several hundred years, many technical advances in methods of production have made it efficient to organize agriculture and manufacturing into large-scale firms organized around a division of labour. There is job specialization within the production process of a particular product.

Mass production In a mass production factory work is divided into specialized tasks using specialized machinery. Each individual repeatedly does one small task that is a small fraction of those necessary to produce any one product. This is an extreme case of the division of labour.

Craft workers and flexible manufacturing Two recent developments have significantly altered the degree of specialization found in many modern production processes. First, individual craft workers have recently reappeared in some lines of production. Craft workers are highly skilled manufacturing workers who are well trained and do much more

than purely routine or repetitive operations. They are responding to a revival in the demand for individually crafted, rather than mass-produced, products. Second, many manufacturing operations have been reorganized along new lines called 'lean production' or 'flexible manufacturing', which was pioneered by Japanese car manufacturers. It has led back to a more craft-based form of organization within the factory. In this technique, which is discussed in more detail in Chapter 9, employees work as a team; each employee is able to do every team member's job rather than one very specialized task at one point on the assembly line.

Globalization

Market economies constantly change, largely as a result of the development of new products and new technologies. One important recent development is referred to as **globalization**. Globalized trade is not new—it has been around for hundreds, and in some areas thousands, of years. Since the industrial revolution, the usual pattern was for manufactured goods to be sent from Europe and North America to the rest of the world, with raw materials and primary products being sent in return. What is new in the last few decades is the globalization of manufacturing.

Behind this phenomenon lie the rapid reduction in transportation costs and the revolution in information technology. The cost of moving products around the world has fallen greatly in recent decades owing to containerization and the increasing size of ships. Our ability to transmit and to analyse data has been increasing even more dramatically, while the costs of doing so have been decreasing equally dramatically. For example, today £1,000 buys a computer that fits into a briefcase and has the same computing power as one that in 1970 cost £5 million and filled a large room. This revolution in information and communication technology (ICT) has made it possible to co-ordinate economic transactions around the world in ways that were difficult and costly fifty years ago and quite impossible a hundred years ago. This, combined with falling costs of transport, has decentralized manufacturing activities. Fifty years ago, if a car was to be assembled in Birmingham, all the parts had to be made nearby. Today it is possible to make parts anywhere in the world and get them to Birmingham exactly when they are required. As a result, manufacturing, which was formerly concentrated in the advanced industrial countries of Europe and North America, now takes place all over the world. A typical CD player, TV set, or car contains components made in literally dozens of different countries. We still know where a product is assembled, but it is becoming increasingly difficult to say where it is *made*.

Many *markets* are globalizing. For example, as some fashions have become universal, we can see the same designer jeans, brand labels, and fast food outlets in virtually all big

Box 1.3 Absolute and comparative advantage

A simple case will illustrate the important principles involved in the gains from specialization.

Absolute advantage

Suppose that, working full time on his own, Peter can produce either 100 sweaters *or* 40 suits per year, whereas Jane can produce 400 sweaters *or* 10 suits. (This may sound like a silly example, but any such example is adequate to illustrate the principles involved. The originator of these ideas, David Ricardo, used two countries, England and Portugal, and the two products were wheat and wine.) These productive abilities are shown in the first two columns of Table I. Jane has an absolute advantage in making sweaters because she can make more per year than Peter can. However, Peter has an absolute advantage over Jane in producing suits, for the same reason. If they both spend *half* their time producing each commodity, the results will be as given in the second pair of columns in Table I.

Now let Peter specialize in suits, producing 40 of them, and Jane specialize in sweaters, producing 400. The final pair of columns in Table I, labelled 'Full specialization', shows that production of both commodities has risen because each person is better than the other person at his or her speciality. Sweater production rises from 250 to 400, while suit production goes from 25 to 40.

Table (I)

	Time spent fully on either one or other		Time divided equally between two		Full specialization	
	Sweaters	Suits	Sweaters	Suits	Sweaters	Suits
Peter	100	40	50	20		40
Jane	400	10	200	5	400	
Total			250	25	400	40

Comparative advantage

Now make things a little less obvious by giving Jane an absolute advantage over Peter in both commodities. We do this by making Jane more productive in suits, so that she can produce 48 of them per year, with all other productivities remaining the same. This gives us the new data for productive abilities shown in the first two columns of Table II. Now, compared with Peter, Jane is four times more efficient at producing sweaters and 20 per cent more efficient at producing suits. The second pair of columns in Table II gives the outputs when Peter and Jane each divide their time equally between the two products.

It is possible to increase their combined production of both commodities by having Jane increase her production of sweaters and Peter increase his

Table (II)

	Time spent fully on either one or other		Time divided equally between two		Peter fully specialized Jane 75/25 on sweaters v. suits	
	Sweaters	Suits	Sweaters	Suits	Sweaters	Suits
Peter	100	40	50	20		40
Jane	400	48	200	24	300	12
Total			250	44	300	52

production of suits. The final pair of columns in Table II gives an example in which Peter specializes fully in suit production and Jane spends 25 per cent of her time on suits and 75 per cent on sweaters. (Her outputs of suits and sweaters are thus 25 and 75 per cent of what she could produce of these goods if she worked full time on one or the other.) Total production of sweaters rises from 250 to 300, while total production of suits goes from 44 to 52.

In this latter example, Jane is absolutely more efficient than Peter in both lines of production, but her margin of advantage is greater in sweaters than in suits.

Jane has a **comparative advantage** over Peter in the line of production in which her margin of advantage is greatest (sweaters, in this case). Peter has a comparative advantage over Jane in the line of production in which his margin of disadvantage is least (suits, in this case).

This example is only an illustration; the principles can be generalized in the following way.

- Absolute advantages are not necessary for there to be gains from specialization.

- Gains from specialization occur whenever there are *differences* in the margin of advantage that one producer enjoys over another in various lines of production.

- Total production can always be increased when each producer becomes more specialized in the production of the commodity in which he or she has a comparative advantage.

A more detailed study of the important concept of comparative advantage and its many applications to international trade and specialization must await our discussion of international trade (Chapter 33). In the meantime, it is worth noting that the comparative advantage of individuals and of whole nations may change. Jane may learn new skills and develop a comparative advantage in suits that she does not currently have. Similarly, whole nations may develop new abilities and know-how that will change their pattern of comparative advantage.

跨国的 (adj)

cities. Many *corporations* are globalized, as more and more of them become what are called transnationals. These are massive firms with a physical presence in many countries. MacDonald's restaurants are as visible in Moscow or Beijing as in London or New York. Many other brands are also virtually universal, such as Coca Cola, Kelloggs, Heinz, Nestlé, Guinness, Toyota, Mercedes Benz, Rolls-Royce, Sony, and Hoover.

Whether globalization is an unambiguously 'good thing' has recently been a subject of great controversy. Notice, however, that globalization is not the only game in town. Globalization has affected financial markets and manufacturing, but an ever-increasing proportion of employment is in service industries, many of which, by the nature of the product, are very local. How far, for example, would you be prepared to travel for an evening meal, an eye test, a haircut, a concert, or to see the doctor?

Markets and money

People who are specialized in doing only one thing, whether they are factory workers or computer programmers, must satisfy most of their needs by consuming things made by other people. In early societies the exchange of goods and services took place by simple mutual agreement among neighbours. In the course of time, however, trading became centred on particular gathering places called *markets*. For example, the French markets or trade fairs of Champagne were well known throughout Europe as early as the eleventh century AD. Even now, many towns have regular market days. Today, however, the term 'market' has a much broader meaning. We use the term **market economy** to refer to a society in which people specialize in productive activities and meet most of their material wants through exchanges voluntarily agreed with others. Most of those in jobs, for example, work for a single employer (at any one time) and buy goods and services in a wide range in outlets (such as shops and restaurants, or by phone and internet).

Specialization must be accompanied by trade. People who produce only one thing must trade most of it to obtain all of the other things they require. 实物交换/物品交换

Early trading was by means of barter, the trading of goods directly for other goods. But barter is costly in terms of time spent searching out satisfactory exchanges. If a farmer has wheat but wants a hammer, he must find someone who has a hammer and wants wheat. A successful barter transaction thus requires what is called a *double coincidence of wants*.

Money eliminates the restrictive system of barter by separating the transactions involved in the exchange of products. If a farmer has wheat and wants a hammer, she

Box 1.4 Some other useful terms frequently used in economics

We define many words used in economics as we proceed in this book. Here are a few expressions that it might be helpful to understand right away.

Arbitrage: trading activity based on buying where a product is cheap and selling where it has a higher price. Arbitrage activity helps to bring prices closer in different segments of the market.

Distortions: outcomes in the economy that are not optimal and arise as a result of some impediment or intervention that prevents market forces delivering the ideal outcome.

Externalities: costs or benefits of an economic activity or transaction that fall on people not directly involved. For example, acid rain generated by a power station in England may generate negative externalities for farmers in Sweden.

Incentives: these are what drive people to make the choices that they do, because responding to an incentive generates a preferred outcome. In economics we generally make assumptions such as that firms attempt to maximize profit and individuals try to maximize their personal satisfaction or utility. Thus, for example, a profitable opportunity would create an incentive for a firm to introduce a new product.

Long run and short run: these concepts are used slightly differently in microeconomics and macroeconomics. In general, however, they relate to what variables we allow to adjust in the time period considered. Long-run adjustment permits more variables to adjust, while the short run is a time period when we can see the impact effects of varying one influence, holding most other things constant.

does not have to find someone who has a hammer and wants wheat. She merely has to find someone who wants wheat. The farmer takes money in exchange. Then she finds a person who wishes to trade a hammer and gives up the money for the hammer.

The existence of 'money' greatly expands the possibilities of specialization and trade.

Some other terms that are commonly used in economics are explained in Box 1.4.

Is there a practical alternative to the market economy?

The answer is: yes and no. 'No' because the modern economy has no practical alternative to reliance on market determination for most of its functions. But 'yes' because a market economy cannot deliver all the outcomes we generally desire without some role for interventions by government.

At the broad level, there are four main types of economic system.

Traditional systems

A **traditional economic system** is one in which behaviour is based primarily on tradition, custom, and habit. Young men follow their fathers' occupations—typically, farming, hunting, fishing, and tool-making. Women do what their mothers did—typically, cooking, mending, and fieldwork. There are few changes in the pattern of production from year to year, other than those imposed by the vagaries of nature. The techniques of production also follow traditional patterns, except when the effects of an occasional new invention are felt. The concept of private property is often not well defined, and property is frequently held in common, such as common grazing land. Finally, production is allocated among the members of society according to long-established traditions. In short, the answers to the economic questions of what to produce, how to produce, and how to distribute are determined by traditions. Such a system works best in an unchanging environment. Under static conditions, a system that does not continually require people to make choices can prove effective in meeting economic and social needs.

Traditional systems were common in earlier times. The feudal system under which most people lived in medieval Europe was a largely traditional society. Today only a few small, isolated, self-sufficient communities still retain mainly traditional systems; examples can be found in the Canadian Arctic, the Himalayas, the Amazon jungle, and isolated parts of Papua New Guinea.

Command systems

We have already seen that in command systems some central authority determines economic behaviour. It makes most of the necessary decisions on what to produce, how to produce it, and who gets it. Because centralized decision-makers usually lay down elaborate and complex plans for the behaviour they wish to impose, the terms **command economy** and **centrally planned economy** are usually used synonymously.

The sheer quantity of data required for the central planning of an entire economy is enormous, and the task of analysing it to produce a fully integrated plan can hardly be exaggerated, even in the age of computers. Moreover, the plan must be a rolling process, continually changing to take account not only of current data but also of future trends in labour supplies, technological developments, and people's tastes for various goods and services. This involves the planners in the notoriously difficult business of forecasting the future.

Little more than two decades ago, over one-third of the world's population lived in countries that relied heavily on central planning to deal with the basic economic questions. Today the number of such countries is small. Even in countries where central planning is the official system, as in China, increasing amounts of market determination are being accepted, even encouraged.

Pure market systems

Earlier in this chapter we discussed the basics of a free-market economy. Millions of consumers decide what products to buy and in what quantities. A large number of firms produce those products and buy the inputs that are needed to make them. Individual decisions collectively determine the economy's allocation of resources among competing uses and the distribution of its output among individual citizens.

In a **pure market economy**, all of these decisions, without exception, are made by buyers and sellers acting through unhindered markets. The state provides the legal structure and external defence, but beyond that markets determine all resource allocation and income distribution.

Mixed systems

Fully traditional, fully centrally controlled, and fully free-market economies are useful concepts for studying the basic principles of resource allocation. When we look in detail at any real economy, however, we discover that its economic behaviour is the result of some mixture of central control and market determination, with a certain amount of traditional behaviour as well. The term **mixed economy** refers to an economy in which both free markets and governments have significant effects on the allocation of resources and the distribution of income.

In practice, every economy is a mixed economy in the sense that it combines significant elements of all three systems—traditional, command, and market—in determining economic behaviour.

The proportions of the mixture of free-market determination and government control vary from economy to economy and over time. There is more free-market determination in the UK and the USA than in France and South Korea. There is more free-market determination in the UK today than there was forty years ago. The mix also varies from sector to sector within any one economy. For example, European agricultural markets have a substantial amount of government control. Under market determination, the average size of a farm would be much larger and agricultural prices much lower than they now are. In contrast, the markets for information and computer technologies are largely free from government intervention. Even the economies closest to free markets have a significant role for government, so it appears that there is no real alternative to a mixed system with major reliance on markets but also a substantial government presence in many aspects of the economy.

Government in the modern mixed economy

Modern market economies in advanced industrial countries are based primarily on market transactions between people who voluntarily decide whether or not to transact. Private individuals have the right to buy and sell what they wish, to accept or refuse work that is offered to them, and to move to where they want when they want. But governments create the legal framework that governs transactions.

Key institutions are private property and freedom of contract, both of which must be maintained by active government policies. The government creates laws of ownership and contract, and then provides the courts to enforce these laws. Governments are also responsible for provision of a stable-valued money which is the measuring rod for all prices.

In modern mixed economies governments go well beyond these important basic functions. They intervene in market transactions to correct what are called 'market failures'. These are identifiable situations in which free markets do not work well. For example, natural resources such as fishing grounds and common pastureland tend to be over-exploited to the point of destruction under free-market conditions. Some products, called *public goods*, are not provided at all by markets because, once produced, no one can be prevented from using them. So their use cannot be restricted to those who are willing to pay for them. Defence and law and order are public goods. In other cases, private agents impose costs called *externalities* on others by their economic activities, such as when factories pollute the air and rivers. The public is harmed but has no part in the producers' decisions about what to make and how to make it. These are some of the reasons why free markets sometimes fail to function as we would like them to. They explain why citizens wish governments to intervene and alter the outcome that would result from leaving everything to the market.

Also, there are important equity (or fairness) issues that arise from letting free markets determine people's incomes. Some people lose their jobs because firms are reorganizing in the face of new technologies. Others may keep their jobs, but the market values their services so poorly that they face economic hardship. The old and the chronically ill may suffer if their past circumstances have not allowed them to save enough to support themselves. For many reasons of this sort, we accept government intervention to redistribute income by taking from the 'haves' and giving to the 'have-nots'. Almost everyone accepts that there should be some redistribution of incomes. Care must be taken, however, not to kill the goose that lays the golden egg. Taking too much from the 'haves' risks eliminating their incentive to work hard and produce income, some of which is to be redistributed to the 'have-nots'.

Governments also play a part in influencing the overall level of prices and in attempting to stabilize the economy against extreme fluctuations in income and employment. A stable price level and full employment are the two major goals of what is called the government's macroeconomic policy. These are dealt with in the second half of this book.

These are some of the reasons why all modern economies are mixed economies. Throughout most of the twentieth century, in advanced industrial societies the mix was altering towards more and more government participation in decisions about the allocation of resources and the distribution of income. In the last two decades of the century, however, there was a worldwide movement to lower the degree of government participation. The details of this shift in the market/government mix, and the reasons for it, are among the major issues that you will study in this book.

SUMMARY

The complexity of the modern economy

■ A market economy is self-organizing in the sense that, when individuals act independently to pursue their own self-interest, responding to prices set on open markets, they produce co-ordinated and relatively efficient economic outcomes.

Resources and scarcity

■ Scarcity is a fundamental problem faced by all economies because not enough resources—land, labour, capital, and entrepreneurship—are available to produce all the goods and services that people would like to consume. Scarcity makes it necessary to choose, among alternative possibilities, what products should be produced and in what quantities.

■ The concept of opportunity cost emphasizes scarcity and choice by measuring the cost of obtaining a unit of one product in terms of the number of units of other products that could have been obtained instead.

■ A production-possibility boundary shows all of the combinations of goods that can be produced by an economy whose resources are fully employed. Movement from one point to another on the boundary shows a shift in the amounts of goods being produced, which requires a reallocation of resources.

Who makes the choices and how

■ Modern economies are based on the specialization and division of labour, which necessitate the exchange of goods and services. Exchange takes place in markets and is facilitated by the use of money. Markets work to co-ordinate millions of individual, decentralized decisions.

Is there a practical alternative to the market economy?

■ Three pure types of economy can be distinguished: traditional, command, and free market. In practice, all economies are mixed economies, in that their economic behaviour responds to mixes of tradition, government command, and price incentives.

■ Governments play an important part in modern mixed economies. They create and enforce important background institutions such as private property. They intervene to increase economic efficiency by correcting situations where markets do not effectively perform their co-ordinating functions. They also redistribute income and wealth in the interests of equity.

TOPICS FOR REVIEW

■ Kinds of resources

■ Self-organization

■ Goods and services

■ Scarcity, choice, and opportunity cost

■ Production-possibility boundary

■ Resource allocation

■ Growth in productive capacity

■ Specialization and the division of labour

■ Command, traditional, market, and mixed economic systems

DISCUSSION QUESTIONS

1 Write down a list of some of the many economic activities that contribute to each of the following: (a) delivering the evening news bulletin to your television or radio, (b) providing cotton shirts on sale in your local high street stores, (c) providing a hamburger in a local fast-food restaurant.

2 What is the opportunity cost to you of each of the following: (a) studying at weekends, (b) doing charity work on two evenings a week, (c) working in paid employment during every vacation?

3 List some of the choices you make on a daily basis in terms of how you spend your time and how you spend your money.

4 Make a list of all the different goods and services you typically buy in a normal week. What does this suggest about the range of goods and services that a typical individual purchases on a regular basis?

5 Explain the concept of opportunity cost and discuss how it relates to the problem of choice between alternatives.

6 Outline the differences between traditional, command, and market economies and give some reasons why the former two have been superseded.

7 In what ways does money facilitate specialization and the division of labour?

8 Why do governments have a role in a market economy? (Revisit this question once you have studied Chapters 19 and 20.)

9 Economics used to be known as the 'dismal science' because it pointed out that, since productive resources were scarce, not enough of everything could be made, so that choices had to be made between alternatives. Assess the prospects of scarcity being eliminated in the foreseeable future.

Chapter 2

HOW ECONOMISTS WORK

In this chapter you will learn some of the language and methods of economics. In particular, you will discover:

- The difference between positive and normative statements
- How economists set out their theories
- How economic data are handled and graphed
- How economic relationships are represented in diagrams
- How marginal values are measured

Economics seeks to understand many important issues in the world around us. What makes some countries grow richer when others seem to get poorer? Why do we sometimes have recessions? When should the government try to influence markets? What are the costs and benefits of globalization? Will new technology eliminate many jobs? In order to get a handle on these big issues, and many more, economists have had to develop ways of setting out and testing their theories. They also seek to use what they have learned in order to provide advice on how things could be improved.

We start this chapter by discussing an important distinction relating to types of statement that might be used in giving advice. We then outline how theories are built in economics and discuss some of the tools that will be used to analyse and illustrate economic relationships not only in this book, but throughout your studies of economics.

Economic advice: positive and normative statements

Economists give advice on a wide variety of topics. If you read a newspaper, watch television, or listen to the radio you will often notice some economist's opinions being reported. Perhaps it is on the prospects for unemployment, inflation, or interest rates, on some new tax, on the case for privatization or regulation of an industry.

Advice comes in two broad types: normative and positive. A commentator might suggest that the government ought to try harder to reduce unemployment or preserve the environment. This is **normative advice.** Economists may be using their expert knowledge to come to conclusions about the costs of various unemployment-reducing or environment-saving schemes, but when they say that the government *ought* to do something, this involves their making judgements about the value of the various things that the government could do with its limited resources. Advice that depends on a value judgement is normative—it tells others what they ought to do.

Another type of advice is illustrated by the statement 'If the government wants to reduce unemployment, this is an effective way of doing so.' This is **positive advice.** It does not rely on a judgement about the value of reducing unemployment. Instead, the adviser is saying, '*If this is what you want to do, here are ways of doing it.*'

It is difficult to have a rational discussion of issues if positive and normative issues are confused. Much of the success of modern science depends on the ability of scientists to separate their views on *what does*, or *might, happen* in the world from their views on *what they would like to happen*. For example, until the eighteenth century almost everyone believed that the Earth was only a few thousand years old. Evidence then began to accumulate that the Earth was thousands of millions of years old. This evidence was hard for most people to accept since it ran counter to a literal reading of many religious texts. Many did not want to believe the evidence. Nevertheless, scientists, many of whom were religious, continued their research because they refused to allow their feelings about what they wanted to believe to affect their search, as scientists, for the truth. Eventually all scientists came to accept that the Earth is about 4,000 million years old.

Table 2.1 **Positive and normative statements**

Positive	Normative
A Higher interest rates cause people to save more.	F People should save more.
B High income tax rates discourage effort.	G Governments should tax the rich to help the poor.
C High taxes on cigarettes discourage smoking.	H Smoking should be discouraged.
D Road use charges would increase traffic.	I The tax system should be used to reduce traffic.
E People are more worried about inflation than unemployment.	J Technical change is a bad thing because it puts some people out of work.

Distinguishing what is true from what we would like to be, or what we feel ought to be, true depends partly on being able to distinguish between positive and normative statements.

Normative statements depend on value judgements. They involve issues of personal opinion, which cannot be settled by recourse to facts. In contrast, **positive statements** do not involve value judgements. They are statements about what is, was, or will be—that is, they are statements that are about matters of fact.

Examples of both types of statement are given in Table 2.1. All five statements listed in the table as 'positive' assert things about the nature of the world in which we live. In contrast, the five statements listed as 'normative' require value judgements.

Notice two things about the positive/normative distinction. First, positive statements need not be true. Statement

D is almost certainly false; yet it is positive, not normative. Second, the inclusion of a value judgement in a statement does not necessarily make the statement normative. Statement E is about the preferences that people hold, that is, about their value judgements. We could, however, check to see if people really do worry more about inflation than unemployment. We can observe their answers to survey questions, and we can observe how they vote for parties that give different priority to these objectives. There is no need to introduce a value judgement in order to check the validity of the statement itself.

You can decide for yourself why each of the other statements is either positive or normative. Remember to apply the two tests. (1) Is the statement only about actual or alleged facts? If so, it is a positive one. (2) Are value judgements necessary to assess the truth of the statement? If so, it is normative.

Economic theorizing

Has the computer and internet revolution of the last few decades led to an increase in the trend growth rate of most major economies? Does globalization help the economies of developing countries? These are important questions. In order to attempt to answer them (and many more such questions), economists have developed an approach that involves developing theories and building models. What do we mean when we use words like 'theory' and 'model'?

Theories

Theories are constructed to explain things. For example, what determines the number of eggs sold in Liverpool in a particular week? As part of the answer to this question, and ones like it, economists have developed a theory of *demand* —a theory that we study in detail in Chapter 3. Like any other theory, the theory of demand is built around definitions, assumptions, and predictions.

Definitions

The basic elements of any theory are its variables. A **variable** is a magnitude that can take on different possible values.

In our theory of egg purchases, the variable *eggs* might be defined as a one-dozen box of large free-range eggs. The variable *price of eggs* is the amount of money that must be given up to purchase the one-dozen carton. The particular values taken on by those two variables might be *2,000 dozen* at a price of *£1.80* on 1 July 2003, *1,800 dozen* at a price of *£2.00* on 8 July 2004, and *1,950 dozen* at a price of *£1.90* on 15 July 2005.

For a theory of the demand for eggs, we define the variable *demand* as the number of cartons of eggs consumers wish to purchase during a particular time-period.

Endogenous and exogenous variables An **endogenous variable** is a variable that is explained within a theory. An **exogenous variable** influences endogenous variables but is itself determined by forces outside the theory. For example, the quantity of eggs purchased is an endogenous variable in our theory of the demand for eggs. The forces at work within the theory determine it. Indeed, the whole point of the theory is to explain what makes the quantity of eggs purchased change. The state of the weather is an exogenous variable. It may affect the number of eggs people demand, but we can safely assume that the state of the weather is not determined by anything going on in the egg market.[1]

Assumptions

A theory's assumptions concern motives, physical relationships, lines of causation, and the conditions under which the theory is meant to apply.

Motives In economics it is generally assumed that individuals pursue their own self-interest when making economic decisions. People are assumed to know what they want, and to know how to go about getting it within the constraints set by the resources at their command. Similarly, firms are assumed to maximize profit. None of this implies that all people are indeed selfish and entirely motivated by their own material well being.

Physical relationships If egg producers buy more chicks and use more labour, land, and chicken feed, they will produce more eggs. This is an example of the most important physical relationship in the theory of markets. It concerns assumptions about how the amount of output is related to the quantities of inputs used to produce it. This relationship is specified in what is called a 'production function'.

Conditions of application Assumptions are often used to specify the conditions under which a theory is meant to hold. For example, a theory that assumes there is 'no government' does not mean literally the absence of government, but only that the theory is meant to hold when governments are not significantly affecting the situation being studied.

Direction of causation When economists assume that one variable is related to another, they are assuming some causal link between the two. For example, when the amount that consumers spend on holiday travel is assumed (and observed) to increase as their incomes increase, the causation is assumed to run from income to holiday travel. Consumers spend more on holiday travel *because* they have more income; they do not get more income because they spend more on holiday travel—it would be great if they did! Two terms are used to indicate this direction of causation. The variable that *does the causing* is called the **independent variable** and the variable that *is caused* is

called the **dependent variable**. In the above example income is the independent variable and expenditure on holiday travel is the dependent variable.

Predictions

A theory's predictions are the propositions that can be deduced from it. For example, a proposition in the theory of demand states, 'If the price of eggs rises, consumers will purchase fewer eggs.' This negative relationship between a product's price and the amount people wish to buy applies to all commodities. These propositions are then taken as predictions about real-world events. For example, if the price of CDs is reduced, consumers will buy more of them. Box 2.1 discusses the distinction between predictions, forecasts, and prophecies.

Models

Economists often proceed by constructing what they call **economic models**. This term has several different but related meanings.

Sometimes the term 'model' is used as a synonym for a theory, as when economists speak of the model of the determination of national income. Sometimes it may refer to a particular subset of theories, such as the Keynesian model or the neoclassical model of income determination.

More often, a model means a specific quantitative formulation of a theory. In this case, specific numbers are attached to the mathematical relationships defined by the theory, the numbers often being derived from observations of the economy. The specific form of the model can then be used to make precise predictions about, say, the behaviour of prices in the potato market, or the course of national income and total employment. Forecasting models used by the Bank of England and the International Monetary Fund (IMF) are of this type.

The term 'model' is often used to refer to an application of a general theory in a specific context. So if we take our theory of consumer demand and apply it to the egg market in southern England, we might speak of a model of the southern English egg market. Finally, a model may be an illustrative abstraction, not meant to be elaborate enough to be tested. The circular flow in Figure 1.3 on page 7 is a model of this sort. By illustrating how income flows between consumers and producers, it helps us to understand how decisions of these two groups influence each other through labour markets and goods markets. However, the actual flows in any real economy are vastly more complex than the simple flows shown in the figure. The

---

[1] Other words are sometimes used to make the same distinction. One frequently used pair is 'induced' for endogenous and 'autonomous' for exogenous. ('Autonomous' means self-governing or independent.)

Box 2.1 **Prediction, prophecy, and forecasting**

A scientific prediction is a conditional statement that takes the form 'If something is done, then such and such will follow.' For example, if the government cuts taxes on firms, then investment will increase.

Prediction versus prophecy

A prediction of this sort is different from the statement 'I prophesy that in two years' time there will be a large increase in investment because I believe the government will decide to cut tax rates.' The government's decision to cut tax rates in two years' time will be the outcome of many influences, both economic and political. If the prophecy about investment turns out to be wrong because in two years' time the government does not cut tax rates, then all that has been learned is that the person was not good at guessing the behaviour of the government. However, if the government does cut tax rates (in two years' time or at any other time) and investment does not then increase, a conditional scientific prediction in economic theory will have been contradicted.

Prediction versus forecasting

Conditional prediction should not be confused with forecasting. Forecasting attempts to predict the future by discovering relationships between economic variables such as that the value of Y at some future date depends primarily on the value of X today. If so, future Y can be predicted by observing present X. Many conditional predictions are not of this form. Some theories relate the *current value* of Y to the current value of X. These theories provide significant and useful relationships that allow us to predict 'if you now do this to X, Y will change now in some specified way', without allowing us to forecast the future. Second, other theories show that the value of X is one important determinant of the future value of Y without being the only determinant. These theories allow us to influence Y in the future without being able to forecast its precise value—because we cannot predict the changes in all the other forces that influence Y. The analogy often drawn between economics and weather forecasting relates to economic forecasting rather than to the wider and more interesting class of conditional *if–then* economic predictions.

 Box 2.2 **An illustrative model**

It has been observed that the amount of research that goes into improving a new product often depends on the product's current sales —since the profits that finance much of a firm's research and development are generated by its sales. To gain insight into some possible consequences of this relationship, we can build a very simple model in which the amount of current research to improve some product is positively related to the amount of that product's current sales. This creates what is called *positive feedback*, because the larger are current sales, the more research is done; the more research is done, the more rapidly the product improves; the more rapidly the product improves, the more current sales rise.

We may then elaborate the model by adding a second product, which competes with the first one. The model then shows that the product that gets the larger sales initially (for whatever reason) will attract more R&D, and hence will be improved more rapidly than the product with the smaller initial sales. This model will reveal one key tendency of positive feedback systems: initial advantages tend to be reinforced, making it more and more difficult for competitors to keep up. No one believes that this simple model catches everything about the complex interactions when various new products compete with each other in the early stages of their development. But it does alert us to certain forces to watch for when we build more complex models or create more general theories of competition among new products and new technologies.

Interestingly, these self-reinforcing characteristics have been observed in many actual cases. These include the competition to be the power source of the first motor cars early in the twentieth century, the competition among alternative technologies to produce nuclear power in the middle of the century, and the recent competition to produce the operating system of personal computers (which was won by Microsoft). All of these are cases in which early success helped a particular technology to build up an unbeatable lead over competing technologies.

used to test a specific prediction of some theory and to provide observations to be explained by theories.

Tests

A theory is tested by confronting its predictions with evidence. Are events of the type contained in the theory followed by the consequences predicted by the theory? For example, is an increase in the price of eggs met by a fall in the quantity of eggs that consumers wish to buy? Generally, theories tend to be abandoned when they are no longer useful. A theory ceases to be useful when it cannot predict more accurately than an alternative theory. When a theory consistently fails to predict better than an available alternative, it is either modified or replaced.

Theory and evidence: which came first?

The old question of the chicken and the egg is often raised when discussing economic theories. In the first instance, it was observation that preceded economic theories. People

model helps us to understand what is going on without being detailed enough to yield specific testable predictions about real-world behaviour. In some ways, a model of this sort is like a political caricature. Its value is in the insights it provides that help us to understand key features of a complex world.

Box 2.2 gives another example of how an illustrative model may be used to understand some tendencies by studying them in isolation.

Evidence

Economists make much use of evidence, or, as they usually call it, empirical observation. Such observations can be were not born with economic theories embedded in their minds: instead, economic theories began to arise when people observed the co-ordination of market behaviour and asked themselves how such co-ordination occurred. But now that a body of economic ideas exists, theories and evidence interact with each other. It has become impossible to say now that one precedes the other. In some cases empirical evidence may suggest inadequacies that require the development of better theories. In other cases an inspired guess may lead to a theory that has little current empirical support but is subsequently found to explain many observations.

Box 2.3 discusses some more detailed aspects of testability.

Theories about human behaviour

So far we have talked about theories in general. But what about theories that purport to explain and predict human behaviour? A scientific study of human behaviour is possible only if humans respond in predictable ways to things that affect them. Is it reasonable to expect such stability? After all, we humans have free will and can behave in capricious ways if the spirit moves us.

Think, however, of what the world would be like if human behaviour were really unpredictable. Neither law, nor justice, nor airline timetables would be more reliable than the outcome of a single spin of a roulette wheel. A kind remark could as easily provoke fury as sympathy. Your landlady might evict you tomorrow or let you off the rent. One cannot really imagine a society of human beings that could work like this. In fact, we live in a world that is a mixture of the predictable, or average, or 'most of the people most of the time', and of the haphazard, contrary, or random.

How is it that human behaviour can show stable responses even though we can never be quite sure what one individual will do? Successful predictions about the behaviour of large groups are made possible by the statistical 'law' of large numbers. Very roughly, this 'law' asserts that (under a carefully specified set of conditions) random movements of a large number of items tend to offset one another.

For example, we might wonder if there is a relationship between motorway speed limits and road accidents. When the speed limit is actually lowered, it will be almost impossible to predict in advance what changes will occur in any single individual's driving record. One individual whose record has been good may have a series of accidents after the speed limit is lowered because of a deterioration in his physical or emotional health. Another person may have an improved accident record for reasons not associated with the alteration in the speed limit, for example because she purchases a more reliable car. Yet others may have altered driving records for no reasons that we can discern.

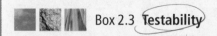 Box 2.3 **Testability**

The way in which a positive statement can be tested against facts varies with the kind of positive statement that is under consideration.

A statement that something exists can be proved by finding a confirming example. But it cannot be conclusively disproved, because it is always possible that we have not looked hard enough and that someone will find a confirming example in the future. For example, the statement that extra-terrestrials exist and frequently visit Earth in flying saucers could be proved if well documented sightings were repeated in situations in which they could be confirmed by scientific measuring techniques—instead of occurring on isolated country roads to single individuals or small groups, as the alleged close-up sightings now do. But it can never be disproved; for, no matter how long we look and wait, there always exists the possibility that in the future sightings will occur in a convincing form. In the meantime believers say the statement is true, while sceptics say 'not proven'.

In contrast, a statement that some relationship always holds true can be refuted by one well documented case in which it is does not hold. But it can never be proved, because there always exists the possibility that in the future we will observe a case in which it does not hold. For example, the theory of consumer demand predicts that the relationship between a commodity's price and the amount consumers wish to purchase is negative—the lower the price, the higher are desired purchases. Occasional exceptions have been alleged (and we will study some of them in later chapters), but they have not been well enough documented or repeated often enough to satisfy contemporary observers. So we can say that the evidence is consistent with the theory, but we cannot say that the theory is proved, because we cannot rule out the possibility that at some future date a case will be documented in which a price reduction reduces desired purchases.

The general point is:

A statement that something exists can be proved but not refuted. A statement that something always exists can be refuted but not proved.

The statement may refer to the existence of some phenomenon or a relationship between two or more variables of the sort that we find in the theories of economics and other fact-based disciplines. In other words, we can show our theories to be consistent with observed facts, but we cannot establish that they are true with certainty.

If we study only a few individuals, we will learn nothing about the effects of the altered speed limit, since we will not know the importance of all the other causes that are at work. But if we observe 1,000 individuals, the effects of the change in the speed limit—if such effects do exist—will tend to show up in the average. If a lowered speed limit does discourage accidents, the group as a whole will have fewer accidents even though some individuals may have more. Individuals may do peculiar things that, as far as we can tell, are inexplicable, but the group's behaviour will none the less be predictable, precisely because the odd things that one individual does will tend to cancel out the odd things that some other individual does.

Why do economists often disagree?

When all their theories have been constructed and all their evidence has been collected, economists still disagree with each other on many issues. If you hear a discussion among economists on *Newsnight* or the *Today Programme*, or if you read about their debates in the daily press or weekly magazines, you will find that economists frequently disagree with each other. What should we make of this disagreement? Here are five of the many possible sources of disagreement.

First, different economists may be using different benchmarks. For example, inflation may be up compared with last year but down compared with the 1980s. When this sort of thing happens the disagreement is more apparent than real, although it can be confusing to observers.

Second, economists often fail to make it clear to their audience whether they are talking about short-term or long-term consequences. For example, one economist may be noting that a tax cut will stimulate consumption at the cost of lowering savings in the short run while another is pointing out that it will stimulate investment and saving in the long run. Here again the disagreement is more apparent than real, since both these short- and long-run effects command much agreement among economists.

Third, economists often fail to acknowledge the full extent of their ignorance. There are many things about which we know little, and even more about which our evidence is far from conclusive. Informed judgements are then required before an economist takes a position on even a purely positive question. If two economists' judgements differ, the disagreement is real. Evidence is not sufficient, and different people can come to different conclusions on the basis of such evidence as is available. What a responsible economist will do in such cases is to make clear the extent to which informed judgement is involved in any position he or she is taking.

Fourth, different economists have different values, and these normative views play a large part in most public discussions of policy. Many economists stress the importance of individual responsibility, while others stress the need for collective action to deal with certain issues. Different policy advice may stem from such differences in value judgements about what is socially important.

A fifth reason lies in the desire of the media to cover both sides of any contentious issue. As a result, the public will usually hear one or two economists on each side of a debate, regardless of whether the profession is divided right down the middle or is nearly unanimous in its support of one side. Thus, the public will not know that in one case a reporter could have chosen from dozens of economists to present each side, whereas in another case the reporter had to spend three days finding someone willing to take a particular side because nearly all the economists supported the other side. In their desire to show both sides of all cases, however, the media present the public with the appearance of a profession equally split over all matters.

Anyone seeking to discredit some particular economist's advice by showing that there is disagreement among economists will have no trouble finding evidence of some disagreement. But on a surprisingly large number of issues a majority view, or even a strong consensus, can be found.

Because the world is complex, and because no issue can be settled beyond any doubt, economists are never in *unanimous* agreement on any issue. None the less, the methods we have been discussing in this chapter have produced an impressive amount of agreement on many aspects of how the economy works and what happens when governments intervene to alter its workings. For example, a survey published in the *American Economic Review* showed strong agreement among economists on many propositions, including 'Rent control leads to a housing shortage' (85 per cent yes). Other examples of these areas of agreement will be found in countless places throughout this book.

Economic data

Economists seek to explain observations made of the real world. Why, for example, did the price of wheat rise in some year even though the wheat crop increased? We would be aware of this issue only if we had numbers for the wheat crop and the price of wheat, and we would need a lot of additional data (such as on incomes and other prices) to come up with a comprehensive answer.

Real-world observations are also needed to test the predictions of economic theories. For example, did the amount that people saved in a particular year rise—as the theory predicts it should have—when a large tax cut increased after-tax incomes? To test this prediction, we need reliable data for people's incomes and their savings.

Political scientists, sociologists, anthropologists, and psychologists all tend to collect the data they use to formulate and test their theories. Economists are unusual among social scientists in using data mainly collected by others, often government statisticians. In economics there is a division of labour between collecting data and using it to generate and test theories. The advantage is that economists do not need to spend much of their scarce research time collecting the data they use. The disadvantage is that they are often not as well informed about the limitations of the data collected by others as they would be if they collected the data themselves.

Once data are collected they can be displayed in various ways, all of which we will see later in this chapter. They can be laid out in tables. They can be displayed in the various types of graph that we study later in this chapter. Where we are interested in relative movements rather than absolute ones, the data can be expressed in index numbers.

Index numbers

Table 2.2 shows how the prices of cocoa and coffee beans varied during five quarters of 2001 and 2002. How do these two sets of prices compare in volatility? It may be difficult to tell from the table because the two prices start at different levels. It is easier to compare the series if we concentrate on relative rather than absolute price changes. (The *absolute change* is the actual change in the price; the *relative change* is the change in the price expressed in relationship to some base price.)

Index numbers as relatives

Comparisons of relative changes can be made by expressing each price series as a set of **index numbers**. To do this we take the price at some point of time as the base to which prices in other periods will be compared. We call this the *base period*. In the present example we choose the first quarter of 2001 (2000 Q1) as the base period for both series. The price in that quarter is given a value of 100. We then take the price of coffee in each subsequent quarter and express it as a ratio of its price in the base year and multiply the result by 100. This gives us an index number of coffee prices. We then do the same for cocoa. The details of the calculations for coffee are shown in Table 2.3.

The results, which are shown in Table 2.4, allow us to compare the relative fluctuations in the two series. It is apparent from the figures that cocoa prices rose by nearly

Table 2.2 **Price of cocoa and coffee**
(average price in each quarter; US cents per kg)

Quarter	Cocoa	Coffee
2001 (1)	100.4	146.7
2001 (2)	104.5	146.4
2001 (3)	100.8	129.7
2001 (4)	121.8	126.4
2002 (1)	149.0	136.6

(*Source*: World Bank; www.worldbank.org)

Table 2.3 **Calculation of an index of coffee prices**

Quarter	Index
2001 (1)	$(146.7/146.7) \times 100 = 100$
2001 (2)	$(146.4/146.7) \times 100 = 99.8$
2001 (3)	$(129.7/146.7) \times 100 = 88.4$
2001 (4)	$(126.4/146.7) \times 100 = 86.2$
2002 (1)	$(136.6/146.7) \times 100 = 93.1$

Index numbers are calculated by dividing the current price by the base-year price and multiplying the result by 100. For example, the coffee price in 2001 (4) was 126.4 cents per kg. Dividing by the base year price of 146.7 cents (in 2001 (1)) and multiplying by 100 gives an index of 86.2 for this quarter.

Table 2.4 **Index of cocoa and coffee prices**

Quarter	Cocoa	Coffee
2001 (1)	100	100
2001 (2)	104.1	99.8
2001 (3)	100.4	88.4
2001 (4)	121.3	86.2
2002 (1)	148.4	93.1

Source: Tables 2.2 and 2.3.

50 per cent over the period while coffee prices fell by nearly 14 per cent before recovering slightly.

The formula of any index number is:

$$\text{Value of index in period } t = \frac{\text{value in period } t}{\text{value in base period}} \times 100.$$

An index number merely expresses the value of some series in any given period as a percentage of its value in the base period. Thus, the 2002 Q1 index of cocoa prices of 148.4 tells us that the 2002 Q1 price of cocoa was 48.4 per cent higher than the 2001 Q1 price. By subtracting 100 from any index, we get the change from the base to the given year, expressed as a percentage of the base year. To take a second example, the coffee index of 93.1 in 2002 Q1 tells us that the price of coffee at this time was only 93.1 per cent of the 1990 price or, what is the same thing, that the price had fallen by 6.9 per cent over the year.

Index numbers as averages

Index numbers are particularly useful if we wish to combine several different series into some average. Say, for example, that we want an index of hot-drinks beans, and cocoa and coffee are the only two commodities we are interested in.

An unweighted index For any one year, we could add the price indexes for cocoa and coffee and average them. This would give us a hot-drinks beans index. But the index would give the two prices equal weight in determining the value of the overall index. Such an index is often called an unweighted index, but that is misleading. Actually it is an equal-weight index. It would be sheer luck if this were the appropriate thing to do.

In practice, we need to weight each price by some measure of its relative importance, letting the more important prices have more weight than the less important prices in determining what happens to the overall index.

An output-weighted index Coffee is a much more important commodity than cocoa in the sense that much greater volume is produced. For purposes of illustration, we assume that 9 kg of coffee is produced for every 1 kg of cocoa. To get our weighted index of bean prices, we multiply the coffee index value in Table 2.4 by 0.9 and the cocoa index by 0.1 and sum the two to obtain the final index. The results are shown in Table 2.5. The quite different behaviour of the two indexes shows the importance of the choice of weights.

An index that averages changes in several series is the weighted average of the indexes for the separate series, the weights reflecting the relative importance of each series.

Price indexes Economists make frequent use of indexes of the price level covering a broad group of prices across the whole economy. One of the most important of these is the retail price index, RPI, which covers goods and services that individuals buy. This is described in detail in the appendix to Chapter 21.

All price indexes are calculated using the same procedure. First the relevant prices are collected. Then a base year is chosen. Then each price series is converted into index numbers. Finally, the index numbers are combined to create a weighted average index series where the weights indicate the relative importance of each price series. For example, in any retail price series, the price of sardines would be given a much smaller weight than the price of living accommodation, because what happens to the price of accommodation is much more important to consumers, all of whom spend much more on accommodation than on sardines.

Graphing economic data

A single economic variable such as unemployment or GDP can come in two basic forms.

Cross-section The first is called **cross-sectional data**, which means a number of different observations on one variable all taken in different places at the same point in time. Figure 2.1 shows an example. The variable in the figure is unemployment as a percentage of the workforce. It is shown for ten selected countries for September 2002.

Time-series

The second type of data is called **time-series data**. This involves observations taken on one variable at successive points in time. The data in Figure 2.2 show the unemployment rate for the UK from 1950 to 2001. The large variations, with two peaks in the mid-1980s and mid-1990s, are readily apparent. Figure 2.3 shows another time-series, this time for the two indexes of hot-drinks beans that we calculated in the section on index numbers.

Table 2.5 **Two indexes of hot drinks beans prices**

Quarter	Equal weights	Coffee = 0.9; cocoa = 0.1
2001 (1)	100	100
2001 (2)	101.9	100.2
2001 (3)	94.2	89.6
2001 (4)	103.7	89.7
2002 (1)	120.7	98.6

Weights really matter. The equal-weight index is calculated for each period by adding the cocoa and coffee indexes from Table 2.4 and dividing by 2. The second index is calculated for each period by multiplying the coffee index by 0.9 and the cocoa index by 0.1 and then adding the results. The two series behave quite differently as a result of using different weights, as can be seen in Figure 2.3.

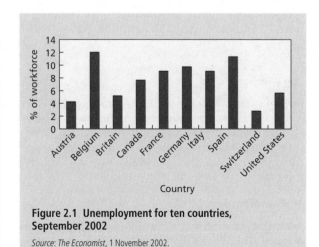

Figure 2.1 Unemployment for ten countries, September 2002

Source: *The Economist*, 1 November 2002.

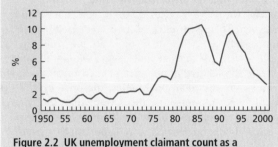

Figure 2.2 UK unemployment claimant count as a percentage of the workforce, 1950–2001

Source: ONS, *Economic Trends annual supplement*, 2002.

Table 2.6 **Income and savings for ten selected households**

Household	Annual income	Annual savings
1	£70,000	£10,000
2	30,000	2,500
3	100,000	12,000
4	60,000	3,000
5	80,000	8,000
6	10,000	500
7	20,000	2,000
8	50,000	2,000
9	40,000	4,200
10	90,000	8,000

Savings tend to rise as income rises. The table shows the amount of income earned by ten selected households together with the amount they saved during the same year.

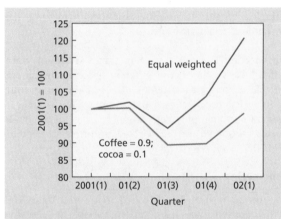

Figure 2.3 Two indexes of hot-drinks bean prices

Weights matter. The two series are constructed from the same prices for cocoa and coffee. The difference is only in the weights. The equal-weighted series is a simple average of the indexes for each type of bean. The output-weighted series is constructed by multiplying the coffee price index by 0.9 and the cocoa price index by 0.1. These weights conform roughly to the relative proportion that each contributes to the total value of production.

Source: Table 2.5.

Logarithmic scales

Box 2.4 shows another type of series that is useful when relative or percentage changes are more important than absolute changes. When data are graphed on a logarithmic scale, equal distances indicate equal percentage changes rather then equal absolute changes. Also, with a log scale a straight line indicates a constant rate of growth.

Scatter diagrams

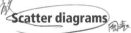

Another way in which data can be presented is in a **scatter diagram**. This type of chart is more analytical than those above. It is designed to show the relationship between two different variables, such as the price of eggs and the quantity of eggs sold. To plot a scatter diagram, values of one variable are measured on the horizontal axis and values of the second variable are measured on the vertical axis. Any point on the diagram relates a specific value of one variable to a corresponding specific value of the other.

The two series plotted on a scatter diagram may be either cross-sectional or time-series. An example of a cross-sectional scatter diagram would be a scatter of the price of eggs and the quantity sold in July 2004 at two dozen different places in England. Each dot would show a price–quantity combination observed in a different place at the same time. An example of a scatter diagram using time-series data would be the price and quantity of eggs sold in Liverpool for each month over the last ten years. Each of the 120 dots would show a price–quantity combination observed at the same place in one particular month.

Table 2.6 shows data for the income and the savings of ten households in one particular year.[2] They are plotted on a scatter diagram in Figure 2.4. Each point in the figure stands for one household, showing its income and its saving. The positive relationship between the two stands out. The higher income is, the higher saving tends to be.

The following two sections are more demanding and can be omitted on first reading by anyone who has a very limited knowledge of maths. However, you should return to them if you have difficulty at a later stage understanding formal statements of relationships between economic variables. It would certainly be helpful to return to them before reading Chapter 6 and beyond.

---

[2] Although our theory refers to individuals, data are often gathered for households, which are defined as groups of individuals who live under the same roof and make joint financial decisions.

Box 2.4 Ratio (logarithmic) scales and graphs

All the graphs in the text use axes that plot numbers on a natural or arithmetic scale. On a **natural scale** the distance between numbers is proportionate to the absolute difference between those numbers. Thus, 200 is placed halfway between 100 and 300. If proportionate rather than absolute changes in variables are important, it is more revealing to use **a ratio or logarithmic scale**. On a ratio scale the distance between two numbers is proportionate to the percentage difference between them (which can also be measured as the absolute difference between their logarithms). Equal distances anywhere on a ratio scale represent equal percentage changes rather than equal absolute changes. On a ratio scale, the distance between 100 and 200 is the same as the distance between 200 and 400, between 1,000 and 2,000, and between any other two numbers that stand in the ratio 1 : 2 to each other. When a time-series is plotted with a natural scale on the horizontal axis (i.e. each year is the same distance apart) but with a ratio scale on the vertical axis, it is said to be plotted on a semi-log scale.

The table shows two series. Series A is growing by a constant absolute amount of 8 units per period, while series B is growing at a constant rate of 100 per cent per period. In the figure, the series are plotted first on a natural scale and then on a semi-log scale.

Time-period	Series A	Series B
0	10	10
1	18	20
2	26	40
3	34	80
4	42	160

The natural scale makes it easy for the eye to judge absolute variations, and the logarithmic scale makes it easy for the eye to judge proportionate variations. Series A, which grows by a constant absolute amount, appears as a straight line on a natural scale but as a curve of diminishing slope on a semi-log scale, because the same absolute growth represents a decreasing percentage growth. Series B, which grows at a rising absolute rate but a constant percentage rate, appears as a curve of increasing slope on a natural scale but as a straight line on a semi-log scale. This is an important relationship: when any economic variable is plotted on a semi-log scale, a constant slope (a straight line) indicates a constant rate of growth; an increasing or a decreasing slope indicates a rising or a falling rate of growth, respectively.

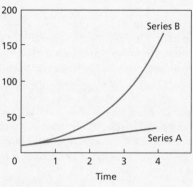

(i) A natural scale

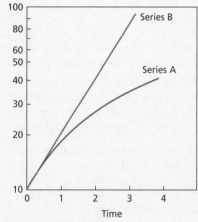

(ii) A semi-log scale

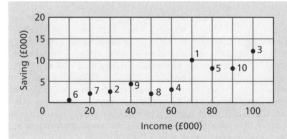

Figure 2.4 Savings and income

Saving tends to rise as income rises. The figure plots the incomes and savings for the ten households listed in Table 2.6. The number on each dot refers to the household in the corresponding row of the table. (Note that the scales are not the same on the two axes.)

Graphing economic theories

Theories are built on assumptions about relationships between variables. For example, the quantity of eggs purchased is assumed to fall as the price of eggs rises, and the total amount an individual saves is assumed to rise as his or her income rises. How can such relationships be expressed? When one variable is related to another in such a way that to every value of one variable there is only one possible value of the second variable, we say that the second variable is *a function of the first*.[3] When we write this relationship down, we are expressing a functional relationship between the two variables.

A functional relationship can be expressed in words, in a numerical schedule, in mathematical equations, or in graphs.

To illustrate, we take a specific example of a relationship between a family's annual income, which we denote by the symbol Y, and the total amount it spends on goods and services during that year, which we denote by the symbol C.

1. **Verbal statement.** When income is zero, the family will spend £800 a year (either by borrowing the money or by consuming past savings), and for every £1 of income that it obtains it will increase its expenditure by £0.80.

2. **Schedule.** This shows selected values of the family's income and the amount it spends on consumption.

Annual income	Consumption	Reference letter
0	800	p
2,500	2,800	q
5,000	4,800	r
7,500	6,800	s
10,000	8,800	t

3. **Mathematical (algebraic) statement.** $C = £800 + 0.8Y$ is the equation of the relationship just described in words. As a check, you can first see that when Y is zero C is £800. Then you can substitute any two values of Y that differ by £1, multiply each by 0.80, and add 800, and see that the corresponding two values of consumption differ by £0.80.

4. **Geometrical (graphical) statement.** Figure 2.5 shows both the points from the schedule above and the line representing the equation given in point 3.

Comparison of the values on the graph with the values in the schedule, and with the values derived from the equation just stated, shows that these are alternative expressions of the same relationship between C and Y. All four of these modes of expression refer to the same relationship between total consumption expenditure and total income.

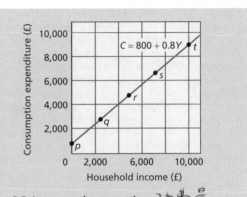

Figure 2.5 Income and consumption

Consumption expenditure rises as income rises. The figure graphs the schedule and the equation for the consumption function discussed in the text.

Functions

Let us look in a little more detail at the algebraic expression of this relationship between income and consumption expenditure. To state the expression in general form, detached from the specific numerical example above, we use a symbol to express the dependence of one variable on another. Using 'f' for this purpose, we write

$$C = f(Y). \tag{1}$$

This is read 'C is a function of Y'. Spelling this out more fully, it reads 'The amount of consumption expenditure depends upon the household's income.'

The variable on the left-hand side is the dependent variable, since its value depends on the value of the variable on the right-hand side. The variable on the right-hand side is the independent variable, since it can take on any value. The letter 'f' tells us that a **functional relationship** is involved. This means that a knowledge of the value of the variable (or variables) within the parentheses on the right-hand side allows us to determine the value of the variable

---

[3] When two variables, X and Y, are related in some way, mathematicians say that there is a *correspondence* between them. When the relationship is such that to any value of the variable X there corresponds one and only one value of the variable Y, then Y is said to be a *function* of X. For example, in the relationship, $Y = a + bX + cX^2$, Y is a function of X because each value of X gives rise to one and only one value of Y. In the text we confine ourselves to functions. It is worth noting that Y being a function of X does not necessarily imply that X is a function of Y. For example, in the equation given in this footnote, X cannot be expressed as a function of Y because to many values of Y there correspond not one but two values of X.

on the left-hand side. Although in this case we have used 'f' (as a memory-aid for 'function'), any convenient symbol can be used to denote the existence of a functional relationship. In practice, Greek letters are often used to denote specific functions.

Functional notation can seem intimidating to those who are unfamiliar with it. But it is helpful. Since the functional concept is basic to all science, the notation is worth understanding.

Functional forms

The expression $C = f(Y)$ states that C is related to Y. It says nothing about the form that this relationship takes. The term 'functional form' refers to the specific nature of the relationship between the variables in the function. The example above gave one specific functional form for this relationship:

$$C = £800 + 0.8Y. \qquad (2)$$

Equation (1) expresses the general assumption that consumption expenditure depends on the consumer's income. Equation (2) expresses the more specific assumption that C rises by 80p for every £1 that Y rises. A second form for the function in (1) would be $C = £600 + 0.9Y$. You should be able to say in words the behaviour implied in this relationship.

There is no reason why either of these assumptions must be true; indeed, neither may be consistent with the facts. But that is a matter for testing. What we do have in each equation is a concise statement of a particular assumption.

Graphing functional relationships

Different functional forms have different graphs, and we will meet many of these in subsequent chapters. Figure 2.5 is an example of a relationship in which the two variables move together. When income goes up, consumption goes up. In such a relationship the two variables are *positively related* to each other. (Figure 23.2 on page 412 shows the actual relationship for the UK over the period 1955–2002.)

Figure 2.6 gives an example of variables that move in opposite directions. As the amount spent on abating smoke pollution goes up, the amount of pollution goes down. In such a relationship the two variables are *negatively related* to each other.[4]

Both of these graphs are straight lines. In such cases the variables are *linearly related* to each other.

The slope of a straight line

Slopes are important in economics. They show you how fast one variable is changing as the other changes. The slope is defined as the amount of change in the variable measured on the vertical or *y*-axis per unit change in the variable measured on the horizontal or *x*-axis. In the case of

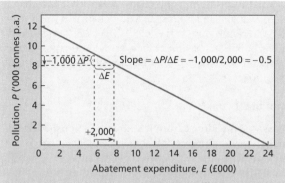

Figure 2.6 Linear pollution abatement
Pollution falls linearly as expenditure on abatement rises. The slope of the line indicates the marginal reduction in pollution for every increase of £1 of abatement expenditure. It is constant at −0.5, indicating that every extra £1 spent on abatement reduces pollution by half a tonne.

Figure 2.6, it tells us how many tonnes of smoke pollution, symbolized by P, are removed per pound spent on pollution control, symbolized by E. As the figure shows, if we spend £2,000 more we get 1,000 tonnes less pollution. This is 0.5 tonne per pound spent. On the graph the extra £2,000 is indicated by ΔE, the arrow indicating that E rises by 2,000. The 1,000 tonnes of pollution reduction is indicated by ΔP, the arrow showing that pollution falls by 1,000. (The Greek uppercase letter delta Δ stands for a change in something.) To get the amount of abatement per pound of expenditure we merely divide one by the other. In symbols this is $\Delta P / \Delta E$.

More generally, if we let X stand for whatever variable is measured on the horizontal axis and Y for whatever variable is measured on the vertical axis, the slope of a straight line is $\Delta Y / \Delta X$.

In Figure 2.5 the two variables change in the same direction, so both changes will always be either positive or negative. As a result their ratio, which is the slope of this line, is positive.

In Figure 2.6 the two variables change in opposite directions: when one increases the other decreases. So the two Δs will always be of opposite sign. As a result their ratio, which is the slope of the line, is always negative.

Notice also that straight lines have the same slope no matter where on the line you measure that slope. This tells

[4] Mathematicians refer to the slopes of curves as *positive* if both variables change in the same direction along the curve (i.e. if either they both increase or they both decrease) and as *negative* if the variables change in opposite directions along the curve (i.e. if one increases while the other decreases). Economists often read curves from left to right, calling negatively sloped curves 'downward-sloping' and positively sloped curves 'upward-sloping'. We stick mainly to the unambiguous terminology of positive and negative slopes.

us what inspection of the chart reveals: that the change in one variable in response to a unit change in the other is the same anywhere on the line. We get 0.5 tonne of additional pollution abatement for every additional £1 that we spend on abatement no matter how much we are already spending.

Nonlinear functions

The world is seldom as simple as linear relationships would make it seem. Although it is sometimes convenient to simplify a real relationship between two variables by assuming them to be linearly related, this is seldom the case over their whole range. Nonlinear relationships are much more common than linear ones. In the case of pollution abatement it is usually quite cheap to eliminate the first units of pollution. Then, as the smoke gets cleaner and cleaner, the cost of further abatement tends to increase because more and more sophisticated and expensive methods need to be used. As a result, the graph relating expenditure on abatement and amount of pollution usually looks more like Figure 2.7 than Figure 2.6. Inspection of this figure shows that, as more and more is spent, the benefit in terms of extra abatement for an additional £1 of abatement expenditure gets smaller and smaller. This is shown by the diminishing slope of the curve as we move rightward along it. As the figure shows, an extra £1 of expenditure yields two-thirds of a tonne of abatement (2,000/3,000) when pollution is 8,000 tonnes but only one-sixth of a tonne of abatement (500/3,000) when pollution is 3,000 tonnes.

Economists call the change in abatement resulting when a bit more or a bit less is spent on abatement the *marginal change*. Figure 2.7 shows that the slope of the curve at each point measures this marginal change. It also shows that, in the type of curve illustrated, the marginal return per pound spent is diminishing as abatement proceeds. There is always a payoff to more expenditure over the range shown in the figure, but the return diminishes as more is spent. This relationship can be described as *diminishing marginal response*. We will meet such relationships many times in what follows, so we emphasize now that diminishing marginal response does not mean that the total response is diminishing. In Figure 2.7 the total amount of pollution continues to fall as more and more is spent on abatement. But diminishing marginal response does mean that the amount of abatement obtained for *each additional unit of expense* is diminishing as more and more pollution is abated.

Figure 2.8 shows a graph where the marginal return is increasing. It relates expenditure on navigational aids to the number of safe passages. At low levels of expenditure

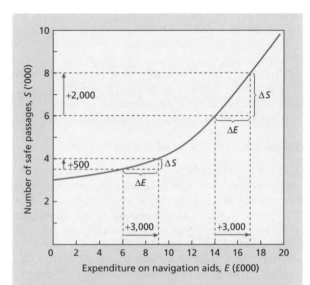

Figure 2.8 Navigation aids

Safe passages increase at an increasing rate as navigation aids are increased. The figure shows the number of safe passages varying positively with the amount spent on navigation aids. Because of network externalities, the number of safe passages increases at an increasing rate as more is spent on navigation aids. An increase in expenditure on navigation aids by £3,000 when expenditure is £6,000 raises safe passages by 500 from 3,500 to 4,000. The marginal return to £1 extra spent on navigation aids is then 500/3,000 or 0.167. In other words, it takes £6 to get one more safe passage (3,000/500). When £14,000 is already being spent, a further increase of £3,000 increases safe passages by 2,000 from 6,000 to 8,000. The marginal return from £1 spent on aids is now 2,000/3,000 or 0.667. In other words, it takes only £1.50 extra spending to get one more safe passage (3,000/2,000).

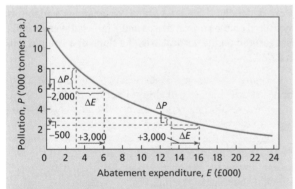

Figure 2.7 Nonlinear pollution abatement

Pollution falls nonlinearly as abatement expenditure rises. When pollution is 8,000 tonnes per year, an additional expenditure of £3,000 reduces pollution by 2,000 tonnes. The marginal return for £1 additional expenditure is $\Delta P/\Delta E$ or 2,000/3,000, which is two-thirds of a tonne per £1 spent on abatement. However, when pollution has already been reduced to 3,000 tonnes, an extra £3,000 spent on abatement reduces pollution by only 500 tonnes. The marginal return for £1 of additional expenditure, $\Delta P/\Delta E$, is now only 500/3,000 or one-sixth of a tonne per £1 spent.

the curve is nearly flat; an additional unit of expenditure does not yield much additional protection. But as more and more is spent, it becomes possible to employ more efficient navigation aids that work together as a whole system. Each extra unit of expenditure yields more additional protection than each previous unit. In this case we have what economists call *increasing marginal response*. The reason is that navigation aids encounter what are called *network externalities*. They are most effective not as single stand-alone bits, such as one lighthouse, but as an integrated whole. Each aid becomes more effective the more complex and interrelated is the whole system of which it is a part.

Functions with maxima and minima

So far all the graphs we have seen have had either a positive or negative slope over their entire range. But many relationships change direction as the independent variable increases. Figures 2.9 and 2.10 extend our navigation and pollution examples over a larger range of the independent variables. We find that as more and more is spent on navigation aids, not only does the marginal contribution of each additional £1 spent begin to decline, but eventually the total safety begins to decline. The reason is that the

signals begin to interfere with each other and confuse rather than aid navigators. So as expenditure on navigation aids increases, eventually the safety reaches a maximum and then begins to decline.

At the maximum point the curve is flat—it has a zero slope. Up to that point each £1 spent does increase safety —it has a positive marginal contribution. But after that point each additional unit lowers safety—it has a negative marginal contribution. At the maximum point the marginal contribution is zero.

Now look at Figure 2.10, which extends the pollution abatement example. Here we see that each £1 spent on pollution control adds to abatement up to the amount E_1, but after that abatement begins to decline. The reason in this case may be that the regulations become so costly that firms find ways of evading them and total enforcement gets less effective. Pollution reaches a minimum when E_1 is spent but rises thereafter. Notice that up to E_1 the curve has a negative slope, indicating that more expenditure is associated with less pollution, but that after E_1 the curve has a positive slope, indicating that more expenditure is associated with more pollution. At the point of minimum pollution the tangent to the curve shown by the line T has a slope of zero. (A *tangent* is a straight line that just touches a curve at some point and lies everywhere above or below the curve near that point.)

These two cases illustrate an important point, which we will see over and over in what follows:

At either a minimum or a maximum value of a function, its marginal value is zero.

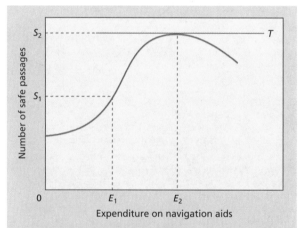

Figure 2.9 Aid saturation

Eventually increases in expenditure on navigation aids serve to reduce the number of safe passages. Up to E_1, expenditure on navigation aids encounters increasing marginal returns. Each additional £1 of expenditure allows a larger increase in safe passages than each previous £1 of expenditure. Between E_1 and E_2, expenditure encounters decreasing marginal returns. Each additional £1 spent increases the number of safe passages by less than the previous £1 of expenditure. At E_2 safe passages reach a maximum of S_2. Further expenditure encounters negative marginal returns. Each additional £1 spent lowers the number of safe passages. At the maximum point the slope of the tangent T (the straight line that just touches the curve at that point) is zero. At that point the number of safe passages shows no response to small changes in expenditure on navigation aids.

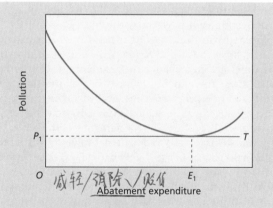

Figure 2.10 Abatement saturation

Beyond a certain point additional abatement expenditure increases pollution. Up to E_1, each additional £1 of expenditure reduces pollution, but at a diminishing amount for each £1. At expenditure E_1, pollution reaches a minimum of P_1. If further amounts are spent, pollution actually rises. At the minimum point the slope of the tangent line T is zero. At that point pollution shows no response to small changes in abatement expenditure.

Measuring marginal values

Economic theory makes much use of the marginal concepts that we have just introduced. Marginal cost, marginal revenue, marginal rate of substitution, and marginal propensity to consume are a few examples of concepts we will use in later chapters. 'Marginal' means on the margin or border, and the concept refers to what will happen when there is a *small change* from the present position.

The last section gave some examples. Now we need to look at marginals a little more generally. A marginal value refers to functional relationships, whether they are written as equations or drawn as graphs. The independent variable, which we call X and draw on the horizontal axis of any graph, determines the value of the dependent variable, which we call Y and draw on the vertical axis of any graph. We wish to know what will be the change in Y when X is changed by a small amount from its present value. The answer is referred to as 'the marginal value of Y' and is given various specific names depending on the economic variables that X and Y stand for.

Figure 2.11 summarizes what we have seen so far. The three lines in part (i) are all positively sloped, making Y positively related to X. The first is a straight line, which means it has a constant slope. The change in Y for a given change in X, i.e. the marginal value of Y, is the same no matter where on the line we measure it. The slope of the second line gets steeper as we move along it to the right. The response of Y to a change in X, the marginal value of Y, is increasing. The third line gets flatter as we move along it. The response of Y to a change in X, the marginal value of Y, is decreasing as we move along the line.

In part (ii) the three lines are all negatively sloped, so that Y is negatively related to X. Along the line labelled (4) the response of Y to a change in X is constant. On the line labelled (5) the response is increasing as the slope gets steeper and steeper. On the line labelled (6) the response of Y to a change in X, its marginal value, is decreasing as we move along it, as shown by the flattening of the curve.

So far we have measured marginal values by taking the ratio of the change in Y to the change in X ($\Delta Y/\Delta X$) between any two points on the curve in which we are interested. Actually, however, there is another, more exact measure, to which the ratios we have been using so far are only approximations. Because the exact measure uses differential calculus (it is called a derivative), introductory texts in economics usually use the ratio approximations, which depend only on simple algebra. This can be confusing, because the language of economic theory refers to the exact measure while introductory examples use the approximation. For this reason we need to explain both of them.

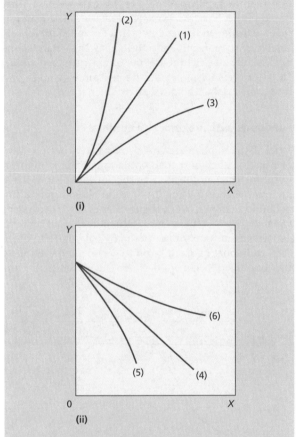

Figure 2.11 Positive and negative relationships

Y is positively related to X in all three curves in part (i) and negatively related in all three curves in part (ii). The lines on the two graphs show the response of Y to a change in X. In curves (1) and (4) this response is constant. In curves (2) and (5) the response is increasing as we move along the curve to the right. In curves (3) and (6) the response is diminishing.

Figure 2.12 relates a firm's monthly output and the revenue that it earns from selling that output. (We assume that the firm produces only as much as it can sell.) The monthly output is designated by Q. It is plotted on the horizontal or x-axis because it is the independent variable—the one that does the determining. The firm's total revenue is denoted by R. It is plotted on the vertical or y-axis because it is the dependent variable—the one that is determined.

This relationship can be expressed as a function, $R = f(Q)$. It can also be expressed on a graph, as line TR in Figure 2.12 shows.

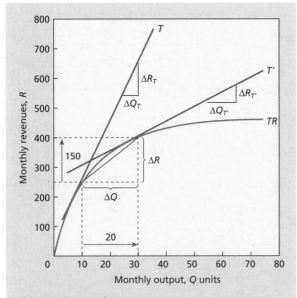

Figure 2.12 A total revenue curve

Total revenue *TR* rises at a diminishing rate, indicating decreasing marginal revenue. Incremental revenue when output goes from 10 to 30 is given by the ratio $\Delta R/\Delta Q$. True marginal revenue is given by the slope of the tangent *T* at 10 ($\Delta R_T/\Delta Q_T$). True marginal revenue at 30 is given by the slope of the tangent *T'* ($\Delta R_{T'}/\Delta Q_{T'}$).

The marginal concept that corresponds to this function is *marginal revenue*. Loosely speaking, it refers to the change in the firm's revenue when output is altered slightly from its present level. But what do we mean by 'altered slightly'? The answer depends on which marginal concept we use.

The approximation to marginal revenue is called the *incremental ratio*, which is the measure we have used so far. In Figure 2.12 let the firm be selling 10 units, with corresponding total revenue of £250. Now the firm decides to increase its output and sales to 30 units. Revenue rises along the *TR* curve to £400. The increase in sales is 20 units and the increase in revenue is £150. Using the Δ notation for changes, we can write this as

$$\Delta R/\Delta Q = £150/20 = £7.50.$$

Thus, incremental revenue is £7.50 per unit of additional sales when sales change from 10 to 30. This means that sales are increasing at an average rate of £7.50 per unit of commodity sold over the range from 10 to 30 units. We may call this the marginal revenue at 10 units of output, but, as we will see, it is only an approximation to the true marginal revenue at that output.

Graphically, as Figure 2.12 shows, incremental revenue is the slope of the line joining the two points in question. (In geometry the line joining two points on a curve is called a *chord*.) In this case the two points are on the revenue function corresponding to outputs of 10 and 30. Look at the

small triangle created by these points. Its base, shown by ΔQ, is 20 units in length and its vertical side, shown by ΔR, is 150 units in height. The slope of the line joining the two points (the hypotenuse of the triangle we are considering) is 150/20 = 7.50, which is the incremental revenue. Visually it is clear that this slope tells us the average gradient or steepness of the revenue function over the range from $Q = 10$ to $Q = 30$. It thus tells us how fast revenue is changing *on average* as output changes over the range of Q from 10 to 30.

Incremental revenue will be different at different points on the function. For example, when output goes from 30 units to 50 units, revenue goes from 400 to 450. Using these changes, we calculate the incremental revenue to be $\Delta R/\Delta Q = £50/20 = £2.50$. This calculation confirms what visual inspection of the figure suggests: the larger is output over the ranges graphed in the figure, the less is the response of revenue to further increases in output. Marginal revenue is positive but declining.

The incremental ratio is an approximation to the true marginal concept, which in the present case measures the tendency for R to change as Q changes at each precise point on the curve (whereas the incremental ratio measures the average tendency over a range of the curve). It is called the derivative of R with respect to Q. The value of this concept of marginal revenue is given by the mathematical procedure of differentiating the function relating R to Q. Geometrically, it is given by the slope of the tangent to the point on the function in which we are interested. Thus, the slope of the line T, which is the tangent to the curve at the point corresponding to 10 units of output, gives the 'true' marginal revenue at 10 units of output.[5] This slope is shown on the figure as $\Delta R_T/\Delta Q_T$, where the subscript T tells us that we are measuring this ratio along the line T. The slope of the line T' is indicated on the figure by the ratio $\Delta R_{T'}/\Delta Q_{T'}$. This tells us the precise marginal revenue at 30 units of output, the point at which T' is tangent to the TR curve. The appendix to this chapter discusses how to find this marginal concept using the tools of calculus.

Figure 2.12 shows that the incremental ratio declines as we measure it at larger and larger values of Q. It should be visually obvious that this is also true for true marginal revenue: the slope of the tangent to the function is smaller the larger is the value of Q at which the tangent is taken.

Now try measuring the incremental ratio starting at 10 units of output but for smaller and smaller changes in output. Instead of going from 10 to 30, go from 10 to 20. This brings the two points in question closer together, and in the present case it steepens the slope of the line joining

---

[5] Because of the thickness of the lines, the tangents in the figure sometimes seem to coincide with the curve over a range. It is of course impossible for a curve and a straight line to do this. The true tangents T and T' touch the curve TR at $Q = 10$ and $Q = 30$ respectively and lie above the curve for all other nearby values of Q.

them. It is visually clear in the present example that, as ΔQ is made smaller and smaller, the slope of the line corresponding to the incremental ratio starting from $Q = 10$ gets closer and closer to the slope of the tangent corresponding to the true marginal value evaluated at $Q = 10$. The degree of approximation of $\Delta R / \Delta Q$ to the slope of the tangent T is improving.

Now we can state our conclusions in general for the function $Y = f(X)$.

1. The marginal value of Y at some initial value of X is the rate of change of Y per unit change in X as X changes from its initial value.

2. The marginal value is given by the slope of the tangent to the curve graphing the function at the point corresponding to the initial value of X.

3. The incremental ratio $\Delta Y / \Delta X$ measures the average change in Y per unit change in X over a range of the function starting from the initial value of X.

4. As the range of measurement of the incremental ratio is reduced (i.e. as ΔX gets smaller and smaller), the value of the incremental ratio eventually approaches the true marginal value of Y. Thus, the incremental ratio may be regarded as an approximation to the true marginal value, the degree of approximation improving as ΔX gets very small.[6]

Moving between marginal and total values

We saw in a previous section that marginal revenue refers to the change in the total revenue as output changes. Figure 2.13(i) draws a new total revenue curve. Figure 2.13(ii) gives the corresponding marginal revenue curve.[7]

From totals to marginals

Assume that we have only the curve in part (i) of Figure 2.13, and that we wish to obtain the curve in part (ii). Mathematically the marginal curve is found by deriving the expression for the derivative of R with respect to Q and plotting it on a graph. Graphically, the curve is derived by measuring the slope of the tangent to the TR curve at each level of output and plotting the value of that slope against the same level of output in part (ii) of the figure. One example is shown in the figure. When output is 60 in part (i), the slope of the tangent to the curve is 40. This value of 40 is then plotted against output 60 in part (ii) of the figure. Looked at either as the slope of the tangent to the TR curve in part (i) or as the height of the MR curve in part (ii), this value tells us that revenue increases at a rate of 40 per unit increase in output when output is 60 units. Repeating this experiment, we could discover the marginal revenue corresponding to each point on the TR curve and plot each

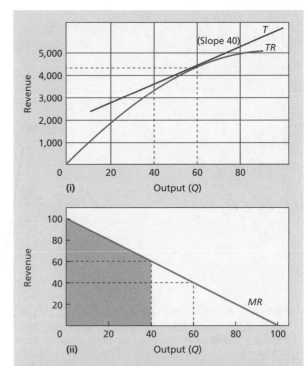

Figure 2.13 Total and marginal revenue curves

Total revenue rises at a diminishing rate, indicating positive but diminishing marginal revenue. In part (i) the slope of the tangent, T, to the TR curve at output 60 is 40. This is plotted in part (ii) as the marginal revenue at output 60. To reverse the procedure and go from marginal to total revenue, the area under the MR curve up to any point is summed, giving total revenue at that point. At output 40 the shaded area is 3,200, which is the total revenue.

value in part (ii). (Fortunately, calculus provides a simpler way of finding the marginal revenue in one step.)

From marginals to totals

Now let us assume that we have only the curve in part (ii) of the figure, and that we wish to derive the curve in part (i). In other words, we know the marginal revenue associated with any specific output and we wish to deduce the

[6] For those who already know some calculus, we must be careful how we state conclusion 4 since, on a wavy function, the degree of approximation may alternately improve and worsen as ΔX gets smaller; but, provided the conditions for a derivative to exist are met, there must be a small neighbourhood around the point in question within which the degree of approximation improves as ΔX gets smaller, with the 'error' going to zero as ΔX goes to zero.

[7] We have drawn a new curve because, in order to make the earlier points visually obvious, we needed a TR curve with a sharply diminishing slope, which we drew freehand. Now we want a TR curve for which we actually know the marginal values at each point. To do this, we take a curve with a specific algebraic formula. For the plotted curve we have chosen the formula $TR = 100Q - 0.5Q^2$.

Table 2.7 Total and marginal revenue associated with various levels of output

Output	Marginal revenue	Total revenue
1	£99.5	£99.5
2	98.5	198.0
3	97.5	295.5
4	96.5	392.0

Summing the marginal revenue yields the total revenue.

corresponding total revenue. This is an operation that is frequently employed in economics and you need to understand it.[8]

If we had a schedule of incremental ratios, all we would have to do is add up the necessary marginal values. This is illustrated in Table 2.7. For example, the total revenue when output is 3 units is calculated in the table as the sum of the contributions to total revenue of the first, second, and third units. This illustrates the fact that, if we know what each unit adds to total revenue, we can calculate the total revenue associated with any amount of output, say 10 units, by summing the separate contributions to revenue of each of the 10 units.

Mathematically, the same operation is done by integrating the function expressing the marginal curve to get the function expressing total curve. Graphically, the same operation is done on a continuous curve by calculating the area under the marginal curve from 0 to any given level of output. For example, at output 40 in part (ii) of Figure 2.13, the shaded area under the MC curve gives total revenue, which is 3,200. The value of this area is the height of the TR curve in part (i) at output 40.[9]

The common sense of this relationship is that the height of the MR curve at any given output tells us how much is being added to revenue by a change in output when output has the value in question. Adding all these heights, from zero to the output in question, means summing all the contributions to revenue from each unit of output from zero to the amount in question. On a continuous curve, this summation yields the area under the curve between zero and that output.

---

[8] We can do this for the revenue that is determined by output but not for any amount that is not. In this case, we can be sure that sales revenue is zero when output is zero so all revenue will be associated with output. But if the firms had other sources of revenue that were independent of output, we could not deduce these from the knowledge of how revenue varied with output. (This is a way of saying that integration is determined only up to an arbitrary constant.)

[9] You may notice that the scale on the vertical axis is different in the two figures. If we plotted MR on the same scale as TR you would hardly see it. Look where 100 would be plotted in part (i)! This is because the entire area in part (ii) is being related to the height of a line in part (i).

SUMMARY

Economic advice: positive and normative statements

- A key to the success of scientific inquiry lies in separating positive questions about the way the world works from normative questions about how one would like the world to work.

Economic theorizing

- Theories are designed to explain and predict what we see. A theory consists of a set of definitions of the variables to be employed, a set of assumptions about how things behave, and the conditions under which the theory is meant to apply.

- A theory provides conditional predictions of the type '*if* one event occurs, *then* another event will also occur'. An important method of testing theories is to confront their predictions with evidence.

- The term 'model' has a number of meanings, including (*a*) a synonym for theory, (*b*) a precise realization of a general theory, with a specific numerical relationship in place of each general relationship posited by the theory, (*c*) an application of a general theory to a specific case, and (*d*) a simplified set of relationships designed to study one specific force in isolation.

Economic data

- Index numbers express economic series in relative form. Values in each period are expressed in relation to the value in the base period, which is given a value of 100.

- Economic data may be graphed in three different ways. Cross-section graphs show observations taken at the same time. Time-series show observations on one variable taken over time. Scatter diagrams show points each one of which refers to specific observations on two different variables.

Graphing economic theories

- A functional relationship can be expressed in words, in a schedule giving specific values, in a mathematical equation, or in a graph.
- A graph of two variables has a positive slope when they both increase or decrease together and a negative slope when they move in opposite directions.

Measuring marginal values

- The marginal value of a variable gives the amount it changes in response to a change in a second variable. When the variable is measured on the vertical axis of a diagram, its marginal value is measured by the slope of the tangent line to the point in question and is approximated by the slope of the line joining two nearby points.

TOPICS FOR REVIEW

- Positive and normative statements
- Endogenous and exogenous variables
- Theories and models
- Variables, assumptions, and predictions
- Time-series and cross-sectional graphs and scatter diagrams
- Functional relationships

- Ways of expressing a relationship between two variables
- Positive and negative relationships between variables
- Positively and negatively sloped curves
- Marginal and incremental values
- Maximum and minimum values

DISCUSSION QUESTIONS

1 Which of the following statements are positive and which are normative?
   (a) The health of poor people is worse than the health of rich people.
   (b) Economic growth in sub-Saharan Africa is affected by the AIDS epidemic.
   (c) Rich countries should provide medicine more cheaply to Africa.
   (d) Protectionist policies in rich countries are hurting poor countries and should be abolished.

2 Draw graphs of the following relationships, where Y is on the vertical axis and X is on the horizontal axis.
   $Y = X$
   $Y = 10X$
   $Y = 0.5X$
   $Y = 100 + 3X$
   $Y = 100 + 3X^2$
   $Y = 100 - 4X$
   $Y = -100 + 4X$

3 The UK retail price index for the four years 1998–2001 was 160.6, 164.3, 170.3 and 171.3, where the base year was 1987 (that is, the RPI in 1987 = 100). Express the RPI for 1998–2001, using 1998 as the base year. If the RPI for 2002, using 1998 as the base year, were 109, what would be the 2002 RPI using 1987 as the base year?

4 A batsman in cricket has had five successive innings where he scored 100. He now scores 50, 20 and 0 in his next three innings. Explain what happens to his total run score for the season, his average score, and his marginal score after the fifth and each subsequent innings. Repeat the exercise using instead the next three scores of 120, 140 and 160. What relationship is revealed between the marginal score and the average?

5 Why does the distinction between a positive and a normative statement matter for economics?

6 Why do economists use models in order to help explain how the economy works?

7 Discuss the view that economic analysis cannot generate predictions because human behaviour is unpredictable.

8 Economists are often criticized for making simplifying assumptions or holding 'other things equal'. Discuss whether you think these criticisms are justified. (You may wish to return to this issue once you have finished the course.)

9 For those who know calculus, what is the mathematical equivalent of 'holding other things equal'?

Mathematical Appendix   The calculus of marginals and totals

In the text we considered several functions. When some variable Y is a function of another variable X, we can write

$$Y = f(X). \tag{A1}$$

For every given value of Y, this function gives us a corresponding value of X. The marginal value of Y is the rate at which Y is tending to change as X changes. Mathematically, this is the derivative of Y with respect to X. We can write

$$Marginal\ value\ of\ Y = dY/dX, \tag{A2}$$

or, in two other common alternative notations,

$$Marginal\ value\ of\ Y = f'(X),$$
$$Marginal\ value\ of\ Y = f_x.$$

If we have only the marginal relationship in (A2), we can derive the relationship of total Y to total X in (A1) up to an arbitrary constant by integrating the marginal function:

$$Y = \int f'(X)dX + C, \tag{A3}$$

where C is the constant of integration.

Consider an example. Let the function be a quadratic:

$$Y = a + bX + cX^2, \quad c < 0 < a,\ b. \tag{A4}$$

The graph of this relationship will show Y rising up to some maximum value and then falling as X increases further.

The marginal value of Y is

$$dY/dX = b + 2cX. \tag{A5}$$

Since $c < 0$, the graph of this marginal relationship is a negatively sloped straight line, starting at the positive value of b when X is zero. This tells us that the increment to Y is positive as X increased from 0 but falls steadily and eventually becomes negative. Where the marginal value is positive the graph of the original relationship is positively sloped, and where it is negative the graph of the original line is negatively sloped.

Letting the values of the parameters be $a = 10$, $b = 2$ and $c = -0.1$, we have

$$Y = 10 + 2X - 0.1X^2. \tag{A6}$$

The marginal value of Y is then given by

$$dY/dX = 2 - 0.2X,$$

which is zero at $X = 10$, positive for smaller X, and negative for larger X. This shows that increments to X up to 10 cause Y to increase while they cause Y to decrease when X exceeds 10.

If all we knew was the marginal revenue relationship of equation (A5), we could determine the total value of Y as

$$Y = \int (2 - 0.2X)dX = 2X - 0.1X^2 + C. \tag{A7}$$

Since the original constant of $a = 10$ in equation (A4) disappears on differentiation, integration can only put back an arbitrary constant, C. In other words, there is no way we can discover the value of the original constant, a. But we can find the equation of the relationship between X and Y and know its shape except for an arbitrary parameter that shifts points on it upwards or downwards by a constant amount.

MICROECONOMICS

 PART ONE

AN INTRODUCTION TO THE MARKET ECONOMY

Chapter 3

DEMAND, SUPPLY, AND PRICE

Why does the price of computers keep falling while house prices keep rising? This is a question about how different markets work and what factors influence the outcome. To answer it we need to understand the functioning of markets. This is one of the most important topics in economics. You will see that we can go a long way in understanding how markets work with some very simple tools. In particular, you will learn about

- The participants in markets and what motivates them

- The main factors that influence how much of a product consumers wish to buy

- The main influences on how much producers wish to sell

- How consumers and producers interact to determine the market price

- You will also learn that, while demand and supply forces are present in all markets, many different institutional structures also affect market outcomes.

Growers of crops come to a town to sell their produce in farmers' markets. High street stores stock a wide range of goods for individuals to buy. Commodity markets determine world-wide prices for products such as oil, copper, and wheat. Potential buyers or renters of housing units deal with sellers of houses or landlords in housing markets. Workers sell their services to employers in labour markets.

Indeed, a market exists whenever buyers and sellers exchange goods or services—usually for money.

Markets do not necessarily happen in one place. The housing markets and the labour market operate throughout the country. The stock market and the foreign exchange market operate globally using computers and telephones. The book market works partly through bookshops and partly by internet or mail order.

We need to understand all of these different types of market. But we start by focusing on a market in which the buyers or demanders are households and the suppliers or producers are firms. The product whose market we analyse is a good that has a physical existence, so it has to be grown or made by the producing firm. Any person who makes decisions relevant to our theory is called an **agent**. To make the study of their behaviour more manageable, we deal with just three types of agent: individuals, firms, and government. In this chapter you will encounter individuals as demanders and firms as suppliers. In a later chapter, when we study the labour market, you will find individuals supplying and firms demanding. Governments also play a role in some markets either as producers or demanders. They can also intervene in markets by taxing transactions (with a sales tax, a value added tax, or an excise tax) or by imposing regulations that impose maximum or minimum prices. In this chapter and the next we ignore the potential role of governments, but we shall return to it later.

Demand

Individuals and motives

In formulating our demand theory, the agents are all assumed to be adult individuals who earn income, and they spend this income purchasing various goods and services.[1]

In economics it is generally assumed that each individual consumer seeks maximum *satisfaction*, or *well-being*, or *utility*, as the concept is variously called. The consumer

'maximizes utility' within the limits set by his or her available resources. Utility cannot be observed directly, but we

[1] When real-world data are studied, the spending unit analysed is often not the individual but the household. A household is defined as all the people who live under one roof and who make joint financial decisions or are subject to others who make such decisions for them. For purposes of developing the elementary theory of market behaviour, however, we view consumers as individuals.

only need to assume that typical consumers know what they like, and make spending choices that give them as much personal satisfaction as possible.

The nature of demand

The amount of a product that consumers wish to purchase is called the **quantity demanded**. There are two important points about this concept. First, quantity demanded is a *desired* quantity. It is how much consumers *wish* to purchase, not necessarily how much they actually succeed in purchasing. We use phrases such as **quantity actually purchased** or **quantity actually bought and sold** to distinguish actual purchases from quantity demanded. Second, the quantity demanded is a *flow*. We are concerned not with a single isolated purchase, but with a continuous flow of purchases. We must, therefore, express demand as so much per period of time—e.g. 1 million oranges *per day*, or 7 million oranges *per week*, or 365 million oranges *per year*. The important distinction between stocks and flows is discussed in Box 3.1.

The concept of demand as a flow appears to raise difficulties when we deal with the purchases of durable consumer goods (often called 'consumer durables'). It makes obvious sense to talk about a person consuming oranges at the rate

---

of 30 per month, but what can we say of a consumer who buys a new television set every five years? This apparent difficulty disappears if we measure the demand for the *services* provided by the consumer durable. Thus, at the rate of a new set every five years, the television purchaser is using the service (viewing TV programmes) at the rate of 1/60 of a set per month.

The determinants of quantity demanded: the demand function

Five main variables influence the quantity of each product that is demanded by each individual consumer:

1. The price of the product
2. The prices of other products
3. The consumer's income and wealth
4. The consumer's tastes
5. Various individual–specific or environmental factors

Making use of the functional notation that was introduced in Chapter 2, the above list is conveniently summarized in what is called a **demand function**:

$$q_n^d = D(p_n, p_1, \ldots, p_{n-1}, Y, S).$$

The term q_n^d stands for the quantity that the consumer demands of some product, which we call product n. The term p_n stands for the price of this product, while $p_1, \ldots, p_{n-1}$ is a shorthand notation for the prices of all other products. The term Y is the consumer's income (including income from assets). The term S stands for a host of factors that will vary from individual to individual, such as age, number of children, place of residence (e.g. big city, small town, country), and other assets. (Car owners for example will demand petrol while non-car owners will demand train tickets.) There are also some environmental factors that will affect demand patterns, such as the state of the weather and the time of year. We need to remember that these factors matter in real markets, but they are not central to our current analysis. Finally, the form of the function D is determined by the tastes of the consumer.

The demand function is just a shorthand way of saying that quantity demanded, which is on the left-hand side, depends on the variables that are listed on the right-hand side. The form of the function determines the nature of that dependence. (Recall that the 'form of the function' refers to the precise quantitative relation between the variables on the right-hand side of the equation and the variables on the left.)

We will not be able to understand the separate influences of each of the above variables if we ask what happens when everything changes at once. To avoid this difficulty, we consider the influence of the variables one at a time.

Box 3.1 Stocks and flows

Economics makes extensive use of both stock and flow variables and it is important not to confuse the two. A *flow variable* has a time dimension: it is so much per unit of time. The quantity of free-range eggs purchased in Glasgow is a flow variable. Being told that the number purchased was 2,000 dozen eggs conveys no useful information unless we are also told the period of time over which these purchases occurred. For example, 2,000 dozen per hour would indicate an active market in eggs, while 2,000 dozen per month would indicate a sluggish market.

A *stock variable* has no time dimension: it is just so much. Thus, the number of eggs in an egg producer's warehouse—for example 20,000 dozen eggs—is a stock variable. All those eggs are there at one time, and they remain there until something happens to change the stock held by the producer. The stock variable is just a number, not a rate of flow of so much per day or per month.

Economic theories use both flow variables and stock variables, and it takes a little practice to keep them straight. The amount of income earned is a flow—so much *per* year or *per* month or *per* hour. The amount of a consumer's expenditure is also a flow—so much spent *per* week or *per* month. In contrast, the amount of money in your bank account is a stock—just so many pounds sterling. The key test for a variable being a flow is that a time dimension is required to give it meaning. Other variables are neither stocks nor flows: they are just numbers, for example the price of eggs.

the law of demand:
the lower price of Product
the larger quantity of demand

CHAPTER 3: DEMAND, SUPPLY, AND PRICE   41

To do this, we use a device that is frequently employed in economic theory. We assume that all except one of the variables on the right-hand side of the above expression are held constant. Then we allow this one variable, say p_n, to change and see how the quantity demanded (q_n^d) changes. We are then studying the effect of changes in one influence on quantity demanded, *assuming that all other influences remain unchanged*, or, as economists are fond of putting it, **ceteris paribus** (which means 'other things being equal').

We can do the same for each of the other variables in turn, and in this way we can come to understand the effect of each variable. Once this is done, we can add up the separate influences of each variable to discover what will happen when several variables change at the same time—as they often do in practice.

Demand and price

We are interested in developing a theory of how products get priced. To do this, we hold all other influences constant and ask, 'How will the quantity of a product demanded vary as its own price varies?'

A basic economic hypothesis is that the lower the price of a product, the larger the quantity that will be demanded, other things being equal.

This negative relationship between the price of a product and quantity demanded is sometimes referred to as the **law of demand.** Why might this law be true? A major reason is that there is usually more than one product that will satisfy any given desire or need. Hunger may be satisfied by meat or vegetables; a desire for green vegetables may be satisfied by broccoli or spinach. The need to keep warm at night may be satisfied by several woollen blankets, or one electric blanket, or a sheet and a lot of oil burned in the boiler. The desire for a holiday may be satisfied by a trip to the Scottish Highlands or to the Swiss Alps, the need to get there by an aeroplane, a bus, a car, or a train; and so on. Name any general desire or need, and there will usually be several products that will contribute to its satisfaction.

Now consider what happens if we hold income, tastes, population, and the prices of all other products constant and vary the price of only one product.

First, let the price of the product rise. The product then becomes a more expensive way of satisfying a want. Some consumers will stop buying it altogether; others will buy smaller amounts; still others may continue to buy the same amount; but no rational consumer will buy more of it. Because many consumers will switch wholly, or partially, to other products to satisfy the same want, less will be bought of the product whose price has risen. For example, as meat becomes more expensive, consumers may switch some of their expenditure to meat substitutes; they may also forgo meat at some meals and eat less meat at others.

Second, let the price of a product fall. This makes the product a cheaper method of satisfying any given want. Consumers will buy more of it and less of other similar products whose prices have not fallen. These other products have become expensive *relative to* the product in question. For example, when a bumper tomato harvest drives prices down, shoppers buy more tomatoes and fewer other salad ingredients, which have now become relatively more expensive than tomatoes.

The demand schedule and the demand curve

An individual's demand A **demand schedule** is one way of showing the relationship between quantity demanded and price. It is a numerical tabulation that shows the quantity that will be demanded at some selected prices.

Table 3.1 shows one consumer's demand schedule for eggs. Alice often eats boiled eggs for breakfast, and, living on her own, she often finds omelettes a convenient evening meal. But she does not have a lot of money, so she keeps an eye on the price of eggs when she does her weekly supermarket shopping. The table shows the quantity of eggs that she wishes to buy each month at six selected prices. For example, at a price of £1.50 per dozen Alice demands 3.5 dozen per month. For easy reference, each of the price–quantity combinations in the table is given a letter.

Next we plot the data from Table 3.1 in Figure 3.1, with price on the vertical axis and quantity on the horizontal axis.[2] The smooth curve drawn through these points is called the demand curve. It shows the quantity that Alice would like to buy at every possible price; its *negative slope* indicates that the quantity demanded increases as the price falls.

A single point on the demand curve indicates a single price–quantity relationship. *The whole demand curve shows the complete relationship between quantity demanded and price.* Economists often speak of the conditions of demand in a particular market as 'given' or as 'known'. When they do so

---

[2] Readers trained in other disciplines often wonder why economists plot demand curves with price on the vertical axis. The normal convention, which puts the independent variable (the variable that does the explaining) on the horizontal axis and the dependent variable (the variable that is explained) on the vertical axis, calls for price to be plotted on the horizontal axis and quantity on the vertical axis. The axis reversal—now enshrined by a century of usage—arose as follows. The analysis of the competitive market that we use today stems from the French economist Leon Walras (1834–1910), in whose theory *quantity* was the dependent variable. Graphical analysis in economics, however, was popularized by the English economist Alfred Marshall (1842–1924), in whose theory *price* was the dependent variable. Economists continue to use Walras's theory and Marshall's graphical representation, and thus draw the diagram with the independent and dependent variables reversed—to the everlasting confusion of readers trained in other disciplines. In virtually every other graph in economics the axes are labelled conventionally, with the dependent variable on the vertical axis.

Table 3.1 Alice's demand schedule for eggs

Reference letter	Price (£ per dozen)	Quantity demanded (dozen per month)
a	0.50	7.0
b	1.00	5.0
c	1.50	3.5
d	2.00	2.5
e	2.50	1.5
f	3.00	1.0

The table shows the quantity of eggs that Alice demands at each selected price, other things being equal. For example, at a price of £1.00 per dozen she demands 5 dozen per month, while at a price of £2.50 per dozen she demands only 1.5 dozen.

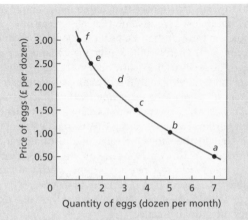

Figure 3.1 Alice's demand curve

This curve relates the price of a commodity to the amount that Alice wishes to purchase. Each point on the figure relates to a row in Table 3.1. For example, when the price is £3.00, 1 dozen eggs are bought per month (point f), while when the price is £0.50, 7 dozen are bought (point a).

they are referring not just to the particular quantity that is being demanded at the moment (i.e. not just to a particular point on the demand curve), but to the whole demand curve. The whole demand curve remains in one place so long as all variables other than the price of the product itself remain unchanged.

The market demand curve So far we have discussed how the quantity of a product demanded by one consumer depends on the price of the product, other things being equal. To explain market behaviour, we need to know the total demand of all consumers. To obtain a market demand schedule, we sum the quantities demanded by each consumer at a particular price to obtain the total quantity demanded at that price. We repeat the process for each price to obtain a schedule of total, or market, demand at all possible prices. A graph of this schedule is called the *market demand curve*.

To avoid unnecessary complication, Figure 3.2 illustrates the summation graphically for only two consumers, Sarah and William. The figure illustrates the proposition that the market demand curve is the horizontal sum of the demand curves of *all* the individuals who buy in the market.

In practice, our knowledge of market demand is usually derived by observing total quantities of sales directly. The derivation of market demand curves by summing individual curves is a theoretical operation. We do it to understand the relation between curves for individual consumers and market curves.

In Table 3.2 we assume that we have data for the market demand for eggs. The schedule tells us the total quantity

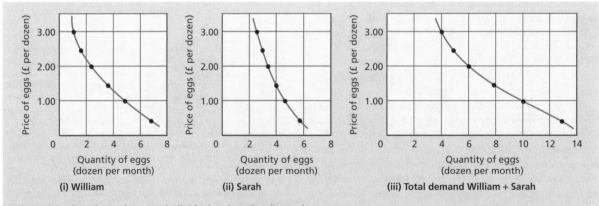

Figure 3.2 The relation between individual and market demand curves

The market demand curve is the horizontal sum of the demand curves of all consumers in the market. The figure illustrates aggregation over two individuals, William and Sarah. For example, at a price of £2.00 per dozen William purchases 2.4 dozen eggs and Sarah purchases 3.6 dozen, a total of 6 dozen.

Table 3.2 A market demand schedule for eggs

Reference letter	Price (£ per dozen)	Quantity demanded ('000 dozen per month)
U	0.50	110.0
V	1.00	90.0
W	1.50	77.5
X	2.00	67.5
Y	2.50	62.5
Z	3.00	60.0

The table shows the quantity of eggs that would be demanded by all consumers at selected prices, *ceteris paribus*. For example, row W indicates that if the price of eggs were £1.50 per dozen, consumers would want to purchase 77,500 dozen per month.

Table 3.3 Two alternative market demand schedules for eggs

	Price of eggs (£ per dozen)	Quantity of eggs demanded at original level of personal income ('000 dozen per month)	Quantity of eggs demanded when personal income rises to new level ('000 dozen per month)	
(1)	(2)	(3)	(4)	(5)
U	0.50	110.0	140.0	U'
V	1.00	90.0	116.0	V'
W	1.50	77.5	100.8	W'
X	2.00	67.5	90.0	X'
Y	2.50	62.5	81.3	Y'
Z	3.00	60.0	78.0	Z'

An increase in total consumers' income increases the quantity demanded at each price. When income rises, quantity demanded at a price of £1.50 per dozen rises from 77,500 dozen per month to 100,800 dozen per month. A similar rise occurs at every other price. Thus the demand schedule relating columns (2) and (3) is replaced by the one relating columns (2) and (4). The graphical representations of these two schedules are labelled D_0 and D_1 in Figure 3.4.

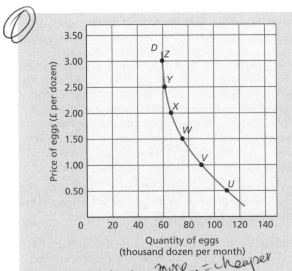

Figure 3.3 A market demand curve for eggs

The negative slope of the curve indicates that quantity demanded increases as price falls. The six points correspond to the six price–quantity combinations shown in Table 3.2. The curve drawn through all of the points and labelled D is the demand curve.

that will be demanded by all buyers of that product at selected market prices. The data are plotted in Figure 3.3, and the curve drawn through these points is the market demand curve.

Market demand: a recap

We now summarize what we have learned about demand.

The total quantity demanded depends on the price of the product being sold, on the prices of all other products, on the incomes of the individuals buying in that market, and on their tastes. The market demand curve relates the total quantity demanded to the product's own price, on the assumption that all other prices, total income, tastes, and all other environmental factors are held constant.

Shifts in the demand curve

The demand schedule and the demand curve are constructed on the assumption of *ceteris paribus* (other things held constant). But what if other things change, as surely they must? What, for example, if consumers find themselves with more income? If they spend their extra income, they will buy additional quantities of many products *even though market prices are unchanged*, as shown in Table 3.3. But if consumers increase their purchases of any product whose price has not changed, the new purchases cannot be represented by the original demand curve. The rise in consumer income *shifts* the demand curve to the right, as shown in Figure 3.4. This shift illustrates the operation of an important general rule.

A demand curve shifts to a new position in response to a change in any of the variables that were held constant when the original curve was drawn.

Any change that increases the quantity of a product that consumers wish to buy at each price will shift the demand curve to the right, and any change that decreases the quantity consumers wish to buy at each price will shift the demand curve to the left.

Changes in other prices We saw that demand curves have negative slopes because the lower a product's price, the

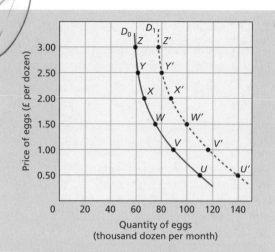

Figure 3.4 Two demand curves for eggs

The rightward shift in the demand curve from D_0 to D_1 indicates an increase in the quantity demanded at each price. The lettered points correspond to those in Table 3.3. When the curve shifts from D_0 to D_1, more is demanded at each price and a higher price is paid for each quantity. For example, at the price of £1.50 the quantity demanded rises from 77,500 dozen (point W) to 100,800 dozen (point W'); while the quantity of 90,000 dozen, which was formerly bought at a price of £1.00 (point V), will be bought at a price of £2.00 after the shift (point X').

cheaper it becomes relative to other products that can satisfy the same needs. Those other products are called **substitutes**. A product becomes cheaper relative to its substitutes if its own price falls. This also happens if the substitute's price rises. For example, eggs can become cheap relative to pizzas either because the price of eggs falls or because the price of pizzas rises. Either change will increase the amount of eggs that consumers are prepared to buy. For example, Alice may eat more omelettes and fewer pizzas whenever she wants a quick meal.

A rise in the price of a product's substitute shifts the demand curve for the product to the right. More will be purchased at each price.

Thus, a rise in the price of pizzas may shift the demand curve for eggs from D_0 to D_1 in Figure 3.4, just as did a rise in income.

Products that tend to be used jointly with each other are called **complements**. Cars and petrol are complements; so are golf clubs and golf balls, bacon and eggs, electric cookers and electricity, an aeroplane trip to Austria and tickets on the ski lifts at St Anton. Since complements tend to be consumed together, a fall in the price of either will increase the demand for both. For example, a fall in the price of cars that causes more people to become car owners will, *ceteris paribus*, increase the demand for petrol.

A fall in the price of one product that is complementary to a second product will shift the second product's demand curve to the right. More will be purchased at each price.

Changes in total income If consumers receive more income, they can be expected to purchase more of most products even though product prices remain the same. Such a shift is illustrated in Table 3.3 and Figure 3.4. A product whose demand increases when income increases is called a **normal good**.

A rise in consumers' incomes shifts the demand curve for normal products to the right, indicating that more will be demanded at each possible price.

For a few products, called **inferior goods**, a rise in consumers' income leads them to reduce their purchases (because they can now afford to switch to a more expensive, but superior, substitute).

A rise in income will shift the demand for **inferior goods** to the left, indicating that less will be demanded at each price.

The distribution of income If total income and all other determinants of demand are held constant while the distribution of income changes (i.e. some people become richer and others become poorer), the demand for normal goods will rise for consumers gaining income and fall for consumers losing income. If both gainers and losers buy a good in similar proportions, these changes will tend to cancel out. This will not, however, always be the case.

When the distribution of income changes, demands will rise for those goods favoured by those gaining income and fall for those goods favoured by those losing income.

Individual characteristics Changes in the characteristics of the individuals who make up the market will cause demand curves to shift. For example, a reduction in the typical number of children per family, as happened in the twentieth century, will reduce the demands for the things used by children or in childcare. If the number of retired people increases, there will be a rise in the demands for goods consumed during leisure times.

Environmental factors Demand for some products is different at different times of year. Some of this is due to weather; for example, demand for electricity is higher in the winter when days are short and the weather is cold,[3] and demand for cold lager and ice cream is higher in the summer during hot weather. Other variations may be due to traditions associated with annual festivals, such as buying presents at Christmas, or to the timing of school holidays. From the point of view of our theory of demand, these are exogenous forces, things that lie outside the

---

[3] In some hot countries, demand for electricity may be even greater in summer than in winter owing to the use of air-conditioners.

Box 3.2 Weather matters

Other things than price and incomes do influence demand, and sellers have to keep abreast of these non-economic causes—which have distinct economic effects.

A recent article in the *Guardian* newspaper quotes a person responsible for getting groceries to the stores at the right time and in the right quantities on the effects of a sudden turn in the weather from cold to hot: 'The trigger point is 80 degrees, especially if it is sustained for more than three days. For products such as ice-cream, soft drinks, and salads, sales can rise by between 70 and 225 per cent on a big change in temperature.' As a result of a sudden upturn in the weather, he had recently had to organize another million cases of soft drinks and additional lorry loads of salad and other fast-selling products 'if the shelves [were] not to be bare by lunchtime'.

Here are some of the ways in which the article said the weather affects UK demand:

- Drink sales respond immediately to temperature change.

- After two days of good weather we might think about buying a bike, but it has to be nice for more than a week before we start buying suntan lotion.

- Curiously, hot weather increases the sales of plain coleslaw much more than coleslaw with pineapple.

- Soft drink sales depend not only on heat but also on humidity.

- Rain and mild temperatures suit insurers best—we drive less and so have fewer and less serious prangs.

- Builders like storms—they interrupt work but generate huge volumes of business repairing and replacing roofs.

- Every one degree colder adds 4 per cent to gas demand and increases electricity demand by about 5,000 megawatts—enough to supply the whole of Sheffield.

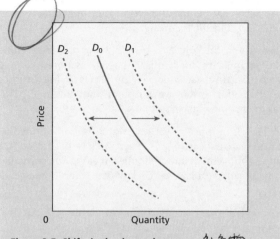

Figure 3.5 Shifts in the demand curve

A shift in the demand curve from D_0 to D_1 indicates an increase in demand; a shift from D_0 to D_2 indicates a decrease in demand. An increase in demand can be caused by a rise in the price of a substitute, a fall in the price of a complement, a rise in income, a redistribution of income towards groups who favour the commodity, or a change in tastes that favours the commodity.

A decrease in demand can be caused by a fall in the price of a substitute, a rise in the price of a complement, a fall in income, a redistribution of income away from groups who favour the commodity, or a change in tastes that disfavours the commodity.

Movements along demand curves versus shifts

Suppose you read in today's newspaper that carrot prices have soared because more carrots are being demanded, perhaps following a report that carrot consumption gives protection against some disease. Then tomorrow you read that the rising price of carrots is greatly reducing the typical consumer's demand for carrots as shoppers switch to potatoes, courgettes, and peas. The two statements appear to contradict each other. The first associates a rising price with a rising demand; the second associates a rising price with a declining demand. Can both statements be true? The answer is that they can be, because they refer to different things. The first refers to a *shift* in the demand curve; the second refers to a movement *along a* demand curve in response to a change in price.

Consider first the statement that the increase in the price of carrots has been caused by an increased demand for carrots. This statement refers to a shift in the demand curve for carrots. In this case, the demand curve must have shifted to the right, indicating more carrots demanded at each price. This shift will, as we will see later in this chapter, increase the price of carrots.

Now consider the statement that fewer carrots are being bought because carrots have become more expensive. This refers to a movement along a given demand curve and reflects a change between two specific quantities being bought, one before the price rose and one afterwards.

theory, affecting demand, sometimes greatly, but not themselves being explained by the theory. Box 3.2 illustrates the major influence that weather can exert on demand.

Changes in tastes If there is a change in tastes in favour of a product, more will be demanded at each price, causing the demand curve to shift to the right. In contrast, if there is a change in tastes away from a product, less will be demanded at each price, causing the entire demand curve to shift to the left.

Figure 3.5 summarizes our discussion of the causes of shifts in the demand curve. Notice that, since we are generalizing beyond our example of eggs, we have relabelled our axes 'price' and 'quantity', dropping the qualification 'of eggs'. The term *quantity* should be understood to mean quantity per period in whatever units the goods are measured. The term *price* should be understood to mean the price measured in pounds per unit of quantity for the same product.

So what lay behind the two stories might have been something like the following.

1. A rise in the perceived health-giving properties shifts the demand curve for carrots to the right as more and more are demanded at each price. This in turn is raising the price of carrots (for reasons we will soon study in detail). This was the first newspaper story.

2. The rising price of carrots is causing each individual consumer to cut back on his or her purchase of carrots. This causes a movement upward to the left along any particular demand curve for carrots. This was the second newspaper story.

To prevent the type of confusion caused by our two newspaper stories, economists have developed a specific vocabulary to distinguish shifts of curves from movements along curves. **Demand** refers to one *whole* demand curve. **Change in demand** refers to a *shift* in the whole curve, that is, a change in the amount that will be bought at *every* price.

An increase in demand means that the whole demand curve has shifted to the right; a decrease in demand means that the whole demand curve has shifted to the left.

Any one point on a demand curve represents a specific amount being bought at a specified price. It represents, therefore, a particular quantity demanded. A movement along a demand curve is referred to as a **change in the quantity demanded**.

A movement down a demand curve is called an increase (or a rise) in the quantity demanded; a movement up the demand curve is called a decrease (or a fall) in the quantity demanded.

To illustrate this terminology, look again at Table 3.3. First, at the original level of income, a decrease in price from £2.00 to £1.50 increases *the quantity demanded* from 67,500 to 77,500 dozen a month. Second, the increase in average consumer income *increases demand* from what is shown by column (3) to what is shown by column (4). The same contrast is shown in Figure 3.4, where a fall in price from £2.00 to £1.50 increases the quantity demanded from the quantity shown by point X to the quantity shown by point W. An increase in total consumers' income increases demand from curve D_0 to curve D_1.

Supply

We now look at the supply side of markets. The suppliers are **firms**, which are in business to make the goods and services that consumers want to buy.

Firms' motives

Economic theory gives firms several attributes.

First, each firm is assumed to make consistent decisions, as though it were run by a single individual decision-maker. This allows the firm to be treated as the agent on the production or supply side of product markets, just as the consumer is treated as the individual unit of behaviour on the consumption or demand side.

Second, firms hire workers and invest capital and entrepreneurial talent in order to produce goods and services that consumers wish to buy. (There are some markets in which firms sell to other firms, or the government, and in the labour market individuals sell their services to firms. But here we focus on consumer goods markets for simplicity.)

Third, firms are assumed to make their decisions with a single goal in mind: to make as much profit as possible. This goal of *profit maximization* is analogous to the consumer's goal of utility maximization.

The nature of supply

The amount of a product that firms are able and willing to offer for sale is called the **quantity supplied**. Supply is a desired flow: how much firms are *willing* to sell per period of time, not how much they actually sell.

Here we make a start on analysis of supply, establishing only what is necessary for a theory of price. In later chapters we study the behaviour of individual firms, and then aggregate individual behaviour to obtain the behaviour of market supply. For present purposes, however, it is sufficient to go directly to market supply, the aggregate behaviour of all the firms in a particular market.

The determinants of quantity supplied: the supply function

Three major determinants of the quantity supplied in a particular market are:

1. The price of the product
2. The prices of inputs to production
3. The state of technology

This list can be summarized in a **supply function;** *shorthand*

$$q_n^s = S(p_n, F_1, \ldots, F_m),$$

where q_n^s is the quantity supplied of product n; p_n is the price of that product; $F_1, \ldots, F_m$ is shorthand for the prices of all inputs into production; and the state of technology determines the form of the function S. (Recall, once again, that the form of the function refers to the precise quantitative relation between the variables on the right-hand side of the equation and the one on the left.)

Supply and price

For a simple theory of price, we need to know how quantity supplied varies with a product's own price, all other things being held constant. We are concerned, therefore, only with the *ceteris paribus* relation, $q_n^s = S(p_n)$. We will have much to say in later chapters about this relationship. For the moment, it is sufficient to state the hypothesis that, *ceteris paribus, the quantity of any product that firms will produce and offer for sale is positively related to the product's own price, rising when price rises and falling when price falls.*

In Chapter 10 we derive this hypothesis from basic assumptions about the firm's behaviour. In the meantime, all we need to note is that the basic reason behind this relationship is the way in which costs behave as output changes. Typically, the cost of increasing output by another unit tends to be higher the higher is the existing rate of output. So, for example, if the firm is already producing 100 units per week, the cost of increasing output to 101 units per week might be £1, while if 200 units were already being produced, the cost of increasing output to 201 units might be £2. Clearly, the firm will not find it profitable to increase output if it cannot at least cover the additional costs that are incurred. As the price of the product rises, the firm can cover the rising costs of more and more additional units of output. As a result, higher and higher prices are needed to induce firms to make successive increases in output. The result is a positive association between market price and the firm's output. Do not worry if this does not seem obvious; we set out a stronger justification in Chapter 10.

The **supply schedule** given in Table 3.4 is analogous to the demand schedule in Table 3.2. It records the quantity all producers wish to produce and sell at a number of alternative prices, rather than the quantity consumers wish to buy.

The six points corresponding to the six price/quantity combinations shown in the table are plotted in Figure 3.6. The curve drawn through the six points is a **supply curve** for eggs. It shows the quantity produced and offered for sale at each price.[4]

The supply curve in Figure 3.6 has a positive slope. This is a graphical expression of the following assumption:

The market price and the quantity supplied are positively related to each other.

Table 3.4 A market supply schedule for eggs

Reference letter	Price (£ per dozen)	Quantity supplied ('000 dozen per month)
u	0.50	5.0
v	1.00	46.0
w	1.50	77.5
x	2.00	100.0
y	2.50	115.0
z	3.00	122.5

The table shows the quantities that producers wish to sell at various prices, *ceteris paribus*. For example, row *y* indicates that if the price were £2.50 per dozen, producers would wish to sell 115,000 dozen eggs per month.

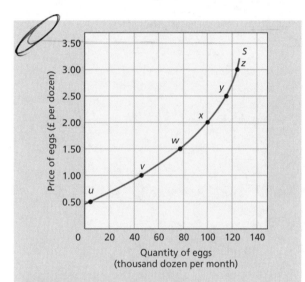

Figure 3.6 A supply curve for eggs

This supply curve relates quantity of eggs supplied to the price of eggs; its positive slope indicates that quantity supplied increases as price increases. The six points correspond to the price–quantity combinations shown in Table 3.4. The curve drawn through these points, labelled *S*, is the supply curve.

Shifts in the supply curve

A shift in the supply curve means that, at each price, a different quantity is supplied. An increase in the quantity supplied at each price is illustrated in Table 3.5 and plotted in Figure 3.7. This change appears as a rightward shift in

[4] Since we are not considering individual firms in this chapter, all supply curves are market curves showing the aggregate behaviour of the firms in the market. Where that is obvious from the context, the adjective 'market' is usually omitted.

Table 3.5 Two alternative market supply schedules for eggs

	Price of eggs (£ per dozen)	Original quantity supplied ('000 dozen per month)	New quantity supplied ('000 dozen per month)	
(1)	(2)	(3)	(4)	(5)
u	0.50	5.0	28.0	u'
v	1.00	46.0	76.0	v'
w	1.50	77.5	102.0	w'
x	2.00	100.0	120.0	x'
y	2.50	115.0	132.0	y'
z	3.00	122.5	140.0	z'

An increase in supply means a larger quantity is supplied at each price. For example, the quantity that is supplied at £2.50 per dozen rises from 115,000 dozen to 132,000 dozen per month. A similar rise occurs at every price. Thus the supply schedule relating columns (2) and (3) is replaced by the one relating columns (2) and (4)

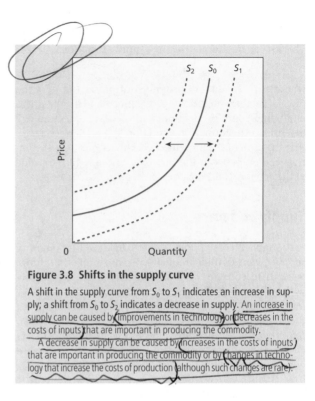

Figure 3.8 Shifts in the supply curve
A shift in the supply curve from S_0 to S_1 indicates an increase in supply; a shift from S_0 to S_2 indicates a decrease in supply. An increase in supply can be caused by improvements in technology or decreases in the costs of inputs that are important in producing the commodity. A decrease in supply can be caused by increases in the costs of inputs that are important in producing the commodity or by changes in technology that increase the costs of production (although such changes are rare).

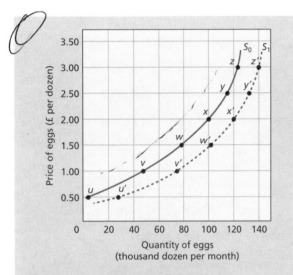

Figure 3.7 Two supply curves for eggs
The rightward shift in the supply curve from S_0 to S_1 indicates an increase in the quantity supplied at each price. For example, at the price of £1.00 the quantity supplied rises from 46,000 dozen to 76,000 dozen per month.

The major possible causes of such shifts are summarized in the caption of Figure 3.8 and are considered briefly below.

Prices of inputs All things that a firm uses to produce its outputs—such as, in the case of an egg producer, chicken feed, labour, and egg-sorting machines—are called the firm's *inputs*. Other things being equal, the higher the price of any input used to make a product, the less will be the profit from making that product. Thus, the higher the price of any input used by a firm, the lower will be the amount that the firm will produce and offer for sale at any given price of the product.

A rise in the price of any input shifts the supply curve to the left, indicating that less will be supplied at any given price; a fall in the price of inputs shifts the supply curve to the right.

Technology At any time, what is produced and how it is produced depend on the technologies in use. Over time, knowledge and production technologies change; so do the quantities of individual products that can be supplied.

A technological change that decreases costs will increase the profits earned at any given price of the product. Since increased profitability leads to increased production, this change shifts the supply curve to the right, indicating an increased willingness to produce the product and offer it for sale at each possible price.

Movements along supply curves versus shifts

As with demand, it is essential to distinguish between a movement along the supply curve (caused by a change in

the supply curve. A decrease in the quantity supplied at each price causes a leftward shift.

For supply-curve shifts there is an important general rule similar to the one stated earlier for demand curves:

When there is a change in any of the variables (other than the product's own price) that affect the amount of a product that firms are willing to produce and sell, the whole supply curve for that product will shift.

the product's own price) and a shift of the whole curve (caused by a change in something other than the product's own price). We adopt the same terminology as with demand: **quantity supplied** refers to a particular quantity actually supplied at a particular price of the product, and **supply** refers to the whole relation between price and quantity supplied. Thus, when we speak of an *increase* or a *decrease in supply*, we are referring to shifts in the supply curve such as those illustrated in Figures 3.7 and 3.8. When we speak of a *change in the quantity supplied*, we mean a movement from one point on the supply curve to another point on the same curve.

The Determination of Price

So far we have considered demand and supply separately. We now outline how demand and supply interact to determine price.

The concept of a market

For present purposes, a **market** may be defined as an area over which buyers and sellers negotiate the exchange of some product or related group of products. It must be possible, therefore, for buyers and sellers to communicate with each other and to make meaningful deals over the whole market.

Individual markets differ in the degree of competition among the various buyers and sellers. In the next few chapters we will confine ourselves to markets in which the number of buyers and sellers is sufficiently large that no one of them has any appreciable influence on price. This is a very rough definition of what economists call *perfectly competitive markets*. Starting in Chapter 11, we will consider the behaviour of markets that do not meet this competitive requirement.

The graphical analysis of a market

Table 3.6 brings together the demand and supply schedules from Tables 3.2 and 3.4. Figure 3.9 shows both the demand and the supply curves on a single graph; the six points on the demand curve are labelled with upper-case letters, while the six points on the supply curve are labelled with lower-case letters, each letter referring to a common price on both curves.

Quantity supplied and quantity demanded at various prices

Consider first the point at which the two curves in Figure 3.9 intersect. Both the figure and Table 3.6 show that

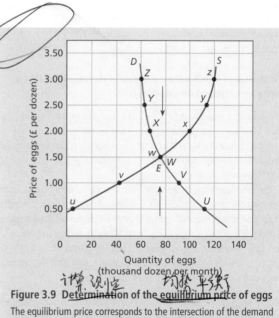

Figure 3.9 Determination of the equilibrium price of eggs
The equilibrium price corresponds to the intersection of the demand and supply curves. Point *E* indicates the equilibrium. At a price of £1.50 per dozen, quantity demanded (point *W*) equals quantity supplied (point *w*). At prices above equilibrium there is excess supply and downward pressure on price. At prices below equilibrium there is excess demand and upward pressure on price. The pressures on price are represented by the vertical arrows.

Table 3.6 Demand and supply schedules for eggs and equilibrium price

Price per dozen (£)	Quantity demanded ('000 dozen per month)	Quantity supplied ('000 dozen per month)	Excess demand (quantity demanded minus quantity supplied) ('000 dozen per month)
0.50	110.0	5.0	105.0
1.00	90.0	46.0	44.0
1.50	**77.5**	**77.5**	**0.0**
2.00	67.5	100.0	−32.5
2.50	62.5	115.0	−52.5
3.00	60.0	122.5	−62.5

Equilibrium occurs where quantity demanded equals quantity supplied so that there is neither excess demand nor excess supply. These schedules are repeated from Tables 3.2 and 3.4. The equilibrium price is £1.50. For lower prices there is excess demand; for higher prices there is excess supply, which is shown as negative excess demand.

the market price is £1.50, the quantity demanded is 77,500 dozen, and the quantity supplied is the same. At that price, consumers wish to buy exactly the same amount as producers wish to sell. Provided that the demand curve is negatively sloped and the supply curve positively sloped throughout their entire ranges, there will be no other price at which the quantity demanded equals the quantity supplied.

Now consider prices below £1.50. At these prices consumers' desired purchases exceed producers' desired sales. It is easily seen, and you should check one or two examples, that at all prices below £1.50 the quantity demanded exceeds the quantity supplied. Furthermore, the lower the price, the larger the excess of the one over the other. The amount by which the quantity demanded exceeds the quantity supplied is called the **excess demand**, which is defined as quantity demanded *minus* quantity supplied ($q^d - q^s$). This is shown in the last column of Table 3.6.

Finally, consider prices higher than £1.50. At these prices consumers wish to buy less than producers wish to sell. Thus, quantity supplied exceeds quantity demanded. It is easily seen, and again you should check a few examples, that for any price above £1.50 quantity supplied exceeds quantity demanded. Furthermore, the higher the price, the larger the excess of the one over the other. In this case there is negative excess demand ($q^d - q^s < 0$). This is also shown in the last column of Table 3.6.

Negative excess demand is usually referred to as **excess supply**, which measures the amount by which supply exceeds demand ($q^s - q^d$).

Changes in price when quantity demanded does not equal quantity supplied

Whenever there is excess demand, consumers are unable to buy all they wish to buy; whenever there is excess supply, firms are unable to sell all they wish to sell. In both cases some agents will not be able to do what they would like to do. How will they react?

There is a key driving force in markets, which might have a stronger claim to be called the law of demand and supply than the laws relating to the slopes of demand and supply curves. To avoid confusion, we refer to this driving force as the **law of price adjustment**. This law predicts what will happen to the market price when there is either excess demand or excess supply.

When supply exceeds demand, the market price will fall. When demand exceeds supply, the market price will rise.

If there is excess supply, it means that producers cannot sell all that they wish to sell at the current price. They may then begin to offer to sell at lower prices, for example through clearance sales or discounts. If purchasers observe the glut of unsold output they may begin to offer lower

prices. For either or both of these reasons, the price in the market will fall.

If, at the current price, consumers are unable to buy as much as they would like to buy, they may offer higher prices in an effort to get more of the available supply for themselves. Suppliers are unable to produce a greater quantity of the product in the short run, but they can ask higher prices for the quantities that they are producing, and will make more profit if they do so. For either or both of these reasons, prices will rise.

This law of price adjustment makes considerable sense and conforms with common experiences of how markets work—shortages of any product tend to lead to price rises while gluts tend to lead to price falls. Most importantly, it implies that prices will move towards the level at which demand and supply will be equal.

This means that the market will exhibit *stability*. Whenever the current price is not the one that equates demand and supply, the law of price adjustment ensures that the price will move towards the market-clearing price rather than away from it. Thus, it is not enough that there exists a price for which demand is equal to supply. Stability of the market also requires some mechanism to return the price to the market-clearing level whenever it is away from that point. The combination of a negatively sloped demand curve and a positively sloped supply curve with the law of price adjustment will guarantee a stable market, so long as any market in this product exists (that is, provided the demand and supply curves intersect at some positive price and quantity).

The equilibrium price

In our hypothetical example, for any price of eggs above £1.50 the price will fall, while for any price below £1.50 the price will rise. At a price of £1.50 there is neither excess demand associated with a shortage, nor excess supply associated with a glut; the quantity supplied is equal to the quantity demanded. Once supply and demand are equal, there is no tendency for the price to change because suppliers are just able to sell all that they want and demanders are just able to buy all that they want. Nobody has any incentive to change the price.

The price of £1.50, where the supply and demand curves intersect, is the price towards which the actual market price will tend. It is called the **equilibrium price**: the price at which quantity demanded equals quantity supplied. The amount that is bought and sold at the equilibrium price is called the **equilibrium quantity**. The term 'equilibrium' means a state of balance; it occurs when desired purchases equal desired sales and there are no forces tending to make anything change. Box 3.3 discusses the implications of inflation for our interpretation of market price.

When quantity demanded equals quantity supplied, we say that the market is in **equilibrium**. When quantity

Box 3.3 **Prices in periods of inflation**

Up to now we have developed the theory of the prices of individual products under the assumption that all other prices remain constant. Does this mean that the theory is inapplicable during an inflationary period when almost all prices are rising? Fortunately, the answer is no.

We have mentioned several times that what matters for demand and supply is the price of the product in question relative to the prices of other products. The price of the product expressed in money terms is called its **money price**; the price of a product expressed in relation to other prices is called its **relative price**.

In an inflationary world changes in a product's relative price can be measured by changes in the product's own price relative to changes in the average of all other prices, which is called the *general price level*. If, during a period when the general price level rose by 40 per cent, the price of oranges rose by 60 per cent, then the price of oranges rose relative to the price level as a whole. Oranges became *relatively* expensive. However, if the price of oranges had risen by only 30 per cent when the general price level had risen by 40 per cent, then their relative price would have fallen. Although the money price of oranges rose, oranges became *relatively* cheap.

In Lewis Carroll's famous story *Through the Looking-Glass*, Alice finds a country where everyone has to run in order to stay still. So it is with inflation. A product's price must rise as fast as the general level of prices just to keep its relative price constant.

It has been convenient in this chapter to analyse a change in a particular price in the context of a constant price level. The analysis is easily extended, however, to an inflationary period. Any force that raises the price of one product when other prices remain constant will, given general inflation, raise the price of that product relative to the average of all other prices. Consider the example of a change in tastes in favour of eggs that would raise their price by 20 per cent when other prices were constant. If, however, the general price level goes up by 10 per cent, then the price of eggs will rise by 32 per cent.* In each case the price of eggs rises 20 per cent *relative to the average of all prices*.

In price theory, whenever we talk of a change in the price of one product, we mean a change *relative to* the general price level.

* Let the price level be 100 in the first case and 110 in the second. Let the price of eggs be 120 in the first case and *x* in the second. To preserve the same relative price, we need *x* such that $120/100 = x/110$, which makes $x = 132$.

---

demanded does not equal quantity supplied, we say that the market is in **disequilibrium**.

Summary

We have now developed one of the most famous and powerful theories in all of economics, and it is worth summarizing it here.

Assumptions concerning a competitive market

• **The law of demand: demand curves have negative slopes throughout their entire range.**

• **The theory of supply: supply curves have positive slopes throughout their entire range.**

• **The law of price adjustment: prices rise when demand exceeds supply, and fall if supply exceeds demand. They remain unchanged when demand and supply are equal.**

Implications

• **There is no more than one price at which quantity demanded equals quantity supplied: equilibrium is unique.**

• **Only at the equilibrium price will the market price remain constant.**

• **When the demand or the supply curve shifts, the equilibrium price and quantity will change.**

• **The market is stable in the sense that forces exist to move the price towards its market-clearing level.**

The predictions of demand and supply analysis

Earlier in this chapter, we studied shifts in demand and supply curves. Recall that a rightward shift in the relevant curve means that more is demanded or supplied *at each market price*, while a leftward shift means that less is demanded or supplied *at each market price*. How does a shift in either curve affect price and quantity?

The answers to this question make up the predictions of our supply and demand theory. We wish to see what happens when an initial position of equilibrium is upset by some shift in either the demand or the supply curve, and a new equilibrium position is then established. This will enable us to derive predictions about what will happen in any market when something changes, and this is why we study economics: so that we can anticipate what will happen in specific markets when some change occurs.

To discover the effects of the demand and supply shifts that we wish to study, we use the method known as **comparative statics**. We start from a position of equilibrium and then introduce the change to be studied. The new equilibrium position is determined and compared with the original one. The differences between the two positions of equilibrium must result from the change that was introduced, for everything else has been held constant.

The four main predictions of demand and supply are derived in Figure 3.10, the caption of which must be carefully

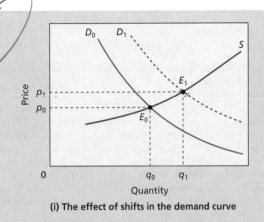

(i) The effect of shifts in the demand curve

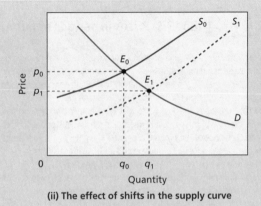

(ii) The effect of shifts in the supply curve

Figure 3.10 The predictions of demand and supply analysis

The predicted effects on equilibrium price and quantity of shifts in either demand or supply are as follows.

An increase in demand. In part (i) assume that the original demand and supply curves are D_0 and S, which intersect to produce equilibrium at E_0, with a price of p_0 and a quantity of q_0. An increase in demand shifts the demand curve to D_1, taking the new equilibrium to E_1. Price rises to p_1 and quantity rises to q_1.

A decrease in demand. In part (i) assume that the original demand and supply curves are D_1 and S, which intersect to produce equilibrium at E_1, with a price of p_1 and a quantity of q_1. A decrease in demand shifts the demand curve to D_0, taking the new equilibrium to E_0. Price falls to p_0 and quantity falls to q_0.

An increase in supply. In part (ii) assume that the original demand and supply curves are D and S_0, which intersect to produce an equilibrium at E_0, with a price of p_0 and a quantity of q_0. An increase in supply shifts the supply curve to S_1, taking the new equilibrium to E_1. Price falls to p_1 and quantity rises to q_1.

A decrease in supply. In part (ii) assume that the original demand and supply curves are D and S_1, which intersect to produce an equilibrium at E_1, with a price of p_1 and a quantity of q_1. A decrease in supply shifts the supply curve to S_0, taking the new equilibrium to E_0. Price rises to p_0 and quantity falls to q_0.

read. The analysis of that figure generalizes our specific discussion about eggs. Because it is intended to apply to any product, the horizontal axis is simply labelled 'quantity' and the vertical axis, 'price'.

The predictions of supply and demand theory are:

1. A rise in the demand for a product (a rightward shift of the demand curve) causes an increase in both the equilibrium price and the equilibrium quantity bought and sold.

2. A fall in the demand for a product (a leftward shift of the demand curve) causes a decrease in both the equilibrium price and the equilibrium quantity bought and sold.

3. A rise in the supply of a product (a rightward shift of the supply curve) causes a decrease in the equilibrium price and an increase in the equilibrium quantity bought and sold.

4. A fall in the supply of a product (a leftward shift of the supply curve) causes an increase in the equilibrium price and a decrease in the equilibrium quantity bought and sold.

In Figures 3.5 and 3.8 we summarized the many events that cause demand and supply curves to shift. Using the four predictions derived in Figure 3.10, we can understand the link between these events and changes in market prices and quantities. To take one example, a rise in the price of butter will lead to an increase in both the price of margarine and the quantity bought. This is because a rise in the price of one product causes a rightward shift in the demand curves for its substitutes, and prediction 1 tells us that such a shift causes price and quantity to increase.

We will see in subsequent chapters that the theory of the determination of price by demand and supply is beautiful in its simplicity and yet powerful in its range of applications. In the meantime, Box 3.4 suggests some simple applications and Box 3.5 details one specific case.

Box 3.4 Demand and supply: what really happens

Just in case you might think at this stage that we are being abstract and theoretical and you feel that the world 'is not like that', here are some examples of recent newspaper headlines or extracts that illustrate how markets actually work. In the last section of this chapter we address some other doubts about how generally applicable our analysis might be.

• OPEC countries once again fail to agree on output quotas. Output soars and prices plummet.

• Oil prices surge on move by producers to cut output.

• The price of cashew kernels has fallen nearly 6 per cent in 10 months as Vietnam has begun to challenge India and Brazil, the world's two largest exporters.

• How deep is the art market's recession? In today's unforgiving economic climate, the sales of contemporary, impressionist, and modern works of art took hits at this week's auctions. Sales totalled just under £60 million compared with £500 million just one year ago. Many paintings on offer went unsold, and those that did sell went for well under their predicted price.

• Coffee prices at the London Commodity Exchange staged another spectacular rise, putting them above their level at the start of the year. The president of the Association of Coffee Producing Countries said that the supply shortages that are underpinning prices would last quite some time.

• Increased demand for macadamia nuts causes price to rise above competing nuts. A major producer now plans to double the size of its orchards during the next five years.

• The effects of deregulation of US airlines were spectacular: cuts in air fares of up to 70 per cent in some cases, record passenger jam-ups at the airports, and a spectacular increase in the average load factor [the proportion of occupied seats on the average commercial flight].

 ## Box 3.5 The market for computer chips

The chart shows the fall in the price of computer chips between 1990 and 2002. Prices are measured as US dollars per megabyte of D-Ram. Here are some components of the explanation of this dramatic price fall.

According to an article in the *Financial Times*,

It is only nine months since the world semiconductor industry was forging ahead. Demand for chips was so great that there was a shortage, analysts were forecasting record growth and manufacturers were unveiling plans for dozens of $1bn chip factories. . . .

The euphoria has been short lived. The shortage rapidly turned into surplus, and the price of dynamic random access memory (D-Ram) chips—the basic memory chips for PCs—has dropped by about 65 per cent over the past six or seven months. . . .

Commodity chip prices normally fall by 20 per cent to 30 per cent each year as manufacturing costs fall. But with manufacturers scrambling to protect market share, international spot market prices have fallen below the break-even point of some Asian manufacturers. (*Financial Times*, 28 June 1996)

The story points to two key elements to the developments in this market. First, the technology of producing computer chips is evolving rapidly. This causes the market supply curve to shift rightwards continually. The second element is the negatively sloped demand curve, which shifts in some periods.

The trend decline of '20 per cent to 30 per cent each year' is clearly shown in the chart. So is the abnormal period between 1992 and 1995, when chip prices actually rose slightly before falling back sharply in 1996, as discussed above. What is the explanation?

In normal times the primary influence is that the shifting supply curve moves to the right along a nearly static demand curve. Chip prices fall and quantity demanded increases. In the 1992–5 period, however, the demand

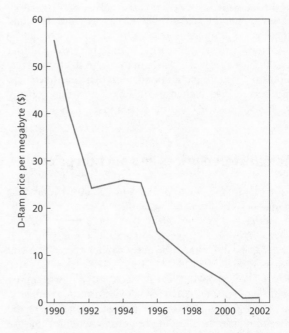

curve shifted sharply to the right. This increase in demand was due to the increased availability and reduced price of such complementary software products as multimedia games and educational programs. By 1996 the demand curve had stopped shifting to the right but the supply curve had not. Hence prices returned to their downward trend.

Notice that the price rises associated with the temporary boom in demand between 1992 and 1995 would have increased the quantity supplied

Box 3.5 (Continued)

on each rightward-shifting supply curve because the high profitability of chip production encouraged higher production at each level of capacity. The fall in price in 1996 no doubt reduced the quantity supplied along the supply curve that existed at that time. However, despite the fall in price, the supply curve continued to shift to the right in successive periods as technical progress continued to reduce costs of production.

A subsequent article (*Financial Times*) showed that the steady decline in prices had continued as expected:

The performance of Japan's leading electronics conglomerates has been hit by the triple blow of a collapse in semi-conductor prices, dire domestic consumer demand and the Asian economic crisis. . . . Both NEC and Mitsubishi Electric were hit by last year's contraction

of the Japanese personal computer market. . . . Poor demand in Asia caused Hitachi's consumer products business to slide into loss and sales of Mitsubishi's consumer products to slide. (*Financial Times*, 29 May 1998)

Ceteris paribus, the fall in prices associated with cost reductions should cause state-of-the-art firms no great difficulty. If their costs fall as fast as prices, they can maintain their profitability. But when demand declined in what had been an expanding industry, even the most efficient producers ran into difficulties. In 2001 prices fell as low as $1 and many producers faced severe difficulties. Prices recovered somewhat early in 2002 on news that one major producer was in difficulties, and this created the expectation that production capacity could be greatly reduced.

But markets are not really like that!

As we built up our analysis of markets in this chapter, you might have been saying to yourself: 'This is all very well in theory, but the markets I know about are not like that.' There is one important respect in which you would be absolutely correct. But we now want to persuade you that the doubts you might have about this analysis are not a real problem. Demand and supply analysis helps us understand *all* markets, even though the details of how they actually work vary considerably from market to market.

Administered prices and auction prices

The worry that we hope you had when reading the analysis of markets is that most of the markets in which consumers, including you and us, operate do not work in the way we describe. For example, if you wish to attend your local cinema for a peak time showing of a much-hyped film you may find queues outside the cinema to buy tickets. There may be more people who want to go at that time than the number of seats available for sale. According to our theory, this means that there is an excess demand and so the price of cinema seats should rise until enough people are discouraged and all those left in the queue are just able to obtain a seat.

Of course, this does not happen. What actually happens is that the cinema continues to sell tickets at its existing prices until it has sold all the seats and it then puts up a notice saying: 'sold out' or 'house full'.

Similarly, if you go into your local supermarket or department store, you will find the prices of all the goods

clearly labelled. You can buy as much of each product as you like at the price set by the store, but the price does not change according to how many people are buying the product on a particular day. If some product is very popular the store will run out and the shelf will be empty, but the store does not adjust the price to ensure that there is just enough supply to meet the demand.

So have we been lying to you when we have said that prices adjust to clear markets? The answer is an overwhelming No! However, we do have to understand that market institutions vary with product and participants. Prices do adjust to clear markets, but they do not do it in the same way in all types of market. Let us think about different ways in which prices are set and then we shall try to give some reasons for these differences.

The prices that most obviously fit our theory are referred to as **flexible prices** or **auction prices**, as they adjust on a continuous basis to equate demand and supply. Prices in the foreign exchange market and the stock market are flexible as they can change minute by minute while the market is open. Prices that are set by the supplier, who then just waits to see how much of the product sells at that price, are known as **administered prices** or **fixed prices**. Most consumer goods and services are sold at administered prices.

Administered prices do adjust

Although prices in most retail outlets are set by the retailer, this does not mean that these prices do not adjust to market forces *over time*. On any particular day we find that all products have a specific price ticket on them. However, this price may be different from day to day or week to week.

If, for example, bad weather leads to a poor potato crop, then the price that supermarkets have to pay for potatoes will go up and this will be reflected in the prices they set for potatoes in their stores. Thus, these prices do reflect the interaction of demand and supply in the wider market place for potatoes. Similarly, fresh strawberries sell at very different prices in mid-winter than in mid-summer. In the summer they are locally grown, but in winter they will have been flown in from the other side of the world.

Even within a supermarket that sets prices on all its produce, there will be times when they mark down prices in order to get rid of stock, perhaps as it approaches its sell-by date, or if they have new lines arriving the next day. Department stores have sales at regular intervals in order to get rid of stock that has not sold at lower prices and to make room for new products. Cinemas will have lower prices at off-peak times. However, in all these cases, the supplier is still setting a price and then (in effect) saying: 'Take it or leave it at this price.'

Why are some prices administered?

If administered prices do eventually adjust to reflect demand and supply conditions, why are they set at a fixed price in the first place? The answer is that this is a more efficient way to organize a retail marketplace. Auction markets work well where all the potential buyers can be assembled in one place (the auction room) or are connected by communication equipment (telephones or computers), so that they can bid simultaneously for the product. The price is set so that the highest bidder gets the goods, and all the goods available are sold.

Imagine the chaos, however, if all the people who ever shop in your local supermarket had to turn up at the same time and make bids for their weekly shopping basket. This is clearly not feasible. Imagine also what the checkout queues would be like if every shopper had to negotiate the price of each item in their shopping trolley as they checked it out. Again, this would be a very time consuming way of shopping. There have been some recent attempts to organize some retail markets by collecting bids through the internet. However, it seems very unlikely that this form of shopping is going to replace the supermarket and the department store any time soon.

Mixed pricing Some markets do have a mixture of administered prices and a degree of price negotiation. This is efficient because these are usually markets for items that are large and/or that you do not buy very often. Motor cars, for example, have 'list prices', but there is usually some leeway for negotiation, either about the price of the car itself, about the extras it includes, or about the trade-in price of your old car. When new models are introduced, stocks of the old models may be sold off at lower than the original list price. Houses too are typically listed at an 'asking price', but there is some negotiation around this price, and if several people are chasing the same house there may be what amounts to an auction where by the house goes to the highest bidder. Indeed, in Scotland a sealed-bid auction system is the norm. Bidders have to enter a written bid on the same day without knowing what others have bid, and the highest bidder gets the property.

Many manufactured goods are put on sale in shops at a fixed price. But these prices already reflect supply factors, such as costs of production and the rent and wages paid by the retailer. Demand influences will certainly affect the price. A very popular item that the retailer is finding hard to get may have its ticket price raised, while unsold items will be marked down for clearance at some stage. Clothing and other fashion items also typically stay on sale for a period at a fixed price but then are sold off in clearance sales to make way for new fashions or new styles. Indeed, while most clothes retailers have 'sales' around twice a year, many also have permanent racks of discounted items within their store. A similar example is wine shops that regularly have 'bin end' sales of unwanted stock to make space for their new stock.

What about goods and services provided free?

Some goods and services are provided free at the point of use, often by the government or by government-funded organizations. Examples include health services in some countries and education in most developed countries. Does demand and supply analysis apply to these markets? The answer is yes and no. 'No' because if a service is provided free to the consumer then the price cannot adjust to equate demand and supply. But 'yes' because demand and supply analysis can still give us insights into the problems of allocation of resources in such markets. At zero price there is likely to be an excess demand for the services involved. So if the price cannot rise to bring demand and supply into equality, then some other method of allocation is going to have to be found to decide who gets what. We discuss this problem further in Chapter 5.

Relationships between different markets

Although each of the individual markets referred to above is distinct, all are interrelated, and we need to see why.

The separation of individual markets

Markets are separated from each other in three main ways: by the product sold, by natural economic barriers, and by barriers created by governments. Here is one example of each type of separation:

1. The market for men's shirts is different from the market for refrigerators because different products are sold in each.

2. The market for cement in the United Kingdom is distinct from the market for cement in the western United States. The costs of transporting cement are so high that UK purchasers would not buy American cement even if its market price in the western United States were very much lower than its market price in Britain.

3. The market for textiles is separated between many countries because government-imposed trade restrictions severely limit the amount that firms in one country can sell to consumers in another.

Because markets are distinct, we can use demand and supply analysis to study the behaviour of markets one at a time, as we have done in this chapter and will do in much more detail in Chapter 5.

The interlinking of individual markets

Although all markets are to some extent separated, most are also interrelated. Consider again the three causes of market separation: different products, spatial separation, and government intervention. First, the markets for different kinds of product are interrelated because all products compete for consumers' income. Thus, if consumers spend more in one market, they will have less to spend in other markets. Second, the geographical separation of markets for similar products depends on transport costs. Products whose transport costs are high relative to their production costs tend to be produced and sold in geographically distinct markets. Products whose transport costs are low relative to their production costs tend to be sold in what amounts to one world market. But whatever the transport costs, there will be some price differential at which it will pay someone to buy in the low-priced market and ship to

the high-priced one. Thus, there is always some potential link between geographically distinct markets, even when shipping costs are high. Third, markets are often separated by policy-induced barriers, such as tariffs (which are taxes paid when goods come into a country from abroad). Although high tariffs tend to separate markets, they do not do so completely. If price differences become large enough, it will pay buyers in the high-price market to import from the low-price market and producers in the low-price market to export to the high-price one, even though they have to pay the tariff as a result.

Because markets are interrelated, we must treat them as a single interrelated system for many purposes. *General equilibrium analysis* studies markets as a single interrelated system in which individual demands and supplies depend on all prices, and what happens in any one market will affect many other markets—and in principle could affect all other markets.

Conclusion

Whatever the market in which we are interested, the analysis of how demand and supply interact to determine the market-clearing price is an essential tool. It is applicable to all situations in which some maker or owner of a product wishes to exchange the product with a potential user.

All the more detailed analysis that we are going to do between now and Chapter 20 is designed to build an increasingly fuller understanding of the forces affecting different types of market and market structure, and the motives and behaviour of market participants. But we have already gone a long way towards an understanding of how markets work.

SUMMARY

- The decision-taking units in economic theory are called agents. They are (*a*) individuals, for demand in goods markets and for supply in labour markets; (*b*) firms, for supply in goods markets and demand in labour and capital markets; and (*c*) governments, for the supply of some goods and for regulation and control of the private sector. Given the resources at their command, each individual is assumed to maximize his or her satisfaction, and each firm is assumed to maximize its profit.

Demand

- An individual consumer's demand curve shows the relation between the price of a product and the quantity of that product

the consumer wishes to purchase per period of time. It is drawn on the assumption that all other prices, income, and tastes remain constant. Its negative slope indicates that the lower the price of the product, the more the consumer wishes to purchase.

- The market demand curve is the horizontal sum of the demand curves of all the individual consumers. The demand curve for a normal good shifts to the right when the price of a substitute rises, when the price of a complement falls, when total income rises, when the distribution of income changes in favour of those with large demands for the product, and when tastes change in favour of the product. It shifts to the left with the opposite changes.

- A movement along a demand curve indicates a change in quantity demanded in response to a change in the product's own price; a shift in a demand curve indicates a change in the quantity demanded at each price in response to a change in one of the conditions held constant along a demand curve.

Supply

- The supply curve for a product shows the relationship between its price and the quantity that producers wish to produce and offer for sale per period of time. It is drawn on the assumption that all other forces that influence the quantity supplied remain constant, and its positive slope indicates that the higher the price, the more producers wish to sell.

- A supply curve shifts in response to changes in the prices of the inputs used by producers, and to changes in technology. The shift represents a change in the amount supplied at each price. A movement along a supply curve indicates that a different quantity is being supplied in response to a change in the product's own price.

The determination of price

- At the equilibrium price the quantity demanded equals the quantity supplied. Graphically, equilibrium occurs where the demand and supply curves intersect. At any price below equilibrium there will be excess demand and price will tend to rise; at any price above equilibrium there will be excess supply and price will tend to fall.

- A rise in demand raises both equilibrium price and quantity; a fall in demand lowers both. A rise in supply raises equilibrium quantity but lowers equilibrium price; a fall in supply lowers equilibrium quantity but raises equilibrium price.

- Price theory is developed most simply in the context of a constant price level. Price changes discussed in the theory are changes relative to the average level of all prices. In an inflationary period, a rise in the relative price of one product means that its price rises by more than the rise in the general price level; a fall in its relative price means that its price rises by less than the rise in the general price level.

But markets are not really like that!

- Most retail markets do not appear to have prices adjusting to differences between demand and supply. Prices are set at a specific level and shoppers can buy as much as they want at this price. Prices are administered by the seller.

- Even administered prices do adjust to demand and supply forces, but it would not be efficient for these prices to be set either by auction or by negotiation, or to change every minute. Price changes do happen in response to persistent changes in the conditions affecting both demand and supply.

TOPICS FOR REVIEW

- Quantity demanded and the demand function
- The demand schedule and the demand curve for an individual and for the market
- The law of demand
- Shifts in the demand curve and movements along the curve
- Substitutes and complements
- Quantity supplied and the supply function

- The supply schedule and the supply curve
- Shifts in the supply curve and movements along the curve
- Excess demand and excess supply
- Equilibrium and disequilibrium prices
- The law of price adjustment
- Auction prices and administered prices

DISCUSSION QUESTIONS

1 What is the equilibrium market price and quantity for each of the following pairs of demand and supply curves:
Demand: $p = £100 - 2q$; supply: $p = £0 + 3q$
Demand: $p = £100 - 2q$; supply: $q = 30$
Demand: $p = £100$;   supply: $p = £20 + 5q$

2 Use demand and supply curves to analyse what is happening in each of the following situations.
(a) The price of coffee has risen because a frost in Brazil has reduced the coffee crop.

(b) A fall in air fares from the UK has raised demand for hotel rooms on the Spanish costas.

(c) Further falls in chip prices have led to a reduction in the price of laptop computers.

(d) An exceptionally cold winter in North America leads to a higher price of oil.

(e) A disease in British beef necessitates the slaughtering of large numbers of cattle.

3 List all the 'markets' in which you regularly buy goods or services. How are the price and quantity determined during your transaction? Do these prices change on a day-to-day basis or only infrequently? If prices do not adjust, what happens when there is an excess demand or supply?

4 Outline the main determinants of quantity demanded and quantity supplied, and explain how these interact to determine the market price.

5 Explain the main differences between administered prices and auction prices, and discuss which markets are most suitable for these two different mechanisms.

6 Outline the conditions that are required to achieve equality between demand and supply at a market-clearing price.

7 Explain the effect on market price and quantity in the market for mobile phone handsets of each of the following circumstances: consumer incomes rise; technical improvements reduce production costs; the price of fixed-line calls falls sharply.

Mathematical Appendix A linear demand and supply model

In this appendix we derive the equilibrium price and quantity when both the demand and supply curves are linear. We then go on to derive the four predictions that are outlined in the text concerning the effects on price and quantity of shifts in these curves.

The model and its solution

$$q^d = a + bp \qquad b < 0 < a \qquad \text{(A1)}$$

$$q^s = c + dp \qquad 0 < d \text{ and } c < a \qquad \text{(A2)}$$

$$q^d = q^s \qquad \text{(A3)}$$

where q^d is quantity demanded, q^s is quantity supplied, p is the product's price and a, b, c, and d are parameters. Equations (A1) and (A2) are behavioural relations while (A3) is the equilibrium condition.[5] The restrictions on the parameters in (A1) ensure that quantity demanded will be positive when the price is zero ($0 < a$) and that the demand curve has a negative slope ($b < 0$). The restrictions on the parameters in (A2) ensure that the supply curve will have a positive slope ($0 < d$), and that more will be demanded than supplied when price is zero ($c < a$).

We many now substitute (A1) and (A2) into (A3) to obtain an expression for the equilibrium price:

$$a + bp = c + dp$$

or

$$a - c = p(d - b)$$

or

$$p = \frac{a - c}{d - b}. \qquad \text{(A4)}$$

We can also eliminate p and solve for q. To do this, we substitute (A4) into (A1), to obtain

$$q = \frac{ad - bc}{d - b}. \qquad \text{(A5)}$$

We now have two equations expressing the two dependant or endogenous variables p and q as a function of the four parameters (also called independent, or exogenous, variables), a, b, c and d.

Predictions

Formally, we derive the four predictions of the model by differentiating the endogenous variables, p and q, in equations (A4) and (A5) with respect to the relevant exogenous variables. This model is so simple that we can do this by inspection.

An increase in demand can be obtained by increasing a, which shifts the demand curve to the right parallel to itself. Inspection of (A4) and (A5) shows that an increase in a raises both p and q. Reduction in demand comes when a is reduced, which, by inspection of (A4) and (A5), reduces p and q.

An increase in supply occurs if c increases, shifting the supply to the right parallel to itself. Inspection of (A4) and (A5) shows that this change lowers the equilibrium price but raises the equilibrium quantity.

[5] Care must be taken when comparing these equations with the graphs in the text. When these equations are plotted naturally, p will be on the x-axis and q on the y-axis. The slope terms refer to this plot and not to the curves in the text where, according to economic convention, the two axes are reversed. This is discussed further in the text footnote 2.

Chapter 4

弹性. 适应性. 灵活性

ELASTICITY OF DEMAND AND SUPPLY

In this chapter we develop some very important concepts that will help you to understand how markets work. In particular, you will learn:

• How the sensitivity of quantity demanded to a change in price is measured by the elasticity of demand and what factors influence it

• How elasticity is measured at a point or over a range

• How income elasticity is measured and how it varies with different types of goods

• How elasticity of supply is measured and what it tells us about conditions of production

• Some of the difficulties that arise in trying to estimate various elasticities from sales data

The demand and supply analysis of the previous chapter helps us to understand the direction in which price and quantity will change in response to shifts in demand or supply. In most real-world situations, economists or busi-ness analysts are not going to get away with saying things like: 'If we raise our price sales will fall' or 'If incomes rise this year our demand will increase'. The question you will need to answer is: 'By how much?' Fortunately, tools exist to help you answer this question in the many different cir-cumstances in which it may be asked. These tools measure the responses of the quantity demanded and the quantity supplied to changes in the variables that determine them, particularly prices and incomes.

To illustrate why we need these measures, consider the effects of a new government tax on each litre of petrol sold (say, to reduce emissions of greenhouse gases). This will shift the supply curve of petrol to the left because less will be offered at each price. If the demand for petrol is as shown in part (i) of Figure 4.1, the effect of the government's pol-icy will be to increase petrol prices slightly, while greatly reducing the quantity refined and consumed. If, however, the demand is as shown in part (ii) of Figure 4.1, the effect of the policy will be to increase petrol prices greatly but to

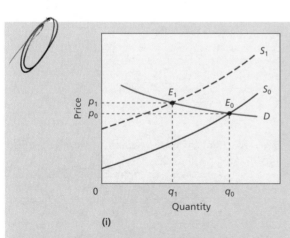

(i)

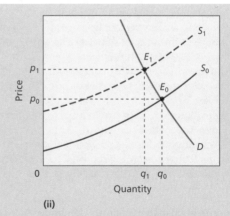

(ii)

Figure 4.1 The effect of the shape of the demand curve

The flatter the demand curve, *ceteris paribus*, the less the change in price and the greater the change in quantity. Both parts of the figure are drawn on the same scale. Both show the same initial equilibrium price p_0 and quantity q_0, the same shift of the supply curve from S_0 to S_1, and a new equilibrium at p_1 and q_1. In part (i) the effect of the shift in supply is a slight rise in the price and a large fall in quantity. In part (ii) the effect of the identical shift in the supply curve is a large rise in the price and a relatively small fall in quantity.

The longer the change in price and the less the change in quantity reduce petrol production and consumption by only a small amount. If the purpose of the tax is to reduce the amount that is produced and consumed, then the policy will be a great success when the demand curve is similar to the one shown in part (i), but a failure when the demand curve is similar to that shown in part (ii). If, however, the main purpose of the tax is to achieve a large increase in the price of petrol, the policy will be a failure when demand is as shown in part (i) but a great success when demand is as shown in part (ii).

This example shows that it is often not enough to know just whether quantity rises or falls in response to some change. It is important to know by how much, and to measure this we use the concept of *elasticity*.

Demand elasticity

In the first part of this chapter we deal with quantity demanded, and we start by considering its response to changes in a product's own price.

Price elasticity of demand

In Figure 4.1 we were able to compare the responsiveness of quantity demanded along the two demand curves because they were drawn on the same scale. You should not try to compare two curves without making sure that the scales are the same. Also, you must not leap to conclusions about the responsiveness of quantity demanded on the basis of the apparent steepness of a single curve. The hazards of so doing are illustrated in Figure 4.2. Both parts of the figure plot the same demand curve, but the choice of scale on the 'quantity' and 'price' axes serves to make one curve look steep and the other flat.

Measuring the responsiveness of demand to price

In order to get a measure of responsiveness that is independent of the scale we use, so that it can be compared across products, we need to deal in percentage changes. A given percentage change in the amount of petrol purchased will be the same whether we measure it in gallons or litres. Similarly, although we cannot easily compare the absolute changes in kilos of carrots and barrels of oil, we can compare their two percentage changes.

These considerations lead us to the concept of the **price elasticity of demand**, which is defined as the percentage change in quantity demanded *divided by* the percentage change in price that brought it about.[1] This elasticity is usually symbolized by the lower-case Greek letter eta, η:

$$\eta = \frac{\text{percentage change in quantity demanded}}{\text{percentage change in price}} \quad (1)$$

Many different elasticities are used in economics. To distinguish η from the others, the full term 'price elasticity of demand' can be used. Since η is by far the most commonly used elasticity, economists often drop the adjective

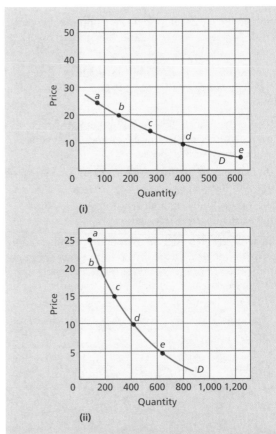

Figure 4.2 One demand curve drawn on two different scales

Suitable choice of scale can make any demand curve appear steep or flat. Parts (i) and (ii) plot the same demand curve. Because the same distance on the quantity axes stands for twice as much in part (ii) as in part (i), and the same distance on the price axes stands for half as much, the curve is steeper when plotted in graph (ii) than when plotted in graph (i).

---

[1] Elasticity is an example of what mathematicians call a *pure number*, which is a number whose value is independent of the units in which it is calculated. Slope, $\Delta p / \Delta q$, is not a pure number. For example, if price is measured in pence, $\Delta p / \Delta q$ will be 100 times as large as $\Delta p / \Delta q$ along the same demand curve where price is measured in pounds sterling.

Table 4.1 Calculation of two demand elasticities

	Original	New	% change	Elasticity
Good A				
Quantity	100	95	−5%	$\left.\begin{array}{c} \\ \end{array}\right\}$ $\dfrac{-5}{10} = -0.5$
Price	£1	£1.10	10%	
Good B				
Quantity	200	140	−30%	$\left.\begin{array}{c} \\ \end{array}\right\}$ $\dfrac{-30}{20} = -1.5$
Price	£5	£6	20%	

Elasticity is calculated by dividing the percentage change in quantity by the percentage change in price. With good A, a rise in price of 10p on £1, or 10 per cent, causes a fall in quantity of 5 units from 100, or 5 per cent. Dividing the 5 per cent reduction in quantity by the 10 per cent increase in price gives an elasticity of −0.5. With good B, a 30 per cent fall in quantity is caused by a 20 per cent rise in price, making elasticity −1.5.

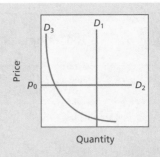

Figure 4.3 Three constant-elasticity demand curves

Each curve has a constant elasticity. D_1 has *zero elasticity*: the quantity demanded does not change at all when price changes. D_2 has *infinite elasticity at price p_0*: a small price increase from p_0 decreases quantity demanded from an indefinitely large amount to zero. D_3 has *unit elasticity*: a given percentage increase in price brings an equal percentage decrease in quantity demanded at all points on the curve; it is a rectangular hyperbola for which price *times* quantity is a constant.

'price' and refer to it merely as *elasticity of demand*, or sometimes just *elasticity*. When more than one kind of elasticity could be involved, however, η should be given its full title.

The sign of the measure Because of the negative slope of the demand curve, the price and the quantity will always change in opposite directions. One change will be positive and the other negative, making the measured elasticity of demand negative. This would pose no problem, except for two unfortunate habits of economists. First, either by carelessness or by design, the minus sign is often dropped and elasticity is reported as a positive number. Second, it is almost universal practice when comparing two elasticities to compare their absolute, not their algebraic, values.[2] For example, if product X has an elasticity of −2 while product Y has an elasticity of −10, economists will say that Y has a greater elasticity than X (in spite of the fact that −10 is *less than* −2). As long as it is understood that absolute and not algebraic values are being compared, this usage is acceptable. After all, the demand curve with the larger absolute elasticity *is* the one where quantity demanded is more responsive to price changes. For example, an elasticity of −10 indicates greater response of quantity to price than does an elasticity of −2.

This need not cause confusion so long as you remember the following:

Demand elasticity is measured by a ratio: the percentage change in quantity demanded divided by the percentage change in price that brought it about. For normal, negatively sloped demand curves, elasticity is negative, but the relative size of two elasticities is usually assessed by comparing their absolute values.

Table 4.1 shows the calculation of two demand elasticities, one that is quite large and one that is smaller. The larger elasticity indicates that quantity demanded is highly responsive to a change in price. The smaller elasticity indicates that the quantity demanded is relatively unresponsive to a change in price.

Interpreting price elasticity

The value of price elasticity of demand ranges from zero to minus infinity. In this section, however, we concentrate on absolute values, and so ask by how much the absolute value *exceeds zero*.

Elasticity is zero if quantity demanded is unchanged when price changes, i.e. when quantity demanded does not respond to a price change. A demand curve of zero elasticity is shown as curve D_1 in Figure 4.3. It is said to be *perfectly* or *completely* inelastic.

As long as there is some positive response of quantity demanded to a change in price, the absolute value of elasticity will exceed zero. The greater the response, the larger the elasticity. Whenever this value is less than one, however, the percentage change in quantity is less than the percentage change in price, and demand is said to be **inelastic**. When elasticity is equal to one, the two percentage changes are then equal to each other. This case, which is called **unit elasticity**, marks the boundary between elastic and inelastic demands. A demand curve having unit elasticity over its whole range is shown as D_3 in Figure 4.3.

[2] The absolute value is the magnitude without the sign. Thus, for example, −3 is smaller in algebraic value than 2 but larger in absolute value.

Box 4.1 The terminology of elasticity

TERM	SYMBOL	NUMERICAL MEASURE OF ELASTICITY	VERBAL DESCRIPTION
Price elasticity of demand (supply)	$\eta(\varepsilon_s)$		
Perfectly or completely inelastic		Zero	Quantity demanded (supplied) does not change as price changes
Inelastic		Greater than zero, less than one	Quantity demanded (supplied) changes by a smaller percentage than does price
Unit elasticity		One	Quantity demanded (supplied) changes by exactly the same percentage as does price
Elastic		Greater than one, but less than infinity	Quantity demanded (supplied) changes by a larger percentage than does price
Perfectly, completely, or infinitely elastic		Infinity	Purchasers (sellers) are prepared to buy (sell) all they can at some price and none at all at a higher (lower) price
Income elasticity of demand	η_y		
Inferior good		Negative	Quantity demanded decreases as income increases
Normal good		Positive	Quantity demanded increases as income increases:
Income-inelastic		Less than one	less than in proportion to income increase
Income-elastic		Greater than one	more than in proportion to income increase
Cross-elasticity of demand	η_{xy}		
Substitute		Positive	The quantity demanded of some good and the price of a substitute are positively related
Complement		Negative	The quantity demanded of some good and the price of a complement are negatively related

When the percentage change in quantity demanded exceeds the percentage change in price, the elasticity of demand is greater than one and demand is said to be **elastic**. When elasticity is infinitely large, there exists some small price reduction that will raise quantity demanded from zero to infinity. Above the critical price, consumers will buy nothing. At the critical price, they will buy all that they can obtain (an infinite amount, if it were available). The graph of a demand curve with infinite price elasticity is shown as D_2 in Figure 4.3. Such a demand curve is said to be *perfectly* or *completely elastic*. (This unlikely looking case will turn out to be important later when we study the demand for the output of a single firm with many competitors all producing an identical product.)

Box 4.1 summarizes the discussion of this and subsequent sections. The terminology in the table is important, and you should become familiar with it at some stage, but you may want to come back to it once you have read the rest of the chapter.

Elasticity and total spending

How does consumers' total spending on a specific product react when the price of the product is changed? The total spending of the product's buyers is equal to the money received by the product's sellers plus any taxes that the government levies on the product. For simplicity, we ignore any taxes, so that sellers' receipts are equal to buyers' spending.

A simple example can be used to show that buyers' total spending and sellers' receipts may rise or fall in response to a decrease in price. Suppose 100 units of a product are being sold for £1 each. The price is then cut to £0.90. If the quantity sold rises to 110, the total spent falls from £100 to £99. But if quantity sold rises to 120, total spending rises from £100 to £108.

The change in total spending brought about by a change in price is directly related to the elasticity of demand. If elasticity is less than unity (so demand is inelastic), the percentage change in price will exceed the percentage change in quantity. The price change will then be the more influential of the two changes, so that total spending will change in the same direction as the price changes. If, however, elasticity exceeds unity (demand is elastic), the percentage change in quantity will exceed the percentage change in price. The quantity change will then be the more influential change, so that the total amount spent will change in the same direction as quantity changes (that is, in the opposite direction to the change in price).

1. When elasticity of demand exceeds unity (demand is elastic), a fall in price increases total spending on the good and a rise in price reduces it.

2. When elasticity is less than unity (demand is inelastic), a fall in price reduces total spending on the good and a rise in price increases it.

3. When elasticity of demand is unity, a rise or a fall in price leaves total spending on the good unaffected.[3]

You should now return to the example in Table 4.1 and calculate what happens to total spending on the product when price changes in each case. In the case of product A, whose demand is inelastic, you will see that a rise in price raises total spending (and thus also the revenue of sellers). In contrast, the rise in the price of good B, whose demand is elastic, lowers total spending (and sellers' revenue).

Some complications

We now need to look a little more closely at the elasticity measure. Let us first write out in symbols the definition that we have been using, which is percentage change in quantity divided by percentage change in price:

$$\eta = \frac{\frac{\Delta q}{q} \cdot 100}{\frac{\Delta p}{p} \cdot 100}.$$

We can cancel out the 100s and multiply the numerator and denominator by $p/\Delta p$ to get

$$\eta = \frac{\Delta q}{q} \cdot \frac{p}{\Delta p}.$$

Since it does not matter in which order we do our multiplication (i.e. $q \cdot \Delta p = \Delta p \cdot q$), we may reverse the order of the two terms in the denominator and write

$$\eta = \frac{\Delta q}{\Delta p} \cdot \frac{p}{q}. \qquad (2)$$

We have now split elasticity into two parts: $\Delta q/\Delta p$, the ratio of the change in quantity to the change in price, which is related to the slope of the demand curve; and p/q, which is the *level* of price and quantity at which we make our measurement.

Figure 4.4 shows a straight-line demand curve. If we wish to measure the elasticity at a point, we take our p and q at

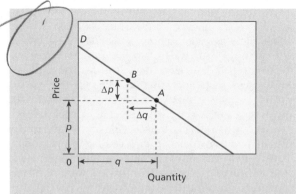

Figure 4.4 Elasticity on a linear demand curve

Elasticity depends on the slope of the demand curve and the point at which the measurement is made. Starting at point A and moving to point B, the ratio $\Delta p/\Delta q$ is the slope of the line, while its reciprocal $\Delta q/\Delta p$ is the first term in the percentage definition of elasticity. The second term is p/q, which is the ratio of the coordinates of point A. Since the slope $\Delta p/\Delta q$ is constant, it is clear that the elasticity along the curve varies with the ratio p/q, which is zero where the curve intersects the quantity axis and 'infinity' where it intersects the price axis.

that point and consider a price change, taking us to another point, and measure our Δp and Δq between those two points. The slope of the straight line joining the two points is $\Delta p/\Delta q$. (If you are not sure about this, see the explanation on page 25.) The term in equation (2), however, is $\Delta q/\Delta p$, which is the reciprocal of $\Delta p/\Delta q$. (This involves just turning the ratio upside down. So the reciprocal of 2/3 is 3/2, and the reciprocal of the whole number is its inverse: the reciprocal of 4 is 1/4.) Thus, the first term in the elasticity formula (2) is the reciprocal of the slope of the straight line joining the two price–quantity positions under consideration. The second term is the ratio of price to quantity at the point where elasticity is measured.

Now we can use the expression in (2) to discover a number of things about our elasticity measure.

First, the elasticity of a negatively sloped straight-line demand curve varies from infinity at the price axis to zero at the quantity axis. A straight line has a constant slope, so that the ratio $\Delta p/\Delta q$ is the same anywhere on the line. Therefore its reciprocal, $\Delta q/\Delta p$, must also be constant. We can now infer the changes in η by inspecting changes in the ratio p/q as we move along the demand curve. At the price axis $q = 0$ and p/q is undefined. However, if we let q

---

[3] Algebraically, total spending is price *times* quantity. If, for example, the equilibrium price and quantity are p_1 and q_1, then total spending is $p_1 q_1$. On a demand-curve diagram, price per unit is given by a vertical distance and quantity by a horizontal distance. It follows that on such a diagram total spending is given by the *area* of a rectangle the length of whose sides represent price and quantity. Total revenue (receipts) to the supplier and total spending by consumers are identical in these examples.

approach zero, without ever quite reaching it, we see that the ratio p/q becomes very large. Thus, elasticity increases without limit as q approaches zero. Loosely, we say elasticity is infinity when q is zero. Now move the point at which elasticity is being measured down the demand curve. As this happens, p falls and q rises steadily; thus, the ratio p/q is falling steadily, so that η is also falling. At the q-axis the price is zero, so the ratio p/q is zero. Thus, elasticity is zero.

Second, with a straight-line demand curve the elasticity measured from any point (p, q), according to equation (2) above, is independent of the direction and magnitude of the change in price and quantity. This follows immediately from the fact that the slope of a straight line is a constant. If we start from some point (p, q) and then change price, the ratio $\Delta q/\Delta p$ will be the same whatever the direction or the size of the change in p.

Our third point takes us back to the beginning of this chapter, where we warned against judging elasticity from the apparent shape of a demand curve. We often want to compare elasticities of two different demand curves, but we have just seen that the elasticity of a straight-line demand curve varies as we move along it. So how can we compare two numbers, both of which are ranging from zero to infinity for every straight-line demand curve? Fortunately, if two demand curves intersect, their elasticity can be compared *at the point of intersection* merely by comparing the slopes of the two curves. The steeper curve is the less elastic. Figure 4.5 shows two intersecting curves and proves that the steeper curve is less elastic than the flatter curve when elasticity is measured at the point where the two curves intersect. The intuitive reason is that at the point of intersection p and q are common to both curves, so all that differs in the elasticity formula is their relative slopes. This is a valuable result, which we will use many times in later chapters.

Measured at the point of intersection of two demand curves, the steeper curve has the lower elasticity.

The fourth point is that, when equation (2) is applied to a nonlinear demand curve, the elasticity measured at any one point varies with the direction and magnitude of the change in price and quantity. Figure 4.6 shows a nonlinear demand curve with elasticity being measured at one point. The figure makes it apparent that the ratio $\Delta q/\Delta p$, and hence the elasticity, will vary according to the size and the direction of the price change. This result is very inconvenient. It happens because the ratio $\Delta q/\Delta p$ gives the average reaction of q to a change in p over a section of the demand curve, and, depending on the range that we take, the average reaction will be different.

A more precise measure

The measure defined in (2) gives the elasticity over some range, or *arc*, of the demand curve. This measure is sometimes

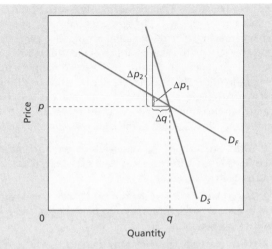

Figure 4.5 Two intersecting demand curves

At the point of intersection of two demand curves, the steeper curve has the lower elasticity. At the point of intersection p and q are common to both curves, and hence the ratio p/q is the same. Therefore, elasticity varies only with $\Delta q/\Delta p$. The absolute value of the slope of the steeper curve, $\Delta p_2/\Delta q$, is larger than the absolute value of the slope, $\Delta p_1/\Delta q$, of the flatter curve. Thus, the absolute value of the ratio $\Delta q/\Delta p_2$ on the steeper curve is smaller than the ratio $\Delta q/\Delta p_1$ on the flatter curve, so that elasticity is lower.

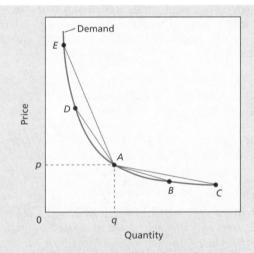

Figure 4.6 Elasticity on a nonlinear demand curve

Elasticity measured from one point on a nonlinear demand curve and using the percentage formula varies with the direction and magnitude of the change being considered. Elasticity is to be measured from point A, so the ratio p/q is given. The ratio $\Delta p/\Delta q$ is the slope of the line joining point A to the point reached on the curve after the price has changed. The smallest ratio occurs when the change is to point C and the highest ratio when it is to point E. Since the term in the elasticity formula, $\Delta q/\Delta p$, is the reciprocal of this slope, measured elasticity is largest when the change is to point C and smallest when it is to point E.

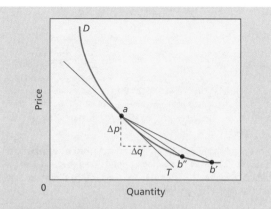

Figure 4.7 Elasticity by the exact method

When elasticity is related to the slope of the tangent to the demand curve at some point, there is a unique measured value of elasticity at that point. In this method the ratio $\Delta q/\Delta p$ is taken as the reciprocal of the slope of the line that is tangent to point a. Thus, there is only one measured elasticity at point a: it is p/q multiplied by $\Delta q/\Delta p$ measured along the tangent T. There is no averaging of changes in p and q in this measure because only one point on the curve is used.

used in empirical work where elasticity is measured between two observed price–quantity situations. In theoretical work, however, it is normal to use a concept that gives a unique measure of the elasticity at each specific point on the demand curve. Instead of using the changes in price (Δp) and quantity (Δq) over some range of the curve, this elasticity measure uses the concept of how quantity is *tending* to change as price changes at each specific point on the curve.

If we wish to measure the elasticity in this way, we need to know the reaction of quantity to a change in price at each point on the curve, not over some range on the curve. We use the symbol dq/dp to refer to this concept and define it as *the reciprocal of the slope of the straight line (i.e. $\Delta q/\Delta p$) that is tangent to the demand curve at the point in question*. Figure 4.7 illustrates the use of this measure to calculate the elasticity of demand at the point a. It is the ratio p/q (as it has been in all previous measures) now multiplied by the ratio $\Delta q/\Delta p$ measured along the straight line that is tangent to the curve at a.[4] This definition may now be written as

$$\eta = \frac{\mathrm{d}q}{\mathrm{d}p} \cdot \frac{p}{q}. \qquad (3)$$

This elasticity measure is the one normally used in economic theory. Elasticity measured by the percentage formula $(\Delta q/\Delta p)(p/q)$ may be regarded as an approximation to this expression. It is obvious from inspecting Figure 4.7 that the elasticity measured from $(\Delta q/\Delta p)(p/q)$ will come closer to that measured by $(\mathrm{d}q/\mathrm{d}p)(p/q)$, the smaller is the price change used to calculate the value of $\Delta q/\Delta p$. Thus, if we consider the percentage definition of elasticity as an

approximation to the precise definition, the approximation improves as the size of Δp diminishes. Box 4.2 further investigates some of the properties of the percentage definition and shows a practical way of avoiding some of its undesirable aspects. The appendix to this chapter sets out in greater detail the mathematics of elasticity.

What determines elasticity of demand?

The main determinant of elasticity is the availability of substitutes. Some products, such as margarine, cabbage, Coca Cola, and the Peugeot 406, have quite close substitutes—butter, other green vegetables, Pepsi, and the VW Passat. When the price of any one of these products changes, *the prices of the substitutes remaining constant*, consumers will substitute one product for another. When the price falls they will buy more of the product and less of its substitutes. When the price rises they will buy less of the product and more of its substitutes. More broadly defined products, such as all foods, all clothing, cigarettes, and petrol, have few if any satisfactory substitutes. A rise in their price can be expected to cause a smaller fall in quantity demanded than would be the case if close substitutes were available.

A product with close substitutes tends to have an elastic demand; one with no close substitutes tends to have an inelastic demand.

Closeness of substitutes—and thus measured elasticity—depends both on how the product is defined and on the time-period under consideration. This is explored in the following sections. One common misconception about demand elasticity is discussed in Box 4.3.

Definition of the product There is no substitute for food; it is a necessity of life. Thus, for food taken as a whole, demand is inelastic over a large price range. It does not follow, however, that any one food, such as Weetabix or Heinz tomato soup, is a necessity in the same sense: each of these has close substitutes, such as Kellogg's Cornflakes and Campbell's tomato soup. Individual food products can have quite elastic demands, and they frequently do.

Durable goods provide a similar example. Durables as a whole have less elastic demands than individual durable goods. For example, after a rise in the price of TV sets, some consumers might replace their personal computer or their hi-fi system instead of buying a new TV. Thus, although their purchases of television sets falls, their total purchases of durables falls by much less.

Because most specific manufactured goods have close substitutes, they tend to have price-elastic demands. Hats, for

---

[4] Although the expression dq/dp, as we have defined it, is the differential-calculus concept of the derivative of quantity with respect to price at the point (p, q), you can understand the concept without knowing calculus. The calculus of elasticity is outlined in the appendix to this chapter.

Box 4.2 Measuring elasticity over a range

We have seen that the percentage formula gives different answers for the elasticity at any point on a nonlinear demand curve depending on the size and the direction of the change being considered. Many textbooks just give the percentage elasticity formula, without warning the reader of this property. Inquisitive students usually discover the property with a shock the first time they try to calculate some elasticities from numerical data.

One common way in which students discover the problem is when they try to calculate the elasticity on a unit-elasticity curve. Using the percentage formula, the answer never comes out to be 1. For example, the demand curve

$$p = £100/q \qquad (A1)$$

is a unit-elastic curve because expenditure, pq, remains constant at £100 whatever the price. But if you substitute any two prices into the above equation and calculate the elasticity according to the percentage formula, you will *never* get an answer of 1, whatever two prices you take. For example, the equation tells us that, if price rises from £2 to £3, quantity falls from 50 to 33.3. If we take the original price as £2, we have a price change of 50 per cent and a quantity change of −33.3 per cent, making an elasticity of −0.667. If we take the original price as £3, the elasticity comes out to be −1.5. This is unsatisfactory. The problem can be avoided when measuring elasticity between two separate points on the curve by taking p and q as the average values between the two points on the curve. This measure has two convenient properties. First, it is independent of the direction of the change and, second, it gives a value of unity for any point on a demand curve whose true value is unity.

In the above example the average p is £2.5 and the average q is 41.667. This makes the percentage change in price 40 per cent ((1/2.5) × 100) and

the percentage change in quantity also 40 per cent ((16.667/41.667) × 100). So elasticity is correctly measured as 1. Whatever two prices you put into equation (A1), you will always get a value of unity for the elasticity, provided you use the average of the two prices and of the two quantities when calculating the elasticity. Readers who enjoy playing with algebra can have fun proving this proposition.*

The best approximation to the correct measure when elasticity is measured between two separate points on a demand curve is obtained by defining p and q as the average of the prices and quantities at the two points on the curve.

The above is the best way to measure elasticities, given readings from any two points on a curve when that is all that is known. As we have seen in the text, for theoretical purposes the way out of the problem is to measure the ratio $\Delta q/\Delta p$ as the slope of the tangent to one point on the curve rather than between two points on the curve. To do this, we need to know a portion of the demand curve around the point in question.

In practice, economists do not usually estimate elasticity on the basis of only one observation. It is more common to report an elasticity measure that is valued at the mean of two p and q data points. This is analogous to the averaging we suggest here.

---

* What you need to prove is that

$$\frac{q_2 - q_1}{p_2 - p_1} \cdot \frac{(p_1 + p_2)/2}{(q_1 + q_2)/2} = 1.$$

 Box 4.3 Elasticity and income

It is often argued that the demand for a product will be more inelastic the smaller the proportion of income spent on it. The argument runs as follows. When only a small proportion of income is spent on some product, consumers will hardly notice a price rise. Hence they will not react strongly to price changes one way or the other.

The most commonly quoted example of this alleged phenomenon is salt. Salt is, however, a poor example for the argument being advanced. Although it does take up a very small part of consumers' total expenditure, it also has few close substitutes. Consider another product, say a type of mint. These mints no doubt account for only a small portion of the total expenditure of mint-suckers, but there are many close substitutes—other types of mints and other sucking sweets. The makers of Polo mints, for example, know that if they raise Polo prices greatly mint-suckers will switch to other brands of mint and to other types of sucking sweets. They thus face an elastic demand for their product.

Similar considerations apply to any one brand of matches. If the makers

of Swan Vesta matches raise their prices significantly, people will switch to other brands of matches rather than pay the higher price.

What this discussion shows is that *goods with close substitutes will tend to have elastic demands, whether they account for a large or a small part of consumers' incomes.*

There is, however, another aspect of the influence of income. To see this, consider any good that has an inelastic demand. A rise in its price causes more to be spent on it. If consumers spend more on that product, they must spend less on all others taken as a group. But the higher is the proportion of income spent on the product, the less likely are they to spend more on it when its price rises. After all, if a consumer spends all of his or her income on potatoes, demand must have unit elasticity. As price rises, purchases must then fall in proportion since the consumer has only a given income to spend. Thus, *for a good to have a highly inelastic demand, it must have few good substitutes, and it must not take up too large a proportion of consumers' total expenditure.*

example, have been estimated to have an elasticity of –3.0. In contrast, all clothing taken together tends to be inelastic.

Any one of a group of related products will tend to have an elastic demand, even though the demand for the group as a whole may be inelastic.

Long-run and short-run elasticity of demand Because it takes time to adjust fully to some price change, a demand that is inelastic in the short run may prove elastic when enough time has passed. For example, before the first OPEC oil price shocks of the mid-1970s, the demand for petrol was thought to be highly inelastic because of the absence of satisfactory substitutes. But the large price increases over the 1970s led to the development of smaller, more fuel-efficient cars and to less driving. The elasticity of demand for petrol was measured as –0.6 soon after the price rose. However, when the first five years of quantity adjustment had been allowed for, the elasticity had become –1.2.

For many products the response of quantity demanded to a given price change, and thus the measured price elasticity of demand, will tend to be greater the longer the time-span considered.

The different quantity responses can be shown by different demand curves. Every demand curve shows the response of consumer demand to a change in price. For such products as cornflakes and ties, the full response occurs quickly and there is little reason to worry about longer-term effects. For these products a single demand curve will suffice. Other products are typically used in connection with highly durable appliances or machines. A change in the price of, say, electricity or petrol may not have its major effect until the stock of appliances and machines using these products has been adjusted. This adjustment may take a long time, making it useful to identify two kinds of demand curve for such products. A *short-run demand curve* shows the response of quantity demanded to a change in price, *given* the existing quantities of the durable goods that use the product, and *given* existing supplies of substitute products. A different short-run demand curve will exist for each such structure of durable goods and substitute products. The *long-run demand curve* shows the response of quantity demanded to a change in price after enough time has passed to allow all adjustments to be made.

The relation between long-run and short-run demand curves is shown in Figure 4.8. Assume, for example, that there is a large rise in the price of electricity. The initial response will be along the short-run demand curve. There will be some fall in quantity demanded, but the percentage drop is likely to be less than the percentage rise in price, making short-run demand inelastic. Over time, however, many people will replace their existing electric cookers with gas cookers as they wear out. New homes will be equipped with gas rather than electric appliances more often than they would have been before the price rise. After

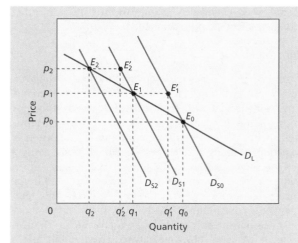

Figure 4.8 Short-run and long-run demand curves

The long-run demand curve is more elastic than the short-run curves. D_L is the long-run demand curve showing the quantity that will be bought after consumers become fully adjusted to each given price. Through each point on D_L there is a short-run demand curve. It shows the quantities that will be bought at each price when consumers are fully adjusted to the price at which that particular short-run curve intersects the long-run curve. So at every other point on the short run curve consumers are not fully adjusted to the price they face, possibly because they have an inappropriate stock of durable goods. When consumers are fully adjusted to price p_0, they are at point E_0 consuming q_0. Short-run variations in price then move them along the short-run demand curve D_{S0}. Similarly, when they are fully adjusted to price p_1 they are at E_1, and short-run price variations move them along D_{S1}. The line D_{S2} shows short-run variations in demand when consumers are fully adjusted to price p_2.

further time, factories will switch to relatively cheaper sources of power. When all these types of long-run adaptation have been made, the demand for electricity will have fallen a great deal. Indeed, over this longer period of time, the percentage reduction in quantity demanded may exceed the percentage increase in price. If so, the long-run demand for electricity will be elastic.

The long-run demand curve for a product that is used in conjunction with durable products will tend to be substantially more elastic than any of the short-run demand curves.

This insight will prove valuable in several of the chapters that follow.

Other demand elasticities

So far we have discussed *price elasticity of demand*, the response of the quantity demanded to a change in the product's own price. The concept of demand elasticity can, however, be broadened to measure the response to changes in *any* of the factors that influence demand. How much, for example, do changes in income and the prices of other products affect quantity demanded?

Income elasticity

Economic growth has raised the real income of the average citizen of Europe and North America quite dramatically over the past two centuries. At low levels of income most money is spent on such basics as food, clothing, and shelter. As income rises, an increasing proportion of expenditure tends to fall on manufactured goods, particularly such durables as cars, TV sets, and refrigerators. At yet higher levels of income, more and more of any additional income goes to services such as foreign travel, entertainment, and education.

The responsiveness of demand for a product to changes in income is termed **income elasticity of demand**, and is defined as

$$\eta_y = \frac{\text{percentage change in quantity demanded}}{\text{percentage change in income}}.$$

(handwritten annotations: Percentage change in income; $\frac{\Delta Income}{\Delta Price}$; Price)

For most products, increases in income lead to increases in quantity demanded, and income elasticity is therefore positive. If the resulting percentage change in quantity demanded is larger than the percentage increase in income, η_y will exceed unity. The product's demand is then said to be **income-elastic**. If the percentage change in quantity demanded is smaller than the percentage change in income, η_y will be less than unity. The product's demand is then said to be **income-inelastic**. In the boundary case, the percentage changes in income and quantity demanded are equal, making η_y unity. The product is said to have a *unit income elasticity of demand*.

While virtually all observed price elasticities are negative, income elasticities are observed to be both positive and negative. *(handwritten: 제곱 제곱이)*

We have already encountered the link between income changes and demand on pages 44–66, where we argued that a change in income would shift the demand curve for a product. If the product is a normal good, a rise in income causes more of it to be demanded, other things being equal, which means a rightward shift in the product's demand curve. If the product is an inferior good, a rise in income causes less of it to be demanded, which means a leftward shift in the product's demand curve. So normal goods have positive income elasticities while inferior goods have negative income elasticities. Finally, the boundary case between normal and inferior goods occurs when a rise in income leaves quantity demanded unchanged, so that income elasticity is zero.

The important terminology of income elasticity is summarized in Figure 4.9 and in Box 4.1 on page 62. You should spend time familiarizing yourself with this terminology. Figure 4.9 illustrates all possible reactions by

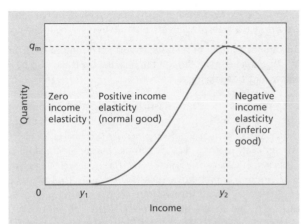

Figure 4.9 The relation between quantity demanded and income

Normal goods have positive income elasticities; inferior goods have negative elasticities. Nothing is demanded at income less than y_1, so for incomes below y_1 income elasticity is zero. Between incomes of y_1 and y_2, quantity demanded rises as income rises, making income elasticity positive. As income rises above y_2, quantity demanded falls from its peak at q_m, making income elasticity negative.

showing a product whose income elasticity goes from zero to positive to negative. No specific good is likely to show a pattern exactly like this. Most goods will have a positive income elasticity at all levels of income—people demand more as they get richer. (It should be obvious that no good can have a negative income elasticity at *all* levels of income.) A graph that directly relates quantity demanded to income, such as Figure 4.9, is called an *Engel curve* after Ernst Engel (1821–96), the German economist who used this device to display the relationship between household income and spending on necessities.

Cross-elasticity

The responsiveness of quantity demanded of one product to changes in the prices of other products is often of considerable interest. Producers of, say, beans and other meat substitutes find the demands for their products rising when cattle shortages force the price of beef up. Producers of large cars found their sales falling when the price of petrol rose dramatically after large oil price rises.

The responsiveness of demand for one product to changes in the price of another product is called **cross-elasticity of demand**. It is defined as

$$\eta_{xy} = \frac{\text{percentage change in quantity demanded of product X}}{\text{percentage change in price of product Y}}.$$

Cross-elasticity can vary from minus infinity to plus infinity. Complementary goods have negative cross-elasticities and substitute goods have positive cross-elasticities.

Box 4.4 **Elasticity matters**

Elasticities are rather boring concepts to learn about and to calculate. But they are powerful tools. Practical people who scorn theory ignore elasticity considerations at their peril. Here are a few cautionary tales.

• Many years ago the government of the former USSR was trying to earn enough US dollars to buy some strategic materials that it lacked at home. It had few exports at the time but it did have large stocks of gold, which it dumped on the world market to earn US dollars. Since it was desperate for the money it adopted desperate measures, selling a large amount quickly. This drove the price down substantially. Indeed, the price fell more than in proportion to the increased quantity brought to the market. If you had been advising the Communist government just after reading this chapter, you would have known enough to point out the error of its ways. Since the world demand for gold was inelastic, it needed to be careful not to try to sell too much. It could have earned more by selling less!

• Not long ago the executive of a professional association introduced a motion at the annual meeting 'to increase dues by 10 per cent so as to increase our revenues by 10 per cent'. You could have told them that they were optimistically assuming the elasticity of demand for membership was zero. If the elasticity differed at all from zero, revenues would rise by less than 10 per cent. If the elasticity proved to be greater than unity, they would actually suffer a loss of revenue as a result of the rise in dues.

• A local bus company fearfully raised its prices two years ago by 10 per cent in an attempt to cover increased costs. It was pleased to see its revenues rise by 5 per cent. This year it confidently raised its prices again, and was surprised and dismayed to find that its revenues fell by 2 per cent. The manager was reported in the local press as saying, 'It is hard to do business when our customers are so erratic.' You could have told him that there was nothing erratic about the customers' behaviour. The manager was unreasonably assuming that the elasticity of demand for bus rides was constant over the whole relevant range. All that happened is that the second increase took fares into the range where the market demand curve was elastic.

Mobile phones and the calls that can be made on them, for example, are complements. A fall in the price of calls causes an increase in the demand for both handsets and calls. Thus, changes in the price of calls and in the quantity of handsets demanded will have opposite signs—price of calls goes down and demand for handsets goes up. In contrast, mobile calls and fixed-line calls are substitutes: a fall in the price of mobile calls increases the quantity of mobile calls made but reduces the quantity of fixed-line calls demanded. Changes in the price of mobile calls and in the quantity of fixed-line calls demanded will, therefore, have the same sign. The terminology of cross-elasticity is also summarized in Box 4.1.

Box 4.4 provides some examples of the importance of taking elasticity into account when making many practical decisions.

Supply elasticity

We have seen that elasticity of demand measures the response of quantity demanded to changes in any of the variables that affect it. Similarly, elasticity of supply measures the response of quantity supplied to changes in any of the factors that influence it. Because we wish to focus on the product's own price as a factor influencing its supply, we will be concerned mainly with *price elasticity of supply*. The usual practice is to drop the adjective 'price', referring to 'elasticity of supply' or 'supply elasticity' whenever there is no ambiguity in this usage.

Supply elasticities are important in economics. Our treatment is brief for two reasons: first, much of what has been said about demand elasticity carries over to the case of supply elasticity and does not need repeating; second, we will have more to say about the determinants of supply elasticity later in this book when we have looked more closely at the production decisions of firms.

A definition

The **price elasticity of supply** is defined as the percentage change in quantity supplied divided by the percentage change in price that brought it about. Letting the lower-case Greek letter epsilon, ε, stand for this measure, its formula is

$$\varepsilon_s = \frac{\text{percentage change in quantity supplied}}{\text{percentage change in price}}.$$

Supply elasticity is a measure of the degree of responsiveness of quantity supplied to changes in the product's own price.

Since supply curves normally have positive slopes, supply elasticity is normally positive.

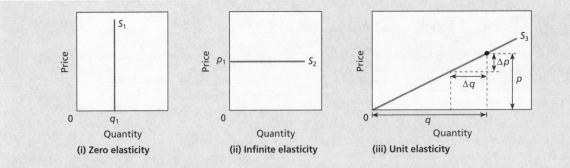

Figure 4.10 Three constant-elasticity supply curves

All three curves have constant elasticity. Curve S_1 has a *zero elasticity*, since the same quantity, q_1, is supplied whatever the price. Curve S_2 has an *infinite elasticity at price p_1*: nothing at all will be supplied at any price below p_1, while an indefinitely large quantity will be supplied at the price of p_1. Curve S_3, as well as all other straight lines through the origin, has a *unit elasticity*, indicating that the percentage change in quantity equals the percentage change in price between any two points on the curve.

Interpreting supply elasticity

Figure 4.10 illustrates three cases of supply elasticity. The case of zero elasticity is one in which the quantity supplied does not change as price changes. This would be the case, for example, if suppliers persisted in producing a given quantity and dumping it on the market for whatever it would bring. Infinite elasticity occurs at some price if nothing is supplied at lower prices but an indefinitely large amount will be supplied at that price. Any straight-line supply curve drawn through the origin, such as the one shown in part (iii) of the figure, has an elasticity of unity. The reason is that, for any positively sloped straight line, the ratio of p/q at any point on the line is equal to the ratio $\Delta p/\Delta q$ that defines the slope of the line. Thus, in the formula $(\Delta q/\Delta p)(p/q)$ the two ratios cancel each other out. A formal proof is available in the mathematical appendix to this chapter.

The case of unit supply elasticity illustrates that the warning given earlier for demand applies equally to supply. Do not confuse geometric steepness of supply curves with elasticity. Since *any* straight-line supply curve that passes through the origin has an elasticity of unity, it follows that there is no simple correspondence between geometrical steepness and supply elasticity. The reason is that varying steepness (when the scales on both axes are unchanged) reflects varying *absolute* changes, while elasticity depends on *percentage* changes. The terminology of supply elasticity is summarized in Box 4.1 on page 62.

What determines elasticity of supply?

What determines the response of producers to a change in the price of the product that they supply? First, the size of the response depends in part on how easily producers can shift from the production of other products to the one whose price has risen. If agricultural land and labour can be readily shifted from one crop to another, the supply of any one crop will be more elastic than if labour cannot easily be shifted. Here also, as with demand, length of time for response is critical. It may be difficult to change quantities supplied in response to a price increase in a matter of weeks or months, but easy to do so over a period of years. An obvious example concerns the planting cycle of crops. Also, new oilfields can be discovered, wells drilled, and pipelines built over a period of years, but not in a few months. Thus, the elasticity of supply of oil is much greater over five years than over one year, and greater over one year than over one month. Second, elasticity is strongly influenced by how costs respond to output changes. This issue will be looked at in more detail in later chapters.

Measurement of demand and supply

Much of what economists do to earn a living uses measurements of demand and supply elasticities. Will a fare increase help to ease the deficit of London Underground or the Panama Canal? The answer requires knowledge of price elasticity of demand. The United Nations Food and Agriculture Organization (FAO), and producers' co-ops, use income elasticities of demand to predict future changes in demand for food. Over the past decade, many industries have estimated their products' cross-elasticities of demand with petroleum in order to predict the effects of sharply changing petroleum prices. Members of the Organization of Petroleum Exporting Countries (OPEC) wish to know supply elasticities in non-member countries in order to predict the reaction to price increases manipulated by OPEC. The methods for obtaining this information are dealt with in econometrics courses. Solutions to two of the most troubling problems concerning demand measurement are discussed below.

Problems of demand measurement

The explosion of knowledge of elasticities in recent decades came about when econometricians overcame major problems in measuring demand (and supply) relationships.

Everything is changing at once

When quantity demanded changes over time, it is usually because *all* of the influences that affect demand have been changing at the same time. How, then, can the separate influence of each variable be determined?

What, for example, is to be made of the observation that the quantity of butter consumed per capita rose by 10 per cent over a period in which average consumer income rose by 5 per cent, the price of butter fell by 3 per cent, and the price of margarine rose by 4 per cent? How much of the change is due to income elasticity of demand, how much to price elasticity, and how much to the cross-elasticity between butter and margarine? If this is all we know, the question cannot be answered. If, however, there are many observations revealing, say, quantity demanded, income, price of butter, and price of margarine every month for four or five years, it is possible to discover the separate influence of each of the variables. The standard technique for doing so is called *multiple regression analysis*.

Separating the influences of demand and supply

A second set of problems concerns the separate estimation of demand and supply curves. We do not observe directly what people wish to buy and what producers wish to sell at each possible price. Rather, we see what they do buy and what they do sell. So in any specific market we observe a price and quantity that is a point on both the supply and demand curve. For example, Marks and Spencer might sell 1,000 white shirts at £30 each in a particular week. These shirts were both demanded and supplied, so the price and quantity combination is a point on the demand curve and on the supply curve. If in the subsequent week 1,100 shirts are sold at £32 each, what can we conclude about elasticity of demand or supply? The answer is 'nothing', unless we know whether it is the demand curve or the supply curve that has shifted. If both have shifted, then the observation tells us nothing about demand or supply elasticity.

The problem of how to estimate demand and supply curves from observed market data on prices and quantities actually traded is called the **identification problem**.

To illustrate the problem, we assume in Figure 4.11 that all situations observed in the real world are equilibrium ones, in the sense that they are produced by the intersection of demand and supply curves. The first two parts of the figure show cases where only one curve shifts. Observations made on prices and quantities then trace out the curve that has not shifted. The third part of the figure, however, shows that when both curves are shifting observations of prices and quantities are not sufficient to identify the slope of either curve.

The identification problem is surmountable. The key to identifying the demand and supply curves separately is to bring in variables other than price, and then relate demand to one set and supply to *some other* set. For example, supply of the product might be related not only to the price of the product but also to its cost of production, and demand might be related not only to the price of the product but also to consumers' incomes. Provided that these other variables change sufficiently, it is possible to determine the relation between quantity supplied and price as well as the relation between quantity demanded and price. The details of how this is done will be found in a course on econometrics.

Econometricians allow for the identification problem when estimating demand curves. In more popular discussions, however, the problem is sometimes ignored. Whenever you see an argument such as 'We know that the foreign elasticity of demand must be very low because the price of whisky rose by 10 per cent last year while whisky exports hardly changed at all', you should ask if the author has really identified the demand curve. If the rise in price was due to a rise in foreign demand for whisky, we may actually have discovered that the short-run *supply curve* of whisky is very inelastic (since whisky takes several years to manufacture). The general proposition to keep in mind is:

Unless we know that one curve has shifted while the other has not, price and quantity data alone are insufficient to reveal anything about the shape of either the demand or the supply curve.

Measurements of specific elasticities

The solution of the statistical problems associated with demand measurement has led to a large accumulation of data on demand elasticities. The value of these data to the applied economist shows the usefulness of demand theory.

Price elasticities

Much of the early work on demand measurement concentrated on the agricultural sector. Large fluctuations in agricultural prices provided both the incentives to study this

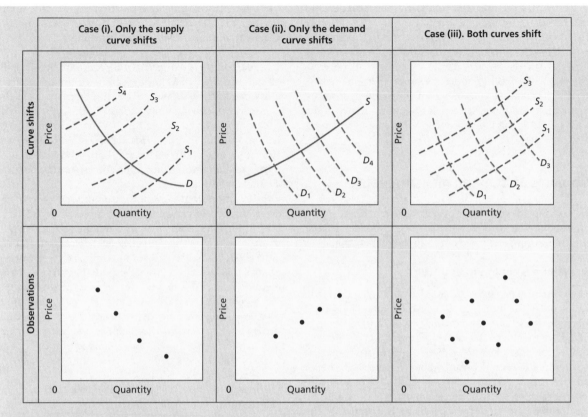

Figure 4.11 The identification problem

Observations on prices and quantities are sufficient to identify the slope of one of the curves only when it is stationary while the other shifts. In each case the curves in the top row shift randomly from one numbered position to another, generating the observations shown by the points in the corresponding bottom row. In case (i) the observations trace out the shape of the demand curve. In case (ii) they trace out the supply curve. In case (iii) neither curve can be identified from the observed prices and quantities.

sector and the data on which to base estimates of price elasticities of demand. Nobel Laureate Professor Richard Stone in the United Kingdom (1913–91) and Professor Henry Schultz (1893–1938) in the United States did much of the pioneering work. Many agricultural research centres extended their work, and even today they are making new estimates of the price elasticities of foodstuffs. The resulting data mostly confirm the existence of low price elasticities for food products as a whole, as well as for many individual products. The policy payoff of this knowledge in terms of understanding agricultural problems has been enormous; it represents an early triumph of empirical work in economics. (See the discussion in Chapter 5.)

Although the importance of the agricultural problem led early investigators to concentrate on the demand for foodstuffs, modern studies have expanded to include virtually the whole range of products on which consumers spend their incomes. The demands for consumer durables such as cars, radios, refrigerators, television sets, and houses are of

particular interest because they constitute a large fraction of total demand, and because they can vary markedly from one year to the next. A durable product can usually be made to last for another year; thus, purchases can be postponed with greater ease than can purchases of non-durables such as food and services. If enough consumers decide simultaneously to postpone purchases of durables for even six months, the effect on the economy can be substantial.

Durables as a whole have an inelastic demand, while many individual brands of durables have elastic demands. This is another example of the general proposition that the broader the category, the fewer the close substitutes and hence the lower the elasticity. Indeed, whether durable or non-durable, many specific manufactured goods have close substitutes, and studies show that they tend to have price-elastic demands. This is why many firms try to build strong brands so that consumers of their product remain loyal. It helps them to raise price without losing substantial market share.

Table 4.2 Price and income elasticities of UK food items

	Price elasticity	Income elasticity
Milk and cream	−0.36	0.05
Cheese	−0.35	0.23
Carcase meats	−0.69	0.2
Fresh fish	−0.69	0.27
Eggs	−0.28	−0.01
Fresh green vegetables	−0.66	0.27
Fresh potatoes	−0.12	0.09
Fresh fruit	−0.29	0.3
Fruit juices	−0.55	0.45
Bread	−0.4	0.12
Beverages	−0.37	0.1

Source: Expenditure and Food Survey, DEFRA 2002; available on www.defra.gov.uk. Data for price elasticities are for 1988–2000 and for income elasticities, 1998–2000. Estimates are derived from panel data, i.e. cross-section data for several periods of time.

Table 4.2 shows some recent measures of price elasticity for food products. Notice that all the price elasticities shown in the table are negative, and staples like potatoes and eggs have relative low price elasticities. What is not clear from the table is that, within categories shown in the table, the elasticity for a subset of that category can be much higher than for the product class as a whole. Carcase meats, for example, have a price elasticity of −0.69, but the price elasticity for lamb is −1.29, for pork −0.82, and for bacon −0.78. This indicates that carcase meats are closer substitutes for each other than are other foods for carcase meats as a whole.

Income elasticities

Table 4.2 also shows some measured income elasticities for the United Kingdom. Note the low income elasticities for all of the food products. The income elasticity for food as a whole (not shown in table) is estimated at 0.2, which says that for every 1 per cent increase in incomes there is only a 0.2 per cent increase in spending on food. Notice, however, that all but one of the estimates in the table show a positive income elasticity. Eggs have a negative income elasticity, but this number is not significantly different from zero, so we should not conclude from this that eggs are an inferior good. The only clear estimate of an inferior good among food products (not shown in the table, but from the same source) is margarine, which has an estimated income elasticity of −0.37.

Cross-elasticities

Cross-elasticities are much harder to estimate as there are many more of them. Each product has only one own-price elasticity and one income elasticity, but it has a (potential) cross-elasticity with every other product. The source for Table 4.2 does report estimates of cross-elasticities for the same food products, but most of them are insignificant. One that is not, however, is the positive cross-elasticity of bread and cheese (at 0.34), which indicates that bread and cheese are substitutes.

Though hard to measure, the concept of cross-elasticity is important. In many countries monopoly is illegal. Measurement of cross-elasticities has helped courts to decide on the allegation that a monopoly exists. To illustrate, assume that the competition authority of a particular country brings a suit against a company for buying up all the firms making aluminium cable, claiming the company has created a monopoly of the product. The company replies that it needs to own all the firms in order to compete efficiently against the several firms producing copper cable. It argues that these two products are such close substitutes that the firms producing each are in intense competition, so that the sole producer of aluminium cable cannot be said to have an effective monopoly over the market for cable. Measurement of cross-elasticity can be decisive in such a case. A cross-elasticity of 10, for example, would support the company by showing that the two products were such close substitutes that a monopoly of either would not be an effective monopoly of the cable market. A cross-elasticity of 0.5, on the other hand, would support the contention that the monopoly of aluminium cable *was* a monopoly over a complete market.

Elasticities and economic growth

One of the most interesting constants in the behaviour of elasticities is the tendency for both income and price elasticities of demand for food to fall as nations get richer. Over the decades, economic growth has been increasing the real incomes of many countries throughout the world. As this happens the demand for foodstuffs increases, but at a slower and slower rate. At the same time, the demand becomes less and less sensitive to price fluctuations. For example, the price elasticity of demand for food is only about 0.1 in the USA, the country with the highest per capita income. As we go down the income scale, price elasticities rise, being about 0.3 in the UK, 0.45 in Israel, 0.55 in Peru, and 0.7 in India. Over the same income range, income elasticities also fall. They go from about 0.15 in the USA 0.2 in the UK, 0.5 in Israel, and 0.65 in Peru to almost 0.8 in India.

This phenomenon of price and income elasticities that fall as economic growth raises per capita income has many important consequences, as we will see in the next chapter.

Other variables

Research shows that demand is often influenced by a wide variety of socioeconomic factors—family size, age, religion, geographical location, type of employment, wealth, and income expectations—that are not included in the traditional theory of demand. Although significant, the total contribution of all these factors to changes in demand tends to be small. Typically, less than 30 per cent of the variations in demand are accounted for by these 'other' factors and a much higher proportion is explained by the traditional variables of current prices and incomes.

Why the measurement of demand is important

The empirical measurements of demand elasticity help to provide the theory of price with empirical content. If we knew *nothing* about demand elasticities, then all of the exercises we have gone through in previous chapters would have very little application to the real world. As time goes by, further evidence accumulates, and economists are far beyond merely wondering if demand curves have negative slopes. Not only do we now know the approximate shape of many demand curves; we also have information about how demand curves shift. Our knowledge of demand relations increases significantly every year.

This knowledge has two general uses. First, in our study of economics it helps us to understand much more about how individual markets and the market economy work. This is helpful in understanding the world around us, and it helps inform debates about whether, for example, the market outcome can be trusted or whether government should intervene. Second, those of you who go on to work in business after you have finished college will find that your employer is competing with other firms in some markets and you may be expected to suggest ways in which the firm can be more successful. This will require you to build a detailed knowledge of the markets in which your firm operates, so that you can analyse issues such as the pricing of existing products and the potential impact of new products.

SUMMARY

Demand elasticity

■ Elasticity of demand (also called price elasticity of demand) is defined as the percentage change in quantity divided by the percentage change in price that brought it about.

■ When the percentage change in quantity is less than the percentage change in price, demand is inelastic and a fall in price lowers the total amount spent on the product. When the percentage change in quantity is greater than the percentage change in price, demand is elastic and a fall in price raises total spending on the product.

■ A more precise measure that gives a unique value for elasticity at any point on any demand curve replaces $\Delta q/\Delta p$ measured between two points on the curve with $\Delta q/\Delta p$ measured along the tangent to the curve at the point in question (symbolized by dq/dp).

■ The main determinant of the price elasticity of demand is the availability of substitutes for the product. Any one of a group of close substitutes will have a more elastic demand than the group as a whole.

■ Elasticity of demand tends to be greater the longer the time over which adjustment occurs. Items that have a few substitutes in the short run may develop ample substitutes when consumers and producers have time to adapt.

■ Income elasticity is the percentage change in quantity demanded divided by the percentage change in income that brought it about. The income elasticity of demand for a product will usually change as income varies.

■ Cross-elasticity is the percentage change in quantity demanded divided by the percentage change in the price of some other product that brought it about. Products that are substitutes for one another have positive cross-elasticities; products that complement one another have negative cross-elasticities.

Supply elasticity

■ Elasticity of supply measures the ratio of the percentage change in the quantity supplied of a product to the percentage change in its price.

■ A commodity's elasticity of supply depends on how easy it is to shift resources into the production of that commodity and how the costs of producing the commodity vary as its production varies.

Measurement of demand and supply

■ Over the years, economists have measured many price, income, and cross-elasticities of demand. This requires the use of statistical techniques to measure the separate influences of each of several variables when all are changing at once. It also requires a solution of the identification problem, which refers to measuring the separate shapes of the demand and supply curves. This cannot be done from price and quantity data alone.

TOPICS FOR REVIEW

- Price, income, and cross-elasticity of demand
- Zero, inelastic, unitary, elastic, and infinitely elastic demand
- The relation between price elasticity and changes in total expenditure
- Determinants of demand elasticity

- Income elasticities for normal and inferior goods
- Cross-elasticities between substitutes and complements
- Long- and short-run elasticity of demand
- Elasticity of supply and its determinants

DISCUSSION QUESTIONS

1 Calculate the elasticity of demand for the demand curve $P = 100 - 5Q$ at each of the following price and quantity levels:
$P = 90$ and $Q = 2$;
$P = 50$ and $Q = 10$;
$P = 5$ and $Q = 19$.

2 Calculate the elasticity of supply for the supply curve $P = 10 + 3Q$ at each of the following price and quantity levels:
$P = 25$ and $Q = 5$;
$P = 40$ and $Q = 10$;
$P = 70$ and $Q = 20$.

3 In one particular month 1.2 million kilos of potatoes are sold at £1.20 per kilo. In the next month 1.5 million kilos are sold at £1.40 per kilo. Which of the following explanations is consistent with this observation? (There may be more than one or none at all.)
(a) The price of carrots has risen and carrots are a close substitute for potatoes.
(b) The price of fish has risen and fish is a complement to potatoes.
(c) Bad weather has reduced the potato crop.
(d) Consumer incomes have risen and potatoes are an inferior good.
(e) Newspapers have reported that potatoes have health giving properties, and this has generated a shift of tastes towards potatoes.

4 Suggest products that you think might have the following patterns of elasticity of demand:
(a) high income elasticity, high price elasticity;
(b) high income elasticity, low price elasticity;
(c) low income elasticity, low price elasticity;
(d) low income elasticity, high price elasticity.

5 Define the elasticity of demand and explain why this concept should be of interest to those in business who have choices to make about the price at which to sell their products.

6 Why is demand for many products likely to be more elastic in the long run than in the short run?

7 Outline the main determinants of demand and supply elasticity.

8 What is the identification problem? How does it affect the interpretation of observed price and quantity changes, and what does it imply that we need to know before we can say whether any specific price and quantity change contains information about either demand or supply elasticity?

9 Explain the concept of income elasticity. Why does the income elasticity of demand for food tend to be low in rich countries? Give examples of types of goods and services the demand for which you would expect to have a high income elasticity in rich countries. How would the last answer differ in poorer countries?

Mathematical Appendix Elasticity

Elasticity defined

Consider a demand function,

$$q^d = q(p). \tag{A1}$$

Elasticity of demand is defined as

$$\eta = \frac{\mathrm{d}q}{\mathrm{d}p} \cdot \frac{p}{q}. \tag{A2}$$

Elasticity of a linear demand curve

If the demand function is linear, i.e. if

$$q^d = a - bp, \tag{A3}$$

we then have

$$\eta = -b\frac{p}{q} \tag{A4}$$

or

$$\eta = -\frac{bp}{a + bp}. \tag{A5}$$

If $p = 0$,

$$\eta = -\frac{0}{a},$$

which is zero.

Now consider the intercept on the quantity axis. If $q = 0$, then from (A3) $a - bp = 0$. Thus,

$$\eta = -\frac{bp}{0},$$

which is undefined.

So as $q \to 0$, $\eta \to \infty$. In words, as q approaches zero, elasticity increases without limit.

Elasticity of a constant expenditure demand curve

Now let a constant amount, K, be spent on the commodity at all prices. The demand function is then

$$pq = K$$

or

$$q = Kp^{-1}.$$

Elasticity is then

$$\eta = (-p^{-2}K)\left(\frac{p}{q}\right),$$

$$\eta = \frac{K}{-pq} = -\frac{K}{K} = -1.$$

So elasticity is constant at unity.

Elasticity and total revenue

Let the demand function be

$$q^d = f(p). \tag{A6}$$

Total revenue is

$$R = pq^d = pf(p). \tag{A7}$$

The change in revenue as p is changed is

$$\frac{\mathrm{d}R}{\mathrm{d}p} = f(p) + pf_p = x. \tag{A8}$$

The last term merely tells us that we have chosen to call the marginal revenue x. So

$$f_p = \frac{x - f(p)}{p} \tag{A9}$$

elasticity is

$$\eta = f_p\frac{p}{q}. \tag{A10}$$

Substituting (A9) gives

$$\eta = \left(\frac{x - f(p)}{p}\right)\left(\frac{p}{q}\right) = \frac{x - f(p)}{q}.$$

So if TR is a maximum, MR $(= x)$ is zero, and since $q = f(p)$, η in the above expression is unity.

Elasticity of a linear supply curve

Now consider a linear supply curve:

$$q^s = c + dp, \quad 0 < d.$$

If this curve passes through the origin, $c = 0$ so

$$q^s = dp$$

or

$$p/q = 1/d.$$

Now

$$\eta = \frac{\mathrm{d}q}{\mathrm{d}p} \cdot \frac{p}{q}$$

$$\eta = (d)\left(\frac{1}{d}\right) = 1.$$

So the elasticity of any straight-line supply curve that passes through the origin is unity, whatever its slope.

Chapter 5

PRICE THEORY IN ACTION

Do demand curves really have negative slopes? Can demand and supply analysis help explain what is going on in real markets? What happens when governments try to intervene in a market? What is it about the agriculture industry that leads to so much government intervention, and what impact does this have on world markets? These are some of the issues we address in this chapter. In particular, you will learn that

• Changes in price really do lead to changes in quantity demanded.

• Market prices do adjust in response to shifts in demand and supply conditions.

• Elasticity of demand can be measured directly so long as other influences can be held constant.

• Intervention in markets by governments to fix prices has important consequences, not all or which can be considered desirable.

• Intervention in agricultural markets has been costly for consumers and for foreign producers.

Demand and supply analysis provides a powerful tool for understanding the world around us. Although there is more to be learned, especially about how firms affect supply, this chapter provides some payoff to what you have learned in the previous chapters. It shows how to use demand and supply to understand real events.

In the first half of this chapter we apply demand and supply analysis to several real-world situations—the world coffee market, admissions to museums, a newspaper price war and the impact of the Channel Tunnel. In the rest of the chapter, we study the effects of various government interventions in specific markets.

Throughout the chapter we use the method of comparative statics. Here is how it works. We start with a market in equilibrium. We then introduce the change in which we are interested. We then determine the new equilibrium. The differences between the two equilibria must be the result of the change we introduced, since that is the only disturbance that is operating. (Appropriate corrections can be made if we wish to apply the results to cases in which the industry is initially in disequilibrium.)

Finish your coffee, we're off to the museum

The coffee market

Judging from the growing number of Starbucks and Costa Coffee outlets, you might think that the market for coffee is booming. So it is for the final product, whether your preference be for a tall skinny latte or a machiatto grande. However, nothing could be further from the truth in the market for coffee beans. As Figure 5.1 shows, the world price of coffee beans fell to a historic low level in late 2001 and early 2002. Indeed, this was the lowest price of coffee in real terms (i.e. adjusted for inflation) in the last hundred years, and the lowest nominal price in at least the last three decades. So what was the reason for this fall?

Not surprisingly, the answer is that although demand has been increasing over time, supply has been increasing even faster. This has had the effect of creating excess supply at whatever is the current market price, which has tended to drive the price down even further.[1]

Demand for coffee has grown over time, but only slowly. The World Bank has estimated that the world-wide income elasticity of demand for coffee was about 0.6 up to the mid-1990s, and that this figure falls as per capita income rises. For example, in the United States, which has the highest

---

[1] Note that we are analysing demand for coffee beans here, and not demand for prepared coffee-based drinks in retail outlets, which has a very different market.

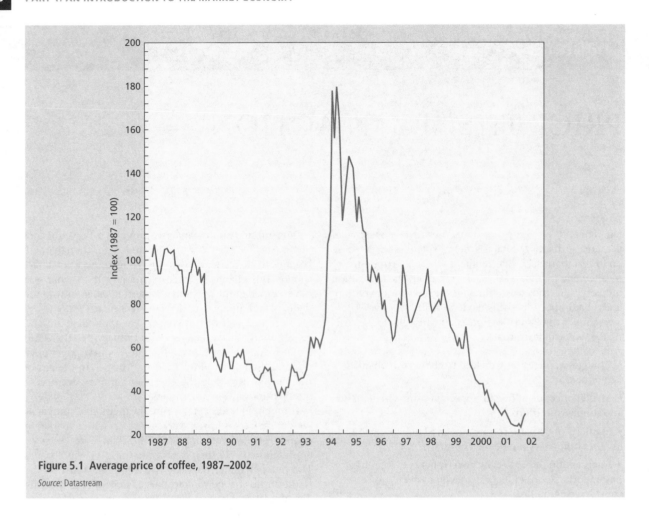

Figure 5.1 Average price of coffee, 1987–2002

Source: Datastream

per capita income in the world, the income elasticity is estimated to be close to zero. This means that demand rises at a slower rate than does income in the coffee importing countries.

On the supply side, there has been a steady increase in output capacity as traditional coffee producing countries such as Brazil have expanded their capacity and newer suppliers such as Vietnam have joined the band of big producers. The excess of supply over demand at current market prices since 1998 (up to 2002) has led to growing stocks of coffee beans in consuming countries. When stocks are already high, consumer countries become increasingly unwilling to take on any more, so only a fall in price can discourage further excess supply. However, the World Bank also estimates that supply elasticities are very low, which means that, despite sharp falls in prices, the quantity supplied falls only slightly. Hence, unless there is a crop failure (typically because of bad weather) in a major producing country such as Brazil (as happened in 1994), the prospects are for low coffee prices for some time to come. However, low prices do little to encourage an increase in quantity

demanded in consumer countries, as the own-price elasticity of demand is also low.

In summary, the demand curve is shifting slowly to the right as income increases, but only slowly (owing to a low income elasticity) and it is a fairly steep curve (owing to a low price elasticity). The supply curve, however, is shifting more quickly to the right over time (because of new production methods and greater planting). This means that prices will be tending to fall in normal times, but will rise sharply in abnormal times, such as when there is a crop failure in a major producer country.

This is a good illustration of the interaction of demand and supply forces. There are other elements to the story, which should not be totally ignored, but we do not have the space to discuss them fully here. First, the low coffee price causes severe problems for many of the world's poorest countries—coffee provides 76 per cent of export revenue for Burundi, 68 per cent for Ethiopia, 62 per cent for Rwanda, and 60 per cent for Uganda. Second, much of the recent growth in capacity has been in 'sun grown' plantations, which have no tree cover (as the forests have been cut down to provide the space), and use chemicals to enhance yields. The plantations can produce high yields quickly, but environmental groups argue that they are bad for the environment as they do not use the tree cover of traditional 'shade grown' coffee plantations and this is harmful to bird life (as well as involving destruction of forests). Third, the low coffee price has been particularly harmful to the traditional 'shade-grown' producers of Central America, who have not been covering costs and so have cut output (but not enough to affect the price significantly) and suffered lower prices, leading to dramatically reduced incomes.

Free museums

In November 2001 the UK government abolished admission charges on many museums. Entrance charges that had been as high as £9 for adults (lower prices for children and pensioners) were all set to zero overnight. What would you expect to happen when charges were abolished? Yes, admissions should rise.

Fortunately for economics textbook writers, admissions really did rise, and quite substantially in many cases. Comparing December 2001 monthly attendances with those in December 2000, and thereby controlling for seasonal influences, a huge increase in museum visits at the lower price is observed. The Victoria and Albert Museum (V&A) experienced the biggest increase, with visitor numbers rising from 42,600 in December 2000 to 174,000 in December 2001, an increase of 309 per cent. Similarly, though not so dramatically, the Museum of London had an 88 per cent increase, the Natural History Museum had an 82 per cent increase, and the Museums of Science and Industry in Manchester had a 75 per cent increase.

You might think that we cannot calculate demand elasticity when a price of zero is involved, as $\Delta P/P$ would be undefined. However, in this case we are measuring the price change over a range, so we would use the price P at the mid-point of the price change and quantity Q at the mid-point of the change. (To review the reasons for this, see Box 4.2 on page 66.)

Let us take the case of the V&A. The entry price fell from £5 to £0 and we know that admissions increased from 42.6 thousand to 174 thousand. We take P to be the mean of the price before and after the change, which is £2.50. The percentage change in price is $(-5/2.5) \times 100 = -200\%$.[2] We take Q to be the mean of admissions before and after the price change $((174 + 42.6)/2)$, which is 108.3 thousand. The change in admissions is 131.4 thousand, so the percentage change in admissions is $(131.4/108.3) \times 100 = 121.3$. The elasticity is the percentage change in quantity divided by the percentage change in price, or $121.3/-200 = -0.61$.

So the elasticity of demand for visits to the V&A on this basis is calculated as -0.61. This might seem very low given the huge increase in attendance; however, note that the price change was large too.

As noted in Chapter 4 (Box 4.2), you would get a different answer if you did the calculation at some other point on the demand curve. Using the initial price and quantity for P and Q, we would get an elasticity of just over (minus) 3 (from a 100 per cent reduction in price and a 309 per cent increase in quantity). However, if we used the after-reduction P and Q the elasticity would be calculated as zero, as we have an infinitely large change in price (5 as a percentage of 0) and a 75 per cent increase in quantity (131.4 thousand as a percentage of 174 thousand). Our actual calculation at the mean of P and Q is somewhere in between these two extremes.

Notice also that we have not, strictly speaking, calculated the demand elasticity for any one museum, as many museums changed their prices at the same time. The response might have been different if one museum had cut its entry charge at a time when no others did. In this case its demand elasticity could have been larger, as the elasticity of demand for a single museum is likely to be larger than that for museums as a whole (see the discussion of elasticity of demand for meat on page 73). On the other hand, numbers may have been boosted by the free publicity that the nationwide cutting of entry charges generated, so these two effects could be offsetting.

We now turn to an example in which one supplier cut its price but no other competitors followed for some time.

Keeping up with *The Times*

In September 1993 the owners of *The Times* newspaper unilaterally lowered the price of *The Times* by one-third. Initially all the major competing newspapers kept their prices constant and carried on as if nothing had happened. Only later did a price war break out.

Table 5.1 provides price and sales figures for the five major national broadsheet newspapers—*The Times*, the *Guardian*, the *Daily Telegraph*, the *Financial Times*, and the

Independent. Since consumers' average incomes changed only slightly over the period and newspapers have a low income elasticity, we would expect total sales to have

---

[2] Among other admission charges abolished, the Natural History Museum had charged £9 and the Science Museum £7.75. So the big increase in numbers attending the V&A was not because it had a higher charge than others before abolition.

Table 5.1   **Changes in demand for newspapers**

	Price		Average daily sales		Percentage change	
	Pre-Sept. '93	Post-Sept. '93	Pre-Sept. '93	Post-Sept. '93	Price	Sales
The Times	45p	30p	376,836	448,962	−40	+17.5
Guardian	45p	45p	420,154	401,705	0.0	−4.5
Daily Telegraph	45p	45p	1,037,375	1,017,326	0.0	−1.95
Independent	50p	50p	362,099	311,046	0.0	−15.2
			2,196,464	2,179,039		

The Times led but no one followed. The table shows the fall in the price of *The Times* and the less-than-proportionate increase in sales. It also shows the constant prices of the other papers, with declining sales as they lost readers to *The Times*. Percentage changes in the last two columns are calculated from the initial position, but calculations of elasticity in the text are made at the mid point between the initial and ultimate position.

Source: Audit Bureau of Circulation. The sales figures are daily average circulation for September 1992 to February 1993 and for September 1993 to February 1994.

remained constant, unless there had been a major change in tastes over the period in question. The data suggest that tastes did not change significantly, since the combined sales of all the newspapers held constant at around 2.5 million copies daily. Hence the existing suppliers were fighting for a share of a stable market. If one gained more customers, it had to be at the expense of rival suppliers.

Observed price elasticities

Table 5.1 shows us that a 40 per cent price reduction in the price of *The Times* led to a 17.5 per cent increase in its sales.[3] This indicates a price elasticity of demand for *The Times* of −0.44 (calculated as percentage change in quantity divided by percentage change in price, or 17.5/−40). As a result, *The Times*'s daily sales revenue fell from £169,576 (376,836 × £0.45) to £134,689 (448,962 × £0.30). Only if the price elasticity had been greater than 1 would total revenue have increased.

The competing papers suffered, and the *Independent* suffered most, with a 15.2 per cent loss of sales. This would suggest that the *Independent* was the closest substitute for *The Times*. The cross-elasticity of demand implied by these figures was −15.2/−40 = 0.38. (This is positive as both the sales and the price changes were negative.) The cross-elasticity for the *Guardian* was −4.5/−40 = 0.11, and the cross-elasticity for the *Daily Telegraph* was −1.95/−40 = 0.05.

Applying demand and supply

The theory of demand and supply developed in Chapters 3 and 4 assumes that there are many buyers and many sellers, each one of whom must accept the price that is determined by overall demand and supply. Newspapers fit this theory on the demand side, since there are tens of

thousands of buyers each of whom can do nothing to affect the price. On the supply side, however, there are only a few newspapers and each sets the price of its own product. In the terminology of Chapter 3, it is an administered price. We can, however, handle the supply side if we note that each newspaper sells all the copies that are demanded at the price that it sets. Graphically, this is shown by a horizontal supply curve at each newspaper's fixed price. The elasticity of supply is effectively infinite at the set price.

Figure 5.2 illustrates the effect of the price cut on both *The Times* and the *Independent*. Notice that, since each newspaper is a distinct product, there is no industry supply curve for newspapers. Each supplier simply sets a price and lets demand determine its sales. Rival newspapers may not have followed *The Times* in cutting prices because they believed that their demand curves would prove as inelastic as that of *The Times*. If so, they would have lost more revenue by cutting their prices than they did by leaving prices unchanged. As it was, the *Independent* suffered a daily loss of revenue of a little over £25,000 (just over 50,000 sales at 50p each).

The puzzle is why *The Times* persisted with its price drop even though it lost sales revenue. One possibility is that the increased circulation led to an increase in advertising revenue. Newspapers' advertising rates are related to their circulation. If *The Times* increased its advertising revenue by more than about £35,000, the price reduction would have increased its profit.

The *Independent* was known to be in financial difficulty, and it is possible that the managers of *The Times* thought that their price cut might force the *Independent* out of business—a strategy sometimes referred to as *predatory pricing*.

[3] Note that we are measuring the price and quantity (*P* and *Q*) used in our elasticity calculations as the mid-point between the initial price and quantity and the ultimate price and quantity. The reasons for doing it this way are explained in Box 4.2 on page 66. Use of the mid-point as the base applies to all calculations in this section.

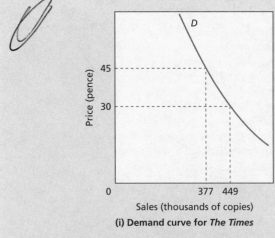
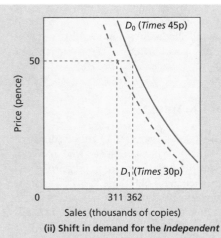

Figure 5.2 Demand for *The Times* and the *Independent*

A cut in the price of *The Times* shifted the *Independent*'s demand curve to the left. Part (i) shows the price cut for *The Times*. When its price was lowered from 45p to 30p, sales rose from 377,000 to 449,000 copies per day. Part (ii) shows the shift in demand for the *Independent* as a result of the fall in the price of *The Times*. At a constant price of 50p, sales fell from 362,000 to 311,000.

Had it succeeded, a high proportion of *Independent* readers would have moved over to *The Times*, since the cross-elasticities show that the *Independent* was the closest substitute for *The Times*. Soon after, however, the *Independent* was taken over by the Mirror Group, which had greater financial resources. Hence if *The Times* had been following a predatory strategy it failed. (Later the Mirror Group sold the *Independent* to an Irish newspaper group.)

A third possibility is that its managers expected that the demand elasticity for *The Times* would increase over time. If so, sales could eventually have risen sufficiently to compensate for the price cut. Indeed, *The Times* did continue to increase its market share beyond the period studied in Table 5.2. In June 1994 the *Telegraph* reacted to *The Times*'s growing market share by cutting its price, and the *Independent* followed. *The Times* responded to this by cutting its own price still further, although prices settled down at slightly higher levels soon after. To some extent this third explanation has proved correct. By July 1998 the price of *The Times* was 35p while the *Guardian*, *Telegraph*, and *Independent*

were selling at 45p. *The Times*'s sales were around 800,000, almost double what they had been just after the first gains following the outbreak of the price war. In contrast, the *Independent*'s sales were 210,000, less than 60 per cent of what they were just before the price war began.

These relative positions stayed more or less unchanged for the next five years. By the spring of 2002 there had been a small decline in the overall market for UK broadsheets. Sales of *The Times* were running at just over 700,000 daily, the *Guardian* at just under 400,000, the *Independent* at about 220,000, while the *Telegraph* remained remarkably stable at just over 1 million. Prices had also remained stable. *The Times* raised its price to 40p in 2001 and the *Guardian*, *Telegraph* and *Independent* set their prices at 50p.

The aggressive pricing strategy adopted by *The Times* in the early 1990s does appear to have had a very long lasting effect on the sales pattern of UK newspapers. The changes in sales patterns established in the mid-1990s were still evident nearly a decade later. We discuss some further episodes of newspaper competition in Chapter 12.

The Channel Tunnel

In 2001 around 7 million passengers took journeys by Eurostar trains through the Channel Tunnel, and about 2.5 million tonnes of freight were shipped on trains. In addition, the Shuttle service carried 2.5 million cars and 75,000 coaches. The equivalent figures for each year before 1994 were zero. The opening of the Channel Tunnel to

full passenger and freight services had a big impact on the cross-Channel travel market as it involved a massive increase in capacity—that is, an increase in supply.

We now know a lot about the impact of the tunnel. However, when we first analysed this issue in the 8th edition of this book the tunnel was not open. We are able to retain our earlier analysis virtually intact as well as using some evidence from our 9th edition, and we do so just to prove that jokes about the failure of economists to make accurate predictions are very far from the truth (at least some of the time).

The impact of the tunnel

We deal with the market in cross-Channel journeys. Although things other than price, such as speed and convenience, will affect the division of demand among the various types of travel, we hold these factors constant and focus on the average price of cross-Channel journeys. The supply comes from the tunnel, several shipping firms, hovercraft, and airlines. [*This is what we wrote in 1994. The hovercraft service ceased in October 2000, and the number of ferry companies has fallen largely in response to competition from the tunnel.*] Although firms operating each of these types of travel have power over price, it is safe to assume that the total amount they will all wish to supply will vary positively with the price, that is to say that the supply curve of cross-Channel transport is positively sloped.

Figure 5.3 analyses the market. Part (i) shows the total demand and supply for cross-Channel journeys. Part (ii) shows the demand for journeys on air and sea services, which were the only suppliers before the tunnel opened. Initially the demand curve facing sea and air operators was the same as the total market demand curve. The opening of the tunnel shifted the market supply curve to the right in part (i) while shifting the demand curve for air and sea journeys to the left in part (ii). (One way to think of the effect on demand for air and sea journeys is that the price of a substitute, tunnel journeys, has fallen from infinity to some positive number.) Notice that it does not matter for the general analysis whether tunnel journeys are cheaper or more expensive than other methods of travel, although the quantitative effects will depend on this. All that matters is that tunnel travel is cheap enough so that some passengers who would have gone by air or sea now go by rail.

The first prediction derived from Figure 5.3 is that the opening of the tunnel will cause a fall in the average price of cross-Channel journeys and an increase in the quantity purchased. The size of the increase depends on the size of the price reduction and the demand elasticity.

The second prediction is that the air and sea operators will experience a fall in demand because a new substitute has come into being. Initially, this would be seen entirely in empty seats and car decks, because prices are set in advance (though some lower prices may have been set in anticipation of a demand fall). Very soon, however, there would be special cut-price deals and, eventually, sustained price-cutting even for regular fares. Prior to the tunnel being built it was estimated that the tunnel might take a market share of about 40 per cent. Up to about half of these journeys were expected to be diverted from air and sea

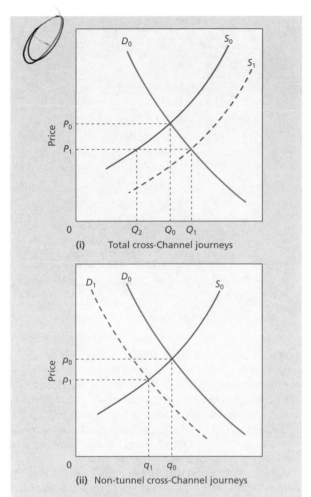

Figure 5.3 The market for cross-Channel journeys

The opening of the tunnel added to total supply but reduced demand for non-tunnel travel. Before the tunnel opened, the demand and supply curves were D_0 and S_0 in both parts of the figure. Price and quantity are thus the same in both parts, shown as P_0, Q_0 in part (i) and p_0, q_0 in part (ii). The opening of the tunnel shifted the supply curve to the right, from S_0 to S_1 in part (i). With a given demand curve D_0, this lowered price and increased quantity from P_0 and Q_0 to P_1 and Q_1. Part (ii) shows the demand and supply curves for non-tunnel journeys (air and sea). The availability of a new substitute, tunnel travel, shifted the demand curve for other forms of travel to the left from D_0 to D_1. The price and quantity accordingly fell to p_1 and q_1. In part (i) the total of cross-Channel journeys Q_1 is split between Q_2, going by air and sea, and $Q_1 - Q_2$, going via rail.

services, and the rest were expected to be new journeys stimulated by the new lower prices.

What happened?

The above predictions, based on the application of simple demand and supply analysis, turned out to be remarkably accurate. In 1998 and 1999 the Channel Tunnel carried almost exactly 40 per cent of passengers and accompanied cars crossing the Channel by surface transport. Passengers travelling to Europe from Thames and Kent ports fell from 23.7 million in 1994 to 16.6 million in 2000, while over the same period passengers travelling on the shuttle rose from 315,000 to 17 million (with around a further 7 million travelling on the Eurostar train service).

Newspaper reports at the time illustrate other aspects of our predictions. In September 1995, shortly after the tunnel came into full operation, the *Financial Times* wrote:

Eurotunnel has grabbed a big slice of the ferry operators' business on the cross-Channel market over the crucial summer months. Stena Sealink, the second largest ferry company on the Dover–Calais route, admitted its passenger volume fell 10 per cent and freight volumes 13 per cent in July compared with the same month last year. These trends have continued during August . . . Eurotunnel's own July traffic figures showed an 11.5 per cent increase over the previous month in the number of cars carried. . . . The price war in the cross-Channel market is growing in intensity, with the ferry companies maintaining discounts of up to 25 per cent on published prices throughout the summer. Eurotunnel has also offered a number of incentives to customers.

A month later *The Economist* had this to say:

In June . . . the number of passengers flying from London's Heathrow to Paris's Charles de Gaulle—traditionally the world's busiest airline route—was down 35 per cent from the same time last year. . . . On the London–Brussels route, the numbers fell by 6 per cent from Heathrow and 22 per cent from Gatwick. Worse still . . . Eurostar has forced down average airline economy fares by 25–30 per cent.

In May 1996 the *Financial Times* wrote:

The cut-throat cross-Channel price war intensified yesterday when Eurotunnel, the Anglo-French operator of the Channel tunnel, announced that it is to halve the standard return fare over the summer to £129. The main ferry companies responded immediately, saying they would match any bargain fares offered by Eurotunnel for comparable trips. . . . Eurotunnel has a market share of Dover–Calais traffic of about 45 per cent . . .

The price war took place in the context of an overall growth in the cross-Channel journey market (as predicted by the negative slope of the overall market demand curve). The *Investors' Chronicle* (12 April 1996, p. 10) estimated that this market had grown by 25 per cent in 1995 and by a further 20 per cent in 1996. Also *The Economist* article referred to above quotes the total seat capacity on the London–Paris/Brussels routes as being 690,000 per week in July 1994 but having risen to 1,297,000 in July 1995. The latter information tells us how much the supply curve shifted.

Assessment

The subsequent data and the events referred to in the newspaper reports show that the predictions of our demand and supply analysis were amply borne out in practice. First, the prices of cross-Channel journeys fell and the quantity demanded increased. Second, the airlines, ferry, and hovercraft companies suffered a fall in demand. They all responded with aggressive price-cutting. The airlines also shifted some of their capacity on to other routes, and air travel to France did not recover to 1994 volumes until 1999.[4] In 1998 the two major ferry companies, P&O and Stena, merged their cross-Channel operations, so that they could co-ordinate their competition with the other forms of transport and manage the needed capacity reduction. In 2000 the hovercraft service closed down owing to lack of demand.

Government intervention in markets

Before we continue in this chapter, we need to introduce a third set of players on the economic stage. We have called decision-takers *agents*, and in Chapter 3 we introduced two sets of agents: consumers and firms. The third set is most accurately called the *central authorities* but is more commonly, if loosely, referred to as the **government** or the state. This broad class of agents includes all public agencies, government bodies, and other organizations belonging to, or owing their existence to, either central or local governments. They exist at the centre of legal and political power and exert some control over the rest of us.[5]

Governments play an important role in modern mixed economies. Among other things, governments sometimes seek to alter market outcomes. They can influence the prices at which goods are sold by taxing or subsidizing either their production or their consumption. They can influence the terms on which goods and services are offered for sale by imposing quality standards or regulating product prices. These, and many other methods that we will encounter

---

[4] This was against a background of rapidly growing demand for air travel. Passenger numbers to all destinations from UK airports doubled between 1990 and 2000.

[5] It is *not* a basic assumption of economics that a central authority always acts in a consistent fashion as if it were a single individual. Indeed, conflict among different central authority agencies is often an important component in theories that analyse government intervention in the economy.

throughout this book, are collectively referred to as *government intervention*.

Price controls

If the government wishes to influence the price at which some product is bought and sold, it has two main alternatives. First, it can change the equilibrium price by altering the product's demand or supply. Second, it can enact legislation that regulates the price. **Price controls** refer to the latter alternative: influencing price by laws, rather than by market forces.

Disequilibrium trading

If controls are used to hold price at a disequilibrium level, what determines the quantity actually traded on the market?

Any voluntary market transaction requires both a willing buyer and a willing seller. Thus, if quantity demanded is less than quantity supplied, demand will determine the amount actually traded, and the excess supply will remain in the hands of the unsuccessful sellers. If quantity supplied is less than quantity demanded, however, supply will determine the amount actually traded and the excess demand will take the form of desired purchases by unsuccessful buyers. This is shown graphically in Figure 5.4.

At any disequilibrium price, quantity exchanged is determined by the lesser of quantity demanded and quantity supplied.

This result is often expressed by the maxim that in disequilibrium the short side of the market dominates (i.e. determines what is bought and sold).

Box 5.1 discusses the problems that arise when governments provide road services at a zero price.

Maximum-price legislation

In this section we concentrate on laws setting *maximum* permissible prices, which are often called 'price ceilings'. Over the years, such laws have had many purposes. Governments of medieval cities sometimes sought to protect their citizens from the consequences of crop failures by fixing a maximum price at which bread could be sold. In modern times, many governments have employed rent controls in an attempt to make housing available at a price that could be afforded by lower-income groups. Governments in many poor countries set the prices of some basic foodstuffs well below their market equilibrium values.

The effects on price and quantity Most price ceilings specify the highest permissible price that producers may legally charge. If the ceiling is set above the equilibrium price it has no effect, since the equilibrium remains attainable. If, however, the ceiling is set below the equilibrium price, it determines the price—in which case the ceiling is said to be *binding*. The key consequences of price ceilings are shown in Figure 5.5.

The setting of a maximum price has no effect if the price is set at or above the equilibrium price. If the maximum price is

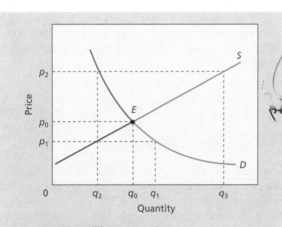

Figure 5.4 Disequilibrium quantity

In disequilibrium, quantity exchanged is determined by the lesser of quantity demanded and quantity supplied. Market equilibrium is at point E. For prices below p_0 the quantity exchanged will be determined by the supply curve. For example, q_2 will be exchanged at price p_1 in spite of the excess demand of $q_1 - q_2$. For prices above p_0 the quantity exchanged will be determined by the demand curve. For example, q_2 will be exchanged at price p_2 in spite of the excess supply of $q_3 - q_2$. Thus, the dark blue and dark red portions of the S and D curves show the actual quantities exchanged at each price.

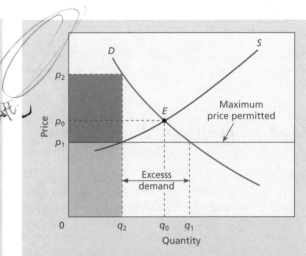

Figure 5.5 Black-market pricing

A price ceiling set below the equilibrium price causes excess demand and invites a black market. Equilibrium price is at p_0. If a price ceiling is set at p_1, the quantity demanded will rise to q_1 and the quantity supplied will fall to q_2. Quantity actually exchanged will be q_2. Excess demand is $q_1 - q_2$. Black marketeers would buy q_2 at the controlled price of p_1, paying the amount shown by the light blue area p_1q_2. They would sell at the price p_2, earning profits shown by the dark blue area between p_1 and p_2.

Box 5.1 **Road pricing**

Some goods and services are provided free, but this does not mean that everyone can have as much as they like all the time. Unless the amount supplied equals the amount demanded at zero price, excess demand will develop. As we have seen in this chapter, allocation of the available quantity will have to be handled by some non-price allocation mechanism. Examples include waiting lists for health services and congestion on the roads.

In the seventeenth and eighteenth centuries, many main roads in Britain were 'turnpikes' and travellers had to pay a fee to travel on them. This fee was used to maintain the road. Throughout the twentieth century, road provision in the United Kingdom has been paid for by the state out of the revenue from general taxation. (Specific taxes on cars such as the road fund licence have not been linked directly to expenditure on roads.) Some other countries have charges on some major roads, such as the autostrade of Italy, the autoroutes of France, some turnpikes in the United States, and new motorways in Mexico.

The recent growth of car ownership has been such that demand for road use continually outstrips supply when the price of using the roads is zero. For example, the M25 orbital motorway around London has had frequent jams from the day it opened. Also, many town centres suffer severe traffic congestion during rush hours, and in some cases for most of the day.

This congestion is, in effect, rationing by queuing. It imposes the highest cost on those whose time is most valuable. Road pricing can be used to reduce the quantity demanded to the available supply. Users are then able to use road services without congestion. Travellers with essential business and other urgent needs will pay. Others will take less crowded routes, use public transport, or postpone their journeys.

Many roads are congested at peak periods but have excess capacity during off-peak periods. If the price for using such roads were higher in periods

of peak demand and lower in off-peak periods, demand would equal the given supply during both periods. A form of this type of pricing has been operating for some time in Singapore—a country with many people but little space. Licences to drive only at weekends are considerably cheaper than licences to drive at any time, and there is a surcharge for driving in the central area during peak traffic times. Also, the number of licences issued is limited. As a result of this and other supporting measures, such as a first-class public transport system, Singapore has one of the few urban road systems in the whole of Southeast Asia that is not heavily congested and polluted. In contrast, Bangkok and Manila are suffering near traffic paralysis from road congestion.

Pricing of specific bits of road with limited access presents no technical problem. Hence, for example, the UK already has tolls on the Severn Bridge, the Dartford Crossing, the Forth Bridge, and the Mersey Tunnel. The pricing of road use in cities presents greater problems. But in February 2001 Mayor of London Ken Livingstone announced that from February 2003 drivers will be charged £5 per day to enter central London. At the same time, he predicted that congestion would be cut by 10 to 15 per cent and delays would drop by between 20 and 30 per cent. Cameras will be used to monitor access. Eventually some form of electronic measurement of road use more generally may be possible.

Free goods can be consumed without restriction only if the supply continues to equal (or exceed) demand at zero price. Where the free good is a gift of nature, pricing soon appears when the resource becomes scarce. Where the free good is provided by the state, pricing is often preferable to other rationing mechanisms. It leads people to economize on the use of the scarce resource and ensures that those who value it most highly will be its most frequent users.

---

set below the equilibrium price a shortage will develop, and quantity actually bought and sold will fall below its equilibrium value.

Allocation of available supply In the case of a binding price ceiling, production is insufficient to satisfy everyone who wishes to buy the product. Since price is not allowed to rise so as to allocate the available supply among would-be purchasers, some other method of allocation must be found. Theory does not predict what this other method will be, but experience has revealed several possibilities.

If shops sell to the first customers who arrive, people are likely to rush to those stores that are rumoured to have any stocks of the scarce product. Long queues will develop, and allocation will be on the basis of luck, or to those knowing enough to gain from the principle of 'first come, first served'. This system was commonly found in the command economies of Eastern Europe during the Communist era, where queuing was a way of life.

Sometimes shopkeepers themselves decide who will get the scarce products and who will not. They may keep products under the counter and sell only to regular customers or to people of a certain colour or religion. Such a system is called allocation by **sellers' preferences**.

If the government dislikes the allocation that results from price ceilings, it can ration the goods, giving out coupons sufficient to purchase the available supply. The coupons might be distributed equally, or on such criteria as age, sex, marital status, or number of dependants. Rationing by coupons was used in Britain and most of the other belligerent countries during the Second World War (1939–45). It persisted in Britain for another nine years after the war, until 1954.

Any official rationing scheme substitutes the government's preferences for the sellers' preferences in allocating a product that is in excess demand because of a binding price ceiling.

Black markets A binding price ceiling, with or without rationing, is likely to give rise to a **black market**. This is a market in which goods are sold illegally at prices that violate the legal restrictions. Many products have only a few manufacturers but many retailers. Although it is easy to police the producers, it is difficult even to locate, much less to control, all those who are, or could be, retailing the product.

Figure 5.5 shows the result of a price ceiling that determines the price that producers get but does not control the price at which retailers sell to the public. Output is restricted by the low price received by producers, while consumers must pay the high price that equates demand to the available supply. The difference between what consumers pay and what producers get goes as profits to the black marketeers.

It is unlikely that all of the output will be sold on the black market—both because there are many honest people in every society and because the government usually has some power to enforce its price ceilings on retailers. Thus, the normal case is not the extreme result shown in the figure. Instead, some of the limited supplies will be sold at the controlled price and some at the black market price.

If the purpose of an intervention policy is to keep prices down, the policy is a failure to the extent that black marketeers succeed in raising prices; it is a success to the extent that sales actually occur at the controlled prices. If, however, the government wishes to restrict production in order to release resources for other, more urgent, needs such as war production, the policy works effectively, if somewhat unfairly.

Evidence There is plenty of evidence confirming these predictions. During the First and Second World Wars governments set binding ceilings on many prices. The legislation of maximum prices was always followed by shortages, then by either the introduction of rationing or the growth of some private method of allocation (such as sellers' preferences), and then by the rise of some sort of black market. The ceilings were more effective in limiting consumption than in controlling prices, although they did restrain price increases to some extent. Until the early 1990s, many of the former socialist countries of Eastern Europe followed a policy of controlling food prices at levels that were below the equilibrium prices. Chronic shortages, queues, allocation by sellers' preferences, and black markets were the result.

Another example of the effects of price controls arises in the market for rented accommodation. Rent controls have now been largely eliminated in the United Kingdom, but rent controls introduced during the First World War distorted the UK housing market for much of the twentieth century. They have also been (and are being) used in other countries. This is discussed in Box 5.2.

 Box 5.2 **Rent controls**

Analysis of the consequences of maximum-price legislation has an important application in rent control legislation, which is just a special case of price ceilings. Controls are usually imposed to freeze rents at their current levels at times when equilibrium rents are rising. Demand may be shifting rightward, owing to forces such as rising population and income, or supply may be shifting leftward, owing to forces such as rising costs. The result is that the controlled rents are soon well below the free-market equilibrium level, and excess demand appears. The further the controlled price falls below the free-market price, the stronger are the consequences. The discrepancy often grows in periods of inflation. Typically, the controlled rents are not increased as fast as the general price level is rising, causing the *relative price* of rented accommodation to fall.

Predictions

The following predictions about rent controls are simply applications to the housing market of the results concerning binding price controls in any competitive market.

1. There will be a shortage of rental accommodation; quantity demanded will exceed quantity supplied.

2. The quantity of accommodation occupied will be less than if free-market rents had been charged.

3. The short-term effects of controls are to lower rents for an unchanged supply of accommodation. The reason is that the short-run supply curve of rental accommodation tends to be quite *inelastic* at the level of the quantity currently supplied. The long-term effects are a growing housing shortage. The reason is that the long-run supply is quite *elastic*, since rental accommodation will not be replaced as it is converted to other uses or wears out unless it offers a market rate of return to its owners.

4. Black markets will appear. Landlords may require large lump-sum entrance fees from new tenants, and may evict existing tenants so as to

collect this fee. Sitting tenants are reluctant to move from their present accommodations, even when they are no longer suitable. If they do move, they may sublet their accommodation, charging the market price while themselves paying only the controlled price.

5. As a political response to the forces just outlined, governments typically pass security-of-tenure laws, which protect the tenant from eviction and thus give existing tenants priority over potential new tenants. By making it harder to evict undesirable tenants, these laws reduce the expected return from any given rental price. Landlords may resort to illegal harassment to evict tenants and become even less willing to replace accommodation as it wears out over the years.

Evidence

These and other consequences have been observed throughout the world wherever binding rent controls have been imposed. Here are a few examples.

UK rent controls were first introduced in 1914 and were gradually extended to cover the entire rental market. Over a period of sixty years, the market for privately owned unfurnished rental accommodation was largely eliminated! From 45 per cent of households in privately owned rental accommodation in 1945, the figure fell steadily until by the 1980s it was only 8 per cent. Finally, in 1989 the British government announced measures to phase out rent controls. They also used subsidies to encourage housing associations, which are non-profit-making providers of rental accommodation. None the less, the long-term consequences of rent controls will persist in the UK housing market well into the twenty-first century because of the small stock of housing available to rent and the high levels of owner-occupation. Both of these influences are the consequences of over half a century of controls that made being a landlord unprofitable and becoming a new tenant nearly impossible.

The problems of agriculture

To the casual observer, the agricultural sector of almost any advanced Western economy presents a series of apparent paradoxes. Food is a basic necessity of life. Yet over the last century agricultural sectors have been declining in relative importance. The number of farmers and farmworkers in the original six EC member states fell from nearly 10.5 million in 1960 to under 3.5 million in 2000, and many of those who have remained on the land have been receiving incomes well below national averages. Were it not for the EU's Common Agricultural Policy (the CAP), the number of farmers in the EU would be much lower than it now is and farm incomes would be even smaller.

Governments of many countries have felt it expedient to intervene in agricultural markets, and have resorted to a bewildering array of controls and subsidies. These have often led to the accumulation of vast surpluses, which have sometimes rotted in storage and sometimes been sold abroad at subsidized prices. The theory of demand and supply can help us gain some insight into these, and other, agricultural problems.

In case you think that we are giving too much attention to agriculture when it is a relatively small industry, notice that it is a very large budget item taking up over one half of the total EU budget, and that European and North American subsidization (and protection) of its agriculture is a major contributor to the poverty of the world's poorer countries.

Support to agricultural producers in advanced countries was $245 billion in 2000, five times total development assistance. In the members of OECD as a whole, a third of farm income came from government mandated support in 2000. (Martin Wolf, Financial Times, 21 November 2001)

Short-term fluctuations in prices and incomes

Agricultural production is subject to large variations resulting from factors that are beyond human control. For example, bad weather reduces output below that planned by farmers (see in Figure 5.1 what happened to the price of coffee in 1994 and 1997 as a result of a poor harvests in Brazil), while exceptionally good weather pushes output above planned levels. Figure 5.6 shows how variations in farm output cause prices to fluctuate in the opposite direction to crop sizes. A bumper crop sends prices down; a poor crop sends them up. The price changes will be larger the less elastic is the demand curve.

Because farm products often have inelastic demands, large price fluctuations accompany unplanned changes in production.

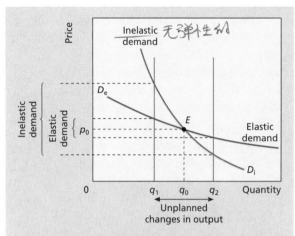

Figure 5.6 Unplanned fluctuations in output

Unplanned fluctuations in output lead to much sharper fluctuations in price if the demand curve is inelastic than if it is elastic. Suppose that the expected price is p_0 and the planned output is q_0. The two curves D_i and D_e are alternative demand curves. If actual production always equalled planned production, the equilibrium price and quantity would be p_0 and q_0 with either demand curve. Unplanned fluctuations in output, however, cause quantity to vary year by year between q_1 (a bad harvest) and q_2 (a good harvest). When demand is inelastic (shown by the red curve), prices will show large fluctuations. When demand is elastic (shown by the blue curve), prices will show much smaller fluctuations. (In both cases elasticity is measured around point E.)

The effects on farmers' incomes follow from the results established on page 62 concerning elasticity and total spending.[6]

When demand is inelastic, unplanned variations in output will cause producers' revenues to vary in the opposite direction as output varies and to fluctuate more the further the elasticity of demand diverges from unity in either direction.

Since most agricultural products have inelastic demands, farmers typically see their incomes dwindling when nature is unexpectedly kind in producing a bumper crop, while their incomes rise when crops are poor. Notice that every individual farmer's income need not rise (after all, some farmers may have nothing to harvest); it follows only that the aggregate revenue earned by *all* farmers must rise.

[6] While we can make predictions in this section only about sales revenues, such receipts are closely related to farmers' incomes. We can therefore, without risk of serious error, extend these predictions to incomes.

Agricultural stabilization programmes

Figure 5.7 shows the required policy to stabilize agricultural prices.[7] Farmers are allowed to sell their whole crop each year. When production unexpectedly exceeds normal output, the government buys in the market. It allows price to fall, but only by the same proportion that production

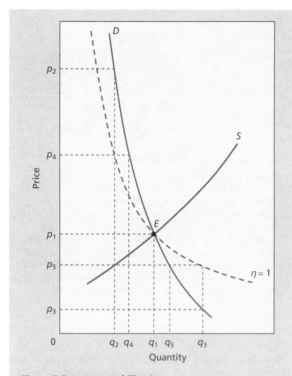

Figure 5.7 Income stabilization

Income stabilization is achieved by allowing prices to fluctuate in inverse proportion to output. D is demand, S is planned supply, and equilibrium is at E. However, actual production fluctuates between q_2 and q_3, and these fluctuations cause the free-market price to fluctuate between p_2 and p_3.

A curve of unit elasticity over its whole range is drawn through E and labelled $\eta = 1$. To stabilize income, any given output must be sold at a price determined by this curve. The government buys or sells an amount equal to the horizontal distance between the $\eta = 1$ curve and the demand curve.

When production is q_3, market price must be held at p_5 if income is to be unchanged. But at market price p_5 the public wishes to purchase only q_5 and the government must buy up the remaining production, $q_3 - q_5$, and add it to its stocks. Farmers' total sales are q_3 at price p_5, and since the broken red curve is a rectangular hyperbola, income $p_5 \times q_3$ is equal to income $p_1 \times q_1$.

When production is equal to q_2, price must be allowed to rise to p_4. (By construction, the area $p_4 q_2$ is equal to the area $p_1 q_1$.) But at price p_4 the public will wish to buy q_4, so the government must sell $q_4 - q_2$ out of its stocks.

has increased. When production unexpectedly falls short of normal output, the government enters the market and sells some of its stocks. It allows price to rise, but only by the same proportion that production has fallen below normal. Thus, as farmers encounter unplanned fluctuations in their output, they encounter exactly offsetting fluctuations in prices, so that their revenues are stabilized. In effect, the government has converted the elasticity of demand from being inelastic to being unitary. With a unit elasticity the total revenue of sellers does not change as quantity changes, because given percentage changes in quantity are offset by equal percentage changes of price but in the opposite direction.

Appropriate government intervention in agricultural markets can reduce price fluctuations and stabilize producers' revenues.

Government schemes of this sort can be self-financing. If we ignore costs of storage, the schemes can show a profit, for the government buys at low prices—the lower the price, the more it buys—and sells at high prices—the higher the price, the more it sells.

The long-term problem of resource allocation If it is possible to even out farm incomes in the face of short-term fluctuations in output and prices, why does agricultural policy run into so many difficulties? The reason is found in the longer-term need to reallocate resources out of agriculture, combined with government policy to ensure farmers a 'reasonable' income. Total output and real incomes have been rising at an average rate of about 2 per cent per year over the last 100 years in the countries that now form the European Union. Assume for simplicity that productivity expands more or less uniformly in all industries. The demand for products with low income elasticities will be expanding more slowly than their output; excess supplies will develop, prices and profits will be depressed, and it will be necessary for resources to move out of these industries. Exactly the reverse will happen for products with high income elasticities: demand will expand faster than supply, prices and profits will tend to rise, and resources will move into those industries.

With continuous productivity increases there will be a continuous tendency towards excess supply of products with low income elasticities and excess demand for products with

---

[7] Stabilization policies are intended to reduce cyclical fluctuations as well as the short-term fluctuation studied in the text. Agricultural markets often show substantial cyclical instability. In periods of prosperity employment and wages are high, which implies a strong demand for most products. In periods of depressed business activity employment and wages are diminished, which implies a weaker demand for most products. Thus, the demand curves for most products rise and fall as business activity ebbs and flows. Given a highly inelastic short-run supply curve, cyclical fluctuations in agricultural prices are often large.

high income elasticities. Adjustment to these changes requires a continuous movement of resources out of industries
producing the former type of products into industries producing the latter.

In a free-market economy, this reallocation will take place
under the incentives of low prices, wages, and incomes in
the declining sector and high prices, wages, and incomes
in the expanding sector. Because of the tendency towards
excess supply in the agricultural sector, prices will fall, taking producers' incomes down with them. There will be a
decline in the demand for farm labour and the other inputs
used in agriculture, and earnings in agriculture will also
decline. At the same time, the opposite tendencies will be
observed in sectors with high income elasticities. Here
demand will be expanding faster than supply; prices will
be rising, taking producers' incomes up with them. The
demand for the inputs used in these industries will be
rising, causing input prices and incomes to increase.

The need to reallocate resources has been strongly felt
in agriculture, where not only is the income elasticity of
demand low, but productivity growth has been high. For
example, between 1970 and 2000 cereal yields per acre
roughly doubled in the EU. Milk yields in France and the
Netherlands, sugar yields in Italy, and rape yields in Germany increased by more than 50 per cent over the same
period. In France and Italy, the potato yield more than
doubled between 1970 and 2000.

Schemes that stabilize farm prices at levels calculated
to guarantee a 'reasonable' income to farmers remove the
incentive for resources to transfer out of the agricultural
sector. Unless other means are found to persuade resources
to transfer, a larger and larger proportion of the resources
currently devoted to agriculture become redundant. The
problems of excess supply that result from governments
resisting price falls are illustrated in Figure 5.8.

Economics cannot prove that governments ought, or
ought not, to interfere with the price mechanism. However, by providing some insight into the workings of that
mechanism, economics can predict some of the gains and
losses resulting from intervention. It can also point out problems that must be solved if intervention is to be successful.

The EU's agricultural policy

The Common Agricultural Policy of the European Union,
nicknamed the CAP, amply illustrates the applicability of
the analysis just outlined. The policy has held agricultural
prices well above their market equilibrium values within
the EU. To prevent the flood of imports that would have
been attracted by these high prices, the imports of all agricultural goods that receive EU price support have been
subject to a high tariff. (The EU imports more agricultural
products than it exports by value, but its imports are
mainly tropical fruits, such as bananas, and those that are
out of season in Europe.) The high European prices cause

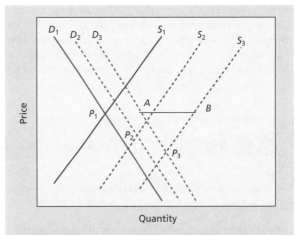

**Figure 5.8 Attempts to protect incomes lead to growing
surpluses**

If supply is increasing rapidly while demand increases more slowly,
then prices will tend to fall. If governments intervene to stop prices
falling, the result will be growing surpluses. The initial demand and
supply curves are D_1 and S_1. Demand shifts slowly from D_2 to D_3, while
supply shifts significantly to S_2 and S_3. With no intervention, price falls
from P_1 to P_2 to P_3. But if government holds the price at P_1, the surplus
in period 3 will be $A - B$.

EU production to exceed EU consumption. Surpluses pile
up, only to be sold abroad at a fraction of their production
costs, or given away. EU farmers gain, while taxpayers,
consumers, and efficient foreign producers lose out. The
payments to farmers have risen so much over the years that
they now place serious strain on the EU budget. Expenditure on agriculture reached a peak of nearly 65 per cent of
the entire EU budget in 1986, but it fell during the 1990s,
reaching around 50 per cent at the end of the century. In
contrast, in 2000 agriculture accounted for a little less than
2 per cent of total EU production of all goods and services
(down from 4.8 per cent in 1973), and just over 4 per cent
of EU civilian employment.

Many of the world's poorer countries have efficient agricultural sectors, and in a world of free trade they would
export large quantities to the EU and the USA, earning
good and rising incomes for their farmers. Instead, farmers
in these developing countries have found their livelihoods
threatened by subsidized exports of surplus EU products.
The attempt to restrain these exports has placed great
strains on the relations between the EU and other agricultural producing countries. These were focused in the long-
running Uruguay Round of trade negotiations, as a result
of which the EU agreed to relatively minor alterations to
the CAP.

A phased reduction in intervention prices started in the
mid-1990s and has helped to reduce the proportion of total
EU budget devoted to agricultural support. Price supports

are being replaced partly by direct subsidies. In some cases these subsidies are payments for non-production. For example, the 'set-aside' policy pays farmers to keep some of their land idle. Thus, while the nature of intervention in the EU is changing, it is not disappearing. Consumers may gain from the price reductions planned (over time), but taxpayers will continue to carry the burden of the costs of intervention.

Box 5.3 provides a recent analysis of the problems of the CAP.

 Box 5.3 **The EU's Common Agricultural Policy**

The CAP has long been criticized by economists, but politicians have either failed to agree with the economists or found reform too difficult to achieve. Here is an extract from a recent newspaper report on the subject.

Radical reform of the CAP is long overdue. This archaic system of farming support absorbs some €41 billion (£27 billion) a year—almost half the European Commission's budget and significantly more than total annual spending by the UK's Department for Education and Skills. For this money, one would expect the CAP to give the economy something substantial. Yet on almost every relevant criterion the policy falls woefully short.

The most obvious negative impact of the CAP—which holds prices for key crops at artificially high levels—is that it increases the cost of food for consumers. According to estimates by the OECD, consumers in industrialised nations pay an average of almost 50 per cent more for food than they would if true markets prices prevailed. Thanks to the CAP, the EU's annual food bill is €48 billion higher than it would otherwise be.

The CAP has also led to widespread economic inefficiency. Many of the subsidies paid to farmers are linked to output—the more you produce, the more you get. This, as the recent White Paper on European Economic Reform rightly highlighted, has led to large-scale production of specific commodities with scant regard for consumer demands on either quantity or quality. Neither do these production-related subsidies take into account the potential environmental impact of large-scale, intensive farming, with its widespread use of chemicals and its potentially adverse effects on animal welfare. The CAP severely damages economies outside Europe, which have to cope with the widespread dumping on international markets of unwanted EU produce. This depresses the international market price and so hurts the revenues of agriculture-exporting developing economies.

What's more, as EU support systems make up the difference between the 'acceptable' price on key products and the international market price, agricultural dumping will tend to make the CAP more expensive by increasing the size of this disparity. But perhaps the most damning indictment of the CAP is that it struggles to satisfy its *raison d'etre*—raising farm incomes. OECD studies suggest that the so-called 'transfer efficiency' of price support systems, which form an important part of the CAP, is about 25 per cent. This means that for every £4 of price support, farmers' incomes are raised by only £1, with the remainder seeping out into the wider economy via higher machinery prices and so forth. In addition, linking support to production, as most CAP payments do, tends to benefit the larger (and typically more prosperous) farmers, who receive about 60 per cent of all financial support within the EU.

But if you think the CAP is bad now, just wait until the EU begins to enlarge. Poland, one of the first candidates for EU accession, has an enormous agricultural sector that employs almost a fifth of the country's workforce. Hungary, another candidate for early entry, has a similarly large farming community. To extend the CAP in its current form to these countries would not only be prohibitively expensive; it would also exacerbate the system's current deficiencies (high consumer prices, agricultural dumping and so forth).

In typical EU fashion, the issue of CAP reform has been side-stepped for the early years of enlargement, although it threatens to come back with a vengeance in four years or so. Under current proposals, new EU entrants would benefit from price support mechanisms and rural development funds immediately, but the more generous direct payments would be phased in over a ten-year period. This has been costed until 2006, when the current CAP budget expires, and is at acceptable levels. The fear is that after 2006, when the CAP budget will be renegotiated, costs of support could spiral out of all control.

That the CAP needs to be reformed is beyond doubt. Much more tricky is identifying the types of reform that EU agricultural policy needs. Key to any change must be a move away from price support and payments based on output—both of which lead to immense market distortions—and towards much more direct forms of assistance. . . .

The move towards a breaking of the link between subsidies and production could also be hastened, were member states to reduce their overall contributions to the CAP. The funds saved could be earmarked for aid for farmers—thereby safeguarding rural incomes—but the distorting effects of the CAP would be in part removed.

There have been some moves towards reform of the CAP in recent years, and in particular a marked reduction in price support schemes. But there is much, much farther to go. The EU cannot postpone discussion of this central issue forever. And the longer politicians delay, the greater will be the global economic cost. (Lea Paterson, *The Times*, 18 March 2002)

Some general lessons about the price system

The cases studied in this chapter suggest four widely applicable lessons.

Costs may be shifted, but they cannot be avoided

The average standard of living depends on the amount of resources available to the economy and on the efficiency with which these resources are used. Production, whether in response to free-market signals or government controls, uses resources; thus, it involves costs to members of society. If it takes 5 per cent of the nation's resources to provide housing at some stated average standard, those resources will not be available to produce other products. If resources are used to produce unwanted wheat, those resources will not be available to produce other goods. For society, there is no such thing as free housing or free wheat. Rent controls or subsidies to agriculture can change the share of the costs paid by particular individuals or groups, lowering the share for some and raising the share for others, but they cannot make the costs go away.

Different ways of allocating the costs may also affect the total amount of resources used and thus the amount of costs incurred. For example, controls that keep prices and profits of some product below free-market levels will lead to increased quantities demanded and decreased quantities supplied. Unless government steps in to provide additional supplies, fewer resources will be allocated to producing the product. If government chooses to supply all the demand at the controlled prices, more resources will be allocated to it, which means that fewer resources will be devoted to other kinds of goods and services.

Free-market prices and profits encourage efficient use of resources

Prices and profits in a market economy provide signals to both demanders and suppliers. Prices that are high and rising (relative to other prices) provide an incentive to purchasers to economize on the product. They may choose to satisfy the want in question with substitutes whose prices have not risen so much (because they are less costly to provide) or to satisfy less of that want by shifting expenditure to the satisfaction of other wants. On the supply side, rising prices tend to create rising profits. Short-term profits that bear no relation to current costs repeatedly occur in market economies. High profits, however, attract further resources into production. They cause resources to move into profitable industries until profits fall to levels that can be earned elsewhere in the economy. Falling prices and falling profits provide the opposite motivations. Purchasers are inclined to buy more; sellers are inclined to produce less and to move resources into more profitable undertakings.

The price system responds to a need for change in the allocation of resources—say, in response to an external event such as the loss of a source of a raw material or the outbreak of a war. Changing relative prices and profits signal the need for change, to which consumers and producers respond.

Government intervention affects resource allocation

Governments intervene in the price system sometimes to satisfy generally agreed-upon social goals and sometimes to help politically influential interest groups. Government intervention changes the allocation of resources that the price system would achieve.

Interventions have allocative consequences because they inhibit the free-market mechanism. Some controls, such as rent controls, prevent prices from rising (in response, say, to an increase in demand with no change in supply). If the price is held down, the signal is not given to consumers to economize on a product that is in short supply. On the supply side, when prices and profits are prevented from rising, the profit signals that would attract new resources into the industry are never given. The shortage continues, and the movements of demand and supply that would resolve it are not set in motion.

Other controls, such as agricultural price supports, prevent prices from falling (in response, say, to an increase in supply with no increase in demand). This leads to excess supply, and the signal is not given to producers to produce less or to buyers to increase their purchases. Surpluses continue, and the movements of demand and supply that would eliminate them are not set in motion.

Intervention requires alternative allocative mechanisms

Intervention typically requires alternative allocative mechanisms. During times of shortages, allocation will be by sellers' preferences, on a first-come, first-served basis, or by some system of government rationing. During periods of surplus there will be unsold supplies unless the government buys and stores the surpluses. Because long-run changes in demand and costs do not induce resource reallocations through private decisions, the government will have to step in. It will have to force resources out of industries in which prices are held too high, as it has tried to do in agriculture, and into industries in which prices are held too low, for example by providing public housing.

Intervention almost always has both benefits and costs. Economics cannot answer the question of whether a particular intervention into free markets is desirable, but it can clarify the issues by identifying benefits and costs and those who will enjoy or bear them. These issues will be discussed in detail in Chapters 19 and 20.

SUMMARY

Finish your coffee, we're off to the museum

■ World commodity prices, such as coffee, change in response to the balance of supply and demand factors. The increase in museum visits following the abolition of admission charge shows that demand curves really do have a negative slope.

Keeping up with *The Times*, and the tunnel

■ Demand and supply theory is a potent tool for analysing many real-world situations, such as the effects of the Channel Tunnel and price-cutting among British newspapers.

Government intervention in markets

■ Effective price ceilings lead to excess demand, black markets, and non-price methods of allocating the scarce supplies among would-be purchasers.

■ Rent controls are a form of price ceiling. Their major consequence is a shortage of rental accommodation that gets worse because of a slow but inexorable decline in the quantity of rental accommodation.

The problems of agriculture

■ On the free market many agricultural prices are subject to wide fluctuations as a result of weather-induced, year-to-year fluctuations in supply operating on inelastic demand curves, and cyclical fluctuations in demand operating on inelastic supply curves.

■ Governments can stabilize agricultural incomes by reducing price fluctuations. They achieve this by holding stocks, which they add to through purchases in times of surplus and sell from in times of shortage.

■ The long-term problems of agriculture arise from productivity growth on the supply side combined with low income elasticity on the demand side. This means that, unless many resources are being transferred out of agriculture fairly rapidly, quantity supplied tends to increase faster than quantity demanded year after year.

■ Stabilization schemes that hold prices above their free-market levels on average, over short-term and cyclical swings, frustrate the long-term adjustment process and lead to ever-growing surpluses—as has the EU's Common Agricultural Policy (the CAP).

Some general lessons about the price system

■ Some major lessons about the price system are that: costs may be shifted, but they cannot be avoided; free-market prices and profits encourage economical use of resources; government intervention affects resource allocation; and intervention requires alternative allocative mechanisms.

TOPICS FOR REVIEW

■ Maximum, or ceiling, prices

■ Alternative allocation systems under excess demand

■ Short- and long-run effects of rent controls

■ Minimum, or floor, prices

■ Causes of fluctuations in agricultural prices and incomes

■ Schemes for income stabilization

■ The CAP

DISCUSSION QUESTIONS

1 Calculate the price elasticity of demand for the Museum of London when admissions rose from 12,965 per month in 2000 to 24,408 per month in 2001 and price fell from £6 to zero.

2 Calculate the price elasticity of demand for the Natural History Museum when its admissions went from 89,650 per month in 2000 to 163,487 per month in 2001 and the price fell from £9 to zero.

3 If the income elasticity of demand for coffee beans is 0.6 and world GDP grows at 2 per cent per year, by how much will demand for coffee beans grow in ten years? What would the answer be if the income elasticity were 1.5?

4 Explain why governments often intervene in agricultural markets. Outline some types of intervention and some of the effects that they will have. Illustrate by reference to the EUs Common Agricultural Policy.

5 Do rent controls help those who wish to find cheap housing?

6 Give some reasons why the price of coffee beans fell to very low levels in 2002.

7 Use demand and supply analysis to discuss some of the problems associated with free provision of health services.

8 Why do black markets often arise during periods of rationing?

PART TWO

CONSUMERS AND PRODUCERS

Chapter 6

DEMAND ANALYSIS I: MARGINAL UTILITY

Why do consumers and producers respond to price and income changes in the way they do? Is it irrational for consumers to spend more on some commodities when their prices fall but to spend less on other commodities when they undergo a similar price reduction? Why are consumers willing to pay high prices for many luxury goods such as diamonds and rare postage stamps, while appearing unwilling to do the same for goods that are necessary to life, such as food and water? These are some of the important questions that we address in this chapter. In particular, you will learn that

- Marginal utility is a key concept underlying demand theory.
- Market price depends on marginal rather than total utility.
- Marginal utility of each product diminishes as additional units are consumed.
- The negative slope of the demand curve is linked to diminishing marginal utility.

- When a consumer has allocated her funds in the best way she can, the marginal utility of each £ worth of spending will be the same for all goods purchased.
- Elasticity of demand depends on marginal, not total, utility.

The history of demand analysis has seen two major breakthroughs. The first was utility theory, which assumed that the utility or satisfaction that people got from consuming products could be measured quantitatively. By distinguishing total and marginal utilities, this theory was able to show that some consumer behaviour that seemed strange or even paradoxical could be seen as rational.

The second breakthrough came with indifference theory, which dispensed with the dubious assumption of quantitatively measurable utility on which marginal utility theory was based. In this new theory, all that was needed was the assumption that consumers could say which of two consumption bundles they preferred without having to say by how much. We deal with these two theories in their historical order.

The utility theory of demand

In this chapter we distinguish marginal from total utility, we see that the shape of the demand curve depends on the former, and we then go on to see how the individual consumer can maximize utility by equating marginal utility to price. From this insight, it is an easy step to derive the negative slope of the demand curve from utility theory and to explain some of what seems like paradoxical behaviour.

Before proceeding with our analysis of demand based upon the assumption that individuals attempt to maximize their personal utility or satisfaction independently of others, it is worth noting that this is not intended to imply that all economic behaviour is selfishly motivated. Box 6.1 contains a discussion of some recent experimental evidence indicating that human beings also have a very strong

sense of fairness, which influences our social and economic interactions.

Marginal and total utility

What we are interested in here is how an individual consumer's satisfaction changes as he or she alters the amount consumed of a single product. The satisfaction a consumer receives from consuming that product is called *utility*. **Total utility** refers to the *total satisfaction* derived from all the units of that product consumed. **Marginal utility** refers to the *change in satisfaction* resulting from consuming one unit more or one unit less of that product. For example, the

Box 6.1 **Experimental economics and the concern for fairness**

In the past decade or so economists and other scientists have co-operated in designing experiments to determine how people actually respond to various choices. This line of enquiry has provided evidence that individuals do not invariably maximize their own utility independent of what others around them are doing. The following extract summarizes the results of one such experiment.

Imagine that somebody offers you $100. All you have to do is agree with some other anonymous person on how to share the sum. The rules are strict. The two of you are in separate rooms and cannot exchange information. A coin toss decides which of you will propose how to share the money. Suppose that you are the proposer. You can make a single offer of how to split the sum, and the other person—the responder—can say yes or no. The responder also knows the rules and the total amount of money at stake. If her answer is yes, the deal goes ahead. If her answer is no, neither of you gets anything. In both cases, the game is over and will not be repeated. What will you do?

Instinctively, many people feel they should offer 50 per cent, because such a division is 'fair' and therefore likely to be accepted. More daring people, however, think they might get away with offering somewhat less that half of the sum.

Before making a decision, you should ask yourself what you would do if you were the responder. The only thing you can do as the responder is say yes or no to a given amount of money. If the offer were 10 per cent, would you take $10 and let someone walk away with $90, or would you rather have nothing at all? What if the offer were only 1 per cent? Isn't $1 better than no dollars? And remember, haggling is strictly forbidden. Just one offer by the proposer: the responder can take it or leave it.

So what will you offer?

You may not be surprised to learn that two-thirds of offers are between 40 and 50 per cent. Only four out of 100 people offer less than 20 per cent. Proposing such small amounts is risky, because it might be rejected. More than half of all responders reject offers that are less than 20 per cent. But here is the puzzle: why should anyone reject an offer as 'too small'? The responder has just two choices: take what is offered, or receive nothing at all. The only rational option for a selfish individual is to accept any offer. Even $1 is better than nothing. A selfish proposer who is also sure that the responder is also selfish will therefore make the smallest possible offer and keep the rest. This . . . analysis, which assumes that people are selfish and rational, tells you that the proposer should offer the smallest possible share and the responder should accept it. But this is not how most people play the game.

The scenario just described, called the Ultimatum Game, belongs to a small but rapidly expanding field called experimental economics. . . . For a long time, theoretical economists postulated a being called *Homo economicus*—a rational individual relentlessly bent on maximizing a purely selfish reward. But the lesson from the Ultimatum Game and similar experiments is that real people are a cross-breed of *Homo economicus* and *Homo emoticus*, a complicated hybrid species that can be ruled as much by emotion as by cold logic and selfishness. . . .

Centuries ago philosophers such as David Hume and Jean-Jacques Rousseau emphasized the crucial role of 'human nature' in social interactions. Theoretical economists, in contrast, long preferred to study the selfish *Homo economicus*. They devoted great energy to theorizing about how an isolated individual—a Robinson Crusoe on some desert island—would choose among different bundles of commodities. We are no Robinson Crusoes. Our ancestors' line has been social for 30 million years. And in social interactions, our preferences turn out to be far from selfish. (Karl Sigmund, Ernst Fehr and Martin A. Nowak, 'The Economics of Fair Play', *Scientific American*, January 2002, pages 82–7)

None of this suggests that it is not useful for many purposes to assume that individuals maximize their own utility or self-interest. However, it is worth bearing in mind that this assumption is not applicable to all forms of behaviour. We care about others as well as ourselves, and we also care about what others think of us; this often affects our behaviour, altering it from what a purely selfish individual would do.

total utility of consuming 14 eggs a week is the sum total satisfaction provided by all 14 eggs. The marginal utility of the fourteenth egg consumed is the addition to total satisfaction provided by consuming that extra egg. Put another way, the marginal utility of the fourteenth egg is the addition to total utility gained from consuming 14 eggs per week rather than 13 per week.

Diminishing marginal utility

A basic assumption of utility theory, which is sometimes called the *law of diminishing marginal utility*, is as follows:

The marginal utility, generated by additional units of any product diminishes as an individual consumes more of it, holding constant the consumption of all other products.

The way in which most of us use water provides a good example of diminishing marginal utility. We consume it in many forms: tap water, soft drinks, bottled water, or water flavoured with such things as tea leaves and coffee grounds. Whatever the form in which we consume it, water is necessary to our very existence. Anyone denied water will not survive very long. So we value the minimum of water needed to sustain life as much as we value life itself. We would be willing, therefore, to pay quite a lot if this were the only way to obtain the amount of water needed to stay alive. Thus, the total utility of that much water is extremely high, as is the marginal utility of the first few units drunk. More than this bare minimum will be drunk, but the marginal utility of successive amounts of water drunk over any period of time will decline steadily.

Furthermore, water has many uses other than for drinking. A fairly high marginal utility will be attached to some minimum quantity for bathing, but much more than this minimum will be used only for more frequent baths or showers. The last weekly gallon used for bathing is likely to have a low marginal utility. Again, some small quantity of water is necessary for tooth brushing, but many people leave the water running while they brush. The water going down the drain between wetting and rinsing the brush surely has a low utility. When all the many uses of water by the modern consumer are considered (washing machines, dishwashers, lawn sprinklers, car washing, etc.), it is certain that the marginal utility of the last, say, 10 per cent of all units consumed is very low and falling, even though the total utility of all the units consumed is extremely high.

Utility schedules and graphs

The schedule in Table 6.1 illustrates the assumptions that have been made about utility, using the number of times one consumer, Carol, attends a performance (gig) by her favourite band each year. The table shows her total utility rising, the more gigs she attends each year. Everything else being equal, more gigs means more satisfaction—at least over the range shown in the table. But Carol's marginal utility of each additional gig per year is less than that of the previous one, even though each gig adds something to her total satisfaction. The schedule shows that marginal utility declines as quantity consumed rises.

Table 6.1 Total and marginal utility schedules

Number of gigs attended per year	Total utility	Marginal utility
0	0.00	
1	15.00	15.00
2	25.00	10.00
3	31.00	6.00
4	35.00	4.00
5	37.50	2.50
6	39.00	1.50
7	40.25	1.25
8	41.30	1.05
9	42.20	0.90
10	43.00	0.80

Total utility rises, but marginal utility declines as consumption increases. The marginal utility of 10, shown as the second entry in the last column, arises because with attendance at the second gig total utility increases from 15 to 25, a difference of 10. Although total utility rises with more attendance, each additional visit adds less to the total.

Maximizing utility

We saw in Chapter 3 that a basic assumption of the theory of consumer behaviour is that consumers try to obtain as much satisfaction as they possibly can in the circumstances in which they find themselves. In other words, consumers seek to maximize their total utility.

Equilibrium for one product

If we hold the consumption of all but one product constant, we can study Carol's maximizing behaviour and derive her demand curve from a marginal utility schedule such as the one shown in Figure 6.1. To help simplify the analysis, we assume that we can identify the money value of each level of utility[1] and we work with money equivalents, and plot these in Figure 6.1.

Now let Carol be faced with a given market price of some product. The price shows what she must sacrifice to obtain each unit of the product. The marginal utility schedule, or graph, shows the additional value of satisfaction she receives from having each additional unit of the product. Clearly, Carol can increase her total utility by adding to her purchases as long as the value that she places on each additional unit (i.e. the value of the additional satisfaction she gets from consuming it) exceeds the amount she must pay for that unit. It follows that our utility-maximizing consumer will adjust her purchases of a product until the marginal utility of the last unit purchased (measured in money) is equal to the price of a unit of that product.

For example, at a price of £6 Carol will attend three gigs per year,[2] since she values the first and second attendance more highly than the price she pays for them and the third just at its price. This is shown in part (ii) of the figure.

When the consumption of all but one product is held constant, the marginal utility schedule for the product in question is that product's demand curve. This is because the consumer will wish to purchase up to the point where price equals the value of marginal utility.

Equilibrium for many products

Now let us drop the simplifying assumption that the consumption of all other products is held constant. How can Carol adjust her expenditure among more than one product so as to maximize her total utility? Should she go to the point where the marginal utility of each product is the same, that is, where she would value equally the last unit of each product consumed? This would make sense only if

---

[1] We could get this by asking how much utility Carol could get if she spent £1 of income on some commodity other than gigs where it would yield her most utility. Say this is CDs, where £1 worth of expenditure yields one unit of utility. Then a unit of utility is worth £1 and we can change all the utility figures in Table 6.1 into pounds.

[2] This not a very good band!

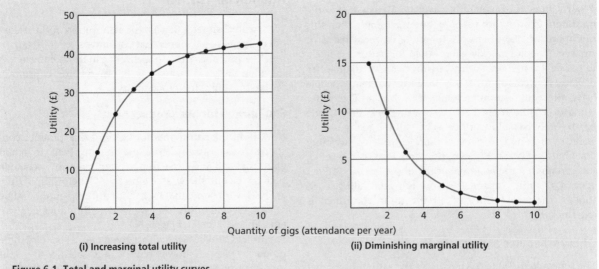

Figure 6.1 Total and marginal utility curves

As consumption increases, total utility rises but marginal utility falls. The dots correspond to the points listed in Table 6.1; smooth curves have been drawn through them. They show total utility rising, while marginal utility is positive but declining, as the amount consumed per period of time rises. The utility-maximizing consumer equates marginal utility to price by attending 2 gigs when the price is £10, 4 when the price is £4, 8 when the price is £1.05, and so on.

each product had the same price per unit. But if Carol must spend £3 to buy an additional unit of one product and only £1 for a unit of another, the first product would represent a poor use of her money if the marginal utility of each were equal. Carol would be spending £3 to get satisfaction she could have acquired for only £1.

To maximize utility, consumers allocate expenditure among products so that equal utility is derived from the last unit of money spent on each.[3]

Imagine that Carol is in a position in which the utility of the last £1 spent on live music yields three times the utility of the last £1 spent on CDs. In this case total utility can be increased by switching £1 of spending from CDs to live-music attendances and gaining the difference between the utilities of £1 spent on each.

Carol will continue to switch spending from CDs to gigs as long as £1 spent on gig attendance yields more utility than £1 spent on CDs. But this switching reduces the quantity of CDs consumed, which raises their marginal utility. At the same time, the switching increases the number of gig attendances consumed, thereby lowering their marginal utility.

Eventually the marginal utilities will have changed enough so that Carol's marginal utility from £1 spent on another gig is just equal to her marginal utility from the last £1 spent on CDs. At this point there is nothing to be gained by a further switch of spending from CDs to gigs. If Carol reallocates her spending even further in the same direction, the marginal utility of gigs will fall (from con-

suming even more of them) and the marginal utility of CDs will rise (from consuming even fewer of them). Total utility will no longer be at its maximum because the marginal utility of the last £1 spent on CDs will exceed the marginal utility of the last £1 spent on gigs.

The conditions for maximizing utility can be stated more generally. Denote the marginal utility of the last unit of product X by MU_X and its price by p_X. Let MU_Y and p_Y refer respectively to the marginal utility of a second product, Y, and its price. The marginal utility per pound spent on X will be MU_X/p_X. For example, if the last unit adds 30 units to utility and costs £2, its marginal utility per pound is $30/2 = 15$.

The condition required for any consumer to maximize utility is that the following relationship should hold, for all pairs of products:

$$\frac{MU_X}{p_X} = \frac{MU_Y}{p_Y}. \tag{1}$$

This merely says in symbols what we earlier said in words. Consumers will allocate spending so that the utilities gained from the last £1 spent on both products are equal. This is the fundamental equation of utility theory. Each consumer demands each good up to the point at which the marginal utility per pound spent on it is the same as the marginal utility of a pound spent on each other good.

[3] By the 'last unit' we do not mean money spent over successive time-periods. Instead, we are talking about buying more or fewer units in the same time period.

When this condition is met, the consumer cannot shift a pound of spending from one product to another and increase total utility.

Now you should be able to see why it does not matter which alternative goods' spending we use for comparison. In our example, we asked what the utility would be of another £1 spent on CDs (as compared with gigs). But when the consumer is in equilibrium the marginal utility of £1 of spending is the same for all the goods and services that are being purchased.

Another view

If we rearrange the terms in equation (1), we can gain additional insight into consumer behaviour:[4]

$$\frac{MU_X}{MU_Y} = \frac{p_X}{p_Y}. \tag{2}$$

The right-hand side of this equation states the relative price of the two goods. This is determined by the market and is beyond Carol's control. She reacts to these market prices but is powerless to change them. The left-hand side of the equation states the relative ability of the two goods to add to her satisfaction if she consumes a little more or a little less of either of them, and this is within her control. In determining the quantities of different goods she buys, Carol determines also what her marginal utilities of the goods will be. Looking at Table 6.1, we see, for example, that if Carol attends three band performances a year the marginal utility of the last performance to her will be 6, while if she attends six performances her marginal utility for the last performance attended will be 1.5.

If the two sides of equation (2) are not equal, Carol can increase her total satisfaction by changing her spending pattern. Assume, for example, that the price of a unit of X is twice the price of a unit of Y ($p_X/p_Y = 2$), while the marginal utility of a unit of X is three times that of a unit of Y ($MU_X/MU_Y = 3$). Under these conditions, it pays Carol to buy more X and less Y. For example, reducing purchases of Y by two units frees enough purchasing power to buy a unit of X. Since one extra unit of X bought yields 1.5 times the satisfaction of two units of Y forgone, the switch is worth making. What about a further switch of X for Y? As Carol buys more X and less Y, the marginal utility of X falls and the marginal utility of Y rises. In this example Carol will go on rearranging purchases—reducing Y consumption and increasing X consumption—until the marginal utility of X is only twice that of Y. At this point, total satisfaction cannot be further increased by rearranging purchases between the two products.

Think about what Carol is doing. She is faced with a set of prices that she cannot change. She responds to these prices and maximizes her satisfaction by adjusting the things that *can* be changed—the quantities of the various goods purchased—until equation (2) is satisfied for all pairs of products.

We see this sort of equation frequently in economics—one side representing the choices the outside world presents to decision-takers and the other side representing the effect of those choices on their satisfaction. It shows the equilibrium position reached when decision-takers have made the best adjustment they can to the external forces that constrain their choices.

When they enter the market, all consumers face the same set of market prices. When they are fully adjusted to these prices, each one of them will have identical ratios of their marginal utilities for each pair of goods. Of course, a rich consumer may consume more of each product than a poor consumer and get more *total utility* from them. However, the rich and the poor consumer (and every other consumer) will adjust their relative purchases of each product so that the relative *marginal utilities* are the same for all. Thus, if the price of X is twice the price of Y, each consumer will purchase X and Y to the point at which his or her marginal utility of X is twice the marginal utility of Y. Consumers with different tastes, however, will have different marginal utility schedules. So they will consume differing relative quantities of products. None the less, when they have maximized their utility, the ratios of their marginal utilities will be the same for all of them.

Box 6.2 illustrates the general applicability of the insight that maximizing behaviour implies balancing things at the margin. Marginal, not average, values are what matter for maximization.

The consumer's demand curve

To derive the consumer's demand curve for some product, say sugar, take equation (2) and let X stand for sugar and Y for all other products. What will happen if, with all other prices constant, the price of sugar rises?

We start by observing that for most consumers sugar absorbs only a small proportion of total budget. If, in response to a change in its price, spending on sugar changes by £2 per month, this might represent a large change in sugar consumption but would require only a negligible change in the consumption of each of many other products. Hence we proceed in the text by assuming that the marginal utilities of other products do not change when the amount spent on sugar changes. The appendix to this chapter looks more closely at this assumption.

Suppose one consumer, Gerry, finds himself in a position where the marginal utility per pound spent on sugar is less than the marginal utility per pound spend on each other good, because the price of sugar has just risen. That is:

$$\frac{MU_X}{p_X} < \frac{MU_Y}{p_Y}, \text{ where good X is sugar and good Y represents all other goods.}$$

---

[4] This is done by multiplying both sides of the equation by p_X/MU_Y.

Box 6.2 Marginals matter

A consumer interested in maximizing utility must allocate expenditure between the things she can buy until the utility of the last penny spent on each is the same. This principle applies to all situations in which something is being maximized. It is one of economists' greatest insights. Yet it is a principle that is often forgotten in practice. Consider the following example.

A firm is allocating workers between two production teams called 'GO' and 'DO'. A manager notices that GO's output per person is higher than DO's. As far as he can see, the workers in each team are more or less the same so the differences must be caused by how each team is organizing its work. He then reasons that, since those working in the GO team are more productive than those working in the DO group, he could increase production by moving some workers from DO to GO. As he does this, he notices that the output per person starts to fall in the GO group and rise in the DO group. But it is still higher in GO than in DO so he continues to transfer workers. Finally he reaches a situation in which the output per worker is the same in both groups. So he reasons that he has found the optimal size of each group since workers are now equally productive in each group.

Can you see what is wrong with the manager's reasoning? What he has done is to equate average output per worker. What he should have done is to equate marginal outputs of a worker in each group. He could do this by transferring workers as long as the reduction in output caused by a worker

leaving the DO group (which is his marginal contribution to DO's output) is less than the increase in output caused by his entry to the GO group (which is his marginal contribution to GO's output). This is another way of saying that the marginal contribution of a worker is higher in the GO group than in the DO group. He should stop moving workers when the last worker causes the output in the DO group to fall by as much as he causes production in the GO group to rise. At this point the manager has equated the marginal contribution of a worker in each group, so there is no gain in any further transfer of workers from one group to the other.

As this example shows, equating averages across groups, whatever the groups are, has a seductive appeal. Yet it does not maximize the total value of whatever the groups are doing.

To help persuade yourself that the rule of equating averages is not the right maximizing rule, work out the following simple illustration. The GO group's output is 20 with one worker, 31 with two workers, and remains at 31 no matter how many further workers are added. The DO group's output is 10 with one worker, 20 with two workers, and rises by ten for every additional worker. Assume that the manager has nine workers to allocate between the two groups. How many would he allocate to each if he came as close as possible to equating the average output per worker in each group? How many would he allocate if he equated the marginal contribution of a worker in each group? Which rule maximizes the total output?

To restore equilibrium, he must buy less sugar, thereby raising his marginal utility until once again equation (1) is satisfied (where X is sugar). The common sense of this is that the marginal utility of sugar per £1 spent on it falls when its price rises. Before the price rise Gerry begins with the utility of the last £1 spent on sugar equal to the utility of the last £1 spent on all other goods, but the rise in sugar prices changes this. Gerry buys less sugar (and more of other goods) until the marginal utility of sugar rises enough to make the utility of a pound spent on sugar the same as it was originally.

This analysis leads to the basic prediction of demand theory, also known as the law of demand.

A rise in the price of a product (with income and the prices of all other products held constant) will lead to a decrease in the quantity of the product demanded by each consumer.

If this is true for each individual consumer, it is also true for all consumers taken together. Thus, the theory predicts a negatively sloped market demand curve.

Consumers' surplus

The concept

The negative slope of the demand curve has an interesting consequence:

All consumers pay less than they would be willing to pay for the total amount of any product that they consume.

The difference between what they would be willing to pay—which is the value of the total utility that they derive from consuming the product—and what they do pay—

which is their total spending on that product—is called **consumers' surplus**.

For example, in Table 6.1 Carol attends gigs five times a year when the price is £2.50 per visit and hence spends £12.50 per year on hearing the band. However, the total value (total utility) to her of these attendances—therefore the maximum Carol would pay for a five-gig ticket—is £37.50. So Carol has £25 worth of enjoyment in excess of what she actually paid (£12.50). Consumers' surplus is the difference between the maximum that a consumer would

Table 6.2 Consumer's surplus

Glasses of milk consumed per week (1)	Total utility (2)	Marginal utility (3)	Consumer's surplus on each glass if milk costs £0.30 per glass (4)
1	£3.00	£3.00	£2.70
2	4.50	1.50	1.20
3	5.50	1.00	0.70
4	6.30	0.80	0.50
5	6.90	0.60	0.30
6	7.40	0.50	0.20
7	7.80	0.40	0.10
8	8.10	0.30	0.00
9	8.35	0.25	—
10	8.55	0.20	—

Consumer's surplus on each unit consumed is the difference between the market price and the maximum price the consumer would pay to obtain that unit. The table shows the value that Ms Green puts on successive glasses of milk consumed each week. As long as she is willing to pay more than the market price for any glass, she obtains a consumer's surplus when she buys it. The marginal glass of milk is the eighth. This is the one she values at just the market price and on which she earns no consumer's surplus.

have paid for a specific set of purchases and he or she actually paid.

This concept is important and deserves further elaboration. Table 6.2 gives hypothetical data for the weekly consumption of milk by one consumer, Ms Green. The second column, labelled 'Total utility', gives the total value she places on consumption of so many glasses per week (when the alternative is zero). The third column, labelled 'Marginal utility', gives the amount she would pay to add the last glass indicated to weekly consumption. Thus, for example, the marginal utility of £0.80 listed against four glasses gives the value Ms Green places on increasing consumption from three to four glasses. It is the difference between the total utilities she attaches to consumption levels of three and four glasses per week.

If Ms Green is faced with a market price of £0.30, she will maximize total utility by consuming eight glasses per week because she values the eighth glass just at the market price, while valuing all earlier glasses at higher amounts. Because she values the first glass at £3.00 but gets it for £0.30, she makes a 'profit' of £2.70 on that glass; that is, she gets £3.00 worth of satisfaction for £0.30. Between her £1.50 valuation of the second glass and what she has to pay for it, she clears a 'profit' of £1.20. She clears £0.70 on the third glass. And so on. These 'profits', which are called her consumer's surpluses on each unit, are shown in the final column of the table. The total surplus is £5.70 per week. In the table, we calculate Ms Green's surplus by summing the surpluses on each glass. We arrive at the same total, however, by first

summing the maximum that Ms Green would pay for all the glasses bought (which is £8.10 in this case) and then subtracting the £2.40 that she does pay.

The value placed by each consumer on his or her total consumption of some product can be estimated in at least two ways. The valuation that the consumer places on each successive unit may be summed, or the consumer may be asked the maximum that he or she would pay to consume the amount in question if the alternative were to have none.[5] While each consumer would put different numerical values into Table 6.2, diminishing marginal utility implies that the figures in the final column would be declining for all of them. Since a consumer will go on buying further units until the value placed on the last unit equals the market price, it follows that there will be a consumers' surplus on every unit consumed except the last one.

The data in columns (1) and (3) of Table 6.2 give Ms Green's demand curve for milk. It is her demand curve because she will go on buying glasses of milk as long as she values each glass at least as much as the market price she must pay for it. When the market price is £3.00 per glass she will buy only one glass; when it is £1.50 she will buy two glasses; and so on. The total consumption value is the area below her demand curve, and consumers' surplus is that part of the area that lies above the price line. This is shown in Figure 6.2.

Figure 6.3 shows that the same relation holds for the smooth market demand curve that indicates the total amount all consumers would buy at each price.[6]

Applications

In subsequent chapters we will find many uses for the concept of consumers' surplus. In this chapter we show how it can be used to resolve some very old puzzles.

The paradox of value

Early thinkers about the economy struggled with the problem of what determines the relative prices of products. They encountered the *paradox of value*: many essential products, without which we could not live, such as water, have relatively low prices. On the other hand some luxury

[5] This is only an approximation, but it is good enough for our purposes. More advanced theory shows that the calculations presented here slightly overestimate consumers' surplus because they ignore the income effect. Although it is sometimes necessary to correct for this bias, none of the corrections that are called for would upset our basic conclusion: when consumers can buy all the units they require at a single market price, they pay much less than they would be willing to pay if faced with the choice between having the quantity they consume and having none.

[6] Figure 6.2 is a bar chart because we allowed the consumer to vary her consumption only in discrete units, one at a time. Had we allowed her to vary her consumption continuously, we could have traced out a continuous curve for Ms Green similar to the one shown in Figure 6.3.

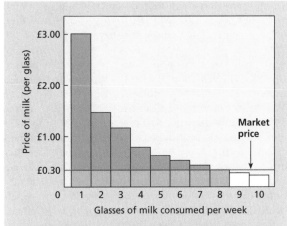

Figure 6.2 Consumer's surplus for an individual

Consumer's surplus is the sum of the extra valuations placed on each unit above the market price paid for each. This figure is based on the data in Table 6.2. Ms Green pays the red area for the 8 glasses of milk she consumes per week when the market price is £0.30 a glass. The total value she places on these 8 glasses of milk is the entire shaded area (red and green). Hence her consumer's surplus is the green area.

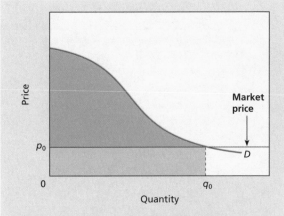

Figure 6.3 Consumers' surplus for the market

Total consumers' surplus is the area under the demand curve and above the price line. The area under the demand curve shows the total valuation that consumers place on all units consumed. For example, the total value that consumers place on q_0 units is the entire area shaded red and green under the demand curve up to q_0. At a market price of p_0 the amount paid for q_0 units is the red area. Hence consumers' surplus is the green area.

products, such as diamonds, have relatively high prices, even though we could easily survive without them. Does it not seem odd that water, which is so important to us, has such a low market value while diamonds, which are much less important, have a much higher market value? It took a long time to resolve this apparent paradox, so it is not surprising that, even today, similar confusions about the determinants of market values persist and cloud many policy discussions.

The key to resolving the 'paradox' lies in the distinction between total and marginal utility. We have already seen in the previous section that the area under the demand curve measures the value of the total utility that consumers place on the sum total of the specific product consumed per period. In Figure 6.3 the total consumption value of q_0 units is the entire shaded area (red and green) under the demand curve.

What about the value that the consumer places on having one more or one less than the q_0 units she is currently consuming? Faced with a market price of p_0, the consumer buys all units on which she puts a value of p_0 or greater, but she does not purchase any units that she values at less than p_0. It follows that the value consumers place on the last unit consumed of any product—its marginal utility—is equal in equilibrium to the product's price.

Now look at the total amount spent to purchase the product—the price paid for it multiplied by the quantity bought and sold—which we can call its total market value or sale value. In Figure 6.3 this is shown by the red rectangle with sides p_0 and q_0. We have seen that the value of the

total utility that consumers derive from a given amount of a product exceeds its total market value. The two values do not, however, have to bear any constant relation to each other. Figure 6.4 shows two goods, one for which total market value is a very small fraction of its total utility and another for which total market value is a much higher fraction of total utility.

The resolution of the paradox of value is that a good that is very plentiful, such as water, will have a low price. It will be consumed, therefore, to the point where all purchasers place a low value on the last unit consumed, whether or not they place a high value on their total consumption of the product; that is, marginal utility will be low whatever the value of total utility. On the other hand, a product that is relatively scarce will have a high market price. Therefore, consumption will stop at a point at which consumers place a high value on the last unit consumed whatever value they place on their total consumption of the good; that is, marginal utility will be high whatever the value of total utility.

We have now reached an important conclusion:

The market price of a product depends on demand and supply. Therefore no paradox is involved when a product from which consumers receive a high total utility sells for a low price, and hence has only a low total market value (i.e. a low amount spent on it).

Total utility, marginal utility, and elasticity

In ordinary discussions people often distinguish between products that are difficult to do without, such as food and

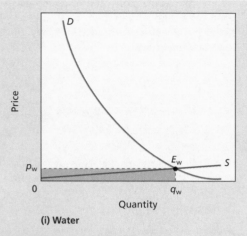
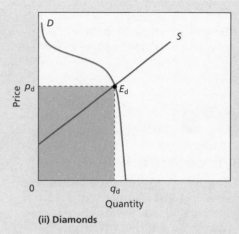

(i) Water

(ii) Diamonds

Figure 6.4 Total utility versus market value

The market value of the amount of some commodity bears no necessary relation to the total utility that consumers derive from that amount. The total utility that consumers derive from water, as shown by the area under the demand curve in part (i), is great—indeed, we cannot possibly show the curve for very small quantities, because people would pay all they had rather than be deprived completely of water. The total utility that consumers derive from diamonds is shown by the area under the demand curve in part (ii). This is less than the total utility derived from water. The supply curve of diamonds makes diamonds scarce and keeps their price high. Thus, when equilibrium is at E_d, the total market value of diamonds sold, indicated by the dark blue area of $p_d q_d$, is high. The supply curve of water makes water plentiful and makes water low in price. Thus, when equilibrium is at E_w, the total market value of water consumed, indicated by the dark blue area of $p_w q_w$, is low.

water, and products that can be fairly easily dispensed with, such as camembert cheese, electric curtain openers, and diamond rings. In the previous section we learned to measure these total utilities by the areas under demand curves. Using this terminology, we could say that an indispensable product has a very large total utility as measured by the area under its demand curve, whereas a dispensable one has a smaller total utility.

A frequent error occurs when people try to use their knowledge of total utilities to predict demand elasticities. It is sometimes argued that since dispensable products can easily be given up they have highly elastic demands—when their prices rise, consumers can stop purchasing them. Conversely, it is argued that indispensable products have highly inelastic demands because, when prices rise, consumers have no choice but to continue to buy them.

But elasticity of demand depends on marginal utilities, not on total utilities. The relevant question for predicting the response to a price change is 'How much do consumers value a bit more of the product?' not 'How much do they value all that they are consuming?' When the price of a product rises, each consumer will reduce his purchases of that product until he values the last unit consumed at the price that must be paid for that unit.

Elasticity of demand depends on the value consumers place on having a bit more or a bit less of the product (marginal utility); it bears no necessary relation to the value they place on total consumption of the product (total utility).

Attitude surveys

Attitude surveys often ask people which of several alternatives they prefer. Such questions measure total rather than marginal utilities. Where the behaviour being predicted involves an either–or decision, such as whether to vote for the Labour or the Conservative candidate, the total utility that is attached to each party or candidate will indeed be what matters, because the voter must choose one and reject the other. However, where the decision is a marginal one regarding a little more or a little less, total utility is not what will determine behaviour. If one attempts to predict behaviour in these cases from a knowledge of total utilities, even if the information is correct, one will be hopelessly wrong.

Here are two examples of how surveys can be misleading. A market research survey asked people to name the household device they thought was most important. Suppliers of a new version of this device used the survey to predict demand but subsequently found that it had failed to do so. A post mortem revealed that most people did not respond to the sales promotion because they already had the product and were unwilling to pay the advertised price for a second one. In other words, although the total utility they got from the device was high, the marginal utility they attached to another unit of it was low.

As a second example, a political party conducted a survey to determine what types of public expenditure people thought most valuable. Unemployment benefits rated very high. The party was subsequently surprised when it aroused great voter hostility by advocating an increase in unemployment benefits. Although the party was surprised, there was nothing inconsistent or irrational in the voters' feeling that protection of the unemployed was a very good thing, providing a high total utility, but that additional payments were unnecessary, and therefore had a low marginal utility.

SUMMARY

The utility theory of demand

■ Marginal utility theory distinguishes between the total utility that each consumer gets from the consumption of all units of some product and the marginal utility each consumer obtains from the consumption of one more unit of the product.

■ The basic assumption in utility theory is that the addition to total utility that the consumer derives from the consumption of successive units of a product diminishes as the consumption of that product increases.

■ Each consumer reaches a utility-maximizing equilibrium at which the utility he or she derives from the last £1 spent on each product is equal. Another way of putting this is that the marginal utilities derived from the last unit of each product consumed will be proportional to their prices.

■ Demand curves have negative slopes because, when the price of product X falls, each consumer restores equilibrium by increasing his or her purchases of X. The increase must be enough to lower the marginal utility of X until its ratio to the new lower price of X is the same as it was before the price fell. This restores the equality of the ratio to what it is for all other products.

Consumers' surplus

■ Consumers' surplus is the difference between (*a*) the value consumers place on their total consumption of some product and (*b*) the actual amount paid for it. The first value is measured by the maximum they would pay for the amount consumed, rather than go without it completely. The second is measured by market price times quantity consumed.

■ It is important to distinguish between total and marginal values because choices concerning a bit more and a bit less cannot be predicted from knowledge of total values. The paradox of value involves confusion between total and marginal values.

■ Elasticity of demand is related to the marginal value that consumers place on having a bit more or a bit less of some product; it bears no necessary relationship to the total value that consumers place on all of the units consumed of that product.

TOPICS FOR REVIEW

■ Marginal and total utility

■ Diminishing marginal utility

■ Derivation of a demand curve

■ Consumers' surplus

■ Paradox of value

DISCUSSION QUESTIONS

1 An individual has allocated income so as to maximize total utility and has a marginal utility of coffee (per cup per week) that is twice that of tea (per cup per week) but only a quarter of that of a pepperoni pizza. If a pepperoni pizza is £8, how much is coffee and tea per cup?

2 You have £120 per week to spend on meals, cinema visits and video rentals. Meals are £20, cinema visits £10 and video rentals £5. If the marginal utility of each is constant, under what circumstance would you consume some of all three, some of only two and all of one and none of the others?

3 Use the same income and prices as in exercise 2. Assume that the marginal utility of successive units (in £ equivalent) is as follows, meals: 50, 20, 18, 16, 14, 12, 9, 7, 6, 4, 2, 1, 0;

cinema visits 25, 20, 15, 12, 10, 8, 6, 5, 4, 3, 2, 1, 0; video rentals: 15, 12, 10, 9, 8, 7, 6, 5, 4, 3, 2, 1, 0. What is the utility-maximizing choice of purchases? What is the value of consumer surplus for each product purchased and for the three combined? Suppose the price of video rentals now rises to £10 (but income and other prices remain unchanged). What is the new outcome?

4 Explain the law of diminishing marginal utility and discuss what this implies for the shape of demand curves.

5 Why do some goods that are vital for life (and thus have high total utility) have a low price, while others that yield lower total utility have a high price?

6 What is consumer surplus and how is it related to utility?

7 Explain why it is the marginal utility, rather than the total utility, of a product that affects its elasticity.

8 What would spending patterns look like if there were some goods or services from which consumers received increasing marginal utility?

Appendix Derivation of a demand curve from marginal utility theory

Marginal utility theory can derive the negatively sloped demand curve for one product only by making some key simplifying assumptions. In this appendix we investigate some of the alternative assumptions that can be used. We consider deriving the demand curve for some product, say sugar (S).

Case 1 In the simplest case we hold the consumption of all other products constant, and the equilibrium is given by

$$p_S = MU_S. \tag{A1}$$

Diminishing marginal utility then yields a negatively sloped demand curve. The problem here is that, if demand has any elasticity other than unity, adjusting sugar purchases to a change in the price of sugar implies altering purchases of other products as well.

Case 2 To deal with the problem just mentioned, we allow for n products. First, we divide (A1) by MU_S to get

$$\frac{p_S}{MU_S} = 1. \tag{A2}$$

Then we observe that there will be a similar equation for each product. Since the right-hand sides of each are all unity, we can equate the left-hand sides to get the following:

$$\frac{p_1}{MU_1} = \frac{p_2}{MU_2} = \frac{p_3}{MU_3} = \ldots = \frac{p_n}{MU_n}. \tag{A3}$$

Sugar is now product one and n is a very large number. The dots indicate the equivalent ratios for all goods other than the four listed.

Since the consumption of each of the goods from 2 to n will change only a little when sugar purchases are altered in response to a change in its price, we can assume that their marginal utilities are constant. In this case, when p_1 changes, MU_1 must change in the opposite direction to keep the ratio of the two values equal to the unchanged ratios of all other MU_s to their respective prices.

Case 3 Next we let money stand for all other goods, since money is general purchasing power. This reduces (A3) to

$$\frac{MU_1}{p_1} = \frac{MU_M}{p_M}. \tag{A4}$$

MU_M is the marginal utility of money,[7] which is the additional utility derived from spending £1 of additional purchasing power distributed optimally among all products. Since the price of £1 of money is by definition £1, cross-multiplication reduces (A4) to

$$MU_1 = p_1 MU_M. \tag{A5}$$

This is the same as (A1) except for the multiple MU_M, the marginal utility of money. Each increment of income permits an increment of consumption of all products, and the utility of this increment must be declining since the utility of successive units of each product that make it up is declining.

A problem now arises because a fall in the price of sugar makes it possible to buy more of all products and hence will reduce the marginal utility of money. This is why, when equations (A1) or (A3) are used, it is necessary to assume that the product in question takes up only a small part of total expenditure so that the change in MU_M caused by a change in p_1 is negligible and therefore can be assumed to be zero.

In marginal utility theory the negative slope of the demand curve is derived using *ceteris paribus* assumptions about the marginal utilities of all other goods or, equivalently, about the marginal utility of money.

These have the effect of eliminating (by assumption) what we will learn in Chapter 7 to call the 'income effect'. There we will see that it is the income effect that prevents us from being able to show in general that the demand curves for each and every product must invariably be negatively sloped.

---

[7] This would be better called 'marginal utility of income', but the term 'marginal utility of money' is commonly used in economics. It is the addition to total utility from having one more pound's worth of income. For most purposes we assume that the marginal utility of money (income) is constant unless we explicitly state otherwise.

Chapter 7

DEMAND ANALYSIS II: INDIFFERENCE THEORY

Is the concept of utility of any use in understanding demand if it cannot be measured? In this chapter we study a different approach, which does not require utility to be measurable but yields equivalent insights into the determinants of demand. In particular, you will learn that:

• A theory of demand can be built by focusing on bundles of goods between which the consumer is indifferent.

• Indifference curves show combinations of goods that give the same level of satisfaction.

• A budget constraint shows what the consumer could buy with a given income.

• A consumer optimizes by trying to get to the highest indifference curve that is available with a given budget constraint.

• The response to a price change can be decomposed into an income and a substitution effect.

• For a good to have a negatively sloped demand curve, it is necessary (but not sufficient) that it be an inferior good.

In this chapter we will first use indifference curves to describe consumers' tastes and will then introduce a budget line to describe the consumption possibilities open to them. After that, we show how consumers reach equilibrium by consuming the bundle that allows them to reach the highest possible levels of satisfaction. We can then see how a consumer alters behaviour when either income or prices change, and go on to derive the negative slope of the demand curve in a more satisfactory fashion than is done with marginal utility theory.

This approach to consumer behaviour has two great advantages.[1] First, it allows us to distinguish between two effects of a change in price, called the income and the substitution effects. This distinction has important practical applications. Second, it allows us to understand the rare but interesting exception to the prediction that all demand curves are negatively sloped, which arises with a so-called Giffen good. Box 7.1 compares the assumptions of the two approaches used in this and the previous chapter.

Box 7.1 Utility and indifference theory contrasted

To explain the difference between the marginal utility and indifference curve approaches, think of a consumer comparing alternative amounts of several goods. A collection that contains a given amount of each good is called a *bundle* of goods. For example, bundle one (signified by b_1) might have 6 apples, 3 oranges, and 5 lemons, while bundle two (signified by b_2) has 8 apples, 2 oranges, and 4 lemons, and bundle three (signified by b_3) has 7 apples, 4 oranges, and 2 lemons.

In utility theory all consumers are assumed not only to be able to say that they are better or worse off when their consumption bundle changes, say, from bundle b_1 to b_2 to b_3, but also to be able to compare the magnitudes of these changes. One consumer might say, for example, that the increase in her utility when going from b_1 to b_2 exceeded the increase in her utility when going from b_2 to b_3. When this can be done, utility is said to be *cardinally measurable*.

Indifference theory uses a much weaker assumption. Consumers are assumed only to be able to *order* various consumption bundles, saying for example that b_3 is preferred to b_2, which is preferred to b_1; they are not assumed to be able to say *by how much* each bundle is preferred to the other. Under this assumption utility is said to be only *ordinally measurable.**

Consider, for example, Table 6.1 on page 99. In marginal utility theory the consumer is assumed to be able to say not only that she prefers attending three gigs per year to two and two to one, but that the increase in utility in going from one to two (10 units in the table) exceeds the increase in going from two to three (6 units in the table). This is the meaning of diminishing marginal utility. In indifference theory, the consumer is assumed to be able to say *only* that she prefers two to one and three to two gigs per year. This is a much weaker assumption, but it is all that is needed to develop demand theory.

---

* Under ordinal measurability the consumer can order bundles, saying for example that $b_3 > b_2 > b_1$, where the > sign indicates the bundle on the left has a larger utility and hence is preferred to the bundle on the right. Under cardinal measurability the consumer can order *first differences*, saying for example $b_3 - b_2 > b_2 - b_1$; that is (in this example), the change in utility in going from b_2 to b_3 *exceeds* the change in going from b_1 to b_2.

---

[1] This approach was originally due to the Italian economist Vilfredo Pareto (1848–1923). It was introduced to the English-speaking world (and greatly elaborated) by two British economists, John Hicks (1904–89) and R. G. D. Allen (1906–83).

Consumer Optimization

The basic assumption about consumer *motivation* does not differ between this and the previous chapter. Consumers try to maximize satisfaction by allocating a given budget between the various goods and services that they wish to buy. Each consumer may be aware of exactly how much satisfaction is delivered by each of the goods consumed (though we doubt it). However, the key thing that is different in this chapter is that the social scientists who are trying to explain the consumer's behaviour do not need to know *how much* satisfaction derives from consumption of each product. Nor indeed does the consumer need to know this. All that is needed is that each consumer can make rational choices between different bundles of goods, and can decide which bundles give him or her more or less satisfaction.

First, we ask how we can find the consumer's equilibrium allocation of spending in this new framework. Once that is done, we will be able to study consumers' responses to changes in such things as prices and incomes.

The consumer's preferences

In the analysis that we are about to develop, the consumer's tastes or preferences, as they are variously called, are shown by indifference curves.

A single indifference curve

We start by deriving a single indifference curve. To do this we give an imaginary consumer, Kevin, some quantity of each of two products, say 18 units of clothing (*C*) and 10 units of food (*F*). This bundle is plotted as point *b* in Figure 7.1. Now think about the alternative combinations of these two products in the two shaded areas created by drawing vertical and horizontal lines through *b*. Would Kevin prefer the bundles of goods in these two shaded areas? To help answer this, we introduce our first assumption about tastes.

Assumption 1. **Other things being equal, the consumer always prefers more of any one product to less of that same product.**

This allows us to rank the bundles of goods represented by the two shaded areas in Figure 7.1. Combinations on the edges of this space to the north east of point *b* all have more of one good and no less of the other, while points inside this area represent bundles containing more of both goods. All points in this space, apart from *b* itself, will thus be preferred to *b*. By similar logic, all points to the south west of

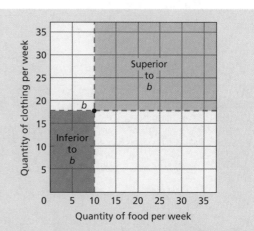

Figure 7.1 Some consumption bundles compared

According to assumption 1, bundle *b* is superior to bundles that have less of both goods and inferior to all bundles that have more of both. All points in the dark blue area are regarded as inferior to bundle *b* because they contain less of both commodities (except on the boundaries, where they have less of one and the same amount of the other).

b represent either fewer of both goods or fewer of at least one and no more of the other. These points will all be inferior for the consumer as they deliver a lower level of satisfaction.

But what about bundles that have more of some products and fewer of others? At point *b*, Kevin consumes 18 units of clothing and 10 of food. Let us ask how much extra clothing we would have to give him to make him equally satisfied if we took away one unit of food. The answer might be that 20 units of clothing and 9 units of food would leave Kevin just as satisfied as the initial combination. If we do this again, taking away another unit of food, there will be some further increase in clothing that could just compensate. Table 7.1 shows that when we have taken away 5 units of food Kevin will require 30 units of clothing to leave him feeling just as satisfied as at point *b*. This is also illustrated by point *a* in Figure 7.2. These combinations of fewer units of food and increased quantities of clothing that leave Kevin just as satisfied trace out the line segment from *b* to *a* in the figure.

Starting again at point *b*, we can now move in the opposite direction and ask how much extra food Kevin would need to leave him equally satisfied as we take successive units of clothing away from him. The answer to this question traces out the line through points *c*, *d*, *e*, and *f*.

By construction, the curved line in Figure 7.2 shows combinations of clothing and food all of which give Kevin the

Table 7.1 **Bundles conferring equal satisfaction**

Bundle	Clothing	Food
a	30	5
b	18	10
c	13	15
d	10	20
e	8	25
f	7	30

Since each of these bundles gives Kevin equal satisfaction, he is indifferent between them. None of the bundles contains more food and more clothing than any of the other bundles. Kevin's assumed indifference among these bundles is not, therefore, in conflict with the assumption that more is preferred to less of each product.

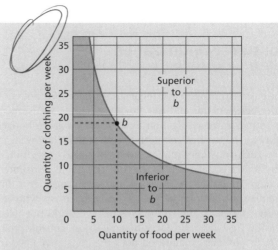

Figure 7.3 **Consumption bundles compared**

The indifference curve allows any bundle such as *b* to be compared with all others. Kevin regards all bundles in the dark blue area as inferior and all bundles in the light blue area as superior to *b*. The indifference curve is the boundary between these two areas. All points on the curve yield equal satisfaction, and Kevin is therefore indifferent among them.

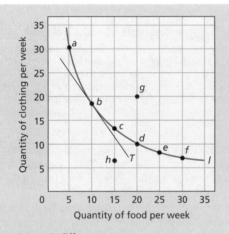

Figure 7.2 **An indifference curve**

The indifference curve shows combinations of food and clothing that yield equal satisfaction and among which the consumer is indifferent. Points *a* to *f* are plotted from Table 7.2 and an indifference curve is drawn through them. Compared with any point on the curve, point *g* is superior while point *h* is inferior. The slope of the tangent *T* gives the marginal rate of substitution at point *b*. Moving down the curve from *b* to *f*, the slope of the tangent flattens, showing that the more food and the less clothing Kevin has, the less willing he will be to sacrifice further clothing to get more food.

same level of satisfaction. He is indifferent between all of the different bundles of goods represented by that line (some specific combinations of which are listed in Table 7.1). For this reason this red line is called an **indifference curve**. The line joining points *a* to *f* in Figure 7.2 is one indifference curve.

An indifference curve shows combinations of products that yield the same satisfaction to the consumer. Thus, a consumer is indifferent between the combinations indicated by any two points on one indifference curve.

Points above and to the right of the indifference curve in Figure 7.2 show combinations of food and clothing that Kevin would prefer to combinations indicated by points on the curve. Consider, for example, the combination of 20F and 20C, which is represented by point *g* in the figure. Although it might not be obvious that this bundle is preferred to bundle *a* (which has more clothing but less food), assumption 1 tells us that *g* is preferred to bundle *c*, because *g* has more clothing *and* more food than *c*. Inspection of the graph shows that *any* point above the curve will be obviously superior to *some* points on the curve, in the sense that it will contain both more food and more clothing than those points on the curve. But since all points on the curve are equally valuable in Kevin's eyes, any point above the curve must, therefore, be superior to *all* points on the curve. By a similar argument, points such as *h*, which are below and to the left of the curve, represent bundles of goods that Kevin regards as inferior to all bundles on the curve. These comparisons are summarized in Figure 7.3.

Diminishing marginal rate of substitution

What is the shape of a typical indifference curve? To answer this we need a second assumption.

Assumption 2. The less of one product that is presently being used by a consumer, the smaller the amount of it that

Table 7.2 Diminishing marginal rate of substitution

Movement	Change in clothing (1)	Change in food (2)	Marginal rate of substitution (3)
From a to b	−12	5	2.4
From b to c	−5	5	1.0
From c to d	−3	5	0.6
From d to e	−2	5	0.4
From e to f	−1	5	0.2

The marginal rate of substitution measures the amount of one product a consumer must be given to compensate for giving up one unit of the other. This table is based on the data in Table 7.1. When Kevin moves from a to b, he gives up 12 units of clothing and gains 5 units of food, a rate of substitution of 12/5 or 2.4 units of clothing sacrificed per unit of food gained. When he moves from b to c, he sacrifices 5 units of clothing and gains 5 of food (a rate of substitution of 1 unit of clothing for each unit of food). Note that the marginal rate of substitution (MRS) is the absolute value of the ratio of ΔC to ΔF. Since these two changes always have opposite signs, the MRS is obtained by multiplying this ratio by −1.

the consumer will be willing to forgo in order to increase consumption of a second product.

This is usually referred to as the assumption of a **diminishing marginal rate of substitution**. The *rate of substitution* tells how much more of one product we need to compensate for successive lost units of the other. The *diminishing* of this rate of substitution may seem intuitively akin to diminishing marginal utility; however, for the latter we hold consumption of all but one good constant, while here we have more of one good compensating for loss of the other.[2]

The diminishing marginal rate of substitution is illustrated in Table 7.2, which is based on the example of food and clothing shown in Table 7.1. As we move down the table through points *a* to *f*, Kevin has bundles with fewer and fewer units of clothing and more and more of food. In accordance with the hypothesis of diminishing marginal rate of substitution, he is willing to give up smaller and smaller amounts of clothing to further increase his consumption of food by one unit. When Kevin moves from *c* to *d*, for example, the table tells us that he is prepared to give up 0.6 unit of clothing to get a further unit of food. When he moves from *e* to *f*, he will give up only 0.2 unit.

The geometrical expression of this hypothesis is found in the shape of the indifference curve. Look closely, for example, at the slope of the curve in Figure 7.2. Its negative slope indicates that, if Kevin is to have fewer units of one product, he must have more of the other to compensate. Diminishing marginal rate of substitution is shown by

the fact that the curve is convex viewed from the origin: moving down the curve to the right, its slope gets flatter and flatter. The absolute value of the slope of the curve is the marginal rate of substitution, the rate at which the consumer is willing to reduce his consumption of the product plotted on the vertical axis in order to increase his consumption of the product plotted on the horizontal axis.

The slope of the indifference curve at any point is measured by the slope of the tangent to the curve at that point. The slope of tangent *T* drawn to the curve at point *b* shows the marginal rate of substitution at that point. It can be seen that, moving down the curve to the right, the slope of the tangent, and hence the marginal rate of substitution at each point, gets flatter and flatter.[3]

The indifference map

So far we have constructed only a single indifference curve. There must, however, be a similar curve passing through any other points in Figure 7.2, in addition to those points on the single curve drawn. Starting at another point, such as *g*, and going through the same exercise, there will be other combinations that will yield Kevin equal satisfaction. If the line joining all of *these* combinations is drawn, another indifference curve will be constructed. This exercise can be repeated many times, generating a new indifference curve each time.

It follows from the comparisons given in Figure 7.3 that the further away any indifference curve is from the origin, the higher is the level of satisfaction given by the consumption bundles that it indicates. We refer to a curve that confers a higher level of satisfaction as a *higher curve*.

A set of indifference curves is called an **indifference map**. An example is shown in Figure 7.4. It specifies Kevin's tastes by showing his complete ordering of preferences between different bundles of these two products, and it shows his rate of substitution between them at each specific point. When economists say that a consumer's tastes are *given*, they do not mean merely that the consumer's current consumption pattern is given: rather, they mean that the consumer's entire indifference map is given.

Of course, there must be an indifference curve through *every* point in Figure 7.4. To graph them we show only a

---

[2] In the mathematical appendix to this chapter we show that diminishing marginal utility is sufficient but not necessary for a diminishing marginal rate of substitution.

[3] Table 7.2 calculates the rate of substitution between distinct points on the indifference curve. Strictly speaking, these are the incremental rates of substitution between the two points. Geometrically, the slope of the chord joining the two points gives this incremental rate. The marginal rate refers to the slope of the curve at a single point and is given by the slope of the tangent to the curve at the point. The discussion of the relation between marginal and incremental rates given on pages 28–31 of Chapter 2 should be read, or reread, at this point.

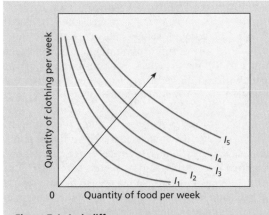

Figure 7.4 An indifference map

A set of indifference curves is called an indifference map. The further the curve from the origin, the higher the level of satisfaction it represents. If Kevin moves along the arrow, he is climbing a 'utility mountain', moving to ever-higher utility levels and crossing ever-higher equal-utility contours, which we call indifference curves.

Table 7.3 **Data for Jessie's budget line**

Quantity of food	Value of food	Quantity of clothing	Value of clothing	Total expenditure
60	£120	0	£0	£120
50	100	5	20	120
40	80	10	40	120
30	60	15	60	120
20	40	20	80	120
10	20	25	100	120
0	0	30	120	120

The table shows combinations of food and clothing available to Jessie when her income is £120 and she faces prices of £4 for clothing and £2 for food. Any row indicates a bundle of food and clothing that exactly exhausts Jessie's income.

few, but all are there. Thus, as Kevin moves upwards to the right starting from the origin, his utility is rising continuously. As he follows a route such as the one shown by the arrow, consuming ever more of both products, he can be thought of as climbing a continuous utility mountain. We show this 'mountain' by selecting a few equal-utility contours, labelled I_1 to I_5. But every point between each of the contours shown must also have a curve of equal utility passing through it. Thus, an indifference map is really like the continuous surface of one half of a cone, rather than a set of discrete lines.

In indifference theory we do not need to make any assumptions about how big the difference is between the level of satisfaction on one indifference curve and the next; that is, we do not need to assume that utility can be quantified. Instead, all we assume is that the utility attached to I_5 exceeds that attached to I_4, which in turn exceeds the utility attached to I_3, and so on. We can say that the consumer is climbing a utility mountain as he moves along the arrow starting from the origin, but we do not need to know if the mountain is gentle or steep.

Box 7.2 shows some specific shapes of indifference curves that correspond to some specific taste patterns.

The choices available to the consumer

An indifference map tells us what any consumer *would like* to do: reach the highest possible indifference curve, that is, be as high up the utility mountain as possible. To see what that consumer *can* do, we need another construction, called the 'budget line'.

We start by considering a single consumer, Jane, who is allocating the whole of her money income between two goods, called food and clothing.[4]

The budget line

The **budget line** shows all those combinations of the goods that are just obtainable given Jane's income and the prices of the products that she buys.[5]

Assume initially that Jane's income is £120 per week, the price of food is £2 per unit, and the price of clothing is £4 per unit. As in the earlier discussion, we denote food by F and clothing by C. Thus, for example, a bundle containing 20 units of food and 10 units of clothing is written as $20F$ and $10C$. Table 7.3 lists a few of the bundles of food and clothing available to Jane, while the blue line running from z to w in Figure 7.5 shows all the possible bundles that she could buy with her income. At point w, for example, Jane is spending all her income to buy $60F$ and no clothing, while a point z indicates that she is spending all her income to buy $30C$ and no food. Points on the line between z and w indicate how much Jane could buy of both products.

---

[4] These assumptions are not as restrictive as they at first seem. Two goods are used so that the analysis can be handled graphically; the argument can easily be generalized to any number of goods with the use of mathematics. Savings are ignored because we are interested in the allocation of expenditure among commodities for current consumption. Saving and borrowing can be allowed for, but doing so affects none of the results in which we are interested here.

[5] A budget line is analogous to the production-possibility boundary shown in Figure 1.1 on page 5. The budget line shows the combinations of commodities available to one consumer given her income and prices, while the production-possibility curve shows the combination of commodities available to the whole society given its supplies of resources and techniques of production.

Box 7.2 **Shapes of indifference curves**

Any taste pattern can be illustrated with indifference curves. This box shows a few examples that will help you to understand how indifference curves work. In each case the curve labelled I_2 indicates a higher utility than the curve labelled I_1.

Perfect substitutes: part (i) Drawing pins that came in red packages of 100 would be perfect substitutes for identical pins that came in green packages of 100 for a colour-blind consumer. He would be willing to substitute one type of package for the other at a rate of one for one. The indifference curves would thus be a set of parallel lines with a slope of −1, as shown in part (i) of the figure. *Indifference curves for perfect substitutes are straight lines whose slopes indicate the rate at which one good can be substituted for the other.*

Perfect complements: part (ii) Left- and right-hand gloves are perfect complements, since one of them is of no use without the other. This gives rise to the indifference curves shown in part (ii) of the figure. There is no rate at which any consumer will substitute one kind of glove for the other when she starts with equal numbers of each. *Indifference curves for perfect complements are 'L-shaped'.*

A good that gives zero utility: part (iii) When a good gives no satisfaction at all, a person would be unwilling to sacrifice even the smallest amount of other goods to obtain any quantity of the good in question. Such would be the case for meat for a vegetarian consumer, whose indifference curves are horizontal straight lines. *Indifference curves for a product yielding zero satisfaction are parallel to that product's axis.*

An absolute necessity: part (iv) There is some minimum quantity of water, w_0, that is necessary to sustain life. As consumption of water falls towards w_0, increasingly large amounts of other goods are necessary to persuade the consumer to cut down on his water consumption. Thus, each indifference curve becomes steeper and steeper as it approaches w_0, and the marginal rate of substitution increases. *The marginal rate of substitution for an absolute necessity approaches infinity as consumption falls towards the amount that is absolutely necessary.*

A good that confers a negative utility after some level of consumption: part (v) Beyond some point, further consumption of many foods and beverages, films, plays, or cricket matches would reduce satisfaction. Figure (v) shows a consumer who is *forced* to eat more and more food. At the amount f_0 she has all the food she could possibly want. Beyond f_0 her indifference curves have positive slopes, indicating that she gets *negative* value from consuming the extra food, and so would be willing to sacrifice some amount of other products to avoid consuming it. *When, beyond some level of consumption, the consumer's utility is reduced by further consumption, the indifference curves have positive slopes.*

This case does not arise if the consumer can dispose of the extra unwanted units at no cost. The indifference curves then become horizontal.

A good that is not consumed: part (vi) Typically, a consumer will consume only one or two of all of the available types of cars, TV sets, dishwashers, or tennis rackets. If a consumer is in equilibrium consuming a zero amount of say, green peas, she is in what is called a *corner solution* (as shown in part (vi) of the figure by the budget line ab and the curve I_1). *When a good is not consumed, the indifference curve cuts the axis of the non-consumed good with a slope flatter than the budget line.*

(i) — Packs of red pins (vertical axis) vs Packs of green pins (horizontal axis); curves I_1, I_2.

(ii) — Left-hand gloves (vertical axis) vs Right-hand gloves (horizontal axis); curves I_2, I_1.

(iii) — Vegetables (vertical axis) vs Meat (horizontal axis); curves I_2, I_1.

(iv) — All other goods (vertical axis) vs Water (horizontal axis), w_0; curves I_2, I_1.

(v) — All other goods (vertical axis) vs Food (horizontal axis), f_0; curves I_2, I_1.

(vi) — All other goods (vertical axis) vs Good X (horizontal axis), points a, b; curves I_1, I_2.

The slope of the budget line

Marked on Figure 7.5 as points x and y are two of the specific spending combinations from Table 7.3. It is clear from the figure that the absolute value of the slope of the budget line measures the ratio of the change in C to the change in F as we move along the line. This ratio, $\Delta C / \Delta F$, is 0.5 in our present example (10/20).

How does the slope of the budget line relate to the prices of the two goods? This question is easily answered if we remember that all points on the budget line represent bundles of goods that just use up Jane's whole income. It follows that, when she moves from one point on the budget line to another, the change in expenditure on C must be of equal value, but opposite in sign, to the change in expenditure on F. Letting ΔC and ΔF stand for the changes

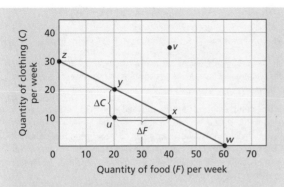

Figure 7.5 Jane's budget line

The budget line shows the quantities of goods available to Jane, given her money income and the price of the goods she buys. With an income of £120 a week and prices of £2 per unit for food and £4 per unit of clothing, the coloured line is Jane's budget line showing all combinations of F and C that are obtainable. Bundle u (10C and 20F) does not use all of her income. Bundle v (35C and 40F) requires more than her present income.

If Jane moves from point y (20F and 20C) to point x (40F and 10C), she consumes 20 more F and 10 fewer C. These amounts are indicated by ΔF and ΔC in the figure. Thus, the opportunity cost of each unit of F added to consumption is 10/20 = 0.5 unit of clothing forgone. This is the absolute value of $\Delta C/\Delta F$, which is the slope of the budget line zw in the figure.

in the quantities of clothing and food respectively, and p_c and p_f stand for the money prices of clothing and food respectively, we can write this relation as follows:

$$\Delta C p_c = -\Delta F p_f.$$

There is nothing difficult in this. All it says is that, if any amount more is spent on one product, the same amount less must be spent on the other. A given income imposes this discipline on any consumer.

If we divide the above equation through, first by ΔF and then by p_c, we get the following:

$$\frac{\Delta C}{\Delta F} = \frac{p_f}{p_c}$$

So the slope of the budget line is the negative of the ratio of the two prices (with the price of the good that is plotted on the horizontal axis appearing in the numerator).

Notice that the slope of the budget line depends only on the ratio of the two prices, not on their absolute values. To check this, consider an example. If clothing costs £4 and food costs £2, then Jane must forgo 0.5 unit of clothing in order to be able to purchase one more unit of food. If clothing costs £8 and food costs £4, Jane must still forgo 0.5 unit of clothing to be able to purchase one more unit of food. As long as the price of clothing is twice the price of food, Jane must forgo half a unit of clothing in order to be able to purchase one more unit of food.

More generally, the amount of clothing that must be given up to obtain another unit of food depends only on *the ratio of* their two prices. If we take the money price of food and divide it by the money price of clothing, we have the opportunity cost of food in terms of clothing (the quantity of clothing that must be forgone in order to be able to purchase one more unit of food). This may be written as

$$\frac{p_f}{p_c} = \text{opportunity cost of food in terms of clothing.}$$

It is apparent that changing income and/or changing both prices in the same proportion leaves the ratio p_f/p_c unchanged.[6]

This discussion helps to clarify the distinction between money prices and relative prices. Both p_f and p_c are money prices, while the ratio p_f/p_c is a relative price.

The consumer's equilibrium

The budget line tells us what consumers *can* do: they can select any consumption bundle on, or below, the line, but not above it. This means that they can spend only within the limits of a given income. To see what consumers *want* to do, we introduce our third assumption.

Assumption 3. **Consumers seek to maximize total satisfaction, which means reaching the highest possible indifference curve.**

We have now developed representations of a consumer's tastes and available choices. Figure 7.6 brings together the budget line and the indifference curves for another consumer, Paul. Any point on the budget line can be attained. Which one will Paul actually choose?

Will Paul choose to consume 25 units of food and no clothing, as he could do with his income? Might he instead choose to consume 30 units of clothing and no food? The answer is no in both cases. By moving away from either of these combinations, he can move to a high indifference curve. Indeed, he can get to higher and higher indifference curves by moving from each of the corners into the middle until he reaches point E, which is just touching, i.e. is tangent to, the highest possible indifference curve. When Paul is at this point of tangency between the indifference curve and the budget line, he cannot reach a higher indifference curve by varying the bundle consumed. Any move from this point that remains within the budget constraint will lead him to a lower indifference curve and thus will lower his satisfaction.

---

[6] Those who prefer an algebraic derivation may refer now to the proof of this proposition on pages 126–7, in the appendix to this chapter.

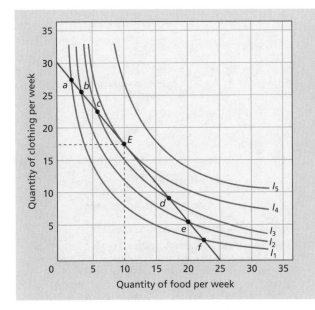

Figure 7.6 The equilibrium of a consumer

Equilibrium occurs at *E*, where an indifference curve is tangent to the budget line. Paul has an income of £150 a week and faces prices of £5 a unit for clothing and £6 a unit for food. A bundle of clothing and food indicated by point *a* is attainable, but by moving along the budget line to points such as *b* and *c*, higher indifference curves can be reached. At *E*, where the indifference curve I_4 is tangent to the budget line, Paul cannot reach a higher curve by moving along the budget line. If he did alter his consumption bundle by moving from *E* to *d*, for example, he would move to the lower indifference curve I_3 and thus to a lower level of satisfaction.

Satisfaction is maximized at the point where an indifference curve is tangent to a budget line. At that point, the slope of the indifference curve—which measures the consumer's marginal rate of substitution—is equal to the slope of the budget line—which measures the opportunity cost of one good in terms of the other as determined by market prices.

Notice that Paul is presented with market prices that he cannot change. He adjusts to these prices by choosing a bundle of goods such that, at the margin, his own relative valuation of the two goods conforms to the relative valuations given by the market. Paul's relative valuation is given by the slope of his indifference curve, while the market's relative valuation is given by the slope of his budget line.

When Paul has chosen the consumption bundle that maximizes his satisfaction, he will go on consuming that bundle unless something changes. The consumer is thus in equilibrium.

The consumer's response to price and income changes

How do consumers change their spending patterns when there is a change in goods prices or in available income? To answer this, we take another hypothetical consumer called Karen. Her tastes are given, and this is represented by an indifference map that does not change. We first show that changes in her income and the prices she faces can be represented as a shift in the budget line. We then investigate the change in spending induced by price and income changes.

Parallel shifts in the budget line

A change in money income

A change in Karen's money income will, other things being equal, shift her budget line. For example, if her income rises, she will be able to buy more of both goods. Her budget line will therefore shift out parallel to itself to indicate this expansion in her consumption possibilities. (The fact that it will be a parallel shift is established by our demonstration on page 114 that the slope of the budget line depends only on the relative price of the two products.) The following proposition is proved in the appendix to this chapter.

Proposition 1 A change in money income, with money prices constant, shifts the budget line parallel to itself—outwards when income rises and inwards when income falls.

The effect of income changes is shown in Figure 7.7. For each level of income, there is an equilibrium position at which an indifference curve is tangent to the relevant budget line. Each such equilibrium position means that Karen is doing as well as she possibly can for that level of income. If we join up all the points of equilibrium, we trace out what

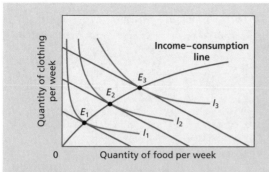

Figure 7.7 An income–consumption line

This line shows how Karen's purchases react to changes in income with relative prices held constant. Increases in income shift the budget line out parallel to itself, moving the equilibrium from E_1 to E_2 to E_3. The blue income–consumption line joins all these points of equilibrium.

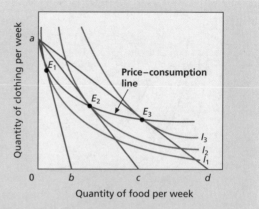

Figure 7.8 The price–consumption line

This line shows how a consumer's purchases react to a change in one price with money income and other prices held constant. Decreases in the price of food (with her money income and the price of clothing constant) pivot Karen's budget line from ab to ac to ad. Her equilibrium position moves from E_1 to E_2 to E_3. The blue price–consumption line joins all such equilibrium points.

is called her **income–consumption line**. This line shows how the consumption bundle changes as income changes, with prices held constant.[7]

A proportionate change in all prices

If all prices are cut in half, Karen can buy twice as much of both products. This causes the same shift in the budget line as when Karen's income doubles with prices held constant. On the other hand, a doubling of all prices will cause her budget line to shift inwards in exactly the same way as if her money income had halved with prices held constant.

This illustrates a general result (which, again, is proved in the appendix to this chapter):

Proposition 2 An equal percentage change in all absolute prices, with money income unchanged, shifts the budget line parallel to itself—inwards towards the origin when prices rise and outwards away from the origin when prices fall.

From this point on, the analysis is the same as in the previous section, since changing money prices proportionately has the identical effect to changing money income.

Offsetting changes in money prices and money incomes

The results in the last two sections suggest that we can have offsetting changes in money prices and money incomes. Consider a doubling of money income, which shifts Karen's budget line outwards. Let this be accompanied by a doubling of all money prices, which shifts her budget line inwards. The net effect is to leave her budget line where it was before the changes in her income and the market prices. This illustrates another general result (which is proved in the appendix to this chapter):

Proposition 3 Multiplying all money prices by the same constant, λ, while holding money income constant has exactly the same effect on the budget line as multiplying money income by $1/\lambda$ while holding money prices constant.

The symbol λ is the lower-case Greek letter lambda, which is often used for some constant multiple. This result is sometimes referred to as the *homogeneity condition*.

Changes in the slope of the budget line

A change in relative prices

We already know that a change in the relative prices of the two goods changes the slope of the budget line. At a given price of clothing, Karen has an equilibrium consumption position for each possible price of food. Connecting these positions traces out a **price–consumption line**, as is shown in Figure 7.8. Notice that, as the relative prices of food and clothing change, the relative quantities of food and clothing purchased also change. In particular, as the price of food falls, Karen buys more food.

Proposition 4 A change in relative prices causes the budget line to change its slope.

---

[7] This income–consumption line can be used to derive the curve relating quantity demanded to income that was introduced on page 68. This is done by plotting the quantity of one of the goods consumed at the equilibrium position against the level of money income that determined the position of the budget line. Repeating this for each level of income produces the required curve.

Box 7.3 **Relative prices and inflation**

Allocation of resources: the importance of relative prices

Price theory shows why the allocation of resources depends on the structure of relative prices. If the money value of all prices, incomes, debts, and credits were doubled, there would, according to our theory, be no noticeable effects. We have already seen that doubling money income and all money prices leaves each consumer's budget line unchanged. So, according to the theory of consumer behaviour, the combination of these changes gives the consumer no incentive to vary any purchases. As far as producers are concerned, if the prices of all outputs and inputs double, the relative profitabilities of alternative lines of production will be unchanged. Thus, producers will have no incentive to alter production rates so as to produce more of some things and fewer of others. The same set of relative prices and real incomes would exist, and there would be no incentive for any reallocation of resources. The economy would function as before. In contrast, a change in *relative* prices will cause resources to be reallocated. Consumers will buy more of the relatively cheaper products and less of the relatively more expensive ones, and producers will increase production of those products whose prices have risen relatively, and reduce production of those whose prices have fallen relatively (since the latter will be relatively less profitable lines of production).

The theory of price and resource allocation is a theory of relative, not absolute, prices.

Inflation and deflation: the importance of absolute prices

The average level of all money prices is called the general price level, or more usually just the **price level**. If all money prices double, we say that the price level has doubled. An increase in the price level is called an **inflation**, a decrease is called a **deflation**. If a rise in all money prices and incomes has little or no effect on the allocation of resources, it may seem surprising that so much concern is expressed over inflation. Clearly, people who spend all their incomes, and whose money incomes go up at the same rate as money prices, lose nothing from inflation. Their real income is unaffected.

Inflation, while having no effect on consumers whose incomes rise at the same rate as prices, does none the less have many serious consequences. These arise mainly because all prices do not rise at the same rate. These consequences are studied in detail later in this book. In the meantime, *we assume that the price level is constant*.

Under these circumstances a change in one money price necessarily changes that price *relative* to the average of all other prices. The theory extends to situations in which the price level is changing. Under inflationary conditions, whenever shifts in demand or supply require a change in a product's relative price, its price rises *faster* (its relative price rising) or *slower* (its relative price falling) than the general price level is rising.

Explaining this each time can be cumbersome. It is therefore simpler to deal with relative prices in a theoretical setting in which the price level is constant. It is important to realize, however, that, even though we develop the theory in this way, it is not limited to such situations. The propositions we develop can be applied to changing price levels merely by making explicit what is always implicit: in the theory of relative prices, 'rise' or 'fall' *always* means rise or fall *relative to the average of all other prices*.

Real and money income

The preceding analysis allows us to look more deeply into the important distinction between two concepts of income. **Money income** measures a consumer's income in terms of some monetary unit, for example so many pounds sterling or so many dollars. **Real income** measures the *purchasing power* of the consumer's money income.

A rise in money income of *x* per cent combined with an *x* per cent rise in all money prices leaves a consumer's purchasing power, and hence his or her real income, unchanged.

When we speak of the real value of a certain amount of money, we are referring to the goods and services that can be bought with the money, that is, to the purchasing power of the money.

Proposition 5 **Equal percentage changes in all absolute prices and in money income leave the budget line unaffected.**

Box 7.3 discusses the importance of relative prices and the problems created by inflation.

The consumer's demand curve

We now establish the link between the above analysis of indifference curves and budget constraints, and the consumer's demand curve. To derive the consumer's demand curve for any product, we need to depart slightly from the world of two products. We are now interested in what happens to the consumer's demand for some product, say petrol, as the price of that product changes, *all other prices being held constant*. We can do this with the tools developed above, simply by making the bundle of 'all other goods' take the place of the second product.

Derivation of the demand curve

In part (i) of Figure 7.9 a new type of indifference map is plotted in which the horizontal axis measures litres of petrol and the vertical axis measures the value of all other goods consumed. We have in effect used *everything but petrol* as the second product. The indifference curves now give the rate at which another hypothetical consumer, Philip, is prepared to substitute petrol for money (which allows him to buy all other goods).

The derivation of a demand curve is illustrated in Figure 7.9. For a given income, each price of petrol gives rise to a particular budget line and a particular spending choice. Plotting the quantity of petrol that Philip consumes for the specific budget line at any given price yields one point on his demand curve. Each other possible price yields a differ-

ent point. The resulting price–quantity combinations trace out Philip's whole demand curve.

The slope of the demand curve

The price–consumption line in part (i) of Figure 7.9 indicates that as price decreases the quantity of petrol demanded increases. But it is possible to draw Philip's indifference curves in such a way that his response to a decrease in price is for less to be consumed rather than more. This possibility of a positively sloped demand curve for a good is referred to as a **Giffen good**, after the Victorian economist Sir Robert Giffen (1837–1910), who is reputed to have documented a case of such a curve. We now show how this case can be analysed using indifference curves.

Income and substitution effects

The key is to distinguish between *the income effect* and *the substitution effect* of a change in price. The separation of the

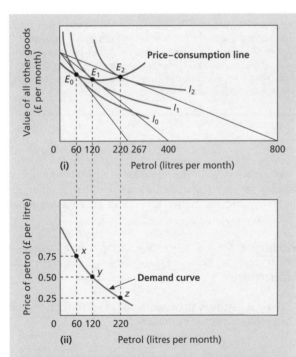

Figure 7.9 Derivation of an individual's demand curve

The points on a price–consumption line provide the information needed to draw a demand curve. In part (i) Philip has an income of £200 per month and alternatively faces prices of £0.75, £0.50, and £0.25 per litre of petrol, choosing positions E_0, E_1, and E_2. The information for the number of litres he demands at each price is then plotted in part (ii) to yield his demand curve. The three points x, y, and z in (ii) correspond to the three equilibrium positions E_0, E_1, and E_2 in (i).

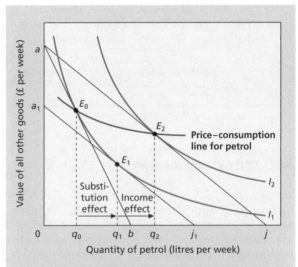

Figure 7.10 The income and substitution effects

The substitution effect is defined by sliding the budget line around a fixed indifference curve; the income effect is defined by a parallel shift of the budget line. The original budget line is *ab* and a fall in the price of petrol takes it to *aj*. The original equilibrium is at E_0 with q_0 of petrol consumed, and the final equilibrium is at E_2 with q_2 of petrol consumed. To remove the income effect, imagine reducing Philip's income until he is just able to attain his original indifference curve at the new price. We do this by shifting the line *aj* to a parallel line nearer the origin until it just touches the indifference curve that passes through E_0. The intermediate point E_1 divides the quantity change into a substitution effect, $q_1 - q_0$, and an income effect, $q_2 - q_1$. The point E_1 can also be obtained by sliding the original budget line *ab* around the indifference curve until its slope reflects the new relative prices.

two effects according to indifference theory is shown in Figure 7.10. We can think of it as occurring in the following way. After the price of the good has fallen, we reduce money income *until the original indifference curve can just be obtained*. Philip is now on his original indifference curve but facing the new set of relative prices. His response is defined as the **substitution effect**: the response of quantity demanded to a change in relative price, real income being held constant (meaning staying on the original indifference curve). Then, to measure the income effect, we restore money income. Philip's response to this is defined as the **income effect**: the response of quantity demanded to a change in real income, relative prices held constant.

Box 7.4 explains an alternative method of isolating the income and substitution effects.

In Figure 7.10 the income and substitution effects work in the same direction, both tending to increase quantity demanded when price falls. Is this necessarily the case? The answer is no. It follows from the convex shape of indifference curves that the substitution effect is always in the same direction: more is consumed of a product whose relative price has fallen. The income effect, however, can be in either direction: it can lead to more or less being consumed of a product whose price has fallen. The direction of the income effect depends on the distinction between normal and inferior goods.

The slope of the demand curve for a normal good For a normal good, an increase in any consumer's real income, arising from a decrease in the price of the product, leads

---

 ## Box 7.4 **The Slutsky decomposition of income and substitution effects**

The discussion of income and substitution effects in the text is based upon the analysis of English Nobel Laureate Sir John Hicks (1904–1989). An alternative approach was developed by the Russian mathematician Evgeny Slutsky (1880–1948).

Hicks's decomposition was derived in the context of developing the concept of indifference curves, so it was natural for him to ask the question: following a price change, how much income must be taken away in order for the consumer to be able to return to the original indifference curve and thus have the same level of utility or satisfaction as before the price change?

Slutsky, when thinking about the same issue, did not have at his disposal the tool of indifference curves. Instead he asked the question: following a price change, how much income must be taken away so that the consumer is just able to buy the initial bundle of goods (and therefore cannot be any worse off than in the initial position)?

The figure illustrates the difference between these two approaches. There is a fall in the price of good 1 holding the price of good 2 constant. The initial consumption point is at A and after the price fall the consumption point is at B.

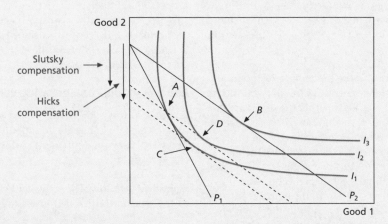

As we saw in the discussion of Figure 7.10, Hicks's decomposition generates an income compensation that returns the consumer to the original indifference curve I_1 following the fall of price of good 1 and the associated shift of the budget constraint from P_1 to P_2. This is achieved by shifting the new budget line P_2 towards the origin until it is just tangent to the original indifference curve. Thus, the Hicks substitution effect takes the consumer from point A to point C, and the income effect takes her from point C to B.

To find the Slutsky decomposition, we shift the new budget constraint inwards parallel to its new position until it just passes through the original consumption bundle at point A. If the consumer had faced this budget con-

straint with the original level of disposable income but at the new relative prices, she would have chosen to be at point D, which is on indifference curve I_2 and is thus at a higher utility level than the initial position.

There is no general reason why one of these methods is to be preferred. They are answering slightly different questions. The Slutsky compensation is easier to calculate as it relies on observable income and prices, but the Hicks compensation is useful for welfare comparisons because it tells us the income change that leaves the consumer *feeling* just as well off as before. The choice of methods should therefore depend on the purpose to which it is put.

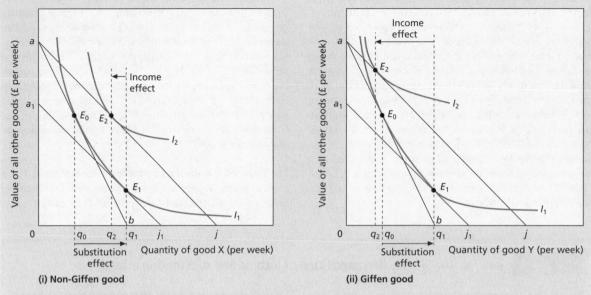

Figure 7.11 Income and substitution effects for inferior goods
A large enough negative income effect can outweigh the substitution effect and lead to a decrease in consumption in response to a fall in price. In each part of the diagram Philip is in equilibrium at E_0, consuming a quantity q_0 of the good in question. The price then decreases and the budget line shifts to aj, with a new equilibrium at E_2 and quantity consumed q_2. In each case the substitution effect increases consumption from q_0 to q_1. In (i) there is a negative income effect of $q_1 - q_2$. Because this is less than the substitution effect, the latter dominates, so good X has a normal, negatively sloped demand curve. In (ii) the negative income effect $q_1 - q_2$ is larger than the substitution effect, and quantity consumed actually decreases. Good Y is a Giffen good.

to increased consumption, reinforcing the substitution effect. Because quantity demanded increases, the demand curve has a negative slope.[8] This is the case illustrated in Figure 7.10.

The slope of the demand curve for an inferior good Figure 7.11 shows indifference curves for inferior goods. The income effect is negative in each part of the diagram. This follows from the nature of an inferior good: as income rises, less of the good is consumed. In each case the substitution effect serves to increase the quantity demanded as price decreases and is offset to some degree by the negative income effect. The final result depends on the relative strengths of the two effects. In part (i) the negative income effect only partially offsets the substitution effect, and thus quantity demanded increases as a result of the price decrease, though not as much as for a normal good. This is the typical pattern for inferior goods, and it too leads to negatively sloped demand curves, often relatively inelastic ones.

In part (ii) the negative income effect outweighs the substitution effect and thus leads to a positively sloped demand curve. This is the Giffen case. For this to happen the good must be inferior. But that is not enough; the change in price must have a negative income effect *strong enough* to more than offset the substitution effect. These circumstances are unusual ones, because strong inferiority

is rarely found. Such goods, if they ever existed, would tend to disappear from use as consumers got richer. Most goods are normal goods. A positively sloped market demand curve is thus a rare exception to the general rule that demand curves have negative slopes.

Equivalent and compensating variations

There are further concepts associated with the income effect of a price change that are commonly used in economics. These are known as **equivalent variation** and **compensating variation**.

Equivalent variation The equivalent variation is the answer to the question: if we had given the consumer a sum of

---

[8] A possible exception to this arises from the *endowment income effect*. This arises in some models where the consumer is assumed to have an initial endowment of goods and may choose to be a net seller of some goods. If the price of these goods rises, the consumer has a higher income and can thus buy more of all normal goods, including the goods for which it is net seller. A practical example would be as follows. Suppose the price of haircuts rises (all other prices remaining constant). For most consumers we would predict that the quantity of haircuts demanded would fall. However, hairdressers are now richer, so for them the price rise has generated a positive rather negative income effect. So for the hairdressers the income effect goes the other way, such that their income rises as the price of haircuts rises.

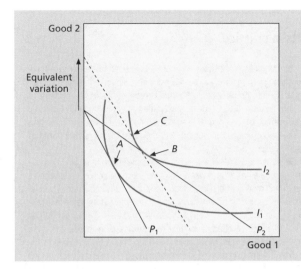

Figure 7.12 Equivalent variation of income

The equivalent variation is the change in income that leaves the consumer just as well off as some specific change in the price of a good. The consumer is initially at point A on budget line P_1. The price of good 1 falls, the budget line shifts to P_2 and the consumer shifts her spending pattern to B, which is on a higher indifference curve. The equivalent variation in income, is given by the size in the parallel shift in the original budget line that would have taken the consumer to the level of utility indicated by the higher indifference curve (which is achieved after the fall in the price of good 1). The equivalent income variation would have generated consumption point C as the optimal choice, but the consumer is indifferent between points B and C.

money instead of a lower price of one product, how much extra income would have made her feel just as well off? This is illustrated in Figure 7.12. It is calculated by shifting outwards the original budget line parallel to itself until it just touches the new indifference curve achieved after a price fall of one good.

Compensating variation This works backwards rather than forwards. It is the same as the income effect shown in Figure 7.10, and is measured by the distance $a - a_1$ in that figure. It is the amount of income that has to be taken away from the consumer following a price fall of one good in order to return the consumer to the initial indifference curve, and thus leave her feeling just as well off as before.

All very well in theory, but is reality different?

Readers new to economics (and some not so new) often find demand theory excessively abstract and/or feel that it is unrealistic. In this section we first discuss whether demand theory is unrealistic and then consider some alleged exceptions to the law of demand. Box 7.5 discusses one of the many practical applications of the distinction between the income and substitution effects of a price change.

Is demand theory in conflict with everyday experience?

It is obvious that most people do not *always* behave in the manner assumed by demand theory. Fortunately, the existence of a relatively stable, negatively sloped market demand curve does not require that all consumers invariably behave in the manner assumed by the theory. Such fully consistent behaviour on the part of everyone at all times is sufficient but not necessary for a stable market demand curve. Consider two other possibilities. First, some consumers may always behave in a manner contrary to

the theory. Consumers who are emotionally disturbed are one obvious possibility. The erratic behaviour of such consumers will not cause market demand curves for normal goods to depart from their downward slope. Provided that the consumers account for a small proportion of purchases of any product, their behaviour will be swamped by the normal behaviour of the majority of consumers. Second, an occasional irrationality on the part of every consumer will not upset the downward slope of the market demand curve for a normal good. As long as these are unrelated across consumers, occurring randomly, their effect will be swamped by the normal behaviour of most consumers most of the time.

The negative slope of the demand curve requires only that at any moment in time most consumers are behaving as is predicted by the theory. This is quite compatible with behaviour contrary to the theory by some consumers all of the time and by all consumers some of the time. Thus, we cannot test the theory of market demand by observing the behaviour of a few isolated consumers.

Box 7.5 **Income and substitution effects in practice**

Although they sound highly abstract and 'theoretical' when first encountered, the income and substitution effects turn out to be useful tools. They help us to deal with many problems such as: Do high rates of income tax act as disincentives to work? Would cutting the rate of income tax increase the amount of work people do? Would raising the wage rate of workers in some industry lead to a reduction in absenteeism?

Such questions frequently face decision-takers and they are often surprised at the results that the market produces. For example, many years ago the National Coal Board, which used to run the UK coal industry, raised miners' wages in an attempt to boost coal production and was surprised to find miners working fewer rather than more hours. In several countries increases in rates of income tax (within a moderate, not a confiscatory, range) have been found to be associated with people working more hours rather than fewer; at other times reductions in tax rates seem to have caused people to work less.

The surprise in all these cases was the same. Intuition suggests that if you pay people more they will work more; experience shows that the result is sometimes the opposite: more pay, less work; less pay, more work.

The explanation of this surprising behaviour lies in distinguishing the income effect from the substitution effect of a change in the reward for work.

Think of Luke, starting with an endowment of 24 hours per day and deciding to consume some of it as 'leisure' (including sleeping time) and to trade the rest for income by working. If Luke works 9 hours a day at an after-tax rate of £10 per hour, he is consuming 15 hours a day of leisure and trading the other 9 hours for £90 worth of income which can be used to buy goods and services.

Now let the after-tax wage rate rise to £12 an hour, either because the wage rate rises or because the rate of personal income tax falls to produce that increase in after-tax earnings. Luke's response to this change will have an income and a substitution component.

The substitution effect works the way intuition suggested: more wages, more work. Gaining income is now cheaper in terms of the leisure Luke must sacrifice per £1 worth of income gained. At the new wage rate, 1/12 of an hour (i.e. 5 minutes) of work earns Luke £1 worth of income, whereas

before it took 1/10 of an hour (6 minutes). Looked at the other way around, consuming leisure is now more expensive per amount of income that Luke must give up. An extra hour of leisure consumed requires sacrificing £12 of income instead of £10. The substitution effect leads to an increased consumption of the thing whose relative price has fallen—income in this case—and a reduced consumption of the thing whose relative price has risen—leisure.

So far so good. The surprise lies in the income effect. The rise in the after-tax wage rate has an income effect, in the sense that Luke can have more goods *and* more leisure. He could, for example, consume an extra hour of leisure by cutting his hours worked from 9 to 8 while at the same time raising his income from £90 a day (9 hours @ £10) to £96 a day (8 hours @ £12). The income effect leads him to consume more goods and more leisure, that is, to work fewer hours.

Only if the substitution effect is strong enough to overcome the income effect will the rise in the wage rate induce Luke to work more. If the substitution effect is strong enough, Luke might for example work 9.5 hours instead of 9 and increase his income from £90 to £114 a day. This means, however, choosing this combination of income and leisure in preference to all combinations that give more income and more leisure, such as 8.5 hours of work (down from 9) and £105 of income (up from £90).

So we should not be surprised if increases in the after-tax hourly wage lead to less work; this merely means that the income effect is stronger than the substitution effect.

The above analysis helps to explain why employers separate higher overtime rates from normal rates of pay. If the normal rate of pay is increased, the income effect is quite large, whereas if only the overtime rate is raised, the income effect is much smaller but the substitution effect is unchanged. In the above example, raising the normal wage rate from £10 to £12 increases Luke's income by £18 if he continues to work an unchanged 9 hours a day. But introducing an overtime rate has an income effect only in so far as overtime hours are already being worked. If, in the previous example, the employer introduced a £15 hourly rate for work of over 9 hours a day, the income effect would be zero; Luke must work more in order to gain any benefit from the higher overtime rate.

Demand and taste changes

Some critics have argued that including changes in tastes as one cause of shifts in demand makes a demand theory untestable. Propositions about tastes are not really testable unless we have some way of measuring them. Since we do not have such a measure, what we usually do is infer tastes from the data for demand. We make such statements as 'In spite of the rise in price, quantity purchased increased, so there must have been a change in tastes in favour of this product.' More generally, we are likely to use prices and incomes to account for as many changes in demand as possible, and then assert that the rest must be due to changes in tastes (and to errors of measurement). Anything that does not seem to agree with our theory can then be explained away by saying that tastes must have changed.

Say, for example, that *incomes and other prices were known to be constant*, while the price of some product X rose and, at the same time, more X was observed to be bought. This gives us observations such as the two illustrated in Figure 7.13(i). The demand curve for X might be positively sloped in this case, but another explanation is that the rise in price coincided with a change in tastes, so that the demand curve shifted just as price changed. With only two observations we are unable to distinguish between these possibilities, since we have no independent way of telling whether or not tastes changed. If however we have many observations, we can get some idea of where the balance of probabilities lies between the two explanations. Consider, for example, a product whose price has changed each week over a period of six months, sometimes increasing and sometimes decreasing. *After using appropriate statistical*

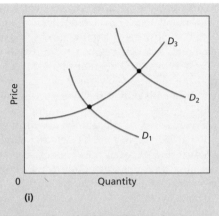

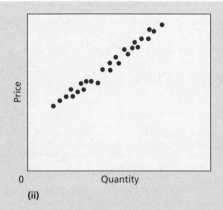

Figure 7.13 Which way does the demand curve slope?

Taste changes may explain isolated contradictions but not repeated ones. These observations may have been generated by changes in taste that shifted a normal demand curve from D_1 to D_2 along an upward-sloping supply curve, or by a supply curve that shifted along a positively sloped demand curve D_3. Part (ii) shows 26 weekly observations over a period when the product's price rose and fell (with incomes and other prices constant). The explanation that supply-curve shifts are operating on a positively sloped demand curve is more likely than the explanation that tastes changed each week to shift a normally sloped demand curve leftwards and rightwards along a upward-sloping supply curve.

procedures to remove the effects arising from changes in income and other prices, we have the 26 observations illustrated in Figure 7.13(ii). We would be hard-pressed to avoid the conclusion that the evidence conflicts with the hypothesis of a negatively sloping demand curve.

Of course, we can always explain away these observations by saying that tastes must have changed in favour of this product each time its price rose and against the product each time its price fell. This 'alibi' can certainly be used with effect to explain away a single conflicting observation, but we would be uncomfortable using the same alibi 26 times in six months. Indeed, we should begin to suspect a fault in the hypothesis that demand and price vary inversely with each other.

We now have a problem in statistical testing. We are not prepared to throw away a theory after only one or two conflicting observations, but we are prepared to abandon it once we accumulate a mass of conflicting observations that were very unlikely to have occurred if the theory was correct. Thus, statistically, the theory is testable. Fortunately, there is, as we have seen, a great deal of evidence that most demand curves do have negative slopes. With a few possible exceptions, the predictions of the theory have been found to be in agreement with the facts.

Alleged exceptions to the law of demand

The prediction that demand curves have negative slopes has long been known as *the law of demand*. Over the years, a number of exceptions to this law have been alleged.

Giffen goods and the law of demand

We have already discussed the Giffen good, which has its origins in the observations reputedly made by Sir Robert Giffen that an increase in the price of wheat led to an increase in the consumption of bread by nineteenth-century English peasants. Assuming that Giffen's observations were correct, this does refute the hypothesis that demand curves *always* have negative slopes. But it does not refute the modern indifference theory of demand because, as we have noted above, this type of rare exception to the normal case is allowed for whenever people spend much of their income on a good that is strongly inferior.

The modern theory of demand makes an unequivocal prediction only when we have extraneous information about income elasticities of demand. Since incomes change continuously as a result of economic growth, we do have such information about many products. When we know that the income effect is positive (income elasticity of demand exceeds zero), as it is for most products, we can predict in advance that the quantity demanded will be negatively related to its price. When we know the income effect is negative (i.e. the good is inferior), we cannot be sure of the result. The only thing we can then say is that, the smaller is the proportion of total expenditure accounted for by this product, the less important the income effect will be, and hence the more likely we are to get the normal result of price and quantity varying negatively with each other. Finally, if we have no knowledge about the income effect, we can still hazard a probabilistic statement:

The great weight of existing evidence suggests that, if we had to guess with no prior knowledge whether the demand for some product X was negatively or positively related to price, the former choice would be the odds-on favourite.

Alternative theories of the sources of consumer satisfaction

The only exception to the law of demand admitted within indifference theory is the Giffen good. Further exceptions all arise from making assumptions that contradict those of indifference theory.

Let us consider another consumer, Rana, and assume that her satisfaction depends not only on the quantities of the various products that she consumes, but also on the prices she has to pay for them. She may, for example, buy diamonds not because she particularly likes diamonds *per se*, but because she wishes to show off her wealth in an ostentatious but socially acceptable way. Rana values diamonds precisely because they are expensive; thus, a fall in price might lead her to stop buying diamonds and switch to a more satisfactory object of ostentatious display. Consumers such as Rana have positively sloping demand curves for diamonds: the lower the price, the fewer they will buy. If enough consumers act similarly, the *market* demand curve for diamonds could be positively sloped as well.

Does this mean that if a jeweller offers a discount to a rich purchaser of diamonds she would be less likely to buy? Not necessarily. The show-off value depends on the price others *think* she paid for the diamonds. Thus, although the demand may be positively associated with published price,

it may also be negatively associated with the price as known only to the buyer and seller.

But a positively sloping *market* demand curve for diamonds and other similar products has never been observed. Why? Think about the industrial uses of diamonds, and the masses of lower-income consumers who would buy diamonds only if they were sufficiently inexpensive. This suggests that positively sloping individual demand curves for a few rich consumers are much more likely than a positively sloping *market* demand curve for the same product. Indeed, even the very rich cannot carry on buying more and more diamonds as they become more and more expensive, because ultimately this will exhaust their income.

Conclusion

The demand curves for most products have negative slopes, and there is good information available about many of their elasticities. Knowledge of the precise nature of the demand curve for a product is obviously important for firms who want to be able to predict the likely quantity demanded at various prices. An understanding of demand is also important for policy-makers who might wish to impose taxes, intervene in markets in other ways, or predict the effects of sudden shortages of such things as food or energy. For economists, an understanding of demand is one important step along the road to understanding the detailed workings of a market economy.

SUMMARY

Consumer optimization

- Indifference theory assumes only that individuals can order alternative consumption bundles, saying which bundles are preferred to which, but not by how much.

- A single indifference curve shows combinations of products that give the consumer equal satisfaction, and among which he or she is therefore indifferent. An indifference map is a set of indifference curves.

- The basic assumption about tastes in indifference curve theory is that of a diminishing marginal rate of substitution: the less of one good and the more of another good the consumer has, the less willing he or she will be to give up some of the first good to get more of the second. This implies that indifference curves are negatively sloped and convex to the origin.

- While indifference curves describe the consumer's tastes and, therefore, refer to what he or she *would like* to purchase, the budget line describes what the consumer *can* purchase.

- Each consumer achieves an equilibrium that maximizes his or her satisfaction at the point at which an indifference curve is tangent to his or her budget line.

The consumer's responses to price and income changes

- The income–consumption line shows how quantity consumed changes as income changes with relative prices constant.

- The price–consumption line shows how quantity consumed changes as relative prices change. The consumer will normally consume more of the product whose relative price falls.

■ The price–consumption line, relating the purchases of one particular product to all other products, contains the same information as an ordinary demand curve. The horizontal axis measures quantity, and the slope of the budget line measures price. Transferring this information to a diagram whose axes represent price and quantity leads to a conventional demand curve.

The consumer's demand curve

■ A change in price of one product, all other prices and money income constant, changes both relative price and the real incomes of those who consume it. The effect of changes on consumption is measured by the substitution effect and the income effect.

■ Demand curves for normal goods have negative slopes because both income and substitution effects work in the same direction, a decrease in price leading to increased consumption.

■ A decrease in price of an inferior good leads to more consumption via the substitution effect and less consumption via the income effect. In the exceptional case of a Giffen good, the income effect more than offsets the substitution effect, causing the product's demand curve to have a positive slope.

All very well in theory, but is reality different?

■ Observed demand curves are negatively sloped in spite of odd behaviour on the part of some people some of the time. Such behaviour tends to cancel out as long as individuals behave independently of each other.

■ The Giffen good, although a genuine exception to the law of demand, is consistent with indifference theory. All these possible exceptions are rarely if ever observed in practice.

TOPICS FOR REVIEW

■ An indifference curve and an indifference map

■ Slope of an indifference curve and diminishing marginal rate of substitution

■ Budget line

■ Absolute and relative prices, and the slope of the budget line

■ Response of a consumer to changes in income and prices

■ Derivation of the demand curve from indifference curves

■ Income and substitution effects

■ Hicks and Slutsky decomposition

■ Normal goods, inferior goods, and Giffen goods

■ Equivalent and compensating variations of income

DISCUSSION QUESTIONS

1 Suppose a consumer's disposable income is £200 per week and she has a choice between spending this on meals and concerts. Concerts are £10 each and meals are £20 each. List or graph the possible combinations of meals and concerts that could be bought with the income.

2 Using the same information as in question 1, the price of meals now falls to £10. What combinations of meals and concerts can now be purchased with the same income?

3 Assuming that (facing the prices in question 1) the consumer chose to consume 10 concerts and 5 meals per week, what change in income would leave the consumer still just able to consume this same combination of meals and concerts while facing the prices set in question 2? Would you expect this

consumer to purchase the same combination of meals and concerts as before, if faced by the new prices but with this amount less income?

4 Which of the following statements is true (there may be more than one or none)?

If the price of good X rises holding all other prices and income constant,

(a) The substitution effect alone will make a consumer buy more of X if X is inferior.

(b) The income effect alone will make a consumer buy more of X if it is a normal good.

(c) The income effect alone will make a consumer buy less of X if it is an inferior good.

(*d*) The substitution effect will make a consumer buy less of X and it is irrelevant whether X is a normal or an inferior good.

(*e*) The consumer will buy less of good X unless it is an inferior good, in which case she will always buy more.

5 Explain the difference between the income effect and substitution effect of a price change.

6 What is a Giffen good? Explain, using indifference curves, how it could arise.

7 'Indifference curve analysis is not much use because it only tells us that demand curves have a negative slope except when they don't.' Discuss.

8 A company that normally pays its workers £400 per week in money decides to pay them instead with £400 worth of a specific good. Assume that there is no second hand market in this good, so they cannot be sold for cash, but also assume that the workers would have chosen to consume some of this good anyway. Using budget constraints and indifference curves, analyse whether the workers are likely to be just as happy with this arrangement as they were when they received their wages in money.

Appendix Mathematics of indifference theory

The algebra of the budget line

In this section we prove the propositions asserted in the chapter.

Let the consumer's money income be M. Let p_x and p_y be the prices of food and clothing, and let X and Y be the quantities of food and clothing. Total expenditure is thus $p_x X + p_y Y$. For a consumer who spends all his income on these two goods,

$$p_x X + p_y Y = M. \tag{A1}$$

Rearrangement yields the equation of the budget line as it is plotted in Figure 7.5. To do this, we subtract $p_x X$ from both sides, and then divide through by p_y to obtain

$$Y = \frac{M}{p_y} - \frac{p_x}{p_y} X. \tag{A2}$$

This is a linear equation of the form

$$Y = a - bX, \tag{A3}$$

where $a = M/p_y$ and $b = p_x/p_y$. The intercept a is the number of units of Y that can be purchased by spending all of M on Y, i.e. money income divided by the price of Y. The slope b is the relative price p_x/p_y.

We first prove that the opportunity cost, the slope of the budget line, and the relative price are identical. First-differencing (A1) yields

$$p_x \Delta X + p_y \Delta Y = \Delta M.$$

This says that the change in the value of purchases of X and Y must be equal to the change in income.

Along a budget line expenditure is constant, so we can write

$$p_x \Delta X + p_y \Delta Y = 0,$$

which says that if income does not change the change in the total value of purchases must be zero. Manipulation yields

$$\frac{p_x}{p_y} = -\frac{\Delta Y}{\Delta X}. \tag{A4}$$

$\Delta Y/\Delta X$ is the opportunity cost of X measured in units of Y, i.e. the amount of Y sacrificed (gained) per unit of X gained (sacrificed). From (A4), this is equal to the relative price of X, which, from (A2), is the slope of the budget line.

We may now prove the five propositions used in the text.

Proposition 1 A change in money income, with money prices constant, shifts the budget line parallel to itself (p. 115).

Proof. If we change the value of M in (A2), we change the value of a in (A3) in the same direction: $\Delta a = \Delta M/p_y$. But b is unaffected since M does not appear in that term. Thus, changing M shifts the budget line inwards ($\Delta M < 0$) or outwards ($\Delta M > 0$) but leaves the slope unaffected.

Proposition 2 An equal percentage change in all absolute prices, with money income unchanged, shifts the budget line parallel to itself (p. 116), inwards towards the origin when prices rise, and outwards away from the origin when prices fall.

Proof. Multiplying both prices in (A2) by the same constant λ gives

$$Y = \frac{M}{\lambda p_y} - \frac{\lambda p_x}{\lambda p_y} X.$$

Since the λ cancel out of the slope term, b is unaffected; the a term, however, is changed. If $\lambda > 1$, a is diminished, while if $\lambda < 1$ a is increased.

Proposition 3 Multiplying all money prices by the same constant, λ, while holding money income constant has exactly the same effect on the budget line as multiplying money income by $1/\lambda$ while holding money prices constant (p. 116).

Proof. Multiply both money prices in (A2) by λ:

$$Y = \frac{M}{\lambda p_y} - \frac{\lambda p_x}{\lambda p_y} X.$$

Cancelling the λ from the slope term gives

$$Y = \frac{M}{\lambda p_y} - \frac{p_x}{p_y}X.$$

Finally, bringing the λ from the denominator to the numerator of the constant term gives

$$Y = \frac{(1/\lambda)M}{p_y} - \frac{p_x}{p_y}X.$$

Proposition 4 A change in relative prices causes the budget line to change its slope (p. 116).

Proof. The relative price p_x/p_y in (A2) is the slope term, b, in (A3). Thus, changing the relative price is necessary and sufficient for changing the slope of the budget line.

Proposition 5 Equal percentage changes in all absolute prices and in money income leave the budget line unaffected (p. 117).

Proof. Multiply M and both prices in (A2) by λ:

$$Y = \frac{\lambda M}{\lambda p_y} - \frac{\lambda p_x}{\lambda p_y}X.$$

Cancel out the λ from the intercept and the slope terms to obtain equation (A2) once again.

Indifference theory

Let the utility function be $U = AF(X,Y)$, where X and Y are quantities of the two goods that are consumed and A is a multiplicative constant.

According to utility theory, the marginal utility of X is $\partial U/\partial X$, which will contain the constant A. If utility is cardinally measurable, as in marginal utility theory, A has a definite meaning in terms of the units in which utility is measured, call them 'utils'.

If utility is only ordinally measurable, as in indifference theory, A is arbitrary and has no economic interpretation.

Totally differentiating of the utility function yields

$$dU = AF_x dx + AF_y dy$$

where F_x and F_y are the partial derivatives of U with respect to X and Y. Since it is an arbitrary number in indifference theory, we can ignore the constant A by setting it at unity. Along any indifference curve, utility is constant so $dU = O$.

Thus

$$F_x dx + F_y dy = 0,$$

or

$$\frac{dy}{dx} = -\frac{F_x}{F_y}.$$

Now, since U is being held constant, dy/dx is the slope of the indifference curve.

We can now show the relation between marginal utility and diminishing marginal utility. If we did have diminishing marginal utility of X and Y the two partials would be negative, and the slope coefficient on the indifference curve would also be negative $(-(-/-) < 0)$. Thus, diminishing marginal utility is sufficient for negatively sloped indifference curves. But it is not necessary, because if both marginal utilities are positive dy/dx is still negative $(-(+/+) < 0)$.

This assumption of a diminishing marginal rate of substitution in indifference theory is a weaker assumption than that of diminishing marginal utility in utility theory. But they do not contradict each other.

Chapter 8

THE COST STRUCTURE OF FIRMS IN THE SHORT RUN

In Chapter 1 we discussed how the price system co-ordinates the actions of independent agents. How does the system ensure that firms produce the things consumers want? Can firms exploit consumers by changing more or less any price they wish? How do firms respond to changes in costs and in demand? These are questions about the supply decisions of firms that we will analyse in this and the next few chapters. In this chapter we focus mainly on the cost structures of firms that have a given stock of capital and available technology. In the next chapter we allow for variations in capital and technical change.

In particular you will learn that:

• Real-world firms can adopt one of several different legal structures, but for most of our analysis in this book firms are assumed to have a very simple structure.

• There is a difference between economists' measure of profit and accountants' measure of profit.

• For economists, profit is the difference between total cost and total revenue, where total cost includes the cost of capital.

• The production function relates physical quantities of inputs to the quantity of output.

• Cost curves show the money cost of producing various levels of output.

• The short-run cost curve is U-shaped because some inputs are being held constant and the law of diminishing returns applies to those that are allowed to vary.

We begin by comparing the firms that we see in the real world with those that we shall assume for the purposes of our analysis throughout this book. Next we introduce the concepts of costs, revenues, and profits, and outline the key role that profits play in determining which goods and services get produced. In order to identify the most profitable level of production for a firm, we need to see how its costs vary with its output. We do this in this chapter for the short run, when a firm can vary only some of its inputs. Output is then governed by the famous 'law of diminishing returns'. In the following chapter we deal with the long run, when the firm can alter all of its inputs, and the very long run, when the firm can change its technology through research and development (R&D) activities.

Production decisions are made by firms

The firm is the agent in the economy that makes decisions about production.

Firms in the reality

Real-world firms come is many sizes and shapes. The most important distinction is between sole traders and ordinary partnerships, where the owners of the firm bear full liability for everything that the firm does, and those firms, mainly joint-stock companies, where the owners' liability is restricted to the amount of money they have invested in the firm. The details of the various ways of organizing firms are covered in more detail in Box 8.1.

The finance that firms need to carry on their business is provided in two basic ways: through equity funds provided by the owners, and debt funds borrowed from outside the firm. For a sole trader and a partnership, the owners provide the equity. A joint-stock company acquires its equity from its owners in return for stocks, shares, or equities (as they are variously called). These are basically ownership certificates. The money goes to the company

Box 8.1 Organization of producers

The majority of production in a market economy is in the hands of firms. These can be organized in any one of five different ways. A **single proprietorship**, or **sole trader**, has one owner–manager who is personally responsible for everything that is done. A **partnership** has two or more joint owners, each of whom is personally responsible for all of the partnership's debts. A **limited partnership**, which is less common than ordinary partnerships, provides for two types of partner. *General partners* take part in the running of the business and are liable for all the firm's debts. *Limited partners* take no part in the running of the business, and their liability is limited to the amount they actually invest in the enterprise.* A **joint-stock company** (called a *corporation* in the United States) is a firm regarded in law as having an identity of its own; its owners are not personally responsible for anything that is done in the name of the firm, though its directors may be.

In the United Kingdom joint-stock companies are indicated either by the initials plc after the firm's name, standing for *public limited company*, or Ltd (limited), which indicates a *private* limited-liability company. 'Private' in this context means that its shares are not traded on any stock exchange, while 'public' means that shares are traded on some public exchange. In the UK many limited companies are wholly owned subsidiaries of plcs, while most plcs own many subsidiary companies. A **public corporation** is set up to run a nationalized industry. It is owned by the state but is usually under the direction of a more or less independent, state-appointed board. Although its ownership differs, the organization and legal status of such a public corporation are similar to those of a joint-stock company.

A sixth type of organization, one that does not involve firms, is governmental or charitable institutions that provide free goods and service, such as hospitals and schools. These are an important part of the economy, but we do not include these in our study of 'firms' as they typically provide their product free, while their costs are met out of general taxation. Their output is thus not part of the market sector of the economy (though many of their input purchases will be).

Joint-stock companies that have operations in more than one country are often called **multinational enterprises (MNEs)**, or **transnational corporations (TNCs)**. Their number has been increasing steadily over the years. Although large firms still dominate the TNC scene, the role of medium-sized and small TNCs is significant and growing.

In 2001 there were about 60,000 TNCs in the world and they controlled about 820,000 foreign affiliates.† Ninety per cent of these TNCs are head-quartered in developed countries, the three major home bases being the EU, Japan, and the United States. Together they owned a stock of about $6 trillion worth of direct foreign investments, about 20 per cent of which are in developing countries.

There are many reasons for a company to transfer some of its production beyond its home base (thus becoming a TNC) rather than producing everything at home and then exporting the output. First, products become more sophisticated and differentiated; locating production in large local markets allows more flexible responses to local needs than can be achieved through centralized production 'back home'. Second, trade barriers make location in large foreign markets, such as the United States and the European Union, less risky than sending exports from the home base. Third, many TNCs are in the rapidly developing service industries such as advertising, marketing, public management, accounting, law, and financial services, where a physical presence is needed to produce a service in any country. Fourth, the computer and communications revolutions have allowed components of any one product to be manufactured in many countries, each component being made where its production is cheapest.

The globalization of production has brought benefits to many less developed countries. They have gained increasing employment at wages that are low by world standards but high by their own. As the United Nations puts it, 'the growth of TNCs is one of the major channels by which economic change is spread throughout the world'.

---

* Limited partnerships are mainly used for high-tech start-ups, where inventors have full liability and backers risk only what they have invested. However, it is in the interest of the general partner (inventor) to convert to 'Ltd' status fairly quickly.

† *Source*: *World Investment Report*, UNCTAD, 2001.

---

and the shareholders become owners of the firm, risking the loss of their money, and gaining the right to share in the firm's profits. Profits that are paid out to shareholders are called dividends.

One easy way for an established firm to raise equity funds is to retain current profits rather than paying them out to shareholders. Financing investment from *undistributed profits* has become an important source of funding in modern times. Reinvested profits add to the value of the firm, and hence raise the market value of existing shares.

The second main way in which funds can be acquired is through borrowing funds from an external lender, which creates debt. Two characteristics are common to all forms of debt. First, there is an obligation to repay the amount borrowed, called the **principal** of the loan. Second, there is an obligation to pay **interest** to the lender. The day when the principal is to be repaid is called the **redemption date** or *maturity date* of the debt. The amount of time between the issue of the debt and its redemption date is called its **term**. There are many different forms of loan agreement. Some involve a financial intermediary such as a bank, which lends money to firms. Others involve the issuance of debt instruments, such as **bonds**. A bond is an IOU that is marketable (i.e. can be sold to others) and specifies a sum of money to be returned at a future date and a number of interest payments to be made between the date of issue and maturity. Box 8.2 discusses a variety of different forms of debt instrument. For simplicity, in this book we refer to all forms of interest-bearing debt instrument (including bank loans) as *bonds*.

Firms are in business to make profits. They earn income by making and selling goods and services, but they must

Box 8.2 **Kinds of debt instruments**

Most debt instruments can be grouped into three broad classes. First, some debt is in the form of *loans* from financial institutions. These are private agreements between the firm and the institution usually calling for the periodic payment of interest and repayment of the principal, either at a stipulated future date or 'on demand', meaning whenever the lending institution requests repayment.

Second, *bills* and *notes* are commonly used for short-term loans of up to a year. They carry no fixed interest payments, only a principal value and a redemption date. Interest arises because the borrowing firm sells the new bills that it issues at a price below their redemption value. If, for example, a bill promising to pay £1,000 in one year's time is sold to a lender for £950, this gives the lender an interest payment of £50 in one year's time when the bill that he bought for £950 is redeemed for £1,000. This makes an interest rate of 5.26 per cent per year ((50/950) × 100). Bills are *negotiable or marketable*, which means they can be bought and sold. So if I buy a 90-day bill

from some firm and want my money back 30 days later, I can sell the bill on the open market. The purchaser must be prepared to assume the loan to the firm for the 60 days that it still has to run, or it can in turn sell it to another party before maturity.

The third type of instrument carries a fixed redemption date, as does a bill, and the obligation to make periodic interest payments, as do most loans. These instruments have many different details and correspondingly many different names, such as *bonds*, *stocks*, and *debentures*. They are commonly used for long-term loans—up to 20 or 30 years. A firm that issues a 7 per cent 30-year instrument of this sort with redemption value of £1,000 is borrowing money now and promising to pay £70 a year for 30 years and then to pay £1,000. All such instruments are negotiable. This is important, because few people would be willing to lend money for such long periods of time if there were no way to get it back before the redemption date.

pay all their costs of production. The cost of labour includes wages, pension contributions, and other payments that must be made whenever labour is employed. In addition to the wage bill, firms have also to pay the cost of interest on debts, the cost of goods and services bought from other firms, and the cost of any rented inputs such as land and buildings. Firms must also impute costs for using their own capital equipment such as buildings, machinery, and office equipment. This cost, which is called *depreciation*, is correctly measured by the reduction in the value of the assets that will occur if firms use them over the period in question. After deducting all these costs, the remainder is what firms call their profits. This is the return on their owners' capital. Some of this may be distributed to the shareholders in the form of dividends while the rest is retained for reinvestment. If the investments are sound, the value of the firm increases and this adds to the owners' capital.

Firms in theory

In Chapter 3 we defined the firm as the unit that takes decisions with respect to the production and sale of goods and services. This theoretical concept of the firm includes all types of business organization, from the sole trader to the joint-stock company. It also covers the whole variety

of business sizes and methods of financing, from the single inventor operating in his garage and financed by whatever he can extract from a reluctant bank manager, to vast undertakings with many thousands of shareholders and customers.

To theorize about the firm, we make two key assumptions.[1] First, all firms are profit-maximizers, seeking to make as much profit for their owners as is possible. Second, each firm can be regarded as a single, consistent decision-taking unit.

The desire to maximize profits is assumed to motivate all decisions taken within a firm, and such decisions are assumed to be unaffected by the peculiarities of the persons taking the decisions and by the organizational structure in which they work.

These assumptions allow us to ignore the firm's internal organization and its financial structure. They also allow us to derive predictions about the behaviour of firms. To do this, we first study the choices open to the firm, establishing the effect that each choice would have on the firm's profits. We then predict that the firm will select the alternative that produces the largest profit.

---

[1] The approach is known as the *neoclassical theory* of the firm.

Production, costs, and profits

We must now define a little more precisely the concepts of production, costs, and profits that we need for our analysis of the firm.

Production

In order to produce the goods or services that it sells, each firm needs inputs. Hundreds of inputs enter into the production of any specific output. Among the many inputs entering into car production, for example, are sheet steel, rubber, spark plugs, electricity, the site of the factory, machinists, cost accountants, spray-painting machines, forklift trucks, painters, and managers. These can be grouped into four broad classes: (1) inputs to the car firm that are outputs to some other firm, such as spark plugs, electricity, and sheet steel; (2) inputs provided directly by nature, such as land and air; (3) efforts of people, such as the services of workers and managers; and (4) the use of plant and machines.

The items that make up the first class of inputs, goods and services produced by other firms, are called *intermediate products*. These appear as inputs only because different firms are involved at different stages of production. For example, one firm mines iron ore and sells it to a steel manufacturer. Iron ore is an intermediate product: an output of the mining firm and an input for the steel plant. The output of the steel maker is then an input for the car manufacturer.

If all production were in the hands of a single firm, there would be no intermediate inputs. In this case, or if we view the entire chain of production as a whole, all production can be accounted for by the services listed as (2)–(4) above. These were first discussed in Chapter 1, as the gifts of nature, such as soil and raw materials, called *land* (item 2 above); physical and mental efforts provided by people, called *labour* (item 3 above); and the services of factories, machines, and other man-made aids to production, called *capital* (item 4 above). These are traditionally called *factors of production*.

The production function relates inputs to outputs. It describes the technological relation between the inputs that a firm uses and the output that it produces. Using functional notation, the production function is written as

---

 Box 8.3 **The boundaries of the firm**

If firms require some specific input such as a specialized part, or a service such as cleaning their shop floor, they have two options. Either they can do it themselves—making the part and providing their own service—or they can buy what they need from some other firm. The boundary between what firms do for themselves and what they buy from outside differs among firms and changes over time. Why is this so?

The answer was provided by British-born economist Ronald Coase, who received the 1991 Nobel Prize in economics for this, and other, path-breaking work. His analysis is based on the concept of **transaction costs**, which are the costs associated with all market transactions. For example, when a firm purchases some good or service, it must identify the market and then find what different quantities and qualities are available at what prices. This takes time and money, and usually involves some uncertainty. When the firm decides to do the job itself 'in house', it uses the *command principle*: it orders the product to be made, or the service to be performed, to its desired specifications. The market transaction costs are avoided, but the advantages of buying in a competitive market are lost. Furthermore, as the firm gets larger, the inefficiencies of the command system tend to rise relative to efficiencies involved in decentralizing decision-taking through the market system.

All firms must choose when to transact internally and when to transact through the market. For example, a car manufacturer must decide whether to purchase a certain component from an independent parts manufacturer or to produce the component itself. Most firms do both, buying many of their components from other firms and producing others for themselves.

Coase's insight was to see the firm as an institution that economizes on transaction costs. The market works best when transaction costs are low. When transaction costs are high, there is an incentive for the firm to reduce these by using the internal mechanisms of the command system in place of market transactions.

Firms exist as an alternative to a pure market structure of transactions. Inside a firm there is a command economy. Managers of firms have always to be asking what activities should be done inside the firm and what should be obtained in the market from other suppliers.

Changes in technology alter the relative advantages of these two types of activity. For example, the modern information and communications revolution, centred on the computer and the internet, has greatly reduced the transactions costs associated with many market activities. So the costs of obtaining things through the market have fallen relative to the costs of doing them in-house. As a result, firms do many fewer things in-house than they used to do. Instead, they 'contract out' both the production of many parts and the performance of many services. Large firms are then able to concentrate on what they call their 'core competencies', the main things they do. Smaller firms that specialize in producing single services, such as lift maintenance, office cleaning, accounting, and product design, are often able to perform these services more efficiently than a large multipurpose business unit can.

$$q = \psi(f_1, \ldots, f_m), \qquad (1)$$

where q is the quantity of output of some good or service and $f_1, \ldots, f_m$ are the quantities of m different inputs used in its production, everything being expressed as rates per period of time. The Greek letter ψ tells us that q is a function of f; that is, f determines q.

When using the production function, remember that it relates flows of inputs to flows of outputs: so many units *per period of time*. For example, if it is said that production rises from 100 to 101 units, this does not mean that 100 units are produced this month and 1 unit next month. Rather, it means that the rate of production has risen from 100 units *each month* to 101 units *each month*.

Costs and profits

Real firms arrive at what they call profits by taking the revenues they obtain from selling their output and deducting all the costs associated with their inputs, including depreciation of their own capital. When all costs have been correctly deducted, the resulting 'profits' are the return to owners' capital.

In economics the concepts of costs and profits differ from those used by firms because economists count the opportunity cost of the owner's capital as part of the firm's costs. This opportunity cost is not just the depreciation of the capital, but also includes an estimate of what the capital, and any other special advantages owned by the firm, could have earned in their best alternative uses. When this larger set of costs is deducted from revenues, the remainder is called **pure** or **economic profits**, or, where there is no room for ambiguity, just profit.

The owners' opportunity cost of the financial capital that they have tied up in their firm can be divided into two parts. The first part can be determined by asking what could be earned by lending the capital to someone else in a riskless loan. For example, the firm could have purchased a government bond, which has no significant risk of default. Suppose the return on this is 6 per cent per annum. This rate is called the pure return, or risk-free rate of return on capital. It is clearly an opportunity cost, since the firm could close down operations, lend out its money, and earn a 6 per cent return. To determine the second part, ask what the firm could earn in addition to this amount by lending its money to another firm where risk of default was equal to the firm's own risk of loss. Say this is an additional 5 per cent. This is called the *risk premium* and it is clearly also a cost. If the firm does not expect to earn this much in its own operations, it could close down and lend its money out to some other equal-risk use earning 11 per cent (6 per cent pure return plus 5 per cent risk premium).[2]

Tables 8.1 and 8.2 compare the concepts of cost and profit as used by firms in practice and in economic analysis.

Table 8.1 Profit and loss account for XYZ Company for the year ending 31 December 1999

Expenditure		Income
Variable costs		
Wages	£200,000	Revenue from sales £1,000,000
Materials	300,000	
Other	100,000	
Total VC	600,000	
Fixed costs		
Rent	50,000	
Managerial salaries	60,000	
Interest on loans	90,000	
Depreciation allowance	50,000	
Total FC	250,000	
Total costs	850,000	
Profit		150,000

The profit and loss account shows profits as defined by the firm. The table gives a simplified version of a real profit and loss statement. The total revenue earned by the firm, minus what it regards as costs, yields profits. (Note that costs are divided into those that vary with output, called variable costs, and those that do not, called fixed costs. This distinction is discussed later in this chapter.)

Table 8.2 Calculation of pure profits

Profit as reported by the firm	£150,000
Opportunity cost of capital	
Pure return on the firm's capital	−100,000
Risk premium	−40,000
Pure or economic profit	10,000

The economist's definition of profit excludes the opportunity cost of capital. To arrive at the economist's definition of profit, the opportunity cost of capital—the return on a riskless investment plus any risk premium—must be deducted from the firm's definition of profit. What is left is pure profit.

(Notice that Table 8.1 divides the firm's costs between those that vary with output, called *variable costs*, and those that do not, called *fixed costs*, a distinction that is considered in detail later in this chapter.)

What firms call profit is the return to the owners' capital. In economics, we deduct from this profit figure the imputed opportunity cost of the owners' capital to obtain pure or economic profits.

---

[2] A firm may also own a valuable patent, a highly desirable location, or a popular brand name such as Gucci, Rolex, Polo, or Porsche. Each of these involves an opportunity cost to the firm in production (even if it was acquired free), because if the firm did not choose to use the special advantage itself *it could sell or lease it to others*. The firm must, therefore, impute a charge to itself for using the special advantage.

Since there are two different concepts, it would be better if two different terms were used to denote them. But since this is not the case it is important to note that economists use a slightly different definition of 'profit' than do firms. When there is any possibility of confusion, we speak of economic or pure profit. But, since this is the standard usage in economics, we shall generally use the word 'profit' to mean the return to the firm over and above all costs including the opportunity costs of capital (the pure risk-free return *and* the risk premium).[3]

Neither of the two alternative definitions of profits is better or worse than the other. Instead, each is appropriate for different purposes. Firms are interested in the return to their owners and seek to maximize this, which is what they call profit. They must also conform to tax laws and accounting standards, which define profit this way. In contrast, in economics we are interested in how profits affect resource allocation, and the definition we use is best for that purpose.[4]

Profits and resource allocation When resources are valued by the opportunity-cost principle, their costs show how much these resources would earn if used elsewhere in the economy. If the revenues of all the firms in some industry exceed opportunity cost, the firms in that industry will be earning pure profits; that is, the returns will be higher than in other industries with comparable risks. Thus, the owners of resources will want to move into this industry, because the earnings potentially available to them are greater there than in alternative activities. If, in some other industry, firms are incurring negative profits (losses), some or all of this industry's inputs will earn higher rewards by moving to new activities.

Profits and losses play a crucial signalling role in the workings of a free-market system.

Positive profits in an industry are the signal that resources can profitably be moved into the industry. Negative profits are the signal that the resources can profitably be moved elsewhere. Only if there are zero economic profits is there no incentive for resources to move into or out of an industry.

Profit-maximizing output

To develop a theory of supply, we need to determine the level of output that will maximize a firm's profit, to which we give the symbol π (the lower-case Greek letter pi). This is the difference between the revenue that each firm derives from the sale of its output, R, and the cost of producing that output, C:

$$\pi = R - C.$$

Thus, what happens to profit as output varies depends on what happens to revenue and to costs. In the rest of this chapter we analyse how costs vary with output. This analysis is common to all firms, irrespective of the market structure in which they operate. In the chapters that follow we consider how revenue varies with output. Costs and revenues are then combined to determine the profit-maximizing equilibrium for firms in various market situations. The resulting theory can then be used to predict the outcome of changes in such things as demand, costs, taxes, and subsidies. This may seem like quite a long route to get to a theory of supply, *and it is*, but the payoff when you get there lies in being able to understand a big part of the working of a market economy.

We start with inputs. Suppose that a firm wishes to increase its rate of output. To do so, it must increase the use of at least some of its inputs. For the rest of this chapter (and the next), we consider a very simple example relating to the production of some manufactured product. However, the approach is the same for any product. Even in service industries, for example, there will be various inputs that are combined to produce the output. A haircut requires the labour of a hairdresser (or barber) plus the services of a chair, shop space, scissors, dryers, basins, mirrors, electricity, hair spray, etc. Virtually any business you can think of involves the combination of human effort (labour), some equipment or tools (capital), and some materials (intermediate inputs).

To keep things as simple as possible, we analyse a hypothetical firm that has only two inputs. The first is labour, to which we give the symbol L. The second is capital, to which we give the symbol K. This means that we are ignoring land and all intermediate inputs[5] and dealing with the simplified version of the production function introduced earlier in this chapter:

$$q = \psi(L, K). \tag{2}$$

In this function q is quantity of output per period of time, L is labour employed in production (measured as worker hours per period—10 men working an 8 hour day is 80 worker-hours per day), and K is units of capital services used (measured as machine hours per period). The Greek letter ψ again stands for the relationship that links the inputs to the outputs; here it links K and L to q.

---

[3] An alternative terminology avoids the potential confusion arising from using the same term to refer to two different things. You may encounter it elsewhere, since it is still used in some elementary textbooks—but seldom in more advanced theory. This terminology calls the opportunity cost of capital *normal profit*. Any excess of revenue over normal profits is then called *supernormal profit*.

[4] Note that any activity that maximizes one of these concepts of profit also maximizes the other. The only difference is that, by subtracting the opportunity cost of capital from the firm's concept of profit, economists make positive or negative pure profit the signal for resources to enter or leave an industry.

[5] Nothing is lost by this simplification, as it is easy to generalize our results to the case of multiple inputs at a later stage.

A firm cannot vary all of its inputs with equal speed. It can usually vary labour at short notice, but time is needed to install more machinery or buildings. To capture the fact that different inputs cannot be varied with the same ease, we abstract from the more complicated nature of real decisions and think of each firm as making three distinct types of decision. These are (1) how best to employ its existing plant and equipment; (2) what new plant, equipment, and production processes to select, using currently available technology; and (3) what to do about encouraging the development of new technology. The first set of decisions is said to be made over the *short run*; and is discussed in the rest of this chapter. The second is made over the *long run*; and the third over the *very long run*. Both of these are discussed in Chapter 9.

Costs in the short run

The **short run** is defined as the period of time over which some inputs, often called **fixed factors** or *fixed inputs*, cannot be varied.[6] The input that is fixed in the short run is usually capital (such as plant and equipment), but it might be land, or the services of management, or even the supply of skilled, salaried labour. What matters for the analysis is that at least one significant input is fixed. The inputs that can be varied in the short run are called *variable inputs*, or **variable factors**.

The short run is not of the same real-time duration in all industries. In the electric power industry, for example, it takes three or more years to build new power stations, so an unforeseen increase in demand must be served as well as possible with the existing capital equipment for several years. At the other end of the scale, a machine shop can acquire new equipment in a few weeks, and thus the short run there is correspondingly short. The length of the short run is influenced by technological considerations such as how quickly equipment can be manufactured and installed. These things may also be influenced to some extent by the price the firm is willing to pay to increase its capacity *quickly*.

Short-run variations in input

In the short run we are concerned with what happens to output and costs as different amounts of the variable input are set to work with a given quantity of the fixed input. In the simplified production function given above, we assume that capital is fixed and labour is variable. In other words, our firm starts with a fixed amount of capital equipment and then contemplates using various amounts of labour to work with it. Table 8.3 shows three different ways of looking at how output varies with the quantity of the variable input. We now need to define some terms.

Total product (*TP*) means just what it says: the total amount produced during some period of time by all the inputs that the firm uses. If all but one of the inputs is held constant, the total product will change as input of the variable factor is changed. This variation is illustrated

Table 8.3 Total, average, and marginal products in the short run

Quantity of labour (L) (1)	Total product (TP) (2)	Average product (AP) (3)	Marginal product (MP) (4)
1	43	43	43
2	160	80	117
3	351	117	191
4	600	150	249
5	875	175	275
6	1,152	192	277
7	1,372	196	220
8	1,536	192	164
9	1,656	184	120
10	1,750	175	94
11	1,815	165	65
12	1,860	155	45

The relation of output to changes in the quantity of the variable factor can be looked at in three different ways. Capital is assumed to be fixed at 10 units. As the quantity of labour increases, the rate of total output increases, as shown in column (2). The average product in column (3) is found by dividing the total product in column (2) by the labour requirement shown in the corresponding row of column (1). The marginal product is shown between the rows because it refers to the change in output from one level of labour input to another.

in column (2) of Table 8.3, which gives a total product schedule. Figure 8.1(i) shows such a schedule graphically. (The shape of the curve will be discussed below.)

Average product (*AP*) is the total product *per unit* of the variable input, which is labour in the present illustration:

$$AP = \frac{TP}{L}.$$

[6] 'Factors' in this context refers to factors of production as defined above, not, as in common usage, to items of influence. We shall more commonly refer to factors of production as 'inputs', as this is a more familiar terminology for most readers.

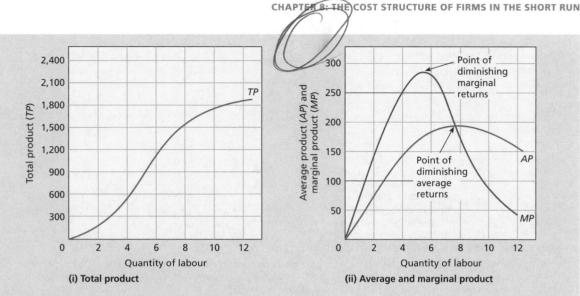

Figure 8.1 Total, average, and marginal product curves

Total product (*TP*), average product (*AP*), and marginal product (*MP*) curves often have these shapes. The curves are plotted from the data in Table 8.3. In part (i) the *TP* curve shows the total product steadily rising, first at an increasing rate, then at a decreasing rate. This causes both the average and the marginal product curves in part (ii) to rise at first and then decline. Where *AP* reaches its maximum, *MP* = *AP*.

Average product is shown in column (3) of Table 8.3. Notice that, as more of the variable input is used, average product first rises and then falls. We argue below that this is one likely pattern, but other patterns are possible. The point where average product reaches a maximum is called the *point of diminishing average returns*. In the table, average product reaches a maximum when 7 units of labour are employed.

Marginal product (*MP*) is the change in total product resulting from the use of one more (or one less) unit of the variable input:[7]

$$MP = \frac{\Delta TP}{\Delta L},$$

where ΔTP stands for the change in the total product and ΔL stands for the change in labour input that caused *TP* to change.

Computed values of the marginal product appear in column (4) of Table 8.3. Marginal product in the example reaches a maximum between $L = 5$ and $L = 6$ and thereafter declines. The level of output where marginal product reaches a maximum is called the *point of diminishing marginal returns*.

Figure 8.1(ii) shows the average and marginal product curves plotted from the data in Table 8.3. Notice, first, that *MP* reaches its maximum at a lower level of *L* than does *AP*, and, second, that *MP* = *AP* when *AP* is a maximum. These relations are discussed in more detail below.

Finally, bear in mind that the schedules of Table 8.3, and the curves of Figure 8.1, all assume a specified quantity

of the fixed input. If the quantity of capital had been, say, 14 units instead of the 10 units that were assumed, there would be a different set of total, average, and marginal product curves. The reason is that, if any specified amount of labour has more capital to work with, it can produce more output. Its total, average, and marginal products will be greater.

The law of diminishing returns

We now consider the variations in output that result from applying different amounts of a variable input to a given quantity of a fixed input. These variations are the subject of a famous hypothesis called the **law of diminishing returns**.

The law of diminishing returns states that, if increasing quantities of a variable input are applied to a given quantity of a fixed input, the marginal product, and the average product, of the variable input will eventually decrease.

[7] Strictly speaking, the text defines what is called 'incremental product', that is, the rate of change of output associated with a discrete change in an input. Marginal product refers to the rate at which output is tending to vary as input varies at a particular output. Students familiar with elementary calculus will recognize the marginal product as the partial derivative of the total product with respect to the variable input. In symbols, $MP = \partial q / \partial L$. In the text we refer only to finite changes, ΔL and ΔTP, but the phrase 'a change of one unit' should read 'a very small change'. At this time it might be helpful to read, or reread, the discussion of the marginal concept on pages 28–31 of Chapter 2.

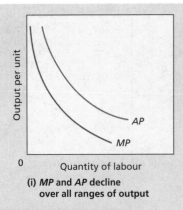
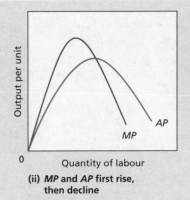

Figure 8.2 Alternative average and marginal product curves

According to the law of diminishing returns, average and marginal product must eventually decline as output increases. The law of diminishing returns permits the average and marginal product curves to decline at all positive levels of output, as shown in part (i). The law also allows the average and marginal products to rise over an initial range of output and only then decline, as shown in part (ii).

The law of diminishing returns is consistent with marginal and average product curves that decline over the whole range of output (as illustrated in part (i) Figure 8.2), or that increase for a while and only later diminish (part (ii) of the same figure). The latter case arises when it is impossible to use the fixed input efficiently with only a small quantity of the variable input (if, say, one man was trying to farm 1,000 acres). In this case, increasing the quantity of the variable input makes possible a more efficient division of labour, so that the addition of another unit of the variable input would make all units more productive than they were previously. According to the hypothesis of diminishing returns, the scope for such economies must eventually disappear, and sooner or later the marginal and average product of additional workers must decline.

Notice that, when various amounts of labour are applied to a fixed quantity of capital, the proportion in which the two types of input are used is being varied.

The law of diminishing returns is also called the 'law of variable proportions', because it predicts the consequences of varying the proportions in which input types are used.

The common sense of diminishing marginal product is that the fixed input limits the amount of additional output that can be obtained by adding more of the variable input. Were it not for the law of diminishing returns, there would be no need to fear that rapid population growth will cause food shortages in poorer countries. If the marginal product of additional workers who were employed on a fixed quantity of land was constant, then a country's food production could be expanded in proportion to the increase in population merely by keeping the same proportion of the population on farms. As it is, diminishing returns implies

that sooner or later there will be an inexorable decline in the marginal product of each additional labourer as an expanding population is applied, with static techniques, to a fixed supply of agricultural land. Thus, unless there is a continual improvement in the techniques of production, a population increase among subsistence farmers in a poor country must bring eventually with it declining living standards.[8]

The relation between marginal and average product curves

Notice that in Figure 8.2(ii) the *MP* curve cuts the *AP* curve at the latter's maximum point. It is important to understand why. The key is that the average product curve slopes upward as long as the marginal product curve is above it; it makes no difference whether the marginal curve is itself sloping upwards or downwards. The common sense of this relationship is that, if an additional worker is to raise the average product of all workers, the worker's addition to total output must be greater than the average output of all existing workers. It is immaterial whether his contribution to output is greater or less than the contribution of the last worker hired immediately before: all that matters is that his contribution to output exceeds the average output of *all* the workers hired previously. Since *AP* slopes upwards or downwards depending on whether *MP* is above

[8] This has not happened everywhere in the world because rapid technological advances have increased productivity in agriculture faster than the increase in population. However, in many poorer countries farmers subsist mainly on what they themselves grow, and they use relatively static techniques. For them, rising population in combination with the law of diminishing returns means declining output per person and hence declining living standards.

or below *AP*, it follows that *MP* must equal *AP* at the highest point on the *AP* curve. The appendix to this chapter explains the mathematical relationship between *MP* and *AP*.

This relationship between marginal and average values is a mathematical one that is thus not restricted to economics. A cricketer, for example, will raises his batting average if his next score is above his current average, and he will lower his average if his next score is below the current average.

Short-run variations in cost

We have now seen how output varies with changes in just one of the inputs in the short run. By costing these inputs, we can discover how the cost of production changes as output varies. For the time being we consider firms that are not in a position to influence the prices of their inputs, so they take the prices of these inputs as given.

We now define cost concepts that are closely related to the product concepts introduced earlier.

Total cost (*TC*) means just what it says. It is the total cost of producing any given rate of output. Total cost is divided into two parts: total fixed costs (*TFC*) and total variable costs (*TVC*). **Fixed costs** are those costs that do not vary with output; they will be the same if output is 1 unit or 1 million units. These costs are also often referred to as *overhead costs*, or *unavoidable costs*. All of those costs that vary positively with output, rising as more is produced and falling as less is produced, are called **variable costs**. In our present example, since labour is the variable input, the cost of labour would be a variable cost. Variable costs are often referred to as *direct costs* or *avoidable costs*. The latter term is used because the costs can be avoided by not hiring the variable factor.

Average total cost (*ATC*) is the total cost of producing any given output divided by the number of units produced, that is, the cost per unit. *ATC* may be divided into **average fixed costs (*AFC*)** and **average variable costs (*AVC*)** in just the same way as total costs were divided.

Marginal cost (*MC*) is the increase in total cost resulting from raising the rate of production by one unit. The marginal cost of the tenth unit, for example, is the change in total cost when the rate of production is increased from nine to ten units per period.

These three measures of cost are merely different ways of looking at a single phenomenon, and they are mathematically interrelated.[9] Which we use depends on the task in hand.

Short-run cost curves

The relations just outlined are most easily understood if we show them as cost curves. To illustrate how this is done, we take the production relationships in Table 8.3 and assume that the price of labour is £20 per unit (worker-hours) and the price of capital is £10 per unit (machine hours). Table 8.4 presents the cost schedules computed for these values. Figure 8.3(i) shows the total cost curves; Figure 8.3(ii) plots the marginal and average cost curves that are derived in Table 8.4.[10]

How cost varies with output

Since total fixed cost (*TFC*) does not vary with output, average fixed cost (*TFC/q*) is negatively related to output, while marginal fixed cost is zero. In contrast, variable cost is positively related to output, since to produce more requires more of the variable input. Average variable cost may, however, be negatively related to output at some levels of output and positively related at others. Marginal variable cost is always positive, indicating that it always costs something to increase output; but, as we will soon see, marginal cost may rise or fall as output rises.

Notice that the marginal cost curve cuts the *ATC* and *AVC* curves at their lowest points. This is another example of the relation (discussed above) between a marginal and an average value. The *ATC* curve, for example, slopes downwards as long as the marginal cost curve is below it; it makes no difference whether the marginal cost curve is itself sloping upwards or downwards.

In Figure 8.3 the average variable cost curve reaches a minimum and then rises. With fixed input prices, when average product per worker is at a maximum, average variable cost is at a minimum. The common sense is that each new worker adds the same amount to cost but a different amount to output, and when output per worker is rising the cost per unit of output must be falling, and vice versa.

Short-run *AVC* curves are often drawn U-shaped. This reflects the assumptions (1) that average productivity is increasing when output is low, but (2) that average productivity eventually begins to fall fast enough to cause average total cost to increase.

The law of diminishing returns implies eventually increasing marginal and average variable cost.

The definition of capacity The output that corresponds to the minimum short-run average total cost is very often called **capacity**. Capacity in this sense is not an upper limit on what can be produced, as you can see by looking again

---

[9] Mathematically, average total cost is total cost divided by output while marginal cost is the first derivative of total cost with respect to output.

[10] The calculation here involves discrete changes, while calculating marginal values requires very small changes. We are thus producing an approximation to the true marginal value calculated over a specific range.

Table 8.4 **Variation of costs with capital fixed and labour variable**

Inputs		Output (q)	Total cost			Average cost			Marginal cost (MC)[d]
Capital (1)	Labour (L) (2)	(3)	Fixed (TFC) (4)	Variable (TVC) (5)	Total (TC) (6)	Fixed (AFC)[a] (7)	Variable (AVC)[b] (8)	Total (ATC)[c] (9)	(10)
10	1	43	£100	£20	£120	£2.326	£0.465	£2.791	£0.465
10	2	160	100	40	140	0.625	0.250	0.875	0.171
10	3	351	100	60	160	0.285	0.171	0.456	0.105
10	4	600	100	80	180	0.167	0.133	0.300	0.080
10	5	875	100	100	200	0.114	0.114	0.228	0.073
10	6	1,152	100	120	220	0.087	0.104	0.191	0.072
10	7	1,372	100	140	240	0.073	0.102	0.175	0.091
10	8	1,536	100	160	260	0.065	0.104	0.169	0.122
10	9	1,656	100	180	280	0.060	0.109	0.169	0.167
10	10	1,750	100	200	300	0.057	0.114	0.171	0.213
10	11	1,815	100	220	320	0.055	0.121	0.176	0.308
10	12	1,860	100	240	340	0.054	0.129	0.183	0.444

The relation of cost to the rate of output can be looked at in several different ways. These cost schedules are computed from the product curves of Table 8.3, given the price of capital of £10 per unit and the price of labour of £20 per unit. Marginal cost (in column (10)) is shown between the lines of total cost because it refers to the *change* in cost divided by the *change* in output that brought it about. Marginal cost is calculated by dividing the increase in costs by the increase in output when one additional unit of labour is used. This gives the increase in cost per unit of output over that range of output. For example, the *MC* of £0.08 is the increase in total cost of £20 (from £160 to £180) divided by the 249 unit increase in output (from 351 to 600). This tells us that when output goes from 351 to 600 (because labour inputs go from 3 to 4), the increase in costs is £0.08 per unit of output. In constructing a graph, marginal costs should be plotted midway in the interval over which they are computed. The *MC* of £0.08 would thus be plotted at output 475.5.

[a] Col. (4) ÷ col. (3). [c] Col. (6) ÷ col. (3)) = col. (7) + col. (8).
[b] Col. (5) ÷ col. (3). [d] Change in col. (5) from one row to the next ÷ corresponding change in col. (3).

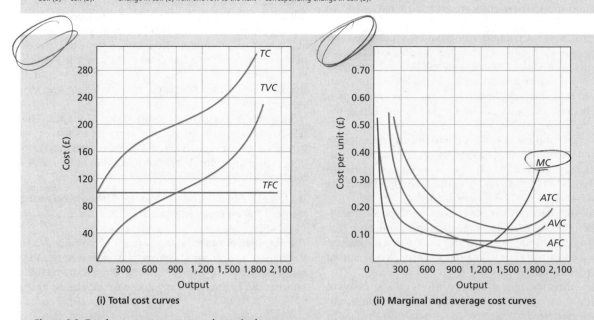

(i) Total cost curves

(ii) Marginal and average cost curves

Figure 8.3 Total cost, average cost, and marginal cost curves

Total cost (*TC*), average cost (*AC*), and marginal cost (*MC*) curves often have the shapes shown here. These curves are plotted from Table 8.4. Total fixed cost does not vary with output. Total variable cost and the total of all costs (*TC = TVC + TFC*) rise with output, first at a decreasing rate, then at an increasing rate. The total cost curves in part (i) give rise to the average and marginal curves in part (ii). Average fixed cost (*AFC*) declines as output increases. Average variable cost (*AVC*) and average total cost (*ATC*) fall and then rise as output increases. Marginal cost (*MC*) does the same, intersecting the *ATC* and *AVC* curves at their minimum points. Capacity output is at the minimum point of the *ATC* curve, which is an output of 1,500 in this example.

at Table 8.4. In the example, capacity output is between 1,536 and 1,656 units, but higher outputs can be achieved. A firm producing *below capacity* is producing at a rate of output less than that for which average total cost is a minimum. A firm producing *above capacity* is producing more than this amount. It is thus incurring costs per unit of output that are higher than the minimum achievable.

Shifts in cost curves

The cost curves in Figure 8.3 are drawn for given prices of the inputs. Since labour is the only variable input in our present example, the cost of an input is some specific hourly wage. Clearly, if the wage per hour of each worker rises, then all of the cost curves that include variable costs will shift upwards. (*TFC* and *AFC* will be unchanged because they depend only on costs that are fixed in the short run.) The total cost line (*TC*) and the total variable cost line (*TVC*) in Figure 8.3(i) will both become steeper, but with the same intersection on the vertical axis. Since labour is the only variable input in the example we are using, the average variable cost curve and the marginal cost curve will shift upwards in the same proportion as the increase in the wage.

A second reason why short-run cost curves might shift is a change in the productivity of the variable factor. This may be brought about by the use of more of the fixed input —capital in this case—or by the introduction of new technologies, both of which we consider in the next chapter. However, productivity can also change, for a given capital stock, if workers learn to produce more as a result of becoming more skilled at the job, that is from learning by doing. When this happens, unit costs of production will fall and the curves will shift in the reverse direction to those outlined in the previous paragraph.

Conclusion

In each period of time when firms are constrained by their existing fixed inputs, there will be some specific production costs for each level of output. These costs affect the output that profit-maximizing firms wish to produce. Once we have discussed the further impact of changing the capital stock and changing technology, we can combine what we have learned about costs with market demand conditions to determine the profit-maximizing output of the firm.

SUMMARY

Production decisions are made by firms

■ Production is organized either by private sector firms, which take four main forms—sole traders, partnerships, limited partnerships, and joint-stock companies—by state-owned enterprises called public corporations and by non-profit units, mostly government-owned bodies, that distribute goods and services free, or at least substantially below cost.

■ Firms are in business to make profits, which they define as the difference between what they earn by selling their output and what it costs them to produce that output. This is the return to owners' capital.

Production, costs, and profits

■ The production function relates quantities of inputs to quantities of outputs.

■ In addition to what firms count as their costs, economists include the imputed opportunity costs of owners' capital. This includes the pure return—what could be earned on a riskless

investment—and a risk premium—what could be earned over the pure return on an equally risky investment. Pure or economic profits are the difference between revenues and all these costs. When there is no ambiguity, these are referred to merely as 'profits'.

■ Pure profits play a key role in resource allocation. Positive pure profits attract resources into an industry; negative pure profits induce resources to move elsewhere.

Costs in the short run

■ Short-run variations in output are subject to the law of diminishing returns: equal increments of the variable input sooner or later produce smaller and smaller additions to total output and, eventually, a reduction in average output per unit of variable input.

■ Short-run average and marginal cost curves are assumed to be U-shaped, the rising portion reflecting diminishing average and marginal returns. The marginal cost curve intersects the average cost curve at the latter's minimum point, which is called the firm's capacity output.

TOPICS FOR REVIEW

- Forms of business organization
- Imputed costs
- Alternative definitions of profits
- The production function

- Short, long, and very long runs
- The law of diminishing returns
- Short-run average, marginal, fixed, and total costs

DISCUSSION QUESTIONS

1 The following series of scores in successive innings is made by a batsman in cricket: 10, 20, 50, 60, 80, 100, 100, 100, 70, 50, 0, 10, 20, 0. Calculate the cumulative total of runs scored after each innings and the average score after each innings. Each successive score tells us the marginal score. Say what happens to the average when the marginal score is above the previous average and what happens to the average when the marginal score is below the average. Notice that these relationships between marginal and average values are not purely applicable to economics.

2 Suppose the production function is $Q = 20(\sqrt{K}\sqrt{L})$ and the value of capital is 100. Calculate the total product for the following values of labour input: 1, 5, 10, 20, 40, 50, 80, 100, 150, 200. Calculate the average product at each of these levels of output. How does marginal product vary for this range of output?

3 Here are data for total production costs of a manufacturing firm at various levels of output:

Output (units)	Total cost (£)
0	1,000
20	1,200
40	1,300
60	1,380
100	1,600
200	2,300
300	3,200
400	4,300
500	5,650
1,000	13,650

(a) Calculate average variable cost (AVC), average total cost (ATC), and average fixed cost (AFC). (Hint: fixed costs have to be incurred even when output is zero, and do not vary with the production level in the short run.)

(b) Calculate marginal or incremental cost over each production range for which data are given.

(c) [You may attempt this and subsequent parts now but you could also return to them after reading Chapter 10.] If this firm can sell as much as it wants at a price of £11, what is its profit-maximizing output?

(d) How much profit is made?

(e) At output levels shown in the table immediately on either side of the profit-maximizing output, what is the level of profit?

4 Explain the difference between economists' and accountants' definition of profit.

5 What is the law of diminishing returns, and what does it imply about the likely shape of short-run cost curves?

6 Using an appropriate diagram, explain the relationship between average variable cost, average total cost, average fixed cost, and marginal cost.

7 Give some reasons why firms exist.

8 Outline the different structures that firms may have, and discuss factors that might influence this choice of structure.

Mathematical Appendix Mathematics of production and costs

Diminishing returns

Let product X be produced by two inputs, labour, L, and capital, K, according to the production function.

$$X = AL^\alpha K^\beta, \qquad 0 < \alpha, \beta, < 1; \qquad \alpha + \beta = 1. \qquad (A1)$$

This is the so-called Cobb–Douglas production function. The marginal products of the two factors are

$$MP_L = \frac{\partial X}{\partial L} = \alpha AL^{\alpha-1}K^\beta > 0$$

and

$$MP_K = \frac{\partial X}{\partial K} = \beta AL^\alpha K^{\beta-1} > 0.$$

So the marginal products are everywhere positive. But do they rise, stay constant or diminish? To answer this question we need the second derivatives of X with respect to L and K.

$$\frac{\partial^2 X}{\partial L^2} = \alpha(\alpha - 1)AL^{\alpha-2}K^\beta < 0$$

and

$$\frac{\partial^2 X}{\partial K^2} = \beta(\beta - 1)AL^\alpha K^{\beta-2} < 0.$$

Since these second derivatives are negative, the total products are rising at a diminishing rate; that is, we have declining *marginal* products.

The relation between average and marginal products

For the production function $Y = q(n)$, where n is the quantity of the variable input, the definitions of total, average and marginal products are $TP = q(n)$, $AP = q(n)/n$, and $MP = q'(n)$, where the single prime mark indicates the first derivative. A necessary condition for the maximum of the AP curve is that its first derivative, $[nq'(n) - q(n)]/n^2$, be equal to zero. Setting the above expression equal to zero, adding $q(n)/n^2$ to both sides, and multiplying through by n yields $q'(n) = q(n)/n$, which is to say $MP = AP$.

The relation between products curves and cost curves

Let L be the quantity of the variable factor labour used and w its prices per unit (a dot indicates multiplication). By definition, $AVC = TVC/q$. But $TVC = L \cdot w$, and $q = AP \cdot L$ (since $AP = q/L$). Therefore

$$AVC = \frac{L \cdot w}{AP \cdot L} = \frac{w}{AP}.$$

In other words, average variable cost equals the price of the variable input divided by the average product of the variable input. Since w is constant, it follows that AVC and AP vary inversely with each other, and when AP is at its maximum value AVC must be at its minimum value.

Chapter 9

THE COST STRUCTURE OF FIRMS IN THE LONG RUN

How are the choices available to firms affected by their ability to change their capital stock and invest in new technology? When will firms choose to replace workers with machines? When will they do the opposite? Here we study these choices and how they affect the costs of producing various levels of output. In particular, you will learn that:

• Profit-maximizing firms use an input mix such that the ratio of marginal products of inputs equals the ratio of input prices.

• If input prices change, methods of production will change to use fewer of those inputs that have become relatively expensive and more of those that have become relatively cheaper.

• There is a family of short-run ATC curves, each one tangent to the long-run ATC curve.

• The long-run cost curve can take on various shapes depending on the scale effects when all inputs are allowed to vary at once.

• Changes in technology are often endogenous responses to changing economic signals.

Varying combinations of inputs

In the short run, with only one input variable, there is only one way to produce a given output: by adjusting the input of the variable factor until the optimal rate of output is achieved. Thus, once the firm has decided on a rate of output, there is only one technically possible way of achieving it.

By contrast, in the long run all inputs can be varied. The firm must decide both on a level of output *and* on the best input mix to produce that output. Specifically, in our two-input example this means that firms must choose the nature and amount of plant and equipment, as well as the size of their labour force. So *long run* in this context means that the capital stock can be changed, while *very long run* means that the technology can change too.

In this chapter we focus largely on how costs are affected by the ability to vary capital as well as labour. However, we do this in a simplified way by assuming that capital can be hired by the hour just as labour can. Some capital can be hired like this, but many decisions to install machines or build a factory commit the firm for many years to come and are to some extent irreversible. This means that evaluating whether an investment should be made necessarily involves evaluating the payoffs over many periods of time. Such investment decisions are risky, because the firm must anticipate what methods of production will be efficient not only today, but for many years in the future, when the costs of labour and raw materials will no doubt have changed. The decisions are also risky because the firm must estimate how much output it will want to produce. Is the industry to which it belongs growing or declining? Will new products emerge to render its existing products less useful than an extrapolation of past sales suggests? By focusing on hiring capital, we avoid some of these problems associated with lumpy investment decisions, but we return to them in Chapter 17.

Profit maximization and cost minimization

In making the choice of inputs, the firm will wish to avoid being technically inefficient, which means using more of *all* inputs than is necessary. Being technically efficient is not enough, however. To be economically efficient, the firm must choose, from among the many technically efficient options, the one that produces a given level of output at the lowest possible cost. This implication of the hypothesis of profit maximization is called **cost minimization**: from the alternatives open to it, the profit-maximizing firm will choose the least costly way of producing whatever specific output it chooses.

Choice of input mix

If it is possible to substitute one input for another in such a way that output remains constant while total cost falls, the firm is not using the least-cost combination of inputs. The firm should then substitute one type of input for another. Such cost-reducing substitutions are always possible whenever the marginal product of one input per £1 spent on it is greater than the marginal product of the other input per £1 spent on it. The firm has not minimized its costs as long as these two magnitudes are unequal. For example, if an extra £1 spent on labour adds more to output than an extra £1 spent on capital, the firm can reduce costs by spending less on capital and more on labour.

If we use K to represent capital, L to represent labour, and P_K and P_L to represent the prices of a unit of each, the necessary condition for cost minimization is as follows:

$$\frac{MP_K}{P_K} = \frac{MP_L}{P_L} \qquad (1)$$

Whenever the two sides of equation (1) are not equal, there are possibilities for input substitutions that will reduce costs.

To see why this equation must be satisfied if costs of production are to be minimized, consider a situation where the equation is not satisfied. Suppose, for example, that the marginal product of capital is 20 and its price is £2, making the left side of equation (1) equal to 10. Suppose that the marginal product of labour is 32 and its price is £8, making the right side of equation (1) equal to 4. Thus, the last £1 spent on capital adds 10 units to output, whereas the last £1 spent on labour adds only 4 units to output. In such a case the firm could maintain its output level and reduce costs by using £2.50 less of labour and spending £1.00 more on capital. Making such a substitution of capital for labour would leave output unchanged and reduce costs by £1.50. Thus, the original position was not cost-minimizing.[1]

We can take a different look at cost minimization by multiplying equation (1) by P_K/MP_L to obtain

$$\frac{MP_K}{MP_L} = \frac{P_K}{P_L}. \qquad (2)$$

The ratio of the marginal products on the left-hand side of the equation compares the contribution to output of the last unit of capital and the last unit of labour. For example, if the ratio is 4, then an additional unit of capital will add four times as much to output as an additional unit of labour. The right-hand side of the equation shows how the cost of one unit more of capital compares with the cost of one unit more of labour. If in this example the ratio is also 4, the firm cannot reduce costs by substituting capital for labour or vice versa. Now suppose that the ratio on the right-hand side of the equation is 2. Capital, which is four times as productive as labour, is now only twice as expensive. It will pay the firm to switch to a method of production that uses more capital and less labour. If, however, the ratio on the right-hand side is 6 (or *any* number greater than 4), it will pay to switch to a method of production that uses more labour and less capital.

We have seen that, when the ratio MP_K/MP_L exceeds the ratio P_K/P_L, the firm will substitute capital for labour. This substitution is measured by changes in the **capital–labour ratio**, which is the amount of capital per worker. So if, for example, the firm uses £1 million worth of capital and employs 100 workers, its capital–labour ratio is 10,000 (1,000,000/100), indicating that there is £10,000 worth of capital for each worker.

How far should the profit-maximizing firm go in making this substitution? The law of diminishing returns tells us that as the firm uses more capital the marginal product of capital falls, and as it uses less labour the marginal product of labour rises. Thus, the ratio MP_K/MP_L falls. When it reaches 2 in this example, the firm does not need to substitute further. The ratio of the marginal products is equal to the ratio of the prices.

Equation (2) shows how the firm can adjust the elements over which it has control (the quantities of inputs used, and thus the marginal products of those inputs) according to the market prices of the inputs. It should substitute one input for the other until the ratio of their marginal products equals the ratio of their prices.

Long-run equilibrium of the firm

The firm has achieved its equilibrium capital–labour ratio when there is no further opportunity for cost-reducing substitutions. This occurs when the marginal product per pound spent on each input is the same (equation (1)) or, equivalently, when the ratio of the marginal products of inputs is equal to the ratio of their prices (equation (2)).

The principle of substitution

Suppose that a firm is meeting the cost-minimizing conditions shown in equations (1) and (2) and that the cost of labour increases while the cost of capital remains unchanged. The least-cost method of producing any output

---

[1] The argument in this paragraph assumes that the marginal products do not change when expenditure changes by a small amount.

will now use less labour and more capital than was required to produce the same output before the factor prices changed.

Methods of production will change if the relative prices of inputs change. Relatively more of the cheaper input and relatively less of the more expensive input will be used.

This is called the **principle of substitution**, and it follows from the assumption that firms minimize their costs.

The principle of substitution plays a central role in resource allocation, because it relates to the way in which individual firms respond to changes in relative input prices that are caused by the changing relative scarcities of factors of production in the economy as a whole. When some resource becomes scarcer to the economy as a whole, its price will tend to rise. This motivates individual firms to use less of that input. When some other input becomes more plentiful to the economy as a whole, its price will tend to fall. This motivates individual firms to use more of it. Firms need never know the relative national scarcities of the various factors of production. As long as relative prices reflect these relative scarcities, firms will tend to substitute inputs that are nationally plentiful for those that are nationally scarce. They do this through their own cost-minimizing responses to the changes in the prices of their inputs. Box 9.1 discusses the broader significance of the principle of substitution.

The next section of this chapter gives a formal analysis of the firm's choice of input proportions and of its substitution in response to changes in relative input prices. The analysis uses *isoquants*, which are the firm's equivalent of consumers' indifference curves: an indifference curve shows all those combinations of products that give the consumer the same satisfaction, while an isoquant shows all those combinations of inputs that give the firm the same output. Those who wish to study this diagrammatic analysis of the subject matter of this section should read on. Those who are content with the intuitive discussion in the text can skip forward to the section entitled 'Cost curves in the long run' on page 147.

Isoquants: an alternative analysis of the firm's long-run input decisions

The long-run choices of factor proportions that we have just studied can also be shown graphically.

A single isoquant Table 9.1 gives a hypothetical illustration of those combinations of two inputs (labour and capital) that will produce a given quantity of output. The data from the table are plotted in Figure 9.1. A smooth curve is drawn through the points to indicate that there are additional ways, not listed in the table, of producing 6 units. The curve is called an **isoquant**. It shows the set of technologically efficient possibilities for producing a given level of output —here it is 6 units. The isoquant in this example is analogous to an indifference curve that shows all combinations of commodities that yield a given utility. It is derived from the production function in equation (2) of the text, by altering L and K in such a way as to keep q constant.

As we move from one point on a single isoquant to another, we are *substituting one input for another* while holding output constant. The **marginal rate of substitution** (MRS) measures the rate at which one input is substituted for another with output held constant. Graphically, this is measured by the absolute value of the slope of the isoquant at a particular point. The table shows the calculation of

---

 Box 9.1 **The economy-wide significance of the principle of substitution**

In free markets, relative input prices reflect the relative scarcities (in relation to demand) of different factors of production. Abundant factors have prices that are low relative to the prices of factors that are scarce. Firms seeking their own private profit and responding to relative input prices will be led to make lavish use of the inputs with which the whole country is plentifully endowed, and to be frugal in their use of those inputs that are in scarce supply.

For example, a country with a great deal of land and a small population will experience a low price of its plentiful land and a high price of its scarce labour. Firms producing agricultural goods will tend to make lavish use of the cheap land and to economize on the expensive labour. In contrast, a small country with a large population will have expensive land and cheap labour. Firms producing agricultural goods will tend to economize on land by using a great deal of labour per unit of land.

In recent decades construction workers' wages have risen sharply relative to the wages of factory labour and the cost of machinery. In response, builders have shifted from on-site construction to panelization, a method of

building that uses standardized modules. The wiring, plumbing, insulation, and painting of these standardized modules are all done at the factory. The bulk of the factory work is performed by machinery and by assembly-line workers whose wages are only half those of on-site construction workers.

These are examples of the price system operating as an automatic control mechanism. No single firm need be aware of national resource surpluses and scarcities. Since these are reflected in relative market prices, individual firms that never look beyond their own private profits are led to economize on inputs that are scarce in the nation as a whole. We should not be surprised, therefore, to discover that methods of producing the same product differ in different countries. In Europe, where labour is highly skilled and very expensive, a manufacturer may use very elaborate equipment to economize on labour. In China, where labour is abundant and capital scarce, a much less mechanized method of production may be appropriate. The Western engineer who feels that the Chinese are behind because they are using methods abandoned in the West as inefficient long ago may be missing the significance of economic efficiency.

Table 9.1 Alternative methods of producing six units of output: points on an isoquant

Method	K	L	ΔK	ΔL	Rate of substitution $\Delta K/\Delta L$
a	18	2			
			−6	1	−6.0
b	12	3			
			−3	1	−3.0
c	9	4			
			−3	2	−1.5
d	6	6			
			−2	3	−0.67
e	4	9			
			−1	3	−0.33
f	3	12			
			−1	6	−0.17
g	2	18			

An isoquant describes the firm's alternative methods for producing a given output. The table lists some of the methods indicated by a production function as being available to produce six units of output. The first combination uses a great deal of capital (K) and very little labour (L). As we move down the table, labour is substituted for capital in such a way as to keep output constant. Finally, at the bottom, most of the capital has been replaced by labour. The rate of substitution between the two factors is calculated in the last three columns of the table. Note that as we move down the table, the absolute value of the rate of substitution declines.

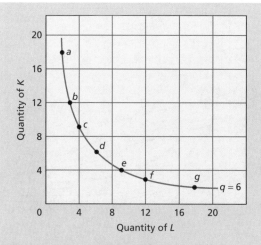

Figure 9.1 An isoquant for output of six units

Isoquants are negatively sloped and convex. The lettered points are plotted from the data in Table 9.1. The convex shape of the isoquant reflects a diminishing marginal rate of substitution; moving along the isoquant to the right, its slope becomes flatter. Starting from point a, which uses relatively little labour and much capital, and moving to point b, 1 additional unit of labour can substitute for 6 units of capital (while holding production constant); but from b to c, 1 unit of labour substitutes for only 3 units of capital; and so on.

some rates of substitution between various points of the isoquant.[2]

Next, consider how the marginal rate of substitution is related to the marginal products of the inputs. An example will illustrate this relationship. Assume that, at the present level of inputs of labour and capital, the marginal product of a unit of labour is 2 units of output while the marginal product of capital is 1 unit of output. If the firm reduces its use of capital and increases its use of labour so as to keep output constant, it needs to add only 0.5 unit of labour for 1 unit of capital given up. If, at another point on the isoquant with more labour and less capital, the marginal products are 2 for capital and 1 for labour, then the firm will have to add 2 units of labour for every unit of capital it gives up. The general proposition this example illustrates is:

The marginal rate of substitution between two inputs is equal to the ratio of their marginal products.

Isoquants satisfy two important conditions: they are negatively sloped, and they are convex viewed from the origin.

The negative slope indicates that each input has a positive marginal product. If the use of one input is reduced and that of the other is held constant, output must fall. Thus, if one input is reduced, production can be held constant only if the other input is increased. This gives the marginal rate of substitution a negative value: decreases in one factor must be balanced by increases in the other input if output is to be held constant.

Now consider what happens as the firm moves along the isoquant in Figure 9.1 downwards and to the right. This movement means that labour is being added and capital reduced so as to keep output constant. If capital is cut by successive increments of exactly one unit, how much labour must be added each time? The key to the answer is that both inputs are assumed to be subject to the law of diminishing returns. Thus, the gain in output associated with each additional unit of labour added is *diminishing*, while the loss of output associated with each additional unit of capital forgone is *increasing*. It therefore takes ever larger increases in labour to offset equal reductions in capital in order to hold production constant. This implies that the isoquant is convex viewed from the origin.

An isoquant map The isoquant drawn in Figure 9.1 referred to 6 units of output. There is another isoquant for 7 units, and one for every other output. Each isoquant refers to a specific output, connecting alternative combinations of inputs that are technologically efficient methods of achieving that output. If we plot a representative set of these isoquants on a single graph, we obtain an **isoquant map**. Such a map is shown in Figure 9.2. The higher the level of output along a particular isoquant, the further away from the origin it will be.

Isoquants and the conditions for cost minimization Finding the efficient way of producing any output requires finding

---

[2] The table shows the incremental rate. The true marginal rate is the partial derivative of K with respect to L, holding output constant.

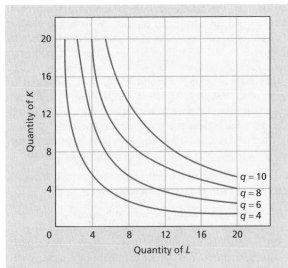

Figure 9.2 An isoquant map

An isoquant map shows a set of isoquants, one for each level of output. The figure shows four isoquants drawn from the production function and corresponding to 4, 6, 8, and 10 units of production. The higher the level of output, the further is the isoquant from the origin.

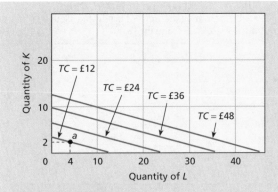

Figure 9.3 Isocost lines

An isocost line shows alternative factor combinations that can be purchased for a given outlay. The graph shows the four isocost lines that result when labour costs £1 a unit and capital £4 a unit and expenditure is held constant at £12, £24, £36, and £48 respectively. The line labelled $TC = £12$ represents all combinations of the two factors that the firm could buy for £12. Point a represents 2 units of K and 4 units of L.

the least-cost input combination. To do this when both inputs are variable, prices of inputs need to be known. Suppose that capital is priced at £4 per unit and labour at £1. We can now draw what is called an **isocost line**, which shows all of the combinations of the two inputs that can be purchased for a given outlay. Four such lines are shown in Figure 9.3. For given factor prices, the parallel isocost lines reflect alternative levels of spending on inputs. The higher the spending, the further from the origin is the isocost line. Note that the isocost line is similar to the budget line introduced in Chapter 7, which shows all the combinations of two goods that can be bought with a given income.

In Figure 9.4 the isoquant and isocost maps are brought together. A careful study of that figure reveals the following important results. If the isoquant cuts the isocost line, it is possible to move along the isoquant and reach a lower level of cost. Where the isoquant is tangent to the isocost line, however, a movement in either direction along the isoquant is a movement to a higher level of cost. Thus:

The least-cost method of producing any given output is shown graphically by the point of tangency between the relevant isoquant and an isocost line.

Notice that point A in Figure 9.4 indicates not only the lowest level of cost for 6 units of output but also the highest output for £24 of cost. This illustrates the general proposition that we find the same solution if we set out either to minimize the cost of producing a given output or to maximize the output that can be produced for a given cost. One problem is said to be a *dual* of the other.

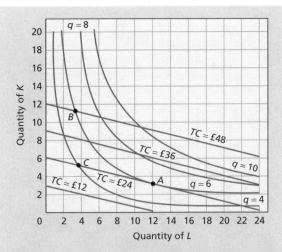

Figure 9.4 The determination of the least-cost method of output

Least-cost methods are represented by points of tangency, such as A, between isoquant and isocost lines. The isoquant map of Figure 9.2 and the isocost map of Figure 9.3 are brought together here. Consider point A. It is on the 6-unit isoquant and the £24 isocost line. Thus, it is possible to achieve an output of 6 units for a total cost of £24. There are, however, other ways to achieve this output. For example, at point B, 6 units are produced, but at a total cost of £48.

Now consider moving along the isocost line, say from point A to point C. Although costs are held constant, output falls from 6 to 4 units.

Point A thus shows both the least-cost method of producing 6 units of output and the maximum output that can be produced for an outlay of £24. Moving along the isoquant from point A in either direction clearly increases cost.

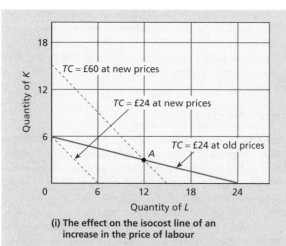

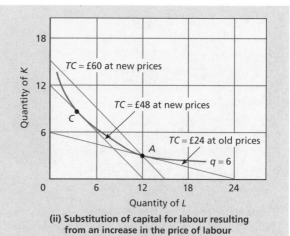

(i) The effect on the isocost line of an increase in the price of labour

(ii) Substitution of capital for labour resulting from an increase in the price of labour

Figure 9.5 The effects of a change in input prices on costs and input proportions

An increase in the price of labour pivots the isocost line inwards and thus increases the cost of producing any given output. It also changes the slope of the isocost line and thus changes the least-cost method of producing any given output. In part (i) the rise in price of L from £1 to £4 a unit (with price of K constant at £4) pivots the $TC = £24$ line inwards. Any output previously produced for £24 will cost more at the new prices if it uses any amount of labour. The new cost of producing at A rises from £24 to £60. In part (ii) the steeper isocost line is tangent to the 6-unit isoquant at C, not A. Total cost at C is £48, which is higher than before the price increase but not as high as it would be if the input substitution had not occurred.

The absolute value of the slope of the isocost line is given by the ratio of the prices of the two inputs. The slope of the isoquant is given by the ratio of their marginal products. (Both statements refer to absolute values.) When the firm reaches its least-cost position, it has equated the price ratio (which is given to it by the market prices) with the ratio of marginal products (which it can adjust by varying the proportions in which it hires the inputs). In symbols,

$$\frac{MP_K}{MP_L} = \frac{P_K}{P_L}.$$

This is equation (2) on page 143 above. We have now derived this result by use of the isoquant analysis of the firm's decisions.

Isoquants and the principle of substitution Suppose that with technology unchanged—that is, with the isoquant map fixed—the price of one input changes. Figure 9.5 shows why the change in price changes the least-cost method of producing a given output. An increase in the price of one input pivots the isocost line inwards and thus increases the cost of producing any output. It also changes the slope of the isocost line and thus changes the least-cost method of production. Costs at the new least-cost point C are higher than they were before the price increase, but not as high as if the input substitution had not occurred. The slope of the isocost line has changed, making it efficient to substitute the now relatively cheaper capital for the relatively more expensive labour.

This result illustrates the principle of substitution stated earlier in the chapter. Of course, substitution of capital for labour cannot fully offset the effects of a rise in the cost of labour, as Figure 9.5 shows. This means that if production is to be held constant higher costs must be accepted—but because of substitution it is not necessary to accept costs as high, as it would be if input proportions remained unchanged.

Cost curves in the long run

When all inputs can be varied, there is a least-cost method of producing each possible level of output. Thus, with given input prices, there is a minimum achievable cost for each level of output; if this cost is expressed as a quantity per unit of output, we obtain the long-run average cost of producing each level of output. When this least-cost method of producing each output is plotted on a graph, the result is called a **long-run average cost curve (LRAC)**. Figure 9.6 shows one such curve.

This cost curve is determined by the industry's current technology and by the prices of the inputs. It is a 'boundary' in the sense that points below it are unattainable;

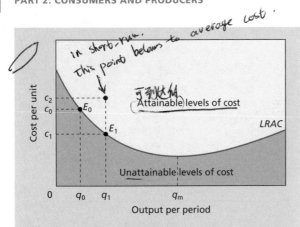

Figure 9.6 A long-run average cost curve

The long-run average cost (LRAC) curve is the boundary between attainable and unattainable levels of cost. Since the lowest attainable cost of producing q_0 is c_0 per unit, the point E_0 is on the LRAC curve. Suppose a firm producing at E_0 desires to increase output to q_1. In the short run it will not be able to vary all inputs, and thus unit costs above c_1, say c_2, must be accepted. In the long run a plant that is the optimal size for producing output q_1 can be built and costs of c_1 can be attained. At output q_m the firm attains its lowest possible per-unit cost of production for the given technology and input prices.

points on the curve, however, are attainable if sufficient time elapses for all inputs to be adjusted. To move from one point on the LRAC curve to another requires an adjustment in all inputs, which may, for example, require building a larger, more elaborate factory.

The LRAC curve is the boundary between cost levels that are attainable, with known technology and given input prices, and those that are unattainable.

Just as the short-run cost curves discussed earlier in this chapter are derived from the *production function* describing the physical relationship between inputs and output, so is the LRAC curve. The difference is that in deriving the LRAC curve there are no fixed factors, so all inputs are treated as variable. Because all input costs are variable in the long run, we do not need to distinguish between average variable cost (AVC), average fixed cost (AFC), and average total cost (ATC), as we did in the short run. In the long run there is only one long-run average cost (LRAC) for any given set of input prices.

The shape of the long-run average cost curve

As the firm varies its output in the long run, average cost may vary for two distinct reasons. First, the prices of its inputs may change. Second, the physical relation between

its inputs and outputs may change. To separate these two effects, we assume for the moment that all input prices remain constant.

Now look at the LRAC curve shown in Figure 9.6. This curve is often described as U-shaped, although empirical studies suggest it is often 'saucer-shaped'.

Decreasing costs

Over the range of output from zero to q_m, the firm has falling long-run average costs: an expansion of output permits a reduction of costs per unit of output. Technologies with this property are said to exhibit **economies of scale**. (Of course, when output is increased, such economies of scale will be realized only after enough time has elapsed to allow changes to be made in all inputs.) Recall that the prices of factors are assumed to be constant for the moment. Thus, the decline in long-run average cost must occur because output is increasing *more than* in proportion to inputs as the scale of the firm's production expands. Over this range of output, the decreasing-cost firm is often said to enjoy long-run **increasing returns**. This is an extremely important phenomenon, and its sources are discussed in the next section. Ouput q_m is called the **minimum efficient scale**, defined as the lowest level of output at which all scale economies are exploited.

Increasing costs

Over the range of outputs greater than q_m, the firm encounters rising long-run unit costs. An expansion in production, even after sufficient time has elapsed for all adjustments to be made, will then be accompanied by a rise in average costs per unit of output. Since input prices are still assumed to be constant, the firm's output must be increasing *less than* in proportion to the increase in inputs. When this happens, the increasing-cost firm is said to encounter long-run **decreasing returns**. Decreasing returns imply that the firm suffers some diseconomy of scale. As its scale of operations increases, diseconomies are encountered that increase its per-unit cost of production.

These diseconomies may be associated with the difficulties of managing and controlling an enterprise as its size increases. For example, planning problems do not necessarily vary in direct proportion to size. At first there may be scale economies as the firm grows, but sooner or later planning and co-ordination problems may multiply more than in proportion to the growth in size. If so, management costs per unit of output will rise. Another source of scale diseconomies concerns the possible alienation of the labour force as firm size increases. Also, providing appropriate supervision becomes difficult as more and more tiers of supervisors and middle managers come between the person at the top and the workers on the shop floor. Control of middle-range managers may also become more difficult. As the firm becomes larger, managers may begin to pursue their own goals rather than devote all of their efforts to making profits for the firm. (This is the principal–agent problem, which is discussed in detail in Chapter 14.)

Constant costs

In Figure 9.6 the firm's long-run average cost falls until output reaches q_m and rises thereafter. Another possibility should be noted. The firm's LRAC curve might have a flat portion over a range of output around q_m. With such a flat portion, the firm would be encountering constant costs over the relevant range of output. This means that the firm's long-run average costs per unit of output do not change as its output changes. Because input prices are assumed to be fixed, the firm's output must be increasing *exactly in proportion to* the increase in inputs. A firm in this situation is said to be encountering **constant returns**.

Sources of increasing returns

Whenever a firm finds that it can increase its output per unit of input, that firm is enjoying economies of large-scale production. These economies are important, and wherever they exist they encourage large plants and/or large firms. Three important sources of scale economies are geometrical relations, one-time costs, and the technology of large-scale production.

Geometrical relations

One important source of scale economies lies in the geometry of our three-dimensional world. To illustrate how geometry matters, consider a firm that wishes to store liquid. The firm is interested in the *volume* of storage space. However, the amount of material required to build the container is related to the *area* of its surface. When the size of a container is increased, the storage capacity, which is determined by its volume, increases faster than its surface area.[3] This is a genuine case of increasing returns—the output, in terms of storage capacity, increases proportionately more than the increase in the costs of the required construction materials. Another of the many other similar effects concerns smelters. The heat loss is proportional to the smelter surface area, while the amount of ore smelted depends on its volume. Thus, there is a scale economy in heat needed per tonne of ore smelted as smelters get larger. In practice, however, the size of the smelter is limited by the need to deliver a smooth flow of air to all of the molten ore. When improved forced-air pumps were invented in the nineteenth century, smelters could be built larger and unit costs fell.

One-time costs

A second source of increasing returns consists of inputs that do not have to be increased as the output of a product is increased, even in the long run. For example, the research and development (R&D) costs to design a new generation of aeroplanes, or a more powerful computer, have to be incurred only once for each product. Hence they are independent of the scale at which the product is subsequently produced. Even if the product's *production costs* increase in proportion to output in the long run, average total costs, including *product development costs*, will fall as the scale of output rises. The influence of such once-and-for-all costs is that, other things being equal, they cause average total costs to be falling over the entire range of output.[4]

The technology of large-scale production

A third and very important source lies in technology. Large-scale production can use more specialized and highly efficient machinery than smaller-scale production. It can also lead to greater specialization of human tasks, with a resulting increase in human efficiency.

Even the most casual observation of the differences in production techniques used in large and small plants will show that larger plants use greater specialization. An example, drawn from the electricity industry, is discussed in Box 9.2.

These differences arise because large, specialized equipment is useful only when the volume of output that the firm can sell justifies employment of that equipment. For example, assembly-line techniques, body-stamping machinery, and multiple-boring engine block machines in car production are economically efficient only when individual operations are repeated thousands of times. Use of elaborate harvesting equipment (which combines many individual tasks that would otherwise be done by hand and by tractor) provides the least-cost method of production on a big farm, but not on a few acres. Typically, as the level of planned output increases, capital is substituted for labour

---

[3] For example, consider a cubic container with metal sides, bottom, and lid, all of which measure 1 metre by 1 metre. To build this container, 6m² of metal is required (six sides, each 1m²), and it will hold 1 cubic metre of gas or liquid. Now increase all of the lengths of each of the container's sides to 2m. Now 24m² of metal is required (six sides, each 4m²), and the container will hold 8m³ of gas or liquid (2m × 2m × 2m). So increasing the amount of metal in the container's walls fourfold has the effect of increasing its capacity eightfold.

[4] This phenomenon is popularly referred to as 'spreading one's overhead'. It is similar to what happens in the short run when average fixed costs fall with output. The difference is that fixed short-run production costs are variable long-run production costs. If the firm increases its scale of output for some product, it will incur more capital costs in the long run when a larger plant is built. However, its costs of developing that product are not affected.

Box 9.2 Economies of scale in the electricity industry

In the 1940s, 1950s, and 1960s, major economies of scale in electricity generation in the UK came from the use of larger and larger generators: from 30 MW (= 30,000 kilowatt) generating sets in 1948 to 100 MW sets in 1956, 200 MW sets in 1959, and 500 MW sets in 1966.

Since the 1970s there has been little increase in the size of generators, with the largest now being installed at 660 MW. Furthermore, total generating capacity has been declining since 1980. The cause is a decline in the demand for energy, because of the decline of British manufacturing and the superior energy efficiency of newer technologies such as chips and fibre optics.

In spite of the absence of further economies in the size of generators after 1970, and in spite of the decline in overall capacity after 1980, methods of gaining scale economies were still being found. The new method was to reduce the *number* of power stations, each station having several generators. As a result, the average capacity of each power station has continued to rise significantly, bringing a different type of economy of scale. The number of power stations fell from 233 in 1965 to 174 in 1978 to 78 in 1987. The average capacity of these stations rose from 147 MW in 1965 to 324 MW in 1974 to 671 MW in 1987.

Costs were also reduced by exploring economies of scale in the bulk transmission of electricity. The 'Supergrid' of 400 kV (= 400,000 volt) transmission lines which was built in the 1960s replaced three lines operating at 275 kV and 18 lines operating at 132 kV, without a corresponding increase in costs.

Economies of scale have allowed the industry to cope with rising *real* prices of its main inputs—coal and labour—without raising the real price of electricity. During the 1960s the real price of oil, the major alternative fuel, was falling owing to the increasing exploitation of economies of scale

in oil tankers delivering crude oil from the Middle East. In response, the UK electricity industry was able to reduce the real price of electricity, which is one of the reasons why electricity was adopted more and more widely in preference to other fuels.

Privatization did not change the cost structure of the industry immediately, partly because producers were locked into three-year contracts to buy coal. After this period shifts were made to cheaper, imported coal and, where new capacity was required, to the adoption of the cheaper technology of combined cycle gas turbines (CCGT). There are mild economies of scale with current technology (in 2002) as size increases from 240 MW to 480 MW, but bigger generators do not deliver significant further scale economies.

Strictly speaking, scale economies refer to the effects of increasing output *along* a negatively sloped LRAS curve as a result of rising output within the confines of known technology, while changes in technological knowledge *shift* the LRAS curve. As this example shows, the two forces usually become mixed in most real-world applications. The rise in demand for electricity in the three decades of the 1950s, 1960s, and 1970s required an increase in output. The rise in output made the use of higher-capacity equipment possible and thus provided an incentive for the development of such equipment. No fundamental new knowledge was required, but the details of the technology of larger generators had to be developed through research rather than being taken from already existing blueprints.

Competitive forces continue to put pressure on producers to reduce costs. The main pressures now are on cutting costs through productivity gains rather than exploiting further economies of even-larger-scale production of individual plants and distribution systems.

and complex machines are substituted for simpler ones. Robotics is a contemporary example. Electronic devices can handle huge numbers of operations quickly, but unless the level of production requires such a large volume of operations, robotics or other forms of automation will not provide the least-cost method of production.

Until very recently large-scale production meant mass production, sometimes referred to as 'Fordism', a system that was introduced early in the twentieth century. It was based on a very detailed division of jobs, often on a production line, in which each person did one repetitive task in co-operation with such very specialized machinery (called 'dedicated machinery'). In this technology, size was very important. Very high rates of output were required in order to reap all the scale economies available to this type of production.

In recent decades production technology has been revolutionized by what is called *flexible manufacturing*. This is a much less specialized type of production, in which workers do many tasks in co-operation with machinery that is also less specialized. One of its most important characteristics is its ability to achieve maximum efficiency with low average costs at much smaller rates of output than are required for

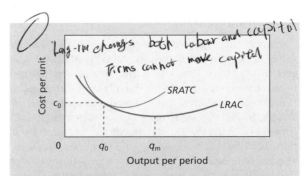

Figure 9.7 Long-run average cost and short-run average total cost curves

The short-run average total cost (*SRATC*) curve is tangent to the long-run average cost (*LRAC*) curve at the output for which the quantity of the fixed factor is optimal. The curves *SRATC* and *LRAC* coincide at output q_0, where the fixed plant is optimal for that level of output. For all other outputs there is too little or too much plant and equipment, and *SRATC* lies above *LRAC*. If some output other than q_0 is to be sustained, costs can be reduced to the level of the long-run curve when sufficient time has elapsed to adjust the size of the firm's fixed capital.

The output q_m is the lowest point on the firm's long-run average cost curve. It is called the firm's *minimum efficient scale* (MES), and it is the output at which long-run costs are minimized.

Box 9.3 **The revolution in flexible manufacturing**

Production techniques have recently been revolutionized by the introduction, in many industries and in many countries, of *flexible manufacturing*, or, as it is sometimes called, *lean production techniques*.* This is the most fundamental change to occur since Henry Ford brought mass production to full development early in the twentieth century.

Mass production methods are based on specialization and division of labour. They use skilled personnel to design products and production methods, and then the employment of relatively unskilled labour to produce standardized parts and assemble them using highly specialized, single-purpose machines. The result is a standardized product, made in a fairly small number of variants and produced at low cost with moderate quality. The work is repetitive, and workers are regarded as variable costs to be laid off or taken on as the desired rate of production varies.

Flexible manufacturing techniques, which were pioneered by the Japanese car industry, combined the flexibility and high quality standards of craft production with the low cost of mass production techniques. They are lean because they use fewer of all inputs, including time, labour, capital, and inventories, compared with either of the other techniques. They are flexible because the costs of switching from one product line to another are minimized. Workers are organized as teams. Each worker is able to do all the tasks assigned to the team, using equipment that is less highly specialized than that used in mass production techniques. This emphasizes individuality and initiative rather than a mind-numbing repetition of one unskilled operation. It also helps workers to identify places where improvements can be made and encourages them to follow up on these.

In mass production plants, stopping an assembly line to correct a problem at one point stops work at all points. So stopping the line is regarded as a serious matter, and keeping the assembly line running is the sole responsibility of a senior line manager. To reduce stoppages, large stocks of each part are held, and defective parts are discarded. Faults in assembly are left to be corrected until after the product has been assembled—often an expensive procedure. Stoppages are none the less frequent to correct materials supply and co-ordination problems.

In flexible manufacturing every worker has the ability to stop production whenever a fault is discovered. Parts are delivered by the suppliers to the work stations 'just in time'. Defective parts are put aside for the source of their problem to be identified. When lean methods are first introduced, stoppages are frequent as problems are identified and investigated. As the sources of such problems are found and removed work stoppages diminish, and the typical mature lean production line—where any worker can stop the line—stops much less frequently than the typical mass production assembly line, where only the line foreman can press the stop button.

Mass production firms try to reduce the costs of product design by using specialist designers. This creates problems both in co-ordinating the work of various designers and in getting good feedback from parts producers and assembly-line workers. The product design must be worked out in detail before the machine makers begin to design the specialized equipment needed to do the work.

Lean producers use design teams that work closely with production engineers and parts producers. As the new product begins to take shape, the tool designers can begin to work on their outline plans; as the product design becomes better specified, the design of the tools can similarly be more fully developed.

Although flexible manufacturing still has scale economies—unit costs fall as the volume of output increases—its main effect is to shift the whole long-run cost curve dramatically downward. These methods are also effective in the very long run in developing successful new products. Japanese motor car manufacturers using these methods have been able to achieve unit costs of production below those of mass production based North American and European car factories, which have twice their volume of output. They have also been able to lead in international competition to design new products efficiently and rapidly.

---

* The material in this box is adapted from J. P. Womack, D. T. Jones, and D. Roos, *The Machine that Changed the World* (New York: Maxwell Macmillan, 1990).

---

mass production techniques. This is further discussed in Box 9.3.

The relationship between long-run and short-run costs

The short-run cost curves and the long-run cost curves are all derived from the same production function. Each curve assumes given prices for all inputs. In the long run all inputs can be varied; in the short run some must remain fixed. The long-run average cost (LRAC) curve shows the lowest cost of producing any output when all inputs are variable. Each short-run average total cost (SRATC) curve shows the lowest cost of producing any output when one or more factors are held constant at some specific level.

No short-run cost curve can fall below the long-run curve, because the LRAC curve represents the lowest attainable cost for each possible output. As the level of output is changed, a different-sized plant is normally required to achieve the lowest attainable cost. This is shown in Figure 9.7, where the SRATC curve lies above the LRAC curve at all outputs except q_0.

As we observed earlier in this chapter, a short-run cost curve such as the SRATC curve in Figure 9.7 is one of many such curves. Each curve shows how costs vary as output is varied from a base output, holding the fixed factor at the quantity most appropriate to that output. Figure 9.8 shows a family of short-run average total cost curves along with a single long-run average cost curve. The long-run average cost curve is sometimes called an **envelope** because it encloses a series of short-run average total cost curves by being tangent to them. Each SRATC curve *is tangent to* the

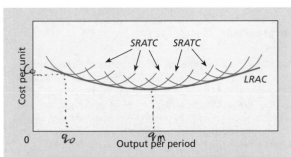

Figure 9.8 The envelope long-run average cost curve

For every point on the long-run average cost (*LRAC*) curve, there is an associated short-run average total cost (*SRATC*) curve tangent to that point. Each short-run curve shows how costs vary if output varies, with the fixed factor held constant at the level that is optimal for the output at the point of tangency. As a result, each *SRATC* curve touches the *LRAC* curve at one point and lies above it at all other points. This makes the *LRAC* curve the envelope of the *SRATC* curves.

This is the reason why the LRAC curve is the envelope of the SRATC curve.

long-run average cost curve at the level of output for which the quantity of the fixed factor is optimal, and lies above it for all other levels of output.

Shifts in cost curves

The cost curves derived so far show how cost varies with output, given constant input prices and fixed technology. Changes in input prices will cause the entire family of short-run and long-run average cost curves to shift. If a firm has to pay more for any input that it uses, the cost of producing each level of output will rise; if the firm has to pay less for any input that it uses, the cost of producing each level of output will fall.

A rise in input prices shifts the family of short-run and long-run average cost curves upward. A fall in input prices, or a technological advance, shifts the entire family of average cost curves downward.

Although input prices usually change gradually, sometimes they change suddenly and drastically. For example, between February 1999 and mid-2000 oil prices rose dramatically from around $10 per barrel to around $35 per barrel. As a result there was a rise in the cost curves of all firms that used oil and oil-related products as inputs. By early 2002 this price had fallen back to around $20 so cost curves shifted back down again.

The very long run: endogenous technical change

In the long run, profit-maximizing firms do the best they can to produce known products with the techniques and the resources currently available. This means being *on*, rather than above, their long-run cost curves. In the very long run, production techniques change. This means that the production function itself alters so that the same inputs produce more output. This in turn causes long-run cost curves to shift.

The decrease in costs that can be achieved by choosing from among the available factors of production, known techniques, and alternative levels of output is necessarily limited. In contrast, improvements by invention and innovation are potentially limitless. Hence sustained growth in living standards is critically linked to *technological change*. This was once thought to be mainly a random process, brought about by inventions made by crackpots and eccentric scientists working in garages and scientific laboratories. However, research over the last few decades has shown that this is an incorrect view.

Changes in technology are often *endogenous responses* to changing economic signals; that is, they result from responses by firms to the same things that induce the substitution of one input for another within the confines of a given technology.[5]

In our discussion of long-run demand curves in Chapter 3, we looked at just such technological changes in response to rising relative prices when we spoke of the development of smaller, more fuel-efficient cars in the wake of rising petrol prices. Similarly, much of the move to substitute capital for labour in manufacturing, transportation, communications, mining, and agriculture in response to rising wage rates has taken the form of inventing new labour-saving methods of production.

Most microeconomic theory analyses only the short- and long-run responses of the firm to various changes. In the short run, firms can change price and output within the confines of fixed plant and equipment. In the long run they can change all inputs, but within the confines of fixed technology. Such an analysis is incomplete whenever technological change is an endogenous response to economic signals. Consider, for example, a rise in the price of an important input in one country. In the short run, firms that use the input will cut back production in response to the rise in costs. In the long run, they will substitute other

[5] Many scholars on both sides of the Atlantic have been influential in establishing this key result. One of the most important books on this issue is N. Rosenberg, *Inside the Black Box: Technology and Economics* (Cambridge University Press, 1982).

inputs for the one whose price has risen. When all adjustments have been made, however, firms still find themselves at a cost disadvantage compared with competitors in other countries who have not suffered the rise in the price of their inputs. In the very long run, the domestic firms may engage in research and development designed to further reduce the use of the newly expensive inputs. If the firms succeed, they may develop processes that allow them to lower costs below those of their competitors in other countries who did not suffer the increased input prices and so did not have the same incentive to innovate.

Modern research into induced technological development has documented many such instances. As a result, the response of firms to changes in such economic signals as output prices and input costs must be studied in three steps:

1. the short-run response that changes the variable input;

2. the long-run response that consists of adjusting *all* inputs; and

3. the research and development (very long-run) response in which firms seek to innovate their way out of difficulties

caused by reductions in their product prices and/or increases in their input prices.

Studies that ignore the third set of responses ignore what are often the most important effects, once several years have elapsed.

In this context it is interesting to note that flexible manufacturing (see Box 9.3 on page 151), which revolutionized production in most industrialized countries, was first developed by Japanese car producers in response to a scale disadvantage. Because they were unable to reach the efficient scale of production when they were selling only in their small, protected, home market, they innovated their way out of these difficulties. They developed techniques that allowed them to produce a superior product at lower prices than those of their American and European competitors and so turned a long-run disadvantage into a very-long-run advantage.

Box 9.4 deals with another revolutionary change, the ability of modern science to design new materials that are appropriate for newly designed products. This ability to create new materials on demand links technological change even more closely to economic incentives than it has been in the past.

 ## Box 9.4 Endogenous materials design: a new industrial revolution?

A new industrial revolution has been in progress since the mid-1980s. It is the 'Materials Revolution'. Throughout history, an important source of technological advancement has been the development of new materials. Indeed, we label stages of history by the materials that were used—the Stone Age, the Bronze Age, the Iron Age. Many key twentieth-century advances in manufacturing would not have been possible without materials such as steel and hydrocarbons. Today, important technical progress is built upon polymers, composites, and ceramics.

Previous materials advances were usually the outcome of a process of trial and error—Edison allegedly tried many thousands of different materials and designs before he 'invented' the light bulb. Today, however, scientists are able to use knowledge of the micro structure of matter, combined with advanced computing power, to design the materials to be used in production simultaneously with the engineering of the production itself. This is having profound effects on the design of most new products and processes.

An example is found in a long-term co-operative venture between Audi and Alcoa to develop an aluminium-intensive car:

The result has been a quantum leap in weight reduction technology and automotive structural manufacturing. This revolution is embodied in the development of the aluminium space frame (ASF) and in the ability to integrate the design of the material, the product, and the manufacturing process. The ASF concept breaks away from design and manufacturing mindsets and requirements associated with steel monocoque car body structures. Moreover, the

aluminium-intensive vehicle introduced by Audi in 1994 represents a significant first step towards the development of a 'green' car which is cost effective, high-performance, low-emission and recyclable. Lower weight facilitates greater fuel efficiency and the reduction of carbon dioxide emissions while at the same time increasing stiffness and passenger safety. . . . Despite a minimum 40 per cent reduction in weight in the spaceframe, it is an extremely strong structure and provides exceptional safety for the car occupants. Aluminium absorbs more energy, on a weight to weight basis, than steel. The aluminium body structure absorbs more energy in a collision than today's steel monocoque body structures. Audi claims that the standard of safety and crashworthiness offered by the ASF has not been seen before in conventional cars.*

Another example of new materials technology can be found in sports equipment. When Björn Borg won the Wimbledon tennis tournament five times in the late 1970s, he was playing with a wooden racket. Jimmy Connors won it in 1982 playing with an aluminium alloy racket. Pete Sampras was the men's champion seven times between 1993 and 2000 playing with a graphite composite racket, a product of the materials revolution.

* Lakis C. Kaounides, 'New materials and simultaneous engineering in the car industry: the Alcoa–Audi alliance in lightweight aluminium car body structures', chapter 1 of *Manufacturing Technology* (London: Institute of Mechanical Engineers, July 1996).

SUMMARY

Varying combinations of inputs

■ In the long run, the firm will adjust all inputs to minimize the cost of producing any given level of output.

■ This requires that the ratio of an input's marginal product to its price be the same for all inputs.

■ The principle of substitution states that, when relative input prices change, firms will substitute relatively cheaper inputs for relatively more expensive ones.

■ An isoquant shows all combinations of inputs that can produce a given output. An isocost line shows all combinations of inputs that can be purchased with a given outlay.

■ Output is maximized for any given cost of inputs and input costs are minimized for any given output when production is at the point of tangency between an isoquant and an isocost line.

Cost curves in the long run

■ Long-run cost curves are often assumed to be U-shaped, indicating decreasing average costs (increasing returns to scale) followed by increasing average costs (decreasing returns to scale).

■ The long-run cost curve may be thought of as the envelope of the family of short-run cost curves, all of which shift when factor prices shift.

The very long run: endogenous technical change

■ In the very long run, innovations introduce new methods of production that alter the production function.

■ These innovations often occur in response to changes in economic incentives such as variations in the prices of inputs and outputs. They cause cost curves to shift downwards.

TOPICS FOR REVIEW

■ Conditions for long-run cost minimization

■ The principle of substitution

■ Isoquants and isocost lines

■ The duality between maximizing output for given input costs and minimizing input costs for a given output

■ The long-run envelope cost curve

■ Constant, increasing, and decreasing long-run costs

■ Invention and innovation in the very long run

DISCUSSION QUESTIONS

1 Using the production function $Q = 20(K^{0.5} L^{0.5})$, where K is machine hours per week, L is worker hours per week, and Q is output per week, calculate five different combinations of capital and labour that will generate each of the following levels of output: 20, 100, 1,000, 2,000.

2 Suppose that capital is £10 per machine hour and labour is £5 per worker-hour. By trying different values, what would be the cost-minimizing combination of capital and labour that could be used to produce each of the four levels of output listed in question 1?

3 Holding capital constant at 100 and varying labour input accordingly, calculate the short-run average cost of producing the levels of output listed in question 1 (and using the input prices set out in question 2). Repeat the exercise for the following levels of capital: 16, 25, 36, 49, 64, 81.

4 Use isoquants to show the combinations of inputs that would minimize a firm's costs, and explain what these mean for the choice of inputs that a profit-maximizing firm will use to produce a specific output.

5 What is the relationship between short-run and long-run cost curves? What is different in the very long run?

6 Explain the principle of substitution. What would be the implications for the relative employment of workers and machines of wage rates rising relative to the cost of capital?

7 Explain the differences between economies of scale, constant returns to scale, and diminishing returns to scale.

Mathematical Appendix Mathematics of scale and substitution

Returns to scale

Diminishing returns relates to the additions to output achieved holding all inputs but one constant. When we can vary all inputs, including capital, this tells us the long-term cost structure and whether there are returns to scale.

To calculate the returns to scale for a specific production function, multiply both inputs in the production function (equation (A1) of the appendix to Chapter 8 on page 141) by some constant, λ:

$$X = A(\lambda L)^{\alpha}(\lambda K^{\beta}),$$

$$X = A\lambda^{\alpha+\beta}L^{\alpha}K^{\beta}.$$

And, since $\alpha + \beta = 1$,

$$X = \lambda A L^{\alpha} K^{\beta}.$$

So multiplying both inputs by some constant, λ, multiplies the output by the same constant. This is a constant returns to scale production function.

Isoquants

To derive the isoquants, take the total derivative of (A1) (from page 141) to obtain

$$\mathrm{d}X = X_L dL + X_K dK$$

$$\mathrm{d}X = (\alpha AL^{\alpha-1}K^{\beta})dL + (\beta AL^{\alpha}K^{\beta-1})dK$$

To hold production constant, set $\mathrm{d}X = 0$. This gives

$$\frac{\mathrm{d}L}{\mathrm{d}K} = -\frac{\beta AL^{\alpha}K^{\beta-1}}{\alpha AK^{\beta}K^{\beta}}$$

$$= -\frac{\beta AL^{\alpha}L^{1-\alpha}}{\alpha AK^{\beta}K^{1-\beta}}$$

$$= -\frac{\beta L}{\alpha K} < 0.$$

So the isoquants are negatively sloped. Taking the second partial with respect to L gives

$$-\frac{\beta}{\alpha K} < 0.$$

Thus, the slope takes on larger and larger negative value as L increases and K decreases; i.e., the slope gets steeper and steeper as the isoquants approaches the L-axis and K gets smaller and smaller.

PERFECT COMPETITION

What determines how much output firms will supply? If firms are out for their own interest, how is it that they end up responding to what consumers desire? If there is competition, how is it that firms can make any profit at all? In particular, in this chapter you will learn that:

• Firms' choices are influenced by the kinds of markets in which they operate.

• In perfect competition firms produce a homogeneous product and are price-takers in their output markets.

• All profit-maximizing firms choose their output to equate marginal cost and marginal revenue.

• Under perfect competition marginal cost will equal the market price, and so the supply curve of firms is determined by the marginal cost curve.

• The long-run supply curve of a competitive industry may be positively sloped, horizontal, or negatively sloped depending on how input prices are affected by the industry's expansion.

Our main task in this chapter is to derive the supply curve for a perfectly competitive industry. We then go on to study how such an industry reacts to various forces that affect it, including changes in demand and costs.

In perfectly competitive industries, all firms produce an identical product and there are so many firms that no one of them can affect the market price by varying its own output. Since each firm can sell as much as it wants at the going price, its sales revenue is proportional to its output. For example, doubling the amount produced and sold at any constant price doubles sales revenue. In contrast, when the sale price changes as more is produced the relationship between production and revenue is more complicated. Firms that can influence their own product price are studied in Chapters 11 and 12.

The degree to which firms can influence the price of their product through their own actions depends upon market structure, a concept that needs discussion at the outset.

Market structure and firm behaviour

Does Shell compete with BP in the sale of petrol? Does HSBC Bank compete with Barclays? Does a wheat farmer from Essex compete with a wheat farmer from Somerset? If we use the ordinary meaning of the word 'compete', the answer to the first two questions is plainly yes, and the answer to the third is no.

Shell and BP both advertise extensively to persuade car drivers to buy *their* products. Gimmicks such as new mileage-stretching additives and free airmiles are used to tempt drivers to buy one brand of petrol rather than another. Most town centres in England and Wales have not only Barclays and HSBC Banks but also others such as LloydsTSB, NatWest, Halifax and Abbey National. In Scotland the choices look to be different, but many of the institutions are linked. Royal Bank of Scotland for example

owns NatWest, and Halifax is merged with the Bank of Scotland. Banks all provide similar services but work hard to attract business from each other. For example, they often offer incentives for students to open bank accounts in the hope that they will stay with that bank for life. If one bank is very successful in attracting business, it will be at the expense of its rival banks.

In the wheat market, however, there is nothing that the Essex farmer can do to affect either the sales or the profits of the Somerset farmer, and the sales and profits of the Somerset farm have no effect on those of the Essex farm.

To understand who is competing with whom and in what sense, it is useful to distinguish between the behaviour of individual firms and the *type of market* in which they operate.

Market structure and behaviour

The term **market structure** refers to the type of market in which firms operate. Markets can be distinguished by the number of firms in the market and the type of product that they sell.

Competitive market structure The competitiveness of the market depends on individual firms' power to influence market prices. *The less power an individual firm has to influence the market in which it sells its product, the more competitive that market is.*

The extreme form of competitive structure occurs when each firm has zero market power. In such a case many firms sell an identical product and each must accept the price set by the forces of market demand and market supply. The firms can sell as much as they choose at the prevailing market price and have no power to influence that price.

This extreme is called a *perfectly competitive market structure*. (Usually the term 'structure' is dropped and economists speak of a *perfectly competitive market*.) In it, there is no need for individual firms to compete actively with one another, since one firm's ability to sell its product does not depend on the behaviour of any other firm. For example, Essex and Somerset wheat farmers operate in a perfectly competitive market over which they have no power. The price of wheat is set in world markets and there are thousands of suppliers to that market in many different countries.[1]

Competitive behaviour In everyday language, the term 'competitive behaviour' refers to the degree to which individual firms actively compete with one another. For example, Shell and BP certainly engage in competitive behaviour. Both companies also have some real power over their market. Either firm could raise its prices and still continue to attract customers. Each has the power to decide, within limits set by buyers' tastes and the prices of competing products, the price that people will pay for their petrol and oil. So although they actively compete with each other, they do so in a market that does not have a perfectly competitive structure.

In contrast, Essex and Somerset wheat farmers do not engage in competitive behaviour, because the only way they can affect their revenues is by changing their outputs of (or their costs of producing) wheat.

Behaviour versus structure The distinction that we have just made explains why firms in perfectly competitive markets (e.g. Essex and the Somerset wheat farmers) do not compete actively with each other, whereas firms that do compete actively with each other (e.g. Shell and BP) do not operate in perfectly competitive markets.

The significance of market structure

The firms that make a product, or a closely related set of products, constitute an **industry**. The market demand curve for any particular product is the demand curve facing the *industry*.

When firms take their production and sales decisions, they need to know what quantity they can sell at various prices. Their concern therefore is not with the *market* demand curve for the whole industry, but rather with the demand curve for their own output. If a firm's managers know the demand curve that their own firm faces, they know the sales that their firm can make and the revenue it will earn at each possible price. If they also know their costs of production, they can calculate the profits that would be associated with each rate of output. With this information, they can choose the output that maximizes their profits.

The structure of the market in which a firm operates determines the relationship between the market demand curve for the product and the demand curve facing each individual firm in that industry. To reduce the analysis of market structure to manageable proportions, we analyse four theoretical market structures. These are called perfect competition, monopoly, monopolistic competition, and oligopoly. Monopoly and perfect competition lie at the two extremes of market structure. In monopoly the industry contains only one firm which can, therefore, set its price without concern about how a competing firm in the industry will react (since there are none). In perfect competition there are so many firms in the industry that no one of them has any any power to influence the market price for its product. Most of the actual markets lie somewhere between these extreme cases and operate in markets that are either monopolistically competitive or oligopolistic.

Perfect competition will be dealt with in the rest of this chapter; the other market structures will be dealt with in the chapters that follow.

[1] Of course government agencies may intervene to influence the price, such as in the EU Common Agricultural Policy, but this does not change the fact that individual farmers are price-takers.

Perfectly competitive markets

The perfectly competitive market structure—usually referred to simply as *perfect competition*—applies directly to a number of real-world markets. It also provides an important benchmark for comparison with other market structures.

Assumptions of perfect competition

Our analysis of **perfect competition** is built on a number of key assumptions relating to the firm and to the industry.

• **Assumption 1.** All the firms in the industry sell an identical or **homogeneous product**.

• **Assumption 2.** Buyers of the product are well informed about the characteristics of the product being sold and the prices charged by each firm.

• **Assumption 3.** The output of each firm, when it is producing at its minimum long-run average total cost, is a small fraction of the industry's total output.

• **Assumption 4.** Each firm is a **price-taker**. This means that each firm can alter its output without significantly affecting the market price of its product. Each firm must passively accept the existing market price, but it can sell as much as it wants at that price.[2]

• **Assumption 5.** There is *freedom of entry and exit*, which means that any new firm is free to enter the industry and start producing if it so wishes, and any existing firm is free to cease production and leave the industry.

The difference between the wheat farmers that we considered earlier and Shell is in *degree of market power*. Each firm that is producing wheat is an insignificant part of the whole market and thus has no power to influence the price of wheat. The oil company does have power to influence the price of petrol because its own sales represent a significant part of the total sales of petrol, even though all the firms in the industry sell a product that is close to homogeneous.[3] Box 10.1 explores further the reasons why each firm producing wheat finds the price of wheat to be beyond its influence.

A perfectly competitive market is one in which individual firms have zero market power.

Demand and revenue for a firm in perfect competition

A major distinction between firms operating in perfectly competitive markets and firms operating in any other

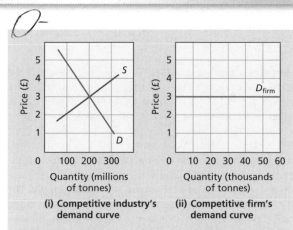

(i) Competitive industry's demand curve

(ii) Competitive firm's demand curve

Figure 10.1 The demand curve for a competitive industry and for one firm

The industry's demand curve is negatively sloped; the firm's demand curve is virtually horizontal. Notice the difference in the quantities shown on the horizontal scale in each part of the figure. The competitive industry has output of 200 million tonnes when the price is £3. The individual firm takes that market price as given and considers producing up to, say, 60,000 tonnes. The firm's demand curve in part (ii) is horizontal because any change in output that this one firm could manage would leave price virtually unchanged at £3.

type of market is in the shape of the firm's own demand curve.

In perfect competition each firm faces a demand curve that is horizontal, because variations in the firm's output have no noticeable effect on price.

The horizontal (perfectly elastic) demand curve does not mean that the firm could actually sell an infinite amount at the going price. What it does mean is that the variations in output *that it will normally be possible for the firm to make* will leave price virtually unchanged because they have only a negligible effect on the industry's total output. Figure 10.1 contrasts the demand curve for the product of a competitive industry with the demand curve facing a single firm in that industry.

---

[2] To emphasize its importance, we identify price-taking as a separate assumption, although strictly speaking it is implied by the first three assumptions.

[3] Even homogeneous commodities come in different types, for example different varieties of wheat or coffee bean. Any firm may produce more than one variety, but across firms each type and grade of a commodity is the same, e.g. super unleaded petrol or number 1 grade durum wheat.

Box 10.1 Demand under perfect competition: firm and industry

Because all products have negatively sloped market demand curves, *any* increase in the industry's output will cause *some* fall in the market price. The calculations given below show, however, that any conceivable increase that one wheat farm could make in its output has such a negligible effect on the industry's price that the farmer correctly ignores it. (For our purposes, the farm is a firm producing wheat.*)

The calculations given below arrive at the elasticity of demand facing one wheat farmer in two steps. Step 1 shows that a 200 per cent variation in the farm's output leads to only a very small percentage variation in the world price. Thus, as step 2 shows, the elasticity of demand for the farm's product is very high: 71,429!

Although the arithmetic used in reaching these measures is unimportant, understanding why the wheat farmer is a price-taker in these circumstances is vital.

Here is the argument that the calculations summarize. The market elasticity of demand for wheat is approximately 0.25. This means that, if the quantity of wheat supplied in the world increased by 1 per cent, the price would have to fall by 4 per cent to induce the world's wheat buyers to purchase the extra wheat.

Even huge farms produce a very small fraction of the total world crop. In a recent year one large farm produced 1,750 metric tonnes of wheat; this was only 0.0035 per cent of the world production of 500 million metric tonnes. Suppose that the farmer decided in one year to produce nothing and in another year managed to produce twice the normal output of 1,750 metric tonnes; this is an extremely large variation in one farm's output. The increase in output from zero to 3,500 metric tonnes represents a 200 per cent variation measured around the farm's average output of 1,750 metric tonnes. Yet the percentage increase in world output is only (3,500/500,000,000) × 100 = 0.0007 per cent. The calculations show that this increase would lead to a decrease in the world price of 0.0028 per cent (2.8p in £1,000) and would give the farm's own demand curve an elasticity of over 71,000. This is an enormous elasticity of demand. The farm would have to increase its output by over 71,000 per cent to bring about a 1 per cent decrease in the price of wheat. It is not surprising, therefore, that the

farmer regards the price of wheat as unaffected by any change in output that his one farm could conceivably make. For all intents and purposes, the wheat-producing firm faces a perfectly elastic demand curve for its product; *it is a price-taker.*

We will now proceed with the calculation of the firm's elasticity of demand (η_f) from market elasticity of demand (η_m), given the following figures:

World elasticity of demand (η_m) = 0.25,
World output = 500,000,000 metric tonnes.

A large farm with an average output of 1,750 metric tonnes varies its output between 0 and 3,500 tonnes. The variation of 3,500 tonnes represents 200 per cent of the farm's average output of 1,750 metric tonnes. This causes world output to vary by only (3,500/500,000,000) × 100 = 0.0007 per cent.

Step 1: Find the percentage change in world price. We know that the market elasticity is 0.25. This means that the percentage change in quantity must be one-quarter as large as the percentage change in price. Put the other way around, the percentage change in price must be four times as large as the percentage change in quantity. We have just seen that world quantity changes by 0.0007 per cent, so world price must change by 0.0007 × 4 = 0.0028 per cent.

Step 2: Find the firm's elasticity of demand. This is the percentage change in its *own output* divided by the resulting percentage change in the world price. This is 200 per cent divided by 0.0028 per cent. Clearly, the percentage change in quantity vastly exceeds the percentage change in price, making elasticity very high. Its precise value is 200/0.0028 or 2,000,000/28, which is 71,429.

* Strictly speaking, this box applies to wheat farmers outside of the EU. It will apply directly when the EU lowers its support price to the world price or removes it altogether. In the meantime, EU wheat farmers *do* face a perfectly elastic demand curve, because the Commission stands ready to buy all the wheat that is legally produced at its support price.

To study the revenues that each firm receives from the sales of its products, we use total, average, and marginal revenue. These are the revenue counterparts of total, average, and marginal cost that we considered in Chapters 8 and 9.

Total revenue (TR) is the total amount received by the seller from the sale of a product. If q units are sold at a price of p pounds each, $TR = p \times q$.[4]

Average revenue (AR) is the amount of revenue per unit sold. This is equal to the market price of the product.

Marginal revenue (MR), sometimes called *incremental revenue*, is the change in a firm's total revenue resulting from the sale by one extra unit. Whenever output changes by more than one unit, the change in revenue must be divided by the change in output to calculate marginal revenue. For example, if an increase in output of three units per month is accompanied by an increase in revenue of

£1,500, the marginal revenue resulting from the sale of *one extra unit* per month is £1,500/3, or £500.[5]

To illustrate each of these revenue concepts, consider a firm that is selling an agricultural product in a perfectly competitive market at a price of £3 per tonne. Because every tonne brings in £3, the average revenue per tonne sold is clearly £3. Furthermore, because each *additional*

[4] Four common ways of indicating that two variables such as p and q are to be multiplied together are $p \cdot q$, $p \times q$, $(p)(q)$ and pq.

[5] Because we use discrete changes in the text, we are, strictly speaking, using *incremental revenues*, $\Delta TR/\Delta q$. Marginal revenue is defined geometrically as the slope of the tangent to the total revenue curve at the point in question. It is defined mathematically as the first derivative of total revenue with respect to output, dTR/dq. For small changes, incremental revenue may be regarded as an approximation of marginal revenue, as we do in the text. The material in Chapter 2 pages 28–31 is once again relevant at this point.

Table 10.1 **Revenue concepts for a price-taking firm**

Quantity sold (units) (q)	Price (p)	TR = p · q	AR = TR/q	MR = ΔTR/Δq
10	£3.00	£30.00	£3.00	
11	3.00	33.00	3.00	£3.00
12	3.00	36.00	3.00	3.00
13	3.00	39.00	3.00	3.00

When price is fixed, average revenue, marginal revenue, and price are all equal to each other. The table shows the calculation of total (TR), average (AR), and marginal revenue (MR) when market price is £3.00 and the firm varies its quantity over the range from 10 to 13 units. Marginal revenue is shown between the lines because it represents the change in total revenue in response to a change in quantity. For example, when sales rise from 11 to 12 units, revenue rises from £33 to £36, making marginal revenue (36 − 33)/(12 − 11) = £3 per unit.

tonne sold brings in £3, the marginal revenue of an extra tonne sold is also £3. Table 10.1 shows calculations of these revenue concepts for a range of outputs between 10 and 13 tonnes.

The important point illustrated in the table is that, as long as the market price is unaffected by the amount the firm sells, its marginal revenue is equal to its average revenue (which is *always* equal to the price at which the output is sold). Graphically, as shown in part (i) of Figure 10.2, average revenue and marginal revenue are the same horizontal line drawn at the level of market price. Because the firm can sell any quantity it chooses at this price, the horizontal line is also the *firm's demand curve*; it shows that any quantity the firm chooses to sell will be associated with this same market price.

> If the market price is unaffected by variations in the firm's output, the firm's demand curve, its average revenue curve, and its marginal revenue curve all coincide in the same horizontal line.

This result can be stated in a slightly different way, which turns out to be important for our later work:

> For a firm in perfect competition, price equals marginal revenue.

This means, of course, that total revenue rises in direct proportion to output, as shown in part (ii) of Figure 10.2.

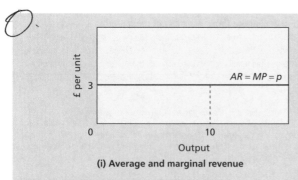
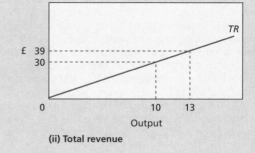

(i) **Average and marginal revenue**

(ii) **Total revenue**

Figure 10.2 Revenue curve for a firm
The demand curve for a perfectly competitive firm is a horizontal straight line. The graph shows the data in Table 10.1. Because price does not change, neither marginal nor average revenue varies with output—both are equal to price. When price is constant, total revenue is a straight line through the origin whose positive slope is the price per unit.

Short-run equilibrium

The next step is to combine information about the firm's costs and revenues to determine the level of output that will maximize its profits. We have just seen how the revenue of each price-taking firm varies with its output. In the short run, the firm has one or more fixed inputs such as its plant and machinery, and the only way in which it can change its output is by altering its variable inputs such as labour. In effect, the firm has to choose where it wants to be on its short-run cost curve (the curve we derived in Chapter 8).

Rules for all profit-maximizing firms

We start by stating three rules that apply to *all* profit-maximizing firms, whether or not they operate in perfectly competitive markets.[6]

[6] Students who know elementary calculus may like to study the mathematical derivation of these rules, given in the appendix to this chapter.

Should the firm produce at all?

The firm always has the option of producing nothing. If it exercises this option, it will have an operating loss that is equal to its fixed costs. If it decides to produce, it will add the variable cost of production to its costs and the income from the sale of its product to its revenue. Therefore, it will be worthwhile for the firm to produce as long as it can find some level of output for which revenue exceeds variable cost. However, if its revenue is less than its variable cost at *every* level of output, the firm will actually lose more by producing than by not producing.

Rule 1. A firm should not produce at all if, for *all* levels of output, the total variable cost of producing that output exceeds the total revenue derived from selling it or, equivalently, if the average variable cost of producing the output exceeds the price at which it can be sold.

The shutdown price The price at which the firm can just cover its average variable cost when producing at its most profitable level of output is called the **shutdown or break-even price**. At that price it is indifferent between producing and not producing. At any price below it, the firm will shut down. Such a price is shown in part (i) of Figure 10.6 on page 163. At the price of £2 the firm can just cover its average variable cost by producing q_0 units. Any other output would not produce enough revenue to cover variable costs. For any price below £2 there is no output at which variable costs can be covered. The price of £2 in part (i) is thus the shutdown price.

Box 10.2 deals with an interesting case of what to do with some parts of a firm's production facilities when their variable costs cannot be covered.

How much should the firm produce?

If a firm decides that (according to rule 1) production is worth undertaking, it must decide how much to produce. Common sense dictates that, on a unit-by-unit basis, if any unit of production adds more to revenue than it does to cost, producing and selling that unit will increase profits. However, if any unit adds more to cost than it does to revenue, producing and selling that unit will decrease profits. Using the terminology introduced earlier, a unit of production raises profits if the marginal revenue obtained from selling it exceeds the marginal cost of producing it; it lowers profits if the marginal revenue obtained from selling it is less than the marginal cost of producing it.

Now let a firm with some existing rate of output consider increasing or decreasing that output. If a further unit of production will increase the firm's profits, the firm should expand its output. However, if the last unit produced reduces profits, the firm should contract its output. From this it follows that the only time the firm should leave its output unaltered is when the last unit produced adds the same amount to costs as it does to revenue. These results yield the following rule.

Rule 2. Whenever it is profitable for the firm to produce some output, it should produce the output at which marginal revenue equals marginal cost.

Maximization not minimization

Figure 10.3 shows that it is possible to fulfil rule 2 and yet have profits at a minimum. Rule 3 is needed to distinguish minimum-profit from maximum-profit positions.

 ## Box 10.2 Scrap or store: what do airlines do in a downturn

The terrorist attack on New York's World Trade Center on 11 September 2001 led to a sharp downturn in demand for air travel. Many airlines soon reduced their number of flights and the number of aircraft in service. Those planes that were not expected to be put back in service for some time, if at all, were parked in the desert in the Southwest of the United States. They are stored there as the dry air means that the metal planes will not rust as they would in a moist climate.

Airlines could consider selling their unwanted planes, but the second-hand value is very low when most other airlines have excess capacity at the same time. The planes that are 'parked' tend to be older models and planes that have already had many years of service. Eventually, decisions will have to be taken about whether the plane should be sold, put back into service or broken up for the value of the spare parts that can be stripped out. This decision will clearly be based on whether the average variable cost of running (and restoring) an old plane will be less than the average variable cost of running other planes in the fleet, which in turn remains less than the average total cost of buying new planes.

The following is an extract from a newspaper article on this subject.

Airlines will be forced to scrap planes worth $1.3 billion [£910 million] that were grounded during the traffic downturn caused by the September 11 terrorist attack.

Research by Boeing, the aircraft maker, reveals that two-thirds of the 2000 planes grounded after the attacks will not return to the skies. They are likely to be used for spares or scrapped altogether.

Airline analysts said the aircraft would be worth about $1m each as scrap. . . . A new aircraft can cost up to $80m.

The cut will be the largest cull of the world's commercial fleet. Usually, about 250 aircraft are scrapped each year. . . . Large American firms have used the downturn to bring forward the retirement of swathes of their fleet. American Airlines, for example, has decided to rationalise its fleet from 11 plane types to six. (Dominic O'Connell, *Sunday Times*, Business Section, 24 March 2002, page 3)

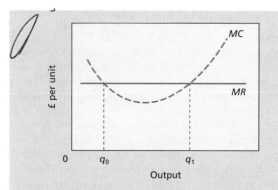

Figure 10.3 Two outputs where marginal cost equals marginal revenue

The equality of marginal cost and marginal revenue is necessary, but not sufficient, for profit maximization. $MC = MR$ at outputs q_0 and q_1. Output q_0 is a minimum-profit position because a change of output in either direction will increase profit: for outputs below q_0 marginal cost exceeds marginal revenue and profits can be increased by *reducing* output, while for outputs above q_0 marginal revenue exceeds marginal cost and profits can be increased by *increasing* output. Output q_1 is a maximum-profit position, since at outputs just below it marginal revenue exceeds marginal cost and profit can be increased by *increasing* output towards q_1; while at outputs just above it marginal cost exceeds marginal revenue and profit can be increased by *reducing* output towards q_1.

Rule 3. An output where marginal cost equals marginal revenue may be either profit-maximizing or profit-minimizing. Profit maximization requires that marginal cost be less than marginal revenue at slightly lower outputs and that marginal cost exceed marginal revenue at slightly higher outputs.

The geometric implication of this condition is that at the profit-maximizing output the marginal cost curve should intersect the marginal revenue curve from below. This ensures that MC is less than MR to the left of the profit-maximizing output and greater than MR to the right of the profit-maximizing output.

The optimum output

The above three rules determine the output that will be chosen by any firm that maximizes its profits in the short run. This output is called the firm's **profit-maximizing output**, and sometimes its **optimum output**.

• The firm's optimum output is zero if total revenue is less than total variable cost at all levels of output; the optimum output is positive if there is any output for which total revenue equals or exceeds total variable cost.

• When the firm's optimum output is positive, it is where marginal cost equals marginal revenue.

• If output is reduced slightly from the optimum level, marginal cost must be less than marginal revenue; if output

is increased slightly from the optimum level, marginal cost must exceed marginal revenue.

Rule 2 applied to price-taking firms

Rule 2 tells us that any profit-maximizing firm that produces at all will produce at the point where marginal cost equals marginal revenue. However, we have already seen that for price-taking firms marginal revenue is the market price. Combining these two results leads us to an important conclusion.

A firm that is operating in a perfectly competitive market will produce the output that equates its marginal cost of production with the market price of its product (as long as price exceeds average variable cost).

In a perfectly competitive industry, the market determines the price at which the firm sells its product. The firm then produces the output that maximizes its profits. This is the output for which price equals marginal cost.

When the firm has reached a position where its profits are maximized, it has no incentive to change its output, because it is doing as well as it can do given the market situation. Therefore, unless prices or costs change, the firm will continue to produce that output. The firm is in *short-run equilibrium*, as illustrated in Figure 10.4. (The long run is considered later in this chapter.) In summary:

In a perfectly competitive market each firm is a price-taker and a quantity-adjuster. It pursues its goal of profit maximization by producing the output that equates its short-run marginal cost with the price of its product that is determined by the market.

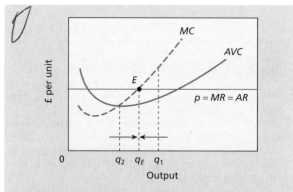

Figure 10.4 The short-run equilibrium of a firm in perfect competition

The firm chooses the output for which $p = MC$ above the level of AVC. When price equals marginal cost, as at output q_E, the firm loses profits if it either increases or decreases its output. At any point to the left of q_E, say q_2, price is greater than marginal cost, and it pays to increase output (as indicated by the left-hand arrow). At any point to the right of q_E, say q_1, price is less than marginal cost, and it pays to reduce output (as indicated by the right-hand arrow).

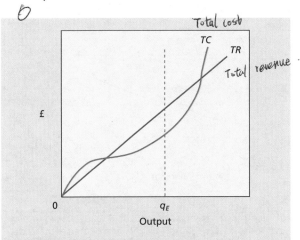

Figure 10.5 Total cost and revenue curves

The firm chooses the output for which the gap between the total revenue and the total cost curves is the largest. At each output the vertical distance between the *TR* and TC curves shows by how much total revenue exceeds or falls short of total cost. In the figure the gap is largest at output q_E, which is thus the profit-maximizing output.

Figure 10.4 shows the equilibrium of the firm using average cost and revenue curves. We can, if we wish, show the same equilibrium using total cost and revenue curves. Figure 10.5 combines the total cost curve first drawn in Figure 8.3 with the total revenue curve first shown in Figure 10.2. It shows the profit-maximizing output as the output with the largest positive difference between total revenue and total cost. This must of course be the same output as we located in Figure 10.4 by equating marginal cost and marginal revenue.

Short-run supply curves

We have seen that in a perfectly competitive market the firm responds to a price that is set by the forces of demand and supply. By adjusting the quantity it produces in response to the current market price, the firm helps to determine the market supply. The link between the behaviour of the firm and the behaviour of the competitive market is provided by the *industry supply curve,* which is also called the *market supply curve.*

The supply curve for one firm

The firm's supply curve is derived in part (i) of Figure 10.6, which shows a firm's marginal cost curve and four alternative prices. The horizontal line at each price is the firm's demand curve when the market price is at that level. The firm's marginal cost curve gives the marginal cost corresponding to each level of output. We require a supply curve that shows the quantity that the firm will supply at each

price. For prices below average variable cost, the firm will supply zero units (rule 1). For prices above average variable cost, the firm will equate price and marginal cost (rule 2, modified by the proposition that $MR = p$ in perfect competition). This leads to the following conclusion.

In perfect competition the firm's supply curve is its marginal cost curve for those levels of output for which marginal cost is above average variable cost.

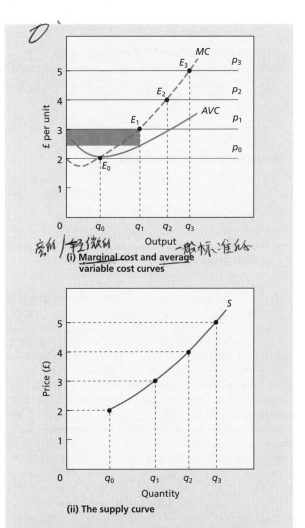

Figure 10.6 The supply curve for a price-taking firm

For a price-taking firm the supply curve has the same shape as its *MC* curve above the level of *AVC*. The point E_0, where price p_0 equals *AVC*, is the shutdown point. As price rises from £2 to £3 to £4 to £5, the firm increases its production from q_0 to q_1 to q_2 to q_3. If, for example, price were £3, the firm would produce output q_1 and be earning the contribution to fixed costs shown by the shaded rectangle.

The firm's supply curve is shown in part (ii). It relates market price to the quantity the firm will produce and offer for sale. It has the same shape as the firm's *MC* curve for all prices above *AVC*.

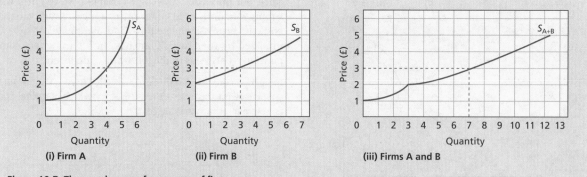

Figure 10.7 The supply curve for a group of firms

The industry supply curve is the horizontal sum of the supply curves of each of the firms in the industry. At a price of £3 firm A would supply 4 units and firm B would supply 3 units. Together, as shown in part (iii), they would supply 7 units. In this example, because firm B does not enter the market at prices below £2, the supply curve S_{A+B} is identical to S_A up to price £2 and is the sum of S_A and S_B above £2.

The supply curve of an industry

To illustrate what is involved, Figure 10.7 shows the derivation of an industry supply curve for an industry containing only two firms. The general result is as follows.

In perfect competition the industry supply curve is the horizontal sum of the marginal cost curves of all firms in the industry (above the level of average variable cost).

The reason for summing the marginal cost curves is that each firm's marginal cost curve shows how much it will supply at each given market price, and the industry supply curve is the sum of what each firm will supply. The reason for the qualification 'above the level of average variable cost' is that, as rule 1 shows, the firm will not produce at all if price is less than its average variable cost.

This supply curve, based on the short-run marginal cost curves of all the firms in the industry, is the industry's supply curve that was first encountered in Chapter 3. We have now established the profit-maximizing behaviour of individual firms that lies behind that curve. It is sometimes called a **short-run supply curve** because it is based on the short-run, profit-maximizing behaviour of all the firms in the industry. This distinguishes it from a *long-run supply curve*, which relates quantity supplied to the price that rules in long-run equilibrium when all inputs are variable (which we study later in this chapter).

Short-run equilibrium price

The price of a product sold in a perfectly competitive market is determined by the interaction of the industry's short-run supply curve and the market demand curve. Although no one firm can influence the market price significantly, the collective actions of all firms in the industry (as shown by the industry supply curve) and the collective actions of consumers (as shown by the market demand curve) together determine the equilibrium price. This occurs at the point where the market demand curve and the industry supply curve intersect.

At the equilibrium price each firm is producing and selling a quantity for which its marginal cost equals price. Given their fixed inputs, all firms are maximizing their profits and so have no incentive to alter output in the short run. Because total quantity demanded equals total quantity supplied, there is no reason for market price to change. Thus, the market and all the firms in the industry are in short-run equilibrium.

Short-run profitability of the firm

We know that when an industry is in short-run equilibrium each firm is maximizing its profits. However, we do not know *how large* these profits are. It is one thing to know that a firm is doing as well as it can, given its particular circumstances; it is another thing to know how well it is doing.

Figure 10.8 shows three possible positions for a firm in short-run equilibrium. In all cases the firm is maximizing its profits by producing where price equals marginal cost, but the size of the profits is different in each case. In part (i) the firm is suffering losses. In part (ii) it is just covering all of its costs—it is just breaking even. In part (iii) it is making pure profits because average revenue exceeds average total cost. In part (i) we could say that the firm is minimizing its losses rather than maximizing its profits, but both statements mean the same thing. In all three cases the firm is doing as well as it can, given its costs and the market price.

(a) No perfect - monopoly - no competitors.
SR = short-Run.

CHAPTER 10: PERFECT COMPETITION   165

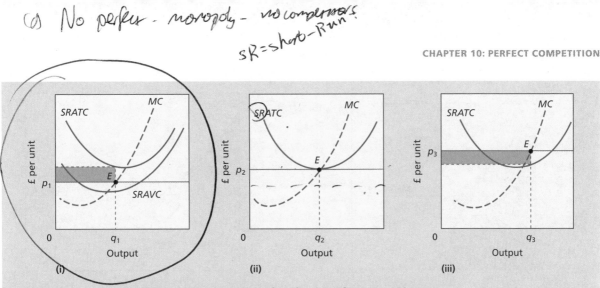

Figure 10.8 Alternative short-run equilibrium positions for a firm in perfect competition

When it is in short-run equilibrium, a competitive firm may be suffering losses, breaking even, or making profits. The diagram shows a firm with given costs faced with three alternative prices, p_1, p_2, and p_3. In each part E is the point at which $MC = MR =$ price. Since in all three cases price exceeds AVC, the firm is in short-run equilibrium.

In part (i) price is p_1. Because price is below average total cost, the firm is suffering losses shown by the light blue area. Because price exceeds average variable cost, the firm continues to produce in the short run. Because price is less than ATC, the firm will not replace its capital as it wears out.

In part (ii) price is p_2 and the firm is just covering its total costs. It will replace its capital as it wears out since its revenue is covering the full opportunity cost of its capital.

In part (iii) price is p_3 and the firm is earning pure profits in excess of all its costs, as shown by the dark blue area. As in part (ii) the firm will replace its capital as it wears out.

The Market price is exactly = the short-run total cost.
The firm will replace its capital as it wears out since its revenue is covering the full opportunity cost of its capital.

The allocative efficiency of perfect competition

We saw in Chapter 1 that resources are allocated by markets in which people make independent decisions motivated by self-interest. Under certain conditions this market outcome is *optimal* or *efficient*. (These two words mean the same thing in this context.) Resources are efficiently allocated if there is no other allocation that would allow someone to be made better off while no one was made worse off. To put this statement the other way around, resources are *inefficiently* allocated if the allocation could be changed in such a way as to make at least one person better off while making no one worse off. For example, if resources could be reallocated so as to make fewer hats and more shoes and someone would be made better off by the change while no one would be made worse off, then the current allocation cannot be efficient.

It can be shown that a perfectly competitive economy would allocate its resources efficiently. However, a number of other conditions also need to be fulfilled, as we will see in Chapter 19. In the meantime we will show one way in which the tendency for perfect competition to produce an optimal allocation of resources can be established. We do this using the concepts of consumers' and producers' surplus.

We saw in Chapter 6 that consumers' surplus is the difference between the total value that consumers place on all the units consumed of some product and the payment that they actually make for the purchase of that product. The total value that they place on the amount they consume is the area under the demand curve, which represents the summation of all the marginal valuations they place on each separate unit consumed. What they pay is the area representing the price multiplied by the quantity consumed. The difference between these two is shown in Figure 10.9 as consumers' surplus.

Producers' surplus is analogous to consumers' surplus. It occurs because all units of each firm's output are sold at the single market price, while, given a rising supply curve, the marginal cost of all but the last unit is less than the market price. **Producers' surplus** is defined as the amount that producers are paid for a product less the total variable cost of production. The total variable cost of producing any output is shown by the area under the supply curve up to that output, which represents the summation of the marginal costs of producing each unit of output.[7] Thus, producers'

---

[7] Recall from Chapter 2 pages 30–1 that the area under a marginal cost curve up to any output is the total variable cost of producing that output. Graphically, taking the area under a marginal cost curve is equivalent to summing all the marginal costs to get total variable cost. Similarly, summing the area under the demand curve yields the total amount that consumers would be willing to pay if offered each unit one at a time, i.e. the total valuation they place on all the units.

[handwritten: The competitive equilibrium E maximizes the sum of consumer's and producer's surplus.]

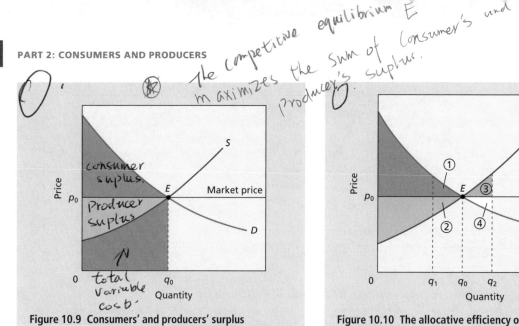

Figure 10.9 Consumers' and producers' surplus

Consumers' surplus is the area under the demand curve and above the market price line. Producers' surplus is the area above the supply curve and below the market price line. The equilibrium price and quantity are p_0 and q_0. The total value that consumers place on q_0 units of the product is given by the sum of the dark red, light red, and dark blue areas. The amount that they pay is p_0q_0, the rectangle that consists of the light red and dark blue areas. The difference, shown as the dark red area, is *consumers' surplus*.

The receipts to producers from the sale of q_0 units are also p_0q_0. The area under the supply curve, the blue-shaded area, is total variable cost, the minimum amount that producers require to supply the output. The difference, shown as the light red area, is *producers' surplus*.

[handwritten: The diff between revenue and variable cost = produce's surplus.]

Figure 10.10 The allocative efficiency of perfect competition

Competitive equilibrium is allocatively efficient because it maximizes the sum of consumers' and producers' surplus. At the competitive equilibrium E consumers' surplus is the dark red area above the price line, while producers' surplus is the light yred area below the price line.

Reducing the output to q_1 but keeping price at p_0 lowers consumers' surplus by area 1 and lowers producers' surplus by area 2. If producers are forced to produce output q_2 and sell it to consumers, who are in turn forced to buy it at price p_0, producers' surplus is reduced by area 3 (the amount by which variable costs exceed revenue on those units), while consumers' surplus is reduced by area 4 (the amount by which expenditure exceeds consumers' satisfactions on those units). Only at the competitive output, q_0, is the sum of the two surpluses maximized.

surplus, which is shown in Figure 10.9, is the area between the supply curve and the market price line. (All firms are either directly or indirectly owned by people, so producers' surplus is really owners' surplus.)

If the total of consumers' surplus and producers' surplus is not maximized, the industry's output could be altered to increase that total. The additional surplus could then be used to make some people better off without making any others worse off.

Allocative efficiency occurs where the sum of consumers' and producers' surpluses is maximized.

The allocatively efficient output occurs under perfect competition where the demand curve intersects the supply curve, that is, at the point of equilibrium in a competitive market. This is shown graphically in Figure 10.10. For any output that is less than the competitive output the demand curve lies above the supply curve, which means that the value consumers put on the last unit of production exceeds its marginal cost of production. Suppose, for example, that an additional pair of shoes costs £60 to make but is valued by consumers at £70. If the shoes are sold at any price between £60 and £70, both producers and consumers

gain; there is £10 of potential surplus to be divided between the two. In contrast, the last unit produced and sold at competitive equilibrium adds nothing to either consumers' or producers' surplus. This is because consumers value it at exactly its market price, and it adds the full amount of the market price to producers' cost.

If production was pushed beyond the competitive equilibrium, the sum of the two surpluses would fall. Assume, for example, that firms were forced to produce and sell further units of output at the competitive market price and that consumers were forced to buy these extra units at that price. (Neither group would do so voluntarily.) Firms would lose producers' surplus on those extra units because their marginal costs of producing them would be above the price that they received for them. Purchasers would lose consumers' surplus because the valuation that they placed on these extra units, as shown by the demand curve, would be less than the price that they would have to pay.

The sum of producers' and consumers' surpluses is maximized when a perfectly competitive industry is in equilibrium with demand equal to supply. The resulting level of output is allocatively efficient.

Long-run equilibrium

In perfect competition, the forces that produce long-run equilibrium of the industry are created by the entry and exit of firms.

The effect of entry and exit

Firms in *short-run equilibrium* may be making profits, suffering losses, or just breaking even. Because costs include the opportunity cost of capital, firms that are just breaking even are doing as well as they could do by investing their capital elsewhere. Thus, there will be no incentive for such firms to leave the industry. Similarly, if new entrants expect just to break even, there will be no incentive for firms to enter the industry, because capital can earn the same return elsewhere in the economy. If, however, existing firms are earning revenues in excess of all costs, including the opportunity cost of capital, new capital will enter the industry attracted by these profits. If existing firms are suffering losses, capital will leave the industry because a better return can be obtained elsewhere in the economy. This process of entry and exit is an important driver of the dynamics of a market economy, so it is worth looking at in a little more detail.

An entry-attracting price

First, suppose that all firms in a competitive industry are in the position of the firm shown in part (iii) of Figure 10.8 on page 165. Attracted by the profitability of existing firms, new firms will enter the industry. If, for example, in response to the high profits that the 100 existing firms are making, 20 new firms enter, the market supply curve that formerly added up the outputs of 100 firms at each price must now add up the outputs of 120 firms. At any price, more will be supplied because there are more producers.

With an unchanged market demand curve, this shift in the short-run industry supply curve means that the previous equilibrium price will no longer prevail. The increase in supply will lower the equilibrium price, and both new and old firms will have to adjust their output to this new price. This is illustrated in Figure 10.11. New firms will continue to enter, and the equilibrium price will continue to fall, until all firms in the industry are just covering their total costs. Firms will then be in the position of the firm shown in part (ii) of Figure 10.8, which is called a *zero-profit equilibrium*.

Profits in a competitive industry create an incentive for the entry of new firms; the industry will expand, pushing price down until the profits fall to zero.

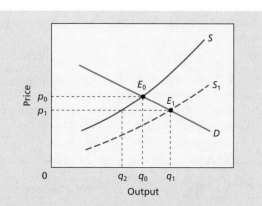

Figure 10.11 New entrants shift the supply curve
The supply curve shifts to the right and the equilibrium price falls. The entry of new firms shifts the supply curve to S_1, the equilibrium price falls from p_0 to p_1, while output rises from q_0 to q_1. Before entry only q_2 would have been produced at this price. The extra output is supplied by the new firms.

An exit-inducing price

Now suppose that the firms in the industry are in the position of the firm shown in part (i) of Figure 10.8. Although the firms are covering their variable costs, the return on their capital is less than the opportunity cost of capital. They are not covering their total costs. This is a signal for the exit of firms. Old plants and equipment will not be replaced as they wear out. As a result the industry's short-run supply curve shifts leftward, and the market price rises. Firms will continue to exit, and the market price will continue to rise, until the remaining firms can cover their total costs, that is, until they are all in the zero-profit equilibrium illustrated in part (ii) of Figure 10.8. The exit of firms then ceases.

Losses in a competitive industry create an incentive for the exit of firms; the industry will contract, driving the market price up until the remaining firms are just covering their total costs.

The break-even price

Firms exit an industry when they are making losses and enter when attracted by positive profits. There is no further entry or exit when firms are just covering all their costs. This means that:

The long-run equilibrium of a competitive industry occurs when firms are earning zero profits.

The firm in part (ii) of Figure 10.8 is in a zero-profit, long-run equilibrium. For that firm, the price p_0 is its shutdown or break-even price. It is the price at which all costs, including the opportunity cost of capital, are being covered. The firm is just willing to stay in the industry. It has no incentive to leave, nor do other firms have an incentive to enter.

Profit seeking generates movement of resources between different industries. Freedom of entry combined with profit seeking tends to push profit towards zero in any industry, whether or not it is perfectly competitive.

Box 10.3 uses the theory just developed to investigate the costs and benefits of changes in input prices.

Marginal and intramarginal firms

If firms have an incentive to exit from an industry, which ones will leave? Here it is useful to distinguish marginal from intramarginal firms. The marginal firm is just covering its full costs and would exit if price fell by even a small amount. The intramarginal firm is earning profits and would require a larger fall in price to persuade it to exit. In the pure abstract model of perfect competition, however, all firms are marginal firms in long-run equilibrium. All firms have access to the same technology, and all, therefore, will have identical cost curves when enough time has passed for full adjustment of all capital to be made. In

---

 Box 10.3   **Who benefits and loses from changes in input costs?**

A fall in the cost of production causes a downward shift in each firm's marginal cost curve. As a result the short-run supply curve, which is the sum of the individual firms' marginal cost curves, shifts downwards. This leads to a higher output and a lower price. The price will fall, however, by less than the fall in costs, while profits will now be earned because of the lower costs of production. These changes are shown in the figure.

A fall in costs in a competitive industry leads to a fall in price, an increase in output, and the emergence of profits. In part (i) the original demand and supply curves of D and S_0 intersect at E_0 to yield a price and quantity of p_0 and q_0. When each firm's production costs fall, the supply curve—which is the sum of the marginal cost curves of all firms in the industry—shifts downward by the amount of the fall in costs, to S_1. If price fell by the full amount that costs had fallen, price would become p_2. Instead, price falls to p_1 while quantity rises to q_1, at the new equilibrium E_1.

In part (ii) the typical firm is shown in equilibrium at price p_0 with cost curves $SRATC_0$ and MC_0. The cost curves then shift to $SRATC_1$ and MC_1. The firm would be willing to produce output q_0 at price p_2. Instead, price falls only to p_1, and the firm increases its output to q_1. At this price–quantity combination it earns profits shown by the dark blue area.

In the short run under perfect competition a fall in variable cost causes price to fall, but by less than the reduction in marginal cost. The benefit of the reduction in cost is thus shared between consumers, in terms of lower prices, and producers, in terms of profits.

In the long run, however, profits cannot persist in an industry with freedom of entry. New firms will enter the industry, increasing output and reducing price until all profits are eliminated. Their entry shifts the short-run supply curve to the right. Now each firm, old and new, just covers its total costs by producing at the minimum point on its average total cost curve.

Under perfect competition, all of the benefits of lower costs are passed on to consumers in terms of higher output and lower prices in the long run.

The case of a rise in costs is just the reverse. In the short run the effects will be shared between consumers, in terms of higher prices, and producers, in terms of losses. In the long run, however, firms will leave the industry until those remaining can cover all their costs. Therefore, the long-run effects of higher costs are fully borne by consumers in terms of lower output and higher prices.

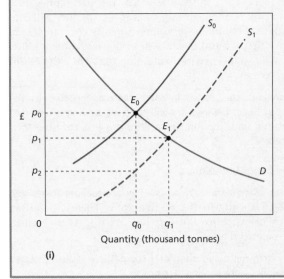

(i)

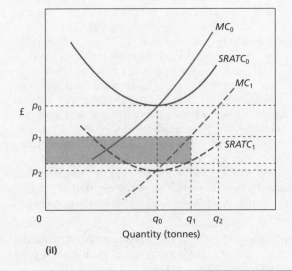

(ii)

long-run industry equilibrium, all firms are thus in position (ii) in Figure 10.8. If price falls below p_2 in that figure, all firms wish to withdraw. Exit must then be by some contrived process, such as random lot, since there is nothing in the theory to explain who will exit first.

In real-world situations firms are not identical, since technology changes continually and different firms have different histories. A firm that has recently replaced its capital is likely to have more efficient, lower-cost plant and hence lower cost curves than a firm whose capital is ageing. The details of each practical case will then determine the identity of the marginal firm that will exit first when price falls. For example, assume that all firms have identical costs and differ only in the date at which they entered the industry. In this case the firm whose capital comes up for replacement first will be the marginal firm. It will exit first because it will be the first to confront the long-run decision about replacing its capital in a situation where no firms are covering long-run opportunity costs.

Box 10.4 shows how the theory can be used to understand some of the effects of technological changes that lower production costs.

A more detailed analysis of the long run

Consider the position of the firms and the industry when both are in long-run equilibrium. There is no change that any firm could make over the short or the long run that would increase its profits. This requirement can be stated as three distinct conditions.

1. *No firm wants to vary the output of its existing plants.* Short-run marginal cost (SRMC) is equal to price.

2. *Profits earned by existing plants are zero.* This implies that short-run ATC is equal to price—that is, firms are in the position of the firm in Figure 10.8(ii).

3. *No firm could earn profits by building a plant of a different size.* This implies that each existing firm must be producing at the lowest point on its long-run average cost curve.

We have already seen why the first two conditions must hold. The reasoning behind the third condition is shown in Figure 10.12. Although the firm with the average cost curve $SRATC_0$ is in short-run equilibrium, it is not in long-run equilibrium because its LRAC curve lies below the market price at some higher levels of output.[8] The firm can, therefore, increase its profits by building a plant of larger size, thereby lowering its average total costs. Since the firm is a price-taker, this change will increase its profits.

A price-taking firm is in long-run equilibrium only when it is producing at the minimum point on its LRAC curve.

All three of the conditions listed above are fulfilled when each firm in the industry is in the position shown in Figure 10.12 by the short-run cost curve $SRATC^*$.[9]

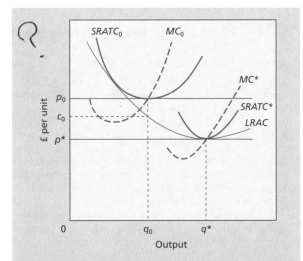

Figure 10.12 Short-run and long-run equilibrium of a firm in perfect competition

A perfectly competitive firm that is not at the minimum point on its LRAC curve cannot be in long-run equilibrium. The firm's existing plant has short-run cost curves $SRATC_0$ and MC_0 while market price is p_0. The firm produces q_0, where MC_0 equals price and total costs are just being covered. Although the firm is in short-run equilibrium, it can earn profits by building a larger plant and so moving downwards along its LRAC curve. Thus, the firm cannot be in long-run equilibrium at any output below q^*, because average total costs can be reduced by building a larger plant.

If all firms do this, industry output will increase and price will fall until long-run equilibrium is reached at price p^*. Each firm is then in short-run equilibrium with a plant whose average cost curve is $SRATC^*$ and whose short-run marginal cost curve, MC^*, intersects the price line p^* at an output of q^*. Because the LRAC curve lies above p^* everywhere except at q^*, the firm has no incentive to move to another point on its LRAC curve by altering the size of its plant. The output q^* is the firm's minimum efficient scale.

Long-run response to a change in demand

What will happen if demand for the product increases? Price will rise to equate demand with the industry's short-run supply. Each firm will expand output until its short-run marginal cost once again equals price. Each firm will earn profits as a result of the rise in price, and the profits will induce new firms to enter the industry. This will shift

---

[8] Because all inputs are variable in the long run, no distinction is needed between variable and fixed costs. There is only one long-run average cost curve.

[9] The text discussion implies that all existing firms and all new entrants face identical LRAC curves. This means that all firms face the same set of input prices and use the same technology. We are in the long run, *where technological knowledge is given and constant*, and where all firms have had a chance to adjust their capital to the best that is available. This is a theoretical construction designed to analyse tendencies. In any industry in which technological change is ongoing, full long-run equilibrium will never be established and a variety of technologies will be used by different firms at each point in time.

Box 10.4 **The effects of changing technology**

A once-and-for-all change

To see the effects of a single advance in an industry's production technology, let the industry start in long-run equilibrium where each firm is earning
zero profits. Some technological development in the industry's production
process now lowers the production costs of newly built plants. In this case,
as with many technological changes, old production facilities cannot use
the technology because it must be embodied in new plant and equipment.
Since initially the price was just equal to the average total cost for the
existing plants, new plants will be able to earn profits and they will be built
immediately. But this expansion in capacity shifts the industry's short-run
supply curve to the right and drives price down.

The expansion in capacity and the fall in price will continue until price is
equal to the average total cost of the new plants. At this price old plants will
not be covering their long-run costs. As long as price exceeds their average
variable cost, however, they will continue in production. As the outmoded
plants wear out, they will gradually disappear. Eventually a new long-run
equilibrium will be established in which all plants use the new technology.
Output will be larger, price will be lower, and the new plants will be just
covering their total costs.

Ongoing changes

Now ask what happens in a competitive industry in which this type of technological change occurs more or less continuously. Plants built in any one
year will tend to have lower costs than plants built in any previous year. The
figure illustrates such an industry. Plant 1 is the oldest plant in operation. It
is just covering its average variable costs, and it will close down when price
falls below p_0. Plant 2 is of intermediate age. It is covering its variable costs
and earning some contribution towards its fixed costs, as shown by the
shaded area in part (ii). Plant 3 is the newest plant with the lowest costs. It
is fully covering its fixed costs as shown by the dark shaded area in (iii). It is

also making additional profits (shown by the light shaded area) which will
offset the losses it expects to suffer later, when firms with newer technology
enter the industry.

Such an industry typically has a number of interesting characteristics.

First, plants in operation will be of many different ages and at different
levels of efficiency. This is dramatically illustrated by the variety of types and
vintages of generator found in any long-established electricity industry.
Critics who observe the continued use of older, less efficient plants and urge
that the industry be modernized miss the point of economic efficiency. If the
plant is already there, it can be operated profitably as long as it can cover its
variable costs.

A second characteristic of such an industry is that price will be governed
by the minimum average total cost of the most efficient plants. Entry
will continue until plants of the latest vintage are just expected to cover the
opportunity cost of their capital over their lifetimes. This means that new
plants must earn pure profits when they enter to balance the losses they
expect later in life when newer firms with superior technologies enter the
industry. The benefits of the new technology are passed on to consumers,
because all units of the product, whether produced by new or old plants, are
sold at a price that is related solely to the average total cost of the new
plants. Owners of older plants find their returns over variable costs falling
steadily as increasingly efficient plants drive the price down.

A third characteristic is that old plants will be discarded when the
price falls below their average total costs. This may occur well before the
plants are physically worn out. In industries with continuous technical
progress, capital is usually discarded because it is economically obsolete,
not because it has physically worn out. This illustrates the economic meaning of 'obsolete'.

**Old capital is obsolete when its average variable cost exceeds the
average total cost of new capital.**

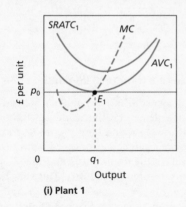

(i) Plant 1

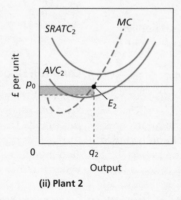

(ii) Plant 2

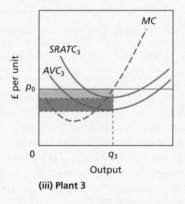

(iii) Plant 3

the short-run supply curve to the right and force down the
price. Entry will continue until all firms are once again just
covering average total costs.

What if demand falls? The industry starts with firms in
long-run equilibrium, as shown in Figure 10.12, and the
market demand curve shifts left and price falls. There are
two possible consequences.

First, the decline in demand may force price below ATC
but leave it above AVC. Firms are then in the position
shown in Figure 10.8(i). They can cover their variable costs
and earn some return on their capital, so they remain in
production for as long as their existing plant and equipment lasts. Exit will occur, however, as old capital wears
out and is not replaced. As firms exit, the short-run supply

Box 10.5 Declining industries

What happens when a competitive industry begins to suffer losses because the demand for its output begins to decline? The market price will begin to fall, and firms that were previously covering average total costs will no longer be able to do so. They find themselves in the position shown in part (i) of Figure 10.8 on page 165. Firms suffer losses instead of breaking even; the signal for the exit of capital is given, but exit takes time.

The economically efficient response to a steadily declining demand is for a firm to continue to operate with existing equipment as long as its variable costs of production can be covered. As equipment becomes obsolete because it cannot cover even its variable cost, it will not be replaced unless the new equipment can cover its total cost. As a result the capacity of the industry will shrink. If demand keeps declining, capacity must keep shrinking.

Declining industries typically give a depressing impression. Revenues are below long-run total costs, and as a result new equipment is not brought in to replace old equipment as it wears out. The average age of equipment in use thus rises steadily. An observer, seeing the industry's plight, is likely to blame it on the old equipment.

The antiquated equipment in a declining industry is often the effect rather than the cause of the industry's decline.

Governments are often tempted to support declining industries because they are worried about the resulting job losses. Experience suggests, however, that propping up genuinely declining industries only delays their demise—at significant national cost. When the government finally withdraws its support, the decline is usually more abrupt and hence more difficult to adjust to than it would have been had the industry been allowed to decline gradually under the market force of steadily declining demand.

Once governments recognize the decay of certain industries and the collapse of certain firms as an inevitable aspect of economic growth, a more effective response is to provide temporary income support and retraining schemes that cushion the impacts of change. These can moderate the effects on the incomes of workers who lose their jobs and make it easier for them to transfer to expanding industries. Intervention that is intended to increase mobility while reducing the social and personal costs of mobility is a viable long-run policy. In contrast, trying to freeze the existing industrial structure by shoring up a declining industry is not viable in the long run.

---

curve shifts left and market price rises. This continues until the remaining firms in the industry can cover their total costs. At this point it will pay to replace capital as it wears out, and the industry will stop declining. This adjustment may take a long time, for the industry shrinks in size only as existing plant and equipment wears out.

The second possibility is that the decline in demand is large enough to push price below the level of AVC. Now firms cannot even cover their variable costs, and some will shut down immediately. Reduction in capital devoted to production in the industry occurs rapidly because some existing capacity is scrapped or shifted to other uses. The decline in the number of firms reduces supply and raises the equilibrium price. Once the price rises enough to allow the remaining firms to cover their variable costs, the rapid withdrawal of capital ceases. Further exit occurs more slowly, as described in the previous paragraph.

Entry of new capital into a profitable industry can take place only as fast as new plants can be built and new equipment installed. Exit of existing capital from an unprofitable industry with losses will occur very quickly when price is less than average variable cost, but only at the rate at which old plant and equipment wears out when price exceeds average variable cost.

Now we can see the answer to one of the questions posed at the beginning of the chapter. Although each firm seeks only its own profit and does not consider the benefit of consumers, it is led to react to consumers' tastes. If tastes for the product rise so that the demand curve shifts to the right, firms produce more output with their given fixed

inputs in the short run and allocate more of all inputs to the production of this product in the long run.

Box 10.5 applies what we have just learned to the case of declining industries.

The long-run industry supply curve

Possible adjustments of the industry to the kind of changes in demand just discussed are shown by the **long-run industry supply (LRS) curve**. This curve shows the relationship between equilibrium market price and the output that firms will be willing to supply after all desired entry or exit has occurred.

The long-run supply curve shows the quantity supplied at each market price in long-run equilibrium, that is, after all demand-induced changes have occurred and the incentives for exit and entry have been eliminated.

For given input prices, the long-run supply (LRS) curve of a competitive industry will be horizontal. But when induced changes in input prices are considered, it is possible for the LRS curve to be positively or negatively sloped. The various cases are illustrated in Figure 10.13.

In Figure 10.13(i) the long-run supply curve is horizontal. This indicates that, given time, the industry will adjust its size to provide whatever quantity is demanded at a constant price. That price is set by the minimum point of the firms' long-run average cost curves. An industry with a horizontal long-run supply curve is said to be a *constant-cost industry*.

This case occurs when a change in the size of the industry leaves the long-run cost curves of existing firms unchanged,

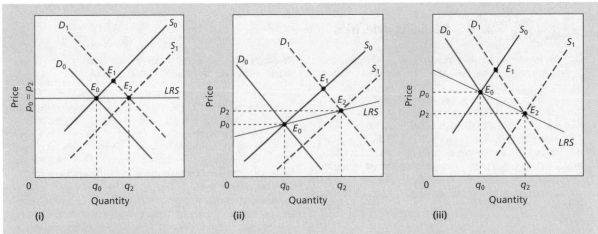

Figure 10.13 Long-run industry supply curves

The long-run industry supply curve may be horizontal, or positively or negatively sloped. In all three parts the initial curves are at D_0 and S_0, yielding equilibrium at E_0 with price p_0 and quantity q_0. A rise in demand shifts the demand curve to D_1, taking the short-run equilibrium to E_1. New firms now enter the industry, shifting the short-run supply curve outwards and pushing price down until pure profits are no longer being earned. At this point the supply curve is S_1 and the new equilibrium is E_2 with price at p_2 and quantity q_2. In part (i) price returns to its original level, making the long-run supply curve horizontal. In part (ii) profits are eliminated before price falls to its original level, giving the *LRS* curve a positive slope. In part (iii) the price falls below its original level before profits return to normal, giving the *LRS* curve a negative slope.

which requires that the industry's input prices do not change as the whole industry's output expands or contracts. Since all firms are assumed to have access to the same technology and face the same input prices, all firms have identical cost curves. Under these circumstances the long-run equilibrium with price equal to minimum long-run average total cost of each and every firm can be re-established after a change in demand only when price returns to its original level.

Changing input prices and rising long-run supply curves
When an industry expands its output it needs more inputs. The increase in demand for these inputs may bid up their prices.[10]

If costs rise with increasing levels of industry output, so too must the price at which the producers are able to cover their costs. As the industry expands, the short-run supply curve shifts outwards but the firms' SRATC curves shift upward because of rising input prices. The expansion of the industry comes to a halt when price is equal to minimum LRAC for existing firms. This must occur at a higher price than ruled before the expansion began, as illustrated in Figure 10.13(ii). A competitive industry with rising long-run supply prices is often called a *rising-cost industry*.

Can the long-run supply curve decline? So far we have suggested that the long-run supply curve may be horizontal or positively sloped. Could it ever decline, thereby indicating that higher outputs are associated with lower prices in long-run equilibrium?

It is tempting to answer 'yes', because of the opportunities of more efficient scales of operation using greater mechanization and more effective specialization of labour. But this answer would not be correct for perfectly competitive industries, because each firm in long-run equilibrium must already be at the lowest point on its LRAC curve. If a firm could lower its costs by building a larger, more mechanized plant, it would be profitable to do so without waiting for an increase in demand. Since any single firm can sell all it wishes at the going market price, it will be profitable to expand the scale of its operations as long as its LRAC is falling.

The scale economies that we have just considered are within the control of the firm; they are said to be **internal economies**. A perfectly competitive industry might, however, have falling long-run costs if industries that supply its inputs have increasing returns to scale. Such effects are outside the control of the perfectly competitive firm and are called **external economies**. Whenever expansion of an industry leads to a fall in the prices of some of its inputs, the firms will find their cost curves shifting downwards as they expand their outputs.

---

[10] In a fully employed economy, the expansion of one industry implies the contraction of some other industry. What happens to input prices depends on the proportions in which the expanding and contracting industries use the inputs. The relative price of the input used intensively by the expanding industry will rise, causing the costs of the expanding industry to rise relative to those of the contracting industry. In a two-sector, two-input model a rising long-run industry supply curve is normal because of the effect that changes in industry outputs have on relative input prices.

As an illustration of how the expansion of one industry could cause the prices of some of its inputs to fall, consider the early stages of the growth of the car industry. As the output of cars increased, the industry's demand for tyres grew considerably. This increased the demand for rubber and tended to raise its price, but it also provided the opportunity for tyre manufacturers to build larger plants, which exploited some of the economies available in tyre production. These economies were large enough to offset any input-price increases, and tyre prices charged to car manufacturers fell. Thus, car costs fell, because of lower prices of an important input. This case is illustrated in part (iii) of Figure 9.13. An industry that has a negatively sloped long-run supply curve is often called a *falling-cost industry*.

Notice that, although the economies were external to the car industry, they were internal to the tyre industry. However, if the tyre industry had been perfectly competitive, all its scale economies would already have been exploited. So this is a case of a perfectly competitive industry using an input produced by a non-competitive industry, whose own scale economies have not yet been fully exploited because demand is insufficient. Another example is provided by perfectly competitive agricultural industries; they buy their farm machinery from the farm-implement industry, which is dominated by a few large firms.

Can perfectly competitive industries have unexploited scale economies?

The key to answering this question lies in the size of the firm relative to the size of the market.

A competitive firm will never be in equilibrium on the falling part of its LRAC—if price is given and costs can be reduced by increasing the scale of output, profits can also be increased by doing so. Thus, firms will grow in size until all scale economies are exhausted. Provided that the output that yields the minimum LRAC for each firm is small relative to the industry's total output, the industry will contain a large number of firms and will remain competitive. If, however, reaching the minimum LRAC makes firms so large that each one has significant market power, they will cease to be price-takers and then perfect competition will cease to exist. Indeed, scale economies may exist over such a large range that one firm's LRAC is still falling when it serves the entire market. That firm will then grow until it monopolizes the entire market. This case, which economists call a *natural* monopoly, is considered further in later chapters.

A necessary condition for a long-run perfectly competitive equilibrium is that any scale economies that are within the firm's control should be exhausted at a level of output that is small relative to the whole industry's output.

Conclusion

Perfect competition is a special case that exists in only a few sectors where the product is homogeneous. This applies to primary commodity industries, but it does not apply to most of the goods and services purchased by consumers. The bread and washing powder in Sainsbury's and Tesco may be identical, but supermarkets are not operating under perfect competition as they have some power over their prices, and their brands make their shopping experience differentiated products. Most other consumer products are even more affected by brands and product differentiation.

Hence the perfect competition model is not directly applicable to most retail markets for goods and services.

However, the perfect competition model gives us some key insights into the working of any market economy. It gives us a simple example within which to understand the principles of profit maximization. It highlights the incentive role played by profits in driving entry and exit of firms. Finally, it provides the benchmark for the optimal allocation of resources. All of these insights have a payoff in later chapters.

SUMMARY

Market structure and firm behaviour

■ Competitive *behaviour* refers to the extent to which individual firms compete with each other to sell their products. Competitive *market structure* refers to the power that individual firms have over the market—perfect competition occurring where firms have no market power and hence no need to react to each other.

Perfectly competitive markets

■ The theory of perfect competition is based on the following assumptions: firms sell a homogeneous product; customers are well informed; each firm is a price-taker; the industry can support many firms, which are free to enter or leave the industry.

Short-run equilibrium

■ Any firm maximizes profits by producing the output where its marginal cost curve intersects the marginal revenue curve from below—or by producing nothing if average variable cost exceeds price at all outputs.

■ A perfectly competitive firm is a quantity-adjuster, facing a perfectly elastic demand curve at the given market price and maximizing profits by choosing the output that equates its marginal cost to price.

■ The supply curve of a firm in perfect competition is its marginal cost curve, and the supply curve of a perfectly competitive industry is the sum of the marginal cost curves of all its firms. The intersection of this curve with the market demand curve for the industry's product determines market price.

The allocative efficiency of perfect competition

■ Perfect competition produces an optimal allocation of resources because it maximizes the sum of consumers' and producers' surplus by producing equilibrium where marginal cost equals price.

Long-run equilibrium

■ Long-run industry equilibrium requires that each individual firm be producing at the minimum point of its LRAC curve and be making zero profits.

■ The long-run industry supply curve for a perfectly competitive industry may be (i) positively sloped, if input prices are driven up by the industry's expansion, (ii) horizontal, if plants can be replicated and factor prices remain constant, or (iii) negatively sloped, if some other industry that is not perfectly competitive produces an input under conditions of falling long-run costs.

TOPICS FOR REVIEW

■ Competitive behaviour and competitive market structure
■ Behavioural rules for the profit-maximizing firm
■ Price-taking and a horizontal demand curve
■ Average revenue, marginal revenue, and price under perfect competition

■ Relation of the industry supply curve to its firms' marginal cost curves
■ The role of entry and exit in achieving long-run equilibrium
■ Exhaustion of scale economies in perfectly competitive long-run equilibrium

DISCUSSION QUESTIONS

1 A firm sells its product at £15 each. Calculate its total, average and marginal revenue at sales levels of 100, 500, and 10,000.

2 Suppose that total fixed costs of the firm in question 1 are £300 and total variable costs for production levels between 100 and 108 units of output are:

100 = £1000
101 = £1010
102 = £1021
103 = £1033
104 = £1046
105 = £1060
106 = £1075
107 = £1091
108 = £1108

What is the profit-maximizing level of output, given a sale price of £15 as in question 1?

3 Calculate the average variable cost and the average total cost associated with the output levels in question 2. How much profit is made at the profit-maximizing level of output? How much profit would be made at the two higher and two lower levels of output? What would be the profit-maximizing output and profit at a sales price of £12?

4 Which of the following observed facts about an industry are inconsistent with its being perfectly competitive? (*a*) Different firms use different methods of production. (*b*) The industry's product is extensively advertised by a trade association.

(*c*) Individual firms devote a large fraction of their sales receipts to advertising their own product brands. (*d*) There are 24 firms in the industry. (*e*) All firms made economic profits in 2003. (*f*) All firms are charging the same price.

5 What are the three rules of profit maximization? Explain these rules in the context of a firm that is in a perfectly competitive market structure.

6 Suppose all of the potentially arable land in some country is currently being used for growing either wheat or barley. Both crop markets are in equilibrium. Discuss exactly how decentralized competitive markets would respond to shift resources following a report that barley helps to reduce cancer risk.

7 Why would the existence of entry barriers make it unlikely that an industry would be perfectly competitive? What types of entry barriers do you think are important in practice? How can the existence of economies of scale affect the degree of competitiveness in a market?

8 How does technical progress affect the equilibrium of a firm and of the perfectly competitive industry in which it operates? Why do some industries decline while others grow? At what point should firms quit a declining industry?

9 What factors determine the shape of the long-run supply curve of an industry?

10 What is allocative efficiency? Why is the outcome under perfect competition allocatively efficient?

Appendix A mathematical derivation of the rules of profit maximization

In this appendix we provide formal derivations of the three rules for profit maximization. The first derivation uses only algebra and can be read by anyone. The second and third use elementary calculus and should not be attempted by those who are unfamiliar with simple derivatives.

Rule 1 Profits, π, are defined as follows:

$$\pi = R - (F + V),$$

where R is total revenue, F is total fixed cost, and V is total variable cost. Now let subscript n stand for a state where there is no production and p for one where there is production. It pays the firm to produce if there is at least one level of production for which

$$\pi_p \geq \pi_n.$$

When the firm does not produce, R and V are zero, so the above condition becomes

$$R - F - V \geq -F$$

or

$$R \geq V.$$

Dividing both sides by output, q, we get

$$price \geq AVC.$$

Rule 2

$$\pi = R - C,$$

where C is total cost $(F + V)$. Both revenues and costs vary with output, i.e. $R = R(q)$ and $C = C(q)$. Thus we may write

$$\pi = R(q) - C(q).$$

A necessary condition for the maximization of profits is[11]

$$\frac{d\pi}{dq} = R'(q) - C'(q) = 0$$

or

$$R'(q) = C'(q).$$

But these derivatives define marginal revenue and marginal cost, so we have

$$MR = MC.$$

Rule 3 To ensure that we have a maximum and not a minimum for profits, we require

$$\frac{d^2\pi}{dq^2} = R''(q) - C''(q) = \frac{dMR}{dq} - \frac{dMC}{dq} < 0$$

or

$$\frac{dMR}{dq} < \frac{dMC}{dq},$$

which means that the algebraic value of the slope of the marginal cost curve must exceed, at the point of intersection, the algebraic value of the slope of the marginal revenue curve. This translates into the geometric statement that the marginal cost curve should cut the marginal revenue curve from below.

---

[11] Note the convenient use of a prime $(')$ for a derivative. Thus, for the function $F(X)$, the two notations d/dX and $F'(X)$ mean the same thing, as do d^2/dX^2 and $F''(X)$.

Chapter 11

MONOPOLY

How does a firm choose its profit-maximizing output when it is the only producer and so faces the downward-sloping market demand curve? What price would this firm set? Does a monopolist have unlimited power to exploit consumers by charging them whatever price it pleases? These are some of the questions that we address in this chapter. In particular, you will learn that:

• A monopolist sets marginal cost equal to marginal revenue, but marginal cost is less than price.

• Output is lower under monopoly than under perfect competition.

• Profit can be increased for a monopolist if it is possible to charge different prices to different customers or in separate markets.

• Pure profits exist in the long run under monopoly, so long as there are entry barriers.

• Cartels can increase the profits of colluding firms, but individual members have an incentive to break away.

Monopoly is at the opposite extreme from perfect competition. A **monopoly** occurs when one firm, called a monopolist or a monopoly firm, produces an industry's entire output. In contrast to perfectly competitive firms, which are price-takers, a monopolist sets the market price.

In the first part of this chapter we show that when a monopoly firm must charge a single price for its output it will produce less, charge a higher price, and earn greater profits than firms operating under perfect competition. Next, we explain why all monopoly firms have an incentive to charge different prices to different classes of users or on different units sold to the same user. We also see that monopoly profits provide a strong incentive for new firms to enter the industry, and that this will happen unless there are effective barriers to entry, of either a natural or a man-made variety. In the final part of the chapter we analyse how groups of firms can band together to form a cartel that raises profits by acting as if it were a monopoly.

In this chapter we analyse mainly the positive implications of monopoly. In Chapter 19 we discuss the normative public policy issues posed by monopoly.

A single-price monopolist

We first analyse the price and output decision of a monopoly firm that charges a single price for its product. The firm's profits, like those of all firms, will depend on the relationship between its production costs and its sales revenues.

Cost and revenue in the short run

We saw in Chapter 8 that U-shaped short-run cost curves are a consequence of the law of diminishing returns. The law of diminishing returns applies to the conditions under which goods are produced rather than to the market structure in which they are sold. Thus, monopoly firms have

U-shaped short-run cost curves just as perfectly competitive firms do.[1]

Because the monopoly firm is the only firm in its industry, there is no distinction between the market demand curve and the demand curve facing a single firm as there is in perfect competition. Thus, the monopoly firm faces a negatively sloping market demand curve and can set its own price. However, this negatively sloped market demand

---

[1] Some monopolies may arise because the minimum efficient scale of production is large relative to the market demand. We discuss this case, which is known as the *natural monopoly*, later in the chapter, and we return to a discussion of the public policy issues that arise in Chapter 19.

curve presents the monopoly firm with a trade-off: sales can be increased only if price is reduced, and price can be increased only if sales are reduced.

Average and marginal revenue

When the monopoly firm charges the same price for all units sold, average revenue per unit is identical to price. Thus, the market demand curve is also the firm's *average revenue curve*. But unlike the firms in perfect competition, the monopoly firm's demand curve is not its marginal revenue curve, which shows the change in total revenue resulting from the sale of an additional (or marginal) unit of production. Because its demand curve is negatively sloped, the monopoly firm must lower the price that it charges on *all* units in order to sell an *extra* unit.

It follows that the addition to its revenue resulting from the sale of an extra unit is less than the price that it receives for that unit (less by the amount that it loses as a result of cutting the price on all the units that it was selling already).

The monopoly firm's marginal revenue is less than the price at which it sells its output.

This proposition is illustrated in Figure 11.1.

To clarify these relationships, we use a numerical example of a specific straight-line demand curve. Some points on this curve are shown in tabular form in Table 11.1 while the whole curve is shown in Figure 11.2. Notice in the table

Table 11.1 Total, average, and marginal revenue

Price $p = AR$	Quantity q	Total revenue $TR = p \cdot q$	Marginal revenue $MR = \Delta TR / \Delta q$
£9.10	9	£81.90	£8.10
9.00	10	90.00	7.90
8.90	11	97.90	

Marginal revenue is less than price because price must be lowered to sell an extra unit. The marginal revenue of the eleventh unit is total revenue when 11 units are sold minus total revenue when 10 units are sold. This is £7.90, which is less than the price of £8.90 at which all 11 units are sold. Marginal revenue is the £8.90 gained from selling the extra unit at £8.90 minus £0.10 lost on each of the 10 units already being sold when their price falls from £9.00 to £8.90.

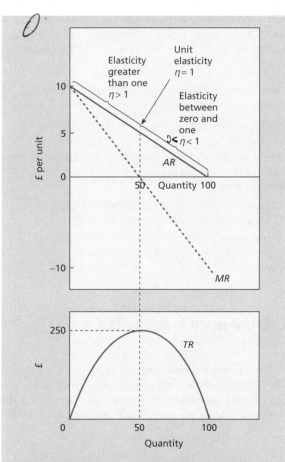

Figure 11.2 Revenue curves and demand elasticity

Rising *TR*, positive *MR*, and elastic demand all go together, as do falling *TR*, negative *MR*, and inelastic demand. In this example, for outputs from 0 to 50 marginal revenue is positive, elasticity is greater than one, and total revenue is rising. For outputs from 50 to 100 marginal revenue is negative, elasticity is less than unity, and total revenue is falling. (All elasticities refer to absolute not algebraic values.)

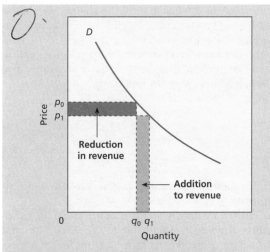

Figure 11.1 The effect on revenue of an increase in quantity sold

Because the demand curve has a negative slope, marginal revenue is less than price. A reduction of price from p_0 to p_1 increases sales by one unit from q_0 to q_1 units. The revenue from the extra unit sold is shown as the medium blue area. But to sell this unit, it is necessary to reduce the price on each of the q_0 units previously sold. The loss in revenue is shown as the dark blue area. Marginal revenue of the extra unit is equal to the *difference* between the two areas.

that the change in total revenue associated with a change of £0.10 in price is recorded between the rows corresponding to three different prices. The data show what happens when the price is changed from the value shown in one row to the value shown in the adjacent row.

Notice also from Figure 11.2 that, when price is reduced starting from £10, total revenue rises at first and then falls. The maximum total revenue is reached in this example at a price of £5. Since marginal revenue is the change in total revenue resulting from the sale of one more unit of output, marginal revenue is positive over the range where total revenue is increasing, and it is negative where total revenue is falling.[2]

The proposition that marginal revenue is always *less than* average revenue, which has been illustrated numerically in Table 11.1 and graphically in Figure 11.2, provides an important contrast with perfect competition. Recall that in perfect competition the firm's marginal revenue from selling an extra unit of output is *equal to* the price at which that unit is sold. The reason for the difference is not difficult to understand. The perfectly competitive firm is a price-taker; it can sell all it wants at the given market price. The monopoly firm faces a negatively sloped demand curve; it must reduce the market price in order to increase its sales.

Marginal revenue and elasticity

In Chapter 4 we discussed the relationship between the elasticity of the market demand curve and the total revenue derived from selling the product. Figure 11.2 summarizes this earlier discussion for a linear demand curve and extends it to cover marginal revenue.[3]

Over the range in which the demand curve is elastic, total revenue rises as more units are sold; marginal revenue must, therefore, be positive. Over the range in which the demand curve is inelastic, total revenue falls as more units are sold; marginal revenue must, therefore, be negative.

Short-run monopoly equilibrium

To show the profit-maximizing equilibrium of a monopoly firm, we bring together information about its revenues and its costs and then apply two rules developed in Chapter 10. First, the firm should not produce at all unless there is some level of output for which price is at least equal to average variable cost. Second, if the firm does produce, its output should be set at the point where marginal cost equals marginal revenue.

When the monopoly firm equates marginal cost with marginal revenue, it reaches the equilibrium shown in Figure 11.3. The profit-maximizing output is the level at which marginal cost equals marginal revenue. The point on the demand curve corresponding to that output determines the price at which that output can be sold.

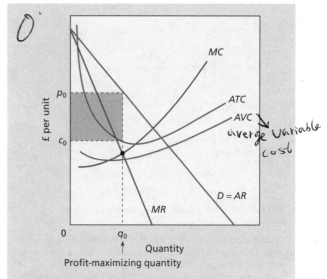

Figure 11.3 The equilibrium of a monopoly

The monopoly maximizes its profits by producing where marginal cost equals marginal revenue. The monopoly produces the output q_0 for which marginal revenue equals marginal cost (rule 2). At this output the price of p_0—which is determined by the demand curve—exceeds the average variable cost (rule 1). Total profits are the profits per unit of $p_0 - c_0$ multiplied by the output of q_0, which is the dark blue area.

When the monopoly firm is in profit-maximizing equilibrium, equating marginal revenue with marginal cost, both are less than the price it charges for its output.

This is because the firm's marginal revenue is always less than the price it charges.

Elasticity of demand for a monopolist

The relationship between elasticity and revenue discussed above has an interesting implication for the monopoly firm's equilibrium. Because marginal cost is always greater than zero, a profit-maximizing monopoly (which must produce where $MR = MC$) will always produce where marginal revenue is positive, that is where demand is elastic. If the firm were producing where demand was inelastic it could reduce its output, thereby increasing its total revenue and reducing its total costs and hence increasing its profits. No such restriction applies in perfect competition. Each

[2] Notice that the marginal revenue shown in the table is obtained by subtracting the total revenue associated with one price from the total revenue associated with another, lower, price and then apportioning the change in revenue among the extra units sold. In symbols, it is $\Delta TR/\Delta q$.

[3] See the appendix to Chapter 4 on page 76 for a mathematical investigation of the relationship between marginal revenue and elasticity.

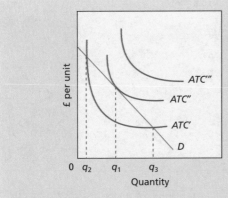

Figure 11.4 Alternative profit possibilities for a monopolist

Profit maximization means only that the monopoly is doing as well as it can do. The figure shows one demand curve and three alternative cost curves. With the curve ATC''' there is no positive output at which the monopolist can avoid making losses. With the curve ATC'' the monopolist covers all costs at output q_1, where the ATC curve is tangent to the D curve. With the curve ATC' profits can be made by producing at any output between q_2 and q_3. (The profit-maximizing output will be some point between q_2 and q_3, where $MR = MC$, which is not shown on the diagram.)

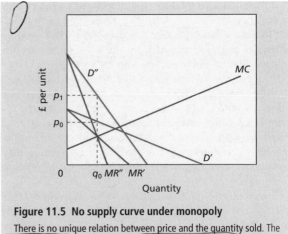

Figure 11.5 No supply curve under monopoly

There is no unique relation between price and the quantity sold. The demand curves D' and D'' both have marginal revenue curves that intersect the marginal cost curve at output q_0. But because the demand curves are different, q_0 is sold at p_0 when the demand curve is D', and at p_1 when the demand curve is D''.

firm faces a perfectly elastic demand curve whatever the elasticity of the market demand curve at that price. Thus, the equilibrium can occur where the market demand curve is either elastic or inelastic.

Monopoly profits

The fact that a monopoly firm produces the output that maximizes its profits tells us nothing about how large these profits will be, or even whether there will be any profits at all. Figure 11.4 illustrates this by showing three alternative average total cost curves: one where the monopoly firm can earn pure profits, one where it can just cover its costs, and one where it makes losses at any level of output.

No supply curve for a monopoly

In perfect competition the industry short-run supply curve depends only on the marginal cost curves of the individual firms. This is true because, under perfect competition, profit-maximizing firms equate marginal cost with price. Given marginal costs, it is possible to know how much will be produced at each price. In contrast, a monopoly firm's output is not solely determined by its marginal cost. Let us see why.

As with all profit-maximizing firms, the monopolist equates marginal cost to marginal revenue; but marginal revenue does not equal price. Hence the monopoly does *not* equate marginal cost to price. In order to know the amount produced at any given price, we need to know the market

demand curve as well as the marginal cost curve. Under these circumstances, it is possible for different demand conditions to cause the same output to be sold at different prices. This is illustrated in Figure 11.5 by an example in which two monopolists facing the same marginal cost curves but different demand curves sell identical outputs at different prices. An important conclusion follows from this.

For a monopoly firm, there is no unique relationship between market price and quantity supplied.

Firm and industry

Because the monopolist is the only producer in an industry, there is no need for separate analysis of the firm and the industry, as is necessary with perfect competition. The monopoly firm *is* the industry. Thus, the short-run, profit-maximizing position of the firm, as shown in Figure 11.3, is also the short-run equilibrium of the industry.

Box 11.1 deals with an interesting variation of monopoly theory, the pricing of limited editions.

A multi-plant monopoly

So far we have implicitly assumed that the monopoly firm produces all of its output in a single plant. The analysis can easily be extended to a multi-plant monopolist. Assume, for example, that the firm has two plants. How will it allocate production between them? The answer is that any given output will be allocated between the two plants so as to equate their marginal costs. Let us assume that plant A was producing 30 units per week at a marginal cost of

Box 11.1 Demand for once-off production

An interesting case of monopoly pricing occurs with 'limited editions'. These are sometimes works of art—such as lithographs, prints, etchings, or woodcuts by famous artists. But limited editions are also produced of everything from cars to T-shirts and briar pipes. In 2001 the Singer Company offered a limited-edition gold coloured sewing machine with a 22k gold badge, to commemorate the 150th anniversary of the invention of the original machine. Our favourite recent example, however, is a limited edition model of a prize-winning goat called Mostyn Minival: 'A beautifully crafted limited edition of 100, each individually numbered. £110 for members and £120 for non-members.' (No we are not kidding—check out the web site www.saanenbreedsociety.org.uk for this or more recent offers!) Indeed, a recent internet search (in 2002) for 'limited edition offers' produced over 700,000 hits. This suggests that limited edition offers are a way of adding value to products, especially collectibles, by creating an image of restricted supply, which may make the product seem unusual and therefore more valuable in future.

So what is the economics of all this? The normal demand curve is for a repeated flow of purchases, period after period. In the case of limited editions, the demand is for a stock to be produced and purchased once only. The smaller the total number of items produced, the more will people value each item and the higher the price that can be charged. This gives rise to a negatively sloped demand curve.

If producers know the curve exactly and know their marginal cost of production, choosing the profit-maximizing price–quantity combination is simple. They equate marginal cost with marginal revenue. But since limited edition production and sales are not repeated period after period, producers have no chance to learn the shape of the demand curve. They must guess on the basis of the sales of earlier, more or less similar, limited editions. If they set the price too low, they will sell all their output but not at its profit-maximizing price. If they set the price too high, they will be left with unsold output, which they must destroy or re-advertise at considerable expense.

Most importantly, perhaps, the limited edition promotion is a way of creating a demand for something that would have very little intrinsic demand in the absence of scarcity value. Selling art work is a hard job for all but the most famous artists, but at least if the work is rare it has a chance of having some market value in future. We do not expect many readers to make their living out of making models of champion goats—why not try something even more unusual!

£20, while plant B was producing 25 units at a marginal cost of £17. Plant A's production could be reduced by one unit, saving £20 in cost, while plant B's production was increased by one unit, adding £17 to cost. Overall output is held constant while costs are reduced by £3. The generalization is that, whenever two plants are producing at different marginal costs, the total cost of producing their combined output can be reduced by reallocating production from the plant with the higher marginal cost to the plant with the lower marginal cost.

A multi-plant, profit-maximizing monopoly firm will always operate its plants so that their marginal costs are equal.

It is worth noting that the message that a multi-plant firm should equate marginal cost in each plant does not apply just to a monopoly: it applies to *any* firm. For any given output and any market structure, if the firm is not equating the marginal cost of production of an identical product between plants, then it is not maximizing profit. It could reduce total cost for the same output by rearranging production between its plants.

How does the multi-plant monopoly firm determine its overall marginal cost? Assume, for example, that both plants are operating at a marginal cost of £10 per unit and one is producing 14 units per week while the other is producing 16. The firm's overall output is 30 units at a marginal cost of £10. This illustrates the following general proposition:

The monopoly firm's marginal cost curve is the horizontal sum of the marginal cost curves of its individual plants.

It follows that the analysis in this chapter applies to any monopolist, no matter how many plants it operates. The marginal cost curve that we use is merely the sum of the marginal cost curves of all the plants. In the special case in which there is only one plant, the *firm's MC* curve is that *plant's MC* curve.

The allocative inefficiency of monopoly

We showed in Chapter 10 that the perfectly competitive equilibrium maximizes the sum of consumers' and producers' surpluses. Output under monopoly is lower and so must result in a smaller total of consumers' and producers' surpluses.

When the monopoly chooses an output below the competitive level, market price is higher than it would be under perfect competition. As a result, consumers' surplus is diminished, and producers' surplus is increased. In this

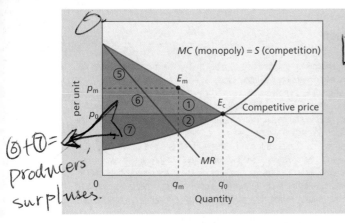

Figure 11.6 The deadweight loss of monopoly

Monopoly is allocatively inefficient because it does not maximize the sum of consumers' and producers' surpluses. At the perfectly competitive equilibrium E_c consumers' surplus is the sum of the red shaded areas 1, 5, and 6. When the industry is monopolized, price rises to p_m and consumers' surplus falls to area 5. Consumers lose area 1 because that output is not produced; they lose area 6 because the price rise has transferred it to the monopolist. Producers' surplus in a competitive equilibrium is the sum of the dark blue areas 7 and 2. When the market is monopolized and price rises to p_m, the surplus area 2 is lost because the output is not produced. However, the monopolist gains area 6 from consumers. Area 6 is known to be greater than 2 because p_m maximizes profits. Thus, areas 1 and 2 are lost to society. They represent the deadweight loss resulting from monopoly and account for its allocative inefficiency.

way, the monopoly firm gains at the expense of consumers. This is not, however, the whole story.

When the output between the monopolistic and the competitive levels is not produced, consumers give up more surplus than the monopolist gains. There is thus a net loss of surplus for society as a whole. This loss of surplus is called the *deadweight loss of monopoly*. It is illustrated in Figure 11.6.

It follows that there is a conflict between the private interest of the monopoly producer and the public interest of all the nation's consumers. This creates a rational case for government intervention to prevent the formation of monopolies if possible or, if that is not possible, to control their behaviour.

A multi-price monopolist: price discrimination

So far in this chapter we have assumed that the monopoly firm charges the same price for every unit of its product, no matter where or to whom it sells that product. We now show that a monopoly firm will also find it profitable to sell different units of the same product at different prices whenever it gets the opportunity.[4]

Raw milk is often sold at one price when it is to be used as fluid milk but at a lower price when it is to be used to make ice cream or cheese. Doctors in private practice often charge for their services according to the incomes of their patients. Cinemas often have lower admission prices for children and pensioners than for adults. Railroads charge different rates per tonne per kilometre for different products. Electricity producers sell electricity at one rate to homes and at a lower rate to firms. Airlines often charge less to people who stay over a Saturday night than to those who come and go on weekdays.

Price discrimination occurs when a seller charges different prices for different units of the same product for reasons not associated with differences in cost. Not all price *differences* represent price *discrimination*. Quantity discounts, differences between wholesale and retail prices, and prices that vary with the time of day or the season of the year may not represent price discrimination, because the same product sold at a different time, in a different place, or in different

quantities may have different costs. If an electric power company has unused capacity at certain times of the day, it may be cheaper for the company to provide service at those hours than at peak demand hours. If price differences reflect cost differences, they are not discriminatory. In contrast, when a price difference is based on different buyers' valuations of the same product, price discrimination does occur.

Some forms of price discrimination may be illegal or contrary to regulations in an industry. We make no moral judgements about whether price discrimination is a good or a bad thing. The analysis is designed merely to show that a firm that has some market power has an incentive to segment its market and charge a different price in each segment of it if it can.

Why price discrimination is profitable

Why should it be profitable for a firm to sell some units of its output at a price that is well below the price that it receives for other units of its output? Persistent price

[4] Because this practice is also prevalent in markets that contain a few large firms, called *oligopolistic* markets, the range of examples quoted covers both types of market structure.

discrimination is profitable either because different buyers are willing to pay different amounts for the same product, or because one buyer is willing to pay different amounts for different units of the same product. The basic point about price discrimination is that, in either of these circumstances, sellers may be able to capture some of the consumers' surplus that would otherwise go to buyers.

Discrimination among units of output

Look back to Table 6.2 on page 103, which shows the consumers' surplus when a person buys eight glasses of milk at a single price. If the supplier could sell each glass separately, it could capture the whole of this surplus. It would sell the first unit for £3.00, the second unit for £1.50, the third unit for £1.00, and so on until the eighth unit was sold for £0.30. The firm would get total revenues of £8.10 rather than the £2.40 obtained from selling eight units at the single price of £0.30 each.

Perfect price discrimination occurs when the firm obtains the entire consumers' surplus. This usually requires each unit to be sold at a separate price, as in the example of the previous paragraph. In practice, perfect discrimination is seldom possible. Suppose, however, that the firm could charge only two different prices, one for the first four units sold and another for the next four units sold. If it sold the first four units for £0.80 and the next four units for £0.30, it would receive £4.40—less than it would receive if it could discriminate perfectly, but more than the £2.40 it would receive if it sold all units eight at £0.30.

Discrimination between buyers in one market

If different buyers have different demand curves for some commodity, a monopoly producer can profitably discriminate by charging more to those with a higher demand for the commodity and less to those with a lower demand. We illustrate with a simple example.

Think of the demand curve in a market that is made up of individual buyers, each of whom has indicated the maximum price that he or she is prepared to pay for the single unit each wishes to purchase. Suppose, for the sake of simplicity, that there are only four buyers, the first of whom is prepared to pay any price up to £4, the second of whom is prepared to pay £3, the third £2, and the fourth £1. Suppose that the product has a marginal cost of production of £1 per unit for all units. If the selling firm is limited to a single price, it will maximize its profits by charging £3, thereby selling two units and earning profits of £4. If the seller can discriminate among each of the buyers, it could charge the first buyer £4 and the second £3, thus increasing its profits from the first two units to £5. Moreover, it could also sell the third unit for £2, thus increasing its profits to £6. It would be indifferent about selling a fourth unit because the price would just cover marginal cost.

Discrimination between markets

Many monopoly firms sell in two different markets. A firm might be the only seller in a tariff-protected home market and a price-taker in foreign markets where there is much competition. The firm would then equate its marginal cost to the price in the foreign market, like any perfect competitor. But in the domestic market it would equate marginal costs to marginal revenue, like any monopolist. As a result, it would charge a higher price on sales in the home market than on sales abroad. This case is elaborated in the appendix to this chapter.

Price discrimination more generally

We saw in Chapter 6 that demand curves have a negative slope because different units are valued differently by an individual. If tastes or incomes differ, the same unit will be valued differently by different individuals. These facts, combined with a single price for a product, are what gives rise to consumers' surplus.

The ability to charge multiple prices gives a seller the opportunity to capture some (or, in the extreme case, all) of the consumers' surplus.

The larger the number of different prices that can be charged, the greater is the firm's ability to increase its revenue at the expense of consumers.

It follows that, if a selling firm is able to discriminate through price, it can increase revenues received (and thus also profits) from the sale of any given quantity. However, price discrimination is not always possible, even if there are no legal barriers to its use.

When is price discrimination possible?

Discrimination among units of output sold to the same buyer requires that the seller be able to keep track of the units that a buyer consumes in each period. Thus, the tenth unit purchased by a given buyer in a given month can be sold at a price that is different from the fifth unit *only* if the seller can keep track of who buys what. This can be done by an electric company through its meter readings or by a magazine publisher by distinguishing between renewals and new subscriptions. It can also be done by distributing certificates or coupons that allow, for example, a car wash at a reduced price on a return visit.

Discrimination between buyers is possible only if the buyers who face the low price cannot resell the goods to the buyers who face the high price. Even though the local butcher might like to charge the banker twice as much for steak as he charges the taxi driver, he cannot succeed in doing so. The banker can always shop for meat in the supermarket, where her occupation is not known. Even if the butcher and the supermarket agreed to charge her twice as much, she could hire someone to shop for her. The surgeon, however, may succeed in discriminating (especially if other reputable surgeons do the same), because it will not do the banker much good to hire the taxi driver to have her operation for her.

Price discrimination is possible if the seller can distinguish either individual units bought by a single buyer or separate buyers into classes such that resale between classes is impossible.

The ability to prevent resale tends to be associated with the character of the product or the ability to classify buyers into readily identifiable groups. Services are less easily resold than goods; goods that require installation by the manufacturer (e.g. heavy equipment) are less easily resold than movable goods such as household appliances.

Of course, it is not enough to be able to separate different buyers or different units into separate classes. The seller must also be able to control the supply going to each group. There is no point, for example, in asking more than the competitive price from some buyers if they can simply go to other firms who will sell the good at the competitive price.

Transportation costs, tariff barriers, and import quotas separate classes of buyers geographically and may make discrimination possible.

Consequences of price discrimination

A monopoly firm that is able to discriminate between two markets will allocate its output between those two markets so as to equate the marginal revenues in the two. If this is not done, total revenue can always be increased by reducing sales by one unit in the market with the lower marginal revenue and raising sales by one unit in the market with the higher marginal revenue. This reallocation of sales raises total revenue by the difference between the two marginal revenues. If the demand curves are different in the two markets, having the same marginal revenues means charging different prices.

Two important consequences of price discrimination follow from this result.

Proposition 1. **For any given level of output, the most profitable system of discriminatory prices will provide higher total revenue to the firm than the profit-maximizing single price.**

Remember that a monopolist with the power to discriminate could produce exactly the same quantity as a single-price monopolist and charge everyone the same price. Therefore, it need never receive *less* revenue, and it can do better if it can raise the price on even one unit sold, as long as the price need not be lowered on any other.

Proposition 2. **Output under price discrimination will generally be larger than under a single-price monopoly.**

Remember that a monopoly firm that must charge a single price for a product will produce less than would all the firms in a perfectly competitive industry because it knows that selling more of a good depresses its price. Price discrimination allows the firm to avoid this disincentive. To the extent that the firm can sell its output in separate blocks, it can sell another block without spoiling the market for the block that is already being sold. In the case of perfect price discrimination, in which every unit of output is sold at a different price, the profit-maximizing monopolist will produce every unit for which the price charged is greater than or equal to its marginal cost. It will therefore produce the same quantity of output as does the perfectly competitive industry.

Figure 11.7 illustrates the output-expanding effects of price discrimination. It shows a case in which a monopoly firm has maximized profits selling at a single price. The firm then finds that it can isolate a group of potential buyers who were unwilling to purchase at the monopoly price.

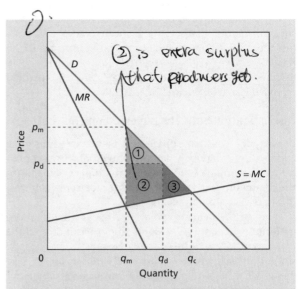

Figure 11.7 A price-discriminating monopolist

Price discrimination reduces the deadweight loss of monopoly. Initially the monopolist produces output q_m where $MC = MR$ instead of the competitive output q_c where MC equals demand (which is consumers' marginal utility). The deadweight loss is the sum of the three blue shaded areas labelled 1, 2, and 3. A second group of consumers is then isolated from the first. This group, who would buy nothing at the original price of p_m, will buy an amount that would increase total output to q_d at a price of p_d. The monopoly firm's profits now rise by the shaded area 2, which is the difference between its cost curve and the price p_d that is charged to the new group who buy the amount between q_m and q_d. Consumers' surplus rises by the shaded area labelled 1 and total deadweight loss falls to the shaded area labelled 3.

Perhaps it forms a buying club from which members of the first group are excluded. A lower price can be used to attract the new group of buyers without having to lower the price charged to its original customers. As long as the new price exceeds the marginal cost of producing the extra output, the monopoly firm will add to its profits. But consumers' surplus is also increased, since a new group of buyers is now in the market. So both the monopolist and consumers earn additional surplus.

Normative aspects of price discrimination

There are two quite separate issues involved in evaluating any particular example of price discrimination. The first concerns the effect of discrimination on the level of output. Discrimination usually results in a higher output than would occur if a single price were charged. As we saw in Figure 11.7, price discrimination tends to reduce the deadweight loss of monopoly and therefore leads to a more efficient allocation of resources than does a single-price monopoly.

Often, however, it is the effect on income distribution that accounts for people's strong emotional reactions to price discrimination. Compared with perfect competition, price discrimination transfers income from buyers to sellers. When buyers are poor and sellers are rich, this may seem undesirable. However, some cases are more complex. For example, doctors in countries with market-based medical systems often vary their charges with their patients' incomes. This enables them to serve their poorer patients in ways that they could not if they had to charge everyone a single price for their services. Another example is the prevalent practice of giving discounts to those of retirement age or airline passengers who stay on over a weekend. These practices often allow lower-income people to buy a product that they would be unable to afford if it were sold at the single price that maximized the producers' profits.

Box 11.2 outlines some interesting cases of price discrimination.

 ### Box 11.2 Examples of price discrimination

The principle of charging different customers different prices has been around for a very long time. The earliest example we have come across is from the Egyptian kingdom of Rameses the Great in the period 1304–1237 BC.* In what is now southern Lebanon, the Egyptians maintained a toll road on an important route across a range of hills. There were other routes, but they were considerably more tortuous. The servant of the Egyptian ruler sent to administer this toll road found that he had some discretion over pricing. He wrote to his employers asking for guidelines on charges. The reply came back: 'Charge what the traffic will bear.' So famous is this instruction that the phrase has become something of a cliché. It is based upon the insight, set out in the text, that setting different prices increases revenue. In practice, the discriminating monopolist charges each traveller the maximum that he or she would be prepared to pay to use the road.

Here are two more recent examples from transport. The first illustrates price discrimination in action. The second shows that problems can arise when price discrimination does not occur.

Air fares

In April 2002 a standard economy fare on British Airways from London Heathrow to Rome was £557. This fare permitted return the same day or within the week. However, if you stayed over Saturday night, the fare was only £209! This difference for the same class of fare on the same planes discriminates between the business traveller and the tourist. Such discrimination is profitable because the elasticities of demand for these two types of travel are different, being lower for business than for leisure travel.

Similar price discrimination applies to transatlantic airfares. In April 2002 a standard economy return fare between London and Chicago on the major airlines (such as British Airways, United and American) cost around £1,050. However, the fare with the same carriers if booked 14 days in advance and for a stay of at least seven days was around £260. Again, these substantial differences reflect a segmentation of the market between business travellers, who presumably get their fares paid by their company, and tourists, who are paying out of their own pocket. Business people do not want to use up more time than is necessary on a business trip, as the opportunity cost of their time is high, so the seven-day minimum keeps them from taking advantage of the low fare.

British Rail

This case illustrates the problems that arise when segmentation is not allowed even though both producers and consumers could be better off if it were. Some years ago British Rail (the nationalized industry that operated all British railways) was not allowed to charge different prices to passengers travelling on different lines. In the interest of equity, a fixed fare per passenger-mile was laid down by government and this had to be charged on all lines, whatever the density of their passenger traffic and whatever the elasticity of demand for their services. In the interests of economy, branch lines were closed down when they could not cover their costs. This meant that some lines closed even though the users preferred rail transport to any of the available alternatives and the strength of their preferences was such that they would voluntarily have paid a price sufficient for the line to cover its costs. The lines were none the less closed because it was thought inequitable to charge the passengers on one line more than the passengers on other lines.

By 2002 (following privatization) differential pricing was permitted. For example, train companies such as the operators of the Gatwick Express were able to charge higher prices for trips from London Victoria to Gatwick Airport than were being charged by other companies running on the same route—the only difference being a non-stop journey.

---

* We are grateful to Professor Arie Melnik of Haifa University for this example.

Long-run monopoly equilibrium

In both monopolized and perfectly competitive industries, profits and losses provide incentives for entry and exit.

If the monopoly firm is suffering losses in the short run, it will continue to operate as long as it can cover its variable costs. In the long run, however, it will leave the industry unless it can find a scale of operations at which its full opportunity costs can be covered.

If the monopoly firm is making profits, other firms will wish to enter the industry in order to earn more than the opportunity cost of their capital. If such entry occurs, the equilibrium position shown in Figure 11.3 will change, and the firm will cease to be a monopolist.

Entry barriers

Impediments that prevent entry are called **entry barriers**; they may be either natural or created.

If a monopoly firm's profits are to persist in the long run, effective entry barriers must prevent the entry of new firms into the industry.

Barriers determined by technology

Natural barriers most commonly arise as a result of economies of scale. When the long-run average cost curve is negatively sloped over a large range of output, big firms have significantly lower average total costs than small firms.

You will recall from Chapter 10 that perfectly competitive firms cannot be in long-run equilibrium on the negatively sloped segment of their long-run average cost curve (see Figure 10.12 on page 169).

Now suppose that an industry's technology is such that any firm's minimum achievable average cost is £10, which is reached at an output of 10,000 units per week. Further, assume that at a price of £10 the total quantity demanded is 11,000 units per week. Under these circumstances only one firm can operate at or near its minimum costs.

A **natural monopoly** occurs when, given the industry's current technology, the demand conditions allow no more than one firm to cover its costs while producing at the minimum point of its long-run cost curve. In a natural monopoly, there is no price at which two firms can both sell enough to cover their total costs.

Another type of technologically determined barrier is *set-up cost*. If a firm could be catapulted fully grown into the market, it might be able to compete effectively with the existing monopolist. However, the cost to the new firm of entering the market, developing its products, and establishing such things as brand image and dealer network might be so large that entry would be unprofitable.

Policy-created barriers

Many entry barriers are created by conscious government action and are, therefore, officially condoned. Patent laws, for instance, may prevent entry by conferring on the patent-holder the sole legal right to produce a particular product for a specific period of time.

A firm may also be granted a charter or a franchise that prohibits competition by law. Regulation and licensing of firms, often in service industries, can restrict entry severely. For example, the 1979 Banking Act required all banks in the UK to be authorized by the Bank of England. The 1986 Financial Services Act required all sellers of investment products to be authorized by the Securities and Investment Board (SIB) or some other recognized regulatory body. Regulation and authorization of all financial firms, including banks, was formally transferred to the Financial Services Authority in December 2001.

Other barriers can be created by the firm or firms already in the market. In extreme cases, the threat of force or sabotage can deter entry. The most obvious entry barriers of this type are encountered in the production and sale of illegal goods and services, where operation outside the law makes available an array of illegal but potent barriers to new entrants. The drug trade is a current example. In contrast, legitimate firms must use legal tactics such as those that are intended to increase a new entrant's set-up costs. Examples are the threat of price-cutting, designed to impose unsustainable losses on a new entrant, and heavy brand-name advertising. (These and other created entry barriers will be discussed in much more detail in Chapter 12.)

The significance of entry barriers

Because there are no entry barriers in perfect competition, profits cannot persist in the long run.

Profits attract entry, and entry erodes profits.

In monopoly, however, profits can persist in the long run whenever there are effective barriers to entry.

Entry barriers frustrate the adjustment mechanism that would otherwise push profits towards zero in the long run.

'Creative destruction'

In the very long run technology changes. New ways of producing old products are invented, and new products are created to satisfy both familiar and new wants. This has important implications for entry. A monopoly that succeeds in preventing the entry of new firms capable of producing its current product will sooner or later find its barriers circumvented by innovations. One firm may be able to use new processes that avoid some patent or other barrier that the monopolist relies on to bar entry of competing firms. Another firm may compete by producing a new product that, although somewhat different, still satisfies the same need as the monopoly firm's product. Yet another firm might get around a natural monopoly by inventing a technology that produces the good at a much lower cost than the existing monopoly firm's technology. (The cost curve may be lowered throughout its range, and/or the minimum level of costs may be reached at a lower output than previously.) The new technology may subsequently allow several firms to enter the market and still cover costs.

Joseph Schumpeter (1883–1950) argued that entry barriers were not a serious problem in the very long run. According to Schumpeter, the possibility of obtaining monopoly profits provides a major incentive for people to risk their money by financing inventions and innovations. The large short-run profits of a monopoly encourage others to try to capture some of these profits for themselves. If a frontal attack on the monopolist's barriers to entry is not possible, the barriers will be circumvented by such means as the development of similar products against which the monopolist will not have entry protection.

Schumpeter called the replacement of an existing monopoly by one or more new entrants through the invention of new products or new production techniques the *process of creative destruction*. He argued that this process precludes the very-long-run persistence of barriers to entry into industries that earn large profits.

It is worth noting that the same argument applies to an oligopolistic industry with a few firms of the sort we will consider in the next chapter. If they are making profits and succeed in barring entry, in the long run new firms may circumvent the entry barriers by inventing new technologies in the very long run.

Cartels as monopolies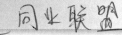

Up to this point in our discussion, a monopoly has meant that there is only one firm in an industry. A second way in which a monopoly can arise is for the firms in an industry to agree to co-operate with one another, to behave as if they were a single seller, in order to maximize joint profits by eliminating competition among themselves. Such a group of firms is called a **cartel**, or sometimes just a producers' association. A cartel that includes *all* firms in the industry can behave in the same way as a single-firm monopoly that owned all of these firms. The firms can agree among themselves to restrict their total output to the level that maximizes their joint profits.[5]

The effects of cartelization

Perfectly competitive firms accept the market price as given and increase their output until their marginal cost equals price. In contrast, a monopoly firm knows that increasing its output will depress the market price. Taking account of this, the monopolist increases its output only until marginal revenue is equal to marginal cost. All the firms in an industry can achieve the same result by grouping together into what is called a cartel to take collective action to reduce output and drive up price. They can agree to restrict industry output to the level that maximizes their joint profits (where the industry's marginal cost is equal to the industry's marginal revenue). One way to do this is to establish a quota for each firm's output. Say that a cartel is formed in what was a perfectly competitive industry

and that the profit-maximizing output is two-thirds of the perfectly competitive output. When the cartel is formed, each firm could be given a quota equal to two-thirds of its competitive output.

The effect of cartelizing a perfectly competitive industry and of reducing its output through production quotas is shown in part (i) of Figure 11.8.

Problems facing cartels

Cartels encounter two characteristic problems. The first is ensuring that members follow the behaviour that will maximize the industry's *joint* profits, and the second is preventing these profits from being eroded by the entry of new firms.

Enforcement of output restrictions

The managers of any cartel want the industry to produce its profit-maximizing output. Their job is made more difficult if individual firms either stay out of the cartel or enter and

---

[5] In this chapter we deal with the simple case, in which *all* of the firms in a perfectly competitive industry form a cartel in order to act as if they were a monopoly. Cartels are sometimes formed by a group of firms that account for a significant part, but not all, of the total supply of some commodity. The effect is to turn the industry into what is called an *oligopoly*. The most famous example of this type is the Organization of Petroleum Exporting Countries, best known as OPEC. We will return to this type of cartel in Chapter 14.

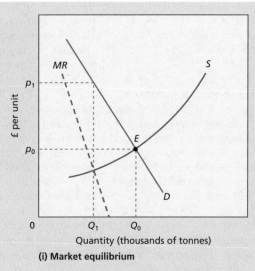

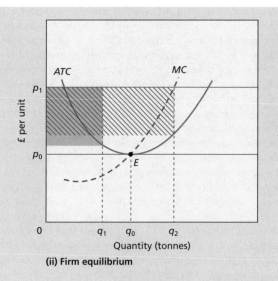

(i) Market equilibrium

(ii) Firm equilibrium

Figure 11.8 Conflicting forces affecting cartels

Co-operation leads to the monopoly price, but individual self-interest leads to production in excess of the monopoly output. Market conditions are shown in part (i), and the situation of a typical firm is shown in part (ii). (Note the change of scale between the two graphs.) Initially the market is in competitive equilibrium, with price p_0 and quantity Q_0. The individual firm is producing output q_0 and is just covering its total costs.

The cartel is formed and then enforces quotas on individual firms that are sufficient to reduce the industry's output to Q_1, the output that maximizes the joint profits of the cartel members. Price rises to p_1. The typical firm's quota is q_1. The firm's profits rise from zero to the amount shown by the dark blue area in part (ii). Once price is raised to p_1, however, the individual firm would like to increase output to q_2, where marginal cost is equal to the price set by the cartel. This would allow the firm to earn profits shown by the blue hatched area. If all firms violate their quotas, industry output will exceed Q_1, and the profits earned by all firms will fall.

then cheat on their output quotas. Any individual firm has an incentive to do just this: to be either the one that stays out of the organization, or the one that enters and then cheats on its output quota. For the sake of simplicity, assume that all firms enter the cartel, so that enforcement problems are concerned strictly with cheating by its members.

If Firm X is the only firm to cheat, it is in the best of all possible situations. All other firms restrict output and hold the industry price near its monopoly level. They earn profits, but only by restricting output. Firm X can then reap the full benefit of the other firms' output restraint and sell some additional output at the high price that has been set by the cartel's actions. However, if *all* of the firms cheat, the price will be pushed back to the competitive level, and all of the firms will return to their zero-profit position.

This conflict between the interests of the group and the interests of the individual firm creates the cartel's dilemma. Provided that enough firms co-operate in restricting output, all firms are better off than they would be if the industry remained perfectly competitive. However, any one firm is even better off if it remains outside the cartel, or joins it and then cheats by exceeding its output quota. If all firms act on this incentive, however, all will be worse off than if they had joined the cartel and restricted output.

Cartels tend to be unstable because of the strong incentives for individual firms to violate the output quotas needed to enforce the monopoly price.

The conflict between the motives for co-operation and for independent action is analysed in more detail in part (ii) of Figure 11.8.

Cartels and similar output-restricting arrangements have a long history. For example, schemes to raise farm incomes by limiting crops bear ample testimony to the accuracy of the predicted instability of cartels. In the past, industry agreements to restrict output often broke down as individual farmers exceeded their quotas. This is why most crop-restriction plans are now operated by governments rather than by private cartels. Production quotas backed by the full coercive power of the state can force monopoly behaviour on existing producers and can effectively bar the entry of new ones.

Restricting entry

A cartel must not only police the behaviour of its members, but must also be able to prevent the entry of new producers. In an industry with no strong natural entry barriers, to maintain its profits in the long run a cartel must create its own barriers; otherwise new firms will enter and force down price until the profits disappear. Successful cartels are often able to license the firms in the industry and to control entry by restricting the number of licences. At other times the government has operated a quota system and has given it the force of law. If no one can produce without a quota and the quotas are allocated among existing producers, entry is precluded.

SUMMARY

A single-price monopolist

- A monopoly is an industry containing a single firm. The monopoly firm maximizes its profits by equating marginal cost to marginal revenue, which is less than price. Production under monopoly is less than it would be under perfect competition, where marginal cost is equated to price.

The allocative inefficiency of monopoly

- Monopoly is allocatively inefficient. By producing less than the perfectly competitive output it transfers some consumers' surplus to its own profits and also causes deadweight loss of surplus that would have resulted from the output that is not produced.

A multi-price monopolist: price discrimination

- If a monopolist can discriminate between either different units or different customers, it will always sell more and earn greater profits than if it must charge a single price.

- For price discrimination to be possible, the seller must be able to distinguish individual units bought by a single buyer or to separate buyers into classes between whom resale is impossible.

Long-run monopoly equilibrium

- A monopoly can earn positive profits in the long run if there are barriers to entry. These may be man-made, such as patents or exclusive franchises, or natural, such as economies of large-scale production.

Cartels as monopolies

- The joint profits of all firms in a perfectly competitive industry can always be increased if they agree to restrict output. After agreement is in place, each firm can increase its profits by violating the agreement. If they all do this, profits are reduced to the perfectly competitive level.

TOPICS FOR REVIEW

- Relationship between price and marginal revenue for a monopolist
- Relationships among marginal revenue, total revenue, and elasticity for a monopolist
- Short- and long-run monopoly equilibrium

- Natural and created entry barriers
- Price discrimination among different units and different buyers
- Individual versus group profits in a cartel

DISCUSSION QUESTIONS

1 Using the same cost information as for the firm described in question 3 of Chapter 8 (page 140), you are now given information about demand. The following table shows the price at which the corresponding quantity can be sold:

Sales (units)	Price (£)
20	19.20
40	18.40
60	17.60
100	16.00
200	12.00
300	8.00
400	4.00
500	0.00
1,000	—

(You might like to know that this is a straight-line demand curve which can be expressed as $p = 20 - 0.04q$, where p is price and q is quantity sold.)

(a) What is the marginal revenue for each level of sales?

(b) What are the approximate profit-maximizing levels of sales and price?

(c) Draw a graph showing total costs, total revenue, and profit at each level of sales.

2 Suppose now that the firm in question 1 has constant marginal costs of £4.00 per unit (i.e. ignore previous information about costs) and that it faces two segmented markets. One has the demand curve as in question 1, and the other has the following demand curve:

Sales (units)	Price (£)
20	9.60
40	9.20
60	8.80
100	8.00
200	6.00
300	4.00
400	2.00
500	0.00
1,000	—

(If it helps, this demand curve can be written $p = 10 - 0.02q$.)

(a) What quantity will the firm sell in each market?

(b) What price will be charged in each market?

3 For the two demand curves given in questions 1 and 2 above, calculate the price elasticity of demand at each of the listed sales levels. What is the elasticity at the sales level that maximizes total revenue? Are there any sales levels for which demand is inelastic? What is total revenue at this level of sales?

4 Compare the price and output levels under monopoly and perfect competition.

5 Explain why monopoly is allocatively inefficient.

6 Explain how a cartel can raise the joint profit of its members, relative to what they would be under competitive conditions. Why are cartels likely to be unstable?

7 If a firm produces an identical product in two separate plants, explain how it should decide the profit-maximizing production levels in each plant.

8 Why can a monopolist increase profit by segmenting its markets and charging different prices in each segment?

9 Explain why a profit-maximizing monopolist will never be selling on an inelastic portion of its demand curve.

Appendix A formal analysis of price discrimination between markets

Consider a monopoly firm that sells a single product in two distinct markets, A and B, with demand, marginal revenue, and cost curves as shown in Figure 11A.1. Resale among customers is impossible and a single price must be charged in each market.

What is the best price for the firm to charge in each market? The simplest way to discover this is to imagine the firm deciding how best to allocate any given total output Q^* between two markets. Since output is fixed arbitrarily at Q^*, there is nothing the monopolist can do about costs. The best thing it can do, therefore, is to maximize the revenue that it gets by selling Q^* in the

two markets. *To do this it will allocate its sales between the markets until the marginal revenues are the same in each market.*

Consider what would happen if the marginal revenue in market A exceeded the marginal revenue in market B. The firm could keep its overall output constant at Q^* but reallocate a unit of sales from B to A, gaining a net addition in revenue equal to the difference between the marginal revenues in the two markets. Thus, it will always pay a monopoly firm to reallocate a given total quantity between its markets as long as marginal revenues are not equal in the two markets.

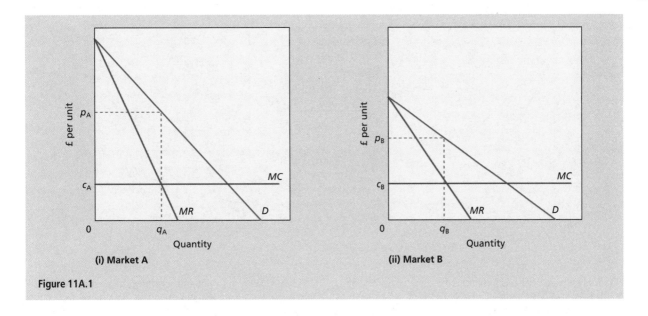

Figure 11A.1

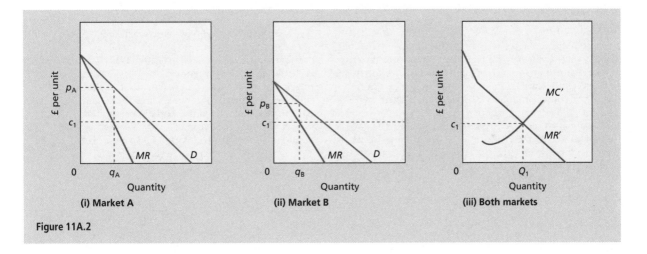

Figure 11A.2

If we assume that marginal cost is constant, we can determine the profit-maximizing course of action from Figure 11A.1. The MC curve in both parts shows the constant marginal cost. The firm's total profits are maximized by equating MR in each market to its constant MC, thus selling q_A at p_A in market A and q_B at p_B in market B. Marginal revenue is the same in each market ($c_A = c_B$) so that the firm has its total output correctly allocated between the two markets, and marginal cost equals marginal revenue, showing that the firm would lose profits if it produced more or less total output.

Next, assume that marginal cost varies with output, being given by MC' in Figure 11A.2(iii). Now we cannot just put the MC curve on to the diagram for each market, since the marginal cost of producing another unit for sale in market A will depend on how much is being produced for sale in market B and vice versa. To determine what overall production should be, we need to

know overall marginal revenue. To find this, we merely sum the separate quantities in each market that correspond to each particular marginal revenue. If, for example, the tenth unit sold in market A and the fifteenth unit sold in market B each have a marginal revenue of £1 in their separate markets, then the marginal revenue of £1 corresponds to overall sales of 25 units (10 units in A and 15 in B). This example illustrates the general principle: the overall marginal revenue curve for a discriminating monopolist is the horizontal sum of the marginal revenue curves in each of its markets. This overall curve shows the marginal revenue associated with an increment to production on the assumption that sales are divided between the two markets so as to keep the two marginal revenues equal.

This overall MR curve is shown in Figure 11A.2(iii) and is labelled MR'. The firm's total profit-maximizing output is at Q_1, where MR' and MC' intersect (at a value of c_1). By construction,

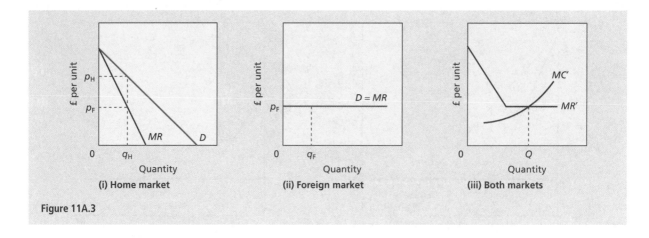

Figure 11A.3

marginal revenue is c_1 in each market although price is different. To find the equilibrium price and quantity in each market, find the quantities, q_A and q_B, that correspond to this marginal revenue; then find the prices in each market that correspond to q_A and q_B. All of this is illustrated in parts (i) and (ii) of the figure.

An application

In some industries firms sell competitively on international markets while enjoying a home market that is protected from foreign competition by tariffs or import quotas. To illustrate the issues involved, consider the following extreme case. A firm is the only producer of product X in country A. There are thousands of producers of X in other countries, so that X is sold abroad under conditions of perfect competition. The government of country A grants the firm a monopoly in the home market by prohibiting imports of X. The firm is now faced with a negatively sloped demand curve at home and a perfectly elastic demand curve abroad at the prevailing world price of X.

What will it do? To maximize profits, the firm will divide its sales between the foreign and the home markets so as to equate marginal revenues in the two. On the world market its average and marginal revenues are equal to the world price. Thus, the firm will equate marginal revenue in the home market with the world price, and, since price exceeds marginal revenue at home (because the demand curve slopes downwards), price at home must exceed price abroad.

The argument is illustrated in Figure 11A.3. The home market is shown in (i), the foreign market in (ii), and the sum of the marginal revenue curves in (iii). Provided that the marginal cost curve cuts the marginal revenue curve to the right of the kink (i.e. MC does not exceed the world price when only the home market is served), the two markets will be served at prices of p_H at home and p_F abroad. The total quantity sold will be Q, of which q_H is allocated to the home market and the rest ($q_F = Q - q_H$) is sold abroad.

Chapter 12

IMPERFECT COMPETITION

Perfect competition and monopoly are extreme cases that do not really involve competition at all. In the former firms have no influence over the market price, while in the latter there is only one producer. So what about the intermediate cases where firms do have some market power but also have competitors? These cases are the subject of this chapter. In particular, you will learn that:

• Concentration of production varies between industries, but firms in all intermediate industry types have some power to influence their price.

• In industries where there are many producers but of differentiated products, free entry will tend to eliminate profits in the long run.

• In industries with two dominant firms (duopoly) but no co-operation, the outcome depends on whether firms compete by price or by quantity.

• Where there is a small group of dominant producers (oligopoly), strategic interaction is important because the market for one is affected by what its rivals do.

• Insights into the choices available and the nature of outcomes can be achieved using game theory.

• Oligopoly can be associated with pure profits in the long run if there are barriers to entry.

Most real firms operate under intermediate market structures rather than the two extremes of perfect competition and monopoly. On the one hand, they are not monopolies because their industries contain several firms, which often compete actively against each other. Firms manufacturing cars, refrigerators, TV sets, breakfast cereals, and many other consumer goods are in industries containing several close rivals, usually both foreign and domestic. Even in small towns, residents find more than one chemist, garage, hairdresser, and supermarket competing for their patronage. On the other hand, these firms do not operate in perfectly competitive markets because the number of competing firms is often small, and, even when the number is large, *the firms are not price-takers*.

In this chapter, we study firm behaviour in two intermediate market structures. One, which is called monopolistic competition, is close to perfect competition with one important difference: firms do not sell a homogeneous product. The second, called oligopoly, deals with industries that typically contain a few large firms that compete actively with each other. A special case of oligopoly is called duopoly. **Duopoly** occurs where there are just two dominant firms competing with each other. This pure form of rivalry rarely arises in this precise form, but the model of duopoly helps to gain insights into the interactions involved.

Patterns of concentration in manufacturing

One measure of the extent to which firms in some industry have potential market power is called a **concentration ratio.** This measures the fraction of total sales in the nation that is controlled by some specified number of the industry's largest sellers. Common types of concentration ratios cite the share of an industry's total market sales made by the three or five largest firms. For example, the UK five-firm concentration ratio for leather and leather products is 43 per cent. This means that the largest five firms in that industry account for 43 per cent of the industry's total sales.

Table 12.1 gives the five-firm concentration ratios for 21 sub-sectors of UK manufacturing. The data show that in many of these industries the five largest firms are too large a part of the total market to be price-takers. Yet none of these industries is a single-firm monopoly. The most concentrated (by this measure) is tobacco products, where the five largest firms account for all of the turnover.

Although national concentration ratios provide useful information, care must be taken in interpreting them. For example, markets often extend across national borders. A single firm operating in the United Kingdom does not have

Table 12.1 **Concentration ratios for UK manufacturing sub-sectors, 2000**

	Turnover of largest five enterprises as a percentage of the turnover of the sector
Food products and beverages	15
Tobacco products	100
Textiles	12
Wearing apparel; dressing and dyeing of fur	16
Leather and leather products	43
Wood and wood products	12
Pulp, paper and paper products, publishing and printing	22
Publishing, printing, and reproduction of recorded media	14
Coke, refined petroleum products, and nuclear fuel	90
Chemicals, chemical products, and man-made fibres	19
Rubber and plastic products	9
Non-metallic mineral products	18
Basic metals	48
Fabricated metal products (excluding machinery and equipment)	6
Machinery and equipment	11
Office machinery and computers	63
Electric machinery and apparatus (not covered elsewhere)	18
Radio, TV, and communication equipment	46
Medical, precision and optical instruments, watches and clocks	20
Motor vehicles, trailers, and semi-trailers	59
Other transport equipment	62

Source: Office of National Statistics, *ABI 2000*.

a monopoly if it is competing in the UK market against products imported from several foreign producers. The globalization of competition, brought about by the falling costs of transportation and communication, has been one of the most significant developments in the world economy in recent decades. Global competition has greatly reduced the number of secure monopolies that exist in national markets. This important development is discussed further in Box 12.1.

The extent of competition in any market depends not just on the number of domestic producers, but also on the ability of foreign producers to compete effectively in that market.

Imperfectly competitive market structures

The market structures that we are now going to study are called *imperfectly competitive*. The word 'competitive' emphasizes that we are not dealing with monopoly, and the word 'imperfect' emphasizes that we are not dealing with perfect competition.

Some patterns of firm behaviour are typical of all imperfectly competitive market structures. We outline these first, before looking at specific models of imperfect competition.

Firms create their own products

If a new farmer enters the wheat industry, the full range of products that can be produced is already in existence. If he decides to produce No. 1 durum wheat, it will be the same as the No. 1 durum wheat produced by all other farmers. In contrast, if a new firm enters the computer software industry, that firm must decide on the characteristics of the new computer programs that it is to produce. It will not produce

Box 12.1 Globalization of production and competition

A mere 150 years ago people and news travelled by sailing ship, so that it took months to communicate across various parts of the world. Advances in the twentieth century sped up both communications and travel. In the past three decades the pace of change in communications technology has accelerated. The world has witnessed a communications revolution that has dramatically changed the way business decisions are made and implemented.

Fifty years ago telephone links were laboriously and unreliably connected by operators; satellites were in the dreams of rocket scientists; photocopying, fax and e-mail were completely unknown, as was the internet. Hand-delivered mail was the only way to send hard copy, and getting it to overseas destinations often took weeks. Computers were in their infancy and accessible to only an elite few academics and military scientists. Jets were just beginning to replace the much slower and less reliable propeller aircraft. Today direct dialling is available to most parts of the world, at a fraction of what long-distance calls cost forty years ago. Internet, faxes, satellite TV links, fast jet travel, e-mail, cheap courier services, and a host of other developments have made communication that is reliable, and often instantaneous, available throughout the world.

The communications revolution has been a major contributor to the development of what has become known as the 'global village', three important characteristics of which are a *disintegration* of production, an increase in competition, and a decline in the power of the nation-state.

Production

The communications revolution has allowed many large international companies, known as transnational corporations (TNCs), to decentralize their production process (see Box [8.1]). They are now able to locate their research and development (R&D) where the best scientists are available. They can produce various components in dozens of places, locating each activity in the country where costs are cheapest for that type of production. They can then ship all the parts, as they are needed, to an assembly factory where the product is 'made'.

The globalization of production has brought employment, and rising real wages, to people in many less developed countries. At the same time, it has put less skilled labour in the developed countries under strong competitive pressures.

Competition

The communications revolution has also caused an internationalization of competition in almost all production industries. National markets are no longer protected for local producers by high costs of transportation and communication or by consumers' ignorance of similar foreign products. Walk into a local supermarket or department store today and you will have no trouble in finding products representing most of the UN member states.

Consumers gain by being able to choose from an enormous range of goods and services. Firms that are successful gain worldwide sales. Firms that fall behind even momentarily, however, may be wiped out by competition coming from many quarters. Global competition is fierce competition, and firms that want to survive must be fast on the uptake of their own and other people's new ideas.

Economic policy

The globalization of production, and consequently of competition, has greatly reduced the scope for individual countries to implement distinctive economic policies. Today firms of all sorts, from large transnationals to individuals operating out of homes through computer links, can relocate production easily. So tough national policies that reduce local profitability are often self-defeating, as firms move production elsewhere. Generous policies that seek to attract production may succeed only in attracting small and specialized parts of it.

Globalization and international capitalism have recently been the object of political demonstrations whenever there is an international economic conference in a vulnerable location. We discuss the economic issues associated with this disquiet in Chapters 33 and 34.

---

programs that are identical to those already in production. Rather, it will develop new programs, each of which will have its own distinctive characteristics. This is true of firms in virtually all consumer and capital goods industries. As a result, firms in these industries sell a range of differentiated products. The term **differentiated product** refers to a group of products that are similar enough to be considered variations on one generic product but dissimilar enough that they can be sold at different prices; for example, Ford and Mercedes both make cars, but their models are different.

Most firms in imperfectly competitive market structures sell differentiated products. In such industries, the firm itself must decide on the characteristics of the products it will sell.

Firms choose their prices

In imperfectly competitive markets firms typically have several product lines that differ more or less from each other and from the competing product lines of other firms. No market sets a single price for blue jeans, television sets, mobile phones, or word-processing packages. Instead, *each variety of the differentiated product has a price that must be set by its maker, and then some mark-up is set by the retailer.* These are the administered prices that we discussed in Chapter 3. Having set the price, firms wait to see how much is sold at that price.

In market structures other than perfect competition, firms set their prices and then let demand determine sales. Changes in market conditions are signalled to the firm by

changes in the quantity that the firm sells at its current administered price.

The changed conditions may then lead firms to change their prices, but they may change their level of production instead.

Short-run price stability

In perfect competition prices change continually in response to changes in demand and supply. In markets for differentiated products, prices often change less frequently. Manufacturers' prices for motor cars, computers, television sets, and CDs do not change with anything like the frequency of price changes in markets for basic materials, company shares, and foreign exchange.

Modern firms that sell differentiated products typically have hundreds, or even thousands, of distinct products on their price lists. Changing such a long list of administered prices involves costs. These include the costs of printing new list prices and notifying all customers, the difficulty of keeping track of frequently changing prices for purposes of accounting and billing, and the loss of customer and retailer goodwill owing to the uncertainty caused by frequent changes in prices.

Because firms producing differentiated products must administer their own prices, they must decide on the *frequency* with which they change these prices.

In making this decision, each firm will balance the cost of making price changes against the revenue lost by not making price changes. Clearly, the likelihood that the firm will make costly price changes rises with the size of the disturbance to which it is adjusting and the probability that the disturbance will not be reversed. Thus, transitory fluctuations in demand may be met by changing output with prices constant, while changes in costs that are thought to be permanent are passed on through price increases.

Non-price competition

Many firms spend large sums of money on advertising. They do so in an attempt both to shift the demand curve for the industry's product and to attract customers from competing firms. Firms often offer competing standards of quality and product guarantees. Any kind of sales promotion activity undertaken by a single firm would not happen under perfect competition, since each firm could sell any amount at the going market price. Any such scheme directed at competing firms in the same industry is, by definition, inconsistent with monopoly. Firms also use advertising to signal their commitment to quality and service, in order to generate customer loyalty to their brand. Again, this is something a perfect competitor would never do, and something a pure monopolist is unlikely to need to do.

Unexploited scale economies

Many firms in imperfectly competitive industries appear to be operating on the downward-sloping portions of their long-run average cost curves.[1] One reason for this is the high development costs and short product lives of many modern products. Many popular software products, for example, did not exist five years ago and will almost certainly have been superseded in five years' time. A computer program takes a lot of time and effort to write, but further copies of it can be run off very cheaply. In such cases firms face steeply falling long-run average total cost curves. The more units that are sold, the lower are the fixed development costs per unit. Given perfect competition, these firms would go on increasing outputs and sales until rising marginal costs of production just balanced their falling average fixed costs, bringing their average total cost to a minimum. As it is, they often face falling average total cost curves throughout each product's life-cycle.

Entry prevention

Firms in many industries engage in activities that appear to be designed to hinder the entry of new firms, thereby preventing existing pure profits from being eroded by entry. We discuss these activities in much more detail later in the chapter.

Monopolistic competition

One easily tractable model of imperfect competition is known as monopolistic competition. Tractability of this model is achieved by limiting the form of interdependence between producers. We deal with this case first before discussing more general types of strategic interaction between firms in oligopolistic market structures.

Monopolistic competition refers to a market in which there are many firms but each sells a differentiated product

---

[1] Although this is also possible under monopoly, firms in perfect competition must, in the long run, be at the minimum point of their long-run average cost curves (see Figure 10.12 on page 169).

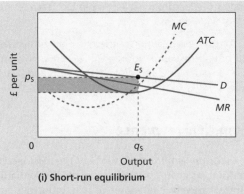
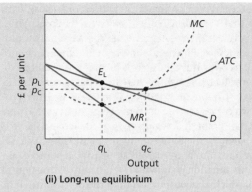

(i) Short-run equilibrium   **(ii) Long-run equilibrium**

Figure 12.1 Equilibrium of a typical firm in monopolistic competition

In the short run a typical firm may make pure profits, but in the long run it will only cover its costs. In part (i) a typical monopolistically competitive firm is shown in short-run equilibrium at point E_S. Output is q_S, where $MC = MR$, price is p_S, and profits are the dark blue area.

In part (ii) the firm is in long-run equilibrium at point E_L. Entry of new firms has pushed the existing firm's demand curve to the left until the curve is tangent to the *ATC* curve at output q_L. Price is p_L, and total costs are just being covered. Excess capacity is $q_C - q_L$. If the firm did produce at capacity, its costs would fall from p_L per unit of output to p_C.

Note that, to make the points q_L and q_C visually distinct, the demand curve in part (ii) has been drawn more steeply sloped than in part (i). The flatter demand curve of part (i) is what is expected in monopolistic competition. If it were drawn on part (ii), q_L would more realistically be closer to q_C, but the differences being illustrated by the figure would be harder to see.

and so faces a downward sloping demand curve for its own product.[2]

The theory

Assumptions

The theory is based on four key assumptions.

1. *Each firm produces one specific variety, or brand, of the industry's differentiated product.* Each firm thus faces a demand curve that, although negatively sloped, is highly elastic, because many close substitutes are sold by other firms.

2. *The industry contains so many firms that each one ignores the possible reactions of its many competitors when it makes its own price and output decisions.* Each firm makes decisions based on its own demand and cost conditions, and does not take any account of potential reactions by other firms.

3. *There is freedom of entry and exit in the industry.* If existing firms are earning profits, new firms have an incentive to enter. When they do, the demand for the industry's product must be shared among more brands.

4. *There is symmetry.* When a new firm enters the industry selling a new version of the differentiated product, it takes customers equally from all existing firms. For example, a new entrant that captured 5 per cent of the existing market would do so by capturing 5 per cent of the sales of each existing firm.

Equilibrium

Short-run equilibrium Because each firm's product has some features that are different from those of competitors, each firm faces a negatively sloped demand curve. But the curve is rather elastic because similar products sold by other firms provide many close substitutes. The negative slope of the demand curve provides the potential for monopoly profits in the short run, as illustrated in part (i) of Figure 12.1.

Long-run equilibrium Freedom of entry and exit forces profits to zero in the long run. If existing firms in the industry are earning profits, new firms will enter. Their entry will mean that the demand for the product must be shared among more and more brands. Thus, the demand curve for each existing firm's brand shifts to the left.[3] Entry continues until profits fall to zero, as shown in part (ii) of Figure 12.1.

Excess capacity

The absence of positive profits requires that each firm's demand curve be nowhere above its long-run average cost

---

[2] US economist Edward Chamberlin (1899–1967) was the originator of the theory of monopolistic competition.

[3] The shift in the demand curve is determined by the *symmetry assumption*: a new entrant takes sales in equal proportion from all existing firms.

curve. The absence of losses, which would cause exit, requires that each firm be able to cover its costs. Thus, average revenue must equal average cost at some output. Together these requirements imply that, when a monopolistically competitive industry is in long-run equilibrium, each firm will be producing where its demand curve is tangent to (i.e. just touching at one point) its average total cost curve. Two curves that are tangent at a point have the same slope at that point. If a negatively sloped demand curve is to be tangent to the long-run average cost (LRAC) curve, the latter must also be negatively sloped at the point of tangency. This situation is shown in Figure 12.1(ii): the typical firm is producing an output less than the one for which its LRAC reaches its minimum point.

This is the **excess capacity theorem** of monopolistic competition. Each firm is producing its output at an average cost that is higher than it could achieve by producing its capacity output. In other words, each firm has *unused* or *excess* capacity. So:

The theory of monopolistic competition shows that an industry can be competitive, in the sense of containing numerous competing firms and no pure profits, and yet contain unexploited scale economies, in the sense that each firm is producing on the negatively sloped portion of its average total cost curve.

This implies that firms typically invest in capacity that is not fully utilized.

Is excess capacity wasteful? The long-run equilibrium of a monopolistically competitive industry might seem inefficient. Production costs are not as low as they could be if firms produced at the lowest point on their average cost curves, and firms typically invest in some capacity that goes unused.

But this is not necessarily inefficient, because people value diversity and are prepared to pay a price for it. For example, each brand of breakfast food, shampoo, car, and blue jeans has its sincere devotees. Increasing the number of differentiated products has two effects. First, it increases the amount of excess capacity in the production of each product, because the total demand must be divided among more products. Second, the increased diversity of available products will better satisfy diverse tastes.

How will consumers' satisfaction be maximized in these circumstances?

Consumers' satisfaction is maximized when the number of differentiated products is increased until the marginal gain in consumers' satisfaction from an increase in diversity

equals the loss from having to produce each existing product at a higher cost.

For this reason, among others, the belief that large-group monopolistic competition would lead to inefficiency in the use of resources is not proven; it might, and it just as well might not.

Empirical relevance

Is there any empirical relevance of the monopolistic competition model? Although product differentiation is an almost universal phenomenon in industries producing consumer goods and capital goods, the monopolistically competitive market structure is found only infrequently in practice. Although many industries produce a vast array of differentiated products, these are often produced by only a few firms. For example, a mere three firms produce most of the many breakfast cereals. Similar circumstances exist in soap powder, chemicals, cigarettes, and numerous other industries. These industries are clearly not perfectly competitive, and neither are they monopolies. Are they monopolistically competitive? The answer is no, because they contain few enough firms for each to take account of the others' reactions when determining its own behaviour (thus violating the second assumption above). Furthermore, these firms often earn large profits without attracting new entry (thus violating the prediction of zero profits in the long run).

One possible example is the restaurant market in a city such as London. Each competes in the 'eating out' market, but no individual restaurant is critically affected by any one other. Each has a slightly different product, and entry into the market is easy. The more entry there is, the smaller the market share of the others is likely to be, but each clearly has some discretion about the prices it charges. Some other retail service providers, such as hairdressers (see Box 12.2), provide similar examples, but good examples in other industries are hard to find.

While not many industries exist that even approximately fit the assumptions of monopolistic competition, there are two ways in which the model is a useful part of the toolbox of economics. First, it gives a simple illustration of the dynamics of competition by which entry of new firms tends to eliminate pure profit in the long run. Second, it shows how any market with differentiated products will involve excess capacity and price unequal to marginal cost, though this apparent inefficiency needs to be set against the benefits of the more diverse choices available with product differentiation.

Box 12.2 The price of haircuts and profits of hairdressers

Suppose that there are many hairdressers and there is freedom of entry into the industry: anyone can set up as a hairdresser. Assume that the going price for haircuts is £7.50 and that at this price all hairdressers believe their incomes are too low.

The hairdressers hold a meeting and decide to form a trade association. The purpose of the association is to impose a price of £10 for haircuts. What is the result?

We need to distinguish between the short-run and the long-run effects of an increase in the price of haircuts. In the short run the number of hairdressers is fixed. Thus, in the short run the answer depends only on the elasticity of the demand for their services. If demand elasticity is less than 1, total expenditure will rise and so will the incomes of hairdressers; if demand elasticity exceeds 1, the hairdressers' revenues will fall. Thus, to answer the question we need some knowledge about the elasticity of demand for haircuts. Assuming it to be inelastic, hairdressers will be successful in raising incomes in the short run.

What about the long run? If hairdressers were just covering costs before the price change, they will now be earning economic profits. Hairdressing will become an attractive trade relative to others requiring equal skill and training, and there will be a flow of new entrants into the industry. As the number of hairdressers rises, the same amount of business must be shared among more and more of them, so the typical hairdresser will find business—and thus earnings—decreasing.

Profits may also be squeezed from another direction. With fewer customers coming their way, hairdressers may compete against one another for the limited number of customers. Their agreement does not allow them to compete through price cuts, but they can compete in service. They may spruce up their shops, offer their customers expensive magazines to read, and so forth. This kind of non-price competition will raise operating costs.

These changes will continue until hairdressers are just covering their opportunity costs, at which time the attraction for new entrants will vanish. The industry will settle down in a new long-run equilibrium in which individual hairdressers make incomes only as large as they did before the price rise. There will be more hairdressers than there were in the original situation, but each one will be working for a smaller portion of the day and will be idle for a larger portion. (The industry will have excess capacity.) Customers will have shorter waits even at peak periods, and they will get to read a wide choice of magazines; but they will be paying £10 for haircuts.

If the association adopted the plan in order to raise the average income of hairdressers, it will have failed. It has created more jobs for hairdressers, but not a higher income for each.

The general lesson is clear: one cannot raise income by raising price above the competitive level unless one can prevent new entry or can otherwise reduce the quantity of the product or service provided.

Oligopoly

Oligopoly is imperfect competition among the few; it applies to an industry that contains only a few competing firms. Each firm has enough market power to prevent its being a price-taker, but each firm is subject to enough inter-firm rivalry to prevent it considering the market demand curve as its own. In most modern economies this is the dominant market structure for the production of consumer and capital goods as well as many basic industrial materials such as steel and aluminium. Services, however, are often produced in industries containing a larger number of firms —although product differentiation prevents them from being perfectly competitive.

In contrast to a monopoly, which has *no* competitors, and to a monopolistically competitive firm, which has *many* competitors, an oligopolistic firm faces *a few* competitors. Because there are only a few firms in an oligopolistic industry, each firm realizes that its competitors may respond to any move it makes. The prudent firm will take such possible responses into account. In other words, oligopolists are aware that all the decisions made by the various firms in the industry affect the other firms.

This is the key difference between oligopolists on the one hand and perfect competitors, monopolistic competitors,

and monopolies on the other hand. The behaviour of oligopolists is **strategic**, which means that they must take explicit account of the impact of their decisions on competing firms and of the reactions they expect from competing firms. In contrast, firms in perfect and monopolistic competition engage in **non-strategic** behaviour, which means they make decisions based on their own costs and their own demand curves without considering any possible reactions from their large number of competitors. The behaviour of a monopolist is also non-strategic. It has no competitors with whom to interact.

Oligopolistic industries are of many types. In some industries there are only a few firms, but oligopoly is also consistent with a large number of small sellers, called a 'competitive fringe', as long as a 'big few' dominate the industry's production. For example, about 500 banks operate in the United Kingdom, but the Big Five—Barclays, LloydsTSB, Royal Bank of Scotland (which owns NatWest), HSBC and HBOS (formed by merger of the Halifax and the Bank of Scotland)—dominate the UK's retail commercial banking industry. Similarly, there are many small shops selling groceries, but a few large nationwide firms, such as Tesco, Sainsbury and Asda, dominate grocery retailing.

In oligopolistic industries prices are typically administered. Products are usually differentiated. Firms engage in rivalrous behaviour, although its intensity varies greatly across industries and over time. This variety has invited extensive theorizing and empirical study.

Why bigness?

Several factors explain why a few large firms dominate so many industries. Some of these factors are 'natural', and some are created by the firms themselves.

Natural causes of bigness

Economies of scale Much manufacturing production applies the principle of the division of labour that we first studied in Chapter 1. The production of a complex product is broken up into hundreds of simple, repetitive tasks. This type of division of labour is the basis of the assembly line, which revolutionized the production of many goods in the early twentieth century and still underlies economies of large-scale production in many industries.[4] The division of labour is, as Adam Smith observed long ago, dependent on the size of the market. If only a few units of a product can be sold each day, there is no point in dividing its production into a number of specialized tasks. So big firms have an advantage over small firms whenever there is great potential for economies based on division of labour. The larger the scale of production, the lower the average variable costs of production.

Fixed costs It is costly to design, prove, and market a new product. In technologically dynamic industries it may be a matter of only a few years before each new version is replaced by some superior version of the same basic product. Yet the fixed costs of product development must be recovered in the revenues from sales of the product. The larger the firm's sales, the lower the cost that has to be recovered from each unit sold. Consider a product that costs £1 million to develop and market. If 1 million units can be sold before the product is replaced by a superior version, £1 of the selling price of each unit must go towards recovering the development costs. If, however, the firm expects to sell 10 million units, each unit need contribute only 10 pence to these costs, and the market price can be lowered accordingly. With the enormous development costs of some of today's high-tech products, firms that can sell a large volume have a distinct pricing advantage over firms that sell a smaller volume. Firms with large product development costs face downward-sloping average total cost curves even if their average variable costs are constant.

Economies of scope Economies of scope apply to a multi-product firm from the fact that some resources of the firms can be shared between different product areas. **Economies of scope** exist if production of several different products within one firm leads to the unit costs of production of each product being lower than if they had been produced in independent firms. Such economies may arise because some functions are shared, such as marketing and distribution, or because of some common skills in the firm that can be applied to more than one product.

Where size confers a cost advantage, through economies of either scale or scope, there may be room for only a few firms, even when the total market is quite large. This cost advantage of size will dictate that the industry be an oligopoly, unless government regulation prevents the firms from growing to their efficient size.

Firm-created causes of bigness

The number of firms in an industry may be decreased while the average size of the survivors rises, as a result of the *strategic* behaviour of the firms themselves. Firms may grow by buying out rivals (acquisitions), or merging with them (mergers), or by driving rivals into bankruptcy through predatory practices. In this way the size and market shares of the survivors increase and may, by reducing competitive behaviour, allow them to earn larger profit margins. But these high profits will attract new entrants unless the surviving firms can create and sustain barriers to entry. Although most firms would like to behave in this manner, it is no easy task to create effective entry barriers when natural ones do not exist. We return to entry barriers later in the chapter.

Is bigness natural or firm-created?

The answer to this question is probably: 'Some of both'. Some industries have production in the hands of few firms because the efficient size of the firm is large relative to the overall size of the industry's market. Other industries may have more concentrated production than efficiency considerations would dictate because the firms are seeking enhanced market power through large size plus entry restriction. What is debatable is the relative importance of these two forces, the one coming from the efficiencies of large scale and scope, and the other coming from the desire of firms to create market power by growing large.

Harvard economist Alfred D. Chandler Jr is a champion of the view that the major reason for the persistence of oligopolies in the manufacturing sector is the efficiency of large-scale production. His monumental work *Scale and Scope*[5] argues this case in great detail for the United States, the United Kingdom, and Germany.

---

[4] This is sometimes referred to as *Fordism*, after Henry Ford who introduced into the modern assembly-line method of production.

[5] A. D. Chandler Jr, *Scale and Scope: The Dynamics of Industrial Capitalism* (Cambridge, Mass.: Harvard University Press, 1990).

The basic dilemma of oligopoly

Oligopolistic behaviour is typically *strategic* behaviour. In deciding on strategies, oligopolists face a basic dilemma between competing and co-operating.

The firms in an oligopolistic industry will make more profits as a group if they co-operate; any one firm, however, may make more profits for itself if it goes it alone while the others co-operate.

This behaviour is similar to that established in Chapter 11 for the cartelization of a perfectly competitive industry.[6] In a perfectly competitive industry, however, there are so many firms that they cannot reach the co-operative solution unless some central governing body is able to force the necessary behaviour on all firms. In contrast, the few firms in an oligopolistic industry will themselves recognize the possibility of co-operating to avoid the loss of profits that will result from competitive behaviour.

The co-operative solution

If the firms in an oligopolistic industry co-operate, either overtly or tacitly, to produce among themselves the monopoly output, they can maximize their joint profits. If they do this, they will reach what is called a **co-operative solution**, which is the position that a single monopoly firm would reach if it owned all the firms in the industry. Of course, explicit co-operation by firms may be forbidden by competition laws. However, even within the range of what is legal, firms can choose whether to compete aggressively or to be more passive. The more passive approach can be equivalent to tacit co-operation.

The non-cooperative equilibrium

The analysis of a cartel in Chapter 11 shows that, if all the firms in an oligopolistic industry are at the co-operative solution, it will be profitable for any one of them to cut its price or to raise its output, as long as the others do not do so. However, if all firms do the same thing, they will be worse off as a group and may all be worse off individually. An equilibrium that is reached by firms when they proceed by calculating only their own gains, without co-operating with others, is called a **non-cooperative equilibrium** or a **Nash equilibrium.** This type of equilibrium is named after the US mathematician John Nash, who developed the concept in the 1950s and received the 1994 Nobel prize in economics for this work.[7] It is an equilibrium in which each firm's best strategy is to maintain its present behaviour, *given the present behaviour of the other firms.*

Nash equilibrium is a concept widely used in *game theory*, which is an approach to formal modelling of strategic interaction. We outline the game theory approach below, but first we turn to an explicit analysis of firm interaction in the special case where there are only two firms and strong assumptions are made about the choices available to them.

Models of strategic interaction

Duopoly

To study the consequences of non-cooperative behaviour among oligopolists in its purest form, we will start with the pathbreaking attack on the oligopoly problem that was made by the French economist A. A. Cournot (1801–76). The non-cooperative equilibrium that he demonstrated has seen a resurgence of interest in the modern industrial organization literature.

Cournot confined his attention to the special case of an industry containing only two firms, called a **duopoly**. He then assumed that the two firms sold an identical product, which was produced at zero marginal cost.[8] Each firm chose its profit-maximizing output *on the assumption that the other firm would hold its output constant.*

Cournot equilibrium

Figure 12.2 shows the situation as it looks to either firm when Cournot's assumptions are made. Let us call the firm we are looking at Firm One, and its rival Firm Two. For any given quantity produced by Firm Two, Firm One only needs to subtract that quantity from the market demand curve to obtain its own demand curve. Firm One can then calculate its profit-maximizing output (for this specific output by Firm Two) by equating its marginal costs to its marginal revenue in the usual way.[9] Repeating this process

---

[6] The basic reason is that, when only one firm increases its output by 1 per cent, the price falls by less than when all firms do the same. Thus, when the point is reached at which profits will be *reduced* if all firms expand output together, it will still pay *one* firm to expand output if the others do not do the same.

[7] Nash was immortalized by Hollywood in the 2002 film of his life, *A Beautiful Mind*, starring Russell Crowe.

[8] The simplifying assumption of zero marginal costs does not restrict the usefulness of the conclusions, none of which are affected in any important way if marginal costs are assumed positive.

[9] Since we have simplified by assuming marginal cost to be zero, the firm will produce at the point where its MR curve cuts the quantity axis, i.e. the output for which marginal revenue is zero.

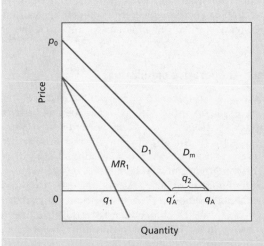

Figure 12.2 Calculation of a firm's own demand curve in Cournot's model

If one firm's output is given, the other firm's demand curve is easily calculated. The market demand curve is D_m. On that curve, quantity demanded is q_A when price is zero, and it falls to zero when price reaches p_0. Firm One assumes that Firm Two will hold its output constant at q_2. Subtracting this fixed quantity from the market demand curve yields Firm One's demand curve which tells Firm One what it can sell at each price. This curve, labelled D_1 in the diagram, is the market demand curve shifted to the left by the amount q_2, which is the distance $q_A - q_A'$ in the figure. Firm One's marginal revenue curve, MR_1, is derived from its own demand curve. Equating MR to zero (since marginal cost is zero in this example) yields Firm One's profit-maximizing output, q_1, *given Firm Two's output of q_2.*

Firm One has its own demand curve, its own marginal cost curve, and its own desired output for each given quantity that it assumes Firm Two will produce.

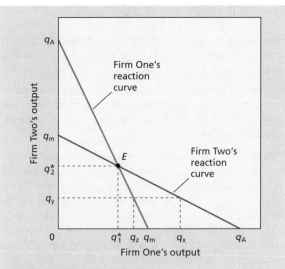

Figure 12.3 Cournot equilibrium

Cournot equilibrium occurs when, given each firm's present output, the other firm's profit-maximizing output is its present output. The figure shows each firm's reaction curve. Firm One's curve shows its profit-maximizing output for each *given* output of Firm Two. Firm Two's reaction curve shows its profit maximizing output for *given* outputs of Firm One. The quantity q_m is the monopoly output measured on both axes because it shows what each firm would like to produce if the other's production were zero. The quantity q_A, measured on both axes, is equal to the intercept on the market demand curve in Figure 12.2 because, when its competitor sells that quantity, the firm in question can sell nothing.

The outputs where the two reaction curves intersect (at E) are the equilibrium output q_1^* and, given q_1^*, Firm Two's desired output, q_2^*.

No other combination of outputs is an equilibrium. For example, if Firm One produces output, q_x, Firm Two will want to produce q_y; but if Firm Two produces q_y, Firm One will want to change its output to q_z.

for each possible output of Firm Two yields a set of corresponding outputs for Firm One. We now have what is called Firm One's **reaction curve**. It shows Firm One's profit-maximizing output for each possible quantity sold by Firm Two. Such a curve is shown in Figure 12.3.

The whole procedure can now be repeated for Firm Two. For each possible output for Firm One, that output can be subtracted from the market demand curve to obtain Firm Two's own demand curve. Firm Two's profit-maximizing output can then be calculated. Repeating the procedure for all possible outputs of Firm One yields a set of corresponding profit-maximizing outputs for Firm Two. This gives us Firm Two's reaction curve, showing its profit-maximizing output for each given output by Firm One. This curve is also given in Figure 12.3.

Figure 12.3 shows the Cournot equilibrium. There is one pair of outputs at the intersection of the reaction curves where the outputs of each firm are mutually consistent. This is an equilibrium in the sense that, if these outputs are

established, neither firm will wish to depart from them, given the assumptions made about their behaviour.

In the Cournot equilibrium, the two firms are making profits that exceed those earned under perfect competition but are less than those that would be earned by a monopoly. They earn less than a monopoly would earn because their joint outputs exceed the monopoly output. They earn more than perfectly competitive firms would make since each is aware that it drives the price down when it increases its own output. Thus, even if each takes its competitor's output as given, the demand curve that they assume they are facing is negatively sloped, so each stops short of the output for which marginal cost equals price.

Bertrand equilibrium

Some time after Cournot's analysis was written, it was criticized by the French mathematician Bertrand (1822–1900). He argued that Cournot's analysis was unrealistic because each firm determined its own best quantity *on the assumption that the other would hold its quantity constant.* Instead, Bertrand had each firm assume that the other would hold its *price* constant, and then ask itself what is the best *price* to charge.

The result was destructive competition, which drove price to the level of short-run marginal cost, so that firms would not be covering their fixed costs. To see why, assume that firms start in the Cournot equilibrium as shown in Figure 12.3. Firm One then follows Bertrand's reasoning and asks: 'If Firm Two holds its price constant, what is my best price?' The answer is to undercut Firm Two's price by a marginal amount. Firm One then gains the whole market in return for a small price cut. For example, if each firm was selling 1,000 units at a price of £1 and Firm One cuts its price to £0.99, it would sell 2,000 units and increase its total revenue from £1,000 (1,000 units at £1) to £1,980 (2,000 units at £0.99). But Firm Two would now reason in the same way. At a price of £1 its sales would now be zero, but at a price of £0.98 it could capture the entire market and earn £1,960 (2,000 units at £0.98).[10]

The incentive for price-cutting is always present as long as each firm can increase its profits by capturing the whole market. The only stable position is when price has been driven to short-run marginal cost (which is zero in the present case). At this price, neither firm has any incentive to cut price. Although it would gain the entire market, selling at a price below the marginal cost of production is never profitable.

Do the theories employ unrealistic assumptions?

For many years it was popular to criticize both Cournot's and Bertrand's theories on the grounds that they employed unrealistic assumptions. Surely, it was argued, each firm would learn that its competitors did not sit idly by, holding their prices, or their outputs, constant, while the firm adopted its own best strategy. Indeed, if these theories were meant to explain how equilibrium was reached, they would be naive. As the process of price or quantity undercutting continued, each firm would learn that it was wrong to assume that the other firm would not react. But the theories are not meant to be about the process by which equilibrium is reached, although many critics have thought otherwise. Instead, they are about the existence of an equilibrium which, if reached by any means, will be self-perpetuating.

The great significance of both Cournot's and Bertrand's equilibria is that they are self-policing.

If firms compete actively with each other by varying the quantities that they sell, and if they reach Cournot's equilibrium by any path whatsoever, they will tend to stay there. Any other combination of outputs is not self-policing, in the sense that each firm will be tempted to vary

its *output*. The same is true of Bertrand's equilibrium. If firms compete with each other by varying prices, and if price is at marginal cost, there is no incentive for any one firm to depart from this *price*. Raising price will reduce sales to zero, while cutting price will capture the entire market but at a price below variable costs.

Implications

It does seem more realistic to assume that firms compete by setting prices rather than quantities. Yet Bertrand's equilibrium cannot be the typical one because, if firms were in Bertrand equilibrium in the short run, they would exit from the industry in the long run—the reason being that, if short-run marginal costs are constant and equal to price, firms cannot be covering their fixed costs.[11]

Examples of Bertrand-style price competition do seem to occur from time to time. In unusually bad recessions, price competition sometimes drives price well below average total costs. Similar behaviour is sometimes found in the aircraft industry, which is close to being a duopoly with Boeing and Airbus being the two dominant producers (and in jet engines, where there are three dominant firms). When the major companies are competing to sell a new generation of aircraft (or jet engines), most of the development costs have already been incurred. Although direct production costs are not zero, they are a small part of average total costs because the costs of developing a new line of aircraft are enormous. Under these circumstances the major companies compete to sell their similar planes to the world's major airlines. If an order is lost, nothing is earned. If an order is gained at any price above variable costs, it contributes something to fixed costs. The resulting competition to obtain large orders can lead to something close to Bertrand's equilibrium. Rather than lose an order, price is cut well below average total cost and little more than marginal production cost is covered. Such competition is costly to firms, but once the fixed costs have been incurred, it is hard to prevent price-cutting when large orders can be won or lost.

Intense price competition tends to produce an equilibrium in which firms are not covering their full costs, while intense quantity competition tends to produce an equilibrium in

---

[10] The figures in this paragraph imply a completely inelastic market demand, since 2,000 units are sold whatever the price. If the demand curve has the normal negative slope, the incentive to undercut the competitor becomes even stronger. The undercutting strategy then increases the firm's sales by the amount that it takes from the other firm, plus the amount that market quantity demanded increases as a result of a fall in the market price.

[11] Under perfect competition in the long run, price is equal to short-run marginal cost and to long-run average total cost because the firms' cost curves are U-shaped. (See Figure 10.12 on page 169.) If short-run marginal costs are constant, and equal to short-run average variable costs, marginal cost will be less than average total cost.

which firms are earning profits that exceed the perfectly competitive result, but are less than the monopoly result.

Price or quantity competition?

The industrial organization literature has investigated circumstances under which each type of competition is more likely to occur. In the aircraft case, where fixed costs are all paid before sales take place and the firms have capacity to fill many more orders than they may get, price competition is likely. In other cases, where the production process takes a long time, firms may commit themselves to some level of output, and then sell it for what they can get. In this case, competition is in quantities.

One important result of these studies, however, concerns capacity.

One firm's temptation to undercut its rival's price and capture all the market, which underlies Bertrand's model, is present only when that firm has the capacity to serve the whole market.

To see this, assume that two firms are in a Cournot equilibrium such as is shown in Figure 12.3. Now also assume that both firms' plants are operating at full capacity: they cannot produce any larger output. Under these circumstances, there is no reason to cut price, since output cannot be increased beyond its present levels in either firm.

Firms will have the ultimate equilibrium in mind when planning how much capacity to install in the first place. Having built their plants, they then compete with each other to sell their outputs. When firms decide on their own best capacity, they know whether the subsequent competition will be in prices (Bertrand) or quantities (Cournot). Under these circumstances, profit-maximizing firms should build plants just big enough to supply the output that would occur in Cournot equilibrium. Then, whether they subsequently compete by deciding on quantities, as in Cournot's theory, or on prices, as in Bertrand's theory, they end up in Cournot's equilibrium. They cover their total costs and make profits that are less than a monopoly but more than a perfectly competitive industry. When they do reach the Cournot equilibrium, they are not tempted to cut prices because they are already producing at full capacity.[12]

The intuitive reason for this result is as follows.

Firms often recognize the self-destructive nature of the price competition that was analysed by Bertrand. Having recognized it, they take steps to avoid it. They do this by limiting their capacity to produce.

This argument leads us to expect Cournot's results when demand is such that firms can just use their capacity, and Bertrand's results when firms unexpectedly (or, as in the case of aircraft, unavoidably) find themselves with large quantities of unused capacity. Thus, for example, when demand falls to unexpectedly low levels during a reces-

sion, firms will have excess capacity and will be tempted to engage in price competition that may drive price below average total costs. But when demand is at its expected level, firms will not find themselves with the excess capacity that tempts them to undercut their competitors, driving price below Cournot's equilibrium level. This is no accident; firms will have planned it that way.

We now discuss a more general approach to the analysis of strategic interaction between a small number of firms.

Game theory applied to oligopoly

Game theory may sound like something trivial or humorous —after all, we play 'games' for fun. However, game theory is a major branch of economic analysis that provides many insights into the real-world behaviour of economic agents in situations where there is an actual or potential conflict of interest. **Game theory** is a theory of rational behaviour in interactive decision-making problems. The 'game' element arises because the outcome depends not only on the choices made by one player, but also on what other players choose to do at the same time (or subsequently).

In a game, several agents aim to maximize their own payoff by choosing specific actions, but the actual outcome also depends on what all the other players do. The game consists of a specified interactive playing field (which in the case of firms would be the market for their product), a specification of all possible courses of action, and a schedule of the payoffs to each of the players under all possible outcomes. Players plan their own courses of action in order to maximize their expected payoff, under the knowledge that the other players are trying to do the same. A player's *strategy* is a complete specification of the actions to be taken in response to outcomes that are discovered as the game proceeds (though a strategy may include some random elements). One player's payoff from choosing a strategy depends on what the other players do, but players cannot make binding agreements with each other.

Given all the players' strategies, there will be a set of possible outcomes to the game. These determine the payoffs for each of the players. A specific outcome is called an *equilibrium* if no player can take actions to improve their own payoff while all other players continue to follow their optimal strategies.

---

[12] The firms are engaged in what is called a two-stage game (discussed in the next section), which uses the equilibrium concept of sub-game perfection. The two stages are the decision on plant size and the competition between the firms once their plants are built. Sub-game perfection means that, in making its first decision on capacity, each firm understands the kind of competitive game it will be playing in the second stage when it competes to sell its output. Recent research has focused on the conditions for Cournot's equilibrium to be the outcome of this two-stage game. The important result, however, is that Bertrand's equilibrium is never the outcome if demand is correctly foreseen.

There is a circularity to the problem that has to be solved, as, in order to select his or her best strategy, a player must know other players will do, but they in turn are in the same position. In **normal** (or **strategic**) **form** games players choose their moves simultaneously. Whenever the choices available are discrete and finite, the game can be represented in the structure of a table setting out the possible outcomes for each of the players depending on what the other players do. In an **extensive form** game players make moves in some order over time, so the analysis of the game needs a specification of the payoffs and information at each point in time. Real business interactions are obviously more closely analogous to an extensive form game, as firms interact dynamically over time; however, whenever the precise timing of moves is not essential to the outcome, a 'game' can often be represented more simply as a normal form game.

A game that is played only once is a 'one-shot' game. Repeated games open possibilities of learning and of acting in order to punish or reward the other players. A **supergame** is a game that is repeated an infinite number of times.

Example 1 Let us think of a simple example in order to give an intuitive feel for the issues involved. Suppose that you are in your first year at university and you are planning for your summer vacation. In all the previous years of your life you have gone on a summer vacation with your parents. This year you would like to go away with your own friends instead. However, you think that your parents will be offended if you say that you do not want to go on holiday with them—after all, they are helping to finance your education. So what do you say when your parents phone up and say that they are booking the summer vacation and are assuming that you will come?

What happens and the payoffs (i.e. the level of happiness of all involved) depend upon what your parents' true preferences are. In one possible case, they would prefer to go on holiday without you, as they have had to have holidays that suit their children for the last 20 years or so. However, they think they should give you the option of going with them even though they hope you will say no, but they do not want to offend you.

Clearly, the best solution for everybody, which would be called the co-operative solution, is for everybody to reveal their true preferences and then you can agree to have separate holidays so that all end up happy. However, a likely outcome in a one shot-game is that each of you tries to avoid the really bad outcome (as you perceive it) of offending the other, so your parents ask you to join them and you agree to go. This is not as bad as everyone feeling offended, but it is inferior for everyone to the best outcome of everybody having the holiday they want. Thus, each choosing a strategy of avoiding the worst possible outcome leads to a solution, but one that is not the best that could be achieved for all concerned.

Of course, if this game were repeated for several years in a row, then the preferences of each side might be revealed more clearly and the optimal solution of separate holidays could be arrived at.

The other possibility is that your parents really would prefer you to come on holiday with them while you really would prefer not to. In this situation there is no way in which both parties can achieve their preferred solution. If you say no to them they really will be upset, but if you say yes you will not have as good a holiday as you could with your friends. Your decision will depend on how you weigh up the psychic cost of offending your parents against the loss of having a good time elsewhere.

This is obviously a rather special case, and in a family situation happily there are other ways of communicating and solving problems where objectives conflict. However, it is hoped that this can give a feel for what is going on in a game structure. Individuals have a range of possible choices, but the outcomes are affected by what other players do at the same time. In business games we normally consider the potential payoffs in terms of profit, but strategy can just as easily be based on other types of preference —such as avoiding offending your parents.

Solutions to games

The first thing to look for in a game is whether each player has a **dominant strategy**. This is a strategy that is the best response independent of what the other players do. If each player has a dominant strategy, this is what they will do, and the outcome of the game will be the payoff associated with all players following this strategy. *Dominated strategies*, which are all those other than the dominant strategy, will not be played, so these can be eliminated from consideration. If there are only two strategies to choose from and one is dominant, the other must be dominated, but it is possible to have dominated strategies with no dominant strategy.

If there is no obvious dominant strategy for each player, it is necessary to look for possible equilibria of the game. A **Nash equilibrium** occurs when each player chooses his or her strategy to maximize the payoff assuming that all other players are playing their Nash equilibrium strategies. In this situation, no player would want to change his or her strategy as it is believed that all other players would not change theirs. The Cournot equilibrium discussed above is an example of a Nash equilibrium.

According to the **Nash Theorem**, every game with a finite number of players and a finite number of strategies will have at least one Nash equilibrium. For this to hold, however, there has to be the possibility of some random element to strategies. A strategy with some random elements is referred to as a *mixed strategy*. Another problem is that there may be multiple Nash equilibria, and it is not always obvious which one will arise. Finally, it is generally true that the Nash equilibrium is not the global optimum in the sense that, if players could co-operate, they could all become better off.

A game theory framework can often help us understand the strategic choices available, but it does not always help predict which of many possible outcomes may occur.

We now discuss a hypothetical example to illustrate the above concepts. Box 12.3 outlines some classic interactive decision dilemmas that can be analysed in the game theory framework.

Example 2 Firms that are competing head-to-head with a small number of other firms have to decide how aggressive

to be. Suppose for example that there are just two firms producing a similar product and that each firm has two possible strategies. One is to act aggressively by increasing output and trying to increase market share. The other is to act passively and keep producing at the current level of output, which involves each firm having roughly half the market and jointly sharing the monopoly profit. The possible outcomes illustrate the relevance of game theory to oligopoly.

When game theory is applied to oligopoly, the players are firms, their game is played in the market, their strategies are their price/output decisions, and the payoffs are their profits.

 ### Box 12.3 **Games and their applications**

The 'prisoner's dilemma'

This is the story that lies behind the above name:

Two men, John and Bill, are arrested for jointly committing a crime and are interrogated separately. They know that if they both plead innocent they will get only a light sentence. Each is told, however, that if either protests innocence while the other admits guilt, the one who claims innocence will get a severe sentence while the other will be let off. If they both plead guilty, they will both get a medium sentence.

The table shows the payoff matrix for that game.

		John's plea	John's plea
		Innocent	Guilty
William's plea	Innocent	J light sentence W light sentence	J no sentence W severe sentence
William's plea	Guilty	J severe sentence W no sentence	J medium sentence W medium sentence

John reasons as follows: 'If Bill pleads innocent, I get a light sentence if I also plead innocent, but no sentence at all if I plead guilty, so guilty is my better plea. Second, if Bill pleads guilty, I get a severe sentence if I plead innocent and a medium sentence if I plead guilty. So once again guilty is my preferred plea.' Bill reasons in the same way, and as a result they both plead guilty and get a medium sentence, whereas if they had been able to communicate, they could both have agreed to plead innocent and get off with a light sentence.

The prisoner's dilemma has many business applications as it is the classic case in which co-operation would maximize joint income, but the strategic interaction of firms is more likely to lead to the non-cooperative outcome, as in Cournot and Nash equilibria.

Battle of the sexes

Imagine a situation where a husband and wife have a choice between going to the theatre and going to a soccer game. John really wants to go to soccer and Jane really wants to go to the theatre. Jane's payoff is the first number in each box and John's is the second. Each would get some satisfaction

		Jane	Jane
		Soccer	Theatre
John	Soccer	100, 200	0, 0
John	Theatre	0, 0	200, 100

from going along with the other's preferred choice, but neither would be at all happy to go alone to either of the potential activities. There are two Nash equilibria in the game as set out here, as both have an incentive to move from the off diagonal outcomes. However, in a one shot game it is not clear which of the two possible equilibria will emerge. In a repeated game the outcome may depend on who moves first and on whether they can agree to alternate the outcome—theatre this time, soccer next time.

The structure of this game illustrates some business situations in which it pays to co-operate rather than compete. The choice between VHS and betamax as a video standard shows that it does not pay to go it alone. Betamax was technically the better standard, but once VHS got to be on top in usage it paid all producers to adopt it. The same applies to cell phones, computer operating systems, and many integrated trading systems.

Zero sum game

As the name suggests, a zero sum game is one in which whatever is won by one player is lost by the other. This is not the normal outcome of economic games, as in most economic interactions both parties can become better off and so there is some positive net gain to be shared out. However, the zero sum game is a frequently used reference point in economics for any interactive situation in which there is a distributional impact but no net increase in income or wealth for the participants.

A sweepstake is a zero sum game, as each player gets one horse in the race or one team in the competition and the winner takes all the stakes put in by others. An auction is also a form of zero sum game, as the article for sale changes hands from seller to winning bidder under all outcomes, but all that has to be decided is how much the buyer pays the seller (and of course which buyer gets the goods). (See page 234.) Many takeover bids are close to a zero sum game, where most of what gets determined is the distribution of gains and losses between shareholders of the bidding and the bid-for firms.

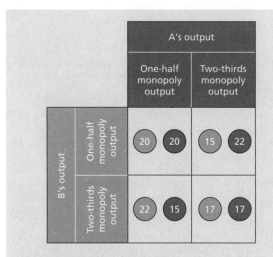

Figure 12.4 The oligopolist's dilemma: to co-operate or to compete

Co-operation to determine the overall level of output can maximize joint profits, but it leaves each firm with an incentive to alter its production. The figure gives what is called a payoff matrix for a two-firm duopoly game. Only two levels of production are considered in order to illustrate the basic problem. A's production is indicated across the top, and its profits (measured in millions of pounds) are shown in the blue circles within each square. B's production is indicated down the left side, and its profits (in millions of pounds) are shown in the green circles within each square. For example, the top right square tells us that if B produces one-half, while A produces two-thirds, of the output that a monopolist would produce, A's profits will be £22 million, while B's will be £15 million.

If A and B co-operate, each produces one-half the monopoly output and earns profits of £20 million, as shown in the upper left box. In this 'co-operative solution', either firm can raise its profits by producing two-thirds of the monopoly output, provided the other firm does not do the same.

Now let A and B behave non-cooperatively. A reasons that, whether B produces either one-half or two-thirds of the monopoly output, A's best output is two-thirds. B reasons similarly. They then reach the non-cooperative equilibrium, where each produces two-thirds of the monopoly output, and each makes less than it would if the two firms co-operated.

The basic dilemma of oligopolists is shown in Figure 12.4 for the case of a two-firm oligopoly. The simplified game, adopted for the purposes of illustration, allows only two strategies for *each firm*. Each firm can produce an output equal to either one-half of the monopoly output (the passive strategy) or two-thirds of the monopoly output (the aggressive strategy). Note that the passive strategy amounts to tacit co-operation while the aggressive strategy is clearly non-cooperative. This simple game is sufficient to illustrate several key propositions in the modern theory of oligopoly.

Figure 12.4 presents the *payoff matrix*. The data in the matrix show the profits that result from the four possible combinations of strategies.

The passive (co-operative) solution If both sides tacitly co-operate, *each producing* one-half of the monopoly output, they share the monopoly profits by *jointly producing* the output that a monopolist would produce. As a group, they cannot do better.

The aggressive (non-cooperative) solution There is one Nash equilibrium in Figure 12.4. In the bottom-right cell, the best decision for each firm, given that the other firm is producing two-thirds of the monopoly output, is to produce two-thirds of the monopoly output itself. Between them they produce a joint output of one-and-a-third times the monopoly output. Neither firm has an incentive to depart from this position, except through co-operation with the other. In any other cell, each firm has an incentive to alter its output, *given the output of the other firm*.

This shows that the basis of a Nash equilibrium is rational decision-making in the absence of co-operation. Its particular importance in oligopoly theory is that it is the only type of equilibrium that is *self-policing*. It is self-policing in the sense that there is no need for group behaviour to enforce it. Each firm has a self-interest to maintain it, because no move that it can make on its own will improve its profits, given what other firms are currently doing.

If a Nash equilibrium is established—by any means whatsoever—no firm has an incentive to depart from it by altering its own behaviour. It is self-policing.

Strategic behaviour The Nash equilibrium will be attained if each firm behaves strategically, by choosing its optimal strategy taking into account what the other firm may do. Let us see how this works.

Suppose that firm A reasons as follows: 'B can do one of two things; what is the best thing for me to do in each case? First, what if B produces one-half of the monopoly output? If I do the same, I receive a profit of 20, but if I produce two-thirds of the monopoly output, I receive 22. Second, what if B produces two-thirds of the monopoly output? If I produce one-half of the monopoly output, I receive a profit of 15, whereas if I produce two-thirds, I receive 17. Clearly, my best strategy is to produce two-thirds of the monopoly output in either case.' Aggressive behaviour is the dominant strategy.

B will reason in the same way. As a result, they end up by jointly producing one-and-a-third times the monopoly output, where each earns a profit of 17.

This type of game, where the non-cooperative equilibrium makes both players worse off than if they were able to co-operate, is like the **prisoner's dilemma** shown in Box 12.3. The important insight following from prisoner's dilemma games is that individual maximization does not always lead to an optimum allocation of resources. In the

Box 12.4 Real-world strategic games

There are many situations in which firms have to make strategic decisions about reactions to their main rival suppliers. Here are some examples.

Supermarket price wars

Major supermarket chains are in competition with each for growth and market share in a relatively static business area—demand for food grows only slowly. They can grow by opening stores in new areas, by trying to attract customers from other stores, by advertising, or by lowering prices.

Managers of supermarkets would like to run their businesses with comfortable profit margins, and in normal times there is a standard mark-up on most products that gives an adequate return on the company's capital employed. From time to time one of the major players decides that it will make a push for more customers and significantly cuts its prices on a wide range of standard products. Frequently the rival players will cut their prices too in order to stem the loss of customers.

This may look like Bertrand competition, and in some respects it is. However, supermarkets are multi-product firms, and the aim of price wars is not to lose money but rather to get more customers into the store so that they will buy a range of other products on which the prices have not been cut. Of course, if other stores also cut their prices, then the price war could reduce the combined profits of all supermarkets. But it is also possible that the big players will end up better off as a result of attracting more customers from smaller grocery shops.

Airline pricing

The European airline business has long had barriers to entry, often designed to protect inefficient state-owned carriers. Deregulation of pricing occurred slowly over time, but some barriers to entry still existed in the form of restriction in the available landing slots at major airports, such as London's Heathrow.

As discussed in Box 11.2 on page 185, established carriers had developed a pricing structure that enabled them to segment the market between business and leisure passengers. This meant that, unless booking ahead (on some routes) or staying over a Saturday night, fairs were very high—for example £500 for an economy flight to Rome if returning within the week, where staying over a weekend might reduce this below £200.

This situation created incentives for new entry into the market. Companies like EasyJet and Ryanair introduced 'no frills' services between various European cities at dramatically lower fares and with no restrictions such as the weekend stay. They circumvented the entry barriers created by

lack of access to landing slots by flying between smaller airports—EasyJet built a hub at Luton and Ryanair built one at Stansted. EasyJet even targeted the business traveller market.

The result was a boom in the business of the low-cost carriers and a decline in the use of traditional carriers such as BA. In April 2002, BA announced that it was slashing its fares on some short-haul domestic routes. A day return from London to Manchester, for example, would be cut from £233 to £69 (on some flights).

The strategic issue for BA was whether to ignore the new players and maintain its old fare structures, which clearly involved some monopoly profit, or to compete on price with the new entrants. For a while BA could ignore the other players as they were small. However, once they started to hit their profitable segment of the market, BA had to fight back. At the time of writing, the battle was only just starting to unfold. But in previous bouts of new entry, in this case into the trans-Atlantic market, the new entrants (such as Laker airways) were driven out by intense price competition from existing carriers. After driving out the upstarts, a new equilibrium was established.

Digital TV

UK satellite TV provider BskyB built up its business by bidding for exclusive coverage of live sporting events such as Premier League football, rugby internationals and cricket test matches. This strategy proved to be successful in attracting subscribers who had to pay a premium for these extra channels.

A new company was set up in 2000 called On Digital (later renamed ITV Digital), paying tried to follow a similar strategy of buying exclusive rights to some live sporting events. Over £300 million for rights to televise Football League games, i.e. lower divisions than the Premier League. However, in this case the strategy failed: there was little demand to watch the games they were showing, and the company went into administration while attempting to renegotiate the terms of its contract with the League.

In effect, the aggressive strategy failed not because of reactions from rivals, but because the revenue to be generated by the aggressive strategy was misjudged. Rival suppliers could just sit back and wait for ITV Digital to fail. The only puzzle is why the managers of this company ever thought that large numbers of consumers would pay a premium to watch lower-division football in the first place. A successful strategy clearly needs a good assessment of the payoffs on which the decision is to be based.

Nash equilibrium of the prisoner's dilemma game, both players can be made better off if they co-operate and so move to the top left-hand box. But if both make individual maximizing decisions, they end up in the bottom right-hand box.

Breakdown of co-operation The Nash equilibrium is attained by the strategic reasoning just outlined. It can, however, be used to give an intuitive argument for why tacit co-operation tends to break down.

Assume that the co-operative position has been attained.

Each firm is producing one-half of the monopoly output and each is earning a profit of 20. The data in Figure 12.4 show that if A cheats by increasing its output its profits will increase. However, B's profits will be reduced. A's behaviour drives the industry's prices down, so B earns less from its unchanged output. Because A's cheating takes the firms away from the joint profit-maximizing monopoly output, their joint profits must fall. This means that B's profits fall by more than A's rise.

Figure 12.4 shows that similar considerations also apply to B. It is worthwhile for B to depart from the joint maximizing output, as long as A does not do so. So both A and B have an incentive to depart from the joint profit-maximizing level of output.

Finally, Figure 12.4 shows that, when either firm departs from the joint-maximizing output, the other has an incentive to do so as well. When each follows this 'selfish' strategy, they reach a non-cooperative equilibrium at which they jointly produce one-and-a-third times as much as the monopolist would. Each then has profits that are lower than at the co-operative solution.[13]

Game theory is an extremely flexible tool that has been applied to many branches of economics. Box 12.4 outlines some real-world situations that illustrate the strategic choices that firms have to make in practice.

Dynamics of oligopoly industries

Suppose that firms in an oligopolistic industry succeed in raising prices above long-run average total costs and earn substantial profits that are not completely eliminated by non-price competition. In the absence of significant barriers to entry, new firms will enter the industry and erode the profits of existing firms, as they do in monopolistic competition. Natural barriers to entry are an important part of the explanation of the persistence of profits in many oligopolistic industries. Where such natural barriers do not exist, oligopolistic firms can earn profits in the long run only if they can create entry barriers.

Entry barriers

We have already discussed the importance of entry barriers on pages 186–7, and here we extend this discussion with some cases that are most relevant to oligopoly.

Brand proliferation

By altering the characteristics of a differentiated product, it is possible to produce a vast array of variations on the general theme of that product. Think, for example, of cars with a little more or a little less acceleration, braking power, top speed, cornering ability, petrol mileage, and so on, compared with existing models.

Although the multiplicity of existing brands is no doubt partly a response to consumers' tastes, it also discourages the entry of new firms. Say, for example, that an industry contains three large firms, each selling one brand of cigarettes, and say that 30 per cent of all smokers change brands in a random fashion each year. If a new firm enters the industry, it can expect to pick up one-third of the smokers who change brands.[14] This would give the new firm 10 per cent (one third of 30 per cent) of the total market the first year merely as a result of picking up its share of the random switchers, and it would keep increasing its share for some time thereafter. If, however, the existing three firms have five brands each, there would be 15 brands already available. A new firm selling one new brand could then expect to pick up only one-fifteenth of the brand-switchers, giving it 2 per cent of the total market the first year, with smaller gains also in subsequent years. This is an extreme case, but it illustrates a general result:

The larger the number of differentiated products sold by existing oligopolists, the smaller the market share available to a new firm entering with a single new product.

An example of brand proliferation drawn from the alcoholic drinks industry is given in Box 12.5.

Advertising

Existing firms can create entry barriers by imposing significant fixed costs on new firms that enter their market. This is particularly important if the industry has only weak natural barriers to entry because the minimum efficient scale occurs at an output that is low relative to the total output of the industry.

Advertising serves the useful function of informing buyers about their alternatives, thereby making markets work more smoothly. Indeed, advertising is essential to make consumers aware of new products, whether produced by existing firms or new entrants.

None the less, advertising can also operate as a potent entry barrier by increasing the set-up costs of new entrants. Where heavy advertising has established strong brand images for existing products, a new firm may have to spend heavily on advertising to create its own brand images in consumers' minds. If the firm's initial sales are small, advertising costs *per unit sold* will be large, and price will have to be correspondingly high to cover those costs.

The combined use of brand proliferation and advertising as an entry barrier helps to explain one apparent paradox

---

[13] This is why we do not speak of the co-operative *equilibrium*. It is a solution to the problem of finding the best co-operative behaviour, but it is not an equilibrium, since, once achieved, each firm has an incentive to depart from it.

[14] Since there are now four brands to choose from, you might think that the new brand would pick up one-quarter of the switchers. But this is not correct because, by definition, the switcher rejects his old brand and chooses one of the others. Each switcher's choice-set therefore consists of three brands—two of the pre-existing brands and the one new brand.

Box 12.5 **Brand proliferation in alcoholic drinks**

Allied Domecq plc is one of Britain's largest companies. It is a major producer of wines and spirits and an owner of restaurants and food outlets including Baskin-Robbins, Dunkin' Donuts, and Togo's.

At one time Allied was a major producer of beers and a retailer of alcohol through pubs, but it sold its beer and pub interests in the late 1990s in order to concentrate on its extensive portfolio of wine and spirits businesses. If you are into scotch whisky, you could try Ballantine's, Teachers, and Laphroaig, or perhaps go for Canadian Club or Maker's Mark bourbon—they are all Allied brands, as are Beefeater gin, Lamb's Navy Rum, Courvoisier brandy, Sauza, Kahlúa, and Tia Maria liqueurs. You may prefer fortified wines like Harvey's and La Ina sherries, or Cockburn's ports—you're still drinking Allied products. If you prefer to drink wine, start the evening with Mumm or Perrier-Jouet champagne then move onto some Montana sauvignon blanc from New Zealand, perhaps followed by Marques de Arienzo Rioja from Spain or an Atlas Peak cabernet from California. You guessed it, these are all Allied products, as are many other wine labels from around the world, including Clos du Bois, Callaway Coastal, William Hill, Buena Vista in California, and Bodegas Balbi in Argentina.

Of course, Allied is not the only multi-brand producer; most of Allied's main competitors also have an extensive portfolio of brands. For example,

Diageo also sells many alcoholic products. In the spirits line they have Archers, Baileys, Bell's scotch whisky, Cacique rum, Captain Morgan rum, Crown Royal Canadian whisky, Cuervo tequila, Gilbey's and Gordon's gin, Hennessy cognac, Johnnie Walker and J&B scotch, Pimms, Smirnoff vodka, and Tanqueray gin. For drinkers of single malts they have Cragganmore, Dalwhinnie, Glenkinchie, Lagavulin, Oban, and Talisker. If you prefer beer they have Guinness, Harp lager, Kilkenny Irish beer, and Red Stripe lager. Wine drinkers are not forgotten, as Diageo owns Beaulieu Vineyard, Blossom Hill and Sterling Vineyards in California and has a significant share in Moet and Chandon champagne.

The production of such a wide range of differentiated products helps to satisfy consumers' clear demand for diversity. It also has the effect of making it more difficult for a new firm to enter the industry. If the new firm wishes to compete over the whole range of differentiated products, it must enter on a massive scale. If it wishes to enter on only a small scale, it faces a formidable task of establishing brand images and customer recognition with only a few products over which to spread the expenses of entry. There may also be significant economies of scope for the big liqueur companies, as they can share distribution channels for most of their products.

---

of business life—one firm often sells multiple brands of the same product, which compete actively against each other as well as against the products of other firms.

The soap and cigarette industries provide classic examples of this behaviour. Because quite small plants can realize all available scale economies, both industries have few natural barriers to entry. Both contain a few large firms, each of which produces an array of heavily advertised products. The numerous existing products make it harder for a new entrant to obtain a large market niche with a single new product. The heavy advertising, although it is directed against existing products, creates an entry barrier by increasing the set-up costs of a new product that seeks to gain the attention of consumers and to establish its own brand image.

Contestable markets and potential entry

The theory of contestable markets shows that pure profits may be eliminated even though the industry contains only a few firms and experiences no actual entry. *Potential* entry can do the job just as well as actual entry, as long as two conditions are fulfilled. First, entry must be easy to accomplish; and, second, existing firms must take potential entry into account when making price and output decisions.

Entry is usually costly to the entering firm. It may have to build a plant, it may have to develop new versions of the industry's differentiated product, or it may have to advertise heavily in order to call attention to its product. These and many other initial expenses are often called **sunk costs of entry**, which are defined as costs that a firm must incur

to enter the market and that cannot be recovered if the firm subsequently exits.

A market that new firms can enter and leave without incurring any sunk costs of entry is called a perfectly **contestable market**. A market can be perfectly contestable even if the firm must pay some costs of entry, as long as these can be recovered when the firm exits. Because all markets require at least some sunk costs of entry, contestability must be understood as a variable. The lower the sunk costs of entry, the more contestable the market.

In a contestable market the existence of profits, even if they are due to transitory causes, will attract entry. Firms will enter to gain a share of these profits and will exit when the transitory situation has changed.

Consider, for example, the market for air travel on the lucrative London–Paris route. This market would become quite contestable once EU regulations are phased out, *if* counter and loading space were easily available to new entrants at the two cities' airline terminals. An airline that was not currently serving the cities in question could shift some of its existing planes to the market with small sunk costs of entry. Some training of personnel would be needed for staff to become familiar with the route and the airport. This is a sunk cost of entry that cannot be recovered if the cities in question are no longer to be served. However, most of the airline's costs of entering the London–Paris market are not sunk costs. If it subsequently decides to leave a city, the rental of terminal space will stop, and the aeroplanes and the ground equipment can be shifted to another location. The former head of the American Civil Aeronautics Board, and architect of airline deregulation, captured this point by referring to commercial aircraft as 'marginal cost with wings'.

Sunk costs of entry constitute an entry barrier. The larger they are, the larger the profits of existing firms can be without attracting new entrants. The flip side of this coin is that firms operating in markets without large sunk costs of entry will not earn large profits. Strategic considerations will lead them to keep prices near the level that would just cover their total costs. They know that if they charge higher prices firms will enter to capture the profits while they last and will then exit.

Contestability, where it is possible, is a force that can limit the profits of existing oligopolists. Even if entry does not occur, the ease with which it could be accomplished may keep existing oligopolists from charging prices that would maximize their joint profits.

Contestability is just another example, in somewhat more refined form, of the key point that the possibility of entry is the major force preventing the exploitation of market power. Notice that the entrants do not have to be new firms. They can be domestic firms entering new domestic markets or foreign firms entering the domestic market.

Oligopoly and the functioning of the economy

Oligopoly is found in many industries and in all advanced economies. It typically occurs in industries where both perfect and monopolistic competition are made impossible by the existence of major economies of scale or of scope (or both). In such industries, there is simply not enough room for a large number of firms, all operating at or near their minimum efficient scales.

Three questions are important for the evaluation of the performance of the oligopolistic market structure. First, do oligopolistic markets allocate resources very differently from perfectly competitive markets? Second, in their short-run and long-run price–output behaviour, where do oligopolistic firms typically settle between the extreme outcomes of earning zero profits and earning the profits that would be available to a single monopolist? Third, how much do oligopolists contribute to economic growth by encouraging innovative activity in the very long run? We consider each of these questions in turn.

The market mechanism under oligopoly

We have seen that under perfect competition prices are set by the impersonal forces of demand and supply, and changes in the market conditions for both inputs and outputs are signalled by changes in the prices of a firm's inputs and outputs. The market signalling system works slightly differently when prices are administered by oligopolists. Changes in prices still signal changes in market conditions for inputs. However, changes in the market conditions for outputs are typically signalled by changes in the volume of their sales at the administered prices.

Increases in costs of inputs will shift cost curves upward, and oligopolistic firms will be led to raise prices and lower outputs. Increases in demand will cause the sales of oligopolistic firms to rise. Firms will then respond by increasing output, thereby increasing the quantities of society's resources that are allocated to producing that output. They will then decide whether or not to alter their administered prices.

The market system reallocates resources in response to changes in demands and costs in roughly the same way under oligopoly as it does under perfect competition.

Profits under oligopoly

Some firms in some oligopolistic industries succeed in coming close to joint profit maximization in the short run. In other oligopolistic industries firms compete so intensely among themselves that they come close to achieving competitive prices and outputs.

In the long run those profits that do survive competitive behaviour among existing firms will tend to attract entry. These profits will persist only in so far as entry is restricted either by natural barriers, such as large minimum efficient scales for potential entrants, or by barriers created, and successfully defended, by the existing firms.

Very-long-run competition

Once we allow for the effects of technological change, we need to ask which market structure is most conducive to the sorts of very-long-run changes that we discussed in Chapter 9. These changes are the driving force of the economic growth that has so greatly raised living standards over the last two centuries. They are intimately related to Schumpeter's concept of creative destruction, which we first encountered in our discussion of entry barriers in Chapter 11 (pages 186–7).

Examples of creative destruction abound. In the nineteenth century, railways began to compete with horse-drawn wagons and barges for the carriage of freight. In the twentieth century, lorries operating on newly constructed highways began competing with rail. During the 1950s and 1960s, aeroplanes began to compete seriously with lorries and rail. In recent years the development of fax transmission and e-mail has eliminated the monopoly of the Royal Mail in delivering hard-copy (as opposed to oral) communications. In their myriad uses, computers for the home and the office have swept away the markets of many once-thriving products and services. For instance, in-store computers answer customer questions, decreasing the need for salespeople. Aided by computers, 'just in time' inventory systems greatly reduce the investment in inventories required of existing firms and new entrants alike. Computer-based flexible-manufacturing systems allow firms to switch production easily and inexpensively from one product line to another, thereby reducing the minimum scale at which each can be produced profitably. Computers are involved in book production, having replaced the author's hand- and typewritten copy and the publisher's laborious page makeup procedures. One day soon the multimedia CD-ROM, or its successor, may replace the textbook altogether.

An important defence of oligopoly relates to this process of creative destruction. Some economists argue that intermediate market structures such as oligopoly lead to more innovation than would occur in either perfect competition or monopoly. Oligopolists face strong competition from existing rivals and cannot afford the more relaxed life of the monopolist. At the same time, however, oligopolistic firms expect to keep a good share of the profits that they earn from their innovative activity.

Everyday observation provides some confirmation of this view. Leading North American firms that operate in highly concentrated industries, such as Kodak, IBM, Microsoft, Du Pont, Intel, General Electric, and 3M, have been highly innovative over many years. UK examples include Rolls-Royce, GlaxoSmithKline, AstraZeneca, and BAE Systems. Also, most of the innovations that have vastly raised agricultural productivity over the last century have come from oligopolistic producers of farm machinery and from government-supported research laboratories, not from perfectly competitive farmers.

Conclusion

Oligopoly is an important market structure in modern economies because there are many industries in which the minimum efficient scale is simply too large to support many competing firms. The challenge to public policy is to keep oligopolists competing, rather than colluding, and using their competitive energies to improve products and lower costs, rather than merely to erect entry barriers.

SUMMARY

Imperfectly competitive market structures

- Firms in market structures other than perfect competition face negatively sloped demand curves and must administer their prices.

Monopolistic competition

- In the theory of large-group monopolistic competition, many firms compete to sell differentiated products. Each may make pure profits in the short run. In the long run, freedom of entry shifts its demand curve until it is tangent to the ATC curve, leading to excess capacity and production at average costs above the minimum possible level.

Oligopoly

- Oligopoly involves competition between a few rivals and the outcome for each is dependent on the behaviour of the others. In planning its production and pricing decisions, each must attempt to anticipate the reactions of the others.

- Competitive behaviour among oligopolists may lead to a non-cooperative equilibrium. It is self-policing in the sense that no one has an incentive to depart from it unilaterally

- Oligopolistic profits can persist only if there are entry barriers. Natural barriers include economies of large-scale production and large fixed costs of entering the market. Artificial barriers include brand proliferation and high levels of advertising.

Models of strategic interaction

- Duopolists can compete with either quantities or by price. Under quantity competition both firms earn profits larger than in perfect competition but smaller than in monopoly. In contrast, price competition leads to an unprofitable outcome unless there are capacity constraints.

- Small group interaction can be analysed using a game theory framework, which sets out the available actions and the payoffs under various actions.

- In a Nash equilibrium each firm is doing the best it can, given the choices that other firms have made.

- A co-operative solution is likely to be the one that maximizes joint profits, but each firm will typically have an incentive to cheat, and explicit co-operation between firms may be proscribed by competition laws.

Dynamics of oligopoly industries

- In qualitative terms, the workings of the allocative system under oligopoly are similar (but not identical) to perfect competition.

- Oligopolistic industries appear to have contributed much more to the technological changes that underlie the long-run growth of productivity than have perfectly competitive industries.

TOPICS FOR REVIEW

- The assumptions of monopolistic competition
- Excess capacity under monopolistic competition
- Cournot and Bertrand duopoly models
- Dominant and dominated strategies in games
- Nash equilibrium

- The prisoners' dilemma
- The co-operative solution and the non-cooperative equilibrium
- Entry barriers
- Resource allocation under oligopoly

DISCUSSION QUESTIONS

1 Consider the following payoff matrixes for the interaction of two firms, A and X. Each has an aggressive or a passive strategy that it could adopt. The first payoff in each pair is for A and the second for X. In each case, attempt to identify
(a) the dominant strategy for each player
(b) the Nash equilibrium
(c) the co-operative equilibrium

(i)

		Firm X choice	
		Aggressive	Passive
Firm A choice	Aggressive	100, 100	150, 50
	Passive	50, 150	175, 175

(ii)

		Firm X choice	
		Aggressive	Passive
Firm A choice	Aggressive	100, 75	160, 60
	Passive	50, 60	110, 80

(iii)

		Firm X choice	
		Aggressive	Passive
Firm A choice	Aggressive	250, 110	320, 120
	Passive	130, 160	300, 240

2 In each of games (i), (ii), and (iii), would the outcome be likely to change if the game were repeated?

3 Explain the short-run equilibrium condition for a firm under monopolistic competition. If this is characterized by the existence of pure profit, what will happen to bring about the long-run equilibrium of the industry?

4 Give examples of barriers to entry and explain why it is beneficial for existing firms to attempt to create such barriers.

5 Explain the difference between Cournot and Bertrand equilibria.

6 What is a Nash equilibrium and why is it self-policing?

7 Why do you think that non-price competition is an important factor where there is a small group of interacting competitors?

Chapter 13

ECONOMICS OF RISK

Nothing in life is certain. So economic transactions, just like everything else we do, involve some element of risk. In some cases the risk does not significantly affect what is done and can be ignored. In other cases the riskiness of the transactions seriously affects the behaviour of those involved in them. It is this impact of risk on economic choices and markets that we need to understand. In particular, you will learn that:

• Diminishing marginal utility of income is sufficient to make people averse to taking risks.

• Risk-averse individuals will rationally wish to buy insurance even if it is not a fair gamble.

• Markets for insurance have to cope with problems of moral hazard—people take more risk because they are insured—and adverse selection—people who know they are most at risk are those most likely to buy insurance.

• Portfolio diversification can reduce financial risks faced by investors.

• Financial intermediaries exist in part because of their ability to spread risk.

We first look at how risk can be characterized and measured. Then we discuss insurance and gambling, both of which involve risk. We find that there appears to be a paradox when people are willing to supply and demand both insurance and gambling activities. After resolving this paradox, we look at two problems that arise in markets for insurance and some other financial transactions. First, the existence of insurance may influence how people behave. Second, the buyers and sellers of insurance may have different amounts of information about the risks that are being insured against. Later in the chapter we consider the problems of investing in financial assets that carry different amounts and types of risk. This leads to the important issues of portfolio diversification and the management of risk by use of appropriate financial instruments.

Risk and consumer choice

In Chapters 6 and 7 we studied the behaviour of consumers who were presented with choices that involve various outcomes. We asked, for example, if a consumer would prefer bundle A, containing 10 units of food and 5 units of clothing, to bundle B, containing 6 units of food and 12 units of clothing. In so doing, we assumed implicitly that the bundle chosen could be obtained with certainty. What happens, however, if the consumer is faced with only a *probability* of obtaining each bundle?

This is not the type of choice that normally faces a shopper. Usually, she knows that if she pays her money she will get what she has paid for with certainty. Sometimes, however, the shopper is uncertain about the quality of the various products offered for sale. She may think that the more expensive brand X will last longer and require less maintenance than the cheaper brand Y. She may not,

however, be sure of how *much* longer it will last, and how *much* less maintenance will be involved.

Other types of choice involve more serious kinds of risk. Buying a flat in area A rather than area B may reduce the chances of being burgled, as may installing a burglar alarm or bars on the ground-floor windows—but by how much? Flats in one area may appreciate in value more than in another—but by how much?

Many of the principles discussed in this chapter were first developed by analysing games of chance such as roulette or coin-tossing.[1] The same principles arise in consumption

---

[1] The first major analysis of choices involving uncertainty was by the Swiss mathematician Daniel Bernoulli (1700–82) in 1738. The subject was greatly advanced by the publication in 1944 of *Theory of Games and Economic Behaviour* by John von Neumann (1903–57) and Oskar Morgenstern (1902–77).

and production decisions involving risk, but they can often be more easily appreciated in the context of games, such as some of those outlined in the previous chapter, where all the possible outcomes and their probabilities are known. Risk in the real world is generally more open-ended and therefore more complex to analyse. This chapter gives only an intuitive overview of the issues involved.

The characterization of risk

How do people make choices when the outcome of any choice is not certain? To study this question we need two important concepts. The first is called **expected value**. It is defined as the most likely outcome if some situation is repeated over, and over, and over. The second is called the **degree of risk.** This is measured by the dispersion of possible outcomes if some situation is repeated over and over. Under certainty, there is only one possible outcome to any given choice. This outcome is thus the expected value and the dispersion of outcomes is zero, indicating no risk. Under uncertainty, more than one outcome is possible and the most likely outcome is the expected value and the spread of possible outcomes is the degree of risk.

Expected value

Suppose that two people, Tom and Jo, play a game in which a coin is tossed *once every minute*. The coin is fair in that there is an equal chance of throwing a head or a tail. The probability of throwing a head is said to be 0.5 or 1/2, and the probability of throwing a tail is also 0.5 or 1/2.[2] Tom pays Jo £1 if the result is a head, and Jo pays Tom £1 if the result is a tail.[3] If they play the game for 10 minutes, one may have a lucky run and win £10 in 10 minutes. There is an equal chance of having an unlucky run and losing £10. It is much more likely, however, that there will be some heads and some tails, so the winnings of one player and losses of the other will be much smaller than £10. The single most likely outcome is that Tom and Jo will exactly break even. This is because there are more sequences of 10 tosses that will end up with 5 heads and 5 tails than any other single combination of heads and tails. For the same reason, the two next most likely results are that Jo will win £2 (6 heads and 4 tails) or that Jo will lose £2 (6 tails and 4 heads). Outcomes with larger gains and larger losses are less likely. The two least likely results are Jo winning £10 or losing £10 (and vice versa for Tom).

Now consider playing the game repeatedly day after day. It is still quite possible that either player will end up winning £10 or losing £10. For example, if they have broken even after many days of play, the chance that they will now encounter 10 heads in a row is the same as it was on their first 10 tosses of the coin. But as they go on playing, the average return *per minute spent playing the game* gets smaller and smaller. This return can be expressed as $(H - T)/n$, where H is the number of heads, T is the

number of tails, and n is the number of minutes they have spent playing the game, which is the same as the number of tosses. Every time the game is played, n increases by one; the only way the numerator can increase by the same amount is if *every* toss is an H, or every toss is a T. So if one player's sequence of losses contains a mixture of heads and tails, the average gain or loss per play will tend to decline. Indeed, it can be shown that, as they go on playing for longer and longer periods of time, so that n increases without limit, the value of $(H - T)/n$ tends to zero. This is the expected value of the game.

The expected value is the most likely outcome for a small number of tosses and the expected earnings on average per toss if the game is repeated many times—in the example above the expected value is zero.

Another way of calculating the expected value of the outcome of any game is to add up the various outcomes, each multiplied by its probability of occurrence. The coin-tossing game above has two possible outcomes for each player on each toss: either he wins £1 with probability 0.5 or he loses £1 with probability 0.5. The expected value of the outcome is £1(0.5) – £1(0.5) = £0.50 – £0.50 = 0.

Degree of risk

In the above game each player stood to win £1 per toss or lose £1 per toss. If they agreed to play for 10 minutes, their maximum possible loss would be £10. Now suppose they play the same game, one toss per minute, but this time Tom pays Jo £100 for each head and Jo pays Tom £100 for each tail. The expected value of the outcome is still zero. But they each risk more if they play it for any given amount of time. There is the same chance that Jo will encounter an unlucky run of 10 tails, but now she stands to lose £1,000 in this event. Clearly there is more risk attached to the second game than to the first. Risk refers to the dispersion of the possible results, that is the range of possible outcomes. In the first game the possible results from 10 minutes play are dispersed over a range running from +£10 to –£10; in the second game the possible results are dispersed over a range running from +£1,000 to –£1,000.

The degree of riskiness associated with a decision is determined by the dispersion in the possible outcomes that could result from making that choice.[4]

---

[2] These are equivalent expressions. The first, 0.5, is the ratio of the expected number of heads to the overall number of tosses. The second, 1/2, says there is one chance in two of throwing a head (since there are two equally likely outcomes on any one toss).

[3] This game is a *zero-sum game*, first mentioned in Box 12.3 on page 206; it is defined as any game in which the sum of the winnings and losses of all the players is always zero. In other words, what someone in the game wins, someone else in the game must have lost.

[4] For many purposes the variation can be satisfactorily measured by the *variance* of the possible results, which is the average of the sum of the squares of the deviations of each result from the average, or most likely, result. It is also often measured by the *standard deviation*, which is the square root of the variance.

Fair and unfair games

The penny-toss game that we have considered so far is a mathematically fair game in the sense that each player has just as much chance of winning as of losing. A lottery in which all of the ticket money is paid out is also a fair game. Say, for example, that 100 lottery tickets are sold for £1 each, and a draw then determines which one of the ticket-holders wins £100. This is a fair game because each ticket-holder has 1 chance in 100 of winning £99 (the person's own £1 back and £99 of winnings) and 99 chances out of 100 of losing £1. To find the expected value of this gamble, we multiply the winnings of £99 by the chance of winning it (1 chance in 100) and subtract the loss multiplied by the chance of losing it (99 chances in 100). This gives

$$£99(1/100) - £1(99/100) = £0.99 - £0.99 = 0.$$

A mathematically fair game is one for which the expected value of the outcome is zero.

If you play a fair game repeatedly, you may end up winning or losing, depending on the 'luck of the toss', but the *average gain or loss per play* calculated over all plays will tend towards zero as time passes.

Now consider playing the coin-tossing game under the following rules: heads we pay you £2, tails you pay us £1. The expected value of the outcome of this game to you is £2(0.5) - £1(0.5) = £1 - £0.50 = £0.50. If you play the game only once, you will either win £2 or lose £1. If you play it repeatedly, however, your average gain will tend towards £0.50 per toss. This is not a fair game. Instead, it is biased in your favour (and hence is biased *against* us). (However, it is still a zero-sum game, since your gain will always be exactly equal to our loss.)

What about the kind of lottery that typically exists? The organizers take a proportion of the ticket revenue as their profit (and perhaps for charity) and distribute the rest as prize money. All such lotteries are not fair games. They are biased against the participants in the sense that the expected value of participating in the game is negative. (Also, they are not zero-sum games, since the losses of those whose tickets are not selected exceed the gains for those whose tickets are winners.)

To illustrate, take our lottery where 100 tickets are sold at £1 each. Now, however, assume that the organizers take £50 as their profit and pay out the other £50 to the winning ticket. The expected value of a lottery ticket is now £49(1/100) - £1(99/100) = £0.49 - £0.99 = -£0.50. The negative value shows that this is not a fair game; instead, it is biased against anyone who plays it.

Another way of seeing this is to ask yourself what would happen if you bought all the tickets. You would spend £100 and win back £50, thus making a loss of £50. This is a loss of £0.50 per ticket, which, we have already seen, is the expected value of each ticket. (Explain why it is irrational to buy two tickets instead of one in order to increase the chances of coming out a winner.)

Consumers' tastes for risk

Economists distinguish three possible patterns of preference when risk is involved. Those who are **risk-neutral** will be indifferent about playing a fair game; they will willingly play one that is biased in their favour, but will not play one that is biased against them. Those who are **risk-averse** will only play games that are sufficiently biased in their favour to overcome their aversion to risk, and will be unwilling to play fair games, let alone ones that are biased against them. Finally, people who are **risk-loving** are willing to play games even when they are biased against them, the extent of the love of risk being measured by the degree of bias that a person is willing to accept. (No one would knowingly buy a ticket in a lottery in which the prize was zero, but some extreme risk-lovers might enter a lottery in which only 10 per cent of the ticket money was paid out as prize money.)

Is it just as likely that any individual will be a risk-lover as that he will be risk-averse? To answer this question, we use a basic assumption that is related to the discussion of diminishing marginal utility in Chapter 6 on pages 98–101.

According to the *assumption of diminishing marginal utility* of income, individuals get less and less satisfaction from successive, equal increases in their income and wealth.

The argument is that if you earn only £1,000 per year you will spend it satisfying your most urgent wants. If your income is increased by £1,000, you will also spend it on quite important needs, but the additional needs will be a little less urgent than those satisfied by the first £1,000. If your income is increased progressively by £1,000 increments, needs that are less and less urgent will be satisfied by the expenditure of each additional £1,000 of income. The general idea, therefore, is that people can arrange their wants in order and will satisfy the ones that give them most utility first, and then, as their incomes increase, those that give them progressively less and less utility. It follows from this assumption that the utility each consumer will attach to successive equal increments of income will decrease steadily as income increases; put the other way around, the utility attached to successive equal reductions of income will increase steadily as income is decreased.

Figure 13.1 shows an illustrative utility curve for income for one hypothetical individual, Amanda. The curve relates any income received with certainty to the utility that Amanda derives from it.

Amanda must now choose between two different occupations. The first is an office job that pays her a definite income of £15,000 per year. The second is as a salesperson

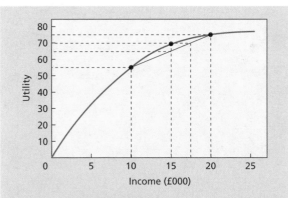

Figure 13.1 The utility of income

Diminishing utility of income implies risk aversion. The curve shows the total utility attached to various incomes to be received with certainty. Amanda's utility from an income of £15,000 for certain is 70. An occupation that gives a 50 per cent chance of either £10,000 or £20,000 has an expected value of £15,000 but an expected utility of only 65. To make her accept a risky income source, its expected value would have to be £17,500 (which yields a utility of 70, as does the certain income of £15,000).

working on commission. If she is good at the job she will earn £20,000, but if she is poor at it she will earn only £10,000. She is uncertain about her sales ability and reckons that she is equally likely to be good or bad at the job. So she assigns a probability of 0.5 to each of the two possible outcomes. Thus, the expected value of the income from the sales job is £15,000—that is, (0.5)(£10,000) + (0.5)(£20,000). If Amanda were risk-neutral, she would be indifferent between these two occupations, since they both yield the same expected income. But the risky alternative yields her either £5,000 more or £5,000 less than the certain one. Because of diminishing utility of income, she assigns a smaller utility to £5,000 more than the office job salary than she assigns to £5,000 less than it. The graph tells us that the utility of the certain income of £15,000 is 70 while the utilities attached to £20,000 and £10,000 are 75 and 55 respectively. Although the expected incomes from the two occupations are the same, the expected utilities are not. The sales job yields either £10,000 with a probability of 0.5 or £20,000 also with a probability of 0.5. So the expected utility associated with this job is only 65—(55)(0.5) + (75)(0.5). So she prefers the job with the certain income of £15,000 to the job with the uncertain income that has the same expected value of £15,000. Amanda is risk-averse.[5]

A moment's reflection will show that this conclusion is independent of the particular utility values that we selected. All that it requires is diminishing marginal utility of income. This means that the addition of utility resulting from an income that is above average by some amount

is less than the subtraction from utility resulting from an income that is below average by the same amount.

What would the expected value of the risky alternative have to be to leave Amanda indifferent between the two occupations? The answer is read off the curve in Figure 13.1. The expected value of the risky income needs to be £17,500 for her to obtain the same utility from the sales job as the office job offers. The difference between the actual expected value of the sales job and the expected value she would need to leave her indifferent between the risky and the riskless job measures her cost of risk. This is what we would have to give her to leave her indifferent between a certain income and an uncertain one with the same expected value.

Diminishing marginal utility of income makes utility-maximizing people risk-averse.

The demand for insurance

The Smiths, who own a house valued at £200,000, estimate that there is 1 chance in 1,000 that it will be destroyed by fire during their period of ownership and 999 chances in 1,000 that there will be no fire. The most likely outcome is that nothing will happen at all, but there is a small chance of a really big loss. Someone offers them a mathematically fair insurance policy that avoids this big loss. The policy costs £200 to be paid now. If they buy the policy, they give up £200. However, if the disaster occurs they will be fully compensated.

So the Smiths have a choice between two alternatives:

- **Alternative A, the status quo.** If they choose not to buy the policy, they have 1 chance in 1,000 of losing £200,000 and 999 chances out of 1,000 of losing nothing. Multiplying these possible losses of £200,000 and zero by their probabilities gives the expected value of this alternative as −£200 (i.e. −£200,000(1/1,000) + £0(999/1,000) = −£200).

- **Alternative B, purchase the policy.** In this case £200 is spent for certain but there is no chance of losing £200,000.

The insurance policy represents a fair bargain because the expected value of the status quo is equal to the certain cost

---

[5] We explain here how expected income and utility vary as Amanda's probability of being good at her sales job varies. Let the probability of Amanda being good at the job be p and of her being bad at it be $1 - p$. The expected value of the income associated with the sales job is then $(£20,000)(p) + (£10,000)(1 - p) = £10,000 + £10,000p$. The expected utility is the utility attached to the high income multiplied by the probability of achieving the high income plus the utility attached to the low income multiplied by the probability of achieving the low income. In the case shown in Figure 13.1, this is $(75)(p) + 55(1 - p) = 55 + 20p$. So, as p varies between 0 and 1, the point showing the expected value of the income and the utility arising from the sales job varies along a straight line joining the two points (£10,000, 55) and (£20,000, 75). This is the straight line shown in Figure 13.1.

of the policy. Not buying the insurance is, however, a much riskier course of action for the homeowners than buying it. If they are lucky, they save the £200 insurance premium; if they are unlucky, they lose £200,000. What should they do?

Risk-averse individuals will buy the policy. The expected value of the outcome is the same as if they did not buy the policy, but they have eliminated the risk of a large monetary loss.

One further complication needs to be mentioned. Since insurance companies must themselves make money, they do not offer their policy-holders mathematically fair policies such as the one just described. In the above case, where the risk to the insurance company is 1 chance in 1,000 of losing £200,000, it would charge a premium of more than £200, possibly £220. The insurance company expects to pay out an average of £200 per policy, so the £20 per policy goes to cover its costs and to earn an income.

For the purchaser the certain cost of buying the policy is now –£220. But the expected value of not buying remains at –£200. A risk-neutral person would not buy the policy, which requires spending £220 to avoid a situation (no insurance) whose expected value is –£200.

People with diminishing marginal utility of wealth are willing to buy insurance policies that are not mathematically 'fair' because they value the reduction of risk more than they value the reduction in their expected wealth when they buy the policy.

Figure 13.2 shows the decision facing our homeowners.[6]

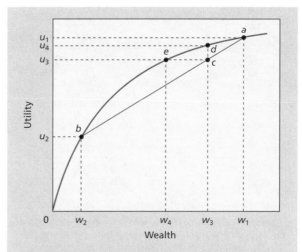

Figure 13.2 Purchasing insurance
Diminishing marginal utility of wealth makes a mathematically unfair insurance policy attractive to utility-maximizing consumers. Without insurance, the homeowners will have *either* wealth of w_1 with utility of u_1 if there is no fire (point *a*) *or* wealth of w_2 and utility u_2 if there is a fire (point *b*). The expected value of their wealth is w_3 with an associated utility of u_3 (point *c*). Point *c* is closer to *a* than to *b* because the fire is an unlikely event. A mathematically fair insurance policy would charge a premium that reduced the owners' wealth to w_3 for certain. The utility associated with w_3 achieved with certainty is u_4, which is higher than u_3. The maximum the owners would be prepared to pay for a mathematically unfair policy is the amount that would reduce their wealth to w_4. Paying that amount would make their wealth w_4 for certain (point *e*), yielding them the same utility as is associated with not buying insurance (point *c*).

The demand to gamble

We now know that diminishing marginal utility of income and wealth lead people to be risk-averse and thus to insure against losses. Why then do people gamble? Why do they buy lottery tickets, enter the football pools, and bet on horse races? These are different from insurance, where one pays money to avoid the risk of a large loss. In gambling one pays money to purchase the chance of a gain. The buyer accepts a large chance of a small loss (the purchase price of the ticket) in return for a small chance of a large gain (the payoff to the winning tickets).

Earlier in this chapter we considered a lottery consisting of 100 tickets sold for £1 each, with a single prize of £100 going to the winning ticket. If you buy a ticket you have 99 chances out of 100 of losing £1 and 1 chance in 100 of winning £99. (If you win, you get your £1 back and £99 more.) This is a mathematically fair game, since the expected value of a ticket is zero (£99(1/100) – £1(99/100)). But, given diminishing marginal utility of income, the utility you get from winning £100 will be less than 100 times the utility you sacrificed by giving up £1. Thus, because the expected value of the ticket measured in money is zero,

the expected value of the ticket measured in utility is negative. If you are a utility maximizer and have diminishing marginal utility of income, you would not buy the ticket.

The lottery above is a mathematically fair gamble. However, most betting games are biased against the player. The organizer of the game takes out some of the stake money to cover costs and provide a profit. Only the remainder is distributed as prize money. This is true of all private and government-run commercial gambling, including lotteries, pools, dog and horse races, and casino gambling. (The gambling games individuals play at home with each other are usually fair in the sense that the value of what is won is equal to the value of what is lost, so that the expected value of playing the game is zero.)

---

[6] Here we deal with wealth rather than the income that we considered in Figure 13.1. Wealth is merely the present value of all current assets including any expected future income. Thus, diminishing marginal utility of either implies diminishing marginal utility of the other.

Gambling on any event in which the organizers take a profit has a negative expected value, and playing such games is thus inconsistent with utility-maximizing risk-averse participants who are subject to diminishing marginal utility of income.

Yet we observe such behaviour every day. How can we explain it? At least four possibilities suggest themselves.

One possibility is that people have increasing marginal utilities of income, over some range of income. This could explain why they gamble on games that have negative expected values. It would, however, be inconsistent with their buying insurance policies with negative expected values.[7] So this explanation would work only if there were one class of people who gambled (those with increasing marginal utility of income) and another class who bought insurance (those with decreasing marginal utility of income). The common observation that there are many people who do both rules out this possibility as a general explanation.

A second possibility is that people derive utility from gambling for its own sake. Although they would not engage in gambling as a way of maximizing the money values of their income and wealth, they get pleasure out of the very act of gambling. In this sense, they are giving up some income to purchase the pleasure of gambling just as if they purchased a ticket to obtain the pleasure of attending the theatre. In the case of gambling games with massive wins, such as the football pools, the appeal may be somewhat different. Diminishing marginal utility of increases in income may not hold for massive wins that could change one's whole life-style in ways that would otherwise be quite beyond the gambler's reach. It may not matter that the average player will lose money over his or her lifetime. The gamblers are sustained by the mere thought that, against all the odds, they might win a sum large enough to transform an otherwise hard life, in the same way that Cinderella's fairy godmother transformed hers.

A third possibility is that people are badly informed. They may not know the expected values of the gambles that they take. It is probably true that many people do not realize the magnitude of the negative expected value of many gambles. (The smaller the *payout ratio*—the ratio of money paid out to money taken in—the larger the magnitude of the negative expected value of the game.)

A fourth possibility is that people are superstitious, as many people are observed to be. They do not believe that the law of averages applies to them. They think that by choosing lucky numbers, or engaging in various rituals, they will beat the odds. These people do not care that they are playing mathematically unfair games. They believe that their personal powers will influence the results in some way or another—as those who choose what they regard as lucky numbers are observed to believe.

Box 13.1 discusses the ethics of gambling.

 Box 13.1 The ethics of gambling

In 2001 UK households spent £6.9 billion on gambling, while in the same year they spent only £3.6 billion on insuring their own homes and contents. Is gambling an activity that should be permitted or even encouraged? Throughout the world both private firms and governments run gambling activities. In many lotteries and pools the payout ratio is quite low. For example, in the UK National Lottery less than 50 per cent of the money wagered is returned in prizes. Also, gambling takes a higher proportion of the income of the poor than of the rich.

Critics argue that this and other similar lotteries are a tax on poverty and ignorance. They argue that those with higher incomes and more knowledge tend to avoid such poor bets. Supporters argue that the poor are the main purchasers of lottery tickets just because, for most of them, escape into a better life-style is beyond anything they could achieve by their own efforts. So they are buying a remote possibility of an otherwise unachievable gain, a dream that gives them utility in itself. The supporters' argument has more weight when fully informed people buy tickets for the value of the dream. It has less weight when badly informed persons buy tickets in the mistaken belief that they are playing either a fair game or one that they can influence by their own supernatural powers.

What do you think?

The supply of gambling

So much for consumers. Why are firms willing to supply such services as insurance and gambling games to consumers who demand them? We first consider the easy case of gambling and then go on to the more difficult, but also more interesting, case of insurance.

There is no difficulty in understanding why firms are willing to provide such gambling opportunities as the pools or betting on horse or dog races. If firms make their own odds after they know the amounts bet, they are on the right side of a mathematically unfair game from which they must win. Assume, for example, that you run a lottery and are free to take for yourself what you wish from the funds raised and then distribute the rest as prizes. You cannot lose.

Firms providing this type of gambling service sometimes have a government monopoly and sometimes are subject to competition from other firms. If there is competition, then there will be pressure to keep the payout ratio high, provided that ticket purchasers are aware of the prizes given out by competing lotteries. If the lottery has a monopoly,

---

[7] Unless there just happened to be diminishing marginal utility of income below some person's current income level and increasing marginal utility of income above it. In which case it would be rational to insure against a significant loss of income and at the same time to gamble to attempt to achieve an increase in income (even in an unfair game).

there will be an optimum payout ratio that will maximize the profits of the firm running the game. As the payout ratio goes to one, profits go to zero, since all money taken in is paid out. As the payout ratio goes to zero, profits will also go to zero, since fewer and fewer people will be willing to bet as the size of the winnings and/or the number of winners get smaller.

Somewhere in between a ratio of zero and one is the optimum payout ratio that maximizes the profits of a mono-poly firm running a lottery or other betting game.

The supply of insurance

In the gambling case, the firm can decide how much to pay out after it knows how much it has taken in. Insurance is a different matter. The insurance firm takes your money and agrees to pay out a certain sum if some unlucky event strikes you. Conceivably, the insurance firm could have a run of bad luck in which, in the limit, all of the people it insures suffer losses at the same time. The basis for profit-able insurance firms is not, therefore, being on the right side of an unfair game. Instead, it lies in the mathematics of what are called *pooled risks*.

Risk-pooling

To see what is involved in the pooling of risks, consider two individuals, John and Jane, who receive incomes that vary according to the toss of a coin. (Once again, the coin toss stands for any source of risk.) Each individual tosses a coin each month. If a head comes up, John gets £500; if a tail, he gets nothing. The same applies to Jane: she gets £500 if she tosses a head and nothing if a tail comes up. The expected value of their income is £500(0.50) = £250 per month. Over a long period of time, their monthly incomes will indeed average close to £250 each. But neither of them may like the possibility of going from £500 to nothing on the toss of a coin each month. Suppose they decide to pool their incomes each month and each take half of the resulting amount. The expected value of the pooled income is £500 while the expected value of each individual income is unchanged at £250 per month.

Importantly, however, the variation from month to month in each income will be diminished. The result is shown in Table 13.1. When they were operating on their own, each income deviated from its expected value by £250 each month; in good months it was £250 over, and in bad months it was £250 below. When the two incomes are pooled, the expected value is reached whenever one is lucky and the other unlucky, which will tend to be about half the time. Only in one-quarter of the outcomes will income be £250 above, and in one-quarter will it be £250 below. These two results require that both John and Jane are lucky at the same time or that both are unlucky.

Table 13.1 Risk-pooling

Coin toss	Risks are not pooled		Risks are pooled:
	John gets	June gets	both get
T–T	0	0	0
T–H	0	500	250
H–T	500	0	250
H–H	500	500	500

Pooling of independent risks reduces risk. Both John and June toss a coin, and each gets an income of £500 if he or she tosses a head (H) and nothing for a tail (T). There are four possible results, in two of which one head and one tail occur. In the other two there are either two tails or two heads. When each accepts his or her own risks, each expects an income of £500 half the time and zero the other half. When the incomes are pooled then split, only one combination in four gives them zero income, while half of the time they will get £250. Pooling leaves the expected value of their incomes unchanged but lowers the average amount of variation around that value.

If three people pool their incomes, the extreme cases of £500 each and zero each occur only when all three are lucky or unlucky at the same time. These cases each occur with a probability of 1 chance in 8. (There is 1 chance in 2 that any one person will get a head, and $(1/2)(1/2)(1/2) = 1/8$ that all three will get heads at once. Similarly, there is 1 chance in 8 that all three will toss tails at the same time.) So the extreme cases in which everyone gets *either* £500 *or* zero occur only one-quarter of the time. If four people pool their incomes, the extreme cases of *either* £500 *or* zero income per person will occur only with probability 2/16. By the time ten people are involved, the two extreme cases will occur only twice in two raised to the tenth power (2^{10}) times,[8] which is a very small fraction indeed.

The larger the number of independent events that are pooled, the less likely is it that extreme results will occur.

The key to this proposition is that the events must be independent; the result of John's coin toss must not be in any way related to the result of Jane's. In the unpooled case, the extreme result occurs to one of them when he or she is unlucky or lucky. The probability of the extreme result is less likely when they pool their incomes because it requires that *both* be unlucky or lucky at the same time.

The same reasoning applies to all kinds of event that may be regarded as chance occurrences, as long as they are independent of each other. There is some probability that any given house in the country will burn down in any given year; let us say it is 1 in 1,000. An insurance company takes a premium from house-owners and offers them full

[8] That is 2 chances in 1024.

compensation if their house burns down. If the company is so small that it insures only ten houses, it may be unlucky in having ten owners who just happen to be careless in the same year and burn their houses down accidentally. This is unlikely, but not impossible. A bad bit of luck over all ten houses insured would ruin the company, which could not then meet all of its insured risks at the same time. But let the company be large enough to insure 100,000 houses. Now it is pooling risk over a large number, and the chances are that very close to 1 house in every 1,000 insured houses will burn down. With 100,000 houses insured, the most likely outcome is that 100 houses will burn down. The company might be unlucky and have 110 burn down or lucky and have only 90 burn down. But to have 200 burn down is very unlikely indeed, as long as a fire in one house is independent of a fire in another.

This requirement of independence explains why insurance policies normally exclude wars and other situations where some common cause acts on all the insured units. A war may lead to a vast number of houses being destroyed. Since the cause of the loss of one house is not independent of the cause of the loss of another, the insurance company has a high probability, should a war break out, of suffering ruinous losses.

The basic feature of insurance is the pooling of independent events, which is what makes extreme outcomes unlikely. A common cause that seriously affects all insured items in the same way defeats the principle on which insurance is based.

The typical insurance company, therefore, deals with repeated events such as fires or death in which the probability of each insured person becoming a claimant is independent of the probability of any other person becoming a claimant.

Risk-sharing

A further practice of insurance companies allows them to extend their coverage to events that are not repeated and where the loss might be large enough to ruin any one company. Say that a famous pianist wants to insure her hands against any event that would stop her from playing the piano. The amount insured could be very large, sufficient to compensate for the loss of all the income she would earn over her lifetime if her hands stayed unharmed. The company can calculate the chances that any randomly chosen female in the population will suffer such a loss of the use of her hands. But it is not insuring the whole population. Only one person is involved. If there is no catastrophe, the company will gain its premium. If there is a catastrophe, the company will suffer a large loss.

The trick in being able to insure the pianist, or any single person or thing where the loss would be large, lies in *risk-sharing* (or re-insurance, as it is sometimes called). One company writes a policy for the pianist and then breaks the policy up into a large number of sub-policies. Each sub-policy carries a fraction of the payout and earns a fraction of the premium. The company then sells the sub-policies to many different firms.

Assume, for illustration, that 100 firms each write one such primary policy—one on a pianist's hands, one on a footballer's legs, one on a rare treasure being flown to Japan for exhibit, etc. Each then breaks its primary policy up into 100 subparts and sells a part to each of the other 99 firms. Each firm ends up holding risks that are independent of each other, no one of which is large enough to threaten the firm should it give rise to a claim. This is what Lloyd's of London does. It is a syndication of a large number of insurance underwriters. Each is prepared to insure almost anything as long as a claim would not break all of the firms when the risk is spread over a large number of them.[9]

We return to risk in the context of financial investments later in this chapter.

Problems with insurance

Two major problems arise in insurance: these are called moral hazard and adverse selection. These problems also arise in many other markets, including those for financial assets and labour services, so the concepts have important general applications.

Moral hazard

If the contents of your home are valuable but are not insured for theft, you are likely to be careful in locking your door every time you leave and will take other sensible, anti-break-in precautions. If you take out an insurance policy, you may be less careful. Say for example that you get ten minutes down the road and realize that you forgot to lock up. You may decide to press on, reasoning that you cannot afford the time you would lose in returning to lock up, that being visited by burglars on any particular day is unlikely, and that anyway you are insured against burglary.

The existence of the insurance policy has altered your behaviour. You take more risks, making a loss from burglary more likely than if you were uninsured.

This behaviour, called **moral hazard**, is defined as an insurance-induced alteration of behaviour that makes the event insured against more likely to occur.

---

[9] This is also what bookmakers do when they cannot control the odds themselves. When they take bets at odds set by others, one large bet could ruin them by requiring a payout greater than their current assets. To avoid such risks, they lay off part of the bet with other bookmakers. In this way no one ends up holding bets that are big enough to threaten their solvency if they suffer an unlucky run of payouts.

Moral hazard occurs in many lines of insurance. For example, people are observed to be more careless about fire prevention when they are insured than when they are not. Fire insurance is clearly socially beneficial in allowing people to pool risks, thus avoiding the chances of a large loss in return for a relatively small payment. However, there is an offsetting social loss if the very existence of fire insurance leads to more destruction by fire than would occur without it.

To deal with moral hazard insurance companies create incentives for purchasers of insurance to be careful. Car drivers, for example, get a no-claims bonus if they have no accident for some number of years. Many policies include an 'excess' clause, which means that the insurer will pay out the value of losses only above some amount. So, for example, a car owner might have to pay the first £100 of a damage claim and the insurer would pay the rest. Home contents policies typically require that homes are fitted with secure locks to doors and windows.

Moral hazard arises in any markets where behaviour can change after a deal has been done. An employer may, for example, agree to a high salary for a star employee in expectation of outstanding performance. But the employee may decide to take the money and shirk. We return to this issue of performance in labour markets in Chapter 16.

Adverse selection

When the person on one side of a bargain knows more about what is being bought and sold than the person on the other side, we have a situation of *asymmetrical information*. This can lead to undesirable consequences.

For example, a person who is considering taking out life insurance may know more about her health than the insurance company can find out in one medical examination and a few life-style questions. The insurance company will quote a rate that covers the average risk for all persons in some category, such as middle-aged female non-smokers in apparent good health. Those who believe their health is better than average know they are being asked for a premium that is high relative to their individual risk. In contrast, those who know they are less healthy than the average in their group know they are being offered a bargain: insurance at a rate that is low relative to their own individual risk. As a result, a higher proportion of people who are above the average risk will insure themselves than those who are below the average risk.

Adverse selection, in the context of insurance, refers to the tendency for people who are more at risk than the average to purchase insurance and for those who are less at risk than the average to reject insurance. This occurs whenever individuals within a group that is offered a common insurance rate know which way their own risk deviates significantly from the average risk within the group. Those at high risk relative to the average are offered a bargain; those at low risk are offered expensive insurance.

This problem would be serious if all people were charged the same rate as the customer with the average risk. Young healthy non-smokers would be heavily penalized and much less inclined to take out insurance. In contrast, older smokers with chronic ailments would be subsidized and would have a strong inducement to insure themselves.

The result would be that the average risk of the group who took out insurance would rise above the average risk in the whole population. Rates would then have to be raised to cover the average risk of the insured groups, and this would provide an even stronger incentive for those who have below-average risks to go uninsured.

Insurance companies try to cope with this problem by defining a number of groups distinguished from each other by characteristics that affect their risk. They then charge each group a different rate based on the average risk of that group. For example, rates for theft insurance in London and other UK cities vary with the postal code. This certainly helps, but it is always true that there will be variations within any one group. Those who know they are more at risk than the average in their group are offered a bargain, while those who know they are less at risk than the average are offered what is, for them, expensive insurance.

Insurance companies sometimes make surprising offers, such as life insurance for people over 55 with no medical examination. When it does this, a company is consciously choosing to avoid obtaining relevant medical knowledge. This increases the degree of knowledge asymmetry between the company and the policy purchaser and thus strengthens the tendency towards adverse selection. If the company is to earn a profit, its rates for this kind of policy will have to be set higher than the rates on otherwise equivalent policies that require a medical examination. For very-high-risk people the policy may still be a bargain—possibly the only way they can get life insurance. For average- and low-risk people the rates must be higher than they could obtain by purchasing a policy that required a medical examination.

Adverse selection also applies in banking. Banks tend to expand their lending business by merger or acquisition, rather than by organic growth. The reason is that the marginal customers obtained by attracting new business are not necessarily the ones banks want to lend to. They are riskier than average.[10] However, when one bank buys another bank it gets the whole set of that bank's existing customers. It knows their average characteristics, and it picks up good customers, as well as bad.

---

[10] This is mainly a problem with unsecured lending. Mortgages are secured on a known property, so less risk is involved for the lender.

Box 13.2 **Used-car prices: the problem of 'lemons'**

It is common for people to regard the large loss of value of a new car in the first year of its life as a sign that consumers are overly style-conscious and will always pay a big premium for the latest in anything. The US economist George Akerlof, winner of the Nobel Prize for economics in 2001, proposed a different explanation. This was based on the proposition that the flow of services expected from a one-year-old car that is *purchased on the used-car market* would be lower than that expected from an *average* one-year-old car on the road.

Any particular model year of motor cars will include a certain proportion of 'lemons'—cars that have one or more serious defects. There were faults in their assembly, or in the parts assembled, that went undetected. Purchasers of new cars of a certain year and model take a chance on their car turning out to be a lemon. Those who are unlucky and get a lemon are more likely to resell their car than those who are lucky and get a well-functioning car. Hence the used-car market will contain a disproportionately large number of lemons for sale. Because it is difficult to identify a lemon or a badly treated used car before buying it, the purchaser is prepared to buy a used car only at a price that is low enough to offset the increased probability that it is of poor quality.

This is a rational consumer response to asymmetric knowledge between the seller of a car and its eventual buyer. It helps to explain why one-year-old cars typically sell for a discount that is somewhat larger than can be explained by the physical depreciation that occurs in one year in the *average* car of that model. The larger discount reflects the lower services that the purchaser can expect from a used car because of the higher probability that it will be a lemon.

All the large UK banks have grown up from mergers of existing banks. None of their major components is less than 150 years old. (The growth of Royal Bank of Scotland, LloydsTSB, Barclays, HBOS, and HSBC fits this story.)

Box 13.2 outlines a different case of moral hazard; in this case it is the sellers who know more about the product than the buyers.

Financial choices and risk

An important function of any financial system is to channel funds from one set of agents, who have money to lend, to another set of agents, who wish to borrow. Those who do this are called financial intermediaries. Savers are investing their own money in the hope of receiving an interest return on that investment. They also have to consider risk, because borrowers may default. Even if default is not likely, many forms of investment involve risks of capital gains and losses, which occur when the market value of the investment changes. Accordingly, all investors have to take into consideration not just the expected return on their investment, but also the risks involved.

The analysis of risk and return as applied to finance has created a vast literature. Here we can develop only a few of the key ideas that help in understanding a wide range of financial behaviour.

Portfolio diversification

'Don't put all your eggs in one basket' is a well-known proverb, which summarizes the message that there are benefits from diversification. If you carry your breakable items in several baskets there is a chance that one will be dropped, but you are unlikely to drop all your baskets on the same trip. Similarly, if you invest all your wealth in the shares of one company, there is a chance that the company will go bust and you will lose all your money. Since it is unlikely that all companies will go bust at the same time, a portfolio of shares in several companies is less risky.

This may sound like the idea of risk-pooling, which we discussed earlier in this chapter, and risk-pooling is certainly an important reason for diversification. We will use the notion of risk-pooling to explain some forms of financial behaviour, but a full understanding of portfolio diversification involves a slightly wider knowledge of the nature of risk than what is involved in coin-tossing.

The key difference between risk in the real world of finance and the risk of coin-tossing is that many of the potential outcomes are not independent of other outcomes. If you and I toss a coin, the probability of yours turning up heads is independent of the probability of my throwing a head. However, the return on an investment in, say, BP is not independent of the return on an investment in Shell. This is because these two companies both compete in the same industry. If BP does especially well in attracting new business, it may be at the expense of Shell. So high profits at BP may be associated with low profits at Shell, or vice versa. On the other hand, all oil companies might do well when oil prices are high and badly when they are low.

The important matter here is that the fortunes of these two companies are not independent of each other.

The fact that the risks of individual investments may not be independent has important implications for investment allocations, or what is now called *portfolio theory*. Investments can be combined in different proportions to produce risk and return characteristics that cannot be achieved through any single investment. As a result, institutions have grown up to take advantage of the benefits of diversification.

Diversified portfolios may produce combinations of risk and return that dominate non-diversified portfolios.

This is an important statement that requires a little closer investigation. That investigation will help to identify the circumstances under which diversification is beneficial. It will also clarify what we mean by the word 'dominate'.

Table 13.2 sets out two simple examples. In both there are two assets that an investor can hold, and there are two possible situations which are assumed to be equally likely. Thus, there is a probability of 0.5 attached to each situation and the investor has no advance knowledge of which is going to happen. The two situations might be a high exchange rate and a low exchange rate, a booming and a depressed economy, or any other alternatives that have different effects on the earnings of different assets.

Consider part (i) of the table. In this case both assets have the same expected return (20 per cent) and the same degree of risk. (The possible range of outcomes is between 10 and 30 per cent on each asset.) If all that mattered in investment decisions were the risk and return of individual shares, the investor would be indifferent between assets A and B. Indeed, if the choice were between holding only A or only B, all investors should be indifferent (whether they were risk-averse, risk-neutral, or risk-loving) because

the risk and expected return are identical for both assets. However, this is not the end of the story, because the returns on these assets are not independent. Indeed, there is a perfect negative correlation between them: when one is high the other is low, and vice versa.

What would a sensible investor do if permitted to hold some combination of the two assets? Clearly, there is no possible combination that will change the overall expected return, because it is the same on both assets. However, holding some of each asset can reduce the risk. Let the investor decide to hold half his wealth in asset A and half in asset B. His risk will then be reduced to zero, since his return will be 20 per cent whichever situation arises. This diversified portfolio will clearly be preferred to either asset alone by risk-averse investors. The risk-neutral investor is indifferent to all combinations of A and B because they all have the same expected return, but the risk-lover may prefer not to diversify. This is because, by picking one asset alone, the risk-lover still has a chance of getting a 30 per cent return and the extra risk gives positive pleasure.

Risk-averse investors will choose the diversified portfolio, which gives them the lowest risk for a given expected rate of return, or the highest expected return for a given level of risk.

Diversification does not always reduce the riskiness of a portfolio, so we need to be clear what conditions matter. Consider the example in part (ii) of Table 13.2. As in part (i), both assets have an expected return of 20 per cent. But asset B is riskier than asset A and it has returns that are positively correlated with A's. Portfolio diversification does not reduce risk in this case. Risk-averse investors would invest only in asset A, while risk-lovers would invest only in asset B. Combinations of A and B are always riskier than holding A alone. Thus, we could say that for the risk-averse investor asset A *dominates* asset B, as asset B will never be held so long as asset A is available. The key difference between the example in part (ii) of Table 13.2 and that in part (i) is that in the second example returns on the two assets are positively correlated, while in the former they are negatively correlated.[11]

The risk attached to a combination of two assets will be smaller than the sum of the individual risks if the two assets have returns that are negatively correlated.

Diversifiable and non-diversifiable risk

Not all risk can be eliminated by diversification. The specific risk associated with any one company can be diversified

---

Table 13.2 **Combinations of risk and return**

	Situation 1	Situation 2
(i) Returns are negatively correlated		
Asset A	10%	30%
Asset B	30%	10%
(ii) Returns are positively correlated		
Asset A	10%	30%
Asset B	0%	40%

Assets differ in expected return and variability in returns. Part (i) illustrates the return on two assets in two different situations. Asset A has a high return in situation 2 and a low return in situation 1. The reverse is true for asset B. A portfolio of both assets has the same expected return but lower risk than a holding of either asset on its own. In (ii) both assets have a high return in situation 2 and a low return in situation 1. For the risk-averse investor asset A dominates asset B.

---

[11] Readers who have studied statistics will recall that if two statistical series A and B are added together, the variance of the combined series is equal to the variance of A plus the variance of B plus twice the covariance of A and B. The covariance of A and B will be negative if A and B are negatively correlated, hence the combined variance will be less than the sum of its parts.

Box 13.3 Conglomerates: not all diversification is beneficial

In the 1960s and 1970s it was fashionable to argue that the benefits of diversification would apply to all firms. Rightly or wrongly, this argument led to the building up of several large conglomerate firms made up of a portfolio of diverse businesses in many different industries. The UK firm Hanson, for example, was a conglomerate that owned a cigarette company, and a brick business in the UK, a coal mining business and a whirlpool bath manufacturer in the US, among dozens of other operations. UK company Tomkins had about fifty different companies ranging from buns (Rank Hovis McDougall) to guns (Smith and Wesson), and including businesses like lawnmower manufacturers and car hose makers.

The most successful firms of the 1980s and 1990s, however, were not conglomerates. Instead they were those who concentrated on being the leading players in one industry, for example Microsoft in software, Glaxo in pharmaceuticals, Intel in semiconductors, BP in oil, GE in electrical engineering.

By the early years of the twenty-first century, most conglomerates had 'de-merged' their businesses into separate companies, and the argument had been accepted (at least for the time being) that it was not efficient for specific non-financial companies to diversify. Financial analysts argue that diversification does not add value to a firm, because investors can achieve their own optimal diversification either through holding a mix of different firms' shares directly, or through investing in mutual funds. A diversified firm is thus not worth any more than the sum of its parts. Indeed, diversification may create diseconomies of scope because the central management of a conglomerate cannot keep fully informed about all the different markets and industries in which it is operating. Hence the conglomerate may be worth less than the sum of its parts, so it will have a greater market valuation if it is split up.

The accepted wisdom at the time of writing is thus that the job of non-financial firms is to maximize the value of the firm, and this cannot be achieved by trying to run diverse businesses within one organization. Certainly the managers should try to manage the business risks that are an unavoidable part of the core business, but there is no value added by trying to run too many different types of business purely as a way of reducing the risks of the combined businesses.

---

away by holding shares of many companies. But even if you held shares in every available traded company, you would still have some risk, because the stock market as a whole tends to move up and down over time. Hence we talk about market risk and specific risk. *Market risk* is non-diversifiable, whereas *specific risk* is diversifiable through risk-pooling.

Box 13.3 discusses the issue of whether all firms should diversify the activities in order to reduce risk.

Beta It is now common to use a coefficient called **beta** to measure the relationship between the movements in a specific company's share price and movements in the market. A share that is perfectly correlated with an index of stock market prices will have a beta of 1. A beta higher than 1 means that the share moves in the same direction as the market but with amplified fluctuations. A beta between 1 and 0 means that the share moves in the same direction as the stock market but is less volatile. A negative beta indicates that the share moves in the opposite direction to the market in general. Clearly, other things being equal, a share with a negative beta would be in high demand by investment managers, as it would reduce a portfolio's risk.

The *capital asset pricing model*, or CAPM, predicts that the price of shares with higher betas must offer higher average returns in order to compensate investors for their higher risk.

For any given market condition there is a trade-off between risk and return. Investments with higher risk will be priced to offer higher expected returns than those with low risk.

Mutual funds

Many small investors do not have enough wealth to invest in company shares to gain the benefits of a diversified portfolio. Yet the average return on investing in shares is higher than that on safe assets, such as government bonds or bank and building society deposits. Hence there is a role for institutions that sell small investors a share in a much bigger and more diversified portfolio.

Such institutions are generally known as mutual funds. They are like clubs in which savers pool their funds and then jointly own a diversified set of investments. In the UK they are known as unit trusts and investment trusts.

Mutual funds play an important role in helping small investors to achieve international diversification. Just as diversification across UK companies is beneficial in improving the risk–return trade-off, so international diversification improves it still further. Small investors find it difficult and costly to buy and sell foreign shares, but mutual funds are able to access foreign markets and spread the costs over large numbers of investors. Investment opportunities for small investors are thereby greatly enhanced.

Financial intermediaries

Mutual funds are a form of financial intermediary. They take in money from savers and invest the money in company shares or bonds. Banks and building societies are also important financial intermediaries. Some other financial instruments that help companies or individuals to manage risk are discussed in Box 13.4.

Box 13.4 **Derivatives: dealing with risk in financial markets**

Many modern financial instruments create markets in various aspects of risk. Agents who wish to avoid or reduce risk can deal on these markets with others who are willing to accept the risk (for a price). The financial products involved can be used to change the risk characteristics of someone's underlying asset or liability position. They are often referred to as 'derivatives'.

Futures and forward contracts *Futures contracts* are contracts traded in standard sizes and maturities on organized exchanges (such as the London International Financial Futures Exchange, LIFFE). They can be resold at any time up to maturity. For example, a farmer might sell his wheat crop six months before it is harvested in order to hedge against the risk of the price falling at harvest time, or a tyre manufacturer might buy rubber ahead of production needs to lock into a particularly favourable current supply price. *Forward contracts* are contracts that are typically made between a customer and a bank and are custom-made in terms of characteristics. (Hence they are said to be traded in the over-the-counter market, or OTC.) They cannot generally be resold before settlement. For example, an importer of American jeans who will have to pay the producer in dollars in nine months' time may buy the US dollars with his local currency in the forward foreign exchange market in order to avoid the risk that the dollar might appreciate in the meantime. The key characteristic of both of these types of arrangement is that they enable agents to buy, at a price agreed today, some product or asset that will be delivered and paid for at some time in the future.

Swaps Swaps are also known as *contracts for differences*, as two parties agree to pay or receive the difference (over some future period) between two different interest rates (typically, one fixed and one floating rate). Swaps are used to manage interest rate risk. Agents who hold assets that pay a fixed interest rate or who have liabilities that pay interest at the current rate will be exposed to losses if interest rates rise, because the cost of borrowing will rise while the return on assets will not. Swapping either the fixed asset rate into a floating rate or the floating liability rate into fixed rate will reduce risk. The principle involved here is referred to as 'matching' because it creates assets and liabilities that will move up or down together.

Options Options come in two varieties. A *call option* is the right (but not the obligation) to buy some commodity or security at a specific price called the *exercise price*. A *put option* is the right (but not the obligation) to sell some commodity or security at a specific price. With a forward or futures contract you are committed to a future transaction; with an option you have the right to go ahead but you can walk away from the deal if you prefer. A wheat farmer who has sold his crop on the futures market must fulfil the contract. (If the size of his crop falls short of the quantity he has sold, he must buy at the market price to make up the shortfall.) With a put option, however, he could choose not to deliver if the market price turned out to be much higher than the exercise price of his contract. Options thus have favourable characteristics. They limit the downside of risk without limiting the upside possibility of gain. Naturally, there is a price that has to be paid for this one-way bet, which is known as the *option premium*. Those who sell options must charge a premium high enough to cover their losses when options are exercised at prices that are much better than the original market price.

The traditional building society takes in deposits from savers and makes loans (mortgages) to house purchasers. Why do savers not lend directly to house-buyers rather than through this intermediary? The building societies' costs could then be avoided and lenders and borrowers could, perhaps, get better terms. (The spread between building society deposit rates and loan rates could be split between the lender and the borrower.)

There are several reasons why both lenders and borrowers prefer not to deal with each other directly. Which of these applies to specific institutions depends on the nature of the business involved.

First, there are transaction or search costs for lenders and borrowers before they can meet. The intermediary provides a 'trading post' where depositors know they can find a willing borrower at all times and borrowers know they can find a willing lender. This applies to both banks and building societies.

Second, the characteristics of the loan that a saver wants to make may differ from those the ultimate borrower would be happy with. A typical saver may want to get her money back at short notice; a typical house buyer will want to borrow money for twenty or twenty-five years. The building society can make long-term loans by taking in a whole series of different short-term deposits. Banks also make long-term loans funded by deposits that can be withdrawn at short notice.

Third, a typical saver could lend to no more than one or two house-buyers. Any single house may collapse, or the borrower may default. A building society can spread the risk over a wide range of different borrowers and a wide range of different types of dwelling. Building societies with nationwide coverage grew up to take advantage of the fact that wide diversification of loans across different industries and regions is safer than, say, lending only to coal miners in South Yorkshire. Banks also spread their risk by making loans to many different borrowers. Hence minimizing overall risk is a central part of any financial intermediary's *raison d'être*.

A fourth reason for the existence of financial intermediaries is the provision of loans that are not secured by any asset, that is personal loans other than mortgages and some business loans. In such cases the lending institutions must make judgements about who is likely to pay them back and who is not. Banks and building societies are well placed to do this because they will normally lend only to people with whom they have an ongoing banking relationship. They can see how much money a customer is earning because it passes through his or her account. They therefore have better information about the creditworthiness of a potential borrower than any other potential lender could have.

Banks and building societies have superior information about the risks involved, and they are in a good position to monitor the financial progress of their customers over time.

Thus, the existence of risk is central to the need for some intermediary to play this role. The nature of the relationship between intermediaries and their customers puts them in an ideal position to monitor (and possibly control) those risks.

Financial intermediaries allow savers to find relatively safe outlets for their savings which pay a competitive rate of interest. (Financial intermediaries compete for business just like the other firms that we have discussed.) Those who wish to borrow are also able to do so in a well developed market for loans. Such savings-and-loans markets are important for the functioning of a market economy. In particular, they enable consumers to move consumption either forward or backward in time, thereby greatly enhancing the range of choices available. Saving postpones consumption for the future. Borrowing permits consumption today that will be paid for in future, or the purchase of large durable product like a house or a car, the services of which will be consumed over future periods.

Conclusion

All economic activity carries some degrees of risk. Goods are produced or bought today for sale in the future. Contracts commit producers, customers, and borrowers to exchange goods and services in the future, and lenders to various actions in the future. Because the future can never be known with certainty, these essential economic activities all carry risks.

One of the triumphs of the market economy is its ability to facilitate a specialization of tasks. For a fee, specialists in risk assume the risks that others must take. In the process, they reduce the total amount of risk because of risk-sharing and their own specialized knowledge of risky situations. Insurance grew up when overseas trade became important

in the post-medieval world. It allowed merchants who were specialists in markets to pass the risks of the voyage on to insurers who were specialists in marine risks. The joint-stock company grew up in the nineteenth century as a way of allowing the accumulation of the vast amounts of capital that were needed to finance the factories of the Industrial Revolution with acceptable risks to the individual investors.

Today's specialists in risks are many and varied. They often act as financial intermediaries, standing between savers and borrowers. They facilitate complex transactions, which among other things allow many economic agents to specialize in what they can best do while allowing others to assume the risks that are inherent in these activities.

SUMMARY

Risk and consumer choice

■ Many economic decisions involve risky choices, which can often be characterized by the expected value of the outcome and the degree of risk as measured by the dispersion of the possible outcomes.

■ Because those providing insurance or gambling must make profits, those who gamble or buy insurance do not take mathematically fair gambles. Diminishing marginal utility explains why people are risk-averse and therefore buy insurance policies, but it also predicts that such people would not gamble. Gambling where there is a small chance of a very large gain may be explained by the value placed on the hope (however

small) of transforming one's life. Gambling where small gains and losses are involved may be explained by enjoyment of gambling in itself.

■ From the firm's point of view, providing gambling games where the odds can be set endogenously is a no-lose situation. Providing insurance is risky, but the pooling of independent risks minimizes the risk.

■ Two problems with insurance are moral hazard, where the existence of insurance alters people's behaviour in a socially costly way, and adverse selection, which arises under conditions of asymmetric information.

Financial choices and risk

■ Portfolio diversification allows investors to reduce their risk by holding a broad spectrum of financial assets. The risk reduction comes partly from the pooling of the return on assets whose risks are independent of each other, and partly from the pooling of assets whose risks are correlated with each other but of different magnitude. Optimum portfolio diversification allows investors to choose a bundle of assets that minimizes the risk on any given expected rate of return.

■ Mutual funds allow even small investors to hold highly diversified portfolios.

■ Financial intermediaries are institutions that stand between savers and borrowers. Their specialized knowledge and large volume of transactions reduce the transaction costs of matching savers and lenders and reduce risk.

TOPICS FOR REVIEW

■ Expected value and risk

■ Fair and unfair games

■ Attitudes to risk

■ Risk-sharing and risk-pooling

■ The demand for insurance

■ Portfolio diversification

■ The beta coefficient

■ Mutual funds

■ Financial intermediaries

DISCUSSION QUESTIONS

1 Calculate the expected return on each of the following sets of returns on an asset when each of the alternative possible outcomes has an equal chance of occurring:
   (a) 5%, 8%, 9%, 12%, 14%
   (b) 2%, 4%, 10%, 14%, 18%
   (c) 20%, 14%, 10%, 4%, 0%

2 Calculate the deviation of each of the five possible alternative outcomes in (a) above from its expected value. Square this deviation and multiply it by the probability of the outcome occurring. Add these terms together. This gives a measure of the variance of returns. Take the square root of the variance to find the standard deviation. Repeat this for (b) and (c). Ranks these outcomes in terms of the standard deviation of returns.

3 Suppose that the returns in question 1 arise in five possible states of the world and are returns on three different assets, (a), (b), and (c), that could be combined in a portfolio. The first number relates to the return on each asset in state 1, the second number to state 2, etc. Each state is equally likely to arise.

   (a) Calculate the expected return and standard deviation of return for a portfolio containing one-third of each asset.
   (b) Calculate the expected return and standard deviation for the following portfolios:
       (i)   half asset (a) and half asset (b)
       (ii) half asset (a) and half asset (c)
       (iii) half asset (b) and half asset (c).

   Which combination of these assets will a risk-averse investor prefer?

4 Can it be rational for a consumer both to gamble and to buy insurance?

5 Explain the problems that arise from moral hazard and adverse selection in insurance or financial markets.

6 Why does the presence of risk help explain the existence of financial intermediaries?

7 Under what circumstances is portfolio diversification beneficial for an investor?

Chapter 14

MARKETS AND FIRMS IN ACTION

In the previous chapters in Part II, we have built up an analysis of the determinant of consumers' demand and producers supply decisions. Is this just abstract theory, or do the analyses help us to understand real markets? Can such simple models give us genuine insights into the complexities of the real world? Here we present some examples of the payoffs from the models that we have built up, and give some other views on the analyses we have developed. In particular, you will learn that:

• A real-world cartel, like OPEC, has periods when it is successful in raising prices, but market responses and the incentive to cheat make co-operation and market control hard to sustain.

• The UK newspaper displays patterns consistent with our analysis of oligopoly, with periods of tacit collusion interspersed with occasional price wars.

• Firms themselves are bought and sold in the market for corporate control.

• Managers of firms may have different objectives from the owners of firms (shareholders), but managerial incentives can be created in order to make their interests coincide.

• Firms may not always succeed in (or even try) maximizing profits, but firms that grow and prosper are most likely to be those that make healthy profits.

As well as helping you to understand some important issues, this chapter provides essential practice in using the theory that has been developed above. Mastering economics lies not in just repeating what you have learned, but in being able to apply the analysis to new situations as they arise.

Markets and competition: some real-world examples

OPEC: a case study of a cartel

Cocoa producers in West Africa, farmers in the European Union, coffee growers in Brazil, oil producers, taxi drivers in many cities, and labour unions throughout the world have all sought to obtain, through collective action, some of the benefits of departing from the price-taking aspects of perfect competition. In all of these cases, the sellers were so numerous that no single one of them had any individual market power. Acting individually, each had to accept the market price that was determined by forces beyond its control. Acting collectively, they were able to influence prices by restricting supply. Cases of this sort are worth studying because they occur frequently and in various guises.

In Chapter 11 on pages 187–8 we studied the behaviour of perfectly competitive firms that organized themselves into a cartel. We reached two important conclusions.

1. It always pays the producers in a perfectly competitive industry to enter into an output-restricting agreement.

2. Each individual cartel member can increase its profits by violating the output restrictions, provided the other members do not violate theirs.

These two conclusions highlight the dilemma of any cartel that is composed of firms that, acting individually, would be price-takers—whether it be the Organization of Petroleum Exporting Countries (OPEC) or a local producers' association. Each firm is better off if the cartel is effective in restricting output and so raising price. But each is even better off if everyone else co-operates while it cheats. Yet if all cheat, all will be worse off.

The behaviour of OPEC provides an example of the cartelization of an industry that contained a large number of price-taking firms. Because it did not cover all of the firms in the industry, it created an oligopoly rather than a monopoly. Its behaviour illustrates both the problems of oligopolistic industries and the general functioning of the competitive price system in all the runs—short, long, and very long.

Early success

OPEC did not attract world attention until 1973, when its members voluntarily agreed to restrict their outputs by negotiating quotas. At the time, OPEC countries accounted for over half of the world's supply of crude oil and an even bigger proportion of world oil exports. So, although it was not quite a complete monopoly, the cartel had substantial market power. As a result of the output restrictions, the world price of oil nearly quadrupled within a year, from about $3 to nearly $12 a barrel. (Oil prices are customarily stated in US dollars.) The demand and supply analysis of what happened (in simplified terms) is analysed in Figure 14.1.

OPEC's policy succeeded for several reasons. First, the member countries provided a significant part of the total world supply of oil. Second, other producing countries could not quickly increase their outputs in response to price increases. Third, as Figure 14.1 shows, the world demand

for oil proved to be highly inelastic in the short run. Data for oil prices over time are shown in Figure 14.2.

The higher prices were maintained for the remainder of the decade. As a result, OPEC countries found themselves suddenly enjoying vast wealth. The increase in their wealth was so great that the temptation to cheat—in order to gain even more—was small during the rest of the 1970s. By the end of the decade, however, the OPEC countries had become used to their vast wealth and were spending more and more on arms, as well as on economic development. Eager for yet more income, they engineered a second output restriction that pushed prices from the $10–$12 range to over $30 a barrel. New income poured in, and OPEC's power to hold the oil-consuming world to ransom seemed limitless.

Longer-term market forces, however, were inexorably working against OPEC.

Pressure on the cartel

Monopolistic producers always face a long-run dilemma. The closer their prices are to the profit-maximizing level, the greater their short-term profits, but also the greater the incentive for market reactions that will reduce their profits in the longer term. In OPEC's case the market reactions came from both the demand and the supply sides of the market.

Increasing world supply The high prices and high profits achieved by the OPEC cartel spurred major additions to the world's oil supply by non-OPEC producers. This was, in effect, new entry and resulted in a rightward shift in the non-OPEC supply curve. In 1973 OPEC produced more than half of the world's oil; by 1979 its share was well under half, and by 1985 it was only just over one quarter (see Figure 14.3)! The increased supply of non-OPEC oil tended to drive the world price down. To maintain the price, OPEC had to reduce its own output more and more.

Declining world demand The market demand curve for oil in Figure 14.1 shows how variations in the price of oil affect purchases, holding other variables constant. Other things being equal, there was little that users could do to reduce their immediate consumption of petroleum products in response to the price rise. Over a longer period of time, however, other things did not remain equal. A host of long-term adaptations—including smaller cars, more efficient insulation on oil-heated buildings, and more economical diesel engines—economized on petroleum products within known technology. The long-run demand curve proved to be much more elastic than the short-run demand curve. (See Figure 4.8 on page 67 for an elaboration of the distinction between short- and long-run demand curves.) UK inland deliveries of petroleum, for example, fell from 107 million tonnes in 1973 to 72 million tonnes in 1981, and

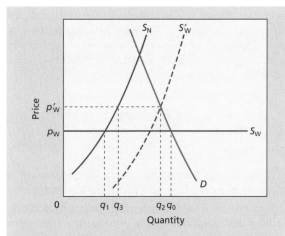

Figure 14.1 OPEC as a successful cartel

Given a rising non-OPEC supply curve of oil, OPEC could determine equilibrium price by choosing its contribution to total supply. The curve S_N represents the non-OPEC supply curve of oil. When the OPEC countries were prepared to supply all that was demanded at the world price p_W, the world supply curve was S_W. At that price production was q_1 in non-OPEC countries and $q_0 - q_1$ in OPEC countries.

By fixing its production, OPEC shifted the world supply curve to S'_W, where the horizontal distance between S_N and S'_W is OPEC's production. The world price rose to p'_W. Production became q_3 in non-OPEC countries and $q_2 - q_3$ in the OPEC countries. OPEC increased its oil revenues because, although sales fell, the price rose more than in proportion. Non-OPEC countries gained doubly because they were free to produce more and to sell it at the new, higher, world price.

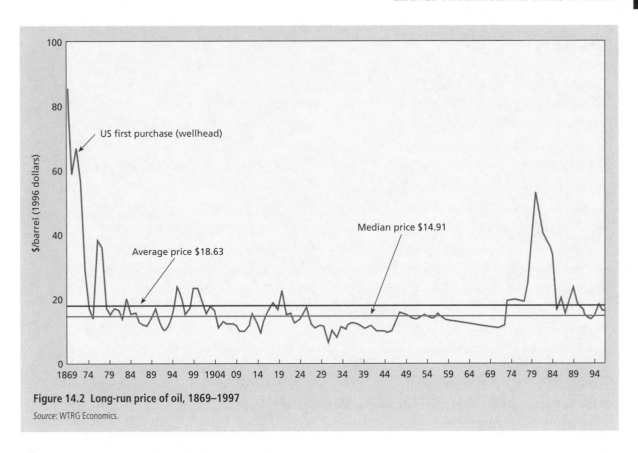

Figure 14.2 Long-run price of oil, 1869–1997

Source: WTRG Economics.

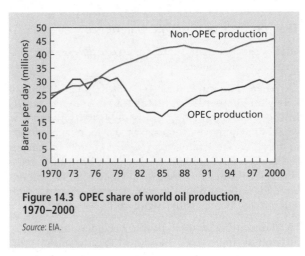

Figure 14.3 OPEC share of world oil production, 1970–2000

Source: EIA.

two decades later in 2000 it had still only recovered to 76 million tonnes.

Very long-run forces were also unleashed. The high price of petroleum led to a burst of scientific research to develop more petroleum-efficient technologies and alternatives to petroleum. Solar-heating technology was advanced, as was technology concerning many longer-term alternatives such as tidal power and heat from the interior of the Earth. Had the price of petroleum remained at its 1980 peak, this research would have continued at an intense pace and would have borne increasing fruits in the decades that followed.

The shrinking market for OPEC oil at the high world price necessitated ever-stiffer production limitations if the cartel was to maintain that price. By 1981 OPEC exports were only 18 million barrels per day, two-thirds of the 1973 level, and by 1985 in order to maintain prices production was cut to just 15 million barrels.

The pressure to cheat As world output of oil grew, OPEC output had to be reduced substantially to maintain the high prices. As a result, incomes in OPEC countries declined sharply and the instabilities inherent in any cartel began to be felt. In 1981 the cartel price was about five times as high as the 1972 price (measured in constant dollars), but production quotas were less than half of OPEC's capacity. Upset by declining incomes, OPEC producers began to violate their quotas. They met every few months to debate quotas, deplore cheating, and argue about strategy. But the agreements that were reached proved impossible to enforce, and at the end of 1985 OPEC eliminated production quotas. The price fluctuated considerably and then

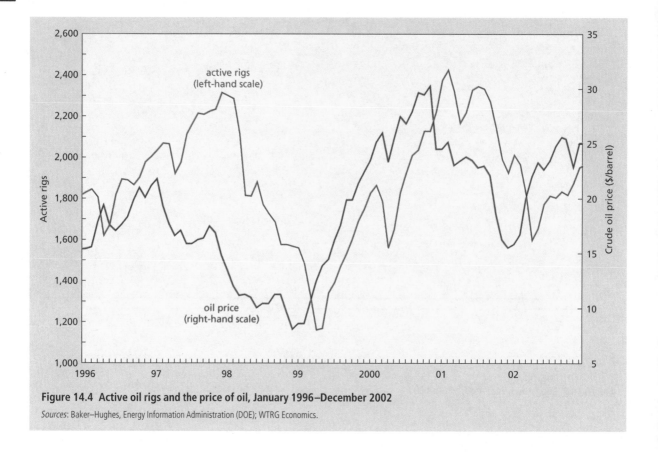

Figure 14.4 Active oil rigs and the price of oil, January 1996–December 2002

Sources: Baker–Hughes, Energy Information Administration (DOE); WTRG Economics.

settled down near $18 a barrel, which is a little higher than the price before OPEC's restrictions began (allowing for inflation)—the slightly higher price being accounted for by the modest output restrictions that OPEC was still able to enforce.

Recently OPEC has got its act together again. This is not surprising, as world consumption, particularly in the United State, rose and discovery of new supplies fell so that non-OPEC production levelled off, and OPEC came to have a rising share of the market. Now it has real market power again and it is using it. It understands this time that if it pushes prices too high it will lose market share and market power over five to seven years as new supplies once again are discovered and come on line.

Figure 14.4 shows just how sensitive oil extraction activity has become to changes in the market price of oil. Between February 1999 and early 2001 the price of oil rose from around $10 to over $30 per barrel. This rise was due partly to new OPEC production restrictions and partly to a boom in activity in the world economy that increased demand. However, in response to this price rise, the number of active oil rigs doubled from 1,200 to 2,400. Not surprisingly, the price then fell back as more production came on stream (and the world economy slowed).

The relevance of the OPEC experience

OPEC's experience illustrates some basic problems of output restriction schemes.

1. **Where demand is inelastic, restriction of output to below the competitive level can lead to immense profits in the short term.** However, supply is likely to increase when, as Schumpeter long ago predicted, new producers find ways of overcoming entry barriers in order to share in the large profits. Furthermore, demand is likely to decrease as new substitutes are invented and produced. These long-term adjustments limit the market power of monopolies and cartels, but only with a significant time-lag.

2. **Maintaining market power becomes increasingly difficult as time passes.** The closer the cartel pushes price to the monopoly level, the higher are the short-run profits, but the greater is the incentive for longer-term, profit-reducing reactions from both the supply side and the demand side of the market.

3. **Producers with market power face a basic trade-off between profits in the short term and profits in the longer term.** When there are many producers, it is difficult to force them all to maintain the output restrictions

because each one has an incentive to cheat. This is particularly so if declining demand and increasing competition from new sources, or new products, lead to a steadily shrinking share of the market and falling profits.

4. Output restriction by voluntary agreement among several producers is difficult to maintain over any long period of time. For a while OPEC massively exploited the non-OPEC world. But in the end the forces of the free market came to the rescue.

Oligopoly in action: newspaper price wars again

In Chapter 5 on pages 79–81 we discussed the impact of a price war between The Times newspaper and the other UK broadsheet newspapers. What was unusual in that case was that one producer cut its price and none of the others followed for quite some time. This makes it a good example of what happens in a market when one price changes and no others do. Eventually, there were some other price reactions as the other producers attempted to protect their market share. It is worth re-reading that example from the perspective of the discussion of oligopoly in Chapter 12. After the burst of price competition in the mid-1990s, the broadsheets settled into a long period of tacit collusion during which they maintained a constant price differential between their various newspapers.

However, another price war did break out in May 2002, but this time between the tabloid papers. The following reports (written for one of the broadsheets) give a good picture of the actions involved.

The Express is the early winner in the latest round of newspaper price wars after unofficial figures showed it has boosted circulation by as much as 14 per cent since it dropped its price to 20p. Owner Richard Desmond slashed the cover price of his daily and Sunday titles two weeks ago and is already seeing significant gains with a 23 per cent rise on weekend sales. The price war intensified yesterday when both the Daily Mirror and the Sun joined him with 20p newspapers.

The Mirror appears to have gained most ground so far in the early stages of the tabloid war. According to unaudited figures the newspaper's sales have risen by 8 per cent, adding 160,000 readers nationwide, since cutting its cover price from 32p to 20p. The Sun, which cut its cover price from 30p to 20p, has seen its sales go up by 5 per cent, adding 200,000 to its circulation. The Daily Star, already the fastest growing newspaper, has also benefited from price-cutting with a 12 per cent rise in sales in the London region. (Jessica Hodgson, media.guardian.co.uk, 14 May 2002)

Notice that this initial report focuses on the apparent increase in sales for all of those involved in price-cutting. This is the impact of the general increase in quantity demanded of a fall in price. However, a month later some winners and losers were emerging, at least from the first round. Also, while the Express initiated the price cutting, the head-to-head competition had shifted to the closer rivalry between the Sun and the Mirror. The Express's closest rival, the Daily Mail, had not reacted.

The Sun has declared itself the undisputed victor in the circulation war, claiming its 'unbeatable mixture of the best news, sport and features' has sent the price-cutting Mirror into crisis. It says the first official circulation figures, including bulk sales, since both papers slashed their cover prices to 20p show the Sun's sales are up by 107,378 year on year, while the Mirror's are down by 64,473.

'The sales disaster is a serious blow for the Mirror', the Sun gloated in Saturday's edition. The Mirror has 'spent £20 million on price cutting, posh telly ads, posters and marketing research and gained NOTHING but a bloody nose and LESS sales', continued the Sun. The latest figures show that the Sun's circulation for May 2002 was 3,458,803, a 0.42 per cent rise since the same time last year. Sales of the Mirror have dropped by 0.53 per cent over the same period to 2,128,755 . . .

By June 6, however, the Mirror was in partial retreat and put its cover price back up to 32p in its northern heartland. In London, Meridian, central, the west and south-west regions, the Mirror is still on sale at 20p, while in Scotland it is selling for 10p.

The tabloid price war between the Sun and the Mirror has taken a particularly bitter twist because of a personality clash between the two editors. (Ciar Byrne, media.guardian.co.uk, 17 June 2002)

Three further points that are worth emphasizing emerge from this second extract. First, price competition is important here but it is only one element of the competitive interface: there are also quality and marketing issues involved. Second, the interaction between the closest rivals can be very explicit and direct. We have not published some of the rude things that the editors of the Sun and Mirror said about each other, but it is clear who they are each competing with and that they are involved in trading insults publicly. Third, notice that the Mirror is using some elements of price discrimination (see pages 182–5) between various segments of its markets. In its heartland it is able to charge a higher price as (presumably) demand there is more inelastic, while in areas where competition is stiffer it sets a lower price.

Price setting in different markets

In Chapters 10–13 we have seen how price setting is influenced by the market structure in which firms operate. In Chapter 3 we also discussed how markets differ between those where prices are administered by suppliers and those where prices are flexible, similar to auction markets. Here we outline some other subtle differences between markets that affect how prices get determined.

We first outline some different types of auction market and then consider various cases in which some element of both an auction and an administered price plays a role.

Auctions

The nature of an auction depends in part on the type of product being sold. If there is only one product to be sold, such as a work of art or a piece of antique furniture, the aim of the auction is to eliminate all potential buyers except one. The person who gets the goods is the highest bidder. In an *English auction* the process involves the auctioneer starting at a low price and raising the price in successive steps until only one bidder remains. In a *Dutch auction*, the price starts very high and is lowered slowly until the first person makes a bid, and this person then gets the goods.

Where there are many of the same products to be sold, as with new issues of shares or government bonds, a system of tender is normally adopted. With a fixed-price tender (commonly used for new issues of shares), the issuer sets the price and bidders submit an application for as many as they want at that price. If there are more bids than shares being issued, the bids will be scaled down in proportion to the excess demand. So if there are twice as many bids as shares on offer, each bidder will get half what they asked. (Or they may all get some fixed number plus some proportion of their bid.) In a flexible-price tender, bidders offer both the number they want to buy and the price they are prepared to pay. The sellers then set the price as the one that just sells all the securities on offer. Some tender systems then allocate all bidders at or above the acceptance price of the stock they bid for but at the market-clearing price. Other systems allocate stock at the price that each bidder offered (so there is not a single market price but each successful bidder pays what he or she bid).

Tenders also apply to bids submitted for contracts such as to build a road or a building. Here the winner of the contract is the bidder who submits to do the work for the lowest price (subject to checks that quality standards will be met).

One famous recent auction was run by the UK government in the spring of 2000. This was to sell the licences for Third Generation mobile phone wave bands. This was a complicated auction that involved 150 rounds of bidding and raised £23 billion for the government. Details can be found on www.spectrumauction.gov.uk. The structure of this auction almost certainly raised far more revenue for the government than would have been achieved by a one-shot tender auction, or indeed by a single bidding process held on one day.

Mixed markets

Many product markets have an auction type market at the wholesale level but administered prices at the retail level. Petrol, for example, sells to motorists at a set retail price, but this price is heavily influenced by crude oil prices which are determined in international auction-style markets where traders bid for contracts on a trading floor or via screen-based trading systems. Fishmongers typically put a set price on the fish in their shops, but they themselves have had to bid for the fish at the dockside earlier the same day.

Foreign exchange (FX) markets work by major traders quoting both the prices at which they will sell and the prices at which they will buy and reporting these on information service computer screens (such as Reuters and Bloomberg). These are like administered prices, as they are set by the trader. However, they are also flexible prices, in the sense that all these traders are watching the prices set by other traders and will all change their prices quoted very quickly if new information arrives. For some small trades FX dealers will guarantee to trade at their posted price; however, for most large deals a negotiation will be conducted over the telephone with a potential buyer or seller. So some bargaining is involved with one other party. Only if a deal cannot be agreed will the trader call another counter-party and start negotiating another deal. Price and quantity are thus negotiated simultaneously in a whole series of bilateral deals.

Bargaining

We have noted in the text that most retail markets have administered prices, and this is more efficient as it involves less negotiation time. In some countries, however, bargaining is a long established tradition and continues to this day. If you want to buy a carpet in Marakesh, for example, you would be foolish to pay the first price asked by the trader in the Suk. The convention is that the first price asked is much higher than the seller would be happy to accept, but it is up to the potential buyer to show his or her skills (and willingness to walk away) in order to get a good deal. This can be good fun and certainly adds to social interaction, but it is very time-consuming so would not be a practical way to organize trading in a modern supermarket.

Bargaining still occurs to some degree in modern market economies, but typically this happens only with infrequent but important transactions. Wage contracts are obvious examples, where the bargaining is delegated by workers in whole firms or industries to trade union representatives. Individuals do sometimes bargain for their own salary, but this typically happens only when they start the job and then much less significantly when it comes to annual pay rises. House purchases also often involve some negotiation. In England offers are received in relation to some asking price. But if there are many potential buyers the price may get bid up in an implicit auction (typically conducted via estate agents), and even an accepted offer may involve subsequent further negotiations, especially if a survey reveals some structural problems with the property. In Scotland, however, a sealed bid auction is the norm. Housing sales have a closing date by which written offers must be received. Bidders do not know what others have bid, but they do know that if they are not the highest bidder they will not get the property. The bidder who submits the highest bid is legally obliged to buy the property at the price bid.

All of these different examples illustrate the subtlety of market institutions and how the way in which the market is structured may have some impact on the specific outcomes achieved. However, at the same time there is a commonality in all markets. They are just the interface between potential buyers and potential sellers, and they facilitate the allocation of goods and services between competing uses and competing consumers.

Alternative views of the firm

After studying some nuances of markets, we now return to the firm. Recall that in Chapter 8 we pointed out that firms can be thought of as alternatives to the market. We began that chapter by observing that there were many forms of business organization, running from the sole trader to the joint-stock company. From then on, however, we have assumed firms to be profit-maximizing agents whose internal structure does not affect their performance. This treats the firm as a black box, since we are unconcerned with what goes on inside it. A great deal can be done in economics using this simple view of the firm as a consistent maximizing agent that acts as if it were run by a single owner–manager. However, it precludes the study of many interesting issues that can be raised only if a more complex view of the firm is taken. It is now time to go beyond the useful simplification and look at the firm in more detail.

Organization as a variable

Different forms and sizes of business organization have varying efficiencies in different circumstances. When the circumstances change, so must the organization change.

The most common cause of changing circumstances to which the firm must react is changes in the technologies of the products it makes (called *product technology*) and in the processes it uses to make them (called *process technology*). At the beginning of the twentieth century, technological changes associated with the electrification of factories made large scale efficient in many—but not all—manufacturing activities. The result was a wave of mergers as many smaller firms were united to make fewer large firms. Not long after, the introduction of mass production made large-scale assembly plants efficient. These plants were made efficient when electric motors were attached to each separate machine tool.

Towards the end of the twentieth century developments in information and communications technology again altered the relative efficiencies of different sizes and forms of business organization. In many activities small size has become efficient. Large firms have shed many peripheral activities that are now undertaken by smaller, more specialized firms. This allows the larger firms to concentrate on what they call their 'core competencies'. Within many large firms, the old hierarchical organization, with hoards of middle managers passing information and commands upwards and downwards, is now obsolete. A newer, more loosely controlled, lateral form of organization is proving more efficient in many situations. In the process of adjustment, many middle-range managers have lost their jobs. In the global economy that has been created by the information and communications revolution, some activities are most efficiently undertaken on a very large scale. For example, banks and other financial institutions have been increasing in size and scope. Also, many specific activities, such as marketing, distribution, and financing, have large-scale economies in the globalized marketplace. These are most efficiently undertaken by large units. In contrast, many production activities are more efficiently undertaken in units that are much smaller than were the typical manufacturing firms in the days of mass production. As a result, many sectors are seeing simultaneous growth in the size of firms, while their internal organizations are becoming less hierarchical.

If the market economy is to function efficiently, these changes in size and structure of firms must be made whenever they are needed. One way in which the size of firms is varied is by combining several existing firms into a larger single unit. Another is in the breaking up of large firms into several separate independent units. Such changes are negotiated in what is called the **market for corporate control**. Instead of the more familiar markets for goods and services, this is a market in which firms themselves are bought and sold, combined and broken up.

The buyers in this market are those who wish to acquire the rights to control a firm. The sellers are the current owners of the firm's equity. As in other markets, the expected outcome is that the assets being bought and sold will wind up in the hands of those who value them most.

The market for corporate control

A **takeover** occurs when company A buys company B (which then becomes a part of A). In a *friendly takeover*, both sides wish to make the transaction. A *hostile takeover* occurs when it is opposed by the current management of the target firm. A **merger** occurs when companies A and B join together, often combining even their names. A **buyout** occurs when a group of investors, rather than an existing firm, buys up a firm or one of its subsidiaries. In a management buyout the existing management buys its firm from the present owners. In one form of management buyout the managers of a wholly owned subsidiary buy their firm from the group that owns it; from then on it becomes an independent firm.

The market for corporate control does not just involve whole firms being bought and sold. It is now very common for parts of firms to be bought and sold. In this respect a modern corporation can be viewed as a portfolio of businesses, and any part of this portfolio can be disposed of at any time if it is thought that its market price is sufficiently high that this asset value can be used more profitably in other activities. Box 14.1 illustrates this point by use of some recent news stories.

The effects of takeovers

Takeovers, mergers, and buyouts tend to come in waves. Some are driven by technological changes that alter the minimum efficient scale of firms in many industries. They tend to have long-lasting effects. Such was the merger wave at the beginning of this century in the United States. Some are based on experiments that prove to be either outright failures or far less valuable than originally thought. Such was the wave of conglomerate mergers in the 1970s that often united firms selling widely different products in widely different markets (hence the name 'conglomerate'). Although a few of the conglomerates formed in that period have survived, most have been dismantled. Some went in the wave of buyouts that occurred in the 1980s. Others were dismantled from within, as when Hanson plc was split into five separate companies in 1996/7 (see Box 13.3 on page 225).

Do takeovers improve economic efficiency? The main argument for answering yes is that after a takeover the new management can make more efficient use of the target firm's assets. The acquiring firm should be able to exploit profit opportunities that the target management was not exploiting. This can be done in many ways after the takeover. The target firm may be operated more efficiently.

 Box 14.1 **The market for parts of companies**

The following are all recent examples of companies selling or buying subsidiary companies. This is an important aspect of the market for corporate control, but it does not involve a full takeover bid. Typically involved is a cash sale or exchange of other assets.

The drinks firm Diageo has finally sold its Burger King fast-food chain, but for a much lower price than originally sought. The chain has been bought for $1.5bn (£950 million) by a consortium of US venture capitalist firms. The price is about a third less than the amount Diageo had previously agreed with the consortium. But the original agreement was changed after the US buyers demanded a review of the price following poor trading at the burger chain.

Burger King has more than 11,000 outlets around the world, with three-quarters of them in the US. Diageo has been keen to sell the chain as part of its strategy of concentrating on its drinks business. The firm is the world's largest drinks group, and includes brands such as Baileys Irish Cream, Smirnoff vodka and Johnnie Walker whisky.

The consortium led by US firm Texas Pacific originally offered $2.26bn (£1.4bn) for Burger King. But the offer was subject to Burger King meeting certain performance targets, and poor trading at the chain led to the original deal being scrapped. (BBC Business News website, 13 December 2002)

Supermarket chain Sainsbury's has sold its Homebase DIY chain in a two-fold deal worth £969 million. The arrangement will see its chain of stores sold to venture capitalist Schroder Ventures for £750 million. A further 28 sites, which were intended to house new Homebase stores, are being sold to Kingfisher, owner of DIY rival B&Q, for £219 million. Sainsbury's chief executive Sir Peter Davis told the BBC he hoped that the change in ownership for Homebase would not lead to job losses.

Sir Peter put Homebase up for sale in August, saying the group needed to be set free to pursue expansion plans which included moves into continental Europe. But the food retailer decided not to fund the DIY division's expansion and chose instead to concentrate on revamping its food stores. (BBC Business News website, 22 December 2000)

British Energy, the beleaguered nuclear generator, is expected to conclude the sale of its Canadian asset, Bruce Power, this week for more than £300 million. Cameco, the world's largest uranium producer, already owns 15 per cent of Bruce Power and will buy British Energy's 82.4 per cent holding as part of a consortium with the Toronto bank Borealis Capital and Trans Canada Pipelines. (*Sunday Times*, 15 December 2002)

These examples are a good illustration of the fact that the market for corporate control is not just about takeover bids for whole quoted companies. Rather, a substantial part of the trading involves inter-firm sales of subsidiary businesses, brands, or other corporate assets.

It may be provided with funds that it could not obtain on its own. It may be able to enter markets that would be too expensive for it to access on its own. Or it might just be moved towards the most efficient size, which may have been changed by technological advances in the industry. If any of these situations hold, the value of the target firm will rise in response to an imminent takeover, reflecting the expectation of increased future profits. Further, it is often argued that, if the acquiring firm's managers are acting in the best interest of its stockholders, the value of the acquiring firm should also rise when it looks as if it is about to succeed in its takeover bid.

Returns to shareholders

Evidence strongly supports the proposition that takeover bids benefit the shareholders of target firms. Estimates of the magnitude of the gains for UK and US shareholders of target firms typically show that on average they sell their shares for about 20 per cent over the pre-takeover share price. Some specific cases have produced gains to shareholders well in excess of this amount.

In contrast, the benefits to shareholders in the acquiring firms vary greatly from takeover to takeover. Sometimes the benefit is large; at other times it is negative. (The takeover lowers the value of the acquiring firm's shares.) However, the accumulated evidence seems to show that the average benefit to acquiring firms in both the United States and the United Kingdom has been very close to zero, or possibly slightly negative.

It may seem strange that firms taking over other firms do not actually benefit from such actions on average. However, this is what we would expect if the market for corporate control were competitive. A typical takeover starts when an existing firm is perceived to be undervalued. This may be for any of the reasons mentioned above. Other firms will want to take the firm over and will bid up the value of its shares to reflect the perceived undervaluation.

The result of bidding wars is a rise in the price of the target firm's shares to the benefit of the owners, whereas the firm that finally makes the successful takeover pays about the price that at best makes its investment yield a normal return (including a risk premium).

However, expectations about the potential profitability of the target firm are subject to a wide margin of error. So some takeovers turn out to be more valuable than expected and the acquiring firm gains, while others turn out to be less valuable than expected and the acquirer loses. Uncertainty about a target firm's value leads to a range of estimates, and the auction process makes it inevitable that the sale always goes to the one with the highest valuation. So if the potential purchasers get the valuation right *on average*

the actual purchasers will pay too much on average. This is known as the 'winner's curse', and is discussed in Box 14.2.

Benefits to the economy?

There is considerable controversy about whether the threat of takeover is always a good thing. Critics of hostile takeovers argue that they encourage 'short-termism'. Managers cannot take appropriate long-term investment decisions because short-term weakness in the share price may lead to the firm being taken over and the management replaced. In Germany and Japan institutional arrangements make hostile takeovers difficult, if not impossible, so managers do not have to worry about being deposed in this way.

Supporters emphasize several positive values. First, the possibility of such hostile takeovers may be a useful discipline on entrenched but inefficient managers. Second, the possibility may restrain managers from acting in non-maximizing ways, for example being more interested in securing their own high salaries than in taking the kind of risk on which long-term business success depends. Third, each new bout of takeovers (whether hostile or friendly) and mergers helps to chart new waters. Changes in technology change the advantages of scale and scope resulting from changes in production techniques, market demand, and market boundaries.

The new forms of organization that are often made necessary by technological changes are sometimes effected through mergers, takeovers, and buyouts (and sometimes through the downsizing of firms—downsizing may require a buyout if existing mangers do not see what is needed). When firms react to rapidly changing circumstances, they must learn by experience. It is not surprising that, even though people generally move in the right direction, some times they make mistakes. In particular, a merger movement may go too far, so that among the profit-increasing mergers, takeovers, or buyouts there are also some profit-reducing ones. Over time the successful ones will be solidified and the unsuccessful ones abandoned.

We would expect to find such experimentation in a world of rapidly changing circumstances where people must learn appropriate responses through experience. This makes assessment of any current wave of mergers, buyouts, or takeovers difficult until the whole process is completed.

Until all the dust has settled, it is hard to distinguish between some spectacular, attention-getting failures that are an inevitable part of the learning process and a more general failure of the concept behind the wave.

One reason why a firm may be taken over by another is that it is not maximizing its profits. The new management may believe that after the takeover it can exploit profitable opportunities that are being ignored by the present management.

Box 14.2 **The winner's curse**

In any auction market the sale price is determined by what the highest bidder is prepared to pay. In a standard auction, the price keeps rising until all but one bidder drops out. The highest bidder, who ends up acquiring the object for sale, is often described as 'the winner'. However, the winner of an auction, especially in the context of the 'winner' of a takeover bid, may not be a winner at all.

The winner of a takeover fight has to pay a price so high that not only are the existing owners prepared to sell, but also all other bidders have dropped out. This means that the so-called winner has paid a price for the target firm that is higher than the valuation placed on it by any other party in the auction.

The winner may know something about the value of the target firm that nobody else knows. More often, however, all bidders have roughly the same information. But there is always some uncertainty about how to assess the importance of this information. The uncertainty gives rise to differences in the potential purchasers' assessments of the true value of the target firm. The auction guarantees that the winner will be the bidder with the most optimistic estimate. If the average of all the bidders' estimates is close to the true value, the firm that wins will always pay more than the true value. Fortunately for the winner, uncertainty is such that sometimes even the most optimistic estimate is less than the true value. Also the target firm is sometimes worth more to the winner than to any other bidder. In such cases the winner really wins.

In other cases, however, the firm that wins a takeover battle does not increase the value of its own company. Indeed, in a hotly contested bidding war in which there are rival bidders and the winning bid is well above the initial bid, the successful bidder may end up paying more than the target

firm is really worth. This is why this phenomenon is known as **the winner's curse**.

The true winners in a takeover war may be not only the shareholders of the target company, but also the rival bidders who failed to 'win'. The shareholders win because they sell their shares for more than they are really worth, at least in the opinion of most potential buyers. The losing bidders win because their rival who 'won' the auction may be saddled with a capital loss that could weaken its ability to compete in other ways.

A good example of this phenomenon is the takeover of the Crocker Bank of California by the UK's Midland Bank. This so weakened Midland that it ended up being taken over itself by HSBC. Another example is the takeover of RJR Nabisco by Kolberg Kravis and Roberts (KKR) in one of the most famous (and biggest—$25 billion) takeover auctions of all time. KKR survived, but the firm's ability to raise capital for other activities was severely dented for most of the following decade.

The winner's curse applies not just to takeover bids but to any transaction in which there is competitive bidding, such as for supply contracts which go to the lowest bidder. That bidder may have underestimated the true costs and hence may lose on the deal.

Telecoms companies such as BT and Vodafone were stock market stars when they entered an auction for 3G telecoms licences in April 2000. They 'won' licences in the auction but at a very high price, and the companies' share prices declined dramatically in the two subsequent years. The beneficiary in this case was the UK government, which received a total revenue for the five licences on offer of £23 billion. Its earlier estimate of the likely revenue was £3 billion.

Conflicts of objectives within firms

One hundred years ago the small firm, whose manager was its owner, was common in many branches of industry. In such firms the single-minded pursuit of profits would be expected. Today, however, ownership of many firms is diversified among thousands of shareholders, and these firms' managers are rarely its owners. Arranging matters so that managers always act in the best interests of shareholders is not straightforward. Thus, there is potential for managers to pursue their own goals in conflict with the shareholder's interest in maximizing the firm's profits.

The separation of ownership from control

In corporations the shareholders elect directors, who appoint managers. Directors are supposed to represent shareholders' interests and to determine the broad policies that the managers will carry out. In order to conduct the complicated business of running a large firm, a full-time professional management group must be given broad powers of decision. Although managerial decisions can be reviewed from time to time, they cannot be supervised in detail.

The links between shareholders, directors, and managers are typically weak enough that it is often top management that really controls the corporation over long periods of time.

Although the managers are legally employed by the shareholders, they remain largely independent from them. This separation of ownership from management does not matter unless the managers pursue interests that are different from the shareholders' interests. Do the interests of the two groups diverge? To study this question, we need to look at what is called principal–agent theory.

Principal–agent theory

If you (the principal) hire a gardener (your agent) to mow your lawn while you are away, all you can observe is how the lawn looks when you come back. He could have mowed it every ten days, as you agreed, or he could have waited until two days before you were due home and mowed it only once. By prevailing on a neighbour to monitor your employee's behaviour, you could find out what he actually did, although at some cost.

When you hire a solicitor, however, it is almost impossible for you to monitor her effort and diligence on your behalf. You have not studied law, and much of what the solicitor does will be a mystery to you.

This latter situation is close to the relationship that exists between shareholders and managers. The managers have information and expertise that the shareholders do not have—indeed, that is why they are the managers. The shareholders can observe profits, but they cannot directly observe the managers' efforts. To complicate matters further, even when the managers' behaviour can be observed, the shareholders do not generally have the expertise to evaluate it. Everyone can see the firm's revenues, but it takes very detailed knowledge to estimate how large those revenues could have been if the managers had acted differently. Boards of directors, who represent the firm's shareholders, can acquire some of the relevant expertise and monitor managerial behaviour, but again this is costly.

These examples illustrate the **principal–agent problem**. This is the problem of designing mechanisms that will induce agents to act in their principals' interests. In general, unless there is costly monitoring of agents' behaviour, the problem cannot be completely solved. Hired managers (like hired gardeners) will generally wish to pursue their own goals. They cannot ignore profits, however, because if they perform badly enough they will lose their jobs. Just how much latitude they have to pursue their own goals at the expense of profits depends on many things, including the degree of competition in the industry and the possibility of takeover by more profit-oriented management.

The principal–agent problem arises within the firm when ownership and control are separated and the self-interest of managers may lead them to act other than in the interest of the shareholders. The problem is to design monitoring or incentive systems that will make managers act in the best interest of the shareholders.

The principal–agent problem in the context of employers and employees more generally is discussed in Chapter 16.

Solutions to the principal–agent problem The way in which agents can be encouraged to act in the interest of principals is by the introduction of incentives to align the goals of the two. There are at least three ways in which this is done in firms today.

The first way to align the interests of shareholders and managers is to ensure that managers themselves have an interest in the value of the shares. This can be done either by ensuring that managers buy (or are perhaps given) some shares or by giving them share options which will create wealth for the managers when the value of the firms' shares rises above some value. Box 14.3 provides some further discussion of this issue. Some companies encourage a wide range of their employees to buy shares in the company via company savings schemes, in order to give these employees an interest in the profit of the company and not just in their own wage.

A second way to give managers a shared interest in profit is by tying some part of their remuneration directly to the firm's profits. This could be an annual bonus that is linked to the previous year's profit of the company as a whole, or it could be some explicit share of the profit of the part of the company in which that manager works.

A third way of achieving the same goal is to make promotion subject to the profits of the company as a whole or to the section in which the person is employed. Those who succeed in increasing profits in their divisions thus will get on well, and those who fail to do so may be let go.

The timing of profits

We have talked so far about profit maximization as though it were a choice that was made in each period of time and there was another independent decision that was made in each other period of time. This is not how it works in practice. Firms are continually making decisions in the current period, such as whether to invest in a new machine or open a new office in another country, that involve costs in the current period but generate revenues in future periods. So should managers today make decisions to maximize profits this year, or should they be planning to maximize profits at some future point in time?

The answer to this question is that firms that seek to maximize their profits in a world that extends over time will be trying to maximize the *present value* of the entire future stream of profits for the firm; in other words, they are trying to maximize the current market value of the firm. We explain how to calculate present values of future income streams and say more about the details of investment appraisal in Chapter 17. The message however is that in each period profit-maximizing firms take actions that increase the value of the firm, and they may rationally sacrifice some profit in one time period for greater profit in another if this succeeds in increasing the value of the firm.

Box 14.3 Share options as a solution to the principal/agent problem

Two American professors, Michael Jensen and William Meckling, proposed that share options could be used to align the interests of managers and shareholders. This proposal was widely adopted but was perceived to have been abused by managers granting themselves over-generous option packages. The following extract from *The Economist* discusses a recent restatement of this scheme by Jensen.

Mr Jensen is best known for work on 'agency' problems—those that arise when somebody (the principal) hires somebody else (an agent). Public firms, with their separation of ownership (shareholders) and control (bosses), have been beset by agency problems for as long as they have existed. Mr Jensen first explored how companies might remedy these problems in a paper written with William Meckling. . . . published in the mid-1970s against a backdrop of depressed share prices and lacklustre corporate performance.

Managers manage in their self-interest, the authors said, a claim that, though often deeply resented by managers, is basically true enough. A rational manager with no investment in his firm would have little incentive to maximize its value, and every incentive to use it for his own ends. . . . Taken to its extreme, a boss without shares might build a comfortable but profitless empire that squandered excess cash flow in shareholder-value-destroying acquisitions. This turned out to be a fairly good description of conglomerates, which were common at the time. . . .

When Mr Jensen first pondered agency issues, the big problem was under-utilization of company assets, and their consequent undervaluation. In the 1990s, the most salient corporate-finance problem was overvaluation—an eventuality seemingly so unlikely that few economists had given it much thought.

Mr Jensen now thinks that the way in which executive pay was typically tied to share performance through options meant that, in the bubble, the carrots became what he calls 'managerial heroin', encouraging a focus on short-term highs with destructive long-term consequences. Once a firm's shares became overvalued, it was in managers' interests to keep them that way, or to encourage even more overvaluation, in the hope of cashing out before the bubble burst. Doing this not only meant being less than honest with shareholders, or being creatively optimistic with corporate accounts. It also encouraged behaviour that actually reduced the value of some firms to their shareholders—such as making an acquisition or spending a fortune on an Internet venture simply to satisfy the whims of an irrational market.

One answer to this problem—the wrong answer, Mr Jensen says—is to increase monitoring by putting many new demands on corporate boards and on how contracts with managers are structured. . . .

A better answer, says Mr Jensen, is to retain the link between pay and share price, but to do it in a way that removes the incentive for managers to exploit and encourage short-term overvaluation. Ideally, bosses should not be able to bank most of the rewards for their performance until it has been proved genuine. . . . [The answer is] to grant a new sort of customized share option, which is profitable only if the share price not only appreciates, but does so by more than a firm's cost of capital; and which can be exercised only after a long period. ('How to pay bosses', *The Economist*, 14 November 2002)

Competition as an evolutionary process

The models of competition that have been used in this book are what can be called 'end-state models', in which what is modelled is the end result of competition between firms that may be operating under conditions of perfect competition, monopoly, or oligopoly. The theory asks: how will things look when equilibrium is reached?

An alternative view of competition is called 'process competition'. Here competition is viewed as an ongoing, never-ending process in which what the firm knows and how it reacts evolves as its experience accumulates and the conditions that it faces change. This view is associated with Austrian economists such as Fredrick von Hayek and Joseph Schumpeter. In process competition,

firms jostle for advantage by price and non-price competition, undercutting and outbidding rivals in the market-place by advertising outlays and promotional expenses, launching new differentiated products, new technical processes, new methods of

marketing and new organizational forms, and even new reward structures for their employees, all for the sake of head-start profits that they know will soon be eroded. . . . [in short,] competition is an active process. (M. Blaug, *Economic Theory in Retrospect, 2nd edn*, Cambridge University Press, 1977, pages 255–6)

A great deal of this kind of competition takes the form of competition in innovation. A firm can survive having made a mistake over prices or over capacity (the two main variables handled in most conventional theories of the firm), but falling behind in innovation is often disastrous.

Importantly, so goes this view, genuine uncertainty, not just risk, pervades the innovative process.[1] When major

---

[1] Risk arises when the possible outcomes of some decision are known and each can be assigned a definite probability. Uncertainty arises when the possible outcomes are not all known, and those that are known cannot be given definite probabilities.

technological advances are attempted, it is typically imposs-ible even to enumerate in advance the possible outcomes of a particular line of research. After all, the search for one breakthrough often produces a breakthrough in some quite unexpected direction. As a result, firms cannot assign probabilities to a known set of possible outcomes in order to conduct standard risk analysis. Of course, most people who make decisions regarding research and development (R&D) do form some kind of subjective expectations and do revise these as experience accumulates. This does not, however, alter the key characteristic of uncertain situations that two equally well-informed agents, presented with the same set of alternative actions, may make different choices. If the choice concerns R&D, one agent may back one line of attack while the other backs a second line, even though both know the same things and are searching for the same technological breakthrough. Although after the results are known one agent may prove to have made a better decision than the other, no one can say which one is making the better choice at the time the decisions are being made.

According to this line of argument, it follows that in-novating agents cannot, and therefore do not, maximize. Because firms are making R&D choices under uncertainty, there is no unique line of behaviour that maximizes their expected profits—if there were, all equally well-informed firms would be seeking the same breakthrough made in the same way. Because of the absence of a unique best line of behaviour, firms are better seen as groping into an uncer-tain future in a purposeful and profit-seeking manner than as maximizing the expected value of future profits.

Profit-seeking in the presence of uncertainty implies that the paths by which technologies are developed are not unique. If we could return to the same initial conditions and play the innovation game again, there is no guarantee that we would then retrace our steps exactly. It then fol-lows that there is no unique optimum way to allocate resources between producing with current technology and searching for new technologies. Instead of maximizing, firms that are operating under uncertainty are seen as groping into an uncertain future in a profit-oriented way. They try various lines of behaviour and learn from their successes and failures. Their idea of what is the best strategy evolves as they experiment and learn; but what they learn depends on what they attempt to do, so firms that try different lines of innovation will learn different things

and will not reach a unique optimal equilibrium line of behaviour.

Although firms may not actually be profit-maximizers, the competitive market does reward the successful line of behaviour and successful types of experiments while pun-ishing the unsuccessful ones. For example, when a wave of merger mania sweeps over investors, both good and bad mergers occur. But the market then sorts out the wheat from the chaff. Those experiments that prove profitable will persist and those that do not will be undone, possibly because the firms who made them fail. Thus, when circum-stances change the market produces results that are not too different from what would occur if all firms were profit-maximizers. This will happen as long as there are enough firms to experiment with many different responses and as long as the market rewards successes and punishes failures. Similarly, firms that have made big profits out of success-ful product innovation will have substantial profits out of which to invest in new R&D, and this in turn should aid the product flow in future periods and thus further enhance future success.

This pushing of profitable and suppressing of unprofit-able behaviour, in spite of each firm (possibly) not being a profit-maximizer, is what Richard Nelson and Sidney Winter call the 'evolutionary hand' view of the competit-ive market:

Whether it is because firms make maximizing decisions inter-nally or because the market sorts out good decisions from bad ones by rewarding the former with profits and punishing the latter with losses, the competitive economy tends to produce behaviour that continually adapts to changing circumstances. (R. Nelson and S. Winter, *An Evolutionary Theory of Economic Change,* Harvard University Press, 1990)

Whether this adaptation of firms is analogous to the evolution of species is controversial. Those who accept that firms are driven by the achievable goal of profit maximiza-tion say that the adaptations that we observe are optimal responses needed to achieve the goal. Those who favour an evolutionary approach say that the adaptations end up being more or less as good as could be expected, but not in any sense perfect. However, both approaches are con-sistent with a similar view of how firms in the market economy work to adapt and innovate as circumstances change.

SUMMARY

Markets and competition: some real-world examples

- OPEC's experience shows the profits that can be earned by restricting output to below the perfectly competitive level, as well as the difficulties of maintaining the co-operative solution over time. It also shows the economy's powerful response to price signals: high relative prices and profits induce increased supplies and long-term reductions in demand.

- The UK newspaper market illustrates key elements of oligopoly behaviour, with periods of tacit collusion interspersed with occasional aggressive price wars.

- Market organizations have many subtle differences from time to time and place to place. Auction markets have several different possible structures, and administered price setting also varies in detail. Some markets have a mixture of auction and administered price characteristics.

Alternative views of the firm

- In the market for corporate control, firms and parts of firms are bought and sold.

- The threat of takeover creates incentives for managers to perform well. Takeovers generally benefit the owners of the firm taken over, but on average bidding firms pay a fair value for their targets and so do not benefit directly from buying firms cheap.

- Principal–agent theory gives support to the idea that corporate managers may pursue their own interests rather than simply maximizing profits, but incentives can be introduced to make managers and shareholders' interests coincide.

- Firms that have profits in many periods will aim to maximize the present value of the firm, rather than seeking to increase profit in any one period at the expensive of profits in other periods.

Competition as an evolutionary process

- Evolutionary theories see innovating firms as making decisions under uncertainty and therefore as profit-oriented but not profit-maximizing.

- Even if individual firms do not always maximize profits, it is possible that the industry will be characterized by behaviour that is approximately profit-maximizing. The reason is that those firms that come closest to maximizing profits will prosper and grow, while those further away from profit maximization will shrink or fail altogether.

TOPICS FOR REVIEW

- OPEC and the dynamics of cartels
- Oligopoly price wars
- Auctions, administered prices and mixed cases
- Mergers, takeovers, and buyouts

- The principal–agent problem
- Maximizing the present value of the firm
- Evolutionary theories

DISCUSSION QUESTIONS

1 What bearing did each of the following events have on the current oil price at the time and on the eventual ability of OPEC to maintain a price for oil well above the competitive equilibrium price?

   (a) Between 1979 and 1985 OPEC's share of the world oil supply decreased by half as new sources of supply came on line.

   (b) During the 1970s government policies in many oil-importing countries protected consumers from oil price shocks by subsidizing domestic prices to hold them well below OPEC's price.

   (c) The former USSR increased its oil exports massively in the 1980s, but exports then dwindled in the 1990s as the industry fell into disrepair.

(d) In the late 1980s Iran became increasingly concerned with maximizing its own oil revenues in order to pay for its war with Iraq.

(e) Iraq occupied Kuwait, and many of Kuwait's large stock of wells were set on fire when Iraq was driven out in 1991.

(f) Other OPEC countries were able to make up for the lost Kuwaiti production by raising their outputs at marginal costs far below the current world price.

2 Explain how the principal–agent problem would arise if teachers wanted to maximize what their students learned while students merely wanted to pass their exams? What incentive structures might induce the agents (students) to come closer to fulfilling the principals' (teachers') goals?

3 Which of the following is an auction market, an administered price market, or some combination of the two?
(a) Your local supermarket
(b) Your local street market
(c) An internet bookseller
(d) The wholesale oil market
(e) The foreign exchange market between major banks
(f) A dockside fish market
(g) The housing market
(h) The second-hand car market

4 Why might a principal–agent problem arise between a firm's shareholders and its senior management? What incentives might be used to alleviate the problem?

5 Discuss the role of cartels such as OPEC in raising the price of oil. What incentives do members have to cheat?

6 What factors would determine the market value of a firm or one of its subsidiaries if it were put up for sale?

7 How might a firm end up better off by initiating a price war with its main rivals?

8 In what ways can the process of competition between firms be viewed as similar to the evolutionary process of species, often summarized as 'survival of the fittest'?

PART THREE

MARKETS FOR INPUTS

Chapter 15

DEMAND AND SUPPLY OF INPUTS

Up to now we have been studying markets for consumer goods where firms are the suppliers and individuals are the demanders. For the next few chapters we focus on the markets for the inputs that firms use to make their outputs, labour, capital, land, and natural resources. In these markets firms are typically the demanders. The suppliers may be other firms or individuals. For example, in labour markets firms are the demanders and individuals are the suppliers. Fortunately, we can analyse these markets with demand and supply tools just as we did for consumer goods.

How do firms decide how many workers to hire? Under what circumstances will employers fire workers and substitute machines that do the work instead? Do input prices determine the prices of final goods or is it the other way round? In this chapter you will learn that:

• Firms' demand for inputs is derived from the demand for their output.

• Firms will hire inputs up to the point where the extra cost is just equal to the extra contribution to revenue.

• Cheaper inputs will be substituted for dearer ones in the long run.

• The supply of inputs is more elastic for one specific use than for the economy as a whole.

• Economic rent is the return achieved in one use in excess of the highest available alternative return in another use.

We study first the forces that determine the demand for inputs, then the forces that determine supply, and finally how these interact in competitive markets to determine the prices of inputs. In subsequent chapters, we allow for market power exercised in these input markets by a few larger sellers and/or buyers.

Overview

Markets for inputs are of interest in their own right. As workers we are interested in the market for our labour; firms want to understand the markets for all the inputs that they buy; and the prices of certain key inputs, such as oil, have important effects on the economy as a whole. However, there is another traditional reason for analysis of input markets, and that is to understand the determinants of the distribution of income. The approach that used to be common was to think of inputs as being divided into groups of resources such as land, labour, and capital, each of which was owned by a different class of society: rentier, workers, and capitalists. The prices assigned to these different resources would then determine the distribution of income between these different classes of society. Hence the analysis of input pricing was also a theory of income distribution between these different groups. Box 15.1 explains some of the concepts associated with distribution theory.

We are still interested in the distributional implications of input pricing, but these are no longer associated with simplistic class divisions. Much of the nation's capital, for example, is now owned by the pension funds of workers rather than by some separate class of capitalists. In this part of the book we will be concerned with, among other things, the forces that determine the degree of income inequality in market societies. Why do some receive high incomes while others receive only low ones? We first look at some facts about income distribution before proceeding to discuss the principles of inputs pricing. The policy implications of income inequalities and attempts by government to redistribute income are discussed in Chapter 20.

Box 15.1 **Theories of the distribution of income**

The term **distribution theory** refers to any theory that explains how the total national income is divided up among the nation's citizens. Any theory that explains distribution on the basis of market forces is a **factor price theory** of distribution, and a **market theory of resource allocation**. Theories of this type use the marginal products of inputs to explain their demands. They are thus often called **marginal productivity theories** after their demand part. Marginal productivity theories were first developed by a group of neoclassical economists writing about a century ago, hence the often-used term **neoclassical theory of distribution**.

Early economists were interested in explaining the distribution of income between the owners of the main resources: labour, land, and capital. This is called the **functional distribution of income** because it divides income by functional classes, the three groups that provide the services of labour, land, and capital.* There was a long and heated debate about how the distribution of income would be affected by rising population, the accumulation of capital, and advancing technological knowledge. Would all three social groups benefit from the progress of society? In contrast, would capitalists and/or landowners receive an ever-larger share of the national income while the workers received an ever-shrinking share?

Modern economists are more concerned with another way of looking at the distribution of incomes, called the **size distribution of income**. This is the distribution of income between different households without reference to the source of their incomes or each individual's social class.

The *functional* distribution of income refers to the share of total national income going to owners of different resources and so

focuses on the source of income, and in particular distinguishes income from employment and income from property. The *size* distribution of income refers to the proportion of total income received by various groups and so focuses on inequality of income between various income earners, irrespective of the source from which that income is derived.

Today economists devote most of their attention to the size distribution of income rather than the functional distribution. If someone is poor, it matters little whether that person is a landowner or a worker. Moreover, some capitalists, such as the owners of small retail stores, are in the lower part of the income scale, and some wage-earners, such as professional footballers, are at the upper end. Furthermore, the vast majority of company shares are owned by wage-earners through pension funds and life insurance policies. This fact alone makes irrelevant to the modern world the old class division between workers who supply labour, the capitalists who own the means of production, and the rentier class (or landed gentry) who owned the land. In most cases, workers are owners and owners are workers. Class distinctions may still exist, but they do not divide those who are and are not the owners of firms or property.

---

* The founders of classical economics, Adam Smith and David Ricardo, were concerned with the distribution of income among what were then the three great social classes of workers, capitalists, and landowners. To match these classes, they defined three *factors of production*: labour, capital, and land. The return to each factor determined the share of total national income going to each social class. This is why the theory of factor pricing is also called the theory of distribution.

Before proceeding, a word of warning is needed. Beware of confusing the terms 'unequal' and 'inequality' with 'unjust' and 'inequitable'. A completely equal distribution of the nation's income among all individuals—between those who worked hard and those who loafed about on the job; those who did dangerous work and those in safe jobs; those on whose skills we relied and those who relied on others' skills—would not satisfy everyone's idea of a *just* distribution of income. The theory we develop here is designed to explain how incomes are determined, not to evaluate whether the outcome is equitable or inequitable, just or unjust.

Income inequalities

Figure 15.1 shows what is called a **Lorenz curve**. It shows how much of total income is received by various proportions of the nation's income earners. We speak of how total income is *distributed* among individuals or groups. (The further the curve bends away from the diagonal, the more unequal are the incomes of the various individuals in society.) The curve shows, for example, that in 1999/2000 the bottom 20 per cent of all UK individuals received only 2.6 per cent of all taxable income earned, while the bottom 80 per cent received only 51 per cent

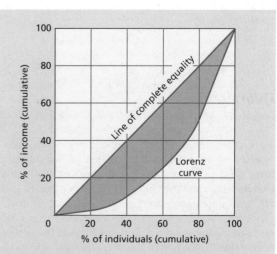

Figure 15.1 A Lorenz curve of individual pre-tax income in the UK, 1999–2000

The size of the shaded area between the Lorenz curve and the diagonal is a measure of the inequality of income distribution. If there were complete income equality, the Lorenz curve would coincide with the diagonal line. The extent of income inequality (e.g. that the lower 40 per cent receive only 10 per cent of the income) determines how far the Lorenz curve lies below the diagonal.

Source: ONS, *Annual Abstract of Statistics*, 2002.

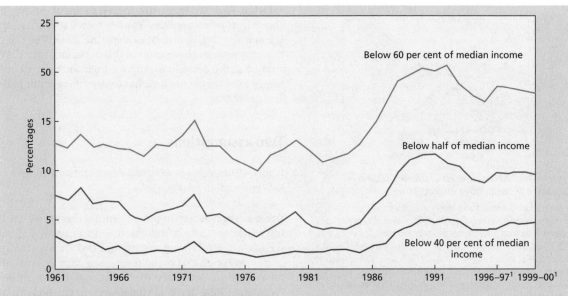

Figure 15.2 Income inequalities in the UK, 1961–2000

The figure shows the percentage of people whose income is below various fractions of median income. The proportions of people below 60 per cent of median income (and below half and 40 per cent) were falling slightly in the 1960s and 1970s, but from the early 1980s these proportions rose sharply. In the 1990s these proportions levelled off or even fell slightly.

[1] Data from 1993–94 onwards are for financial years; data for 1994–95 onwards exclude Northern Ireland.
Source: ONS, *Social Trends*, 2002.

of total taxable income; the remaining 49 per cent went to the top 20 per cent of income-earners. The income measured is taxable income, measured before taxes and benefits.[1] After the impact of taxes and benefits is included, the share of the bottom 20 per cent rises to 9 per cent and the share of the top 20 per cent falls to 39 per cent.

Figure 15.2 shows how UK income inequalities have changed over time. Average income has been rising over time, so it does not tell us anything about the level of income. But it does tell us that inequalities have increased over time. For example, while about 13 per cent of the population had incomes that were less than 60 per cent of median income in 1961, the figure was close to 18 per cent in 1999/2000.

The link between output and input decisions

In Chapters 8 and 9 we showed how firms' costs vary with their output and how they can achieve cost minimization by finding the least costly combination of inputs to produce any given output. In Chapter 10 we saw that firms in perfect competition decide how much to produce by equating their marginal cost to the market price. We also saw how the market supply curve interacts with the market

demand curve in each goods market. This interaction determines the market price as well as the quantity that is produced and consumed.

These events in goods markets have implications for input markets. The decisions of firms on how much to produce and how to produce it imply specific demands for various quantities of inputs. These demands, together with the supplies of inputs (which are determined by the owners of resources), come together in markets for inputs. Together they determine the quantities of the various inputs that are employed, their prices, and the incomes earned by their owners.

The above discussion shows that there is a close relationship between the production and pricing of the goods and services produced by firms on the one hand, and the pricing, employment, and incomes earned by the owners of inputs that they hire on the other hand. These are two related aspects of how the market economy determines the production of goods and services and the allocation of the nation's resources among their various possible uses. This discussion provides a brief introduction to one of the great insights of economics:

[1] The data refer only to income with some tax liability and therefore exclude all income that escapes the notice of the tax authorities or is otherwise exempt from income tax.

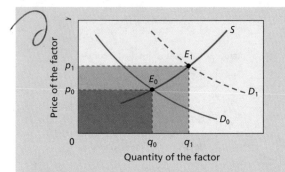

Figure 15.3 Income of owners of primary resources determined in competitive markets

The interaction of demand and supply in competitive input markets determines resource owners' equilibrium price and quantity, and hence their income. The original demand and supply curves are D_0 and S. Equilibrium is at E_0, with price p_0 and quantity employed q_0. The resource owners' incomes are shown by the dark blue area in the figure. When the demand curve shifts to D_1, equilibrium shifts to E_1, with price p_1 and quantity q_1. The resource owners' incomes rise by the amount of the medium blue area.

When demand and supply interact to determine the allocation of resources between various lines of production, they also determine the incomes of the owners of inputs that are used in making the outputs.

The way this works can be summarized as follows.

1. The income of owners of different types of input depends on the price that is paid for these inputs and the amount that is used.

2. Demands and supplies in input markets determine input prices and quantities in exactly the same way that the prices and quantities of goods and services are determined in product markets.

3. All that is needed to explain input pricing is the identification of the main determinants of the demand for, and supply of, various inputs (and adjustment for any distortion in free markets caused by governments, unions, or monopoly firms).

Figure 15.3 illustrates the theory of input pricing by showing how competitive market forces determine the income accruing to owners of a specific input. The rest of this chapter is an elaboration of this important theme. We study first the demand for inputs, then their supply, and finally how they come together to determine input prices and quantities.

Two assumptions

Before we begin, we need to make explicit two assumptions that will underlie our analysis.

Other prices constant In order to ensure that we are speaking of relative and not just absolute prices and quantities, we make the following assumption. When the changes studied in Figure 15.3 occur, *the prices of all other inputs, the prices of all goods, and the level of national income are held constant.*[2] Under these circumstances fluctuations in an input's equilibrium price and quantity cause fluctuations (*a*) in the money earnings of the owners of that input, (*b*) in their earnings relative to owners of other inputs, and (*c*) in the share of national income going to those owners.

Competitive markets In this chapter we confine ourselves to perfectly competitive markets. This means that individual firms are price-takers in both output and input markets. On the one hand they face a given price for the product they produce, and that price is both their average and marginal revenue. On the other hand they face a given price of each input that they buy, and that price is both the average and marginal cost of the input. These input and output prices may change, but they cannot be influenced by the actions of any single firm (or any single seller of inputs).

Dealing first with firms that are price-takers in product and input markets allows us to study the principles of input price determination in the simplest context. Once these are understood, it is relatively easy to allow for monopolistic elements in either or both types of market. This is done in Chapter 16.

The demand for inputs

Firms use the services of land, labour, capital, and natural resources[3] as inputs. They also use products, such as steel, plastics, and electricity, that are produced by other firms. These products are in turn made by using land, labour, capital, natural resources, and other produced inputs. If we continue following through the chain of outputs of some firms that are used as inputs by other firms, we can account for all of the economy's output in terms of inputs of the

[2] We make these assumptions because we are interested in resource owners' relative share of total national income. These assumptions are only a simplifying device for our analysis; they do not prevent it from being applied to inflationary situations.

[3] Although natural resources are often included with land as a single type of resource, they have so many important special characteristics that it is sometimes worthwhile treating them as a separate type of primary input. Some of the issues involved with pricing natural resources are discussed in Chapter 17.

Box 15.2 **Economics of produced inputs**

It may seem strange that throughout this and the next few chapters we concentrate on analysing demand and supply of primary resource inputs: land, labour, capital, and natural resources. Most firms buy many of their inputs from other firms. A car manufacturer, for example, will buy in many of the components that go into its cars as well as hiring assembly workers, designers, marketing experts, accountants, etc., and using its own capital and land for its factory. So why not analyse the markets for these other produced inputs?

The answer is that we do, but only indirectly. The principles that are set out in this chapter apply just as easily to manufactured inputs as they do to land, labour, capital, and raw materials. Demand for produced inputs is a derived demand depending on demand for the final product. Profit-maximizing firms (as we shall see below) will buy these inputs up to the point where the extra cost of the last unit is just equal to the value of the extra output that input generates. The demand curve for produced inputs will be negatively sloped as it is for all inputs (as we can rule out the Giffen-good case that arises with consumer demand), so markets for produced inputs can be analysed with demand and supply tools just like any other market.

By focusing on demand for primary resource inputs, we are aggregating across the entire supply chain of produced goods and services, and focusing on the inputs for industry as a whole rather than on each link in that supply chain. We do this because we are interested in resource allocation for the economy as a whole. But analysis of each intermediate market between firms and their suppliers of produced inputs is straightforward.

Individual firms do have some issues to resolve relating to their produced inputs. First, should they buy in the input or make it for themselves? So long as quality and reliability of supply are guaranteed, the answer will be: buy from another firm if they can make the product more cheaply than we can make it ourselves. Second, if the product is bought in, should the firm simply set up a long-term supply contract with the input producer, or should it try to buy on the market from the cheapest supplier in each period? The answer here will depend on whether this is a standardized product that is widely available at short notice, or a highly specific input that needs special skills or equipment to produce. In the latter case, a longer-term supply contract is more likely.

basic resources—land, labour, capital, and natural resources. The theory of input pricing applies to *all* inputs used by a firm, as explained in Box 15.2.

Firms require inputs not for their own sake but as a means to produce goods and services. For example, the demand for computer programmers and technicians is growing as more and more computers are used. The demand for carpenters and building materials rises and falls as the amount of housing construction rises and falls. Thus, demand for any input is derived from the demand for the goods and services that it helps to produce; for this reason, the demand for all inputs is called a **derived demand**.

Derived demand provides a link between the markets for output and the markets for inputs.

An important point to note is that the quantity demanded of any input *always* varies negatively with its price. As its price falls more is demanded, and as its price rises less is demanded. In other words,

The demand curve for any input is negatively sloped, with price and quantity demanded always varying in the opposite direction.

This is an important result, which we explain below. It means that we can rule out Giffen goods so far as demand for inputs is concerned. The reasons for the negative slope to input demand curves differ in the long and the short run.

Input demand in the long run

In the long run all inputs are variable. In this case, both the substitution and the income effects contribute to the negative slope of the demand curve. We consider the case of a price reduction and leave a price rise as a simple variation, which is easy to work through for yourself.

The substitution effect

A fall in an input's price makes it less expensive relative to other inputs, and more of it will be used relative to those whose price has not fallen. This is true at all levels of aggregation. It is true if the price of all labour falls relative to capital, or if the price of one type of labour falls relative to other types of labour. We showed in Chapters 8 and 9 that a fall in the price of all types of labour will lead profit-maximizing firms to substitute labour for capital. According to the principle of substitution (see page 143), they will use more of the now cheaper input and less of the relatively more expensive ones. A fall in the wage of one type of labour will lead to more of that type being used as a replacement for other types of labour whose wage has not fallen. For example, some time ago the wages of building labour rose dramatically. This led builders to substitute prefabricated parts made in factories for parts made to order on the building site. Window frames, door jambs, walls, and a host of other parts of buildings that used to be custom-made on the site were prefabricated to standard designs in factories where wages were much lower than those on construction sites. In effect, factory labour whose price had not risen was substituted for building labour whose price had risen.

The income effect

A fall in the price of one input reduces the cost of making all products that use that input. The cost curves of these products thus shift downwards, shifting the sum of the marginal cost curves—which is the industry supply curve. As a result more will be produced and sold. To make more output, an increase in all the inputs is required. This leads to a rise in the amount demanded of the input whose price has fallen, as well as a rise in the demand for all other inputs that co-operate with it in production.

Input demand in the short run

In the short run some inputs are fixed and only some can be varied. If we think of an extreme situation in which only one input can be varied, we can derive a famous proposition that is true for each and every input as long as the firms that hire them are maximizing their profits.

The maximizing firm

In Chapter 10 we set out the rules for the maximization of a firm's profits in the short run. When one input is fixed and another is variable, the profit-maximizing firm increases its output until the last unit produced adds just as much to cost as to revenue, that is until marginal cost equals marginal revenue. An equivalent way of stating that the firm maximizes profits is to say that *the firm will increase production up to the point at which the last unit of the variable input employed adds just as much to revenue as it does to cost.*

The addition to total cost resulting from employing one more unit of an input is its price. (The firm is buying its inputs in a competitive market, so the extra purchase does not affect the market price.) So if one more worker is hired at a wage of £15 per hour, the addition to the firm's costs is £15 (and other workers' wages remain unchanged).

The amount that a unit of a variable input adds to revenue is the amount that the unit adds to total output multiplied by the change in revenue resulting from selling an extra unit of output.

In Chapter 8 we called the variable input's addition to total output its *marginal product*. When dealing with demand for inputs, we use the term **marginal *physical* product** (MPP) to avoid confusion with the revenue concepts that we also need to use.

The change in revenue resulting from selling one extra unit of output is just the price of the output, p (since the firm is a price-taker in the market for its output). The resulting amount, which is $MPP \times p$, is called the input's **marginal revenue product** and given the symbol MRP.

For example, if the variable input's marginal physical product is two widgets per hour and the price of a widget is £7.50, then the input's marginal revenue product is £15 (£7.50 × 2).

We can now state the firm's profit maximization condition in two ways. First,

| Addition to total costs caused by hiring another unit of the variable input | = | the input's marginal revenue product (MRP). | (1) |

First note that, if the firm is a price-taker in input markets, the left-hand side is just the price of a unit of the variable input, which we now call w (as the variable input is often labour and its price is the wage rate). Also note that, as long as the firm is a price-taker in the market for its output, the right-hand side is the input's marginal physical product, MPP, multiplied by the price at which the output is sold, which we call p. We can now restate (1) as follows:

| Price of a unit of the variable input | = | the input's marginal physical product multiplied by the product's market price | (2) |

and in symbols,

$$w = MPP \times p. \qquad (2')$$

Here is an example to clarify the meaning of equation (2). Suppose that the extra labour is available to the firm at a cost of £10 an hour (w = £10). Suppose also that employing another hour's work adds three units to output (MPP = 3). Suppose further that output units sell for £5 each (p = £5). Thus, the additional hour of input adds £15 to the firm's revenue and £10 to its costs. Hiring one worker for an extra hour brings in £5 more than it costs. *The firm will take on more of the variable input whenever its marginal revenue product exceeds its price as this adds more to revenue than to cost.*

Now suppose that the last hour of work by the variable input has a marginal physical product of one unit of output—it adds only one extra unit to output—and so adds only £5 to revenue. Clearly, the firm can increase profits by reducing its use of the input, since hiring for one hour less reduces revenues by £5 while reducing costs by £10. *The firm will hire less of the variable input whenever its marginal revenue product is less than its price.*

Finally, suppose that the last hour of a worker hired has an MPP of two units, so that it increases revenue by £10. Now the firm cannot increase its profits by altering its employment of the variable input in either direction. *The firm cannot increase its profits by altering employment of the variable input whenever the input's marginal revenue product equals its price.*

We are doing nothing new here. We are merely looking at the firm's profit-maximizing behaviour from the point of view of its inputs rather than its output. In Chapter 10 we analysed the firm varying its output until the marginal cost of producing the last unit of output was equal to the marginal revenue derived from selling that unit. The same profit-maximizing behaviour involves the firm varying its inputs until the marginal cost of the last input hired is just equal to the revenue derived from selling the marginal product of that extra input. These are exactly the same, because the variable input is the only component of marginal cost (and its MRP is the same as the MR for the firm).

The firm's demand curve for the input

It is now easy to see why in the short run, with only one variable input, the firm's demand curve for that input is negatively sloped. Suppose the firm starts in equilibrium. The relationship shown in (2) above must hold, which means that that input's marginal revenue product is equated to its price. Now the price of the input falls. The unchanged marginal revenue product is now higher than the lowered price. So it pays the firm to hire more of the input. As it hires more inputs the marginal physical product falls, and since the firm is a price-taker so does the marginal revenue product. The firm goes on hiring more of the variable input until the marginal revenue product falls to the level of the new lower price.

What this tells us is that

In the short run, with only one variable input, the firm's demand for its variable input is negatively sloped as a result of the operation of the law of diminishing returns.

This is all we need to know about the short-run demand for an input. The appendix to this chapter, however, gives a more elaborate graphical derivation of the short-run demand curve for those who would like to study it.

The industry's demand curve for an input

So far we have seen how a single firm that takes its market price as given will vary its quantity demanded for an input as that input's price changes. But when an input's price changes and *all firms* in a competitive industry vary the amount of the input that they demand in order to vary their output, the price of the industry's product changes. That change will have repercussions on desired output and on the quantity of the input demanded. For example, a fall in carpenters' wages will reduce the cost of producing houses, thus shifting the supply curve of houses to the right. Price-taking construction firms will plan to increase construction, and hence increase the quantity of carpenters demanded, by some specific amount if the price of houses does not change. Because the demand curve for houses is negatively sloped, however, the increase in output leads to a fall in the market price of houses. As a result, each individual firm will increase its desired output *by less* than it had planned to do before the market price changed.

An increase in carpenters' wages has the opposite effect. The cost of producing houses rises, the supply curve shifts to the left, and the price of houses rises. As a result, the individual firm will cut its planned output and employment of inputs by less than it would have done if market price had not changed.

The industry's demand curve for an input is steeper when the reaction of market price is allowed for than it would be if firms faced an unchanged product price.

It may be useful to summarize the argument so far.

1. In the short run, the derived demand curve for an input on the part of a *price-taking* firm will have a negative slope because of the law of diminishing returns. As more of the input is employed in response to a fall in its price, its marginal product falls. No further units will be added once its marginal revenue product falls to the input's new price.

2. An industry's short-run demand curve for an input is less elastic than suggested by point 1. As the industry expands output in response to a fall in an input's price, the price of the firm's output will fall, causing the final increase in each firm's output, and hence its demand for employment of inputs, to be less than it would be if the output price remained unchanged.

Elasticity of demand for inputs

The elasticity of demand for an input measures the *degree* of the response of the quantity demanded to a change in its price. The influences that were discussed in the preceding sections explain the *direction* of the response; that is, the quantity demanded is negatively related to price. You should not be surprised, therefore, to hear that the amount of the response depends on the strength with which these influences operate. This section describes the four principles of derived demand that were first set out by the British economist Alfred Marshall (1842–1924).

Diminishing returns

The first influence on the slope of the demand curve is the diminishing marginal productivity of an input. If marginal productivity declines rapidly as more of a variable input is employed, a fall in the input's price will not induce many more units to be employed. Conversely, if marginal productivity falls only slowly as more of a variable input is employed, there will be a large increase in quantity demanded as price falls.

The faster the marginal productivity of an input declines as its use rises, the lower is the elasticity of each firm's demand curve for the input.

For example, both labour and fertilizers are used by market gardeners who produce vegetables for sale in nearby cities. For many crops additional doses of fertilizers add significant amounts to yields over quite a wide range of fertilizer use. Although the marginal product of fertilizer does decline, it does so rather slowly as more and more fertilizer is used. In contrast, although certain amounts of labour are needed for planting, weeding, and harvesting, there is only a small range over which additional labour can be used

Box 15.3 Electricity generation: substitution in practice

The principle of substitution has been important in the choice of fuels used to generate electricity, but it has not always worked in the same direction.

During the 1950s and 1960s increasing economies of scale in shipping crude oil from the Middle East to Western Europe made oil-based fuels more and more competitive. The relative price of fuels for industrial use fell by even more than the production cost of petrol, as it was the demand for petrol that was mainly responsible for the derived demand for crude oil. Other outputs of the oil-refining process were byproducts. The Central Electricity Generating Board (CEGB), as it was then called (it has since been privatized as National Power and Powergen), responded to the falling relative price of 'bunker' oil by building more and more oil-fired power stations and gradually closing down (or converting) the older coal-fired stations. From 85–7 per cent of electricity generated from coal and 11–14 per cent from oil in 1962–5, the CEGB steadily changed the 'mix', so that by 1971–4 it was generating 63–6 per cent from coal and 24–6 per cent from oil.

Then came the 'oil shocks' of 1973–4 and 1979–80, when the OPEC countries dramatically raised the price of crude oil, leading to correspondingly dramatic increases in the prices of all oil products. Even though people

in coal mining saw an opportunity to raise coal prices substantially, the *relative* price of oil was significantly higher in the 1980s than it had been in the 1960s and early 1970s. The CEGB accordingly reverted to an increasing reliance on coal-firing, generating 77–81 per cent of its electricity from coal and only 5–7 per cent from oil in 1982–4.

Nevertheless, the CEGB clearly retained the ability to switch back to oil rapidly if required. In 1984–5 a coal miners' strike which lasted almost the whole year led to an amazing 41 per cent of electricity being generated from oil (with total output slightly higher than the previous year) and only 42 per cent from coal. After the strike, the figures quickly returned to their 1982–4 levels. However, the proportion of coal used declined in the late 1980s and 1990s owing to the growing use of natural gas and nuclear power (and environmental problems caused by high sulphur content of UK coal). By 2000 the percentages of fuels used in electricity generation were coal 33, nuclear 23, gas 38, oil 1, and hydroelectric plus wind 1.*

---

* The 4 per cent unaccounted for was imported by cable connections from France and the Republic of Ireland.

---

productively. The marginal product of labour, although high for the first units, declines rapidly as more and more labour is used. Under these circumstances, market gardeners will have an elastic demand for fertilizer and an inelastic demand for labour.

Substitution

In the long run all inputs are variable. If one input's price rises, firms will try to substitute relatively cheaper inputs instead. For this reason, the slope of the demand curve for an input is influenced by the ease with which other inputs can be substituted for the input whose price has changed.

The greater the ease of substitution, the greater is the elasticity of demand for the input.

The ease of substitution depends on the substitutes that are available and on the production technology. It is often possible to vary input proportions in surprising ways. For example, in car manufacturing and in building construction glass and steel can be substituted for each other simply by varying the dimensions of the windows. As another example, construction materials can be substituted for maintenance labour in the case of most durable consumer goods. This is done by making the product more or less durable and more or less subject to breakdowns, and by using more or less expensive materials in its construction.

Such substitutions are not the end of the story. Plant and equipment are being replaced continually, which allows more or less capital-intensive methods to be built into new plants in response to changes in input prices. Similarly,

engines that use less petrol per mile tend to be developed when the price of petrol rises significantly.

Box 15.3 provides an example of substitution in the electricity industry.

Importance of the input

Other things being equal, the larger the fraction of the total costs of producing some product that are made up of payments to a particular input, the greater is the elasticity of demand for that input.

To see this, suppose that wages account for 50 per cent of the costs of producing a good and raw materials for 15 per cent. A 10 per cent rise in the price of labour raises the cost of production by 5 per cent (10 per cent of 50 per cent), but a 10 per cent rise in the price of raw materials raises the cost of the product by only 1.5 per cent (10 per cent of 15 per cent). The larger the increase in the cost of production, the larger is the shift in the product's supply curve, and hence the larger the decreases in quantities demanded of both the product and the inputs used to produce it.

Elasticity of demand for the output

The fourth, and last, principle of derived demand is this:

Other things being equal, the more elastic the demand for the product that the input helps to make, the more elastic is the demand for the input.

If an increase in the price of the product causes a large decrease in the quantity demanded—that is, if the demand

Box 15.4 **The principles of derived demand**

This box demonstrates two of the four principles of derived demand using demand and supply curves.

1. The larger the proportion of total costs accounted for by an input, the more elastic is the demand for it.

Consider part (i) of the figure. The demand curve for the *industry's product* is *D* and, given the input's original price, the *industry supply curve* is S_0. Equilibrium is at E_0 with output at q_0.

Suppose that the input's price then falls. If the input accounts for a small part of the industry's total cost, each firm's marginal cost curve shifts downward by only a small amount. So also does the industry supply curve, as illustrated by the supply curve S_1. Output expands only a small amount to q_1, which implies only a small increase in the quantity of the variable input demanded.

If the input accounts for a large part of the industry's total costs, each firm's marginal cost curve shifts downward a great deal. So also does the industry supply curve, as illustrated by the curve S_2. Output expands greatly to q_2, which implies a large increase in the quantity of variable input demanded.

2. The more elastic the demand curve for the product, the more elastic is the demand for the input.

Consider part (ii) of the figure. The original demand and supply curves for the industry's product intersect at E_0 to produce an industry output of q_0. A fall in the price of an input causes the industry's supply curve to shift downward to S_1.

When the demand curve is relatively inelastic, as shown by the curve D_i, the industry's output increases by only a small amount to q_1. The quantity of the variable input demanded will increase by a correspondingly small amount.

When the demand curve is relatively elastic, as shown by the curve D_e, the industry's output increases by a large amount to q_2. The quantity of the variable input demanded will then increase by a correspondingly large amount.

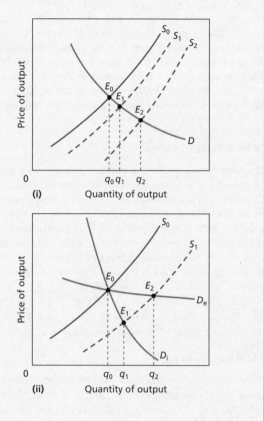

for the product is elastic—there will be a large decrease in the quantity of an input needed to produce it in response to a rise in the input's price. However, if an increase in the price of a product causes only a small decrease in the quantity demanded—that is, if the demand for the product is inelastic—there will be only a small decrease in the quantity of the input required in response to a rise in its price.

In Box 15.4 the forces affecting the elasticity of the derived demand curves that have just been discussed are related more specifically to the market for the industry's output.

The supply of inputs

When we consider the supply of any input, we must consider the amount supplied to the economy as a whole, to each industry and occupation, and to each firm. The elasticity of supply of an input will normally be different at each of these levels of aggregation. We start with the highest level of aggregation, the total supply of each resource input to the economy as a whole.

The total supply of resources

At any one time, the total quantity of inputs of each resource is given. For example, in each country the labour force is of a certain size, there is so much arable land available, there is so much machinery installed in factories, and there is a given supply of discovered petroleum. However, these supplies can and do change in response to both economic and non-economic forces. Sometimes the change is very gradual, as when climatic changes slowly turn arable land into desert, or when a medical discovery lowers the rate of infant mortality and hence increases the rate of population growth. Sometimes the changes can be quite rapid, as when the UK discovered oil in the North Sea, or when a boom in business activity brings retired people back into the labour force, or when a rise in the price of agricultural produce encourages the draining of marshes to add to the supply of arable land.

Total supply of capital

The supply of capital in a country consists of the stock of existing machines, factories, equipment, and so on. Capital is a manufactured input, and its total quantity is in no sense fixed, although it changes only slowly. Each year the stock of capital goods is diminished by the amount that becomes physically or economically obsolete and is increased by the amount that is newly produced. The difference between these is the net addition to, or net subtraction from, the capital stock. On balance, the trend has been for the capital stock to grow from decade to decade over the past few centuries. In Chapter 17 we will discuss the determinants of investment in capital.

Total supply of land

The total area of dry land in a country is almost completely fixed, but the supply of *fertile* land is not fixed. Considerable care and effort are required to sustain the productive power of land. If farmers earn low incomes they may not provide the necessary care, and the land's fertility may be destroyed within a short time. In contrast, high earnings from farming may provide the incentive to increase the supply of arable land by irrigation and other forms of reclamation.

Total supply of labour

The number of people willing to work is called the *labour force*; the total number of hours they are willing to work is called the **supply of effort** or, more simply, the **supply of labour**. The supply of effort depends on three influences: the size of the population, the proportion of the population willing to work, and the number of hours worked by each individual. Each of these is partly influenced by economic forces.

Population Populations vary in size, and these variations are influenced to some extent by economic forces. There is some evidence, for example, that the birth rate and the net immigration rate (immigration minus emigration) are higher in good times than in bad. Much of the variation in population is, however, explained by factors outside economics.

The labour force The proportion of the total population, or of some subgroup such as men, women, or teenagers, that is willing to work is called that group's **labour force participation rate**. This rate varies in response to many influences. One non-economic influence is change in attitudes and tastes. The enormous rise in female participation rates in the second half of the twentieth century is a case in point. One economic influence is change in the demand for labour. A rise in demand is usually accompanied by a rise in earnings. This then leads to an increase in the proportion of the population willing to work. More married women and elderly people enter the labour force when the demand for labour is high. For the same reasons, the labour force tends to decline when earnings and employment opportunities decline.

Hours worked Not only does the wage rate influence the number of people in the labour force (as we observed above), but it is also a major determinant of hours worked. By giving up leisure in order to work, workers obtain the incomes they need to buy goods. They can, therefore, be thought of as trading leisure for goods.

A rise in the wage rate implies a change in the relative prices of goods and leisure. Goods become cheaper relative to leisure, since each hour worked buys more goods than before. The other side of the same coin is that leisure becomes more expensive, since each hour of leisure consumed is at the cost of more goods forgone.

This change in relative prices has both the income and the substitution effects that we studied on pages [107–9]. The substitution effect leads the individual to consume more of the relatively cheaper goods and *less* of the relatively more expensive leisure—that is, to trade more leisure for goods. The income effect, however, leads the individual to consume more goods and *more* leisure, since the rise in the wage rate makes it possible for the individual to have more of both. For example, if the wage rate rises by 10 per cent and the individual works 5 per cent fewer hours, more leisure and more goods will be consumed.

Because the income and the substitution effects work in the same direction for the consumption of goods, we can be sure that a rise in the wage rate will lead to a rise in income earned and goods consumed. However, because the two effects work in opposite directions for leisure,

a rise in the wage rate leads to less leisure being consumed (more hours worked) when the substitution effect is the dominant force and to more leisure being consumed (fewer hours worked) when the income effect is the dominant force.

Box 15.5 provides an optional analysis of these two cases using indifference curves. Much of the long-run evidence tends to show that, as real hourly wage rates rise for the economy as a whole, people wish to reduce the number of hours they work.

Box 15.5 **The supply of labour**

The discussion in the text can be formalized using indifference curves. The key proposition is the following.

Because a change in the wage rate has an income effect and a substitution effect that pull in opposite directions, the supply curve of labour may have a positive or a negative slope.

Part (i) of the figure plots leisure (in hours) on the horizontal axis and the consumption of goods (measured in pounds) on the vertical axis. The budget line always starts at 24, indicating that everyone is endowed with 24 hours a day which may be either consumed as leisure or traded for goods by working.

At the original wage rate the individual could obtain q_a of goods by working 24 hours (i.e. the hourly wage rate is $q_a/24$). Equilibrium is at E_0, where the individual consumes l_0 of leisure and works $24 - l_0$ in return for q_0 of goods.

The wage rate now rises, so that q_b becomes available if 24 hours are worked (i.e., the hourly wage rate is $q_b/24$). Equilibrium shifts to E_1.

Consumption of leisure falls to l_1, and the individual works $24 - l_1$ hours in return for a consumption of q_1 goods. The rise in wages increases hours worked.

The hourly wage rate now rises further to $q_c/24$, and equilibrium shifts to E_2. Consumption of leisure rises to l_2, whereas $24 - l_2$ hours are worked in return for an increased consumption of q_2 goods. This time, therefore, the rise in the wage rate lowers hours worked.

Part (ii) of the figure shows the same behaviour as in part (i), using a supply curve. It plots the number of hours worked against the wage rate. At wage rates of up to w_1 the individual is not in the labour force, since no work is offered. As the wage rate rises from w_1 to w_2, more and more hours are worked, so the supply curve of effort has the normal, positive slope. The wage rates that result in E_0 and E_1 in part (i) of the figure lie in this range. Above w_2 the quantity of effort falls as wages rise, so that the supply curve has a negative slope. This latter case is often referred to as a *backward-bending supply curve of labour*. The wage that gives rise to equilibrium E_2 in part (i) lies in this range.

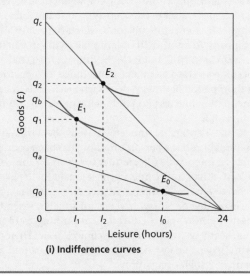

(i) **Indifference curves**

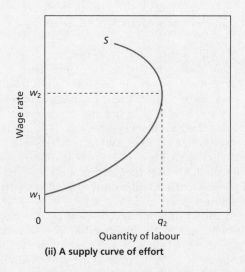

(ii) **A supply curve of effort**

The supply of inputs for a particular use

Most primary resources have many uses. A piece of land can be used to grow any one of several crops, or it can be subdivided for a housing development. A computer programmer in Oxford can work for one of several firms, for the government, or for the university. A lathe can be used to make many different products, and it requires no adaptation when it is turned for one use or another. Plainly, it is easier for any one user to acquire more of a scarce resource than it is for all users to do so simultaneously.

One user of an input can bid resources away from another user, even though the total supply of that input may be fixed.

When we are considering the supply of an input for a particular use, the most important concept is *resource mobility*. An input that shifts easily between uses in response to small changes in incentives is said to be *mobile*; its supply to any one of its uses will be elastic, because a small increase in the price offered will attract many units of the input from other uses. Inputs that do not shift easily from one use to another, even in response to large changes in remuneration, are said to be *immobile*; it will be in inelastic supply in any one of its uses, because even a large increase in the price offered will attract only a small inflow from other uses. Often a specific input may be immobile in the short run but mobile in the long run.

An important key to input mobility is time. The longer the time interval, the easier it is to convert an input from one use to another.

Consider the mobility between uses of each of the three key types of input.

Capital Some kinds of capital equipment—lathes, lorries, and computers for example—can be shifted easily between uses; many others are difficult to shift. A great deal of machinery is quite specific: once built, it must be used for the purpose for which it was designed, or it cannot be used at all. (It is the immobility of much fixed capital equipment that makes the exit of firms from declining industries the slow and difficult process.)

In the long run, however, capital is highly mobile. When capital goods wear out, a firm may simply replace them with identical goods, or it may exercise other options. It may buy a newly designed machine to produce the same goods, or it may buy machines to produce totally different goods. Such decisions lead to changes in the long-run allocation of a country's stock of capital between various uses.

Land Land, which is physically the least mobile of inputs, is one of the most mobile in an economic sense. On agricultural land one crop can be harvested and a totally different crop can be planted. A farm on the outskirts of a growing city can be sold for a housing development at short notice—as long as planning permission is forthcoming. Once land is built on, its mobility is much reduced. A site on which a hotel has been built can be converted into a warehouse site, but it takes a large differential in the value of land use to make that transfer worthwhile, because the hotel must be torn down.

Although land is highly mobile between alternative uses, it is completely immobile as far as location is concerned. There is only so much land within a given distance of the centre of any city, and no increase in the price paid can induce further land to be located within that distance. This locational immobility has important consequences, including high prices for desirable locations and the tendency to build tall buildings to economize on the use of scarce land, as in the centre of large cities.

Labour Labour is a unique input, as supply of the services of labour usually requires the physical presence of the person who owns it. Most people in employment have to attend their place of work each day. In other cases, however, labour services, such as consulting, designing a product, or writing advertising copy, can be supplied at a distance and their product communicated to the purchaser by such means as phone, fax, email, or post.

Absentee landlords, while continuing to live in the place of their choice, can obtain income from land or buildings located in another part of the world. While physical capital needs to be present at the production site, its owner need not be. However, when a worker who is employed by a firm that produces men's ties in York decides to supply labour service to a firm that produces women's shoes in Northampton, the worker must physically travel to Northampton. This has an important consequence.

Because of the need for labour's physical presence when its services are provided for the production of many commodities, non-monetary considerations are much more important for the supply of labour than for other inputs.

People may be satisfied with, or frustrated by, the kind of work that they do, where they do it, the people with whom they do it, and the social status of their occupation. Since these considerations influence their decisions about what they will do with their labour services, they will not always move just because they could earn a higher wage. Nevertheless, labour does move between industries, occupations, and areas in response to changes in the signals provided by wages and opportunities for employment. The ease with which movement occurs depends on many forces. For example, it is not difficult for a secretary to shift from one company to another in order to take a job in Cheltenham instead of in Hull, but it can be difficult for a coal miner to become an editor, a model, a machinist, or a doctor within a short period of time. Workers who lack skills, training, or inclination find certain kinds of job moves to be difficult or impossible.

Some barriers to movement may be virtually insurmountable once a person's training has been completed. It may be impossible for a farmer to become a surgeon or for a lorry-driver to become a professional athlete, even if the relative wage rates change greatly. However, the *children* of farmers, doctors, lorry-drivers, and athletes, when they are deciding how much education or training to obtain, are not nearly as limited in their choices as are their parents, who have already completed their education and are settled in their occupations.

In any year some people enter the labour force directly from school or further education, and others leave it through retirement or death. The turnover in the labour force owing to these causes is 3 or 4 per cent per year. Over a period of ten years the allocation of labour can change dramatically merely by directing new entrants to jobs other than the ones that were left vacant by workers who left the labour force.

The role of education in helping new entrants adapt to available jobs is important. In a society in which education is provided to all, it is possible to achieve large increases in the supply of any needed labour skill within a decade or so. These issues are discussed at greater length in the first part of Chapter 16.

The labour force as a whole is mobile, even though many individual members of it are not.

The supply of inputs to individual firms

Most firms usually employ a small proportion of the total supply of each input that they use. As a result they can usually obtain their inputs at the going market price. For example, a firm of accountants can usually augment its clerical staff by placing an advert in the local paper and paying the going rate for accounts clerks. In hiring just one more person, the firm will not affect the rate of pay earned by accounts clerks in its area. Similarly, most individual firms are price-takers in markets for their inputs.

The operation of input markets

The determination of the price, quantity, and income of an input in a single market poses no new problem. Figure 15.3 on page 250 has already shown a competitive market for an input in which the intersection of the demand and supply curves determines the input's price and the quantity of it that is employed. As we saw at that time, the input's price times its quantity employed is its total income, and that amount, divided by the total income earned by all resource owners in the economy, represents that specific resource owner's share of the nation's total income. (We will study total national income and total national output in some detail in later chapters.)

Reward differentials

If every worker were the same, if all benefits were monetary, and if workers moved freely between markets, then wage rates would tend to be the same in all jobs. Workers would move from low-priced jobs to high-priced ones. The quantity of labour supplied would diminish in occupations in which wages were low, and the resulting labour shortage would tend to force those wages up; the quantity of labour supplied would increase in occupations in which wages were high, and the resulting surplus would force wages down. The movement would continue until there were no further incentives to change occupations, that is until wages were equalized in all uses.

As it is with labour, so it is with other types of input. If all units of capital or land were identical and moved freely between markets, all units would have the same market price in equilibrium.

In reality, of course, different units of any specific input type receive very different rewards. These differentials may be divided into two distinct types: those that exist only in disequilibrium situations, and those that persist in equilibrium.

Disequilibrium differentials lead to, and are eroded by, movements of inputs between alternative uses; equilibrium differentials are not eliminated by mobility.

Disequilibrium differentials

Some price or wage differentials reflect a temporary state of disequilibrium. They are brought about by circumstances such as the growth of one industry and the decline of another. The differentials themselves lead to reallocation of inputs, and such reallocations in turn act to eliminate the differentials.

Over the past century there has been a steady rise in the demand for products of information and communications technology (ICT for short) firms and a decline in the demand for output of some traditional industries such as coal mining. In input markets, the ICT industry's demand has increased while the mining industry's demand has decreased. Relative wages and return on capital have gone up in ICT and down in mining. The differential in rewards caused a net movement of resources from mining (and other traditional industries) to the new ICT industries, and this movement itself caused the differentials to lessen. How long such a process takes depends on how easily factors can be reallocated from one industry to the other, that is on resource mobility. Of course, not many coal miners became computer engineers or internet designers. What did happen, however, was that the UK coal mining industry went from employing over 1 million in the 1930s to under 10,000 in 2002, while ICT in the UK went from employing around zero in the 1930s to around 2 million in 2002.[4]

The behaviour that causes the erosion of disequilibrium differentials is summarized in the assumption of the *maximization of net benefit:*[5] the owners of inputs will allocate them to uses that maximize the net benefit to themselves, taking both monetary and non-monetary rewards into consideration. If net benefits were higher in occupation A than in occupation B, inputs would move from B to A. The increased supply in A, and the lower supply in B, would drive earnings down in A and up in B until net benefits

---

[4] Precise numbers depend on definitions adopted, but that there has been a general decline in jobs in production industries and strong rise of jobs in ICT-related industries is not in doubt.

[5] This is just another form of 'utility' maximization and 'profit' maximization. Here the payoff is a mixture of financial reward and (especially in the case of labour) non-financial reward, such as status and job satisfaction.

were equalized, after which no further movement would occur. This analysis gives rise to the prediction of *equal net benefit*:

In equilibrium, inputs will be allocated among alternative possible uses in such a way that the net benefits in all uses are equalized.

Although non-monetary benefits are important in explaining differences in levels of pay for labour in different occupations, they tend to be quite stable over time. As a result it is monetary rewards, which vary with market conditions, that lead to changes in *net benefits*:

A change in the relative price paid for the same inputs in any two industries will change the net benefits to the owner and create an incentive to shift some inputs into the activity in which relative rewards have increased.

This implies a positively sloped supply curve for an input in any particular use. When the price of an input rises in that use, more will be supplied to that use. This input supply curve (like all supply curves) can also *shift* in response to changes in other variables. For example, an improvement in the safety record in a particular occupation will shift the labour supply curve to that occupation.

Equilibrium differentials

Some price differentials persist in equilibrium without generating any forces that will eliminate them. These **equilibrium differentials** can be explained by intrinsic differences in the type and quality of inputs and, for labour, by differences in the cost of acquiring skills and by different non-monetary advantages of different occupations. These were first called *compensating differentials* by Adam Smith over two hundred years ago.

Intrinsic differences If some inputs of the same general type have different specific characteristics, their market prices will differ. For example, if intelligence and dexterity are required to accomplish a task, intelligent and manually dextrous workers will earn more than less intelligent and less dextrous workers. If land is to be used for agricultural purposes, highly fertile land will command a higher rental value than poor land. These differences will persist even in long-run equilibrium.

Acquired differences It takes time and money to acquire qualifications. If this did not lead to higher expected future earnings, there would be no incentive to invest the time and money. So those employers that wish to hire highly qualified people will have to pay sufficiently higher salaries to compensate for that investment. Obtaining an MBA, for example, can cost well over £50,000 in terms of fees and lost earnings. Few people would study for this qualification unless they thought it would sufficiently enhance their earnings prospects.

Non-monetary benefits Whenever working conditions differ, workers will earn different equilibrium amounts in different occupations. The difference between a test pilot's wage and a chauffeur's wage is only partly a matter of skill; the rest is compensation to the worker for facing the higher risk of testing new planes compared with driving a car. If both were paid the same, there would be an excess supply of chauffeurs and a shortage of test pilots.

Academics commonly earn less than they could earn in the world of commerce and industry because of the substantial non-monetary advantages of academic employment, such as flexible working and long breaks from teaching, which can be devoted partly to research and partly to leisure. If chemists, for example, were paid the same in universities and in industry, many chemists would prefer academic to industrial jobs. Excess demand for industrial chemists and excess supply of academic chemists would then force chemists' wages up in industry until the two types of jobs seemed equally attractive on balance.

The same forces account for equilibrium differences in regional earnings of otherwise identical workers.[6] People who work in remote logging or mining areas are paid more than people who do jobs requiring similar skills in large cities. Without the higher pay, not enough people would be willing to work at sometimes-dangerous jobs in unattractive or remote locations.

Pay equity

The distinction between equilibrium and disequilibrium wage differentials raises an important consideration for policy. Trade unions, governments, and other bodies often have explicit policies about earnings differentials, sometimes seeking to eliminate them in the name of equity. The success of such policies depends to a great extent on the kind of differential that is being attacked. Policies that attempt to eliminate equilibrium differentials will encounter severe difficulties.

Some government legislation seeks to establish *equal pay for work of equal value*, or *pay equity*. These laws can work as intended whenever they remove pay differentials that are due to prejudice. They run into trouble, however, whenever they require equal pay for jobs that have different non-monetary advantages.

To illustrate the problem, say that two jobs demand equal skills, training, and everything else that is taken into account when deciding what is work of equal value but that, in a city with an extreme climate, one is an outside job and the other is an inside job. If some pay commission

---

[6] Many regional wage differences are disequilibrium phenomena where a wage in a declining industry is not yet sufficiently low to compensate for costs of moving.

requires equal pay for both jobs, there will be a shortage of people who are willing to work outside and an excess of people who want to work inside. Employers will seek ways to attract outside workers. Higher pensions, shorter hours, longer holidays, overtime paid for but not worked, and better working conditions may be offered. If these are allowed, they will achieve the desired result but will defeat the original purpose of equalizing the monetary benefits of the inside and outside jobs. They will also cut down on the number of outside workers that employers will hire, since the total cost of an outside worker to an employer will have

risen. If the authorities prevent such 'cheating', the shortage of workers for outside jobs will remain.

In Chapter 16 we discuss the effects of discrimination on wage differentials. Although discrimination is often important, it remains true that many wage differentials are a natural market consequence of supply and demand conditions that have nothing to do with inequitable treatment of different groups in society.

Policies that seek to eliminate wage differentials without considering what caused them or how they affect the supply of specific types of worker are likely to have perverse results.

Economic rent

Economic rent is one of the most important concepts in economics. The owner of an input must earn a certain amount in its present use to prevent her from moving that input to another use. This is called its **reservation price**. (Alfred Marshall called it the input's *transfer earnings*.) If there were no non-monetary advantages in alternative uses, the input's reservation price would equal what it could earn elsewhere (its opportunity cost). This usually holds for capital and land. Labour, however, gets non-monetary advantages that differ between jobs. It must earn enough in one use to equate the two jobs' total benefits—monetary and non-monetary.

Any excess that the owner of an input earns over its reservation price is called its **economic rent**. Economic rent is analogous to economic profit as a surplus over the opportunity cost of capital. The concept of economic rent is crucial in predicting the effects that changes in earnings have on the movement of inputs between alternative uses. However, the terminology of rent is confusing because economic rent is often called simply *rent*, which can of course also mean the full price paid to hire something, such as a house or a piece of land. How the same term came to be used for these two different concepts is explained in Box 15.6.

  ## Box 15.6 Origin of the term 'economic rent'

In the early nineteenth century there was a public debate about the high price of wheat in England. The price was causing great hardship because bread was a major source of food for the working class. Some people argued that wheat had a high price because landlords were charging high rents to tenant farmers. In short, it was argued that the price of wheat was high because the rents of agricultural land were high. Some of those who held this view advocated restricting the rents that landlords could charge.

David Ricardo, a great British economist who was one of the originators of classical economics, argued that the situation was exactly the reverse. The price of wheat was high, he said, because there was a shortage, which was caused by the Napoleonic Wars. Because wheat was profitable to produce, there was keen competition among farmers to obtain land on which to grow wheat. This competition in turn forced up the rent of wheat land. Ricardo advocated removing the tariff so that imported wheat could come into the country, thereby increasing its supply and lowering both the price of wheat and the rent that could be charged for the land on which it was grown.

The essentials of Ricardo's argument were these. The supply of land was fixed. Land was regarded as having only one use, the growing of wheat. Nothing had to be paid to prevent land from transferring to a use other than growing wheat because it had no other use. No landowner would leave

land idle as long as some return could be obtained by renting it out. Therefore, all the payment to land—that is, rent in the ordinary sense of the word—was a surplus over and above what was necessary to keep it in its present use.

Given a fixed supply of land, the price of land depended on the demand for land, which depended on the demand for wheat. *Rent*, the term for the payment for the use of land, thus became the term for a surplus payment to a resource owner over and above what was necessary to keep the resource in its present use.

Later two facts were realized. First, land often did have alternative uses, and, from the point of view of any one use, part of the payment made to land would necessarily have to be paid to keep it in that use. Second, owners of resources other than land also often earned a surplus over and above what was necessary to keep them in their present use. Television stars and great athletes, for example, are in short and fairly fixed supply, and their potential earnings in other occupations are often quite moderate. However, because there is a huge demand for their services as television stars or athletes, they may receive payments greatly in excess of what is needed to keep them from transferring to other occupations. This surplus is now called *economic rent*, whether the input is land, labour, or a piece of capital equipment.

How much of earnings is rent?

In most cases economic rent makes up part of the actual earnings. The distinction is most easily seen, however, by examining two extreme cases. In one case all of earnings is rent; in the other none is rent.

The possibilities are illustrated in Figure 15.4. When the supply curve is perfectly inelastic (vertical), the same quantity is supplied whatever the price. Evidently, there is no minimum that the owners of this input need to be paid to keep it in its present use, since the quantity supplied does not decrease no matter how low the price goes. In this case the whole of the payment is economic rent. The price actually paid allocates the fixed supply to those who are most willing to pay for it.

When the supply curve is perfectly elastic (horizontal), none of the price paid is economic rent. If any lower price is offered, nothing whatsoever will be supplied. All units of the input will be transferred to some other use.

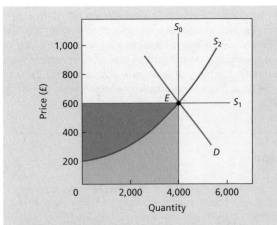

Figure 15.4 The determination of rent in resource owners' incomes

The amount of rent in earnings depends on the shape of the supply curve. A single demand curve is shown with three different supply curves. In each case the competitive equilibrium price is £600, and 4,000 units of the input are hired. The total payment (£2.4 million) is represented by the entire dark and medium blue areas.

When the supply curve is vertical (S_0) the whole payment is economic rent, because a decrease in price would not lead any units of the input to move elsewhere.

When the supply curve is horizontal (S_1) none of the payment is rent, because even a small decrease in price offered would lead all units of the input to move elsewhere.

When the supply curve is positively sloped (S_2) part of the payment is rent. Although the 4,000th unit is receiving just enough to persuade it to offer its services in this market, the 2,000th unit is earning well above what it requires to stay in this market. The aggregate of economic rents is shown by the dark blue area, and the aggregate of what must be paid to keep 4,000 units in this market is shown by the light blue area.

The more usual situation is that of a gradually rising supply curve. A rise in the price paid for an input serves the allocative function of attracting more resources into the market in question, but the same rise provides additional economic rent to all units of the input that are already employed. We know that the extra pay that is going to the units already employed is economic rent because the owners of these units were willing to supply them at the lower price. The general result for a positively sloped supply curve is as follows:

If there is an upward shift in the demand for a specific input in some sector, its price will rise. This will serve the allocative function of attracting additional inputs into that sector. It will also increase the economic rent going to all the owners of the inputs already employed in that sector.[7]

Determinants of the division

The proportion of earnings that is economic rent varies from situation to situation. We cannot point to owners of any specific resource and assert that some fixed fraction of their income is always economic rent. The proportion of earnings that is rent depends on the alternatives that are available.

Focus first on a narrowly defined use of a specific input, say the use of a worker by a particular firm. From that firm's point of view the worker will be highly mobile, since she could readily move to another firm in the same industry. The firm must pay the going wage or risk losing that worker. Thus, from the perspective of the *single firm*, a large proportion of the payment made to a worker is needed to prevent her from transferring to another use.

Consider now a more broadly defined use, for example the worker's use in an entire industry. From the industry's point of view the worker is less mobile, because it would be more difficult for her to gain employment quickly outside the industry. From the perspective of the particular *industry* (rather than the specific *firm* within the industry), a larger proportion of the payment to an input is economic rent.

From the even more general perspective of a particular *occupation*, mobility is likely to be less, and the proportion of earnings that is economic rent is likely to be more. The often controversial large salaries that are received by some highly specialized types of labour, such as superstar singers and professional athletes, illustrate these distinctions. These performers have a style or a talent that cannot be duplicated, whatever the training. The earnings that they receive are mostly economic rent from the viewpoint of the occupation: these performers enjoy their occupations and would pursue them for much less than the high remuneration that they actually receive. For example, Michael Owen would choose football over other alternatives even at a much

---

[7] In this context the term 'sector' can stand for occupation, industry, or geographical area.

lower salary than he was earning in 2003. However, because of Owen's skills as a football player, most teams would pay handsomely to have him, and he is able to command a high salary from the team he does play for. From the perspective of the firm, Liverpool FC, most of Owen's salary is required to keep him from switching to another team and hence is not economic rent. From the point of view of the 'football industry', however, much of his salary is economic rent. Similar arguments apply to top pop stars, who may earn several million pounds from record sales and concerts but would earn little in alternative occupations.

The notion of *rent seeking* is also commonly in use in the business world. Modern businesses are all trying to find products that give them some advantage over their rivals so that they can generate economic profits and not be quickly competed away. Patent protection of a new invention can give such an advantage for a time, but reputation and brand loyalty may also create economic rents for some companies.

Conclusion

The key driving force of resource allocation in a market economy is that inputs are attracted into uses where they receive the highest rewards. In the case of capital and other non-human inputs, the reward sought is typically financial. However, in the case of labour financial rewards are only part of the story, as working conditions, job satisfaction, and other psychic benefits may also matter. Firms will demand inputs in relation to the value that those inputs add to output. Hence inputs will tend to be drawn towards those industries in which they are most productive and for which output demand is highest—the demand for inputs is derived from the demand for the outputs that they help produce. Thus, there is a direct link from consumer demand for final products to demand for inputs and the rewards that the owners of those inputs receive.

SUMMARY

Overview

- The determination of prices in input markets depends on demand and supply, just like markets for final goods and services.

- The distribution of income is determined in input markets.

- The income of owners of inputs depends on the price paid per unit of the input and the quantity used.

The demand for inputs

- The firm's decisions on how much to produce and how to produce it imply demands for inputs, which are derived from the demand for goods that they help to produce.

- A profit-maximizing firm equates an input's marginal cost to its marginal revenue product, which is its marginal physical product multiplied by the marginal revenue associated with the sale of another unit of output. When the firm is a price-taker in input markets, the marginal cost of the input is its price per unit. When the firm sells its output in a competitive market, the marginal revenue product is the input's marginal physical product multiplied by the market price of the output.

- A firm's demand for an input is negatively sloped in the long run because cheaper inputs will be substituted for dearer ones and a fall in an input's price will lead to an increase in the output of the commodities it is used to make. It is negatively sloped in the short run because of the law of diminishing returns.

- The industry's demand for an input will be more elastic: (a) the slower the marginal physical product of the input declines as more of it is used, (b) the easier it is to substitute one input for another, (c) the larger is the proportion of total variable costs accounted for by the cost of the input in question, and (d) the more elastic is the demand for the good that the input helps to make.

The supply of inputs

- The total supply of land and capital is fixed at any moment but can vary over time. The total supply of labour varies with the size of the population, the participation rate, and hours worked. The latter two vary with the wage rate. A rise in the wage rate has a substitution effect, which tends to induce more work, and an income effect, which tends to induce less.

■ The supply of an input to a particular use is more elastic than its supply to the whole economy because one user can bid units away from other users. The elasticity of supply to a particular use depends on resource mobility, which tends to be greater the longer the time allowed for a reaction to take place.

The operation of input markets

■ Disequilibrium price differentials induce resource movements that eventually remove the differentials. Equilibrium differentials persist indefinitely.

Economic rent

■ Whenever the supply curve is positively sloped, part of the total return going to owners of a resource is needed to prevent them from transferring it to another use, and the rest is economic rent. The proportion of each depends on the potential mobility of the resource.

TOPICS FOR REVIEW

■ The distribution of income
■ Derived demand
■ Marginal physical product
■ Marginal revenue product

■ Input mobility between alternative uses
■ Disequilibrium and equilibrium differentials
■ Equal net benefit
■ Economic rent

DISCUSSION QUESTIONS

1 A firm making lawnmowers has an existing factory and machinery but it can vary the number of workers it hires. The following are data for total numbers of lawnmowers produced per week when hiring between 7 and 16 workers.

Workers per week	Lawnmowers produced per week
7	99
8	110
9	120
10	129
11	137
12	144
13	150
14	155
15	159
16	162

(a) Calculate the marginal physical product of workers numbering 8 to 16.

(b) Calculate the marginal revenue product of each worker if the lawnmowers can all be sold at £100.

(c) How many workers will this firm wish to hire if it is profit-maximizing and the going wage is £500 per week?

2 Suppose that the firm has the same production relationships as in question 1 but faces a downward-sloping demand curve for lawnmowers. The demand curve is $P = 400 - 1Q$ (so the marginal revenue curve is $MR = 400 - 2Q$), where Q is the output of lawnmowers per week. If workers can again be hired at £500 per week, how many workers will be hired?

3 If the firm were faced with an upward-sloping supply curve of labour: $W = 300 + 20M$ (where W is the wage per week and M is the number of men hired per week) and the demand conditions in question 2 obtain, how many men will be hired?

4 Explain how demand for inputs is linked to the demand for the final outputs that those inputs help produce.

5 What determines the elasticity of demand for an input in one specific use and in general use?

6 Is the high price of hotel rooms in central London determined by high demand or by the scarcity of land on which hotels can be built (or something else)?

7 Rank the following occupations in terms of the likely proportion of rent (as compared to transfer earnings) in typical earnings: pop stars, professional footballers, taxi drivers, computer consultants, university teachers, shop assistants, doctors.

8 What are the implications for input markets of rising demand for the following products: mobile phones, cheap flights, organic vegetables?

Appendix Marginal productivity and input demand

In this appendix we derive the firm's demand curve for an input in the short run. This was done intuitively in the text but is now set out more formally.

One variable input

Equation (2′) on page 252 in the text is repeated below as equation (A1):

$$w = MPP \times p. \tag{A1}$$

(Here we use an × to indicate multiplication.) This equation tells us what determines the quantity of a variable input that a firm will demand when faced with some specific price of the input and some specific price of its output. The firm's demand curve shows how much the firm will buy at *each* price of the variable input. To derive this curve, we start by considering the right-hand side of equation (A1), which tells us that the input's marginal revenue product is composed of a physical component and a value component.

The physical component of MRP As the quantity of the variable input used changes, output will vary. The hypothesis of diminishing returns, first discussed in Chapter 8, predicts what will happen. As the firm adds further units of the variable input to a given quantity of the fixed input, the additions to output will eventually get smaller and smaller. In other words, the input's marginal physical product will decline. This is illustrated

in part (i) of Figure 15A.1, which uses hypothetical data that have the same general characteristics as the data in Table 8.3 on page 134. The negative slope of the MPP curve reflects the operation of the law of diminishing returns: each unit of labour adds less to total output than the previous unit.

The value component of MRP To convert the marginal physical product curve of Figure 15A.1(i) into a curve showing the marginal revenue product of the variable input, we need to know the value of the extra physical product. As long as the firm sells its output on a competitive market, this value is simply the marginal physical product multiplied by the market price at which the firm sells its product.

This operation is illustrated in part (ii) of Figure 15A.1, which shows a marginal revenue product curve for labour on the assumption that the firm sells its product in a competitive market at a price of £5 a unit. This curve shows how much would be added to revenue by employing one more unit of the input *at each level of total employment of the input.*

Profit-maximizing firms should equate the addition to cost of buying another unit of a variable input with the addition to revenue caused by selling the output of that unit, which we call the input's marginal revenue product, MRP. The MRP is always composed of a physical component, which is the input's MPP, and a value component, which is the marginal revenue of selling those extra physical units of output. Because our firms are price-takers in their output markets, the marginal revenue is just the price

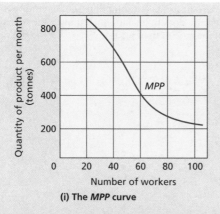

(i) The *MPP* curve

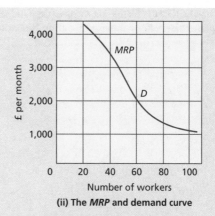

(ii) The *MRP* and demand curve

Figure 15A.1 From marginal physical product to demand curve

Each additional unit of the input employed adds a certain amount to total product (part (i)) and hence a certain amount to total revenue (part (ii)), and this determines the amount of the input that firms will demand at each price. Part (i) assumes data that are consistent with marginal productivity theory; it shows the addition to the firm's *output* produced by additional units of labour hired. The curve is negatively sloped because of the law of diminishing returns.

Part (ii) shows the addition to the firm's *revenue* caused by the employment of each additional unit of labour. It is the marginal physical product from part (i) multiplied by the price at which that product is sold. In this case the price is assumed to be £5. (The multiplication is by market price because the firm is assumed to be a price-taker in the market for its output.)

Since the firm equates the price of the variable input, which in this case is labour, to the input's marginal revenue product, it follows that the *MRP* curve in part (ii) is also the demand curve for labour, showing how much will be employed at each price.

that they face in that market. If the firms faced a negatively sloped demand curve for their output, we know from Chapter 10 that the addition to revenue from selling further units is not the market price, because marginal revenue is less than price.

From MRP to the demand curve Equation (A1) states that the profit-maximizing firm will employ additional units of the input up to the point at which the MRP equals the price of the input. If, for example, the price of the variable input were £2,000 per month, then it would be most profitable to employ 60 workers. There is no point in employing a sixty-first, since that would add just under £2,000 to revenue but a full £2,000 to costs. So the profit-maximizing firm hires the quantity of the variable input that equates the marginal revenue product with the price of the variable input. Thus, the curve that relates the quantity of the variable input employed to its MRP is also the curve that relates the quantity of the variable input the firm wishes to employ to its price.

The MRP curve of the variable input is the same as the demand curve for that input.

More than one variable input

When a firm can vary the amounts of several inputs that it uses, profit maximization requires that the last £1 it spends on each input brings in the same amount of revenue.

To see how this works out for two inputs, call their prices p_A and p_B and their marginal revenue products MRP_A and MRP_B. The amount of extra revenue per £1 spent on hiring more of input A is MRP_A/p_A, while the amount of extra revenue per pound spent on hiring more of input B is MRP_B/p_B. For example, if one more unit of A costs £3 and adds £6 to revenue, it yields £2 of revenue per £1 spent on it. If one more unit of B costs £5 and adds £10 to revenue, it too yields £2 of revenue per £1 spent on it. If the firm wants to equate these MRPs per pound spent on the inputs, it must set

$$\frac{MRP_A}{p_A} = \frac{MRP_B}{p_B}. \tag{A2}$$

The marginal revenue product is the marginal physical product multiplied by the product's selling price. We now have three prices: two for the variable inputs and one for output. To prevent confusion, we call the output price p_S, which stands for selling price. So $MRP = MPP \times p_S$. So we can rewrite equation (A2) as

$$\frac{(MPP_A)(p_s)}{p_A} = \frac{(MPP_B)(p_s)}{p_B}. \tag{A3}$$

If we eliminate the common p_S term, we have

$$\frac{MPP_A}{p_A} = \frac{MPP_B}{p_B}. \tag{A4}$$

This is equation (1) in the text of Chapter 9 page 143, except that we are now calling the input's marginal product MPP (to distinguish it from MRP), whereas we called it MP in the text treatment, because there was no possibility of confusion there.

Equation (A4) can be rewritten as follows:

$$\frac{MPP_A}{MPP_B} = \frac{p_A}{p_B}. \tag{A5}$$

In Chapter 9 the analysis given here was carried out with isoquants, where the slope of the isoquant is given by the ratio of the two inputs' marginal physical products.

Equation (A5) should be compared with equation (2) on page 101 of Chapter 6. In (A5) the firm is given prices of the two inputs, and it adjusts to these by altering the quantities of the two inputs until it has the profit-maximizing amount of each. This behaviour is similar to that of the consumer described on page 90. The consumer is given the prices of two commodities and she adjusts her consumption until her utility is maximized (which she does by making the ratios of the marginal utilities equal the ratio of their prices).

Chapter 16

THE LABOUR MARKET

Labour markets are the most important markets for most people, as this is where they find employment and earn their living. Can labour markets be analysed just like any other market? How do we explain wide differences in pay between different occupations? How do potential employers select employees when their quality is uncertain? What incentives are there for workers to perform once in the job? These are some of the questions we address in this chapter. In particular, you will learn that:

- Some long-lasting wage differentials arise from differences in skills and educational attainments; some arise for differences in age and sex.

- Some wage differentials arise from the type of market in which labour is sold; different wages are likely to be produced by competitive markets, where there are many buyers and sellers, in monopoly markets, in which unions control the supply, and in markets in which there are so few employers that each has power to influence the outcome.

- The full characteristics of many of today's workers are hard to ascertain in advance, so labour market practices evolve to cope with imperfect and asymmetric information.

- Efficiency wages are above the minimum that would be required to hire a worker as they contain an incentive for the employee to perform well.

- Selection and management procedures evolve to provide effective monitoring and incentive mechanisms.

- Internal labour markets within firms are like tournaments in which employees compete for promotion to more senior and better paid jobs.

The first part of the chapter is devoted to explaining wage differentials between different types of labour.[1] These are due partly to different skills and educational attainments, partly to age and sex, and partly to the type of market in which labour services are supplied. Workers can improve upon free market outcomes if they are organized as a single seller dealing with a large number of buyers, but they do worse when unorganized and selling to a single buyer.

The first part of the chapter uses theories that assume that wages are set in competitive markets. These markets clear, in the sense that neither excess demand nor excess supply persists unless strong buyers or sellers are able to exercise power over the market to prevent it from clearing. These theories can explain quite a bit about the forces that create wage differentials in the real world. But they are not the whole story, since they treat labour as a homogeneous commodity, which is far from the truth.

Today more and more employees are hired for their brain rather than their brawn. This adds many complications to the labour market. Because people are heterogeneous, their individual contributions to the firm's success are difficult to assess and their motives may not always conform to the firm's objective of maximizing its profits. In the final part of the chapter we study the many institutions and practices that have evolved to deal with these modern labour market problems.

Wage differentials

We noted in the previous chapter that, if labour were homogeneous, jobs all had the same non-financial characteristics, and labour markets were perfectly competitive, every person would earn the same income in equilibrium. Disequilibrium differentials in wages would arise whenever demand or supply curves shifted. However, workers would then move from lower-wage to higher-wage jobs until the differentials had disappeared. In reality, some workers

---

[1] By 'labour' we mean all human resources of both workers and management, and by 'labour income', or 'wages', we mean all income earned from work, whether in the form of wages or salaries.

receive low rates of pay, others receive modest but higher wages, while yet others are paid very high wages (or salaries). These are equilibrium differentials that persist even after all markets have reached equilibrium. For full-time employees who work a standard week and have no income from assets, rates of pay translate into incomes.

• **Incomes vary with the type of job.** Cleaners and casual staff in fast-food restaurants, for example, earn less than electricians and IT support staff.

• **Incomes vary with education.** Average earnings of people with university degrees exceed the average earnings of those with only A-levels, which in turn exceed the average earnings of those with only GCSEs, which exceed the average earnings of those with no qualifications at all.

• **Incomes vary with age.** Average earnings tend to rise until a person's mid-40s and fall thereafter (though this pattern varies with occupation).

• **Incomes vary with years on the job.** Generally, the longer one stays with one firm, the higher the income one earns.

• **Incomes vary with sex and race.** On average, men earn more than women, and members of some minority ethnic groups earn less than members of majority groups—even when differences in education and experience are allowed for.

• **Incomes vary with the type of market in which labour sells its services.** Workers who sell their labour in markets dominated by trade unions often earn more than similar people who sell their labour in more non-unionized, hence competitive, markets.

We now discuss some of the major causes of these equilibrium differentials in the earnings of various types of labour.

Differentials arising from basic differences: non-competing groups

More highly skilled jobs pay better wages than less highly skilled jobs. Why does a movement from the latter to the former not erode these differentials?

One obvious answer lies in human differences that are either innate or acquired so early in life as to be beyond each individual's personal control. Some people are brighter than others; some are more athletic; some are blessed with a good singing voice; others are better endowed with manual skills. People might be separated by their natural endowments of intelligence, skills, and abilities into separate groups between which no movement was possible. We would then have many *non-competing groups*. They would be selling their services in a number of *segmented labour markets*.

Figure 16.1 shows that wage differentials between non-competing groups arise from the positions of both the demand and the supply curves. One group will earn higher incomes than another only if its supply is low *relative to the demand for it*. It is not good enough to have a rare skill: that skill must be rare in relation to the demand for it.

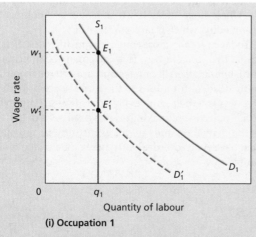

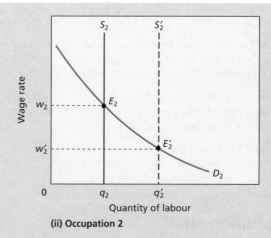

(i) Occupation 1   **(ii) Occupation 2**

Figure 16.1 Wage differentials in segmented labour markets

When labour cannot move from one market to another, wage differentials of any size can persist. Because of basic differences in abilities, the supply of labour is fixed at q_1 in occupation 1 and at q_2 in occupation 2. Demand and supply curves intersect at E_1 and E_2 to produce the high wage of w_1 in occupation 1 and the low wage of w_2 in occupation 2.

A fall in demand from D_1 to D_1' in occupation 1 takes equilibrium to E_1', lowering its wage to w_1'. A rise in supply in occupation 2, to q_2', takes equilibrium to E_2', lowering its wage to w_2'.

Over time, wage differentials change. On the demand side, economic growth constantly alters the derived demand for many specific groups of labour, creating new differentials and eroding old ones. On the supply side, there may be exogenous shifts. For example, a new group of immigrants may alter the mix of skills available in the local market. Furthermore, human differences notwithstanding, substantial mobility between groups does occur —particularly in the long run, when older people with specific skills leave the labour force and young people with different skills enter.

None the less, one lesson of the simple theory of non-competing groups is important:

Some income differentials arise because basic human characteristics cause the supplies of some types of labour to remain low relative to the demand for them, even in the long run.

Differentials arising from human capital

The key to mobility among occupations is education. Many skills are learned rather than inherited. These may be thought of as a stock of human capital acquired by each worker.

A machine is physical capital. It requires an investment of time and money to create it, and once built yields valuable services over a long time. In the same way, the acquisition of labour skills requires an investment of time and money, and once acquired these skills yield an increased income to their owner over a long time. Since investment in labour skills is similar to investment in physical capital, acquired skills are called **human capital**.

Because acquiring human capital is costly, the more highly skilled the job, the more it must pay if enough people are to be attracted to train for it.

The stock of skills acquired by individual workers is called human capital; investment in this capital is usually costly, and the return is higher labour productivity and hence higher earning power.

The two main ways in which human capital is acquired are through formal education and on-the-job training.

Formal education

Compulsory education provides some minimum human capital for all citizens. Some people, either through luck in the school they attend or through their own efforts, profit more from their early education than do others. Those who decide to stay in school beyond the years of compulsory education are deciding to invest voluntarily in acquiring further human capital.

Costs and benefits The cost of further education is the income that could have been earned if the person had

entered the labour force immediately after compulsory education, plus any out-of-pocket costs for such things as fees and equipment, minus any student grant or scholarship. The return is the difference between the income that would have been earned if one had left school and the income that is earned as a result of going on to higher education. (There is also a consumption return whenever higher education is something that students enjoy more than work.) These costs and benefits are analysed in Figure 16.2.

Changes in costs and benefits If the demand for labour with low amounts of human capital falls, as it has in recent

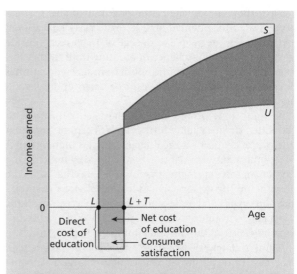

Figure 16.2 The costs and benefits of formal education

Acquiring human capital through formal education beyond minimum school-leaving age implies costs now and benefits later. Age is plotted on the horizontal axis and income earned on the vertical axis. Income is zero until age L, which is the minimum school-leaving age. After that the red line U shows the income of a typical person who leaves school at age L and takes the relatively unskilled job for which his or her human capital is suitable.

The blue line S shows the more complicated stream of payments and income receipts of someone who stays on for T years of formal training after age L. At first receipts are negative, reflecting the net out-of-pocket expenses related to attending school and university. Deducting the consumption value placed on being at school rather than at work (light red area) yields the net cost associated with being in school. Adding this to the income that could have been earned by going directly into the labour force at age L yields the total cost of the education, which is the medium red area.

The benefit is shown by the dark red area, representing the difference between the income earned in the skilled job that is acquired at year $L + T$ (line S) and the income that would have been earned if the labour force had been entered at age L (line U). The investment in human capital could not possibly be worthwhile unless the dark red benefit area exceeded the medium red cost area. The net benefit to a particular individual depends on how much he or she discounts the more distant gain in order to compare it with the more immediate costs.

times, the earnings of such people will fall. This will lower the costs of staying on in school, since the earnings forgone by not going to work are reduced. A rise in unemployment will also lower the costs, because the probability of earning a steady income will be reduced, and this will reduce the expected loss from not entering the labour force early. If the demand for labour having more human capital rises, the earnings of such labour will rise. This will raise the expected return to those currently deciding whether or not to make the investment themselves.

Individual decisions For any *given* state of these incentives, why do some people decide to acquire human capital while others do not?

First, there are differences among individuals. For reasons related to inherited abilities or to early educational experience, some people at the age of 16 correctly decide that they have a low chance of profiting from further formal education. For them the return from such education is lower than for others who have the necessary aptitudes and inclination.

Second, some people have special talents for types of work that do not require further human capital. For them the cost of acquiring more human capital is higher than it is for others; the earnings they would forgo by not entering the labour force are higher than the earnings that would be forgone by the average school-leaver. Obvious examples are pop singers and professional football players—Sir Mick Jagger did not suffer any loss of income by quitting his economics degree at the LSE and joining the Rolling Stones!

Third, different people have different time-preferences. The cost of acquiring human capital is forgone income *now*, and the return is a *probability* of higher income *later*. Tastes differ. Some people put a high value on income now and are not willing to pay the cost of postponing it. Others place a higher value on income to be earned later in life and are willing to have less now in return for the chance of much more later on.

Fourth, different people put different values on the consumption aspects of education. Those who enjoy the experience find the costs of acquiring human capital lower than those who do not. Those who would prefer to be at work rather than at school find the cost increased by the negative value they place on the educational experience.

Market forces adjust the overall costs and benefits of acquiring human capital, while individuals respond according to their varying personal evaluation of the costs and the benefits.

In the long run, decisions to acquire human capital help to erode disequilibrium differentials in incomes. Market signals change the costs and benefits of acquiring human capital in such specific forms as skill in electronics, accountancy, law, or medicine. By reacting to these signals, young people increase the supplies of high-income workers and

reduce the supplies of low-income workers, thus eroding existing disequilibrium differentials.

On-the-job education

Wage differentials according to age are readily observable in most firms and occupations. To a significant extent these differentials are a response to human capital acquired on the job. This type of human capital falls into two types.

Firm-specific human capital Learning how one firm does such things as recording and retrieving its information, how it makes decisions, and how the personal relations among its employees are to be used to advantage are all firm-specific. As employees acquire this knowledge, they become more valuable to the firm. But the knowledge is not valuable to other firms; workers who move to similar jobs with other firms will have to learn the new firm-specific characteristics of their new jobs.

Firms do not want to lose long-term employees with large amounts of firm-specific human capital, since other employees will then have to be trained to take their place. But, being firm-specific, the capital is of no value to other firms. So if the firm pays its employees a wage that reflects the productivity conferred by this capital, they will have an incentive to stay in the job rather than to move to another firm where their value would initially be much less.

General human capital If a firm trains a clerical assistant through various ranks up to becoming the PA of the managing director, able to run his office efficiently, the PA's skills will be potentially useful to other firms. Some of the PA's human capital can be acquired only through on-the-job training; hence it must be acquired within the firm. However, unlike the firm-specific capital, a PA who is paid the value of his or her marginal product has no monetary incentive to stay with the firm that taught these transferable skills, as he or she could earn the same elsewhere. The same is true of any non-firm-specific human capital acquired through on-the-job experience by any of the firm's employees.

So why would firms invest in training employees if the employees on whom the human capital is invested are free to walk out of the door and move to another employer? Firms have no incentive to provide training when they cannot capture the benefit itself because it accrues to the individual employee. One solution is to pay each worker less than her marginal product in the early years and more later on. The low pay can be seen as the employee's payment to the firm for helping her to acquire marketable human capital. The high pay later in life is a return on that capital, and in part is a reward for loyalty to the firm.

Human capital acquired through on-the-job experience provides a reason why earnings rise with the length of time spent with a firm. Firms tend to pay employees the value of

their current marginal products for firm-specific capital, but for general human capital they pay less than the marginal products early in life and more later in life.

Another reason for the same pattern of lifetime wages is that competition tends to be strongest at the initial point of entry into the firm and to weaken thereafter, when promotion posts typically go to internal candidates. This will tend to hold wages down to competitive levels at entry points but allow them to drift above those levels for personnel with years of seniority and experience. This pattern does not always hold of course—in universities for example new faculty members are often paid more than those who have been in place for some time. This is because the university is trying to recruit the brightest and best on the market and has to pay high rates to attract them, while the existing staff have some job security (so cannot easily be fired) but might not be strong candidates if applying in the current market situation.

Market solutions The above discussion illustrates the subtlety of market solutions to the issues posed by the human capital acquired through on-the-job experience. What may look arbitrary, or unfair, to the casual observer is often a rational response that has evolved to handle some aspect of the employment relationship—such as the fact that on-the-job training creates capital that is sometimes firm-specific and sometimes transferable, but in all cases is embodied in the employee.

To illustrate the importance of these insights, consider two jobs that employ people with equal initial requirements. One provides on-the-job training that is mainly firm-specific, and the wage follows the time-path of the employee's evolving marginal product fairly closely. The second job provides training that builds up transferable skills, and the wage paid is less than marginal product for younger employees and higher for older ones. Now assume that government policy-makers get worried about the discrimination between workers in different jobs and introduce legislation requiring equal pay for 'work of equal value'. Both types of employee must now be paid the value of their marginal products. Firms then become reluctant to invest in training their employees to acquire transferable human capital, because it is now illegal to use a time-pattern of wages that allows the firm to recover the cost of providing this capital. However fair it may appear to some, this government policy, designed to enhance equity, may not be in the interests of the workers affected by it.

Differentials resulting from sex and race

Aggregate statistics show that incomes vary by race and sex. More detailed studies suggest that much of these differences can be explained by such influences as amount of human capital acquired through both formal education and on-the-job experience. When these influences are taken into account, however, a core of difference remains that is consistent with discrimination based on race and sex. This is further discussed with respect to male–female earnings differentials in Box 16.1.

Some forms of discrimination make it difficult, or impossible, for particular groups to take certain jobs, even if skill and education equip them for these jobs. Until fairly recently, non-whites and women found many occupations closed to them. Even today, when overt discrimination is illegal, many feel that more subtle forms of discrimination are applied.

To the extent that such discrimination occurs, it reduces the supply of labour in the exclusive jobs—by keeping out the groups that are discriminated against. It also increases the supply in non-exclusive jobs, which are the only ones open to groups that are subject to discrimination. This raises the wages in the exclusive jobs and lowers them in the non-exclusive jobs. Since discrimination prevents movement from the lower to the higher-wage jobs, the resulting wage differences are equilibrium, not disequilibrium, differentials.

A model of labour market discrimination

To isolate the effects of discrimination, we begin by considering a non-discriminating labour market. We then introduce discrimination between two groups of equally qualified workers, group X and group Y. The analysis applies to workers who are distinguished on any grounds other than their ability, such as female and male, black and white, alien and citizen, Catholic and Protestant.

Suppose that, except for the fact that the people in one group are marked with X and those in the other are marked with Y, the groups are the same. Each has the same number of members, the same proportion educated to various levels, identical distributions of talent, and so on. Suppose also that there are two occupations. Occupation E (for elite) requires people of above-average education and skills, and occupation O (ordinary) can use anyone. If wages in the two occupations are the same, employers in occupation O will prefer to hire the above-average worker. Finally, suppose that the non-monetary advantages of the two occupations are equal.

In the absence of discrimination, the wages in E occupations will be bid up above those in O occupations in order that the E jobs attract the workers of above-average skills. Both Xs and Ys of above-average skill will take the E jobs, while the others, both Xs and Ys, will have no choice but to seek O jobs. Because skills are equally distributed, each occupation will employ one-half Xs and one-half Ys.

Now discrimination enters in an extreme form. All E occupations are hereafter open only to Xs; all O occupations are hereafter open to either Xs or Ys. The immediate effect is to reduce by 50 per cent the supply of job

Box 16.1 **Why are women paid less than men?**

Wage discrimination can affect women (or any other group that is discriminated against) in at least two ways: (1) they may earn less than men when doing the same job, or (2) they may be forced into jobs that typically pay lower wages than the jobs from which they are excluded. Non-discriminatory wage differentials arise when men and women differ on average in relevant labour market characteristics. For example, men and women differ significantly in their average educational qualifications and their labour market experience, with women typically spending somewhere between five and ten years out of the labour market raising children.

Across the whole economy, the average pay of women is less than that of men. This has been known since at least the 1880s, when reliable records started. Indeed, at the Trades Union Congress of 1888 a motion was passed stating that where men and women do the same jobs they should get the same pay. However, it was 1970 before the Equal Pay Act finally legislated that pay must be the same 'for the same or broadly similar work'.

Up to 1970, the data show that on average women were paid just over 60 per cent of the average male wage. However, by the late 1970s this had narrowed to a little over 70 per cent, and by the end of 2001 the figure was 81.6 per cent. Researchers have been unable to explain this narrowing in any way other than as a result of the legislation. This suggests that some previously existing discrimination has been eliminated, and confirms the continued narrowing of this differential in the UK since the mid-1980s.

Research has looked at the remaining differentials. Correcting for differing lengths of labour market experience would increase average female pay to over 85 per cent of the average male wage. Other differences between the sexes, such as years of schooling, account for another 5 or 6 percentage points, leaving fewer than 10 percentage points unexplained. This could be due to discrimination.

On a narrow interpretation, the pay differentials according to different labour market experiences are a reflection of the resulting lower marginal products. On a wider view of discrimination, however, these different experiences are merely convenient excuses for paying women less. This wider view is given some plausibility by the fact that in Sweden, the most egalitarian country in Europe, female earnings average fully 90 per cent of male earnings.

It is harder to estimate the effects of discrimination that excludes women from certain jobs and crowds them into others. Studies suggest, however, that if the discrimination in type of employment were eliminated, wages in occupations that are currently dominated by females would rise by as much as 50 per cent! In contrast, wages in male-dominated jobs would fall by only a few percentage points.

These estimates put *upper bounds* on the effects of discrimination. To some extent, the crowding of women into certain types of jobs may reflect their own preferences for these types of jobs, and the amount of human capital that they are willing to acquire. To the extent that this is true, the crowding into certain occupations and the resulting lower female earnings represent the outcome of female preferences. However, to the extent that crowding is due to discriminatory practices on the part of employers, the wage differentials are not an efficient market outcome.

All of the research results reported here are tentative, since this type of estimation is no easy matter. However, the evidence does suggest two things. First, there is almost certainly some discrimination against women remaining in labour markets today. Second, we have to be very careful in interpreting the raw data. The measured average differentials have to be adjusted for labour force characteristics in order to identify any residual that is due to discrimination.

---

candidates for E occupations; candidates must now be *both* X and above average. The discrimination also increases the supply of applicants for O jobs by 50 per cent; this group now includes *all* Ys and the below-average Xs.

Wage-level effects As shown in Figure 16.3, wages now rise in E occupations and fall in O occupations.

Discrimination, by changing supply, can decrease the wages and incomes of a group that is discriminated against.

In the longer run, further changes may occur. Notice that total employment in the E industries falls. Employers may find ways to utilize slightly below-average labour and thus lure the next-best-qualified Xs out of O occupations. Although this will raise O wages slightly, it will also make these occupations increasingly 'Y occupations'. If discrimination has been in effect for a sufficient length of time, Ys will learn that it does not pay to acquire above-average skills: regardless of ability, Ys are forced by discrimination to work in unskilled jobs.

Now suppose that a long-standing discriminatory policy is reversed. Because they will have responded to discrimination by acquiring fewer skills than Xs, many Ys will be locked into the O occupations, at least for a time. Moreover, if both Xs and Ys come to expect that Ys will have less education than Xs, employers will tend to look for Xs to fill the E jobs. This will reinforce the belief of Ys that education does not pay. This, and other kinds of subtle discrimination, can persist for a very long time, making the supply of Ys to O jobs higher than it would be in the absence of the initial discrimination, thus depressing the wages of Ys and poor Xs.

The kind of discrimination that we have considered in our model is extreme. It is similar to South Africa's former apartheid system (which was eliminated by 1994), in which blacks were excluded by law from prestigious and high-paying occupations. In most Western countries labour market discrimination against a specific group usually occurs in somewhat less obvious ways. First, it may be difficult (but not impossible, as in our model) for members of the group to get employment in certain jobs. Second, members of groups subject to discrimination may receive lower pay for a specific kind of work than members of groups not subject to discrimination.

It is interesting to note that falling transport and communication costs over the past century have expanded

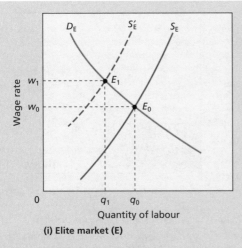
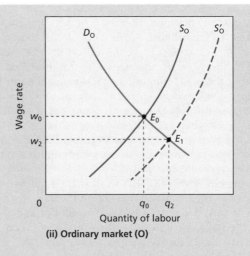

Figure 16.3 Economic discrimination

If market E discriminates against one group and market O does not, the supply curve will shift to the left in E and to the right in O. Market E requires above-average skills, while market O requires only ordinary skills. When there is no discrimination, demands and supplies are D_E and S_E in market E, and D_O and S_O in market O. Initially the wage rate is w_0 and employment is q_0 in each market. (The actual wage in market E will be slightly higher than the wage in market O.) When all Ys are barred from E occupations, the supply curve shifts to S_E' and the wage earned by the remaining workers, all of whom are Xs, rises to w_1. Ys put out of work in the E occupations now seek work in the O occupations. The resulting shift in the supply curve to S_O' brings down the wage to w_2 in the O occupations. Because all Ys are in O occupations, they have a lower wage than many Xs. The average X wage is higher than the average Y wage.

firms' choice of location for the production of goods—from local markets to national markets, to wider regional markets, and now often to global markets. This has greatly reduced the power of local prejudices to impose discriminatory employment policies on firms. If firms are unhappy about local pressures to employ one group rather than another, production can be transferred to other sites and the customers will quickly lose any concern about, or even awareness of, the nature of the far-distant workforce that makes the products they consume.

Differentials resulting from labour market structures

In this section we see how differences in the degree of competition can contribute to income differentials across markets. We then go on to study unions in a little more detail.

The determination of wages without unions

When labour is supplied competitively, each worker must take the existing wage rate as given and decide how many hours to work at that wage.[2] Each worker has a supply curve showing how much effort he will supply at each wage (see page 256). The sum of these curves yields a market supply curve showing the total supply of effort to this market as a function of the real wage rate. The determination of wages under competitive supply now falls into three cases,

distinguished by whether labour is bought by competitive purchasers, by a single-wage monopsonist, or by a discriminating monopsonist.

Case 1: a competitive market We first assume that there are so many purchasers of labour services that no one of them can influence the market wage rate. Instead, each merely decides how much labour to hire at the current rate. Since both demanders and suppliers are price-takers and quantity-adjusters, this labour market is perfectly competitive. Demand and supply as shown in Figure 15.3 on page 250 then determine the wage rate and volume of employment.

Case 2: a single-wage monopsonist—a single purchaser Now consider a labour market containing only a few firms. For simplicity we deal with a case in which the few purchasers form an employers' association and act as a single decision-taking unit in the labour market. In this section the single buyer is restrained to paying a single wage to all workers of one type that it employs.

When there is a single purchaser in any market, that purchaser is called a **monopsonist**. A monopsonist can offer any wage rate it chooses, and workers must either work for that wage or move to other markets (i.e. change occupation or location).

[2] In practice, the individual decision may be whether or not to work the standard working week at the going wage.

Suppose that the monopsonist decides to hire some specific quantity of labour. The labour supply curve shows the wage that it must offer. To the monopsonist this wage is the *average cost curve* of labour. In deciding how much labour to hire, however, the monopsonist is interested in the marginal cost of hiring additional workers. It wants to know how much its costs will rise if it takes on more labour.

Whenever the supply curve of labour has a positive slope, the marginal cost of employing extra units will exceed the average cost (the wage) because the increased wage rate necessary to attract an extra worker must also be paid to *everyone already employed*.

Consider an example. If 100 workers are employed at £10 per hour, then total cost is £1,000 and average cost per worker is £10. If an extra worker is employed and this drives the wage rate up to £11, then total cost becomes £1,111 (101 × £11); the average cost per labourer is £11, but the total cost has increased by £111 as a result of hiring one more labourer.

Monopsony results in a lower level of employment and a lower wage rate than when labour is purchased competitively.

The reason is that the monopsonistic purchaser is aware that, by purchasing more, it is driving up the price against itself. It will, therefore, stop short of the point that is reached when the input is purchased by many different firms, none of which can exert an influence on its price.

Case 3: a discriminating monopsonist What happens if the monopsonist can discriminate between different units of a single type of labour that it hires? By discrimination here we mean that the employer negotiates a different contract with each individual employee. We do not imply that this is related to any ethnic and gender characteristics whose impact we discussed above. As with the discriminatory monopolists that we studied in Chapter 11, the ability to discriminate has two effects:

A discriminating monopsonist will (1) hire more labour and (2) earn more profits than will a monopsonist who must pay the same wage to everyone.

In Figure 16.4 the monopsonist who had to pay the same wage to all did not hire more labour, because doing so would have driven up the wage of its existing workers. For this reason the monopsonist's marginal cost of hiring labour exceeds the average costs. If the monopsonist can split its labour into groups, it can hire a second group without driving up the price of the first group. Consider the extreme case in which the monopsonist can make a separate bargain with each worker, paying just what is needed to persuade that person to accept a job. The supply curve is then the marginal cost curve of labour and the monopsonist employs the same amount of labour as would a perfectly competitive industry, but only the last worker hired gets the equivalent of the competitive wage—all others get less.

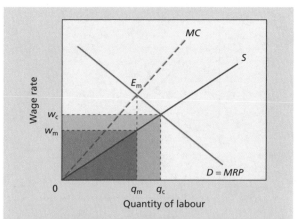

Figure 16.4 A monopsonist facing many sellers

Under monopsony employment and wages are less than under competition. The competitive wage and employment are w_c and q_c, where the demand and supply curves intersect. The monopsonist that must pay the same wage to all equates the marginal cost of hiring labour with labour's marginal revenue product, which occurs at point E_m. The firm hires q_m workers at a wage of w_m. (According to the supply curve, w_m is the wage at which q_m workers will be supplied.) Labour's income is shown by the dark red and dark blue areas enclosed by q_m and w_m.

A perfectly discriminating monopsonist can pay each worker his or her supply price, so the S curve is also its marginal cost curve. It will hire q_c labour and pay labour a total income equal to the dark and medium blue areas *under* the S curve. The light red area between w_m and w_c is now part of the monopsonist's profits, as is the dark red area between w_m and the S curve (whereas under perfect competition both red areas are part of labour's income).

A perfectly discriminating monopsony is the extreme case. However, whenever the monopsonist can discriminate between two or more groups, employment and profits will be higher than when a single wage must be paid to all.

The determination of wages with unions

Unions affect wages and employment in two ways, depending on whether labour is hired competitively or monopsonistically.[3]

Case 4: monopoly—a single seller Suppose a union enters a competitive labour market and raises the wage above its equilibrium level. By so doing, it is establishing a minimum wage below which no one will work. The industry can hire as many units of labour as are prepared to work at the union wage, but none at a lower wage. Thus, the industry (and each firm) faces a supply curve that is horizontal at the level of the union wage up to the quantity of labour willing to work at that wage.

---

[3] For simplicity we deal here with only the single-wage monopsonist. Combining a union with a discriminating monopsonist complicates the analysis substantially without adding any new insights.

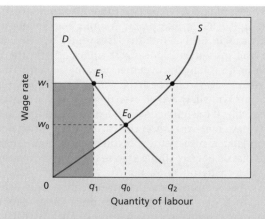

Figure 16.5 A single union facing many employers

A union that faces many employers can raise wages above the competitive level. Competitive equilibrium is at E_0. When the union sets the wage at w_1, it creates a perfectly elastic supply curve of labour up to the quantity q_2, which is the amount of labour willing to work at the wage w_1. Equilibrium is at E_1, with q_1 workers employed and $q_2 - q_1$ willing to work at the going wage rate but unable to find employment. Labour income is shown by the dark blue area.

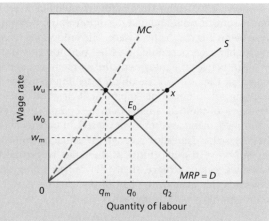

Figure 16.6 A single union facing a single employer

A union can raise both the wage and employment above their monopsonistic levels. The monopsonist facing competitively supplied labour is in the equilibrium analysed in Figure 15.4, with q_m workers employed at a wage of w_m. If a newly entering union sets its wage at w_0, the supply curve runs from w_0 to E_0 and then rises along the line S. Equilibrium is at E_0 with employment at q_0.

If the union seeks a wage higher than w_0, it must accept a lower level of employment than q_0. The union can, for example, set a wage of w_u, creating a supply curve that runs from w_u to x then up the S curve. This yields the same level of employment, q_m, as when the monopsonist dominated the market, but at the much higher wage of w_u. At that wage rate there are $q_2 - q_m$ people who would like to work but who are unable to find employment.

This is shown in Figure 16.5. The intersection of this horizontal supply curve and the demand curve establishes a higher wage rate, and a lower level of employment, than would occur at the competitive equilibrium.

There will be a group of workers who would like to obtain work in the industry or occupation but cannot. Pressure to cut the wage rate may develop among the unemployed, but the union must resist this pressure if the higher wage is to be maintained.

A union can raise wages above the competitive-market level, but only at the costs of lowering employment and creating an excess supply of labour with its consequent pressure for wage-cutting.

Case 5: a monopsony versus a monopoly We now consider the effects of introducing a union into the monopsonistic labour market first illustrated in Figure 16.4.

The (single-wage) monopsonistic employers' organization now faces a monopoly union, and the two sides will settle the wage through collective bargaining. The outcome of this bargaining process will depend on the objective that each side sets and on the skill that each has in bargaining for its objective. We have seen that, left to itself, the employers' organization will set the monopsonistic wage shown in Figure 16.4.

To understand the range over which the wage may be set after the union enters the market, let us ask what the union would do if it had the power to set a wage below which its members would not work. There is now no point in the employers' holding off hiring for fear of driving the wage

up, or reducing the quantity demanded in the hope of driving the wage rate down. Here, just as in the case of a wage-setting union in a competitive market, the union presents the employer with a horizontal supply curve (up to the maximum number of workers who will accept work at the union wage). As demonstrated in Figure 16.6, the union can raise wages *and employment* above the monopsonistic level.

Because the union turns the firm into a price-taker in the labour market, it can stop a firm from exercising its monopsony power and thus raise both wages and employment to the competitive level.

The union may not be content merely to neutralize the monopsonist's power. It may choose to raise wages further. If it does, the outcome will be similar to that shown in Figure 16.5. If the wage is raised above the competitive level, the employer will no longer wish to hire all the labour that is offered at that wage. The amount of employment will fall, and unemployment will develop. This is also shown in Figure 16.6. Notice, however, that the union can raise wages substantially above the competitive level before employment falls to a level as low as it was in the pre-union monopsonistic situation.

So now we know that the employer would like to set the monopsonistic wage and that the union would not want a wage below the competitive wage. The union may target a still higher wage depending on what trade-off it is willing to make between employment for its members and the wage that they earn. If the union is willing to accept the resulting low amount of employment, it could target a wage rate substantially higher than the competitive wage.

Simple demand and supply analysis can take us no further. As we have already observed, the actual outcome will depend on such other things as the target wage that the two sides seek to achieve, their relative bargaining skills, how each side assesses the cost of concessions, and how serious a strike would be for each.

Differentials arising from product market structures

The ability of a union to raise wages above the competitive level depends partly on the profitability of the industry in which it is operating. Some industries are highly competitive because they contain a large number of small firms and entry and exit are easy. Typically, firms in such industries will be earning enough to cover the opportunity cost of their capital, but no pure profits. A strong union might still raise wages in such an industry. This would increase costs and lead to exit until prices rose sufficiently for the remaining firms fully to cover their now higher costs. Thus, the rise in wages would be accompanied by a fall in output and employment. However, even this limited gain may not be possible. If the union does not have a closed shop, new firms may enter, with lower costs achieved by hiring non-union labour. Also, if there is competition from foreign firms that do not face strong unions, the domestic industry may suffer a drastic contraction.

In other industries scale economies allow only a few firms, each one of which may earn significant profits. Government regulation that restricts competitive behaviour can also create profits over and above the opportunity cost of capital. Evidence suggests that unions can appropriate a share of these profits for their members through aggressive collective bargaining. Wages fell significantly in the UK newspaper industry after new technology gave the opportunity to break the union monopoly on print workers.

Box 16.2 discusses the case of earnings differentials associated with super-stars.

 Box 16.2 The earnings of superstars

Small groups of people in many professions are often paid extraordinarily large salaries. In May 2002 David Beckham signed a new contract with Manchester United reported to be worth £90,000 per week for three years. Roy Keane had already been given a contract with the same club reported to be worth £80,000 per week. In the spring of 2002 Ferrari raised its annual pay for Michael Schumacher from £21m to £25m. At around the same time, pop singer Robbie Williams was reported to have signed a £40 million five-record deal with EMI. These rewards for pop stars and top sports stars are not new. Michael Jordon the basketball player made US$100m in 1998, Mike Tyson the boxer made US$75m in 1996, and singer/songwriter Sir Paul McCartney amassed a nearly £1bn fortune out of his career in popular music.

Why are superstars so highly paid? Should not market incentives encourage others to compete for these large rewards, with the end result that the massive rewards for a few would fall and be replaced by more modest rewards for the many? Conversely, forces in the modern economy appear to be increasing the gap between superstars and the rest. There are three components to the explanation.

First, the general increase in real wealth over time has created an increase in demand for output in the sectors in which superstars perform.

Second, in some of these activities there is a premium to being the very best over what the merely competent can command. For example, if you are wealthy and need a lawyer or a heart surgeon, you are going to pay for the best; someone who is good but not the best will not do. Equally, if you want your team to win the Premier League, you need the best striker in the country; coming second is commendable but not good enough. Hence those who are 'the best' may be only, say, 10 per cent better than a bunch behind them, but they may command a substantial wage premium just because there is no one better. (The MRP of being the best greatly exceeds the MRP of being second.)

Tiger Woods, for example, the world's number one ranked golfer, in 2001 earned about US$6m in prize money and over US$60m in endorsements. He is on average only about two shots per 18-hole round better than the player ranked number 100. Yet the 100th ranked player earned less than $1 million in prize money and endorsements combined. So Tiger, who was less than 2 per cent better at golf than the 100th ranked player, earned 66 times as much.

Third, modern communications have increased the size of the market over which stars compete. What used to be a series of local markets, where the person who was the best in each market earned a moderately high income, have become a single global market in which people compete to be the best in the world. The winners earn huge sums because they serve huge markets. TV, movie, and pop stars are the obvious examples. Why listen to a local opera company when you can listen to Pavarotti and Domingo on a CD? Why listen to a local band when you can access the latest global music hits, played by those who wrote them? The marginal revenue products of top stars have been vastly increased by modern communications media which allow them to reach audiences thousands of times larger than could be reached a century ago.

Minimum-wage laws

When unions set wages for their members, they are in effect setting a minimum wage. Governments can cause similar effects by legislating specific *minimum wages*, which define the lowest wage rates that may legally be paid. Such minimum wages are common in the United States and Canada and in some EU countries. The UK introduced a minimum wage on 1 April 1999 of £3.60 an hour for adult workers and £3.00 for 18–21-year-olds (16- and 17-year-olds are exempt). In October 2002 the adult rate rose to £4.20 while that for 18–21-year-olds rose to £3.60 per hour.

To the extent that minimum wages are effective, they raise the wages of employed workers. However, as our analysis in Chapter 5 indicated, an effective floor price (which is what a minimum wage is) may well lead to a market surplus—in this case, unemployment. Thus, minimum wages benefit some groups of workers while hurting others.

The problem is more complicated than the analysis of Chapter 5 would suggest, both because not all labour markets are competitive and because only a small proportion of the labour force is affected by minimum-wage laws. Moreover, some groups in the labour force, especially youths and minorities, are affected more than the average worker. It is also worth bearing in mind that labour is not a homogeneous commodity (even though much of our demand and supply analysis assumes that it is). A change in employment conditions that encourages workers to work harder or to invest in improving their skills may have effects that differ from those that would occur in a market where the 'product' is unchanging.

A comprehensive minimum wage

Consider a minimum-wage law that, like the UK one, applies uniformly to all occupations. The occupations and the industries in which minimum wages are effective will be those paying the lowest wages. They will usually involve unskilled or, at best, semi-skilled labour. In most of them the workers will not be members of unions. Thus, the market structures in which minimum wages are likely to be most effective include both those in which competitive conditions obtain and those in which employers exercise monopsony power. The effects on employment are different in the two cases.

Competitive labour markets The consequences for employment of an effective minimum wage are unambiguous when the labour market is competitive and labour is homogeneous. By raising the wage that employers must pay, minimum-wage legislation leads to a reduction in the quantity of labour that is demanded and an increase in the quantity of labour that is supplied. As a result, the actual level of employment falls, and unemployment is generated.

This situation is exactly analogous to the one that arises when a union succeeds in setting a wage above the competitive equilibrium wage, as was illustrated in Figure 16.5. The excess supply of labour at the minimum wage also creates incentives for people to evade the law by working below the legal minimum wage.

In competitive labour markets, effective minimum-wage laws raise the wages of those who remain employed but also create some unemployment.

Monopsonistic labour markets By effectively flattening out the labour supply curve, a minimum-wage law can simultaneously increase both wages and employment in monopsonistic labour markets. The circumstances in which this can happen are the same as those in which a union that is facing a monopsonistic employer succeeds in setting a wage above the wage that the employer would otherwise pay, as was shown in Figure 16.6. Of course, if the minimum wage is raised above the competitive wage, employment will start to fall, as in the union case. When it is set at the competitive level, however, the minimum wage can protect workers against monopsony power *and* lead to increases in employment.

Evidence from North America

Empirical work on the effects of minimum-wage laws in North America, where they are commonly used, reflects these mixed theoretical predictions. There is some evidence that those who keep their jobs gain when the minimum wage is raised. There is also evidence that some groups suffer a decline in employment consistent with the effect of a minimum wage in a competitive market. At other times and places, there is evidence that both wages earned and employment rise when the minimum wage rises, as is consistent with monopolistic labour markets.

The gains and losses are not neatly segregated by group. Within any affected group, such as the young and inexperienced, those who keep their jobs gain while those who are unable to find work because of a high minimum wage lose. Supporters tend to stress the benefits to those who gain, while detractors stress the losses of those who suffer.

One worrying problem arises because critical job experience is gained from one's first job, particularly for those with minimum school training. Only part of a young inexperienced person's wage is in the form of money, the rest comes in the form of training. Those who have their first employment postponed because of the unemployment created by a minimum wage lose time before they get their critical first-job training. The long-term effects on these people can be serious. So, as with any group, the policy helps some and can seriously hurt other young and inexperienced workers.

Impact in the UK

It is still too early for a comprehensive assessment of the impact of the national minimum wage (NMW) in the UK; however, by the summer of 2002 no clear evidence had emerged of harmful effects on levels of employment. In part this is because the NMW was introduced at a time of generally rising demand for labour, so employment in most sectors continued to grow from 1999 to 2002. Only one sector showed a sharp decline in employment (clothing and footwear), and employment in this sector was already declining before the NMW was introduced. Indeed, the NMW may have encouraged more people to join the labour force, as female participation in the labour market rose significantly during the first two years of the NMW. At least initially, the NMW narrowed pay differentials between the highest and lowest paid, between men and women, and between regions of the country. The wage rates of about 1.3 million people, or around 5 per cent of the workforce, were raised as a result of the NMW.

While many academic studies will no doubt appear in future, a government report assessing the impact of the NMW after its first full year concluded:

The minimum wage has had a substantial impact in increasing the earnings of those in the bottom decile and removing the worst excesses of low pay. At the same time, the announcement and implementation of the NMW appears to have had minimal adverse impact on the aggregate levels of employment, unemployment, average earnings growth and inflation. Developments in the labour market appear to have continued to follow the underlying trends rather than responses to the NMW.[4]

Heterogeneity, incentives, and monitoring costs

In the first part of this chapter we studied the broad forces that create wage differentials between different groups of workers. For some purposes, it is a useful simplification to assume that workers of each type are identical individuals. But to understand other labour market issues, we need to recognize that no two workers are identical, while each can choose how to behave on the job. Labour market institutions evolve in subtle ways to cope with the following problems that arise from heterogeneity of employees and incomplete information about worker characteristics.

Heterogeneity Individuals differ from each other. They all respond to the same incentives, but they respond differently. Given the same wage, some will work harder than others; some have more ability than others; with the same amount of effort, some will produce more and get better results than others. This applies to all employees, whether working in production, design, planning, or supervision.

Asymmetric information Firms might like to reward good workers more than indifferent workers, but it is difficult to know one from the other in many work situations. Generally, workers know more about their effectiveness than does their employer.

Adverse selection We first met the problem of adverse selection in Chapter 13, where, faced with the same rates, high-risk persons were more inclined to take insurance than low-risk persons. In labour markets, a firm seeking to hire people usually advertises a particular job with an associated pay, or pay range. From the pool of those who meet the paper specifications, applicants are more likely to be lower-quality workers who find such a wage a good bargain than higher-quality workers who know they can get a better wage elsewhere. This would be no problem if the employer knew as much about his prospective employees as did the employees themselves. But this is an obvious case of asymmetric information. You know more about yourself —your work habits, and your strengths and weaknesses— than any outsider.

Costly monitoring It is difficult and costly for management to monitor its employees to find out how well each is contributing to the production process.

The principal–agent problem The management wishes to motivate employees to work in the firm's best interest, while employees often have different and conflicting motivations. Management would like to design incentive systems that motivate workers to provide the type of effort that the firm requires. This is the principal–agent problem that we first encountered in Chapter 14, where we used it to study the relationship between shareholders and senior management. Here we use the same theory to help us understand the relationship between senior management and all other employees.

Contracts and performance monitoring

When you purchase a haircut, you have a clear idea of what you expect to get and you can accurately judge the quality of the service you receive. When a firm hires a divisional manager, it knows that it wants good work, but it cannot say specifically what the manager should be doing at each

---

[4] *Government evidence to the Low Pay Commission*, December 2000, p. 42. Available on www.dti.gov.uk/er/nmw/evidence2000.pdf.

moment in her work day. Furthermore, it is not easy to judge how much of the division's subsequent performance will be due to the manager's efforts and how much to forces beyond the manager's control.

Many modern employment situations are better thought of as an ongoing relationship rather than as the equivalent of a purchase of a specific, exactly definable labour service. Hence employment contracts are often referred to as *relational contracts*. These contracts do not attempt to cover all of the many contingencies that could arise in a job. Instead, they set out general functions to be fulfilled in the post and leave the details to be decided by an evolving interaction between employer and employee. In many modern jobs it is not even desirable in principle to establish an exact job description, because the nature of the work is continually evolving. For example, as recently as the 1980s a secretary's job involved taking handwritten manuscripts and creating hard copy using a typewriter. Today the same job typically involves taking draft documents on a floppy disc and reformatting them using a word-processor package. Instead of typing memos, the secretary will now be sending email messages. A precise 1980 job description would have been a hindrance to needed changes.

Under relational contracts neither employer nor employee has an exact or agreed expectation of each other's detailed behaviour.

The firm does not know the marginal product of each employee. The employees do not know precisely what they need to do to get promoted and avoid being sacked. Neither workers nor firms can make accurate decisions based upon full information.

An obvious principal–agent problem that arises with relational contracts, from the perspective of the firm, is that employees have some range of discretion about how hard they work, and they may have objectives of their own that are different from those of the employer.

The firm (the principal) cannot monitor accurately the performance of many of its employees (the agents). It is often too costly even to try, and in many jobs it is impossible even if money were no object. In such circumstances, the firm needs to design mechanisms that will induce its employees to act in the firm's interests. In general, unless there is costly monitoring of the agents' behaviour, the problem cannot be completely solved.

Principal–agent analysis shows that, when employees have some range of discretion, their self-interested behaviour will make profits lower than in a 'perfect', frictionless world in which principals act as their own agents, or agents always do exactly what the principals want.

Much labour market behaviour that seems odd at first sight has evolved to deal—more or less effectively—with the principal–agent problem. For example, people put in positions of trust are often paid much more than is needed to induce them to take these jobs. Why should principals pay their agents more than they need to pay to fill the jobs? The explanation is that agents who are paid much more than they could earn in other jobs have an incentive not to violate the trust placed in them. If they do violate the trust and are caught, they lose the premium attached to the job.

Efficiency wages

The theory of competitive markets predicts that excess supply causes price to fall until the excess supply is eliminated —that is, until demand equals supply. Often this does not happen in labour markets. In the face of excess supply, firms do not typically cut wages, even though such a move would seem to enhance profits. Why?

Employers are worried about the quality and performance of the heterogeneous workers that they hire as well as their price. The wage that yields the best combination of price and quality of worker is known as the **efficiency wage**.

The theory of the *efficiency wage* helps to explain why it may be optimal for firms to set wages that are permanently above the level that would clear the labour market. Efficiency wage theory applies to hiring, to productivity on the job, and to worker turnover.

Efficiency in hiring Firms do not know the characteristics of specific workers until after they have sunk costs into hiring and training them. Good workers know who they are and are likely to have a higher reservation wage than bad workers. The reservation wage is the lowest wage at which a person is prepared to work for a particular firm. By lowering the wage that it offers, a firm will significantly lower the average ability of the workers who apply for its jobs. This tendency for a firm that pays lower wages to attract poor-quality workers is a case of adverse selection. As a result, paying lower wages can make the firm worse off.

In labour markets with informational asymmetries, where unobserved characteristics of workers are correlated with the reservation wage, it will generally be optimal for firms to pay wages that exceed their employees' reservation wages.

Productivity on the job If wages are so low that workers are just indifferent between staying and losing their job, they are unlikely to do more than the minimum required. Workers are likely to give greater effort if they feel they are being well rewarded. They will then expect to be much worse off if they lose their current job, and they will be aware of a queue of good-quality workers prepared to work for the high wage. The high wage improves on-the-job efficiency.

Minimizing turnover Many firms find that high quit rates are costly because they must invest in training their workers. Firms are thus reluctant to lower wages for existing workers, even in the face of an excess supply of labour. Workers who are already inside the company and know its work practices are worth retaining, even at premium wages. New workers, though possibly cheaper, may not be as good, and will be costly to train.

Efficiency wage theory says that firms will find it advantageous to pay high enough wages that working is a clearly superior alternative to being laid off. This will minimize labour turnover and improve the quality of workers' effort.

When considering the supply curve of labour, we saw that high wages may induce less work from workers who can choose their hours—because of an income effect that is stronger than the substitution effect (see page 118). High efficiency wages give the workers a different choice, which is to work hard for a high reward or not to work at all (or, perhaps, to work in another job at the much lower average wage). By posing an all-or-nothing choice, employers alleviate the disincentive effects of high wages. Workers who do not work hard enough risk losing their high-paying job. This *potential-loss-of-income effect* reinforces the substitution effect, and for many workers encourages them to adopt the hard-work/high-pay solution—at least among those who are fortunate enough to have this choice.

Signalling

Participants in markets with asymmetric information will develop informal criteria for signalling information about some of these unseen characteristics. Employers who pay a high efficiency wage signal that they are interested in high-quality staff and are prepared to pay them well. Educational qualifications provide a signal from potential employees. Hopefully your university degrees, or higher education certificate, will indicate that you have acquired some useful knowledge and skills. However, another important function of the degree you will acquire is to convince potential employers that you are ambitious, hard working, intelligent, and committed to self-improvement —just the kind of person that every employer is looking for! The degree creates a signal about your personal characteristics that is independent of the subject of the degree. In selection situations the signal about who you are may play as important a role as what you have learned.

Internal labour markets

Most manual and other unskilled workers have little or no expectation of advancement or even of long-term employment. They are often paid an hourly rate and have little job security. In contrast, many skilled manual workers, most white-collar workers, and virtually all technical, managerial, and professional staff have a long-term employment relationship, which provides a career path within the firm. Typically, there are limited entry points into the firm and most senior posts are filled by promotions from within the firm. These workers operate in what is known as an **internal labour market**, composed of a firm and its long-term employees; that is, the market is internal to the firm. Such a market has only limited connections with external labour markets, and its structure reflects the needs and traditions of each specific firm. The market offers a *job ladder* for the firm's long-term employees, with most employees starting somewhere near the bottom of the ladder and working their way up throughout their career.

Pay and promotion

Firms with internal labour markets do not generally try to assess their employees' marginal productivity and then pay them accordingly. Instead, they have a number of defined job grades with pay rates being attached to the job rather than to any individual's productivity. Individuals generally improve their pay by moving up the ladder of promotion. Good work in the current job has a potential payoff more in terms of promotion prospects than in terms of dramatically increased current pay.

There are at least three reasons why internal labour markets may be more efficient than tying individuals' pay to their individual performance. First, most of the covered jobs involve a great deal of learning. A long-term employment relationship, with a potential for promotion, creates an incentive for employees to invest in acquiring skills that will benefit the firm. These firm-specific skills will take time to acquire and will take even longer to generate a payoff to the firm. Hence to achieve the benefits of this learning effect, firms have to offer the prospect of both long-term employment and future promotion.

The second reason why internal labour markets may be efficient derives from efficiency wage theory. The incentives for good performance built into the efficiency wage require a long-term employment relationship. The 'good' workers are attracted to the firm by high rewards and also by a commitment on the part of the firm to a high degree of employment stability and 'good prospects'. Hence both employees and employer are likely to generate a more productive relationship via mutual longer-term commitment, than via temporary employment contracts and minimal mutual commitment.

The third factor supporting internal labour markets is that successful firms require long-term strategic thinking from their senior staff. The ability to take and implement long-term strategies is not something that shows up or can be tested over a short horizon. Hence successful firms have significant numbers of senior managers who have been selected as a result of observing their performance within the company, and who have sufficient expectation of continuing employment that they are prepared to take a long-term view. A manager who does not expect to stay with a firm very long may postpone important investments, while one who sees his own future as tied to the success of the firm will want to ensure its continued survival.

The internal labour market increases the convergence of interests between the employee and the firm, thereby reducing principal–agent problems.

Tournaments

One way to think of an internal labour market is as a *tournament*. Workers enter the tournament when they join a firm on the lower rungs of the ladder. Workers at each level compete with each other to show the senior management that they are most worthy of promotion. Periodically, when a more senior job becomes vacant, someone from the grade immediately below the vacant post is chosen to progress up the ladder. As there are fewer senior jobs than junior jobs, not everybody can progress up the ladder at the same pace. The winner of the tournament is the one who reaches the post of chief executive.

In an internal labour market tournament the pay of senior executives is as much about motivating everybody in the organization as it is about paying a 'fair' compensation for the incumbent of a specific post. The £1 million salary paid to a chief executive officer (CEO) may be more

important in terms of motivating junior staff to strive to rise to that exalted post than in terms of rewarding the current CEO for his efforts. Even though those who enter a golf or tennis tournament know that they cannot all win, tournaments offering the greatest prize to the winner still attract the best players and tend to bring out the best in them. The issue of CEO pay is discussed further in Box 16.3.

The tournament structure of rewards has three advantages for firms. First, when a candidate is selected for promotion, only enough information is needed to make relative judgements among potential candidates—no absolute or detailed performance measures are needed. This economizes on the need to acquire costly information, which may in any case be unreliable.

The second advantage is that pay ranges are set in advance for each job, so time is not wasted on individual pay negotiations with each and every employee. An employee who wants more pay must work for a promotion. So bargaining time is saved. Equally, there is no incentive for employers to argue about performance in order to avoid having to pay bonuses.

The third advantage is that tournaments reduce the problems of asymmetric information. Employees who are chosen for promotion from within the firm will have become well known to their superiors, and so there will be little uncertainty about their characteristics. Equally, employees who are promoted already know a great deal about the functioning of the company, so they can become

---

 Box 16.3 CEO pay—fat cats or optimal incentives?

Can chief executives of large companies possibly be 'worth' their very large salaries? Multi-million dollar salaries are not uncommon in the United States, as are salaries of £1m or more for UK chief executives and chairmen. Some people believe that these high salaries for British and American CEOs are an inefficiency caused by the principal–agent problem. In this view, CEOs have escaped shareholders' control. Their high pay is evidence that shareholders are being ripped off. If this were true, the solution would be either to give genuinely independent non-CEOs more power in setting compensation, or to give shareholders a vote on CEO pay. There are good economic reasons, however, why high payments to CEOs are needed for the incentives they create within the company. There are three elements to the incentive issue.

One is the tournament model of internal incentives. High pay for CEOs provides an incentive for all the workers in the firm to aspire to the top job. Hence the pay is not justified solely by the performance of the specific incumbent CEO: rather, it is desirable for the extra effort it motivates from those who have any serious prospects of eventually becoming CEO. For them, high CEO pay may increase loyalty and the ambition to achieve promotion.

The second element is that the CEO does have to be motivated by his rewards, because there is no further promotion available. Hence, while

middle-managers may be motivated partly by the prospect of moving up the promotion ladder, the CEO needs other motivation.

The third element relates to the incentives to take risks. If employees are risk-averse, they will take the safe option rather than take a chance of being fired for making a risky decision that goes wrong. However, in a modern dynamic economy, firms need to be at least risk-neutral, if not risk-taking. This means that CEOs need an incentive to take risks in the interest of the long-term health of the company. One way to encourage them to do this is to offer a reward if risk-taking pays off, while imposing no penalty when failures occur. Just such a reward profile is offered by share options. These options become valuable if the company's shares rise in value, but carry no cost to the CEO if the options expire worthless. Share options may encourage senior executives to take risks. A significant proportion of CEO compensation does involve just such incentives. (See also Box 14.3 on page 240.)

One further important use of employment-contingent options to buy shares in the future is to bind managers to the firm. A young firm in a dynamic industry may not be able to pay its executives a large current salary. It thus risks their leaving, taking their firm-specific experience with them. As well as providing an incentive to take risks, options to buy the firm's shares in the future reduce a manager's incentive to leave for a higher-paying job. After all, the stock options become worthless when the individual leaves.

effective in their new position more quickly than would be likely with an outsider.

The promotion path in an internal labour market can be thought of as a tournament in which higher pay rates in more senior jobs create an incentive for employees to progress up the career ladder.

Seniority and MRP

The incentive issues discussed above suggest that, where there is a long-term relationship between firm and workers, firms will find it efficient to reward loyalty and long service. Hence it will generally be true that longer-serving workers will get higher rewards than younger workers. The rewards for long service will come via higher wages and company pension schemes, which will naturally reward long service with a higher pension. A pension can be thought of as deferred wages.

The need to reward long service means that on average there is a cross-subsidy passing from young workers, who get less than their current marginal revenue products, to older workers, who get more. However, the young workers have the encouragement of knowing that they themselves will eventually benefit from this cross-subsidy when they become older workers. Thus, *ceteris paribus*, expectations of lifetime earnings will be the same for both groups.

Conclusion

Labour is the most important input into any modern firm. A hundred years ago it was mainly the manual effort of workers that was being hired. Today, however, the vast majority of workers are hired not for their physical strength, but for their mental skills. Today brain power rather than muscle power drives business success.

Brain power is a much more complicated input to manage than was muscle power. The mental ability of potential new employees is difficult to assess and the effort of brain workers is hard to monitor accurately. Yet the success of a firm in the long term depends crucially upon selecting, keeping, and motivating a stock of brain power. The institutions and practices discussed in this section have evolved to provide the structure within which a company's most talented employees are nurtured, motivated, and developed.

SUMMARY

Wage differentials

- Equilibrium wage differentials can arise between jobs because (a) each requires different degrees of physical or mental abilities, (b) each requires different amounts of human capital acquired through costly formal education or on-the-job training, (c) some jobs are closed to people who could fill them as a result of discrimination, and (d) the markets for the types of worker needed in different jobs have different competitive structures.

- In perfectly competitive input markets, wages are set by demand and supply and there is no unemployment in equilibrium. In monopsonistic markets wages and employment are less than their competitive levels, but there is no unemployment in equilibrium.

- If a union enters a perfectly competitive market, it can raise wages above the competitive level at the cost of lowering employment and creating a pool of people who would like to work at the union wage but cannot. If a union enters a monopsonistic labour market, it can raise wages *and* employment to the competitive level. If it raises wages beyond that point, employment will fall.

- Unions and professional associations can sometimes restrict the supply of labour and thereby achieve wages above the competitive equilibrium without creating a pool of unemployed.

- Minimum-wage laws have a similar effect to the setting of wages by unions. If the market was monopsonistic before the minimum wage is imposed, both wages and employment can be raised. If it was competitive, wages can be raised only at the expense of increased unemployment.

Heterogeneity, incentives, and monitoring costs

- Today's labour markets are complicated by the fact that brainpower is extremely heterogeneous, but it is hard for employers to discern the full characteristics of individual workers.

- Many employment contracts are relational contracts, which do not specify in detail what workers have to do. This creates the potential for principal–agent problems, where the hired employees act, in part, in their own interest rather than that of the employer.

- Solutions to the principal–agent problem involve some combination of incentives and monitoring.

- Most skilled, managerial, and professional workers now find themselves in internal labour markets that have some of the characteristics of a tournament. Here the main incentive for lower and middle-ranking staff is to achieve promotion. Higher pay generally attaches to more senior jobs, and the competition to gain promotion can be thought of as a tournament.

TOPICS FOR REVIEW

- Causes of equilibrium wage differentials
- Human capital
- Formal education and on-the-job training
- Wage differentials due to departure from perfect competition on the demand and the supply sides of labour markets

- Relational contracts
- Principal–agent problems in labour markets
- Efficiency wages
- Signalling in the labour market
- Internal and tournament labour markets

DISCUSSION QUESTIONS

1 Using the MRP data and the supply curve of labour from learning exercises 2 and 3 of Chapter 15, calculate how many workers would be hired and what wage would be paid if the hiring firm were a profit-maximizing monopsonist.

2 How would the outcome in question 1 differ if the monopsonist could price-discriminate and pay each worker the minimum wage at which he or she would work?

3 How would the outcome in question 1 change if a trade union were able to impose a going wage of £500 per week for all workers?

4 Why are wage rates not equal in different jobs even in equilibrium?

5 What would be the effect on carpenters' wages of (a) a rise in the demand for houses and (b) a fall in the wages of bricklayers?

6 What are the main differences between labour markets and markets for homogeneous commodities?

7 How does the efficiency wage help to solve the problems of recruitment, monitoring, and retention?

8 In what ways is the principal–agent problem manifested in employment relationships, and what measures are available to ameliorate the problem?

9 How does asymmetric information affect labour hiring decisions, and what role might signalling play in this process?

10 What is different about an internal labour market (compared with the goods markets that we have studied earlier in this book)?

Chapter 17

CAPITAL AND NATURAL RESOURCES

After studying human resources, we now turn to physical resources. How do firms decide how much capital equipment they need? How fast should we utilize non-renewable natural resources? Can the market be left alone to allocate these resources optimally? These are some of the questions we address in this chapter. In particular, you will learn that:

• In order to evaluate capital investments, firms need to calculate the present value of the income stream generated.

• Firms will invest up to the point where the present value of the increase in revenue is just equal to the present value of the cost.

• The socially optimal rate of usage of a completely non-renewable resource occurs when its price rises at a rate equal to the rate of interest. Rising prices of non-renewable resources act as a conservation device.

• The market mechanism will not always deliver the socially optimal rate of usage, so some government intervention or co-ordination may be needed.

Resources that can be replaced, either by being manufactured, as is the case with machines, or by reproducing themselves, as do people or fish, are called **renewable resources.** Resources that cannot be replaced, such as fossil fuels, are called **non-renewable** or **exhaustible resources.** Physical capital and non-renewable resources are similar inputs in that each is a stock of valuable things that gets used up in the process of producing goods and services. They are different in that physical capital can be replaced while non-renewable resources cannot. A new machine can always be created to replace one that wears out, but when a barrel of oil is used there is a permanent reduction in the world's total stock of oil.

Capital

The capital stock consists of all those produced goods that are used in the production of other goods and services. Factories, machines, tools, computers, roads, bridges, houses, and railways are a few examples. Because capital is a produced input, it is a renewable resource.

The pure return on capital

For a firm, the decision to invest in capital will be guided by whether the extra revenue that the capital generates justifies the cost.[1] To calculate the *return on capital*, we take the receipts from the sale of the output that the capital helps to make and subtract all variable costs of production. This gives us the **gross return on capital.**[2] It is convenient to divide this gross return into four components using concepts defined in Chapter 8 (see pages 131–4).

1. *Depreciation* is an allowance for the decrease in the value of a capital good over time resulting from its use in production and its obsolescence. Depreciation is often assumed to occur at a constant rate.

2. The *pure return on capital* is the amount that capital could earn in a riskless investment in equilibrium. When expressed as a return per £1 worth of capital invested, the result is called the **pure rate of interest.**

3. The *risk premium* compensates the owners for the actual risks of the enterprise.

4. *Pure* or *economic profit* is the residual after all other deductions have been made from the gross return. It may be positive, negative, or zero.

---

[1] Households and governments may have slightly different reasons for investing, but firms can be assumed to wish to maximize profits.
[2] This simplified example assumes that capital is the only fixed input.

The *gross return* on capital is the sum of these four items. The *net return* is the sum of the last three—that is, the gross return minus depreciation.

In a competitive economy positive and negative pure profits are a signal that resources should be reallocated, because earnings exceed opportunity costs in some lines of production and fall short of costs elsewhere. Economic profits thus occur only in disequilibrium.

To study the return to capital in its simplest form, we consider an economy that is in equilibrium with respect to the allocation of existing resources between their possible uses. Thus, economic profits are zero in every productive activity. This does not mean that the owners of capital get nothing; it means only that the gross return to capital does not include an element signalling the need to reallocate resources. The *equilibrium* net return on capital is the sum of components 2 and 3 above minus component 1.

To simplify things further at the outset, we deal with a world of perfect certainty: everyone knows what the return to an existing new unit of capital will be in any of its possible uses. Since there is no risk, the gross return to capital does not include a risk premium.

We have now simplified to the point where the net return to capital is all pure return (item 2 on the above list), while the gross return is pure return plus depreciation (items 1 and 2). We are interested in what determines this pure return on capital. This is the return that varies from time to time and from place to place under the influence of economic forces. Broadly speaking, it will be determined by the overall balance between saving and investment in the economy as a whole. Risk and disequilibrium differentials are merely additions to that pure return.[3]

Implications of durability

Next we consider an important issue that arises because capital is durable—a machine or a factory building lasts for years. To understand this, it is helpful to think of a capital good's lifetime as being divided into short periods that we refer to as production periods, or rental periods. The present time is the current period; future time is one, two, three (etc.) periods hence.

The durability of capital goods makes it necessary to distinguish between the capital good itself and the flow of services that it provides in a given production period. A firm could, for example, rent a building for some period of time, or it could buy the building outright. This distinction is just a particular instance of the general distinction between flows and stocks that we first encountered in Box 3.1 on page 40. Here we are interested in capital investment decisions, but Box 17.1 discusses some of these issues as they apply to labour.

If a firm hires a piece of capital equipment for some period of time—for example one lorry for one month—it

---

 Box 17.1 The rental and purchase price of labour

If you wish to farm a piece of land, you can buy it yourself, or you can rent it for a specific period of time. If you want to set up a small business, you can buy your office and equipment, or you can rent them. The same is true for all capital and all land; a firm often has the option of either buying or renting.

Exactly the same would be true for labour if we lived in a slave society. You could buy a slave to be your assistant, or you could rent the services either of someone else's slave or of a free person. Fortunately, slavery is illegal throughout most of today's world. As a result, the labour markets that we know deal only in the services of labour; we do not go to a labour market to *buy* a worker, only to hire his or her services.

You can, however, buy the services of a labourer for a long period of time. In professional sports, multi-year contracts are common, and ten-year contracts are not unknown. The late Herbert von Karajan was made conductor for life of the Berlin Philharmonic Orchestra. Publishers sometimes tie up their authors in multi-book contracts, and film and television production firms often sign up their actors on long-term contracts. In all cases of such *personal service contracts*, the person is not a slave, because his or her personal rights and liberties are protected by law. The purchaser of the long-term contract is none the less buying ownership of the person's services for an extended period of time. The price of the contract will reflect the person's expected earnings over the contract's lifetime. If the contract is transferable, the owner can sell these services for a lump sum or rent them out for some period. As with land and capital goods, the price paid for this *stock* of labour services depends on the expected rental prices over the contract period.

---

pays a price for the privilege. If the firm buys the lorry outright, it pays a different (and higher) price for the purchase. Consider in turn each of these prices.

Rental price

The *rental price of capital* is the amount that a firm pays to obtain the services of a capital good for a given period of time. The rental price of one week's use of a piece of capital is analogous to the weekly wage rate that is the price of hiring the services of labour.

Just as a profit-maximizing firm operating in competitive markets continues to hire labour until its marginal revenue product (MRP) equals its wage, so the firm will go on hiring capital until its MRP equals its rental price, which we call R. Since in a competitive market all firms will face the same rental price, all firms that are in equilibrium will have the same MRP of each type of capital.

---

[3] We are implicitly assuming a constant price level. Under inflationary conditions we need to distinguish the nominal return on capital, where everything is measured in nominal monetary units, from the real return, where nominal values are deflated by a price index. This distinction is discussed in Chapter 3.

A capital good may also be used by the firm that owns it. In this case the firm does not pay out any rental fee. However, the rental price is the amount that the firm could charge if it leased its capital to another firm. It is thus the *opportunity cost* to the firm of using the capital good itself. This rental price is the *implicit* price which reflects the value to the firm of the services of its own capital that it uses during the current production period.

Whether the firm pays the rental price explicitly or calculates it as an implicit cost of using its own capital, the profit-maximizing firm will hire capital up to the point where the rental price of a capital good is just equal to its marginal revenue product.

Purchase price

The price that a firm pays to buy a capital good, say a machine, is the *purchase price of capital*. When a firm buys such a machine outright, it obtains the machine's expected marginal revenue product over its lifetime. The firm's willingness to buy the machine is, naturally enough, related to the value that it places now on this stream of *expected* receipts over future time-periods, compared with the cost of the machine.

The term 'expected' emphasizes that the firm is usually uncertain about the prices at which it will be able to sell its outputs in the future. For the sake of simplicity, we assume that the firm knows the future MRPs.

Present value of future returns

Let us put capital goods aside for a short while and ask how a firm values income in the future compared with income today. This question is relevant to the issue of how to value bonds and shares as well as to the issue of how much capital firms should install.

How much is an asset that generates a particular income stream in the future worth *now*? How much would someone be willing to pay now to buy the right to receive that flow of future payments? The answer is called that asset's *present value*. In general, **present value** (PV) refers to the value *now* of one or more payments to be received *in the future*.

Present value of a single future payment

One period hence Let us start with the simplest possible case. How much would a firm be prepared to pay *now* to purchase an asset that will produce a single payment of £100 in one year's time? One way to approach this question is to ask how much the firm would have to lend out in order to have £100 a year from now. Suppose for the moment that the interest rate is 5 per cent, which means that £1.00 invested today will be worth £1.05 in one year's time.[4]

If we use PV to stand for this unknown amount, we can write $PV(1.05) = £100$. (The left-hand side of this equation means PV multiplied by 1.05.) Thus, $PV = £100/1.05 = £95.24$. This tells us that the present value of £100 receivable in one year's time is £95.24 when the interest rate is 5 per cent: anyone who lends out £95.24 for one year at 5 per cent interest will get back £95.24 plus £4.76 in interest, which makes £100 in total. When we calculate this present value, the interest rate is used to *discount* (i.e. reduce to its present value) the £100 to be received one year hence. The maximum price that a firm would be willing to pay for this asset is £95.24 (assuming that the interest rate relevant to the firm is 5 per cent).

To see why, let us start by assuming that the firm is offered the asset at some other price. Say that it is offered at £98. If, instead of paying this amount for the asset, a firm lends its £98 out at 5 per cent interest, it would have at the end of one year more than the £100 that the asset will yield. (At 5 per cent interest, £98 yields £4.90 in interest, which, together with the principal, makes £102.90.) Clearly, no profit-maximizing firm would pay £98—or, by the same reasoning, any sum in excess of £95.24—for the asset. It could do better by using its funds in other ways.

Now suppose that the good is offered for sale at £90. A firm could borrow £90 to buy the asset and would pay £4.50 in interest on its loan. At the end of the year, the asset yields £100. When this is used to repay the £90 loan and the £4.50 in interest, £5.50 is left as profit to the firm. Clearly it would be worthwhile for a profit-maximizing firm to buy the asset at a price of £90 or, by the same argument, at any price less than £95.24.

The actual present value that we have calculated depended on our assuming that the interest rate was 5 per cent. What if the interest rate is 7 per cent? At that interest rate, the present value of the £100 receivable in one year's time would be $£100/1.07 = £93.46$.

These examples are easy to generalize. In both cases we have found the present value by dividing the sum that is receivable in the future by 1 plus the rate of interest.[5] In general, the present value of £R one year hence at an interest rate of i per year is

$$PV = \frac{R}{(1+i)}. \tag{1}$$

Several periods hence The next step is to ask what would happen if the sum were receivable at a later date. What, for example, is the present value of £100 to be received *two* years hence when the interest rate is 5 per cent? This is $£100/(1.05 \times 1.05) = £90.70$. We can check this by seeing

---

[4] The analysis in the rest of this chapter assumes *annual* compounding of interest.

[5] Notice that in this type of formula the interest rate, i, is expressed as a decimal fraction; for example, 7 per cent is expressed as 0.07, so $(1+i)$ equals 1.07.

Box 17.2 **The future value of a present sum**

In the text we have concentrated on the present value of amounts to be received in the future. We can, however, turn the question around and ask, 'What is the future value of an amount of money that is available in the present?'

Assume that you have £100 available to you today. What will that sum be worth next year? If you lend it out at 5 per cent, you will have £105 in one year. Letting *PV* stand for the sum you have now and *FV* for the value of the sum in the future, we have $FV = PV(1.05)$ in this case. Writing the interest rate as we have in the text, we get

$$FV = PV(1 + i).$$

If we divide through by $(1 + i)$, we get equation (1) in the text. (In the text we denote the future value by *R*.)

Next, if we let the sum build up by reinvesting the interest each year, we get

$$FV = PV(1 + i)^t.$$

If we divide both sides by $(1 + i)^t$, we get equation (2) in the text.

This tells us that what we did in the text is reversible. If we have an amount of money today, we can figure out what it will be worth if it is invested at compounded interest for some number of future periods. Similarly, if we are going to have some amount of money at some future date, we can figure out how much we would need to invest today to get that amount at the specified date in the future.

Our argument tells us that the two sums, *PV* and *FV*, are linked by the compound interest expression $(1 + i)^t$. To go from the present to the future, we *multiply PV* by the interest expression, and to go from the future to the present we *divide FV* by the interest expression.

The so-called 'Rule of 72' is a convenient way of going from *PV* to *FV* by finding out how long it takes for *FV* to become twice the size of *PV* at any given interest rate. According to this rule, the time it takes for any amount to double in size is given approximately by $72/100i$. So, for example, if *i* is 0.1 (an interest rate of 10 per cent), any present sum doubles in value in $72/10 = 7.2$ years.

what would happen if £90.70 were lent out for two years. In the first year the loan would earn an interest of $(0.05)(£90.70) = £4.54$, and so after one year the firm would receive £95.24. In the second year the interest would be earned on this entire amount; interest earned in the second year would equal $(0.05)(£95.24) = £4.76$. Therefore in two years the firm would have £100. (The payment of interest in the second year on the interest income earned in the first year is known as *compound interest*.)

In general, the present value of £*R* after *t* years at *i* per cent is

$$PV = \frac{R}{(1 + i)^t}. \qquad (2)$$

All that this formula does is discount the sum, *R*, by the interest rate, *i*, repeatedly, once for each of the *t* periods that must pass until the sum becomes available. If we look at the formula, we see that the higher is *i* or *t*, the bigger is the whole term $(1 + i)^t$. This term, however, appears in the denominator, so *PV* is *negatively* related to both *i* and *t*.

The formula $PV = R/(1 + i)^t$ shows that the present value of a given sum payable in the future will be smaller the more distant the payment date and the higher the rate of interest.

Present value of a stream of future payments

Now consider the present value of a stream of receipts that continues indefinitely.[6] At first glance that PV might seem very high, because the total amount received grows without reaching any limit as time passes. The previous section suggests, however, that people will not value the far-distant money payments very highly.

To find the PV of £100 a year, payable for ever, we ask how much you would have to invest now, at an interest rate of *i* per cent per year, to obtain £100 each year. This is simply $iPV = £100$, where *i* is the interest rate and *PV* the investment required. Dividing through by *i* shows the present value of the stream of £100 a year for ever to be

$$PV = \frac{£100}{i}. \qquad (3)$$

For example, if the interest rate were 10 per cent, the present value would be £1,000. This merely says that £1,000 invested at 10 per cent will yield £100 per year, for ever. Notice that, as in the previous sections, PV is negatively related to the rate of interest: the higher the interest rate, the less is the present value of the stream of future payments.

In the text we have concentrated on finding the present value of amounts available in the future. Box 17.2 reverses the process and discusses the future value of sums available in the present.

Implications for firms' desire to invest in capital

Firms will want to invest in capital so long as it offers a return that is at least as good as could be achieved by investing a similar sum of money at the going market interest rate. Equivalently, if firms are borrowing the funds to finance the investment, they will want to purchase capital that offers a return in terms of revenue that exceeds the

---

[6] Some government securities, known as 'perpetuities', have the characteristic that they pay out a specific sum at regular intervals with no terminal (or maturity) date.

cost of the loan. Clearly, the costs of the capital and the revenues that arise from using the capital will accrue at different points in time. In order to compare payments and receipts at different points in time, the firm simply calculates the present value of the extra revenues and deducts the present value of the costs. This gives the **net present value** of the investment project.

Profit-maximizing firms should undertake any investment project for which the net present value is positive, as this means that it is increasing the present value of profits and thus adding value to the firm. On the very plausible assumption that firms are faced with diminishing returns to capital, firms will invest up to the point where the net present value of investment is zero. Beyond this point, further investment is adding more to the present value of costs than to the present value of revenues, and thus is lowering the value of the firm.

Firms will undertake projects that have a positive net present value.

Investment decisions are very important for firms, so we now look in more detail at the investment decisions for profit-maximizing firms and what this implies for demand for capital.

Equilibrium of the firm

When putting a present value on future income flows, each firm will discount these flows at a rate that reflects its own opportunity cost of capital, often called its *internal rate of discount*. With perfect capital markets in which the firm can borrow all that it needs, the internal rate of discount will equal the market rate of interest (suitably adjusted for risk in each case). The evidence suggests, however, that most firms do not face perfect capital markets and have internal rates of return that exceed market rates. They thus have internal rates of discount that exceed the relevant market rate of interest. The general points made in the text are not affected by this complication, as long as i is interpreted in each case to mean the 'appropriate rate of discount'. In what follows we assume, for simplicity, that firms face perfect capital markets so that the internal rate of discount is equal to the market rate of interest.

In adjusting to market forces, an individual firm faces a given interest rate and given purchase prices of capital goods. The firm can vary the quantity of capital that it employs, and as a result the marginal revenue product of its capital varies. The law of diminishing returns tells us that the more capital the firm uses, the lower is its capital's MRP.

The decision to purchase capital

A firm is deciding whether or not to add to its capital stock. It can borrow (and lend) money at an interest rate of, say,

10 per cent per year. The first thing the firm needs to do is to estimate the expected marginal revenue product of the new piece of capital over its lifetime—for example, the addition to revenue generated by the extra output in each period of time made possible by installing the extra machine. Then it discounts this at the appropriate rate, 10 per cent in this example, to find the present value of that stream of receipts the machine will create.[7] Let us say it is £5,000.

The present value, by construction, tells us how much the flow of future receipts is worth today. If the firm can buy the machine for less than the PV *of the extra revenue stream it generates*, the machine is a good buy. If it must pay more, it is not worth buying.

It is always worthwhile for a firm to buy another unit of capital whenever the present value of the stream of future MRPs that the capital provides exceeds its purchase price.

The size of the firm's capital stock

The MRP of each addition to the firm's capital stock is likely to decline as the amount of capital is increased. The firm will go on adding to its capital stock until the *present value* of the flow of MRPs conferred by the last unit added is equal to the purchase price of that unit. The firm then has its equilibrium amount of capital.

The equilibrium capital stock of the firm is such that the present value of the stream of net income that is provided by the marginal unit of capital is equal to its purchase price.

This is yet another example of the condition that, for equilibrium, marginal cost will equal marginal revenue.

Now let the firm be in equilibrium with respect to its capital stock and ask what would cause it to buy more capital. Given the price of the machines, anything that increases the present value of the flow of income that the machines produce will have that effect. Two things will do this job. First, the MRPs of the capital may rise. That will happen, for example, if technological changes make capital more productive so that each unit produces more than before. (This possibility is dealt with later in the chapter.) Second, the interest rate may fall, causing an increase in the present value of any given stream of future MRPs. For example, suppose that next year's MRP is £1,000. This has a PV of £909.09 when the interest rate is 10 per cent and £952.38 when the interest rate falls to 5 per cent.

---

[7] Suppose that the machine has an MRP of £1,000 each period. First, suppose the machine only lasts one period. The present value is then £1,000. Next, suppose it lasts two periods. The PV is then £1,000 + £1,000/1.10 = £1,909.09. If it lasts three periods, the PV is £1,000 + £1,000/1.10 + £1,000/(1.10)^2 = £2,735.53; and so on. Each additional period that it lasts produces an MRP of £1,000, but at a more and more distant date, so that the *present value* of that period's revenue gets smaller owing to heavier discounting.

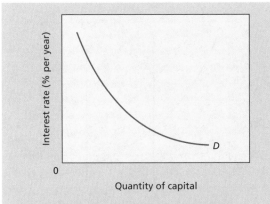

Figure 17.1 The firm's demand curve for capital

The firm's desired capital stock is negatively related to the rate of interest. The lower the interest rate, the higher is the present value of any given stream of marginal revenue products, and hence the more capital the firm will wish to use.

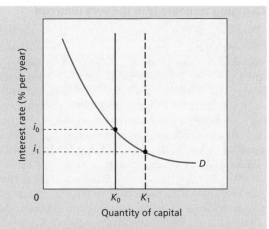

Figure 17.2 The equilibrium interest rate

In the short run the interest rate equates the demand for capital with its fixed supply. The economy's desired capital stock is negatively related to the interest rate, as shown by the curve D. In the short run, when the stock is K_0, the equilibrium interest rate is i_0. When the capital stock grows to K_1 in the long run, the equilibrium interest rate falls to i_1.

So when the interest rate falls, the firm will wish to add to its capital stock. It will go on doing so until the decline in the MRPs of successive additions to its capital stock, according to the law of diminishing returns, reduces the present value of the MRP, at the new lower rate of interest, to the purchase price of the capital.

The size of a firm's desired capital stock increases when the rate of interest falls, and it decreases when the rate of interest rises.

This relationship is shown in Figure 17.1. It can be considered as the firm's demand curve for capital plotted against the interest rate. It shows how the desired stock of capital varies with the interest rate. (It is sometimes called the *marginal efficiency of capital curve*.)

Equilibrium for the whole economy

The term **capital stock** refers to some aggregate amount of capital. The *firm's capital stock* has an MRP, showing the net increase in the firm's revenue when another unit of capital is added to its existing capital stock. The *economy's capital stock* can also be thought of as having a marginal revenue product; this is the addition to total national output (GDP) that is caused by adding another unit of capital to the economy's total stock. This capital stock also has an average product, which is total output divided by the total capital stock (i.e. the amount of output per unit of capital).

The same analysis that we used for one firm in the previous section applies to the whole economy. The lower the rate of interest, the higher is the desired stock of capital that all firms will wish to hold. Such a curve is shown as the economy's demand curve in Figure 17.2.

Short-run equilibrium

In the short run the economy's capital stock is given, but for the economy as a whole the interest rate is variable.[8] Whereas the firm reaches equilibrium by altering its capital stock, the whole economy reaches equilibrium through variations in the interest rate.

For the economy as a whole, the condition that the present value of the MRPs should equal the price of capital goods determines the equilibrium interest rate.

Let us see how this comes about. If the price of capital were less than the present value of its stream of future MRPs, it would be worthwhile for all firms to borrow money to invest in capital. For the economy as a whole, however, the stock of capital cannot be changed quickly. As a result, the main effect of this demand to borrow would be to push up the interest rate until the present value of the MRP equals the price of a unit of capital goods. Conversely, if the price of capital is above its present value, no one would wish to borrow money to invest in capital, and the rate of interest would fall. This too is illustrated in Figure 17.2.

Accumulation of capital in the long run

In an economy with positive saving, more capital is accumulated over time and the stock of capital grows slowly. As this happens, the MRP falls. This will cause the equilibrium interest rate to fall over time, as is also shown in Figure 17.2.

---

[8] We know that the central bank sets the short-term nominal interest rate; however, we are talking here about long-term real interest rates. These are set by market forces, and are the rates relevant for long-term investment decisions.

Changing technology in the very long run

In the very long run technology changes. As a result the capital stock becomes more productive as the old, obsolete capital is replaced by newer, more efficient capital. This shifts the MRP curve outward, which in turn tends to increase the equilibrium interest rate associated with any particular size of the capital stock. This, of course, is also the equilibrium return on capital. However, the accumulation of capital moves the economy downward to the right along any given MRP curve, and that tends to lower the return on capital associated with any one MRP curve. The net effect on the return on capital of both of these changes may be to raise it, to lower it, or to leave it unchanged, as shown in Figure 17.3. The very-long-run effects of changing technology, combined with a growing capital stock, are studied further in Chapter 22.

So we see that the income going to owners of capital is the pure rate of return (multiplied by the amount of capital in use), plus a risk premium, plus any pure profits or minus any pure losses. The pure return serves to allocate capital to its most productive uses. All uses that yield more than the pure rate of return (plus any necessary risk premium) will be exploited; all uses that earn less than the pure rate will not be taken up.

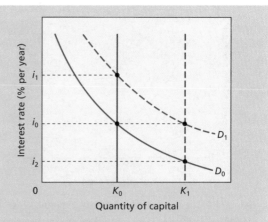

Figure 17.3 Changes in technology and the capital stock

Increases in technological knowledge and in the capital stock have opposing effects on the interest rate. The original demand curve D_0 and capital stock K_0 produce an interest rate of i_0. Technological improvements shift the desired capital stock curve to D_1 and, with a constant stock of capital, would raise the interest rate to i_1. However, the capital stock increases to K_1, which *ceteris paribus* would lower the interest rate to i_2. In the figure the two effects exactly offset each other, and the interest rate remains unchanged at i_0, where K_1 and D_1 intersect.

Non-renewable resources

The world's minerals and fossil fuels are examples of non-renewable resources; the total amount in existence is fixed. However, since some of the world's total stock is as yet undiscovered, the *known* stock of each resource is not fixed over time. New discoveries increase the known stock, and current use reduces it.

Are we exhausting our supply of non-renewable resources too quickly? Some people advocate conserving more of our resources to pass on to our children and grandchildren. Others are willing to let future generations take care of themselves. 'After all,' they argue, 'they will be richer than we are in any case.'

How does the price system regulate the use of a non-renewable resource? Does it lead to overly rapid exploitation? Does it lead to too much conservation of a resource, which may in any case be rendered less useful by future technological change?

Determining the rate of extraction

To focus on the basic issues, it helps to begin with a few simplifying assumptions. First, assume that all the petroleum in existence has already been discovered, so that every unit that is used permanently diminishes the stock by one unit. Second, assume that many different firms own the land that contains the oil supply, so that each must accept the world price as given. Third, assume that their current extraction costs are virtually zero. They have invested money in discovering the oil, drilling wells, and laying pipelines. All they have to do now is turn their taps on, and the oil flows at any desired rate to the petroleum markets.

The last two of these assumptions are close to reality for the oil industry. Although large groups of producers, such as OPEC, can influence the price of oil by agreeing to alter the rate of current production, no one producer has that kind of market power—and even OPEC's power is quite limited over any longish period of time. Also, most of the costs of producing oil are incurred discovering fields, proving them, drilling wells, and building such transport facilities as pipelines and oil ports. Once all this has been done, the variable cost of producing another barrel from established fields is quite small. The only one of our three assumptions that is far from the mark for oil is that the total existing supply has already been discovered and developed. As we will see, much new oil is continually being discovered. This has important consequences, but to understand them we need first to see what happens with any non-renewable resource whose total supply is already known and available for current production.

Optimal firm behaviour

What should each firm do if it wishes to maximize its profits? It could extract all of its oil in a great binge of production this year, or it could husband the resource for some future rainy day and produce nothing this year. In practice, it is likely to adopt some intermediate policy, producing and selling some oil this year and holding stocks of it in the ground for extraction in future years. But *how much* should it extract this year and *how much* should it carry over for future years?

Its profit-maximizing course of action depends on three things: the current market price, the price the firm expects to rule next year, and the interest rate. Let us see why. Each firm can do two things with its oil. It can leave it in the ground to be available for extraction next year; if the price rises next year, the firm will have gained the difference between the current price and next year's price. Or it can extract and sell the oil at the current price, yielding revenue this year. How does the firm compare these two amounts, one earned now and one available next year?

There are two ways of arriving at the answer.[9] One is to take the expected gain in value of a barrel of oil over the coming year and discount that amount to get its present value today. The other is to turn the value of the revenue from the sale of the oil now into an amount available next year which can be compared with the estimated value of the oil in the ground next year. If the money earned by selling the oil now is invested at the current rate of interest, it will be increased in value next year by the interest that it earns. The firm will decide whether to extract the oil now or leave it in the ground depending on which of two values is the greater. The first is the amount it could earn by selling the oil now and investing the revenue for a year. The second is the increase in the value of the oil if it is left in the ground.

To illustrate this important result, assume that next year's price is expected to be £1.05 per barrel and that the rate of interest is 5 per cent. Now suppose the current price is £1.04 per barrel. Clearly, it pays to produce more now, since the £1.04 that is earned by selling a barrel now can be invested to yield approximately £1.09 (£1.04 × 1.05), which is more than the £1.05 that the oil would be worth in a year's time if it is left in the ground. Next, suppose that the current price is £0.90 per barrel. Now it pays to reduce production, since oil left in the ground will be worth 16.66 per cent more next year ((1.05/0.90) × 100). Extracting it this year and investing the money will produce a gain of only 5 per cent. Finally, let the current price be £1.00. Now oil producers make the same amount of money whether they leave £1.00 worth of oil in the ground to be worth £1.05 next year or sell the oil for £1.00 this year and invest the proceeds at a 5 per cent interest rate.

The price response

How will the world market price for oil respond if all firms decide their current production by making the comparison just outlined?

First, suppose the price of oil is expected to rise by less than the interest rate. Oil extracted and sold now will have a higher value than oil left in the ground. All firms will therefore extract more oil this year. But, although no one firm is large enough to affect the world price, the price will react when they *all* decide to produce more. Because the demand curve for oil has a negative slope, raising the world extraction rate will lower the current price. Production will rise, and the current price will fall until the expected price rise between this year and next year is equal to the interest rate.[10] The firms will then be indifferent at the margin between producing another barrel this year and leaving that barrel in the ground for next year. (Of course, next year each firm can make the same calculation and decide to leave some of its oil in the ground for a further year.)

Second, suppose that the price is expected to rise by more than the interest rate. Firms will prefer to leave their oil in the ground, where they earn a higher return than could be earned by selling the oil this year and investing the proceeds at the current interest rate. Thus, firms will cut their current rate of production, which will raise this year's price. When the current price has risen so that the gap between the current price and next year's expected price is equal to the interest rate, firms will put equal value on a barrel of oil extracted and one left in the ground.

In a perfectly competitive industry, the profit-maximizing equilibrium for a completely non-renewable resource occurs when the last unit currently produced earns just as much for each firm as it would if it had been left in the ground for future use.

The actual price

What we have established so far determines the pattern of prices over time: if stocks are given and unchanging, prices should rise over time at a rate equal to the rate of interest. But what about the level of prices? Will they start low and rise to only moderate levels over the next few years, or will they start high and then soar to even higher levels? The answer depends on the total stock of the resource that is

---

[9] Box 17.2 shows that these two methods are equivalent. In the text we use the second method.

[10] The discussion is simplified by assuming next year's expected price to be given. The decision to produce more this year may also affect next year's price. If the total supplies are small, next year's expected price might rise. The argument proceeds exactly as in the text, except that the equilibrium gap between two prices is achieved by the present price falling and the expected future price rising, rather than by having next year's expected price remaining constant and all the adjustment coming through this year's price.

available (and, where some new discoveries are possible, on the expected additions to that stock in the future). The scarcer is the resource relative to the demand for it, the higher will its market price be at the outset.

Profit-maximizing behaviour on the part of many producers will cause the resource's price to rise over time at a rate equal to the rate of interest, while the height of that whole price profile will depend on the resource's scarcity relative to current demand.

Optimal social behaviour

Petroleum is a valuable resource. The value to consumers of one more barrel produced now is the price that they would be willing to pay for it, which is the current market price of the oil (in this example assumed to be £1.00). If the oil is extracted this year and the proceeds are invested at the rate of interest (the proceeds might be used to buy a new capital good), they will produce £1.05 worth of valuable goods next year. If that barrel of oil is not produced this year and is left in the ground for extraction next year, its value to consumers at that time will be next year's price of oil. It is not socially optimal, therefore, to leave the oil in the ground unless it will be worth £1.05 to consumers next year. More generally, society obtains increases in the value of what is available for consumption by conserving units of a non-renewable resource only if the price of the units is expected to rise at a rate that is at least as high as the interest rate.

How much of a non-renewable resource is it socially optimal to consume now? The US economist Harold Hotelling (1895–1973) provided the answer to this question many years ago. His answer is very simple, yet it specifically determines the optimal profile of prices over the years. It is interesting that the answer applies to all non-renewable resources. It does not matter whether there is a large or a small demand, whether that demand is elastic or inelastic, or whether the remaining stock is large or small. In all cases the answer is the same:

The socially optimal rate of extraction of any non-renewable resource should be such that its price increases at a rate equal to the interest rate.

For example, if the rate of interest is 4 per cent, then the price of the resource should be rising at 4 per cent per year. If it is rising by more, there is too little current extraction; if it is rising by less, then there is too much current extraction. We have already seen that this is the rate of extraction that will be produced by a competitive industry.

The actual rate of extraction

What about the actual rate at which the resource will be extracted *if the competitive market fulfils Hotelling's rule for optimal extraction rates*? The answer to this question does depend on market conditions. Specifically, it depends on the position and the slope of the demand curve. If the quantity demanded at all prices is small, the rate of extraction will be small. The larger the quantity demanded at each price, the higher the rate of extraction will tend to be.

Now consider the influence of the slope of the demand curve. A highly inelastic demand curve suggests that there are few substitutes and that purchasers are prepared to pay large sums rather than do without the resource. This will produce a relatively even rate of extraction, with small reductions in each period being sufficient to drive up the price at the required rate. A relatively elastic demand curve suggests that people can easily find substitutes once the price rises. This will encourage a great deal of consumption now and a rapidly diminishing amount over future years, since large reductions in consumption are needed to drive the price up at the required rate.

Figure 17.4 illustrates this working of the price mechanism with a simple example in which the whole stock of oil of 200,000 barrels must be consumed in only two periods, this year and next year. At a 10 per cent interest rate, the price in the second year must be 10 per cent higher than the price in the first year. With a relatively elastic curve this requires that the quantities differ substantially over the two years, while on the relatively inelastic curve the quantity in the second year need be only slightly smaller than in the first year. (Because the two curves are drawn on the same scale, the steeper curve is also the more inelastic at each price.) The general point is as follows:

The more inelastic the demand curve, the more even the rate of extraction (and hence the rate of use) will be over the years; the more elastic the demand curve, the more uneven the rate of extraction will be over the years.

An elastic demand curve will lead to a large consumption now and a rapid fall in consumption over the years. An inelastic demand curve will lead to a smaller consumption now and a less rapid fall in consumption over the years. In each case, quantities consumed are varying over time in such a way as to equate the rate of price increase with the rate of interest. The difference between the two lies in the different patterns of quantity variation that are required along demand curves of different slopes if prices are to rise at the same rate.

Rents to natural resources

The incomes earned by the owners of the oil resources are *rents* in the sense defined in Chapter 15. This is because the owners would be willing to produce the oil at a price that covers the direct costs of extraction, which in this example is zero. (In real cases the direct cost of extracting the resource is positive, and the rent is the income earned above that amount.) Thus, the incomes they do earn over their costs of extraction are not needed to get the product

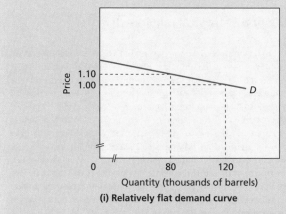
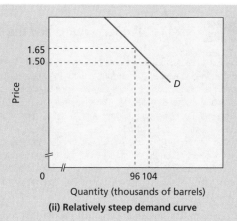

Figure 17.4 The extraction rate for non-renewable resources

The shape of the demand curve determines the extraction profile over time. The two conditions—that the whole supply be used over two periods and that the price rise by 10 per cent between the two periods—determine price and quantities. In part (i), with a relatively flat demand curve, quantity and price are 120,000 barrels at £1.00 in the first period and 80,000 barrels at £1.10 in the second period. In part (ii), with a relatively steep demand curve, the values are 104,000 barrels at £1.50 in the first period and 96,000 barrels at £1.65 in the second.

produced, since any non-zero price would do that. They do, however, fulfil the important function of determining the extraction rate, and hence the use of the resource, *over time*. As we have seen, the price profile determines the use of the resource and hence the amount of resources allocated to its production *over time*.

The price system as a conservation mechanism

In the above discussion we see the price system playing its now familiar role of co-ordinator. By following private profit incentives, firms are led to conserve the resource in a manner that is consistent with society's needs.

The role of rising prices

We have seen that from society's viewpoint the optimal extraction pattern of a totally non-renewable resource occurs when its price rises each year at a rate equal to the interest rate. The rising price fulfils a number of useful functions.

First, the rising price encourages conservation. As the resource becomes scarcer and its price rises, purchasers will be motivated to be more and more economical in its use. Uses of oil that yield low returns may be abandoned altogether, and uses that yield high returns will be pursued only as long as their value at the margin is enough to compensate for the high price.

Second, the rising price encourages the discovery of new sources of supply—at least in cases in which the world supply is not totally fixed and already known. Unlike our simple example given above, the world's supply of petroleum is not completely known. High prices, when they do occur, encourage exploration, which adds to known reserves; low prices discourage it.

Third, the rising price encourages innovation. New products that will do the same job may be developed, as well as new processes that use alternative resources.

How might the price system fail?

Three basic ways in which the price system might fail to produce the optimal rate of resource extraction are discussed below. We look at examples of each of these and ask if each justifies government intervention.[11]

Ignorance Private owners might not have sufficient knowledge to arrive at the best estimate of the rate at which prices will rise. If they do not know the world stocks of their commodity and the current extraction rate, they may be unable to estimate the rate of the price rise and thus will not know when to raise or lower their current rates of extraction. For example, if all firms mistakenly think that prices will not rise greatly in the future, they will all produce too much now and conserve too little for future periods.

The government could not do better, unless it had access to some special knowledge that private firms do not possess. If it did have such knowledge, the government could make it public, leaving the firms to do the rest. In practice, whatever knowledge does exist about both the proven reserves of non-renewable resources and their current extraction rates is usually freely and openly available.

---

[11] This discussion partly anticipates Chapter 19, which studies market successes and market failures in more general terms.

 Box 17.3 Property rights and the destruction of tropical rain forests

A key factor leading to the destruction of tropical rain forests has been the lack of property rights assigned to these forests. With lack of ownership, nobody has an incentive to plan for the long-term preservation of the trees and the sustainability of forest industries. Rather, the incentive is to cut down the trees, sell the timber and then move on—that is, take what money can be made immediately and 'run'.

The following two extracts from the 2003 World Development Report give examples of how Brazilian state authorities are creating incentives for preservation of the Amazon forest. In the first, tax rebates on value added tax (ICMS) are related to the areas of protected forest. The second has introduced tradable conservation permits.

The ICMS Ecologico is a unique Brazilian mechanism that uses state-to-municipality transfers to reward the creation and maintenance of protected areas for biodiversity conservation and watershed protection. The intent is to counteract the local perceptions that maintenance of protected areas reduces municipal revenue. . . . Since the programs were adopted, about 1 million hectares have been placed under environmental zoning restrictions in Parana, and about 800,000 in Minas Gerais.

The Brazilian state of Parana has created a market for conservation by allowing trade in landholder obligations to maintain forests. A long-standing Brazilian law has required that property owners maintain 20 percent of each property under native vegetation (50 percent to 80 percent in the Amazon region). But noncompliance was common. . . . A preliminary analysis of a hypothetical similar program for the nearby state of Minas Gerais illustrates how efficiency-enhancing programs such as this might increase biodiversity conservation and economic output. . . . When landholders are free to trade within the biome, compliance costs drop by almost three-quarters, while the proportion of higher-ecological-quality forest reserve increases to 72 percent. (World Bank, *World Development Report 2003*, page 173)

This illustrates the point that socially suboptimal exploitation of resources can arise when property rights are not appropriately assigned. However, incentives can be introduced to encourage a socially efficient outcome.

Inadequate property rights Some non-renewable resources have the characteristics of what is called a *common property resource*. Such property cannot be exclusively owned and controlled by one person or firm. For example, one person's oil-bearing land may be adjacent to another person's, and the underground supplies may be interconnected. If one firm holds off producing now, the oil may end up being extracted by the neighbour. In such cases, which are sometimes encountered with petroleum, there is a tendency for a firm to extract the resource too quickly, because a firm's oil that has been left in the ground may not be available to that firm at a future date. Similar issues arise with any common property resource such as fishing grounds, and they are discussed in more detail in Chapter 19. Box 17.3 discusses the related issue of the destruction of tropical rain forests.

This problem arises because of inadequate property rights. Since the resource will be worth more in total value when it is exploited at the optimal extraction rate than when small firms exploit it too quickly, there will be an incentive for individual owners to combine until each self-contained source of supply is owned by only one firm. After that the problem of over-exploitation will no longer arise. Government ownership is not necessary to achieve this result. What is needed, at most, is intervention to ensure that markets can work to provide the optimal size of individual units so that the private owners can apply proper extraction management.

Political uncertainty can provide another source of inadequate property rights. For example, the owners of the resource may fear that a future election or a revolution will establish a government that will confiscate their property. They will then be motivated to exploit the resource too quickly, on the grounds that certain revenue now is more valuable than highly uncertain revenue in the future. The current rate of extraction will tend to increase until the expected rate of price rise exceeds the interest rate by a sufficient margin to compensate for the risks that supplies left in the ground may be confiscated at some future date. The problem arises here because property rights are not secure over time.

Unequal market and social values Normally in a competitive world the real interest rate indicates the rate at which it is optimal to discount the future over the present. Society's investments are valuable if they earn the market rate of return, and are not valuable if they earn less (because the resources could be used in other ways to produce more value to consumers). In certain circumstances, however, the government may have reasons to adopt a different rate of discount. It is then said that the *social rate of discount* —the discount rate that is appropriate to the society as a whole—differs from the private rate, as indicated by the market rate of interest. In such circumstances there is reason for the government to intervene to alter the rate at which the private firms would exploit the resource. If the government owns the resources, it must be careful to use the social rate of discount in all of its decisions about exploiting the resource.

Critics are often ready to assume that profit-mad producers will despoil most non-renewable resources by using them up too quickly. They argue for government intervention to conserve the resource by slowing its rate of extraction. Yet unless the social rate of discount is *below* the private rate, there is no clear social gain in holding the resources in the ground.

Since governments must worry about their short-term popularity and their chances of re-election, there is no presumption that government intervention will slow down the rate of extraction, even if the social discount rate is below the private rate. Instead, governments often extract resources faster than would free markets. This is because governments, being concerned primarily with the next election, may have a rate of discount much higher than either the social or the market rate.

A good example is provided by the Hybernia oil field, which lies off the Newfoundland coast of Canada. When development began, the costs of developing the field and extracting the oil exceeded its current market value. It would thus not have been developed under free-market conditions. Instead, Canadian taxpayers' money was used to produce oil whose market value was less than its full costs of production. If left in the ground, the field would one day have developed a positive value, if either the price of oil rose or the costs of production fell.

Actual price profiles

Many non-renewable resources do not seem to have the steadily rising profile of prices that the theory predicts. The price of petroleum, having been raised artificially by the OPEC cartel, returned in the late 1990s to an inflation-adjusted level that was at or a little below where it was in 1970. It has risen somewhat since, but not in a smooth way linked to the interest rate as suggested above. The price of coal has not soared; nor has the price of iron ore.

In many cases the reason lies in the discovery of new supplies, which have prevented the total known stocks of many resources from being depleted. In the case of petroleum, for example, the ratio of known reserves to one year's consumption is no lower now than it was two or even four decades ago. Furthermore, most industry experts believe that large quantities of undiscovered oil still exist under both land and sea.

In these cases the amount firms spend on exploration depends on their expectations of future prices. Even a small rise in the expected price can lead to a large increase in exploration activity. As a result, the proven supply rises. In such an industry the price behaves more as it would in a competitive industry with a very elastic long-run supply curve. Eventually, if an oil substitute is not developed, undiscovered supplies will diminish. Then the price will begin to behave as predicted by the theory of the pricing of non-renewable resources with completely fixed supplies. In the meantime 'non-renewable' resource prices behave more like those of renewable resources. If the price rises, it pays firms to invest more in discovering new supplies, just as it pays them to produce more of renewable resources. The end result is the same: a rise in price leads to more of the resource being produced/discovered, and this prevents the price from rising further.

In other cases the invention of new substitute products has unexpectedly reduced the demand for some of these resources. For example, plastics have replaced metals in many uses, fibre optics have replaced copper wire in many types of message transmission, and newer fuels have replaced coal in many of its uses. The interesting case of the coal industry's decline in the face of massive unused resources is discussed in Box 17.4.

 Box 17.4 The abdication of king coal

The British coal industry has witnessed a dramatic decline in output and employment stretching over most of this century. Many have argued that this decline must be the outcome of a political decision designed to reduce the power of the National Union of Mineworkers. However, the underlying economics of the industry has had more influence on events than have political vendettas.

Peak output for the coal industry was achieved immediately before the First World War, when 290 million tonnes were produced and over 1 million workers were employed. About a third of this output was exported. A significant decline in production during the inter-war period (1919–39) resulted from the loss of export markets. However, in 1955 output was still 225 million tonnes; there were 850 working collieries and nearly 750,000 miners.

Substitution in favour of oil and natural gas, combined with a sharp decline in demand for coal for domestic heating (following the Clean Air Act of 1956), caused coal output to decline to 125 million tonnes, produced in 133 pits by just over 150,000 workers, in 1975. Substitution towards cheaper imported coal, combined with greater use of other energy sources, including electricity imported from France and hydroelectric power, caused output to fall by 1991/2 to just over 30 million tonnes, produced by only 50 pits, employing fewer than 50,000 workers. By 2002, output was around the same level at 32 million tonnes, but there were only 11,000 employees and only 10 deep mines still in operation.

The main driving force behind this decline in demand for British coal was the availability of imported coal at a cheaper price. A second reason for the industry's decline is that coal is a greater producer of harmful gases than most alternative fuels. Furthermore, British coal has nearly twice the acid-rain-producing sulphur content of imported coal. Gas turbine generation produces about half the greenhouse gas emissions of coal. The high costs of building clean coal technology (such as flue gas desulphurization) will induce a continued decline in the already low demand for British coal.

Thus, the decline in the British coal industry was the result of fundamental economic and environmental pressures.

In yet other cases the reason is to be found in government pricing policy. An important example of this type is the use of *non-renewable* water for irrigation in much of the United States. Vast underground reserves of water lie in aquifers beneath many areas of North America. Although these reserves were accumulated over millennia, they are being used up at a rate that will exhaust them in a matter of decades. The water is often supplied by government water authorities at prices that cover only a small part of total costs and that do not rise steadily to reflect the dwindling stocks.

Such a constant-price policy for *any* non-renewable resource creates three characteristic problems. First, the resource will be exhausted much faster than if price were to rise over time. A constant price will lead to a constant rate of extraction to meet the quantity demanded at that price until the resource is completely exhausted. Second, no signals go out to induce conservation, innovation, and exploration. Third, when the supply of the resource is finally exhausted, the adjustment will have to come all at once. If the price had risen steadily each year under free-market conditions, adjustment would have taken place little by little each year. The controlled price, however, gives no signal of the ever-diminishing stock of the resource until all at once the supplies run out. The required adjustment will then be much more painful than it would have been if it had been spread over time in response to steadily rising prices.

SUMMARY

Capital

- Because capital goods are durable, it is necessary to distinguish between the stock of capital goods and the flow of services provided by them, and thus between their purchase price and their rental price. The linkage between them relies on the ability to assign a present value to future returns. The present value of a future payment will be lower when the payment is more distant and the interest rate is higher.

- Firms will hire capital goods up to the point where the rental price of capital in each period equals its marginal revenue product in that period. The rental price is the amount that is paid to obtain the flow of services that a capital good provides for a given period. The purchase price is the amount that is paid to acquire ownership of the capital, and firms will buy capital goods up to the point where their price is just equal to the present value of the future net income stream generated by the capital. This is the present value of capital's future stream of marginal revenue products.

- An individual firm will invest in capital goods as long as the present value of the stream of future net incomes that are provided by another unit of capital exceeds its purchase price. For a single firm and for the economy as a whole, the size of the total capital stock demanded varies negatively with the rate of interest.

Non-renewable resources

- The socially optimal rate of exploitation for a completely non-renewable resource occurs when its price rises at a rate that is equal to the rate of interest. This is also the rate that will be established by a profit-maximizing, competitive industry.

- Resources for which the demand is highly elastic will have a high rate of exploitation in the near future and a fairly rapid fall-off over time. Resources for which the demand is highly inelastic will have a lower rate of exploitation in the near future and a smaller fall-off over time.

- Rising prices act as a conservation device by rationing the consumption over time according to people's preferences. As prices rise, conservation, discovery of new sources of supply, and innovation to reduce demand are all encouraged.

- The price system can fail to produce optimal results if (a) people lack the necessary knowledge, (b) property rights are inadequate to protect supplies left for future use by their owners, or (c) the social rate of discount differs significantly from the market rate.

- Controlling the price of a non-renewable resource at a constant level speeds up the rate of exploitation and removes the price incentives to react to the growing scarcity.

TOPICS FOR REVIEW

- Rental price and purchase price of capital
- Present value
- The interest rate and the capital stock

- Hotelling's rule
- The role of rising prices of non-renewable resources

DISCUSSION QUESTIONS

1 An extra tractor will lead to an increase in revenue for a farmer in successive years of £500, £4,000, £3,000, £3,000 and £1,000, after which the tractor is sold for £1,000. Assuming that the first revenue is treated as current and the interest rate is 8 per cent, what is the present value of the extra income stream?

2 If a new tractor costs £10,000 in the current period, would the purchase of the tractor increase the present value of profit?

3 If the tractor could be paid for in five equal instalments of £2,000 in each of the five years, would this make the purchase of the tractor more attractive?

4 Suppose you are offered, free of charge, one from each of the following pairs of assets: (a) a perpetuity that pays £20,000 per year for ever, or an annuity that pays £100,000 per year for five years; (b) an oil-drilling company that earned £100,000 after corporate taxes last year, or British government bonds that paid £100,000 in interest last year; (c) a 1 per cent share in a new company that has invested £10 million in a new cosmetic that is thought to appeal to middle-income women, or a £100,000 bond that has been issued by the same company. What considerations would determine your choice in each case?

5 How would you go about evaluating the present value of each of the following?

(a) The existing reserves of a relatively small oil company
(b) The total world reserves of an exhaustible natural resource with a known, completely fixed supply
(c) A long-term bond, issued by a very unstable Third World government, that promises to pay the bearer £1,000 per year for ever
(d) A lottery ticket that your neighbour bought for £10 which was one of one million tickets sold for a draw to be held in one year's time that will pay £2 million to the single winner

6 List some resources that are renewable if they are exploited at one rate and non-renewable if they are exploited at other, higher rates.

7 Species that are on the verge of extinction—beluga whales, African elephants, mountain gorillas, and California condor—might be classified as non-renewable resources; once they disappear, there will be no regeneration. Does the market create appropriate incentives to ensure that extinction will not occur? How might market signals be devised to do so?

8 What determines the optimal rate for the extraction of non-renewable resources?

9 How can a profit-maximizing firm decide if an investment that incurs costs now in exchange for higher future revenues is worthwhile?

Chapter 18

RESOURCE ALLOCATION IN ACTION

In this chapter we illustrate the power of the market mechanism in allocating the resources of the economy (land, labour, capital, and natural resources) between competing uses. Is there a rational explanation of some of the apparently outrageous prices that are paid for some goods and services? Why, for example, are houses so expensive in desirable parts of major cities? Why are some branded goods expensive while almost identical but unbranded goods are cheaper? Are the principles of resource allocation more or less stable or are they changing rapidly over time? Is there, for example, a New Economy associated with rapid change in information and communications technology (ICT)? Is this just the latest example of technical change that has been going on for hundreds of years? In particular, you will learn that:

• Resources move between uses in response to market prices because owners of resources are trying to maximize their net return.

• The market allocates resources efficiently so long as prices reflect the underlying demand and supply conditions, and resources are free to move between uses in response to price signals.

• Rising demand and fixed supply explain why prices of land in the centre of growing cities continue to rise relative to the prices on the outskirts.

• Some brands of goods are priced more highly than competitors because their producers have managed to create a high demand based on status or influence on tastes.

• Resources do move in response to price signals but adjustment is often slow.

• The recent revolution in communications technology has important implications for the way firms work and the economy in general, but it is only a modest step in the evolution of ICT over time.

We start by restating our market-based analysis of resource allocation, that is the allocation of the inputs of the economy into the process of production of goods and services. We then look at some of the impressive evidence, first, that market conditions do strongly influence input prices and, second, that owners of resources do respond to the price incentives created by markets so that resources move towards uses in which they are most highly valued. In doing this, we give a number of examples in which market analysis explains commonly observed events which seem strange at first sight.

Resource pricing and allocation: a summary

The previous three chapters have developed the neoclassical theory of resource allocation in several contexts, repeating what is basically the same analysis in applications to labour, capital, and natural resources (including land). This repetition helps to develop a 'feel' for the workings of the price system that is central to understanding economics. It has the disadvantage, however, of making the analysis appear to be more complex than it actually is. In fact, the whole theory depends on a very few basic hypotheses about the behaviour of resource owners and

firms. Before going on, it may be useful to repeat its underlying structure.

The neoclassical theory of resource allocation maintains that prices can be explained by supply and demand. The analysis of resource supply is based on the assumption that resource owners will seek occupations, industries, and places that yield the highest net return, taking both monetary and non-monetary rewards into account. Resources will move between these uses until the net returns in all uses are equalized. Because there are impediments to mobility, there may be lags in the movement of resources in response to changes in prices. The elasticity of resource supply will depend not only on the type of resource being considered but also on the time allowed for adjustment.

The demand side of the neoclassical theory is based on profit maximization and is called the marginal productivity theory (of input demand). The demand for an input is a derived demand. It depends for its existence on the demand for the product made by the input. The elasticity of an industry's demand curve for an input is higher in the long run than in the short run, since more substitution is possible the longer the time considered. Also, as we saw in Chapter 3, the demand for any product made by the input will itself be more elastic in the long run than in the short run—thus making the derived demand for the inputs that it uses correspondingly more elastic.

In equilibrium, *all* profit-maximizing firms will employ their variable inputs up to the point at which the marginal unit of each type of input adds as much to cost as to revenue. When firms are *price-takers in the markets for their inputs*, they employ inputs up to the point at which the price paid for the last unit of each variable input is equal to the increase in revenue resulting from the sale of that input's additional contribution to output. When firms are *price-takers in the markets for their outputs*, the increase in revenue is the marginal physical product times the price. When firms face *negatively sloped demand curves* for their products, the increase in revenue is marginal physical product times marginal revenue.

The relationships just described all hold in equilibrium. They apply to all firms that succeed in maximizing their profits, and can be stated in two equivalent ways. First, a firm that is not equating the marginal revenue product of each of its inputs with that input's price is not maximizing its profits. Second, a firm that is maximizing its profits is necessarily equating each input's price to its marginal revenue product, whether or not it knows it is doing so. Thus, the theory of input demand is merely an implication of profit maximization. We spell it out in detail because this helps us to develop interesting and useful insights into the effects of various changes in the economy on the markets for the various types of resource.

If markets are to allocate the nation's productive resources in the way that the theory says they do, two things are necessary. First, prices must be determined by demand and supply conditions in resource markets, changing in response to changes in these conditions. Second, resources must move in response to changes in their relative prices and earnings. We consider these in turn.

Markets determine prices

To see how market conditions determine prices, it is convenient to look separately at markets for raw materials, land, capital, and labour, and then at some special factors that sometimes influence the outcome.

Raw materials

The prices of copper, tin, rubber, petroleum, and hundreds of other basic commodities fluctuate daily in response to changes in their demands and supplies (see also the discussion of coffee prices on pages 77–9). Prices fluctuate in response to several different types of force. First, short-term fluctuations in demand and supply create shortages and gluts that are almost always signalled by price changes. Second, there is often a distinct seasonal pattern in these prices. For example, the price of fuel oil is higher in winter, when demand is high, and lower in summer. Furthermore, a really cold and prolonged winter results in significantly higher prices than a mild winter. These prices also show a strong cyclical component. They rise on the upswing of the business cycle, when their (derived) demand rises, and fall on the downswing, when their (derived) demand falls.

They also show long-term secular shifts. For example, traditional materials, such as copper and nickel, are displaying weak prices as their demands fall in response to the development of many new materials that are part of the materials revolution (see Box 9.4 on page 153).

Of course, if monopoly elements arise, the models of pricing under monopoly or monopsony need to be applied. For example, OPEC's drastic restriction of oil supplies in the 1970s and early 1980s led to a large rise in the prices of petroleum and its derivatives, which are inputs into many production processes (see discussion on pages 229–33). This in turn led to rapid rises in the prices of such diverse products as fertilizers and plastics.

Land values

Values of land in the centres of growing cities rise in response to increasing demand. The London and New York skylines are monuments to the high value of urban land. The increase in the price of land on the periphery of every growing city is another visible example of the workings of the market.

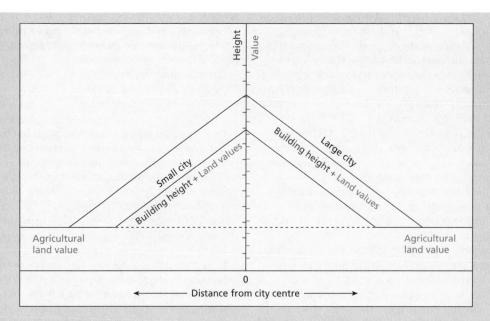

Figure 18.1 Rent and height profiles

Both land rents and building heights tend to be highest at the city centre. The figure shows two typical rent gradients for cities of two different sizes. Rents are highest at the city centre and fall towards the periphery. At the boundary between the city and the countryside, the rent that urban uses can pay just equals the rent that can be paid for the same land in agricultural uses. Building heights will show a similar profile, being highest at the centre and tending to fall as one moves towards the periphery.

Case study 1: the economics of land prices and skyscrapers

The larger is a city's population, the larger is the demand for all the inputs that are required to run its industries and to service its residents. One of these inputs is land. So, according to the principles of derived demand, the larger the city, the higher the demand for land on which to site all of its activities. A high demand for labour in the city will attract more people to come to the city. But land cannot move from one place to another. So the higher the demand for land, the higher its rental and purchase price.

Since land in the centres of cities is a more desirable location for almost all commercial activities than land on their periphery, the demand for central land is higher than that for land on the outskirts. As a result virtually all cities show a 'rent gradient', with rents and property prices looking like a tent, highest in the centre and declining towards the edges. Figure 18.1 shows typical gradients for two cities, one larger than the other. If land were physically mobile, it would be reallocated until these gradients disappeared. Since it is immobile, the gradients persist indefinitely.

It follows from what has just been said that the margin between the price of land in the centre of the city and on the edges will increase as the city grows. So the margin is higher in London than in Bristol and higher in Bristol than in Shrewsbury.

Case study 2: New York and London skylines

What determines the height of buildings? Construction costs per square metre of usable space rise as the height of buildings rises. There are many reasons for this, including the requirements that higher buildings be stronger, and have more and faster lifts than smaller buildings. Profit-maximizing developers will go on adding to a building's designed height until the extra cost per square metre can just be covered by rentals. So for any piece of land, the larger the city and the closer to the centre is its location, the higher the demand for the space it provides—and so the higher the building that can be profitably erected on it. For this reason most large cities display a profile of average height of building that is similar to their rent profile, highest in the centre and lowest at the peripheries.

Why is this predicted profile much clearer in New York than in London? The reason is that until the last half of the twentieth century construction technology did not permit the erection of very high buildings on the clay that underlies London. In contrast, New York is built largely on rock, and for more than a hundred years technology has been adequate for the construction of very high buildings on rock. When the technology of construction improved in the last half of the twentieth century, the average height of new London buildings began to increase, just as the theory predicts.

Why, when the technology changed, did London's profile not immediately change to mimic New York's? One reason is related to sunk costs. We saw in Chapter xx that it takes a long time for physical capital to exit a declining industry. Similarly, it takes a long time for old buildings to wear out and be replaced. The buildings are already there, and all the associated construction costs, are sunk. They cannot be recovered by exiting. A new building must earn, over and above what the old building can earn, enough to repay the full costs of construction. So, as the theory predicts, we see large variations in the sizes of buildings, even on the most expensive land in the centre of the city. But old buildings are eventually demolished, either because they reach the limit of their age, or because their productivity falls sufficiently below what a new building would earn on the same site. So old and new coexist, but gradually the old go and new higher buildings take their place.

A second reason is related to government regulations. Many of the older London boroughs and hamlets had long-standing restrictions on building heights. These tended to push the new higher buildings away from the very centre of the city to the nearest convenient location where these restrictions do not apply. Canary Wharf and Docklands are, literally and figuratively, monuments to the new construction technologies and the response of the market to economic and political forces.

What these case studies tell us is that a city is an evolving entity whose past history determines much of its present character. None the less, its evolution over time is determined to a great extent by the size and type of buildings that the market shows to be currently most profitable.

Case study 3: the evolution of agricultural land prices

Writing in the early nineteenth century, the classical economists predicted that, as population and the demand for agricultural products grew, the price of the fixed supply of land would rise enormously. To the contrary, however, the free-market price of agricultural land has not skyrocketed world-wide. The demand for agricultural produce *did* expand in the predicted fashion because of the rise in population. However, the productivity of agricultural land increased in quite unexpected ways with the invention of the vast range of new machines, crops, and farming techniques that characterize modern agriculture. A century ago over half of the workforce of Western nations was producing food to feed the rest; today a mere 3–5 per cent of the workforce produces enough to feed everyone in the Western nations, with substantial margins left over for export. The prediction of rising land prices and increasing food shortages in advanced countries was falsified not because the price of agricultural land is insensitive to market forces, but because some of the market forces were incorrectly foreseen. Technological advances in food production caused supply of agricultural produce to expand much faster than rising populations and incomes caused demand to grow.

Case study 4: policy-created high prices

The European Union's Common Agricultural Policy (CAP) has insulated the European market from cheap foreign imports and has held up food prices. As a result, the prices of agricultural land in Europe, and the gross earnings of landowners, have been much higher than prices and incomes for comparable land in such other food-producing countries as Australia and Canada. For example, when Ireland entered the European Union and became eligible for CAP subsidies and market restraints, prices of Irish agricultural land increased by between 100 and 500 per cent, a strong testimony both to the power of the CAP and to the applicability of the theory of derived demand.

Capital

We saw in the previous chapter that the return to capital is made up of a pure return, which responds to demand and supply, plus a risk premium. The effect of risk is easily observable. Interest rates are high in countries where economic and political conditions are unstable. Interest rates are higher on unsecured loans to consumers than on loans secured on property, because the risk of default is larger.

In past centuries loans to the major European governments commanded very high rates. In more recent times, however, such loans have commanded the lowest rates in the market. The reason is that the risk of default on loans to governments was enormous in most previous centuries, while the risk of lending to modern governments has fallen dramatically. Governments have developed high capacity to tax their citizens, so loans to them are safer than loans to individuals or firms who cannot impose taxes on others to pay their bills.

It is interesting to note, however, that by making capital and enterprise extremely mobile, the information/communication revolution is making it increasingly difficult for one government to charge taxes that are out of line with those ruling in other jurisdictions. As a result, governments will have either to curtail their borrowing or face rising interest rates on their large debts.

Supply and demand conditions determine the pure rate of interest. For example, over the past few decades Japan has had remarkably low interest rates. The Japanese were exceptionally high savers. Although their economy was booming, the domestic supply of funds was more than adequate to meet the high demand for capital to invest. The result was interest rates that were much lower than those typically found in Europe and North America.

Labour

We saw in Chapter 16 that we can explain most of the pay differentials between major classes of labour.

Non-competitive elements can also be handled. For example, strong unions succeed in raising wages and incomes when they operate in small sections of the whole economy. The high earnings attract others to enter the occupation or industry. Thus, the privileged position can be maintained only if entry can be effectively restricted. Closed-shop laws are one obvious way of doing this. With the end of much of the power of unions to restrict entry, union-induced wage differentials have narrowed substantially in the UK, as shown in Table 18.1.

Not only can monopoly elements raise incomes above their competitive levels, they can also prevent incomes from falling and reflecting decreases in demand. Of course, if demand disappears more or less overnight unions cannot

Table 18.1 **Union wage differentials, UK, 1984–1990**

% extra for union in	1984	1990
Unskilled	10.5	7.5
Semi-skilled	10.5	6.5
Skilled	3.5	1.5

Unions' power has diminished over recent decades. The fall in union power is manifested in the reduced differentials between union and non-union wages in each of the three skill categories.

Source: M. Stewart, 'Union wage differentials in an era of declining unionisation', *Oxford Bulletin of Economics and Statistics*, 1995.

maintain incomes. But the story may be different if, as is more usual, demand shrinks slowly over a few decades. In this case unions that are powerful enough to stop new labour from entering the industry can often hold wages up in the face of declining demand. The industry's labour force thus declines, through death and retirement, despite the relatively high wage being paid to the employees who remain.

Wages also respond to long-term changes in demand and supply that are driven by new technologies. Consider some examples from the past. With the advent of the motor car, many skilled carriage-makers found the demand for their services declining rapidly. Earnings fell, and many craftsmen who were forced to leave the industry found that they had been earning substantial rents for their scarce, but highly specific, skills. When the demand for silent films grew, music-hall stars whose talents did not project on to the flat, flickering screen of the early silent films suffered disastrous cuts in income and sank into oblivion. A similar fate later hit many silent-screen actors whose voices were unsuitable for the 'talkies'. Later still, falling incomes beset many radio personalities who were unable to make the transition to television and had to compete in a greatly reduced market for radio talent.

This type of variation in earnings is caused by changes in market conditions, not by changes in our notions of the intrinsic merit of various activities. To illustrate, ask yourself why, if you have the ability, you can make a lot of money writing copy for a London advertising agency, whereas even if you have great talent you are unlikely to make a lot of money writing books of poetry. This is not because any economic dictator or group of philosophers has decided that advertising is more valuable than poetry. Instead, the explanation lies in the large demand for advertising and the tiny demand for poetry.

Two extreme cases of earnings differentials—for chief executives and for rock and other superstars—were discussed in Box 16.2 on page 276 and Box 16.3 on page 281.

Special factors: legal restrictions on production

The right to produce is sometimes restricted by regulations enforced by governments. The instrument that gives the right to produce, whether it is a licence, a quota, or a patent, generates a rent to the owner, just like any other resource that is limited in supply. When the right to produce is saleable, its market value becomes the present value of the monopoly profits that arise from the output restriction.

Suppose, for example, that each tonne of a crop that is produced under quota restriction earns £1,000 of pure profit per year, that is, £1,000 of revenue in excess of the return necessary to persuade farmers to go on producing it. People who obtain the quota to produce a tonne of the product can make £1,000 per year more than they could by producing in some other industry where freedom of entry and exit forces pure profits to zero. The quota will thus sell in the open market for the present value of a flow of £1,000 per year, which is $1,000/i$. At a 10 per cent rate of interest, this is £10,000.[1] As the demand for the product fluctuates and the supply restriction is held constant, the profits, and hence the present value of the quota, fluctuate.

New entrants do not earn pure profits because they must buy the quota, whose price is the present value of those profits. So entry becomes even more costly since, in addition to the normal expenses of setting up in business, the price of the quota must be found. Farmers do gain in the long run, however, as long as the market in which they operate is expanding. If demand is growing while the supply of quotas is held constant, prices and profits will rise. These extra profits are reflected in an enhanced value of the quotas, increasing the wealth of their present owners. In contrast, if there were no restrictions, a rise in demand would induce new entry until profits' were pushed back to zero. So the existing farmers would get no long-term gain from a rise in demand. The big losers are consumers, who must pay higher prices than they would have to pay if entry were free.

Case study 5: price differentials and branded goods

Why is a Rolex watch more expensive than a similar watch that looks as good and tells the time just as well? Why are Gucci shoes more expensive than similar leather shoes from a less well-known shoemaker? Why are specific designer labels associated with higher priced fashion items in clothing shops? This is to do with the economics of branding. Designers and manufacturers of cars, clothes, watches, and many other consumer items attempt to create a distinctive image of quality

---

[1] Where, as we saw in Chapter 17, i is the rate of interest expressed as a decimal fraction; for example, $i = 0.1$ means a 10 per cent rate of interest. In practice, there will be a further discounting because of the risk that government policy will change.

associated with their own product that creates consumer loyalty and adds value to the product that is additional to the cost of the materials that go to make the product. Establishing a valuable brand is not straightforward, but it is clearly something that many producers would wish to do. In part it may be achieved by advertising, which establishes a good image of the product and perhaps gives the impression that the product is used by top media stars or sports personalities.

How to establish a good brand is a topic for business studies courses. From the perspective of economics, what matters is that a good brand adds a dimension to a product for which consumers are prepared to pay. In effect, they have a taste for specific brands and are prepared to pay extra to buy those brands. A brand is thus a capital asset that is of value to the firm that owns it, and it can be valued just like any other capital asset.

Case study 6: patents and products

A patent confers a monopoly right to the exclusive use of an invention. Patent laws differ from one country to another. In the UK, to be patentable an invention must be new, must involve an inventive step, must be capable of industrial application, and must not be 'excluded'. Among exclusions are all discoveries, such as scientific theories or mathematical methods, that have no specific products as an outcome. Also excluded are works of art and literature (though these may be covered by copyright laws) and new designs that have no function other than appearance. Patents are granted for an initial four-year period, renewable annually for up to twenty years.

The benefits of patent protection is that it gives an inventor several years of monopoly trading and thus creates an incentive to invest in R&D that can generate some patentable product. Drugs companies, for example, invest large sums in searching for the new drugs.

Patents also have drawbacks. First, they create a tension because there are social pressures to provide a potentially life-saving drug as cheaply as possible and available to as many people as possible once it has been invented. For example, there has recently been considerable pressure on Western drugs companies to provide anti-aids drugs to poor countries in Africa at their marginal cost of production, rather than at the monopoly price charged to the richer countries.

Second, the patent may hold up the spread of technology. One of the most famous examples in history is the patent protection granted to James Watt for his invention of the steam engine. This patent applied to any process using steam to drive a piston, and no one could infringe the patent until it ran out in 1800. This greatly inhibited the spread of existing engines by holding up their prices. It also held up the development of more effective engines, because Watt had no faith in the potential of high-pressure engines. After his patent ran out others showed how wrong he was by developing high-pressure engines without which steam could be only a stationary source of power. Steam engines powerful and light enough to be used for railways and ships had to be of the high-pressure variety.

Furthermore, patents provide strong protection only in a fairly narrow range of products—pharmaceuticals are one of the modern industries where they work best. In many other industries firms do not even bother to prosecute believed patent violations, owing to the cost of legal proceedings. Rather, they rely on secrecy and a short product cycle to keep potential competitors out of the field, so that by the time imitations come along some newer product will have been developed.

Thus, patent protection has only a limited role in creating monopolies and this is at best temporary. Perhaps a more important product protection device derives from laws relating to *trademarks* and to *passing off*. For example, there is no patent protection to stop a soft-drinks manufacturer making a drink identical to Coca Cola. However, this firm would not be allowed to sell this product under the Coca Cola label or sell it in red cans that might fool customers into believing that they were buying genuine Coca Cola. Here it is the brand that has commercial value rather then the specific product itself.

Case study 7: taxis in Toronto and London

The system of regulating taxicabs in London is very different from the one in use in Toronto. The theory successfully predicts the consequences of these different regulatory rules.

The supply of Toronto taxicabs, and the fares they charge, are rigidly controlled by a licensing system. The number of cabs is kept well below what it would be in a free-market situation. The medallion that confers the right to operate a cab acquires a scarcity value. In 2002 it sold for about C\$100,000 and there were only about 4,000 licences available. As the population increases and people earn higher incomes, the demand for the services of taxicabs rises. In a free market fares would rise, increasing the earnings of taxi owners; the higher earnings would attract new entrants until earnings had been reduced to what could be earned in other comparable lines of activity. But neither of these things can happen, so existing cabs spend less time empty and hence earn more for their owners. Since investment in a taxi would now earn more than comparable other investments, investors would like to enter the industry. The only way to do so, however, is to buy one of the fixed supply of medallions. So the market price of medallions is bid up. The price rises to equal the present value of the extra earnings that can be obtained by investing in a taxicab rather than other comparable lines of activity. As a result, new entrants earn only normal returns on their investment, which includes the price of the medallion. Eventually the regulating authority raises fares in response to the excess demand. If the demand proves inelastic, the gross income from operating a cab rises. But the price of the medallion is bid up correspondingly. The fare increase thus amounts to a free gift to the current holders of medallions; it does nothing to raise the net incomes of cab operators newly entering the industry, or to make it more attractive to enter.

In London the fares of black cabs are rigidly regulated, but entry is free to anyone who can pass a set of tests.[2] The fares of minicabs are completely unregulated and entry is free (but they are prohibited from cruising the streets in search of fares). Periodically black cab fares are raised in an effort to raise incomes. If demand is inelastic, incomes do rise in the short run. But this attracts new entrants, who continue to enter until each existing cab is carrying just enough fares to cover its full opportunity cost, at which price economic profits have been reduced to zero. This case is analytically identical to the case of hairdressers discussed in Box 12.2 on page 199.

---

[2] The main test is known as 'the Knowledge', as it involves learning street names and locations.

Resources move in response to changes in relative prices

Changes in earnings are signals that induce resources to move from where they are not needed to where they are needed. Once again, the details of how this works differ between various types of resource.

Land

Does land move between uses according to economic signals? One might at first think the answer would be no, because land is physically immobile. Yet land is observed to be highly mobile in its economic uses. Land is transferred from one crop to another in response to changes in the relative profitability of the crops. Land on the edge of town is transferred from rural to urban uses as soon as it can earn substantially more as a building site than as a corn field (and provided planning permission can be obtained).

Case study 8: support policies and land allocation

When free markets determine agricultural prices, farmers often plant more than one crop as insurance against expected price fluctuations. This is the kind of risk-sharing that we studied in Chapter 13. Instead of having all their eggs in one product basket, farmers diversify among several products. This reduces the risk of extreme income fluctuations, which, under diversification, require unexpectedly high or low prices for several crops at the same time, rather than for just one.

The agricultural support policies adopted by many governments, including the European Union's CAP, remove much of this uncertainty. Farmers can then calculate the most profitable crop to plant with something close to certainty. The incentive is to produce the single crop, or small set of crops, that promises the highest monetary rewards. The results can be unfortunate. Gluts of crops whose support prices are out of line can often occur. More importantly, the land can suffer from exhaustion of specific minerals and other valuable properties as a result of repeated planting of one crop rather than a diversified set of crops. Overproduction has led EU policy-makers to pay farmers not to produce. Set-aside policies give an income to farmers so long as they leave their land idle or perhaps plant trees.

Although these responses to price and profit signals are undesirable, they provide strong evidence that agricultural resources do move according to price and profit incentives. This type of response is what makes government intervention into otherwise competitive markets so fraught with danger. Economists cannot prove that governments ought not to try, but they can reveal the difficulties inherent in such attempts. Difficulties typically arise when some excellent-sounding scheme provides unsuspected incentives to behave in ways that are then seen to be undesirable.

This is also the reason for the maxim that 'controls breed controls'. The government is likely to react to these unexpected events by introducing new measures to prevent them. These new measures may in turn create unsuspected incentives with further undesirable consequences. Further schemes are then introduced to remove these consequences. Such a progression is not inevitable but it often does occur. Where it does, it is a monument to the fact that owners of resources do respond to incentives and that such incentives are often subtle in nature.

Natural resources

Markets for the use of natural resources often do not work efficiently. In many cases this is not because resource owners are unresponsive to incentives, but because the incentives themselves are perverse. An important source of perverse incentive is imperfect or non-existent property rights. We will discuss these in more detail in Chapter 19. In the meantime we can note that the incentive to use resources efficiently over the long run is absent if the users do not themselves have a property right to the resource over the long run.

Case study 9: imperfect property rights

We noted in Chapter 17 that when individual properties within one oil field are too small, owner A can extract the oil under owner B's land by pumping extra oil out of B's well. Neither owner then has an incentive to extract at the socially optimal rate, preserving most of the oil for future extraction. After all, the oil may not be there when owner B plans to extract it—his neighbour may have got there first. This is a case of imperfect property rights.

Case study 10: property rights that reside with the wrong agents

It has been seriously argued that some of the incentives for non-sustainable logging in the vast forests of western Canada are created by the system of property rights in place there.[3] The government owns the forests and leases them out to the lumber companies for specific periods of time. As a result the company logging a particular area has little incentive to act in a way that is compatible with efficient reforestation. So laws are needed to force the companies to behave as they would if they owned the land themselves. Once the laws are in place

---

[3] Much of the concern of environmentalists is with another issue: whether or not the remaining first-growth lands should be logged at all. Our concern here is with the efficient management of those areas that it is agreed will be logged. See also Box 17.2 on page 294.

they must be enforced, which is not always easy, particularly in remote areas. If the logging companies owned the land, they would have a self-interest in preserving the forests for their own future logging. More efficient logging practices and more effective reforestation would be the result.

Capital

The location of, and the products produced by, a country's factories have changed greatly over the last two centuries. Over a period of fifty years or so the change can be dramatic. From one year to the next it is small. Most plant and machinery is relatively specific. Once installed, it will be used for the purpose for which it was designed, as long as the variable costs of production can be covered. But if full long-run opportunity costs are not covered, the capital will not be replaced as it wears out. Investment will take place in other industries instead.

Long-run movements in the allocation of physical capital clearly occur in response to market signals.

The mechanism works as long as there is freedom of entry and exit. Exit is difficult to prevent (other than by government legislation and subsidy), but monopolies and oligopolies, government regulations, and nationalized industries do erect barriers to entry. Where entry is blocked, profits of monopolists or oligopolists do not induce flows of new investment. Thus, such barriers serve no apparent long-run allocative function.

Case study 11: underinvestment by nationalized industries

After the end of the Second World War in 1945, many industries were nationalized in the UK and other European countries. Many nationalized public utilities typically did not invest enough to produce the quantity that was demanded at the prices that were being charged. The telephone industry was a good case in point. For most of the post-war period service was poor; phones were hard to get, with long waiting-lists; and in many areas private lines were almost impossible to obtain. Customers had to put up with shared lines serving two or more private residences. When the industry was privatized in the 1980s, whatever else good or bad happened, the waiting-lists vanished very quickly. Motivated by the profits that could be earned by satisfying customer demands, investment in telephone capacity rose to meet consumer requirements.

Although the profits that arise from the market power of private firms do not cause capital to move when entry is blocked in the long run, we cannot be so sure about this in the very long run. Profits may cause other firms to develop competing products and to innovate in other ways so as to attack the firms with market power. This is a process that

Joseph Schumpeter called 'creative destruction'. Because this incentive is important, monopoly profits do influence the allocation of capital in the very long run. Furthermore, creative destruction takes place not only when there is monopoly, but also when oligopolistic firms compete through the development of new product and process technologies. In such cases the market allocates capital investment into research and development when firms anticipate that they can better satisfy consumers' wants by creating new products or new ways of producing old products.

Case study 12: creative destruction—an endless process

The steel-nibbed pen eliminated the quill pen with its sharpened bird's feather nib. The fountain pen eliminated the steel pen and its accompanying inkwell. The ball-point pen or 'biro' virtually eliminated the fountain pen. Rolling-ball and fibre-tipped pens have partly replaced the biro. Who knows what will come next in writing implements.

The hand-cranked adding machine replaced the Dickensian clerk adding up long columns of figures in his head. (This *was* an all-male occupation.) The electrically driven mechanical desk calculator eliminated the hand-cranked version. The electronic desk calculator eliminated the mechanical calculator, while the pocket calculator eliminated the slide rule (which was a device for doing calculations based on logarithms). The mainframe computer largely replaced the electronic calculator during the 1960s and 1970s (except for pocket use). In the late 1980s and early 1990s the increasingly powerful personal computer (PC) largely replaced the mainframe. IBM, then the world's largest producer of computer equipment, suffered seriously from its misjudgement of this shift in demand. Each step vastly increased the speed and accuracy with which calculations could be completed. A modern PC will do in a fraction of a second what the Dickensian clerk did in a week, and what a desk calculator could do in half a day.

The silent film eliminated vaudeville. The 'talkies' eliminated the silent film, and colour largely eliminated black-and-white films. The TV seriously reduced the demand for films (and radio) while not eliminating either of them. Satellites reduced the demand for terrestrial TV reception by offering better pictures and a more varied selection. For a while it looked like fibre optic cable might do the same to satellite transmission, but at the time of writing it seems that cable will be made redundant both by simpler satellite systems and by technical changes in the ability to deliver fast signals (suitable for broad band internet) down telephone lines.

In the 1920s and 1930s the American supermarket threatened the small grocery store as the main shopping place for the typical family. The small store fought back with assistance from the courts and the regulators, and was able to slow the advance of the supermarkets. But in the end the big stores were seen to offer a superior product, and they pushed the small operations into the niche of the convenience store or corner shop. In the 1960s supermarkets spread throughout Britain. In the 1980s and 1990s out-of-town shopping malls and hypermarkets threatened town-centre supermarkets. But by the late 1990s and early 2000s major supermarket groups had slowed their out-of-town expansion and focused on town centre 'metro' stores close to where people live or work.

For long-distance passenger travel by sea, the steamship eliminated the sailing vessel around the late nineteenth century. The aeroplane eliminated the ocean liner in the 1950s and 1960s. For passenger travel on land the train eliminated the stagecoach, while the bus competed with the train without eliminating it. The aeroplane wiped out the passenger train in most of North America while leaving the bus still in a low-cost niche used mainly for short and medium distances. In Europe distances are such that bus, train, and plane all compete over many routes while air transport dominates the longer trips.

The above are all *product* innovations. But *production* processes undergo the same type of creative destruction. The laborious hand-setting of metal type for printing was replaced by the linotype, which allowed the type to be set by a keyboard operator but still involved a costly procedure for making corrections. The linotype was swept away by computer typesetting, and many of the established printing shop operations have recently been replaced by desktop publishing.

Masses of assembly-line workers, operating highly specialized and inflexible machines, replaced the craftsman when Henry Ford perfected the techniques of mass production at the beginning of the twentieth century. A smaller number of less specialized flexible-manufacturing workers, operating sophisticated and less specialized machinery, have now replaced the assembly-line workers who operated the traditional factory in many industries.

The list of such cases can be extended almost indefinitely, and they all illustrate the same general lesson. Creative destruction transforms the products we consume, how we make those products, and how we work. It continually sweeps away positions of high income and economic power established by firms that were in the previous wave of technological change and by those who work for them. It is an agent of dynamism in our economy, an agent of change and economic growth. But it is not without its negative side. Some firms go bust, owners lose wealth, and workers become redundant.

Labour

Labour clearly moves in response to monetary incentives. High relative wages attract and hold labour in such unattractive parts of the world as the North Sea oil fields, the Canadian North, Siberia, and the Amazon jungle, while occupations with much leisure and pleasant working conditions pay lower wages, *ceteris paribus*. There is a supply as well as a demand element at work here. Unpleasant but unskilled jobs are often poorly paid because anyone can do them; but even so, electricians working in the frozen Canadian North are paid more than electricians working in Vancouver, because otherwise they would not choose to work in the unattractive climate.

At the risk of grossly oversimplifying a complex situation, the following generalizations seem consistent with the evidence.

1. There exists a fairly mobile component of labour in any group. It tends to consist of the younger and more adaptable members of the group.

2. This mobile group can be attracted from one area, occupation, or industry to another by relatively small changes in economic incentives. It can also be induced to invest in skills that are newly in high demand and hence are being highly remunerated.

3. Provided that the pattern of demand for resources does not shift too quickly, this mobile group can accomplish most of the necessary reallocation. Of course, the same individual need not move over and over again. New entrants into the labour force are constantly replenishing this group.

4. As we go beyond this very mobile group, we get into ranges of lower and lower mobility until, at the very bottom, we find those who are completely immobile. The most immobile are the old, those with capital sunk in non-marketable assets, the timid, the weak, and those who receive high rents in their present occupation or location. In extreme cases even the threat of starvation may not be enough to induce movement, since some people believe they will starve even if they do move.

Thus, shifts in earnings may create substantial inflows of workers into an expanding occupation, industry, or area and an outflow of workers from a depressed occupation, industry, or area. Over long periods of time, outflows have been observed from depressed areas such as the Highlands of Scotland, the former Welsh mining areas, the Appalachian region in the United States, the Maritime Provinces of Canada, southern Italy, and the rural parts of central France. Although some out-migration occurs readily, it is difficult for large transfers to take place in short periods of time. When demand falls rapidly, pockets of poverty tend to develop. Workers have been leaving each of the geographical areas mentioned above, but poverty there has increased too. This is because the rate of exit has been slower than the rate of decline of the economic opportunities in these areas. Indeed, the exit itself causes further decline, because when a family migrates all the locally provided goods and services that it once consumed suffer a reduction in demand, leading to a further decline in the demand for labour.

Unemployment

Our analysis does well in explaining earnings and resource allocations, but it has one implication that seems to conflict with observations. A competitive market should clear, in the sense that there should be neither excess demand nor excess supply. So in labour markets there should be no one who is willing to work at the prevailing wage but cannot find a job. Yet we observe what appear to be substantial amounts of this type of unemployment from time to time and place to place. Theories that seek to explain why are studied in Chapter 32. Some theories deny that such involuntary unemployment exists. Other theories accept its existence and seek to explain why modern methods of wage determination do not yield the type of wage flexibility that would quickly remove involuntary unemployment. Broadly speaking, the answer seems to be that wages in labour markets do not fluctuate with sufficient rapidity to prevent large pockets of unemployment from persisting. Over the long term relative wages do respond to the conditions of demand and supply. Over the long term labour does move in response to market signals. But over shorter periods of time, which may be several years, wages respond to many influences other than demand and supply. As a result, pockets of excess demand and excess supply can persist.

So markets do work in providing incentives and in allocating labour between its various uses, but they do not seem to work in such a way as to prevent long-term persistent unemployment among some groups of workers.

It is one thing to say that resources move in response to price signals, for which there is much evidence; it is quite another thing to say that they always move fast enough that equilibrium theory is all we need to understand what we see in the world. There is much evidence that resource movements are quite sluggish at various times and in various markets. Sluggish movement can give rise to many effects, some of which come under the heading 'hysteresis'.[4] The amount of human capital that workers acquire depends, among other things, on the time that they are employed. Long bouts of unemployment not only may reduce their accumulated experience, but also can create attitudes that would lower their future ability to get work and to command high wages even if they were to find employment. It is quite possible for resource markets to work qualitatively in the directions that we have discussed above while in many cases working slowly enough that their behaviour can be regarded as less than satisfactory. Quantitative studies of how well and how fast labour markets work are important in modern labour economics. This problem is briefly discussed in Chapter 32, and it is discussed in detail in books and courses devoted to labour economics.

The Information and Communication Technology (ICT) Revolution and the 'New Economy'

To understand what is meant by the ICT revolution and the New Economy, we need to consider a few basic facts about technological change and economic growth. Long-term economic growth is driven by technological change: that is, by changes in the products that are produced, the process by which they are produced, and the ways in which productive activities are organizational—what are called product, process, and organizational technologies. Although each person living in Western Europe and North America has about five times as much 'real purchasing power' as did their forebears who lived 100 years ago, they consume it largely in the form of *new commodities* made with *new techniques* and *new organizations*. Those who lived at the beginning of the twentieth century could not have imagined modern dental and medical equipment, penicillin, painkillers, bypass operations, safe births, control of genetically transmitted diseases, personal computers, compact discs, DVDs, television sets, efficient motor cars, opportunities for cheap fast world-wide travel, affordable universities, safe food of great variety free from ptomaine and botulism, or the elimination of endless kitchen drudgery through the use of detergents, washing machines, electric cookers, vacuum cleaners, refrigerators, dishwashers, and a host of other labour-saving household products that we take for granted today. Nor could they have imagined

the clean, robot-operated, computer-controlled modern factories that have largely replaced their noisy, dangerous, predecessors that spewed coal smoke and other pollutants over the surrounding countryside.

The point is important. Technological advance not only raises our incomes; it transforms our lives through the invention of new, hitherto undreamed of, things that are made in new, hitherto undreamed of, ways.

General Purpose Technologies

The technological changes that drive long-term economic growth range from small incremental improvements in existing technologies to the introduction of what are called 'general purpose technologies' (GPTs). GPTs share some important characteristics. They begin as fairly crude technologies with a limited number of uses. As they diffuse throughout the economy they evolve into much more complex technologies, with dramatic increases in their efficiency, in the range of their use, in the range of economic

[4] In economics hysteresis relates to persistence or irreversibility of effects.

outputs that they help to produce, and in the range of new product and process technologies that incorporate, or otherwise depend on, them.

Throughout history the most important new GPTs have had major impacts on the economic, social, and political structures, creating what may be called a series of 'New Economies'. Here are some of the main ones.

• **Information and communication technologies (ICTs):** *Writing*; *printing* with movable type; the *computer*, which along with several related technologies is driving the current ICT Revolution

• **Materials:** *Bronze*; *iron*; the current ability to create *made-to-order materials* invented specifically for use in newly developed products and processes

• **Power delivery systems:** *Domesticated animals*; the *water wheel*; the *steam engine*; *electricity*; the *internal combustion engine*

• **Transportation:** the *three-masted sailing ship*; *railways*; the *iron steam ship*; the *motor vehicle*; *commercial aircraft* (the latter two of which were enabled by the internal combustion engine)

• **Organizational technologies:** the *factory system*; *mass production*; *flexible manufacturing* (or lean production or Toyotaism, as it is variously called—see Box 9.3 on p. 151).

As each new GPT diffuses through the economy, it creates a research programme from which entrepreneurs can apply its principles to create new processes and new products and to improve old ones. These, in turn, create other new opportunities, and so on in a chain reaction that stretches over decades, even centuries. Note, for example, all of the myriad ways that innovators have found to use electronic chips; how these ways have multiplied as the power and reliability of chips have increased; and how some of these ways have in turn enabled other developments; and so on in a complex linking of related innovations.

GPTs typically greatly reduce the cost of providing some good or service. Power GPTs reduced the cost of power while information GPTs reduced the cost of creating, storing, transmitting, and analysing information. It is also important to note that some of the most important consequences to any new GPT depend on purely technological relations and not on how a given technology responds to a change in price. The use of water power, the main source of non-human power for manufacturing until well into the nineteenth century, requires that factories be located near fast running water. The introduction of steam power freed manufacturing from that constraint and allowed it to locate in the industrial cities that grew up in the nineteenth century. No fall in the price of water power—even to zero—could have given rise to this transforming relocation of industry.

The ICT Revolution

For the last few decades, the West has been living through a set of major structural adjustments associated with the so-called revolution in information and communication technologies (ICTs). Like all transforming GPTs, the ICT revolution has roots that go a long way back in techno-logical history. This one began with the development of commercially useful electricity in the nineteenth century. True 'tele' communications started in the 1840s with the introduction of the telegraph and its associated commun-ications language, the Morse Code. Submarine telegraphy started in 1851 with the first line from England to France. In 1866 the first commercial submarine cable came into regular use between Britain and the United States. The tele-phone was invented in 1876, and the wireless telegraph followed twenty years later. Wireless speech commun-ication was first established in 1906, and in 1920 the first commercial radio station went on the air. Television first appeared in the late 1930s but was widely available, at prices most households could afford, only after 1945.

The modern ICT revolution is based on a new GPT that is driven by a cluster of technologies centred around the electronic computer, but including efficient long-distance STD telephonic communication, faxes, satellite transmis-sions, lasers, fibre optics and the internet (most of which either use computers directly, or were developed with their assistance). These technologies are changing product de-sign, production, marketing, finance, and the organization of firms. By managing information flows more effectively than did the old, hierarchically organized mass of middle managers, computers have caused a major reorganization in the management of firms. They have also created a wide range of new products incorporating hard coded chips, computers and/or software. Computers are used to design products, fly aeroplanes, drive trains, operate machines, run buildings systems, facilitate scientific research, warn of unsafe driving practices, monitor health, and facilitate communication through the internet, e-mail, and desktop publishing.

When computers were initially introduced, they entered structures designed for the paper world, merely substitut-ing for human hands and minds. Before they could really begin to pay off, administration and production facilities had to be redesigned both physically and in their com-mand structures. Slowly, as it was with electricity, the whole process of producing, designing, delivering, and marketing goods and services was, and still is, being reorganized along lines dominated by computing technologies.

ICT not only affects every industry and service but also every function within each industry, that is R&D, design, produc-tion, marketing, transport, and general administration. It is systemization rather than automation, integrating the various previously separate departments and functions. In design and development every industry now depends on computers. This is not just a question of Computer-Aided-Design (CAD), although this is of great importance, especially in complex products, such as large buildings chemical plants, aircraft, and ships as well as the products of the electronics industry itself. It is also a question of the accuracy, speed and volume of all kinds of calculations and access to data banks at all stages of the R&D process. Christopher Freeman, Ch. 2 in Robin Mansell (ed.) *Management of Information and Communications Technologies*, London: Association of Information Management, 1994, pp. 14–15.

New Economies

Each of the GPTs mentioned earlier issued in a set of economic, social, and political transformations that could be called the creation of a 'New Economy'. Two examples from earlier ICT revolutions illustrate that this is not a new phenomenon.

Writing The invention of writing around 3500 BC caused a radical transformation of the societies of the Tigris–Euphrates valley. Written records permitted the development of sophisticated systems of taxation and public spending that were quite impossible when all records were held in memory. The new public savings financed the West's first irrigation works, the technology of which evolved rapidly. The area under cultivation increased and agricultural surpluses rose. The populations of the largest settlements, which typically had been measured in the hundreds for millennia, increased over the span of a mere two centuries into the tens of thousands.

Printing In the fifteenth century the invention of printing with movable type greatly lowered the total cost of reproducing a manuscript. It also altered the ratio of variable to fixed costs—the major cost of manuscript reproduction was the variable cost of the scribe's time, whereas the major cost involved in printing was the high fixed cost of typesetting, while the marginal cost of printing an extra copy was low. This new cost structure made mass communication feasible. Costs of large-scale publications fell and learning exploded. Monopolies of knowledge were upset. The results of new scientific experiments were quickly disseminated and results duplicated and expanded upon at a speed that would have seemed miraculous a century earlier. Mass communication helped the Protestant Revolution, since its direct appeal to the people would have been impossible without the many low-cost printed pamphlets written in the vernacular.

In the sixteenth century the tiny country of the Netherlands rose to become a world power. A key contributor to its success was its liberal attitude towards the technology of printing that it embodied—unlike the Islamic nations, which had suppressed it and stayed with hand-copied manuscripts for centuries. The creation of the Dutch information network, which was based on low-cost reproduction of the printed word, greatly increased the Dutch economy's productive efficiency and the government's tax revenues. Between 1590 and 1620, multinational corporations, the stock exchange, efficient year-round financial intermediation, the federal state, and a systematically drilled army all made their first appearances in Holland.

The current New Economy

The current ICT revolution is similarly transforming many economic, social, and political relations. The term 'New Economy' is however used in more than one sense, which can be a cause of confusion. Some use the term to refer to an economy in which the laws of supply and demand no longer hold and there are neither business cycles nor inflations. Not many academic economists are gullible enough to believe that the ICT revolution can so alter normal economic behaviour. Others define the New Economy as the sector producing computing power and related things. By this supply-side definition, the New Economy covers only a small fraction of the whole economy. Still others define a New Economy as something that occurs only when there is a sustained acceleration in the rate of growth of productivity. In contrast, we follow a well established procedure of using the term in a wider sense to refer to the social, economic, and political changes bought about by the current ICT revolution. It is an economy-wide *process*, not located in just one hi-tech sector any more than the 'New Economy' initiated by electricity was confined to the electricity-generating sector.

Below we list just a few of the many changes that have been driven by the ICT revolution since 1970. They are grouped loosely under the headings of process, product, and organizational technologies, and social and political implications, although the categories clearly overlap.

Process technologies

• Computerized robots and related technologies have transformed the modern factory and eliminated most of the high-paying, low-skilled jobs that existed in the old Fordist assembly line factories.

• Computer assisted design (CAD) is revolutionizing the design process and eliminating much of the need for 'learning by using', whereby complex products such as new aircraft had to be built before their behavioural characteristics could be fully established.

• Surgery on hips, knees, and other delicate parts of the body is more and more done by computers, which will soon facilitate long-distance surgery, permitting specialists working in major urban hospitals to operate on patients in remote parts of the world.

• Research in everything from economics to astronomy has been changed dramatically by the ability to do complex calculations that were either impossible or prohibitively time-consuming before electronic computers.

• Computer-age crime detection is much more sophisticated than it was in the past. Here the biological and the ICT revolutions complement each other, as is so often the case with co-existing GPTs.

• Traffic control in the air and on the ground has been revolutionized in many ways, while navigation at sea is now so easy that lighthouses, the sailor's friend for several millennia, are slowly being phased out as unnecessary, now that ships can determine their distance to within a few yards using satellites and computers.

Product technologies

• Many goods now contain chips that allow them to do new things, or old things more efficiently. New applications continue to be developed. For example, cars will soon be equipped with systems that warn drivers of oncoming dangers and take over control if the driver fails to take evasive action.

• ATMs have enormously facilitated accessing one's bank account and obtaining funds in any currency in almost any part of the world.

• Email has largely replaced conventional mail with a resulting large increase in volume and also in speed of transmission—from days or weeks in the past, depending on the locations, to minutes today.

• Computerized translation is a now a reality and will progress from its present crude form to high degrees of sophistication within the lifetimes of most of us. We are witnessing the arrival of Douglas Adam's vision in *The Hitch Hiker's Guide to the Galaxy*: the ability to hear in one's own language words spoken in any other, and to be understood in any other language while speaking one's own. The only difference is that, instead of inserting a fish into one's ear, a small computer will be attached to one's body.

• Distant education is growing by leaps and bounds and many are enrolled in education courses where they never (or only rarely) set foot inside the institution that they are attending.

• Cars will soon receive real-time information on traffic conditions at all points in their projected journey, just as Tokyo taxis now do.

• Smart buildings and factories already exist and will grow rapidly in number. Among many other things, power consumption can be adjusted continually in response to real-time price signals sent out by the electricity supply company and calculated in response to current loads.

• The electronic book looks like it might defeat consumer resistance to reading books on screen. The book's blank pages fill up on demand with any one of a hundred or more books stored in a chip that is housed in its cover. A touch of a button, and one is reading a physics text in what looks like a conventional book; with another touch, an art history text replaces it on the book's pages.

Organizational technologies

• The management of firms has been reorganized as direct lines of communication opened up by computers have eliminated the need for the old pyramidal structure in which middle managers processed and communicated information. Today's horizontally organized loose management structure bears little resemblance to the management structure of the 1960s.

• Firms are increasingly disintegrating their operations. Virtually no firm in Silicon Valley, California's pioneering hi-tech sector, now produces physical products. In other industries, the main firm is increasingly becoming a co-ordinator of subcontractors who do everything from designing products, to manufacturing them, to distributing them.

• The e-lance economy—groups of independent contractors who come together for a single job then disperse—is growing and, incidentally, becoming difficult for authorities to track.

• Just as the first Industrial Revolution took work out of the home, the ICT revolution is putting much of it back, as more and more people find it increasingly convenient to do all sorts of jobs at home rather than 'in the office'.

• ICTs have been central to the globalization of trade in manufactured goods, and of the market for unskilled workers. This has shifted the location of much manufacturing and has allowed poorer countries to industrialize, creating new opportunities and challenges for both developed and developing nations.

• Digitalized special effects have changed the movie industry in many ways, for example by reducing the need for shooting on location or for myriad extras, whose presence can now often be produced digitally.

Political and social technologies

• The computer-enabled internet is revolutionizing everything from interpersonal relations to political activity. Chat rooms form the basis for new forms of community,

CHAPTER 18: RESOURCE ALLOCATION IN ACTION

making interpersonal relations possible on a scale never seen before. Non-governmental organizations (NGOs) are able to organize activities to protest against such things as clear-cut logging, WTO efforts to reduce trade barriers, and the push for a Free Trade Area of the Americas (FTAA). Never again will trade negotiations take place in relative obscurity.

• Dictators find it much harder to cut their subjects off from knowledge of what is going on in the outside world, and hence to maintain their power.

• Driven by the internet, English is becoming a *lingua franca* for the world and, unlike Latin in the Middle Ages, its use is not limited to the intelligentsia.

• In former times, a physical presence was required from virtually everyone providing a service. With computers, email links, and a host of other ICTs, this link between physical presence and provision has been broken in many services, with profound social and political effects on such things as place of residence and the ability to regulate and tax many activities.

Falling cost curves

Most of the firms that we have looked at in earlier chapters are assumed to have U-shaped cost curves—after a declining portion, the curves slope upwards. However, many ICT firms are working with cost curves that decline over their whole range. Typically, there are very large fixed costs associated with the R&D and setup costs of creating and establishing a new technology in the ICT sector. In contrast, marginal costs of producing another unit of output are very small or virtually zero. As a result, the average total cost curve (ATC) declines throughout its whole relevant range. Microsoft, for example, spent a lot of money and effort developing its Windows software (and MS DOS before that), but once it existed an extra copy could be made at virtually no cost. Similarly, modern telephone cables have very high capacity, so once the lines are in place the extra cost of delivering a marginal call is virtually zero.

Increasing returns tend to generate natural monopolies. (This is discussed in the following chapter.) Such industries tend to be characterized by *winner takes all* outcomes, as new entrants find it virtually impossible to break into an industry where an established player is selling its product at very low marginal cost. This is reinforced by the *network externalities* that arise from the adoption of common standards. For example, computer compatibility is helpful so that computers can exchange messages and software.

When Microsoft Windows emerged as the standard platform, most software was developed to be compatible with it and new operating systems found it hard to break in. Similarly, because a telephone network is more useful to any one user the more other users are on the same system, new phone companies found it hard to break into the UK telephone market while BT owned all the lines. Regulators tried to offset this advantage by insisting that BT give other companies access to the network. Later, in an example of Schumpeter's creative destruction, the new technology of mobile phones made traditional phone lines less important.

Increasing returns are not unique to ICT industries. Pharmaceuticals also have some products, such as major drugs, that incur huge costs to develop but then can often be produced at low marginal cost. These products tend to gain a dominant position while patent protection lasts (see above) and the companies making them hope to recoup their development cost during the patent period. Once the patent expires, such drugs are typically copied and sold by other drug companies at close to marginal cost.

It is not always the best product that obtains the winner-take-all advantage. The VHS format became the dominant standard for videotapes because it established a critical mass ahead of Betamax, even though the latter was a better system.

The nature of competition is different in constant or falling marginal cost industries. Where costs are rising, firms are competing at the margin—a small price change or quality initiative will take a bit of business at the margin from several main rivals. Market share may rise or fall, but only by a small amount at a time (see the example of newspapers on page 79–82, and of supermarkets on page 208). However, constant or falling marginal cost industries tend to have big jumps from one dominant player to another. Companies like Intel, Microsoft, Amazon, AOL, Nokia, and Vodafone grew to be huge within less than two decades. They may disappear just as quickly if some new and better technology removes their edge. In contrast, traditional retailers, banks, and manufacturers tend to grow up slowly and fade slowly. They may merge or be taken over and so lose their name, but they are rarely made redundant by the sudden appearance of a new technology.

In these and many other ways, new ICTs have already revolutionized society and will continue to do so well into the twenty-first century. Some of these are minor while others are transforming—e.g. globalization and its many ramifications, the dramatic changes in the organization of firms, the end of mass production and its associated labour and management requirements, the alternations in the political power structure, the emergence of the civil society and its effects on the conduct of international negotiations.

SUMMARY

Resource pricing and allocation: a summary

- The neoclassical theory of resource allocation is an implication of profit maximization. Each resource owner is paid the value of the marginal revenue product of that resource, and resources move between uses to equalize net returns, taking monetary and non-monetary rewards into account.

- The satisfactory working of resource markets depends on two conditions: prices must reflect market conditions; and resources must move in response to changes in relative prices.

Markets determine prices

- Urban land values respond to demand by showing a typical tent shape, highest in the city centre and lowest in the suburbs. Rural land values have not risen to the extent predicted by the classical economists because rising agricultural productivity has increased food supplies faster than rising population and rising incomes have increased food demand.

- Brands are like a capital asset that adds to the income stream of the firms that own them.

- Saleable production quotas have market values that eliminate monopoly profits once the cost of the quota is included as a cost of production.

Resources move in response to changes in relative prices

- Land and natural resources are constantly being reallocated between their various possible uses in response to changes in market prices.

- Inefficiencies can arise when property rights do not confer long-term ownership of resources on those currently making use of them. These are particularly serious in the use of natural resources.

- In the long and very long runs, capital moves into industries making pure profits, using creative destruction to break down entry barriers when necessary.

- Problems arise when resources do not move with sufficient speed even though they do move in the directions indicated by market signals. Early experience of prolonged unemployment can affect a person's ability to gain employment and earn a satisfactory wage for the rest of her life.

The Information Communication Technologies (ICT) Revolution and the 'New Economy'

- The revolution in information and communication technologies (ICTs) has roots that go back to the nineteenth century, but it accelerated in the latter part of the twentieth century when a new general purpose technology, the electronic computer, and a few related technologies began to transform much of the economic, social, and political structure of society.

- The revolution has been associated with many new products, new production processes, and new forms of organization.

- None the less, resources still move in response to price signals and profit motives, and recessions and inflations have not been banished for ever.

- Two of the special features of ICT industries are increasing returns and network externalities. These generate a winner-take-all competition between firms.

TOPICS FOR REVIEW

- The neoclassical theory of resource allocation
- The effect of licences and quotas
- The effect of market conditions on resource prices
- The effect of prices on the allocation of resources between alternative uses
- The ICT revolution

- General purpose technologies
- Declining cost curves arising from the high costs of R&D and setup for entry
- Network externalities
- Winner takes all

DISCUSSION QUESTIONS

1 Governments around the world frequently seek to raise the incomes of groups of producers by imposing a minimum price that is well above the free-market price for their products.
   (a) Who benefits and who loses?
   (b) Why are such schemes difficult to maintain in the long run?

2 Concern is sometimes expressed that serious food shortages will arise because urban growth is taking so much land out of food production.
   (a) Explain how the market mechanism determines how much land is allocated to urban and to agricultural uses.
   (b) Explain why serious food shortages are unlikely to arise for the reason alleged above.

3 Suppose that the earnings of top footballers were legally capped at £200,000 per annum. What would be the consequences for the clubs and players?

4 What would be the consequences of a policy of controls that fixed the rents of unfurnished accommodation on the basis of construction and operating costs but did not allow them to reflect local conditions of demand and supply (a policy followed for decades in the UK)?

5 How do effective property rights provide incentives to conserve resources? How do ineffective ones provide incentives to squander them?

6 How does the market ensure that resources move into uses that are most highly valued?

7 Why is city-centre land more valuable than suburban land?

8 List some of the ways in which increasing-returns industries differ from traditional diminishing-returns industries.

PART FOUR

THE GOVERNMENT IN THE ECONOMY

Chapter 19

MARKET SUCCESS AND MARKET FAILURE

So far our main aims have been to understand how individual markets work, and how the market economy as a whole allocates resources between competing uses. We now ask what happens if markets are left alone entirely. Do markets always generate efficient outcomes? If they do not, in what circumstances do they fail to do so? Where markets fail, what alternative methods are available to deliver desired outcomes? In particular, you will learn that:

• A perfectly competitive economy is allocatively efficient since it operates where price equals marginal cost.

• Free markets can fail to achieve an efficient outcome for one of several possible causes of 'market failure'.

• Private markets will tend to overexploit common property resources.

• Goods that are jointly consumed by more than one person are called public goods and cannot be provided efficiently by the market.

• The costs and benefits of production that are external to the producer cause the level of production that is achieved by the free market to deviate from the socially optimal level.

• Government policy towards competition is designed to encourage competitive practices and to discourage monopoly.

In this chapter we first look at the basic functions that all governments have undertaken since the dawn of history: to provide institutions that protect the security of life, limb, and property. We see that if those functions are reasonably well performed the free-market economy will allocate resources with relative efficiency. Indeed, an idealization of the free market, in which there is perfect competition in all markets, allocates resources optimally. We go on to see that in the real world markets fail to perform efficiently under a number of well-defined circumstances, involving common property resources, public goods, harmful externalities, and excessive market power. These market failures provide the potential for government intervention to improve market efficiency. We consider what government policies could achieve this objective under ideal circumstances. In Chapter 20 we study how well or poorly actual governments manage to improve market efficiency.

Basic functions of government

Organized governments are as old as organized economic activity. They arose shortly after the Neolithic agricultural revolution turned people from hunter–gatherers into settled farmers. An institution that has survived that long must be doing something right! Over the intervening one hundred centuries, the functions undertaken by government have varied enormously. But through all that time the function that has not changed is to provide what is called a *monopoly of violence*. Violent acts can be conducted by the military and civilian police arms of government; and through its judicial system the government can deprive people of their liberty by incarcerating them or, in extreme cases, executing them. This is a dangerous monopoly that

is easily abused—as is any monopoly, but with more serious consequences than when monopolies over production are abused. For these reasons satisfactory governments have systems of checks and balances designed to keep the use of their monopoly power directed to the general good rather than to the good of a narrow government circle.

The importance of having a monopoly of violence can be seen in those countries whose governments do not have it. Somalia and Afghanistan in recent decades and China in the 1920s provide examples of countries in which individual warlords commanded armies that could not vanquish each other. Colombia, and to some extent Russia, provide examples of countries in which organized crime has substantial power to commit violence that the government cannot control. In extreme cases where many groups have almost equal ability to exert military violence, power struggles can create havoc with normal economic and social life. Life then becomes 'nasty, brutish, and short'—to use the words of the seventeenth-century English political philosopher Thomas Hobbes.

The importance of having checks on the arbitrary use of its monopoly by a selfish government is seen in the disasters that ensue in the many dictatorships that misuse their power. The USSR under Stalin, Uganda under Idi Amin, Nigeria under Sanni Abacha, and Cambodia under Pol Pot are a few of the many modern-day examples.

When the government's monopoly of violence is secure and functions with reasonable restraints against its arbitrary use, citizens can safely carry on their ordinary economic and social activities.

So governments are, as they always have been, institutions to which people give over a monopoly of violence in return for the enforcement of 'law and order'. A related

government activity is to provide security of property. Governments define and enforce property rights that give people a secure claim to the fruits of their own labour. These property rights include clear definition and enforcement of the rights and obligations of institutions such as joint-stock companies, banks, insurance companies, and stock exchanges, as well as provisions for bankruptcy and protections against the rise and/or abuse of monopoly power over markets.

As the founder of British classical economics, Adam Smith, put it a long time ago:

The first duty of the sovereign [is] that of protecting the society from the violence and invasion of other independent societies. . . . The second duty of the sovereign [is] that of protecting, as far as possible, every member of the society from the injustice or oppression of every other member of it.[1]

In a modern complex economy, providing these 'minimal' government services is no simple task. Countries whose governments are not good at doing these things have seldom prospered economically.

Market efficiency

Within a secure framework of law and order, and well-defined and enforced property rights and other essential institutions, a modern economy can function at least moderately well without further government assistance. In this section we see how and why this is so. In subsequent sections we study government functions that arise when free markets fail to produce results that are regarded as acceptable.

Free markets are impressive institutions. Consumers' tastes and producers' costs help to generate price signals. These signals co-ordinate the separate decisions taken by millions of independent agents, all pursuing their own self-interest and oblivious to national priorities. In doing so, they allocate the nation's resources without conscious central direction. Markets also determine the distribution of income by establishing the prices of resources (such as land, labour, and capital) that provide incomes for their owners. Furthermore, in modern market economies firms compete to get ahead of each other by producing better goods more cheaply, and in the process they generate the technological changes that have raised average living standards fairly steadily at least over the past two centuries.

How markets work

The most general case in support of market economies is that they fulfil their functions better than any known

alternative. We observed that this *was* so in Chapter 1, but now we have developed a deeper insight into *why* this is so.

Better information Market-generated prices convey an enormous amount of information about constantly changing market conditions. The central planners of the former Soviet Union found that generating this information by conscious planning was a massive job. For example, the Soviet authorities had to set prices for over 5 million items. Yet their economy was much simpler than any Western economy because the planners suppressed most of the vast range of differentiated products available to consumers in modern industrial economies.

Greater flexibility Compared with any known alternative, the decentralized market system is more flexible and leaves more scope for personal adaptation at any moment in time. If, for example, a scarcity of oil raises its price, one individual can elect to leave her heating on full and economize on her car's petrol consumption, while another may wish to do the opposite. In order to obtain the same overall reduction in consumption by non-price rationing, the government typically forces the same reduction in heating and driving on both individuals, independent of their tastes, doctor's advice, and other perceived needs.

[1] Adam Smith, *The Wealth of Nations*, 1776 (New York: Random House, 1937 edn, pp. 653, 669).

适应性.

Better adaptability In market economies prices change as conditions change. Decentralized decision-takers can react continuously to these changing signals, whereas government quotas, allocations, and rationing schemes are slower to adjust. Millions of adaptations to millions of changes in tens of thousands of markets are required every year. The Eastern European planners discovered that it is a Herculean task to anticipate these and plan the necessary adjustments.

Decentralization of power The market economy decentralizes power and thus requires less coercion of individuals than do other types of economy. Governments must coerce if markets are not allowed to allocate people to jobs, and products to consumers. The power to allocate creates major opportunities for bribery, corruption, and allocation according to the tastes of the central administrators. If, at the going prices and wages, there are not enough flats or coveted jobs to go around, the bureaucrats must allocate them. Some will go to those who pay the largest bribe, some to those with religious beliefs, hairstyles, or political views that they like, and only the rest to those whose names come up on the waiting-list.

Of course, large firms and large unions exercise substantial economic power in market economies. However, that power tends to be constrained both by the competition of other large entities and by the emergence of new products and firms.

The efficiency of perfect competition

While they accept the general case for the superiority of the market economy outlined above, many professional economists want to be more precise about just what the market economy does so well. They do this by proving that an idealization of the market economy (perfect competition) leads, in equilibrium, to an optimum, or efficient, allocation of resources. This is often referred to as **Pareto optimality** after the great Italian economist Vilfredo Pareto (1848–1923), who studied it in great detail.

In Chapter 10 we showed that perfect competition is efficient because it maximizes the sum of producers' and consumers' surplus. In Chapter 11 we showed that monopoly is not efficient because it restricts output below what is required to maximize these surpluses. In this section we develop an alternative proof of the proposition that perfect competition leads to efficient allocation of resources. As a first step, we inquire in a little more depth into the meaning of the term *efficiency*.

Productive efficiency

Production is efficient when it is impossible to reallocate resources so as to produce more of some product without producing less of some other product. Watch the double negative! An allocation of resources is productively inefficient when it is possible to produce more of some product without producing less of any other product. It is efficient when this cannot be done—in other words, when the only way to produce more of one product is to produce less of some other product.

Productive efficiency has two aspects, one concerning the allocation of resources within each firm, and the other concerning the allocation of resources among the firms in an industry. The first condition for productive efficiency is that each firm should produce any given output at the lowest possible cost. Any firm that is not being productively efficient is producing at a higher cost than is necessary. This must reduce its profits. Thus, any perfectly competitive profit-maximizing firm will be productively efficient.[2]

The second condition for productive efficiency is that all firms producing the same product should have the same marginal cost. This ensures that the total output of each industry is allocated among its individual firms in such a way that the total cost of producing the industry's output is minimized. If firms' marginal costs were not all the same, resources could be transferred from the firm with the highest marginal cost to the firm with lowest. The same output would be produced but at a lower cost.

Perfect competition produces productive efficiency. First, all firms are motivated to produce at the lowest possible cost. Second, since firms in any one industry face the same price to which they equate their marginal cost, all firms have the same marginal cost. Market price = M<.

Look again at the production-possibility curve in Figure 1.1 on page 5. An economy that is productively inefficient will be at some point inside the curve, such as point *c*. It will be possible to produce more of some goods without producing less of others.

Productive efficiency implies being on, rather than inside, the economy's production-possibility curve.

Allocative efficiency 分配效率

Allocative efficiency relates to the allocation of resources among the production of all the goods and services that are produced. In other words,

Allocative efficiency relates to the choice among alternative points on the production-possibility curve.

---

[2] This result is restricted to price-taking firms because inefficient production, using more fixed capital than is necessary, can be an entry-barring strategy for oligopolistic firms. It may pay firms in such markets to produce above the minimum attainable cost in order to maximize profits in the long run by restricting entry.

It concerns, for example, the choice between points such as *a* and *b* in Figure 1.1 on page 5. Changing the allocation of resources implies producing more of some goods and less of others, which in turn means moving from one point on the production-possibility curve to another.

Allocative inefficiency means that resources can be reallocated from their present uses so as to make at least one person better off while making no other person worse off. Conversely, **allocative efficiency** means that it is impossible, by producing a different bundle of goods, to make any one person better off without making at least one other person worse off.

How do we find the allocatively efficient point on the production-possibility curve? For example, how many shoes, dresses, and hats should be produced to achieve allocative efficiency?

The economy's allocation of resources is efficient when the marginal cost of producing each good is equal to its market price.

To understand the reasoning behind this answer, we need to look at the significance of price and marginal cost. First, look at price. Recall a point that was established in our discussion of consumers' surplus in Chapter 6. The price of any product indicates the value that each consumer places on the last unit purchased of that product. Faced with the market price of some product, the consumer goes on buying units until the last one is valued exactly at its price. Consumers' surplus arises because each consumer would be willing to pay more than the market price for all but the last unit bought. On the last unit bought (i.e. the marginal unit), however, the consumer only 'breaks even', because the valuation placed on it is just equal to its price.

Now consider marginal cost. This is the value of the resources used to produce the last unit of output. Thus, when marginal cost is equated to price, the value that consumers place on the last unit they consume is exactly equal to the value of the resources required to produce that unit of output.

For the next step in the argument, suppose that the entire economy is perfectly competitive. Marginal cost will then equal price in all lines of production. The value that consumers place on the last unit of each and every commodity that they consume will be equal to the cost of producing that unit.

In a perfectly competitive economy, £1 worth of resources reallocated from the production of any one product would produce £1 worth of value for consumers, whatever product it was then used to produce.

To illustrate, assume that marginal cost equals price in all lines of production except blue jeans. Jeans sell for £25 but initially cost £30 to produce at the margin. If one less pair of jeans is produced, consumers lose the £25 of value that they place on it. But resources worth £30 are freed. If those resources move to any industry in which marginal cost equals price, they will produce £30 worth of value. Society will have gained £5 in total value and it will be possible to make someone better off by £5 worth of consumption without making anyone else worse off.

Now let the output of jeans fall until they cost only £20 to produce at the margin but still sell for £25. If one more pair of jeans is now produced, resources worth £20 will have to be withdrawn from some other line of production. But since marginal cost equals price in all other lines, only £20 worth of consumer satisfaction will be lost when these resources move. When they produce one more pair of jeans, consumers get a product they value at £25. So there is a net gain of £5 on the transfer.

Finally, let the output of jeans increase until the marginal cost of the last pair produced is equal to its £25 price. If *one less pair of jeans* is produced, £25 worth of value is sacrificed and the £25 worth of resources that are freed could produce £25 worth of value anywhere else in the economy. If *one more pair of jeans* is produced, the producers of jeans create £25 of value but £25 worth of value is lost when the resources are taken from some other industry. So there is no gain in reallocating resources either into or out of the production of blue jeans. The current allocation is efficient.

When marginal cost equals price in all industries, it is impossible to reallocate resources between alternative lines of production and increase consumer satisfaction. The economy is allocatively efficient.

A perfectly competitive economy is allocatively efficient because it equates marginal cost to price in all lines of production, and (as we saw in earlier chapters) because it maximizes the sum of producers' and consumers' surpluses.

How markets fail

The term **market failure** describes the failure of the market economy to achieve an efficient allocation of resources. We observed in Chapter 12 that firms in most lines of production have some market power over their prices because they face negatively sloped rather than perfectly elastic demand curves for their products. When firms face negatively sloped demand curves, price will exceed marginal cost in equilibrium. Thus, no real market economy has ever achieved perfect allocative efficiency. The conditions for efficiency are meant only as a benchmark to help in identifying sources of allocative inefficiency, called market failures. These sources provide scope for possible government intervention designed to improve market efficiency—even if not to achieve complete efficiency. (But there are also costs of such intervention, which we consider later in this chapter.)

There are several important circumstances under which markets fail to allocate resources with reasonable efficiency, let alone achieve the optimal allocation of resources:

1. where producers with excess capacity set positive prices;

2. where there are resources that can be used by everyone but belong to no one—called *common property resources*;

3. where there are goods whose consumption cannot be restricted to those who are willing to pay for them—called *public goods*;

4. where people not party to some market bargain are none the less significantly affected by it—called *externalities*;

5. where one party to a market transaction has fuller knowledge of its consequences than is available to the other party—a situation referred to as *asymmetric information*;

6. where needed markets do not exist;

7. where substantial monopoly power causes prices to diverge from marginal costs.

Coping with these market failures provides governments with major functions in addition to the law and order functions discussed earlier. In the rest of this chapter we study these sources of market failure and how government policies could conceivably alleviate them. In Chapter 20 we study the costs of government intervention which must be set against the possible benefits before an intervention is justified on economic grounds. This raises the question of how well government policies actually work in coping with market failures as well as in achieving all the other goals that governments set for themselves.

Rivalrous and excludable goods

Economies must allocate resources between the production and consumption of the four major classes of goods and services that are shown in Table 19.1. A good is **rivalrous** if no two people can consume the same unit. For example, if you buy and eat an apple, no one else can buy and eat *that same* apple. A good is **excludable** if people can be prevented from obtaining it. Excludability requires that an owner be able to exercise effective property rights over the good or service in order to determine who uses it—typically, only those who pay for the privilege.

Most of the goods and services that you and I buy are rivalrous and excludable. If I buy a chocolate bar and eat it, no one else can buy and eat that same bar, and the owner can prevent me from having it if I am unwilling to pay for it (unless I steal it). If an airline sells you a seat on a particular flight, it cannot let another person occupy that seat as well as you.

Obvious though these characteristics may seem, there are important classes of goods and services that lack one or both of them. Goods and services are **non-rivalrous** when the amount that one person consumes does not affect the amount that other people can consume. They are **non-excludable** when, once produced, there is no way to stop anyone from consuming them.

What determines which is which?

Rivalrousness is usually fixed once and for all by the nature of the good or service. An apple is rivalrous; a work of art is not. In contrast, excludability depends on the specific circumstances and the state of technology.

Circumstances The Fastnet lighthouse guides all shipping making a landfall on southwest Ireland, and there is no way to force passing ships to pay for its services. The New Brighton lighthouse, on the other hand, illuminates the entrance to the River Mersey and the Port of Liverpool, and if its operators had turned it off (prior to the invention of radar) many ships would have simply passed on to another, better lit, harbour entrance. In this case the private owners of the lighthouse could sell its services—not to passing ships, but to the port authorities, who knew they needed it in order to compete with rival ports.

Table 19.1 **Four types of goods**

	Excludable	Non-excludable
Rivalrous	*Normal goods* Apples Dresses TV sets Computers A seat on an aeroplane	*Common property* Fisheries Common land Wildlife Air Streams
Non-rivalrous (up to capacity)	Art galleries Museums Fenced parks Roads Bridges	*Public goods* Defence Police Public information Broadcast signals Some navigation aids

Markets cope best with rivalrous excludable goods. The table gives examples of items in each of the four categories. The market can produce goods that are excludable but non-rivalrous, but their efficient use requires a zero price. Goods that are non-excludable but rivalrous are common property resources, which get overused by free markets. Goods that are non-rivalrous and non-excludable are public goods, which will usually not be produced at all by the free market.

Technology Early TV programmes were all broadcast openly to anyone who had a set. But the development of satellites, encoded signals, and cable transmission now allows some forms of TV signals to be provided only to those who pay for the service. The programmes are still non-rivalrous, in the sense that there is no limit to the number of people who can watch a given programme. But the new technologies have made them excludable, so that private companies are willing to provide them. As another example, until recently it has been impracticable to charge tolls for the use of urban roads and exclude non-payers because of the excessive costs involved in the many tollbooths needed to service a road in a densely populated urban area. Today it is possible to implant in each car a device that tracks its location at very small cost. Fees for the use of urban roads can now be assessed and non-payers denied use of the roads.

Cost In some cases it is technically possible to make a good excludable but too costly to do so. One could put a fence around the Lake District National Park and charge hikers a fee for walking in the area, but the cost of erecting and policing the fence makes it uneconomic.

In what follows, we look at the characteristics of goods and services that fall into the four possible combinations of excludable and non-excludable and rivalrous and non-rivalrous as shown in Table 19.1.

Excludable goods

Private agents who produce goods and services for sale on the free market must be able to prohibit the consumption of their output by those who will not pay for the privilege. Otherwise the producers cannot gain the revenue they need to cover their production costs.

So excludability is necessary for a good to be produced by a firm for sale on the market.

Ordinary goods: excludable and rivalrous

The market works best when goods and services are rivalrous and excludable.

Private firms can produce and sell them. Furthermore, these firms will fulfil the condition for allocative efficiency by operating where marginal cost equals price as long as they are price-takers.

Art galleries, museums, and parks: excludable but non-rivalrous

Some excludable goods and services are non-rivalrous, at least up to a large capacity constraint. This is the first reason on our list of market failures. A park with a fence around it provides an excludable service, but one person's use does

not interfere with another person's use—at least, not until there are so many users that overcrowding becomes a serious problem. Such goods can be provided by private firms, but since the marginal cost of adding another user is zero (until capacity is reached) any admission fee that the owner charges will result in a non-optimal use of the facility. It costs nothing to add another user, but to cover their costs the providers must charge each user a fee. Thus, under private provision price will exceed marginal cost, and some people who are willing to pay more than this marginal cost but less than the current price will not use it. This market failure is called **inefficient exclusion**.

To avoid inefficient exclusions, the government often provides non-rivalrous but excludable goods and services.

The costs are then met out of taxation, and the service is provided free. Parks, art galleries, roads, and bridges often come under this category. Box 19.1 reviews the debate that arose in the early 1990s when the Conservative government in the UK reduced the grants to galleries and museums and the trustees of some felt they had little option but to levy charges for admission. The subsequent Labour government abolished admission charges. (See also the evidence on what happened when these charges were abolished—in Chapter 5 on page 179.)

Non-excludable goods

This class provides the next two sources on our list of major market failures: those associated with common property resources and with public goods.

Common property: non-excludable but rivalrous

If *you* catch a fish in the open ocean, *I* cannot catch it, so it is rivalrous. But in a free market there is no way for you to exclude me from trying to catch it, so it is non-excludable. This is the second reason on our list of causes of market failures. A **common property resource** is one that is rivalrous but non-excludable. No one has an exclusive property right to it, and it can be used by anyone. No one owns the ocean's fish until they are caught. No one owns common grazing land. The world's international fishing grounds are common property for all fishermen, as is common grazing land for all livestock owners. If, by taking more fish, one fisherman reduces the catch of other fishermen, he does not count this as a cost, although it is a cost to society. If, by grazing her own sheep, a peasant reduces the feed available for other people's goats, she does not count this as a cost. The result has been called *the tragedy of the commons*—the tendency for commonly held property to be over-exploited, often to the extent of destruction.

It is socially optimal to add to a fleet that is fishing any given fishing area until the last boat increases the *value of*

Box 19.1 Pricing of galleries and museums

Art galleries, museums, fenced parks, bridges, and similar public institutions are examples of goods that are excludable—admission is easily controlled at entrances—but non-rivalrous, at least up to substantial capacity. Except on crowded days, one person's use does not reduce another person's ability to use the facility. The efficient solution is to allow everyone to use the facility free of charge on non-crowded days but to charge a price on days on which the crowds do make the facility's use a rivalrous activity.

The argument *against* the policy of free admission runs along the following lines. Many taxpayers who never use the facility, and do not even care that it exists, are forced to help to pay for it. Many of these people may have lower-than-average incomes and be less well educated. So the free-admission policy is to a great extent a subsidy for middle-class persons with particular tastes. In times of financial stringency, those who want the facility should pay for it.

Whatever the reasons, in the early 1990s the Conservative government in the UK decided to curtail its support for the arts drastically. In response, many museum and gallery trustees decided that the only course open to them was to institute admission charges, although some others did not. Controversy was sustained and often bitter.

Those who opposed the imposition of charges argued several points. The admission fees would lead to inefficient exclusion. Institutions that were underused and could add more visitors would be excluding potential users by their not-insignificant charges. Those excluded would be from lower-income classes that had contributed little to the costs of operation in the past because they paid little in income tax.

There is no easy resolution of such debates. They tend to pit those who worry about equity against those who worry about efficiency. But even that is not always a clear division. It is an equity argument that those who benefit from the facilities should pay for them. But it is also an equity argument that positive admission fees should not be used to preclude the poor from taking part in an activity that has a zero marginal cost.

In the latest development in this saga the UK Labour government abolished admission charges in 2001. (See the evidence of the increase in admissions that followed the price reductions on page 79.) What is not clear is whether the government was swayed more by concerns about equity or about efficiency in reaching this decision.

---

the fleet's total catch by as much as it costs to operate the boat. Similarly, it is optimal to add another sheep to the flock that grazes on the commons as long as the total supply of meat (and milk) is increased by as much as the cost of maintaining the extra animal. These are the sizes of fishing fleet and flock of sheep that a social planner or a private monopolist would choose.

The socially optimal exploitation of a common property resource occurs when the marginal cost of the last user equals the value of the marginal addition to total output.

The free market will not, however, produce that result. Consider the fishery. Potential new entrants will judge entry to be profitable if the *value of their own catch* is equal to the costs of operating their boats. But a new entrant's catch is *partly* an addition to total catch and *partly* a reduction of the catch of other fishermen—because of congestion, each new boat reduces the catch of all other boats. Thus, under competitive free entry there will be too many boats in the fleet and too many sheep on the common.

How does a potential new fisherman judge the value of entering the industry? He will expect to do about as well as the average boat. So it will pay to enter, adding a new boat to the fleet, until the *average* value of the catch of a typical boat in the fleet is equal to the cost of running the newly entering boat.[3]

The free market will add users to a common property resource until the marginal cost of the last entrant equals the *average* output of all existing producers.

At this point, however, the *net* addition to the *total* catch brought about by the last boat will be substantially less than the cost of operating the boat, and it may even be negative.

With common property resources the level of output will be too high because each new entrant will not take account of the cost that he is imposing on existing producers.

This tendency to overexploit a common property resource is illustrated by the example in Figure 19.1. Free-market entry proceeds until the cost of the last boat, which is average total cost per boat, equals the revenue it expects, which is the average revenue per boat. This is the same as saying that total cost equals total revenue—so there are no economic profits to attract further entrants. The surplus over cost that could be earned with a smaller fleet is dissipated by entry. In this example, the fishing fleet is 100 vessels. Each boat costs £10,000 to run and catches £10,000 worth of fish. If the fleet were restricted to 35 boats, each £10,000 boat would catch fish worth just over £14,000. The new technology reduces the cost of running each. Entry then proceeds well beyond the 140-boat level where each additional boat actually begins to reduce the total catch.

---

[3] This subtle point is the same as the difference between the perfectly competitive producer and the monopolist. The monopolist knows that if it sells more it will reduce the market value of what it is already selling. The perfect competitor must take the market price as given and so will value a marginal unit of production at the market price, i.e. at the *average value* of all units already being sold.

Market efficiency : MR = MC.

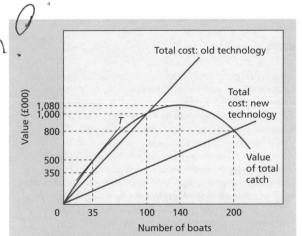

Figure 19.1 Overfishing of a common property fishery

A common property resource is exploited beyond the socially optimal level. Adding boats to the fleet adds to the total catch but at a diminishing rate up to 140 boats, after which additional boats lower the total catch. With the old technology, the cost (capital and current) of running each boat is £10,000, giving the steeper of the two total cost curves. The socially optimal level is 35 boats, where the addition to total catch, as shown by the slope of the tangent to the total catch curve, just equals the addition to the total cost of running one more boat, as shown by the slope of the total cost curve. At that point there is a surplus of revenue over total cost of £150,000. At that fleet size, a new boat expects to catch about £14,300 (i.e. £500,000/35) worth of fish, so entry is profitable from the private point of view. When the fleet reaches 100 boats, a new boat expects to catch £10,000 worth of fish, which just matches its cost. With new technology, each boat costs only £4,000 to run. The fleet expands to 200 boats catching £800,000 worth of fish. This yields revenue of £4,000 per boat, which just matches cost. Production has been pushed beyond the point of negative marginal returns.

Fishing grounds, common pastures, and other common property resources often show a pattern of overexploitation.

This is true of almost all of today's fishing grounds, except where the catch is effectively regulated by government intervention. Box 19.2 considers this case in more detail.

One solution to the common property problem is to agree on the optimal level of use and then police the resource to reduce its use to that level. This is done with such items as fishing quotas and hunting licences. The problem here is to enforce the restrictions. It is possible to control the number of fish caught in the high seas, but doing so is difficult and costly, as is attested by the frequent international disputes over alleged quota violations.

Another method is for the state to create property rights that make the resource excludable. Its private owners then have an incentive to exploit it efficiently. The English enclosure movement that peaked between 1793 and 1815 did just that. Although those who had previously used the common grazing land were hurt by the measure, the land

was used much more efficiently under private ownership. Issuing licences for the use of each particular wavelength can control the airwaves. State forests, which are being destroyed by excessive wood gathering, can be sold to private owners. Property rights to wildlife can be given to local villages. And so on. This last case is controversial and is further discussed in Box 19.3. (The problem of the tropical rainforests is discussed in Box 17.3 on page 294.)

All of these cases exemplify the common problem of a trade-off between efficiency and equity. When a common property resource is 'privatized', the efficiency of its use typically rises but the former users typically suffer some losses. The difficult issue of trading off efficiency of the resource's use against justice for the present users has no easy resolution. What is sure however is that, if the resource is being exploited to the point of destruction, little is achieved for either equity or efficiency by preserving its common property status.

Public goods: non-excludable and non-rivalrous

Goods that are neither excludable nor rivalrous are called **public goods,** or sometimes **collective consumption goods.** They provide the third reason on our list of causes for market failure. The classic case is national defence. An army of a given size protects all the nation's citizens equally, no matter how many citizens there are and whether or not a particular individual pays taxes to support it. Similarly, a police force that keeps the public streets safe protects all of the street's users, no matter how many there are. If some do not pay their share of the costs, they cannot be denied protection as long as they continue to use the safe street. Information is often a public good. It is clearly non-rivalrous and often non-excludable. Suppose a certain food additive causes cancer. The cost of discovering this needs to be borne only once. The information is then of value to everyone who might have used the additive. Once it is in the public domain, no one can be stopped from learning about the information. Other public goods include lighthouses (in most but not all circumstances) and publicly available weather forecasts.

Because public goods are non-excludable, private firms will not provide them.

The obvious remedy in these cases is for the government to provide the good and pay for its provision out of general tax revenue.

When should a public good be provided? To illustrate the basic principle, consider a community composed of just two consumers. The government is considering whether or not to provide a park. Arthur is prepared to pay up to £200 for use of the park, while Julia is willing to pay up to £100. The total value to the two individuals of having the park is £300. If it can be produced for £225, there is a £75 gain on

Box 19.2 **Endangered fish**

The fish in the ocean are a common property resource, and theory predicts that such a resource will be overexploited if there is a high enough demand for the product and suppliers are able to meet that demand. In past centuries there were neither enough people eating fish nor efficient enough fishing technologies to endanger stocks. Over the last fifty years, however, the population explosion has added to the demand for fish and advances in technology have vastly increased the ability to catch fish. Large boats, radar detection, and more murderous nets have tipped the balance in favour of the predator and against the prey. As a result, the overfishing prediction of common property theory has been amply borne out. Today fish are a common property resource; tomorrow they could become no one's resource.

Overfishing

Since 1950 the world's catch has increased fivefold. The increase was sustained only by substituting smaller, less desirable fish for the diminishing stocks of the more desirable fish and by penetrating ever further into remote oceans. Today all available stocks are being exploited, and now even the total tonnage is beginning to fall. The UN estimates that the total value of the world's catch could be increased by nearly $30 billion if fish stocks were properly managed by governments interested in the total catch, rather than exploited by individuals interested in their own catch.

The developed countries have so overfished their own stocks that Iceland and the European Union could cut their fleets by 40 per cent and catch as much fish as they do today. This is because more fish would survive to spawn, allowing each boat in a smaller fleet to catch about 40 per cent more than does each boat in today's large fishing fleet.

The problem became so acute that Canada shut down its entire Atlantic cod fishing industry in 1985 and its Pacific salmon industry in 1988. Tens of thousands of Newfoundland residents lost their livelihoods in the demise of what had been the province's largest industry—the catching, freezing, and canning of fish—an industry that had flourished for five centuries (see the chart). Canada and the European Union have since been in conflict over what Canada claims is predatory overfishing by EU boats just outside Canadian territorial waters.

The Mediterranean has been so overfished that seafood, which was once the staple for the poor, is now an expensive luxury eaten mainly by rich tourists.

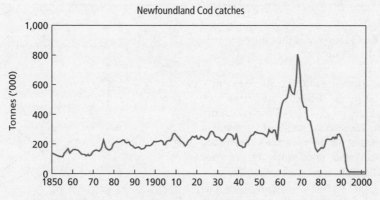

Newfoundland Cod catches

Source: Dr R. Meyers, Canadian Department of Fisheries and Oceans, St John's, Newfoundland.

Policy response

The European Union has a Common Fisheries Policy covering the territorial waters of its member countries. Since 1983, total allowable catches for all main species have been set annually and divided up into catch quotas for each member country. Minimum mesh size on nets and other ways of protecting young fish are also imposed. Inspection and monitoring measures are applied to give force to the regulations. However, measures in place up to 2002 failed to solve the problem. In May 2002, the EU announced a new radical plan:

Dwindling fish stocks, diminishing catches, too many vessels chasing too few fish, steady job losses and a lack of effective control and sanctions . . . the Common Fisheries Policy (CFP) needs fundamental change. . . . The Commission proposes to do away with the annual ritual of setting fishing quotas at too high levels. In future, total admissible catches would be fixed within a multi-annual management plan, on the basis of the most recent scientific advice to ensure that enough fish stay in the sea to replenish stocks. . . . the necessary cut in fishing effort (between 30 and 60% according to the state of stocks and the regions) under multi-annual plans would result in an estimated withdrawal of some 8,600 vessels which represents 8.5% of the number of EU fishing vessels and about 18% in tonnage. . . . To achieve sustainable fisheries beyond EU waters on the basis of stronger international co-operation, the reform package includes an action plan against illegal fishing and a strategy for EU fisheries development partnerships with third countries.*

The UN World Summit on Sustainable Development, held in Johannesburg in September 2002, agreed that there should be a strategy for restoring fish stocks at the global level. It was agreed to implement an action plan to address illegal fishing, and to set up a network of marine protected areas by 2012. The longer-term target was to restore fisheries to their maximum sustainable yields by 2015.

It remains to be seen how many types of fish will be caught to extinction and how many will recover as nations slowly learn the lesson of economic theory. Common property resources need central management if they are not to be overexploited to an extent that risks extinction.

* *Source*: press release, 28 May 2002; see: europa.eu.int/comm/fisheries.

Box 19.3 **Buffaloes, cows, and elephants**

For centuries North American bison—commonly called 'buffaloes'—were a common property resource for the Plains Indians, whose populations were small enough that they could kill all they needed without endangering the ability of the herds to reproduce themselves. However, in a little over a decade following the end of the American Civil War in 1865, white hunters decimated the herds. Buffalo Bill Cody may have been a folk hero, but he, and those like him, were the buffalo's executioners.

The buffalo was replaced by cattle, which did not follow the buffalo into extinction. The difference was that cattle were the private property of the ranchers. Rustlers and other predators attacked the herds, but the self-interest of ranchers made it worthwhile for them to protect their cattle.

Many people, watching the decimation of wildlife in Africa and Asia, have argued that property rights should be used to turn these animals from the modern equivalent of the buffalo into the modern equivalent of cattle. Wildlife is a common property resource. When it becomes endangered, laws are passed to prevent predatory hunting. But no one has any profit motive in enforcing these laws. Government officials are employed to do this job,

but they are often few in number and poorly paid. Some become corrupted by the large sums that poachers are willing to pay to avoid enforcement. Others find the policing job impossible, given the inadequate resources that their governments devote to enforcement.

Some African governments have dealt with the problem by giving ownership of the wild animals to local villages and allowing them to use the animals as a commercial asset. The animals are the subjects of camera safaris whose organizers pay the locals for the privilege. They are also prey for hunters who pay large sums for licences to kill a selected number of animals. Local tribesmen control poachers and keep the licensed kill rate below the reproduction rate, because they have a profit motive in protecting what has become their very valuable property.

These schemes have many opponents as well as many supporters. Some opponents object to any permissible 'sports hunting' and other commercial use of wild animals. They argue for more effective public enforcement of anti-poaching laws. Supporters counter that leaving the animals as common property is bound to result in their extinction. Farming them is, they argue, better than presiding over their extinction.

---

its production since it provides services that the community values at £300 at a cost of only £225.

The optimal quantity of a public good The above example reveals a key point about public goods. If one person consumes a unit of an ordinary good, another person cannot also consume that unit. Thus, to satisfy all the demand at any given price, the sum of all the quantities demanded must be produced. With a public good, however, everyone can consume any specific unit. A new defence system, for example, protects everyone in the country, and the fact that one person is protected does not reduce the protection received by all others.

The demand for a unit of the good is represented by the sum of the prices that each individual consumer would be willing to pay for that unit. Therefore, the community's demand curve for a public good is the vertical sum of the demand curves of the individual consumers.

If the amount of a public good can be varied continuously, the optimal quantity to produce is that quantity for which the marginal cost of the last unit is just equal to the sum of the prices all consumers would be willing to pay for that unit.

This equilibrium, which is analysed in Figure 19.2, guarantees that the last unit of the public good costs as much to produce as the value that it gives to all of its consumers.

Who pays? One way to pay for a public good is to charge each person the same proportion of the maximum amount she would be prepared to pay rather than go without the good, while fixing that proportion so as to cover the total

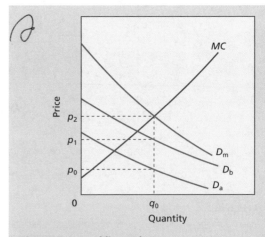

Figure 19.2 A public good

The society's demand curve for a public good is the vertical sum of all the individuals' demand curves. The demand curves D_a and D_b refer to two individuals. Their collective demand is shown by D_m, which is the vertical summation of D_a and D_b. For example, individual a would pay p_0 for quantity q_0, while individual b would pay p_1 for the same quantity. Together they are willing to pay the sum of p_0 and p_1, which is p_2.

The optimal quantity of the good to produce is q_0, where the marginal cost curve MC cuts the collective demand curve. At this point the marginal cost of another unit is just equal to the sum of the values that each person places on that unit.

costs of production. In the two-person community discussed above, Arthur is prepared to pay £200 and Julia £100 for the park rather than go without. If it costs £150 to produce, then each person can be charged one-half of their own maximum, making £100 for Arthur and £50 for Julia. Each of them gets the use of the park for half of what they are prepared to pay. Their payments just cover total costs of production, leaving £150 of total consumers' surplus.

The practical problem in using any formula based on what people are willing to pay for the public good lies in getting people to reveal their preferences. Suppose, for example, that the government is considering building a public park to serve a community of 1,000 people. It asks each of them how much he or she is prepared to pay. If I am one of those 1,000, it is in my interests to understate my true valuation, as long as everyone else does not do the same. Indeed, I might say I valued the park at zero, while others reported enough value to cover the costs. The public good would then be produced, and I would get the use of it for no payment at all.

The **free rider problem** refers to each person's motivation to understate the value of a non-rivalrous good in the hope that others will end up paying for it. This motivation makes it difficult to cover the costs of such goods by any formula based on people's individual valuations.

The free rider problem can be avoided by covering the costs of public goods out of tax revenue.

Goods such as national defence, weather forecasts, navigation aids, police, and fire protection are typically paid for from tax revenue and provided free to all users. This allows the goods to be produced above the levels at which the free market would produce them. (Often the free market would produce nothing.) It also avoids the problem of *inefficient exclusion* that we encountered in the context of discussion of the first source of market failure above. Those who value a particular good more than the average valuation gain more than those who value it less than the average valuation. The hope is that, over a large number of public goods, these individual differences will cancel out. Everyone will then gain on balance as a result of the government's provision of public goods out of tax revenue.

Externalities

A perfectly competitive economy allocates resources optimally because price equals marginal cost in all lines of production. For this outcome to happen, it is necessary that all costs are incurred by the producers and all benefits are reaped by their customers. This localization of costs does not occur when there are **externalities,** which are costs or benefits of a transaction that are incurred or received by other members of the society but not taken into account by the parties to the transaction. They are also called *third-party effects* and sometimes *neighbourhood effects*, because parties other than the primary participants in the transaction (the consumers and the producers) are affected. Externalities are the fourth item on our list of causes of market failure.

Externalities arise in many different ways, and they may be beneficial or harmful. A harmful externality occurs, for example, when a factory generates pollution. Individuals who live and work in the neighbourhood bear costs arising from the factory's production, including adverse health effects and clean-up costs. Profit-maximizing factory owners do not take these effects into account when they decide how much to produce. The element of social cost that they ignore is external to their decision-making process.

A beneficial externality occurs, for example, when I paint my house and enhance my neighbours' views and the values of their properties. Other cases arise when some genius—an Einstein, a Mozart, a van Gogh—gives the world discoveries and works of art whose worth is far in excess of what he is paid to create them.

Externalities create a divergence between the private benefits and costs of economic activity and the social benefits and costs. **Private costs** are those costs that are incurred by the parties directly involved in some economic activity. When a good is produced, the private costs are those borne by the producing firm. **Social costs** are the costs incurred by the whole society. These are the private costs *plus* any costs borne by third parties. **Private benefits** are the benefits received by those involved in the activity. In the case of a marketed good, these are the utilities obtained by buyers. **Social benefits** are the benefits to the whole society. They are the private benefits *plus* any benefit to third parties.

Society's resources are optimally allocated when social marginal cost equals social marginal benefit.

When this is so, there can be no social benefit in reallocating resources among different lines of production. Free markets will not produce social optimality when there are discrepancies between private and social costs and private and social benefits. The reason is that under perfect competition *private* marginal cost is equated to *private* marginal benefit (the price of the product).

Two important results follow immediately.

1. The outputs of firms that create harmful externalities will exceed the socially optimal levels.

When marginal private cost is equated to price and hence to marginal private benefit, marginal social cost, which is higher because of harmful externalities, will excee marginal social benefit. Thus there is social gain from reducing the level of output. The reason for this discrepancy is that the private firm takes no account of the costs imposed on others,

2. The outputs of firms that create beneficial externalities will be less than the socially optimal levels.

When marginal private cost is equated to price and hence to marginal private benefit, the marginal social benefit, which is higher because of beneficial externalities, will exceed marginal social cost. Thus, there is social gain from increasing the level of output. The reason is that the private firm takes no account of the benefits received by others.

Consider a simple example in which an electric power station produces 1 million units of electricity per day at a marginal cost of 5p per unit, and sells power for 5p per unit to consumers. If there are no externalities this is the socially optimal output, because the 5p valuation that each consumer puts on the last unit consumed is equal to the 5p opportunity cost of producing that unit. Now let there be 2p of negative externalities created when each unit is produced (perhaps from pollution of the atmosphere from a coal or gas fired station). Marginal social cost of 7p exceeds the marginal social benefit of 5p on the last unit produced. To move towards the social optimum, output should be reduced. Alternatively, suppose the externality is beneficial instead of harmful, conferring external benefits valued at 3p a unit on third parties. Now marginal social benefit of 8p exceeds marginal social cost of 5p. To approach a social optimum, output should be increased.

To achieve the optimal allocation of resources in the face of externalities, the production of goods with positive externalities needs to be encouraged and the production of those with negative externalities discouraged, compared with what would be produced under free-market conditions.

Figure 19.3 illustrates the market failures caused by externalities as well as their optimal correction.

Externalities and the Coase theorem

Externalities arise because of a lack of property rights. A factory throws its liquid waste into the river and its smoke into the atmosphere because no one owns them. Both the river and the air are common property resources. If they were in private hands, the owners would have a self-interest in preserving them. Let us see how this might come about.

An example

Say, for example, that a manufacturing plant needs pure water for one of its processes. It gets this from a short mountain stream that then tumbles into the ocean. A

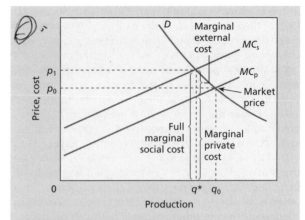

Figure 19.3 Private and social cost

Negative externalities cause marginal social cost to exceed price in competitive equilibrium. Marginal social cost, MC_s, exceeds marginal private cost, MC_p, by the amount of the external cost imposed on others. At the competitive output, q_0, marginal private cost equals price, but marginal social cost exceeds it. The socially optimal output is q^*, where $MC_s =$ price. For every unit between q^* and q_0 marginal social cost exceeds price and hence its production involves a social loss.

chemical plant is established upstream and dumps its waste into the river. The river is a common property resource so the plant cannot be stopped from imposing negative externalities on the downstream user, who must now set up an expensive water purification system.

A downstream owner Assume that the downstream plant owns the stream. Its owner might say to the chemical plant's managers, 'Do not dump *your* waste into *my* stream.' The managers might counter that they were willing to pay for the privilege. The downstream owner asks, 'How much?' After considering the cost of alternative waste-disposal mechanisms, the chemical plant's managers answer, '£6 per tonne of waste'. The owner of the downstream plant determines that the cost of purifying the water in the stream is £8 per tonne of waste. 'No deal,' she says. The upstream chemical plant opens an alternative waste-disposal system at a cost of £6, and the least costly method of dealing with the waste is thus used.

Later, technological improvements in water purification allow the downstream plant to purify its water for only £3 per tonne. The owner calls the upstream managers and says, 'I hear your disposal plant is coming up for renewal next year. I am prepared to let you dump the waste in my stream for a fee of £4 per tonne.' 'Done,' say the upstream managers, and next year the waste is disposed of in the river. The water is then cleaned up by the downstream user at a cost of £3 per tonne, instead of the cost of £6 when the chemical plant treated the waste. Once again, the cheapest method of disposal and use is adopted.

An upstream owner What if the river had been owned by the chemical plant instead of the downstream user? The managers of the chemical plant decide to use their stream for disposing of their waste. But the downstream users of water complain and offer to pay for the use of the fresh water. Their costs of making the water usable are £8 per tonne of waste. So they can offer up to that much to dissuade the chemical plant from dumping its waste. The plant can use an alternative waste-disposal method at a cost of £6 per tonne. So the managers say, 'Yes, how about giving us £7 for every tonne of our waste that we do not dump into our river?' A deal is struck and the cheapest method is undertaken.

Later, when the new water purification technology is developed, the downstream users can purify the water at a cost of only £3 per tonne. So they will offer no more than that to prevent the chemical plant from dumping its waste. When the upstream plant's alternative waste-disposal system wears out, it will not be replaced. The waste will be dumped and the downstream plant will purify its water at a cost of £3 per tonne. Once again, the cheapest method of dealing with the waste will have been adopted.

The theorem

This example illustrates a remarkable result developed some years ago by the British-born economist Ronald Coase, who received the 1991 Nobel Prize in economics. The result is now called the **Coase theorem:**

If the two sides to an externality—the one causing it and the one suffering from it—can bargain together with zero transactions costs, they will produce the efficient use of resources.

What is needed is that one of the two has a property right that forces the other side to bargain. Surprisingly, however, it does not matter which side has the property right. We saw this in the above example, where the same result was arrived at independently of who owned the river. Property rights will determine who gets most of the consumers' surplus on the bargain, because they determine who has to pay whom. But, given that both sides bargain for their own self-interest, the allocation of resources to deal with the externality will be independent of where the property right resides.

High transaction costs

What makes the Coase theorem work is that someone has a property right over what is affected by the externality *and* that both sides can bargain effectively together. This latter condition is a matter of transaction costs. It was easy enough for the owners of the two plants to talk on the phone and reach an efficient bargain. It is another matter for all the citizens of the cities of London or São Paulo to bargain with the hundreds of factory owners, car drivers, and other producers of pollution in order to reach an efficient solution to dealing with air and water pollution in and around their cities.

In cases where property rights cannot be assigned and/or where transaction costs are excessive, there are only two possibilities. We may accept the externality and learn to live with it, *or* governments may intervene on our behalf to deal with it.

We will see however, that although governments often do improve matters somewhat, arriving at the most efficient solution is no easy task.

The control of pollution

In this section we illustrate government policies with respect to negative externalities in the context of one of their most important applications: environmental damage caused by pollution. Steel plants produce heat and smoke in addition to steel. Farms produce chemical runoff as well as food. Household consumption produces human waste and refuse. Indeed, there are few human activities that do not produce some negative pollution externalities.

For this reason, it is impossible to reduce pollution to zero. Instead, the optimal amount of pollution abatement occurs when the marginal benefit of a unit of abatement is just equal to the marginal cost of abatement.

Unregulated markets tend to produce excessive amounts of environmental damage. Zero environmental damage, however, is neither technologically possible nor economically efficient.

Pollution control through direct regulation

Direct controls are a common method of environmental regulation. For example, UK car emissions standards must be met by all new cars, and by all cars over three years of age when they take their annual MOT test. Many cities and towns prohibit the private burning of leaves and other rubbish because of the air pollution problem that the burning would cause. The 1956 UK Clean Air Act obliged people in city centres to switch from coal to smokeless fuels. Similarly, the government gradually reduced the amount of lead allowed in petrol and provided tax incentives for drivers to switch to unleaded petrol. Since the mid-1970s, UK petrol consumption has increased by about 50 per cent while lead emissions have fallen by about 75 per cent.

Problems with direct controls

Direct controls are often economically inefficient. This is because controls typically mandate the same response from different polluters independently of their costs of pollution abatement. Although these requirements may seem reasonable, they will be inefficient unless the polluters face the same pollution abatement costs. Alternative, more flexible, methods can often provide the same amount of abatement at a lower cost.

Direct pollution controls are usually inefficient because, by mandating the same response from all agents, they do not minimize the cost of any given amount of pollution abatement.

Efficient allocation of pollution abatement between firms with different prevention costs is analysed in Figure 19.4. As long as one firm has a lower abatement cost than another firm, it pays to reallocate a given amount of abatement. The lower-cost firm should abate more and the higher-cost firm less. The general conclusion is:

Efficient abatement requires that each firm have the same marginal cost of pollution abatement activity.

None the less, direct controls are effective when it is important not to exceed certain dangerous thresholds. They are also useful in situations where production is undertaken by a very small number of publicly owned natural

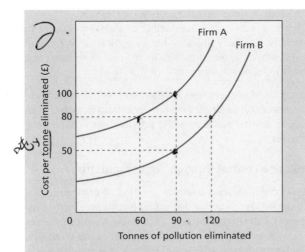

Figure 19.4 Pollution abatement

Efficient methods of abating pollution take account of differences in costs of abatement among firms. The figure shows the different marginal costs of pollution abatement for two firms. For any given amount of abatement, firm A has a higher cost of a further unit of abatement than has B. When they are both mandated to reduce pollution by 90 units, A's marginal cost of £100 exceeds B's marginal cost of £50. This is inefficient. A could cut its abatement by one unit, saving £100, while B increased its abatement by one unit, adding £50 to its costs. Total abatement would then be unchanged but costs would fall by £50.

An emissions tax of £80 per tonne of pollution is now imposed. Low-cost firm B now abates pollution by 120 tonnes, while high-cost firm A abates by 60 tonnes. This is the efficient way of producing 180 tonnes of abatement since the two firms have the same abatement costs at the margin, thus minimizing the total cost of reducing pollution by 180 tonnes.

monopolies. In other cases, policies that create economic incentives not to pollute are more effective than those that operate on the command principle.

Control through emissions taxes

The great British economist A. C. Pigou (1877–1959), who did path-breaking work on externalities of all sorts, was a pioneer in developing public policy tools for their control. His name is associated particularly with pollution taxes, which provide an alternative method to direct controls. The advantage of such taxes is that they *internalize the externality*, which means that they increase the firm's private cost by the amount of the external cost. This makes private and social costs the same, with the result that efficient outcomes can result from decentralized decisions made by individual producers.

Look again at the example in Figure 19.4. If all firms are required to pay a tax of £80 on each unit of pollution, profit maximization will lead them to reduce emissions to the point at which the marginal cost of further reduction is equal to the tax. This means that firm B will reduce emissions much more than firm A, and that in equilibrium both will have the same marginal cost of further abatement, which is required for efficiency.

A second great advantage of using emissions taxes is that they do not require the regulators to specify how polluters should abate pollution. Firms can be left to find the most efficient abatement techniques. The profit motive will lead them to do so, because they will want to minimize their tax bill.

In principle, emissions taxes can perfectly internalize pollution externalities, so that profit-maximizing behaviour on the part of firms will lead them to produce the efficient amount of pollution abatement at minimum cost.

Emissions taxes in practice Emissions taxes can work only if it is possible to measure emissions accurately. In some cases this does not pose much of a problem, but in many other cases there are no effective measuring devices that can be installed at reasonable cost. One important example is automotive pollution. Today (but possibly not at some future date) it would be very expensive to attach a reliable monitor to every car and lorry and then to assess taxes based on readings from the monitor. In this case, as in many others, direct controls are the only cost-effective method.

Another problem involves setting the tax rate. The regulatory agency needs to estimate the marginal social damage caused per unit of each pollutant and to set the tax equal to this amount. This would perfectly internalize the pollution externality. However, the required information is often difficult to obtain. If the regulatory agency sets the tax rate too high, too many resources will be devoted to pollution control. If the tax is set too low, there will be too much pollution. Furthermore, if technological change causes the social damage to change, the optimal tax rate is also changed.

Control through tradable emissions permits

Tradable emissions permits can solve many of the problems associated with direct controls and emissions taxes. To use them, the regulator must decide how much pollution to permit. In Figure 19.4 the original regulations required each firm to reduce its total pollution by 90 tonnes. This is exactly the same as permitting firms to pollute by their original amount of pollution *minus* 90 tonnes. Presenting the problem in this way, the regulators issue to each firm a right to pollute by that amount. To illustrate, if each firm had been generating 150 tonnes of pollution, exactly the same reduction would occur if firms were ordered to reduce pollution by 90 tonnes or if they were permitted to pollute to a maximum of 60 tonnes.

Tradable permits in theory Now, however, comes the new twist. A large efficiency gain can be achieved by making these rights to pollute tradable. This allows the firm with the low cost of pollution abatement to sell its right to pollute to the high-abatement-cost firm. Total pollution and total pollution abatement will be unchanged, but more abatement will be done by the firm with the low abatement cost (which sold its rights to pollute to the other firm), thus reducing the total cost of meeting the target for any given amount of pollution reduction.

Figure 19.5 illustrates this case. Where Figure 19.4 showed the amount of abatement, Figure 19.5 shows the amount of emissions. The cost curves now rise to the left instead of to the right as in Figure 19.4. Starting from the 150 tonnes of pollutants that each firm is emitting with zero abatement, the abatement cost rises as less and less pollution is allowed. Production with zero pollution is impossible, so the costs rise rapidly as very low pollution levels are achieved. The government wishes to cut pollution from its existing level of 300 tonnes to 120 tonnes. So it gives each firm 60 tonnes' worth of pollution permits. When they each cut their pollution to 60 tonnes, firm A has a much higher marginal cost than firm B. So B sells A some permits. B abates more and A pollutes more. Total pollution is unchanged but total abatement costs fall. Trade will be profitable as long as A's marginal abatement costs exceed B's. In the final equilibrium, both firms have the same marginal cost of abatement, which equals the price of a permit to abate by 1 tonne. Now each firm is indifferent between abating by 1 tonne and buying a permit to avoid abating by 1 tonne. The cost of abatement is minimized and both firms have gained. A has saved more clean-up costs than the cost of the permits it has bought. The prices of the permits that B sells exceed the cost of the extra abatement it must incur because it has fewer permits.

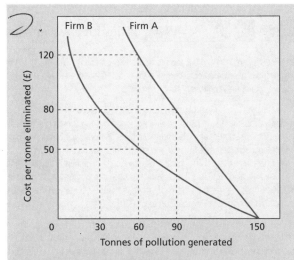

Figure 19.5 Tradable pollution permits

Tradable permits achieve the same results as the most efficient tax. Each firm produces 150 tonnes of pollution when no abatement procedures are followed. Abatement reduces the amount of pollution but at a rising marginal cost. Each firm is originally given an endowment of permits to emit 60 tonnes of pollution. If no trading is allowed, the marginal costs of abatement are then £120 for A and £50 for B. With trading, B sells 30 tonnes' worth of permits to A. Firm A then pollutes by 90 tonnes and firm B by 30 tonnes. The price of a permit is £80, which is the same as both firms' marginal cost of abatement at their new levels of pollution.

Everyone is better off. Society gets its abatement at the least cost in terms of valuable resources. Both firms have more money in their pockets than if each had been ordered to cut pollution by an identical amount.

Notice that the £90 price of a permit to produce 1 tonne of pollution is the same as the pollution tax required to induce 150 tonnes of abatement at the least cost. The difference is that permits require less information than taxes. The authorities just issue the number of permits they decide upon and let the market fix the price. If taxes are to be used, the government must determine the best tax rate and then impose it.

Tradable emissions permits can be used to achieve the same allocation of resources as would occur with emissions taxes, while reducing the amount of information required by the regulatory authorities.

Tradable emissions permits in practice Tradable permits and emissions taxes pose difficult problems of implementation. Some of these involve technical difficulties in measuring pollution and in designing mechanisms to ensure that firms and individuals comply with regulations. None the less, their use is growing in the USA as firms and governments become more used to them. One interesting phenomenon has been the steady fall in the price of pollution

Box 19.4 **Policies for environmental regulation**

Governments throughout the world are experimenting with many of the methods of environmental control discussed in the text. Here is a sampling of some of these policies.

• In the United Kingdom the Environmental Protection Act of 1989 lays down minimum standards for all emissions from thousands of chemical, waste incineration, and oil-refining factories. Performance is monitored by HM Inspectorate of Pollution, the costs of which are paid for by the factory owners themselves. The release of genetically engineered bacteria and viruses is also regulated. Strict regulations are imposed on waste-disposal operations and on most forms of straw and stubble burning. Litterers are subject to on-the-spot fines of up to £1,000.

• The 'Sixth Environmental Action Programme' of the European Union covers policies to be implemented in the period 2001–10. It includes a wide range of actions on many aspects of the environment (see reference in footnote 4 on this page).

• In the 1992 Copenhagen Agreements, nearly 100 countries agreed to phase out chlorofluorocarbons (CFCs) by the year 1996, four years earlier than had previously been agreed. The Copenhagen Agreements also regulated other ozone-damaging substances, such as methyl bromide, used in preserving fruit and grain, the output of which was to be held at 1991 levels by the year 1995.

• The Kyoto Protocol signed in 1998 called for major reductions in greenhouse gas emissions over the following fifteen years. Once again, the developed countries had more success in agreeing on reductions among themselves than in persuading developing nations to follow suit. Many observers wondered if the reductions agreed to by some of the developed nations could be realized at an acceptable cost. Following the conference, the UK environment minister was quoted (on the government's web site) as saying that measures such as voluntary agreements, adoption of best practice, regulations, and market instruments such as trading or taxation would all have a part to play. Until such measures could be devised, he called on business to co-operate voluntarily in meeting objectives for reductions in emissions. The 2002 UN World Summit on Sustainable Development further reinforced the Kyoto targets and established new targets for improvement of sanitation and clean water supply in poor countries.

• Under the United States Clean Air Act, utilities had to cut emissions of sulphur dioxide from a national total of 19 million tonnes to 9 million tonnes by the year 2000. This was accomplished by issuing 9 million tonnes' worth of tradable permits to pollute.

• According to the 'polluter-pays' principle used by the OECD, the polluter is to bear the cost of government-imposed measures designed to reduce pollution. This principle has been adopted in all member states so as to avoid the distortions in trade flows that could arise if countries tackled environmental problems in widely different ways with widely different effects on prices. In other cases it is the sufferer who is paying. For example, Sweden is helping Poland to reduce the acid rain that is damaging Swedish lakes and forests. Similarly, the Montreal Protocol includes provisions by which developing countries are to be compensated by richer countries for agreeing to limit their use of CFCs.

• The UK strategy for water pricing gives water companies the freedom to pass on any extra costs of environmental improvements and ensures that those companies have an economic incentive to undertake such improvements. The policy violates the 'polluter-pays' principle by putting the costs on the consumer. Non-market incentives are also widely applied to water. Under the UK Control of Pollution Act, a licence is required for the discharge of pollutants into rivers and coastal waters. These licences, called Discharge Consents, are issued by the National Rivers Authority. They specify the type and quantity of substances that may be discharged.

---

permits, particularly for SO$_2$ emissions. This reflects the development of newer, less polluting technologies under the incentive of having to pay for polluting by purchasing a pollution permit. As less and less pollution is produced, the price of the rights to produce a fixed amount of pollution is declining.

European governments until recently have shown a preferences for 'ecotaxes' over tradable pollution permits. However, the EU has recently outlined a plan[4] that includes the introduction of tradable emissions permits in preparation for the international scheme agreed in the Kyoto Protocol, which is to be introduced in 2008.

Conclusion

Much environmental pollution is caused by the failure of markets to account for externalities. At the same time, market-like mechanisms can be used to internalize the externalities. Pollution is an example of a problem in which markets themselves can be used to correct market failure.

The problem of externalities arises because of the absence of property rights. For example, the polluting firm uses the free air to dump its waste. If it owned the air, it would worry about the loss of the value of its property caused by the pollution. If those affected by the pollution owned the air, they would not allow it to be used unless they were paid sufficient compensation.

Since many externalities arise from an absence of property rights, externalities can often be internalized if appropriate property rights can be created.

Box 19.4 outlines some of the main policies that governments have used to give effect to desired environmental control.

---

[4] Sixth Environment Action Programme of the European Community, 'Environment 2010: Our future, our choice', available on: europa.eu.int/scadplus/leg/en/lvb/l28027.htm.

Asymmetric information

Markets work best when everyone is well informed. People cannot make maximizing decisions if they are poorly informed about the things they are buying or selling. Lack of relevant information is the fifth item on our list of reasons for market failure.

Rules requiring that products and prices be described correctly are meant to improve the efficiency of choices by providing people with correct and relevant information. In many cases where the consequences of errors are not dramatic, consumers can be left to discover, through trial and error, what is in their own best interests. In other cases, however, the results of error can be too drastic to allow consumers to learn from their own experiences which products are reliable and which unreliable. For example, botulism, caused by poorly preserved foods, can cause death. In such cases the state intervenes to impose standards and testing requirements in the consumers' own best interests.

Standards are also set in the workplace. Some people argue that firms should be left to set their own safety standards. High-risk firms would then have to pay wage premiums to induce workers to accept these risks voluntarily. Those who favour government regulation of work standards argue it on two grounds. First, firms are often better informed than workers about changing safety conditions in work, particularly in small factories. Government regulation then compensates for the inefficiencies caused by this unequal access to information. Second, people who are desperate for work will take risks that are socially unacceptable, or that their own desperation causes them to assess imperfectly. In this case the purpose of government intervention is either to impose social values not held by specific individuals, or to act paternalistically in the belief that the state can assess the self-interests of the workers better than the workers can do for themselves.

In some situations governments cannot easily remove the differences in information that is available to buyers and sellers. The party with the superior knowledge can then use it to change the nature of the transaction itself. For example, doctors, lawyers, and other specialists typically know much more than their clients about what they are doing. They can, therefore, influence the demand for their services by what they do and do not tell their clients. In countries where doctors are paid for on a fee-for-service basis—whether by the government, private insurers, or individual patients—elective surgery is often observed to vary with doctors' other workloads. It is low in regions where doctors are busy and high in regions where they are underemployed. The explanation lies not in the different needs of patients in these various areas, but in the varying demands for these services created by the different advice that doctors give to their patients.

Two important sources of market failure that arise when privately held information is bought and sold have already been discussed in Chapter 13. (The discussion on pages 221–3 should be reviewed at this point.) These are *moral hazard* and *adverse selection*. Since they were discussed earlier, we need say little more here beyond two observations. First, when insurance leads people to take risks that they would avoid in the absence of insurance (*moral hazard*), social costs are unnecessarily high. For example, more houses are destroyed by fire because insured people take risks that they would avoid if they had to bear the full cost of any fire losses themselves. Second, when buyers and sellers have unequal knowledge about their transactions, *adverse selection* may cause the outcome to be less efficient than if they were equally well informed. This happens, for example, when some types of insurance are bought heavily by those who know better than the insurers that they are bad risks, and is avoided by those who know better than the insurers that they are good risks.

Missing markets

In the 1950s two American economists, Kenneth Arrow and Gerard Debreu, who were subsequently awarded Nobel Prizes in economics, studied the necessary conditions for optimality in resource allocation. One of the conditions is that there must exist a separate market in which each good and service can be traded to the point where the marginal benefit equals the marginal cost. Missing markets are the sixth item on our list of causes of market failure.

Not only do markets not exist for such prominent things as public goods and common property resources; they are also absent in a number of less obvious but equally important cases.

One important set of missing markets involves risk. You can insure your house against its burning down. This is because your knowledge of the probability of this occurrence is not much better than your insurance company's, and because the probability of your house burning down is normally independent of the probability of other houses burning down.

If you are a farmer, you cannot usually insure your crop against bad weather. This is because the probabilities of your crop and your neighbour's suffering from bad weather are interrelated. If the insurance company has to pay you, the probabilities are that it will also have to pay your neighbour and everyone else in the county—perhaps even throughout the country. An insurance company survives by pooling independent risks. It cannot survive if the same event affects all its clients in the same way. (This is why, although you can insure your house against a fire from ordinary causes, you cannot insure it against fires caused by war.)

If you are in business, you cannot insure against bankruptcy. Here the problem is adverse selection. You know much better than does your would-be insurance company the chances that your business will fail. If insurance were offered against such failure, it would mainly be taken out by people whose businesses had recently developed a high chance of failure.

Another set of missing markets concerns future events. You can buy certain well-established and unchanging products, such as corn or oil, on futures markets. But you cannot do so for most manufactured products, such as cars and TV sets, because no one knows the precise specifications of future models. Futures markets for these products are missing, so there is no way that the costs and benefits of planned future expenditure on these products can be equated by economic transactions made today.

Public policy towards monopoly and competition

The seventh and last item on our list of reasons for market failure concerns market power. Cartels and price-fixing agreements among oligopolists, whether explicit or tacit, have long met with public suspicion and official hostility. These, and other non-competitive practices, are collectively referred to as 'monopoly practices'. Note that these are not just what monopolists do. They include non-competitive behaviour of firms that are operating in other market structures such as oligopoly. The laws and other instruments that are used to encourage competition and discourage monopoly practices make up competition policy and are used to influence both the market structure and the behaviour of individual firms.

The goal of controlling market power provides rationales both for competition policy and for economic regulation. Competition can be encouraged and monopoly practices discouraged by influencing either the *market structure* or the *market behaviour* of individual firms. By and large, UK competition policy has sought to create more competitive market structures where possible. Where such structures could not be established, policy has sought to discourage monopolistic practices and to encourage competitive behaviour. In addition, the government employs economic regulations, which prescribe the rules under which firms can do business, and in some cases determine the prices that businesses can charge for their output.

We study three aspects of these policies: the direct control of natural monopolies, the direct control of oligopolies, and the creation of competitive conditions. The first is a necessary part of any competition policy, the second has been important in the past but is less so now, and the third constitutes the main current thrust of UK competition policy.

Direct control of natural monopolies

The clearest case for public intervention arises with a **natural monopoly**, which is an industry in which economies of scale are so dominant that there is room for only one firm to operate at the minimum efficient scale. UK policy makers have not wanted to insist on the establishment of several smaller, less efficient producers whenever a single firm would be much more efficient; nor have they wanted to give a natural monopolist the opportunity to restrict output, raise prices, and reap monopoly profits.

One response to natural monopoly is for government to assume ownership of the single firm, setting it up as a nationalized industry. Another response has been to allow private ownership but to regulate the monopoly firm's behaviour. Until the 1980s UK policy favoured public ownership. Recently such industries have been privatized—that is, sold to members of the public—and then to some extent regulated; examples are telecommunications, gas, water, and electricity. Whichever choice the government makes, it will be able to exert an influence on the behaviour of these industries.

Short-run price and output

What is the correct price–output policy that the government should encourage these industries to adopt?

Marginal cost pricing Sometimes the government dictates that price should be set equal to short-run marginal cost so as to maximize consumers' plus producers' surpluses. According to economic theory, this policy, which is called marginal cost pricing, provides the efficient solution.

Marginal cost pricing does, however, create some problems. The natural monopoly may still have unexploited economies of scale and hence may be operating on the falling portion of its average total cost curve. In this case marginal cost will be less than average total cost and pricing at marginal cost will lead to losses, as shown in Figure 19.6.

A falling-cost natural monopoly that sets price equal to marginal cost will suffer losses.

Average cost pricing Sometimes natural monopolies are directed to produce the output that will just cover total costs, thus earning neither profits nor losses. This means that the firm produces to the point where average revenue equals average total cost, which is where the demand curve cuts the average total cost curve. Figure 19.6 shows that for a falling-cost firm this pricing policy requires producing at

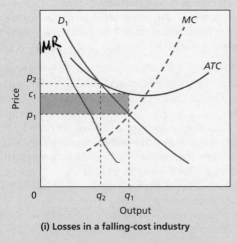
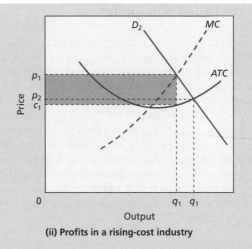

Figure 19.6 Pricing policies for natural monopolies

Marginal cost pricing leads to profits or losses; average cost pricing is inefficient. In each part the output at which marginal cost equals price is q_1 and price is p_1.

In part (i) average costs are falling at output q_1, so marginal costs are less than the average cost of c_1. There is a loss of $c_1 - p_1$ on each unit, making a total loss equal to the dark blue area.

In part (ii) average cost of c_1 is less than price at output q_1. There is a profit of $p_1 - c_1$ on each unit sold, making a total profit equal to the dark blue area.

In each part of the diagram the output at which average cost equals price is q_2 and the associated price is p_2. In part (i) marginal cost is less than price at q_2, so output is below its optimal level. In part (ii) marginal cost exceeds price at q_2, so output is greater than its optimal level.

less than the optimal output in order to avoid the losses that would occur under marginal cost pricing.

Average cost pricing is usually allocatively inefficient.

The very long run

Natural monopoly is a long-run concept, meaning that, given existing technology, there is room for only one firm to operate profitably. In the very long run, however, technology changes. Not only does today's competitive industry sometimes become tomorrow's natural monopoly, but also, today's natural monopoly sometimes becomes tomorrow's competitive industry.

A striking example is the telecommunications industry. Not long ago the transmissions of voice and hard-copy messages were natural monopolies. Now technological developments such as satellite transmission, electronic mail, the internet, and fax machines have made these activities highly competitive. Also, new firms can be given access to existing infrastructure such as cables, thus greatly lowering setup costs and encouraging competition from new entrants. As a consequence, in many countries an odd circumstance arose: nationalized industries, such as the UK Post Office and the nationalized telephone system, sought to maintain their profitability by prohibiting entry into what would otherwise have become a fluid and competitive industry. Since it has the full force of the legal

system behind it, the public firm may be more successful than the privately owned firm in preserving its monopoly long after technological changes have destroyed its 'naturalness'.

Government policies need to be adjusted frequently to keep them abreast with more or less continuous technological change.

Regulation of natural monopolies

Now that most UK nationalized industries have been privatized, those that are natural monopolies are regulated by public regulatory authorities, such as OFCOM (telecoms and media), OFGEM (gas and electricity), and OFWAT (water). In the United States, such regulatory bodies were often captured by the firms they were supposed to regulate and ended up working against the interests of consumers. An opposing pitfall that some worry about in the United Kingdom is that prices may be pushed so far down in the short-term interests of consumers that the regulated industries will have little incentive to invest in technological innovations. In response to this worry, firms were given the right to appeal if they feel prices are being pushed too low. In today's world of rapid technological change, this could work to the long-term disadvantage of consumers.

Direct control of oligopolies

Governments have intervened from time to time in industries that were oligopolies, rather than natural monopolies, seeking to enforce the type of price and entry behaviour that was thought to be in the public interest. Such intervention has typically taken two distinct forms. In the United Kingdom from 1945 to 1980 it was primarily nationalization of whole oligopolistic industries such as airlines, railways, steel, and coal mining, which were then run by government-appointed boards. In the United States firms in such oligopolistic industries as airlines, railways, and electric power were left in private hands, but their decisions were regulated by government-appointed bodies that set prices and regulated entry.

Deregulation and privatization

The last two decades of the twentieth century witnessed a movement in virtually all advanced industrial nations, and the vast majority of less developed nations as well, to reduce the level of government control over industry.

Causes

A number of forces had been pushing in this direction.

• Expectations that nationalized industries would be superior to private firms in the areas of efficiency, productivity growth, and industrial relations were falsified by experience.

• Falling transportation costs, and the information and communications revolutions, have exposed domestic industries to much more international competition than they had previously experienced. This has lowered concern over high national concentration ratios.

• Regulatory bodies sometimes had the effect of reducing, rather than increasing, competition.

• In spite of being allocatively inefficient because price exceeds marginal cost (by virtue of each firm's negatively sloped demand curve), oligopolistic market structures provided much of the economic growth of the twentieth century. New products, and new ways of producing old products, have followed each other in rapid succession, all leading to higher living standards and higher productivity. Many of these innovations have been provided by firms in oligopolistic industries such as motor cars, agricultural implements, steel, petroleum refining, chemicals, and telecommunications. As long as governments can keep oligopolists competing with each other rather than co-operating to produce monopoly profits, most economists see no need to regulate such things as the prices at which they sell their products and the conditions of entry into their industries.

The worldwide movement towards privatization and deregulation is part of a growing belief among policy makers that private firms operating in free markets are more efficient producers and innovators than governments.

The call is for a diminished role of government in resource allocation compared with what it was through most of the second half of the twentieth century—but not for a zero role. Although the belief that government intervention has been excessive is almost worldwide, there are many reasons why the public interest may still require significant intervention. Externalities and other market failures are just two of the reasons why it is not necessarily efficient to leave the free market to decide all issues of resource allocation.

The natural outcome of these revised views has been the privatization of nationalized industries and the deregulation of privately owned ones. This latter policy was intended, among other things, to return price-setting and entry decisions to market determination.

Privatization has gone a long way in the United Kingdom. The majority of the nationalized industries have been returned to private ownership. Some details are given in Box 19.5.

 Box 19.5 Privatization in the United Kingdom

Privatization has been a complex development in the United Kingdom. Some nationalized industries were sold outright; in others, the government maintained substantial holdings while selling off the rest of its shares. Sometimes the profitable parts of unprofitable enterprises were separated off and sold. In still other cases, the government sold shares held in private companies that had never been nationalized.

The first step towards UK privatization was the sale of council houses, which began in 1979. Over the succeeding decade there was a major reduction in the stock of publicly owned housing, with almost 700,000 dwellings being sold to their occupiers.

The next phase covered a number of relatively small operations in markets where competition was strong. These included the British Sugar Corporation, British Rail Hotels, Sealink Ferries, British Ports, Jaguar, and British Aerospace. These companies have operated successfully, under relatively competitive conditions, since their privatization.

The third phase covered the great industrial giants. It began with British Telecom in 1984 and continued with British Gas in 1986, British Airways in 1987, and British Steel in 1988. Sale of shares in the publicly owned electricity industry began in 1990, with water following soon thereafter. Sale of the remaining coal pits was completed in 1994. The privatization of British Rail was completed by 1997, with the track going to Railtrack and the train services going to several private operators (though owing to financial problems Railtrack was temporarily taken back under government control in 2001/2).

Outcomes

The evidence on the effects of privatization is largely encouraging. Prices have fallen markedly in the gas, electricity, and telecommunications industries. Some former state-owned companies have become world leaders in a manner that did not occur under state control; the most obvious examples are BT and British Airways. Many have been attractive targets for takeover bids by foreign utilities. All of this is strong evidence that their performance has been improved by being transferred to private ownership.

Privatization has also spread to other EU countries; for example, Deutsche Telekom was privatized in 1996. Part of the pressure to privatize has come from stiff competition from efficient foreign firms and part from the Maastricht Treaty, which limits public spending and government borrowing. There has also been a trend towards deregulation of many markets. Major pressure in this direction has been exerted by the Single Market Act, which is discussed in Chapter 33. A notable example is air travel, where state-imposed restrictions, often designed to protect stateowned national airlines, are being phased out. Many new private carriers are entering the industry, such as easyJet and Ryanair in the UK. The ensuing competition has pushed many fares down.

Intervention to keep firms competing

The least stringent form of government intervention is designed to create conditions of competition by preventing firms from merging unnecessarily or from engaging in certain anti-competitive practices such as colluding to set monopoly prices. Such policies seek to create the most competitive market structure possible and then to prevent firms from reducing competition by engaging in certain forms of co-operative behaviour.

Why worry?

For some time up until the early 1990s, industrial concentration increased in Britain, with the percentage of industrial production accounted for by the five largest firms growing steadily. Two major causes were the growth of large firms at the expense of smaller ones, and mergers of existing firms. Although very recent data are difficult to come by, those that exist suggest that recent developments have been mixed. Concentration increased, for example, in pharmaceuticals when Glaxo merged with Wellcome, and then again with Smithkline-Beacham to form GlaxoSmithKline; and Zeneca merged with Astra to form AstraZeneca. In other industries, however, large firms have been broken up by their owners, reducing concentration ratios.

Globalization—the growing internationalization of competition—is one reason why this increasing domestic

 Box 19.6 UK competition policies

Ultimate responsibility for competition policy in the United Kingdom lies with the Secretary of State for Trade and Industry, but application of the policy is in the hands of two main institutions (plus the utility regulators mentioned in the text): the Office of Fair Trading (OFT) and the Competition Commission (CC).* The goal of the OFT is to make markets work well for consumers. It has powers of enforcement of competition and consumer protection rules; it can initiate investigations into how any specific market is working; and it is involved in communication to explain and improve awareness of competition rules and policy. The OFT may refer mergers that it deems to be anti-competitive to the CC and it may also refer markets where competition is perceived to be not working well.

The CC was established by the 1998 Competition Act and it replaced the Monopolies and Mergers Commission (MMC) on 1 April 1999. The CC has two main functions: 'On its reporting side, the Commission has taken on the former MMC role of carrying out inquiries into matters referred to it by the other UK competition authorities concerning monopolies, mergers and the economic regulation of utility companies. Secondly, the newly established Appeal Tribunals hear appeals against decisions of the Director General of Fair Trading and the Regulators of utilities in respect of infringements of the prohibitions contained in the [1998] Act concerning anti-competitive behaviour and abuse of a dominant position.'†

 * For more information see their respective web sites: www.oft.gov.uk and www.competition-commission.org.uk
 † www.competition-commission.org.uk.

concentration in production has not necessarily implied less market competition. (Globalization is further discussed in Chapters 33 and 34.) The size of most markets now extends well beyond the boundaries of a single nation. A firm with an apparent monopoly in the United Kingdom may well be operating in a highly competitive international market that includes German, French, and Japanese firms. None the less, some intervention to keep firms competing rather than colluding is still thought necessary in most countries.

Unsettled questions: market structure in the very long run

The case against monopoly and monopolistic practices is based on the allocation of resources with a given technology. In the very long run, however, technology is constantly changing as a result of both the discoveries of lower-cost methods of producing old products and the introduction of new and improved products. Does market structure affect the rate of innovation in the very long run?

The incentive to innovate

Who gets the profits? Both the monopolist and the perfect competitor have a profit incentive to introduce cost-reducing innovations. A monopoly can always increase its profits if it can reduce costs. Furthermore, since it is able to prevent the entry of new firms into the industry, these additional profits will persist into the long run. Thus, a firm that is either a monopoly or an oligopolist with entry barriers has both a short- and a long-run incentive to reduce its costs.

Firms in perfect competition have the same incentive in the short run, but not in the long run. In the short run a reduction in costs will allow a firm that was just covering costs to earn profits. In the long run other firms will be attracted into the industry by these profits. Existing firms will copy the cost-saving innovation, and new firms will enter the industry using the new techniques. This will go on until the profits of the innovator have been eliminated.

Monopolies and oligopolists with entry barriers have both a short- and a long-run incentive to innovate; perfectly competitive firms have only a short-run incentive.

Funds for research and development The large profits available to oligopolistic firms provide a ready fund out of which research and development can be financed. The typical perfectly competitive firm, however, is earning only enough to cover all its production costs, and it will have few funds to spare for research and development. As an empirical illustration, farmers producing under perfect competition did not develop the innovations that have vastly raised agricultural productivity over the last century. Rather, they were developed by a few oligopolistic manufacturers of farm equipment and by researchers in universities and in government-financed research institutions.

Schumpeter's defence of oligopoly and monopoly

In Joseph Schumpeter's theory (mentioned previously on page 187), monopolistic and oligopolistic market structures are more conducive to growth than is perfect competition.[5] He claimed that, since it is the incentive of profits that leads individuals and firms to take the great risks of innovation, market power is much more important than perfect competition in providing the climate under which

innovation occurs. The large short-run profits earned by firms with market power provide the incentive for others to try to usurp some of these for themselves. Oligopolistic firms compete for each other's profits, as well as for the new profits that will be generated by major innovations. If they do not compete, or if they have a genuine monopoly, outsiders will seek to enter in order to share in the profits of the sitting firm or firms. If a frontal attack on the major barriers to entry is not possible, then the barriers will be circumvented by such dodges as the development of similar products against which the established firms will not have entry protection. Schumpeter called the replacing of one entrenched position of market power by another through the invention of new products or new production techniques the *process of creative destruction.*

Perfect competition is not only impossible but inferior, and there is no case for taking it seriously as a model. Hence it is a mistake to base the theory of government regulation of industry on the principle that big business should be made to work as the respective industry would work in perfect competition.[6]

Schumpeter's theory is not easy to test. None the less, business school studies of firm behaviour show that much, probably most, inter-firm competition is in product and process innovation. Firms rarely fail because they set the wrong prices—for one reason, it is easy to alter prices that turn out to be uncompetitive. Firms do fail, however, when they fall behind their competitors in the constant battle to produce new and better products by ever more cost-efficient methods.

The future of competition policy

Even though governments on the whole are no longer in the business of owning industries or tightly controlling their pricing and output decisions, government has an important role as both rule-maker and referee of the market economy. Even the strongest advocates of Schumpeter's theory of creative destruction accept that the public interest is better served when oligopolists are induced to compete with each other instead of colluding to avoid such rivalrous activity.

Conclusion

Some see everything that the government does as useless, and would do away altogether with its activities in respect to the free market. The all-important function of providing the background against which the free market can effectively function—by maintaining a monopoly of violence and defining and protecting property rights—discredits this case.

[5] At the time that Schumpeter first wrote, economists recognized only two market structures: perfect competition and monopoly. He thus applied his arguments about creative destruction to monopolies. Now that oligopoly is seen to be the dominant market form in manufacturing, it is clear that his arguments apply with more force in oligopoly, where the threat of competition is more immediate, than in monopoly.

[6] Joseph Schumpeter, *Capitalism, Socialism and Democracy*, 3rd edn (New York: Harper & Row, 1950), p. 106.

Others see a very limited role for government but would take government activity no further than absolutely necessary. Just provide an effective basis for law and order, they say, and the miracle of Adam Smith's hidden hand will do the rest. Most people, although not quite all, reject this view. The case against the minimalist state lies in what we observed at the outset of this chapter: although markets work—and work very effectively much of the time—markets also fail—and sometimes fail quite seriously.

We have devoted much space to explaining the *why*, *how*, and *where* of these market failures. We have also explained what might be done to alleviate the most serious of these failures.

In the next chapter we will raise concerns about how well governments actually deal with these market failures. Whatever the conclusion about those concerns, there is no doubt about three points. First, markets do fail in many important ways. Second, governments provide the only institutions available to deal with many of these failures. Third, economists have designed many instruments, some of them highly subtle, by which governments can deal with these failures.

As Adam Smith long ago observed (see Chapter 1), altruism, no matter how valuable a motive in many situations, cannot be the basis for the day-to-day functioning of a market economy, which must be founded on the pursuit of self-interest. Similarly, altruism, although often a highly effective motive behind locating and publicizing market failures, cannot be the basis for a systematic and sustained handling of these failures. Instead, market failures are best coped with by creating incentives for self-interested behaviour to alleviate them.

SUMMARY

Basic functions of government

- Effective governments have a monopoly of violence. They also define and protect the rights and obligations of property owned by individuals and institutions.

- Key characteristics of market economies are (*a*) their ability to co-ordinate decentralized decisions without conscious control, (*b*) their determination of the distribution of income, and (*c*) compared with the alternatives, their minimization of arbitrary economic power.

Market efficiency

- A perfectly competitive economy is allocatively efficient because it produces where price, which measures the value consumers place on the last unit produced, equals marginal cost, which measures the value to consumers that the resources used to produce the marginal unit could produce in other uses. Equating price to marginal cost maximizes the sum of producers' and consumers' surpluses.

- Free markets can fail to achieve efficiency because of inefficient exclusion of users from facilities with excess capacity, common property resources, public goods, externalities, asymmetric information, missing markets, and market power.

Rivalrous and excludable goods

- The optimal price for the service of a facility with excess capacity is zero. Since private owners will charge a positive price, their facility will be inefficiently underused.

- The private market will exploit a common property resource to the point where the average revenue per producer equals the production cost of a new entrant instead of to the socially optimal level, where the marginal addition to total product caused by a new entrant equals its production cost.

- The optimal quantity of a public good is provided when the marginal cost of production is equal to the sum of the prices that all its consumers would be willing to pay for the marginal unit produced. This is difficult to attain because of the free rider problem—the incentive for individuals to understate the true value that they place on a public good.

Externalities

- The Coase theorem shows that, if those parties that create an externality and those that are affected by it can bargain together with minimal transaction costs, all inefficiencies can be removed.

- Where private bargaining is impossible, the government can alleviate externalities by imposing rules and regulations or, more efficiently, by internalizing externalities through such measures as taxes and tradable permits to pollute.

Public policy towards monopoly and competition

- Government policy with respect to market power is designed to encourage competitive practices and discourage monopolistic ones.

- Direct control of pricing and entry conditions of some key oligopolistic industries has been common in the past, but deregulation is reducing such control.
- An important issue concerns the effect of market structure on economic growth. The productively inefficient resource allocation that results whenever firms have market power may be more conducive to the technological change than is the productively efficient allocation that results from perfect competition.

TOPICS FOR REVIEW

- Government as a monopolist of violence and a protector of property rights
- The efficiency of a perfectly competitive economy
- Rivalrous and non-rivalrous goods
- Excludable and non-excludable goods
- Inefficient exclusion
- Common property resources and the tragedy of the commons
- Rules for providing and pricing public goods

- Harmful and beneficial externalities
- Emissions taxes
- Tradable emissions permits
- Government control of market power
- Marginal and average cost pricing
- Competition policy
- Privatization
- Deregulation

DISCUSSION QUESTIONS

1 Your local authority undoubtedly provides a police station, a fire brigade, and a public library.
   (a) What are the market imperfections, if any, that each of these seeks to correct?
   (b) Which of these is closest to being a public good?
   (c) Which is furthest from being a public good?
   (d) What would happen if governments were prevented from offering these services?

2 Not counting the ones mentioned in the text, how many goods and services can you think of that are
   (a) non-rivalrous but excludable?
   (b) non-excludable but rivalrous?
   (c) non-rivalrous and non-excludable?

3 An industry consists of two firms producing the same product but using different technologies. Each emits 50 tonnes of pollution each year. One can clean up the first tonne at a cost of £1,000, while the cost of each additional tonne cleaned up rises by £1,000 per tonne until the last tonne costs £50,000. The second firm's cost for the first tonne cleaned up is £20,000, and the cost rises by £1,000 per tonne until the fiftieth tonne is cleaned up at a cost of £70,000. The government wishes to cut the industry's total emissions from 100 to 50 tonnes a year.

It gives each firm 25 tradable permits, each one allowing 1 tonne of pollution.
   (a) What will be the equilibrium price of a permit to pollute by 1 tonne?
   (b) How many permits will be traded?
   (c) By how much will each firm clean up its own pollution?
   (d) What would you infer if, in a subsequent year, the price of a pollution permit fell by 50 per cent?

4 Why do we worry about the behaviour of natural monopolies and about collusion among oligopolists? What can be done to prevent the undesirable effects of their behaviour without stifling technological advance?

5 'There would be no externalities, harmful or beneficial, if everyone were well informed and could bargain with each other with no transactions cost.' Explain why you agree or disagree.

6 What are public goods, and why cannot markets easily provide such goods?

7 Why do common property resources tend to be overexploited, and what solutions are available?

8 Why would it be inefficient to exclude people from using a facility that had excess capacity?

Chapter 20

GOVERNMENT SUCCESS AND GOVERNMENT FAILURE

In Chapter 19 we established three important results. First, free markets are effective ways of co-ordinating decentralized decision-taking. Second, although markets work quite well most of the time, they fail in the presence of certain well defined circumstances. Third, government policy can alleviate some of these market failures, either by imposing more efficient behaviour by rules, regulations, and public ownership or by internalizing externalities. But, while government interventions may have the potential to improve the workings of markets, this does not mean that governments always get it right. What objectives do governments actually have for their economic actions? Do they usually succeed in improving economic outcomes by their interventions, or do they often make outcomes worse? What costs does government intervention impose on the private sector? Do governments sometimes pursue objectives of their own, objectives that do not reflect the interests of the community as a whole? In particular, you will learn that:

- Governments have objectives for stability, growth, and equity as well as for efficiency.
- Equity, efficiency, and growth objectives may often conflict.

- Tools of government policy include taxation and spending, the law, and regulation as well as public ownership of enterprises.
- Government interventions usually involve both direct costs of administration and indirect costs associated with interference with the price mechanism.
- The incentives facing specific governments may deviate from those needed to deliver economic efficiency.

We start by outlining the objectives that governments may have in addition to correcting market failures. We then outline the many tools that are available to the government to achieve its policies, showing how these tools can be applied to areas other than market failure. After that, we allow for the *costs* of government activity. These must be offset against the benefits in order to assess the net value of any proposed government intervention. Finally, we deal with government failure, which occurs when governments consciously act in ways that encourage either inefficiency in resource allocation or undesirable inequities in income distribution.

Government objectives

Governments have multiple objectives, only some of which we studied in the previous chapter. Aside from looking after the welfare of elected officials and civil servants—which we will consider later in the chapter—governments seek many more socially acceptable objectives. The main ones are as follows:

1. to protect life and property by exercising a monopoly of force and establishing property rights;

2. to improve economic efficiency by addressing the various causes of market failure;

3. to achieve some accepted standard of equity;

4. to protect individuals from others and from themselves;

5. to influence the rate of economic growth;

6. to stabilize the economy against income and price level fluctuations.

The first two of these objectives were considered in the previous chapter. The next three are considered in this chapter. (Chapter 22 is also devoted to the fifth objective.) The last is a major subject of the second half of this book, which deals with macroeconomic theory and policy.

Policies for equity

Markets generate reasonably efficient allocations of the nation's resources because, most of the time, the information that they need to allow them to perform well is derived from agents' desires to improve their private circumstances. No one should be surprised, therefore, that markets do not efficiently allocate resources towards achieving such broad social goals as establishing an 'equitable' distribution of income and promoting shared community values. Markets do not directly foster these goals, precisely because individuals do not seek to achieve them when they are purchasing goods and services in markets. Instead, they look to the political system to achieve desired outcomes in this respect.

The distribution of income

An important characteristic of any market economy is the *distribution* of income that it determines. People whose skills are scarce relative to supply earn large incomes, whereas people whose skills are plentiful relative to supply earn much less.

As we have seen in earlier chapters, differentials in earnings serve the important function of motivating people to adapt. The advantage of such a system is that individuals can make their own decisions about how to alter their behaviour when market conditions change. The disadvantage is that temporary rewards and penalties are dealt out as a result of changes in market conditions that are beyond the control of the affected individuals. The resulting differences in incomes will seem inequitable to many—even though they are the incentives that make markets work.

Concerns about equity have two dimensions: horizontal and vertical equity. **Horizontal equity** means that people in similar circumstance should be treated similarly. Although this type of equity appears to many people as desirable, it is not always a goal of government policies. For example, people who are exposed to similar natural risks are given more government assistance when they are planting crops than when they are mining ore, cutting trees, or extracting oil. This may be because farmers have more political power than others, or it may stem from a gut feeling on the part of the electorate that food production is more basic than any other economic activity. **Vertical equity** concerns the different treatment of people in different economic situations in order to reduce inequalities between them.

Redistributive policies are of two general types. Some, such as the progressive income tax, are concerned with vertical equity. They seek to alter the size distribution of income in quite general ways. High marginal rates of income tax, combined with a neutral expenditure system that benefits all income groups more or less equally, will narrow income inequalities.

Other policies seek to mitigate the effects of markets on particular individuals. They seek not to narrow income gaps in general, but to deal with specific unfortunate events. Should farmers bear all the losses associated with the destruction of livestock after an outbreak of foot and mouth or mad cow disease? Should heads of households be forced to bear the full burden of their misfortune if they lose their jobs through no fault of their own? Even if they lose their jobs through their own fault, should they and their families have to bear the whole burden, which may include starvation? Should the ill and the aged be thrown on the mercy of their families? What if they have no families? Policies designed to deal with such situations usually seek horizontal equity in treating similarly all those who fall into some group.

Both private charities and a great many government policies are concerned with modifying the distribution of income that results from such things as one's parents' abilities, luck, and how one fares in the labour market.

The distribution of wealth

It is sometimes argued that egalitarian economic policy should devote more attention than it does to the distribution of wealth and less to the distribution of income. Wealth confers economic power, and wealth is more unequally distributed than is income. Heavy estate duties in the United Kingdom, however, caused a gradual reduction in the inequality of wealth distribution during the twentieth century. The trend has slowed, if not reversed, over the last two decades, but largely because of the buildup of pension wealth in the hands of 50–70-year-olds. None the less, at the end of the twentieth century just less than 20 per cent of all marketable wealth was held by the top 1 per cent of people in the UK wealth distribution, and a little over 90 per cent of all marketable wealth was owned by those in the top half of the distribution.

There are two main ways in which inequalities in the distribution of wealth can be reduced. The first is to levy taxes on wealth at the time that wealth is transferred from one owner to another, either by gifts during the lifetime of the owner or by bequest after death. In Britain such transfers used to be subject to a capital transfer tax. The rate of tax was progressive and rose to 60 per cent on taxable transfers in excess of £2 million. Currently, however, gifts among individuals during their lifetime are potentially exempt from tax. They become taxable only if made within seven years of the donor's death. In 2002/3, UK inheritance tax was set at the rate of 40 per cent on all estates over £250,000.[1]

The second method is an annual tax on the value of each person's wealth. A wealth tax of this sort has been

---

[1] The Inland Revenue estimates that only 4 in 100 deaths involve estates sufficiently large to pay inheritance tax.

considered in the past but it has never been instituted, and it has not been actively debated in the past two decades.

Equity versus efficiency

Problems arise when government measures designed to improve equity seriously inhibit the efficient operation of the price system.

Often the goal of a more equitable distribution conflicts with the goal of a more efficient economy.

Say that we were so extreme as to believe that equity demanded that everyone receive the same income. All incentives to work hard and to move from job to job would be eliminated. Some command economies came close to this extreme position, and the results were predictably disastrous. Suppose that, to be less extreme, we believed that earnings received by some owners of resources should not reflect short-term fluctuations in demand and supply. The UK controls on rented accommodation did just that during much of the twentieth century, as do controls in several other countries today. When such intervention is effective, the incentive system for resource allocation is eliminated. A rise in demand creates extra earnings, which attract resources to meet the demand. Remove the price reaction, and there is no reason for the resources to be reallocated.

Policies to protect individuals

Protection from others

People can use and even abuse other people for economic gain in ways that the members of society find offensive. Child labour laws and minimum standards of working conditions are responses to such actions. In an unhindered free market, the adults in a household usually decide how much education to buy for their children. Selfish parents might buy no education, while egalitarian parents might buy the same education for all of their children, regardless of their abilities. The members of society may want to interfere in these choices, both to protect the child of the selfish parent and to ensure that some of the scarce educational resources are distributed according to ability rather than family wealth. All households are forced to provide a minimum of education for their children, and a number of inducements are offered—through public universities, scholarships, and other means—for talented children to consume more education than they or their parents might choose if they had to pay the entire cost themselves.

Protection from oneself

Members of society, acting through the government, often seek to protect adult (and presumably responsible) individuals not from others, but from themselves. Laws prohibiting the use of heroin, crack cocaine, and other drugs, and laws prescribing the installation and use of car seat belts, are intended primarily to protect individuals from their own ignorance or short-sightedness. This kind of interference in the free choices of individuals is called **paternalism**. Whether such actions reflect the wishes of the majority in society or the interference of overbearing governments, there is no doubt that the market will not provide this kind of protection. Buyers do not buy what they do not want, and sellers have no motive to provide it.

Paternalism is often closely related to **merit goods**. Merit goods are goods that society, operating through the government, deems to be especially important or that those in power feel individuals should be encouraged to consume. Housing, education, health care, and certain cultural activities are often cited as merit goods. Critics argue that the concept is merely a way of imposing the tastes of an elite group on others.

Policies to promote social obligations

In a free-market system, if you can persuade someone else to clean your house in return for £40, both parties to the transaction are presumed to be better off. You prefer to part with £40 rather than to clean the house yourself, and the person you hire prefers to have £40 than to avoid cleaning your house. Normally society does not interfere with people's ability to negotiate mutually advantageous contracts.

Most people do not feel this way, however, about activities that are regarded as social obligations. For example, during major wars when military service is compulsory, contracts similar to the one between you and your housekeeper could also be negotiated. Some persons, faced with the obligation to do military service, could no doubt pay enough to persuade others to do their tour of service for them. By exactly the same argument we just used, we can presume that both parties will be better off if they are allowed to negotiate such a trade. Yet such contracts are usually prohibited as a result of widely held values that cannot be expressed in the marketplace. In times of major wars, of the sort that were experienced twice in the twentieth century, military service by all healthy males is held to be a duty that is independent of an individual's tastes, income, wealth, or social position.

Military service is not the only example of a social obligation. Citizens are not allowed to buy their way out of jury duty or to sell their votes, even though in many cases they could find willing trading partners. Even if the price system allocates goods and services with complete efficiency, members of a society do not wish to rely solely on the market for all purposes, since they have other goals that they wish to achieve.

Policies for economic growth

Over the long haul, economic growth is the most powerful determinant of living standards (see Chapter 22). Whatever their policies concerning efficiency and equity, people who live in economies with rapid rates of growth find their living standards rising on average faster than those of people who live in countries with low rates of growth. Over a few decades, these growth-induced changes tend to have much larger effects on living standards than any policy-induced changes in the efficiency of resource allocation or the distribution of income.

For the last half of the twentieth century, most economists viewed growth mainly as a macroeconomic phenomenon related to total savings and total investment. Reflecting this view, most textbooks do not even mention growth in their chapters on microeconomic policy.

More recently there has been a shift back to the perspective of earlier economists, who saw technological change as the engine of growth, with individual entrepreneurs and firms as the agents of innovation. This is a microeconomic perspective, which is meant to add to, not replace, the macroeconomic stress on capital accumulation.

Governments are aware of this microeconomic perspective on growth. Today few microeconomic policies escape being exposed to the question, 'Even if this policy achieves its main goal, will it have unfavourable effects on growth?' Answering yes is not a sufficient reason to abandon a specific policy. But it is a sufficient reason to think again. Is it possible to redesign the policy so that it can still achieve its main objective, while removing its undesirable side-effects on growth?

Tools and performance

The main sets of tools available to governments to achieve their goals are taxes, expenditure, rules, and public ownership. In this section we discuss these tools and show how they are used to achieve the specific objectives outlined earlier.

Taxation

Taxes and expenditures are by far the most important items on this list. Governments spend money to achieve many purposes, and that money must be either borrowed or raised through taxes. We leave borrowing aside as it is only a temporary measure. Interest must be paid on borrowed money and, if that too is borrowed, the total government debt eventually explodes to unmanageable proportions.

So sooner or later all government expenditure must be paid for out of taxes. Borrowing only postpones the need to tax.

Table 20.1 shows the major sources of tax revenues, along with the major classes of government expenditures, for the UK in 2001.

As well as providing the revenues needed to finance all of the government's activities, taxes are also used as tools in their own right for a wide range of purposes. They can be used to alter the incentives to which private maximizing agents react, and to alter the distribution of income.

Indirect taxes

Taxes are divided into two broad groups, depending on whether persons or transactions are taxed. An **indirect**

Table 20.1 **Expenditure and revenue of UK central and local government, 2001**

Expenditure	£bn	Revenue	£bn
Health	61.5	Taxes on products	140.1
Education	46.7	Taxes on income and wealth	165.8
Defence	27.7	Social contributions	63.5
Social protection	159.2	Other capital taxes	2.5
Other	103.1	Total taxes and social	
Total	398.2	contributions	371.9

Source: ONS, Blue Book, 2002.

tax is levied on a transaction and is paid by an individual by virtue of being involved in that transaction. Taxes and stamp duties on the transfer of assets from one owner to another are indirect taxes, since they depend on the assets being transferred. Inheritance taxes, which depend on the size of the estate being inherited and not on the circumstances of the beneficiaries, are also an indirect tax.

The most important indirect taxes in today's world are those on the sale of currently produced products. These taxes are called excise taxes when they are levied on manufacturers, and sales taxes when they are levied on the sale of goods from retailer to consumer. The EU countries levy a comprehensive tax of this sort on all transactions, whether at the retail, wholesale, or manufacturer's level, called the value added tax (VAT). Value added is the difference between the value of inputs that the firm purchases from other firms and the value of its output. It therefore represents the value that a firm adds by virtue of its own activities. VAT is an indirect tax because it depends on the value of what is made and sold, not on the wealth or income of the maker or seller. Thus, two self-employed fabric designers, each with a value added of £50,000 in terms of designs produced and sold, would pay the same VAT even if one had no other source of income while the other was independently wealthy.

Indirect taxes may be levied in two basic ways. An **ad valorem tax** is a percentage of the value of the transaction on which it is levied. The UK's 17.5 per cent VAT on most transactions is an ad valorem tax. A **specific** or **per-unit tax** is a tax expressed as so many pence per unit, independent of the commodity's price. Taxes on cinema and theatre tickets, and on each litre of petrol or alcohol, and on each packet of cigarettes are all specific, indirect taxes. Box 20.1 outlines the main impact of a per-unit tax on the output of firms.

从价税

单位税

Direct taxes

纳税人.

Taxes in the second broad group are called **direct taxes**. These are levied on people and they vary with the status of the taxpayer. The most important direct tax is the income tax. The personal income tax falls sometimes on the income of households and sometimes separately on each member of the household. It varies with the size and source of the taxpayer's income and various other characteristics, such as marital status and number of dependants.

Firms also pay taxes on their incomes. UK companies are subject to corporation tax, which is levied on their profits. This is a direct tax, both in the legal sense that the company is an individual in the eyes of the law, and in the economic sense that the company is owned by its shareholders so that a tax on the company is a tax on them. The impact of taxes on profits is discussed in Box 20.2. An expenditure tax—as advocated some years ago for the United Kingdom by the Royal Commission headed by Nobel Prize-winning

---

Box 20.1 **The impact of a per-unit tax**

Many kinds of taxes affect the costs of firms. We illustrate here a tax that is levied on each unit produced.

From the firm's point of view, the tax on each unit produced is just another cost of production. It shifts each firm's marginal cost curve vertically upwards by the amount of the tax, where marginal cost now refers to the firm's total outlay—costs and taxes—associated with each additional unit of production.

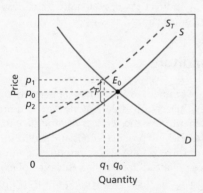

The figure shows a competitive market in equilibrium with the demand and supply curves D and S intersecting at E_0 to produce equilibrium price and output of p_0 and q_0. A tax of T per unit is then placed on the product. We show the effect of the tax by adding it to the supply curve. The 'costs' of producers now comprise production costs plus the tax that must be paid to the government. Every point on the supply curve shifts vertically upwards by the amount of the tax. The intersection of the new supply curve S_T and the demand curve D yields the new quantity and market price of q_1 and p_1. Producers' after-tax receipts are read from the original supply curve S and are $p_2 (= p_1 - T)$ per unit.

The upward shift in marginal cost curves makes the industry's supply curve shift upward by the amount of the tax. Now recall the results established in Chapter 10 on cost changes.

A per-unit tax on the output of a competitive industry will:

1. **raise price in the short run, but by less than the amount of the tax, so that the burden will be shared by consumers, who pay a higher price, and by producers, who do not cover their average total costs;**

2. **cause the industry to contract in the long run until the losses disappear, and the whole burden falls on consumers;**

3. **if the cost curves of firms remaining in the industry are unaffected by the contraction in the size of the industry, cause the price to rise in the long run by the full amount of the tax.**

The second of the above consequences is an example of a most important general proposition. This is that, in an industry with freedom of entry or exit and where there is room for a large number of firms, profits will always be pushed to zero in the long run. Thus, any temporary advantage or disadvantage given to the industry by any public policy or private action must be dissipated in the long run—free entry and exit always ensures that surviving firms earn zero pure profits.

Government intervention in a competitive industry can influence the size of the industry, the total volume of its sales, and the price at which its goods are sold; but intervention cannot influence the long-run profitability of the firms that remain in the industry.

Many a government policy has started out to raise the profitability of a particular industry and ended up only increasing the number of firms, each operating at an unchanged level of profits. This illustrates that any policy by any group will fail to secure economic profits in the long run.

Box 20.2 **The effect of taxes on profits**

A famous prediction is that a tax levied as a percentage on what economists call profits will have no effect on price and output under any market structure. Let us first see how the prediction is derived, and then consider its application to real-world situations.

Given free entry, there will be no profits in long-run equilibrium. Thus, the firms in a perfectly competitive industry will pay no profit tax in the long run. (X per cent of zero is zero.) It follows that the tax does not affect any firm's long-run behaviour and hence has no effect on industry price and output.

A tax on profit as defined in economics affects neither price nor output of a competitive industry in equilibrium. Hence it does not affect the allocation of resources.

Does this prediction apply to those taxes on firms' profits that are actually levied in many countries? The answer is no, because profits are defined in tax law according to accountants' rather than economists' usage. In particular, the tax-law definition includes the opportunity cost of capital and the reward for risk-taking. To economists this is a cost; for tax purposes it is profit. (To review economists' definition of profit, see pages 132–3.)

A tax on the return to capital will have some effects. First, perfectly competitive firms will pay such taxes even in long-run equilibrium, since they use capital and must earn enough money to pay a return on it. Second, the tax will affect costs differently in different industries. To see this, compare two industries. One is very labour-intensive, so that 90 per cent of its costs of production go to wages and only 10 per cent to capital and other factors. The other is very capital-intensive, so that fully 50 per cent of its costs (in the economist's sense) are a return to capital. The tax on the return to capital will take a small part of the total earnings of the first industry and a large part of those of the second industry. If the industries were equally profitable (in the economist's sense) before the tax, they would not be afterwards, and producers would be attracted into the first industry and out of the second one. This would cause prices to change until both industries became equally profitable (post-tax), after which no further movement would occur.

A tax on profits as they are defined in tax law does affect price and output and hence alters the allocation of resources. It also implies a higher effective tax rate in capital-intensive industries (though the impact of real tax systems would have to look at the entire range of taxes, including those on labour).

economist James Meade (1909–96)—is also a direct tax. It is based on what a person spends, rather than on what he or she earns, and has exemptions that are specific to the individual taxpayer. A poll tax, which is simply a lump-sum tax levied on each person, is also a direct tax.

It is important for many purposes to distinguish average from marginal rates of any tax. The *average rate* of income tax paid by a person is that person's total tax divided by her income. The *marginal rate* of tax is the rate she would pay on another unit of income.

Progressivity The general term for the relation between the level of income and the percentage of income paid as a tax is **progressivity**. A **regressive tax** takes a *smaller percentage* of people's incomes the larger is their income. A **progressive tax** takes a *larger percentage* of people's incomes the larger is their income. A **proportional tax** is the boundary case between the two since it takes the *same percentage* of income from everyone. Taxes on food, for example, tend to be regressive, because the proportion of total income spent on food tends to fall as income rises. Taxes on alcoholic spirits tend to be progressive, since the proportion of income spent on spirits tends to rise with income. Taxes on cigarettes, on the other hand, are regressive. Different types of progressivity are shown in Figure 20.1.

Progressivity can be defined for any one tax or for the tax system as a whole. Different taxes have different characteristics. Inevitably, some will be progressive and some regressive. The impact of a tax system as a whole on high-, middle-, and low-income groups is best judged by looking

at the progressivity of the whole set of taxes taken together. For example, income taxes are progressive in the United Kingdom, rising to a maximum marginal rate of 40 per cent. The overall tax system is also progressive, but much less so than one would guess from studying only the income tax rates. This is because a great deal of revenue is raised by indirect taxes, which are much less progressive than income taxes.

Expenditure

Some government expenditures are in return for goods and services that count as part of current output. When the government buys the services of land, labour, or capital, and uses them to produce goods and services in the public sector of the economy, these resources are unavailable to produce private sector output. This type of expenditure is sometimes called **exhaustive expenditure**. Among their many uses, exhaustive expenditures are the tool for filling in gaps in what the free market provides. For example, public goods, such as national defence, the legal system, and coastal navigation aids, must be produced by the government or not at all. In those cases the failure of the free market, and the potential for a remedy by government action, are obvious.

The remainder of government expenditure consists of **transfer payments**, which are payments *not* made in return for any contribution to current output. Old-age pensions, unemployment insurance and supplementary benefits,

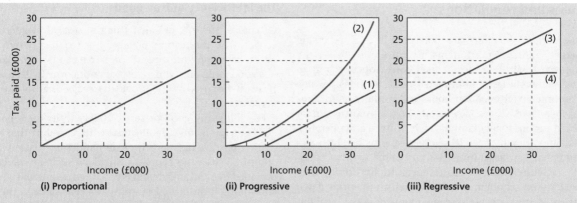

Figure 20.1 Income taxes with different progressivities

Income taxes may be proportional, progressive, or regressive. In part (i) the proportional tax's average and marginal rates remain unchanged at 50 per cent as income changes. In part (ii) tax (1) has a constant marginal rate of 50 per cent. But the average rate rises with income, from zero at income £10,000 to 25 per cent at income £20,000, and to 33.3 per cent at income £30,000. With tax (2), both the marginal and the average tax rates rise as income rises. In part (iii) tax (3) has a constant marginal rate of 50 per cent; but the average rate falls as income rises, from 150 per cent at £10,000 to 100 per cent at £20,000, and to 83.3 per cent at £30,000. With tax (4), both the marginal and the average rates fall as income rises.

welfare payments, disability payments, and a host of other expenditures made by the modern welfare state are all transfer payments. They do not add to current marketable output; they merely transfer the power to purchase output from those who provide the money (usually taxpayers) to those who receive it. Their main purpose, therefore, is to alter the *distribution* of income. Tax-induced redistributions are not just from rich to poor. They also make transfers from those working to those retired and unemployed, from the healthy to the sick, and from city-dwellers to farmers (through CAP subsidies in the EU). None of these transfer payments represents a claim by the government on real productive resources. Revenue must none the less be raised to finance them. Table 20.2 shows UK government spending expressed as a proportion of the nation's output.

Figure 20.2 shows the overall redistributive effect of the UK tax—expenditure system. The system redistributes incomes from rich to poor. The main benefits to lower-income groups come from cash payments, such as welfare

and unemployment benefits, and in-kind benefits, mainly education and the NHS. High-income groups contribute to the income redistribution because, although they receive many benefits, they pay even higher amounts of both direct and indirect taxes.

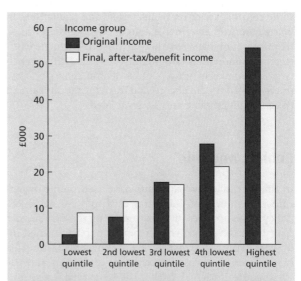

Figure 20.2 UK households' original and final income per year, 2001

The distribution of original income is much more unequal than the distribution of final income. Original income obtained from private sector activities is altered by the subtraction of direct and indirect taxes and the addition of cash benefits and benefits in kind to obtain final, or after-tax/benefit, income.

Table 20.2 **UK government spending as a percentage of GDP**

Spending on	1956	1976	1997	2001
Goods and services	20.7	25.9	20.8	20.5
Transfer payments	13.2	21.0	18.6	19.6
Total spending	33.9	46.9	39.2	40.1

Source: ONS, UK national accounts.

Rules and regulations

Rules and regulations are potent tools for redressing market failures. Governments use rules both to set the framework within which market forces operate and to alter the workings of unhindered markets. Rules pervade economic activities. Shop hours and working conditions are regulated. Rules govern the circumstances under which various types of union can be formed and operated. Discrimination between labour services provided by males and females is illegal in the UK and in many other countries. Children cannot be served alcoholic drinks; they must attend school in most countries, and be inoculated against communicable diseases in many. Laws prohibit people from selling or using certain drugs. Prostitution is prohibited in many societies even though it usually involves a willing buyer and a willing seller. In many countries you are forced to purchase insurance for the damage you might do to others with your private motor car. In some countries people who offer goods for sale cannot refuse to sell them to someone just because they do not like the customer's colour or religion. There are rules against fraudulent advertising and the sale of substandard, adulterated, or poisonous food. In some countries, such as the United States, anyone can purchase a variety of firearms ranging from pistols to machine-guns; in other countries, such as the United Kingdom, it is difficult for a private citizen to obtain a handgun.

As we saw in Chapter 19, most business practices have some control exerted on them by rules and regulations. In many countries agreements among oligopolistic firms to fix prices, or divide up markets, are illegal. The mere existence of monopoly is outlawed in some countries. When large economies of scale create a natural monopoly, the prices that a firm can charge, and the return it can earn on its capital investment, are often regulated.

Public ownership

In the past many governments have used public ownership of nationalized industries as a tool for achieving policy goals. In the UK today most of these industries have been privatized. The remaining publicly owned industries in the UK (as of 2002) are the Royal Mail Group plc (which owns the Post Office), state education, and the National Health Service (NHS). The Royal Mail Group is in the market sector in the sense that it finances its activities by selling its services on the open market. We say nothing more about it here. We deal briefly with education and then in more detail with the NHS. The provision of both of these services—education and health—has been largely removed from the UK private sector and is provided free to consumers.

The inefficiency of free goods

Of course, there is no such thing as a costless good or service. The production of anything requires resources, which have opportunity costs. So a 'free good' is not a costless good, only one whose costs are not borne by its users. Instead, the costs of state-provided free goods are borne by taxpayers.

Providing any good or service freely to its users poses efficiency problems. We illustrate with a product that has neither positive nor negative externalities, so that private and social costs and benefits coincide. If such a product is provided free and all demand is met, then people will go on consuming it until the last unit has a zero value to them. But that unit will have a positive marginal cost of production, which represents the value to consumers that the resources used in its production could have created in other lines of activity.

The provision of free goods is allocatively inefficient because its price (of zero) is less than its marginal cost.

Figure 20.3 shows the resource waste. It is obvious that the size of the waste will depend on the elasticity of the demand curve for the subsidized product. With a highly inelastic demand curve the policy induces only a small increase in output, so only a small quantity of resources is inefficiently allocated. With a highly elastic demand, the quantity of misallocated resources is large.

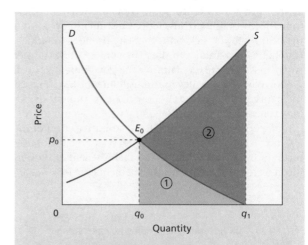

Figure 20.3 The inefficiency of free goods

Consumption of a free good exceeds what it would be at the efficient competitive equilibrium. Competitive equilibrium is at E_0 with price p_0 and quantity q_0. At a zero price q_1 is consumed. Since each extra unit that is produced adds its marginal cost to the total cost of production, total costs rise by the area under the industry's marginal cost curve (its supply curve). The two shaded areas 1 and 2 show this extra cost. The additional consumers' surplus is given by the medium blue shaded area 1. So the efficiency loss is the dark shaded area 2.

Positive

From the point of view of improving equity in income distribution, free goods also have major shortcomings. Much of the money spent goes to subsidize their consumption by higher-income groups. Since there are few goods that are not bought by all income groups, the policy is much like shooting at a target with a shotgun—the bull's-eye will be hit, but so will almost everything else.

Transfer payments can be targeted at specific income groups; free goods cannot.

This lack of targeting makes the free-good policy an unnecessarily expensive way of helping low-income groups.

A further problem with free goods is that the government often does not provide a sufficient quantity to meet the demand at zero price. Some alternative rationing scheme must therefore arise. Sometimes queues do the rationing. At other times sellers' preferences do the job, as first discussed in Chapter 5. This happens, for example, when those considered most worthy by administrators or doctors are given expensive health care while others get cheaper alternatives.

Education

Education could be left completely to the private sector. Those who were willing to pay would choose from the many schools at all levels that the private sector would no doubt provide. Most countries leave a substantial amount of education to be provided in this way. In the UK in 2001 about 6 per cent of 5–16-year-olds were being educated in the private sector. Thus, state schools still account for the vast majority of pupils. This raises three questions that are distinct although often confused. First, why is education made compulsory? Second, who should pay for education? Third, who should provide it?

Why compulsion? There are three main reasons for making education compulsory up to some allowable school-leaving age, which is 16 in the UK. The first is protection of children. If selfish parents decided to spend money on themselves and nothing on their children, they would hamper their children's ability to function in the economy when they grew up. The second is income redistribution. It is held that no one should be prevented from gaining some minimum level of education because of lack of parental income. The third reason is externalities. Everyone gains from living in a society where everyone else has some minimum level of education. A well-trained person is seldom of value on his own. One machinist in a society with no others would not be able to take most of the jobs that machinists do because they are done with other similarly trained workers. Because of externalities, we insist that everyone attend school up to some legal leaving age.

Who should pay for it? If an expensive service is made compulsory because it is of benefit to everyone, the obvious way to pay for it is through taxes. This is more acceptable because the proposition that free goods are consumed in inefficient amounts does not apply to any good or service whose consumption is compulsory. Because everyone of school age must attend school, the elasticity of demand for such education is zero. Thus, the amount of resources allocated to compulsory education is independent of who pays for it. The method of payment will affect the distribution of income but will not cause any allocative inefficiency.

Who should provide it? There is no universal agreement on the question of provision. In the UK many parents opt out of the system and provide private education for their children. For this they must pay (in addition to the taxes that they already pay to support the state system). Those who go through the state system have little choice. They must go to the local school (possibly choosing between two nearby ones if space is available). They must accept the current curriculum and whatever educational practices are currently being mandated. They cannot purchase an alternative educational experience that does not currently have ministry approval (without opting out of the state sector entirely). In short, as with any other nationalized industries, there is little market choice available and innovation is centralized.

There are several arguments commonly advanced for state provision of education. It creates a desirable uniformity of standards. Pay and working conditions will be the same throughout the system. The state with all its educational experts knows better than the child and its parents what educational experience is in the child's best interest. Ministries can research new methods and techniques, and institute them efficiently when they seem to be improvements on current practices.

Opponents of the state monopoly in the provision of state-funded education argue for more market determination. The state could give every child education vouchers to the value of what the state is providing; these vouchers could be used to purchase education in any establishment that accepts them. Proponents of this type of system argue several alleged advantages. It would give parents more choice among various schools. Parents and their children usually have a better idea of what kind of education is needed and of whether or not they are getting it at the school currently being attended. This would penalize schools with poor academic and discipline records. Salaries would not be uniform across all schools; instead, the earnings of schools and the salaries of teachers would vary with the success of individual schools in attracting students. Poorer schools would get few vouchers and hence would have little revenue out of which to pay their staff. The system would also encourage experimentation. Anyone with a new idea could try it out, provided only that she could fill one classroom with students. The small amount of current centralized experimentation would be replaced with a large amount of decentralized experimentation. If some new educational ideal or fad gained majority acceptance it would not be forced on all students. Anyone who disagreed with it would need only find a school that was not following the herd.

These are some of the arguments advanced by some for exposing education to market forces while ensuring that it remains available to everyone. Many others worry about exposing education to market forces and prefer the system of state monopoly.

Although state financing of education is not in dispute in modern countries, the value of a state monopoly in providing free education is debated. Some think it the best system; others wish to inject market competition into the provision of free education.

Health and medical care

The case for providing hospital and medical services at a price below cost (zero in the limit) rests on three considerations. First, private provision is prone to market failure. Second, it is alleged that the inefficiencies of free medical care are not large. Third, serious equity issues arise when health care is left to private markets.

Market failure In the previous chapter we studied the types of market failure that emerge when all sides to a transaction are not equally informed. So we merely need note how these failures apply to the market for medical and health care. First, doctors are better informed about their patients' needs than are the patients themselves. So doctors are in a position to influence the demand for their services rather than responding to the demands of their patients. As a result, elective surgery and other treatments of non-life-threatening medical conditions are observed to vary with the supply of doctors. Second, patients are better informed than their medical insurers on the state of their own health. This creates the problem of adverse selection first studied in Chapter 13, page 222. Third, people who are fully insured are likely to be more careless with their health than those who must pay themselves. This is the problem of moral hazard also studied in Chapter 13. It is worth noting that the first problem exists with any fee-for-service system, no matter who pays the bill. The second exists only when insurance companies pay the bill, while the third exists in all systems where anyone but the patient pays.

With medical care, social and private costs and benefits are thought to diverge substantially. If I do not cure my infectious disease, the effects will not be felt by me alone. More generally, everyone gains by living in a healthy rather than a disease-ridden society. Thus, there are arguments for reducing the private costs of these services below the market rate by means of a subsidy.

Insurers can do little to avoid some adverse selection, but they will not insure those whom they know to be already ill or at serious risk for other reasons. This means that a considerable number of people just cannot get medical insurance under free-market provision. This group includes those who were born with serious health problems or acquired them while still living at home. It also includes those with serious health problems whose medical coverage runs out when they leave their present employer to change firms or retire; when they try to reinsure themselves in a private plan, they often find themselves uninsurable.

Small inefficiencies? Recall that the magnitude of the resource cost of a free-good policy depends on the slope of the demand curve between the free-market price and the subsidized price. Studies suggest low incidence of unnecessary hospitalization in free-hospital systems. If the demand for services is not much larger than it would be in the free market (where most people would be privately insured), then the magnitude of the waste caused by divergence between the zero price and the positive marginal cost will be small.

Other potential inefficiencies also exist. Governments typically do not provide facilities to meet all the demand for free services. So scarce funds must be allocated within the system. However, bureaucratic decisions are seldom efficient in allocating scarce funds, so that their marginal benefits are the same in all uses. In the mid-1990s a controversial internal-market mechanism was introduced into the NHS. Patients got treatment free, but doctors had a notional budget that they used to buy services from hospitals. Hospitals priced operations, and these prices varied substantially over the country. This internal-market system was abolished by the Labour government in 1999. A ten-year plan was embarked upon in 2000 to improve health service resources and the efficiency of the internal allocation mechanisms. The impact of this plan can only be judged in future years, but it seems unlikely that it will solve the problem created by virtually permanent excess demand at a zero price.

Equity considerations There are also more subtle arguments about social values. It has been argued that in richer societies decisions about basic medical care should be taken out of the economic arena. It is degrading for a person to have to balance medical care for a child against the other family needs. Therefore, it is argued, the inefficiency cost of freely provided basic medical care is worth accepting in order to produce a society where choices about basic medical services are eliminated.

Notice the use of the word 'basic' in the previous paragraph. The above position is arguable if it is confined to basic services for all. Modern medical technology is so expensive that the state could not afford to make all conceivable services freely available to all. The more expensive services must be rationed. This can be done either by prices or by decisions about need taken by medical and hospital authorities.

For all its problems, the NHS remains one of the most popular of the government's many activities. It seems likely, therefore, to stay in place for a long time to come. As a result, understanding its shortcomings and using economic analysis to alleviate the worst of its inefficiencies is an important social activity.

Economic growth

We saw earlier that modern concern about the interface between microeconomic policies and economic growth is relatively new. Concern is largely about unintentional side-effects on the growth of policies with other primary objectives. Concern is directed to a lesser extent at micro policies that are directly focused on growth. But, as we will see below, both types of concerns are relevant when policy tools are chosen.

Taxation policies for growth

Almost all taxes can affect growth by altering incentives either to save, to work, or to take risks.

Taxation of consumption or income Income taxes apply to income when it is earned; spending taxes (such as VAT) apply only to that part of income that is spent on consumption.

Consider a woman in the 40 per cent marginal tax bracket who earns an extra £1,000 and pays £400 income tax. If she spends her after-tax income, she will be able to buy £600 worth of goods. If she saves the money, she will be able to buy a £600 bond. If the bond pays, say, a 4 per cent real return, she will earn £24 interest per year. But a 40 per cent tax must then be paid on the interest earnings, leaving only a £14.40 annual income. This is a 2.4 per cent after-tax return on the bond and a 1.44 per cent after-tax return on the original £1,000 income!

This 'double taxing' of savings is a disincentive. Economists who wish to encourage saving, which helps to finance growth-creating investment, argue for taxes on consumption, not income. Under an expenditure tax any income that is saved is untaxed. Our saver in the previous paragraph would be taxed only when the interest earned on the savings was actually spent on consumption.

Steeply progressive rates of tax Steeply progressive tax rates are an incentive to emigrate or at least move one's business abroad. They also penalize people with fluctuating incomes, such as authors, self-employed builders, and small-scale innovators. Consider an innovator who tries to introduce one new product each year. She just covers costs on her first four attempts, and then has a success that yields £250,000 over costs in the fifth year. Her income over the five years is the same as a salaried employee who earns £50,000 for each of these five years. Yet under a steeply progressive tax regime she will pay much more tax than he will. This was a really serious problem when the maximum rate of tax in the United Kingdom was 70 per cent. (Right after the Second World War in 1945 it was well over 90 per cent!) In the 1980s the maximum rate was cut to the present rate of 40 per cent, which greatly reduced the tax penalty paid by someone with a highly fluctuating income. But it did not eliminate it. In 2002/3 our innovator above would have paid £92,542 in taxes, while over the same five-year period the salaried man would have paid £62,708 (assuming each had no dependants).

Here we see one of the many possible conflicts between growth and equity. One may favour steeply progressive tax rates on grounds of equity but be persuaded to moderate the degree of progressivity in the interest of encouraging the risk-taking that is necessary for promoting growth.

Adjustment policies for growth

The innovations in products and production processes that underlie growth require continual changes and adaptations throughout the economy. If government policies discourage change, growth will be slowed. The realization that many policies designed to improve equity can discourage change has led to some policy re-evaluations.

Labour market policies When people lose jobs because of economic change, the various measures that constitute the welfare safety net provide them with income support. Although such passive support provides immediate relief, it gives no incentive for recipients to change their situation and can sometimes even discourage such efforts.

An alternative is to make some or the entire support conditional on adjusting to change, for example by re-training or relocating. The UK government, for example, has funded the Learning and Skills Council, to encouraged young people to undergo a period of training or work experience.

Support of firms and industries Governments are always tempted to support declining industries. Over the past century both Labour and Conservative governments have done a lot of this. Such policies reduce unemployment in the short run, but if economic forces are leading to a continual decline, the policies are only costly ways of postponing the inevitable. Furthermore, when it finally becomes necessary, the adjustment often comes suddenly. This is because government support will be withdrawn all at once when the growing cost of the support finally becomes unacceptable.

Box 20.3 **The great Microsoft anti-trust case**

Some of the greatest innovations in information and communications technology have been due to Bill Gates and his firm Microsoft. Now in his late thirties, Gates is one of the world's wealthiest people. He is a classic entrepreneur who entered the PC software industry when it was new, fiercely competitive, and rapidly developing. His Windows operating system achieved instant customer approval and now dominates the industry.

In 1998 the US Department of Justice brought an anti-trust suit against Microsoft for alleged monopoly practices. The firm was accused of tactics designed to make entry difficult for smaller firms selling specialized products that competed with some parts of Microsoft's array. In particular, when customers buy any new version of the Windows operating system, they are automatically provided with Microsoft's Internet browser. This bundling of Microsoft products undoubtedly makes competition more difficult for smaller firms producing one type of product.

The suit reveals all the conflicting views that can be taken about competition and technical change.

• Technological innovations have transformed the lives of ordinary people several times since the first industrial revolution in the mid-eighteenth century.

• A new industry producing a wholly new range of products typically starts off as highly competitive as did cars, aircraft, and computers. Soon, however, the winners in the race to expand and improve the range of products eliminate most of the weaker competitors. They emerge as oligopolists in a mature industry.

• The dominant firm in the technological race often establishes something close to a monopoly position. This dominance is partly a result of continued successful innovation—established oligopolies have been the source of much growth-inducing technological change over the past 150 years. It is also partly a result of the firm's ability to suppress competition from smaller upstart firms.

• Over the long haul, even if the oligopolist becomes something close to a monopolist, it cannot perpetuate its position indefinitely—new firms with

new products eventually arise to challenge and unseat the established firms.

So how should the US government react? Should it constrain Microsoft in order to create more growth-enhancing competition? Or should it accept Microsoft's dominant position in the industry as the reward for its amazing record as an innovator? Should it accept Schumpeter's argument that, in the very long run, neither Microsoft nor any other dominant firm will be able to maintain its position unless it outperforms actual and potential competitors in the race to provide consumers with more, better, and cheaper products?

Faced with that decision, the US Department of Justice took the line that Microsoft's behaviour was designed to stifle competition. Later a US appeals court took the opposite line. Whatever the final outcome, these early differences in legal opinions illustrate the difficulty in distinguishing successful competitive behaviour from behaviour designed to suppress competition. The legal arguments are complicated and the case was still running in 2002. Later court hearings had found Microsoft guilty in some aspects of anti-competitive behaviour but not in others. The US Justice Department proposed a final judgement that

will stop recurrence of Microsoft's unlawful conduct, prevent recurrence of similar conduct in the future, and restore competitive conditions in the personal computer operating system market by, among other things, prohibiting actions by Microsoft to prevent computer manufacturers and others from developing, distributing or featuring middleware products that are threats to Microsoft's operating system monopoly; creating the opportunity for independent software vendors to develop products that will be competitive with Microsoft's middleware products; requiring Microsoft to disclose interfaces and license protocols in order to ensure that competing middleware and server operating system products can interoperate with Microsoft's desktop operating systems; and ensuring full compliance with the. [final judgment]

[For details of the final outcome, see www.usdoj.gov/atr/cases/ms_index.htm.]

Patents If an innovation can be easily copied, new firms may enter an industry so quickly that the innovating firm is not compensated for the costs and risks of innovation. The innovation is, in effect, a public good, and private firms are not motivated to produce it. Patent laws are designed to provide the needed incentives by creating a temporary property right over the invention allowing the invention's owner to earn profits as a reward for inventing. Once the patent expires, others can legally copy the innovation and production will expand until profits fall to normal.

Reduction of entry barriers Those who accept Schumpeter's theory hold that anti-monopoly policy and public utility regulations are unnecessary as policies to influence behaviour in the very long run. They worry that state intervention will inadvertently create entry barriers that will

protect existing firms from the growth-creating process of creative destruction. They believe that government policies directed at minimizing entry barriers are the only industrial and competition policies that are needed.

Nationalization Those who reject Schumpeter's theory often support anti-monopoly and public utility regulation policies. They feel that such policies are required to prevent monopolies from earning large profits at the expense of consumers.

Supporters of Schumpeter's theory argue that nationalization and public regulation will defeat their own purposes in the long term by inhibiting the process of creative destruction. A government monopoly provides the most enforceable entry barrier. It may inhibit the introduction of new products, or new ways to produce old products, that would have occurred when new firms attacked the entrenched positions of existing firms. Supporters of this view point to the former Soviet Union's need to buy technology from Western countries, and argue that the rapid development of new products and processes in the oligopolistic and monopolistic industries operating in market-oriented economies gives support to Schumpeter's view. Box 20.3 deals with an important court case in which different groups took different positions on the issue of the importance of monopoly power and creative destruction.

A short-term/long-term trade-off? Economists who accept both the force of the argument that monopolistic firms can earn large exploitative profits in the short term *and* Schumpeter's argument about the very long run face a policy dilemma. In the short term, firms that gain monopoly power may earn very large profits at the expense of consumers. In the very long term, however, attempts to control these monopolies may inhibit the creative destruction that helps to raise living standards through productivity growth.

The policy world is not a simple place, and policies that help to achieve desired goals over one time-span must be constantly scrutinized for undesired effects over other time-spans.

The costs of government intervention

We have seen that governments have many reasons to take action and many tools that help them to achieve their goals. However, to evaluate government intervention, we need to consider costs as well as benefits.

Large potential benefits do not necessarily justify government intervention, nor do large potential costs necessarily make it unwise. What matters are net benefits—the balance between benefits and costs.

Three types of cost of government intervention are important. These are costs that are internal to the government, costs that are external to the government but directly paid by others in the sector where the intervention occurs, and costs that are external to the government and felt more generally throughout the entire economy.

Internal costs

Everything the government does uses resources. It costs money when government inspectors visit plants to check on compliance with government-imposed health standards, industrial safety, or environmental protection. The inspectors and their support staff must be paid and their offices maintained. The salaries of the judges, the clerks, and the court reporters that are needed when an anti-monopoly case is heard are costs imposed by the regulation.

Armies of office workers, backed up by computers and other modern equipment, keep track of income tax and VAT receipts. Inspectors take the field to enforce compliance, and the courts deal with serious offenders. Unemployment and other benefits must be administered.

Direct external costs

External costs are costs that the government's action imposes on others; they may be either direct or indirect.

Direct external costs fall on agents with whom the government is directly interacting. Regulation and control often add directly to the costs of producing goods. For example, firms must inspect machinery to ensure that it meets government safety standards.

Much business activity is devoted to understanding, reporting, and contesting regulatory provisions. Occupational safety and environmental control have increased the number of employees not working on the shop floor. The costs of complying with tax laws can run to large sums each year. Firms, and wealthy individuals, spend substantial sums on lawyers and accountants to help them to comply with tax laws and chose tax-minimizing courses of action.

Quite apart from the actual expenditures, government intervention may reduce the incentive for experimentation, innovation, and the introduction of new products. Requiring advance government clearance before introducing a new method or product (on grounds of potential safety hazards or environmental impact) can reduce the incentive to develop it. New lines of investment may be chosen more for their tax implications than for their potential for reducing production costs and so contributing to productivity growth.

Indirect external costs

Indirect external costs are costs of the government's action that spread beyond those immediately affected by it—sometimes to the entire economy. Here is a sampling of the many costs of this type.

Externalities

Ironically, government intervention to offset adverse externalities can create new adverse externalities. For example, government regulations designed to ensure the safety of new drugs delay the introduction of all drugs, including those that are safe. The benefits of these regulations are related to the unsafe drugs kept off the market. The cost includes the delayed availability of new safe drugs.

The shifting of taxes often causes major externalities. **Shifting** refers to the passing of the incidence of a tax from the person who initially pays it to someone else. **Incidence** refers to who actually bears the tax. One major problem with the use of taxes to achieve a social goal such as redistributing income is that market forces may shift the burden of the tax from the person who initially pays it to others. In Box 20.1 we studied the effects of a tax levied in a single market and concluded:

If the supply curve is positively sloped, and the demand curve negatively sloped, the burden of a tax is shared between producers and consumers.

This outcome does not depend on who actually makes the tax payment to the government. If producers initially pay the tax, the upward shift in the market supply curve will raise the price and pass some of the tax burden on to consumers. If consumers initially pay the tax, the downward shift in their after-tax demand curve will lower the price received by producers. This passes some of the burden on to producers.

There will also be repercussions in other markets. As the price of one product rises, the demand curves for substitutes will shift to the right, while the demand curves for complements will shift to the left. The resulting changes in their market prices will induce changes in other related markets. The effects of a tax on one market will thus spread throughout the economy, making the final distribution of the burden difficult to ascertain.

Inefficiencies

Almost all government interventions have some adverse efficiency effects. These have played an important part in the so-called supply-side criticisms of government policy, and we need to look at them in some detail.

First, consider a *sales tax* on one specific good. The tax raises the relative price that consumers face for that good, so they will buy less of it and more of other products. Production falls below the competitive equilibrium level, which is the one that maximizes the sum of consumers' and producers' surplus. The result, as shown in Figure 20.4, is a loss of consumers' surplus exactly analogous to the deadweight loss of monopoly.

This result applies to any taxes that affect the prices of products in different proportions and hence change relative prices. It thus applies to VAT whenever different products are taxed at different rates. The key is that

Consumers equate their marginal utilities to prices including tax, while producers equate their marginal costs to the price net of the tax. Hence the tax causes inefficiency, since the

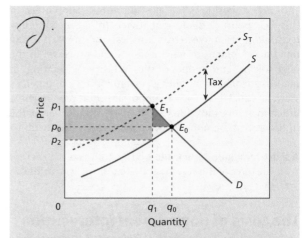

Figure 20.4 The efficiency loss from an indirect tax
The tax causes a loss of consumers' surplus, which is a deadweight loss. The tax shifts the supply curve from S to S_T. This moves equilibrium from E_0, with price p_0 and quantity q_0, to E_1, with price p_1 and quantity q_1. Consumers pay p_1, while the after-tax receipts of producers are p_2. The government gains tax revenue equal to the light red area, which is p_1 minus p_2 (the tax) multiplied by q_1. Part of this comes from producers and part from consumers. Consumers also lose surplus of the dark red area. Producers also lose surplus of the medium shaded area. Since no one gets the surpluses that consumers and producers lose, they are the deadweight loss of the tax.

value that consumers place on the last unit consumed exceeds the marginal cost of making it.

Next consider the *income tax*. This creates inefficiency by distorting the work–leisure choice. Employers pay one wage (pre-tax) and employees receive another wage (post-tax). Employees, reacting to after-tax wage rates, see a rate of substitution between work and leisure that differs from the rate implied by the pre-tax wage the employer is prepared to pay.

To understsand the source of the inefficiency, compare the income tax with a **poll tax**, which takes the same lump sum from everyone. Because it is not related to income, a poll tax leaves the marginal rate of substitution between goods and leisure unaffected. The tax exerts no disincentive to work at the margin, and thus is more efficient than income tax.

Figure 20.5 demonstrates the inefficiency of the income tax. It shows that each individual achieves a higher indifference curve when forced to pay a given amount of tax revenue through a poll tax, rather than through an income tax. The poll tax is more efficient because it leaves each person facing a choice at the margin that reflects the wage rate actually paid by employers in the labour market.

The importance of the figure lies in its demonstration that any practical tax does have negative efficiency effects, because it distorts relative price signals. The only tax that

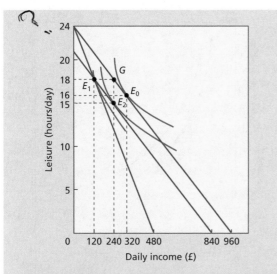

Figure 20.5 An income tax and the work–leisure choice

An income tax results in an inefficient choice between work and leisure. This person earns £40 an hour. His budget line runs from 24 hours (no work) to £960 (no sleep!). He maximizes utility at E_0 with 16 hours of leisure (8 hours of work) and income of £320 per day. An income tax of 50 per cent shifts his after-tax budget line to run from 24 hours to £480 (no sleep). He maximizes utility by moving to E_1 with 18 hours of leisure (6 hours of work) and a gross pay of £240. This yields him an after-tax income of £120.

The government could raise its £120 through a tax that did not alter the income–leisure trade-off (say a poll tax). The after-tax budget line in this case shifts in to 21 hours (the tax is the equivalent of 3 hours' work) and £840. The individual now moves from E_0 to E_2, consuming 15 hours of leisure (working 9 hours) and consuming £240 worth of goods. E_2 is superior to E_1 because it lies on a higher indifference curve.

does not do so, under normal conditions, is the poll tax. It has no negative efficiency effects because the amount paid does not vary with the taxpayer's economic income or wealth or any of his economic decisions. It is precisely for this reason that most people find it *unacceptable* on equity grounds as anything other than a minor source of revenue.[2]

Disincentive effects

If we consider a 'closed economy' where there is no possibility of emigration, then marginal rates of up to 40 or 50 per cent do not seem to have strong disincentive effects. Economic theory makes no general prediction about how altering income tax rates in this range will affect the supply of effort. On page 257 and in Box 15.5 we showed that a rise in the wage rate might increase, or decrease, the supply of effort, and, similarly, that a fall in the wage rate might have either effect. Now observe that the after-tax wage rate is lowered by a rise in the rate of income tax, and is raised by a fall in the rate. It follows immediately that any given change in the rate of income tax may either raise or

lower the supply of effort. At some point, however, high marginal tax rates begin to have more serious disincentive effects. As marginal rates approach 100 per cent, the disincentive effect becomes absolute.

In an open society where emigration is possible, very high marginal rates of tax have major effects. Authors, artists, pop groups, and others who 'strike it rich' are strongly tempted to emigrate to countries that will allow them to keep a higher proportion of their incomes. Emigration of successful people of this type from the United Kingdom to the United States was significant between 1945 and 1980, when UK marginal rates of income tax were often double those in the United States.

From the point of view of maximizing tax revenues and reducing tax burdens on middle- and lower-income groups it would be better to have high-income people still in the country paying tax rates of 40–50 per cent than out of the country avoiding higher tax rates.

Governments throughout the world have come to accept that very high marginal rates of tax do exert various important disincentive effects. Table 20.3 shows marginal

Table 20.3 UK marginal rates of income tax (tax rate on an extra £1 of income)

Taxable income*	Marginal tax rate (%)	
	1978–79	2002–3
1,500	34	10
6,000	34	22
18,000	45	22
24,000	50	22
30,000	65	40
36,000	70	40
54,000	83	40

UK income taxes are much less progressive than they used to be. The figures have been converted to 1990 pounds to make them comparable. Currently, the maximum marginal rate of 40 per cent sets in at about £30,000 taxable income. Twenty years earlier the marginal rate at that level of income was a full 65 per cent.

* Income after deducting allowances.

Source: ONS Financial Statement and Budget Report.

[2] The argument in the text assumes a closed economy in which everyone actually pays the tax. In practice, however, even the poll tax will have some efficiency effects. A large enough poll tax will cause people to emigrate. It will also cause some people to choose jobs, and life-styles, that facilitate evasion. People with no fixed addresses, and no regular jobs, find evasion easier than people who are stuck with one job and own their own houses or flats. Thus, at the margin, the poll tax will influence some people's job and residence decisions, which means that it does have some adverse efficiency effects.

rates of income tax in the UK for 1978–79 and 1997–98 and 2002–03. It is worth noting that the higher rate in 1978 was much lower than the highest marginal rate of 97.5 per cent levied in the UK in the period shortly after the Second World War. (This enormous rate included a surtax on investment income.)

Taxes are not the only government measure that have disincentive effects. Payments designed to help certain low-income groups are often means-tested. Sometimes the welfare payments are reduced by £1 for every £1 of income received by welfare recipients. The person in effect faces a marginal tax rate of 100 per cent on every unit of income earned up to the level of the benefit payments. The effect, called the 'poverty trap', is a severe disincentive to work, and we should not be surprised when people respond rationally to these market signals.

Say, for example, that benefit payments are £25 a day and are cut by £1 for every £1 of income earned. If the person makes £5 a day, benefits fall to £20; if £10 is earned, benefits fall to £15, and so on. Only when more than £25 per day is earned will the person's disposable income begin to rise. Even if the benefits are reduced at a less sharp rate, say 50p per £1 earned, the disincentive of the high implicit tax rate is strong. Figure 20.6 illustrates this disincentive effect by showing how such schemes induce many people to reject employment that they would have accepted if the schemes had not existed.

Benefit payments are required to help those in real need. If they are income-related, however, they tend to discourage recipients from working.

This does not argue against welfare payments. It does, however, suggest that welfare schemes should be designed to minimize their effects on efficiency.

Costs versus benefits

It is difficult to estimate the overall direct and indirect costs of general government activity. About the most that can be said is that they are not insignificant. The level of uncertainty is great enough that those who wish to reduce the scope of government activity can argue that these costs are high, while those who wish to maintain or enlarge the present scope of government can argue that the benefits greatly outweigh the costs.

The costs are often clearer when government activities are considered separately, rather than taking everything in one lump. For example, when it became generally accepted that high marginal rates of income tax had serious consequences, governments (eventually) moved to lower these rates. When it became accepted that government-run business enterprises were no more efficient than privately run ones, and often much less efficient, many governments

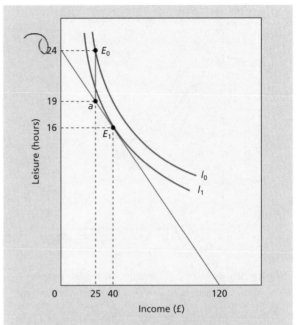

Figure 20.6 Disincentives of welfare schemes

Income-tested benefits provide disincentives to work. The individual is not employed but is receiving benefits of £25 per day from some income-related scheme. This puts him at point E_0, consuming 24 hours of leisure and receiving £25 pounds of income. He is now offered work at £5 per hour, presenting him with a budget line that ends at £120 (for 24 hours' work). In the absence of the benefit he would locate at E_1, consuming 16 hours of leisure (working 8 hours) and earning £40 of income. But for every £1 he earns he loses £1 of benefit, so the budget line starts at E_0 and is vertical to point a, where he is working 5 hours and still getting £25 but now all from work. Further work nets him £5 an hour, so the budget line has its normal slope below a. Since the indifference curve through E_1 is lower than the curve through E_0, his rational choice is not to work.

moved to privatize the industries that they owned. A great debate has raged over the costs of environmental regulation. Although full indirect costs are hard to measure, most estimates do not show these costs to be prohibitive. But the costs and inefficiencies of direct mandates to specific firms have seemed large enough that governments have searched for more efficient, less costly methods. In many cases the best solution seems to be tradable pollution permits.

So the lesson is that there is no general lesson about too much or too little government, but that government activity *is* costly and in some circumstances can be very costly. So every activity, existing or projected, needs to be assessed on its individual merits. Only if the benefits appear to outweigh the measurable costs and the best guess about the unmeasurable costs should the activity be initiated or continued.

Government failure

So far we have dealt with a government that is trying its best to achieve the goals that we laid out at the beginning of this chapter. It may impose costs, some expected and some unexpected, but it is seeking, as best it can, to achieve socially acceptable goals.

Is this too naïve a view of government and the political process? Today many observers of the political scene, including not a few economists, would answer with an emphatic yes.

Without doubt, governments are far from perfect. This is not because bureaucrats and politicians are worse than other people—more stupid, more rigid, or more venal. Instead, it is because they are like others, with flaws as well as virtues and with motives of their own. So, having found potential net benefits from perfect but costly government intervention, the final issue is whether the imperfect governments that we encounter in the real world can achieve some of these benefits. Where they do not succeed in attaining potential benefits that exceed the full direct and indirect costs, we speak of **government failure**.

Governments may sometimes make isolated mistakes just as private decision-makers do. What is interesting, however, are the reasons why governments tend, under certain circumstances, to be more systematically in error than unhindered markets. Here are a few of the many possible causes of systematic government failure.

Rigidities

Rules and regulations, tax rates, and expenditure policies are hard to change. Market conditions, however, change continually and often rapidly. A rule requiring the use of a certain method to reduce pollution may have made sense when the cost of that method was low. It may, however, become a wasteful rule when some alternative becomes a less costly method.

Today's natural monopolies are often made into tomorrow's competitive industries by technological innovations. For example, the near monopoly of the early railways was eliminated by the development of cheap road transport, and the falling cost of air transport is currently providing potent competition for surface transport in the movement of many products.

A centralized decision-taking body has difficulty in reacting to changing conditions as fast as decentralized decision-takers react to market signals.

Governments are often slow to admit mistakes even when they become aware of them. It is often politically easier to go on spending money on a project that has turned sour than to admit fault. A classic example was the development of Concorde. Successive governments realized it was an enormous money-loser, but they went on supporting it long after there was any chance of commercial success.

Markets are much harsher in judging success. When people are investing their own money, the principle that bygones are bygones is usually followed. No firm can raise fresh financial capital for what is currently a poor prospect just because the prospects seemed good in the past. Nor can it do so because much money has already been spent on it, or because those who have supported it in the past will lose face if it is now dropped.

Decision-makers' objectives

By far the most important cause of government failure arises from the nature of the government's own objectives. Why is economists' advice followed closely in some cases but systematically ignored in others? Governments are not faceless robots, doing whatever economic analysis shows to be in the social interest. Instead they have their own objectives, which they seek to maximize.

Governments undoubtedly do care about the social good to some extent; but public officials have their careers, their families, and their prejudices as well. Elected MPs and local councillors no doubt care about the public good, but they must also worry about being re-elected. The resulting problems are similar to the principal–agent issues mentioned earlier as a source of market failure. In the present case the *principals* are the public: they want governments to do certain things. However, their *agents*—elected and appointed—are motivated by considerations that sometimes pull against those of the electorate.

Modelling governments as maximizers of their own welfare, and then incorporating them into theoretical models of the working of the economy, was a major breakthrough. One of the pioneers of this development was the American economist James Buchanan, who was awarded the 1986 Nobel Prize in economics for his work in this field. The theory that he helped to develop is called *public choice theory*.

The key idea is to view the government as just another economic agent engaging in its own maximizing behaviour. When this view is adopted, there is still room for many competing theories, depending on what variables are in the government's preference function (i.e. what things the government cares about). Consider the other two main decision-taking bodies in orthodox economics. Firms have only profits in their utility functions, and they seek to maximize these. Consumers have only goods and services in their utility functions, and they seek to maximize their satisfactions from consuming them. An analogous theory of the government allows only one variable in its utility function, the variable being votes! Such a government takes all its decisions with a view to maximizing its votes at the next election.

Public choice theory

Full-blown public choice theory deals with three maximizing groups. Elected officials seek to maximize their votes. Civil servants seek to maximize their salaries (and hence their positions in the hierarchy). Voters seek to maximize their own utility. To this end, voters look to the government to provide them with goods and services and income transfers that raise their personal utility. No one cares about the general interest!

On the one hand, this surely is not a completely accurate characterization of motives. Elected statesmen have acted in what they perceive to be the public interest, hoping to be vindicated by history even if they know they risk losing the next election. Some civil servants have exposed inside corruption even though it cost them their jobs. And some high-income individuals vote for the political party that advocates the most, not the least, income redistribution.

On the other hand, the characterization is close to the mark in many cases. Most of us have read of politicians whose only principle is 'What will get me most votes?' And many voters ask only 'What's in it for me?' This is why the theory can take us a long way in understanding what we see, even though real behaviour is more complex.

Here is one example. Why, in spite of strong advice from economists, have governments persisted in subsidizing agriculture for decades, until many governments now have major farm crises on their hands? Public choice theory looks at the gainers and the losers among the voters.

The gainers from agricultural supports are farmers. They are a politically powerful group, and are aware of what they will lose if farm supports are reduced. They would show their disapproval of such action by voting against any government that even suggested it. The losers are the entire group of consumers. Although they are more numerous than farmers, and although their total loss is large, each individual consumer suffers only a small loss. For example, a policy that gives £50 million a year to British farmers need only cost each citizen £1 per year.[3] Citizens have more important things to worry about, and so do not vote against the government just because it supports farmers. As long as the average voters are unconcerned about, and often unaware of, the losses they suffer, the vote-maximizing government will ignore the interests of the many and support the interests of the few. The vote-maximizing government will consider changing the agricultural policy only when the cost of agricultural support becomes so large that ordinary taxpayers begin to count the cost. What is

required for a policy change, according to this theory, is that those who lose become sufficiently aware of their losses for this awareness to affect their voting behaviour.

The ability of elected officials and civil servants to ignore the public interest is strengthened by a phenomenon called **rational ignorance**. Many policy issues are extremely complex. For example, even the experts are divided when assessing the pros and cons of the UK's decision to stay out of the first wave of membership in the euro, the common European currency. Much time and effort is required for a layperson even to attempt to understand the issue. Similar comments apply to the evidence for and against capital punishment or lowering the age of criminal liability. Yet one person's vote has little influence on which party gets elected or on what they really will do about the issue in question once elected. So the costs are large, the benefits small. Thus, a majority of rational, self-interested voters will remain innocent of the complexities involved in most policy issues.

Who will be the informed minority? The answer is: those who stand to gain or lose a lot from the policy, those with a strong sense of moral obligation, and those policy junkies who just like this sort of thing.

Inefficient public choices

A major principle in most people's idea of democracy is that each citizen's vote should have the same weight. One of the insights of public choice theory is that resource allocation based on the principle of one-person–one-vote will often be inefficient because it fails to take into account the *intensity of preferences*.

To illustrate this problem, consider three farmers, Al, Bob, and Charles. Farmers Al and Bob want the government to build an access road to each of their farms, each road to cost £6,000. Suppose that the road to Al's farm is worth £7,000 to Al and that the one to Bob's farm is worth £7,000 to Bob. (Charles's farm is on the main road and so requires no new access road.) Suppose that, under the current taxing rules, the cost of building each road would be shared equally among the three farmers—£2,000 each. It is efficient to build both roads, since each generates net benefits of £1,000 (£7,000 gross benefits to the farmer helped, less £6,000 total cost). But each would be defeated 2–1 in a simple majority vote: Bob and Charles would vote against Al's road; Al and Charles would vote against Bob's road.

Now suppose that we allow Al and Bob to make a deal: 'I will vote for your road if you vote for mine.' Although

[3] 'Why worry?' you may ask. 'Isn't the small loss to each consumer a reasonable price to pay?' It may be in this one case. The problem, however, lies not in one such policy, but in the cumulative effects of many. If each of many special-interest groups secures a policy that costs each member of the public a small amount, the total bill over all such policies can be, and in many countries is, very large indeed.

political commentators often decry such deals, the deal enhances efficiency. Both roads now get 2–1 majorities, and both roads get built. However, such deals can just as well reduce efficiency. If we make the gross value of each road £5,000 instead of £7,000 and let Al and Bob make their deal, each road will still command a 2–1 majority because the total cost is £4,000 to each farmer while Al and Bob each gain £5,000 worth of road. It is, however, socially inefficient to build the roads, since the gross value of each road is now only £5,000, while the cost is still £6,000. Al and Bob will be using democracy to appropriate resources from Charles while reducing economic efficiency.

This case can be interpreted in a different way. Instead of being the third farmer, Charles might be all of the other voters in the county. Instead of bearing one-third of the costs, Al and Bob might each bear only a small portion of the costs. To the extent that Al and Bob are able to go to the local government and forcefully articulate the benefits that they would derive from the roads, they may be able to use democracy to appropriate resources from taxpayers in general. Much of the concern with the power of 'special interests' stems from the fact that the institutions of representative democracy tend to be responsive to benefits that focus on particular, identifiable, and articulate groups. Often the costs are diffused among all taxpayers, who hardly notice them and in any case are rationally ignorant about them.

The effects of government failure

Suppose that, for any of the reasons discussed above, the government makes a mistake in regulation. Say it mistakenly specifies a method of pollution control that is less effective than the best method. If it insists on the level of control appropriate to the best method, but chooses the poorer method, it can convert a social gain from control into a social loss. This possibility is illustrated in Figure 20.7.

If governments pursue their own objectives, such as vote-maximizing, they may sometimes fail to act in the voters' interest by design rather than by mistake. If government economists foresee that a politically popular policy will

increase the degree of market failure in the long term while seeming beneficial in the short term, the government may adopt the harmful policy, in spite of the unfavourable long-run consequences. The government could plead in such cases that it was only being democratic in following the public will. But if governments always follow public opinion blindly, this may lead to policies being adopted whose consequences are undesirable—and which could have been avoided by taking expert advice.

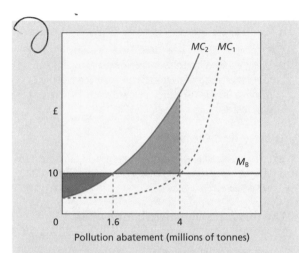

Figure 20.7 Government failure

Choice of an unnecessarily costly method of control reduces the optimal amount of abatement. Each tonne of pollution imposes a social cost of £10, so the marginal social benefit of abatement is £10 per tonne as shown by the M_B line. The most efficient method of control has a marginal cost curve of MC_1, making it socially optimal to prevent 4 million tonnes of pollution. The government misguidedly chooses an abatement procedure that has a marginal cost curve of MC_2. Optimal abatement is now only 1.6 million tonnes. If the government insists on having 4 million tonnes abated, there is a loss of the light shaded area above marginal benefit curve and below the MC_2 curve. That loss may exceed the benefit, which is given by the dark shaded area between the M_B curve and the MC_2 curve. If so, the programme causes a net social loss. Having no programme would then be better than having the inefficient one imposed at too high a level of abatement.

Conclusion

Do governments intervene too little, or too much, in response to market failure? This question reflects one aspect of the continuing debate over the role of government in the economy.

Since the early 1980s, in most of the advanced industrial countries the mix of free-market determination and government ownership and regulation has been shifting towards more market determination. No one believes that

government intervention can, or should, be reduced to zero. Have we still got a long way to go in reversing the tide of big intrusive government that flowed through most of the twentieth century? Or have we gone too far and given some things to the market that governments could do better? These will be some of the great social debates of the early decades of the twenty-first century.

SUMMARY

Government objectives

- Governments seek to protect life and property, improve economic efficiency, protect individuals from others and (sometimes) from themselves, influence the rate of economic growth, and stabilize the economy against fluctuations in national income and the price level.

- Policies for equity include making the distribution of income and wealth somewhat less unequal.

- Equity, efficiency, and growth often come into conflict. Policies to increase equity can reduce efficiency and/or growth, while policies to increase efficiency or growth can make some situations less equitable.

Tools and performance

- Governments may seek to achieve their policies using the tools of taxes, expenditure, rules and regulations, and public ownership.

The costs of government intervention

- Government activity incurs many types of cost. Internal costs refer to the government's own costs of administering its policies. Direct external costs refer to the costs imposed on those directly affected by these policies in such terms as extra production costs, costs of compliance, and losses in productivity. Indirect external costs refer to the efficiency losses that spread throughout the whole economy as a result of the alteration in price signals caused by government tax and expenditure policies.

Government failure

- As well as showing the potential for benefits to exceed costs in a world where the government functioned perfectly, it is necessary to consider the likely outcome in the imperfect world of reality. Government failure—not achieving some possible gains—can arise because of rigidities causing a lack of adequate response of rules and regulations to changing conditions, poorer foresight on the part of government regulators than private participants in the market, and government objectives—such as winning the next election—that conflict with such objectives as improving economic efficiency.

TOPICS FOR REVIEW

- Direct and indirect taxes
- Progressive, regressive, and proportional taxes
- Benefits and costs of government intervention

- Sources of government failure
- Public choice theory
- Rational ignorance

DISCUSSION QUESTIONS

1 What inefficiencies will be caused by (*a*) VAT, (*b*) the personal income tax, (*c*) farm subsidies, (*d*) free health care, (*e*) free elementary school education, (*f*) welfare payments to non-working persons? Explain why such inefficiencies do not provide *sufficient* reasons to end the activity.

2 How many rules, regulations, prohibitions, and other 'command-type' tools of government policy can you think of that could be replaced by market-based incentive schemes?

3 Can you think of government programmes that would have effects on all three goals of *equity*, *efficiency*, and *growth*? Select those programmes that have desirable effects on some and undesirable effects on others of these three goals. (Assume that your equity criterion is to have a less unequal distribution of income.) Discuss the trade-offs involved in these policy conflicts.

4 Discuss the relative efficiency and equity effects of two programmes designed to assist certain needy groups. One

programme provides coupons that reduce the purchase price of groceries by 50 per cent. (The shop returns the coupons to the government and gets back the discount that it gave to the coupon-holder.) The other programme gives a money income supplement that has the same value as the food coupons.

5 List some things that *only* governments can do and some things that the government can do better than the private sector. Can you think of anything that the British government did thirty years ago, or that it does now, that the private sector could probably do better? Can you think of anything that the private sector did thirty years ago, or is doing now, that the government could probably do better?

6 Discuss the distinction between the initial incidence of a tax and the ultimate bearer of the tax.

7 Why is a role for government inevitable even in a market economy?

8 What difficulties arise in determining and implementing an optimal government intervention in the economy?

9 What are the arguments for and against government provision of (*a*) health and (*b*) education?

10 What government policies might encourage economic growth?

MACROECONOMICS

PART FIVE

MACROECONOMICS: GROWTH AND CYCLES

Chapter 21

MACROECONOMIC ISSUES AND MEASUREMENT

So far we have been analysing individual markets or firms. Now we look at the economy as a whole. Why do some economies grow with steady increases in their living standards while others do not? Why are there cycles in economic activity with jobs being scarce and unemployment high at some times and plentiful with jobs for all at other times? What can governments do to reduce such fluctuations? Will inflation erode that value of savings? What is the Bank of England trying to achieve when it sets interest rates? These are all issues addressed by macroeconomics and will be covered in the chapters ahead.

Here we start to analyse the economy as a whole and set out some key issues and concepts. In particular you will learn that:

• Macroeconomics is about aggregate phenomena such as growth, business cycles, inflation, unemployment and the balance of payments.

• The total output of the economy as a whole is the sum of the value added by each firm or enterprise.

• GDP can be measured as the sum of value added by all producers, as the sum of income claims generated in producing goods and services, or as the spending on all final goods and services produced.

• GDP measures the value of what is produced in this country, while GNI (or GNP) measures the income accruing to UK residents, including net income from overseas.

• GDP is a specific measure of output in the market economy, and is not a measure of welfare or happiness.

In this chapter we explain how macroeconomics differs in approach from the microeconomics of the first half of this book, and outline the main issues addressed. We then look in detail at how the activity of the economy as a whole is measured before discussing the interpretation of these measures. In subsequent chapters we are concerned with explaining how the national product or national income is determined, and what government policy can do to influence it. Growth theory, which we discuss in the next chapter, is about what determines the long-term trend in national output. The traditional focus of macroeconomic analysis, which we explain in subsequent chapters, is mainly on the short run and on the issue of what explains deviations of output from its long-run trend level.

What is macroeconomics?

Macroeconomics is the study of how the economy behaves in broad outline without dwelling on much of its interesting, but sometimes confusing, detail. Macroeconomics is largely concerned with the behaviour of economic *aggregates*, such as total national product, total investment, and exports for the entire economy. It is also concerned with the average price of all goods and services, rather than the prices of specific products. These aggregates result from activities in many different markets and from the behaviour of different decision-makers such as consumers, governments, and firms. In contrast, *microeconomics* (as outlined in Chapters 3–20) deals with the behaviour of individual markets, such as those for wheat, computer chips, or strawberries, and with the detailed behaviour of individual agents, such as firms and consumers.

In macroeconomics we add together the value of cornflakes, beer, cars, strawberries, haircuts, and restaurant meals along with the value of all other goods and services produced, and we study the aggregate *national product*. We also average the prices of all goods and services consumed and discuss the *general price level* for the entire economy—usually just called the price level. In practice, the averages of several different sets of prices are used. For example, one important index measures the average price of the goods and services bought by the typical consumer. In Britain it is known as the **retail price index** (RPI), while the equivalent in some other countries is called the *consumer price index* (CPI). An appendix to this chapter discusses how the RPI is calculated.

We know full well that an economy that produces much wheat and few cars differs from one that produces many cars but little wheat. We also know that an economy with cheap wheat and expensive cars differs from one with cheap cars and expensive wheat. Studying aggregates and averages often means missing such important differences, but in return for losing valuable detail we are able to view the big picture.

In macroeconomics we look at the broad range of opportunities and difficulties facing the economy as a whole. When national product rises, the output of most firms, and the incomes of most people, usually rise with it. When interest rates rise, most borrowers, including firms and homeowners, have to make bigger payments on their debts, though many savers will get a higher return on their savings. When the price level rises, virtually everyone in the economy is forced to make adjustments, because of the lower value of money. When the unemployment rate rises, workers are put at an increased risk of losing their jobs and suffering losses in their incomes. These movements in economic aggregates are strongly associated with the economic well-being of most individuals: the health of the sectors in which they work and the prices of the goods that they purchase. These associations between the health of the macroeconomy and the economic fortunes of many people are the reason why macroeconomic aggregates (particularly inflation, unemployment, interest rates, and the balance of payments) are often in the news.

Why do we need macroeconomics?

We need a separate subject called macroeconomics because there are forces that affect the economy as a whole that cannot be fully or simply understood by analysing individual markets and individual products. A problem that is affecting all firms, or many workers, in different industries may need to be tackled at the level of the whole economy. Certainly, if circumstances are common across many sectors of the economy, then analysis at the level of the whole economy may help us to understand what is happening. Let us look at some of the issues that are best thought about in a macroeconomic context.

Major macroeconomic issues

Economic growth

Both total and per capita output have risen for many decades in most industrial countries. These long-term trends have produced rising average living standards. In the United Kingdom the real value of the average wage doubled in the twenty years between 1953 and 1973. It stagnated for a while in the 1970s but then grew steadily again in the 1980s, the 1990s and into the early years of the twenty-first century.

Although long-term growth gets less media attention than does the current inflation or unemployment rate, it is the predominant determinant of living standards and the material constraints facing a society from decade to decade and generation to generation. We discuss some of the influences on long-term growth in Chapter 22. Macroeconomics has traditionally taken the trend in output as given and looked at how to minimize deviations from that trend. However, in recent years there has been discussion of whether the policies used to stabilize activity may also influence the long-term trend. Among the most important issues in macroeconomics is identifying policies that increase the chances that world-wide growth will continue without the type of slowdown that happened in the 1970s or the serious recessions of the early 1980s and early 1990s. Growth is thus a clear objective of macroeconomic policy.

Business cycles

The economy tends to move in a series of ups and downs, called *business cycles*, rather than in a steady pattern. The 1930s saw the greatest world-wide economic depression in the twentieth century, with nearly one-fifth of the UK labour force unemployed for an extended period. In contrast, the twenty-five years following the Second World War were a period of sustained economic growth, with only minor interruptions caused by modest recessions. Then the business cycle returned in more serious form. There have been three major recessions in the United Kingdom during the last three decades (1973–5, 1979–81, and 1990–2), and most other major countries have experienced a similar pattern.

An understanding of business cycles is important for the owners and managers of firms. During recessions many businesses go bust, while profits fall for the survivors. In contrast, during a boom, demand for most products rise, profits rise, and most businesses find it easy to expand. Understanding the business cycle is, thus, important for successful businesses. Expanding capacity during the onset of a recession could be a recipe for disaster, while having too little capacity during a boom may be a lost opportunity.

Most importantly, although business cycles are beyond the control of individual firms, firms do need to understand that the economy moves in cycles. Governments sometimes claim that their policies will bring stable growth and the end to cycles, but business cycles have been around for a long time, and they are likely to be with us for much longer yet.

Macroeconomics as a subject was invented to help produce policies that could ameliorate economic fluctuations. Much of what follows is devoted to explanations of why the economy goes through these ups and downs, and what, if anything, the government can do about them.

Inflation

The annual UK inflation rate was over 25 per cent in 1975. This was the highest level reached in peacetime for at least three centuries, and at that rate inflation halves the purchasing power of money in three years. The government of Margaret Thatcher was elected in 1979 on the promise of eliminating inflation from the British economy. Inflation did fall below 5 per cent by 1984, but it rose again to around 10 per cent before the end of the decade. By the late 1990s the annual rate of inflation had fallen to around 2–3 per cent, which was the lowest level since the early 1960s. In May 1997 the incoming Labour government set a target level of inflation of 2.5 per cent and gave the Bank of England the power to set interest rates in order to achieve this target. From 1997 to 2002 inflation stayed within one percentage point of the target as intended. (We will discuss monetary policy in the UK and euro area in Chapter 28 below.)

Swings in economic activity have usually accompanied swings in inflation. Generally, attempts by governments to control high inflation have tended to bring about recessions. However, the pattern of booms and recessions has been very similar across many different countries, so it cannot all be attributed to domestic government policy alone. Also, the relationship between inflation and recession seems to change over time. The 1979–81 UK recession was accompanied by inflation in the mid-teens, while the 1990–2 recession was accompanied by only single-figure inflation. The slowdown in major economies in 2000–2 was accompanied by very low levels of inflation, so was unrelated to anti-inflation policies.

An important policy problem for governments is how to stimulate economic activity without causing inflation. The rise in inflation during boom times often leads policy-makers to tighten their policies in order to bring inflation under control. When inflation falls after a recession, policy-makers often feel that they have the leeway to stimulate the economy again. Hence they have to tread carefully to achieve a suitable balance between stimulus and contraction, and we will learn below that timing policy interventions in order to achieve a desired outcome is not a simple matter.

Unemployment

A downturn in economic activity causes an increase in unemployment. Indeed, it was the high unemployment of the 1930s that led to the establishment of the subject now known as macroeconomics, and unemployment is still a central concern of economics. During the Great Depression of the 1930s UK unemployment rose to nearly 20 per cent of the labour force, and even higher levels were reached in some other countries. Although in the 1950s and 1960s unemployment was consistently very low in most industrial countries, higher unemployment returned in the 1980s and 1990s. UK unemployment[1] reached peaks of 12.2 per cent in 1986 and of 10.8 per cent in 1993 in the two recessions, while unemployment in France and Germany reached post-war highs of 12.5 and 11.7 per cent, respectively, in 1997. Japanese unemployment in June 2002 reached a level of 5.4 per cent, not seen there since the Second World War. By 2000 unemployment had fallen in Britain and the United States, but it was still relatively high in several European countries, such as Spain, Germany, and France (and it started to rise again in the United States in 2001/2). Accordingly, the analysis of the causes of, and potential cures for, unemployment is still very high on the agenda of macroeconomics today, especially in the EU and Japan. A new bout of high unemployment can never be ruled out, even for those countries where it has been low for some time.

The main method of reducing unemployment that economists developed early in the twentieth century was for governments to increase their spending and reduce taxes. Such deliberate use of government spending and taxes to influence the economy is known as **fiscal policy**. In Chapter 33 we will discuss why this long accepted policy no longer seems promising.

Government budget deficits

With the exception of two brief periods (1970 and 1988–9), the British government has had a *budget deficit* since the Second World War—it was spending more than it was raising in taxation. In the mid-1970s the budget deficit rose to around 8 per cent of the value of the nation's total annual output. In the early years of the twenty-first century the budget was again in deficit; and, with high government spending commitments, it seems likely to stay in deficit for the foreseeable future. Deficits have to be financed by government borrowing, which raises the national debt.

At one time it was thought that budget deficits might be good for the economy because government spending

---

[1] There are two main measures of unemployment. The *claimant count* measures those registered for unemployment benefits, while the *Labour Force Survey (LFS)* asks a sample of people if they are actively seeking employment. The LFS number is usually higher than the claimant count. Numbers in the text refer to the LFS measure, but charts of UK unemployment usually use the claimant count, as this measure has been available for longer.

created jobs. Nowadays there is more concern about the potential burden of the debt, in the form of interest, which has to be paid by taxpayers and which, therefore, keeps taxes high. In later chapters we will discuss how the budget deficit affects the economy, and the conflict over the role of the government budget that is central to macroeconomics. We will also discuss the implications of the limitations on budget deficits imposed on EU member states by the Maastricht Treaty and the Stability and Growth Pact.

Interest rates

In addition to fiscal policy, government (or the monetary authority, where this is independent of government) has available the tools of monetary policy. Monetary policy involves changing interest rates, or the money supply, in order to influence the economy. High interest rates are a symptom of a tight monetary policy. When interest rates are high firms find it more costly to borrow, and this makes them more reluctant to invest in expanding their business. Individuals with mortgages or bank loans are also hit by high interest rates since it costs more to make their loan repayments. Hence high interest rates tend to reduce demand in the economy—firms invest less, and those with mortgages have less to spend. Low interest rates tend to stimulate demand.

Another important channel of monetary policy is via the exchange rate, at least for countries whose exchange rates are flexible. Exchange rate changes can affect the relative prices, and thereby the competitiveness, of domestic and foreign producers. A significant appreciation of the domestic currency makes domestic goods expensive relative to foreign goods. This may lead to a shift of demand away from domestic goods towards foreign goods. Such shifts have an important influence on domestic economic activity.

Targets and instruments

The issues that we have just discussed are of two types. First, there are the things that really matter for their own sake. These are the things that affect living conditions and the state of the economic environment. Living standards, unemployment, business cycles, and inflation are outcomes that matter. Almost everyone wants rising living standards, high employment, and low unemployment, as well as avoidance of recessions and inflation. These things are known as the **targets** of policy. 'Good' values of these variables are what governments would like to achieve.

Fiscal and monetary policies (government spending, taxes, interest rates, and the money supply) are not so much valued for their own sake: rather, they are the **instruments** of policy and are valued for the effect they have on the targets. *Instruments* are the variables that the government can change directly in order to change the *targets*, which are the things that it would like to change.

The macroeconomic policy problem is to choose appropriate values of the policy instruments in order to achieve the best possible combination of the outcomes of the targets. This is a continually changing problem because the targets are perpetually being affected by shocks from various parts of the world economy.

We now turn to a discussion of the measurement of aggregate economic activity before returning to explanations of how that activity is determined.

National output concepts

Macroeconomics has as its central goal the explanation of the determinants of national income and output. In the next chapter we discuss the forces that determine how national income and output change over long periods of time. Starting in Chapter 23, we then build an analytical framework that helps us to understand the forces that influence these variables over shorter time periods. First, however, we have to understand what it is we are talking about. What exactly do we mean by national income and the national product? What do people mean when they refer to GDP, and how does it differ from GNI (or GNP)?

We start by discussing the measurement of national output, and find that by summing the *value added* for each industry or sector we arrive at a standard measure of national product. We then discuss how it is that we can arrive at the same measure of national product both from

the spending side of the economy and from adding up factor (inputs) incomes. An explicit result of this discussion is a demonstration of the equivalence of the concepts of national income and national product.

The national output, or national product, is related to the sum of all the outputs produced in the economy by individuals, firms, and governmental organizations. To obtain it, however, we cannot just add up all of the outputs of individual production units.

Value added as output

The reason why getting a total for the nation's output is not quite so straightforward as it may seem at first sight is that one firm's output may be another firm's input. A maker of clothing buys cloth from a textile manufacturer and buttons, zips, thread, pins, hangers, etc., from a range of other producers. Most modern manufactured products have many ready-made inputs. A car or aircraft manufacturer, for example, has hundreds of component suppliers.

Production occurs in stages: some firms produce outputs that are used as inputs by other firms, and these other firms in turn produce outputs that are used as inputs by yet other firms.

If we merely added up the market values of all outputs of all firms, we would obtain a total that was greatly in excess of the value of the economy's actual output. The error that would arise in estimating the nation's output by adding all sales of all firms is called **double counting**. 'Multiple counting' would be a better term, since, if we added up the values of all sales, the same output would be counted every time it was sold from one firm to another.

The problem of double counting is solved by distinguishing between two types of output. **Intermediate goods and services** are the outputs of some firms that are in turn inputs for other firms. **Final goods and services** are goods that are not used as inputs by other firms in the period of time under consideration. The term **final demand** refers to the purchase of final goods and services for consumption, for investment (including inventory accumulation), for use by governments, and for export. It does not include goods and services that are purchased by firms and used as inputs for producing other goods and services.

If the sales of firms could be readily separated into sales for final use and sales for further processing by other firms, measuring total output would still be straightforward. Total output would equal the value of all *final goods and services* produced by firms, excluding all intermediate goods and services. However, when a steel maker sells steel to Ford UK it does not care, and usually does not know, whether the steel is for final use (say, construction of a new warehouse) or for use as an intermediate good in the production of cars. The problem of double counting must therefore be resolved in some other manner. To avoid double counting, statisticians use the important concept of **value added**. Each firm's value added is the value of its output minus the value of the inputs that it purchases from other firms (which were in turn the outputs of those other firms). Thus, a steel mill's value added is the value of its output minus the value of the ore that it buys from the mining company, the value of the electricity and fuel oil that it uses, and the values of all other inputs that it buys from other firms. A bakery's value added is the value of the bread and cakes it produces minus the value of the flour and other inputs that it buys from other firms.

The total value of a firm's output is the *gross* value of its output. The firm's value added is the *net* value of its output. It is this latter figure that is the firm's contribution to the nation's total output. It is what its own efforts add to the value of what it takes in as inputs.

Value added measures each firm's own contribution to total output, the amount of market value that is produced by that firm. Its use avoids the statistical problem of double counting.

The concept of value added is further illustrated in Box 21.1. In this simple example, as in all more complex cases, the value of total output of final goods is obtained by summing all the individual values added.

The sum of all values added in an economy is a measure of the economy's total output. This measure of total output is called *gross value added*. It is a measure of all final output that is produced by all productive activity in the economy.

Table 21.1 gives the gross value added by major industrial sectors for the UK economy in 2001. You will see from this table that gross value added becomes GDP by the addition of a further term (taxes on products minus subsidies). We will explain this step in moving from value added to GDP below.[2]

Notice that we have used 'gross' in two different senses above—first in comparing the gross and net values of a firm's output, and then in the term 'gross value added'. The first usage relies on the common meanings of 'gross' and 'net'. The gross value of the firm's output is the total output before making any deductions, while the net value deducts inputs made by other firms. In 'gross value added' the usage is different. Value added is already defined as firms' net output; the word 'gross' is added because of its specific meaning in national accounts statistics. This distinction is important to understand, as we will be using the word from here on in terms such as *gross* domestic product and *gross* national income.

'Gross' in national accounts aggregates refers to the fact that we are measuring currently produced outputs or incomes without taking into account the wearing out, or *depreciation*, of capital goods during their production. Thus, gross value added is the value added of the economy as a whole *before* any allowance for depreciation, and gross domestic product is the nation's output *before* allowing for depreciation.

---

[2] Gross value added at basic prices is similar to what used to be called 'GDP at factor cost', but the latter term fell out of the national accounts in 1998.

Box 21.1 **Value added through stages of production**

Because the output of one firm often becomes the input of other firms, the total value of goods sold by all firms greatly exceeds the value of the output of final goods. This general principle is illustrated by a simple example in which firm R starts from scratch and produces goods (raw materials) valued at £100; the firm's value added is £100. Firm I purchases these raw materials valued at £100 and produces semi-manufactured goods which it sells for £130. Its value added is £30 because the value of the goods is increased by £30 as a result of the firm's activities. Firm F purchases the semi-manufactured goods for £130 and works them into a finished state, selling them for £180. Firm F's value added is £50. The value of final goods, £180, is found either by counting the sales of firm F or by taking the sum of the values added by each firm. This value is less than the £410 that we obtain by adding up the market value of the commodities sold by each firm. The table summarizes the example.

Transactions between firms at three different stages of production

	Firm R	Firm I	Firm F	All firms
A: Purchases from other firms	£0	£100	£130	£230 = Total interfirm sales
B: Purchase of factors of production				
(wages, rent, interest, profits)	100	30	50	180 = Value added
Total A + B = value of product	100	130	180 = Value of final goods and services	410 = Total value of all sales

Table 21.1 **Gross value added at current basic prices, by sector, UK, 2001**

Sector	£ m	% of GDP
Agriculture, hunting, forestry and fisheries	8,241	0.9
Mining and quarrying	25,665	2.6
Manufacturing	153,132	15.6
Electricity, gas and water supply	15,713	1.7
Construction	47,327	4.8
Wholesale and retail trade	106,766	10.8
Hotels and restaurants	29,359	3.1
Transport and communications	70,252	7.2
Financial intermediation and real estate	209,837	21.2
Public administration and defence	42,096	4.4
Education	52,659	5.4
Health and social work	61,410	6.2
Other services	45,101	4.6
Gross value added at current basic prices	**874,227**	
Plus adjustment to current basic prices (taxes minus subsidies on products)	113,787	11.5
= GDP at market prices	**988,014**	**100**

The table shows gross value added by industrial sector in the UK for 2001 at current basic prices. The sector values added combine to make gross value added. Gross value added is equal to the total output of goods and services minus the purchase of intermediate goods. It is also the sum of the factor rewards attributable to each sector.

Source: ONS, *UK National Accounts* (the Blue Book), 2002.

Gross national Income
Gross national Product
Gross domestic Product

GDP, GNI, and GNP

The measures of national income and national product that are used in Britain derive from an accounting system that has recently been standardized by international agreement and is thus common to most major countries. It is known as the System of National Accounts. A more detailed specification of this accounting system applies to all EU member states under the European System of Accounts 1995 (which was applied by all EU countries by April 1999 and was introduced into UK accounts in 1998). These accounts have a logical structure, based on the simple yet important idea that all output must be owned by someone. So whenever national output is produced, it must generate an equivalent amount of claims to that output in the form of national income.

Box 21.2 explains how the process that determines national income and national output simultaneously can be represented by a diagram illustrating the circular flow of spending (or expenditure) and income. The right half of the figure in that box focuses on spending to purchase the nation's output in product markets, and the left half focuses on input markets through which the receipts of

producers are distributed to owners of inputs, such as workers and the owners of capital and land.

Corresponding to the two halves of the circular flow are two ways of measuring national income: by determining the value of what is produced, and by determining the value of the income claims generated by production. Both measures yield the same total, which is called **gross domestic product (GDP)**. When it is calculated by adding up the total spending for each of the main components of final output, the result is called *GDP spending-based*. When it is calculated by adding up all the incomes generated by the act of production, it is called *GDP income-based*.

All value produced must be accounted for by a claim that someone has to that value. For example, any spending you make when you buy a TV set must also be received by the supplier of that set. The value of what you spend is the spending; the value of the product sold to you is the output. Thus, the two values calculated on income and spending bases are identical conceptually and differ in practice only because of errors of measurement. Any discrepancy arising from such errors is then reconciled so

---

 Box 21.2 The circular flow of income, output, and spending

Consider an economy that is made up of domestic individuals and domestic firms. For a moment we assume that the economy has no imports or exports and no government. The individuals provide labour for the firms and they buy the firms' output. The income that flows to individuals is represented by the black line running up the left-hand side of the diagram, and the spending on the final output of firms is represented by the black line running down the right-hand side. National output (or national income) can be measured either from the spending side in terms of spending on final goods produced, or on the income side. These factor incomes can be measured either as the sum of values added in the economy or as the sum of individual incomes.

In practice, final spending is not made up just of individuals' consumption spending, so when we approach the explanation of GDP from the spending side we need to add in investment spending, government consumption, and exports (the green lines). However, it is still true that the national product is equal to the sum of these total final spending components. It is also true that this final spending creates incomes that can be added up to generate the equivalence between national income and national output. The flows on the left side of the diagram have to be equal to the flows on the right. Any flow that generates spending also generates income.

We will refer back to this diagram several times in future chapters. When we do so we will point out that, for the level of income and output to be constant (rather than rising or falling), the injections of spending from outside the circular flow must just equal the withdrawals (or leakages) from the circular flow. In the model to be developed in subsequent chapters, we call the

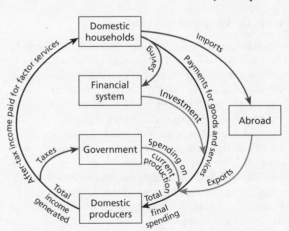

injections *exogenous* or *autonomous* spending. These are investment, government consumption, and exports, and are shown in the diagram in green. The leakages are taxes, saving, and imports, shown in blue.

For present purposes, the key point is that

Domestic production creates an income claim on the value of that production, and when all of the claims are added up, they must be equal to the value of all the production.

that one common total is given as *the* measure of GDP. Both calculations are of interest, however, because each gives a different and useful breakdown. Also, having two independent ways of measuring the same quantity provides a useful check on statistical procedures and on unavoidable errors in measurement.

GDP spending-based

GDP spending-based for a given year is calculated by adding up the spending going to purchase the final output produced in that year. Total spending on final output is expressed in the national accounts as the sum of three broad categories of spending: consumption, investment, and net exports. However, consumption is further divided into the consumption spending of government and that of private individuals (and non-profit organizations serving households). So there are four important categories of spending that we will discuss in considerable detail: private consumption, government consumption, investment, and net exports. In Chapter 23 we explain why these particular categories have received more attention in macroeconomics than have the net sector outputs listed in Table 21.1 and the income categories discussed below (Table 21.3). Here we define what these spending categories are and how they are measured. Throughout it is important to remember that they are exhaustive: they are defined in such a way that *all* spending on final output fall into one of the four categories.

Private consumption spending

Private consumption spending includes spending by individuals on goods and services produced and sold to their final users during the year. It includes services, such as haircuts, medical care, and legal advice; nondurable goods, such as fresh meat, clothing, cut flowers, and fresh vegetables; and durable goods, such as cars, television sets, and microwave ovens. However, it excludes purchases of newly built houses as these are counted as investment.[3] Also measured in the national accounts as part of private consumption is the final consumption spending of non-profit-making institutions serving households (NPISH). These are institutions, such as charities, that are neither firms nor governmental organizations but do contribute some spending and so have to be included somewhere in the national accounts. We denote actual, measured, private consumption spending by the symbol C^a.

Government consumption spending

When governments provide goods and services that their citizens want, such as health care and street lighting, it is obvious that they are adding to the sum total of valuable output in the same way as do private firms that produce

cars and video cassettes. With other government activities the case may not seem so clear. Should spending by the UK government to negotiate over the political situation in Northern Ireland, or to pay a civil servant to help draft legislation, be regarded as contributions to the national product? Some people believe that many (or even most) activities in Whitehall and in town halls are wasteful, if not downright harmful. Others believe that governments produce many of the important things of life, such as education, law and order, and pollution control.

National income statisticians do not speculate about which government spending is worthwhile. Instead, they include all government purchases of goods and services as part of national income and output. (Government spending on investment goods appears as public sector capital formation, which is a part of total investment spending.) Just as the national product includes, without distinction, the outputs of both gin and Bibles, it also includes refuse collection and the upkeep of parks, along with the services of judges, members of Parliament, and even Inland Revenue inspectors.

However, the UK national accounts do distinguish two different categories of government consumption. When government pays for the goods and services that are consumed by private individuals, this is referred to in the national accounts as *individual government final consumption*. This applies to health spending and education. If, for example, National Health Service doctors perform an operation, it is paid for by the government but the service is received by an identifiable individual. In contrast, the government also pays for street lighting, national defence, and law and order, but the benefit is consumed by the population at large rather than some specific individual. This is spending on *public goods*, which we discussed in Chapter 19. Spending by the government but where the consumption cannot be assigned to specific individuals is referred to in the national accounts as *collective government final consumption*. As a simplification (which we explain further in Chapter 23) in macroeconomics, we lump together individual government final consumption and collective government final consumption into one term: *government consumption*, sometimes just called government spending. Actual government consumption spending is denoted by the symbol G^a.

Government output is typically valued at cost rather than at the market value. In most cases there is really no choice. The output of public services is not (generally) sold in the marketplace, so government output is not observed independently of the spending that produces it. What, for example, is the market value of the services of a court of law? No one knows. We do know, however, what it costs

---

[3] Private consumption does not include purchases of existing houses as these are not part of current production. Rather, this involves a transfer of an existing asset.

the government to provide these services, so we value them at their cost of production.

Although valuing at cost is the easiest way to measure many government activities, it does have one curious consequence. If, owing to an increase in productivity, one civil servant now does what two used to do, and the displaced worker shifts to the private sector, the government's measured contribution to the national product will register a decline. On the other hand, if two workers now do what one worker used to do, the government's measured contribution will rise. Both changes could occur even though the services the government actually provides have not changed. This is an inevitable consequence of measuring the value of the government's output by the cost of the inputs, mainly labour, that are used to produce it, rather than by the value of outputs.[4]

It is important to recognize that only government spending *on currently produced goods and services* is included as part of GDP. A great deal of government spending is not a part of GDP. For example, when the Department of Health and Social Security (DHSS) makes a payment to an old-age pensioner, the government is not purchasing any currently produced goods or services from the retired. The payment itself adds to neither employment nor total output. The same is true of payments on account of unemployment benefit, income support, student grants, and interest on the national debt (which transfers income from taxpayers to holders of government bonds). All such payments are examples of **transfer payments**, which is government spending not made in return for currently produced goods and services. It is not a part of spending on the nation's total output, and therefore is not included in GDP.[5]

Thus, when we refer to government spending as part of GDP or use the symbol G^a, we include all government spending on currently produced goods and services, and we *exclude* all government transfer payments. (The term *total government spending* or *total government expenditure* is often used to describe all government spending, including transfer payments.)

Investment spending

Investment spending is defined as spending on the production of goods not for present consumption but rather for future use. The goods that are created by this spending are called **investment** (or **capital**) **goods**. Investment spending can be divided into three categories: changes in inventories, **fixed capital formation**, and the net acquisition of valuables.

Changes in inventories Almost all firms hold stocks of their inputs and their own outputs. These stocks are known as inventories. Inventories of inputs and unfinished materials allow firms to maintain a steady stream of production in spite of short-term fluctuations in the deliveries of inputs

bought from other firms. Inventories of outputs allow firms to meet orders in spite of temporary fluctuations in the rate of output or sales. Modern 'just-in-time' methods of production pioneered by the Japanese aim to reduce inventories held by manufacturing plants to nearly zero by delivering inputs just as they are needed. Most of the economy, however, does not achieve this level of efficiency and never will. Retailing, for example, would certainly not be improved if shops held no stocks.

An accumulation of stocks and unfinished goods in the production process counts as current investment because it represents goods produced (even if only half-finished) but not used for current consumption. A drawing down of inventories, also called *de-stocking*, counts as negative investment because it represents a reduction in the stocks of finished goods (produced in the current period) that are available for future use. Inventories are valued at what they will be worth on the market, rather than at what they have cost the firm so far. This is because the expenditure-based measure of GDP includes the value of what final spending on these goods would be if they were sold, even though they have not been sold yet.

Fixed capital formation All production uses capital goods. These are manufactured aids to production, such as machines, computers, and factory buildings. Creating new capital goods is an act of investment and is called *fixed investment* or **fixed capital formation**. The economy's total quantity of capital goods is called the **capital stock**. Much of the capital stock is in the form of equipment or buildings used by firms or government agencies in the production of goods and services. This includes not just factories and machines, but also hospitals, schools, and offices. A house or a flat is also a durable asset that yields its utility (housing services) over a long period of time. This meets the definition of fixed capital formation, so (as we pointed out above) housing *construction* is counted as investment spending rather than as consumption spending. When a family purchases a house from a builder or another owner, the ownership of an already produced asset is transferred, and that transaction is not a part of current GDP.

Net acquisition of valuables Some productive activity creates goods that are neither consumed nor used in the production process. Rather, they are held for their intrinsic beauty or for their expected appreciation in value. Examples

---

[4] UK national income statisticians are developing some new measures of the output of government that will help improve measurement of productivity, but this exercise is in its infancy.

[5] When the recipients of transfer payments spend these on buying goods and services, their spending is measured as consumption spending, and thus as part of GDP, in the same way as any other consumption spending. We do not want to measure it twice, which we would be doing if we included in GDP both the government transfer and the spending by the recipient.

are jewellery and works of art. Such works are known as *valuables*. Acquisitions less disposals of valuables are treated as investments in the national accounts.

Gross and net investment Total investment spending is called **gross investment** or **gross capital formation**. Gross investment is divided into two parts: replacement investment and net investment. **Replacement investment** is the amount of investment that just maintains the level of existing capital stock; in other words, it replaces the bits that have worn out. Replacement investment is classified as the **capital consumption allowance**, or simply **depreciation**. Gross investment minus replacement investment is **net investment**. Positive net investment increases the economy's total stock of capital, while replacement investment keeps the existing stock intact by replacing what has been used up or worn out.

All of gross investment is included in the calculation of GDP. This is because all investment goods are part of the nation's total output, and their production creates income (and employment) whether the goods produced are a part of net investment or are merely replacement investment. Actual total investment spending is denoted by the symbol I^a.

Net exports

The fourth category of aggregate spending, one that is very important to the UK economy, arises from foreign trade. How do imports and exports affect the calculation of GDP?

Imports A country's GDP is the total value of final goods and services produced *in that country*. If you spend £15,000 on a car that was made in Germany, only a small part of that value will represent spending on UK production. Some of it represents payment for the services of the UK dealer and for transportation within this country; much of the rest is the output of German firms and spending on German products, though there may be component suppliers from several countries. If you take your next holiday in Italy, much of your spending will be on goods and services produced in Italy and thus will contribute to Italian GDP.

Similarly, when a UK firm makes an investment expenditure on a UK-produced machine tool that was made partly with imported materials, only part of the spending is on British production; the rest is on production by the countries supplying the materials. The same is true for government spending on such things as roads and dams; some of the spending is for imported materials, and only part of it is for domestically produced goods and services.

Private consumption, government consumption, and investment all have an import content. To arrive at total spending on UK output, we need to subtract from total UK residents' spending actual spending on imports of goods and services, which is represented below by the symbol IM^a.

Exports If UK firms sell goods or services to German consumers, the goods and services are a part of German consumption spending, but they also constitute spending on UK output. Indeed, all goods and services that are produced in the United Kingdom and sold to foreigners must be counted as part of UK GDP: they are produced in the United Kingdom, and they create incomes for the UK residents who produce them. They are not purchased by UK residents, however, so they are not included as part of C^a, I^a, or G^a. Therefore, to arrive at the total value of spending on the domestic product, it is necessary to add in the value of UK exports. Actual exports of goods and services are denoted by the symbol X^a.

It is convenient to group actual imports and actual exports together as **net exports**. Net exports are defined as total exports of goods and services minus total imports of goods and services ($X^a - IM^a$), which will also be denoted by NX^a. When the value of exports exceeds the value of imports, the net export term is positive. When the value of imports exceeds the value of exports, the net export term becomes negative.

Market prices and basic prices

There is one important difference that arises when calculating the level of GDP from the spending side of the economy compared with calculating it by summing the value added in production. This difference arises because the price paid by consumers for many goods and services is not the same as the sales revenue received by the producer. There are taxes that have to be paid, which place a wedge between what consumers pay and what producers receive. Taxes attached to transactions are known as *indirect taxes*. Examples of UK indirect taxes include VAT and excise duties.[6] Thus, if you pay £100 for a meal in a restaurant, the restaurateur will receive only £82.50 and £17.50 will go to the government in the form of VAT.

In cases where products are subsidized by the government, the producer receives more than the consumer pays. In 2001 subsidies on UK products were minimal, amounting to only 0.8 per cent of GDP.

The term **basic prices** is used in the national accounts to refer to the prices of products as received by producers. **Market prices** are the prices as paid by consumers. Thus, basic prices are equal to market prices *minus* taxes on products *plus* subsidies on products. In the example of the meal bill above, the market price was £100 but the basic price was £82.50.

If you look again at Table 21.1, you will see that the sum of sectoral values added presented there is referred to as gross value added at *basic prices*. You should also notice that, by

---

[6] The rate of VAT was 17.5 per cent in the UK in 2002/3 and applied to a wide range of goods and services. Excise duties applied mainly to tobacco, alcohol, and petrol.

Table 21.2 **Expenditure-based GDP and its components, UK, 2001**

Expenditure categories	£ m	% of GDP
Individual consumption		
Household final consumption	631,010	64
Final consumption of non-profit institutions serving households	24,255	2.5
Individual government final consumption	117,941	11.9
Total actual individual consumption	773,206	78.3
Collective government final consumption	72,722	7.4
Total final consumption	**845,928**	**85.6**
Gross capital formation		
Gross fixed capital formation	162,244	16.4
Change in inventories	1,441	0.2
Acquisition less disposals of valuables	363	0
Total gross capital formation	**164,048**	**16.6**
Exports of goods and services	268,451	27.2
Less imports of goods and services	−290,912	−29.5
External balance of goods and services (net exports)	**−22,461**	**−2.3**
Statistical discrepancy	499	0.1
Gross domestic product at market prices (money GDP)	**988,014**	**100**

Expenditure based GDP is made up of consumption, investment, and net exports. Consumption is by far the largest expenditure category, equal to about 85 per cent of GDP. Private consumption makes up most of this, around 66 per cent of GDP, and government consumption makes up the rest. Investment accounts for about 17 per cent of GDP. Whereas exports and imports are both quite large (each over 27 per cent of GDP), net exports are small—in 2001 they represented (negative) 2.3 per cent of GDP. Government consumption is reported in two parts: that which is paid for by government but is consumed by individuals, such as health services and education; and that which is consumed collectively, such as defence and the legal system.

Source: ONS, *UK National Accounts* (the Blue Book), 2002.

adding to gross value added at basic prices a term labelled 'adjustment to current basic prices', we arrived at the total for GDP at market prices. This adjustment to current basic prices is made up of taxes minus subsidies on products.

Since our final spending categories are all measured at market prices—as they measure what is spent by purchasers rather than what is received by producers—we can proceed by adding up this final spending to arrive at GDP *at market prices* directly.

Total spending

The spending-based measure of gross domestic product at market prices is the sum of the four spending categories that we have discussed above; in symbols,

$$GDP = C^a + I^a + G^a + (X^a - IM^a).$$

The actual spending components of GDP for the United Kingdom in 2001 are shown in Table 21.2.

GDP spending-based is the sum of private consumption, government consumption, investment, and net export spending on currently produced goods and services. It is GDP at market prices.

GDP income-based

The production of a nation's output generates income. Labour must be employed, land must be rented, and capital must be used. The calculation of GDP from the income side involves adding up incomes of owners of resource inputs (land, labour, capital, etc.) so that all of that value is accounted for. In essence, we are taking the value added displayed for the economy as a whole in Table 21.1 and dividing it up by types of income rather than by industrial sector. We have already noted that, because all value produced must be owned by someone, the value of production must equal the value of income claims generated by that production.

National income accountants distinguish three main categories of income: operating surplus, mixed incomes, and compensation of employees.

Operating surplus Operating surpluses are net business incomes after payment has been made to hired labour and for material inputs, but before *direct taxes* (such as corporation tax) have been paid. Direct taxes are those taxes levied on individuals or firms, usually in relation to their income.

Table 21.3 **Income-based GDP and its components, UK, 2001**

Income type	£ m	% of GDP
Operating surplus, gross (profits)	238,625	24.2
Mixed incomes	60,073	6.1
Compensation of employees	556,371	56.3
Taxes on production and imports	140,447	14.2
less subsidies	−7,884	−0.8
Statistical discrepancy	382	0.0
GDP at market prices	**988,014**	**100**
Employees' compensation		
Receipts from rest of world	1,049	
less payment to rest of world	−869	
Total	**180**	
less taxes on production paid to rest of world *Plus* subsidies received from rest of world	−3,704	
Other subsidies on production	298	
Property and entrepreneurial income		
Receipts from rest of world	138,831	
less payments to rest of world	−129,849	
Total	**8,982**	
Gross national income (GNI) at market prices	**993,770**	

The income-based measure of GDP is made up of gross operating surplus (profit), mixed incomes, compensation of employees, and net taxes on goods. Mixed incomes are largely incomes of the self-employed or non-incorporated businesses, where it is hard to distinguish profits from employee compensation. By far the largest income category is compensation of employees, which makes up 56.3 per cent of GDP. GNI is GDP at market prices plus various net income receipts from the rest of the world.

Source: ONS, *UK National Accounts* (the Blue Book), 2002.

Operating surpluses are in large part the profits of firms, but they also include the financial surplus of organizations other than companies, such as universities. Some profits are paid out as **dividends** to owners of firms; the rest are retained for use by firms. The former are called *distributed profits*, and the latter are called *undistributed profits* or *retained earnings*. Both distributed and undistributed profits are included in the calculation of GDP.

Mixed incomes This category covers the many people who are earning a living by selling their services or output but who are not employed by any organization. It includes some consultants and those who work on short contracts but are not formally employees of an incorporated business. They are self-employed individuals who are running sole-trader businesses. Also included are some partnerships where the partners own the business. The reason why the incomes of this group are referred to as *mixed incomes* is that it is not clear what proportion of their earnings is equivalent to a wage or salary and what proportion is the profit or surplus of the business. They are a mixture of the two.

Compensation of employees This is wages and salaries (usually just referred to as *wages*). It is the payment for the services of labour. Wages include take-home pay, taxes withheld, National Insurance contributions, pension fund contributions, and any other fringe benefits. In other words, wages are measured gross. In total, wages represent that part of the value of production that is attributable to hired labour.

The various components of UK income-based GDP in 2001 are shown in Table 21.3. Notice that the three income categories in this table add up to gross value added at basic prices, as shown in Table 21.1. These income-based and output- or value-added-based measures are showing the same thing: the sum of factor incomes for the whole economy. In both cases we add taxes on production less subsidies to arrive at GDP at market prices. Note also that one of the terms in the table is a 'statistical discrepancy'. This is a small 'fudge factor' (which also appears with a different value in Table 21.2). It is there to make sure that the independent measures of income and product come to the same total. The statistical discrepancy is a clear indication that national accounting is not error-free.

Income produced and income received

GDP at market prices provides a measure of total output produced in the United Kingdom and of the total income generated as a result of that production. However, the total income received by UK residents differs from GDP for two reasons. First, some domestic production creates factor earnings for non-residents who either do some paid work for UK residents or have previously invested in the United Kingdom; on this account, income received by UK residents will be less than UK GDP. Second, many UK residents earn income from work for overseas residents or on overseas investments; on this account, income received by UK residents will be greater than GDP.

While GDP measures the output, and hence the income, that is *produced in* this country, the **gross national income (GNI)** measures the income that is *received by* this country. To convert GDP into GNI, it is necessary to add three terms that combine to account for the difference between the income received by this country and the income produced in this country. The first term is employees' compensation receipts from the rest of the world minus payments to the rest of the world. Thus, if a UK-based consultant sells her services to a French firm and does the work in France, the income received will contribute to UK GNI but will be part of French GDP.

The second term is (minus) net taxes on production paid to the rest of the world plus subsidies received from the rest of the world. The logic of this is that we are measuring GNI (as with GDP) at market prices. If some element of the market prices paid is an indirect tax that generates revenue for a foreign government, then that tax represents a loss of income for the domestic economy as a whole and reduces domestic gross national income. Equally, if the product is subsidized by a foreign government, this raises domestic incomes by enabling us to consume a given amount of goods at lower prices.

The third component of the difference between GDP and GNI is property and entrepreneurial income receipts from the rest of the world minus payments to the rest of the world. If for example you live in Manchester and own a holiday home in Spain that you rent out for part of the year, the revenue earned will count as part of GDP in Spain (as it is produced there), but the income accrues to a UK resident, so it adds to UK GNI. Similarly, many UK firms have subsidiaries located in other countries. The value added of those subsidiaries counts as part of GDP in the host country, but, if remitted to the parent, counts as part of GNI in the UK. Conversely, a Japanese firm located in the UK contributes all its value added to UK GDP, but profits remitted back to Japan are deducted from GDP in order to arrive at GNI (as they are not part of UK income).

Total output produced in the economy, measured by GDP, differs from total income received, measured by GNI, owing to net income from abroad.

It is important to note that the term 'gross national income' was introduced as recently as 1998 to replace the term gross national product or GNP. GNI and GNP are conceptually identical, but the latter has been in use for several decades all over the world, so readers will continue to come across it for many years to come even if it is replaced by GNI in a number of new publications. This minor difference in terminology is not important for understanding macroeconomics, which is concerned primarily with GDP, but it is important not to be confused when both terms are encountered.

GDP and GNI (or GNP) at market prices are the most commonly used concepts of national output and national income. Once we move on to theory in the next chapter, we ignore the small difference between GDP and GNI and refer to GDP at all times unless stated otherwise. This is true even though we talk sometimes about 'national income' and sometimes about the 'national product', depending on the context. For analytical purposes, they are the same thing.

Reconciling GDP with GNI

Table 21.3 shows the reconciliation of GDP with GNI. UK GNI was greater than GDP in 2001, but only by about half of 1 per cent. This reflects slightly greater income from abroad for UK residents than is being paid out to foreigners. Clearly, GNI could be smaller than GDP if outward payments were greater than income earned from abroad.

Figure 21.1 provides a visual representation of the information in Tables 21.1–21.3. It shows (*a*) the relations between gross value added at basic prices and GDP at market prices, and (*b*) the difference between GDP and GNI at market prices. Components of the three possible decompositions of GDP are also displayed.

Other income concepts

Personal income is income that is earned by or paid to individuals, before allowing for personal income taxes on that income. Some personal income goes for taxes, some goes for savings, and the rest goes for consumption. **Personal disposable income** is the amount of current income that individuals have available for spending and saving; it is personal income minus personal income taxes and National Insurance contributions.

Personal disposable income is GNI *minus* any part of it that is not actually paid to persons (such as retained profits of companies) minus personal income taxes plus transfer payments received by individuals.

Personal ___ GNI ___ taxes
disposable   (incomes)
income

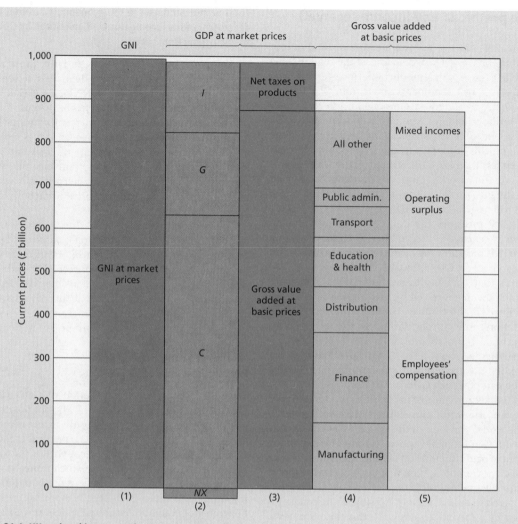

Figure 21.1 UK national income and output measures, 2001

Measurement of national income and output can be approached in three different ways, but they are all related. The figure shows the actual UK aggregates GNI at market prices, GDP at market prices, and gross value added at basic prices for 2001. Column (1) is GNI at market prices. Columns (2) and (3) add up to GDP at market prices. Columns (4) and (5) add up to gross value added at basic prices (or what used to be called GDP at factor cost).

Column (1) exceeds column (2) by about half of 1 per cent. This difference is net income from abroad, which in 2001 was positive but small. Column (2) shows that GDP is made up of the spending components: consumption (C), investment (I), government spending (G), and net exports (NX). Notice that in 2001 net exports were negative, so NX has to be subtracted from the sum of $C + I + G$ to arrive at GDP. Columns (3) and (4) show that gross value added at basic prices is equal to GDP at market prices minus net taxes on production.

Column (4) shows that gross value added is made up of the sum of the values added of each of the production sectors of the economy; manufacturing, for example, produces about 17.5 per cent of gross value added. Column (5) shows that gross value added can also be broken down by income type. Employees' compensation amounts to about 56 per cent of GDP at market prices.

Source: ONS, *UK National Accounts* (the Blue Book), 2002.

Interpreting national income and output measures

The information provided by national accounts data is useful, but unless it is carefully interpreted it can be misleading. Furthermore, each of the specific measures gives different information. Each may be the best statistic for studying a particular range of problems, but it is important to understand these differences if you are going to use the data for analytical purposes. Here we discuss some of the caveats to bear in mind.

Real and nominal measures

It is important to distinguish between *real* and *nominal* measures of national income and output. When we add up money values of outputs, spending, or incomes, we end up with what are called *nominal values*. Suppose we found that a measure of nominal GDP had risen by 70 per cent between 2000 and 2010. If we wanted to compare *real GDP* in 2010 with that in 2000, we would need to determine how much of that 70 per cent nominal increase was due to increases in the general level of prices and how much was due to increases in quantities of goods and services produced. Although there are many ways of doing this, the basic principle is always the same: it is to compute the value of output, spending, and income in each period by using a common set of *base-period prices*. When this is done, we speak of real output, spending, or income as being measured in *constant pounds* or, say, 2000 *prices*.

GDP valued at current prices (i.e. money GDP) is a nominal measure. GDP valued at base-period prices is a real measure of the volume of national output and national income.

Any *change* in nominal GDP reflects the combined effects of changes in quantities and changes in prices. However, when real income is measured over different periods by using a common set of base-period prices, changes in real income reflect only changes in real output.

The implicit deflator

If nominal and real GDP change by different amounts over some time-period, this must be because prices have changed over that period. Comparing what has happened to nominal and real GDP over the same period implies the existence of a price index measuring the change in prices over that period. We say 'implies' because no price index was used in calculating real and nominal GDP. However, an index can be inferred by comparing these two values. Such an index is called an *implicit price index* or an *implicit deflator*. It is defined as follows:

$$\text{Implicit deflator} = \frac{\text{Nominal GDP at current prices}}{\text{GDP at base-period prices}} \times 100\%.$$

The implicit GDP deflator is the most comprehensive index of the price level because it covers all the goods and services that are produced by the entire economy. Although some other indexes use fixed weights, or weights that change only periodically, implicit deflators are variable-weight indexes. They use the current year's 'bundle' of production to compare the current year's prices with those prevailing in the base period. Thus, the 2000 deflator uses 2000 output weights, and the 2005 deflator uses 2005 output weights. Box 21.3 illustrates the calculation of real and nominal GDP and an implicit deflator for a simple hypothetical economy that produces only wheat and steel. The appendix to this chapter contains a discussion of the construction of the retail price index.

A change in any nominal measure of GDP can be split into a change resulting from prices and a change resulting from quantities. For example, in 2001 UK nominal GDP ('money' GDP) was 4 per cent higher than in 2000. This increase was due to a 2.1 per cent increase in prices and a 1.9 per cent increase in real GDP. Table 21.4 presents nominal and real GDP and the implicit deflator for selected years since 1900.

Table 21.4 **Nominal and real GDP at market prices, 1900–2001**

	Money GDP (£ billion)	Real GDP (1990 prices) (£ billion)	Implicit GDP deflator (1990 = 100)
1900	1.9	109.5	1.7
1930	4.7	138.6	3.4
1950	13.1	200.4	6.5
1970	51.6	350.9	14.7
1980	231.2	426.8	54.2
2001	988	708	137.9

The data in the table are money GDP, real GDP, and the implicit GDP price deflator for selected years. The first column shows that money (nominal) GDP increased 520-fold between 1900 and 2001. However, the second column shows that there was only a 6.5-fold increase in real GDP over the same period. The difference between the two is accounted for by the final column, which shows that the implicit price deflator for GDP rose 81-fold in this period. Since 1950, real GDP has seen a just-over-3.5-fold increase, while the GDP price deflator has increased over 20-fold.

Sources: Economic Trends and *100 Years of Economic Statistics* (London: The Economist).

Box 21.3 **Calculation of nominal and real GDP**

To understand what is involved in calculating nominal GDP, real GDP, and the implicit deflator, an example may be helpful. Consider a simple hypothetical economy that produces only two commodities, wheat and steel. Table I gives the basic data for output and prices in the economy for two years.

Table I

	Quantity produced		Prices	
	Wheat (bushels)	Steel (tons)	Wheat (£ per bu.)	Steel (£ per ton)
Year 1	100	20	10	50
Year 2	110	16	12	55

Table II shows nominal GDP, calculated by adding the money values of wheat output and of steel output for each year. In year 1 the value of both wheat and steel production was £1,000, so nominal income was £2,000. In year 2 wheat output rose and steel output fell; the value of wheat output rose to £1,320, and that of steel fell to £880. Since the rise in value of wheat was greater than the fall in value of steel, nominal GDP rose by £200.

Table II

Year 1	$(100 \times 10) + (20 \times 50) = £2,000$
Year 2	$(110 \times 12) + (16 \times 55) = £2,200$

Table III shows real GDP, calculated by valuing output in each year by year 2 prices; that is, year 2 becomes the base year for weighting purposes. Using year 2 prices, the value of the fall in steel output between years 1 and 2 exceeded the value of the rise in wheat output, and real GDP fell.

Table III

Year 1	$(100 \times 12) + (20 \times 55) = £2,300$
Year 2	$(110 \times 12) + (16 \times 55) = £2,200$

In Table IV the ratio of nominal to real GDP is calculated for each year and multiplied by 100. This ratio implicitly measures the change in prices over the period in question and is called the *implicit deflator* or *implicit price index*. The implicit deflator shows that the price level increased by 15 per cent between year 1 and year 2 (calculated as $(13.04/86.96) \times 100$, where 13.04 is $(100 - 86.96)$).

Table IV

Year 1	$(2,000/2,300) \times 100 = 86.96$
Year 2	$(2,200/2,200) \times 100 = 100.00$

In Table IV we used year 2 as the base year for comparison purposes, but we could have used year 1. The implicit deflator would then have been 100 in year 1 and 115 in year 2, and the increase in price level would still have been 15 per cent. Or the base year could be some earlier year. No matter what year is picked as the year in which the index had a value of 100, the change in the implicit deflator between year 1 and year 2 is 15 per cent.

International comparisons of GDP

One purpose to which GDP measures are often put is international comparison of living standards or real income. It is natural to want to know if people have higher living standards in Britain or in, say, Germany or France. However, comparisons using measures such as GDP must be conducted with great care. There are many dimensions to living standards that are not measured by GDP or GNI.

For some purposes we may want to compare the absolute size of one economy with that of another, but normally we are interested in how well off the average individual is in each country. For this purpose we want to look at GDP per head or per capita (or perhaps GNI per capita). To get this figure, we divide GDP by the total population of the country. This tells us the share of total GDP that is available for the average citizen.

GDP in each country is measured in the local currency. So to make comparisons we have to convert different countries' nominal GDPs into the same currency. To do this, we have to use an exchange rate. This is problematic because exchange rates fluctuate, sometimes dramatically. Even in normal conditions it is not unusual for exchange rates to move by 10 per cent in a few weeks, but the move could easily be reversed a little later.

To solve the problem of making comparisons using unreliable or atypical exchange rates, economists compare GDPs using the exchange rate that equates the prices of a representative bundle of goods in two countries. This is known as the *purchasing power parity (PPP)* rate. We will discuss this concept more fully in Chapter 29.

Some comparisons of GNI per capita in 13 different countries (using PPP exchange rates) are given in Table 21.5. Figures are all expressed in US dollars. Several other indicators of material well-being are included in the table. Broadly speaking, they tell the same story as the GNI figures—the inhabitants of the richer countries can purchase more goods and services and tend to have a longer life expectancy. However, the rankings will be different for each possible indicator of well-being. The significance of this is that GNI per capita contains some useful information but other important indicators sometimes tell a slightly different story.

What GDP does not measure

GDP measures the flow of economic activity in organized markets in a given year. But much economic activity takes place outside the market economy. Although these activities

Table 21.5 **International comparisons of living standards**

	GNI per capita 2001 (US$)	Average annual real GDP growth per capita 1990–2000 (%)	Fixed line and mobile telephones per 1,000 pop. 2000	Infant mortality per 1,000 live births, 2000	Personal computers per 1,000 pop. 2000	Life-expectancy at birth 2000	Cars per 1,000 pop. 2000	Doctors per 1,000 pop. 1999 (or most recent year available)
USA	34,870	2.2	1,098	7	585.2	77	478	2.7
Japan	27,430	1.1	1,112	4	315.2	81	395	1.9
France	22,690	1.3	1,073	4	304.3	79	469	3
Canada	21,340	1.9	961	5	390.2	79	458	2.1
Germany	23,700	1.2	1,196	4	336	77	508	3.5
UK	24,230	2.2	1,316	6	337.8	77	373	1.8
Australia	19,770	2.9	972	5	464.6	79	450*	2.5
Spain	14,860	2.3	1,030	4	142.9	78	389	3.1
Mexico	5,540	1.4	267	29	50.6	73	102	1.7
Brazil	3,060	1.5	534	32	44.1	68	na	1.3
Russia	1,750	−4.6	240	16	42.9	65	120	4.2
China	890	9.2	178	32	15.9	70	1*	1.7
India	460	4.1	36	69	4.5	63	5	0.2

The table shows eight different indicators of living standards for 13 countries. Most of the indicators tell the same story—wealthy countries have more goods and better life expectations. However, there are some interesting anomalies. Russia has more doctors per 1,000 people than any other country in the table, yet life expectancy is lower than in China, which has less than half as many doctors per person.

* indicates 1990 figure as 2000 data not available

Sources: *World Bank Atlas*, 2002, and *World Development Indicators*.

are not typically included in GDP or GNI, they nevertheless use real resources and satisfy real wants and needs.

Unreported activities A significant omission from measured GDP is the so-called underground or black economy. The transactions that occur in the underground economy are perfectly legal in themselves; the only illegality involved is that such transactions are not reported for tax purposes. One example of this would be a carpenter who repairs a leak in your roof and takes payment in cash or in kind in order to avoid taxation. Because such transactions go unreported, they are omitted from GDP.

The growth of the underground economy can be encouraged by high rates of taxation and is facilitated by the rising importance of services in the nation's total output. The higher the tax rates, the more there is to be gained by 'going underground'. Also, it is much easier for a carpenter or plumber to pass unnoticed by government authorities than for a manufacturing establishment to do so.

Studies of the scale of the underground economy show that its importance has been growing in recent years. Estimates have put the underground economy in Britain at about 7 per cent of GDP. A Canadian study concluded that 15 per cent of Canadian GDP went unreported because it was in the black economy. In other countries the figures are even higher. The Italian underground economy, for example, has been estimated at about 20 per cent of GDP; for Spain estimates are close to 25 per cent, and for Greece 30 per cent!

Non-marketed activities If homeowners hire a firm to do some landscaping, the value of the landscaping enters into GDP; if they do the landscaping themselves, the value of the landscaping is omitted from GDP. Other non-marketed activities include the services of those who do housework at home, any do-it-yourself activity, and voluntary work such as canvassing for a political party, helping to run a volunteer day-care centre, or coaching an amateur football team.

One important non-marketed activity is leisure itself. If a lawyer voluntarily chooses to work 2,200 hours a year instead of 2,400 hours, measured GDP will fall by the lawyer's hourly wage rate times 200 hours. Yet the value to the lawyer of the 200 hours of new leisure, which is enjoyed outside of the marketplace, must exceed the lost wages (because she has voluntarily chosen the leisure in preference to the extra work), so total economic welfare has risen rather than fallen. Until recently one of the most important ways in which economic growth benefited people was by permitting increased amounts of time off work. Because the time off is not marketed, its value does not show up in measures of GDP.

Economic bads When a coal-fired electricity generator sends sulphur dioxide into the atmosphere, resulting in acid rain and environmental damage, the value of the electricity sold is included as part of GDP, but the value of the damage done by the acid rain is not deducted. Similarly, the petrol that we use in our cars is part of GDP, but the damage to the atmosphere from burning that petrol is not deducted. To the extent that economic growth brings with it increases in pollution, congestion, and other disamenities of modern living, GDP measures will overstate the value of the growth. They measure the increased economic output and income, but they fail to deduct the increased 'bads', or negative outputs, that generally accompany economic growth.

Do the omissions matter?

GDP does a reasonable job of measuring the flow of goods and services through the market sector of the economy. Usually an increase in GDP implies greater opportunities for employment for those households that sell their labour services in the market. Unless the importance of unmeasured economic activity changes rapidly, *changes* in GDP will do an excellent job of measuring *changes* in economic activity and well-being. However, when the task at hand is measurement of the overall flow of goods and services

available to satisfy people's wants, regardless of the source of the goods and services, then the omissions that we have discussed above become undesirable and potentially serious. Still, in the relatively short term, changes in GDP will usually be good measures of the direction, if not the exact magnitude, of changes in economic welfare.

The omissions cause serious problems when GDP measures are used to compare living standards in structurally different economies, as was discussed above. Generally the non-market sector of the economy is larger in rural than in urban settings and in less developed than in more developed economies. Be cautious, then, when interpreting data from a country with a very different climate and culture. When you hear that the per capita GNI of India is about US$1,580 per year, you should not imagine living in Manchester on that income; but although the average Indian is undoubtedly poorer than the average Briton, he is probably not twelve times poorer, as the GNI figures suggest.

SUMMARY

What is macroeconomics?

■ Macroeconomics is about the economy as a whole. It studies aggregate phenomena, such as growth, business cycles, living standards, inflation, unemployment, and the balance of payments. It also asks how governments can use their monetary and fiscal policy instruments to help stabilize the economy.

Why do we need macroeconomics?

■ Macroeconomics is useful because it enables us to study events that affect the economy as a whole without getting into too much detail about specific products and sectors.

National output concepts

■ Each firm's contribution to total output is equal to its value added, which is the gross value of the firm's output minus the value of all intermediate goods and services—that is, the outputs of other firms—that it uses. Goods that count as part of the economy's output are called final goods; all others are called intermediate goods. The sum of all the values added produced in an economy is called gross value added at basic prices. Basic prices are the prices received by producers net of taxes on products (plus subsidies).

GDP, GNI, and GNP

■ Gross domestic product (GDP) can be calculated in three different ways: (1) as the sum of all values added by all producers of both intermediate and final goods; (2) as the income claims generated by the total production of goods and services; and (3) as the spending needed to purchase all final goods and services produced during the period. By standard accounting conventions these three aggregations define the same total, so long as we add taxes on products (minus subsidies) to the first two in order to measure GDP at market prices. Market prices are the prices paid by consumers.

■ From the spending side of the national accounts, $GDP = C^a + I^a + G^a + (X^a - IM^a)$. C^a comprises private consumption spending. I^a is investment in fixed capital (including residential construction), inventories, and valuables; gross investment can be split into replacement investment (necessary to keep the stock of capital intact) and net investment (net additions to the stock of capital). G^a is government consumption. $(X^a - IM^a)$ represents net exports, or exports minus imports; it will be negative if imports exceed exports.

■ GDP income-based adds up all factor rewards in production. The main income categories making up GDP are operating surpluses, mixed incomes, and compensation of employees.

■ UK GDP measures production that is located in the United Kingdom, and UK gross national income (GNI) measures income accruing to UK residents. The difference is due to net income from overseas. GNI is the same thing as what used to be called gross national product (GNP).

$$GDP = C + I + G + (X - IM)$$

出口 − 进口 = 净出口 (Net Export)

个人消费　投资　政府投资

- Real GDP is calculated to reflect changes in real volumes of output and real income. Nominal GDP reflects changes in both prices and quantities. Any change in nominal GDP (or GNI) can be split into a change in real GDP and a change that is due to prices. Appropriate comparisons of nominal and real measures yield implicit deflators.

- Personal income is income received by individuals before any allowance for personal taxes. Personal disposable income is the amount actually available for individuals to spend or to save—that is, income minus taxes.

Interpreting national income and output measures

- GDP and related measures of national income and output must be interpreted with their limitations in mind. GDP excludes production that takes place in the underground economy or does not pass through markets. Moreover, GDP does not measure everything that contributes to human welfare.

- GDP is one of the best measures available of the total economic activity within a country. It is particularly valuable when changes in GDP are used to indicate how economic activity has changed over time.

TOPICS FOR REVIEW

- Targets and instruments of macroeconomic policy
- Value added
- Intermediate and final goods
- Spending-based and income-based GDP

- GNI and GNP
- Personal disposable income
- Implicit deflator
- What GDP does and does not measure

DISCUSSION QUESTIONS

1. Assuming an economy with no government and no foreign trade, calculate GDP for the following output scenario. There are three firms: firm A is a mining company, firm B is a steel producer and firm C is a car manufacturer. In a specific year, firm A sells £100 million worth of iron ore to firm B, firm B sells £200 million worth of steel to firm C, and firm C sells £500 million worth of cars to the general public. If there are no changes in inventories, no taxes, and no other producers in the economy, what is GDP?

2. How would the answer to question 1 change if firm B had increased its inventories of iron ore by £20 million during this year, having bought £120 worth of ore from firm A?

3. How would the answer to question 2 change if firm C had sold £50 million worth of lorries to firm A in addition to its car sales, all other purchases remaining unchanged?

4. Suppose again there are only three companies in an economy. Company A grows crops and extracts minerals from its land with no inputs from other companies. Its sales are £100 million per year, half of which goes to consumers and half to companies B and C in equal amounts. Company B buys inputs from A and sells its entire output of £200 million to company C. Company C buys inputs from A and B and sells its £450 million output directly to consumers (though 20 per cent of this is overseas). What is gross value added at basic prices?

   If there is only one indirect tax, value added tax, levied at 10 per cent, what is the value of GDP at market prices?

5. If the price index in February 2004 is 165 and by February 2005 has risen to 171, what is the annual rate of inflation? If over the same time period nominal GDP has risen from £1,000 billion to £1,080 billion, what is the growth rate of real GDP?

6. Explain why we cannot calculate the national product simply by adding up the production values of all firms.

7. What is the difference between real GDP and nominal GDP, and why does this distinction matter? Which measure would be appropriate for judging changes in standard of living?

8. What are the limitations of GDP per head as a measure of the quality of life?

9. What would it mean to be told that a country's GNI was greater than its GDP?

10. Using the expenditure-based definition $(C + I + G + NX)$, explain where each of the following expenditures appears in the national income accounts measure of GDP, if at all: state pensions; company pensions; student grants; theatre receipts; judges' salaries; unsold cars in showrooms; receipts from beer sales in a students' union bar; receipts from purchases of new copies of this book; receipts from purchases of second-hand copies of this book.

Appendix   How the RPI is constructed

Two important questions must be answered when any price index is constructed. First, what group of prices should be used? This depends on what the index is intended to measure. The retail price index (RPI), which is calculated by the Office for National Statistics (ONS), covers prices of goods and services that are commonly bought by households. Changes in the RPI are meant to measure changes in the typical household's *cost of living*. (Other indexes, such as the wholesale price index or the producer price index, cover the prices of different baskets of commodities. The implicit deflator for GDP covers all of the nation's output, not just consumer prices.)

Second, how should the movements in consumer prices be added up and summarized in one price index? If all prices changed in the same proportion, this would not matter: a 10 per cent rise in every price would mean a 10 per cent rise in the average of all prices, no matter how the average was constructed. However, different prices usually change in different proportions. It then matters how much importance we give to each price change. Changes in the price of bread, for example, are much more important to the average consumer than changes in the price of caviar. In calculating a price index, each price is given a *weight* that reflects its importance.

Let us see how this is done for the RPI. Government statisticians periodically survey a representative group of households in what is called the Family Expenditure Survey. This shows how consumers spend their incomes. The average bundle of goods that is bought is determined, along with the proportion of spending that is devoted to each good. These proportions become the weights attached to the individual prices in calculating the RPI. As a result, the RPI weights rather heavily the prices of commodities on which consumers spend much of their income, and weights rather lightly the prices of commodities on which consumers spend only a little of their income. Table 21A.1 provides a simple example of how these weights are calculated.

Once the weights are chosen, the average price can be calculated for each period. This is done, as shown in Table 21A.2, by multiplying each price by its weight and summing the resulting figures. However, a single average price is not informative. Suppose, for example, you were told that the average price of all goods that were bought by consumers last year was £89.35. 'So what?' you might well ask, and the answer would be: 'So, not very much. By itself, this tells you nothing useful.' Now suppose you are told that this year's average price for the same set of consumers' purchases is £107.22. Now you know that, on average, prices paid by consumers have risen sharply over the year—in fact, by 20 per cent.[7]

The average for each period is divided by the value of the average for the base period and multiplied by 100. The resulting series is called an index number series. By construction, the base-period value in this series equals 100; if prices in the next period average 20 per cent higher, the index number for that period will be 120. A simple example of how these calculations are carried out is given in Table 21A.2.

Price indexes are constructed by assigning weights to reflect the importance of the individual items being combined. The value is set equal to 100 in the base period.

Table 21A.1 **Calculation of weights for a price index**

Commodity	Price (£)	Quantity	Spending (£) (price × quantity)	Proportional weight
A	5	60	300	0.50
B	1	200	200	0.33
C	4	25	100	0.17
Total			600	1.00

The weights are the proportions of total spending that are devoted to each commodity. This simple example lists the prices of three commodities and the quantities bought by a typical household. Multiplying price by quantity gives spending on each, and summing these gives the total spending on all commodities. Dividing spending on each good by total spending gives the proportion of total spending that is devoted to each commodity, as shown in the last column. These proportions become the weights for the price indexes that are calculated in Table 21A.2.

Table 21A.2 **Calculation of a price index**

Commodity	Weight	Price (£) 1980	1985	1990	Price × weight (£) 1980	1985	1990
A	0.50	5.00	6.00	14.00	2.50	3.00	7.00
B	0.33	1.00	1.50	2.00	0.33	0.495	0.66
C	0.17	4.00	8.00	9.00	0.68	1.36	1.53
Total	1.00				3.51	4.855	9.19

Index		
	1980	$\dfrac{3.51}{3.51} \times 100 = 100$
	1985	$\dfrac{4.855}{3.51} \times 100 = 138.3$
	1990	$\dfrac{9.19}{3.51} \times 100 = 261.8$

A price index expresses the weighted average of prices in the given year as a percentage of the weighted average of prices in the base year. The prices of the three commodities in each year are multiplied by the weights from Table 21A.1. Summing the weighted prices for each year gives the average price in that year. Dividing the average price in the given year by the average price in the base year and multiplying by 100 gives the price index for the given year. The index is, of course, 100 when the base year is also taken as the given year, as is the case for 1980 in this example.

---

[7] The change is £17.87, which is 20 per cent of the initial average price of £89.35.

Table 21A.2 shows the calculation of what is called a *fixed-weight index*. The weights are the proportion of income that is spent on each of the three goods in the base year. These weights are then applied to the prices in each subsequent year. The value of the index in each year measures exactly how much the base-year bundle of goods would cost at that year's prices.[8] Fixed-weight indexes are easy to interpret, but problems arise because consumption patterns change over the years; the fixed weights represent with decreasing accuracy the importance that consumers *currently* place on each of the commodities.

The RPI used to be calculated using fixed weights that were changed only every decade or so. Now they are revised annually. This avoids the problem of the fixed-weight index becoming steadily less representative of current spending patterns.

Measuring the rate of inflation

At the end of May 2002 the RPI was 176.2. (The value for January 1987 equals 100.) This means that at the end of May 2002 it cost just over 76 per cent more to buy a representative bundle of goods than it did in the base period, which in this case is January 1987.[9] In other words, there was a 76 per cent *increase* in the price level over that period as measured by the RPI. The *percentage change* in the cost of purchasing the bundle of goods that is covered by any index is thus the level of the index minus 100.

The *inflation rate* between any two periods of time is measured by the percentage increase in the relevant price index from the first period to the second period. In the rare event of a drop in the price level, we speak of a *deflation*. When the amount of the rise in the price level is being measured from the base period, all that needs to be done is to subtract the base-period index (100) from the later index, as we have just done. When two other periods are being compared, we must be careful to express the change as a percentage of the index in the first period.

If we let P_1 indicate the value of the price index in the first period and P_2 its value in the second period, the inflation rate is merely the difference between the two, expressed as a percentage of the value of the index in the first period.

$$\text{Inflation rate} = \frac{(P_2 - P_1)}{P_1} \times 100.$$

When P_1 is the base period its value is 100, and the expression shown above reduces to $P_2 - 100$. In other cases the full calculation must be made. For example, suppose the index went to 144.7 in June 2005 from 141.0 in June 2004 (using a hypothetical base year later than 1987). The rise of 3.7 points in the index is a 2.6 per cent rise over its initial value of 141.0, indicating a rate of inflation of 2.6 per cent over the year.

If the two values being compared are less than or more than a whole year apart, it is common to convert the result to an *annual rate*. For example, suppose the RPI is 135.2 in January 2004 and 135.6 in February 2004 (on a base of, say, 1995 = 100). This is an increase of 0.296 per cent over the month $[(0.4/135.2) \times 100]$. It is also an *annual rate* of approximately 3.55 per cent (0.296 per cent × 12) over the year.[10] This means that, if the rate of increase

that occurred between January and February 2004 did persist for a year, the price level would rise by approximately 3.55 per cent over the year.

Variations on RPI

There are three additional, often-quoted, variations on RPI in use in the United Kingdom.

1. *RPIX* is an index calculated using the same components as RPI except that it excludes mortgage interest payments. This was the index that was used as the basis for the inflation target set by the government for the Bank of England's Monetary Policy Committee from 1997 to 2003.

2. *RPIY* is RPIX but with the further modification that it excludes the effects of indirect tax changes on prices. RPIY is sometimes referred to as 'underlying inflation' because it excludes the effects on inflation induced by changes in monetary *and* fiscal policies.

3. *HICP* is another measure of UK retail price inflation calculated on a different basis from the RPI in order to conform with EU statistical practices. It is the harmonized index of consumer prices. (This has some differences in components and is calculated as a geometric rather than arithmetic average. This is the index that the UK government proposed to use as the basis for its inflation target from November 2003.

In April 2003 the annual inflation rate according to each of these measures was:

- RPI = 3.1
- RPIX = 3.0
- RPIY = 2.9
- HICP = 1.5

Thus, these different measures can diverge, and these differences have been much greater at times.

The European Central Bank uses the HICP for the euro zone as a whole to judge whether it is meeting its objective of price stability.

---

[8] To verify this, calculate the total spending required to buy 60 units of commodity A, 200 units of commodity B, and 25 units of commodity C in each of the three years for which price data are given in Table 21A.2. Divide the resulting amounts by £600, multiply by 100, and you will get exactly the index values shown in the table.

[9] Notice that the base year on which the RPI is calculated is changed periodically, so it is likely that the base year in current use will be more recent than 1987. The latter was the base year in use up to 1998 for RPI calculations.

[10] We say *approximately* because a 0.296 per cent rise each month that is *compounded* for 12 months will give rise to an increase over the year that is greater than 3.55 per cent. The appropriate procedure is to increase the index in January by 0.296 per cent 12 times (calculate $[(1.00296)^{12} - 1] \times 100$) rather than just to multiply it by 12. The two results are the difference between simple and compound interest rates.

Chapter 22

ECONOMIC GROWTH

Why are some countries getting richer while others seem to be getting poorer? Why are we so much better off than our grandparents? Will our children be better off than us? These are questions about economic growth and what determines it. This is one of the most important topics in economics, as it affects how well off people are, and how this changes over time. In particular, you will learn that:

• Economic growth theory studies the determinants of the long-run trend in GDP, while macroeconomics was developed to explain the cycle about this trend.

• Even small differences in growth rate can lead to big differences in living standard between generations.

• While growth has many benefits, it also brings with it significant costs and serious risks.

• Growth of output depends on growth in inputs (capital and labour force, etc.) plus changing technology, which raises productivity (i.e. output per unit of input).

• Continued growth puts pressure on supplies of non-renewable resources and the environment.

In this chapter we first discuss the distinction between the long-term growth in the productive capacity of the economy and the cycle about that long-term trend. We then emphasize the importance of growth, and discuss the costs and benefits of economic growth. After that we outline some of the theories that economists use to understand the growth process. We deal with these first at a highly aggregated (or macro) level, then at a more disaggregated (or micro) level. We end with a brief discussion of possible limits to growth.

Growth and cycles

Potential GDP and the GDP gap

Economic growth is about the long-term trend in GDP. The cycle about this long-term trend is the topic on which much of the rest of macroeconomics focuses, and is what we shall be studying from the next chapter onwards. In order to facilitate this distinction between growth and cycles, we use the concepts *actual* and *potential GDP*, and we refer to the difference between them as the *GDP gap*.

Actual GDP represents what the economy does in fact produce. An important related concept is **potential GDP**, which measures what the economy could produce if all resources—land, labour, and productive capacity—were fully employed at their normal levels of utilization. This concept is also referred to as *potential income* and is sometimes called *full-employment income* (or *high-employment income*).[1] We give it the symbol Y^* to distinguish it from actual GDP (or national income), which is indicated by just Y.

What is variously called the **output gap** or the **GDP gap** measures the difference between what would have been produced if potential, or full-employment, GDP had been produced and what is actually produced, as measured by the current GDP. The gap is calculated by subtracting actual GDP from potential GDP ($Y^* - Y$).

When potential GDP exceeds actual GDP, the gap measures the market value of goods and services that *could have been produced* if the economy's resources had been fully employed but that actually went unproduced. The goods and services that are not produced when the economy is operating below Y^* are permanently lost to the economy. Because these losses occur when employable resources are unused, they are often called the *deadweight loss* of

[1] In everyday usage the words *real* and *actual* have similar meanings. In the national accounts, however, their meanings are distinct. *Real* GDP is distinguished from *nominal* GDP, and *actual* GDP is distinguished from *potential* GDP. The latter two refer to real measures, so that the full descriptions are actual real GDP and potential real GDP.

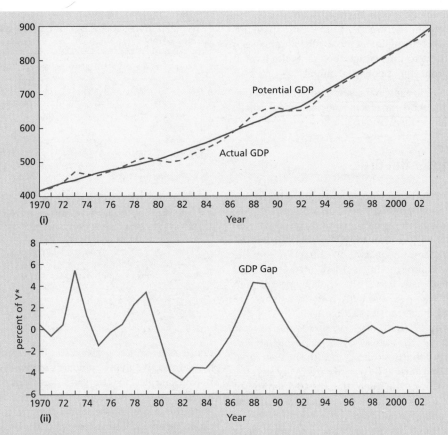

Figure 22.1 UK potential GDP and the output gap, 1970–2003

Potential and actual GDP have both displayed an upward trend in recent years, but actual GDP fluctuates around its potential level.

(i) Growth in the economy has been such that both potential and actual GDP have nearly doubled since 1970. Both series are in real terms and are measured in 1995 pounds sterling. Measurement of potential GDP is controversial and there is no official UK series at present. These figures were calculated by the IMF. The data for 2002–03 are IMF forecasts.

(ii) The cycles in the economy are apparent from the behaviour of the output gap. Slumps in economic activity produce large recessionary gaps, and booms produce inflationary gaps. The zero line indicates where actual and potential GDP are the same. The shaded areas below the zero line indicate the deadweight loss that arises from unemployment during periods when there is a recessionary output gap. Notice the large recessionary gaps in the early 1980s and the early 1990s.

Source: International Monetary Fund.

unemployment. When the economy is operating below its potential level of output—that is, when Y is less than Y^*— the output gap is called a **recessionary gap**.

In booms actual GDP may *exceed* potential GDP, causing the output gap to become negative. Actual output can exceed potential output because potential GDP is defined for a *normal rate of utilization* of factors of production, and these normal rates can be bettered temporarily. Labour may work longer hours than normal; factories may operate an extra shift, or not close for routine repairs and maintenance. Although many of these expedients are only temporary, they are effective in the short term. When actual GDP exceeds potential GDP, there is generally upward

pressure on prices. For this reason, when Y exceeds Y^*, the output gap is called an **inflationary gap**.

Figure 22.1(i) shows one estimate of UK potential GDP for the years 1970–2003.[2] The rising trend reflects the growth in productive capacity of the UK economy over this period. The figure also shows actual real GDP, which has kept approximately in step with potential GDP. The distance between the two, which is the GDP gap, is plotted in Figure 22.1(ii). Fluctuations in economic activity are apparent from fluctuations in the size of the gap. The deadweight

[2] Note that in both parts of Figure 22.1 the data for 2002 and 2003 are IMF projections as of mid-2002 rather than actual outturns.

loss from unemployment over any time-span is indicated by the overall amount of the gap over that time-span. It is shown in part (ii) of the figure by the shaded area between the curve and the zero line, which represents the level at which actual output equals potential output.

> Growth theory aims to explain the long-term trend in potential GDP, while the short-run macroeconomic model usually focuses on explaining the GDP gap.

Growth in potential GDP

Economic growth is the economy's most powerful engine for generating long-term increases in living standards. Throughout most of the nineteenth and twentieth centuries, per capita GDP rose steadily while its distribution became somewhat less unequal. As a result, citizens of the countries in the European Union, the United States, and Japan became materially better off decade by decade, and children typically were substantially better off on average than their parents had been at the same age.

At times in the 1970s, 1980s, and 1990s there was a perception that growth was slowing. Certainly growth rates fell in many countries compared with the very rapid growth experienced during the period of recovery after the Second World War. At the same time the distribution of income became somewhat more unequal. As a result, the real incomes of many European and Japanese families grew less fast than in the early postwar years. In contrast, there was a feeling in some other countries, like the USA, that from the mid-1990s onwards we were entering a new age of rapid growth linked to new technology (see pages 307–11).

Whatever has actually happened or will happen in the future, the key point to note is how important steady growth has been in people's minds and hearts over the previous decades of the nineteenth and twentieth centuries.

Continued annual growth has a big impact over long periods

Since 1885, the annual average growth rate of real output (GDP) per head of population in the UK has been around 2 per cent. Two per cent per year may not sound like much, and may not seem much from one year to the next, but it has very big effects over the average person's lifetime. A 2 per cent growth rate doubles real incomes every 36 years and quadruples it every 72 years. This means that each generation has on average been twice as well off as its parents, and there has been, on average, a four-fold increase in living standards during each person's lifetime!

> What look like quite modest annual growth rates have a powerful effect in raising living over the decades *because growth can go on indefinitely and its effects accumulate.*

Table 22.1 illustrates the cumulative effect of what seem to be very small differences in growth rates. Notice

Table 22.1 How national incomes change when growth rates differ

Year	Country (rate of growth per year)				
	A (1%)	B (2%)	C (3%)	D (5%)	E (7%)
2000	100	100	100	100	100
2010	110	122	135	165	201
2030	135	182	246	448	817
2050	165	272	448	1,218	3,312
2070	201	406	817	3,312	13,429
2100	272	739	2,009	14,841	109,660

Small differences in growth rates cause enormous differences in national incomes over even a few decades. In the year 2000 all five countries shown in the table have the same level of national income equal to 100 but they have different growth rates. Within ten years there are large differences between the national incomes of the various countries, and by 2070, the span of one lifetime, there are massive differences. By 2070 even the country with a 2 per cent growth rate has twice the income of the country with the 1 per cent rate, while the others have vastly more.

that if one country grows faster than another the gap in their respective living standards will widen progressively. If, for example, two countries start from the same level of income, and the first country grows at 2 per cent per year while the second grows at 1 per cent, the first country's per capita income will be twice that of the second country's in about 70 years. Having started from equality, within one lifetime the occupants of the second country will come to look poor and backward to the citizens of the first country.

Figure 22.2 shows the level of UK real GDP since 1885. The steady upward trend throughout this period is clearly evident. Total national output increased more than eight-fold between 1885 and 2001 while the population increased by only about 60 per cent over the same time, which means that incomes per head rose by over five-fold. In terms of levels of real GDP, the strong upward trend has shown only a few small blips around an otherwise relentless upward drift. There were periods of faster growth during the two world wars as national resources were mobilized for the war effort, and these periods were both followed by postwar recessions (periods of negative growth). Since the Second World War, however, growth has always been positive except for three short periods of negative growth (1974–5; 1980–2; 1991–2).

While growth throughout the past 116 years has been generally positive, and this is what generates the upward drift in incomes, the annual growth rates have been quite variable. Figure 23.1 on page 406 shows the same data as those that lie behind Figure 22.2 but expressed as annual growth rates. UK economic growth was extremely volatile in the interwar period. Growth has generally been positive since 1950 and has been much less variable, with most annual growth rates falling in the range of 0 to 5 per cent.

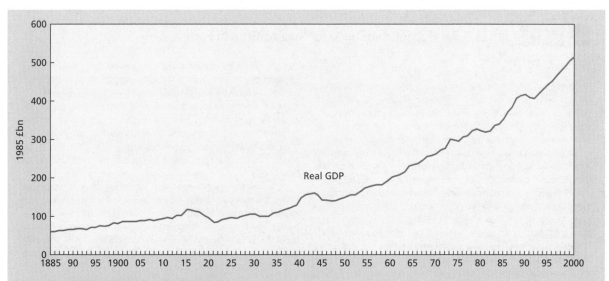

Figure 22.2 UK Real GDP growth, 1885–2001

Real GDP, which measures the total production of goods and services for the whole economy over a year, has grown steadily over the past century. Long-term growth is reflected in the upward trend of real GDP. There were significant declines in real GDP after each of the world wars, there was a recession in the 1930s, and there have been three notable recessions since 1970. Otherwise the trend dominates the cycle in the long term.

Benefits and costs of growth

We now look at the benefits of growth, and we then consider the costs. Boxes 22.1 and 22.2 outline some of the popular arguments on both sides of the growth debate. Each puts only one side of the case, and each has some valid points to make.

Benefits of growth

Growth and living standards For those who share in it, growth is a powerful weapon against poverty. A family that is earning £25,000 today can expect an income of about £30,500 within ten years (in constant pounds and with no promotion) if it shares in a 2 per cent growth rate, and £37,000 if that rate is 4 per cent.

The transformation of the life-style of ordinary workers in advanced industrial countries over the last two centuries is the result of the massive improvements in living standards and the quality of life that growth makes possible. Much of the recent concern over economic problems facing European families stems from the decline of growth that occurred in the mid-1970s, and in the recessions of the early 1980s and early 1990s. Partly because growth slowed in those periods and partly because the distribution of income has changed unfavourably for them, the real incomes of many working families grew little in the 1970s and only modestly in the 1980s and 1990s.

Growth and life-style A family often finds that a big increase in its income can lead to a major change in the pattern of its consumption—that extra money buys important amenities of life. In the same way, members of society as a whole may change their consumption patterns as their average income rises. Not only do markets in a country that is growing rapidly make it profitable to produce more cars, but also the government is led to construct more roads and provide more recreational areas for its newly affluent and mobile citizens. At yet a higher level of income, a concern about litter, pollution, and congestion may become important, and their correction may then begin to account for a significant fraction of GDP. Such 'amenities' usually become matters of social concern only when growth has ensured the provision of the basic requirements for food, clothing, and housing of a substantial majority of the population.

More subtle, but in the long term more important, are the effects of technological change on the whole nation's life-style. Today's real incomes are five to ten times those of Victorians who lived in the second half of the nineteenth century. But we do not spend this higher purchasing power on more of what Victorians consumed: instead, we buy new and better products made in new and better ways. We return to this point later, and Box 22.4 on page 397 expands on this.

The new products created by technological change transform our entire ways of living.

Box 22.1 **An election manifesto for the Pro-Growth Party**

Dear Voter:

You live in the world's first civilization that is devoted principally to satisfying *your* needs rather than those of a privileged minority. Past civilizations have always been based on leisure and high consumption for a tiny upper class, a reasonable living standard for a small middle class, and hard work with little more than subsistence consumption for the great mass of people.

The continuing industrial revolution is based on mass-produced goods for you, the ordinary citizen. You were born in a period of sustained economic growth that has dramatically raised the consumption standards of ordinary citizens. Reflect on a few examples: travel, live and recorded music, art, good food, inexpensive books, universal literacy, and a genuine chance to be educated. Most important, there is leisure to provide time and energy to enjoy these and thousands of other products of the modern industrial economy.

Would any ordinary family seriously prefer to go back to the world of 150 or 500 years ago in its same relative social and economic position? Surely the answer is no. However, for those with incomes in the top 1 or 2 per cent of the income distribution, economic growth has destroyed much of their privileged consumption position. They must now vie with the masses when they visit the world's beauty spots, and, while lounging on the terrace of a palatial mansion, suffer the sound of charter flights carrying ordinary people to inexpensive holidays in far places. Many of the rich complain

bitterly about the loss of exclusive rights to luxury consumption, and it is not surprising that they find their intellectual apologists. Whether they know it or not, the anti-growth economists are not the social revolutionaries that they think they are. They say that growth has produced pollution and the wasteful consumption of all kinds of frivolous products that add nothing to human happiness. However, the democratic solution to pollution is not to go back to where so few people consumed luxuries that pollution was trivial, but rather to learn to control the pollution that mass consumption tends to create.

It is only through further growth that the average citizen can enjoy consumption standards (of travel, culture, medical and health care, etc.) now available only to people in the top 25 per cent of the income distribution— a group that includes the intellectuals who earn large royalties from the books they write in which they denounce growth. If you think that extra income confers little real benefit, just ask those in the top 25 per cent to trade incomes with average citizens.

Ordinary citizens, do not be deceived by disguised élitist doctrines. Remember that the very rich and the élite have much to gain by stopping growth, and even more by rolling it back—but you have everything to gain by letting it go forward.

VOTE FOR GROWTH. VOTE FOR US.

 Box 22.2 **An election manifesto for the Anti-Growth Party**

Dear Voter:

You live in a world that is being despoiled by a mindless search for ever-higher levels of material consumption at the cost of all other values. Once upon a time men and women knew how to enjoy creative work and to derive satisfaction from simple activities. Today the ordinary worker is a mindless cog in an assembly line that turns out more and more goods and services which the advertisers must work overtime to persuade the workers to consume.

Statisticians count the increasing flow of material output as a triumph of modern civilization. You arise from your electric-blanketed bed, clean your teeth with an electric toothbrush, and pop into your electric toaster a slice or two of bread baked from super-refined and chemically refortified flour; you climb into your car to sit in vast traffic jams on exhaust-polluted roads.

Television commercials tell you that by consuming more you are happier, but happiness lies not in increasing consumption, but in increasing the ratio of *satisfaction of wants* to *total wants*. Since, the more you consume, the more the advertisers persuade you that you *want* to consume, you are almost certainly less happy than the average citizen in a small town in 1955, whom we can visualize standing at the front gate, chatting with neighbours, and watching the local children skipping with pieces of old clothesline.

Today the landscape is dotted with endless factories that produce the plastic trivia of the modern industrial society. They drown you in a cloud of noise, air, and water pollution. The countryside is despoiled by open-cast mines, petroleum refineries, acid rain, and dangerous nuclear power stations, producing energy that is devoured insatiably by modern factories and motor vehicles. Worse, our precious heritage of natural resources is being rapidly depleted.

Now is the time to stop this madness. We must stabilize production, reduce pollution, conserve our natural resources, and seek justice through a more equitable distribution of existing total income.

A long time ago Malthus taught us that if we do not limit population voluntarily nature will do it for us in a cruel and savage manner. Today the same is true of output: if we do not halt its growth voluntarily, the halt will be imposed upon us by a disastrous increase in pollution and a rapid exhaustion of natural resources.

Citizens, awake! Shake off the worship of growth, learn to enjoy the bounty that is yours already, and reject the endless, self-defeating search for increased happiness through ever-increasing consumption.

VOTE AGAINST GROWTH. VOTE FOR US.

Growth and income redistribution Not everyone benefits equally from growth. Many of the poorest are not even in the labour force and thus are unlikely to share in the higher wages that, along with higher profits, are the primary means by which the gains from growth are distributed. Others lose their jobs as a result of technical change, and the older people may find it difficult to retrain for anything like as good a job as they lost. For this reason, even in a growing economy, redistribution policies will be needed if poverty and extreme hardship are to be averted.

If a constant total of national income is redistributed, someone's standard of living will actually have to be lowered. However, when there is economic growth, and when only the increment in income is redistributed (through government intervention), it is possible to reduce income inequalities without actually having to *lower* anyone's income.

It is much easier for a rapidly growing economy to be generous towards its less fortunate citizens—or neighbours—than it is for a static economy to do so.

Costs of growth

Other things being equal, most people would probably regard a fast rate of growth as preferable to a slow one; but other things are seldom equal.

The opportunity cost of growth In a world of scarcity almost nothing is free. Growth requires heavy investment of resources in capital goods, as well as in activities such as education. Often these investments yield no immediate return in terms of goods and services for consumption; thus, they imply that sacrifices have been made by the current generation of consumers.

Growth, which promises more goods tomorrow, is achieved by consuming fewer goods today. For the economy as a whole, this sacrifice of current consumption is the primary cost of growth.

Social and personal costs of growth A growing economy is a changing economy. Innovation renders some machines obsolete and also leaves some people partly obsolete. No matter how well trained workers are at age 25, in another twenty-five years many will find that their skills are at least partly obsolete. A rapid growth rate requires rapid adjustments, which can cause much upset and misery to the people who are affected by them.

It is often argued that costs of this kind are a small price to pay for the great benefits that growth can bring. Even if this is true in the aggregate, these personal costs are very unevenly borne. Indeed, many of those for whom growth is most costly (in terms of lost jobs) share least in the fruits that growth brings.

Growth creates new jobs and destroys some old jobs. Those who were trained for the jobs that are lost can, and often do, suffer. Box 22.3 deals with a less-well-founded worry: that growth may destroy more jobs than it creates, leading to long-term heavy unemployment for a growing body of structurally unemployed workers.

 Box 22.3 **The end of work?**

From time immemorial, people have observed that technological change destroys particular jobs and have worried that it will destroy jobs in general. Two points are important in assessing this issue.

First, technological change does destroy particular jobs. When waterwheels were used to automate the fulling of cloth in twelfth-century Europe, there were riots and protests among the fullers who lost their jobs. A century ago, half of the labour force in North America and Europe was required to produce the enough food to feed the population. (The figure was a little lower in the UK because British-manufactured goods were exported in return for imported foodstuffs.) Today less than 3 per cent of the labour force is needed in the high-income countries to feed all their citizens. In other words, out of every 100 jobs that existed in 1900, 50 were in agriculture, and 47 of those jobs have been destroyed by technological progress over the course of the last century.

The second point is that new technologies create new jobs just as they destroy old ones. The displaced agricultural workers did not join the ranks of the permanently unemployed—although some of the older ones may have done, their children did not. Instead they, and their children, took jobs in manufacturing and service industries and helped to produce the mass of new goods and services that have raised living standards over the century—such as cars, refrigerators, computers, foreign travel, and so on over a vast list of new things.

New technologies usually require new skills. Those who are unable to retrain may suffer, but their children will be able to train appropriately from the outset.

Technological change raises living standards by destroying jobs in existing lines of production and freeing labour to produce new commodities as well as more of some existing commodities.

Modern technologies have two new aspects that worry some observers. First, they tend to be knowledge-intensive. A fairly high degree of literacy and numeracy, as well as familiarity with computers, is needed to work with many although not all of these new technologies. Second, owing to the globalizing of world markets—through falling costs of transporting goods and co-ordinating their production worldwide—unskilled workers in advanced countries have come into competition with unskilled workers everywhere in the world. Both of these forces are decreasing the relative demand for unskilled workers in developed countries, and may lead to falling relative wages for the unskilled and also, if labour markets are sufficiently inflexible, to some structural unemployment.

For these reasons some people blame the high unemployment rates in Europe on the new technologies. This is hard to reconcile, however, with the fact that the lowest unemployment rates in the industrialized countries are currently being recorded in the United States, which is the most technologically dynamic of all countries and the one in which policy-makers have worried least about the unemployment effects of new technologies. This suggests that the cause of high European unemployment rates may be not enough technological change and too much government interference, rather than too much technological change.

Worries that technological change will cause general unemployment have been recorded for at least 200 years, but, so far at least, there is no sign that those displaced by technological change or their children are being forced into the ranks of the permanently unemployed.

Over all of recorded history so far, technological change has created more jobs than it has destroyed.

Time-distribution of costs and benefits The costs of technological change tend to be borne immediately. Jobs are lost, and people trained in the old technologies lose their jobs and find their skills obsolete. The forgone consumption needed to finance the investment that embodies the new technologies happens right away. In contrast, the benefits are felt by many in the present generation and by almost everyone in the future. We are all better off for having most of the new products that are created by technological change, even though those who made the older competing products probably suffered when the new ones were first introduced. As a result, everyone is a beneficiary of past growth-inducing technological change—the costs have been paid and the benefits are still with us. But not everyone is a beneficiary of current change. Most benefit but some suffer, and some of those would have been better off if the change that affected them adversely had never happened.

Theories of economic growth

In this section we study some of the theories that attempt to explain economic growth. This is an exciting area. Ideas are changing rapidly as both theoretical and empirical research expands our knowledge.

Before going further, it is helpful to clarify the distinction between what has been called *extensive growth* and *intensive growth*. Extensive growth relates to the growth of total GDP, whereas intensive growth is about GDP per head. The former is thus relevant to discussions of total market size and income of the economy as a whole, but the latter is relevant to understanding the real living standard of average individuals in the economy. The former tells us about the size of cake, while the latter tells us how much cake is available for each citizen.

Determinants of growth

The four of the most important determinants of growth of total output are:

1. *growth in the labour force*, such as occurs when the population grows or participation rates rise;

2. *investment in human capital*, such as formal education and on-the-job experience;

3. *investment in physical capital*, such as factories, machines, transportation, and communications facilities;

4. *technological change*, brought about by innovation that introduces new products, new ways of producing existing products, and new forms of business organization.

One line of investigation studies how these four forces operate in what is called the **aggregate production function**. This is an expression for the relationship between the total amounts of labour (L), physical capital (K), and human capital (H) that are employed[3] and the nation's total output, its GDP:

$$\text{GDP} = f(L, K, H).$$

This is an aggregate function because it relates the economy's total output, its GDP, to the total amount of the three main inputs that are used to produce that output. (A micro production function, such as is discussed in Chapter 8, relates the output of one firm to the inputs employed by that firm.) The function, indicated by the letter 'f', shows the relation between the inputs of L, K, and H and the output of GDP. The production function tells us how much GDP will be produced for given amounts of labour and capital employed. For example, the function may tell us that, when 200 million units of labour per period[4] of time, 400 million units of physical capital per period, and 100 million units of human capital per period are used, the GDP will be 4,000 million units of output per period.[5]

In growth theory we ignore short-term fluctuations of output around its trend. Thus, the GDP in the above production function can be interpreted as the trend level of GDP, that is potential GDP.

We may now use this aggregate production function to discuss some theories of economic growth.

Neoclassical growth theory

One branch of neoclassical theory deals with growth when the stock of technological knowledge remains unchanged.

---

[3] Growth theory focuses on the production of manufactured goods and services, where, in contrast to agriculture, land is rarely a limiting factor. All the relatively small amounts of land that are needed can be obtained, and hence nothing significant is lost by ignoring land in the analysis of an industrialized economy—although this is not the case for an agricultural economy.

[4] These would be flows of inputs and flows of outputs, so for example labour input would be measured as worker-hours or worker-weeks.

[5] A simple example of a production function is GDP = $z(LKH)^{1/3}$. This equation says that, to find the amount of GDP produced, multiply the amount of labour by the amount of physical capital and the amount of human capital, take the cube root, and multiply the result by the constant z. This production function has positive but diminishing returns to each factor. This can be shown using calculus by evaluating the first and second partial derivatives and showing that the first derivatives are positive while the second derivatives are negative. In the numerical example in the text z is taken as 20, making $20[(200)(400)(100)]^{1/3} = 4,000$.

There are no innovations—no new ways of making things, and no new products. As a result, the relation between inputs and output, as shown by the production function, does not change. The key aspects of what is called the neoclassical model are that the aggregate production function displays *decreasing returns* when any factor is increased on its own, and *constant returns* when all factors are increased together and in the same proportion. We explain these concepts below.

Decreasing returns to a single input

To start with, suppose the population of the country grows while the stocks of physical and human capital remain constant. More and more people go to work using the same fixed quantity of physical capital and knowledge. The amount that each new unit of input adds to total output is called its *marginal product*. The operation of the famous **law of diminishing returns** tells us that the successive employment of equal additional amounts (or units) of labour will eventually add less to total output than the immediately previous unit of labour. In other words, sooner or later each additional unit of labour will produce a diminishing marginal product. This is referred to as *diminishing returns to a single input*. We first met it in Chapter 8, and it is illustrated in Figure 22.3.

The law of diminishing returns applies to any input that is varied while the other inputs are held constant. Thus,

successive amounts of capital added to *a fixed supply of labour* will also eventually add less and less to GDP.

According to the law of diminishing returns, the increment to total production will eventually fall whenever equal increases of a variable input are combined with another input whose quantity is fixed.[6]

Constant returns to scale

The other main property of the neoclassical aggregate production function is **constant returns to scale**. This means that, if the amounts of labour and physical and human capital are all changed in equal proportion, the total output will also change in that proportion. For example, a 10 per cent increase in the amounts of labour and physical and human capital used will lead to a 10 per cent increase in GDP. We first met this relationship in Chapter 9.

Sources of growth in the neoclassical model

Now consider each of the sources of growth listed above. To begin with, we let each source operate with the others held constant.

Labour force growth In the long term we can associate labour force growth with population growth (although in the short term the labour force can grow if participation rates rise, even though the population remains constant). As more labour is used, there will be more output and, consequently, a growth in total GDP. The law of diminishing returns tells us that sooner or later each further unit of labour to be employed will cause a smaller and smaller addition to GDP. Eventually, not only will the marginal product of labour be falling, but the average product will fall as well. Beyond that point, although economic growth continues in the sense that total output is growing, living standards are falling in the sense that average GDP per head of population is falling. If we are interested in the growth in living standards, we are concerned with increasing GDP *per person*.

Whenever diminishing average returns apply, increases in population on their own are eventually accompanied by falling living standards.[7]

Physical capital Increases in the amount of physical capital on their own affect GDP in a manner similar to population

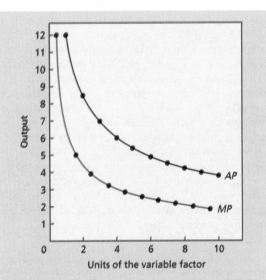

Figure 22.3 The average and marginal products of a variable input

The average and marginal products of any variable input decline as successive units of that input are added to a fixed amount of another input. This figure shows the marginal and average products of the variable input declining as more and more units of that input are used. The marginal products are plotted between the units of the variable input since they apply to a change from one amount to the next.

[6] In some production functions marginal product may rise at first and begin to decline only after a certain critical amount of the variable input is used. In the neoclassical, constant-returns production function, however, marginal product declines from the outset, as shown in Figure 22.2.

[7] In the neoclassical model diminishing returns set in from the outset, so that there is no range over which population increases cause rising marginal or average product of labour. The issue of when diminishing returns set in need not concern us here, since all that matters for the text discussion is that increases in any one input, other things held constant, must eventually encounter diminishing returns.

growth alone. Eventually, each successive unit of physical capital will add less to total output than each previous unit of physical capital.

There is, however, a major contrast with the case of labour growth, because it is output per person that determines living standards, not output per unit of capital. Thus, as physical capital increases, living standards increase because output is rising while the population is constant. Indeed, per capita output can be increased by adding more physical capital as long as its marginal product exceeds zero. However, since the increases in output are subject to diminishing returns, successive additions to the economy's capital stock bring smaller and smaller increases in per capita output.

In the neoclassical model, the operation of diminishing returns implies that equal increases in physical capital on its own bring smaller and smaller increases in per capita GDP.

Human capital Human capital has several aspects. One involves improvements in the health and longevity of the population. Of course, these are desired as ends in themselves, but they also have consequences for both the size and the productivity of the labour force. There is no doubt that improvements in the health of workers have increased productivity per worker-hour by cutting down on illness, accidents, and absenteeism.

A second aspect of the quality of human capital concerns technical training—from learning to operate a machine to learning how to be a scientist. This training depends on the current state of knowledge, and advances in knowledge allow us not only to build more productive physical capital, but also to create more effective human capital. Training is clearly required if a person is to operate, repair, manage, or invent complex machines. More subtly, there may be general social advantages to an educated population. Productivity improves with literacy. The longer a person has been educated, the more adaptable, and thus the more productive in the long run, that person is in the face of new and changing challenges.

A third aspect of human capital is its contribution to growth and innovation.

Not only can current human capital embody in people the best current technological knowledge, but, by training potential innovators, it leads to advances in our knowledge and hence contributes to growth.

Balanced growth Now consider what happens if labour and physical and human capital all grow at the same rate. In this case the neoclassical assumption of constant returns to scale means that GDP grows at the same rate. As a result, per capita output (GDP/L) remains constant.[8] This is called a **balanced growth path**. It is one in which all inputs and output are growing at the same constant rate. Per capita GDP, however, is unchanged.

This is not the kind of growth that concerns those interested in living standards. It is just more of the same: larger and larger economies, with more capital and more labour, doing exactly what the existing capital and the existing labour were already doing. There is nothing new.

Growth and living standards In this constant-technology neoclassical model, the only way for growth to add to living standards is for the per capita stocks of physical and human capital to increase. However, the law of diminishing returns dictates that the rise in living standards brought about by successive equal increases in capital will inexorably diminish. Raising living standards becomes more and more difficult as capital accumulation continues.

Technological change in the neoclassical growth model

So far we have held technology constant. In fact, over the centuries (and even decades) economic growth is dominated by technological changes. As we have already observed, we are not better off than our Victorian ancestors because we have more Victorian factories making more Victorian commodities: we are better off because technological change has provided us with new commodities often made in radically new ways. Box 22.4 discusses some of the many new products that have literally transformed life-styles over the past century. In the neoclassical model technological change can be shown as shifting the production function so that the same amount of labour, physical capital, and human capital produces more GDP. This result is depicted in Figure 22.4 by rightward shifts in the MP curves of each input: the same amount of input produces more output.[9]

The neoclassical growth model can accommodate technological change along balanced growth paths if the changes increase the efficiency of labour, making labour grow at a constant exponential rate when measured in *efficiency units*. This is called labour-augmenting, or Harrod-neutral, technical change. The result is that there is no increase in output per efficiency unit of labour, but there is an increase in output *per worker*. Along such a balanced growth path labour is constant, measured in number of workers employed, while human and physical capital, the efficiency of labour, and total and per capita output are all growing at a constant rate.

---

[8] In all of these models, a constant fraction of the population is assumed to be in the labour force, so that output per employed person and output per head of population always change in the same direction.

[9] In the neoclassical production function which allows for growth we have GDP = $z(L^{\alpha}K^{\beta}H^{1-\alpha-\beta})$, $0 < \alpha, \beta, \alpha + \beta < 1$. The parameter z is a constant that relates given inputs of L, K, and H to a specific GDP. Increases in factor productivity cause z to rise, so the given amounts of L, K, and H are associated with higher GDP. Exogenous technical progress at a constant rate can be shown as GDP$_t = z_t(L^{\alpha}K^{\beta}H^{1-\alpha-\beta})$, where z grows at a constant rate as time passes.

Box 22.4 **Technical change and living standards**

Why are our material living standards higher than those of our Victorian ancestors who lived in the 1890s, and why were *they* better off than their Georgian ancestors who lived in the 1790s were? We are better off today not because we consume more of the same goods than our predecessors did: we are better off because we have new goods made in different ways.

Today we enjoy five to ten times as much purchasing power as did Victorians (measured in constant pounds), but we consume it largely in terms of new commodities produced with new techniques. We are better off, in largest part, *not* because we have accumulated more polluting Victorian factories that produce yet more horse carriages, penny-farthing bicycles, and other Victorian commodities. We are better off because we have a vast array of new goods and services to choose from, and those goods are produced in much more efficient ways.

Victorians could not have imagined modern dental and medical equipment, penicillin, pain-killers, bypass operations, safe births and abortions,

personal computers, the internet, compact discs, TV, cars, aeroplanes, opportunities for cheap, fast worldwide travel, affordable universities, food of great variety and free of the risk of ptomaine poisoning and botulism, central heating, the elimination of endless domestic drudgery by either wives or masses of servants through the use of detergents, washing machines, vacuum cleaners, and a host of other new household products that their great-grandchildren take for granted.

Nor could they have imagined the modern automated, air-conditioned factory free of noisy, smelly steam engines and unsafe pulleys, belts, and cogs. Nor could they have imagined the modern office dominated by computers and free of Bob Cratchits adding up long columns of figures and recording them with quill pen and bottled ink.

The point is important. Technological advance transforms our lives by inventing new, undreamed-of things and making them in new, undreamed-of ways.

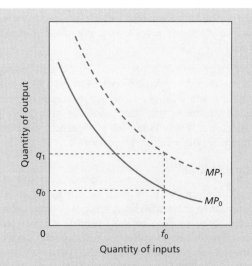

Figure 22.4 Shifts in marginal product curves
Technological change shifts the marginal product curve of each input so that any given amount will produce more. In this example technological change shifts the marginal product curve of the input from MP_0 to MP_1. The amount f_0 of the input formerly produced a marginal product of q_0, but after the change it produces the larger amount q_1.

Kinds of technological change Increases in productive capacity that are created by installing new and better capital goods are called **embodied technical change**. The historical importance of embodied technical change is clear: the assembly line and automation transformed most manufacturing industries, the aeroplane revolutionized transportation, and electronic devices now dominate the information and communications industries. These innovations, plus

lesser known but no less profound ones—for example improvements in the strength of metals, the productivity of seeds, and the techniques for recovering basic raw materials from the ground—create new investment opportunities.

Less obvious but none the less important changes occur through **disembodied technical change**, that is, changes in the organization of production that are not embodied in particular capital goods. Examples are improved techniques of management, design, marketing, organization of business activity, and feedback from user experience to product improvement.

The modern understanding that technological innovation is at the heart of the growth process has led to two important developments in many economists' views on growth. The first is that technological change is largely endogenous to the economic system. The second is that investment that increases the capital stock may encounter increasing rather than diminishing returns. These insights have led to new growth theories that go far beyond the neoclassical growth model.

Endogenous growth

In the neoclassical model, innovation shifts the production function but is itself unexplained. In other words, technological change is treated as being *exogenous*. It has profound effects on economic variables, such as GDP, but it is not influenced by economic causes. It just happens.

Yet microeconomic research by many scholars over the last several decades has established that technological change *is* responsive to such economic 'signals' as prices and profits. In other words, technological change is *endogenous* to the economic system. Much of the earliest work on this issue was done in the United Kingdom by scholars associated with the Science Policy Research Unit (SPRU) at Sussex University. The most influential overall single study, however, was by the American professor Nathan Rosenberg, whose path-breaking book *Inside the Black Box* argued this case in great detail.[10]

Technological change stems from research and development (R&D) and from innovating activities that put the results of R&D into practice. These are costly and highly risky activities, undertaken largely by firms and usually in pursuit of profit. It is not surprising, therefore, that these activities respond to economic incentives.

Rosenberg establishes two key relationships. First, R&D designed to apply known basic principles to new problems is responsive to economic signals. For example, if the price of some particular input such as petroleum or skilled labour goes up, R&D and innovating activities will be directed to altering the production function to economize on these inputs. This process does not involve a substitution of less expensive inputs for more expensive ones within the confines of known technologies: rather, it is the development of new technologies in response to changes in relative prices. Second, *basic research* itself is also responsive to economic incentives. One reason for this is that the basic research agenda is strongly influenced by practical issues of the day. For example, basic research in solid-state physics became popular, and was heavily funded, only after the development of the transistor.

There are many important implications of this new understanding that, to a great extent, growth is achieved through costly, risky, innovative activity that occurs to a significant extent in response to economic signals. We will discuss a few of these below.

The complexity of the innovation process

The pioneering theorist of innovation Joseph Schumpeter developed a model in which innovation flowed in one direction, starting from a pure discovery 'upstream', to more applied R&D, then to working machines, and finally to output 'downstream'.

In contrast, modern research shows that innovation involves a large amount of 'learning by doing' at all of its stages. (This phenomenon, whereby costs per unit of output fall steadily over time as firms learn how to manage new technologies, is discussed in more detail in Chapter 33.) What is learned 'downstream' then modifies what must be done 'upstream'. The best innovation-managing systems encourage feedback from the more applied steps to the purer researchers and from users to designers.

The location of innovation

Innovation typically takes place in different parts of the producer–user chain in different industries—as shown, for example, by the research of Eric von Hippel of the Massachusetts Institute of Technology (MIT) in his book *The Sources of Innovation*. Von Hippel describes how, while in some industries manufacturers make most of the product innovations, in other industries it is users who make most of them, and in yet others the innovating is done by those who supply components or materials to the manufacturer.

Unless these differences are appreciated, public policy designed to encourage innovation can go seriously astray. An example is provided by von Hippel:

Consider the current concern of US policy-makers that the products of US semiconductor process equipment firms are falling behind the leading edge. The conventional assessment of this problem is that these firms should somehow be strengthened and helped to innovate so that US semiconductor equipment users (makers of semiconductors) will not also fall behind. But investigation shows that most process equipment innovations in this field are, in fact, developed by equipment users. Therefore, the causality is probably reversed: US equipment builders are falling behind because the US user community they deal with is falling behind. If this is so, the policy prescription should change. Perhaps US equipment builders can best be helped by helping US equipment users to innovate at the leading edge once more.[11]

More recent events suggest that the US semiconductor industry did improve its performance in the 1990s, but the message for economists and policy-makers is important: an understanding of the details of the innovating process in each industry is needed if successful innovation-encouraging policies are to be developed.

Costly diffusion

The *diffusion* of technological knowledge from those who have it to those who want it is not costless (as it was assumed to be in Schumpeter's model). Firms need research capacity just to adopt the technologies developed by others. Some of the knowledge needed to use a new technology can be learned only through experience by plant managers, technicians, and operators. (Such knowledge is called *tacit knowledge*.) We often tend to think that once a production process is developed it can easily be copied by others. Indeed, some advanced economic theories adopt the hypothesis of replication, which holds that any known process can be replicated in any new location by using the same factor inputs and management as are used in the old location. In practice, however, the diffusion of new technological knowledge is not so simple.

[10] N. Rosenberg, *Inside the Black Box: Technology and Economics* (Cambridge University Press, 1982). See also the same author's *Exploring the Black Box: Technology, Economics, and History* (Cambridge University Press, 1994).

[11] Eric von Hippel, *The Sources of Innovation* (New York: Oxford University Press, 1988), pp. 9–10.

For example, US economists Richard Nelson and Sidney Winter have argued that most industrial technologies require technology-specific organizational skills that can be 'embodied' neither in the machines themselves, nor in instruction books, nor in blueprints. Acquiring tacit knowledge requires a deliberate process of building up new skills, work practices, knowledge, and experience.

The fact that diffusion is a costly, risky, and time-consuming business explains why new technologies take considerable time to diffuse, first through the economy of the originating country and then through the rest of the world. If diffusion were simple and virtually costless, the puzzle would be why technological knowledge and best industrial practices do not diffuse very quickly. As it is, decades can pass before a new technological process is diffused everywhere that it could be employed.

Market structure and innovation

Because it is highly risky, innovation is encouraged by a strongly competitive environment and is discouraged by monopoly practices. Competition among three or four large firms often produces much innovation, but a single firm, especially if it serves a secure home market protected by trade barriers, seems much less inclined to innovate.[12]

Although the ideas of Joseph Schumpeter lie behind much of modern growth theory, this emphasis on competition seems on the surface to conflict with his ideas. The apparent conflict arises because the theories available to Schumpeter in his time offered only two market structures: perfect competition and monopoly. He chose monopoly as the structure more conducive to growth on the grounds that monopoly profits would provide the incentive to innovate, and innovation itself would provide the mechanism whereby new entrants could compete with established monopolies. (He called this latter process 'creative destruction'.) Modern economists, faced with a richer variety of theoretical market structures, find that competition among oligopolists is usually more conducive to growth-enhancing technological change than is either monopoly or perfect competition.

Government interventions that are designed to encourage innovation often allow the firms in an industry to work together as one. Unless great care is exercised, and unless sufficient foreign competition exists, the result may be a national monopoly that will discourage risk-taking rather than encourage it, as the policy intends.

The United Kingdom provides many examples of this mistaken view of policy. For example:

[UK policy in the 1960s] operated under the faulty theory that encouraging British companies to merge would create world-class competitors. Consolidation of steel, automobiles, machine tools, and computers all led to notable failures. A program of research support for industry . . . proved disastrous. The British government tried to choose promising technologies and

gave direct grants to firms to develop them. Most of the choices were failures. . . . [In contrast] unusually low levels of regulation in some service industries have avoided disadvantages faced by other nations and allowed innovation and change . . . in auctioneering . . . trading and insurance. British firms in these industries have been among the most innovative in the world.[13]

Shocks and innovation

One interesting consequence of endogenous technical change is that shocks that would be unambiguously adverse to an economy operating with fixed technology can sometimes provide a spur to innovation that proves a blessing in disguise. A sharp rise in the price of one input can raise costs and lower the value of output per person for some time. But it may lead to a wave of innovations that reduce the need for this expensive input and, as a side-effect, greatly raise the productivity of labour.[14]

Sometimes individual firms will respond differently to the same economic signal. Those who respond by altering technology may do better than those who concentrate their efforts on substituting within the confines of known technology. For example, in *The Competitive Advantage of Nations* Michael Porter tells of how US consumer electronics firms decided to move their operations abroad to avoid high, and rigid, labour costs. They continued to use their existing technology and went where labour costs were low enough to make that technology pay. Their Japanese competitors, however, stayed at home. They innovated away most of their labour costs—and then built factories in the United States to replace the factories of US firms that had gone abroad!

Innovation as a competitive strategy

Managing innovation better than one's competitors is one of the most important objectives of any modern firm that wishes to survive. Firms often fail because they do not keep up with their competitors in the race to develop new and improved products and techniques of production and distribution. Success in real-world competition often depends more on success in managing innovation than on success

---

[12] This is an important theme in much contemporary research, supported by evidence from such authors as Alfred D. Chandler, Jr (*Scale and Scope: The Dynamics of Industrial Capitalism*, Harvard University Press, 1990), David Mowrey and Nathan Rosenberg (*Technology and the Pursuit of Economic Growth*, Cambridge University Press, 1989), and Michael Porter (*The Competitive Advantage of Nations*, New York: Free Press, 1990).

[13] Porter, *The Competitive Advantage of Nations*, p. 507.

[14] This is why in microeconomics we study three runs: the short run, the long run, and the very long run. Often the very-long-run response to a change in relative prices is much more important than either the short-run response, limited by fixed capital, or the long-run response, limited by existing technology.

in adopting the right pricing policies or in making the right capacity decisions from already-known technological possibilities.

Increasing returns theories

We saw earlier that neoclassical theories assume that investment is always subject to diminishing returns. Some new growth theories emphasize the possibility of *historical increasing returns to investment*. This means that, as investments in some new areas—products, power sources, or production technologies—proceed through time, each new increment of investment is more productive than previous increments. A number of sources of increasing returns have been noted. These fall under the general categories of once-and-for-all costs, and ideas.

Fixed costs

There are three ways in which once-and-for-all costs can cause increasing returns to investment.

1. Investment in the early stages of development of a country or region may create new skills and attitudes in the workforce that are then available to all subsequent investors, whose costs are therefore lower than those encountered by the initial investors. In the language of Chapter 19, the early firms are conferring an externality on those who follow them.

2. Each new investor may find the environment more and more favourable to its investment because of the infrastructure that has been created by those who came before.

3. The first investment in a new product will encounter countless problems, both technical problems of production and problems of product acceptance among customers. Once the technical problems are overcome, they do not exist for subsequent investors. When a new product is developed, customers will often resist adopting it, partly because they may be conservative and partly because they know that new products often have teething troubles. Customers also need time to learn how best to use the new product—they need to do what is called 'learning by using'. The first firms in the field with a truly new idea, such as personal computers, usually meet strong customer resistance, but this resistance is eroded over time.

All of these cases, and many more that could be mentioned, are examples of a single phenomenon:

Many investments require fixed costs, the advantages of which are then available to subsequent investors; hence the investment costs for 'followers' can be substantially less than the investment costs for 'pioneers'.

More generally, many of the sources of increasing returns are variations on the following theme:

Doing something really new is difficult, both technically and in terms of customer acceptance, whereas making further variations on an accepted and developed new idea becomes progressively easier.

The implications of these ideas have been the subject of intense study ever since they were first embedded in modern growth models by Paul Romer of the University of California and Maurice Scott of Oxford University.[15]

Ideas

An even more fundamental change in the new theories is the shift from the economics of goods to the economics of ideas.

Physical goods, such as factories and machines, exist in one place at one time. The nature of this existence has two consequences. First, when physical goods are used by someone, they cannot be used by someone else. Second, if a given labour force is provided with more and more physical objects to use in production, sooner or later diminishing returns will be encountered.

Ideas have different characteristics. In the first place, ideas can be used by one person without reducing their use by others. Thus, once someone has an idea and develops it, it can be used simultaneously by everyone. For example, if one firm is using a certain van, another firm cannot use that van at the same time; but one firm's use of a revolutionary design for a new suspension on a van or lorry does not prevent other firms from using that design as well. Ideas are not subject to the same use restrictions as goods. (In the language of Table 19.1 on page 321, physical goods are rivalrous; ideas are non-rivalrous.)

Second, ideas are not necessarily subject to decreasing returns. As our knowledge increases, each increment of new knowledge does *not* inevitably add less to our productive ability than did each previous increment. A year spent improving the operation of semiconductors may be more productive than a year spent improving the operation of vacuum tubes (the technology used before semiconductors).

Modern growth theories stress the importance of ideas in producing what can be called knowledge-driven growth. New knowledge provides the input that allows investment to produce constant or increasing rather than diminishing returns. Furthermore, the evidence from modern research is that new technologies are usually absolutely input-saving—they typically use less of all inputs per unit of output. Since there are no practical boundaries to human knowledge, there need be no immediate boundaries to

---

[15] As with so many innovations, these new views have many historical antecedents, including a classic article in the 1960s by Nobel Prize winner Kenneth Arrow of Stanford University: 'The Economic Implications for Learning by Doing', *Review of Economic Studies*, 29 (1962).

finding new ways to produce more output using less of all inputs.[16]

> Classical and neoclassical growth theories gave economics the name 'dismal science' by emphasizing that diminishing returns under conditions of given technology put a cap on growth based on capital accumulation. Modern growth theories are more optimistic, because they emphasize the unlimited potential of knowledge-driven technological change to economize on all resource inputs, and because they display increasing or constant returns to investment with constant population.

However, these theories refer to long-term trends. For reasons that are not fully understood, the dynamics of market systems cause growth rates to vary from decade to decade, fluctuating about their long-term trend which is the subject of growth theory. Over the long haul, however, there seems no reason to believe that equal increments of human inventive effort must inevitably be rewarded by ever-diminishing increments to material output.

Further causes of growth

So far we have looked at increases in labour and capital and at technological change as causes of growth. Contemporary studies suggest that other causes of growth are also important. The effects of these other causes appear as shifts in the production function, so that any given number of hours of labour operating with a given amount of capital produces more and more output as time passes.

Institutions

Almost all aspects of a country's institutions can foster or deter the efficient use of a society's natural and human resources. Social and religious habits, legal institutions, and traditional patterns of national and international trade are all important. So, too, is the political climate.

Historians of economic growth, such as Paul David and Nathan Rosenberg, attribute much of the growth of Western economies in the post-medieval world to the development of *new institutions*, such as the joint-stock company, limited liability, efficient forms of insurance, effective patent laws, and double entry bookkeeping (which allowed the firm's value to be assessed by those who wished to invest in it—at least until modern managers began to manipulate these figures.). Many students of modern growth suggest that institutions are as important today as they were in the past. They suggest that the societies that are most successful in developing the new institutions that are needed in today's knowledge-intensive world of globalized competition will be those that are at the forefront of economic growth.

The role of the government

Governments play an important role in the growth process.

First, the government needs to provide the framework for the market economy, which is given by such things as well-defined property rights secure from arbitrary confiscation, security and enforcement of contracts, law and order, a sound money, and the basic rights of the individual to locate, sell, and invest where and how he or she decides.

Second, governments need to provide infrastructure. For example, transportation and communication networks are critical to growth in the modern globalized economy. Some of these facilities, such as roads, bridges, and harbours, are usually provided directly by governments; others, such as telecommunications, rail, and air services, can be provided by private firms, but government regulations and competition policy may be needed to prevent the emergence of growth-inhibiting monopolies in these areas.

Education and health (especially for the disadvantaged) are important forms of government expenditure. Creating the appropriate inputs to production is critical to creating comparative advantages in products that can be exported. This requires general education, trade schools, and other appropriate institutions for formal education as well as policies to increase on-the-job training within firms. These activities are even more important today than they were in the past, because so much of a nation's capacity to grow, and to compete in a world of rapidly developing ideas, lies in the quality of its human capital —both in those who produce goods and services and in those who carry out research and development (R&D) on new goods and services that can be produced in the future.

Other possible government policies include favourable tax treatment of saving, investment, and capital gains; R&D tax incentives and funding assistance; and policies to encourage some portion of the large pools of financial capital held by pension funds and insurance companies to be used to finance innovation.

Finally, emphasis can be placed on poverty reduction for at least two reasons. First, poverty can exert powerful anti-growth effects. People living in poverty will not develop the skills to provide a productive labour force, and they may not even respond to incentives that are provided. Malnutrition in early childhood can affect a person's capacities for life. Second, although economic growth tends to reduce the incidence of poverty, it does not eliminate it.

---

[16] At some distant date we may know everything there is to know, but if that time ever comes, it is clearly going to be a long, long way in the future.

Are there limits to growth?

Many opponents of growth argue that sustained world growth is undesirable; some argue that it is impossible. Of course, all terrestrial things have a limit. After all, astronomers predict that the solar system itself will die when the sun burns out in another five billion or so years. But to be of practical concern, a limit must be within our planning horizons.

Resource exhaustion

The years since the Second World War have seen a rapid acceleration in the consumption of the world's resources, particularly fossil fuels and basic minerals. World population has increased from under 2.5 billion to over 6 billion in that period; this increase alone has intensified the demand for the world's resources. Furthermore, as economic development spreads to more and more countries, living standards are rising, in some cases rapidly. As people attain higher incomes, they consume more resources. So not only are there more people in the world, but many of those people are consuming increasing quantities of resources.

Most economists believe that the technology and resources available at the beginning of the twenty-first century cannot possibly support the world's population at a standard of living equal to that currently enjoyed by the average European family. To do so, for example, the annual consumption of oil would have to increase more than ten-fold. It seems evident that resources and our present capacity to cope with pollution and environmental degradation are insufficient to accomplish such a rise in living standards with the technology available at present.

Most economists, however, agree that *absolute* limits to growth, based on the assumptions of constant technology and fixed resources, are not relevant. As modern growth theory stresses, technology changes continually, as do stocks of resources. For example, forty years ago few would have thought that the world could produce enough food to feed its present population of around 6 billion people, let alone the 10 billion at which the population is projected to stabilize sometime in the mid-twenty-first century. Yet this task now seems feasible, and major famines are associated not with our inability to produce enough but (often) with political upheavals which reduce food production well below what could be achieved by existing technology.

At the beginning of the twenty-first century, the developed world is struggling not with a food shortage, but with a food glut. Farm support policies in the European Union have turned the countries of Europe into food exporters rather than food importers, as they had been in the past. A mere 3 per cent of European, US, and Canadian labour applied to limited farmland with modern technology is producing more food than the world markets can consume. The problem in the early 2000s is how to reduce subsidized production, not how to produce more.

Although globally there is enough food for everyone, severe problems arise when primarily agricultural economies suffer drought and other natural disasters, or wars and other man-made disasters. The problem, then, is not to produce more food worldwide, but to be sure that it is available where it is needed.

It is possible that fifty years from now the global energy problem will be as much a thing of the past as the global food shortage problem is today. Technology could by then have produced a cheap, non-polluting energy source to replace our present reliance on fossil fuels. There are many candidates, most of which are used somewhere today and require only further R&D to reduced their costs to competitive levels. These include solar energy, geothermal heat, wind power, hydrogen-based fuel cells, and possibly nuclear fusion.

The typical innovation in production processes uses less of all inputs per unit of output. Thus, technological change is part of the *solution*, as well as part of the problem. The problem is too many people aspiring to levels of consumption that cannot be sustained *with existing technologies*.

The future is always uncertain, and it is instructive to recall how many things that we accept as commonplace today would have seemed miraculous a mere twenty-five years ago.

Yet there is surely also cause for concern. Although many barriers can be overcome by technological advances, such achievements are not instantaneous and are certainly not automatic. There is a critical problem of timing: how soon can we discover and put into practice the knowledge required to solve the problems that are made ever more imminent by the growth in the population, the affluence of the rich nations, and the aspirations of the billions who now live in poverty? There is no guarantee that a whole generation will not be caught in transition between technologies, with enormous social and political consequences.

Renewable resources

One possible limitation to growth relates to renewable resources. The demands placed on them threaten to destroy their natural recuperative cycle. Throughout history, for example, fishermen were a small part of the predatory process. Now the demands of 6 billion people have made fish a scarce resource, threatening to destroy the fish-generating capacity of many oceans, as we saw in Box 19.2 on page 325.

Pollution

A major problem is how to cope with pollution. Air, water, and earth are polluted by a variety of natural activities, and over billions of years the environment has coped with these. The Earth's natural processes had little trouble dealing with the pollution generated by its 1 billion inhabitants in 1800. But the 6 billion people who now exist put demands on pollution abatement system become unsustainable. Smoke, sewage hydrocarbon emissions, spent nuclear other pollutants threaten to overwhelm regenerative processes. Detailed analysis of some which these problems may be dealt with was given in Chapters 19 and 20.

Conscious management of pollution and renewable resources was unnecessary when the world's population was 1 billion people, but such management has become a pressing matter of survival now that over 6 billion people are seeking to live in the same space and off the world's limited resources.

Conclusion

Growth has raised the average citizens of advanced countries from poverty to plenty in the course of two centuries —a short time in terms of human history. Yet the world still faces many problems. Starvation and poverty are the common lot of citizens in many countries and are not unknown in the European Union and the United States, where average living standards are high. Further growth is needed if people in less developed countries are to escape material poverty, and further growth would help advanced countries to deal with many of their pressing economic problems. (The problems of producing growth in less developed countries are further considered in Chapter 34.)

Rising population and rising per capita consumption, however, put pressure on the world's natural ecosystems, especially through pollution and congestion. Further growth must be sustainable growth, which in turn must be based on idea-driven technological change. Past experience suggests that new technologies will use less of all resources per unit of output. However, if they are to reduce dramatically the demands placed on the Earth's ecosystems, price and policy incentives will be needed to direct technological change in more 'environmentally friendly' ways. Just as present technologies are much less polluting than the technologies of a hundred years ago, the technologies of the twenty-first century must be made much less polluting than today's.

There is no guarantee that the world will solve the problems of sustainable growth, but there is nothing in modern growth theory and existing evidence to suggest that such an achievement is impossible.

SUMMARY

Growth and cycles

- Growth theory studies the long-term trend in real output and living standards, while macroeconomics studies cycles about that trend.

- Growth is the most important determinant of changes in living standards over time.

Benefits and costs of growth

- The most important benefit of growth lies in its contribution to the long-run struggle to raise living standards and to escape

poverty. The cumulative effects of what may appear to be small growth rates become large over periods of a decade or more.

- Small differences in national growth rates can cumulate into large national differences in living standards over a few decades.

- It is easier to redistribute income in a growing society than in a static one.

- The opportunity cost of growth is the diversion of resources from current consumption to capital formation. For individuals who are left behind in a rapidly changing world, the costs can be high and more personal.

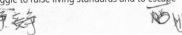

Theories of economic growth

■ The aggregate neoclassical model displays diminishing returns when one input is increased on its own and constant returns when all inputs are increased together. In a balanced growth path, labour, capital, and national output all increase at a constant rate, leaving living standards unchanged. When labour-augmenting productivity growth occurs, a balanced growth path is consistent with rising per capita output and income.

■ In the long term, technological change is the major cause of growth, together with the new capital investment that is needed to embody new technologies. Modern growth theory treats technological change as an endogenous variable that responds to market signals. The diffusion of technology is also endogenous. It is costly and often proceeds at a relatively slow pace.

■ Some modern growth theories display increasing returns as investment increases on its own. This is because investment creates externalities so that successive increments of investment may add constant or even successively *increasing* amounts to total output.

■ The critical importance of increasing knowledge and new technology to the goal of sustaining growth is highlighted by the great drain on existing natural resources that has resulted from the explosive growth of population and output in recent decades. Without continuing technological change, the present needs and aspirations of the world's population cannot come anywhere close to being met.

Are there limits to growth?

■ Rising population and rising real incomes place pressure on resources. Although resources in general will not be exhausted, particular resources, such as petroleum, will be. Furthermore, resources that renewed themselves without help from humans when the world's population was 1 billion people will be exhausted unless they are consciously conserved now that the world's population exceeds 6 billion.

■ The enormous increase in population also creates severe problems of pollution. The Earth's environment could cope naturally with most of the pollution caused by humans 200 years ago, but the present population is so large that pollution has outstripped nature's coping mechanisms in many cases. Technological advance is needed to reduce the amount of pollution created by each unit of output.

TOPICS FOR REVIEW

■ Short-run and long-run effects of investment and saving

■ The cumulative nature of growth

■ Benefits and costs of growth

■ The neoclassical aggregate production function

■ Balanced growth

■ Endogenous technical change

■ Increasing returns to investment

■ Embodied and disembodied technical change

■ The economics of goods and of ideas

■ Resource depletion and pollution

DISCUSSION QUESTIONS

1 GDP per head of population in the UK in 2001 was a little over £17,000. Supposing that there is no inflation and zero population growth, what will GDP per head be in 2011, 2021 and 2031 if the rate of economic growth continues at its long-term trend rate of 2 per cent per annum?

2 How would your answers to question 1 change if the average rate of growth over these periods rose to: (a) 3%; (b) 4%; (c) 5%?

3 Using the actual data for GDP growth in Table 21.4 on page 381 and the GDP per head figure for 2001 given in question 1, and assuming the same population as today, calculate the real GDP per head in 1900 (at 2001 prices). In reality, the UK population was about 41 million in 1900, while it had grown to about 58 million in 2001. Recalculate your figure for real GDP per head in 1900 using this information.

4 Outline some of the costs and benefits of economic growth.

5 What actions by (a) governments, (b) firms, and (c) individuals might increase the rate of economic growth?

6 What are the main determinants of economic growth?

7 List products that were not available when (a) your parents, and (b) you grandparents were born. What does the process of product innovation tell us about the nature of economic growth?

8 Must economic growth inevitably come to an end when various non-renewable energy (and commodity) sources are depleted?

Chapter 23

A BASIC MODEL OF THE DETERMINATION OF GDP IN THE SHORT RUN

In Chapter 22 we studied the determination of the growth of potential output or potential GDP. This can be thought of as the behaviour of GDP over the long term or long run. In the next several chapters we are going to build a model that explains the causes and consequences of deviations of GDP from its potential level. This is the behaviour of what we defined in Chapter 22 as the GDP gap. At some times GDP rises above its potential level, creating a negative GDP gap, and at other times it falls below it, creating a positive GDP gap. These variations can be thought of as the behaviour of GDP in the short term or short run. Because the first macroeconomic models of the economy were developed to explain this short-term behaviour of GDP, they are often called *macroeconomics* without qualification, and also *the theory of national income determination* also without qualification. But 'short term' should always be understood to apply to these models and theories. This is in contrast to growth theories, which deal with the determination of potential GDP over the long term. So when we speak of macroeconomics and the theory of the determination of national income below, we refer to *short-run macroeconomics* and *the theory of the determination of GDP gaps in the short run*.

Although the long-term economic health of nations is determined by the long-term growth of their potential GDPs, short-term deviations from the long-run trend also have important consequences. For example, the period in which the great UK economist, John Maynard Keynes, first developed macroeconomics was a period (the 1930s) when the actual GDPs of the industrialized countries stayed below their potential levels for almost a decade, with the consequence of massive levels of unemployment. In more recent times, actual GDP has several times stayed above its potential level for several years during which periods major inflations ensued. As a result, much of macroeconomic theory is devoted to examining the causes and consequences of such deviations. Also as a result, much economic policy is aimed at preventing the onset of the major bouts of unemployment and inflation that are associated with deviations of actual GDP from its potential, and in mitigating these consequences when they do occur.

So we are now going to build a model of how GDP is determined in relation to its potential level, which level we can take as given. This model will help us to study the forces that determine how actual GDP and the price level are determined from year to year. We seek to answer questions such as 'Why are there sometimes booms in activity and slowdowns at other times?' 'What happens to GDP when government spending is increased?' and 'Under what conditions do we get inflation?'

In this chapter, you will learn that:

• The macroeconomic theory that we now study explains the deviation of actual from potential GDP, that is the GDP gap.

• The determination of GDP in the short run depends on the behaviour of key categories of aggregate spending: consumption, investment, government spending, and net exports.

• Consumption spending depends on disposable income and wealth.

• Investment spending depends on real interest rates and business confidence.

• A necessary condition for GDP to be in equilibrium is that desired domestic spending equals actual output.

We start by setting out some of the conceptual foundations of the short-term analysis of macroeconomic activity. We then build the simplest possible model of GDP determination, under some very special assumptions. Later chapters make our model increasingly realistic.

The macro problem: inflation and unemployment

Actual economies do not expand slowly and steadily as the level of potential GDP grows. Instead, virtually all economies have some periods when actual GDP is growing faster than potential and other periods when it is growing more slowly than potential, or even falling. In other words, actual economies exhibit cycles about the trend growth path.

The growth rate of UK GDP since 1886 is shown in Figure 23.1 (and the GDP gap since 1970 is shown in Figure 22.1 on page 389). This makes clear that, while growth is generally positive, year-to-year changes in actual GDP are quite volatile. There are some periods of very strong positive growth and others when growth is negative. The terminology associated with such cycles in economic activity is set out in Box 23.1.

Periods of decline in actual GDP (or even periods where growth in actual GDP is below potential) are costly because they are associated with a loss of output that is gone for ever. This is what we have referred to above as a *deadweight loss*. Economic downturns do not typically lead to all citizens losing some equal amount of income. Rather, they lead to some people losing their jobs (or their businesses) and thus suffering a quite substantial loss of income and well-being. Unemployment is thus highly undesirable,

and all are agreed that policy-makers should aim to sustain unemployment at as low a level as possible. Indeed, macroeconomics as a subject was invented in order to explain why there was mass unemployment in the 1930s and to discover what could be done to eliminate it.

Another problem arises, however, when policy-makers try to make their economies grow too fast. This is especially so when governments try to encourage a growth of spending in the economy that is faster than the growth in productive capacity. The outcome of an excessive growth in demand relative to supply is that it generally causes inflation, and inflation itself is disruptive to the economy (for reasons that we discuss in Chapter 31).

Thus, the central problem for macroeconomic policy-makers is to decide how to manage the economy in such a way that inflation is kept under control while unemployment is also kept to a minimum.

This is not a trivial task, and many mistakes have been made in the past. Our aim in the next several chapters is to understand how the macroeconomic system works in the short term and what policy-makers can do to keep the economy stable, that is, as close to potential as possible.

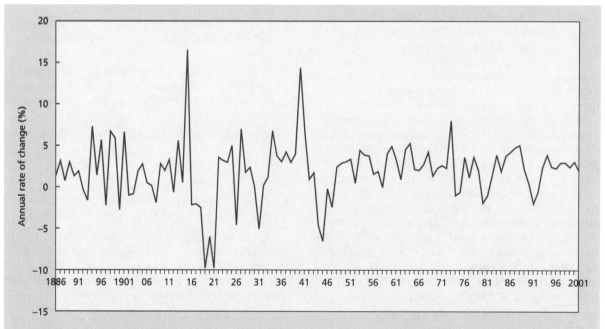

Figure 23.1 UK real GDP growth, 1886–2001

Actual growth in real GDP has displayed considerable volatility over time.

Source: 100 Years of economic statistics, The Economist, and UK National Accounts, ONS.

Box 23.1 **The terminology of business cycles**

The red line shows the hypothetical path of national output relative to trend, or potential, over time. Although the phases of business fluctuations are described by a series of commonly used terms, no two cycles are the same.

Trough A trough is characterized by high unemployment and a level of demand that is low in relation to the economy's capacity to produce. There is thus a substantial amount of unused productive capacity. Business profits are low; for some individual companies they are negative. Confidence about economic prospects in the immediate future is lacking, and as a result many firms are unwilling to risk making new investments.

Recovery The characteristics of a recovery, or expansion, are many—run-down equipment is replaced; employment, income, and consumer spending all begin to rise; and expectations become more favourable as a result of increases in production, sales, and profits. Investments that once seemed risky may be undertaken as the climate of business opinion starts to change from one of pessimism to one of optimism. As demand rises, production can be increased with relative ease merely by re-employing the existing unused capacity and unemployed labour.

Peak A peak is the top of a cycle. At the peak existing capacity is utilized to a high degree; labour shortages may develop, particularly in categories of key skills; and shortages of essential raw materials are likely. As shortages develop in more and more markets, a situation of general excess demand develops. Costs rise, but since prices also rise business remains profitable.

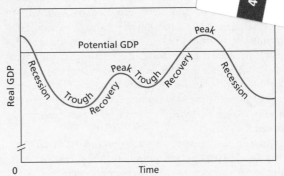

Recession A recession, or contraction, is a downturn in economic activity. Common usage defines a recession as a fall in real GDP for two quarters in succession. Demand falls off, and as a result production and employment also fall. As employment falls so do personal incomes. Profits drop, and some firms encounter financial difficulties. Investments that looked profitable with the expectation of continually rising demand now appear unprofitable. It may not even be worth replacing capital goods as they wear out, because unused capacity is increasing steadily. In historical discussions, a recession that is deep and long-lasting is often called a **depression**.

Booms and slumps Two non-technical but descriptive terms are often used. The bottom of an abnormally deep recession is called a *slump*, and the top of an abnormally strong recovery is called a *boom*.

Macroeconomics as theory

Our task is to understand what *causes* macroeconomic variables to behave as they do in the short term, and how they are interrelated. It is important to realize that we are about to discuss *theory*. In this process we will build up a conceptual model of the economy. This model will be simple. It needs to be simple so that we can understand how it works. This branch of macroeconomics has been around for well over half a century. It has developed and changed a great deal in this time. It is going to take several chapters before

we get close to understanding contemporary macroeconomics. Hence readers should be patient and not rush to draw policy conclusions too soon.

We will proceed by starting from a very simple structure and then adding features to it as we go along. Some clearly stated *assumptions* will define our macroeconomic model. Some of these assumptions will be relaxed as we go along, others will remain throughout. The permanent or temporary nature of individual assumptions will be indicated as they are introduced.

Key assumptions

In Chapter 21 we learned that 'national income' and 'national output' are the same thing, and can be measured by 'GDP'. From now on we will use these three terms equivalently. However, we refer to national income most frequently when discussing the determinants of domestic spending, as incomes are one of the most important determinants of consumers' spending. We refer to national output, or GDP, more commonly when discussing the

responses of producers to changes in spending. Remember, though, that the actual values of these three concepts are identical.[1]

[1] As we have seen, there is a small difference between GDP and GNI; however, we are now assuming that this difference can be ignored. Recall also that GNI used to be called GNP, but GNI became standard in the UK national accounts in 1998. You will no doubt see references to GNP in the economics literature for many years to come.

We also saw in Chapter 21 that we could arrive at a measure of GDP by three different routes. We could add up incomes of owners of resource inputs, we could add up the values added of each industrial sector, or we could add up total final spending. Now that we want to *explain* GDP determination rather than just describe it, we have to decide which of these three classifications we are going to rely on to structure our theories. We will learn very shortly that macroeconomics, as a subject, has developed by attempting to explain the major categories of final spending in the economy. We need to understand why this approach was adopted.

Suppose that we were to start our theory of GDP by trying to explain the net output (value added) of each major industrial sector—manufacturing, agriculture, etc.—as listed in Table 21.1. We could establish the capital stock and employment in each sector, and we could analyse demand forces for the output of each sector. In essence we would be building a theory around demand and supply forces in each industry in the economy, and we would then add up the results to get total output.

One reason we do not do this in macroeconomics is that such an approach would not really be dealing with the aggregate economy at all. Models that explain output industry by industry do exist in economics, but they are microeconomic and not generally regarded as part of macroeconomics. Such models require so much detail that they make it difficult to handle the many important issues that affect the whole economy simultaneously.

A second reason why we do not apply the tools of demand and supply on an industry-by-industry basis in macroeconomics is that the founders of macroeconomic theory thought that those tools were not appropriate for handling the most important macro problems. In particular, macroeconomics as a subject was originally invented to explain why an economy might have unemployment and excess capacity for some time. In contrast, the microeconomic analysis of markets suggests that prices will move to clear markets. Macroeconomists also want to be able to study simultaneous (or near simultaneous) movements in output that are common to all sectors—the business cycle. An important question in macroeconomics is 'What causes the cycle in GDP, and can government policy stabilize it, that is, smooth out the cycles?'

Aggregation across industries

In macroeconomics we take the industrial structure of the economy as fixed. When national output expands or contracts, all sectors expand and contract together. No consideration is given to relative prices of different goods or services. In this respect the economy is best thought of as being made up of many competitive firms, all producing the same type of product. These firms are all aggregated into a single productive sector. It is the behaviour of this sector that will determine national output and national income.

In macroeconomics we assume the existence of a single productive sector producing a homogeneous output.

This assumption will remain throughout our study of macroeconomics. We will also analyse the behaviour of this single sector as if it were a manufacturing industry, though this is only a matter of convenience.

The fact that we assume a single production sector explains why we approach the determination of GDP by focusing on spending categories: there are no subdivisions of output by type of product. However, an important implication for final spending is that *in our model* it is all spent on the same final good—the product of United Kingdom plc. This means that, while different categories of spending may be differently motivated, they all have the same effect once implemented.

From time to time we use concrete examples, such as 'suppose the government increases spending on road building', or 'suppose firms decide to buy more machines (invest)'. The point to bear in mind is that changes in spending of any type have the same effect. They are all demands for the output of the single-product industrial sector.

The government sector Confusion can arise out of the assumption of a single sector when we come to discuss the role of government. In reality, part of government activity involves producing goods and services, such as health and education. However, in order to maintain the simplicity of the assumption that there is only one sector, in macroeconomics we ignore the fact that government is a producer and treat government as a purchaser of the output of the private industrial sector. In other words, we make no exceptions to our assumption about the homogeneity of productive activity. Such exceptions can be accommodated, but we do not do so in this book.

Justification The extreme assumption that there is only one output is of course not meant as a description of reality. It is a theoretical abstraction, meant to simplify our study without losing the essence of the problem in which we are interested. In this case the one-product model captures the assumption that, for what we are interested in, the similarities between the effects of £1 spent in each sector of the real-world economy are more important than the differences. Note that it is only similarities with respect to the effects of spending that are in question. Causes of spending are not assumed to be the same. Indeed, much of our effort is directed to developing consumption, investment, and net export functions that explain the *different* motives that determine the various spending flows.

Time-scale

The part of macroeconomics that we are about to study has traditionally been concerned with the short-run behaviour of an economy, while growth theory has been concerned with long-run trends. It is important to note, however, that the concepts of 'short run' and 'long run' have a different meaning in macroeconomics from the usage in microeconomics. Indeed, 'long run' itself will be used in two different senses, even within macroeconomics.

Short run In microeconomics 'short run' is used to analyse the behaviour of firms during the period in which their capital stock is taken as given and they can change only their variable inputs (labour and materials). In other words, the short run is a period during which the capital stock is fixed; none the less, firms are in equilibrium because they are producing their optimal output given their capital stock. In macroeconomics the short run is the period during which the economy maintains a deviation of actual from potential output, or a GDP gap. This deviation is associated with the existence of either excess capacity and unemployment, in the case of recession, or unsustainable output and inflation, in the case of a boom. In practice, the short run may be measured in terms of several years, so it is not really short in the common sense meaning of the term.

In its early days as a discipline, macroeconomics concentrated entirely on the short run as we have just defined it. Recent developments, however, have increasingly emphasized longer-run considerations.

Analysis of the short run in macroeconomics is concerned with explaining why national output can deviate from its potential level. It is about the GDP gap and how to reduce it.

Long run The long run is a period sufficient to allow time for the automatic adjustment mechanisms (discussed below) to return economic activity to equilibrium after it has been disturbed by an exogenous shock. This equilibrium is reached when the economy returns to producing the level of potential (or full-employment) output. For analytical purposes, we will assume that the long-run level of output is constant and is associated with a fixed capital stock and a fixed level of technical knowledge. This contrasts markedly with the usage of 'long run' in microeconomics, where it relates to a period within which the capital stock can vary. Even in macroeconomics there is really a 'long run' and a 'longer run', where the latter permits growth in productive capacity and, therefore, growth in potential output. For the most part we use the static concept of long run, unless we are explicitly discussing growth, as in Chapters 22 and 34.

The long run in macroeconomics is the period it takes the economy to return to the level of potential GDP once it has been disturbed.

Temporary assumptions

In order to get us started in building a theory of macroeconomics, we need to make a few additional assumptions, but these will be relaxed in succeeding chapters.

The price level At the outset we will assume that the price level, that is the money price of the output good produced by the economy, is fixed. All input prices are also fixed. Permitting the price level to vary simultaneously with output will be the main task addressed in Chapters 25 and 26. While the price level is held constant, all variables must necessarily be measured in real terms. But it is important to notice for the future that all spending (consumption, investment, government spending, and net exports) will continue to be defined in real terms, even when the price level is permitted to vary.

Excess capacity Initially we will think of the economy as having excess capacity; it is not constrained from producing more output by shortages of capital stock or labour. One reason we make this assumption is that this is the context in which macroeconomics as a subject got started. It was trying to explain how an economy could get stuck (for some time at least) with high unemployment and excess capacity. When unemployment is approaching 20 per cent and GDP has fallen sharply, as in the early 1930s, this is a reasonable assumption to make. It would not be regarded as a reasonable assumption for analysing an economy at potential GDP and full employment.

Another reason we start with the twin assumptions of a fixed price level and excess capacity is that it is helpful to begin in an environment where all changes in GDP are changes in real GDP. Explaining how changes in money GDP are divided between changes in the price level and changes in real GDP requires a more complicated model, which we come to in Chapter 25.

Closed economy In this chapter alone we will ignore the fact that the output of our economy could be sold overseas and that domestic consumers could buy foreign-produced goods. We assume an economy with no foreign trade, so domestic spending and domestic output are the same thing. This is not an assumption we will need very long. It will be dropped in the next chapter.

No government Government enters into macroeconomics in two ways: first, through decisions relating to taxation and spending, and second, through the setting of interest rates. A final simplifying assumption in this chapter is that there is no government sector either demanding goods (spending) or raising money through taxes; but we will drop this assumption in the next chapter.

Interest rates are one of the most important tools by which modern governments control the macroeconomy.

Interest rates have their main impact via influencing various categories of private spending and asset prices. In this and subsequent chapters we point out the impact that interest rate changes have on private spending. In Chapter 28 we provide a comprehensive analysis of the transmission mechanism of monetary policy, that is, of how changes in interest rates affect the GDP gap and inflation. Throughout, we treat the official interest rate as determined by policy-makers outside our model.

It is worth summarizing all these assumptions. We have a closed economy with a single industrial sector, producing a homogeneous output, at a fixed price, with no government. There is also excess capacity, so there are no resource constraints preventing the expansion of national output. By now readers may be wondering what is left after we have assumed away so many potentially important things. The answer is: final demand or spending on the output of the economy. Explaining final spending will explain what determines the national product and national income, that is, GDP.

There is a good reason for starting with an explanation of spending. This is that the original inventors of macroeconomics believed that the explanation of recessions was to be found in *demand failure*. Hence they focused explicitly on categories of spending. The theory was not developed to explain the measured values of spending. Rather, the way in which we now measure these spending categories (see Table 21.2 on page 377) was influenced by the theory.

Accordingly, we now turn to the task of explaining aggregate spending.

What determines aggregate spending?

Before we can answer this question, we must deal with a few more important preliminaries.

Some important preliminaries

From actual to desired spending In Chapter 21 we discussed how statisticians divide actual GDP, calculated from the spending side, into its components: private consumption, investment, government consumption, and net exports.

In this chapter and the next we are concerned with a different concept. It is variously called *desired, planned*, or *intended* spending. Of course, all people would like to spend virtually unlimited amounts, if only they had the resources. Desired spending does not refer, however, to what people would like to do under imaginary circumstances: it refers to what people want to spend out of the resources that are at their command. The *actual* values of the various categories of spending are indicated by C^a, I^a, G^a, and $(X^a - IM^a)$. We use the same letters without the superscript *a* to indicate the *desired* spending in the same categories: $C, I, G,$ and $(X - IM)$.

Everyone with income to spend makes spending decisions. Fortunately it is unnecessary for our purposes to look at each of the millions of such individual decisions. Instead, it is sufficient to consider four main groups of decision-makers: individual consumers (or households), firms, governments, and foreign purchasers of domestic output. The actual purchases made by these four groups account for the four main categories of spending that we studied in the previous chapter: private consumption, investment, government consumption, and net exports. These groups' desired spending—desired private consumption, desired investment, desired government consumption, and desired exports—account for total desired spending. (To allow for the fact that many of the commodities desired by each group have an import content, we subtract spending on imports to arrive at the value of spending on domestic output.) The result is total desired spending on domestically produced goods and services, called **aggregate spending**, or AE:[2]

$$AE = C + I + G + (X - IM).$$

Desired spending need not equal actual spending, either in total or in any individual category. For example, firms may not *plan* to invest in the accumulation of unsold stock this year but may do so unintentionally. If they produce goods to meet estimated sales but demand is unexpectedly low, the unsold goods that pile up on their shelves are undesired, and unintended, inventory accumulation. In this case actual investment spending, I^a, exceeds desired investment spending, I.

> The national accounts measure actual spending in each of the four categories: private consumption, investment, government consumption, and net exports. The theory of GDP determination deals with desired spending in each of these four categories.

Recall, however, that these spending categories differ because different agents are doing the spending and have different motivations for that spending. They are not different in the effects of their spending, because they all generate spending on the final output of the single productive sector.

---

[2] We use AE, which is short for 'aggregate expenditure', as we reserve AS to refer to 'aggregate supply'.

Autonomous and induced spending In what follows it will be useful to distinguish between *autonomous* and *induced* spending. Components of aggregate spending that *do not* depend on current domestic incomes are called **autonomous**, or sometimes *exogenous*.[3] Autonomous spending can and does change, but such changes do not occur systematically in response to changes in income. Components of aggregate spending that *do* change in response to changes in income are called **induced**, or *endogenous*. As we will see, the induced response of aggregate spending to a change in income plays a key role in the determination of equilibrium GDP.

A simple model To develop a theory of GDP determination, we need to examine the determinants of each component of desired aggregate spending. In this chapter we focus on desired consumption and desired investment. Private consumption is the largest single component of aggregate spending (about 64 per cent of UK GDP in 2001), and, as we will see, it provides the single most important link between desired aggregate spending and actual GDP. Investment is national output that is not used either for current consumption or by governments, and it is motivated by firms' desire to increase the capital stock.[4]

Desired private consumption spending

We are now ready to study the determinants of desired spending flows. We start with private consumption.

People can do one of two things with their disposable income: spend it on consumption, or save it. **Saving** is all disposable income that is not consumed.

By definition there are only two possible uses of disposable income: consumption and saving. So when each individual decides how much to put to one use, he or she has automatically decided how much to put to the other use.

What determines the division between the amount that people decide to spend on goods and services for consumption and the amount that they decide to save? The factors that influence this decision are summarized in the consumption function and the saving function.

The consumption function

The **consumption function** relates the total desired consumption spending of the personal sector to the factors that determine it. It is, as we will see, one of the central relationships in macroeconomics.

Although we are interested ultimately in the relationship between consumption and *national* income (GDP), the underlying behaviour of consumers depends on the income that they actually have to spend—their disposable income. Under the simplifying assumptions that we have

made in this chapter, there are no taxes. Individuals receive all income that is generated.[5] Therefore, disposable income, which we denote by Y_d, is equal to national income, Y. (Later in our discussion Y and Y_d will diverge, because taxes are a part of national income that is not at the disposal of individuals.)

Consumption and disposable income

It should not surprise us to hear that a consumer's spending is related to the amount of income available. There is, however, more than one way in which this relationship could work. To see what is involved, consider two quite different types of individual.

The first behaves like the proverbial prodigal son. He spends everything he receives and puts nothing aside for a rainy day. When overtime results in a large pay cheque, he goes on a binge. When it is hard to find work during periods of slack demand, his pay cheque is small and spending has to be cut correspondingly. This person's spending each week is thus directly linked to each week's take-home pay, that is to his current disposable income.

The second individual is a prudent planner. She thinks about the future as much as the present, and makes plans that stretch over her lifetime. She puts money aside for retirement and for the occasional rainy day when disposable income may fall temporarily—she knows that she must expect some hard times as well as good times. She also knows that she will need to spend extra money while her children are being raised and educated and that her disposable income will probably be highest later in life when the children have left home and she has finally reached the peak of her career. This person may borrow to meet higher expenses earlier in life, paying back out of the higher income that she expects to attain later in life. A temporary, unexpected windfall of income may be saved. Spending the savings that were put aside for just such a rainy day may cushion a temporary, unexpected shortfall. In short, this person's current spending will be closely related to her expected average *lifetime income*. Fluctuations in her *current income* will have little effect on her current spending, unless such fluctuations also cause her to change her expectations of lifetime income—as would be the case, for example, if an unexpected promotion came along.

John Maynard Keynes (1883–1946), the famous English economist who developed the basic theory of macroeconomics—and gave his name to 'Keynesian economics'—

---

[3] 'Autonomous' means self-motivated, or independent. 'Exogenous' means determined outside the model.

[4] In practice, government and consumers are responsible for some of the nation's investment, but for simplicity we focus mainly on the investment behaviour of firms. The principles involved can be generalized.

[5] We are assuming here that all firms pass on all their profits to the people who own them, so there is no retained profit.

populated his theory with prodigal sons. For them current consumption spending depended only on current income. To this day, a consumption function based on this assumption is called a *Keynesian consumption function*.

Later two US economists, Franco Modigliani and Milton Friedman, both of whom were subsequently awarded the Nobel Prize in economics, analysed the behaviour of prudent consumers who take a longer-term view in determining their consumption. Their theories, which Modigliani called the *life-cycle theory* and Friedman called *the permanent-income theory*, explain some observed consumer behaviour that cannot be explained by the Keynesian consumption function. Most modern approaches to private consumption behaviour are based upon the life-cycle or permanent-income approaches, in which rational consumers plan their consumption over a broad time-horizon, and may even build in plans to leave money to their children (thus planning consumption *beyond* their own lifetimes).

However, the differences between the modern theories and the Keynesian consumption function are not as great as they might seem at first sight. To understand why this is so, let us return to our two imaginary individuals and see why their actual behaviour may not be quite so divergent as we have described it.

Even the prodigal son may be able to do some smoothing of spending in the face of income fluctuations. Most people have some money in the bank and some ability to borrow, even if it is just from friends and relatives. As a result, not every income fluctuation will be matched by an equivalent spending fluctuation.

In contrast, although the prudent person wants to smooth her pattern of consumption completely, she may not have the borrowing capacity to do so. Her bank may not be willing to lend money for consumption when the security consists of nothing more than the expectation that income will be much higher in later years. This may mean that in practice her consumption spending fluctuates more with her current income than she would wish.

This suggests that the consumption spending of both types of individual will fluctuate to some extent with their current disposable incomes and to some extent with their expectations of future disposable income. Moreover, in any economy there will be some people of both extremes, spendthrifts and planners, and a mix of the two types will determine aggregate consumption. As we develop our basic theory, we will often find it useful to make the simplifying assumption that consumption spending is determined primarily by current disposable income. That is, we will often use a Keynesian consumption function and then indicate how things change if we consider more sophisticated theories of consumer spending. Figure 23.2 shows real personal disposable income and real consumers' spending in the UK from 1955 to 2002. It is clear that the two series are closely related.

The term 'consumption function' describes the relationship between private consumption and the variables that influence it. In the simplest theory, consumption is determined primarily by current personal disposable income.

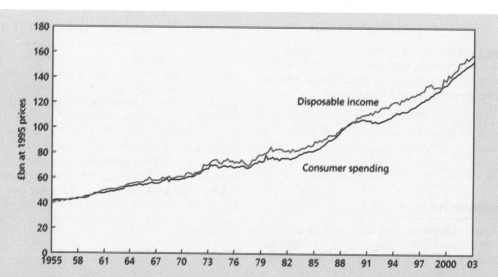

Figure 23.2 Consumers' spending and personal disposable income, UK, quarterly, 1955–2002 (£ bn at constant 1995 prices, seasonally adjusted)

Consumer spending and income are closely related over time.

Source: ONS.

[handwritten top margin:] disposable Income (Y_d)

Table 23.1 The calculation of average and marginal propensity to consume (APC and MPC) (£ million)

Disposable income (Y_d) (1)	Desired consumption (C) (2)	$APC = C/Y_d$ (3)	Change in Y_d (ΔY_d) (4)	Change in C (ΔC) (5)	$MPC = \Delta C/\Delta Y_d$ (6)
0	100	—			
			100	80	0.80
100	180	1.800			
			300	240	0.80
400	420	1.050			
			100	80	0.80
500	500	1.000			
			500	400	0.80
1,000	900	0.900			
			500	400	0.80
1,500	1,300	0.867			
			250	200	0.80
1,750	1,500	0.857			
			250	200	0.80
2,000	1,700	0.850			
			1,000	800	0.80
3,000	2,500	0.833			

APC measures the proportion of disposable income that households desire to spend on consumption; MPC measures the proportion of any increment to disposable income that households desire to spend on consumption. The data are hypothetical. We call the level of income at which desired consumption equals disposable income the break-even level; in this example it is £500 million. APC, calculated in the third column, exceeds unity—that is, consumption exceeds income—below the break-even level; above the break-even level APC is less than unity. It is negatively related to income at all levels of income. The last three columns are set between the lines of the first three columns to indicate that they refer to *changes* in the levels of income and consumption. MPC, calculated in the last column, is constant at 0.80 at all levels of Y_d. This indicates that, in this example, £0.80 of every additional £1.00 of disposable income is spent on consumption, and £0.20 is used to increase saving.

When income is zero, a typical individual will still (via borrowing, or drawing down savings) consume some minimal amount.[6] This level of consumption spending is *autonomous* because it persists even when there is no income. The higher a person's income, the more he will want to consume. This part of consumption is *induced*; that is, it varies with disposable income and hence, in our simple model, with national income (GDP).

Consider the schedule relating personal disposable income to desired private consumption spending for a hypothetical economy that appears in the first two columns of Table 23.1. In this example autonomous consumption spending is £100 million, whereas induced consumption spending is 80 per cent of disposable income. In what follows we use this hypothetical example to illustrate the various properties of the consumption function.

Average and marginal propensities to consume To discuss the consumption function concisely, economists use two technical expressions.

The **average propensity to consume (APC)** is total consumption spending divided by total disposable income: $APC = C/Y_d$. The third column of Table 23.1 shows the APC calculated from the data in the table. Note that APC falls as disposable income rises.

[handwritten:] $APC = \dfrac{C}{Y_d}$

The **marginal propensity to consume (MPC)** relates the *change* in consumption to the *change* in disposable income that brought it about. MPC is the change in disposable income divided into the resulting consumption change: $MPC = \Delta C/\Delta Y_d$ (where the capital Greek letter delta, Δ,

[handwritten:] 平均 MPC

[handwritten bottom:] $MPC = \dfrac{\partial C}{\Delta Y_d}$

means 'a change in'). The last column of Table 23.1 shows the MPC that corresponds to the data in the table. Note that, by construction, MPC is constant.

The slope of the consumption function Part (i) of Figure 23.3 shows a graph of the consumption function, derived by plotting consumption against income using data from the first two columns of Table 23.1. The consumption function has a slope of $\Delta C/\Delta Y_d$, which by definition is the marginal propensity to consume. The positive slope of the consumption function shows that the MPC is positive; increases in income lead to increases in spending.

Using the concepts of average and marginal propensities to consume, we can summarize the assumed properties of the short-term consumption function as follows:

1. There is a break-even level of income at which APC equals unity ($APC = 1$). Below this level APC is greater than unity; above it APC is less than unity. Below the break-even level consumption exceeds income, so consumers run down savings or borrow. Above the break-even level income exceeds consumption, so there is positive saving.

[6] Many individuals have no income but continue to consume, for example dependent children or non-working partners. In this case there is normally at least one earner in a household and it is the household income that is relevant. The household would be the decision unit in that context. Such distinctions are important if we want to study the behaviour of individual spending units, but they are not critical in macroeconomics, which studies the aggregate behaviour of all consumers and relates their total spending to their total income.

$$APS = \frac{S}{Y_d}$$

$$MPS = \frac{\Delta S}{\Delta Y_d}$$

2. MPC is greater than zero, but less than unity, for all levels of income. This means that, for each additional £1 of income, less than £1 is spent on consumption and the rest is saved. For a straight-line consumption function, the MPC is constant at all levels of income.

The 45° line Figure 23.3(i) contains a line that is constructed by connecting all points where desired consump-tion (measured on the vertical axis) equals disposable income (measured on the horizontal axis). Because both axes are given in the same units, this line has a positive slope of unity; that is, it forms an angle of 45° with the axes. The line is therefore called the **45° line**.

The 45° line makes a handy reference line. In part (i) of Figure 23.3 it helps to locate the break-even level of income at which consumption spending equals disposable income. The consumption function cuts the 45° line at the break-even level of income, in this instance £500 million. (The 45° line is steeper than the consumption function because MPC is less than unity.)

The saving function

Individuals decide how much to consume and how much to save. As we have said, this is a single decision: how to divide disposable income between consumption and saving. It follows that, once we know the dependence of consumption on disposable income, we also automatically know the dependence of saving on disposable income. (This is illustrated in Table 23.2.)

There are two saving concepts that are exactly parallel to the consumption concepts of APC and MPC. The **average propensity to save (APS)** is the proportion of disposable income that households want to save, derived by dividing total desired saving by total disposable income: $APS = S/Y_d$. The **marginal propensity to save (MPS)** relates the *change* in total desired saving to the *change* in disposable income that brought it about: $MPS = \Delta S/\Delta Y_d$.

There is a simple relationship between the saving and consumption propensities. APC and APS must sum to unity, and so must MPC and MPS. Because income is either spent or saved, it follows that the fractions of incomes consumed and saved must account for all income ($APC + APS = 1$).

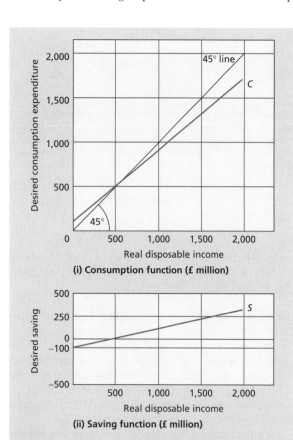

(i) Consumption function (£ million)

(ii) Saving function (£ million)

Figure 23.3 The consumption and saving functions

Both consumption and saving rise as disposable income rises. Line C in part (i) relates desired consumption spending to disposable income by using the hypothetical data from Table 23.1. Its slope, $\Delta C/\Delta Y_d$, is the marginal propensity to consume (MPC). The consumption line cuts the 45° line at the break-even level of disposable income, £500 million in this case. Note that the level of autonomous consumption is £100 million.

Saving is all disposable income that is not spent on consumption ($S = Y_d - C$). The relationship between desired saving and disposable income is derived in Table 23.2, and it is shown in part (ii) by line S. Its slope, $\Delta S/\Delta Y_d$, is the marginal propensity to save (MPS). The saving line cuts the horizontal axis at the break-even level of income. The vertical distance between C and the 45° line in part (i) is by definition the height of S in part (ii); that is, any given level of disposable income must be accounted for by the amount consumed plus the amount saved. Note that the level of autonomous saving is –£100 million. This means that at zero income consumers will draw down existing assets by £100 million a year or will borrow this amount.

Table 23.2 Consumption and saving schedules (£ million)

Disposable income	Desired consumption	Desired saving
0	100	−100
100	180	−80
400	420	−20
500	500	0
1,000	900	+100
1,500	1,300	+200
1,750	1,500	+250
2,000	1,700	+300
3,000	2,500	+500
4,000	3,300	+700

Saving and consumption account for all household disposable income. The first two columns repeat the data from Table 23.1. The third column, desired saving, is disposable income minus desired consumption. Consumption and saving both increase steadily as disposable income rises. In this example the break-even level of income is £500 million. At this level all income is consumed.

It also follows that the fractions of any increment to income consumed and saved must account for all of that increment ($MPC + MPS = 1$). Calculations from Table 23.2 will allow you to confirm these relationships in the case of the example given. MPC is 0.80 and MPS is 0.20 at all levels of income, while, for example, at an income of £2,000 million, APC is 0.85 and APS is 0.15.

Figure 23.3(ii) shows the saving schedule given in Table 23.2. At the break-even level of income, where desired consumption equals disposable income, desired saving is zero. The slope of the saving line $\Delta S/\Delta Y_d$ is equal to the MPS.

Wealth and the consumption function

The Keynesian consumption function that we have been analysing can easily be combined with the permanent-income or life-cycle theories of consumption. According to these theories, households save in order to accumulate wealth that they can use during their retirement (or pass on to their heirs[7]). Suppose that there is an unexpected rise in wealth. This will mean that less of current disposable income needs to be saved for the future, and it will tend to cause a larger fraction of disposable income to be spent on consumption and a smaller fraction to be saved. Thus, the consumption function will be shifted upward and the saving function downward, as shown in Figure 23.4. A fall in wealth increases the incentive to save in order to restore wealth. This shifts the consumption function downward and the saving function upward.

The interest rate and consumer spending

Higher interest rates will generally lead to lower consumer spending. Higher interest rates encourage saving, as the rewards for saving are increased. Higher interest rates also discourage borrowing, as the cost of credit rises. Many households have purchased houses with borrowed money in the form of a mortgage. Most mortgages in the UK have a variable interest rate, so that monthly mortgage payments will increase as interest rates increase. Higher mortgage payments will thus leave less out of any given income for spending on current consumption. Higher interest rates also tend to lead to lower asset values (for reasons we discuss in Chapter 28), and this then generates a fall in wealth that lowers consumption as discussed above.

When we fully incorporate interest rates into our model in Chapter 28, we will have the main impact running from interest rates to investment. But it is also consistent with our analysis to think of higher interest rates as lowering autonomous consumption.[8]

Desired investment spending

Investment spending is the most volatile component of GDP, and changes in investment spending are strongly

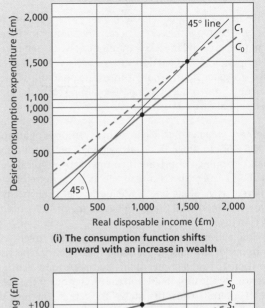

(i) The consumption function shifts upward with an increase in wealth

(ii) The saving function shifts downward

Figure 23.4 Wealth and the consumption function

Changes in wealth shift the consumption function. In part (i) line C_0 reproduces the consumption function from Figure 23.3(i). An increase in the level of wealth raises desired consumption at each level of disposable income, thus shifting the consumption line up to C_1. In the figure the consumption function shifts up by £200 million; so with disposable income of £1,000 million, for example, desired consumption rises from £900 million to £1,100 million. As a result of the rise in wealth, the break-even level of income rises to £1,500 million.

The saving function in part (ii) shifts down by £200 million from S_0 to S_1. Thus, for example, at a disposable income of £1,000 million, saving *falls* from +£100 million to −£100 million.

associated with economic fluctuations. For example, the Great Depression witnessed a major fall in investment. Total investment fell by nearly a quarter between 1929 and 1932. A little less dramatically, at the trough of the UK recession of the early 1990s (in 1992), investment spending was 13 per cent less than the level two years earlier.

[7] Empirical evidence suggests that there is a significant 'bequest motive' for saving. This means that some individuals plan even further ahead than their own lifetime, because they want to leave money to their children.

[8] UK monetary policy-makers' own perception of how monetary policy works also includes an effect of interest rates working on consumer spending (see the appendix to Chapter 30).

Investment and the real interest rate

Other things being equal, the higher is the real interest rate,[9] the higher is the cost of borrowing money for investment purposes and the less is the amount of desired investment spending. This relationship is most easily understood if we disaggregate investment into three parts: inventory accumulation, residential house building, and business fixed capital formation.[10]

Inventory accumulation Changes in inventories of finished goods, work in progress, or raw materials represent only a small percentage of private investment in a typical year, but their average size is not an adequate measure of their importance. They are one of the more volatile elements of total investment and therefore have a major influence on shifts in investment spending.

When a firm ties up funds by holding bigger inventories of inputs or outputs, those same funds cannot be used elsewhere to earn income. As an alternative to investing in inventories, the firm could lend the money out at the going rate of interest. Thus, the higher the rate of interest, the higher will be the opportunity cost of holding inventories of a given size; the higher that opportunity cost, the smaller the inventories that will be desired.

The higher the real rate of interest, the lower is the desired inventory of goods and materials. Changes in the rate of interest cause temporary bouts of investment (or disinvestment) in inventories.

Residential housing construction Spending on new houses is also volatile. Because spending for housing construction is both large and variable, it exerts a major impact on the economy. Notice that what matters for investment is the demand for new housing. House purchases that involve the exchange of ownership of an existing house do not affect the demand for currently produced output and are, therefore, not relevant to determining current GDP.

Most houses are purchased with money that is borrowed by means of a mortgage. Interest on the borrowed money typically accounts for over half of the purchaser's annual mortgage payments; the rest is repayment of the original loan, called the principal. Because interest payments are so large a part of mortgage payments, variations in interest rates exert a substantial effect on the demand for housing. During the mid-1980s UK interest rates fell sharply and there was a boom in the demand for housing; that boom persisted until late 1988, when interest rates started to rise again. The housing market then collapsed and house prices fell. The lower interest rates that arrived in 1992 and 1993 permitted the beginning of a recovery in the housing market; however, it was very slow and house prices did not pick up until the second half of the 1990s. In the 2000–02 period, however, interest rates again fell to low levels and a further house price boom ensued.

Spending for residential construction tends to vary negatively with interest rates.

Business fixed capital formation Investment by firms in fixed capital (factories, offices, and machines) is the largest component of domestic investment. Over one-half of such investment is financed by firms' retained profits (profits that are not paid out to their shareholders). This means that current profits are an important determinant of investment.

The rate of interest is also a major determinant of investment. In the United Kingdom, both in the early 1980s and during 1989–92, high interest rates greatly reduced the volume of investment, as more and more firms found that their expected profits from investment did not cover the interest on borrowed investment funds. Other firms who had cash on hand found that purchasing interest-earning assets provided a better return than investment in factories and machinery. For them the increase in real interest rates meant that the opportunity cost of investing in fixed capital had risen. The monetary authority sets short-term interest rates. In the UK case, this is the Monetary Policy Committee of the Bank of England. We analyse monetary policy-making more fully in Chapter 28.

Expectations and business confidence

Investment takes time. When a firm invests, it increases its future capacity to produce output. If the new output can be sold profitably, the investment will prove to be a good one. If the new output does not generate profits, the investment will be a bad one. When the investment is undertaken, the firm does not know if it will turn out well or badly—it is betting on a favourable future that cannot be known with certainty.

When firms expect good times ahead, they will want to invest in order to reap future profits. When they expect bad times, they will not invest because, given their expectations, there would be no payoff from doing so. For future reference, it is worth noting that one of the influences on firms' expectations and confidence will be the actions and credibility of the government and monetary policy-makers.

---

[9] The *real* rate of interest is approximately equal to the nominal (money) rate of interest minus the expected rate of inflation.

[10] These represent different motives for investment, and in practice would create demand for different kinds of goods. However, recall that they will all end up creating demand for the output of the single production sector. Thus, in our model, the impact of £1 worth of inventory accumulation is the same as £1 worth of fixed capital formation and, indeed, of £1 worth of consumption. The reason we distinguish investment from consumption is that it is affected by different factors, the most important of which will be the interest rate. Note also that house building is part of gross fixed capital formation in the national accounts. We ignore here the net acquisition of valuables, as this is very small.

Business investment depends in part on firms' forecasts of the future state of the economy.

Investment as autonomous spending

We have seen that many things influence investment. For the moment we treat investment as exogenous, meaning only that it is not influenced by changes in GDP. But obviously, the policy-determined rate of interest is one of the things that could make investment change. The treatment of investment as exogenous allows us to study, first, how GDP is determined when there is an unchanged amount of desired investment spending and, second, how alterations in the amount of desired investment cause changes in equilibrium GDP.

The aggregate spending function

The aggregate spending function relates the level of desired real spending to the level of real national income, that is, real GDP. Generally, total desired spending on the nation's output is the sum of desired private consumption, investment, government consumption, and net export spending. In the simplified economy of this chapter, aggregate spending is just equal to $C + I$:

$$AE = C + I.$$

Table 23.3 shows how the AE function is calculated, given the consumption function of Tables 23.1 and 23.2 and a constant level of desired investment of £250 million. In this specific case all of investment spending is autonomous, as is the £100 million of consumption that would be desired when national income is zero (see Table 23.1). Total autonomous spending is thus £350 million—induced spending is just equal to induced consumption, which is equal to $0.8Y$. Thus, desired aggregate spending, whether thought of as $C + I$ or as autonomous plus induced spending, can be written as $AE = £350$ million $+ 0.8Y$. This aggregate spending function is illustrated in Figure 23.5.

The propensity to spend out of national income The fraction of any increment to national income (GDP) that will be spent on purchasing domestic output is called the economy's **marginal propensity to spend**. It is measured by the change in aggregate spending divided by the change in income, or $\Delta AE/\Delta Y$, the slope of the aggregate spending function. In this book we will denote the marginal propensity to spend by the symbol z, which will typically be a number greater than zero and less than one.

Similarly, the **marginal propensity not to spend** is the fraction of any increment to national income that does not add to desired aggregate spending. This is denoted $(1 - z)$—if z is the part of any £1 of incremental income that

Table 23.3 The aggregate spending function in a closed economy with no government (£ million)

GDP (national income) (Y)	Desired consumption spending ($C = 100 + 0.8Y$)	Desired investment spending ($I = 250$)	Desired aggregate spending ($AE = C + I$)
100	180	250	430
400	420	250	670
500	500	250	750
1,000	900	250	1,150
1,500	1,300	250	1,550
1,750	1,500	250	1,750
2,000	1,700	250	1,950
3,000	2,500	250	2,750
4,000	3,300	250	3,550

The aggregate spending function is the sum of desired consumption, investment, government, and net export spending. In this table government and net exports are assumed to be zero, investment is assumed to be constant at £250 million, and desired consumption is based on the hypothetical data given in Table 23.2. The autonomous components of desired aggregate spending are desired investment and the constant term in desired consumption spending (£100 million). The induced component is the second term in desired consumption spending $0.8Y$.

The marginal response of consumption to a change in national income is 0.8, the marginal propensity to consume. The marginal response of desired aggregate spending to a change in national income, $\Delta AE/\Delta Y$, is also 0.8, because all induced spending in the economy is consumption spending.

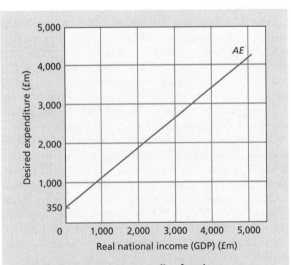

Figure 23.5 An aggregate spending function

The aggregate spending function relates total desired spending to national income. The *AE* line in the figure plots the data from the first and the last columns of Table 23.3, which are repeated in Table 23.4. Its intercept (which in this case is £350 million) shows autonomous spending, which in this case is the sum of autonomous consumption of £100 million and investment of £250 million. Its slope (which in this case is 0.8) shows the marginal propensity to spend.

is spent, then $(1 - z)$ is the part that is not spent.[11] In the example given in Table 23.3, z, the marginal propensity to spend, is 0.8. If national income increases by £1, then 80p will go into increased spending. Twenty pence (£1 × 0.2, the value of $(1 - z)$) will go into increased saving and will not be spent.

The marginal propensity to spend, which we have just defined, should not be confused with the marginal propensity to consume, which we defined earlier in the chapter. The marginal propensity to spend is the amount of extra total spending induced when *national* income rises by £1,

while the marginal propensity to consume is the amount of extra consumption spending induced when *personal disposable income* rises by £1. In the simple model of this chapter, the marginal propensity to spend is equal to the marginal propensity to consume, and the marginal propensity not to spend is equal to the marginal propensity to save. In later chapters, when we add government and the international sector, the marginal propensity to spend differs from the marginal propensity to consume. Both here and in later chapters, it is the more general measures z and $(1 - z)$ that are important for determining equilibrium GDP.

Equilibrium GDP

We are now ready to see what determines the *equilibrium* level of national income and output, that is, GDP. When something is in equilibrium, there is no tendency for it to change; forces are acting on it, but they balance out, and the net result is *no change*. Any conditions that are required for something to be in equilibrium are called *equilibrium conditions*. Here we determine the level of GDP that is consistent with spending decisions; we will discover the full story about GDP determination only after we have added the supply behaviour of firms (Chapters 25 and 26). Thus, the conditions we analyse here are necessary for an equilibrium of GDP, but others will contribute to determine the total picture later.

Table 23.4 illustrates the determination of equilibrium GDP for our simple hypothetical economy. Suppose that firms are producing a final output of £1,000 million, and thus GDP is £1,000 million. According to the table, at this level of national income aggregate desired spending is £1,150 million. If firms persist in producing a current output of only £1,000 million in the face of an aggregate desired spending of £1,150 million, one of two things must happen.[12]

One possibility is that consumers and investors will be unable to spend the extra £150 million that they would like to spend, so queues and unfulfilled order books will appear. These will send a signal to firms that they can increase their sales if they increase their production. When the firms increase production, GDP rises. Of course, the individual firms are interested only in their own sales and profits, but their individual actions have as their inevitable consequence an increase in GDP.

The second possibility is that consumers and investors will spend everything that they want to spend. Then, however, spending will exceed current output, which can happen only when some spending plans are fulfilled by purchasing stocks of goods that were produced in the past. In our example, the fulfilment of plans to purchase £1,150 million worth of commodities in the face of a current output of only £1,000 million will reduce inventories

Table 23.4 The determination of equilibrium GDP (£ million)

GDP (national income) (Y)	Desired aggregate spending ($AE = C + I$)	
100	430	
400	670	
500	750	Pressure on Y
1,000	1,150	to rise
1,500	1,550	↓
1,750	**1,750**	**Equilibrium Y**
2,000	1,950	↑
3,000	2,750	Pressure on Y
4,000	3,550	to fall

GDP is in equilibrium where aggregate desired spending equals national output. The data are copied from Table 23.3. When GDP is below its equilibrium level, aggregate desired spending exceeds the value of current output. This creates an incentive for firms to increase output and hence for GDP to rise. When GDP is above its equilibrium level, aggregate desired spending is less than the value of current output. This creates an incentive for firms to reduce output and hence for GDP to fall. Only at the equilibrium level of GDP is aggregate desired spending equal to the value of current output.

by £150 million. As long as stocks last, more goods can be sold than are currently being produced.[13]

[11] More fully, these terms would be called the marginal propensity to spend *on the national product* and the marginal propensity not to spend *on the national product*. The marginal propensity not to spend, $(1 - z)$, is sometimes referred to as the *marginal propensity to withdraw*. Not spending some part of income amounts to a *withdrawal* or a *leakage* from the circular flow of income, as illustrated in Box 22.3 on page 373.

[12] A third possibility—that prices could rise—is ruled out by assumption in this chapter.

[13] Notice that in this example actual national income (GDP) is equal to £1,000 million. Desired consumption is £900 million and desired investment is £250 million, but the reduction of inventories by £150 million is unplanned negative investment; thus, actual investment is only £100 million.

Eventually stocks will run out. But before this happens, firms will increase their output as they see their sales increase. Extra sales can then be made without a further depletion of inventories. Once again the consequence of each individual firm's behaviour, in search of its own individual profits, is an increase in the national product and national income. Thus, the final response to an excess of aggregate desired spending over current output is a rise in GDP.

At any level of GDP at which aggregate desired spending exceeds total output, there will be pressure for GDP to rise.

Next, consider the £4,000 million level of GDP in Table 23.4. At this level desired spending on domestically produced goods is only £3,550 million. If firms persist in producing £4,000 million worth of goods, £450 million worth must remain unsold. Therefore, stocks of unsold goods must rise. However, firms will not allow unsold goods to accumulate indefinitely; sooner or later they will reduce the level of output to the level of sales. When they do, GDP will fall.

At any level of GDP for which aggregate desired spending is less than total output, there will be pressure for GDP to fall.

Finally, look at the GDP level of £1,750 million in Table 23.4. At this level, and only at this level, aggregate desired spending is equal to national output (GDP). Purchasers can fulfil their spending plans without causing inventories to change. There is no incentive for firms to alter output. Because everyone wishes to purchase an amount equal to what is being produced, output and income will remain steady; GDP is in equilibrium.

The equilibrium level of GDP occurs where aggregate desired spending equals total output.

This conclusion is quite general and does not depend on the numbers that are used in the specific example.

Figure 23.6 shows the determination of the equilibrium level of GDP. In the figure the line labelled 'AE' graphs the aggregate spending function given by the first and last columns of Table 23.3, also shown in Table 23.4. The line labelled '45° line $(AE = Y)$' graphs the equilibrium condition that aggregate desired spending equals national output. Since in equilibrium the variables measured on the two axes must be equal, the line showing this equality is a 45° line. Anywhere along that line the value of desired spending, which is measured on the vertical axis, is equal to the value of national output, which is measured on the horizontal axis.[14]

Graphically, equilibrium occurs at the level of GDP at which the aggregate desired spending line intersects the 45° line. This is the level of GDP at which desired spending is just equal to total national output and therefore is just sufficient to purchase that output. Exactly the same

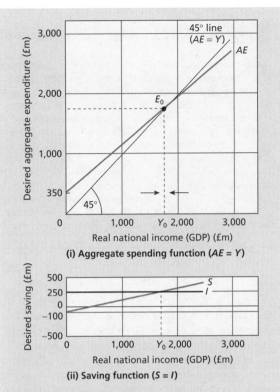

(i) Aggregate spending function ($AE = Y$)

(ii) Saving function ($S = I$)

Figure 23.6 Equilibrium GDP

Equilibrium GDP occurs at E_0, where the desired aggregate spending line intersects the 45° line. If real GDP is below Y_0, desired aggregate spending will exceed national output, and production will rise. This is shown in part (i) by the arrow to the left of Y_0. If GDP is above Y_0, desired aggregate spending will be less than national output, and production will fall. This is shown by the arrow to the right of Y_0. Only when real GDP is Y_0 will desired aggregate spending equal real national output.

When saving is the only withdrawal and investment is the only injection, the equilibrium Y_0 is also the level of GDP at which saving equals investment, shown in part (ii). At levels of GDP greater than Y_0 saving exceeds investment (withdrawals exceed injections), so aggregate spending is less than output and the economy contracts. At levels of GDP below Y_0, investment exceeds saving (injections exceed withdrawals), so spending exceeds output and the level of GDP increases. Parts (i) and (ii) are just two different ways of looking at the same phenomenon.

[14] Because it turns up in many different guises, the 45° line can cause a bit of confusion until one gets used to it. The main thing about it is that it can be used whenever the variables plotted on the two axes are measured in the same units, such as pounds, and are plotted on the same scale. In that case equal distances on the two axes measure the same amounts. One centimetre may, for example, correspond to £1,000 on each axis. In such circumstances the 45° line joins all points where the values of the two variables are the same. In Figures 23.3 and 23.4 the 45° line shows all points where *desired consumption spending in real terms* equals *real disposable income*, because these are the two variables that are plotted on the two axes. In Figure 23.6 and all those that follow it, the 45° line shows all points at which *desired total spending in real terms* equals *real national output (GDP)*, because those are the variables that are measured on the two axes of these figures.

Box 23.2 **A hydraulic analogue of GDP determination**

The key concept to understand in this chapter is how it is that GDP achieves its equilibrium level (for given values of exogenous spending). This is one of the most important ideas in macroeconomics, because it explains how GDP can be in equilibrium even when there is excess capacity in the economy.

Think of the economy as a water container, say a bath, which has inflows and outflows on a continuous basis—the tap is turned on and there is no plug in the plughole. Although the water is always changing, there is some condition under which the level of water in the bath will remain unchanged. This is when the volume of the inflow and the volume of the outflow are exactly equal.

Call the inflow 'investment', the outflow 'saving', and the level of water in the bath 'GDP'. GDP will stay at one level so long as the volume of investment just equals the volume of saving. (The same principle can be viewed in terms of the circular flow diagram in Box 22.3 on page 373 when there is no foreign trade and no government. Only when $I = S$ will the level of the circular flow be stable.)

What happens if the bath fills up to overflowing? That is the problem of capacity constraints and full employment that we discuss in later chapters. Hopefully, the bath will never run empty, because that would mean that national income and output have fallen to zero—though the problem of the water getting undesirably low is what macroeconomics was invented to study.

Note also that in later chapters we will see that investment is not the only inflow, or injection (government spending and exports will be added), and saving is not the only leakage, or withdrawal (taxes and imports are also leakages).

equilibrium is illustrated in panel (ii), but in terms of the saving–investment balance. The line labelled 'S' is equal to aggregate saving. In an economy without government and without international trade—the case we are studying here—aggregate saving is just equal to $Y - C$, the difference between national income and consumption. The line labelled 'I' is investment, in this case assumed to be constant at all levels of income.

Notice that the vertical distance between S and I is just equal to the distance between the 45° line and AE. When desired investment exceeds desired saving, desired aggregate spending exceeds national output by the same amount.

When desired investment is less than desired saving, desired aggregate spending is less than national output by the same amount.

Now we have explained the determinants of the equilibrium level of GDP at a *given price level*. A simple analogue, which will help us to understand why it is that equilibrium GDP is associated with equality of desired investment and saving, is set out in Box 23.2. In the next section we will study the forces that cause equilibrium income to change. We will see that shifts in autonomous consumption and investment spending cause changes in equilibrium GDP.

Changes in GDP

Because the AE line plays a central role in our explanation of the determination of the equilibrium value of GDP, you should not be surprised to hear that shifts in the AE line play a central role in explaining why GDP changes. (Remember that we continue to assume for the moment that the price level is constant.) To understand this influence, we must recall an important distinction first encountered in Chapter 3—the distinction between *shifts* in a curve and *movements along* a curve.

Suppose desired aggregate spending rises. This may be a response to a change in GDP (and therefore in incomes), or it may be the result of an increased desire to spend at each level of GDP. A change in GDP causes a *movement along* the aggregate spending line. An increased desire to spend at each level of GDP causes a *shift* in the aggregate spending line. Figure 23.7 illustrates this important distinction.

Shifts in the aggregate spending function

For any specific aggregate spending line, there is a unique level of equilibrium GDP. If the aggregate spending line shifts, the equilibrium will be disturbed and GDP will change. Thus, if we wish to find the causes of changes in GDP, we must understand the causes of shifts in the AE line.

The aggregate spending line shifts when one of its components shifts, that is, when there is a shift in the consumption function, in desired investment spending, in desired government spending on goods and services, or in desired net exports. In this chapter we consider only shifts in the consumption function and in desired investment spending. Both of these are changes in desired aggregate spending at every level of income. Such changes could, for

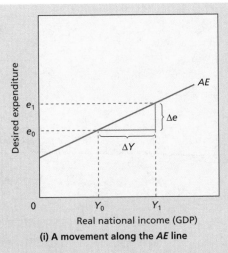

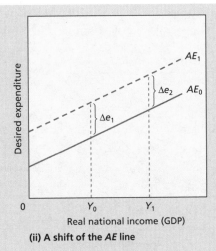

(i) A movement along the *AE* line   **(ii) A shift of the *AE* line**

Figure 23.7 Movements along and shifts of the *AE* function

A movement along the aggregate spending line occurs in response to a change in income; a shift of the *AE* line indicates a different level of desired spending at each level of income. In part (i) a change in income of ΔY, from Y_0 to Y_1, changes desired spending by Δe, from e_0 to e_1. In part (ii) a shift in the spending function from AE_0 to AE_1 raises the amount of spending associated with *each level* of income. At Y_0, for example, desired aggregate spending is increased by Δe_1; at Y_1 it is increased by Δe_2. (If the aggregate spending line shifts parallel to itself, $\Delta e_1 = \Delta e_2$.) (Notice that from here on we drop 'aggregate' from the vertical axis label and write 'Desired spending'. The term 'aggregate' is always understood, even when we omit it to save space.)

example, be induced by a change in the level of the interest rate set by the monetary authorities.

Upward shifts

What will happen if individuals permanently increase their levels of consumption spending at each level of disposable income, or if a major company invests in more fixed capital because of improved confidence about the future health of the economy? (Recall that an increase in any component of spending has the same effect, because it is an increase in demand for the output of the single production sector.) In considering these questions, remember that we are dealing with continuous flows measured as so much per period of time. An upward shift in any spending function means that the desired spending associated with each level of national income rises to and stays at a higher amount.

Because any such increase in desired spending shifts the entire aggregate spending function upward, the same analysis applies to each of the changes mentioned. Two important types of shift in AE need to be distinguished. First, if the same addition to spending occurs at all levels of income, the *AE* line shifts parallel to itself, as shown in part (i) of Figure 23.8. Second, if there is a change in the propensity to spend out of national income, the slope of the *AE* line changes, as shown in part (ii) of Figure 23.8.

(Recall that the slope of the *AE* curve is *z*, the marginal propensity to spend.) A change such as the one illustrated would occur if consumers decided to spend more of every £1 of disposable income, that is, if MPC rose.

Figure 23.8 shows that upward shifts in the aggregate spending line increase equilibrium GDP. After the shift in the *AE* line, output is no longer in equilibrium at its original level, because at that level desired spending exceeds national output. Equilibrium GDP now occurs at the higher level, indicated by the intersection of the new *AE* line with the 45° line, along which aggregate spending equals national output.

Downward shifts

What happens to GDP if there is a decrease in the amount of consumption or investment spending desired at each level of income? These changes shift the aggregate spending line downward. A constant reduction in desired spending at all levels of income shifts AE parallel to itself. A fall in the marginal propensity to spend out of national income reduces the slope of the AE line. When we use the saving–investment relation, we must note that a downward shift in the consumption function causes an upward shift in the saving function, reducing the equilibrium level of income and output, at which saving equals investment.

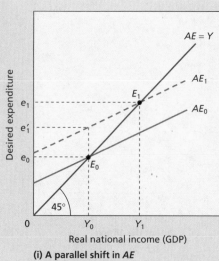

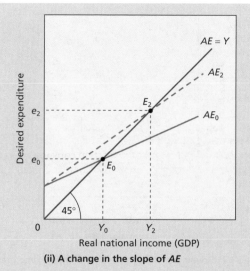

Figure 23.8 Shifts in the *AE* line

Upward shifts in the *AE* line increase equilibrium income and output; downward shifts decrease equilibrium income and output. In parts (i) and (ii) the aggregate spending line is initially AE_0 with national income Y_0. In part (i) a parallel upward *shift* in the *AE* line from AE_0 to AE_1 means that desired spending has increased by the same amount at each level of national income. For example, at Y_0 desired spending rises from e_0 to e_1' and therefore exceeds national output. Equilibrium is reached at E_1, where output is Y_1 and spending is e_1. The increase in desired spending from e_1' to e_1, represented by a *movement along* AE_1, is an induced response to the increase in GDP from Y_0 to Y_1.

In part (ii) a non-parallel upward shift in the *AE* line, say from AE_0 to AE_2, means that the marginal propensity to spend at each level of national income has increased. This leads to an increase in equilibrium GDP. Equilibrium is reached at E_2, where the new level of spending e_2 is equal to output Y_2. Again, the initial *shift* in the *AE* line induces a *movement along* the new *AE* line. Downward shifts in the *AE* line, from AE_1 to AE_0 or from AE_2 to AE_0, lead to a fall in equilibrium GDP to Y_0.

The results restated

We have derived two important general propositions of the theory of GDP determination.

1. A rise in the amount of desired aggregate spending that is associated with each level of national income will increase equilibrium national output (GDP).

2. A fall in the amount of desired aggregate spending that is associated with each level of national income will lower equilibrium national output (GDP).

The multiplier

We have learned how to predict the direction of the changes in GDP that will occur in response to various shifts in the aggregate spending function. We would like also to predict the *magnitude* of these changes.

During a recession the monetary authorities often lower interest rates in order to stimulate the economy. If this action has a larger effect than estimated, demand may rise too much and potential GDP may be reached with demand still rising. (We will see in Chapter 26 that this outcome will have an inflationary impact on the economy.) If the monetary authorities overestimate the effect of interest rate change, the recession will persist longer than is necessary. In this case there is a danger that the policy will be discredited as ineffective, even though the correct diagnosis is that too little of the right thing was done.

Definition

The *multiplier* provides a measure of the magnitude of changes in GDP. We have just seen that a shift in the aggregate spending curve will cause a change in equilibrium GDP. Such a shift could be caused by a change in any autonomous component of aggregate spending, for example an increase or decrease in desired investment. We will soon see that an increase in desired aggregate spending increases equilibrium GDP by a multiple of the initial increase in autonomous spending. The **multiplier** is the ratio of the change in GDP to the change in spending, that is, the change in GDP *divided by* the change in autonomous spending that brought it about.

Why the multiplier is greater than unity

What will happen to GDP if GlaxoSmithKline PLC spends £100 million per year on new factories? Initially the construction of the factories will create £100 million worth of new demand for the output of the production sector (recall that there is only one type of output) and £100 million of new national income, and a corresponding amount of extra wages for workers and profits for firms (the income components of GDP). But this is not the end of the story. The increase in national income of £100 million will cause an increase in disposable income, which in turn will cause an induced rise in consumption spending.

Workers who gain new income directly from the building of the factory will spend some of it on consumer goods. (In reality they will spend it on many different goods, such as beer and cinema visits; in the simplified world of our model, all spending is on the final output of the single industrial sector.) When output and employment expand to meet this demand, further new incomes will then be created for workers and firms. When they then spend their newly earned incomes, output and employment will rise further. More income will be created, and more spending will be induced. Indeed, at this stage we might wonder whether the increases in income would ever come to an end. To deal with this concern, we need to consider the multiplier in somewhat more precise terms. 滚雪球

The simple multiplier defined

Consider an increase in autonomous spending of ΔA, which might be, say, £100 million per year. Remember that ΔA stands for any increase in autonomous spending, from an increase in investment to the autonomous component of consumption. The new autonomous spending shifts the aggregate spending function upward by that amount. GDP is no longer in equilibrium at its original level, because desired aggregate spending now exceeds output. A movement along the new AE line restores equilibrium.

The **simple multiplier** measures the change in equilibrium GDP that occurs in response to a change in autonomous spending *at a constant price level*.[15] We refer to it as 'simple' because we have simplified the situation by assuming that the price level is fixed. Figure 23.9 illustrates the simple multiplier. Box 23.3 provides a numerical example.

The size of the simple multiplier

The size of the simple multiplier depends on the slope of the AE function, that is, on the marginal propensity to spend, z. This is illustrated in Figure 23.10.

A high marginal propensity to spend means a steep AE line. The spending induced by any initial increase in income is large, with the result that the final rise in GDP is correspondingly large. In contrast, a low marginal propensity to spend means a relatively flat AE line. The spending induced by the initial increase in income is small, and the final rise in GDP is not much larger than the initial rise in autonomous spending that brought it about.

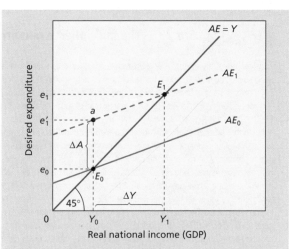

Figure 23.9 The simple multiplier

An increase in the autonomous component of desired aggregate spending increases equilibrium GDP by a multiple of the initial increase. The initial equilibrium is at E_0, where AE_0 intersects the 45° line. At this point desired spending, e_0, is equal to national output, Y_0. An increase in autonomous spending of ΔA then shifts the desired spending function upward to AE_1. If GDP stays at Y_0, desired spending rises to e_1'. (The coordinates of point a are Y_0 and e_1'.) Because this level of desired spending is greater than national output, GDP will rise.

Equilibrium occurs when GDP rises to Y_1. Here desired spending, e_1, is equal to output, Y_1. The extra spending of e_1 represents the induced increases in spending. It is the amount by which the final increase in income and output, ΔY, exceeds the initial increase in autonomous spending, ΔA. Because ΔY is greater than ΔA, the multiplier is greater than unity.

The larger the marginal propensity to spend, the steeper is the aggregate spending function and the larger is the multiplier.

The precise value of the simple multiplier can be derived by using elementary algebra. (The derivation is given in the appendix to this chapter.) The result is that the simple multiplier, which we call K, is

$$K = \frac{\Delta Y}{\Delta A} = \frac{1}{1 - z},$$

where z is the marginal propensity to spend out of national income. (Recall that z is the slope of the aggregate spending function.)

As we saw earlier, the term $(1 - z)$ stands for the marginal propensity not to spend out of national income. For example, if £0.80 of every £1.00 of new national income is

---

[15] Recall that we have assumed that there is excess capacity in the economy, so an increase in spending *can* lead to extra real activity. The situation is very different when we begin with resources already fully employed. We consider this situation in later chapters.

Box 23.3 **The multiplier: a numerical example**

Consider an economy that has a marginal propensity to spend out of national income of 0.80. Suppose that autonomous spending increases by £100 million per year because a large company spends an extra £100 million per year on new factories. National income (and output) initially rises by £100 million, but that is not the end of it. The workers involved in factory building that received the first £100 million spend £80 million. This second round of spending generates £80 million of new income. This new income, in turn, induces £64 million of third-round spending; and so it continues, with each successive round of new income generating 80 per cent as much in new spending. Each additional round of spending creates new income (and output) and yet another round of spending.

The table carries the process through ten rounds. Students with sufficient patience (and no faith in mathematics) may compute as many rounds in the process as they wish; they will find that the sum of the rounds of spending approaches a limit of £500 million, which is five times the initial increase in spending.

The graph of the cumulative spending increases shows how quickly this limit is approached. The multiplier is thus 5, given that the marginal propensity to spend is 0.8. Had the marginal propensity to spend been lower, say 0.667, the process would have been similar, but it would have approached a limit of three, instead of five, times the initial increase in spending. Notice that, since our model has only a single productive sector, it makes no difference what the initial spending goes on. That, and all subsequent spending, is on the output of this single industry. In reality, the impact of spending increases may vary slightly depending on the product first demanded.

Round of spending	Increase in expenditure (£m)	Cumulative total (£m)
Initial increase	100.0	100.0
2	80.0	180.0
3	64.0	244.0
4	51.2	295.2
5	41.0	336.2
6	32.8	369.0
7	26.2	395.2
8	21.0	416.2
9	16.8	433.0
10	13.4	446.4
11–20 combined	47.9	494.3
All others	5.7	500.0

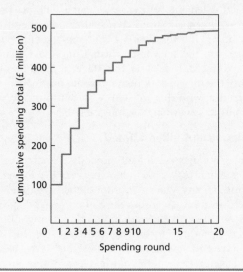

spent ($z = 0.80$), then £0.20 is the amount not spent. The value of the multiplier is then calculated as $K = 1/0.20 = 5$.

The simple multiplier equals the reciprocal of the marginal propensity not to spend.

From this we see that if $(1 - z)$ is small (that is, if z is large), the multiplier will be large (because extra income induces much extra spending). What if $(1 - z)$ is large? The largest possible value of $(1 - z)$ is unity, which arises when z equals zero, indicating that none of any additional national income is spent. In this case the multiplier itself has a value of unity; the increase in equilibrium GDP is confined to the initial increase in autonomous spending. There are no induced additional effects on spending, so GDP increases only by the original increase in autonomous spending. The relation between $(1 - z)$ and the size of the multiplier is illustrated in Figure 23.10.

To estimate the size of the multiplier in an actual economy, we need to estimate the value of the marginal propensity not to spend out of national income in that economy, that is, $(1 - z)$. Evidence suggests that in the United Kingdom the value of the marginal propensity not to spend is much larger than the 0.2 used in the above example. This is because there are 'leakages' from the circular flow of income other than saving—income taxes and import spending (which will be added to our model in the next chapter). Allowing for these extra withdrawals leads to a realistic estimate of something around 0.65 for $(1 - z)$.[16] Thus, the simple multiplier for the United Kingdom is just over 1.4, rather than 5 as in the above example.

The simple multiplier is a useful starting-point for understanding the effects of spending shifts on GDP. However, as we will see in subsequent chapters, many qualifications will arise, so you should not place too much policy significance on its value at this stage.

[16] This 0.65 is calculated using a marginal propensity to save of 0.2, a marginal propensity to import of 0.25, and an income tax rate of 0.25 (25p in the pound).

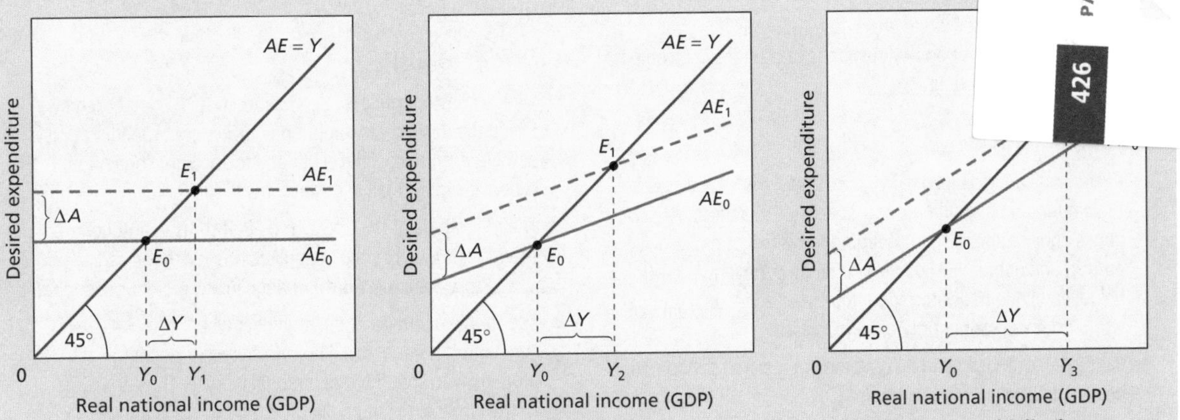

$K = \frac{\partial Y}{\partial A} = \frac{1}{1-z}$

(i) Flat AE, multiplier unity   **(ii) An intermediate case**   **(iii) A steep AE, multiplier large**

Figure 23.10 The size of the simple multiplier

The larger is the marginal propensity to spend out of national income (z), the steeper is the AE line and the larger is the multiplier. In each part of the figure the initial aggregate spending function is AE_0, equilibrium is at E_0, with income Y_0. The AE line then shifts upward to AE_1 as a result of an increase in autonomous spending of ΔA. ΔA is the same in each part. The new equilibrium is at E_1. In part (i) the AE line is horizontal, indicating a marginal propensity to spend of zero ($z = 0$). The change in GDP, ΔY, is only the increase in autonomous spending, because there is no induced spending by those who receive the initial increase in income. The simple multiplier is then unity, its minimum possible value.

In part (ii) the AE line slopes upward but is still relatively flat (z is low). The increase in GDP to Y_2 is only slightly greater than the increase in autonomous spending that brought it about.

In part (iii) the AE line is quite steep (z is high). Now the increase in GDP to Y_3 is much larger than the increase in autonomous spending that brought it about. The simple multiplier is quite large.

MPC = Marginal propensity of Consume.
MPS = Marginal propensity of Saving.

SUMMARY

The macro problem: inflation and unemployment

- Models of the short-term determination of GDP explain why actual GDP deviates from potential GDP. $Y > Y^*$

- Actual GDP above potential can be associated with inflation, while actual GDP below potential is associated with unemployment and lost output. $Y < Y^*$ unemployment

Key assumptions

- For simplicity we aggregate all industrial sectors into one, so the economy produces only one type of output good. We explain GDP determination through the major spending categories: private consumption, investment, government consumption, and net exports. $GDP = C + I + G + (X - IM)$

What determines aggregate spending?

- Desired aggregate spending includes desired consumption, desired investment, and desired government spending, plus desired net exports. It is the amount that economic agents want to spend on purchasing the national product. In this chapter we consider only consumption and investment.

- A change in personal disposable income leads to a change in private consumption and saving. The responsiveness of these changes is measured by the marginal propensity to consume (MPC) and the marginal propensity to save (MPS), which are both positive and which sum to one. This indicates that, by definition, all disposable income is either spent on consumption or saved.

- A change in wealth tends to cause a change in the allocation of disposable income between consumption and saving. The change in consumption is positively related to the change in wealth, while the change in saving is negatively related to this change.

- Investment depends, among other things, on real interest rates and business confidence. In our simple theory investment is treated as *autonomous*, or exogenous, as is the constant term in the consumption function, called *autonomous* consumption.

change Consumption → change Wealth Positive.
change Saving → change Wealth Negative

■ The part of consumption that responds to changes in income is called *induced* spending.

诱导消费

Equilibrium GDP

■ At the equilibrium level of GDP, purchasers wish to buy exactly the amount of national output that is being produced. At GDP above equilibrium, desired spending falls short of national output, and output will sooner or later be curtailed. At GDP below equilibrium, desired spending exceeds national output, and output will sooner or later be increased.

■ In a closed economy with no government, desired saving equals desired investment at equilibrium GDP.

■ Equilibrium GDP is represented graphically by the point at which the aggregate spending curve cuts the 45° line: that is, where total desired spending equals total output. This is the same level of GDP at which the saving function intersects the investment function.

相交·交叉

GDP > Equilibrium. desired spending < National out

GDP < Equilibrium. desired spending > National output

Changes in GDP

■ With a constant price level, equilibrium GDP is increased by a rise in the desired consumption or investment spending that is associated with each level of national income. Equilibrium GDP is decreased by a fall in desired spending.

■ The magnitude of the effect on GDP of shifts in autonomous spending is given by the multiplier. This is defined as $K = \Delta Y/\Delta A$, where ΔA is the change in autonomous spending.

■ The simple multiplier is the multiplier when the price level is constant. It is equal to $1/(1 - z)$, where z is the marginal propensity to spend out of national income. Thus, the larger z is, the larger is the multiplier. It is a basic prediction of macroeconomics that the simple multiplier, relating £1 worth of increased spending on domestic output to the resulting increase in GDP, is greater than unity.

TOPICS FOR REVIEW

■ Aggregation across sectors

■ Actual and potential GDP

■ The GDP gap

■ Desired spending

■ Consumption function

■ Average and marginal propensities to consume and to save

■ Aggregate spending function

■ Marginal propensities to spend and not to spend

■ Equilibrium GDP at a given price level

■ Saving−investment balance

■ Shifts of, and movements along, spending curves

■ The effect on GDP of changes in desired spending

■ The simple multiplier

■ The size of the multiplier and slope of the *AE* curve

DISCUSSION QUESTIONS

1 Calculate GDP using the following information (where there is no government and no foreign trade and C = consumption, I = investment and Y = GDP). $C = 100 + 0.8Y$; $I = 1,000$.

2 How will the answer to question 1 change if I increases to (a) 2,000, (b) 4,000, and (c) 10,000?

3 How would the answers to questions 1 and 2 change if the consumption function were (a) $C = 1,000 + 0.6Y$, (b) $C = -200 + 0.9Y$, and (c) $C = -200 + 1Y$?

4 Why is there a close relationship between personal disposable income and consumer spending?

5 Explain why a specific increase in autonomous spending leads to a greater increase in GDP.

6 What factors do you think would put limits on how far increases in spending can lead to increases in real GDP?

7 What do you think are likely to be some of the main determinants of investment by firms?

8 Is it likely that individual consumers' marginal propensities to spend out of disposable income will vary with the age of the consumer? If so, how would you expect it to vary?

Appendix The algebra of the multiplier

In models of short-run GDP determination, aggregate spending is divided into autonomous spending, A, and induced spending, N. In the simple model of this chapter, A is just investment plus autonomous consumption, and N is just induced consumption. When we add imports and government in the next chapter, N will include induced imports, and A will include government spending and exports. The derivation here is quite general, however. All that matters is that desired aggregate spending can be divided into one class of spending, N, that varies with income and another class, A, that does not.

Thus, we can write

$$E = N + A. \qquad (A1)$$

Because N is spending on domestically produced output that varies with income, we can write

$$N = cY, \qquad 0 < c < 1 \qquad (A2)$$

where c is the marginal propensity to spend out of national income. (In the simple model of this chapter, with no government and no foreign sector, it is equal to the marginal propensity to consume.) Substituting (A2) into (A1) yields the equation of the aggregate spending curve:

$$E = cY + A. \qquad (A3)$$

Now we write the equation of the 45° line,

$$E = Y, \qquad (A4)$$

which states the equilibrium condition that desired aggregate spending equals GDP. Equations (A3) and (A4) are two equations with two unknowns, E and Y. To solve them, we substitute (A3) into (A4) to obtain

$$Y = cY + A. \qquad (A5)$$

Subtracting cY from both sides, factoring out Y, and dividing through by $1 - c$ yields

$$Y = \frac{A}{1 - c}. \qquad (A6)$$

To discover how GDP changes when autonomous spending changes, i.e. the multiplier K, we merely differentiate (A6) to obtain

$$\frac{dy}{dA} = \frac{1}{(1 - c)} = K. \qquad (A7)$$

Since this is a constant expression, we can write

$$\Delta Y = \frac{\Delta A}{1 - c}.$$

This tells us that the change in GDP is equal to the change in autonomous spending multiplied by the multiplier from equation (A7).

Chapter 24

GDP IN AN OPEN ECONOMY WITH GOVERNMENT

In this chapter we continue building a model of the short-run determination of GDP. When we began to build this model in Chapter 23, we maintained four simplifying, but temporary, assumptions: no government, no foreign trade, a fixed price level, and excess capacity. The current chapter relaxes the first two of these. The following chapter relaxes the last two. In particular, you will learn that:

• Government consumption contributes to aggregate spending in the same way as any other component of autonomous spending.

• Taxes affect private consumption via their effect on disposable income.

• Net exports are negatively related to domestic income.

• A necessary condition for GDP to be in equilibrium is that desired aggregate domestic spending is equal to national output.

• The size of the multiplier is negatively related to the income tax rate and the marginal propensity to import.

In what follows we first add government and then a foreign sector to our simple model. Adding the government sector allows us to study *fiscal policy*, which is the ability of the government to use its taxing and spending powers to affect the level of GDP. In an open economy, net foreign demand for domestic output is an important source of final spending, so it has to be included in any complete treatment of the spending components of GDP. After adding the government and the foreign trade sector, we examine how these additions change both the structure of the model

and its behaviour in response to changes in autonomous spending.

As we proceed, it is important to remember that the key elements of our theory of GDP determination in the short run are unchanged. The most important of these that will remain true, even after incorporating government and the foreign sector, are restated here.

1. Aggregate desired spending can be divided into autonomous spending and induced spending. Induced spending is spending that depends on the level of national income, and thus on GDP.

2. The equilibrium level of GDP (national income and output) is the level at which the sum of autonomous and induced desired spending in the domestic economy is equal to the level of output. Graphically, this is where the aggregate spending line intersects the 45° line.

3. The simple multiplier measures the change in equilibrium GDP that takes place in response to a unit change in autonomous domestic spending, with the price level held constant.

Recall that the spending-based measure of GDP is made up of private consumption, investment, government consumption spending, and net exports. We have already built a model of GDP determination that includes private consumption and investment. We are about to extend this model to include government consumption and net exports. Recall also that 'national income', 'national output', and 'GDP' are all equivalent terms for our purposes.

Government spending and taxes

Government spending and taxation policies affect equilibrium GDP in two important ways. First, government spending is part of autonomous spending in our model; that is, it is an exogenous element of spending in the economy. Second, in deriving disposable income, taxes must be

subtracted from national income, and government transfer payments must be added. Because disposable income determines private consumption spending, the relationship between desired private consumption and national income becomes more complicated when a government is added. A government's plans for taxes and spending define its *fiscal policy*, which has important effects on the level of GDP in both the short and the long run.

Government spending

In Chapter 21 we distinguished between *government consumption spending on goods and services* and government *transfer payments*. The distinction bears repeating here. Government consumption is part of GDP. When the government hires a civil servant, buys a paper clip, or purchases fuel for the navy, it is directly adding to the demand for the economy's current output of goods and services. Thus, desired government purchases, G, are part of aggregate spending. As explained in Chapter 23, in our model we assume government consumption spending buys the output from the single industrial sector. This makes government spending have the same effect on GDP as any other component of autonomous spending.

The other part of government spending, transfer payments, also affects desired aggregate spending, but only indirectly. Consider for example state pensions or unemployment benefit. These are payments (transfers) made by government to individuals, who will spend at least some of the money. Since that spending is recorded as personal consumption, we do not want to count it twice by recording it under G as well. Government transfer payments affect aggregate spending only through the effect that these payments have on personal *disposable* income. Transfer payments increase disposable income; and increases in disposable income, via the consumption function, increase desired consumption spending.

This distinction (between transfers and government consumption) is important when it comes to issues such as determining the amount of GDP that is accounted for by government. Measuring the size of government to include transfers makes it look as though government's share of GDP is much bigger than it really is. However, looking only at G makes the government's revenue needs look smaller than they are, since transfers must be financed by taxes or borrowing, just as spending on goods and services must be. In what follows, government spending always excludes transfers, unless the contrary is clearly stated.

Tax revenues

Tax revenues may be thought of as negative transfer payments in their effect on desired aggregate spending. Tax payments reduce disposable income relative to national income; transfers raise disposable income relative to national income. For the purpose of calculating the effect of government policy on desired consumption spending, it is the net effect of the two that matters.

We define *net taxes* to be total tax revenues received by the government *minus* total transfer payments made by the government, and we denote net taxes as T. (For convenience, when we use the term 'taxes' we will mean *net* taxes unless we explicitly state otherwise.) Since transfer payments are smaller than total taxes, net taxes are positive, and personal disposable income is less than national income. Personal disposable income was a fraction under 70 per cent of GDP at market prices in 2001.

The budget balance

The **budget balance** is the difference between total government revenue and total government spending—or, equivalently, net taxes minus government spending, $T - G$. When revenues exceed spending, the government is running a *budget surplus*. The government will then reduce the national debt, since the surplus funds will be used to pay off old debt. When spending exceeds revenues, as it has for much of the period since the Second World War (1969–70, 1988–9, and 1998–2001 were the only exceptions in the United Kingdom between 1945 and 2001), the government is running a *budget deficit*. The government must then add to the national debt, since it must borrow to cover its deficit.[1] When the budget surplus (and deficit) is zero, the government has a *balanced budget*. Since the budget deficit is simply a negative budget surplus, we generally use 'budget surplus' to cover both cases, so bear in mind that the budget surplus can be negative.

Tax and spending functions

We treat government spending as autonomous. It is assumed that the government decides on how much it wishes to spend in real terms and holds to these plans whatever the level of GDP. We also treat *tax rates* as autonomous. The government sets its tax rates and does not vary them as GDP varies. This makes *tax revenues* endogenous. As GDP rises with given tax rates, the tax revenue will rise. For example, when incomes rise, people pay more total tax, even though tax rates are unchanged.

Table 24.1 and Figure 24.1 illustrate these assumptions with a specific example. They show the size of the government's surplus when its desired purchases (G) are constant at £170 million and its net tax revenues are equal to 10 per

---

[1] It does this by selling government bonds (known as 'gilts' in the UK). When the government runs a surplus, it uses the excess revenue to purchase outstanding government bonds. The stock of outstanding bonds is termed the *national* or *public debt*. (Public debt is the debt of the entire public sector, which includes local authorities and nationalized industries; national debt is the debt of the central government only.)

Table 24.1 **The budget surplus function (£ million)**

GDP (Y)	Government expenditure (G)	Net taxes ($T = 0.1Y$)	Government surplus ($T - G$)
500	170	50	−120
1,000	170	100	−70
1,750	170	175	5
2,000	170	200	30
3,000	170	300	130
4,000	170	400	230

The budget surplus is negative at low levels of GDP and becomes positive at high levels of GDP. The table shows that the size of the budget surplus increases with GDP, given constant expenditure and constant tax rates. For example, when GDP rises by £1,000 million, the deficit falls or the surplus rises by £100 million.

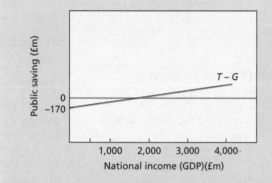

Figure 24.1 Budget surplus function

The budget surplus function increases as GDP increases. This figure plots the $T - G$ column from Table 24.1. Notice that the slope of the surplus function is equal to the income tax rate of 0.1.

cent of GDP (national income). Notice that the government budget surplus (or public saving) increases with GDP. This relationship occurs because net tax revenues rise with GDP but, by assumption, government spending does not. The slope of the budget surplus function is just equal to the income tax rate. The *position* of the function is determined by fiscal policy, as we discuss later in this chapter.[2]

For given tax rates, the government budget surplus (public saving) increases as GDP rises and falls as GDP falls.

Net exports

The UK's foreign trade sector is significant in relation to its GDP. Exports of goods and services in 2001 were just over 27 per cent of GDP at market prices. Although the total volume of trade is important for many purposes, such as determining the amount by which a country gains from trade (see Chapter 33), the balance between exports and imports (the current account balance) is particularly important in determining GDP.

The net export function

In macroeconomics we are interested in how the balance of trade responds to changes in GDP, the price level, and the exchange rate. Our theory covers trade in goods *and services*. The effect on GDP of selling a service to a foreigner is identical to that of selling a physical commodity. (Recall that we have only one type of product in our economy, and that all desired spending is treated as a demand for this product.)

Exports depend on spending decisions made by foreign consumers or overseas firms that purchase domestic goods and services. We assume, therefore, that exports are determined by influences outside of the home economy. This is autonomous, or exogenous, spending from the point of view of the determination of domestic GDP.

Imports, however, depend on the spending decisions of domestic residents. Most categories of spending have an import content; British-made cars, for example, use large quantities of imported components and raw materials in their manufacture. Thus, imports rise when the other categories of spending rise. Because consumption rises when the income of domestic consumers rises, imports of foreign-produced consumption goods, and of materials that go into the production of domestically produced consumption goods, also rise with domestic income. Total domestic (national) income, of course, rises identically with GDP.

Desired net exports are negatively related to GDP because of the positive relationship between desired imports and GDP.

[2] The numerical example used here is designed only to illustrate the principles of GDP determination developed in this chapter. To avoid the appearance of direct applicability of overly simplified models, we have deliberately chosen not to use 'realistic' numbers. The example produces GDP of £2,000 million, whereas UK money GDP in 2001 was around £988,000 million.

Table 24.2 **The net export function (£ million)**

GDP (Y)	Exports (X)	Imports ($IM = 0.25Y$)	Net exports
0	540	0	540
1,000	540	250	190
2,160	540	540	0
3,000	540	750	−210
4,000	540	1,000	−460
5,000	540	1,250	−710

Net exports fall as GDP rises. We assume that exports are constant and that imports are 25 per cent of GDP. In this case net exports are positive at low levels of GDP and negative at high levels of GDP.

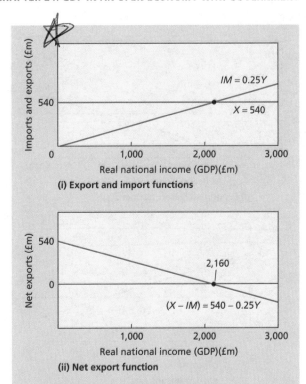

(i) Export and import functions

(ii) Net export function

Figure 24.2 The net export function

Net exports, defined as the difference between exports and imports, are inversely related to the level of GDP. In part (i) exports are constant at £540 million, while imports rise with GDP. Therefore net exports, shown in part (ii), decline with GDP. The figure is based on hypothetical data in Table 24.2. With GDP equal to £2,160 million, imports are equal to exports at £540 million and net exports are zero. For levels of GDP below £2,160 million, imports are less than exports, and hence net exports are positive. For levels of GDP above £2,160 million, imports are greater than exports, and hence net exports are negative.

This negative relationship between net exports and GDP is called the *net export function*. Data for a hypothetical economy with constant exports and with imports that are assumed to be 25 per cent of GDP are given in Table 24.2 and illustrated in Figure 24.2. In this example exports form the autonomous component and imports form the induced component of the desired net export function. The formulation in the table implicitly assumes that all imports are for final consumption. Imports rise when income rises, but imports do not change when *other* categories of autonomous spending change, so there is no direct import content of G, I, and X. This simplification will prove useful in our development of the determination of equilibrium income and does not affect the essentials of the theory.

Shifts in the net export function

We have seen that the net export function relates net exports ($X - IM$), which we also denote by NX, to GDP. It is drawn on the assumption that everything that affects net exports, except domestic GDP, remains constant. The major factors that must be held constant are foreign GDP, relative international price levels, and the exchange rate. A change in any of these factors will affect the amount of net exports that will occur at each level of GDP and hence will shift the net export function.

Notice that anything that affects domestic exports will change the values in the 'Exports' column in Table 24.2 and so will shift the net export function parallel to itself, upward if exports increase and downward if exports decrease. Also notice that anything that affects the proportion of income that home consumers wish to spend on imports will change the values in the 'Imports' column in the table, and thus will change the slope of the net export function by making imports more or less responsive to changes in domestic income. What factors will cause such shifts?

Foreign GDP An increase in foreign GDP, other things being equal, will lead to an increase in the quantity of domestic-produced goods demanded by foreign countries, that is, to an increase in our exports. This is because, as foreign GDP rises, foreign residents will receive higher incomes and will buy more of all goods, including imports. But foreign imports are domestic exports. Because the same amount more is sold at each level of domestic GDP, the increase is in the constant of the domestic net export function, X. This causes NX to shift upward, parallel to its original position. A fall in foreign GDP leads to a parallel downward shift in the net export function.

Relative international prices Any change in the prices of home-produced goods relative to those of foreign goods will cause both imports and exports to change. This will shift the net export function. Consider first a rise in

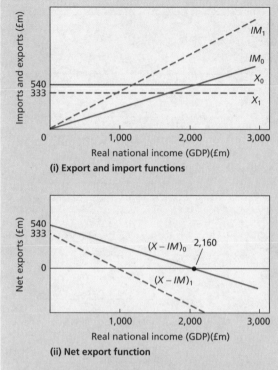

(i) Export and import functions

(ii) Net export function

Figure 24.3 Shifts in the net export function

An upward shift in imports and/or a downward shift in exports shifts the net export function downward. A rise in the domestic price level relative to foreign price levels, or a rise in the exchange rate, lowers exports from X_0 to X_1 and raises the import function from IM_0 to IM_1. This shifts the net export function downward from $(X - IM)_0$ to $(X - IM)_1$. (In the figure imports are 25 per cent of Y along IM_0 and are assumed to rise to a third of Y when domestic goods become more expensive relative to foreign goods, while exports fall from £540 million to £333 million.)

domestic prices relative to prices in foreign countries. On the one hand foreigners will now see domestically produced goods as more expensive relative both to goods produced in their own country and to goods imported from other countries. As a result domestic exports will fall. On the other hand, domestic residents will see imports from foreign countries become cheaper relative to the prices of home-produced goods. As a result they will buy more foreign goods, and imports will rise. Both of these responses will cause the net export function to shift downwards and change its slope, as shown in Figure 24.3.

Second, consider the opposite case of a fall in UK prices relative to prices of foreign-made goods. On the one hand, potential UK exports will now look cheaper in foreign markets relative both to their home-produced goods and to goods imported from third countries. As a result UK exports will rise. On the other hand, the same change in relative prices—British-made goods becoming cheaper relative to

foreign-made goods—will cause UK imports to fall. Thus the net export function will shift upwards, in exactly the opposite way to the movement in Figure 24.3.

What circumstances will cause relative international prices to change? Two important causes of changes in competitiveness for a country as a whole are: international differences in inflation rates, and changes in exchange rates.

Consider inflation rates first, and assume that the UK is the home country. If the sterling exchange rate remains constant, UK prices will rise relative to foreign prices if the UK inflation rate is higher than the inflation rates in other major trading countries. In contrast, UK prices will fall relative to foreign prices if the UK inflation rate is lower than the rates in other major trading countries.

Now consider the exchange rate. Holding domestic and foreign price levels constant, a depreciation of sterling will make imports more expensive for domestic residents and UK exports cheaper for foreigners. This is because UK residents will get less foreign currency for each pound sterling and foreigners will get more pounds for each unit of their own currency. Both foreigners and domestic consumers will shift spending towards the UK-produced goods, which have become cheaper relative to foreign goods. The net export function will thus shift upward.

An appreciation of sterling (holding price levels constant) has the opposite effect. It makes UK goods relatively expensive, thus shifting the net export function downward.[3]

Exchange rate changes may be brought about by changes in interest rates implemented by the monetary authorities. The domestic currency will generally appreciate (other things being equal) when the domestic interest rate is raised, and *vice versa*. This is because more people will wish to buy assets denominated in the home currency to take advantage of the high domestic interest rates, and a high demand for anything including currency tends to push its price upwards. As we shall see, changes in the exchange rate are an important way in which monetary policy can exert leverage over domestic aggregate spending in an open economy with a floating exchange rate. We discuss these influences in more detail in Chapters 28–30.

The results of this important chain of reasoning are summarized below (continuing with the UK home country example).

---

[3] A depreciation of sterling that is exactly proportional to the excess of UK inflation over foreign inflation will leave the relative price of UK exports and imports unchanged. This would be referred to as a constant *real exchange rate*, or as preserving purchasing power parity (PPP). The real exchange rate is the relative price of home- and foreign-produced goods. It is also referred to as 'competitiveness' or the 'terms of trade'. A rise in the real exchange rate (fall in competitiveness) shifts the net export function down because it lowers exports and increases imports at each level of GDP. These concepts are discussed more fully in Chapter 29.

①UK prices rise relative to foreign prices if either the UK inflation rate exceeds the rate in other major trading countries (with exchange rates fixed) or the pound sterling appreciates (with price levels constant). This discourages exports and encourages imports, causing the net export function to shift downwards.

②UK prices fall relative to foreign prices if either the UK inflation rate is less than the rates in competitor countries (with exchange rates fixed) or the pound sterling depreciates (with price levels constant). This encourages exports and discourages imports, causing the net export function to shift upwards.

Equilibrium GDP

We are now ready to see how equilibrium GDP is determined in our new model which includes a government and a foreign sector. As in Chapter 23, we can determine the equilibrium in two ways, both of which come to the same thing in the end: by relating output and spending, and by relating saving and investment.

The income–spending approach

In Chapter 23 we determined equilibrium GDP by finding the level of GDP at which desired aggregate spending is equal to national output. The addition of government and the foreign sector changes the calculations we must make but does not alter the basic principles that are involved. Our first step is to derive a new aggregate spending function that incorporates the effects of government consumption and foreign trade.

Relating desired consumption to national income

Our theory of GDP determination requires that we relate each of the components of aggregate spending to national income, Y. Personal income taxes cause personal disposable income to differ from national income (by the proportion of income taxation net of transfers). We simply assume that disposable income is always 90 per cent of national income.[4] Thus, whatever the relationship between C and Y_d, we can always substitute $0.9Y$ for Y_d. For example, if changes in consumption were always 80 per cent of changes in Y_d, changes in consumption would always be 72 per cent (80 per cent of 90 per cent) of changes in Y.

Table 24.3 illustrates how we can write desired consumption as a function of Y as well as of Y_d. We can then derive the marginal response of consumption to changes in Y by determining the proportion of any change in *national income* (GDP) that goes to a change in desired consumption.

The marginal response of consumption to changes in national income ($\Delta C/\Delta Y$) is equal to the marginal propensity to consume out of disposable income ($\Delta C/\Delta Y_d$) multiplied by the fraction of national income (GDP) that becomes personal disposable income ($\Delta Y_d/\Delta Y$).

Table 24.3 Comsumption as a function of disposable income and national income (GDP) (£ million)

National income (GDP) (Y)	Disposable income ($Y_d = 0.9Y$)	Desired private consumption ($C = 100 + 0.8Y_d$)
100	90	172
1,000	900	820
2,000	1,800	1,540
3,000	2,700	2,260
4,000	3,600	2,980

If desired private consumption depends on disposable income, which in turn depends on national income, desired consumption can be written as a function of either income concept. The second column shows deductions of 10 per cent of any level of national income to arrive at disposable income. Deductions of 10 per cent of Y imply that the remaining 90 per cent of Y becomes disposable income. The third column shows consumption as £100 million plus 80 per cent of disposable income.

By relating the second and third columns, one sees consumption as a function of disposable income. By relating the first and third columns, one sees the derived relationship between consumption and national income. In this example the change in consumption in response to a change in disposable income (i.e. *MPC*) is 0.8, and the change in consumption in response to a change in national income is 0.72.

Table 24.3 shows how desired consumption spending varies as national income varies, including the effects of taxes and transfer payments ($C = 100 + 0.72Y$; arrived at from $C = 100 + 0.8Y_d$ by substituting $0.9Y$ for Y_d). This equation is part of the aggregate spending function.

The aggregate spending function

In order to determine the equilibrium level of GDP, we start by defining the aggregate spending function,

$$AE = C + I + G + NX.$$

---

[4] In this case T, desired net taxes, would be given by the function $T = 0.1Y$. Recall that for simplicity we ignore indirect taxes.

Table 24.4 The aggregate expenditure function (£ million)

National income (GDP) (Y)	Desired private consumption spending ($C = 100 + 0.72Y$)	Desired investment spending ($I = 250$)	Desired government spending ($G = 170$)	Desired net export spending ($IM = 540 - 0.25Y$)	Desired aggregate spending ($AE = C + I + G + (X - IM)$)
0	100	250	170	540	1,060
100	172	250	170	515	1,107
500	460	250	170	315	1,195
1,000	820	250	170	290	1,530
2,000	1,540	250	170	40	**2,000**
3,000	2,260	250	170	−210	2,470
4,000	2,980	250	170	−460	2,940
5,000	3,700	250	170	−710	3,410

The aggregate spending function is the sum of desired private consumption, investment, government, and net export spending. The autonomous components of desired aggregate spending are desired investment, desired government spending, desired export spending, and the constant term in desired consumption (first row). These sum to £1,060 million in the above example. The induced components are the second terms in desired consumption spending ($0.72Y$) and desired imports ($0.25Y$).

The marginal response of consumption to a change in national income is 0.72, calculated as the product of the marginal propensity to consume (0.8) and the fraction of national income that becomes disposable income (0.9). The marginal response of desired aggregate spending to a change in national income, $\Delta AE/\Delta Y$, is 0.47.

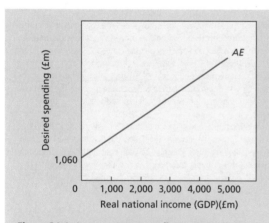

Figure 24.4 An aggregate spending curve

The aggregate spending line relates total desired spending to national income. The *AE* line in the figure plots the data from the first and last columns of Table 24.4. Its intercept shows £1,060 million of autonomous spending (£100 million autonomous consumption plus £250 million investment plus £170 million government spending plus £540 million autonomous net exports). Its slope is the marginal propensity to spend (which, following the calculations in Table 24.4, is 0.47 in this case).

Table 24.4 illustrates the calculation of this function. It shows a schedule of desired spending for each of the components of aggregate spending, and it shows total desired *aggregate* spending at each level of national income (GDP). Figure 24.4 shows this aggregate spending function in graphical form.

The marginal propensity to spend

The slope of the aggregate spending function is the *marginal propensity to spend* on national output (z). With the addition of taxes and net exports, however, the marginal propensity to spend is no longer equal to the marginal propensity to consume.

Suppose that the economy produces £1 of extra income (and output) and that the response to this is governed by the relationships shown in Tables 24.1 and 24.2, and summarized in Table 24.4. Since £0.10 is collected by the government as net taxes, £0.90 is converted into disposable income, and 80 per cent of this amount (£0.72) becomes consumption spending. However, import spending also rises by £0.25, so spending on domestic goods, that is, aggregate spending, rises by only £0.47. Thus z, the marginal propensity to spend out of national income (GDP), is 0.47. What is not spent on domestic output includes the £0.10 in taxes, the £0.18 of disposable income that is saved, and the £0.25 of import spending, a total of £0.53. Hence the marginal propensity not to spend, $(1 - z)$, is $1 - 0.47 = 0.53$.

Determining equilibrium GDP

The logic of GDP determination in our (now more complicated) hypothetical economy is exactly the same as in the closed economy without government discussed in Chapter 23. We have added two new components of aggregate spending, G and $(X - IM)$. We have also made the calculation of desired private consumption spending more complicated: taxes must be subtracted from national income in order to determine personal disposable income. However, *equilibrium GDP is still the level of GDP at which desired aggregate spending equals national output (and income).*

The aggregate spending function can be used directly to determine equilibrium GDP. In Table 24.4 the equilibrium is £2,000 billion. When GDP is equal to £2,000 billion, it is also equal to desired aggregate spending.

Suppose that GDP is less than its equilibrium amount. The forces leading back to equilibrium are exactly the same as those described on pages 418–20 of Chapter 23. When domestic consumers, firms, foreign consumers, and governments try to spend at their desired amounts, they will try to purchase more goods and services than the economy is currently producing. Thus, some of the desired spending must either be frustrated or take the form of purchases of inventories of goods that were produced in the past. As firms see that they are (or could be) selling more than they are producing, they will increase production, thereby increasing the level of national output (and income).

The opposite sequence of events occurs when national output is greater than the level of aggregate desired spending at that level of GDP. Now the total of personal consumption, investment, government spending, and net foreign demand for the economy's output is less than the national product. Firms will be unable to sell all of their output. Their unsold stocks will be rising, and they will not let this happen indefinitely. They will seek to reduce the level of output until it equals the level of sales, and GDP (national output and income) will fall.

Finally, when national output is just equal to desired aggregate spending (£2,000 billion in Table 24.4), there is no pressure for output to change. Private consumption, investment, government consumption, and net exports just add up to the national product. Firms are producing exactly the quantity of goods and services that purchasers want to buy, given the level of income.

Equilibrium GDP is determined where desired aggregate spending equals national output. In our extended model aggregate spending includes private consumption, investment, government consumption, and net exports.

Graphical exposition Figure 24.5 illustrates the determination of equilibrium GDP and the behaviour of the economy when it is not in equilibrium. The line labelled 'AE' is simply the aggregate spending function shown in Figure 24.4. The slope of AE is the marginal propensity to spend out of national income (0.47 in our example). Recall that AE plots the behaviour of desired purchases. It shows demand for the domestic product at each level of national income (GDP). (The AE line is sometimes referred to as the 'aggregate demand curve' in this context. However, we reserve this term for another, related construct that we use in the next chapter, once we have permitted the price level to be variable.)

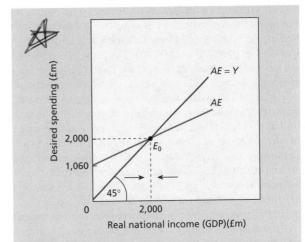

Figure 24.5 Equilibrium GDP

Equilibrium GDP occurs at E_0, where the desired aggregate spending line intersects the 45° line. Here the aggregate spending line is taken from Table 24.4; autonomous spending is £1,060 million, and the slope of AE is 0.47. If real GDP is below £2,000 million, desired aggregate spending will exceed national output and production will rise. This is shown by the arrow to the left of $Y =$ £2,000 million. If GDP is above £2,000 million, desired aggregate spending will be less than national output and production will fall. This is shown by the arrow to the right of $Y =$ £2,000 million. Only when real GDP is £2,000 million will desired aggregate spending equal real national output.

The line labelled '$AE = Y$' (the 45° line) depicts the equilibrium condition that desired aggregate spending be equal to actual national output (and income). Any point on this line *could* be an equilibrium, but only one is. Equilibrium occurs where behaviour (as depicted by the AE function) is consistent with equilibrium (as depicted by $AE = Y$). At the equilibrium level of GDP, desired spending is just equal to national output (GDP) and is, therefore, just sufficient to purchase the total domestic product.

The augmented saving–investment approach

An equivalent way of determining equilibrium GDP is analogous to finding the point where desired saving equals desired investment. Finding the level of income where $S = I$ was appropriate in Chapter 23, where we were dealing with a closed economy with no government. Now we have to take account of government as well as private saving, and net exports that provide an injection of spending that plays a similar role to investment.

Additional injections and leakages

Saving and investment had to be equal for GDP to be in equilibrium, as this provided a balance of inflows and outflows (injections and leakages). It may be helpful to re-view both the hydraulic analogue in Box 23.2 on page 420 and the circular flow of income and spending, illustrated in Box 21.2 on page 373, at this stage. The principles involved are unchanged. Now, however, we have two additional sources of leakages and two additional sources of injections.

In Chapter 23 saving was the only leakage of spending from the circular flow. The marginal propensity to save told us how much was not spent out of each additional £1 of income received. Now we add personal income taxes. These are levied on individuals' gross incomes, and so they also represent a proportion of income earned that cannot be spent. The second additional leakage is imports. Imports are a leakage because they create demand for foreign output. This does not generate domestic income. Investment was the only injection in our model in Chapter 23. In this chapter we have added government spending. This is received as income by the private sector, and this extra income leads to further spending as before. Similarly, ex-port demand comes from other countries, but it generates domestic incomes. Hence export demand is our second new injection.

The condition for GDP to be in equilibrium is now that the sum of desired injections should equal the sum of desired leakages. We can write this condition as an equa-tion, with the sum of all leakages (saving, S, plus taxes, T, plus imports, IM) equal to the sum of all injections (invest-ment, I, plus government spending, G, plus exports, X):

$$S + T + IM = I + G + X.$$

An equivalent equilibrium condition to $AE = Y$ for the deter-mination of equilibrium GDP is that injections (investment plus government spending plus exports) must equal leak-ages (saving plus income taxes plus imports).

Graphical exposition In order to illustrate the determina-tion of GDP via the equality of injections and leakages, it is convenient to rearrange the above equation. The graphical expression is made simpler, and the economic explanation more intuitive.

Subtracting G and IM from both sides of the above equa-tion gives

$$S + (T - G) = I + (X - IM).$$

The brackets do not change the meaning of anything, but they do identify two terms we are already familiar with. $(T - G)$ is the government budget surplus. In this context

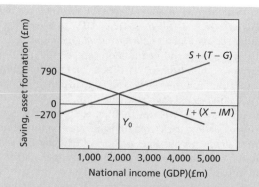

Figure 24.6 National saving and national asset formation
The economy is in equilibrium at Y_0, where desired national saving, $S + (T - G)$, equals desired national asset formation, $I + (X - IM)$. To the left of Y_0 desired national asset formation exceeds desired national saving. This implies that desired aggregate spending exceeds national output. Firms will respond to the imbalance by producing more, mov-ing the economy towards equilibrium. To the right of Y_0 desired national asset formation is less than desired national saving, and aggregate spend-ing is less than national output. Firms will cut back on output in order to avoid accumulating excess inventories, and the economy will move towards equilibrium.

it can be thought of as public sector (government) saving. Since S is private saving, $S + (T - G)$ is total domestic sav-ing, or national saving. $(X - IM)$ is our old friend net exports. When there is no net income from abroad—that is, when GNI (or GNP) and GDP are equal (as was approxim-ately true in the United Kingdom in 2001)—net exports equal the net accumulation of claims on foreigners. This is because, if we sell to foreigners more than we buy from them, we must either acquire a new foreign asset or reduce some foreign liability. Hence net exports cause the net acquisition of foreign assets, or overseas investment. I is domestic investment, so $I + (X - IM)$ is domestic plus over-seas investment, or national asset formation. Thus, the equation $S + (T - G) = I + (X - IM)$ can be interpreted as a generalization of the condition that saving equals invest-ment, since it says that national saving equals national asset formation.

Figure 24.6 illustrates how GDP is determined by the intersection of the national saving and national asset formation schedules. Notice that this is exactly the same level of GDP at which $AE = Y$.

Changes in aggregate spending

Changes in any of the autonomous components of planned aggregate spending will cause changes in equilibrium GDP. In Chapter 23 we investigated the consequences of shifts in the consumption function and in the investment function. Here we discuss fiscal policy—the effects of government spending and taxes. We also consider shifts in the net export function. First, we show that the simple multiplier is reduced by the presence of taxes and the marginal propensity to import.

The simple multiplier revisited

In Chapter 21 we saw that the *simple multiplier*, the amount by which equilibrium GDP changes when autonomous spending changes by £1, was equal to $1/(1 - z)$. In the example considered throughout Chapter 23, z, the marginal propensity to spend, was equal to 0.8, and the multiplier was equal to 5, or $1/0.2$. In the example that we have developed in this chapter, with a marginal propensity to import of 0.25 and a marginal (net) income tax rate of 0.1, the marginal propensity to spend is 0.47. (Ten per cent of a £1 increase in autonomous spending goes to taxes, leaving 90p of disposable income. With a marginal propensity to consume of 0.8, 72p is spent. Of this, 25p is spent on imports, leaving a total of 47p to be spent on domestically produced consumption goods.) Thus, $(1 - z)$ is (0.53), and the simple multiplier is $1/0.53 = 1.89$.

Fiscal policy

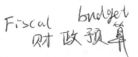

Fiscal budget
财 政 预 算

Fiscal policy involves the use of government spending and tax policies to influence total desired spending in order to achieve any specific goal set by the government.

Since government spending increases aggregate desired spending and taxation decreases it, the *directions* of the required changes in spending and taxation are generally easy to determine once we know the direction of the desired change in GDP. But the *timing*, *magnitude*, and *mixture* of the changes pose more difficult issues.

Any policy that attempts to stabilize GDP at or near any desired level (usually potential GDP) is called **stabilization policy**. The basic idea of stabilization policy follows from what we have already learned. A reduction in tax rates or an increase in government spending shifts the *AE* curve upward, causing an increase in equilibrium GDP. An increase in tax rates or a decrease in government spending shifts the *AE* curve downward, causing a decrease in equilibrium GDP.

If the government has some target level of GDP, it can use its taxation and spending as instruments to push the economy towards that target. First, suppose the economy is in a serious recession. The government would like to increase GDP. The appropriate fiscal tools are to raise spending and/or to lower tax rates. Second, suppose the economy is 'overheated'. In the next two chapters we will study what this means in detail. In the meantime we observe that an 'overheated' economy has such a high level of GDP (relative to potential) that shortages are pushing up prices and causing inflation. Without worrying too much about the details, just assume that the current level of GDP is higher than the target level that the government judges to be appropriate. What should the government do? The fiscal tools at its command are to lower government spending and to raise tax rates, both of which have a depressing effect on GDP.

The proposition that governments can avoid recessions by deliberately stimulating aggregate demand created a major revolution in economic thought. This is still known as the Keynesian revolution. We have already done enough macroeconomics to understand what this was all about. According to the theory we have developed so far, an economy can reach an equilibrium level of GDP well below its full-employment or potential level. According to Keynesian theory, governments could then use fiscal policy to increase aggregate spending by increasing government spending or reducing taxes (or both).

The expenditure model of national income and output determination predicts that GDP can get stuck at a level below its full potential. It also suggests how fiscal policy might be used to return an economy to its potential level of GDP.

Now let us look in a little more detail at how this might work out. Bear in mind, however, that we are still dealing with a special case in which prices are fixed and there is excess capacity, so we are just looking at how our present model works, not yet at how the real world works.

Changes in government spending

Suppose the government decides to increase its road-building programme by £10 million a year.[5] Desired government spending (G) would rise by £10 million at every level of income, shifting *AE* upwards by the same amount. By how much would equilibrium GDP change? This can be calculated, in our simple model, using the multiplier. Government purchases are part of autonomous spending,

[5] It does not matter what we assume the extra spending goes on. In our model it is always spent on the output of the single homogeneous industrial sector. Notice also that the value of the multiplier used in this section is hypothetical and is based on the numerical example in Table 24.4

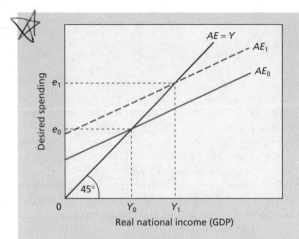

Figure 24.7 The effect of a change in government spending

A change in government spending changes GDP by shifting the AE line parallel to its initial position. The figure shows the effect of an increase in government spending. The initial level of aggregate spending is AE_0, and the equilibrium level of GDP is Y_0, with desired spendings e_0. An increase in government spending shifts aggregate spending upwards to AE_1. As a result GDP rises to Y_1, at which level desired spendings are e_1. The increase in GDP from Y_0 to Y_1 is equal to the increase in government spending times the multiplier.

A reduction in government spending can be analysed in the same figure if we start with aggregate spending function AE_1 and GDP Y_1. A reduction in government spending shifts the AE function downwards from AE_1 to AE_0, and as a result equilibrium GDP falls from Y_1 to Y_0. The fall is equal to the change in government spending times the multiplier.

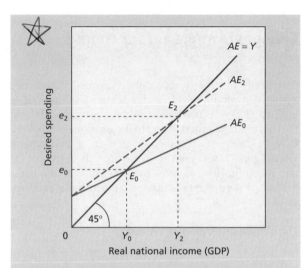

Figure 24.8 The effect of changing the tax rate

Changing the tax rate changes equilibrium GDP by changing the slope of the AE line. A reduction in the tax rate pivots the AE line from AE_0 to AE_2. The new line has a steeper slope, because the lower tax rate withdraws a smaller amount of national income from the desired consumption flow. Equilibrium GDP rises from Y_0 to Y_2, because at every level of national income desired consumption, and hence aggregate spending, is higher. If we take AE_2 and Y_2 to be the initial equilibrium, an increase in tax rates will reduce the slope of the AE line, thereby reducing equilibrium GDP, as shown by AE_0 and Y_0.

so a *change* in government consumption of ΔG will lead to a *change* in equilibrium GDP of the multiplier times ΔG. In this numerical example equilibrium GDP would rise by £10 million times the simple multiplier, or £18.9 million. Figure 24.7 shows the effect on GDP of an increase in government spending. It shows an upward parallel shift of the aggregate spending function, and a resulting increase in GDP. The same analysis could be applied equally to an increase in any other autonomous spending, such as investment or exports.

Reducing government spending has the opposite effect of shifting the AE line downwards, parallel to itself, and re-ducing equilibrium GDP. For example, if the government were to spend £2 million less on new roads, equilibrium GDP would fall by £2 million times the simple multiplier, or £3.78 million.

A change in government spending, in this model, changes the equilibrium level of GDP by the size of the spending change times the simple multiplier.

Changes in tax rates

If tax rates change, the relationship between disposable income and national income changes. As a result, the

relationship between desired consumption spending and national income also changes. For any given level of national income there will be a different level of disposable income, and thus a different level of consumption. Con-sequently, a change in tax rates will also cause a change in z, the marginal propensity to spend out of national income.

Consider a decrease in the tax rate. If the government decreases its rate of income tax so that it collects 5p less out of every £1 of national income, then disposable income rises in relation to national income. Thus consumption, which depends on disposable income, will also rise at every level of national income. This results in a non-parallel upward shift of the AE line, that is, an increase in the slope of the line, as shown in Figure 24.8. The result of this shift will be a rise in equilibrium GDP.

A rise in the tax rate has the opposite effect. It causes a given percentage decrease in disposable income, and hence consumption spending, at each level of national income. This results in a (non-parallel) downward shift of the AE line and thus decreases the level of equilibrium GDP.

Tax rates and the multiplier We have seen that the *simple multiplier* is equal to the reciprocal of one minus the mar-ginal propensity to spend out of national income. That is, the multiplier equals $1/(1 - z)$. The simple multiplier tells us how much equilibrium GDP changes when autonomous spending changes by £1 and there is no change in prices.

When tax rates change, the multiplier also changes. Suppose that *MPC* is 0.8 and the tax rate *falls* by 5p per pound of national income. This would increase the marginal propensity to spend by 4p per pound of national income. (Disposable income would rise by 5p per pound at each level of national income, and consumption would rise by the marginal propensity to consume, 0.8, times 5p, which is 4p.) The increase in the value of z, the marginal propensity to spend, would cause the multiplier to rise, making equilibrium GDP more responsive to changes in autonomous spending from any source. In our example the multiplier has gone up from 1.89 to 1.96 (($1 - z$) has fallen from 0.53 to 0.51).

The lower is the income tax rate, the larger is the simple multiplier.

GDP may change as a result of a shift in any of the other exogenous components of spending—net exports, investment, and autonomous consumption. An increase in any of these would increase GDP by the shift times the multiplier, as illustrated (for the case of a government spending increase) in Figure 24.7. An increase in any exogenous spending shifts the *AE* line vertically upwards by the amount of the spending increase. The new intersection with the 45° line determines the new level of GDP, and its increase is measured relative to the original position on the horizontal axis. A reduction in any of these exogenous spendings would shift the *AE* line downwards by the amount of the fall in spending.

Changes that would alter the slope of the *AE* line are a shift in the marginal propensity to consume, a shift in the rate of income tax, and a shift in the propensity to import. A fall in the marginal propensity to save (hence a rise in MPC, the marginal propensity to consume), a fall in the income tax rate, and a fall in the propensity to import all make the *AE* line steeper and increase the multiplier, as illustrated in Figure 22.8. A rise in any of these three has the opposite effect.

Balanced budget changes

Another policy available to the government is to make a balanced budget change by altering spending and taxes equally. Say the government increases tax rates enough to raise an extra £100 million, which it then uses to purchase goods and services. Aggregate spending would remain unchanged if, and only if, the £100 million that the government takes from the private sector would otherwise have been spent by that sector. If so, the government's policy would reduce private spending by £100 million and raise its own spending by £100 million. Aggregate demand, and hence national income and employment, would remain unchanged.

But this is not the case in our model. When an extra £100 million in taxes is taken away from households, they reduce their spending on domestically produced goods by less than £100 million. If the marginal propensity to consume out of disposable income is, say, 0.75, consumption spending will fall by only £75 million. If the government spends the entire £100 million on domestically produced goods, aggregate spending will increase by £25 million. In this case the balanced budget increase in government spending has an expansionary effect, because it shifts the aggregate spending function upwards and thus increases GDP.

A balanced budget increase in government spending will have a mild expansionary effect on GDP, and a balanced budget decrease will have a mild contractionary effect.

The **balanced budget multiplier** measures these effects. It is the change in GDP divided by the balanced budget change in government spending that brought it about. Thus, if the extra £100 million of spending (combined with the tax increases to finance it) causes GDP to rise by £50 million, the balanced budget multiplier is 0.5; if GDP rises by £100 million, it is 1.0.

When government spending is increased with no corresponding increase in tax rates, we say it is deficit-financed. Because there is no increase in tax rates, there is no consequent decrease in consumption to offset the increase in government spending. With a balanced budget increase in spending, however, an offsetting increase in the tax rate and decrease in consumption does occur. Thus, the balanced budget multiplier is much lower than the multiplier that relates the change in GDP to a deficit-financed increase in government spending (with the tax rate constant).

Monetary policy

Monetary policy influences aggregate spending through several channels that we study in detail in Chapter 28. We have already mentioned the most important of these in this and the previous chapter. **Monetary policy** works via the effects of interest rates on aggregate spending. The monetary authorities set a specific short-term interest rate. Interest rate changes affect consumption. Higher interest rates encourage people to cut their spending in order to save more and discourage borrowing in order to spend more. They also generate wealth effects on consumption via changes in the value of financial assets and property. Interest rates also affect investment, as higher interest rates discourage firms from borrowing in order to invest in such things as new equipment. Another channel from interest rates to aggregate spending is via the effect on the exchange rate to net exports (discussed further below).

Interest rate changes lead to a shift in autonomous spending (whether it be consumption, investment, or net exports) and can be analysed in the same way as a change of government spending shown in Figure 24.7. A rise in interest rates reduces autonomous spending and thus shifts the *AE* line downwards. A cut in interest rates raises autonomous spending and shifts the *AE* line upwards. There is thus a negative relationship between the interest rate and aggregate spending, and between interest rates and GDP from the spending side of the economy. We make use this relationship again in Chapter 28.

Monetary authorities will aim to lower aggregate spending if actual GDP is above potential, that is if demand in the economy is running ahead of the capacity to produce. They will wish to stimulate spending if actual GDP is below potential, that is if demand is low compared with supply capacity. For the moment, however, the key point to note is that monetary policy works through influencing one or more of the categories of aggregate spending that we have studied in this and the previous chapter.

Net exports and equilibrium GDP

As with the other elements of desired aggregate spending, if the net export function shifts upward equilibrium GDP will rise; if the net export function shifts downward equilibrium GDP will fall. Again, we take the UK as the home country.

Autonomous net exports

Net exports have both an autonomous component and an induced component. We have assumed that exports themselves are autonomous (exogenous) with respect to domestic GDP. Foreign demand for UK goods and services depends on foreign income, on foreign and UK prices, and on the exchange rate, but it does not depend on UK domestic income. Export demand could also change because of a change in tastes. Suppose that foreign consumers develop a taste for British-made goods (perhaps in reality Jaguars or Land Rovers, but in the model it is for the output of the single sector) and wish to purchase £500 million more per year of such goods than they had in the past. The net export function (and the aggregate spending function) will shift up by £500 million, and equilibrium GDP will increase by £500 million times the multiplier.

Induced net exports

The domestic demand for imports depends in part on domestic income. The greater is domestic income, the greater will be UK residents' demand for goods and services in general, including those produced abroad. Because imports are subtracted to obtain net exports (net exports equal $X - IM$), the greater is the marginal propensity to import, the lower will be the marginal propensity to spend on the domestic product, and the lower will be the multiplier, $1/(1 - z)$.

The exchange rate regime

We have noted above that foreign demand for domestic exports will depend upon the exchange rate (and that this can be affected by the interest rate set by the monetary authorities). The way in which the exchange rate interacts with net exports will vary according to the exchange rate regime in operation at the time. For example, the adjustment of net exports will be different if the exchange rate is floating (determined by market forces) rather than pegged. It may be different again for countries that share a common currency, such as in the euro zone. We discuss the implication of various exchange rate regimes for external adjustment in some detail in Chapter 29, once we have added money to the model. For now we assume that there are no endogenous exchange rate changes affecting net exports, so our economy can best be thought of as one with a fixed exchange rate regime. The importance of this assumption will become apparent later.

Lessons and limitations of the income–spending approach

In this and the preceding chapter we have discussed the determination of the four categories of aggregate spending and seen how, simultaneously, they determine equilibrium national income and output (GDP). The basic approach, which is the same no matter how many categories are considered, was first presented in Chapter 23 and has been restated and extended in this chapter.

Any factor that shifts one or more of the components of desired aggregate spending will change equilibrium GDP *at a given price level*. Holding the price constant has been necessary because we have not yet added a supply side to our analysis. So the level of GDP that we have been determining is the one that would be determined by demand conditions alone. The true outcome will depend on supply behaviour as well as on demand behaviour, so what we have done so far is only part of the story.

In the following chapters we augment the income–spending model by allowing the price level to change, in both the short run and the long run. That is, we explicitly add a relationship that determines aggregate supply. When prices change, real GDP will change by amounts different from those predicted by the simple multiplier. We will see that changes in desired aggregate spending generally change both prices *and* real GDP. This is why the simple multiplier, derived under the assumption that prices do not change, is too simple.

However, there are three ways in which the simple income–aggregate spending model developed here remains useful, even when prices are incorporated. First, the simple multiplier will continue to be a valuable starting-place when calculating actual changes in GDP in response to changes in autonomous spending. Second, no matter what the price level, the components of aggregate spending add up to GDP in equilibrium. Third, no matter what the price level, equilibrium requires that desired aggregate spending must equal output (GDP) in equilibrium, or equivalently that injections equal leakages.

Net taxes = Taxes - transfer Payments .

SUMMARY

Government spending and taxes

- Government consumption is part of autonomous aggregate spending. Taxes minus transfer payments are called net taxes and affect aggregate spending indirectly. Taxes reduce disposable income, whereas transfers increase disposable income. Disposable income, in turn, determines desired private consumption, according to the consumption function. *Gover spending*
- The budget balance is defined as government revenues minus government spending. When this difference is positive the budget is in surplus; when it is negative the budget is in deficit. *= Govern revennes - Gover spending*
- When the budget is in surplus, there is positive public saving, because the government is spending less on the national product than the amount of income that it is withdrawing from the circular flow of income and spending. When the government budget is in deficit, public saving is negative.

Net exports

- Since desired imports increase as national income increases, desired net exports decrease as national income (GDP)

increases, other things being equal. Hence the net export function is negatively sloped. (Net exports fall as GDP rises.)

Equilibrium GDP

- GDP is in equilibrium when desired aggregate spending, $C + I + G + (X - IM)$, equals national output.
- The sum of investment and net exports is called national asset formation, because investment is the increase in the domestic capital stock and net exports result in investment in foreign assets. At the equilibrium level of GDP, desired national saving, $S + T - G$, is just equal to national asset formation, $I + X - IM$.

$$S + T - G = I + X - IM.$$

Changes in aggregate spending

- The size of the multiplier is negatively related to the income tax rate.
- A shift in exogenous spending changes GDP by the value of the shift times the simple multiplier.
- A shift in aggregate spending can be brought about by fiscal policy changes or by a change in the official interest rate.

TOPICS FOR REVIEW

- Taxes and net taxes
- The budget balance
- Public saving
- The net export function
- The marginal propensity to spend

- National asset formation
- National saving
- Calculation of the simple multiplier
- Fiscal policy and equilibrium GDP
- Monetary policy

DISCUSSION QUESTIONS

1 Using the same notation as in the text, solve for the value of GDP, given the following relationships and values of exogenous variables: $C = 100 + 0.8(Y - T)$; $IM = 0.25Y$; $I = 1,000$; $G = 100$; $T = 100$; $X = 500$ (where T is a lump-sum income tax).

2 Repeat question 1 where income tax is a proportion of income, so that the consumption function can be written $C = 100 + 0.8(1 - t)Y$ where t is the income tax rate that can be taken as 0.2 (i.e. 20 per cent).

3 How does the answer to question 1 change if (*a*) *G* rises to 200, (*b*) *X* rises to 600, (*c*) *I* rises to 1,100? (Take all other exogenous variables to be at their initial value in each case.)

4 Using the relationships in question 1, calculate (*a*) the impact on GDP of an equal increase in *G* and *T*, (*b*) the impact of an equal increase in *X* and *IM*. (Hint: increase each by the same number, say 100. In the case of *IM*, add the chosen number as an intercept to its equation.)

5 Explain how governments might try to use their fiscal policy instruments to end a recession. What practical difficulties might be encountered in implementing such a policy?

6 Why does the trade balance deteriorate as domestic income increases?

7 How is the size of the multiplier related to (*a*) the income tax rate, (*b*) the marginal propensity to import, (*c*) the marginal propensity to consume?

8 Explain how a change in foreign demand for UK goods will affect the level of UK GDP.

9 For the model of GDP determination set out above to be adequate, what must be assumed about the supply side of the economy? Are the necessary assumptions plausible?

Chapter 25

GDP AND THE PRICE LEVEL IN THE SHORT RUN

In this chapter we allow the price level to be determined in our model. Virtually all shocks to the economy affect both real GDP and the price level; that is, they affect both the volume of goods and services produced, and the money values of those goods and services, at least initially. Such shocks have both *real* and *nominal* effects. To understand these effects, we need to develop some further tools called the *aggregate demand curve* and the *aggregate supply curve*. In particular, you will learn that:

• Aggregate demand is the level of desired real domestic spending at each price level.

• The aggregate demand curve plots the negative relationship between GDP and the price level.

• A change in autonomous spending shifts the aggregate demand curve horizontally by the multiplier times the initial change in spending.

• The aggregate supply curve reflects a positive relationship between output and the price level, for given input prices.

• The equilibrium level of GDP and the price level are determined where aggregate demand and supply are equal.

In order to determine the price level as well as real GDP, we need an explicit description of the supply side of our economy. No longer will we maintain the assumption that national output is purely demand-determined.

We make the transition to a variable price level in two steps. First, we study the consequences for GDP of *exogenous* changes in the price level—changes that happen for reasons that are not explained by our present model of the economy. This gives us what we call the aggregate demand curve. Then we develop a theory of aggregate supply which, when combined with aggregate demand to expand our model, explains simultaneous movements in both GDP and the price level. As a result, we will be able to analyse more realistic situations where an economy operates close to potential GDP.[1]

Aggregate demand

What happens to real GDP when all money prices change for some exogenous reason? We look at this question first from the spending side of the economy, then from the production side, and we finally put the two together. To find out what happens on the demand side, we need to understand how the change affects desired aggregate spending.

Shifts in the *AE* curve

There is one key result that we need to establish:

A rise in the price level shifts the aggregate spending curve downward, while a fall in the price level shifts it upward.

In other words, the price level and desired aggregate spending are negatively related to each other. A major part of the explanation lies in the way the change in the price level affects desired private consumption spending and desired net exports.

Changes in private consumption

The link between a change in the price level and changes in desired consumption is provided by wealth. This link is in two parts.

The first part is provided by the effect of changes in the price level on the wealth of the private sector. Much of this

[1] Recall that potential GDP may sometimes be referred to as *full-employment* or *capacity output*. Each of these concepts may have slightly different meanings in different contexts. The key feature for present purposes, however, is that we are talking about the maximum level of GDP that is currently sustainable without generating inflation.

wealth is held in the form of assets with a fixed nominal money value. One obvious example is money itself—cash and bank deposits. Other examples include many kinds of financial instruments, such as government bonds (gilts) and bills. When a bill or a bond matures, the owner is repaid a stated sum of money. What that money can buy—its real value—depends on the price level. The higher the price level, the less that sum of money can purchase. For this reason, a rise in the domestic price level lowers the real value of all assets that are denominated in money units.

How does this affect individuals? An individual who holds a bond has loaned money to the agent that issued it. When the real value of the asset falls the holder has his or her wealth reduced. However, the real wealth of the issuer of the bond has increased. This is because the money value of the bond buys fewer real goods and services as a result of the rise in the price level. So the agent that has to repay the bond will part with less purchasing power to do so, and so will have more wealth. For example, if you are owed £100 in one year's time, this will be worth less to you if prices rise by 20 per cent over the year than if they remain unchanged. However, the person who owes you the £100 will be better off by an amount equal to your loss if prices rise rather than remain unchanged, in that he or she will have to give up fewer goods to repay you.

A change in the price level affects the wealth of holders of assets denominated in money terms in exactly the opposite way to how it affects the wealth of those who issued the asset.

Inside assets An *inside asset* is one that is issued by someone (an individual or a firm) in the private sector and held by someone else in the private sector. It follows that for inside assets a rise in the price level lowers the real wealth of a bond-holder but raises the real wealth of the bond-issuer, who will have to part with less purchasing power when the bond is redeemed. With inside assets, therefore, the wealth changes are exactly offsetting. A rise in the price level lowers the real wealth of the person who owns any asset that is denominated in money, but it raises the real wealth of the person who must redeem the asset. So with inside assets a change in the price level has no net effect on private sector wealth.

Outside assets Outside *assets* are those held by someone in the domestic private sector but issued by some agent outside that sector. In practice, this usually means the government or any foreign issuer. In this case the only private sector wealth-holders to experience wealth changes when the price level changes are the holders of the outside assets. There are no offsetting private sector wealth changes for the issuers of the assets since they are not in the private sector. It follows that a change in the price level does cause a change in net private wealth held in outside assets

denominated in nominal money units. A rise in the price level lowers the real wealth of holders of these assets.[2]

A change in the price level causes no net change in the wealth of the private sector with respect to inside assets, but it does cause a change with respect to outside assets since the issuers are not in the private sector.

The second link in the chain running from changes in the price level to changes in desired consumption is provided by the relationship between wealth and consumption that we stressed in Chapter 23 (see Figure 23.4 on page 415). Whenever individuals suffer a decrease in their wealth, they increase their saving so as to restore their wealth to the level that they desire for such purposes as retirement. At any level of income, of course, an increase in desired saving implies a reduction in desired consumption. Conversely, whenever individuals get an increase in their wealth, they reduce their saving and consume more, causing an upward shift in the line that relates desired consumption spending and national income.

A rise in the domestic price level lowers the real value of total private sector wealth by lowering the real value of outside assets denominated in money units; this leads to a fall in desired private consumption, which in turn implies a downward shift in the aggregate spending curve. A fall in the domestic price level leads to a rise in wealth and desired private consumption, and thus to an upward shift in the aggregate spending curve, *AE*.

We have concentrated here on the direct effect of a change in wealth on desired private consumption spending. There is also an indirect effect that operates through the interest rate. Although this effect is potentially very powerful, we cannot study it until we have studied the macroeconomic role of money and interest rates. Further discussion of this point must therefore be postponed until Chapter 28.

Changes in net exports

When the domestic price level rises, domestically produced goods become more expensive relative to foreign goods. This change in relative prices causes domestic consumers to reduce their purchases of domestically produced goods (which have now become relatively more expensive) and to increase their purchases of foreign goods (which have now become relatively less expensive). At the same time, consumers in other countries reduce their purchases of the now relatively expensive domestic goods. We saw in

---

[2] We are assuming that taxpayers do not include in their wealth calculations the real value of future tax liabilities. Taxpayers must pay taxes to service the national debt, and when a rise in the price level lowers its real value, it also lowers the real value of future tax liabilities by exactly the same amount. We ignore this possible offsetting change.

Chapter 24 that these changes can be summarized as a downward shift in the net export function.

A rise in the domestic price level shifts the net export line downward, which shifts the aggregate spending curve downward. A fall in the domestic price level shifts the net export function and the aggregate spending line upward.

To summarize, if home-produced goods and services become more expensive, fewer of them will be bought, so total desired spending on UK output will fall; if home-produced goods and services become cheaper, more will be bought, and total desired spending on them will rise.[3]

Demand-induced changes in GDP

Because it shifts both the net export function and the consumption function downwards, a rise in the price level also shifts the aggregate desired spending line downwards, as shown in Figure 25.1. This figure also allows us to reconfirm what we already know from Chapter 24: when the *AE* line shifts downward, the level of GDP falls.

A rise in the domestic price level reduces GDP because it causes the aggregate spending line to shift downward—all other exogenous variables being held constant.

Since a fall in the domestic price level is the opposite of the case that we have just studied, we can quickly summar-

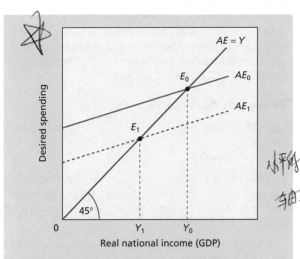

Figure 25.1 Aggregate spending and the price level

Changes in the price level cause the *AE* line to shift and GDP to change. At the initial price level the *AE* line is given by the solid line AE_0, and hence the level of GDP consistent with injections equal to leakages is Y_0. An increase in the price level reduces desired aggregate spending and thus causes the *AE* line to shift downward to the dashed line AE_1. As a result GDP falls to Y_1. Starting with the dashed line AE_1, a fall in the price level increases desired aggregate spending, shifting the *AE* line up to AE_0 and raising GDP to Y_0.

ize the two key effects. First, domestic goods become relatively cheaper internationally, so net exports rise. Second, the real value of some money assets increases, so consumers spend more. The resulting increase in desired spending is represented by an upward shift of the *AE* line which raises GDP, as shown in Figure 25.1.

A fall in the domestic price level increases real GDP because it shifts the aggregate spending line upward—all other exogenous variables being held constant.

Notice that the level of GDP determined by aggregate spending (and the condition that injections equal leakages) would have been described in Chapter 24 as the 'equilibrium' level of GDP. This certainly would be the equilibrium for GDP if only demand-side forces mattered, but we are soon going to combine demand-side and supply-side forces. Demand and supply combined will then determine the equilibrium level of GDP (and the price level). So only when we put aggregate demand and aggregate supply together will we have the full 'equilibrium' outcome.

The aggregate demand curve

We now know from the behaviour underlying the aggregate spending line (*AE*) that the price level and real GDP (as determined on the spending side of the economy) are negatively related to each other. That is, a change in the price level changes GDP in the opposite direction, holding all other exogenous variables (such as government consumption, tax rates, exports, and investment) constant. This negative relationship can be shown in an important new construct called the *aggregate demand curve*.

Recall that the *AE* line relates national income (GDP) to desired spending for a given price level, plotting income on the horizontal axis. The **aggregate demand (*AD*) curve** relates GDP to the price level, again plotting GDP on the horizontal axis.[4] Because the horizontal axes of both the *AE* line and the *AD* curve measure real GDP (national income), the two can be placed one above the other so that the level of GDP on each can be compared directly. This is shown in Figure 25.2.

Now let us see how the *AD* curve is derived. Given a value of the price level, equilibrium GDP is determined in part (i) of Figure 25.2 at the point where *AE* crosses the 45° line. In part (ii) of the figure the combination of the level of GDP

---

[3] This assumes that the price elasticity of demand for traded goods exceeds unity, so that a fall in price leads to both a greater volume and a greater value being bought.

[4] Don't forget that 'GDP' and 'national income' are the same thing. It is income that determines aggregate spending, and that spending in turn determines output. But any level of output generates an equivalent level of income. So income, output, and spending must all be consistent.

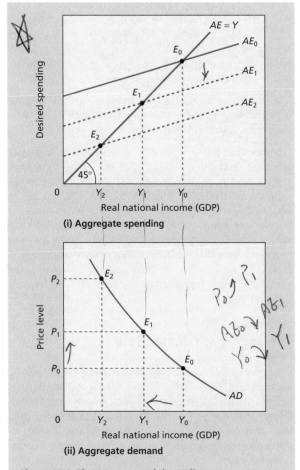

Figure 25.2 The *AD* curve and the *AE* line

GDP consistent with spending decisions is determined by the *AE* line for each given price level; the level of GDP and its associated price level are then plotted to yield a point on the *AD* curve. When the price level is P_0, the *AE* line is AE_0, and hence demand-determined GDP is Y_0, as shown in part (i). (This reproduces the initial position from Figure 25.1.) Plotting Y_0 against P_0 yields the point E_0 on the *AD* curve in part (ii).

An increase in the price level to P_1 causes AE_0 in part (i) to shift downward to AE_1 and thus causes GDP to fall to Y_1. Plotting this new, lower, level of GDP Y_1 against the higher price level, P_1, yields a second point, E_1, on the *AD* curve in part (ii). A further increase in the price level to P_2 causes the *AE* line in part (i) to shift downward further, to AE_2, and thus causes GDP to fall further, to Y_2. Plotting Y_2 against P_2 yields a third point, E_2, on the *AD* curve in part (ii).

Thus, a change in the price level causes a shift in the *AE* line in part (i) and a movement along the *AD* curve in part (ii).

(for which injections equal leakages) and the corresponding value of the price level is plotted, giving one point on the *AD* curve.

When the price level changes, the *AE* line shifts, for the reasons just seen. The new position of the *AE* line gives rise to a new level of GDP that is associated with the new price

level. This determines a second point on the *AD* curve, as shown in Figure 25.2(ii).

Any change in the price level leads to a new *AE* line and hence to a new level of GDP consistent with injections and leakages being in balance. Each combination of GDP and its associated price level defines a particular point on the *AD* curve.

Note that, because the *AD* curve relates real GDP to the price level, changes in the price level that cause *shifts in* the *AE* curve cause *movements along* the *AD* curve. A movement along the *AD* curve thus traces out the response of the level of GDP to a change in the price level that would be determined by aggregate spending alone. Notice also that the only exogenous change we are permitting at present is a change in the price level. All other exogenous spending is held constant along a given *AD* curve.

The aggregate demand curve shows, for each price level, the associated level of GDP for which aggregate desired spending equals total output, and is consistent with the level of income generated at that output.

In Chapter 24 we showed that points for which aggregate desired spending is equal to output are equivalent to points for which injections equal leakages (or, in the model of Chapter 23, for which investment equals saving). This equivalence carries through to the *AD* curve. Hence points on the *AD* curve are combinations of real GDP and the price level (for given values of all exogenous spending) for which injections equal leakages, that is, for which $I + G + X = S + T + IM$. Recall that this equation can be rearranged to make clear the further equivalence to the condition that national saving is equal to national asset formation: $S + (T - G) = I + (X - IM)$.

The slope of the *AD* curve

Figure 25.2 shows that the *AD* curve is negatively sloped. Starting from some specific point on the *AD* curve, two changes are possible.

1. A rise in the price level causes the aggregate spending line, *AE*, to shift downward and hence leads to a movement upward and to the left along the *AD* curve, reflecting a fall in the associated level of GDP.

2. A fall in the price level causes the aggregate spending line, *AE*, to shift upward and hence leads to a movement downward and to the right along the *AD* curve, reflecting a rise in the associated level of GDP.

In Chapter 3 we saw that demand curves for individual goods such as carrots and cars are negatively sloped. However, the reasons for the negative slope of the *AD* curve are different from the reasons for the negative slope of the individual demand curves that are used in microeconomics. This important point is discussed further in Box 25.1.

Box 25.1 **The shape of the aggregate demand curve** *answer of lecture 11.*
P31 tutorial topic

In Chapter 3 we studied the demand curves for individual products. It is tempting to think that the properties of the aggregate demand curve arise from the same behaviour that gives rise to those individual demand curves. However, this would involve committing the fallacy of composition, that is, to assume that what is correct for the parts must be correct for the whole.

Consider a simple example of the fallacy. An art collector can go into the market and add to her private collection of nineteenth-century French paintings provided only that she has enough money. However, the fact that any one person can do this does not mean that everyone could do so simultaneously. The world's stock of nineteenth-century French paintings is fixed. It is not possible for *all* of us to do what any *one* of us with enough money can do.

How does the fallacy of composition relate to demand curves? An individual demand curve describes a situation in which the price of one commodity changes while the prices of all other commodities and consumers' money incomes are constant. Such an individual demand curve is negatively sloped for two reasons. First, as the price of the commodity rises, each con-

sumer's given money income will buy a smaller *total* amount of goods, so a smaller quantity of each commodity will be bought, other things being equal. Second, as the price of the commodity rises, consumers buy less of it and more of the now relatively cheaper substitutes.

The first reason has no application to the aggregate demand curve, which relates the total demand for all output to the price level. All prices and total output are changing as we move along the *AD* curve. Because the value of output determines income, consumers' money incomes will also be changing along this curve.

The second reason does apply to the aggregate demand curve, but in a limited way. A rise in the price level entails a rise in *all* domestic commodity prices. Thus, there is no incentive to substitute among domestic commodities whose prices do not change relative to each other. However, it does give rise, as we saw earlier in this chapter, to some substitution between domestic and foreign goods and services. Domestic goods and services rise in price relative to imported goods and services, and the switch in spending will lower desired aggregate spending on domestic output and hence will lower equilibrium GDP.

Points off the *AD* curve

The *AD* curve depicts combinations of GDP and the price level at which aggregate desired spending is equal to actual output (and income). These points are said to be *consistent* with spending decisions.

> The level of GDP given by any point on the aggregate demand curve is such that, *if* that level of output is produced, aggregate desired spending at the *given price level* will exactly equal total output.

We do not yet know if producers will really want to produce that output, as we have not modelled the supply decision, but we can say that the incomes generated by that level of GDP will be such as to generate the exact level of spending (via consumption and net exports, etc.) that purchases all the output.

Points to the left of the *AD* curve show combinations of GDP and the price level that cause aggregate desired spending to exceed output; there is thus pressure for output to rise, because firms could sell more than their current output. Points to the right of the *AD* curve show combinations of GDP and the price level for which aggregate desired spending is less than current output; there is thus pressure for output to fall, because firms will not be able to sell all of their current output. These relationships are illustrated in Figure 25.3.

Shifts in the *AD* curve

Because the *AD* curve plots demand-determined GDP as a function of the price level, anything that alters this

outcome for GDP *at any specific price level* must shift the *AD* curve. In other words, any change in exogenous spending that we have been holding constant causes the aggregate spending curve to shift, and will also cause the *AD* curve to shift. (Recall that a change in the price level causes a *movement along* the *AD* curve.) Such a shift is called an *aggregate demand shock*.

Demand shocks can originate by changes in spending by the private sector, but they may also be induced by changes in monetary or fiscal policy. Higher interest rates will lower aggregate spending and thus shift the *AD* curve to the left; lower rates will increase aggregate spending and shift the *AD* curve to the right. Higher government spending shifts the *AD* curve to the right, while higher taxes shift *AD* to the left, and vice versa for cuts in government spending and cuts in taxes.

One example of a *positive* aggregate demand shock comes from the United Kingdom. A lowering of tax rates in the 1987 Budget led to an increase in the amount of UK consumption spending associated with each level of UK national income. This was an expansionary demand shock that shifted the UK *AD* curve to the right. This stimulated a boom in the domestic economy. The extra domestic demand also spilled over into the balance of payments. Some of the increased domestic demand went on to imports, and the balance of payments went into deficit. In the context of our model, the net export function shifted downwards. Later, policy was aimed at shifting the *AD* curve down again. This was a contributory factor in the 1990–2 recession.

A more recent positive demand shock occurred in July 2002 when the UK government announced substantial

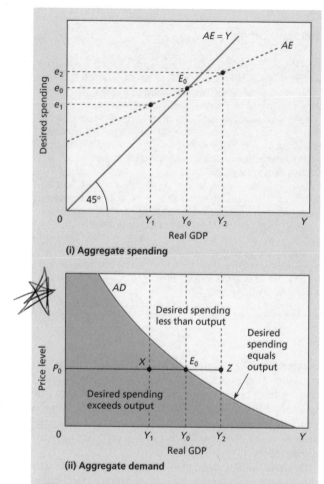

(i) Aggregate spending

(ii) Aggregate demand

Figure 25.3 The relationship between AE and the AD curve

The AD curve plots the price level against the level of GDP consistent with spending decisions at that price level. With the price level P_0, GDP is Y_0, shown by the intersection of AE and the 45° line at E_0 in part (i) and by the point E_0 on the AD curve in part (ii).

With the price level constant at P_0, consider a level of GDP of Y_1, which is less than Y_0. As can be seen in part (i), if GDP were equal to Y_1, desired aggregate spending would be e_1, which is greater than Y_1. Hence Y_1 is not a level of GDP consistent with spending decisions when the price level is P_0, and the combination (P_0, Y_1) is not a point on the AD curve in part (ii), as shown by point X. Now consider a level of GDP of Y_2, which is greater than Y_0. As can be seen in part (i), if GDP were equal to Y_2, desired aggregate spending would be e_2, which is less than Y_2. Hence Y_2 is not a level of GDP consistent with spending decisions when the price level is P_0, and the combination (P_0, Y_2) is not a point on the AD curve in part (ii), as shown by point Z.

Repeating the same analysis for each given price level tells us that, for all points to the left of the AD curve (dark blue shaded area) output is tending to rise, because desired spending exceeds output, whereas for all points to the right of the AD curve (light blue shaded area) output is tending to fall, because desired aggregate spending is less than output.

increases in spending on education and health. This is a rightward shift of the AD curve, and you will soon be able to work out for yourself what other change should follow from this demand shock. (At the time of writing it is too early to say what has actually happened.)

An example of a *negative* aggregate demand shock can be found in Germany in the early 1990s. The high costs for the German government associated with reunification of East and West Germany required a sharp rise in German income tax rates. Although this was associated with higher spending in East Germany, there was a downward shift of the AD curve for West Germany, which led to a downturn in output and a substantial rise in unemployment. The situation was made worse by a simultaneous fiscal tightening in several other European countries, such as France, Belgium, and Italy, as they attempted to reduce their budget deficits to below 3 per cent of GDP to satisfy the Maastricht criteria for entry into the single European currency system in 1999. A simultaneous negative AD shock in, say, France would reinforce the fiscally generated AD shock in Germany, because it would lead to a downward shift in the German net export function, causing a further downward shift in Germany's AD curve.

Demand shocks also resulted from big wealth effects associated with swings in stock markets. In the years up to March 2000, there was a boom in technology stocks that led to a huge increase in financial wealth, especially in the United States. This was associated with a consumer boom, as people whose wealth was rising felt little need to save. By the summer of 2002, however, stock markets had collapsed. At the time of writing this seems likely to lead to a fall in consumer confidence and an autonomous downward shift in the consumption function, and thus also of aggregate demand.

We now summarize the factors that shift the AD curves as follows.

A rise in the amount of (autonomous) desired private consumption, investment, government consumption, or net export spending that is associated with each level of GDP shifts the AD curve to the right. A fall in any of these spending categories shifts the AD curve to the left.

The simple multiplier and the AD curve

We saw in Chapter 24 that the simple multiplier measures the magnitude of the *change* in (what we then called) equilibrium GDP in response to a change in autonomous spending when the price level is constant. It follows that this multiplier gives the magnitude of the *horizontal* shift in the AD curve in response to a change in autonomous spending. This is shown in Figure 25.4.

The simple multiplier measures the horizontal shift in the AD curve in response to a change in autonomous spending.

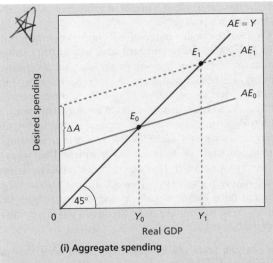

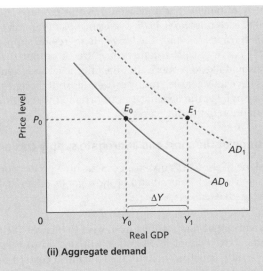

(i) Aggregate spending   (ii) Aggregate demand

Figure 25.4 The simple multiplier and shifts in the *AD* curve

A change in autonomous spending changes GDP for any given price level, and the simple multiplier measures the resulting horizontal shift in the aggregate demand curve. The original desired spending curve is AE_0 in part (i). The initial position is at E_0, with GDP Y_0 at price level P_0. This yields point E_0 on the curve AD_0 in part (ii).

The *AE* line in part (i) then shifts upwards from AE_0 to AE_1 because of an increase in autonomous spending of ΔA. Output now rises to Y_1, with the price level still constant at P_0. Thus, the *AD* curve in part (ii) shifts to the right to point E_1, indicating the higher output Y_1 associated with the same price level P_0. The magnitude of the shift, ΔY, is given by the simple multiplier.

A fall in autonomous spending can be analysed by shifting the *AE* line from AE_1 to AE_0, which shifts the *AD* curve from AD_1 to AD_0 at the price level of P_0. The value of GDP determined by spending decisions falls from Y_1 to Y_0.

If the price level were to remain constant and firms were willing to supply everything that was demanded at that price level, the simple multiplier would still show the change in equilibrium GDP that would occur in response to a change in autonomous spending. However, this will not normally be the case. To see how producers will actually respond to a shift in aggregate demand, we need to model supply responses.

Aggregate supply and macroeconomic equilibrium

So far we have explained how the level of GDP is determined *when the price level is given*, and how that outcome changes as the price level is changed exogenously. We are now ready to take an important further step: to take account of the supply decisions of producers. Once we have done this, we will be able to combine aggregate demand and supply to provide an *explanation* for the simultaneous determination of the price level and real GDP.

The aggregate supply curve

Aggregate supply is the total output of goods and services that firms wish to produce, assuming that they can sell all they wish to sell at the going price level. Recall, however,

that in our simple model there is only one type of output, so *in our model* aggregate supply is the final output of the single good produced by all the firms in the economy. In the real world the national output is made up of thousands of different types of goods and services. Both in our model and in the real world, aggregate supply is the outcome of the decisions of all producers in the economy to hire workers and buy other inputs in order to produce goods (and services) to sell to consumers, governments, and other producers, as well as for export.

The *aggregate supply curve* relates the quantity of output supplied to the price level. It is useful to define two types of such curve, in order to allow for different stages of adjustment of the production sector to external shocks. The **short-run aggregate supply (*SRAS*) curve** shows the quantity of output that firms would like to produce and to sell at each price level *on the assumption that the prices of all inputs remain constant*. The **long-run aggregate supply (LRAS) curve** plots the desired quantity of output that firms would like to produce after the price level and input prices have fully adjusted to any exogenous shift of aggregate demand. For the remainder of this chapter we confine our attention to the *SRAS* curve.

The slope of the short-run aggregate supply curve

The slope of the *SRAS* curve depends on how production costs are related to output and on how goods prices and output are related.

Costs and output Suppose that firms wish to increase their outputs above current levels. What will this do to their costs per unit of output—often called their **unit costs**? The short-run aggregate supply curve is drawn on the assumption that the prices of all inputs that firms use, such as labour, remain constant. This does not, however, mean that unit costs will be constant. As output increases, less efficient standby machinery may have to be used, and less efficient workers may have to be hired, while existing workers may have to be paid overtime rates for additional work. For these reasons unit costs will tend to rise as output rises, even when input prices are constant.[5]

Unit costs and output are positively related in the short run.

Prices and output To understand the relationship between price and output, we need to think about firms that sell in two distinct types of market: those in which firms are price-takers, and those in which firms are price-setters. Some industries contain many individual firms selling a homogeneous product. In these cases each one is too small to influence the market price, which is set by the overall forces of demand and supply. So each firm must accept whatever price is set on the open market and adjust its output to that price. The firms are said to be *price-takers* and *quantity-adjusters*. When the market price changes, these firms will react by altering their production.

Price-taking firms produce more only if price rises and will produce less if price falls. This is because their unit costs rise with output.

Many other industries, including most of those that produce manufactured goods, are not price-takers. Whether there are few large firms or many small ones, each can influence the market price of its output. Most such firms sell differentiated products, although all are similar enough to be thought of as the product of one industry. For example, no two makes of car are identical, but all cars are sufficiently alike that we can talk about 'the car industry' and the commodity 'cars'. In such cases each firm typically sets the price at which it is prepared to sell its products; that is, the firm is a *price-setter*.

Over some (small) range of output, price-setting firms will keep their prices constant and will satisfy changes in demand by running down or building up inventories, such as numbers of cars in the showroom. However, if the demand for the output of price-setting firms increases sufficiently to take their production level into the range at which their unit costs start to rise (for example, because overtime is worked and standby equipment is brought into production), profit-maximizing firms will not want to increase production further unless they can pass on at least some of these extra costs through higher prices. When demand falls, they will reduce output, and competition among them will tend to cause a reduction in prices whenever unit costs fall.

Price-setting firms will increase their prices when they expand production into the range where unit costs are rising.

This is the basic behaviour of firms in response to changes in demand and prices when input prices are constant, and it explains the slope of the *SRAS* curve, such as the one shown in Figure 25.5.[6]

The actions of both price-taking and price-setting firms cause the price level and the desired supply of output to be positively related—the short-run aggregate supply curve is positively sloped.

Real and nominal wages Another way of explaining why the *SRAS* curve is positively sloped involves real wages. Consider price-taking firms selling in competitive markets. With given money prices of their inputs—we will concentrate on the labour input—and a given price at which they can sell their output, each firm will produce output at the level where its marginal cost equals its marginal revenue (and average revenue, which is also equal to the market price of its output, as shown in Chapter 10).

Now what happens if an increase in total demand for final output leads to a rise in the output price? Firms will find that their marginal revenue curves (and average revenue) have shifted upwards. They will increase profits by expanding output up to the point where their new marginal revenue curve cuts their marginal cost curve. In the process they will also increase employment. Thus, as

---

[5] The law of diminishing returns (see Chapter 8) is one reason why costs rise in the short run, as firms try to produce more output with a fixed stock of capital equipment.

[6] Notice that our argument here relating to two different types of firm is not really consistent with our assumption that there is only one type of output. However, since both price-takers and price-setters generate a positively sloped supply curve, for the purpose of building our macro model this does not cause any difficulties. It is worth bearing in mind, however, that in reality price-setting behaviour varies with product type and market structure.

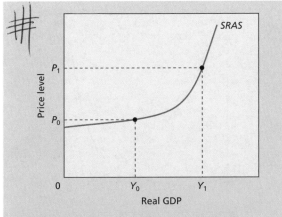

Figure 25.5 A short-run aggregate supply curve

The *SRAS* curve is positively sloped. The positive slope of the *SRAS* curve shows that, with the prices of labour and other inputs given, total desired output and the price level will be positively associated. Thus, a rise in the price level from P_0 to P_1 will be associated with a rise in the quantity of total output supplied from Y_0 to Y_1. The slope of the *SRAS* curve is fairly flat at low levels of output and very steep at higher levels.

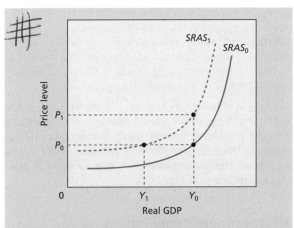

Figure 25.6 Shifts in the *SRAS* curve

A shift to the left of the *SRAS* curve reflects a decrease in supply; a shift to the right reflects an increase in supply. Starting from (P_0, Y_0) on $SRAS_0$, suppose there is an increase in input prices. At price level P_0 only Y_1 would be produced. Alternatively, to get output Y_0 would require a rise to price level P_1. The new supply curve is $SRAS_1$, which may be viewed as being above and to the left of $SRAS_0$. An increase in supply—caused, say, by a decrease in input prices—would shift the *SRAS* curve downward and to the right, from $SRAS_1$ to $SRAS_0$.

the price level rises, output increases. This is the positively sloped *SRAS* curve.

Notice, however, what is happening to the real wage rate. Money wages are fixed (by assumption, in the short run) in money terms. As the price of final output goes up, workers' money wages will buy fewer goods. The *real wage* has fallen. This is why firms choose to hire more labour and expand output. The relative price of their inputs has fallen in comparison with the price of their output.

Of course, this will not be the end of the story. Workers will resist a permanent fall in their real wage, and their representatives will bargain for higher wage rates. Money wages will eventually start to rise, and as they do the relative input and output prices faced by firms will tend to return to their initial level. So firms' output and employment will return to their original level. But this is the long-run story, to which we return in Chapter 26.

> As we move upwards along a given *SRAS* curve, the rise in the price level and output is associated with a fall in the real wage—that is, a rise in output prices relative to input prices.

Shifts in the *SRAS* curve

Shifts in the *SRAS* curve, which are shown in Figure 25.6, are called *aggregate supply shocks*. Two sources of aggregate supply shocks are of particular importance: changes in the price of inputs, and increases in productivity.

Changes in input prices Input prices are held constant along the *SRAS* curve. When they change, the curve shifts. If input prices rise, firms will find the profitability of their

current production reduced. If output prices do not rise, firms will react by decreasing production. For the economy as a whole this means that there will be less output at each price level than before the increase in input prices. Thus, if input prices rise the *SRAS* curve shifts upward. (Notice that when a positively sloped curve shifts upward, indicating that any given quantity is associated with a higher price level, it also shifts to the left, indicating that any given price level is associated with a lower quantity.)

Similarly, a fall in input prices causes the *SRAS* curve to shift downward (and to the right). More will be produced and offered for sale at each price level.[7]

Increases in productivity If labour productivity rises, meaning that each worker can produce more per hour, the unit costs of production will fall, as long as wage rates do not rise sufficiently to offset fully the productivity rise. Lower costs generally lead to lower prices. Competing firms cut prices in an attempt to raise their market shares, and the net result of such competition is that the fall in production costs is accompanied by a fall in prices. Because the same output is sold at a lower price, the increased productivity

---

[7] Note that, for either the *AD* or the *SRAS* curve, a shift to the right means an increase, and a shift to the left means a decrease. Upward and downward shifts, however, have different meanings for the two curves. An upward shift of the *AD* curve reflects an increase in aggregate demand, but an upward shift in the *SRAS* curve reflects a decrease in aggregate supply.

causes a downward shift in the *SRAS* curve. This shift is an increase in supply, as illustrated in Figure 25.6.

A rightward shift in the *SRAS* curve, brought about, for example, by an increase in productivity with no increase in input prices, implies that firms will be willing to produce more output with no increase in the price level.

A change in either input prices or productivity will shift the *SRAS* curve, because any given output will be supplied at a different price level than previously. An increase in input prices or a decrease in productivity shifts the *SRAS* curve to the left; an increase in productivity or a decrease in input prices shifts it to the right.

Macroeconomic equilibrium

We have now added the *SRAS* curve to our model, and we are ready to see how both real GDP and the price level are simultaneously determined by the interaction of aggregate demand and aggregate supply.

The equilibrium values of real GDP and the price level occur at the intersection of the *AD* and *SRAS* curves, as shown by the pair Y_0 and P_0 at point E_0 in Figure 25.7. We call the combination of real GDP and price level at the intersection of the *AD* and *SRAS* curves a *macroeconomic equilibrium*.

To see why the pair of points (Y_0, P_0) is the only macroeconomic equilibrium, first consider what Figure 25.7 shows would happen if the price level were below P_0. At this lower price level the desired output of firms, as given by the *SRAS* curve, is less than desired aggregate spending at that level of GDP. The excess desired aggregate spending will cause prices to be bid up, and output will increase along the *SRAS* curve. Hence there can be no macroeconomic *equilibrium* when the price level is below P_0.

Similarly, Figure 25.7 shows that when the price level is above P_0 the behaviour underlying the *SRAS* and *AD* curves is not consistent. In this case producers will wish to supply more than the output that is demanded at that price level. Desired spending will not be large enough to purchase everything that firms wish to produce at that price level.

Only at the combination of GDP and price level given by the intersection of the *SRAS* and *AD* curves are spending (demand) behaviour and production (supply) activity consistent.

When the price level is less than its equilibrium value, spending behaviour is consistent with a level of GDP that is greater than the desired output of firms. When the price level is greater than its equilibrium value, spending beha-

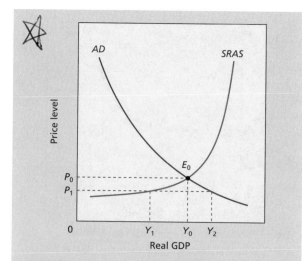

Figure 25.7 Macroeconomic equilibrium

Macroeconomic equilibrium occurs at the intersection of the *AD* and *SRAS* curves and determines the equilibrium values for GDP and the price level. Given the *AD* and *SRAS* curves in the figure, macroeconomic equilibrium occurs at E_0, with GDP equal to Y_0 and the price level equal to P_0. At P_0 the desired output of firms, as given by the *SRAS* curve, is equal to the level of GDP that is consistent with spending decisions, as given by the *AD* curve.

If the price level were equal to P_1, less than P_0, the desired output of firms, given by the *SRAS* curve, would be Y_1. However, at P_1 the level of output that is consistent with spending decisions, given by the *AD* curve, would be Y_2, greater than Y_1. Hence when the price level is P_1, or any other level less than P_0, the desired output of firms will be less than the level of output that is consistent with spending decisions.

Similarly, for any price level above P_0, the desired output of firms, given by the *SRAS* curve, will exceed the level of output that is consistent with spending decisions, given by the *AD* curve.

viour is consistent with a level of GDP that is less than the desired output of firms.

Macroeconomic equilibrium thus requires that two conditions be satisfied. The first is familiar to us because it comes from Chapters 23 and 24: at the prevailing price level, desired aggregate spending must be equal to national output (and consistent with the income generated by that output), which means that agents must be just willing to buy all that is produced. The *AD* curve is constructed in such a way that this condition holds everywhere on it. The second requirement for equilibrium is introduced by consideration of aggregate supply: at the prevailing price level, firms must wish to produce the prevailing level of national output, no more and no less. This condition is fulfilled everywhere on the *SRAS* curve. Only where the two curves intersect are both conditions fulfilled simultaneously.

Changes in GDP and the price level

The aggregate demand and aggregate supply curves can now be used to understand how various shocks to the economy change both real GDP and the price level.

A shift in the *AD* curve is called an **aggregate demand shock**. A *rightward* shift in the *AD* curve results from an *increase* in aggregate demand; this means that at all price levels spending decisions will now be consistent with a *higher* level of real GDP. Similarly, a *leftward* shift in the *AD* curve indicates a *decrease* in aggregate demand; this means that at all price levels spending decisions will now be consistent with a *lower* level of real GDP.[8]

A shift in the *SRAS* curve is called an **aggregate supply shock**. A *rightward* shift in the *SRAS* curve represents an *increase* in aggregate supply: at any given price level *more* real national output will be supplied. A *leftward* shift in the *SRAS* curve is a *decrease* in aggregate supply: at any given price level *less* real national output will be supplied.[9]

What happens to real GDP and to the price level when either the aggregate demand or aggregate supply curve shifts?

A shift in either the *AD* or the *SRAS* curve leads to changes in the equilibrium values of the price level and real GDP.

Box 25.2 deals with the special case of a perfectly elastic *SRAS* curve. In that case, the aggregate supply curve determines the price level, while the aggregate demand curve determines real GDP. This is a special case that is unlikely to arise in practice, but it is the only case where the model of Chapter 22 (with a fixed price level) would be adequate to explain the determination of real GDP.

Aggregate demand shocks

Figure 25.8 shows the effects of an increase in aggregate demand. This increase could have occurred because of, say, increased investment or government spending; it means that more national output will be demanded at any given

[8] The factors that could shift *AD* are the same as those that could shift *AE* (*apart from the price level*). An autonomous increase in private consumption, government consumption, investment, or net exports, or a reduction in tax rates, will all shift *AD* upwards to the right. The opposite shift in any of these will move *AD* downwards to the left.

[9] The distinction between movements along curves and shifts of curves, which we encountered in studying demand and supply in Chapter 3, is also relevant here. A *movement along* an aggreate demand curve indicates a change in the quantity demanded, whereas a *shift* in an aggregate demand curve indicates a 'change in demand'. A similar distinction applies to the supply curve.

 Box 25.2 **The Keynesian *SRAS* curve**

One extreme version of the *SRAS* curve, which is horizontal over some range of GDP, is called the Keynesian short-run aggregate supply curve. The reference is to John Maynard Keynes, who in his famous book *The General Theory of Employment, Interest and Money* (1936) pioneered the study of the behaviour of economies under conditions of high unemployment.

The following behaviour gives rise to the Keynesian *SRAS* curve. When real GDP is below potential GDP, individual firms are operating at less than normal-capacity output, and they hold their prices constant at the level that would maximize profits if production were at normal capacity. They then respond to demand variations below that capacity by altering output. In other words, firms will supply whatever they can sell at their existing prices as long as they are producing below their normal capacity. This means that the firms have horizontal supply curves and that their output is *demand-determined*.*

Under these circumstances, the economy has a horizontal aggregate supply curve, indicating that any output up to potential will be supplied at the going price level. The amount that is actually produced is then determined by the position of the aggregate demand curve, as shown in the figure. Thus, we say that real GDP is demand-determined. If demand rises by enough that firms are trying to squeeze more than normal output out of their plants, their costs will rise, and so will their prices. Thus, the horizontal Keynesian *SRAS* curve applies only to situations below potential GDP.

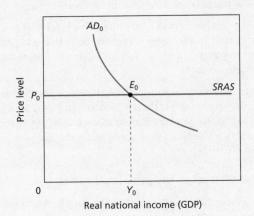

* The evidence is strong that firms, particularly in the manufacturing sector, do behave like this in the short run. One possible explanation for this is that changing prices frequently is too costly, so firms set the best possible (profit-maximizing) prices when output is at normal capacity and then do not change prices in the face of short-term fluctuations in demand.

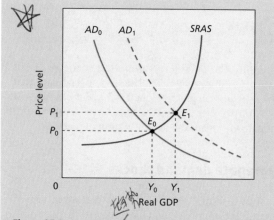

Figure 25.8 Aggregate demand shocks

Shifts in aggregate demand cause the price level and real GDP to move in the same direction. An increase in aggregate demand shifts the AD curve to the right—say, from AD_0 to AD_1. Macroeconomic equilibrium moves from E_0 to E_1. The price level rises from P_0 to P_1 and real GDP rises from Y_0 to Y_1, reflecting a movement along the $SRAS$ curve.

A decrease in aggregate demand shifts the AD curve to the left—say, from AD_1 to AD_0. Equilibrium moves from E_1 to E_0. Prices fall from P_1 to P_0, and real GDP falls from Y_1 to Y_0.

price level. For now we are not concerned with the source of the shock; we are interested in its implications for the price level and real GDP. As is shown in the figure, following an increase in aggregate demand, both the price level and real GDP rise.

Figure 25.8 also shows that both the price level and real GDP fall as the result of a decrease in aggregate demand.

Aggregate demand shocks cause the price level and real GDP to change in the same direction; both rise with an increase in aggregate demand, and both fall with a decrease in aggregate demand.

An aggregate demand shock means that there is a shift in the AD curve (for example from AD_0 to AD_1 in Figure 25.8). Adjustment to the new equilibrium following an aggregate demand shock involves a movement along the $SRAS$ curve (for example from point E_0 to point E_1).

The multiplier when the price level varies

We saw earlier in this chapter that the simple multiplier gives the extent of the horizontal shift in the AD curve in response to a change in autonomous spending. If the price level remains constant, and if firms are willing to supply all that is demanded at the existing price level (that is, if the aggregate supply curve is horizontal), then the simple multiplier gives the increase in equilibrium GDP.

Now that we can use aggregate demand and aggregate supply curves, we can answer a more interesting question:

what happens in the more usual case where the aggregate supply curve slopes upward?

Figure 25.8 shows that, when the $SRAS$ curve is positively sloped, the change in GDP that is caused by a change in autonomous spending is no longer equal to the size of the horizontal shift in the AD curve. A rightward shift of the AD curve causes the price level to rise, which in turn causes the rise in GDP to be less than the horizontal shift of the AD curve. Part of the expansionary impact of an increase in demand is dissipated by a rise in the price level, and only part is transmitted to a rise in real output. Of course, there is still an increase in output, so there is still a positive multiplier effect, but its value is not the same as that of the simple multiplier.

When the $SRAS$ curve is positively sloped, the multiplier is smaller than the simple multiplier.

Why is the multiplier smaller when the $SRAS$ curve is positively sloped? The answer lies in the behaviour that is summarized by the AE curve. To understand this, it is useful to think of the final change in GDP as occurring in two stages, as shown in Figure 25.9. First, with prices remaining constant, an increase in autonomous spending shifts the AE curve upward (part (i) of the figure) and therefore shifts the AD curve to the right (part (ii)). The horizontal shift in the AD curve is measured by the simple multiplier, but this cannot be the final equilibrium position because firms are unwilling to produce enough to satisfy the extra demand at the existing price level.

Second, we take account of the rise in the price level that occurs owing to the positive slope of the $SRAS$ curve. A rise in the price level, via its negative effect on net exports and on wealth, leads to a downward shift in the AE curve. This second shift of the AE curve partially counteracts the initial rise in GDP and so reduces the size of the multiplier. The second stage shows up as a downward shift of the AE curve in part (i) of Figure 25.9 and a movement upward and to the left along the AD curve in part (ii).

The importance of the shape of the $SRAS$ curve

The shape of the $SRAS$ curve has important implications for how the effects of an aggregate demand shock are divided between changes in real GDP and changes in the price level. Figure 25.10 highlights this point by considering AD shocks in the presence of an $SRAS$ curve that exhibits three distinct ranges. Box 25.3 explores some possible reasons for such an increasing slope of the $SRAS$ curve.

Over the *flat* range in Figure 25.10, from 0 to Y_0, any change in aggregate demand leads to no change in prices and a response of output equal to that predicted by the simple multiplier.

Over the *intermediate* range along which the $SRAS$ curve is positively sloped, from Y_1 to Y_4, a shift in the AD curve

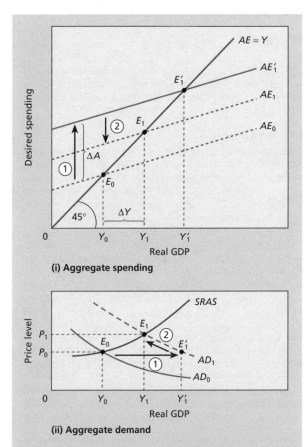

(i) Aggregate spending

(ii) Aggregate demand

Figure 25.9 The *AE* line and the multiplier when the price level varies

An increase in autonomous spending causes the *AE* line to shift upward, but the rise in the price level causes it to shift part of the way down again. Hence the multiplier effect on GDP is smaller than when the price level is constant. Originally equilibrium is at point E_0 in both part (i) and part (ii), with real GDP at Y_0 and price level at P_0. Desired aggregate spending then shifts by ΔA to AE_1', taking the aggregate demand curve to AD_1. These shifts are shown by arrow 1 in both parts. If the price level had remained constant at P_0, the new equilibrium would have been E_1' and real GDP would have risen to Y_1'. The amount Y_0Y_1' is the change called for by the simple multiplier.

Instead, however, the shift in the *AD* line raises the price level to P_1 and shifts the aggregate spending curve down to AE_1, as shown by arrow 2 in part (i). This is shown as a movement along the *AD* curve, as indicated by arrow 2 in part (ii). The new equilibrium is thus at E_1. The amount Y_0Y_1 is ΔY, the actual increase in real GDP, whereas the amount Y_1Y_1' is the shortfall relative to the simple multiplier owing to the rise in the price level.

The multiplier is the ratio $\Delta Y/\Delta A$ in part (i).

gives rise to appreciable changes in both real GDP and the price level. As we saw earlier in this chapter, the change in the price level reduces the response of GDP to a change in autonomous spending.

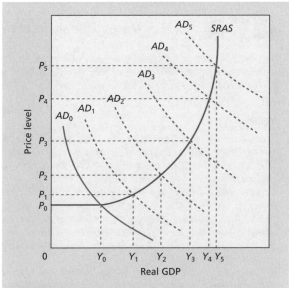

Figure 25.10 The effects of increases in aggregate demand

The effects of increases in aggregate demand are divided between increases in real output and increases in prices, depending on the shape of the *SRAS* curve. Increases in aggregate demand up to AD_0 have virtually no impact on the price level. When aggregate demand increases from AD_0 to AD_1, there is a relatively small increase in the price level, from P_0 to P_1, and a relatively large increase in output, from Y_0 to Y_1. Successive further increases bring larger price increases and relatively smaller output increases. By the time aggregate demand is at AD_5, virtually all of the effect is on the price level.

Over the *steep* range, for GDP above Y_4, the economy is near its capacity constraint. Any change in aggregate demand leads to a sharp change in the price level and to little change in real GDP. The multiplier in this case is nearly zero.

How do we reconcile what we have just discovered with the analysis of Chapters 23 and 24, where shifts in *AE* *always* change real GDP? The answer is that each *AE* curve is drawn on the assumption that there is a constant price level and plenty of excess capacity. A rise in *AE* shifts the *AD* curve to the right. However, a steep *SRAS* curve means that the price level rises significantly (because there is little excess capacity), and this shifts the *AE* curve downward, offsetting some of its initial rise.

This interaction is seen most easily if we study the extreme case, shown in Figure 25.11, in which the *SRAS* curve is vertical. An increase in autonomous spending shifts the *AE* curve upward, thus raising the amount demanded. However, a vertical *SRAS* curve means that output cannot be expanded to satisfy the increased demand. Instead, the extra demand merely forces prices up, and as prices rise the *AE* curve shifts downward once again. The rise in prices continues until the *AE* curve is back to where it started.

Box 25.3 More on the shape of the *SRAS* curve

The *SRAS* curve relates the price level to the quantity of output that producers are willing to sell. Notice two things about the shape of the *SRAS* curve that is reproduced in Figure 25.8: it has a positive slope, and the slope increases as output rises.

Positive slope

The most obvious feature of the *SRAS* curve is its positive slope, indicating that a higher price level is associated with a higher volume of real output, other things being equal. Because the prices of all of the inputs to production are being held constant along the *SRAS* curve, why is the curve not horizontal, indicating that firms would be willing to supply as much output as might be demanded with no increase in the price level?

The answer is that, even though *input prices* are constant, *unit costs of production* eventually rise as output increases. Thus, a higher price level for increasing output—rising short-run aggregate supply—is necessary to compensate firms for rising costs.

The preceding paragraph addresses the question of what has to happen to the price level if national output increases, with the price of inputs remaining constant. Alternatively, one could ask what will happen to firms' willingness to supply output if product prices rise with no increase in input prices. Production becomes more profitable, and since firms are interested in making profits they will usually produce more. Thus, when the price level of final output rises while input prices are held constant, firms are motivated to increase their outputs. This is true for the individual firm and also for firms in the aggregate. This increase in the amount produced leads to an upward slope of the *SRAS* curve.

Thus, whether we look at how the price level responds in the short run to increases in output or at how the level of output responds to an increase in the price level with input prices being held constant, we find that the *SRAS* curve has a positive slope.

Increasing slope

A less obvious, but in many ways more important, property of a typical *SRAS* curve is that its slope *increases* as output rises. It is rather flat to the left of potential output and rather steep to the right. Why? Below potential output, firms typically have unused capacity—some plant and equipment are idle. When firms are faced with unused capacity, only a small increase in the price of their output may be needed to induce them to expand production—at least up to normal capacity.

Once output is pushed far beyond normal capacity, however, unit costs tend to rise quite rapidly. Many higher-cost expedients may have to be adopted. Standby capacity, overtime, and extra shifts may have to be used. Such expedients raise the cost of producing a unit of output. These higher-cost methods will not be used unless the selling price of the output has risen enough to cover them. The further output is expanded beyond normal capacity, the more rapidly unit costs rise and hence the larger is the rise in price that is needed to induce firms to increase output even further.

This increasing slope is sometimes called the *first important asymmetry* in the behaviour of aggregate supply. (The second, 'sticky wages', will be discussed in the next chapter.)

The analysis of Chapter 10 shows how a firm in a perfectly competitive market, when faced with a higher output price, expands output *along* its marginal cost curve until marginal cost is once again equal to price.

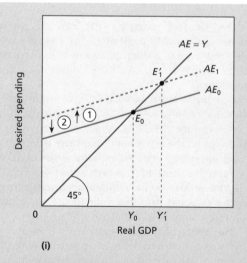
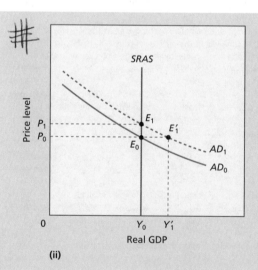

Figure 25.11 Demand shocks when the *SRAS* curve is vertical

If the *SRAS* curve were vertical, the effect of an increase in autonomous spending would be solely a rise in the price level. An increase in autonomous spending shifts the *AE* line upwards from AE_0 to AE_1, as shown by arrow 1 in part (i). Given the initial price level P_0, equilibrium would shift from E_0 to E_1' and real GDP would rise from Y_0 to Y_1'. However, the price level does not remain constant. This is shown by the *SRAS* curve in part (ii). Instead, the price level rises to P_1. This causes the *AE* line to shift back down all the way to AE_0, as shown by arrow 2 in part (i), and equilibrium output stays at Y_0. In part (ii) the new equilibrium is at E_1, with GDP at Y_0 and price level P_1.

Thus, the rise in prices offsets the expansionary effect of the original shift and, as a result, leaves both real aggregate spending and equilibrium real GDP unchanged.

The discussion of Figures 25.10 and 25.11 illustrates a general proposition:

The effect of any given shift in aggregate demand will be divided between a change in real output and a change in the price level, depending on the conditions of aggregate supply. The steeper the *SRAS* curve, the greater is the price effect, and the smaller is the output effect.

For reasons discussed in Boxes 25.2 and 25.3, the *SRAS* curve probably has the shape shown in Figure 25.10, that is, relatively flat for low levels of output and becoming steeper as the level of GDP increases (relative to potential GDP). This shape of the *SRAS* curve implies that at low levels of GDP (well below potential) shifts in aggregate demand primarily affect output, and at high levels of GDP (above potential) shifts in aggregate demand primarily affect prices.

Of course, as we have noted already, treating wages and other input prices as constant is appropriate only when the time-period under consideration is short. Hence the *SRAS* curve is used to analyse only short-run, or *impact*, effects. In the next chapter we will see what happens in the *long run* when input prices (especially wages) respond to changes in GDP and the price level. First, however, our analysis of the short run needs to be completed with a discussion of aggregate supply shocks.

Aggregate supply shocks

A decrease in aggregate supply is shown by a shift to the left of the *SRAS* curve and means that less national output will be supplied at any given price level. An increase in aggregate supply is shown by a shift to the right of the *SRAS* curve and means that more national output will be produced at any given price level.

Figure 25.12 illustrates the effects on the price level and real GDP of aggregate supply shocks. Following a decrease in aggregate supply, the price level rises and real GDP falls. This combination of events is called *stagflation*, a rather inelegant word that has been derived by combining *stagnation* (a term that is sometimes used to mean slow growth or even falling output) and *inflation*.

Figure 25.12 also shows that an increase in aggregate supply leads to an increase in real GDP and a decrease in the price level.

Aggregate supply shocks cause the price level and real GDP to change in opposite directions: with an increase in supply the price level falls and output rises; with a decrease in supply the price level rises and output falls.

An aggregate supply shock means that there is a shift in the *SRAS* curve (for example from $SRAS_0$ to $SRAS_1$ in Figure 25.12). Adjustment to the new equilibrium following the shock involves a movement along the *AD* curve (for example from E_0 to E_1).

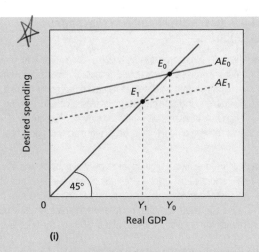
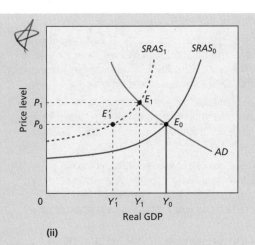

Figure 25.12 Aggregate supply shocks

Shifts in aggregate supply cause the price level and real GDP to move in opposite directions. The original equilibrium is at E_0 with GDP of Y_0 in both parts of the figure. The price level is P_0 in part (ii), and at that price level the desired aggregate spending line is AE_0 in part (i).

An aggregate supply shock now shifts the *SRAS* curve in part (ii) to $SRAS_1$. At the original price level of P_0, firms are now willing to supply only Y_1'. The fall in supply, with no corresponding fall in demand, causes a shortage that leads to a rise in the price level along $SRAS_1$. The new equilibrium is reached at E_1, where the *AD* curve intersects $SRAS_1$. At the new, and higher, equilibrium price level of P_1, the *AE* line has fallen to AE_1, as shown in part (i), which is consistent with equilibrium GDP of Y_1.

Oil prices have provided three major examples of aggregate supply shocks in recent decades. The major industrial economies have been especially responsive to changes in the market for oil, because, in addition to being used to produce energy, oil is an input into plastics and many other materials that are widely used in production. Massive increases in oil prices during 1973–4 and 1979–80 caused leftward shifts in the *SRAS* curve for virtually all major economies. GDP fell while the price level rose, causing stagflation. During the mid-1980s oil prices fell substantially and stayed low for most of the 1990s (except for a blip after Iraq invaded Kuwait in 1990). This shifted the *SRAS* curve to the right, increasing GDP and putting downward pressure on the price level. However oil prices rose sharply again after the spring of 1999, reversing some of the earlier positive supply shock (see discussion on pages xxx–xx). We can see now how a rightward shift in the *SRAS* curve, which is brought about by an increase in productivity or a fall in input prices, raises real GDP and lowers the price level.

In the late 1990s it was thought that there might be a positive supply shock associated with productivity gains delivered by new technologies, and especially by computers and the internet. This is associated with the debate about whether there was a 'new economy'. Certainly significant productivity gains would generate a positive supply shock; however, at least in the UK, there remains some doubt about whether this has really happened. (See also our discussion of the new economy on pages 307–11.)

Conclusion

GDP and the price level are determined by the interaction of aggregate demand and aggregate supply. The aggregate demand curve is drawn for given values of exogenous expenditures. The aggregate supply curve is drawn for a given technology and given input prices. Demand and supply shocks disturb an existing equilibrium and lead to new values of GDP and the price level. In this chapter we have analysed the short run response. We now turn to the long run.

SUMMARY

Aggregate demand

- A change in the price level shifts the *AE* curve upward when the price level falls and downward when the price level rises. A new level of GDP results. This would be the equilibrium level of GDP if it were demand-determined.

- The *AD* curve plots the level of GDP (for which injections equal leakages) that corresponds to each possible price level. A change in GDP following a change in the price level is shown by a *movement along* the *AD* curve.

- A rise in the price level lowers exports and lowers private consumption spending (because it decreases consumers' wealth). Both of these changes lower GDP and cause the aggregate demand curve to have a negative slope.

- The *AD* curve *shifts* when any element of autonomous spending changes, and the simple multiplier measures the magnitude of the shift. This multiplier also measures the size of the change in equilibrium GDP when the price level remains constant *and* firms produce everything that is demanded at that price level.

Aggregate supply and macroeconomic equilibrium

- The short-run aggregate supply (*SRAS*) curve, drawn for given input prices, is positively sloped because unit costs rise with increasing output and because rising product prices make it profitable to increase output. An increase in productivity or a decrease in input prices shifts the curve to the right. A decrease in productivity or an increase in input prices has the opposite effect.

- Macroeconomic equilibrium refers to equilibrium values of real GDP and the price level, as determined by the intersection of the *AD* and *SRAS* curves. Shifts in the *AD* and *SRAS* curves, called aggregate demand shocks and aggregate supply shocks, change the equilibrium values of real GDP and the price level.

Changes in GDP and the price level

- When the *SRAS* curve is positively sloped, an aggregate demand shock causes the price level and real GDP to move in the same direction, the division between these effects depending on the shape of the *SRAS* curve. The main effect is on real GDP when the *SRAS* curve is flat and on the price level when it is steep.

- An aggregate supply shock moves equilibrium real GDP along the *AD* curve, causing the price level and output to move in opposite directions. A leftward shift in the *SRAS* curve causes a

stagflation—rising prices and falling output. A rightward shift causes an increase in real GDP and a fall in the price level. The division of the effects of a shift in *SRAS* between a change in real GDP and a change in the price level depends on the shape of the *AD* curve.

TOPICS FOR REVIEW

- Effects of a change in the price level
- Relationship between the *AE* and *AD* curves
- Negative slope of the *AD* curve
- Positive slope of the *SRAS* curve
- Macroeconomic equilibrium

- Aggregate demand shocks
- The multiplier when the price level varies
- Aggregate supply shocks
- Stagflation

DISCUSSION QUESTIONS

1 Explain what happens to the UK *AD* curve in response to each of the following exogenous changes: (*a*) a rise in optimism leads to higher investment; (*b*) the government decides to build some new schools; (*c*) there is a recession in the United States; (*d*) consumers become cautious about the future and decide to save more; (*e*) GDP in France and Germany rises; (*f*) new computer technology increases productivity in manufacturing industry.

2 Show what will happen to the *SRAS* curve if (*a*) investment in transport infrastructure lowers costs of shipping goods and raw materials; (*b*) oil prices rise; (*c*) workers agree to work for lower wages; (*d*) there is an increase in export demand; (*e*) there is technical innovation in manufacturing industry.

3 Outline how the interaction of the *AD* and *SRAS* curves determines the course of GDP and the price level in response to (*a*) a rise in wage rates; (*b*) an increase in investment;

(*c*) a reduction in government consumption; (*d*) a boom in demand in neighbouring economies.

4 Explain why changes in the price level lead to changes in desired aggregate expenditure for each level of GDP.

5 Explain why the change in GDP in response to an increase in export demand is smaller than that suggested by the simple multiplier. What happens to the size of this effect as GDP gets above its potential level?

6 Explain how the shifts in *AD* set out in question 1 are consistent with the condition that injections equal leakages.

7 What determines the slope of the *SRAS* curve?

8 How do you think changes in interest rates would affect aggregate demand?

Chapter 26

GDP AND THE PRICE LEVEL IN THE LONG RUN

Employees know that the best time to ask for a pay rise is during a boom, when the demand for labour is high. They also know that it is difficult to get significant wage increases during a recession, when high unemployment signals a low demand for labour. Managers in industry know that the cost of many materials tends to rise rapidly during business expansions and to fall—often dramatically—during recessions. In short, input prices change with economic conditions, and we need to allow for these effects. In particular, you will learn in this chapter that:

• Output gaps will stimulate changes in both output and input prices.

• If actual output is greater than potential output, there is an inflationary gap associated with a high level of activity and a tendency for the price level to rise.

• If actual output is less that potential output, there is a recessionary gap associated with low levels of activity and a tendency for the price level to fall.

• The long-run aggregate supply curve is vertical at the level of potential output.

• Economic growth determines the position of the long-run aggregate supply curve.

• Shocks to aggregate demand and aggregate supply are associated with business cycles.

• In principle, fiscal and monetary policies can stabilize cycles and keep GDP close to its potential level.

In Chapter 25 we studied aggregate supply holding input prices constant. In this chapter we analyse what happens when changes in GDP *induce* changes in input prices. Once we have completed this task, we can use our model of the short-run behaviour of the macroeconomy to investigate the causes and consequences of business cycles and to further our study of fiscal policy. In the following two chapters we study monetary policy.

Induced changes in input prices

We begin by revising two key concepts that we first encountered in Chapter 22: potential output and the GDP gap.

Another look at potential output and the GDP gap

Recall that potential output is the total output that can be produced when all productive resources are being used at their *normal rates of utilization*. When a nation's actual output diverges from its potential output, the difference is called the GDP gap or output gap. (See Figure 22.1 on page 389.)

Although growth in potential output has powerful effects from one decade to the next, its change from one *year* to the next is small enough to be ignored when studying the year-to-year behaviour of GDP and the price level. (See Chapter 22 for a discussion of the determinants of the growth of potential output.) Therefore in this discussion we will continue with the convention, first adopted in Chapter 23, of ignoring the small changes in potential GDP caused by year-to-year changes in productivity. Variations in the output gap are then determined solely by variations in actual GDP around a given potential GDP.

Figure 26.1 shows actual GDP being determined by the intersection of the *AD* and *SRAS* curves. Potential GDP is constant, and it is shown by identical vertical lines in the two parts of the figure. In part (i), the *AD* and *SRAS* curves intersect to produce an equilibrium GDP that falls short of potential GDP. The result is called a *recessionary gap* because recessions often begin when actual output falls below potential output. In part (ii) the *AD* and *SRAS* curves

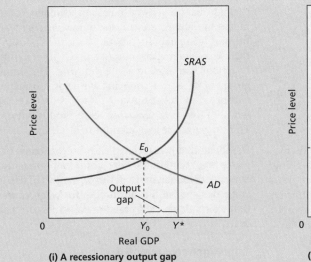
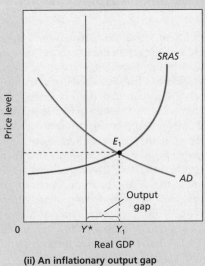

(i) A recessionary output gap

(ii) An inflationary output gap

Figure 26.1 Actual GDP, potential GDP, and the output gap

The output gap is the difference between potential GDP, Y^*, and actual GDP, Y. Potential GDP is shown by a vertical line because it refers to a given, constant level of real GDP. Actual GDP is determined by the intersection of the aggregate demand (AD) and short-run aggregate supply ($SRAS$) curves.

In part (i) the positions of the AD and $SRAS$ curves result in a recessionary gap: equilibrium is at E_0, so actual GDP is given by Y_0, which is less than potential output. The output gap is thus $Y^* - Y_0$. In part (ii) the positions of the AD and $SRAS$ curves result in an inflationary gap. Although potential output is unchanged at Y^*, equilibrium is now at E_1, so actual GDP is given by Y_1, which is greater than potential output. The output gap is $Y_1 - Y^*$.

intersect to produce an equilibrium GDP that exceeds potential output, resulting in an *inflationary gap*. The way in which an inflationary output gap puts upward pressure on prices will become clear in the following discussion.

Input prices and the output gap

The output gap provides a convenient measure of the pressure of demand on input prices. When actual GDP is high relative to potential GDP, demand for inputs will also be high. When actual GDP is low relative to potential GDP, demand for inputs will be relatively low. This relationship is true of all inputs. The discussion that follows is simplified, however, by focusing on one key input, labour, and on its price, the wage rate.

When there is an inflationary gap, actual output exceeds potential, and the demand for labour services will be relatively high. When there is a recessionary gap, actual output is below potential, and the demand for labour services will be relatively low.

Each of these situations has implications for wages. Before turning to a detailed study of these, we first consider a benchmark for the behaviour of wages. Earlier we referred to average costs per unit of output as *unit costs*; to focus on

labour costs, we now use average wage costs per unit of output, which we refer to as *unit labour costs*.

Upward and downward wage pressures

Consider the *upward* and *downward* pressures on wages that are associated with various output gaps. Most wage bargaining starts from the assumption that, other things being equal, workers will get the benefit of increases in their own productivity by receiving higher wages. Thus, when GDP is at its potential level, wages will tend to be rising at the same rate as productivity is rising.[1] When wages and productivity change proportionately, *unit labour costs* remain unchanged. For example, if each worker produces 4 per cent more and earns 4 per cent more, unit labour costs will remain constant. This, then, is the benchmark:

When there is neither excess demand nor excess supply in the labour market, wages will tend to be rising at the same

[1] Ongoing inflation will also influence the normal pattern of wage changes. Wage contracts often allow for changes in prices that are expected to occur during the life of the contract. For now, we make the simplifying assumption that the price level is expected to be constant; hence changes in money wages also are expected to be changes in real wages. The distinction between changes in money wages and in real wages, and the important role played by expectations of price level changes, will be discussed later.

rate as labour productivity; as a result, unit labour costs will remain constant.

Note that, with unit labour costs remaining constant, there is no pressure coming from the labour market for the *SRAS* curve to shift. Hence there is no pressure for the price level to change. Indeed, a key characteristic of the definition of potential GDP is that there is no pressure for unit labour costs to rise or fall. So the state of the labour market and the level of potential GDP are inextricably connected.

In comparison with this benchmark of constant unit labour costs, *upward pressure on wages* means that there is pressure for wages to rise faster than productivity is rising. Thus, unit labour costs will also be rising. For example, if money wages rise by 8 per cent while productivity rises by only 4 per cent, labour costs per unit of output will be rising by about 4 per cent. In this case the *SRAS* curve will be shifting to the left, reflecting upward pressure on wage costs coming from the labour market.

Downward pressure on wages means that there is pressure for wages to rise more slowly than productivity is rising. When this occurs, unit labour costs will be falling. For example, if productivity rises by 4 per cent while money wages rise by only 2 per cent, labour costs per unit of output will be falling by about 2 per cent. In this case the *SRAS* curve will be shifting to the right, reflecting downward pressure on wage costs coming from the labour market.

Actual GDP exceeds potential GDP

Sometimes the *AD* and *SRAS* curves intersect where actual output exceeds potential, as illustrated in part (ii) of Figure 26.1. Firms are producing beyond their normal-capacity output, so there is an unusually large demand for all inputs, including labour. Labour shortages will emerge in some industries and among many groups of workers, particularly skilled workers. Firms will try to bid workers away from other firms in order to maintain the high levels of output and sales made possible by the boom conditions.

As a result of these tight labour market conditions, workers will find that they have considerable bargaining power with their employers, and they will put upward pressure on wages relative to productivity. Firms, recognizing that demand for their goods is strong, will be anxious to maintain a high level of output. Thus, to prevent their workers from either striking or quitting and moving to other employers, firms will be willing to accede to some of these upward pressures.

The boom that is associated with an inflationary gap generates a set of conditions—high profits for firms and unusually large demand for labour—that exert upward pressure on wages.

Actual GDP is less than potential GDP

Sometimes the *AD* and *SRAS* curves intersect where actual output is less than potential, as illustrated in part (i) of Figure 26.1. In this situation firms are producing below their normal-capacity output, so the demands for all inputs, including labour, are unusually low. The general conditions in the market for labour will be the opposite of those that occur when actual output exceeds potential. There will be labour surpluses in some industries and among some groups of workers. Firms will have below-normal sales, and will not only resist upward pressures on wages, but also tend to offer wage increases below productivity increases. They may even seek reductions in money wages.

The slump that is associated with a recessionary gap generates a set of conditions—low profits for firms, unusually low demand for labour, and a desire on the part of firms to resist wage demands and even to push for wage concessions—that exerts downward pressure on wages and unit labour costs.

Adjustment asymmetry

Boom conditions, along with severe labour shortages, cause wages, unit labour costs, and the price level to rise rapidly. When there is a large excess demand for labour, wage (and price) increases may well run ahead of productivity increases. Money wages might be rising by, say, 6 per cent, while productivity is rising at only 2 per cent, so that unit labour costs will be rising by around 4 per cent.

However, the experience of most European economies (and other industrial economies, such as the United States and Canada) suggests that the downward pressures on wages during slumps often do not operate as quickly as do the upward pressures during booms. Even in quite severe recessions, when the price level is fairly stable, money wages may continue to rise, although their rate of increase tends to fall below that of productivity. For example, productivity might be rising at, say, 1.5 per cent per year while money wages are rising at 0.5 per cent. In this case unit labour costs are falling, but only by about 1 per cent per year. The rightward shift in the *SRAS* curve and the downward pressure on the price level are correspondingly slight. Money wages may actually fall, reducing unit wage costs even more, but the reduction in unit labour costs in the times of deepest recession has not been as fast as the increases that have occurred during several of the strongest booms. This suggests that there is an asymmetry in the way in which the economy responds to each of the output gaps.

Both upward and downward adjustments to unit labour costs do occur, but there is a difference in the speed at which they typically operate. Excess demand can cause unit labour costs to rise very rapidly; excess supply normally causes unit labour costs to fall only slowly.[2]

---

[2] This is the second asymmetry in aggregate supply that we have encountered. The first refers to the variable slope of the *SRAS* curve, as discussed in Box 25.3.

Inflationary and recessionary gaps

Now it should be clear why the output gaps are named as they are. When actual GDP exceeds potential GDP there will normally be rising unit costs, and the *SRAS* curve will be shifting upward. This in turn will push the price level up. Indeed, the most obvious event accompanying these conditions is likely to be a significant inflation. The larger is the excess of actual output over potential output, the greater will be the inflationary pressure. The term *inflationary gap* emphasizes this salient feature.

When actual output is less than potential output, as we have seen, there will be unemployment of labour and other productive resources. Unit labour costs will fall only slowly, leading to a slow downward shift in the *SRAS* curve. Hence the price level will be falling only slowly, so that *unemployment* will be the output gap's most obvious result. The term *recessionary gap* emphasizes this salient feature that high rates of unemployment occur when actual output falls short of potential output.

The induced effects of output gaps on unit labour costs and the consequent shifts in the *SRAS* curve play an important role in our analysis of the long-run consequences of aggregate demand shocks, to which we now turn.

Long-run consequences of aggregate demand shocks

We can now extend our study to cover the longer-run consequences of aggregate demand shocks, by incorporating changes in input prices. We need to examine separately the effects of aggregate demand shocks on input prices for expansionary and contractionary shocks, because, as we have just seen, the behaviour of unit costs is not symmetrical for the two cases.

Expansionary shocks

Suppose that the economy starts with a stable price level at full employment, so actual GDP equals potential GDP, as shown by the initial equilibrium in part (i) of Figure 26.2.

Now suppose that this stable situation is disturbed by an increase in autonomous spending, perhaps caused by a

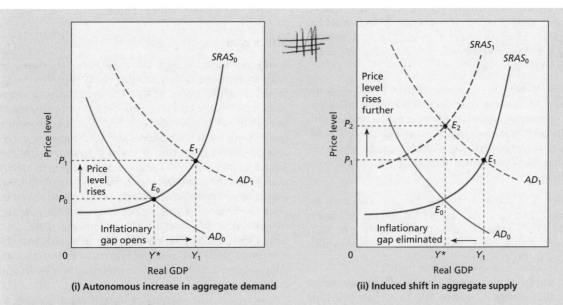

(i) Autonomous increase in aggregate demand (ii) Induced shift in aggregate supply

Figure 26.2 Demand-shock inflation

A rightward shift of the *AD* curve first raises prices and output along the *SRAS* curve. It then induces a shift of the *SRAS* curve that further raises prices but lowers output along the *AD* curve. In part (i) the economy is in equilibrium at E_0, at its level of potential output Y^* and price level P_0. The *AD* curve then shifts to AD_1. This moves equilibrium to E_1, with GDP Y_1 and price level P_1, and opens up an inflationary gap of $Y^* - Y_1$.

In part (ii) the inflationary gap results in an increase in wages and other input costs, shifting the *SRAS* curve leftward. As this happens, output falls and the price level rises along AD_1. Eventually, when the *SRAS* curve has shifted to $SRAS_1$, output is back to Y^* and the inflationary gap has been eliminated. However, the price level has risen to P_2.

sudden boom in investment spending. Figure 26.2(i) shows the effects of this aggregate demand shock in raising both the price level and GDP. Now actual GDP exceeds potential GDP; i.e., there is an inflationary gap.

We have seen that an inflationary gap causes wages to rise faster than productivity, which raises unit costs. The *SRAS* curve shifts to the left as firms seek to pass on their increases in costs by increasing their output prices. For this reason the initial increases in the price level and in real GDP shown in part (i) of Figure 26.2 are *not* the final effects of the demand shock. As seen in part (ii) of the figure, the upward shift of the *SRAS* curve causes a further rise in the price level, but this time the price rise is associated with a fall in output.

The cost increases (and the consequent upward shifts of the *SRAS* curve) continue until the inflationary gap has been removed, that is, until output returns to Y^*, its potential level. Only then is there no excess demand for labour, and only then do wages and unit costs, and hence the *SRAS* curve, stabilize.

This important expansionary demand-shock sequence can be summarized as follows:

1. Starting from full employment, a rise in aggregate demand raises the price level and raises output above its potential level as the economy expands along a given *SRAS* curve.

2. The expansion of output beyond its normal-capacity level puts pressure on input (especially labour) markets; input prices begin to increase faster than productivity, shifting the *SRAS* curve upward, such that prices are higher at every level of output.

3. The shift of the *SRAS* curve causes GDP to fall along the *AD* curve. This process continues *as long as* actual output exceeds potential output. Therefore, actual output eventually falls back to its potential level. The price level, however, is now higher than it was after the initial impact of the increased aggregate demand, but inflation will have come to a halt.

The ability to wring more output (and income) from the economy than its underlying potential output (as in point 2 above) is only a short-term possibility. GDP greater than Y^* sets into motion inflationary pressures that tend to push GDP back to Y^*.

A once-and-for-all demand shock sets off an adjustment process that eventually returns GDP to its potential level but (normally) at a different price level.

Contractionary shocks

Let us return to that stable economy with full employment and steady prices. It appears again in part (i) of Figure 26.3,

which is similar to part (i) of Figure 26.2. Now assume that there is a *decline* in aggregate demand, perhaps owing to a major reduction in investment spending, or to a fall in exports as a result of a fall in overseas demand.

The first effects of the decline are a fall in output and some downward adjustment of the price level, as shown in part (i) of the figure. As output falls, unemployment rises. The difference between potential GDP and actual GDP is the recessionary gap that is shown in the figure.

Flexible wages

What would happen if severe unemployment caused a rapid fall in wage rates relative to productivity? For example, with productivity rising by 1 per cent per year, suppose that money wages fell by 4 per cent. Unit costs would then *fall* by 5 per cent. Falling wage rates would lower unit costs, causing a rightward shift of the *SRAS* curve. As shown in part (ii) of Figure 26.3, the economy would move along AD_1, with falling prices and rising output, until full employment was restored at potential GDP, Y^*. We conclude that, if wages were to fall whenever there was unemployment, the resulting fall in the *SRAS* curve would restore full employment.

Flexible wages that fell during periods of unemployment would provide an automatic adjustment mechanism that would push the economy back towards full employment whenever output fell below potential.

Sticky wages

Boom conditions, along with severe labour shortages, do cause wages to rise rapidly, shifting the *SRAS* curve upward. However, as we noted earlier, the experience of many economies suggests that wages typically do not fall rapidly in response to recessionary gaps and their accompanying unemployment. It is sometimes said that wages are 'sticky' in a downward direction. This does not mean that wages never fall. In recession money wages often rise more slowly than productivity and some money wages actually fall. But during recessions there is typically only a small difference between the rate at which money wages are changing and the rate at which productivity is changing. Thus, unit labour costs fall only slowly. This in turn implies that the downward shifts in the *SRAS* curve occur slowly, and the adjustment mechanism that depends on these shifts will act sluggishly.

One reason why wage rates do not adjust quickly to clear labour markets will be discussed in Chapter 32. This explanation is associated with the idea of *efficiency wages* that we first encountered in Chapter 16 (page 279). Because labour is not a standardized commodity, employers face both a problem of attracting the best workers and a problem of motivating those workers who have been hired. Employers are reluctant to lower wages for their workforce,

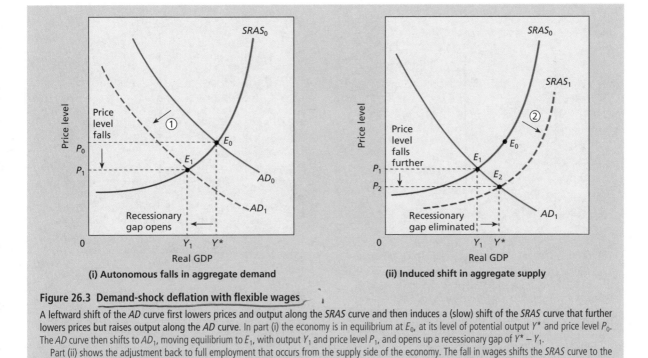

Figure 26.3 Demand-shock deflation with flexible wages

A leftward shift of the AD curve first lowers prices and output along the $SRAS$ curve and then induces a (slow) shift of the $SRAS$ curve that further lowers prices but raises output along the AD curve. In part (i) the economy is in equilibrium at E_0, at its level of potential output Y^* and price level P_0. The AD curve then shifts to AD_1, moving equilibrium to E_1, with output Y_1 and price level P_1, and opens up a recessionary gap of $Y^* - Y_1$.

Part (ii) shows the adjustment back to full employment that occurs from the supply side of the economy. The fall in wages shifts the $SRAS$ curve to the right. Real GDP rises, and the price level falls further along the AD curve. Eventually the $SRAS$ curve reaches $SRAS_1$, with equilibrium at E_2. The price level stabilizes at P_2 when GDP returns to Y^*, eliminating the recessionary gap.

even when there is an excess supply of potential new workers, because lower wages are more likely to attract lower-quality workers at the margin, and existing staff would be discouraged by such actions.

The weakness of the adjustment mechanism does not imply that slumps must always be prolonged. It only requires that speedy recovery back to full employment be generated mainly from the demand side. If the economy is to avoid a lengthy period of recession or stagnation, the force leading to recovery must usually be a rightward shift of the AD curve rather than a downward drift of the $SRAS$ curve.

The $SRAS$ curve shifts to the left fairly rapidly when GDP exceeds Y^*, but it shifts to the right only slowly when GDP is less than Y^*.

Could government *stabilization policy* accomplish the needed shift in AD? This is one of the more important and contentious issues in macroeconomics, and one that we will return to later.

The asymmetry

This difference in speed of adjustment is a consequence of the important asymmetry in the behaviour of aggregate supply that was noted earlier in this chapter. The asym-

metry helps to explain two key facts about our economy. First, unemployment can persist for quite long periods without causing decreases in unit costs and prices of sufficient magnitude to remove the unemployment. Second, booms, along with labour shortages and production beyond normal capacity, do not persist for long periods without causing increases in unit costs and the price level.

The long-run aggregate supply (LRAS) curve

The **long-run aggregate supply (LRAS) curve** shows the relationship between the price level and real GDP after wage rates and all other input costs have been fully adjusted to eliminate any unemployment or overall labour shortages.

Shape of the *LRAS* curve Once all the adjustments that are required have occurred, the economy will have eliminated any excess demand or excess supply of labour. In other words, full employment will prevail, and output will necessarily be at its potential level, Y^*. It follows that the aggregate supply curve becomes a vertical line at Y^*, as shown in Figure 26.4. The $LRAS$ curve is sometimes called

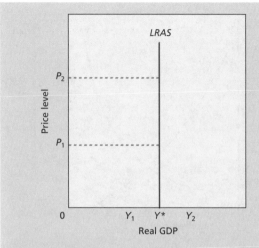

Figure 26.4 The long-run aggregate supply (*LRAS*) curve

The long-run aggregate supply curve is a vertical line drawn at the level of GDP that is equal to potential GDP, Y^*. It is a vertical line because the total amount of goods that the economy produces when all factors are efficiently used at their normal rate of utilization does not vary with the price level. If the price level were to rise from P_1 to P_2 and wages and all other factor prices were to rise by the same proportion, the total desired output of firms would remain at Y^*.

If output were Y_1, which is less than Y^*, wages would be falling and the *SRAS* curve would be shifting rightward; hence the economy would not be on its *LRAS* curve. If output were Y_2, which is greater than Y^*, wages would be rising and the *SRAS* curve would be shifting leftward; hence, again, the economy would not be on its *LRAS* curve.

the classical aggregate supply curve because the classical economists were concerned mainly with the behaviour of the economy in long-run equilibrium.

Notice that the vertical *LRAS* curve does not represent the same thing as the vertical portion of the *SRAS* curve (see Figure 25.10). Over the vertical range of the *SRAS* curve, the economy is at the utmost limit of its existing productive capacity, as might occur in an all-out war effort. No more can be squeezed out. The vertical shape of the *LRAS* curve is due to the workings of an adjustment mechanism that brings the economy back to its potential output, even though actual output may differ from its potential level for considerable periods of time. It is called the long-run aggregate supply curve because it arises as a result of adjustments that take a significant amount of time.

Along the *LRAS* curve, the prices of all outputs and all inputs have been fully adjusted to eliminate any excess demands or supplies. Proportionate changes in money wages and the price level (which, by definition, will leave real wages unaltered) will also leave equilibrium employment and total output unchanged. In the next section we will ask what does change when we move from one point on the *LRAS* curve to another.

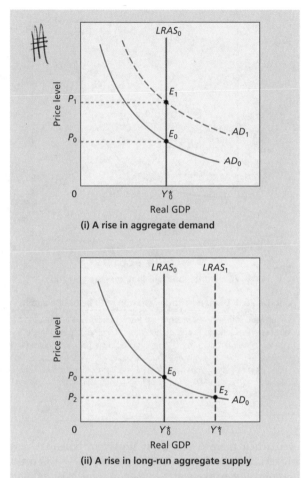

(i) A rise in aggregate demand

(ii) A rise in long-run aggregate supply

Figure 26.5 Long-run equilibrium and aggregate supply

When the *LRAS* curve is vertical, aggregate supply determines the long-run equilibrium value of GDP at Y^*. Given Y^*, aggregate demand determines the long-run equilibrium value of the price level. In both parts of the figure the initial long-run equilibrium is at E_0, so the price level is P_0 and GDP is Y_0^*.

In part (i) a shift in the *AD* curve from AD_0 to AD_1, with the *LRAS* curve remaining unchanged, moves the long-run equilibrium from E_0 to E_1. This raises the price level from P_0 to P_1 but leaves GDP unchanged at Y_0^* in the long run.

In part (ii) a shift in the *LRAS* curve from $LRAS_0$ to $LRAS_1$, with the aggregate demand curve remaining constant at AD_0, moves the long-run equilibrium from E_0 to E_2. This raises GDP from Y_0^* to Y_1^* but lowers the price level from P_0 to P_2.

Long-run equilibrium

Figure 26.5 shows equilibrium GDP and the price level as they are determined by the intersection of the *AD* curve and the vertical *LRAS* curve. Because the *LRAS* curve is vertical, shifts in aggregate demand change the price level but not the level of equilibrium GDP, as shown in part (i).

By contrast, a shift in aggregate supply changes both GDP and the price level, as shown in part (ii). For example, a rightward shift of the *LRAS* curve increases real GDP and leads to a fall in the price level.

With a vertical *LRAS* curve, in the long run total output is determined solely by conditions of supply, and the role of aggregate demand is simply to determine the price level.

What does change when the economy moves from one point on the *LRAS* curve, such as E_0 in part (i) of Figure 26.5, to another point, such as E_1? Although total output and total desired spending do not change, their *compositions* do change. The higher the price level, the lower is personal wealth (for a given nominal stock of assets) and hence the lower is private consumption. (Recall from Chapter 23 that private consumption is positively related to wealth.) Also, the higher the price level, the lower are exports and the higher are imports, and hence the lower are net exports.

Suppose the economy starts at a point on the *SRAS* curve and an increase in government spending then creates an inflationary gap. Money wages and the price level rise until the gap is removed. At the new long-run equilibrium, the higher level of government spending is exactly offset by lower private consumption and net exports, leaving total output unchanged. A similar analysis holds for an increase in investment. In the new long-run equilibrium, the higher level of investment spending will be exactly offset by lower consumption spending and net exports.

The vertical *LRAS* curve shows that, given full adjustment of input prices, potential GDP, Y^*, is compatible with any price level although its composition among private consumption, investment, government consumption, and net exports may vary with different price levels.

In Chapter 28 we will discover circumstances under which a rise in the price level has *no real effects*, so that not only are real GDP and total spending the same at all points on the *LRAS* curve, but also the composition of spending among C, I, G, and $(X - IM)$ is the same. We will also learn, once we have added a monetary sector, that interest rate changes have important effects on the composition of spending.

Real GDP in the short and long run

We have now identified two distinct equilibrium conditions for the economy:

1. In the short run the economy is in equilibrium at the level of GDP and the price level where the *SRAS* curve intersects the *AD* curve.

2. In the long run the economy is in equilibrium at potential GDP, the position of the vertical *LRAS* curve. The price level is that at which the *AD* curve intersects the *LRAS* curve.

The *position* of the *LRAS* curve is at Y^*, which is determined by past economic growth. Deviations of actual output from potential output—GDP gaps—are generally associated with business cycles. Changes in total real output (and hence in employment, unemployment, and living standards) may take place as a result of either growth or the business cycle.

We refer to a change in any exogenous variable that shifts the aggregate demand curve as a **demand shock**, and we refer to any change in an exogenous variable that shifts the aggregate supply curve as a **supply shock**. Demand and supply shocks may be positive or negative. Such shocks may result from policy changes by the government or monetary authorities, or they may result from autonomous changes in private sector behaviour, such as an autonomous change in consumer spending. They may also result from changes in other countries, which affect the domestic economy via a shift in net exports.

This discussion above suggests a need to distinguish three ways in which GDP can be increased. These are illustrated in Figure 26.6.

Increases in aggregate demand As shown in part (i) of Figure 26.6, an increase in aggregate demand will yield a one-time increase in real GDP. If that increase occurs when there is a recessionary gap, it pushes GDP towards its potential level. It thus short-circuits the working of the automatic adjustment mechanism that would eventually have achieved the same outcome by depressing unit costs, as discussed earlier in this chapter.

If the demand increase pushes GDP beyond its potential level, the rise in GDP will be only temporary; the inflationary gap will cause wages and other costs to rise, shifting the *SRAS* curve to the left. This drives GDP back towards its potential level, so that the only lasting effect is on the price level. Box 26.1 presents a number of reasons why we might expect the effect of demand shocks on GDP to be cyclical, that is, to cause GDP to move first one way, then the other.

Temporary and permanent increases in aggregate supply Increases in aggregate supply will also lead to increases in GDP. Here it is useful to distinguish between two possible kinds of increase that might occur: those that leave the *LRAS* curve unchanged, and those that shift it.

Part (ii) of Figure 26.6 shows the effects of a positive shock to short-run aggregate supply that leaves potential

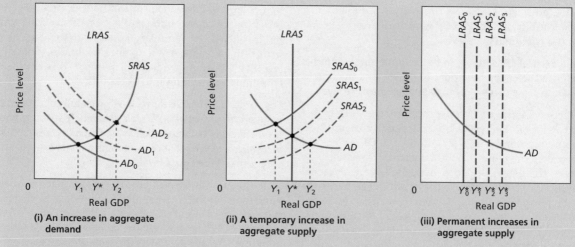

Figure 26.6 Three ways of increasing GDP

GDP will increase in response to an increase in aggregate demand or an increase in aggregate supply. The increase will be permanent if the *LRAS* curve shifts, but if the *LRAS* curve does not shift, any divergences of GDP from potential will be only temporary; the output gap that is created will set in motion the wage adjustments that we studied earlier in this chapter. In part (i) of the figure the *AD* curve shifts to the right. If the initial level of output is Y_1, then the shift from AD_0 to AD_1 eliminates the recessionary gap and raises GDP to Y^*. If the initial level of GDP is Y^*, then the shift from AD_1 to AD_2 raises GDP to Y_2 and thereby opens up an inflationary gap.

In part (ii) the *SRAS* curve shifts to the right. If the initial level of output is Y_1, then the shift from $SRAS_0$ to $SRAS_1$ eliminates the recessionary gap and raises GDP to Y^*. If the initial level of output is Y^*, then the shift from $SRAS_1$ to $SRAS_2$ raises GDP to Y_2 and thereby opens up an inflationary gap.

In the cases shown in parts (i) and (ii) any increase in output beyond potential is temporary, since, in the absence of any additional shocks, the inflationary gap will cause wages and other factor prices to rise; this will cause the *SRAS* curve to shift upward and, hence, GDP to converge to Y^*.

In part (iii) the *LRAS* curve shifts to the right, causing potential GDP to increase. Whether or not actual output increases immediately depends on what happens to the *AD* and *SRAS* curves. Since, in the absence of other shocks, actual GDP eventually converges to potential GDP, a rightward shift in the *LRAS* curve eventually leads to an increase in actual GDP. If the shift in the *LRAS* curve is recurring, then GDP will grow continually.

 Box 26.1 Demand shocks and business cycles

Aggregate demand shocks are a major source of fluctuations in GDP around Y^*. As we have seen, an expansionary demand shock, starting from a position of full employment, will lead to an increase in output, followed by a fall in output accompanied by an increase in prices, as the adjustment mechanism restores the economy to equilibrium. Depending on the nature and magnitude of the shock, the adjustment will take many months, often stretching into one or two years.

Suppose that the government increases spending on roads or that economic growth in Germany leads to an increase in demand for UK exports. No matter what the source of growth in demand, the economy will not respond instantaneously. In many industries it takes weeks or months, or even longer, to bring new or mothballed capacity into production and to hire and train new workers. The multiplier process itself also takes time, as people and firms respond to the change in income that results from an initial increase in autonomous spending.

Because of these lags in the economy's response, changes in demand give rise to changes in output that are spread out over a substantial period of time. An increase in demand may lead to a gradual increase in output

that builds up over several months. Then, as output does change, the adjustment mechanism comes into play. As an inflationary gap opens up, wages and costs start to rise, shifting the *SRAS* curve to the left.

Thus, a once-and-for-all positive demand shock gives rise to a *cyclical* output response, with GDP first rising because of the rightward shift in the *AD* curve, and then falling because of the upward shift in the *SRAS* curve. A negative demand shock is likely to play out even more slowly because of the asymmetry of response. Again, however, the behaviour of output will be cyclical: starting from potential output, GDP will fall over a period of time because of a leftward shift in the *AD* curve, and then will rise slowly as the adjustment mechanism shifts *SRAS* to the right.

Each major component of aggregate spending—private consumption, investment, net exports, and government consumption—is subject to continual random shifts, which are sometimes large enough to disturb the economy significantly. Adjustment lags convert such shifts into cyclical oscillations in GDP.

GDP unchanged. This will shift the *SRAS* curve to the right but will have no effect on the *LRAS* curve. The shock will thus cause GDP to rise towards potential if it starts out below, but an increase that takes GDP beyond potential will eventually be reversed.

Part (iii) of Figure 26.6 shows the effects of permanent increases in aggregate supply that shift the *LRAS* curve. A once-and-for-all increase due to, say, a labour market policy that reduces the level of structural unemployment will lead to a one-time increase in potential GDP. A recurring increase that is due to, say, population growth, capital accumulation, or ongoing improvements in productivity will cause a continual rightward shift in the *LRAS* curve, giving rise to a continual increase in the level of potential GDP.

Economic growth

A gradual but continual rise in potential GDP, or what we have called *economic growth*, is the main source of improvements in the standard of living over the long term.

Eliminating a severe recessionary gap could cause a once-and-for-all increase in GDP of, say, 4 per cent, while eliminating structural unemployment will raise it by somewhat less. However, a growth rate of 3 per cent per year raises GDP by 10 per cent in 3 years, *doubles* it in 24 years, and *quadruples* it in 48 years.

In any given year, the position of the *LRAS* curve is at potential GDP, Y^*. The 'long run' to which the *LRAS* curve refers is thus one in which the resources available to the economy do not change, but in which all markets reach equilibrium. Economic growth moves the *LRAS* curve to the right, year by year. Here the long run is not a period in which everything settles down, because growth is a continuing process: rather, the movement in *LRAS* causes a continuing movement in Y^*.

Determinants of long-run shifts in potential GDP, or economic growth, used to be regarded as beyond the scope of macroeconomics. However, it is clearly one of the most important factors in determining living standards. There is now a much stronger case for treating growth as an integral part of macroeconomics. This is that the forces of growth may be endogenous; that is, apparently short-term policies may have implications for long-term growth. No longer is

it safe to assume that the determinants of growth are independent of the determinants of the short-term cycle.

Cyclical fluctuations

Figure 26.6 distinguishes the causes of trend growth in potential GDP, which is the gradual rightward shifting of the *LRAS* curve, from the causes of cyclical fluctuations, which are deviations from that trend.

Cyclical fluctuations in GDP are caused by shifts in the *AD* and *SRAS* curves that cause actual GDP to deviate temporarily from potential GDP.

These shifts in turn are caused by changes in a variety of factors, including interest rates, exchange rates, consumer and business confidence, and government policy. Although the resulting deviations of actual from potential GDP are described as 'temporary', recall from the discussion above that the automatic adjustment mechanism may work slowly enough that the deviations can persist for some time, perhaps several years.

It is worth looking back at this stage to Figures 22.2 on page 390 and 23.1 on page 406. The first shows the level of UK real GDP since 1885. The dominant feature of this graph is the continued upward trend that has led to a more than five-fold increase in real GDP in just over 100 years. The average year-to-year increase is only about 2 per cent, but the cumulative effect of this slow but steady growth has been spectacular. This long-term trend reflects the steady rightward shift in the *LRAS* curve associated with sustained increases in potential GDP.

Figure 23.1 shows the year-to-year percentage changes in UK real GDP. Fluctuations in the annual rate of growth reflect the effects of aggregate demand and supply shocks. The two largest positive shocks derive from the increases in aggregate demand associated with the First and Second World Wars. The two largest negative demand shocks appear to be associated with the ends of those two wars, though there were sharp recessions in the early 1920s and early 1930s. The three post-1970 recessions look trivial in comparison with these earlier events, even though many who lived through them suffered severe loss of income and/or employment.

Government policy and the business cycle

The short-run analysis of the macroeconomy that we set out in this and the previous three chapters was developed not just to explain business cycles, but also to suggest policies that could be used to avoid the worst occurrences of recessions—where there is persistent high unemployment

and excess capacity. Central to the so-called Keynesian revolution in economic policy making was the idea that government policy could be used in a countercyclical manner to stabilize the economy. Accordingly, in the remainder of this chapter we discuss how changes in governments' taxing and spending policies and interest rates might be used as tools of stabilization policy. The use of taxes and spending by the government in an attempt to control the economy is known as discretionary *fiscal stabilization policy*, which is defined as *deliberate* changes in tax rates or government spending that are targeted at stabilizing the economy. We discuss monetary policy only briefly in this section, as the monetary system and monetary policy are the topic of the next two chapters.

Since increases in government spending increase aggregate demand and increases in taxation decrease it, the *directions* of the required changes in spending and taxation are generally easy to determine, once we know the direction of the desired change in GDP—cutting taxes and raising expenditure will tend to increase GDP, while the opposite policy changes will tend to lower it. However, the *timing*, *magnitude*, and *mixture* of the changes pose more difficult issues.

There is no doubt that the government can exert a major influence on GDP. Prime examples are the massive increases in military spending during major wars. British government spending during the Second World War rose from 13.4 per cent of GDP in 1938 to 49.2 per cent of GDP in 1944. At the same time, the unemployment rate fell from 9.2 per cent to 0.3 per cent. Most observers agree that the increase in government spending helped to bring about the rise in GDP and the associated fall in unemployment. Similar experiences occurred during the rearmament of most European countries before, or just following, the outbreak of the Second World War in 1939 and in the United States during the Vietnam War in the late 1960s and early 1970s.

It might seem from what we have just said that fiscal policy can be an important tool for stabilizing the economy. In the heyday of fiscal policy activism, from about 1945 to about 1970, many economists were convinced that the economy could be stabilized adequately just by varying the size of the government's taxes and spending. That day is past. Today most economists are aware of the many limitations of fiscal policy.

The basic theory of fiscal stabilization

A reduction in tax rates or an increase in government spending will shift the *AD* curve to the right, causing an increase in GDP. An increase in tax rates or a cut in government spending will shift the *AD* curve to the left, causing a decrease in GDP.

A more detailed look at how fiscal stabilization works will provide a useful review. It will also help to show some of the complications that arise in using fiscal policy.

A recessionary gap

The two possible ways in which a recessionary gap can be removed are illustrated in Figure 26.7.

First, the gap may eventually drive wages and other input prices to rise sufficiently more slowly than productivity growth to shift the *SRAS* curve to the right and thereby reinstate full employment and potential GDP (at a lower price level). The evidence, however, is that this process takes a substantial period of time.

Second, the *AD* curve could shift to the right, restoring the economy to full employment and potential GDP (at a higher price level). The government can cause such a shift by using expansionary fiscal policy, lowering taxes or raising spending (or the monetary authorities might cut interest rates in order to stimulate spending). The advantage of using fiscal policy is that it may substantially shorten what would otherwise be a long recession. One disadvantage is that the use of fiscal policy may stimulate the economy just before private sector spending recovers on its own. As a result, the economy may overshoot its potential output and an inflationary gap may open up. In this case fiscal policy that is intended to promote economic stability can actually cause instability.

An inflationary gap

Figure 26.8 shows the ways in which an inflationary gap can be removed. First, wages and other input prices may be pushed up by the excess demand. The *SRAS* curve will therefore shift to the left, eventually eliminating the gap, reducing GDP to its potential level, and raising the price level.

Second, the *AD* curve could shift to the left, restoring equilibrium GDP. The government, by raising taxes or cutting spending, can induce such a shift, reducing aggregate demand sufficiently to remove the inflationary gap. The advantage of this approach is that it avoids the inflationary increase in prices that accompanies the first method. One disadvantage is that if private sector spending falls GDP may be pushed below potential, thus opening up a recessionary gap.

A key proposition This discussion suggests that, in circumstances in which the economy fails to adjust quickly enough on its own, or gives rise to undesirable side-effects such as rising prices, there is a potential stabilizing role for fiscal policy.

Government taxes and spending shift the *AD* curve and hence can be used to remove persistent GDP gaps.

Automatic stabilizers

The government budget surplus increases as GDP increases. This is because tax revenues rise, some transfer payments, especially unemployment-related benefits, fall, while government consumption is generally unaffected by cyclical fluctuations. Thus, net taxes move in the same direction as

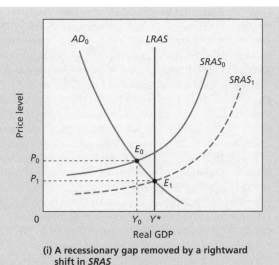

(i) A recessionary gap removed by a rightward
shift in *SRAS*

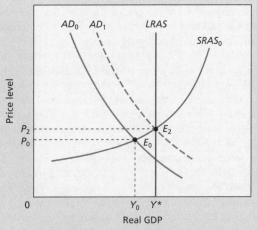

(ii) A recessionary gap removed by a rightward
shift in *AD*

Figure 26.7 Removal of a recessionary gap

A recessionary gap may be removed by a (slow) rightward shift of the *SRAS* curve, a natural revival of private sector demand, or a fiscal-policy-induced increase in aggregate demand. Initially equilibrium is at E_0, with GDP at Y_0 and the price level at P_0. The recessionary gap is $Y^* - Y_0$.

In part (i) the gap might be removed by a shift in the *SRAS* curve to $SRAS_1$, as a result of reductions in wage rates and other input prices. The shift in the *SRAS* curve causes a movement down and to the right along AD_0 and establishes a new equilibrium at E_1, achieving potential GDP, Y^*, and lowering the price level to P_1.

In part (ii) the gap might also be removed by a shift of the *AD* curve to AD_1. That occurs either because of a natural revival of private sector spending or because of a fiscal-policy-induced increase in spending. The shift in the *AD* curve causes a movement up and to the right along $SRAS_0$ and shifts the equilibrium to E_2, raising GDP to Y^* and the price level to P_2.

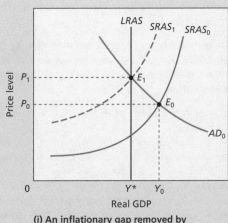

(i) An inflationary gap removed by
a leftward shift in *SRAS*

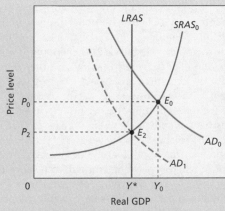

(ii) An inflationary gap removed by
a leftward shift in *AD*

Figure 26.8 Removal of an inflationary gap

An inflationary gap may be removed by a leftward shift of the *SRAS* curve, a reduction in private sector demand, or a fiscal-policy-induced reduction in aggregate demand. Initially equilibrium is at E_0, with GDP at Y_0 and the price level at P_0. The inflationary gap is $Y^* - Y_0$.

In part (i) the gap might be removed by a shift in the *SRAS* curve to $SRAS_1$, which occurs as a result of increases in wage rates and other input prices. The shift in the *SRAS* curve causes a movement up and to the left along AD_0 and establishes a new equilibrium at E_1, reducing GDP to its potential level, Y^*, and raising the price level to P_1.

In part (ii) the gap might also be removed by a shift of the *AD* curve to AD_1, which occurs either because of a fall in private spending or because of contractionary fiscal policy. The shift in the *AD* curve causes a movement down and to the left along $SRAS_0$. This movement shifts the equilibrium to E_2, lowering GDP to Y^* and the price level to P_2.

472   PART 5: MACROECONOMICS: GROWTH AND CYCLES

GDP (unless there are changes in policy that involve, for example, changes in tax rates). This means that there are increases in leakages as the economy expands and reductions in leakages as the economy contracts.

For example, in Chapter 24 we assumed that the net income tax rate was 10 per cent. This implies that a £1 rise in autonomous spending would increase disposable income by only 90p, dampening the multiplier effect of the initial increase. Generally, the wedge that income taxes place between national income and disposable income reduces the marginal propensity to spend out of national income, thereby reducing the size of the multiplier. The lower the multiplier, the less will equilibrium GDP tend to change for a given change in autonomous spending. The effect is to stabilize the economy, reducing the fluctuations in GDP that are caused by changes in autonomous spending. Because no policies need to be changed in order to achieve this result, the properties of the government budget that cause the multiplier to be reduced are called **automatic fiscal stabilizers**.

Even when the government does not undertake to stabilize the economy via discretionary fiscal policy, the fact that net tax revenues rise with GDP means that there are fiscal effects that cause the budget to act as an *automatic stabilizer* for the economy.

Of course, a government might try to follow a balanced budget policy, which means tying its spending in each period to the tax revenue it raises. This would change the impact of fiscal policy in a major way by making it *pro-cyclical*. With a pro-cyclical fiscal policy the government will restrict its spending during a recession because its tax revenue is low, and will increase its spending during a recovery when its tax revenue is rising. In other words it moves with the economy, raising and lowering its spending in step with everyone else, exactly counter to the theory of fiscal stabilization that we just discussed. Some politicians have proposed changing the law so that governments must balance their budget every year. However, most economists rarely call for anything more restrictive than a policy whereby governments aim to balance their budget on average over the course of the business cycle. A budget that was balanced on average would still permit the automatic stabilizer that is built into fiscal policy to work.

Limitations of discretionary fiscal policy

The discussion of the previous few pages might suggest that returning the economy to potential is simply a matter of changing taxes and government spending. However, many economists argue that such policies would be as likely to harm as to help. Part of their reasoning is that the execution of successful discretionary fiscal policy is anything but simple.[3]

Lags Changing fiscal policy in response to GDP gaps requires changing taxes and government spending. First, statistics take time to collect and process; so some time passes before the size of the current gap can be discerned. This reason for delay is known as an **information lag**.

There is then a much more serious delay caused by the policy making process itself. In the UK case the changes must be agreed upon by the Cabinet and passed by Parliament. Major changes in taxes are normally announced only once a year, in the spring Budget Statement, although 'mini-budgets' are possible if 'crisis' measures need to be taken at other times of year. In July 2002 the Chancellor of the Exchequer announced spending plans for the succeeding three years. In the United States and most European countries the budgetary process involves an annual round of policy proposals and legislation, though many spending programmes are for much longer horizons.

The political stakes in such changes are usually very large. Taxes and spending are called 'bread-and-butter issues' precisely because they affect the economic well-being of almost everyone. Thus, even if experts agreed that the economy would be helped by a tax cut, politicians might spend a good deal of time debating *whose* taxes should be cut and *by how much*. The delay between the initial recognition of a recession or inflation and the enactment of legislation to change fiscal policy is called a **decision lag**.

Once policy changes are agreed upon, there is still an **execution lag**, adding time between the enactment and the implementation of the change. Furthermore, once policies are in place, it usually takes still more time for their economic consequences to be felt.

Because of these lags, it is quite possible that, by the time a given policy decision has any impact on the economy, circumstances will have changed such that the policy is no longer appropriate.

Figure 26.9 illustrates the problems that can arise in these circumstances.

To make matters even more frustrating, tax measures that are known to be temporary are generally less effective than measures that are expected to be permanent. If consumers know that a given tax cut will last for only a year or so, they may recognize that the effect on their long-run consumption possibilities is small and they may adjust their short-run consumption relatively little. The more closely household consumption spending is related to lifetime (or 'permanent') income rather than to current income, the

---

[3] Another part has to do with the long-term consequences of budget deficits. Governments that run deficits for long periods build up substantial debts. These debts require significant tax revenues just to pay the interest, and this limits the ability of governments to spend on other programmes. Also, depending on the exchange rate regime, international considerations may reduce (but not eliminate) fiscal policy's effectiveness as a stabilization tool.

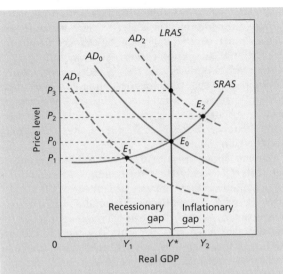

Figure 26.9 Effects of fiscal policies that are not reversed
Fiscal policies that are initially appropriate may become inappropriate when private spending shifts. The initial position is on AD_0, at Y^* and price level P_0. Suppose a slump in private investment shifts aggregate demand to AD_1, lowering GDP to Y_1 and causing a recessionary gap of $Y^* - Y_1$.

The government now introduces fiscal expansion to restore aggregate demand to AD_0. But private investment then recovers, raising aggregate demand to AD_2. If fiscal policy can be quickly reversed, aggregate demand can be returned to AD_0 and GDP stabilized at Y^*. If the policy is not quickly reversed, the economy is at E_2 with an inflationary gap $Y^* - Y_2$. This gap will cause wages to rise and thus will shift the $SRAS$ curve leftward and eventually restore Y^* at price level P_3.

smaller will be the effects on current consumption of tax changes that are known to be of short duration.

The role of discretionary fiscal policy Fine-tuning refers to the use of fiscal and monetary policy to offset virtually all fluctuations in private sector spending and so hold GDP at, or very near, its potential level at all times. However, the lags just discussed prevent policy-makers from undoing the consequences of every aggregate demand shock.

None the less, many economists would still argue that, when a recessionary gap is large enough and persists for long enough, gross-tuning may be appropriate. **Gross-tuning** refers to the occasional use of fiscal and monetary policy to remove large and persistent GDP gaps. Advocates of gross-tuning hold that fiscal policy can and should be used to push the economy towards full employment when a GDP gap is large and has persisted for a long time. Other economists believe that fiscal policy should not be used for economic stabilization under any circumstances. They argue that tax and spending behaviour should be the outcome of public choices regarding the long-term size and

financing of the public sector and should not be altered for short-term considerations.

Economic policy, economic stability, and economic growth

The desirability of using fiscal policy to stabilize the economy depends a great deal on the speed with which the automatic adjustment mechanisms return the economy to potential GDP. If the automatic adjustment mechanisms work quickly, there is no role for discretionary fiscal policy. If the automatic adjustment mechanisms work slowly, there may well be a role for policies that can be used to shift aggregate demand. Fiscal policy is one such policy; monetary policy, which we take up in Chapter 28, is another. Only when we have completed our study of the way in which money fits into the overall macroeconomy can we fully outline the choices available to governments wishing to stabilize their economies.

EU fiscal policy and the single currency

Since the 1992 Maastricht Treaty, which established limits on fiscal deficits and public debt for EU member states that wished to join the euro single-currency zone, those member states have operated fiscal policy under severe constraints. The Treaty required almost all EU member states to initiate tight fiscal polices, even though many of their economies were in recession. This extra negative shock to aggregate demand made the resulting recession worse and drove EU unemployment up to levels not seen since the Second World War.

Following the introduction of the euro in 1999, fiscal constraints on member states have remained in place in the form of the so-called Stability and Growth Pact. This puts limitations on fiscal deficits similar to those imposed by the Maastricht criteria. The limits ensure that fiscal policy at the level of individual member states will have only a minor role in the control of their national aggregate demands. A fiscal policy role may develop for the EU central budget. However, that budget is very small in comparison with the budgets of governments of member states, making it unlikely that the EU will exert significant fiscal leverage in the near future. This could be a severe problem for members of the euro zone. As we shall see in a later chapter, the creation of the euro itself takes away monetary policy power from individual member governments, and the Stability and Growth Pact limits fiscal freedom even in the face of very persistent recessionary gaps. Accordingly, governments appear to have very few tools left with which to deal with persistent gaps. This could be an especially severe problem for member states that find their economies persistently out of phase with the cycle in the majority of other states. We will return to this issue in Chapter 35.

Monetary policy

The difficulties in using fiscal policy to fine-tune the economy have caused current fiscal policy to be targeted on funding long-term government spending plans rather than being used as a tool for stabilizing the economy over the business cycle (other than from the perspective of automatic stabilizers). This means that **monetary policy**, that is the setting of interest rates in order to influence output or inflation, has become the main tool for short-run demand management.

Many monetary authorities have been given the authority to set the official interest rate, but they have not been given the task of stabilizing macroeconomic activity. Rather, they have been set the objective of stabilizing inflation. The UK Monetary Policy Committee (MPC), for example, is charged with targeting an inflation rate of 2.5 per cent, while the ECB is charged with achieving 'price stability'. Fortunately, stabilizing inflation and offsetting aggregate demand shocks requires the same policy actions. Thus, where demand shocks are the main source of disturbances, stabilizing inflation and stabilizing output will amount to the same thing. For example, a positive demand shock that takes actual GDP above potential GDP will cause inflation. To control inflation, interest rates will generally need to rise. This will lower domestic spending and thus lower actual relative to potential GDP, and thereby will reduce inflationary pressures.[4]

Monetary policy has some advantages over fiscal policy. Although the information lag is the same, the other two lags are much shorter. Policy can be changed frequently. The UK MPC, for example, meets every month, the ECB meets every two weeks, and the US Federal Open Market Committee meets every six weeks (but can react more quickly if necessary via a video conference). The execution lag is even shorter. Once a policy decision has been made, interest rates can be changed within minutes of the policy decision being taken.

However, monetary policy is subject to a further time lag before its full effect is felt on the economy. The traditional rule of thumb is that a change in monetary policy today takes about one year to have its maximum impact on output and a further year to have its maximum impact on the inflation rate. As we shall see in the Appendix to Chapter 30, lags of this magnitude are nevertheless considered by monetary policy-makers to be plausible.

The next two chapters focus entirely on these issues: how does the monetary system influence real activity and inflation, and how does monetary policy work?

---

[4] Deciding how to respond to supply shocks is more difficult, as a shock that raises prices will lower output and vice versa. Tightening monetary policy (raising interest rates) to control inflation would make the output loss even worse. We postpone a discussion of this case to Chapter 28.

SUMMARY

- Potential GDP is represented by a vertical line at Y^*, which means that it does not vary with the price level.

- The output gap is equal to the horizontal distance between Y^* and the actual level of GDP, as determined by the intersection of the *AD* and *SRAS* curves.

Induced changes in input prices

- An inflationary gap means that actual GDP, Y, is greater than Y^*, and hence there is excess demand in the labour market. As a result wages rise faster than productivity, causing unit labour costs to rise. The *SRAS* curve shifts leftward, and the price level rises.

- A recessionary gap means that Y is less than Y^*, and hence demand in the labour market is relatively low. Although there is some resulting tendency for wages to fall relative to productivity, this force is much weaker than in the case of an inflationary gap. Unit labour costs fall only slowly, so the output gap persists for a considerable length of time.

- An expansionary demand shock creates an inflationary gap.

- A contractionary demand shock creates a recessionary gap.

Long-run consequences of aggregate demand shocks

- The long-run aggregate supply (*LRAS*) curve relates the price level and real GDP after all wages and other costs have been adjusted fully to long-run equilibrium. The *LRAS* curve is vertical at the level of potential GDP, Y^*.

- Because the *LRAS* curve is vertical, output in the long run is determined by the position of the *LRAS* curve, and the only long-run role of the *AD* curve is to determine the price level. Economic growth determines the position of the *LRAS* curve.

Real GDP in the short and long run

- GDP can increase (or decrease) for any of three reasons: a change in aggregate demand, a change in short-run aggregate supply, or a change in long-run aggregate supply (which is called economic growth). The first two changes are typically associated with business cycles.

Government policy and the business cycle

■ In principle, fiscal policy can be used to stabilize the position of the *AD* curve at or near potential GDP. To remove a recessionary gap, governments can shift *AD* to the right by cutting taxes and increasing spending. To remove an inflationary gap, governments can pursue the opposite policies.

■ Because government tax and transfer programmes tend to reduce the size of the multiplier, they act as automatic stabilizers. When national income changes in either direction, disposable income changes by less because of taxes and transfers.

■ Discretionary fiscal policy is subject to information, decision, and execution lags that limit its ability to take effect quickly.

■ Monetary policy-makers can react quickly, but the impact of interest rates changes is also subject to a lag.

TOPICS FOR REVIEW

- GDP gap and the labour market
- Inflationary gaps
- Recessionary gaps
- Asymmetry of wage adjustment
- Changes in aggregate demand and induced wage changes
- Wages, productivity, and unit costs
- Adjustment mechanism

- Long-run aggregate supply (*LRAS*) curve
- Economic stabilization
- Information, decision, and execution lags
- Automatic stabilizers
- Fiscal policy
- Monetary policy

DISCUSSION QUESTIONS

1 Starting with the economy at Y^*, explain what happens to the price level and real GDP in the short run and in the long run in response to (*a*) an increase in export demand; (*b*) an increase in oil prices (assuming that oil is an input into production); (*c*) a permanent increase in productivity; (*d*) an increase in income tax rates.

2 Starting with the economy below Y^*, (*a*) explain how the economy will eventually adjust back to Y^*; (*b*) explain how fiscal and monetary policy could help speed up the return to Y^*.

3 Repeat question 2 but starting from a position where current GDP is above Y^*.

4 Set out the reasons why fiscal policy was once thought to be able to offset shocks to the economy. Why is the effectiveness of fiscal policy now thought to be much more limited?

5 Outline the reasons for asymmetry in the adjustment mechanism to external shocks. How would the response to a positive demand shock differ from the response to a negative demand shock?

6 Explain what is meant by 'automatic stabilizers'. How do these help to reduce the amplitude of the business cycle?

7 Explain the differences between the adjustment of the economy in a recessionary gap and an inflationary gap.

8 Why is the *LRAS* curve vertical? What does this imply about the impact of aggregate demand shifts on equilibrium real GDP in the long run?

MACROECONOMIC POLICY IN A MONETARY ECONOMY

Chapter 27

MONEY AND MONETARY INSTITUTIONS

What role does money play in the economy and how did it evolve? How does money get into the economy and how is the total amount of money determined? What role do banks play in the creation of money? These are some of the questions that we address in this chapter. In the following chapter we add a monetary sector to our macro model and analyse how monetary policy works. In this chapter you will learn that:

• Money is neutral in the economy when it has no impact on real activity.

• Money acts as a medium of exchange, a unit of account, and a store of value.

• The existence of money facilitates a wider range of transactions than would otherwise be feasible.

• Money has evolved from being based on commodities such as gold and silver.

• Paper currency was originally convertible into gold or silver, but now has nothing backing it except its acceptability in payment.

• The money multiplier is the ratio of broad money to high-powered money.

• Bank deposits are now the biggest part of the total amount of money in the economy, so the behaviour of the banking system is central to determining that amount.

Many people believe that money is one of the more important things in life, and that there is never enough of it. However, increasing the amount of money in any one country or in the world overall would not make the average person better off. Although money allows those who have it to buy someone else's output, the total amount of goods and services available for everyone to buy depends on the total output produced, not on the total amount of money that people possess. In the terminology of Chapter 26, an increase in the total quantity of money will not increase Y^*, the level of *potential* GDP. However, the link between money and real activity has been a source of considerable debate.

Money and the economy

The classical view

Money's role in the economy has been a controversial topic for some time. Early theories in this area argued for the independence of Y^* from monetary factors in terms of an economic analysis that distinguished sharply between the 'real sector of the economy' and the 'monetary sector'. This approach led to a view of the economy that is now referred to as the *classical dichotomy*, which meant that the real sector of the economy (the production and consumption of real goods and services) could be analysed separately from the monetary sector. In other words, economic forces originating in the monetary sector did not affect real activity.

According to this view, the allocation of resources, and hence the determination of real GDP, is fully determined in the real sector. It is *relative prices*, including the level of wages relative to the price of commodities, rather than money (nominal) prices, that matter for this process.

According to the classical dichotomy, the price *level* is determined in the monetary sector of the economy. If the quantity of money were doubled, other things being equal, the prices of all commodities and money incomes would double. Relative prices would remain unchanged, and the real sector would be unaffected.

According to the classical dichotomy, an increase in the total amount of money leads to a proportionate increase in all

money prices, with no change in the allocation of resources or the level of real GDP.

The doctrine that the quantity of money influences the level of money prices but has no effect on the real part of the economy is called the **neutrality of money**. Because early economists believed that the most important questions—How much does the economy produce? What share of it does each group in society get?—were answered in the real sector, they spoke of money as a 'veil' behind which occurred the real events that affected material well-being. Of course, if the classical dichotomy were correct, we would not need to study monetary factors in order to explain the determination of real GDP.

The modern view

Most contemporary economists still accept the insights of the early economists that relative prices are a major determinant of the allocation of resources and that the quantity of money has an association with the absolute level of prices. They accept the neutrality of money in long-run equilibrium when all the forces causing change have fully worked themselves out. However, they do not accept the neutrality of money when the economy is adjusting to shocks, that is, when the economy is not in a state of long-run equilibrium. Thus, they reject the classical dichotomy.

Money and the price level It is widely accepted today that there is a clear link between money and the price level, especially over long periods of time, when the conditions of long-run equilibrium are apt to be most relevant. However, many would argue that the causation runs from prices to money rather than from money to prices. What is generally agreed is that it is desirable to keep inflation under control and that it is the job of the monetary authorities to achieve this.

We now focus on how the monetary system works before returning to the issue of monetary policy in the next chapter.

The nature of money

There is probably more widespread misunderstanding of money and the monetary system than of any other aspect of the economy. In this section we describe the functions of money and briefly outline its history.

Before we proceed, it is important to note that the amount of money in an economy is a *stock* (in the UK it is so many billions of pounds), not a *flow* of so many pounds per unit of time. Previously we have been talking about flows of output or spending *per period*. It is also important to notice that the money supply is a nominal variable measured in money units, whereas the other variables in our macro model are real variables measured in purchasing power units, or holding prices constant.

What is money?

Money is defined as any generally accepted medium of exchange. A *medium of exchange* is anything that will be widely accepted in a society in exchange for goods and services. Although being a medium of exchange is usually regarded as money's defining function, money can also serve other roles:

Money acts as a medium of exchange and can also serve as a store of value and a unit of account.

A medium of exchange

As we saw in Chapter 1, if there were no money, goods would have to be exchanged by barter (one good being swapped directly for another). The major difficulty with barter is that each transaction requires a double coincidence of wants; anyone who specialized in producing one commodity would have to spend a great deal of time searching for satisfactory transactions. Thus, a thirsty economics lecturer would have to find a brewer who wanted to learn economics before he could swap a lesson in economics for a pint of beer.

The use of money as a medium of exchange alleviates this problem. People can sell their output for money and subsequently use the money to buy what they wish from others. So a monetary economy typically involves exchanges of goods and services for money and of money for goods and services, but not of goods and services for other goods and services.

The double coincidence of wants, which is required for barter, is unnecessary when a medium of exchange is used.

By facilitating transactions, money makes possible the benefits of specialization and the division of labour, which in turn contribute to the efficiency of the economic system. It is not without justification that money has been called one of the great inventions contributing to human freedom and well-being.

To serve as an efficient medium of exchange, money must have a number of characteristics. It must be readily acceptable and therefore of known value. It must have a high value relative to its weight (otherwise it would be a nuisance to carry around). It must be divisible, because money that comes only in large denominations is useless for transactions having a small value. Finally, it must be difficult, if not impossible, to counterfeit.

A store of value

Money is a convenient way to store purchasing power; goods may be sold today, and the money taken in exchange for them may be stored until it is needed. To be a satisfactory store of value, however, money must have a relatively stable value. A rise in the price level leads to a decrease in the purchasing power of money, because more money is required to buy a typical basket of goods. When the price level is stable, the purchasing power of a given sum of money is also stable; when the price level is highly variable, this is not so, and the usefulness of money as a store of value is undermined.

Although in a non-inflationary environment money can serve as a satisfactory store of accumulated purchasing power for a single individual, even in those circumstances it cannot do so for society as a whole. A single individual can accumulate money and, when the time comes to spend it, can command the current output of some other individual. However, if all individuals in a society were to save their money and then retire simultaneously to live on their savings, there would be no current production to purchase and consume. Society's ability to satisfy wants depends on goods and services being available. If some of this want-satisfying capacity is to be stored up for society as a whole, some goods that are produced today must be saved for future periods. In other words, money may be accumulated as savings to help individuals buy future goods, but it is the future real capital stock and labour resources that will determine future real output. Money and real wealth should not be confused.

Money is a store of value for individuals, but not for society as a whole.

A unit of account

Money also may be used purely for accounting purposes, without having a physical existence of its own. For instance, a government store in an imaginary centrally planned society might say that everyone had so many 'pounds' to spend or save each month. Goods could then be assigned prices and each consumer's purchases recorded, the consumer being allowed to buy until his allocated supply of pounds was exhausted. These pounds need have no existence other than as entries in the store's books, yet they would serve as a perfectly satisfactory unit of account.

Whether they could also serve as a medium of exchange between individuals depends on whether the store would agree to transfer credits from one customer to another at the customer's request. Banks will transfer pounds credited to current account deposits in this way, and so a bank deposit can serve as both a unit of account and a medium of exchange. Notice that the use of 'pounds' in this context suggests a further sense in which money is a unit of account. People think about values in terms of the monetary unit with which they are familiar.

A related function of money is that it can be used as a standard of deferred payments. Payments that are to be made in the future, on account of debts and so on, are reckoned in money. Money's ability to serve as a unit of account over time in this manner can be diminished if there is significant inflation.

The origins of money

The origins of money go far back in antiquity. Many primitive tribes seem to have made some use of it.

Metallic money

All sorts of commodities have been used as money at one time or another, but gold and silver proved to have great advantages. They were precious because their supplies were relatively limited, and they were in constant demand by the wealthy for ornament and decoration. Thus these metals tended to have a high and stable price. Further, they were easily recognized, they were divisible into extremely small units, and they did not easily wear out.

Before the invention of coins, it was necessary to carry the metals in bulk. When a purchase was made, the requisite quantity of the metal was carefully weighed on a scale.

The invention of coinage eliminated the need to weigh the metal at each transaction, but it created an important role for an authority, usually a monarch, who made the coins by mixing gold or silver with base metals to create convenient size and durability, and affixed his or her seal, guaranteeing the amount of precious metal that the coin contained. This was clearly a great convenience, as long as traders knew that they could accept the coin at its 'face value'. The face value was nothing more than a statement that a certain weight of gold or silver was contained therein.

However, coins often could not be taken at their face value. A form of counterfeiting—clipping a thin slice off the edge of the coin and keeping the valuable metal—became common. This, of course, served to undermine the acceptability of coins, even if they were stamped. To get around this problem, the idea arose of minting the coins with a rough edge; the absence of the rough edge would

 **Box 27.1 Gresham's Law**

The early experience of currency debasement led to the observation known as Gresham's Law, after Sir Thomas Gresham, an adviser to the Elizabethan court, who stated that 'bad money drives out good'.

When Queen Elizabeth I came to the throne of England in the middle of the sixteenth century, the coinage had been severely debased. Seeking to help trade, Elizabeth minted new coins that contained their full face value in gold. However, as fast as she fed these new coins into circulation, they disappeared. Why?

Suppose that you possessed one new and one old coin, each with the same face value, and had a bill to pay. What would you do? Clearly, you would use the debased coin to pay the bill and keep the undebased one. (You part with less gold that way.) Again, suppose that you wanted to obtain a certain amount of gold bullion by melting down the gold coins (as was frequently done). Which coins would you use? Clearly, you would use new, undebased coins because you would part with less 'face value' that way. For these reasons, the debased coins would remain in circulation and the undebased coins would disappear.

Gresham's insights have proven helpful in explaining the experience of a number of modern high-inflation economies. For example, in the 1970s inflation in Chile raised the value of the metallic content in coins above their face value. Coins quickly disappeared from circulation as private citizens sold them to entrepreneurs who melted them down for their metal. Only paper currency remained in circulation and was used even for tiny transactions such as purchasing a box of matches. Gresham's Law is one reason why modern coins, unlike their historical counterparts, are merely tokens that contain a metallic value that is only a minute fraction of their face value.

Gresham's Law has had another modern interpretation, in regimes of pegged exchange rates, where the values of two currencies are pegged together artificially. If one currency is overvalued and is widely expected to have to be devalued, this causes people to spend it fast, while building up their holdings of the undervalued currency. The combination of hoarding one currency and running down balances of the other often brings about the devaluation that was feared—as when the pound sterling was forced to leave the European Exchange Rate Mechanism (ERM) in September 1992 and when Argentina was forced to break the link of its currency to the US dollar in 2001.

---

immediately indicate that the coin had been clipped. This practice, called milling, survives on some coins (such as the current UK 5p, 10p, £1, and £2 coins) as an interesting anachronism to remind us that there were days when the market value of the metal in the coin was equal to the face value of the coin.

Not to be outdone by the cunning of their subjects, some rulers were quick to seize the chance of getting something for nothing. The power to mint placed rulers in a position to work a really profitable fraud. They often used some suitable occasion—a marriage, an anniversary, an alliance—to re-mint the coinage. Subjects would be ordered to bring their coins into the mint to be melted down and coined afresh with a new stamp. Between the melting down and the recoining, however, the rulers had only to toss some further inexpensive base metal in with the molten coins. This debasing of the coinage allowed the ruler to earn a handsome profit by minting more new coins than the number of old ones collected, and putting the extras in the royal vault.

The result of debasement was inflation. The subjects had the same number of coins as before, and hence could demand the same quantity of goods. When rulers paid their bills, however, the recipients of the extra coins could be expected to spend them. This caused a net increase in demand, which in turn bid up prices.

Debasing the coinage was a common cause of increases in prices.

It was the experience of such inflations that led early economists to stress the link between the quantity of money and the price level. The relationship, known as the 'quantity theory of money', will be discussed in Chapter 28. A famous law in economics that owes its origins to the era of metallic money is set out in Box 27.1.

To this day, the revenue generated from the power to create currency is known as *seigniorage*. Today the possibility of debasement does not enter. The term applies to the revenue that accrues from the powers to print banknotes (which have very low production costs relative to their face value) and to require private banks to place non-interest-bearing deposits at the central bank.

The benefits of seigniorage could arise simply because the monetary authorities print money and spend it, so its value would be equal to the increase in note issue each period. In practice, central banks typically buy interest-bearing bonds with each new issue of notes. The seigniorage from the note in circulation is thus equal to the interest per period on those bonds. So, for example, if the note issue was £100 and the central bank had bought £100 worth of bonds in issuing those notes, and the yield on the bonds was 5 per cent, then seigniorage would be £5 per year. Some seigniorage also arises from the policy of many central banks in forcing commercial banks to place non-interest-bearing deposits, which the central bank can also use to purchase interest-bearing securities. In the United Kingdom the Bank of England returns most of the revenue from seigniorage to HM Treasury; only an amount to cover the Bank's running costs is retained.[1]

---

[1] In 2002 the Bank of England paid around £1.5 billion to HM Treasury from this source.

Paper money

The next important step in the history of money was the evolution of paper currency, one source of which was goldsmiths. Since goldsmiths had secure safes, the public began to deposit their gold with them for safekeeping. Goldsmiths would give their depositors receipts promising to hand over the gold on demand. When any depositor wished to make a large purchase, she could go to her goldsmith, reclaim some of her gold, and hand it over to the seller of the goods. If the seller had no immediate need for the gold, he would carry it back to the goldsmith for safekeeping on his own behalf.

If people knew the goldsmith to be reliable, there was no need to go through the cumbersome and risky business of physically transferring the gold. The buyer needed only to transfer the goldsmith's receipt to the seller, who would accept it as long as he was confident that the goldsmith would pay over the gold whenever it was needed. If the seller wished to buy a good from a third party who also knew the goldsmith to be reliable, passing the goldsmith's receipt from the buyer to the seller too could effect this transaction. The deposit receipt was 'as good as gold'. The convenience of using pieces of paper instead of gold is obvious.

When it came into being in this way, paper money represented a promise to pay so much gold on demand. In this case the promise was made first by goldsmiths and later by banks.[2] Such paper money, which became banknotes, was backed by precious metal and was convertible on demand into this metal.[3]

Fractionally backed paper money

Early on many goldsmiths and banks discovered that it was not necessary to keep a full ounce of gold in the vaults for every claim to an ounce circulating as paper money. At any one time, some of the bank's customers would be withdrawing gold, others would be depositing it, and most would be trading in the bank's paper notes without indicating any need or desire to convert them into gold.

As a result, the bank was able to issue more money (initially notes, but later deposits) redeemable in gold than the amount of gold that it held in its vaults. This was good business, because the money could be invested profitably in interest-earning loans (often called advances) to individuals and firms. The demand for loans arose, as it does today, because some customers wanted credit to help them over hard times or to buy equipment for their businesses. To this day, banks have many more claims outstanding against them than they actually have in reserves available to pay those claims. We say that the currency issued in such a situation is *fractionally backed* by the reserves.

The major problem with a fractionally backed, convertible currency was maintaining its convertibility into the precious metal by which it was backed. The imprudent bank that issued too much paper money would find itself unable to redeem its currency in gold when the demand for gold was even slightly higher than usual. It would then have to suspend payments, and all holders of its notes would suddenly find that the notes were worthless. However, the prudent bank that kept a reasonable relationship between its note issue and its gold reserve would find that it could meet a normal range of demand for gold without any trouble.

If the public lost confidence and demanded redemption of its currency *en masse*, however, the banks would be unable to honour their pledges. The history of nineteenth- and early-twentieth-century banking around the world is full of examples of banks that were ruined by 'panics', or sudden runs on their gold reserves. When this happened, the banks' depositors and the holders of their notes would find themselves with worthless pieces of paper.[4]

Fiat money

As time went on, note issue by private banks became less common, and **central banks**, which are (usually) state-owned institutions, took control of the currency. Over time central banks have assumed a monopoly in the provision of money to the economy.[5] As a result they have the job of controlling monetary conditions and are ultimately responsible for determining the value of a nation's (or group of nations') currency.

Originally central banks issued paper currency that was fully convertible into gold. In those days gold would be brought to the central bank, which would issue currency in

---

[2] Banks grew out of at least two other trades in addition to that of the goldsmiths. There were scriveners, who had writing skills and sold their services managing other people's financial affairs; there were also merchant bankers, who started trading in commodities but ended up specializing in trade finance—Barings and Rothschilds started this way, and are still referred to as 'merchant banks' today. (In US terminology they are called 'investment banks'.)

[3] One of the earliest issuers of formal banknotes was the Riksbank of Sweden, established in 1668. It is thus twenty-six years older than the Bank of England, which was established in 1694. The Riksbank, which is now the central bank of Sweden, instituted the Nobel Prize for economics in 1968 to commemorate its tercentenary.

[4] In the early 1930s about 10,000 banks, or a third of the total, went bust in the United States. The personal and corporate losses involved were a major contributor to the Great Depression.

[5] In England and Wales no new banks have been permitted to issue notes since the 1844 Bank Charter Act, though in Scotland banks such as the Bank of Scotland, the Royal Bank of Scotland, and the Clydesdale Bank still issue the main notes in circulation. (Since 1845, however, the Scottish note issue has had 100 per cent backing with Bank of England liabilities, and hence has been fully under Bank of England direction.) In 2002 euro notes were issued by the European Central Bank to replace the previous currencies of the 11 member states of the euro zone (see pages 512–13 below).

the form of 'gold certificates' asserting that the gold was available on demand. The gold supply thus set some upper limit on the amount of currency. However, central banks, like private banks before them, could issue more currency than they had in gold, because in normal times only a small fraction of the currency was presented for payment at any one time. Thus, even though the need to maintain convertibility under a **gold standard** put an upper limit on note issue, central banks had substantial discretionary control over the quantity of currency outstanding.

During the first half of the twentieth century almost all the countries of the world abandoned the gold standard; their currencies were thus no longer convertible into gold. Money that is not convertible by law into anything else derives its value from its acceptability in exchange. *Fiat money* is widely acceptable because government order, or fiat,[6] declares it to be legal tender. Legal tender is anything that by law must be accepted when offered either for the purchase of goods or services or to discharge a debt. Bank of England notes have been legal tender in England and Wales since 1833.

Today almost all currency is fiat money.

Bank of England notes still say on them 'I promise to pay the bearer on demand the sum of *x* pounds', and they are signed by the chief cashier. Until 1931 (apart from occasional temporary suspensions of convertibility) you could take these notes into the Bank of England and demand gold of equivalent value in return for your notes. Today, however, the promise is a quaint tradition rather than a real contract. The pound sterling, like all major currencies, is a fiat currency that is not backed by gold or any other commodity (though some people still argue for the return to a gold standard).

Fiat money is valuable because it is accepted by convention and in law in payment for the purchase of goods or services and for the discharge of debts.

Many people are disturbed to learn that present-day paper money is neither backed by, nor convertible into, anything more valuable—that it consists of nothing but pieces of paper whose value derives from common acceptance. Many people believe that their money should be more substantial than this. Yet money is, in fact, nothing more than pieces of paper.

If fiat money is acceptable, it is a medium of exchange. Further, if its purchasing power remains stable, it is a satisfactory store of value. And if both of these things are true, it will also serve as a satisfactory unit of account.

How does money get into the economy?

When gold was the basis of money, it was not too difficult to see how more gold got into circulation. It was either produced from gold mines, converted from non-monetary uses (such as jewellery), or imported from other countries. In effect, it was received in payment for some transaction from the owners of gold mines or from the previous owner of the gold, wherever in the world they happened to be. However, it is not so obvious how fiat money gets into the economic system. In fact, as suggested above, it comes from the central bank—in the UK the Bank of England, in the USA the Federal Reserve, in the euro area the European Central Bank (ECB).

The central bank does not just drop money from the sky, or even just give it to the government to spend. What the central bank has direct control over is referred to as **high-powered money**, *the cash base*, or **the monetary base**. (In the United Kingdom it is also defined as M0; see Box 27.2 below.) This consists of currency (banknotes and coin) held by the public and the banks, and deposits held by the banks with the central bank.[7] The monetary base is referred to as high-powered money because it is the basis upon which a much bigger stock of monetary assets is built (including the biggest component of the money stock, bank deposits). High-powered money is an asset to anyone in the private sector who holds it, but to the central bank it is a liability.

The central bank gets high-powered money into the economy simply by buying securities (usually government debt instruments). It pays for these purchases with newly issued high-powered money.

Hence in creating new high-powered money, the central bank is expanding both sides of its own balance sheet. At the same time as it increases its liabilities, it purchases assets of equal value. Of the two components of high-powered money, in the UK case, bankers' deposits are the liability of the Banking Department of the Bank of England and currency is the liability of the Issue Department. The balance sheets of these two departments are shown in Table 27.1.

It is simplest to think of the process of high-powered money creation in two steps. First, we will discuss, using

---

[6] Fiat means 'let there be' in Latin, and hence 'by decree'.
[7] M0 includes bankers' working balances at the Bank of England but it excludes compulsory cash ratio deposits. The latter are a form of tax on the banks that finance the Bank of England while making it not reliant on government funding.

Table 27.1 **Bank of England balance sheet, June 2002**

Assets	(£m)	Liabilities	(£m)
(i) *Balance sheet of Issue Dept*			
Government securities	13,491	Notes in circulation	29, 946
Other securities	16,459	Notes in Banking Department	4
Total assets	29,950	Total liabilities	29,950
(ii) *Balance sheet of Banking Dept*			
Government securities	1,760	Public deposits	404
Advances	5,717	Bankers' deposits	1,635
Premises	5,766	Reserves and other accounts	11,193
Notes and coin	4	Balancing item	15
Total assets	13,247		13,247

The Bank of England is divided into the Issue Department and the Banking Department. The table shows the balance sheets of these two departments at June 2002. The only function of the issue department is to issue currency (bank notes). It does this in exchange for purchases of securities, normally through a transaction with the Banking Department. The Banking Department acts as banker to the government and also holds deposits from the banks.

Source: Bank of England, *Monetary and Financial Statistics*.

the UK example, how the purchase of securities by the Bank of England creates bankers' deposits. Then we will see how currency gets into circulation.

Bankers' deposits

Consider a situation in which there are initially no net transactions between the Bank of England and the rest of the economy. The Bank now buys £1 million worth of securities from an agent in the private sector. The seller receives a cheque for £1 million from the Bank of England which is paid into the recipient's bank account at, say, Barclays Bank. Barclays' deposits rise by £1 million, but at the same time Barclays receives an increase of £1 million in its deposits at the Bank of England. The balance in Barclays' account at the Bank of England is an example of what are called *bankers' deposits*. This increase in its bankers' deposits at the Bank of England arises when Barclays clears the cheque drawn on the Bank of England. (A cheque deposited in Barclays drawn on HSBC Bank would simply transfer bankers' deposits from HSBC to Barclays, but a cheque drawn on the Bank of England creates new bankers' deposits at the central bank.)

This is not the end of the story so far as Barclays is concerned, because as we shall see bankers' deposits constitute reserves against which the commercial banks can create new deposits. We will soon explain how this is done. In the meantime, this is most of what we need to know about how the Bank of England expands the monetary base, though we will look more closely below at how the Bank of England uses its money market operations to set interest rates. Contraction of the monetary base simply

reverses the process—the Bank sells securities. A member of the public then writes a cheque drawn on, say, NatWest Bank, payable to the Bank of England, and NatWest transfers bankers' deposits to the Bank of an equivalent amount. The monetary base falls.

Currency

The above discussion explains how central banks, such as the Bank of England, create or destroy high-powered money. The division of high-powered money between bankers' deposits and currency is determined by the demand for currency on the part of the general public. If private individuals (or firms) choose to increase their currency holdings, relative to bank deposits, they simply go to their bank and withdraw deposits in cash. The bank (if it did not have enough cash in its tills) would go to the Bank of England and withdraw some bankers' deposits in cash from the Banking Department. The Banking Department, in turn, would replenish its own stock of cash by selling securities to the Issue Department. The Issue Department prints the new currency. Currency is made available on demand to the economy in this way and is not restricted in supply by the Bank of England.

The stock of currency in circulation is determined entirely by the demands of the economy and is not set by any policy-makers.

In the current UK financial system, the total stock of high-powered money is also demand-determined. This is because the authorities choose to set short-term interest rates and supply whatever high-powered money is demanded at

Box 27.2 **Definitions of UK monetary aggregates**

The way in which 'money' is defined has changed a great deal over time and is likely to change again in future. In 1750 money would almost certainly have been defined as the stock of gold in circulation (specie). By 1850 it would probably have been defined as gold in the hands of the non-bank public plus banknotes in circulation. In 1950 the most likely definition would have been currency held by the public plus current account bank deposits. In 2003 money was usually defined to include currency held by the public plus all deposits (current and savings) in banks and building societies. By 2050, who knows? Perhaps money on the internet will be included.

There have been many changes in the definition of money even in the last few years. Many of these are the result of the financial innovations of the 1980s. We should not expect this to be the end of the story. UK money measures such as M1 and £M3 (sterling M3), which were at the centre of monetary policy debates into the first half of the 1980s, have disappeared. These had to be dropped after 1989, when the Abbey National Building Society converted into a bank (and other conversions followed later). Thereafter, any monetary aggregate that contained bank deposits but not building society deposits became distorted. M0 contains neither; M2 and M4 contain both.

The money measures current in 2002 were as follows:

• **M0 (the monetary base)** This measure refers to all the currency in circulation outside the Bank of England plus bankers' deposits (in excess of their cash ratio deposits) with the Bank of England.

• **M2** This encompasses UK non-bank and non-building society holdings of notes and coins, plus sterling retail deposits with UK banks and building societies. The definition of M2 was changed in 1992 to make it a subset of M4, and it is now referred to in official statistics as 'retail M4'.

• **M4** M4 is M2 plus all other private sector sterling interest-bearing deposits at banks and building societies, plus sterling certificates of deposit (and other paper issued by banks and building societies of not more than five years' original maturity). (£M3 was effectively M4 minus building society deposits.)

• **M3H** This is a new harmonized measure created to have standard money definitions throughout the EU. It is equal to M4 plus residents' foreign currency deposits in UK banks and building societies plus public corporations' sterling and foreign currency deposits in UK banks and building societies.

The accompanying table presents data for these monetary aggregates for November 2002.

UK money supply, November 2002
(£ million, not seasonally adjusted)

Notes and coin outside Bank	37,080	
Bankers' deposits	87	
M0	37,167	
Notes and coins with public (part of M0)		29,622
Non-interest-bearing bank deposits		49,368
Other bank retail deposits		487,668
Building society retail deposits		133,322
M2 (retail M4)		699,980
Wholesale bank deposits + CDs, etc.		292,005
Wholesale building society deposits + CDs		9,648
M4		1,001,632
M3H		1,084,920

Note: M0 is not a subset of M2 and M4 because it includes notes and coin held by banks, which are excluded from M2 and M4. If notes and coin held by banks were included in the latter, there would be double counting, because notes and coin held by banks are assets, and the deposits (liabilities) that are counterparts to those assets are included in M2 and M4 already. CDs are certificates of deposit.

Source: Bank of England, *Monetary and Financial Statistics*.

---

those rates. A discussion of the implementation of monetary policy follows later in this chapter.

Modern money

The total amount of money in the economy is called the **money supply** or the **money stock**.[8] The creation of high-powered money is only part of the story of how the money supply is created, because most measures of the money supply include a wider range of assets than just the monetary base. In particular, money is usually defined to include bank deposits.

Deposit money

Today's bank customers frequently deposit coins and paper money with the banks for safekeeping, just as in former times they deposited gold. Such a deposit is recorded as a credit to the customer's account. A customer who wishes to pay a debt may come to the bank, claim the money in currency, and then pay the money to other persons, who may themselves re-deposit the money in a bank.

As with gold transfers, this is a tedious procedure. It is more convenient to have the bank simply transfer claims to money on deposit. As soon as cheques, which are written instructions to the bank to make a transfer, became widely accepted in payment for commodities and debts,

---

[8] Those who have studied microeconomics should note that the concept of a money supply is different from the concept of the supply of some commodity. In microeconomics supply refers to a desired quantity: how much producers would like to make and sell. In macroeconomics the money supply is the actual amount of money that is in existence..

bank deposits became a form of money called 'deposit money'. Deposit money is defined as money held by the public in the form of deposits in commercial banks that can be withdrawn on demand. Cheques, unlike banknotes, do not circulate freely from hand to hand; thus, cheques themselves are not currency. However, a balance in a current account deposit is money; the cheque simply transfers that money from one person to another. Because cheques are easily drawn and deposited, and because they are relatively safe from theft, they have been widely used. New technology has recently replaced many cheque transactions by computer transfer. Plastic cards such as Visa, Mastercard, and Switch enable holders of bank accounts to transfer money to another person's account in new ways.[9] The principle is the same, however: the balance in the bank account is the money that is to be transferred between customers—not the cheque or the plastic card.

When commercial banks lost the right to issue notes of their own, the form of bank money changed, but the substance did not. Today banks have money in their vaults (or on deposit with the central bank) just as they always did. Once it was gold; today it is the legal tender of the times—fiat money. It is true today, just as in the past, that most of the banks' customers are content to pay their bills by passing among themselves the banks' promises to pay money on demand. Only a small proportion of the value of the transactions made by the banks' customers involves the use of cash.

Bank deposits are money. Today, just as in the past, banks can create money by issuing more promises to pay (deposits) than they have cash reserves available to pay out.

The main reason that we are interested in the money stock is that if money grows too fast it will cause inflation. For this purpose, it is the broad measure of the money stock—the one that includes bank deposits—that is most relevant, as bank deposits can be used in payment for goods and it is often said that 'too much money chasing too few goods' is the source of inflation. Which specific measure of broad money we choose to use is of second-order importance.

Box 27.2 shows the various measures of the money stock that were in use in the United Kingdom in 2002. The main aggregates are M0, a narrow measure that excludes all private sector bank and building society deposits, and M4, a broad measure that includes all such bank and building society deposits. Notice also that there is now an EU harmonized measure of broad money known in the UK as M3H. This is slightly larger than M4 because it adds residents' foreign currency deposits (and some public sector deposits) to M4. The only other monetary aggregate current in the UK is M2, which is also known as 'retail M4' as it excludes the wholesale deposits in M4.

We now turn to a discussion of the role of banks in determining the broad money supply and in transmitting policy-determined interest rate changes to the economy.

Two models of banking

We now present two models of the creation of deposit money. The first shows how banks can create a large volume of deposit money on the basis of a given amount of reserves. It is called the ratios approach to the creation of money. The second shows how banks work in a competitive environment to attract the reserves they need in order to create deposit money. This model is better suited to understanding both the forces of competition between banks themselves and the competition between banks and other channels of financial intermediation (such as securities markets).

The ratios approach to the creation of deposit money

If you deposit cash with a bank, that deposit is an asset to you and a liability to the bank—because the bank owes that amount to you. Because the bank has the cash as an asset, its assets equal its liabilities. If a bank gives you a loan, it writes an extra balance into your account. This creates a

deposit for you, but it is also a loan that you have to repay. So the process of overdraft or loan creation creates both deposits and loans simultaneously. In general, banks' deposits are their liabilities, and whatever loans they make or securities they purchase constitute their assets. We will see below how banks can create deposits (and loans) that are some multiple of their cash reserves. This *fractional reserve* banking is analogous to the fractional backing of the note issue discussed above. Notice two slightly different meanings of the term cash. 'Cash' held by the banks can be currency in their tills or deposits at the central bank; 'cash' for the public means currency.

[9] With credit cards such as Visa or Mastercard, if you buy, say, petrol today, the petrol company will receive a credit in its bank account after a few days and you will have to settle with the credit card company once a month. With so-called EFTPOS (Electronic Funds Transfer at the Point Of Sale) cards like Switch, however, the funds are transferred directly from your account to the account of the petrol company very quickly. The technology is likely to keep changing, but it does not fundamentally alter the nature of the bank account transfer that is involved.

Table 27.2 A new cash deposit

Liabilities	(£)	Assets	(£)
Deposit	100	Cash	100

A new cash deposit has 100 per cent backing. The balance sheet shows the changes in assets and liabilities resulting from a new cash deposit. Both cash assets and deposit liabilities rise by the same amount.

Table 27.3 Deposit expansion in expection of a cash drain

Liabilities	(£)	Assets	(£)
Deposit	190	Cash	100
		Loans	90
	190		190

If a bank expands deposits in the expectation of a cash drain, it will end up with excess reserves. The table shows the position if a bank expands deposits on the basis of receiving £100 in new cash deposits and in the expectation that 90 per cent of any new deposits will drain out of the bank in a cash flow. The bank obtains new assets of loans and bonds of £90 by creating new deposits of that amount. It expects £81 of these to be withdrawn in cash, leaving it with £19 to provide a 10 per cent reserve against £190 of deposits.

Suppose that, in a system with many banks, each bank obtains new deposits in cash. Say, for example, that there are ten banks of equal size and that each receives a new deposit of £100 in cash. Each bank now has on its books the new entries shown in Table 27.2. The banks are on a fractional reserve system, and we assume for purposes of this illustration that they wish to hold 10 per cent cash reserves against all deposits. The new deposits put the banks into disequilibrium, since they each have 100 per cent reserves against these new deposits.

First, suppose that only one of the ten banks begins to expand deposits by making new loans (advances). When a bank makes a loan to a customer, it simply writes a larger balance into the customer's account, thereby increasing the size of its deposits. Now when cheques are written on these deposits, the majority will be deposited in other banks. If, for example, this one bank has only 10 per cent of the total deposits held by the community, then, on average, 90 per cent of any new deposits it creates for its customers—and thus much of its £100 in cash—will drain away to other banks. On this basis the bank will make loans of £90, expecting that it will suffer a cash drain of £81 on account of these loans, leaving it with a £19 cash reserve (£100 new deposit minus the £81 cash drain). This is the position shown in Table 27.3.

One bank in a multi-bank system cannot produce a large multiple expansion of deposits based on an original accretion of cash when other banks do not also expand their deposits.

Now assume, however, that all ten banks begin to expand their deposits based on the £100 of new reserves that each received. On the one hand, since each bank does one-tenth of the total banking business, 90 per cent of the value of any newly created deposits will find its way into other banks as customers make payments by cheque to various members of the community. This represents a cash drain to these other banks. On the other hand, 10 per cent of the new deposits created by each other bank should find its way into this bank. Thus, if all banks receive new cash, and all start creating deposits simultaneously, no bank should suffer a significant cash drain to any other bank. Instead of finding itself with its surplus cash drained away, a bank with the balance sheet shown in Table 27.3 would have cash reserves of close to 53 per cent (£100 reserves against £190 deposits) rather than only 10 per cent as desired.

When all banks can go on expanding deposits without losing cash to each other, they need only worry about keeping enough cash to satisfy those depositors who occasionally require cash. Thus the expansion can go on, with each bank watching its own ratio of cash reserves to deposits, expanding its deposits as long as the ratio exceeds 1:10 and ceasing to do so when it reaches that figure. Assuming no cash drain to the public, the process will not come to a halt until each bank has created £900 in additional deposits, so that, for each initial £100 cash deposit, there is now £1,000 in deposits backed by £100 in cash. Now each of the banks will have new entries in its books similar to those shown in Table 27.4.

A multi-bank system creates a multiple increase in deposit money when all banks with excess reserves expand their deposits in step with each other.

A complication: cash drain to the public

So far we have ignored the fact that the public actually divides its money holdings in a fairly stable proportion between cash and deposits. This means that, when the banking system as a whole creates significant amounts of new deposit money, the system will suffer a cash drain as the public withdraws enough cash from the banks to maintain its desired ratio of cash to deposits.

An example Assume that the public wishes to hold a proportion of cash equal to 10 per cent of the size of its bank deposits. This means that, for a given stock of cash in the system, the amount that will be held in bank reserves is reduced, so the maximum amount of deposit creation is also reduced. In this special case in which banks have a reserve ratio of 10 per cent and the public holds cash to the

Table 27.4 **Restoration of a 10 per cent reserve ratio**

Liabilities	(£)	Assets	(£)
Deposit	1,000	Cash	100
		Loans	900
	1,000		1,000

With no cash drain, a new cash deposit will support a multiple expansion of deposit liabilities. The table shows the changes in assets and liabilities when all banks engage in deposit expansion after each has received a new cash deposit of £100. New assets are £900 and new deposits are £900. The accretion of £100 in cash now supports £1,000 in deposits, thus restoring the 10 per cent reserve ratio.

Table 27.5 **Deposit creation with a cash drain to the public**

Liabilities	(£)	Assets	(£)
Deposit	500	Cash	50
		Loans	450
	500		500

A cash drain to the public greatly reduces the amount of new deposits that can be created on the basis of a given amount of cash. The table shows the balance sheet of the banking system on the assumption that there is £100 of cash in the system but the public desires cash holdings equal to 10 per cent of their bank deposits. The outcome which satisfies both banks' desired reserve ratio and the public's cash to deposit ratio is such that the banks hold £50 in reserves and issue £450 worth of loans. Total deposits are £500, and £50 is held in cash by the public. The total money stock is £550 (deposits plus cash held by the public). An example in which the banks' reserve ratio differs from the public's cash to deposits ratio is given in Table 27.6.

value of 10 per cent of the size of its bank deposits, the outcome will be as in Table 27.5. Half of the cash in existence (assumed to be £100 in total) will be held in banks' reserves, and the public will hold the other half. On the basis of their £50 reserves, banks will extend £450 of loans, so total deposits will be £500. This is only half of the value of deposits that were created when the entire £100 of cash was held in bank reserves (as shown in Table 27.3).

A cash drain to the public reduces the expansion of deposit money that can be supported by the banking system.

The general case of deposit creation

The two ratios that we have discussed (the banks' reserve ratio and public's ratio of cash to deposits) can now be used to determine the total level of deposit creation in a formal way. Let R be the cash held in bank reserves, C be the cash held by the non-bank public, H (for high-powered money) be the total cash in the economy, and D be the size of bank deposits. Thus,

$$C + R = H. \qquad (1)$$

This says that the total cash in the economy is held either by the banks or by the public. Let the desired reserve ratio of banks be x. This allows us to write

$$R = xD. \qquad (2)$$

Finally, let the public hold a fraction, b, of its bank deposits in cash:

$$C = bD. \qquad (3)$$

Substituting the second and third equations into the first gives

$$bD + xD = H,$$

and solving for D yields

$$D = \frac{H}{(b + x)}. \qquad (4)$$

Equation (4) shows that, if the public's desired cash ratio is zero, deposits rise by the reciprocal of the cash reserve ratio. (If the banks' reserve ratio were 0.1 (10 per cent), then deposits would be ten times the cash in the economy.) A positive value of b, however, means that the resulting cash drain lowers the increase in deposits since it raises the value of the denominator in (4).

The money multiplier

The total money supply in an economy with a banking system is defined as $D + C$. (It does not include R because the deposit that created the original bank reserves is already counted in with deposits, D, and should not be counted twice.) Hence the money supply, M, is

$$M = C + D. \qquad (5)$$

We can arrive at an expression that links M and H by substituting (2) into (5) for C and then (4) into (5) for D. This gives

$$M = \frac{b + 1}{b + x} H. \qquad (6)$$

Expression (6) is known as the money multiplier, because it tells us how much bigger is the money supply than the cash base of the system. In the modern UK banking system, where reserve ratios and cash ratios are very small, the money multiplier could be of the order of 27, since M4 was 27 times greater than M0 in 2002 (Q1).

The money multiplier should not be confused with the multiplier that links changes in exogenous spending with changes in GDP. The same term is used for two different concepts.

The size of the money multiplier is greater, the smaller is the banks' desired reserve ratio x and the smaller is the public's desired cash ratio b.

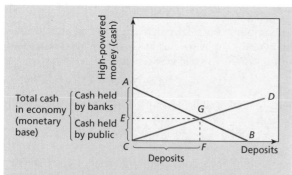

Figure 27.1 The ratios approach to the determination of the money supply

The money supply is determined by the stock of high-powered money (monetary base), the reserve ratio of the banks, and the cash–deposit ratio of the non-bank public. The diagram illustrates the size of deposit creation, given the banks' reserve ratio x ($= AC/CB$), the public's cash–deposit ratio b ($= EC/CF$), and the total cash in the economy AC. Deposits plus cash held by the public make up the total money supply. The total stock of high-powered money, or cash, in the economy has to be held by either the banks or the public. At point A the public holds all the cash available, so there are no bank deposits, and the total money supply is just AC, which is all cash. At point C the banks hold all the cash, and on that reserve base they create deposits of CB. The line AB thus plots the level of deposit creation resulting from each level of cash reserves (where point A represents the point where banks have no cash or deposits and point C represents the point where all the cash in the economy is held in bank reserves and CB is the value of bank deposits created on that reserve base). The banks' reserve ratio AC/CB is thus equal to (minus) the slope of AB.

The line CD represents the cash—deposit ratio for the non-bank public. Its slope, measured by EC/CF, is equal to that cash—deposit ratio. For a given base of high-powered money (cash), deposit creation will be determined at the point where these two ratios are both satisfied. This will be where CD and AB intersect. So the actual outcome is at point G, where banks have AE cash in reserves and create CF of deposits. The public holds EC of cash and CF of deposits. The total money supply at G is given by CF plus EC.

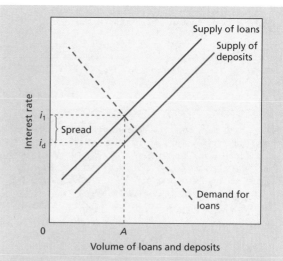

Figure 27.2 Competitive banking: supply of and demand for loans

The volume of bank loans is determined by the intersection of the supply curve of loans and the demand curve for loans. The diagram shows the positively sloped supply curve of loans and the negatively sloped demand curve for loans. The supply curve of loans is determined by the supply curve of deposits and the spread, or the interest margin that banks require to cover costs and risk. For given interest rates elsewhere in the economy, the supply curve of deposits is positively sloped because higher interest will attract more savings. The demand curve for loans is negatively sloped—high interest rates discourage borrowing and low rates encourage borrowing. Competition in banking drives the margin between deposit and loan rates to a level such as $i_1 - i_d$, where the spread is just enough to allow banks to cover costs and make a normal return on capital. With the demand and supply curves shown, there will be $0A$ deposits and loans, and depositors will receive an interest rate of i_d while borrowers pay the loan rate i_1.

A diagrammatic exposition of the above algebra is given in Figure 27.1. It shows that the two ratios, combined with a given cash base, can be used to determine the level of deposits that result and also the money supply. A numerical example of the same ideas is given in Table 27.6.

A competitive banking system

The ratios approach to bank behaviour gives us important insights into how deposit money is created as some multiple of high-powered money, but it does not provide an accurate picture of how modern banks work. They do not just sit around waiting for cash deposits to be made, and then lend some multiple of the deposit (though it is certainly true that their deposits are some multiple of their reserves, and since equation (6) above is an identity it cannot be 'wrong'). Instead, modern banks usually start from the other end. They wait until they have found a profitable lending opportunity, and they then take steps to make sure that funds are available to make the loan. This they can do either by offering higher interest on deposits, or by borrowing from other banks.

In the ratios world, banks passively receive deposits and then use these to make loans. In the modern world, however, banks are trading in highly competitive markets for both deposits and loans. In a competitive market there will be a market-clearing interest rate for both deposit money and loans. Banks cannot expand their activity in either of these markets without taking into account the supply curve of deposits and the demand curve for loans that they face.

The market for bank loans is illustrated in Figure 27.2. This shows a positively sloped supply curve for the loans that banks are willing to make to the public and a negatively sloped demand curve for the loans that the public is willing to take out. The supply curve of loans is determined

Table 27.6 High-powered money, deposits, and the money supply

Banks		Non-bank public		High-powered money ($H = C + R$)	Money supply ($M = C + D$)
Reserves (R)	Deposits (D) ($R \times 20$)	Cash (C) ($1,000 - R$)	Deposits (D) ($C \times 10$)		
(1)	(2)	(3)	(4)	(5)	(6)
1,000	20,000	0	0	1,000	
600	12,000	400	4,000	1,000	
400	8,000	600	6,000	1,000	
333.3	**6,666.6**	**666.6**	**6,666.6**	**1,000**	**7,333.3**
200	4,000	800	8,000	1,000	
100	2,000	900	9,000	1,000	
0	0	1,000	10,000	1,000	

For a given stock of high-powered money the amount of bank deposits created will be the amount which is consistent with the banks' reserve ratio and the non-bank public's cash–deposit ratio. The table sets out a range of desired positions for banks and the non-bank public independently. Only one of these positions satisfies the desired positions for both the banks and the public, such that the deposits the banks wish to create are the same as the deposits the public wishes to hold.

The example assumes that high-powered money (the cash base or monetary base) is fixed at £1,000. This can be held in some proportion between the banks and the public, but it cannot be changed other than by the monetary authorities. Banks are assumed to have a reserve ratio of 5 per cent, and the non-bank public is assumed to wish to hold cash at a level 10 per cent of their holding of bank deposits. Column (1) shows a range of possible levels of reserve holding for the banks, ranging from all of the £1,000 to none of it. Column (2) shows the level of deposits they would like to create (by making loans) in order to satisfy their desired reserve ratio for each level of reserve holding in column (1). Column (3) shows the cash holding by the public that is implied by the number in column (1), so it is equal to £1,000 minus the number in column (1). Column (4) shows the level of deposits that the public would like to hold given their cash holdings in column (3). Column (5) reminds us that the stock of high-powered money is fixed at £1,000 throughout. Column (6) shows the value of the money supply for the unique position that satisfies the desires of both the banks and the public.

The actual outcome is the single position where the deposits that the banks wish to create are exactly equal to the deposits the public wishes to hold. This is where the level of deposits is £6,666.6. At this point the banks hold £333.3 in reserves and the public holds £666.6 in cash. The money supply is £7,333.3 (deposits plus cash held by the public) and the money multiplier is 7.333 (MIH). We could also calculate this from equation (6) on p. 489: $(b + 1)/(b + x)$ is 1.1/0.15 (where $b = 0.1$ and $x = 0.05$); this is 7.333.

---

by two factors: the supply curve of deposits, and the spread. The **spread** is the difference between what the banks have to pay to borrow money and what they get by lending it (which has to provide a margin to cover staff costs, return on capital employed, and default risk). Remember that banks have to take in deposits in order to make loans. They borrow from one set of people or firms and lend to another.

The supply curve of deposits is positively sloped because, for given interest rates elsewhere in the economy, banks can attract more deposits by offering higher interest rates. (Not all deposits in banks pay interest, but the deposits that banks can increase by offering high interest rates—their marginal deposits—do.) To make the explanation easier, we assume that the spread is a constant absolute size, so that the supply curve of loans is drawn parallel to the supply curve of deposits, but above it by the constant amount of the spread.[10]

The public's demand curve for loans is negatively sloped because, the higher the interest rate being charged, the less will customers wish to borrow. Equilibrium in the market for bank loans occurs where the demand and supply curves intersect, that is, where the amount customers wish to borrow is equal to the amount banks wish to lend.

Money supply and competitive banking

The ratios approach to money supply creation and the competitive model of banking present two rather different ways of looking at the banking system, but they are compatible. Indeed, each helps us understand the other better, and both are necessary for a complete understanding of modern monetary control techniques.

The ratios approach tells us that the total money supply is related to the stock of high-powered money, this relationship being determined by the reserve ratio of banks and the cash–deposits ratio of the public. For given reserve ratios, the total money supply would be determined if the authorities fixed the supply of high-powered money. However, the UK monetary authorities (and most other central banks, including the ECB) do not operate this way.

---

[10] Although, the spread may vary from loan to loan depending, among other things, on the size of the loan and the creditworthiness of the customer, on average the spread over all loans is driven down by competition among banks to an amount that will just cover costs with no pure profits. Hence its average value can be reasonably assumed to be a constant.

Box 27.3 **The implications of electronic money for the monetary system**

Some people have argued that electronic money will fundamentally change the nature of the monetary system and perhaps even eliminate the power of central banks to control the stock of high-powered money or to set the short-term interest rate in money markets. Is this likely?

Our answer is that this is possible but very unlikely. There are two main forms of electronic money.

First, there is what is sometimes called an 'electronic purse', which involves loading some prepaid credits on to a plastic card (which has either a magnetic strip or a computer chip recording information). The carrier of the card can then use this to make retail payments in various shops where some of the balance on the card can be transferred to the retailer. Such cards are just a more general form of pre-paid telephone card that carries some credit paid for in advance. They are certainly feasible methods of facilitating some payments. But whether they catch on remains to be seen. The key thing to note is that they offer no difference in principle from earlier payment methods. In effect, they are just a new way of transferring ownership of bank deposits from one person to another. They may lead to the general public needing to hold less cash, but they do not change the reality that bank deposits are the main component of money. The amount of cash loaded on to one of these cards is in effect a bank deposit, and this is transferred to the retailer when a purchase is made. This is just a new way of ordering your bank to transfer money from your account to that of someone from whom you buy goods.

Second, there are some forms of money that are transferred via the internet. Here the answer depends on the nature of the transaction involved. If all you are doing is using an internet message to transfer funds from your bank account to someone else's, then again this is just a new way of writing a cheque and no new principles are involved. If, however, new types of institution become able to issue tokens that become widely accepted in payment, this would be a new departure and these new forms of money could provide a substitute for existing moneys. However, if such new moneys did emerge it is most likely that governments would regulate them. The money issuers would be regulated like banks, and as banks they would have to hold deposits with the central bank. In that case, again, no new principles would be involved. Indeed, most large payments, in both the domestic and the international economy, have been made electronically for many years. This trend started with the invention of the telegraph in the 1830s and continued with the opening of the trans-Atlantic telegraph cable in the 1880s. The internet is a new technology for authorizing payments, but the monetary principles involved are not new.

This all suggests that e-money is not going to break the monopoly of central banks to issue high-powered money and so is not going to weaken their ability to set interest rates in wholesale money markets. Nor is e-money going to affect the ability of central banks to control inflation, as that depends on the impact of interest rates on spending decisions, which is not affected in any obvious way by the nature of the payments technology.

Rather, they aim to control total deposits via the demand for bank loans. If they wish to lower deposits (and loans), they force up short-term interest rates, as shown in Figure 27.2. In other words, the authorities use the knowledge of the market demand curve for loans to influence the total stock of deposits and, therefore, also the money supply. Box 27.3 discusses whether the evolution of electronic money, sometimes called e-money, will have an impact on the way the monetary system works.

Having chosen what they think is the correct interest rate to generate the desired demand for loans, the UK monetary authorities supply whatever high-powered money is demanded at that going interest rate. So the authorities do not fix the supply of high-powered money; rather, this is demand-determined at the interest rate that policy-makers have set. The competitive model of banking helps us to see how this can be done by moving up or down the market demand curve for bank loans. We will return to this issue in more detail below.

Before moving on, however, there are two other important insights provided by the competitive model of banking. First, in the absence of reserve requirements imposed on the banking system by the monetary authorities,[11] we can see that the reserve ratio that banks will choose will be the outcome of an internal optimization process. Banks will try to keep the level of reserves as low as possible, subject to the need to supply cash on demand when customers wish to withdraw deposits. This is because reserves earn no interest and banks would like to devote as much as possible of the funds that are available to them to profitable uses. Thus, in the absence of high legal reserve requirements, banks' chosen reserve ratios tend to be very small, especially where they can access liquid funds very quickly by borrowing in the interbank market. The money multiplier has, as a result, become quite large (as mentioned above).

Second, the competitive model helps us to understand that the banking system as a whole is in competition with other financial channels in the economy for the available amount of borrowing and lending (intermediation) business at any point in time. The real size of the banking sector, relative to other channels of finance (and, indeed, other industries), is determined by how efficient it is in channelling funds from savers to borrowers in the economy. Issues relating to the nominal size of bank deposits and the money supply should be kept separate from the question of the real relative size of the banking system compared with other channels of borrowing and lending flows (such as through securities markets).

In the next chapter we look at how money fits into our short-term model of the macroeconomy.

---

[11] In the UK in July 2002 reserves (known as the cash-ratio deposit, or CRD) held with the Bank of England were required to be around 0.15 per cent of deposits.

SUMMARY

Money and the economy

- In the classical dichotomy, money affected the price level but it did not affect real activity.

The nature of money

- Money is a medium of exchange, a unit of account, and a store of value.
- Money avoids the need for a double coincidence of wants and thus facilitates a wider range of transactions.

The origins of money

- Money has evolved from being based primarily on a precious metal to being mainly in the form of bank deposits.
- Early moneys were based on commodities, and especially precious metals like gold and silver.

- Paper currency started as a claim to a deposit of precious metal.
- Bank deposits account for most of modern money.

How does money get into the economy?

- Central banks create the monetary base or high-powered money, which is made up of notes and coins and bankers' deposits at the central bank.
- Banks create deposit money by expanding loans and deposits.

Two models of banking

- Banks create deposits to some multiple of their cash reserves.
- In a competitive market in which banks pay interest on deposits and charge interest on loans, banks' behaviour is best understood in terms of demand and supply curves of deposits and loans. Banks must pay competitive interest rates to attract deposits, and they must charge competitive rates on their loans.

TOPICS FOR REVIEW

- Neutrality of money
- Medium of exchange
- Unit of account
- Store of value
- Gold standard

- Reserve ratio
- Fiat money
- Money multiplier
- Competitive banking systems
- Interest rate spread

DISCUSSION QUESTIONS

1. Suppose that the monetary base is £20 billion, that the general public wish to hold 20 per cent of their money in cash and the remaining 80 per cent in bank deposits, and that banks wish to hold a 5 per cent cash reserve. What will be the size of the broad money stock (M4)?

2. How does the answer to question 1 change for bank reserve ratios of (a) 0%, (b)1%, and (c)10%?

3. How does the answer to question 1 change for general public cash holdings of (a) 0%, (b) 5%, (c) 100%?

4. How would the answers to questions 2 and 3 change if the monetary base were £40 billion?

5. How is the broad money stock determined in a system where the monetary base is demand-determined, the central bank sets an interest rate, and the banking system is competitive?

6. Why do people hold money when higher yielding assets are available?

7. What role does money play in a market economy?

8. What difference would it make to the economy if there were no money? What types of commodity might serve as money instead?

Chapter 28

THE ROLE OF MONEY IN MACROECONOMICS

How do interest rates influence aggregate demand and inflation? Does the money stock matter? Do inflation-targeting central banks stabilize output? These are some of the important questions addressed in the chapter. In particular, you will learn that:

• The price of bonds is inversely related to the interest rate.

• Monetary equilibrium occurs where people are willing to hold the existing stock of money and bonds at the current interest rate.

• A rise in interest rates reduces aggregate demand, and vice versa.

• Monetary and fiscal polices may assist the stabilization of the economy and control of inflation, but inappropriate policies can make things worse.

• Central banks have the power to set interest rates because they are the monopoly supplier of high-powered money (notes and coin plus bankers' deposits at the central bank).

• UK monetary policy is focused on an inflation target.

• The goal of European Central Bank monetary policy is price stability across the euro zone.

In this chapter we add money to our model of the short-term determination of GDP and the price level. We want to know how monetary forces affect economic activity and how we can ensure that inflation is kept under control. We approach this issue in a number of steps. First, we discuss the factors that influence the demand for and supply of money balances in the economy. Second, we ask how monetary factors spill over into real activity. We are then able to accomplish the final task of integrating money and monetary policy into the aggregate demand and aggregate supply framework of Chapters 23–26. Then we can see how monetary and fiscal policy can be used to influence the GDP gap and the price level.

In previous chapters we have discussed the determinants of *flows* of output and spending. When we incorporate money and financial markets, we are also talking about *stocks* of assets and financial instruments. The central issue is then how markets for financial assets and liabilities interact with markets for goods. This occurs through two important prices—the interest rate, which is the price we pay to borrow money, and the exchange rate, which is the price we pay to obtain foreign currency—and through wealth effects that arise when the real value of assets changes. First, we need to understand some important characteristics of financial assets and interest rates.

Financial assets

At any particular moment people have a stock of wealth that they can hold in many forms. Some of it may be money in the bank or building society; some may be cash in hand or under the mattress; some may be in shares; and some of it may be in property, such as a house.

In order to concentrate on money, we group wealth into just two categories: *money*, and everything else which we call *bonds*. By 'money' we mean the assets that serve as a medium of exchange, that is, paper money, coins, and deposits on which cheques may be drawn. We outlined the various definitions of money in Chapter 27 (see Box 27.2 on page 486). For present purposes it is adequate to think of money as including cash held by the public plus deposits in banks and building societies. By 'bonds' we mean all other forms of financial wealth; these include interest-earning financial assets *plus* claims on real capital. For simplicity, however, our analysis of bonds will assume an asset that is exactly like the debt of the central government (known in the UK as a *gilt*), rather than having the characteristics of corporate bonds or equities.[1]

Money and bonds have different characteristics as assets. The market price of bonds can rise or fall, but the price of money is fixed in money terms. (Obviously, £1 is always worth £1.) The price of bonds is related to market interest rates, so our first task is to understand this relationship.

---

[1] This simplification can take us quite a long way and is necessary in order to keep our model straightforward.

The rate of interest and present value

A bond is a financial asset that promises to make one or more interest payments and to repay a capital sum at a specified date in the future. The **present value (*PV*)** of a bond, or of any asset, refers to the value now of the future payment or payments to which the asset represents a claim. The concept of present value was discussed in more detail in Chapter 17 on pages 286–8. For those of you who have read Chapter 17 what follows is a review; for the rest it is essential reading.

Present value depends on the rate of interest, because when we calculate present value the interest rate is used to *discount* the future payments. Two extreme examples help illustrate this relationship between the rate of interest and present value.

A single payment one year hence We start with the simplest case. How much would someone be prepared to pay *now* to purchase a bond that will produce a single payment of £100 in one year's time?

Suppose that the interest rate is 5 per cent, which means that £1.00 invested today will be worth £1.05 in one year's time. Now ask how much someone would have to lend out in order to have £100 a year from now. If we use *PV* to stand for this unknown amount, we can write *PV*(1.05) [which means *PV multiplied by* 1.05] = £100. Thus, *PV* = £100/1.05 = £95.24.[2] This tells us that the present value of £100 receivable in one year's time is £95.24; anyone who lends out £95.24 for one year at 5 per cent interest will get back the £95.24 plus £4.76 in interest, which makes £100.

What if the interest rate had been 7 per cent? At that interest rate the present value of the £100 receivable in one year's time would be £100/1.07 = £93.46, which is less than the present value when the interest rate was 5 per cent.

A perpetuity Now consider another extreme case—a perpetuity that promises to pay £100 per year to its holder *for ever*. The *present value* of the perpetuity depends on how much £100 per year is worth, and this again depends on the rate of interest.

A bond that will produce a stream of income of £100 per year for ever is worth £1,000 at 10 per cent interest, because £1,000 invested at 10 per cent per year will yield £100 interest per year for ever. However, the same bond is worth £2,000 when the interest rate is 5 per cent per year, because it takes £2,000 invested at 5 per cent per year to yield £100 interest per year. The lower the rate of interest obtainable on the market, the more valuable is a bond paying a fixed amount of interest.

Similar relations apply to bonds that are more complicated than single payments but are not perpetuities. Although in such cases the calculation of present value is more complicated, the same negative relationship between the interest rate and present value still holds.

The present value of any asset that yields a given stream of money over time is negatively related to the interest rate.

Present value and market price

Present value is important because it establishes the market price for an asset.

The present value of an asset is the amount that someone would be willing to pay now to secure the right to the future stream of payments conferred by ownership of the asset.

To see this, return to our example of a bond that promises to pay £100 one year hence. When the interest rate is 5 per cent, the present value is £95.24. To see why this is the maximum that anyone would pay for this bond, suppose that some sellers offer to sell the bond at some other price, say £98. If, instead of paying this amount for the bond, a potential buyer lends her £98 out at 5 per cent interest, she will have at the end of one year more than the £100 that the bond will produce: at 5 per cent interest, £98 yields £4.90 in interest, which when added to the principal makes £102.90. Clearly, no well-informed individual would pay £98—or by the same reasoning any sum in excess of £95.24—for the bond.

Now suppose that the bond is offered for sale at a price less than £95.24—say £90. A potential buyer could borrow £90 to buy the bond and would pay £4.50 in interest on the loan. At the end of the year the bond yields £100. When this is used to repay the £90 loan and the £4.50 in interest, £5.50 is left as profit. Clearly, it would be worthwhile for someone to buy the bond at the price of £90—or by the same argument at any price less than £95.24. But at £90 no holder would want to sell the bond. If she needed £90 she could borrow it for a year then cash in the bond at the end of the year, pay back the £90 plus £4.50 interest, and be £5.50 better off than if she had sold the bond at the beginning of the year.

Thus, *all* bondholders would want to sell at £98 and *none* would want to sell at £90, so £95.24 is the only price at which there are both buyers and sellers—it is the market price. This discussion should make clear that the present value of an asset determines its market price. If the market price of any asset is greater than the present value of the income stream that it produces, no one will want to buy it, and the market price will fall. If the market value is below its present value, there will be a rush to buy it, and the market price will rise. These facts lead to the following conclusion:

In a free market, the equilibrium price of any asset will be the present value of the income stream that it produces.

---

[2] Notice that in this type of formula the interest rate, *i*, is expressed as a decimal fraction. For example, 5 per cent is expressed as 0.05, so (1 + *i*) equals 1.05.

The rate of interest and market price

The discussion above leads us to three important propositions. The first two stress the negative relationship between interest rates and asset prices:

1. If the rate of interest falls, the value of an asset producing a given income stream will rise.

2. A rise in the market price of an asset producing a given income stream is equivalent to a decrease in the rate of interest earned by the asset.

Thus, a promise to pay £100 one year from now is worth £92.59 when the interest rate is 8 per cent and only £89.29 when the interest rate is 12 per cent: £92.59 at 8 per cent interest (£92.59 × 1.08) and £89.29 at 12 per cent interest (£89.29 × 1.12) are both worth £100 in one year's time.

The third proposition focuses on the term to maturity of the bond:

3. The nearer the maturity date of a bond, the less the bond's value will change with a change in the rate of interest.

To see this, consider an extreme case. The present value of a bond that is redeemable for £1,000 in one week's time will be very close to £1,000 no matter what the interest rate is. Thus, its value will not change much even if the rate of interest leaps from 5 to 10 per cent during that week. Note that any interest-earning components of *money* are so short-term that their values remain unchanged when the interest rate changes.

As a second example consider two bonds, one that promises to pay £100 next year and one that promises to pay £100 in ten years. A rise in the interest rate from 8 to 12 per cent will lower the value of £100 payable in one year's time by 3.6 per cent, but it will lower the value of £100 payable in ten years' time by 37.9 per cent.[3]

The supply of money and the demand for money

We now return to our central task of adding a monetary sector to the macro model built up over Chapters 23–26. We proceed in several small steps. In this chapter we make some simplifying assumptions about the international financial environment in which our economy operates. In effect, we assume that the exchange rate is fixed, and that there is some segmentation of domestic and international financial markets. This will enable us to analyse domestic monetary equilibrium without fully incorporating international influences. In Chapter 29 we introduce international transactions explicitly, and in Chapter 30 we incorporate the influences of international financial markets and the exchange rate regime.

The supply of money

In a modern economy the supply of money is determined by the interaction of the banking system and the non-bank private sector. We have already discussed the variety of definitions of the money stock and the way in which the money supply is determined in detail in Chapter 27. For present purposes we use the broad definition of money, M4 (see page 486).

In most major countries the authorities implement monetary policy by setting interest rates and letting the money stock be determined by how much is demanded at that interest rate. We say more about how the authorities set interest rates later in this chapter. But for now we just assume that the authorities set the interest rate and focus on the implications of this fact for money demand. We can then

see how policy-determined changes in interest rates affect the real economy. Our analysis, therefore, now focuses on the factors influencing money demand because at the set interest rate the money stock is demand-determined.

The demand for money

The amount of wealth that everyone in the economy wishes to hold in the form of money balances is called the **demand for money**. Because people are choosing how to divide their given stock of wealth between money and bonds, it follows that if we know the demand for money, we also know the demand for bonds. With a *given level of wealth*, a rise in the demand for money necessarily implies a fall in the demand for bonds; if people wish to hold £1 billion more money, they must wish to hold £1 billion less of bonds. It also follows that, if households are in equilibrium with respect to their money holdings, they are in equilibrium with respect to their bond holdings.

When we say that in first quarter of 2002 the quantity of money demanded was £950 billion (the approximate value of the broad money stock, M4, at that time), we mean that at that time the public wished to hold money balances that

---

[3] The example assumes annual compounding. The first case is calculated from the numbers of the previous example: (92.58 – 89.29)/92.58. The ten-year case uses the formula

$$\text{Present value} = \text{principal}/(1 + i)^n,$$

which gives £46.30 at 8 per cent and £28.75 at 12 per cent. The percentage fall in value is thus (46.30 – 28.75)/46.30 = 0.379, or 37.9 per cent.

totalled £950 billion. But why do firms and individuals wish to hold money balances at all? There is a cost to holding any money balance. The money could have been used to purchase bonds, which earn higher interest than does money.[4] For the present we assume no ongoing inflation, so there is no difference between real and nominal interest rates.

The opportunity cost of holding any money balance is the extra interest that could have been earned if the money had been used instead to purchase bonds.

Clearly, money will be held only when it provides services that are valued at least as highly as the opportunity cost of holding it. Three important services that are provided by money balances give rise to three motives for holding money: the transactions, precautionary, and speculative motives.

The transactions motive

Most transactions require money. Money passes from consumers to firms to pay for the goods and services produced by firms; money passes from firms to employees to pay for the labour services supplied by workers to firms. Money balances that are held to finance such flows are called **transactions balances**.

In an imaginary world in which the receipts and disbursements of consumers and firms were perfectly synchronized, it would be unnecessary to hold transactions balances. If every time a consumer spent £10 she received £10 as part payment of her wages, no transactions balances would be needed. In the real world, however, receipts and payments are not perfectly synchronized.

Consider the balances that are held because of wage payments. Suppose, for purposes of illustration, that firms pay wages every Friday and that employees spend all their wages on goods and services, with the spending spread out evenly over the week. Thus, on Friday morning firms must hold balances equal to the weekly wage bill; on Friday afternoon the employees will hold these balances.

Over the week, workers' balances will be drawn down as a result of their purchasing goods and services. Over the same period, the balances held by firms will build up as a result of their selling goods and services until, on the following Friday morning, firms will again have amassed balances equal to the wage bill that must be met on that day.

The transactions motive arises because payments and receipts are not synchronized.

What determines the size of the transactions balances to be held? It is clear that in our example total transactions balances vary with the value of the wage bill. If the wage bill doubles for any reason, the transactions balances held by firms and households for this purpose will also double, on average. As it is with wages, so it is with all other trans-

actions: the size of the balances held is positively related to the value of the transactions.

It is the average value of money balances that people choose to hold over a particular period that is relevant for macroeconomics, but we need to know how money demand relates to GDP rather than to total transactions. In fact, the value of all transactions exceeds the value of the economy's final output. When the miller buys wheat from the farmer and when the baker buys flour from the miller, both are transactions against which money balances must be held, although only the value added at each stage is part of GDP. Generally there will be a stable, positive relationship between transactions and GDP. A rise in GDP also leads to a rise in the total value of all transactions and hence to an associated rise in the demand for transactions balances. This allows us to relate transactions balances to GDP.

The larger the value of GDP, the larger is the value of transactions balances that will be held.

The precautionary motive

Many reasons for spending arise unexpectedly, such as when your car breaks down, or when you have to make an unplanned journey to visit a sick relative. As a precaution against cash crises, when receipts are abnormally low or disbursements are abnormally high, firms and individuals carry money balances. **Precautionary balances** provide a cushion against uncertainty about the timing of cash flows. The larger such balances are, the greater is the protection against running out of money because of temporary fluctuations in cash flows.

The seriousness of the risk of a cash crisis depends on the penalties that are inflicted for being caught without sufficient money balances. A firm is unlikely to be pushed into insolvency, but it may incur considerable costs if it is forced to borrow money at high interest rates in order to meet a temporary cash crisis.

The precautionary motive arises because individuals and firms are uncertain about the degree to which payments and receipts will be synchronized.

The protection provided by a given quantity of precautionary balances depends on the volume of payments and

---

[4] Many of the bank and building society deposits that are included in M4 now yield interest. This complicates, but does not fundamentally alter, the analysis of the demand for money. In particular, it means that the opportunity cost of holding those interest-bearing components of money is not the *level* of interest rates paid on bonds, but the *difference* between that rate and the rate paid on money. Because the interest earned on deposits tends to fluctuate less than rates on marketable securities, the difference tends to move with the level of interest rates in the economy, rising when rates rise and falling when rates fall. For simplicity we talk of the demand for money responding to the *level* of interest rates, although in reality it is the *difference* that is the opportunity cost of money.

receipts. A £100 precautionary balance provides a large cushion for a person whose volume of payments per month is £800 and a small cushion for a firm whose monthly volume is £250,000. As the value of transactions rises, more money is necessary to provide the same degree of protection.

The precautionary motive, like the transactions motive, causes the demand for money to vary positively with the money value of GDP.

For most purposes the transactions and precautionary motives can be merged, as they both show that desired money holdings are positively related to GDP. Indeed, they both show money being held in relation to transactions, either planned or potential.

The speculative motive

Money can be held for its characteristics as an asset. Firms and individuals may hold some money in order to provide a hedge against the uncertainty inherent in fluctuating prices of other financial assets. Money balances held for this purpose are called **speculative balances**. This motive was first analysed by Keynes. Professor James Tobin, the 1981 Nobel Laureate in economics, developed the modern analysis.

Any holder of money balances forgoes the extra interest income that could be earned if bonds were held instead. However, market interest rates fluctuate, and so do the market prices of existing bonds. (Their present values depend on the interest rate.) Bonds are risky assets, because their prices fluctuate. Many individuals and firms do not like risk; they are said to be *risk-averse*.[5]

In choosing between holding money and holding bonds, wealth-holders must balance the extra interest income that they could earn by holding bonds against the risk that bonds carry. At one extreme, if individuals hold all their wealth in the form of bonds, they earn extra interest on their entire wealth, but they also expose their entire wealth to the risk of changes in the price of bonds. At the other extreme, if people hold all their wealth in the form of money, they earn less interest income, but they do not face the risk of unexpected changes in the price of bonds. Wealth-holders usually do not take either extreme position. They hold part of their wealth as money and part of it as bonds; that is, they *diversify* their holdings. The fact that some proportion of wealth is held in money and some in bonds suggests that, as wealth rises, desired money holdings will also rise.

The speculative motive implies that the demand for money varies positively with wealth.

Although one individual's wealth may rise or fall rapidly, the total wealth of a society changes only slowly. For the analysis of short-term fluctuations in GDP, the effects of changes in wealth are fairly small, and we will ignore them for the present. Specific individuals may undergo large wealth changes in response to bond price changes, but with inside wealth the total effect is small.[6] When lenders gain, borrowers lose; and when lenders lose, borrowers gain. Over the long term, however, variations in aggregate wealth can have a major effect on the demand for money.

Wealth that is held in cash or deposits earns less interest than could be earned by holding bonds; hence the reduction in risk involved in holding money carries an opportunity cost in terms of forgone interest earnings. The speculative motive leads individuals and firms to add to their money holdings until the reduction in risk obtained by the last pound added is just balanced (in each wealth-holder's view) by the cost in terms of the interest forgone on that pound. A fall in the rate of return on bonds for the same level of risk will encourage people to hold more of their wealth as money and less in bonds. A rise in their rate of return for a given level of risk will cause people to hold more bonds and less money.

The speculative motive implies that the demand for money will be negatively related to the rate of interest.

The precautionary and transactions motives may also be negatively related to interest rates at the margin, because higher returns on bonds encourage people to economize on their money holding. However, in practice we observe only total money holdings, so we cannot distinguish the components held for different motives. Hence demand for money, as a whole, is likely to be positively related to GDP and wealth, and negatively related to the interest rate.

Real and nominal money balances

The money supply is a nominal quantity, but it is important to distinguish *demand* for real money balances from nominal money demand. Real money demand is the number of units of purchasing power that the public wishes to hold in the form of money balances. For example, in an imaginary one-product (wheat) economy, the number of bushels of wheat that could be purchased with the money balances held would be the measure of their real value. In a more complex economy it could be measured in terms of the number of 'baskets of goods', represented by a price index such as the RPI, that could be purchased with the money balances held. When we speak of the demand for money in real terms, we speak of the amount demanded in constant pounds (that is, with a constant price level).

[5] A person is risk-averse when he or she prefers a certain sum of money to an uncertain outcome for which the expected value is the same. See Chapter 13 for a discussion of risk aversion.

[6] 'Inside wealth' is not net wealth for the economy *as a whole*—one agent's assets are another agent's liabilities.

Box 28.1 **The quantity theory of money**

The quantity theory of money can be set out in terms of four equations. Equation (i) states that the demand for money balances depends on the value of transactions as measured by nominal GDP, which is real GDP multiplied by the price level:

$$M^D = kPY. \tag{i}$$

Equation (ii) states that the supply of money, M, is exogenously determined:

$$M^S = M. \tag{ii}$$

Equation (iii) states the equilibrium condition that the demand for money must equal the supply:

$$M^D = M^S. \tag{iii}$$

Substitution from (ii) and (iii) into equation (i) yields

$$M = kPY. \tag{iv}$$

The original classical quantity theory assumes that k is a constant given by the transactions demand for money and that Y is constant because full employment (equilibrium GDP) is maintained. Thus, increases or decreases in the money supply lead to proportional increases or decreases in prices.

Often the quantity theory is presented by using the *equation of exchange*:

$$MV = PY, \tag{v}$$

where V is the **velocity of circulation**, defined as nominal GDP divided by the quantity of money:

$$V = PY/M. \tag{vi}$$

Velocity may be interpreted as the average amount of 'work' done by a unit of money. If annual money GDP is £600 billion and the stock of money is £200 billion, on average, each pound's worth of money is used three times to create the values added that compose GDP.

There is a simple relationship between k and V. One is the reciprocal of the other, as may be seen immediately by comparing (iv) and (vi). Thus, it makes no difference whether we choose to work with k or V. Further, if k is assumed to be constant, this implies that V must also be treated as being constant.

An example may help to illustrate the interpretation of each. Suppose the stock of money that people wish to hold equals one-fifth of the value of total transactions. Thus, k is 0.2 and V, the reciprocal of k, is 5. If the money supply is to be one-fifth of the value of annual transactions, each pound must be 'used' on average five times.

The modern version of the quantity theory does not assume that k and V are exogenously fixed. However, it does argue that they will not change in response to a change in the quantity of money.

The real demand for money (or the demand for real money balances) is the nominal quantity demanded divided by the price level.

In the twenty years from March 1982 to March 2002, on the M4 definition, the nominal quantity of money balances held in the United Kingdom increased nearly seven-fold, from just over £140 billion to around £950 billion. Over the same period, however, the price level, as measured by the RPI, rose by about 130 per cent (that is, it more than doubled). This tells us that the real quantity of money rose from £140 billion to about £410 billion, measured in constant 1982 prices, a nearly three-fold increase.

Up to now we have held the price level constant, and so we have identified the determinants of the demand for real money balances as real GDP, real wealth, and the interest rate. Now suppose that with the interest rate, real wealth, and real GDP held constant, the price level doubles. Because the demand for real money balances will be unchanged, the demand for nominal balances must double. If the public previously demanded £300 billion in nominal money balances, it will now demand £600 billion. This keeps the real demand unchanged at £600/2 = £300 billion. The money balances of £600 billion at the new, higher price level represent exactly the same purchasing power as £300 billion at the old price level.

Other things being equal, the nominal demand for money balances varies in proportion to the price level; when the price level doubles, desired nominal money balances also double.

This is a central proposition of the quantity theory of money, which is discussed further in Box 28.1.

Total demand for money

Figure 28.1 summarizes the influences of the nominal rate of interest, real GDP, and the price level, the three variables that account for most of the short-term variations in the nominal quantity of money demanded. The function relating money demanded to the rate of interest is often called the **demand for money function**, even though the demand for nominal money depends also on GDP, wealth, and prices.

We have seen that the public has a fixed stock of wealth at any point in time. When it decides how much money to hold, for the reasons just mentioned, it is also deciding how many bonds to hold. So the public can be seen as adjusting the balance of its portfolio of wealth between the two assets, money and bonds. When it is in disequilibrium, it is trying to alter that balance either by selling bonds and getting money, or by buying bonds and giving up money. When it is in equilibrium, it has the desired balance between the two assets.

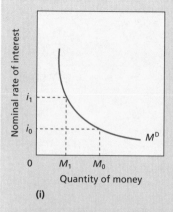
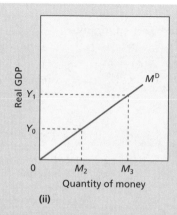
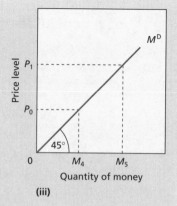

Figure 28.1 The demand for money as a function of interest rates, GDP, and the price level

The quantity of money demanded varies negatively with the nominal rate of interest and positively with both real GDP and the price level. In part (i) the quantity of money demanded varies negatively with the interest rate. When the interest rate rises from i_0 to i_1, the quantity of money demanded falls from M_0 to M_1. In part (ii) the quantity of money demanded is positively related to real GDP. When GDP rises from Y_0 to Y_1, the quantity demanded rises from M_2 to M_3. In part (iii) the quantity of money demanded is proportional to the price level. When the price level doubles from P_0 to P_1, the quantity demanded doubles from M_4 to M_5. In the text we refer to the M^D curve in (i) as the money demand function. It is drawn for given values of real GDP, wealth, and the price level.

Monetary forces and aggregate demand

We are now in a position to examine the relationship between monetary forces on the one hand, and the equilibrium values of GDP and the price level on the other. The first step in explaining this relationship is a new one: the link between monetary equilibrium and aggregate demand. The second is familiar from earlier chapters: the effects of shifts in aggregate demand on equilibrium values of GDP and the price level. We set out the first step in this section and we analyse the second in the last section of this chapter, where we compare monetary and fiscal polices as tools for controlling the economy.

Monetary equilibrium and the interest rate

Monetary equilibrium occurs when the demand for money equals the supply of money. In Chapter 3 we saw that in competitive markets the price will adjust so as to ensure equilibrium. The rate of interest is the relevant price in the money markets. However, in UK and European money markets (as well as those of most other major countries) the monetary authorities set the level of interest rates and the money supply adjusts to become equal to the quantity of money demanded at the policy-determined rate of interest.[7]

The easiest way to understand how this works is to start by showing how interest rates would adjust to clear the money market (equate demand and supply) if there were a given money supply. We then show how the money stock adjusts to equate demand and supply when the authorities choose to change the interest rate for macro policy reasons.

Equilibrium interest rate

Figure 28.2 shows supply and demand curves for money. The supply of money that is in existence at the initial point in time is shown as a vertical line, indicating that the money supply is a given nominal quantity. The money demand curve is based upon the speculative demand illustrated in Figure 28.1(i). It is negatively sloped because people desire to hold less money as interest rates rise. The money demand curve is drawn for given levels of real GDP, the price level, and wealth, and will shift to the right if any of these variables increases.

Figure 28.2 also shows how the interest rate would move in order to equate the demand for money with its supply,

---

[7] The authorities actually set a specific rate at which they trade with the wholesale money markets. All other rates are determined relative to this policy rate by market forces. We will talk as if there is only one interest rate and this is the one the authorities set. More institutional detail on the process of interest rate setting was set out in the last section of this chapter.

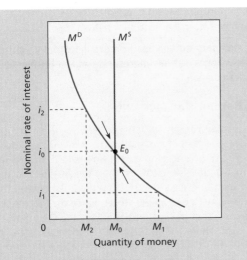

Figure 28.2 The equilibrium interest rate

The equilibrium interest rate arises where demand for money equals the supply of money. A given quantity of money, M_0, is shown by the vertical supply curve M^S. The demand for money is M^D; its negative slope indicates that a fall in the rate of interest causes the quantity of money demanded to increase. Equilibrium is at E_0, with a rate of interest i_0.

If the interest rate is i_1, there will be an excess demand for money of $M_1 - M_0$. Bonds will be offered for sale in an attempt to increase money holdings. This will force the rate of interest up to i_0 (the price of bonds falls), at which point the quantity of money demanded is equal to the fixed supply, M_0. If the interest rate is i_2, there will be an excess supply of money $M_0 - M_2$. Bonds will be demanded in return for excess money balances. This will force the rate of interest down to i_0 (the price of bonds rises), at which point the quantity of money demanded has risen to equal the fixed money supply, M_0.

given the initial money stock and the existing stock of bonds. When a few people find that they have less money than they wish to hold, they can sell some bonds and add the proceeds to their money holdings. This transaction simply redistributes given supplies of bonds and money among individuals—it does not change the total supply of either money or bonds.

Now suppose that all of the firms and households in the economy have excess demands for money balances. They all try to sell bonds to add to their money balances, but what one person can do, all cannot necessarily do. At any one moment the economy's total supply of money and bonds is fixed; there is just so much money and there are just so many bonds in existence. If everyone tries to sell bonds there will be no one to buy them, and the price of bonds will fall.

We saw earlier in this chapter that a fall in the price of bonds means a rise in the rate of interest. As the interest rate rises, people economize on money balances, because the opportunity cost of holding such balances is rising. This is what we saw in Figure 28.1(i), where the quantity of money demanded falls along the demand curve in

response to a rise in the rate of interest. Eventually the interest rate will rise enough that people will no longer be trying to add to their money balances by selling bonds. At that point there will no longer be an excess supply of bonds, and the interest rate will stop rising. The demand for money will again equal the supply.

Suppose now that all firms and households hold larger money balances than they would like. A single household or firm would purchase bonds with its excess balances, achieving monetary equilibrium by reducing its money holdings and increasing its bond holdings. However, just as in the previous example, what one individual can do, all cannot do. At any one moment the total quantity of bonds is fixed, so everyone cannot simultaneously add to personal bond-holdings. When all agents enter the bond market and try to purchase bonds with unwanted money balances, they bid up the price of existing bonds, and the interest rate falls. Individuals and firms then become willing to hold larger quantities of money; that is, the quantity of money demanded increases along the money demand curve, in response to a fall in the rate of interest. The rise in the price of bonds continues until firms and households stop trying to convert bonds into money. In other words, it continues until everyone is content to hold the existing supply of money and bonds.

Monetary equilibrium occurs when the rate of interest is such that the demand to hold money equals the supply of money available to be held, and hence the demand to hold bonds equals the supply of bonds available to be held.

The determination of the interest rate depicted in Figure 28.2 is often called the *liquidity preference theory* of interest and sometimes the *portfolio balance theory*.

As we will see, a monetary shock—an autonomous shift in the demand for money or a change in the policy-determined interest rate—will lead to an adjustment in the money supply. However, the critical factor is that aggregate spending—especially investment, but also consumption and net exports (as we saw in Chapters 23 and 24)—is sensitive to changes in the interest rate. Here, then, is a link between monetary factors and real spending flows.

Interest rates as the monetary policy instrument

In the section above we have seen how the interest rate would adjust to clear the money market for a given level of the money stock and a given money demand curve. In most industrial countries, including the UK and the euro zone, the monetary authorities set the interest rate and then let the money supply adjust to whatever interest rate is set.

Figure 28.3 illustrates how this works. If the authorities wished to relax monetary policy they *could do so* by increasing the money supply. If they did this, there would initially be an excess supply of money. Holders of this

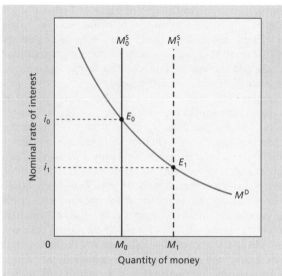

Figure 28.3 Interest rates and money supply changes

A change in the policy-determined interest rate requires the money supply to change. In the figure the initial money supply is shown by the vertical line M_0^S, and the demand for money is shown by the negatively sloped curve M^D. The initial equilibrium is at E_0, with corresponding interest rate i_0. The monetary authorities choose to lower the interest rate from i_0 to i_1. In order to achieve this they must generate an increase in the money supply, from M_0^S to M_1^S. The new equilibrium is at E_1. Starting at E_1, with M_1^S and i_1, it can be seen that a decrease in the money supply to M_0^S would be required to achieve an increase in the interest rate from i_1 to i_0.

money would demand more bonds, and via the process discussed above this would raise the price of bonds and lower the interest rate.

However, this is not what happens. Rather than setting a level of the money supply, the authorities set the level of the interest rate. When the central bank decides to loosen monetary policy, it lowers the interest rate. At this lower interest rate the public wishes to hold more money. So there is excess demand for money. In order to achieve portfolio balance (that is, the desired composition of asset holding), the public tries to sell bonds for money. If the Bank did nothing, the sales of bonds would raise the interest rate. However, the Bank is setting the interest rate, so, in order to maintain that rate, it accommodates the public's desire to switch from bonds to money by buying bonds and supplying money.[8] The money supply thus increases to whatever is demanded at the new interest rate.[9]

Notice that the outcome in Figure 28.3 is exactly the same when the authorities fix interest rates and let the money supply adjust as it is when they fix the money supply and let interest rates adjust. It makes no difference to the equilibrium of our macro model which way it is done. We will see, however, that when the authorities are responding to an exogenous shock to aggregate demand,

fixing interest rates and fixing the stock of money can lead to widely different adjustment paths.

The monetary authorities in most industrial countries (or currency zones) set the interest rate and let the money stock adjust to demand.

The transmission mechanism

The mechanism by which changes in monetary policy affect aggregate demand is called the **transmission mechanism**. The transmission mechanism operates in two stages: the first is the link between the interest rate and investment spending, and the second is the link between investment spending and aggregate demand. For this discussion we assume that the authorities are setting the interest rate. The case where the authorities set the exchange rate is discussed in Chapter 30. The views of the UK Monetary Policy Committee on the transmission mechanism of their interest rate decisions are set out as an appendix to that chapter.

From changes in the interest rate to shifts in investment

The first step in the transmission mechanism relates interest rates to aggregate spending. For simplicity we shall focus here only on the link via changes in investment. We saw in Chapter 23 that investment, which includes spending on inventory accumulation, residential construction, and business fixed investment, responds to changes in the real rate of interest. Other things being equal, a decrease in the real rate of interest makes borrowing cheaper and generates new investment spending.[10] This negative relationship between investment and the rate of interest is called the **investment demand function**.

This link between the interest rate and investment is shown in Figure 28.4. In part (i) we see that, if the authorities wish to lower the interest rate, they can do so (as discussed above) by buying all the extra bonds offered for sale at the new interest rate and thereby increasing the money supply. In part (ii) we see that a change in the interest rate causes the level of investment spending to change in the

[8] The central bank's money market operators are instructed to buy or sell whatever short-term securities are necessary to keep that rate at the target level. So, in effect, they are making up any discrepancy between the stock demand and the current stock supply by altering the stock in existence.

[9] In practice it is the monetary base, M0, that the authorities supply in order to maintain interest rates. Broader monetary aggregates are then determined by demand at whatever level the set interest rate determines (as a result of the public's demand for loans and deposits). This complication does not change the principles involved.

[10] Consumption, too, may respond to changes in the real interest rate, and there may also be an impact on net exports via the exchange rate. In this chapter we concentrate on investment spending, which may be taken to stand for *all* interest-sensitive spending, and we maintain our simplifying assumption that expected inflation is zero so that the real and nominal interest rates are equal.

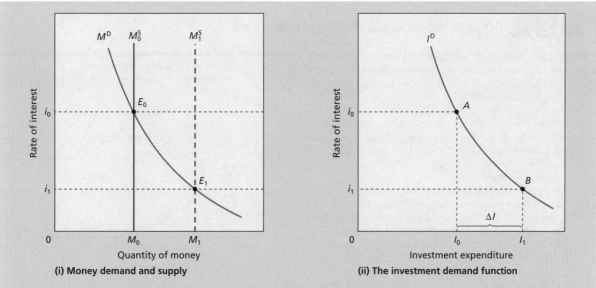

Figure 28.4 The effect of changes in the interest rate on investment spending

A reduction in the rate of interest increases desired investment spending. Initial equilibrium is at E_0, with a quantity of money M_0 (shown by the vertical money supply curve M_0^S), an interest rate of i_0, and an investment spending of I_0 (point A in part (ii)). The monetary authorities then lower the rate of interest to i_1 (and increase the money supply to M_1), and this increases investment spending by ΔI to I_1 (point B). A policy-induced rise in the interest rate from i_1 to i_0 is accompanied by a fall in the money stock from M_1 to M_0 and leads investment to fall by ΔI from I_1 to I_0.

opposite direction.[11] A fall in the interest rate causes investment to rise, and a rise in the interest rate causes investment to fall.

A fall in the interest rate leads to an increase in investment spending. A rise in the interest rate leads to a decrease in investment spending.

The change in investment spending shifts the aggregate spending curve, AE, as shown in Chapters 23 and 24. Box 28.2 discusses some forces additional to interest rates that help explain investment.

From shifts in aggregate spending to shifts in aggregate demand Now we are back on familiar ground. In Chapter 25 we saw that a shift in the aggregate spending curve leads to a shift in the AD curve. This is shown again in Figure 28.5.

A change in the interest rate, by causing a change in desired investment spending (which in previous chapters was assumed to be exogenous) and hence a shift in the AE curve, causes the AD curve to shift. A fall in the interest rate

causes an increase in investment spending and hence an increase in aggregate demand. A rise in the interest rate causes a decrease in investment spending and therefore a decrease in aggregate demand.

The transmission mechanism connects monetary forces and real spending flows. A change in the interest rate causes a change in investment spending, which in turn leads to a shift in the aggregate demand curve.

Thus, a lowering of the interest rate increases investment, and this shifts the AD curve to the right. A raising of interest rates lowers investment and shifts AD to the left. Later we will see that another important channel of the transmission mechanism is provided by the exchange rate. A discussion of how the openness of the economy affects the transmission mechanism is presented in Chapter 30.

---

[11] Recall that we have assumed that real and nominal interest rates are the same. Generally, as long as inflation expectations are constant, the change in the nominal interest rate determined in part (i) of Figure 28.4 is equal to the change in the real interest rate in part (ii).

Box 28.2 **The accelerator theory of investment**

In our macroeconomic model, investment changes in response to changes in interest rates. The **accelerator theory of investment** relies on another determinant of investment, which can be formalized only in a dynamic model. This theory relates investment to GDP. The possibility of systematic fluctuations arises because the *level* of investment is related to *changes* in GDP.

The demand for machinery and factories is obviously derived from the demand for the goods that the capital equipment is designed to produce. If there is a demand that is expected to persist, and that cannot be met by increasing production with existing industrial capacity, then new plant and equipment will be needed.

Investment expenditure occurs while the new capital equipment is being built and installed. If the desired stock of capital goods increases, there will be an investment boom while the new capital is being produced. But if nothing else changes, and even though business conditions continue to look rosy enough to justify the increased stock of capital, investment in new plant and equipment will cease once the larger capital stock is achieved. This makes investment depend on changes in final demand, and hence on changes in GDP, as illustrated in the table.* The figure illustrates what happens to investment under the accelerator theory when GDP rises from one constant level to another.

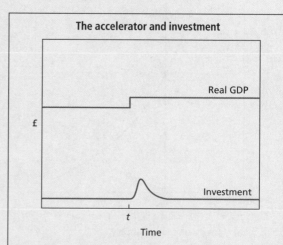

The accelerator and investment

When there is a change in the level of final output, there is a much bigger percentage change in the rate of investment. The figure illustrates the path over time of GDP and investment. We assume that GDP is constant but that at time *t* it jumps to a new, higher level and then continues at this level. Replacement investment carries on at some constant level, but the increase in output requires a higher capital stock. This in turn requires a burst of *new investment*. Once this burst of new investment is over (shown as being spread out over time), the level of new investment returns to zero.

An illustration of the accelerator theory of investment

Year	Annual sales	Change in sales	Required stock of capital[a]	Net investment increase in required capital stock
(1)	(2)	(3)	(4)	(5)
1	£10	£0	£50	£0
2	10	0	50	0
3	11	1	55	5
4	13	2	65	10
5	16	3	80	15
6	19	3	95	15
7	22	3	110	15
8	24	2	120	10
9	25	1	125	5
10	25	0	125	0

With a fixed capital–output ratio, net investment occurs only when it is necessary to increase the stock of capital in order to change output. Assume that it takes £5 of capital to produce £1 of output per year. In years 1 and 2 there is no need for investment. In year 3 a rise in sales of £1 requires investment of £5 to provide the needed capital stock. In year 4 a further rise of £2 in sales requires an additional investment of £10 to provide the needed capital stock. As columns (3) and (5) show, the amount of net investment is proportional to the *change* in sales. When the increase in sales tapers off in years 7–9, investment declines. When sales no longer increase in year 10, net investment falls to zero because the capital stock of year 9 is adequate to provide output for year 10's sales.

[a] Assuming a capital–output ratio of 5:1.

The main insight that the accelerator theory provides is its emphasis on the role of net investment as a *disequilibrium* phenomenon—something that occurs when the stock of capital goods differs from what firms and

households would like it to be. This makes the accelerator a possible explanation of *fluctuations* in GDP. As we will see, it can itself contribute to those fluctuations.

Taken literally, the simple accelerator assumes a mechanical and rigid response of investment to changes in sales (and thus, in the aggregate, to changes in GDP). It does this by assuming a proportional relationship between changes in output and changes in the desired capital stock. It also assumes that there is a fixed ratio between the level of output and the level of the capital stock. This ratio is called the *capital–output ratio*. Both assumptions are to some degree questionable.

The accelerator does not by itself give anything like a complete explanation of variations in investment in capital goods, and it should not be surprising that a simple accelerator theory provides a relatively poor overall explanation of changes in investment. Yet accelerator-like influences do exist, and they play a role in the cyclical variability of investment. Modern investment theories often include a flexible version of the accelerator, in which the capital–output ratio (coefficient α in the footnote to this box) varies with other factors such as interest rates.

* A more formal derivation is: let the relationship between the GDP level and the amount of capital needed to produce it be

$$K = \alpha Y, \tag{i}$$

where K is the required capital stock. The coefficient α is the capital–output ratio; $\alpha = K/Y$ and is also called the accelerator coefficient. Taking changes in (i), and noticing that investment is, by definition, the change in the capital stock, yields

$$I = \Delta K = \alpha \Delta Y.$$

This says that investment is some constant times *the change* in GDP. This is called the 'simple', or sometimes the 'naïve', accelerator.

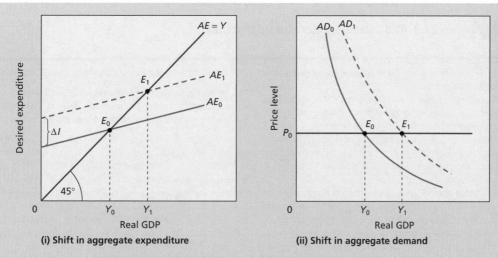

Figure 28.5 The effects of changes in the interest rate on aggregate demand

Changes in the interest rate cause shifts in the aggregate spending and aggregate demand functions. In Figure 28.4 a fall in the interest rate increased desired investment spending by ΔI. Here, in part (i) the aggregate spending function shifts up by ΔI, from AE_0 to AE_1. At the fixed price level P_0, equilibrium GDP rises from Y_0 to Y_1, shifting the aggregate demand curve horizontally from AD_0 to AD_1 in part (ii).

When the interest rate rises (as from i_1 to i_0 in Figure 28.4), investment falls by ΔI, thereby shifting aggregate spending from AE_1 to AE_0. At the fixed price level P_0 this reduces equilibrium income from Y_1 to Y_0 and shifts the AD curve from AD_1 to AD_0.

Macroeconomic cycles and aggregate shocks

In Chapter 26 we discussed how fiscal policy could be used to return GDP to its potential level following an inflationary or deflationary shock. Now that we have added a monetary sector to our model, we are able to tell a much more detailed story about how shocks work their way through the economy and about the policy options available to the authorities to respond to those shocks.

Aggregate demand and supply shocks

Let us now return to our complete model, in which we add the long-run and short-run aggregate supply curves developed in Chapters 25 and 26 to the aggregate demand curve. We want, first, to study how the economy responds to shocks to aggregate demand and supply and, second, to discuss what monetary and fiscal policy can do to 'improve' the response.

Aggregate demand shocks

How does the economy respond to an aggregate demand shock? Such shocks could come from a change in world demand for domestic exports, or from an autonomous shift in investment or consumption coming, perhaps, from

a wave of optimism or a wave of pessimism. Some of the detail of the resulting changes will depend upon the precise nature of the shock, but the general principles will be the same. For simplicity, we assume that the shock is an autonomous shift in domestic investment. Box 28.3 discusses why the interaction of the multiplier and accelerator tends to be associated with cumulative responses to specific exogenous shocks.

Positive demand shock Figure 28.6 shows how the economy responds to an autonomous increase in investment. Starting at point A, the AD curve shifts to the right. This rightward shift of AD has two components. First, the rise in investment shifts the AD curve to the right. With a given money supply, that would be the end of the story. However, the increase in GDP brought about by the increase in investment increases the transactions demand for money, and this puts upward pressure on interest rates. If the monetary authorities are to hold the initial level of the interest rate, they must buy bonds and so permit the money stock to rise. This increase in the money stock imparts a further rightward shift to AD (such that the total horizontal shift is equal to the initial shift in investment times the simple multiplier).

Box 28.3 Multiplier–accelerator interaction

The theory linking systematic fluctuations in GDP to systematic fluctuations in investment expenditure combines the accelerator theory discussed in Box 28.2 with the multiplier.

This **multiplier–accelerator theory** of the cycle is divided into three steps. First, a theory of cumulative upswings and downswings explains why, once started, movements tend to carry on in the same direction. Second, a theory of floors and ceilings explains why upward and downward movements are eventually brought to a halt. And third, a theory of instability explains how, once a process of upward or downward movement is brought to a halt, it tends to reverse itself.

Why does a period of expansion or contraction, once begun, tend to develop its own momentum? First, the multiplier process tends to cause cumulative movements. As soon as a revival begins, some unemployed people find work again. These people, with their newly acquired income, can afford to make much-needed consumption expenditures. This new demand causes an increase in production and creates new jobs for others. As incomes rise, demand rises; as demand rises, incomes rise. Just the reverse happens in a downswing. Unemployment in one sector causes a fall in demand for the products of other sectors, which leads to a further fall in employment and a further fall in demand.

A second major factor is the accelerator theory. New investment is needed to expand existing productive capacity and to introduce new methods of production. When consumer demand is low and there is excess capacity, investment is likely to fall to a very low level; once demand and output start to rise and entrepreneurs come to expect further rises, investment expenditure may rise very rapidly. Furthermore, when full employment of existing capacity is reached, new investment becomes one of the few ways available for firms to increase their output.

A third major explanation for cumulative movements is expectations. All production plans take time to fulfil. Current decisions to produce consumer goods and investment goods are very strongly influenced by business expectations. Such expectations can sometimes be volatile, and sometimes self-fulfilling. If enough people think, for example, that equity prices are going to rise, they will all buy equities in anticipation of the price rise, and these purchases will themselves cause prices to rise. If, on the other hand, enough people think that equity prices are going to fall, they will sell quickly at what they regard as a high price, and thereby will actually cause prices to fall. This is the phenomenon of *self-realizing expectations*. It applies to many parts of the economy. If enough managers think the future looks rosy and begin to invest in increasing capacity, this will create new employment and income in the capital goods industries, and the resulting increase in demand will help to create the rosy conditions whose vision started the whole process. There is a bandwagon effect. Once things begin to improve, people expect further improvements, and their actions, based on this expectation, help to cause further improvements. On the other hand, once

things begin to worsen, people often expect further worsening, and then their actions, based on this expectation, help to make things worse.

The multiplier–accelerator process, combined with changes in expectations that cause autonomous shifts of expenditure, can explain the cumulative tendencies of recessions and recoveries.

The next question that arises is why these upward and downward processes ever come to an end.

A very rapid expansion can continue for some time, but it cannot go on for ever because eventually the economy will run into bottlenecks (or ceilings) in terms of some resources. This will happen when firms cannot take on more workers without paying much higher wages to attract them from other firms. Inflation will pick up, and either the monetary authorities will put interest rates up or firms will cut investment in anticipation of a downturn. This expectation itself may become self-fulfilling.

A rapid contraction, too, is eventually brought to an end. Firms can postpone investment and run down stocks, and consumers can put off buying new clothes and new cars. Eventually some kinds of spending can be postponed no longer. Even a modest increase in sales can cause confidence to return. The small upturn in spending then leads to further spending and the start of an upswing of the cycle, through the interaction of the multiplier and accelerator.

Indeed, the accelerator can explain how expansions and contractions reverse direction. We have seen that the accelerator causes the desired level of *new* (not replacement) investment to depend upon the rate of change of GDP. If GDP is rising at a constant rate, then investment will be at a constant *level*; if there is a slackening in the speed at which GDP is rising, the level of investment will decline. This means that a *levelling-off* in GDP at the top of a cycle may lead to a *decline* in the amount of investment. The decline in investment at the upper turning-point will cause a decline in the level of GDP. This will be intensified through the multiplier process.

The accelerator theory explains why a slowdown in the growth of GDP can lead to negative growth in subsequent periods, via a fall in investment spending.

Recessions do not go on for ever. Investment theory predicts that sooner or later an upturn will begin. If nothing else causes an expansion of business activity, eventually there will be a revival of replacement investment. As existing capital wears out, the capital stock will fall below the level required to produce current output. At this stage new machines will have to be bought to replace those that are wearing out. The rise in the level of activity in the capital goods industries will then cause, by way of the multiplier, a further rise in incomes and output. The economy will have turned the corner. An expansion, once started, may trigger the sort of cumulative upward movement already discussed.

With given initial input prices, the economy expands from point *A* to point *B* along the short-run aggregate supply curve $SRAS_0$. The economy is in a boom. In the first phase of this boom prices may be slow to respond, but as GDP moves further above its potential level the price level will start to rise. Real wages fall because money wages are assumed to be fixed, at least initially. However, workers will

not for long be happy to see their real wages fall while the economy is booming. Also, unemployment will be falling and excess demand for certain types of labour will develop. Soon workers will demand, and employers will concede, increases in money wage rates. Once money wages start to rise, the $SRAS$ curve starts to shift upwards to the left, the wage rises are partly passed on in the form of higher prices,

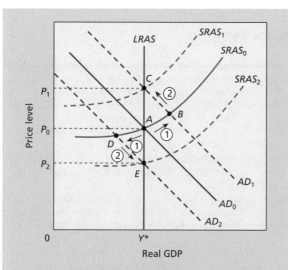

Figure 28.6 Aggregate demand shocks

A positive demand shock leads to a temporary boom in GDP and a permanent rise in the price level, while a negative demand shock leads to a temporary fall in output and (ultimately) lower prices. Consider an initial position at point A with the economy at Y^* with an initial price level P_0. A positive demand shock shifts the AD curve from AD_0 to AD_1. This shift will be greater with a pegged interest rate than with a fixed money stock, as the money supply will increase, reinforcing the rightward shift. The economy will move from point A to a point such as B. The inflationary gap will now lead to upward pressure on money wages. As wages rise, the rise is partly passed on in higher prices, and the $SRAS$ curve shifts leftward from $SRAS_0$ to $SRAS_1$. At the equilibrium, point C, the economy has returned to the initial level of potential GDP, Y^*, but at a higher price level.

A negative demand shock shifts the AD curve from AD_0 to AD_2, and the economy moves from point A to a point such as D. The recessionary gap eventually leads to wage cuts, and, as these are passed on into prices, output recovers and the economy moves to a point such as E with price level P_2.

and output starts to fall. The economy moves from B to C in the figure.

Once the economy has returned to point C it is back in equilibrium, with GDP returned to its potential level but at a higher price level. This price level will be higher in the case where interest rates are pegged than it would be if the money stock were fixed, because the authorities have permitted an increase in the money stock to prevent interest rates from rising.

Negative demand shock Suppose instead there was an autonomous fall in investment, starting from the same initial position as above. This is shown in Figure 28.6 as a leftward shift in the AD curve from AD_0 to AD_2. The economy now moves into recession as GDP falls along the path from A to D. As GDP falls, the transactions demand for money also falls, and with a fixed money stock this leads to a fall in

interest rates. However, if the monetary authorities are pegging interest rates, they will reduce the money supply in order to stop interest rates falling. This imparts two steps to the leftward shift in AD (as above but in reverse).

The major difference in this case (apart from the direction of change) is that, because the $SRAS$ curve is flatter to the left of Y^* than to the right, more of the initial adjustment falls on GDP and less falls on the price level. Indeed, if prices and money wages are slow to adjust downwards (as is often claimed), in the absence of a policy response the economy may get stuck for some time in the neighbourhood of point D. Only as higher unemployment leads to *falling* money wages and these decreases get passed on into lower prices (so that the $SRAS$ curve shifts down to $SRAS_2$ along the path D to E) will the economy return to its potential level of output at a point like E.

The ultimate fall in the price level from point A to point E (assuming the economy returns smoothly to this point) will be greater in the case where interest rates are held constant than in the case where the money stock is fixed. This is because in the former case the money stock has been allowed to fall relative to its initial level. What then could policy makers have done to moderate these responses to demand shocks?

Policy responses In order to understand the problem faced by policy-makers, we have to be clear that the economy is being hit by various shocks of differing strength more or less continuously. Also, the economy is continuing to respond in complex ways to past shocks. However, in order to get some insights into the nature of the policy problem, we study single discrete shocks, even though we know that in reality the authorities have to cope with a continually changing situation.

Let us consider first what could be done to offset the effects of a positive demand shock. Again we refer to Figure 28.6. If the authorities had known that investment was about to rise and had been able to implement a policy change that had immediate effect (a very big IF), they could have acted to shift the AD curve straight back down again so that it never shifted from AD_0 and the economy stayed put at point A. The monetary authorities could do this by raising interest rates, and the fiscal authorities could do this by increasing taxes or cutting government spending.

Even here there would still be a slight difference, depending upon whether it was the monetary or the fiscal authorities that acted. With higher interest rates, the reversal of the AD shift would be achieved by lowering investment (or other interest-sensitive spending) relative to the level it would otherwise have achieved. Higher taxes shift AD down to the left via a fall in personal consumption, while lower government spending obviously leads to a fall in G. Thus, although monetary and fiscal policies have identical effects on the price level and aggregate GDP, they have different effects on the composition of GDP. We will learn in

Box 28.4 **Monetary policy reactions and the Taylor Rule**

Professor John B. Taylor of Stanford University noticed that the interest rates set by the US Federal Reserve could be explained in terms of a fairly simple rule. The authorities raise interest rates when inflation is above target and when actual GDP is above potential, and vice versa. This rule can be expressed in the following equation:

$$i_t = 2 + \pi_t + g_n(\pi_t - \pi^*) + g_x(Y_t - Y^*),$$

where i_t the official interest rate that monetary policy-makers set, π_t is the latest annual inflation rate, π^* is the target inflation rate, Y_t is actual GDP, Y^* is potential GDP, g_n and g_x are weights attached to the inflation target and GDP gap, respectively. Taylor estimated that these weights for the United States during the period 1987–1992 were both 0.5. Some recent UK evidence indicates that the UK authorities' weight on inflation increased between the 1970s and the 1990s as the inflation target came to have an explicit role in policy.* The constant (i.e. 2) in the equation is the long-run average real interest rate.

Policy-makers do not admit to operating any simple policy—as they say, 'we look at everything'. However, it is very plausible that we should find some policy reaction of this sort. The UK Monetary Policy Committee, for example, is charged with targeting a specific inflation rate, so it should be expected that they would raise interest rates if actual inflation were above target. The reaction to the GDP gap can be interpreted in two ways. Either the authorities also care directly about keeping GDP close to potential, or the GDP gap is an important predictor of future inflationary pressure, so by responding to the current GDP gap they are in effect reacting to control future inflation.

The behaviour summarized in the Taylor Rule is consistent with our explanation of monetary policy in the text, but the actual process of making policy decisions is rather more complex than this simple rule suggests.

* Latest evidence on the Taylor Rule and its application to many countries can be found via John Taylor's website: www.stanford.edu/~johntayl/

Chapter 30 that changes in net exports are also part of this story, once exchange rate adjustments are incorporated.

Of course, it is not realistic to think that policy-makers can react at the same time as shocks occur or that they can implement policy changes immediately. We discussed the problems created by information lags and policy lags for fiscal policy in Chapter 26. These problems also apply to monetary policy. Indeed, Milton Friedman said many years ago that the impact of monetary policy was subject to 'long and variable lags'. Box 28.4 explains the **Taylor Rule**, which explains the policy changes made by monetary authorities as a reaction to deviation of inflation from target and of GDP from its potential.

If the monetary authorities respond in a timely way to the positive demand shock, they may be able to improve the outcome. This could be accomplished by helping the economy return from point *B* to point *A*, or at least to some point between *A* and *C*, thereby reducing the inflation that results from the positive demand shock. However, the danger of mistimed policy interventions is a serious one. Suppose, for example, the impact of a monetary tightening only starts to bite just as the economy is arriving at point *C*. This tightening will force the economy to the left of point *C* and will *cause* a recession that would not otherwise have occurred. The same error could obviously arise from badly timed fiscal policy, and this is the main case against attempts to use active monetary or fiscal fine-tuning of the economy.

The case for an active policy response may be much stronger in the event of a negative demand shock than in the above case. This is because there is good reason to believe that the automatic adjustment processes are much slower working in a downward than an upward direction—because of the asymmetry in the aggregate supply curve

and the (possible) fact that money wages are slower to adjust down than up. If this is true, with the economy stuck for some time around point *D* in Figure 28.6, a lowering of interest rates would help shift production back towards point *A*, as would a cut in taxes or an increase in government spending. Again there would be differences in the composition of GDP but not the level (in equilibrium).

Aggregate supply shocks

Let us now consider shocks to aggregate supply instead of shocks to demand. For the purpose of this analysis, we will assume that the supply shock affects only the *SRAS* curve and does not affect Y^*, the level of potential output. In many cases supply shocks will have long-run effects causing Y^* to change—a productivity shock, for example, will increase aggregate supply in both the short and the long run. Where there are long-run effects, there is no potential for monetary and fiscal policies to influence the long-run outcome, as these policy tools only influence aggregate demand. It is for this reason that nothing is lost if we assume that the position of the *LRAS* curve is unchanged. This is equivalent to assuming that the position of *LRAS* is invariant to monetary and fiscal policy; but bear in mind that this assumption will not generally be true.[12]

Positive supply shock Figure 28.7 illustrates the effect of a positive supply shock. Starting at the initial point *A* at Y^* and on $SRAS_0$, the supply shock, such as a fall in world raw material prices, shifts the *SRAS* curve down to the right. The

[12] Indeed, some economists have proposed distinguishing supply shocks from demand shocks by the condition that demand shocks have no long-run effects on output while supply shocks do.

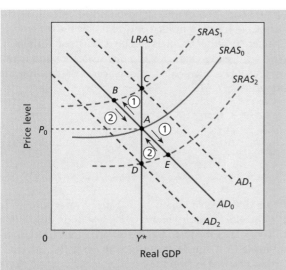

Figure 28.7 Supply shocks

A positive supply shock increases output and lowers prices temporarily, while a negative supply shock lowers output and raises prices temporarily. The economy starts at point A as in Figure 28.6. A positive supply shock shifts the SRAS curve from $SRAS_0$ to $SRAS_2$. This stimulates output and lowers the price level as the economy moves from A to E. However, if the monetary authorities peg the interest rate, they will resist the interest rate fall necessary to increase investment and instead will reduce the money supply, taking the economy from A to D. With a fixed money stock the move from A to E will eventually be reversed as the inflationary gap leads to money wage rises and $SRAS_2$ shifts back to its original position.

A negative supply shock shifts the SRAS curve from $SRAS_0$ to $SRAS_1$. This raises prices and lowers output as the economy moves from A to B. With a fixed money stock, the recessionary gap will eventually lead to lower wages and prices, SRAS will shift back to $SRAS_0$, and the economy will return to point A. However, with pegged interest rates, the money stock will increase (as the authorities accommodate the supply shock) and the economy will move from A to C.

economy will experience a rise in GDP and falling prices as it starts to move from A to E. Both of these would be not unwelcome events, but a move to point E would not be the end of the story.

First, as the price level falls below P_0 the real money supply starts to rise (for a given nominal money stock), and this in turn leads to lower interest rates. It is this fall in interest rates, causing an increase in investment, that tends to increase real GDP. However, if the monetary authorities were pegging interest rates they would tend to reduce the money stock rather than let interest rates fall, and this would make the economy follow a path closer to $A \rightarrow D$ rather than $A \rightarrow E$.

Second, to the extent that the economy did move to the right of Y^*, this would set up inflationary pressure which would tend to make prices rise again until SRAS had shifted back up to its initial position at point A. Thus, with a fixed

money stock, the economy would tend to move from A to E and back again to A, while with a fixed interest rate it would tend to move from A to D and then stop. (Here the assumption of unchanged Y^* is important, as it is quite likely that the ultimate effect of a positive supply shock would be a new level of potential output to the right of Y^*.)

Negative supply shock Suppose we start from the same initial equilibrium at point A and there is now a rise in raw material prices, such as a rise in the price of oil. Here the short-run aggregate supply curve shifts upward to the left from $SRAS_0$ to $SRAS_1$. With the given initial aggregate demand curve AD_0, the economy will tend to move from point A to point B. This situation is characterized by both a rising price level and falling output—known (when it occurred in the 1970s) as *stagflation*. In practice, the move from A to B along a given AD curve will only occur if the money stock is held constant. Then the logic would be that the rising price level reduces the real money supply, forcing up interest rates and thus leading to lower investment, which in turn lowers GDP. However, if the monetary authorities peg the interest rate, they will resist the rise in interest rates by increasing the money supply, and this will shift the AD curve to the right, causing the economy to move along a path more like $A \rightarrow C$ than $A \rightarrow B$.

The contrast between the effects of supply shocks and demand shocks is worth emphasizing. The outcomes also differ depending on whether the monetary authorities are setting interest rates or fixing the money supply.

A monetary policy that sets the interest rate stabilizes the effects of supply shocks on real GDP but amplifies the effects of demand shocks.

Notice that this applies to the automatic effects of the policy and *not* to discretionary policy changes, which could have quite different effects.

Policy responses The optimal policy response to supply shocks is far from clear, especially if mistiming is possible. With a fixed interest rate there will automatically be a stabilizing change in the money supply, although if policy-makers are fixing the money stock there may be a role for temporary countercyclical monetary or fiscal changes to aid the return to equilibrium. However, these will have to be reversed rapidly as the economy returns to equilibrium; otherwise policy action could lead to deviations from Y^* that could have been avoided. That is, policy that is intended to return the economy to equilibrium could end up leading it to overshoot in the opposite direction. Indeed, the possibility that policy-makers might do more harm than good is much debated.

As we have discussed above, getting macro policy right is a difficult task in a complex world. Often, for example, the authorities do not know what shocks are hitting the economy until some time after the event, and even then they are uncertain about the quantitative significance of specific shocks. Stabilization policy is therefore an imperfect art, and the correct role of policy has been (and continues to be) a source of great controversy.

The appendix to this chapter outlines an alternative way of deriving the aggregate demand curve known as the *IS/LM* model. This can be skipped on first reading, as the material in it will be needed only to follow the contents of Chapter 30. Other chapters can be understood without it. We conclude this chapter with a discussion of how monetary policy is implemented in practice in the UK and the euro zone.

Implementation of monetary policy

How is monetary policy implemented by the Bank of England in the United Kingdom, and by the European Central Bank (ECB) for the twelve members of the euro zone? In both cases the main objective of monetary policy is to maintain price stability, that is to control inflation, and in both cases this is done by setting a specific short-term interest rate which then influences other local-currency interest rates. The same is generally true also of other central banks in the major industrial countries. The institutional details vary from place to place. They are also likely to change over time. Indeed, the arrangements we describe were introduced in the UK only in 1997 and by the ECB in January 1999.

The Bank of England

The Bank of England started life as a privately owned joint-stock company, but in 1946 it was nationalized. From 1946 to 1997 the Bank had a key role in implementing monetary policy, but the decisions about policy were all taken by the elected government of the day, in the person of the Chancellor of the Exchequer. However, in May 1997 the incoming Labour government decided to delegate the power to set interest rates to the Bank of England with effect from June 1997, and the new arrangements were embodied in the Bank of England Act of 1998. This formally established the Monetary Policy Committee and the framework within which it operates. First, we outline the make-up and procedures of this committee; then we explain what it tries to achieve; and finally, we describe how its interest rate decisions are transmitted to the financial markets.

The Monetary Policy Committee

The Monetary Policy Committee (MPC) is made up of nine members. Five of these are senior Bank of England officials and four are outsiders appointed by the Chancellor of the Exchequer. The Governor of the Bank of England chairs the committee. The outside members are each appointed for a three-year period, while the term of the Bank insiders depends upon the length of their Bank contract.

The MPC meets formally to set interest rates once every month, with announcements coming at noon on the first Thursday after the first Monday of each month. Decisions are made by a simple majority vote, with the Governor having a casting vote in the event of a tie. Prior to making this decision, MPC members have three days of meetings to evaluate the latest data on the state of the economy and debate among themselves the appropriate course of action. A record of the debate is published two weeks later in the form of the minutes of the meeting.

Four times a year the Bank also publishes its *Inflation Report*, which gives an in-depth assessment of the state of the economy. It contains the Bank's forecast of inflation and GDP growth over the succeeding two-year period. Members of the MPC are also summoned from time to time by the Treasury Select Committee of the House of Commons (the elected parliament) to answer questions about how and why they reached the decisions they did on monetary policy in the past.

Policy goals The government sets the target for inflation that the MPC is meant to achieve. The target set originally in 1997 was to keep inflation at 2.5 per cent using RPIX as the measure of inflation targeted, and this remained the goal until November 2003. RPIX is constructed by removing mortgage interest payments from the standard RPI (see the appendix to Chapter 21). The logic of using this measure was that, if inflation were expected to rise and the MPC tightened monetary policy in order to control it, this rise in interest rates would itself raise RPI, but not RPIX.

Because it is impossible to hit an inflation target exactly, the MPC was given a band of plus or minus 1 per cent. If RPIX inflation turns out at more than 3.5 per cent or less than 1.5 per cent, the MPC had to write an open letter to the Chancellor of the Exchequer explaining why this deviation had happened and setting out what it intended to do about it. In June 2003 the UK Chancellor announced that from November 2003 the target would be specified in terms of the HICP inflation measure. The new target level and bands had not been announced when the book went to press.

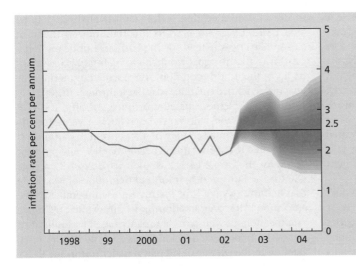

Figure 28.8 Bank of England RPIX inflation forecast
The Bank of England forecasts the probability distribution of inflation up to a two-year horizon. Each level of shading represents 10 per cent of the probability distribution. There are nine bands, so the bank is 90 per cent sure that inflation will lie somewhere in the shaded area. The mean of the forecast is in the dark area at the centre of the distribution. The target inflation rate is 2.5 per cent.

Source: Bank of England, *The Inflation Report*, November 2002.

The MPC has been given *instrument independence*, in that it can set the interest rate at whatever level it thinks appropriate, but it does not have *goal independence*, as the government sets the inflation target.

Choosing an interest rate to achieve an inflation target is not a simple matter. It requires a detailed quantitative understanding of the transmission mechanism in the economy, which we will discuss in the following chapters. (We set out the MPC's own view of the monetary transmission mechanism as an appendix to Chapter 30.) Because of time lags, the full effect of any policy change is spread over many months. This means that policy has to be forward-looking. In effect, policy-makers are targeting an inflation forecast rather than current inflation, because there is nothing they can do about inflation already reported, but they can take actions that will influence inflation in the future.

Figure 28.8 shows a 'fan chart' for inflation as published in the Bank of England *Inflation Report*. This shows a probability distribution of future inflation over a two-year period looking forward. The Bank estimates this on the basis of previous forecasting errors. Each shaded band represents 10 per cent probability, and the shaded area represents 90 per cent of the potential possibilities. Clearly, an important piece of information in the policy process is the mean of this probability distribution, which expresses the most likely outcome for the inflation rate. If the mean forecast inflation rate is well above the target of 2.5 per cent, the MPC will be likely to raise interest rates in order to bring inflation down. If the mean forecast inflation rate is well below 2.5 per cent, it will be likely to bring interest rates down because inflation is well under control. If the mean forecast is very close to target, there is likely to be a fine balance between raising and lowering interest rates, with a strong likelihood of an unchanged policy.

The monetary regime in the United Kingdom is one in which interest rates are adjusted in order to hit an inflation target looking up to about two years forward. A key intermediate target is the inflation forecast, which determines whether monetary policy needs to be tightened or loosened.

Implementation Suppose that the MPC has decided to change interest rates. How does it act in order to make this change stick? In practice, it announces the new rate to the media and this rate appears on Reuters and Bloomberg screens around the City at noon on the announcement day. Banks then change their base rates[13] more or less immediately. Why do money markets have to adjust their interest rates in this way?

The reason is that they know that the Bank of England has raised the interest rate at which it will lend high-powered money (M0) to the banks. And they also know that *the Bank of England can force them to borrow from it on a regular basis*. Thus, the general level of money market rates is set by the rate at which the central bank will provide base money (cash plus bankers' deposits at the Bank of England in the UK case) to participants in the money markets.

The Bank of England can force other banks to borrow from it because it is the monopoly supplier of high-powered money and it can conduct security sales or purchases (open-market operations) to ensure that the banks are short of cash.

The standard instrument through which the Bank of England now lends money to the banks is known as a **repo**. 'Repo' is short for 'sale and repurchase agreement'.

---

[13] The base rate is an interest rate set by each bank as a reference point for the loan rates charged to customers. For example, a large corporate client may be charged interest at the base rate plus 1 per cent, while a (more risky) smaller business may be charged base rate plus 4 per cent.

It sounds complicated, but it is actually very simple. The basic problem is that the Bank of England needs to be able to lend high-powered money to private banks, but it does not want to take on any credit risk—it does not want the risk that some counter-party (some institution to which it has lent money) may go bust and not be able to repay. Accordingly, it makes only secured loans. 'Secured' means that the borrower gives up the claim to some asset as security for the loan. (A mortgage on a house is a secured loan—if you do not repay the loan, the lender can take your house.) A repo is a loan secured upon a government security.

A repo has two parts. Suppose the Bank of England does a repo transaction with NatWest for £100 million. NatWest needs cash but it starts with some government securities (gilts) on its balance sheet. It is going to borrow money from the Bank using the gilts as security. Step one: it sells £100 million of gilts to the Bank of England in exchange for a credit in NatWest's account at the Bank. Step two: it agrees to buy back the gilts on some future date. But it will not pay back £100 million: rather, it will pay back a bit more—the extra representing the interest rate for the loan over that period. This interest rate is known as the repo rate, *and this is the interest rate that the Bank of England sets*. The two steps in the repo deal are both agreed at the outset, so the sale and repurchase are structured as part of a single contract. A *reverse repo* would involve a bank lending, rather than borrowing, in the same way. In practice, it is the two-week repo rate that is set by the Bank of England.

Interest rate decisions of the MPC are implemented by the Bank of England fixing the interest rate at which it will do two-week repos. In effect, this is just the rate at which the Bank will lend high-powered money to private banks.

The European Central Bank

The ECB runs monetary policy for the twelve EU countries that adopted the euro in place of their former currencies.[14] The ECB is at the centre of the European System of Central Banks (ESCB), which includes also the central banks of other EU member countries. For monetary policy purposes, only central banks of euro zone members have a say in ECB monetary policy. The ECB has an Executive Board of six members responsible for implementation of monetary policy decisions. The Governing Council of the ECB is responsible for taking monetary policy decisions, and it is made up of the Executive Board plus the governors of the member central banks (of the euro zone).

The Maastricht Treaty defined as the primary objective of the ESCB 'to maintain price stability'. But 'without prejudice to the primary objective of price stability', the ESCB has to support the general economic policies of the European Union. In October 1998 the Governing Council of the ECB decided that 'price stability shall be defined as a year-on-year increase in the Harmonized Index of Consumer Prices (HICP) for the euro area of below 2 per cent', and that the goal would be to maintain price stability according to this criterion over the medium term. This goal has remained unchanged at least through to 2002.

In order to achieve its goal of price stability, the ECB in December 1998 announced a reference value for the growth rate of broad money of 4.5 per cent per annum. It also defined the monetary aggregate that it would monitor as M3 for the euro area as a whole. (See Box 27.2 on page 486 for the European harmonized definition of M3. Note that definitions may vary slightly for each member of the euro zone.) However, in addition to this explicit reference rate for monetary growth, 'a broadly based assessment of the outlook for price developments and the risks to price stability in the euro area will play a major role in the ECB's strategy'.

The ECB has both target and instrument independence, but with a general objective to maintain price stability.

Implementation

The general principles of how the ECB operates are very similar to those for the Bank of England, though the ECB currently operates through its member central banks (just as the US Federal Reserve Board operates mainly through the Federal Reserve Bank of New York). There are three main elements to the operating procedures.

Open-market operations This involves repo-style secured lending and borrowing operations *vis-à-vis* the money markets. This is the main day-to-day operating procedure; and it is the rate at which the ECB lends to the money markets (on secured terms) that determines the general level of short-term interest rates within the euro area. As with the Bank of England, repo operations are the key activity, and this is similar to the way that many other central banks already operate.

Standing facilities The ECB also offers a standing facility for participating banks to make deposits with and take loans from the ECB for overnight duration. The deposit and loan rates so specified in effect put upper and lower bands around the short-term interest rate that can rule in the market for overnight money, and are in themselves an adequate instrument for setting very-short-term market rates even without participation in the repo market. The lending facility must be secured on eligible assets (such as government securities). These facilities are open on a daily

---

[14] The twelve countries are France, Germany, Italy, Spain, Portugal, Belgium, the Netherlands, Luxembourg, Austria, Finland, Greece and the Republic of Ireland.

basis and provide and absorb overnight liquidity as well as providing a tool for signalling monetary policy stance.

Minimum reserves The ECB has the power to set minimum reserves required from private banks within the system. In October 1998 the ECB announced that the required reserve would initially be 2 per cent of bank deposits. This is much larger than the scale of the cash-ratio deposits required in the United Kingdom. However, the ECB pays interest on these reserves at a level determined by its repo rate. A change in reserve requirements may be used from time to time to influence the money supply, as we explained in our discussion of the money multiplier earlier in this chapter, but this has not been used up to spring 2003.

But the target of maintaining euro zone inflation at less than 2 per cent over the medium term is likely to endure for the foreseeable future. The reference rate for monetary

growth will no doubt be adjusted from time to time, and the ECB will use other information about the state of the economy, including economic forecasts, in order to inform its decisions.[15]

The success of the new monetary arrangements in the United Kingdom and the euro zone will be judged by how well the respective monetary authorities do in controlling inflation, as well as by the price that has to be paid, if any, in terms of lost output and employment. Up to 2002 the verdict was very positive. UK inflation from 1997 to 2002 was consistently within the target range. Euro zone inflation had exceeded its target for a while but was very close to the 2 per cent ceiling in late 2002.

[15] The latest information about policy statements from the Bank of England can be found via the internet at www.bankofengland.co.uk, and at www.ecb.int for the ECB.

SUMMARY

- For simplicity, we group all forms in which wealth is held into money, which is a medium of exchange, and bonds, which earn a higher interest return than money and can be turned into money by being sold at a price that is determined on the open market.

- The price of existing bonds varies negatively with the rate of interest. A rise in the interest rate lowers the prices of all outstanding bonds. The longer a bond's term to maturity, the greater the change in its price will be for a given change in interest rate.

The supply of money and the demand for money

- The value of money balances that the public wishes to hold is called the *demand for money*. It is a stock (not a flow), measured in the United Kingdom as so many billions of pounds.

- Money balances are held, despite the opportunity cost of bond interest forgone, for transactions, precautionary, and speculative motives. They have the effect of making the demand for money vary positively with real GDP, the price level, and wealth, and negatively with the nominal rate of interest. The nominal demand for money varies proportionally with the price level.

- When there is an excess demand for money balances, people try to sell bonds. This pushes the price of bonds down and the interest rate up. When there is an excess supply of money balances, people try to buy bonds. This pushes the price of bonds up and the rate of interest down. Monetary equilibrium

is established when people are willing to hold the existing stocks of money and bonds at the current rate of interest.

Monetary forces and aggregate demand

- With given inflationary expectations, changes in the nominal interest rate translate into changes in the real interest rate. A change in the real interest rate causes desired investment to change along the investment demand function. This shifts the aggregate desired spending function and causes equilibrium GDP to change.

- A rise in interest rates (or a decrease in the supply of money) reduces aggregate demand; that is, it shifts *AD* to the left. A cut in interest rates (or an increase in the money supply) increases aggregate demand; that is, it shifts *AD* to the right.

- The negatively sloped aggregate demand curve indicates that the higher the price level, the lower the equilibrium GDP. The explanation lies in part with the effect of money on the adjustment mechanism: other things being equal (for a given money stock), the higher the price level, the higher the demand for money and the rate of interest, the lower the level of investment, and therefore the lower the aggregate spending function, and thus the lower the level of GDP (for which injections equal leakages).

Macroeconomic cycles and aggregate shocks

- A positive demand shock (starting at potential GDP) will trigger a temporary boom in output and lead to a permanent increase in the price level. The latter will be greater if interest rates are pegged than if the money stock is fixed.

■ A negative demand shock will cause a recession, and the automatic adjustment mechanisms may be slow to return the economy to equilibrium.

■ A positive supply shock will increase output and reduce the price level temporarily, but inflationary pressure will eventually return the economy close to its initial position (where there is no permanent impact on potential GDP).

■ A negative supply shock is associated with rising prices and falling output—a situation known as stagflation.

■ Monetary and fiscal policies can assist the return of the economy to equilibrium, but inappropriate policies can also make things worse.

■ Monetary authorities' reactions are well described by the Taylor Rule: interest rates are raised when inflation exceeds target and when GDP exceeds potential, and *vice versa*.

Implementation of monetary policy

■ Central banks are the ultimate suppliers of cash to the monetary system, and they have the power to set short-term interest rates in the money markets.

■ The Bank of England uses the two-week repo rate as its policy instrument.

■ The UK inflation target is set by the government, and the Monetary Policy Committee has been delegated the responsibility to keep inflation close to target.

TOPICS FOR REVIEW

■ Interest rates and bond prices

■ Transactions, precautionary, and speculative motives for holding money

■ Negative relationship between the quantity of money demanded and the interest rate

■ Monetary equilibrium

■ Transmission mechanism

■ Investment demand function

■ Demand and supply shocks

■ Monetary and fiscal policy reactions

■ The Taylor Rule

DISCUSSION QUESTIONS

1 Suppose a bond is issued that is a perpetuity; it pays £5 per year and is issued for £100. What will this bond be worth if the current interest rate is (a) 2 per cent, (b) 10 per cent and (c) 20 per cent.

2 At an interest rate of 5 per cent, what is the present value of £1,000 in (a) one year's time, (b) 5 years' time, and (c) 10 years' time?

3 Starting from a given price level and with GDP at its potential, explain what happens to real GDP and the price level in the short term and long term in response to (a) a rise in the interest rate, (b) an increase in export demand, (c) a fall in government spending, and (d) a fall in income tax rates.

4 Explain how a change in monetary policy works its way through the economy to influence GDP and the price level in both the short and long term.

5 Compare and contrast monetary and fiscal policies as tools for controlling output and inflation.

6 When the monetary authorities set interest rates, what role does the money stock play in monetary policy?

7 Why does the *AD* curve have a negative slope, and what factors determine this slope?

8 What factors cause the *AD* curve to shift?

Appendix An alternative derivation of the *AD* curve: *IS/LM*

We show here a slightly more detailed exposition of the monetary sector and its links with aggregate spending. This helps us derive the aggregate demand curve explicitly. There are no new economic relationships or even different assumptions involved here.

This particular diagrammatic exposition was devised by the English Nobel Laureate Sir John Hicks (1904–89). It is so familiar to economists who have trained over the last half century that it is frequently quoted. If you have followed the macroeconomics chapters this far, you already know the economics behind the *IS/LM* model, but it is also helpful to know what specific bit of analysis '*IS/LM*' refers to. The diagrammatic apparatus has one important additional payoff. It shows the differences between the transmission mechanisms of monetary and fiscal policy. The only place where we use this apparatus again in this book is in Chapter 30.

For purposes of the present analysis, we assume that real wealth is constant and that there are no relative price changes between domestic and foreign goods—these were the factors that gave us a negatively sloped aggregate demand curve in Chapters 25 and 26. By eliminating them, we focus on the way in which money markets, acting through interest rates on spending, contribute to the negative slope of the *AD* curve.

The *IS* curve

Figure 28.4(ii) on page 503 plots the negative relationship between interest rates and investment, called the investment demand function. We have also seen (in Figure 28.5 on page 505) that an increase in investment shifts the *AE* curve upwards and that this is associated with an increase in equilibrium GDP (a rightward shift of *AD*).

The *IS* curve shows the equilibrium[16] level of GDP that is associated with each possible interest rate. Recall that GDP is in equilibrium when desired expenditure equals actual output, or—what is the same thing—when injections equal withdrawals (and, in the simplest possible closed economy model, investment equals saving).

An *IS* curve is plotted in Figure 28A.1. It is negatively sloped because higher interest rates cause investment to fall, which shifts *AE* down and lowers equilibrium GDP. In contrast, lower interest rates cause investment to rise, which shifts *AE* up and raises equilibrium GDP.

In all cases, the *IS* curve shows the relationship between interest rates and the level of income at which desired expenditure flows are equal to actual output, or—what is the same thing—desired withdrawals are equal to desired injections. But, because, the flows of withdrawals and injections are different in a closed and in an open economy, the relationship given by the *IS* curve can be stated somewhat differently for each. In a closed economy with no government, the *IS* curve shows the combinations of the interest rate and GDP for which saving and investment are equal. In an open economy with a government, the *IS* curve shows the combinations of the interest rate and GDP for which withdrawals in the form of saving, taxes, and imports ($S + T + IM$) are equal to injections in the form of investment, government purchases, and exports ($I + G + X$). In this case the *IS* curve is

drawn for given values of government spending, exports, and autonomous consumption as well as the tax rate.

The *IS* curve is the locus of interest rates and levels of GDP that are consistent with equality between desired spending and output; or, what is the same thing, injections and leakages. It is drawn for given values of government spending, exports, and autonomous consumption as well as for given tax rates and a given price level.

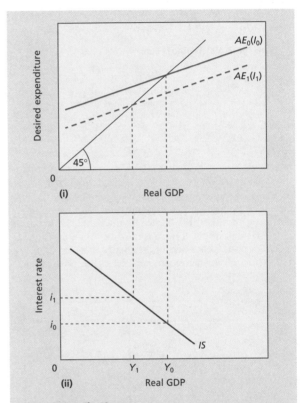

Figure 28A.1 The *IS* curve

The *IS* curve shows the equilibrium level of GDP associated with each given rate of interest. It shows combinations of the interest rate and GDP for which desired spendings equal actual national output, and for which injections equal withdrawals. Part (i) shows a fall in *AE* resulting from a fall in investment from I_0 to I_1. This fall in *I* is caused by a rise in the interest rate from i_0 to i_1. The fall in investment produces a fall in GDP from Y_0 to Y_1.

Part (ii) shows the resulting combinations of the interest rate and real GDP. For given values of exogenous spendings, i_0 leads to a level of GDP Y_0, and i_1 leads to level of GDP Y_1. Choosing any other level of the interest rate and following through its effect on GDP via investment produces another point on the *IS* curve.

---

[16] 'Equilibrium' in this section should be taken to mean the level of GDP that would be determined by aggregate spending if there were no supply constraints, that is, if there were no aggregate supply curve and GDP were entirely demand-determined at an exogenously given price level. This is the level of GDP where injections and leakages are equal.

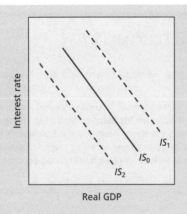

Figure 28A.2 Shifts in the *IS* curve

An increase in exogenous spendings shifts the *IS* curve to the right, while a decrease shifts it to the left. The initial *IS* curve is IS_0. Suppose there is an autonomous increase in government consumption. The *IS* curve shifts right to IS_1. This means that for each level of the interest rate there is a higher level of GDP consistent with injections being equal to withdrawals. Increases in any other autonomous spendings give the same shift. In contrast, if the change is a fall in autonomous spendings, the *IS* curve shifts left to IS_2.

Now let us see what shifts the *IS* curve. In particular, we are interested in the effects of shifts in exogenous spending. An increase in exogenous spending shifts the *AE* curve up in Figure 28.6(i), so it shifts the *IS* curve to the right. The size of the horizontal shift in the *IS* curve is the same when measured on the GDP axis as is the effect of the change in *AE* on GDP. This change (for a given interest rate, and holding the price level con-

stant) is simply equal to the increase in exogenous spending times the multiplier. This means that there is nothing new here, just a new way of representing what we knew already. A fall in exogenous spending shifts the *AE* curve down, so it shifts the *IS* curve to the left. These shifts in the *IS* curve are illustrated in Figure 28.7.

The *LM* curve

The *LM* curve shows the combination of GDP and interest rates that will produce equilibrium in the money market so that people are just willing to hold the stocks of money and bonds that are in existence. Initially we assume that there is a given money supply and that interest rates are free to vary. Later we show how this can be used to handle an interest rate that is set by the monetary authorities.

Figure 28.2 on page 501 illustrates equilibrium in the money market at the point where the money demand curve intersects the money supply curve. The money demand curve is plotted for given levels of real GDP, the price level, and wealth. We continue to assume that wealth and the price level are constant, but what happens in that figure when real GDP increases? The answer is shown in Figure 28A.3(i). As GDP increases, the transactions and precautionary demands for money both increase, and so the money demand curve shifts to the right. People will now try to sell bonds to get more money. But the stock of money is fixed so that the price of bonds must fall, which means that the interest rate rises, until the quantity of money demanded returns to its original level. This requires that the quantity of money demanded for speculative purposes falls by just enough to offset the increase in the amount of money demanded for transactions purposes.

The *LM* curve is shown in Figure 28A.3(ii). This curve is drawn for given values of the price level, wealth, and the money supply.

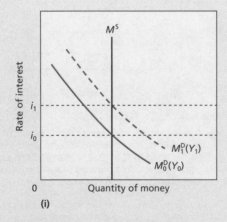

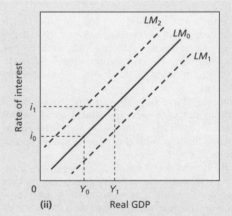

Figure 28A.3 The *LM* curve

The *LM* curve shows the combinations of real GDP and interest rates that are consistent with the equality of money demand and supply for a given nominal money supply and given price level. Part (i) shows equilibrium in the money market with a given money supply and an M^D function that is negatively sloped. At an initial level of GDP Y_0, the demand curve for money is given by M_0^D and the equilibrium interest rate is i_0. At higher levels of GDP the M^D curve shifts to the right. (Higher levels of GDP cause higher transactions demand for money.) When GDP increases to Y_1, the money demand curve shifts to M_1^D and the associated equilibrium interest rate rises to i_1.

In part (ii) the *LM* curve LM_0 plots out the equilibrium interest rate associated with each possible Y and the given money stock M^S. This is a positively sloped curve. An increase in the nominal money supply shifts the *LM* curve parallel to the right, such as to LM_1, and a decrease in the nominal money supply shifts the *LM* curve to the left, such as to LM_2.

The curve is positively sloped because, for reasons outlined in the previous paragraph, a rise in income must lead to a rise in the interest rate if people are to be made willing to hold only the same amount of money in spite of needing more for transactions purposes.

The *LM* curve plots combinations of GDP and the interest rate, for a given money supply and given price level, that are consistent with the equality of money demand and money supply.

Now let us see how the curve shifts. As with any other curve, a change in any of the variables held constant along the curve causes the curve to shift. We focus here on the effect of a change in the money supply. An increase in the money supply shifts the *LM* curve to the right, while a decrease in the money supply shifts the *LM* curve to the left. To see this, shift the vertical money supply curve in part (i) of Figure 28A.3.

An increase in the money supply produces a lower equilibrium interest rate for each level of Y (and therefore for each M^D curve). This is shown as a shift of the *LM* curve from LM_0 to LM_1 in Figure 28A.3(ii). People try to buy bonds with their newly acquired money, but the stock is fixed so their price must rise, which means that the interest rate must fall until they are willing to hold the larger stock of money and the unchanged stock of bonds. A decrease in the money supply produces a higher equilibrium interest rate for each level of real GDP, as shown by a shift of the *LM* curve from LM_0 to LM_2.

IS/LM and aggregate demand

The *IS* and *LM* curves each tell part of the story of the determination of aggregate demand. The *IS* curve determines GDP for given interest rates, while the *LM* curve determines the interest rate for given levels of GDP. In effect, they are two simultaneous equations in GDP and the interest rate. One (*IS*) represents the set of points for which desired spending equals national output (and injections equal leakages). The other (*LM*) represents the set of equilibrium points for which money demand equals money supply. Equilibrium for the whole economy (but still excluding the aggregate supply side) must be on both the *IS* and *LM* curves. This will be where they intersect. This is shown in Figure 28A.4.

In the past the *IS/LM* model was widely used to analyse the effects on GDP of either changes in monetary policy that altered the quantity of money (shifts in *LM*) or changes in fiscal policy (shifts in *IS*). However, this framework has the limitation that it can be used (on its own) only for the case where the price level is fixed and real GDP is variable. We could equivalently analyse the case where real GDP is fixed and the price level is variable, but we do not do this here. When output and prices are simultaneously variable, we need to use the *AS/AD* model.

There is nothing wrong with the *IS/LM* model. It is just incomplete. Indeed, it can be used to derive the *AD* curve (thereby illustrating that the *IS/LM* model is consistent with our approach to *AD*). The *AD* curve implied by our *IS/LM* model is derived in Figure 28A.4(ii).

To derive *AD*, we take a given *IS* and *LM* curve and ask what happens to the level of GDP (determined by their intersection) as the price level rises. The answer is that a higher price level shifts the *LM* curve to the left (as it reduces the real money supply for a given nominal money supply, and given all exogenous spending) and leads to a lower level of equilibrium GDP.

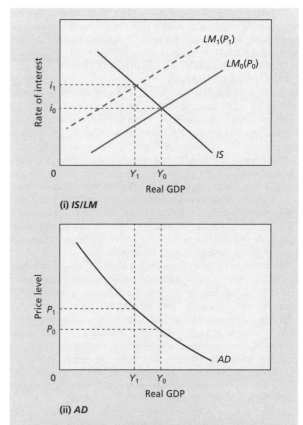

(i) *IS/LM*

(ii) *AD*

Figure 28A.4 *IS/LM* and aggregate demand

The *AD* curve plots the *IS/LM* equilibrium level of GDP for each given price level (holding all exogenous spendings and the nominal money supply constant). Part (i) has the initial position at the intersection of LM_0 (which is drawn with price level P_0) with the *IS* curve. This gives the overall equilibrium levels of real GDP and the interest rate as Y_0 and i_0. At higher price levels the *LM* curve shifts to the left (because the real money supply falls). At price level P_1 the *LM* curve is given by LM_1, and this leads to equilibrium GDP and interest rate of Y_1 and i_1. Part (ii) plots out the resulting combinations of the price level and GDP. This is the aggregate demand curve, *AD*.

The reason why an increase in the price level shifts the *LM* curve to the left is that the given money supply is *nominal* but money is demanded in relation to its *real* purchasing power. This means that, as the price level rises, there is an increase in the nominal quantity of money demanded to finance a given volume of real transactions. This leads to an upward shift in the M^D curves in Figure 28A.3(i) and so leads to a higher equilibrium interest rate for each level of real GDP. This shifts the *LM* curve (upwards) to the left. An alternative way of making the same point (that a higher price level shifts the *LM* curve to the left) is to draw Figure 28A.3(i) with the *real* money stock on the horizontal axis. Then, an increase in the price level simply reduces the real money supply and shifts the money supply curve to the left. These two different ways of expressing the point are equivalent and lead to the same impact of price level changes on the *LM* curve.

By taking different values of the price level, we plot out the aggregate demand curve. Notice that the *AD* curve is drawn for given levels of the money supply and exogenous spending, but *not* for given levels of endogenous variables like the interest rate, consumption, investment, net exports, and GDP.

This derivation also helps us to understand the determinants of the slope of the *AD* curve. Since it is determined by the intersection of the *IS* and *LM* curves, its slope depends upon the slopes of both *IS* and *LM*. These in turn depend on four factors: the interest and income elasticities of demand for money, the interest elasticity of investment, and the size of the multiplier.

This reinforces our earlier argument that the reason for the slope of the *AD* curve is not logically the same as that for the slope of any micro demand curve. The logic here is more tortuous: a higher price level lowers real money supply; this raises equilibrium interest rates; this lowers investment; this lowers GDP via the multiplier. In addition, there is the wealth effect and the effect of relative prices (domestic and foreign) on net exports, which we explained in Chapter 24.

We now show that an increase in the money supply will shift the *AD* curve to the right while a decrease in the money supply will shift the *AD* curve to the left. This is done in Figure 28A.5 simply by shifting the *LM* curve. With a given *IS* curve, each level of the money supply will be associated with a different equilibrium level of GDP for any given price level. A reduction in the money supply is represented by a leftward shift of the *LM* curve, and this leads to a leftward shift of the *AD* curve. Hence an exogenous fall in the nominal money supply shifts the *AD* curve to the left. An exogenous increase in the nominal money supply shifts the *AD* curve to the right.

So far we have assumed when using the *LM* curve that the monetary authorities controlled the amount of money, leaving interest rate to be determined in the market. Now let us allow for the fact that they usually fix the interest rate and let the amount of money be determined by the demand for it. When the central bank lowers interest rates it needs to permit the money stock to increase, since more money will be demanded the lower is the interest rate. When it raises interest rates it needs to lower the money stock, which it does by selling bonds and accepting high-powered money in return. Thus, changes of monetary policy can be interpreted as shifts of the *LM* curve irrespective of whether the authorities are fixing the interest rate or the money supply. Hence once we are in the *IS/LM* framework, we have an analytical tool that is just as suitable for either policy environment. The reason this is true is that the *LM* curve represents equilibrium states in the money market. It does not matter whether that equilibrium is achieved by the interest rate adjusting to the money stock or by the money stock adjusting to the interest rate—the outcome is the same either way. A relaxation of monetary policy involves the *LM* curve shifting to the right, while a tightening of monetary policy involves the *LM* curve shifting to the left.

We now look more closely at how we can use our macro model to understand the role of monetary and fiscal policies in stabilizing activity.

Monetary policy and aggregate demand

We have already explained in this chapter that the aggregate demand curve is drawn for a given money stock. However, since most monetary authorities set the interest rate and not the

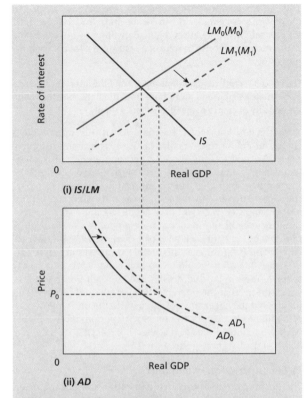

(i) *IS/LM*

(ii) *AD*

Figure 28A.5 Shifts in the *AD* curve

A change in the money supply leads to a shift in the *AD* curve. The curves are drawn with an initial money stock M_0 leading to *LM* curve LM_0 and *AD* curve AD_0. An increase in the money stock to M_1 shifts the *LM* curve right to LM_1 and with a given *IS* curve produces *AD* curve AD_1. Thus, a higher GDP is associated with each level of *P*. The reverse happens for a fall in the money stock—*LM* and *AD* shift left.

money supply, we need to understand how monetary policy changes work in our model.

We saw in Figure 28A.4 on page 517 how the *AD* curve can be derived from the intersection of the *IS* and *LM* curves as we vary the price level. And we also saw in Figure 28A.5 that a change in the money stock shifts the *AD* curve. We now want to make the connection between shifts of the *AD* curve and changes in monetary policy, that is, changes in the interest rate. This is shown in Figure 28A.6.

The initial position is shown in part (i) by the intersection of *IS* and LM_0 and in part (ii) by the aggregate demand curve AD_0. Suppose now the monetary authorities decide to relax monetary policy by lowering interest rates. To do this they buy bonds. This raises the price of bonds and, what is the same thing, lowers the rate of interest. Their purchases provide the extra money supply that will be demanded at the lower interest rate. In providing this money, they shift the *LM* curve to the right. At each price level this gives us a point on the new *AD* curve, which has shifted to the right. Notice that the size of the horizontal shift in *AD* depends not only on the size of the shift in *LM* (necessary to equate demand and supply of money at the new lower interest

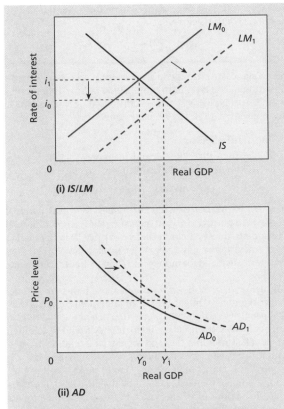

Figure 28A.6 Interest rate changes and aggregate demand

A policy-induced fall in the interest rate shifts the AD curve to the right. In part (i), from an initial position with interest rate i_0 at the intersection of IS and LM_0, which is associated with aggregate demand curve AD_0 in part (ii), a fall in the interest rate to i_1 requires an increase in the money stock, which shifts the LM curve rightward to LM_1. In part (ii) this implies that the AD curve has shifted from AD_0 to AD_1, and at a price level such as P_0 there has been an increase in GDP from Y_0 to Y_1. A rise in interest rates would have the reverse effect, requiring a lowering of the money stock and a leftward shift of AD.

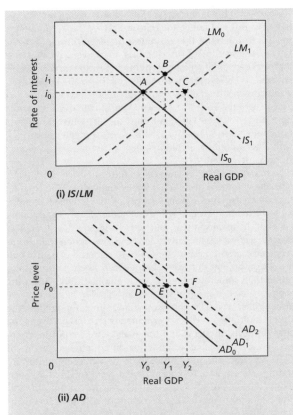

Figure 28A.7 Fiscal policy changes and aggregate demand

An expansionary fiscal policy shifts the AD curve to the right, but the shift is greater if the monetary authorities peg interest rates than if they fix the money stock. The initial position is shown in part (i) by point A and in part (ii) by point D, with a given price level of P_0 and initial values of the interest rate of i_0 and of GDP of Y_0. The introduction of an expansionary fiscal policy shifts the IS curve to the right from IS_0 to IS_1. With a given money stock the LM curve would stay put at LM_0 and the interest rate would rise to i_1, illustrated by point B. Accordingly, the new AD curve would now pass through point E, reflecting an increase in GDP from Y_0 to Y_1.

However, if the monetary authorities act to prevent interest rates rising, they will permit an increase in the money supply, represented by a shift of the LM curve to LM_1 where it intersects IS_1 at point C. The associated AD curve passes through point F, so the new AD curve is AD_2. At the given price level P_0 GDP has increased to Y_2. This shift in AD is equal to the change in government spending that triggered it, times the simple multiplier. A contractionary fiscal policy change would lead to a symmetrical leftward shift in AD.

rate) but also on the slope of the IS curve. The slope of the IS curve is important, because it is determined by the amount of the increase in investment in response to a fall in the interest rate and by the multiplier. And it is the change in investment times the multiplier that determines how much real GDP increases. (This will not be the actual increase in GDP, as we do not have the aggregate supply curves in this figure.)

A monetary policy-loosening that involves a policy-induced lowering of interest rates shifts the AD curve to the right. A monetary policy-tightening involves raising interest rates and shifts the AD curve to the left.

Fiscal policy and aggregate demand

We have seen in Chapter 26 how fiscal policy can be used to shift the aggregate demand curve. However, now that we have added a monetary sector to our model, we can see more clearly how the size of that shift is determined. In particular, it turns out that the

effects of a fiscal policy change depend in part on what the monetary authorities are doing.

The initial position is shown in Figure 28A.7(i) by the intersection of IS_0 and LM_0, and in part (ii) of the figure by the aggregate demand curve AD_0. An expansionary fiscal policy, for example an increase in government spending, shifts the IS curve to the right in part (i). With a given LM curve associated with a fixed money supply, interest rates will rise, and this rise in interest rates will *crowd out* some investment expenditure. The AD curve will shift from AD_0 to AD_1 and GDP will increase from Y_0 to Y_1 for a price level such as P_0.

However, if the monetary authorities are pegging the interest rate at i_0, this will not be the outcome. Once the IS curve starts to shift to the right, this will put upward pressure on interest rates (because the rise in spending increases GDP and this increases demand for money). To obtain the extra money, people sell bonds. The monetary authority purchases the bonds, thus stabilizing the interest rate and supplying the extra money that people require. Accordingly, the LM curve will also shift to the right and so the AD curve will shift to AD_2, which involves a horizontal shift of $Y_0 - Y_2$. This is clearly a greater horizontal shift than would have obtained in the case where the money stock is unchanged.

Notice that when the monetary authorities peg the interest rate, the effect of a given fiscal policy change on GDP is larger than when they fix the money supply. With a fixed money stock a rise in the interest rate will offset some of the expansionary effect of the fiscal stimulus. But with a pegged interest rate this offsetting effect is eliminated. Of course, the monetary authorities could *choose* to raise interest rates in response to a fiscal policy relaxation, but this would be an independent policy choice rather than something that happens automatically within the economy. Notice also that the shift in *AD when interest rates are held constant* is equal to the direct change in spending times the simple multiplier. In effect, the monetary sector is passive to the changes in fiscal policy, and the analysis we set out in Chapters 23–26 is adequate for understanding the determinants of GDP. In reality, of course, although the monetary authorities are setting interest rates, they do not hold them constant for ever. Rather, they change them in an attempt to control inflation and (perhaps) to avoid large deviations of GDP from its potential level.

The Algebraic Derivation of *IS-LM* and *AD*

In this section we linearize all the behavioural equations and use them to show the explicit derivation of the AD curve from the IS and LM curves.

The production sector

We first look at the income/spending part of the model and use it in the form in which aggregate spending, E, is divided into only two parts: consumption, C, and investment, I.

$$E = C + I \tag{A1}$$

$$C = a_0 + cY \qquad 0 < c < 1, 0 < a_0 \tag{A2}$$

$$I = a_1 + bR \qquad b < 0 < a_1 \tag{A3}$$

$$E = Y \tag{A4}$$

The first equation is a definition that divides total spending, E, between consumption, C, and investment, I. The second is a behavioural equation that divides consumption spending between an autonomous component, a_0, and an induced component that depends on income, cY. The third is a behavioural equation that divides investment spending between an autonomous component, a_1, and an induced component that depends on the interest rate, bR. The fourth equation is the equilibrium condition that desired spending equals actual output.

Substituting for C and I in (A1), and then for E in the equilibrium condition of (A4), yields

$$Y = a_0 + cY + a_1 + bR. \tag{A5}$$

These terms can then be rearranged to produce the equation (in linear form) of the IS curve:[17]

$$[IS] \quad R = \frac{1-c}{b}Y - \frac{A}{b}, \tag{A6}$$

where A stands for all exogenous expenditure and is equal in this case to $a_0 + a_1$. It is clear from (A6) that the IS curve is negatively sloped. Since c is positive but less than unity, $1 - c$ is also positive. But b is negative, so $(1 - c)/b$ is also negative.

The Monetary Sector

First, we assume that the demand for money balances varies positively with income and negatively with the interest rate:

$$M_D = dY + eR, \qquad e < 0 < d, \tag{A7}$$

where M_D is the real demand for money, Y is real national income, d is a positive constant indicating the fraction of annual income desired to be held in money balance, R is the market rate of interest, and e is a negative constant showing how responsive the demand for money is to changes in the market rate of interest.

The demand for money is measured in real terms. In our one-product economy Y might be, say 20 million bushels of wheat, and if people wished to hold transaction balances equal to 1/10 of other incomes, the real demand for money would be 2 million bushels. (The nominal demand would be 2 million bushels multiplied by the price of a bushel.) The supply of money is measured in nominal money units, and to make it comparable with the demand we need to divide by the price level, P. For example, if the price of wheat is £5 a bushel in our one-product economy and the nominal supply of money is £10 million, the real supply, measured in units of wheat, will be $10/5 = 2$ million bushels. So we write

$$M_S = \frac{\bar{M}}{p}, \tag{A8}$$

where M_S stands for the money supply, $\bar{M}$ is the fixed quantity of money as determined by the central bank, and P is the price level.

The equilibrium conditions is

$$M_S = M_D, \tag{A9}$$

which merely says that people are willing to hold the supply of money that is available to be held .

Substituting (A7) and (A8) into (A9) gives

$$dY + eR = \frac{\bar{M}}{P}. \tag{A10}$$

To derive the LM curve, we manipulate (A10) to obtain[18]

$$[LM] \quad R = \frac{\bar{M}}{P} \cdot \frac{1}{e} - \frac{d}{e}Y. \tag{A11}$$

---

[17] The steps are: (i) subtract cY, a_0 and a_1 from both sides; (ii) factor out the Y to obtain $Y(1 - c)$; (iii) divide through by b; and (iv) write A for $a_0 + a_1$.

[18] This is done by subtracting dY from both sides and dividing through by e.

As e is negative and d is positive, d/e is negative so $-(d/e)$ is positive and the LM curve has a positive slope.

Equation (A6) and (A11) constitute the equations of the IS/LM model. By substituting one into the other, we can solve for Y. The solution for Y is[19]

$$Y = \frac{1}{(1-c)+bd/e}A + \frac{1}{d+e(1-c)/b}\frac{\bar{M}}{P}. \qquad \text{(A12)}$$

The IS/LM multiplier

In Chapter 23 we developed a simple multiplier that took the form

$$\frac{\Delta Y}{\Delta A} = \frac{1}{1-c}, \qquad \text{(A13)}$$

where c is the marginal propensity to spend out of GDP. This number is often called the *simple multiplier*. But if the money supply is constant, a rise in GDP will raise the demand for money, which will bid up interest rates, which will reduce or 'crowd out' interest-sensitive expenditure. Thus, the multiplier that allows for induced changes in the interest rate, sometimes called the *interest-variable multiplier*, will be smaller than the simple multiplier.

Algebraically, the interest effect can be seen by first differencing equation (A12), which is the equilibrium solution for Y. Doing this, and assuming that $\Delta M = \Delta P = 0$, i.e. holding the real money supply and hence the LM curve constant, yields

$$\frac{\Delta Y}{\Delta A} = \frac{1}{(1-c)+bd/e}. \qquad \text{(A14)}$$

This is the IS/LM, the interest-variable multiplier. To understand it, assume first that spending is totally insensitive to interest rates, which means $b = 0$. The multiplier then becomes $1/(1-c)$, which is the interest-constant multiplier. If however expenditure does respond to interest rates, then b takes on a negative value. Now, since d and e, the responses of the demand for money to income and to interest rates, are respectively positive and negative, the whole term $(bd)/e$ is positive. The term then increases the value of the denominator in (A14) and hence reduces the value of the whole expression. *The crowding-out term lowers the value of the multiplier.*

The interest-constant multiplier is shown by the horizontal shift in the IS curve in response to a shift in autonomous spending. The interest-variable IS/LM multiplier is always smaller than the interest-constant multiplier.

For formal derivation of the AD curve, we return to (A12), which gives the solution of the IS/LM model for equilibrium GDP when autonomous expenditure, A, the nominal money supply, M, and the price level, P, are all treated as exogenous variables. We then treat the price level P as an endogenous variable making equation (A12) one equation in two variables. It thus defines a locus of P, Y combinations that satisfy the twin equilibrium condition $E = Y$ and $M_D = M_S$. It is a negatively sloped curve with the equation

$$Y = \frac{A}{(1-c)+bd/e} + \frac{\bar{M}}{d+e(1-c)/b}\frac{1}{P}.$$

It shows that the price level is negatively associated with the equilibrium level of GDP that follows from the IS/LM model.

This aggregate demand curve is plotted in Figure 28A.4 above. Note that, following the Marshallian convention, when price and quantity variables are involved we plot price on the vertical and quantity on the horizontal axis.

---

[19] Straightforward manipulation of (A6) and (A11) produces the solution shown in (A12). Here are the steps: (i) eliminate R by equating the LHSs of (A6) and (A11); (ii) multiply through by bc; (iii) gather the two terms containing Y on the LHS and the other terms on the RHS; (iv) factor out the Y to obtain $Y[bd + (1-c)e]$ on the LHS; (v) divide through by the coefficient of Y just given; (vi) clear the e from the numerator of the term containing A by dividing denominator by e; and divide the term in front of $\frac{M}{P}$ by b; this gives equation (A12).

Chapter 29

THE BALANCE OF PAYMENTS AND EXCHANGE RATES

Is a balance of payments deficit a sign of economic failure? Why are floating exchange rates so volatile? These are two of the questions we address in this chapter. In particular, you will learn that:

- Balance of payment accounts measure the net transactions between domestic residents and the rest of the world over a specific period.

- The current account balance is identically equal and opposite to the capital and financial account balance.

- There is nothing inherently 'good' or 'bad' about a current account deficit or surplus.

- The exchange rate is determined by the demand and supply of domestic currency, in a floating exchange rate regime.

- Exchange rates often overshoot the long-run equilibrium and they can be volatile as they react to 'news'.

We now focus on the linkages between the economy and the rest of the world. We have mentioned some of these linkages before, but here they are the main concern. There are financial (or monetary) linkages, through the international money and capital markets, and there are 'real' linkages, through international trade and travel. The real and the monetary links are not independent of each other. Real transactions cannot take place without money and finance, and are influenced by monetary forces; equally, money markets are influenced by the fundamentals of the real economy.

The discussion of these issues will bring together much material from elsewhere in this book: the theory of supply and demand (Chapter 3), the nature of money (Chapter 27), international trade (yet to come in Chapter 33), and short-run macroeconomics (Chapters 23–28). Indeed, we have had the balance of payments (net exports of goods and services, *NX*) explicitly in our macroeconomic model since Chapter 23. We now need to look at these issues in much greater detail, to prepare the ground for our policy discussions in the next chapter.

In the first part of this chapter we discuss the balance of payments. This is an important concept concerned with net transactions between one country and the rest of the world. We ask what the 'balance of payments' means, how it is measured, and why it matters. In the second part we discuss the exchange rate—what role it plays in connecting the domestic economy with foreign economies, and what economic forces determine its value.

The balance of payments

The economy's balance of payments has had a high profile in political arguments over economic policy throughout the past century in countries like the United Kingdom that had recurrent balance of payments problems. However, in the past decade or so balance of payments issues have been most problematic for developing and transition economies. We will first explain how the balance of payments is recorded, using the United Kingdom as an example, and we will then ask in what ways the balance of payments matters.

Balance of payments accounts

In order to know what is happening to international payments, governments keep track of the transactions between countries. The record of such transactions is made in the *balance of payments accounts*. Each transaction, such as a shipment of exports or the arrival of imported goods, is classified according to the payments or receipts that would typically arise from it.

Table 29.1 **UK Balance of payments, 2001 (£ million)**

	Credits	Debits	Balances
1 Current Account	**424,514**	**444,967**	**−20,453**
A Goods and services			
1 Goods	191,644	225,178	−33,534
2 Services	76,807	65,734	11,073
B Income			
1 Compensation of employees	1,049	869	180
2 Investment income	138,831	129,849	8,982
C Current transfers			
1 Central government	4,912	7,403	−2,491
2 Other sectors	11,271	15,934	−4,663
2 Capital and financial accounts	**304,168**	**283,378**	**20,790**
A Capital account	**2,825**	**1,326**	**1,499**
1 Capital transfers	2,706	985	1,721
2 Acquisition/disposal of non-produced, non-financial assets	119	341	−222
B Financial account	**301,343**	**282,052**	**19,291**
1 Direct investment	43,775	23,710	20,065
2 Portfolio investment	44,182	93,284	−49,102
3 Financial derivatives (net)		−8,432	8,432
4 Other investment	213,386	176,573	36,813
5 Reserve assets		−3,083	3,083
Total			**337**
Net errors and omissions			−337

Transactions that lead to a receipt of payment from foreigners, such as a commodity export or a sale of an asset abroad, are recorded in the balance of payments accounts as a *credit*. In terms of our later objective of analysing the market for foreign exchange, these transactions represent the supply of foreign exchange and the demand for sterling on the foreign exchange market. This is because foreigners have to buy our currency in order to pay us in sterling for the goods or assets they have bought. Transactions that lead to a payment to foreigners, such as a commodity import or the purchase of a foreign asset, are recorded as a *debit*. These transactions represent the demand for foreign exchange and the supply of sterling on the foreign exchange market, because we have to buy foreign currency with sterling in order to pay for our overseas purchases.[1] In calculating the *balance*, credits are positive and debits are negative, so the overall balance is simply credits minus debits.

Balance of payments accounts are divided into two broad parts. One part deals with payments for goods and services, income, and transfers. This is known as the **current account**. The other part records transactions in assets and is, accordingly, known as the **capital and financial account**. A summary of the balance of payments accounts of the United Kingdom for 2001 is given in Table 29.1.[2]

Current account

The current account records transactions arising from trade in goods and services, from income accruing to residents of one country from another, and from transfers by residents of one country to residents of another. The current account is divided into three main sections.

The first of these is the *goods and services account*. This has two parts. The component of this relating to 'goods' trade is often called the **visible account**, the **trade account**, or the **merchandise account**. It records payments and receipts arising from the import and export of tangible goods, such as computers, cars, wheat, and shoes. UK imports require payments to be made to foreign residents in foreign exchange, and hence are entered as debit items on

[1] In the euro zone it is the payments for the euro zone as whole *vis à vis* the rest of the world that matter for the exchange market of the euro. In this chapter we assume that external payments or receipts generate demands or supplies of foreign exchange. However, for countries within a single currency area or for regions of a single country, this would not be true.

[2] This format for balance of payments accounts was introduced in 1998, so earlier accounts may look different. This is now an international standard format, so balance of payments accounts for other countries have a similar structure.

the visible account. In 2001 UK residents spent just over £225 billion on buying goods imported from overseas. UK exports earn payments from foreign residents in foreign exchange (though the foreign exchange will be converted into sterling through the foreign exchange market), and hence are recorded as credit items. In 2001 UK exports amounted to about £192 billion. Exports represent goods leaving the country, but payment for those goods passes in the opposite direction. With imports, goods enter the country and payment has to be made to the foreign manufacturers. We can see that in 2001 there was a goods trade deficit of nearly £34 billion, which is the difference between the value of exports and imports.

The second part of the goods and services account is services. Trade in services covers transactions that do not involve a physical commodity (or asset) changing hands, such as insurance, banking, shipping, and tourism.[3] Trade in services showed a surplus of just over £11 billion in 2001; however, this was smaller than the deficit in goods trade, so that trade in goods and services had a (negative) balance of a little over £20 billion.

The second element of the current account is the *income account*. This again has two components. The first is employee compensation. Credit items involve UK residents being paid for working for non-residents, while the debit items result from UK residents employing non-residents. The second component is investment income. Credit items involve interest and dividend income received by UK residents from assets overseas, while debits reflect similar payments to non-resident owners of assets in the UK. The income component of the current account showed a surplus of £9.2 billion in 2001.

The third element in the current account is *current transfers*. This is subdivided into central government and other transfers. An example of a central government transfer is payment of a UK old-age pension to a former UK resident now living in Spain. An Italian restaurant owner in London sending money to his mother in Milan is an example of an 'other' transfer. Current transfers contributed a deficit of around £7 billion to the UK current account in 2001.

All components of the current account *other than trade in goods* are sometimes referred to as **invisibles**, because you can see goods entering the country but you cannot see, for example, the services of a consultant crossing borders.

Overall, the current account of the UK balance of payments showed a negative balance (or deficit) of about £20 billion in 2001.

Capital and financial accounts

The other major component in the balance of payments is the capital and financial accounts, which record transactions related to international movements of ownership of financial assets. It is important to notice right away that the 'capital' and financial accounts do not relate to imports

and exports of physical capital: trade in such things as machine tools and construction equipment is part of the *goods trade account*. Rather, the capital and financial accounts of the balance of payments relate only to cross-border movements in ownership of assets, a large part of which involves financial instruments such as ownership of company shares, bank loans, or government securities.

The entire capital and financial accounts used to be referred to just as the 'capital account', and we will continue this usage below. However, in the UK accounts shown in Table 29.1, the 'capital account' and 'financial account' are itemized separately. In the accounting conventions used today, the item labelled 'capital account' is a relatively insignificant one. It is made up of 'capital transfers' and 'acquisition/disposal of non-produced, non-financial assets'. Included in the former are items such as a government investment grant to build a hospital overseas, and debt forgiveness between the UK government and an overseas government. The latter includes overseas sales or purchases of patents, trade marks, or copyrights.

The second component of the capital and financial accounts is the financial account. This is made up of four elements: direct investment, portfolio investment, other investment, and reserve assets. **Direct investment** relates to changes in non-resident ownership of domestic firms and resident ownership of foreign firms. One form of direct investment, called greenfield investment, is the building of a factory in the United Kingdom by a foreign firm—for example the Toyota car factory near Derby. Another form of direct investment, called brownfield investment,[4] is a takeover in which a controlling interest in a firm previously controlled by residents is acquired by foreigners—such as when Ford acquired Jaguar from its domestic owners. **Portfolio investment**, on the other hand, is investment in bonds or a minority holding of shares that does not involve legal control. Direct and portfolio investment combined is sometimes referred to as the *long-term capital* element of the capital and financial accounts.

'Other investments' is made up mainly of what are called *short-term capital flows*. These include transfers into overseas banks, and sales or purchases of short-term financial instruments, such as Treasury bills or commercial bills. The large size of these other investment flows in the UK balance of payments accounts reflects in part the role of the City of London as an international financial centre. 'Reserve assets' reflects changes in the official foreign exchange reserves that are held by the Bank of England.

---

[3] The symbols *X* and *IM* as used in this book refer to exports and imports of both tangible goods *and* services, but do not include payments of interest, dividends and profits, or transfers.

[4] The terms are used slightly differently in the context of, for example, housebuilding. Here 'greenfield' building means building on what used to be agricultural or park land, while 'brownfield' means building on land that had previously had an industrial or commercial use.

From now on we adopt the convention that the terms 'capital flows' and 'capital account' refer to all items in the 'capital and financial accounts' of the balance of payments. UK purchases of foreign investments (which then become assets to the UK) are called a *capital outflow.* They use foreign exchange in order to buy the foreign investment, and so they are entered as a debit item in the UK payments accounts.[5] Foreign investment in the United Kingdom (which thereby increases UK liabilities to foreigners) is called a *capital inflow.* It earns foreign exchange and so is entered as a credit (positive) item.

As shown in Table 29.1, in 2001 UK residents increased their investments abroad by nearly £282 billion, while foreigners increased their investments in the United Kingdom by just under £301 billion. These may seem like very large amounts, and indeed they are. However, as already mentioned, a high proportion of this activity stems from the international borrowing and lending of the financial institutions in the City of London. The net capital inflow resulted in a surplus in the capital account of about £19 billion. This means that there was a net decrease in foreign assets (or increase in borrowing from foreigners) of £19 billion.[6]

The meaning of payments balances and imbalances

We have seen that the payments accounts show the total of receipts of foreign exchange (credit items) and payments of foreign exchange (debit items) on account of each category of payment. It is also common to calculate the *balance* on separate items or groups of items. Interest in 'the balance of payments' and its interpretation has a number of aspects, so we approach this issue in a series of steps.

The balance of payments must balance overall

The notion that the balance of payments accounts must balance should present no great mystery. The accounts are constructed so that this has to be true. The idea behind this proposition is quite general. Take your own personal income and spending. Suppose you earn £100 by selling your services (labour) and you buy £90 worth of clothing. You have exports (of services/labour) worth £100, and imports (of clothing) worth £90. Your current account surplus is £10. However, that £10 surplus must be invested in holding a financial claim on someone else—if you hold cash, it is a claim on the Bank of England; if you deposit the money in a bank, it becomes a claim on the bank; and so on.

Whichever way you look at it, the £10 you have acquired is the acquisition of an asset. It represents a capital outflow from your personal economy that is the inevitable consequence of your current account surplus. So you have a current account surplus of £10 and a capital account deficit

(outflow) of £10. The main difference between your accounts and those for the UK economy as a whole is that, with the latter, payments across the foreign exchange markets are involved.[7] A country with a current account surplus in its balance of payments must, at the same time, have acquired net claims on foreigners to the same value.

The current and capital account balances are necessarily of equal and opposite size. When added together, they equal zero.

There is one important caveat to the above statement with regard to actual official accounts. This is that, while conceptually the current and capital accounts are defined to be equal and opposite, in practice the national income statisticians are not able to keep totally accurate records of all transactions, and hence there are always errors in measurement. This means that a balancing item, called 'net errors and omissions', is included in the balance of payments table. The balancing item stands for all unrecorded transactions and is defined to be equal to the difference between the measured current account and the measured capital and financial account. So in practice it is the sum of the current account, the capital and financial accounts, and net errors and omissions that is always zero by construction.

Does the balance of payments matter?

The *balance of payments on current account* is the sum of the balances on the visible and invisible accounts. As a carry-over from a long discredited eighteenth-century economic doctrine called *mercantilism*, a credit balance on current account (where receipts exceed payments) is often called a *favourable balance*, and a debit balance (where payments exceed receipts) is often called an *unfavourable balance*. Mercantilists, both ancient and modern, hold that the gains from trade arise only from having a favourable balance of

---

[5] Capital outflows are sometimes also referred to as *capital exports*. It may seem odd that, whereas a merchandise export is a credit item on current account, a capital export is a debit item on capital account. To understand this terminology, consider the export of UK funds for investment in a German bond. The capital transaction involves the purchase, and hence the *import*, of a German bond, and this has the same effect on the balance of payments as the purchase, and hence the import, of a German good. Both items involve payments to foreigners, and both use foreign exchange. Both are thus debit items in UK balance of payments accounts.

[6] Note that this figure relates only to transactions in assets. It does not account for capital gains or losses resulting from valuation changes of existing asset holdings. Thus, the capital and financial accounts balance is *not* a measure of the total change in indebtedness between the United Kingdom and the rest of the world.

[7] Areas that do not have their own currency still have a balance of payments. The member countries of the euro zone, for example, have balance of payments accounts even though they share a common currency. We could in principle also construct balance of payment accounts for Wales or Scotland.

Box 29.1   Trade and the new mercantilism

Media commentators, political figures, and much of the general public often judge the national balance of payments as they would the accounts of a single firm. Just as a firm is supposed to show a profit, the nation is supposed to secure a balance of payments surplus on current account, with the benefits derived from international trade measured by the size of that surplus.

This view is related to the exploitation doctrine of international trade: one country's surplus is another country's deficit. Thus, one country's gain, judged by its surplus, must be another country's loss, judged by its deficit.

People who hold such views today are echoing an ancient economic doctrine called *mercantilism*. The mercantilists were a group of economists who preceded Adam Smith. They judged the success of trade by the size of the trade balance. In many cases this doctrine made sense in terms of their objective, which was to use international trade as a means of building up the political and military power of the state, rather than as a means of raising the living standards of its citizens. A balance of payments surplus allowed the nation (then and now) to acquire foreign exchange reserves. (In those days the reserves took the form of gold. Today they are a mixture of gold and claims on the currencies of other countries.) These reserves could then be used to pay armies, to purchase weapons from abroad, and generally to finance colonial expansions.

People who advocate this view in modern times are called *neo-mercantilists*. In so far as their object is to increase the military power of the state, they are choosing means that could achieve their ends. In so far as

they are drawing an analogy between what is a sensible objective for a business, interested in its own material welfare, and what is a sensible objective for a society, interested in the material welfare of its citizens, their views are erroneous, because their analogy is false.

If the object of economic activity is to promote the welfare and living standards of ordinary citizens, rather than the power of governments, then the mercantilist focus on the balance of trade makes no sense. The law of comparative advantage shows that average living standards are maximized by having individuals, regions, and countries specialize in the things that they can produce comparatively best and then trading to obtain the things that they can produce comparatively worst. The more specialization there is, the more trade occurs.

On this view, the gains from trade are to be judged by the volume of trade. A situation in which there is a *large volume* of trade but in which each country has a *zero balance* of trade can thus be regarded as quite satisfactory. Furthermore, a change in commercial policy that results in a balanced increase in trade between two countries will bring gain, because it allows for specialization according to comparative advantage, even though it causes no change in either country's trade balance.

To the business interested in private profit, and to the government interested in the power of the state, it is the *balance* of trade that matters. To the person interested in the welfare of ordinary citizens, it is the *volume* of trade that matters.

trade. This misses the point of the doctrine of comparative advantage, first introduced in Box 1.4. It states that countries can gain from a *balanced increase* in trade because this allows each country to specialize according to its comparative advantage. The modern resurgence of mercantilism is discussed in Box 29.1.

It would be tempting to refer to a deficit on capital account as an unfavourable balance as well. However, by now it should be clear that this would be nonsense, because a current account surplus is the same thing as a capital account deficit. Hence it is impossible for one to be 'good' and the other 'bad'. However, this discussion does have one important implication.

The terms 'balance of payments *deficit*' and 'balance of payments *surplus*' must refer to the balance on some part of the payments accounts. In the United Kingdom these terms almost always apply to the current account.

A current account deficit is just as likely to be the product of a healthy growing economy as of an unhealthy economy. Suppose, for example, that an economy has rapidly growing domestic industries that offer a high rate of return on domestic investment. Such an economy would be attracting investment from the rest of the world, and as a result it would have a capital account surplus (capital inflows) and a current account deficit. Far from being a sign

of weakness, the current account deficit would indicate economic health. True, the economy is acquiring external debt; but if this debt is being used to finance rapid real growth, it can be repaid out of higher future output.[8]

In contrast, another economy may indeed have inefficient and unproductive domestic industry, and may be in a situation where domestic spending exceeds domestic output. (Recall from Chapter 22 that the balance of trade in goods and services is equal to the difference between total domestic spending and total domestic production.) Therefore, it will have a trade deficit and will be borrowing from abroad to finance the extra consumption.[9]

The existence of a current account balance of payments deficit tells us only that an economy's total spending exceeds its total income and that it has a capital inflow. The existence of such a deficit is consistent both with healthy, growing economies and with unhealthy, inefficient economies.

---

[8] 'Debt' is used here in its general sense to refer to foreign liabilities rather than in the context of debt versus equity. These external debts can be in any specific form, including equity, bonds, or bank loans.

[9] It is assumed here that the balance of trade in goods and services and the current account balance are the same. The balance of trade is the difference between domestic spending and GDP, while the current account balance is the difference between domestic spending and GNI.

Box 29.2 Balance of payments crises

Many countries have experienced crises in the last decade that have been linked to external payments problems. The Mexican crisis of 1994, the Asian crisis of 1997, the Russian crisis of 1998, and the Argentina crisis of 2001–2 are but a few examples. We discuss the problems in Argentina and the Asian crisis in Chapter 35 below. Here we summarize some common features of these crises and discuss who bears the costs of the adjustments necessary to eliminate the problem.

We argued in the text that a current account deficit can be a healthy sign when it indicates that a country is borrowing from abroad to finance investment in real economic growth. But a current account deficit can be unhealthy if it involves borrowing to finance current consumption so that debts build up but there is no investment in real assets that can help repay the debt.

The most common reason for balance of payments crises is that potential investors in a specific economy revise their analysis of an economy's prospects and come to believe that the level of international borrowing has become unsustainable. At this point capital inflows turn into outflows, as foreigners try to get their money out and domestic residents try to move their funds abroad. If the exchange rate is pegged by the domestic government (see the next section, on the market for foreign exchange, for a discussion of how this is done) there will be a run on official foreign exchange reserves and this will put pressure on the domestic authorities to change their monetary and/or fiscal policies. If the currency is floating, the exchange rate will fall sharply and this will lead to a sharp increase in domestic inflation.

There could be many reasons for the change in assessment of an economy that triggers a crisis. It could be political instability or the introduction of profligate government spending plans; it could be a sharp fall in market price of the country's main export commodity; it could be a general rise in world interest rates that sharply increases the costs of servicing foreign debts.

Countries hit by such crises generally seek loans from the International Monetary Fund (IMF) which are intended to help provide finance while policies are put in place to correct the underlying problem. As a condition of the loan, the IMF usually requires a significant tightening of domestic monetary and fiscal policies, that is higher interest rates, cuts in spending and higher taxes.

Two main groups suffer from the after-effects of the crisis. International banks and other investors who have lent to the country may find that the value of their investments has fallen sharply or in some cases that there is a debt default. The main sufferers, however, are typically domestic residents, who often suffer sharp falls in their income and wealth and may lose their jobs or their businesses. Critics of IMF policies have argued that the IMF loans and the conditions attached help to bail out international investors but do little to ease the adjustment pains felt by domestic residents. This is controversial, but it seems unlikely that countries suffering such crises could be better off with no source of international financial support, even if it is conceded that the handling of such crises by the IMF could be improved.

There are some times when balance of payments problems are associated with crises. The causes of these differ from place to place and time to time. Some of the issues that arise are discussed in Box 29.2.

Actual and desired transactions The discussion in this section has focused on *actual* transactions as measured in the balance of payments accounts. It is the actual capital inflow that must equal the actual current account deficit. There is no reason at all, however, why *desired* (or planned) current account transactions should equal desired capital account transactions. In practice, it is movements in the exchange rate that play a key role in reconciling actual and desired transactions (at least for a country that has its own currency and a flexible exchange rate). We now turn to a discussion of the exchange rate and how it is determined.

The market for foreign exchange

The foreign exchange markets are the markets in which one currency can be traded for another. We are used to thinking about markets in which goods are exchanged for money. In a foreign exchange market, it is one country's money that is exchanged for another country's money. As with all markets, the foreign exchange market can be analysed with the tools of demand and supply developed earlier in this book. Before proceeding with this exercise, it is helpful to remind ourselves why we need such markets.

Money is central to the efficient working of any modern economy that relies on specialization and exchange. Yet fiat money as we know it is a *national* matter, one that is closely controlled by national governments. Until recently each nation-state had its own currency, though in 1999 twelve EU nations adopted a common currency, the euro. For purposes of the following discussion we treat the euro zone countries as if they were a single country, as they have a single external exchange rate. Other nation-states each have their own currency. If you live in Sweden, you earn kronor and spend kronor; if you run a business in Australia, you borrow Australian dollars and meet your wage bill with Australian dollars. The currency of a country is acceptable within the bounds of that country, but usually it will not be accepted by people and firms in another country.

The Stockholm buses will accept kronor for a fare, but not Australian dollars; the Australian worker will not take Swedish kronor for wages, but insists on being paid in Australian dollars.

UK producers require payment in pounds sterling for their products. They need pounds to meet their wage bills, to pay for their raw materials, and to reinvest or distribute their profits. There is no problem when they sell to UK-based purchasers. However, if they sell their goods to, say, Indian importers, either the Indians must exchange their rupees to acquire pounds to pay for the goods, or the UK producers must accept rupees;[10] and they will accept rupees only if they know that they can exchange the rupees for pounds. The same holds true for producers in all countries; they must eventually receive payment in the currency of their own country.

Trade between nations typically requires the exchange of one nation's currency for that of another. The major exception is the euro zone, where member states have a common currency.

International payments involve the exchange of currencies between people who have one currency and require another. Suppose that a UK firm wishes to acquire ¥3 million for some purpose. (¥ is the currency symbol for the Japanese yen.) The firm can go to its bank and buy a cheque, or money order, that will be accepted in Japan as ¥3 million. How many *pounds* the firm must pay to purchase this cheque will depend on the value of the yen in terms of pounds.

The exchange of one currency for another is a *foreign exchange transaction*. The term 'foreign exchange' refers to the actual foreign currency or various claims on it, such as bank deposits or promises to pay that are traded for each other. The UK *exchange rate* is the value of the domestic currency in terms of foreign currency; it is the amount of foreign currency that can be obtained with one unit of the domestic currency. For example, if £1 will buy ¥150, the yen–pound exchange rate is 150. Most other countries, however, express their exchange rate the other way round, that is, as the number of units of domestic currency that it takes to buy one unit of foreign currency (usually expressed in term of US dollars). In economic theory we also usually express the exchange rate in the latter format (i.e. as quantity of domestic currency per unit of foreign currency).

A rise in the external value of the pound (that is, a rise in the exchange rate) is called an **appreciation** of the pound; for example, if one can now obtain ¥175 for £1, the pound has *appreciated*. A fall in the external value of the pound (that is, a fall in the exchange rate) is called a **depreciation** of the pound; for example, if one can now obtain only ¥125 for £1, the pound has *depreciated*.[11]

Because the exchange rate expresses the value of one currency in terms of another, when one currency appreciates, the other must depreciate.

The demand for and supply of pounds

The exchange rate is just a price, albeit a very important price. As with other prices, we will approach the explanation of exchange rates from the perspective of demand and supply. However, the exchange rate is potentially influenced by (and influences) all payments into and out of the national economy from abroad. Hence we must first be clear about what those payments are.

For the sake of simplicity, we use an example involving trade between the United Kingdom and the United States and the determination of the exchange rate between their two currencies, the pound sterling and the US dollar, for which we use the shorthand forms 'pound' and 'dollar'. The two-country example simplifies things, but the principles apply to all foreign transactions. Thus, 'dollar' stands for foreign exchange in general, and the value of the pound in terms of dollars stands for the foreign exchange rate in general.[12]

When £1 = $1.50, a US importer who offers to buy £1 million with dollars must be offering to sell $1.5 million. Similarly, a UK importer who offers to sell £1 million for dollars must be offering to buy $1.5 million.

Because one currency is traded for another in the foreign exchange market, it follows that a demand for foreign exchange (dollars) implies a supply of pounds, while a supply of foreign exchange (dollars) implies a demand for pounds.

For this reason, a theory of the exchange rate between the pound and the dollar can deal either with the demand for and the supply of pounds or with the demand for and the supply of dollars: both need not be considered. We will concentrate on the demand, supply, and price of the pound (quoted in dollars).

We develop our example in terms of the demand-and-supply analysis first encountered in Chapter 3. To do so, we need only recall that, *in the market for foreign exchange*, transactions that generate a receipt of foreign exchange (a credit in the balance of payments) represent a demand for pounds, and transactions that require a payment of foreign exchange represent a supply of pounds. We focus on the demand and supply of pounds arising from both the current and capital accounts. Later we turn to the important role of official intervention by the domestic government.

---

[10] Some trade, especially in primary commodities such as wheat and oil, is conducted in US dollars even when US residents are not involved. In this respect, the US dollar has a special role as an international medium of exchange or unit of account.

[11] When the external value of the currency changes as a result of an explicit policy of the central bank, it is often said to have been *devalued* when it falls and *revalued* when it rises.

[12] The foreign exchange market between the pound and the dollar is referred to in the market as 'cable', because it grew to its present structure by use of one of the first transatlantic telegraph cables.

The demand for pounds

The demand for pounds arises from all international transactions that generate a receipt of foreign exchange, that is, credits in the balance of payments.

UK exports One important source of demand for pounds in foreign exchange markets is foreigners who do not currently hold pounds but wish to buy UK-made goods and services. A German importer of Scotch whisky is such a purchaser; an Austrian couple planning to take a holiday in Cornwall is another; the Chinese national airline seeking to buy Rolls Royce engines for its passenger aircraft is yet another. All are sources of demand for pounds, arising out of international trade. Each potential buyer wants to sell their own currency and buy pounds for the purpose of purchasing UK exports.

Income payments and transfers A UK resident who owns shares in, say, General Motors receives dividend payments on those shares. The dividend is paid by GM in dollars. But the UK resident wants to use the money for a meal out in London, so converts the dollars into pounds, thereby creating a demand for pounds. Thus, credit items in the balance of payments accounts for income or transfers create demand for pounds.

Capital inflows A third source of a demand for pounds comes from foreigners who wish to purchase UK assets. In order to buy UK assets, holders of foreign currencies must first buy pounds in foreign exchange markets.[13]

Reserve currency Governments often accumulate and hold foreign exchange reserves, just as individuals maintain savings accounts. The government of Nigeria, for example, may decide to increase its reserve holdings of pounds and reduce its reserve holdings of dollars; if it does so, it will be a demander of pounds (and a supplier of dollars) in foreign exchange markets. The pound sterling used to be a very important reserve currency, particularly for countries that were formerly British colonies. This role has been greatly reduced (relative to the US dollar and euro), but there is still a significant overseas demand for pounds. Currency reserves are almost always held in an interest-bearing asset, so it is the expected return on these assets that is likely to influence the choice, just as with private sector capital flows.

The total demand for pounds

The demand for pounds by holders of foreign currencies is the sum of the demands for all of the purposes just discussed—for purchases of UK exports of goods and services, for income payments and transfers, for capital movements, or for adding to currency reserves. Furthermore, because people, firms, and governments in all countries purchase goods from, and invest in, many other countries, the

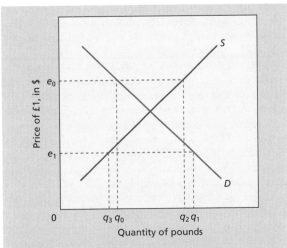

Figure 29.1 The market for foreign exchange

The demand curve for pounds is negatively sloped, and the supply curve of pounds is positively sloped. The demand for pounds is D. It represents the sum of transactions giving rise to receipts of foreign exchange. When the exchange rate is e_0, the quantity of pounds demanded is q_0. A depreciation of the pound is indicated by a fall in the exchange rate to e_1; foreign demand for UK goods and assets rises, and hence the quantity of pounds demanded also rises, from q_0 to q_1. An appreciation has the opposite effect; a rise in the exchange rate from e_1 to e_0 causes the quantity of pounds demanded to fall from $q1$ to q_0.

The supply of pounds is given by line S. It represents the sum of transactions that require payments of foreign exchange. When the exchange rate is e_0, the quantity of pounds supplied is q_2. If the exchange rate falls to e_1, UK demand for foreign goods and assets falls, and hence the quantity of pounds supplied also falls, from q_2 to q_3. An appreciation has the opposite effect; a rise in the exchange rate from e_1 to e_0 causes the quantity of pounds supplied to rise from q_3 to q_2.

demand for any one currency will be the aggregate demand of individuals, firms, and governments in a number of different countries. Thus, the total demand for pounds, for example, may include Germans who are offering euros, Japanese who are offering yen, Australians who are offering Australian dollars, and so on. For simplicity, however, we continue with our two-country example and use only the United Kingdom and the United States.

The demand curve for pounds

The demand for pounds in terms of dollars is represented by a negatively sloped curve, such as the one shown in Figure 29.1. This figure plots the price of the pound (measured in dollars) on the vertical axis and the quantity of

---

[13] Capital inflows also arise when UK citizens sell foreign assets, because they enter the foreign exchange market and sell the foreign currency received for the assets and buy pounds.

pounds on the horizontal axis. Moving down the vertical scale, the pound is worth fewer dollars and hence is depreciating in the foreign exchange market. Moving up the scale, the pound is appreciating.

Why is the demand curve for pounds negatively sloped? Consider the demand for pounds for foreign purchases of UK exports. If the pound depreciates, the dollar price of UK exports will fall because holders of dollars require fewer of them to buy £1. US citizens will buy more of the cheaper UK goods and will require more pounds for this purpose. The quantity of pounds demanded will therefore rise. In the opposite case, when the pound appreciates, more dollars are required to buy £1, and so the price of UK exports rises in terms of dollars. US citizens will buy fewer UK goods and therefore will demand fewer pounds.

Similar considerations affect other sources of demand for pounds. When the pound is cheaper UK assets become attractive purchases, and the quantity purchased will rise. As it does, the quantity of pounds demanded to pay for the purchases will increase.

The demand curve for pounds in the foreign exchange market is negatively sloped when it is plotted against the dollar price of £1.

The supply of pounds

The supply of pounds in the foreign exchange market is merely the opposite side of the demand for dollars. (Recall that the *supply* of pounds by people who are seeking dollars is the same as the *demand* for dollars by holders of pounds.)

Who wants to sell pounds? UK residents seeking to purchase foreign goods and services or assets will be supplying pounds and purchasing foreign exchange for this purpose. In addition, holders of UK assets may decide to sell their UK holdings and shift them into foreign assets, and if they do they will sell pounds; that is, they will be supplying pounds to the foreign exchange market. Similarly, a country with some sterling reserves of foreign exchange may decide that the sterling-denominated assets offer a poor return and that it should sell pounds in order to buy another currency.

The supply curve of pounds

When the pound sterling depreciates, the sterling price of US exports to the United Kingdom rises. It takes more pounds to buy the same US goods, so UK residents will buy fewer of the now more expensive US goods. The quantity of pounds being offered in exchange for dollars in order to pay for US exports to the United Kingdom (UK imports) will therefore fall.[14]

In the opposite case, when the pound appreciates, US exports to the United Kingdom become cheaper, more are sold, and a greater quantity of pounds is spent on them. Thus, more pounds will be offered in exchange for dollars to obtain the foreign exchange that is needed to pay for the extra imports. The argument also applies to purchases and sales of assets.

The supply curve of pounds in the foreign exchange market is positively sloped when it is plotted against the dollar price of £1.

This too is illustrated in Figure 29.1.

The determination of exchange rates

The demand and supply curves in Figure 29.1 do not include official foreign exchange market intervention by the domestic government (or by the monetary authorities,[15] depending on the institutional arrangements in the country concerned), though they do include any transactions in pounds by foreign monetary authorities. In order to complete our analysis, we need to incorporate the role of domestic official intervention.[16] Three important cases need to be considered.

1. When there is no official intervention by the monetary authorities or the government, the exchange rate is determined by the equality between the supply and demand for pounds arising from the capital and current accounts. This is called a *flexible* or *floating exchange rate regime*.

2. When official intervention is used to maintain the exchange rate at (or close to) a particular value, there is said to be a *fixed* or *pegged exchange rate regime*.

3. Between these two 'pure' regimes are many possible intermediate cases, including the *adjustable peg* and the

---

[14] As long as the demand for imports is elastic (price elasticity greater than 1 (in absolute terms)), the fall in the volume of imports will swamp the rise in price, and hence fewer pounds will be spent on imports. If the elasticity of demand for imports is less than 1 (in absolute terms), the volume of imports will fall but the amount of domestic money spent on them will still rise. In what follows, we adopt the case of elastic demand, which is usual in this area. In a more general form this is called the *Marshall–Lerner condition*, after two famous British economists who first studied the problem.

[15] In the UK the official reserves used to be owned entirely by the government but managed by the Bank of England. However, following the 1998 Bank of England Act, the Bank was given some of the UK reserves, so foreign exchange market intervention could be performed with either the Treasury's or the Bank's reserves. The European Central Bank can also intervene in foreign exchange markets, as it has its own foreign exchange reserves.

[16] Official intervention is included in the balance of payments accounts in Table 29.1 under 'reserve assets'.

managed float. Under an adjustable peg governments set and attempt to maintain par values for their exchange rates, but they explicitly recognize that circumstances may arise in which they will change the par value. In a managed float the authorities seek to have some stabilizing influence on the exchange rate but do not try to fix it at some publicly announced par value.

Flexible exchange rates

Consider an exchange rate that is set in a freely competitive market, with no intervention by the authorities. Like any competitive price, this rate fluctuates according to the conditions of demand and supply.

Suppose that the current price of the pound is so low (say, at e_1 in Figure 29.1) that the quantity of pounds demanded exceeds the quantity supplied. Pounds will be in scarce supply in the foreign exchange market; some people who require pounds to make payments to the United Kingdom will be unable to obtain them; and the price of the pound will be bid up. The value of the pound *vis-à-vis* the dollar will appreciate. As the price of the pound rises, the dollar price of UK exports to the United States rises and the quantity of pounds demanded to buy UK goods decreases. At the same time as the sterling price of imports from the United States falls, a larger quantity will be purchased and the quantity of pounds supplied will rise. Thus, a rise in the price of the pound reduces the quantity demanded and increases the quantity supplied. Where the two curves intersect, quantity demanded equals quantity supplied and the exchange rate is in equilibrium.

What happens when the price of the pound is above its equilibrium value? The quantity of pounds demanded will be less than the quantity supplied. With pounds in excess supply, some people who wish to convert pounds into dollars will be unable to do so. (Equivalently, we could say that there is an excess demand for dollars.) The price of the pound will fall, fewer pounds will be supplied, more will be demanded, and an equilibrium will be re-established.

A foreign exchange market is like other competitive markets in that the forces of demand and supply lead to an equilibrium price at which quantity demanded equals quantity supplied.

In a floating exchange rate regime it is exchange rate adjustment that determines the actual current and capital account transactions, even though planned, or desired, trade and investment decisions may have been inconsistent. Suppose that at the beginning of some period importers and exporters had plans that would have created a current account deficit and domestic investors had plans to buy foreign securities (while foreigners had no such plans). The attempt to implement these plans would create a massive excess supply of pounds (demand for dollars).

This would force a sterling depreciation, which would continue until it moved far enough to force changes in plans. Indeed, it would depreciate just far enough so that any supply of pounds generated by a current account deficit was just balanced by a capital inflow (or any current account surplus was just balanced by a capital outflow).

Fixed exchange rates

When there is official intervention in the foreign exchange market to maintain a particular exchange rate, this stops some movement in the exchange rate that would otherwise have happened. In this way it may prevent the exchange rate from adjusting sufficiently to guarantee that the current account balance and the (private sector) capital account balance are equal and opposite. In this situation the authorities must satisfy any private-sector excess demand or supply of pounds. In the process of intervention the authorities will be building up or running down their foreign exchange reserves.

The official foreign exchange reserves are the stock of foreign-currency-denominated assets that the monetary authorities hold in order to be able to intervene in the foreign exchange markets.

When the authorities peg the exchange rate, they do not do so at one specific rate, but rather within some range. In the postwar exchange regime that existed until 1972 (in the UK case) exchange rates were pegged within one percentage point on either side of a central (or 'par') rate. This was known as the Bretton Woods regime, after the town in the United States where the agreement was drawn up. In the European Exchange Rate Mechanism (ERM) of the 1980s and early 1990s, the range of permitted fluctuation was 2.25 per cent for some countries and 6 per cent for others (including the United Kingdom from October 1990 to September 1992), though the band was widened to 15 per cent after a crisis in 1993.

Let us consider a simplified analysis of how such pegged exchange rate regimes operate. Assume for simplicity that the domestic authorities peg the UK exchange rate between, say, $1.50 and $1.60. This case is illustrated in Figure 29.2. The authorities would then enter the market to prevent the rate from going outside this range. At the price of $1.50 the authorities offer to buy pounds (in exchange for dollars) in unlimited amounts; at the price $1.60 the authorities offer to sell pounds (in exchange for dollars) in unlimited amounts. When the authorities buy dollars (sell pounds) their exchange reserves rise, but when they sell dollars (buy pounds) their foreign exchange reserves fall.

If on average the demand and supply curves intersect in the range $1.50–$1.60, then exchange reserves will be relatively stable. However, if demand for pounds intersects the supply curve below $1.50, the authorities will find

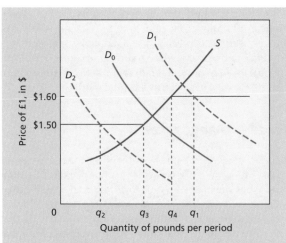

Figure 29.2 Managing fixed exchange rates

Under a fixed exchange rate regime, the authorities intervene in the foreign exchange market to ensure that the exchange rate stays within specified bands. The supply curve is S, and the exchange rate is pegged within the range $1.50–$1.60. If the demand curve is given by D_0, the equilibrium exchange rate is within the bands so no intervention by the authorities is required. With demand curve D_1 the equilibrium exchange rate would be above $1.60. To stop the exchange rate rising above $1.60, the authorities have to sell q_4q_1 pounds per period and buy dollars of equivalent value. (For every £100 sold, they will acquire $160.) If the demand curve were D_2, the exchange rate would fall below $1.50 in a free market, so the authorities have to buy q_2q_3 pounds per period with dollars.

themselves losing reserves each period, and such a situation cannot be sustained indefinitely (because the authorities will run out of reserves). They must then either move the bands of fluctuation (devalue), or take action to shift the demand or supply curves. This could be done, for example, by trade restrictions, or by raising interest rates to attract short-term capital inflows.

In a fixed exchange rate regime with an overvalued currency, the balance of payments becomes a problem. In this case it is not necessarily a current account deficit that is the problem: rather, it is the overall excess supply of domestic currency (excess demand for foreign currency) in the foreign exchange market that could arise from any of the components of the balance of payments.

With fixed exchange rates and an overvalued currency, the monetary authorities will be suffering a loss of reserves. It is this that causes balance of payments crises for governments operating under fixed exchange rate regimes.

The problems associated with fixing the exchange rate provide a further example of the difficulties of government price fixing studied in Chapter 5. In the remainder of this chapter we focus on flexible exchange rates, which is the regime under which sterling, the euro, the US dollar, and most other major currencies operate today.

Changes in exchange rates

What causes flexible exchange rates to move? The simplest answer to this question is: changes in demand or supply in the foreign exchange market. Anything that shifts the demand curve for pounds to the right or the supply curve of pounds to the left leads to an appreciation of the pound. Anything that shifts the demand curve for pounds to the left or the supply curve of pounds to the right leads to a depreciation of the pound. This is nothing more than a restatement of the laws of supply and demand, applied now to the market for foreign currencies; it is illustrated in Figure 29.3.

What causes the shifts in demand and supply that lead to changes in exchange rates? There are many causes, some of which are transitory and some of which are persistent. We will discuss some of the most important ones.

A rise in the domestic price of exports

Suppose that the sterling price of UK-produced telephone equipment rises. The effect on the demand for pounds depends on the price elasticity of foreign demand for the UK products.

If the demand is inelastic (say, because the United Kingdom is uniquely able to supply the product for which there are no close substitutes), then more will be spent; the demand for pounds to pay the bigger bill will shift the demand curve to the right, and the pound will appreciate. This is illustrated in Figure 29.3(i).

If the demand is elastic, perhaps because other countries supply the same product to competitive world markets, the total amount spent will decrease and thus fewer pounds will be demanded; that is, the demand curve for pounds will shift to the left, and the pound will depreciate. This too is illustrated in Figure 29.3(i), by a reverse of the previous shift.

A rise in the foreign price of imports

Suppose that the dollar price of US-produced videos increases sharply. Suppose also that UK consumers have an elastic demand for US videos because they can easily switch to UK substitutes. In this case they will spend fewer dollars on US videos than they did before. Hence they will supply fewer pounds to the foreign exchange market. The supply curve of pounds will shift to the left, and the pound will appreciate. If the demand for US videos is inelastic, spending on them will rise and the supply of pounds will shift to the right, leading to a depreciation of the pound. This is illustrated in Figure 29.3(ii).

Changes in price levels

Suppose that, instead of a change in the price of a specific exported product, there is a change in *all* prices because of

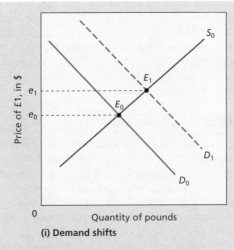
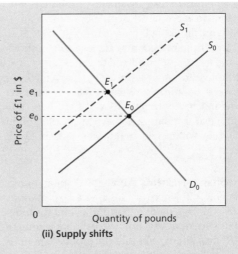

(i) Demand shifts   **(ii) Supply shifts**

Figure 29.3 Changes in exchange rates

An increase in the demand for pounds or a decrease in the supply will cause the pound to appreciate; a decrease in the demand or an increase in supply will cause it to depreciate. The initial demand and supply curves, D_0 and S_0, are shown as solid lines. Equilibrium is at E_0 with an exchange rate of e_0. An increase in the demand for pounds, as shown by a rightward shift in the demand curve from D_0 to D_1 in part (i), or a decrease in the supply of pounds, as shown by a leftward shift in the supply curve from S_0 to S_1 in part (ii), will cause the pound to appreciate. In both parts the new equilibrium is at E_1, and the appreciation is shown by the rise in the exchange rate from e_0 to e_1.

A decrease in the demand for pounds, as shown by a leftward shift in the demand curve from D_1 to D_0 in part (i), or an increase in the supply of pounds, as shown by a rightward shift in the supply curve from S_1 to S_0 in part (ii), will cause the pound to depreciate. The equilibrium will shift from E_1 to E_0, and the depreciation is shown by the fall in the exchange rate from e_1 to e_0 in both parts.

inflation. What matters here is the change in the UK price level *relative to* the price levels of its trading partners. (Recall that in our two-country example the 'United States' stands for the rest of the world.)

If UK inflation is higher than that in the United States, UK exports are becoming relatively expensive in US markets while imports from the United States are becoming relatively cheap in the United Kingdom. This will shift the demand curve for pounds to the left and the supply curve to the right. Each change causes the dollar price of £1 to fall, that is, causes the pound to depreciate.

If the price level of one country is rising relative to that of another country, the equilibrium value of its currency will be falling relative to that of the other country.

Indeed, the price level and the exchange rate are both measures of a currency's value. The price level is the value of a currency measured against a typical basket of goods, while the exchange rate values a currency against other currencies.

Capital movements

Major capital flows can exert a strong influence on exchange rates, especially as the size of capital flows (in the modern globalized financial system) can swamp trade payments on any particular day. An increased desire by UK residents to invest in US assets will shift the supply curve for pounds to the right, and the pound will depreciate. This is illustrated in Figure 29.3(ii).

A significant movement of investment funds has the effect of appreciating the currency of the capital-importing country and depreciating the currency of the capital-exporting country.

This statement is true for all capital movements—short-term and long-term. Because the motives that lead to large capital movements are likely to be different in the short and long terms, however, it is worth considering each separately.

Short-term capital movements A major motive for short-term capital flows is a change in interest rates. International traders hold transactions balances just as domestic traders do. These balances are usually lent out on a short-term basis rather than being left in a non-interest-bearing deposit. Naturally, other things being equal, the holders of these balances will tend to lend them in those markets where interest rates are highest. Thus, if one major country's short-term rate of interest rises above the rates in most other countries, there will tend to be an inflow of short-term capital into that country (or at least of deposits in major financial centres denominated in that country's currency) in an effort to take advantage of the high rate, and this will tend to appreciate the currency. If these short-term interest rates should fall, there will most likely be a sudden shift away from that country as a location for short-term funds, and its currency will tend to depreciate.

A second motive for short-term capital movements is speculation about a country's exchange rate. If foreigners expect the pound to appreciate, they will rush to buy assets denominated in pounds; if they expect the pound to depreciate, they will be reluctant to buy or to hold UK financial assets.

Long-term capital movements Long-term capital movements are largely influenced by long-term expectations about another country's profit opportunities and the long-run value of its currency. A US firm will be more willing to purchase a UK firm if it expects that the profits in pounds will buy more dollars in future years than the profits from investment in a US factory. This could happen if the UK business earned greater profits than the US alternative, with exchange rates remaining unchanged. It could also happen if the profits were the same but the US firm expected the pound to appreciate relative to the dollar.

Structural changes

An economy can undergo structural changes that alter the equilibrium exchange rate. 'Structural change' is an all-purpose term for a change in technology, the invention of new products, or anything else that affects the pattern of comparative advantage. For example, when a country's products do not improve in quality as rapidly as those of some other countries, that country's consumers' demand (at fixed prices) shifts slowly away from its own products and towards those of its foreign competitors. This causes a slow depreciation in the first country's currency, because the demand for its currency is shifting slowly leftward, as illustrated in Figure 29.3(i).

An important example of a structural change in recent UK history was the production of oil and gas from the North Sea. This reduced UK demand for imported oil, leading to a reduced supply of pounds in the foreign exchange market and an appreciation of the UK exchange rate.

The behaviour of exchange rates

The degree of exchange rate variability experienced since the advent of floating in the early 1970s has been greater than was expected.

Why have exchange rates been volatile? This question remains at the centre of debate and controversy among researchers and policy commentators. In this section we provide only a cursory view of this and related questions about the behaviour of exchange rates. First, we look at one

measure of the value that the exchange rate would take on if it were subject to the influence of what might be called the underlying, or fundamental, market determinants. We can then compare this with the actual value of the exchange rate. Second, we provide one explanation for the divergence of the exchange rate from the path determined by these fundamentals.

Purchasing power parity

Purchasing power parity (PPP) theory holds that over the long term the average value of the exchange rate between two currencies depends on their relative purchasing power. The theory holds that a currency will tend to have the same purchasing power when it is spent in its home country as it would have if it were converted to foreign exchange and spent in the foreign country.

If, at existing values of relative price levels and the existing exchange rate, a currency has a higher purchasing power in its own country, it is said to be undervalued. There is then an incentive to sell foreign exchange and buy the domestic currency in order to take advantage of this higher purchasing power (that is, the fact that goods seem cheaper) in the domestic economy. This will put upward pressure on the domestic currency.

Similarly, if a currency has a lower purchasing power in its own country, it is said to be overvalued; there is then an incentive to sell the domestic currency and buy foreign exchange in order to take advantage of the higher purchasing power (cheaper goods) abroad. This will put downward pressure on the domestic currency.

The PPP exchange rate is determined by relative price levels in the two countries.

For example, assume that the UK price level rises by 20 per cent, while the US price level rises by only 5 per cent over the same period. The PPP value of the dollar then appreciates by approximately 15 per cent against sterling. This means that in the United States the prices of all goods (both US-produced and imported UK goods) will rise by 5 per cent, measured in dollars, while in the United Kingdom the prices of all goods (both UK-produced and imported US goods) will rise by 20 per cent, measured in pounds.

The PPP exchange rate adjusts so that the relative prices of the two nations' goods (measured in the same currency) are unchanged, because the change in the relative values of two currencies compensates exactly for differences in national inflation rates.

If the actual exchange rate changes along with the PPP rate, the competitive positions of producers in the two countries will be unchanged. Firms that are located in countries with high inflation rates will still be able to sell their outputs on international markets, because the

Box 29.3 **Exchange rates and the quantity theory of money**

A simple expression for the exchange rate can be derived from the quantity theory of money (as set out in Box 28.1) when there are two countries and an exchange rate that follows its PPP value.

Let the foreign country be denoted by an asterisk (*), so that it has an equation linking money, prices, income, and velocity:

$$M^*V^* = P^*Y^*. \qquad \text{(i)}$$

Using values for home money supply, prices, velocity, and income, we already had

$$MV = PY. \qquad \text{(ii)}$$

All we need to add is the relationship implied by PPP. This is that prices will be the same in both economies when converted at the current exchange rate:

$$PE = P^*, \qquad \text{(iii)}$$

where P is the home country price level, P^* is the foreign country price level, and E is the exchange rate (number of units of foreign currency per unit of home currency). Now all we do is rearrange (i) and (ii) as expressions for P and P^*, then substitute into (iii), and arrange as an expression for E. This gives†

$$E = \frac{M^*}{M} \cdot \frac{Y}{Y^*} \cdot \frac{V^*}{V}. \qquad \text{(iv)}$$

This is an important equation, which gives us some new insights into the exchange rate. The first term is the ratio of the home and foreign money supplies. E falls in proportion to the home money supply and rises in proportion to the foreign money supply. This means that when the home money supply rises, the exchange rate depreciates in the same proportion. The logic of this has two steps. First, a rise in home money supply leads to a proportional increase in the home price level (for given levels of Y and V). Second, a rise in the home price level leads to a proportional depreciation of the home currency to preserve PPP.

The second term in (iv) has a very important implication. Domestic real national income is positively related to E. This means that, other things being equal, a rise in domestic national income leads to an appreciation of the home currency. The reason for this is that an increase in Y leads to an increased transactions demand for the home currency. As we have learned in this chapter, anything that increases demand for the home currency will tend to appreciate its exchange rate.

This simple model of exchange rates gives important insights, but it is only a beginning. Many more complicated factors affecting interest rates and expectations can easily be incorporated by a more detailed specification of the determinants of V. However, the main elements of (iv) are recognizable in many of the empirical exchange rate models of the last two decades.

†The steps are as follows: (1) $P^* = M^*V^*/Y^*$ and $P = MV/Y$; (2) substitute into (iii), $E(MV/Y) = M^*V^*/Y^*$; (3) rearranging gives (iv).

exchange rate will adjust to offset the effect of the rising domestic prices. An exchange rate that adjusts in line with the PPP exchange rate is also referred to as a constant *real exchange rate*.[17] A simple model of the exchange rate implied by the quantity theory of money and PPP is set out in Box 29.3.

Figure 29.4 shows an index of the real exchange rate for the United Kingdom, the United States, and Germany for 1980–2002. PPP requires that the real exchange rate should be constant in the long term. This is broadly true. Notice also, however, the large fluctuations around the PPP rate. The United Kingdom had a high real exchange rate in the early 1980s, associated with its emergence as an oil producer. This led to a sharp loss of competitiveness of the non-oil sectors of the economy (especially manufacturing), causing a sharp decline in UK manufacturing output which in turn contributed to the 1979–81 recession. The UK real exchange rate fell significantly between 1981 and 1986. The UK real exchange was high again at the end of the 1990s and in the early years of the twenty-first century. The most dramatic swing in the 1980s, however, was in the US real exchange rate, which increased 50 per cent between 1980 and 1985, and then fell back to its 1980 level by 1987.

PPP governs exchange rate behaviour in the long term, but there often are significant deviations from PPP in the short to medium term.

Why have these wide fluctuations occurred? One of the most important reasons is associated with international differences in interest rates. Another, related reason— responses to new information—is discussed in Box 29.4.

Exchange rate overshooting

Differences in interest rates between countries, arising from differences in monetary and fiscal policies, among other factors, can trigger large capital flows as investors seek to place their funds where returns are highest. These capital flows will in turn result in swings in the exchange rate between the two countries. Some economists argue that this is the fundamental reason for the wide fluctuations in exchange rates that have been observed.

To illustrate, suppose that an exogenous change in monetary policy causes UK interest rates to rise 4 percentage points above those in New York. The interest rate differential will lead to a capital inflow into the United Kingdom. UK and foreign investors alike will sell assets denominated

---

[17] The real exchange rate is the inverse of competitiveness. A country whose goods are becoming relatively cheap in world markets can be said to be improving its competitiveness but to be having a falling real exchange rate, and vice versa. The real exchange rate is not an actual price of currency: it is an index number of the relative prices of home and foreign goods.

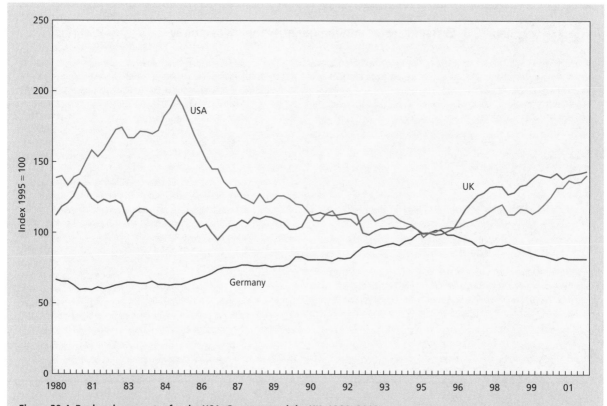

Figure 29.4　Real exchange rates for the USA, Germany, and the UK, 1980–2002

Deviations from PPP can be substantial in the short run, but over the long run exchange rates tend to converge to their PPP values. At the PPP exchange rate the real exchange rate would be constant. The chart shows real exchange rates for three countries, calculated by adjusting actual exchange rates by indexes of consumer prices, and set to a value of 100 in 1995.

The UK real exchange rate rose between 1980 and early 1981. It then fell in stages. It rose again at the end of the 1980s but fell sharply after September 1992, when Britain left the ERM. It rose again in 1996 and stayed high for some time. The USA experienced a dramatic appreciation of its real exchange rate from 1980 to 1985, after which time it fell back. The real exchange rate of Germany fell in the early 1980s but then rose to the mid-1990s before easing again after Germany tied its currency with those of other euro zone members.

Source: Datastream.

in US dollars and will buy UK assets that earn higher interest. These capital inflows will lead to an increased demand for pounds on the foreign exchange market as investors exchange dollars for pounds to buy UK assets. The increased demand will in turn lead to an appreciation of sterling.

A relative rise in domestic interest rates will cause a capital inflow and an appreciation of the home currency.

When will the process stop? It will stop only when expected returns on UK and foreign assets are again roughly equalized; as long as the return on UK assets is above that on foreign assets, the capital inflows will continue, and the upward pressure on the pound will continue. The key is that the expected return includes not only the interest earnings, but also the expected gains or losses that might

arise because of changes in the exchange rate during the period of the investment. A foreign investor holding a UK asset will receive pounds when the asset is sold, and will at that time want to exchange pounds for foreign exchange. If the value of the pound has fallen, that will be a source of loss that has to be balanced against the interest income in assessing the net return on holding the asset.

Equilibrium in the above example occurs when the rise in value of the pound sterling in foreign exchange markets is large enough that investors will expect a future depreciation which just offsets the interest premium from investing funds in sterling-denominated assets.

Suppose investors believe that the PPP rate is £1 = $1.50, but as they rush to buy pounds to take advantage of higher

Box 29.4 'News' and the exchange rate

Foreign exchange markets are different from markets for consumer goods in that the vast bulk of trading takes place between professional foreign exchange dealers of banks. These dealers do not meet each other face to face. Rather, they conduct their transactions over the telephone, and the other party to the deal can be anywhere in the world. The structure of this market has one interesting implication: exchange rates respond to news. Let us see why this is and what it means.

Deals done by the professional dealers are all on a large scale, typically involving sums no smaller than £1 million and often very much larger. Each dealer tends to specialize in deals between a small number of currencies, say the pound sterling and the euro. But the dealers in all currencies for each bank sit close together, in a dealing room, so that they can hear what is going on in other markets. When a big news event breaks, anywhere in the world, this will be shouted out to all dealers in the room simultaneously.

Each dealer is also faced with several computer screens and many buttons which will connect him or her very quickly by telephone to other dealers. Speed of transaction can be very important if you are dealing with large volumes of money in a market that is continuously changing the prices quoted. Latest price quotes from around the world appear on the screens. However, contracts are agreed over the telephone (and nowadays are recorded in case of disagreement) and the paperwork follows within two days.

As exchange rates are closely related to expectations and to interest rates, the foreign exchange dealers have to keep an eye on all major news events affecting the economic environment. Since all the players in the foreign exchange markets are professionals, they are all well informed—not just about what has happened, but also about forecasts of what is likely to happen. Accordingly, the exchange rate, at any point in time, reflects not just history but also current expectations of what is going to happen in future.

As soon as some future event comes to be expected, it will be reflected in the current exchange rate. Events expected to happen soon will usually be given more weight than distant events. The only component in today's news that will cause the exchange rate to change is what was *not* expected to happen. Economists attribute the unforecastable component of news to a random error. It is random in the sense that it has no detectable pattern to it and it is unrelated to the information available before it happened.

Some events are clearly unforecastable, like an earthquake in Japan or a head of state having a heart attack. Others are the production of economic statistics for which forecasts have generally been published. In the latter case it is the deviation of announced figures from their forecast value that, if large, tends to move exchange rates.

Exchange rates are moved by news. Since news is random and unpredictable, changes in exchange rates will tend to be random.

Some people, observing the volatility of exchange rates, conclude that foreign exchange markets are inefficient. However, with well-informed professional players who have forward-looking expectations, new information is rapidly transmitted into prices. Volatility of exchange rates may, therefore, reflect the volatility of relevant, but unexpected, events around the world.

UK interest rates they drive the rate to, say, £1 = $1.75. (Because £1 now buys more dollars, the pound has appreciated, and because it takes more dollars to buy £1, the dollar has depreciated.) They do not believe that this rate will be sustained, and instead expect the pound to lose value in future periods. If foreign investors expect the pound to depreciate by 4 per cent per year, they will be indifferent between lending money in London and doing so in New York. The extra 4 per cent per year of interest that they earn in London is exactly offset by the 4 per cent that they expect to lose when they turn their money back into their own currency.

A policy that raises domestic interest rates above world levels will cause the external value of the domestic currency to appreciate enough to create an expected future depreciation that will be sufficient to offset the interest differential.

While interest differentials persist, the exchange rate must deviate from its equilibrium or PPP value; this is often referred to as exchange rate *overshooting*, because, at the time interest rates are raised, the exchange rate will jump beyond its long-run equilibrium level. This is illustrated in Figure 29.5.

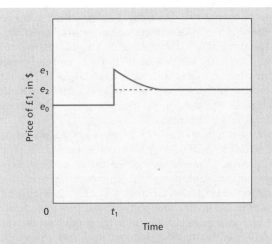

Figure 29.5 Exchange rate overshooting

The adjustment of exchange rates to policy changes often involves overshooting the long-run equilibrium. The figure illustrates how the exchange rate may move over time after a monetary policy tightening. The initial exchange rate is e_0. At time t_1 the central bank raises domestic interest rates and the exchange rate appreciates to e_1. Over time it then depreciates back towards the new long-run equilibrium level of e_2.

The argument that a rise in domestic interest rates will cause an appreciation of the home currency requires an important proviso. The interest rate rise has to occur with all other factors—especially long-run inflation expectations—held constant. If, for example, it was a rise in expectations of future inflation that triggered off events, the story would be quite different. In that case the interest rate rise would be responding to these expectations and to the consequent expectation of a long-run *depreciation* in the home currency. Now the change in the exchange rate would depend upon the size of the interest rate rise relative to the size of the expected long-run depreciation. In short, we need to be careful when applying economic analysis that works, *holding other things constant*, to a world where many things are changing simultaneously.

Implications of overshooting One policy implication of exchange rate theory is that a central bank that is seeking to use its monetary policy to attain its domestic policy targets may have to put up with large fluctuations in the exchange rate. Indeed, overshooting of the exchange rate in response to interest rate changes may be one of the most important elements of the monetary transmission mechanism.

In the case of a tightening of monetary policy, which raises interest rates, the overshooting (appreciation) of the pound beyond its PPP rate would put export- and import-competing industries under temporary but severe pressure from foreign competition, because UK goods would become expensive relative to imported goods. The resulting fall in demand for UK goods would open up a recessionary gap, thus providing a further mechanism by which the restrictive monetary policy would be transmitted to the rest of the economy. This is discussed further in Chapter 30.

The two recessions in the United Kingdom in the early 1980s and early 1990s illustrate this mechanism at work. Both were associated with tight monetary policy and an overvalued exchange rate, although, as there were worldwide recessions at roughly the same time, domestic factors cannot be the whole story.

In the run-up to the 1979–81 recession the pound had appreciated strongly. In 1979 interest rates were raised sharply and the pound appreciated further, as the Thatcher government implemented its commitment to control inflation by tight monetary policy. The high exchange rate meant that domestic producers became very uncompetitive, and so imports of cheaper foreign goods rose. Between late 1979 and early 1981, domestic manufacturing output fell by nearly 20 per cent and unemployment subsequently rose to over 3 million.

The high exchange rate cannot be blamed on tight monetary policy alone, because this was also the time when the

United Kingdom was emerging as an oil producer (and the price of oil had doubled in 1979). However, monetary policy—especially the sharp rise in interest rates in 1979—certainly contributed to the overshooting of sterling, and the extremely high exchange rate was undoubtedly a central element in the transmission mechanism between the monetary sector and the real economy.

The recession of 1990–2 was made worse by an attempt to maintain an overvalued exchange rate. From 1981 to 1988 the economy had seen a sustained recovery, and by 1988 inflationary pressures had built up. The government tightened monetary policy in the autumn of 1988 by raising interest rates. Higher interest rates created a higher foreign exchange value of the pound than would otherwise have happened. Then in October 1990 the pound was pegged in the European Exchange Rate Mechanism (ERM). The onset of recession and fall of inflation, which was evident from 1991, would normally have permitted a reduction in interest rates (and a subsequent decline in the foreign exchange value of sterling), but ERM membership prevented such a reduction. This was because of the need to keep interest rates consistent with those of other ERM members, notably Germany, in order to defend the exchange rate. In September 1992 sterling was forced to leave the ERM by speculative pressure which caused reserve losses (as illustrated in Figure 29.2). This permitted a sharp fall in UK interest rates, which was associated with a fall in the exchange rate. (Sterling fell from nearly $2.00 per pound in the summer of 1992 to around $1.50 after September, and stayed around that level for the next couple of years.) The fall in interest rates and in the exchange rate led fairly quickly to economic recovery by the spring of 1993.

The UK exchange rate experienced another period of overvaluation from mid-1996 until (at least) 2002. Initially it is likely that the strength of sterling was due to the uncertainty affecting other EU currencies (especially the Deutschmark) over prospects for creation of a single currency. Sterling was regarded as something of a 'safe haven' for investors of funds. This was reinforced by the extra credibility attached to the UK monetary policy regime once the Bank of England was given monetary policy independence in May 1997 (see Chapter 28). The strength of the pound in this period made UK exporters (and producers of import-competing goods) less competitive, and was associated with the large balance of trade deficit reported in Table 29.1.

A more detailed analysis of the role of the exchange rate in macroeconomic adjustment follows in the next chapter. What we have learned in this chapter is that the exchange rate is an essential element of the transmission mechanism that turns monetary policy shocks into real shocks in an open economy under flexible exchange rates.

SUMMARY

- International trade normally requires the exchange of the currency of one country for that of another. The major exception is trade within the euro zone. The exchange rate between two currencies is the amount of one currency that must be paid in order to obtain one unit of another currency.

The balance of payments

- Actual transactions among the firms, consumers, and governments of various countries are recorded in the balance of payments accounts. In these accounts any transaction that uses foreign exchange is recorded as a debit item, and any transaction that produces foreign exchange is recorded as a credit item. If all transactions are recorded, the sum of all credit items necessarily equals the sum of all debit items, because the foreign exchange that is bought must also have been sold.

- The two major categories in the balance of payments accounts are the current account and the capital and financial accounts. When we talk about a balance of payments surplus or deficit, we are normally referring to the current account balance alone. A balance on the current account must be matched by a balance on the capital and financial accounts of equal magnitude but opposite sign.

- There is nothing inherently good or bad about deficits or surpluses on the current account. Persistent deficits or surpluses involve a build-up or run-down of a country's net foreign assets.

The market for foreign exchange

- The demand for pounds arises from UK exports of goods and services, income payments from overseas, capital inflows, and the desire of foreign governments to use sterling assets as part of their reserves.

- The supply of pounds to purchase foreign currencies arises from UK imports of goods and services, income payments to overseas, capital outflows, and the desire of holders of sterling assets to decrease the size of their holdings.

- The demand curve for pounds is negatively sloped and the supply curve of pounds is positively sloped when the quantities demanded and supplied are plotted against the price of pounds, measured in terms of a foreign currency.

The determination of exchange rates

- When the authorities do not intervene in the foreign exchange market, there is a flexible exchange rate. Under fixed exchange rates, the authorities intervene in the foreign exchange market to maintain the exchange rate within a specified range. To do this, they must hold sufficient stocks of foreign exchange reserves.

- Under a flexible (or floating) exchange rate regime the exchange rate is market-determined by supply and demand for the currency.

- Fluctuations in exchange rates can be understood as fluctuations around a trend value that is determined by the purchasing power parity (PPP) rate. The PPP rate adjusts in response to differences in national inflation rates. Deviations from the PPP rate are related, among other things, to international differences in interest rates.

- Exchange rates tend to overshoot their long-run equilibrium in response to shocks. A relaxation of monetary policy, which lowers domestic interest rates, will cause the exchange rate to depreciate. However, it will tend to depreciate to a point from which it can then appreciate at a rate sufficient to compensate for the interest rate fall. A rise in domestic interest rates will tend to make the exchange rate overshoot in the opposite direction (upwards).

TOPICS FOR REVIEW

- Balance of trade in goods and services
- Balance of income payments and transfers
- Current and capital accounts
- Mercantilist views on the balance of trade and volume of trade
- Foreign exchange and exchange rates
- Appreciation and depreciation

- Sources of the demand for and supply of foreign exchange
- Effects on exchange rates of capital flows, inflation, interest rates, and expectations about exchange rates
- Fixed and flexible exchange rates
- Adjustable pegs and managed floats
- Purchasing power parity
- Exchange rate overshooting

DISCUSSION QUESTIONS

1   If PPP holds and the same basket of goods that is priced at $100 in the USA costs £80 in the UK, what will be the exchange rate between £ and $?

2   Starting from the position in question 1, if UK prices now rise by 10 per cent while US prices rise by 5 per cent, what will the new exchange rate be?

3   Where (if at all) do each of the following appear in the balance of payments accounts: (*a*) money earned by an Italian waiter in London that is sent to his family in Italy? (*b*) a purchase by a UK resident of a house in France financed entirely by a loan from a French bank? (*c*) a purchase of shares in an American company by a UK pension fund? (*d*) the cost of an airline flight from the UK to USA on a US airline? (Would it change if it were a UK airline?)

4   Does the balance of payments matter? If so, how?

5   What are the advantages and disadvantages of having a strong currency?

6   Why do floating exchange rates tend to overshoot?

7   'Capital outflows are a bad thing for the home economy as they mean that we are investing in jobs overseas.' Critically evaluate this statement.

8   Is it desirable to have a current account surplus in the balance of payments?

9   Would you expect PPP to hold in the short run?

Chapter 30

MACROECONOMIC POLICY IN AN OPEN ECONOMY

How is macroeconomic policy affected by international influences? Do domestic policy-makers have any power over their own economy, or is it the world economy that matters? How do macro policy choices change with the exchange rate regime adopted? Should stabilization policy be conducted at the world level? These are some of the questions we study in this chapter. In particular, you will learn that:

• Openness of the economy matters, as international factors directly affect real demand, world financial forces influence domestic financial markets, and the exchange rate regime affects the policy choices that are available.

• Monetary policy is powerless to affect domestic aggregate demand under a fixed exchange rate regime when capital is perfectly mobile.

• The exchange rate is an important element of the monetary transmission under a floating exchange rate regime.

• The effects of fiscal policy depend on the exchange rate regime and the monetary policy rule that is used.

• The long-run impact of fiscal policy is mainly on the trade balance.

• Financial and spending linkages between economies cause business cycles to have similar patterns in many major economies.

We now focus on how the exchange rate regime and the explicit incorporation of international financial capital flows affect the impact of fiscal and monetary policies. This will give us a much better grasp of how the transmission mechanism works in a world of globalized finance. An appendix to this chapter sets out in full how the UK Monetary Policy Committee (MPC) perceives the transmission mechanism of monetary policy to work in an economy that has a floating exchange rate and in which the MPC sets a specific interest rate in order to hit the inflation target. We shall also gain some understanding of the macroeconomies of those twelve EU countries that have become members of the euro currency system.

In Chapter 28 we expanded our model of the economy to incorporate monetary forces in the determination of aggregate demand. In that analysis we did make some allowances for openness, as net exports were a component of aggregate demand. Chapter 29 discussed the determinants of the exchange rate, and capital flows were an important part of that analysis. In this chapter we incorporate financial capital flows explicitly into our model and then go on to reconsider the impact of monetary and fiscal policies, under the alternative regimes of fixed and floating exchange rates.

Before proceeding, it might help to revise Chapter 28. It is also necessary to understand the IS/LM model, so it is advisable to read the appendix to Chapter 28 before proceeding (if you have not already done so). In Chapter 28 we neglected the role of external influences, such as capital flows and the exchange rate, in the adjustment process. Now they must be incorporated in order to complete our formal development of the short-run model of the macroeconomy.

Why does openness matter?

There are three main reasons why we have to take a much closer look at the interactions between our macro model and the rest of the world. First, while we have always had net exports in our model, we have not paid attention to all the possible implications of trade imbalances. Second, as we have mentioned several times in earlier chapters, financial markets have become more integrated around the world. This is often referred to as the globalization of financial markets, and Box 30.1 discusses some of its causes. The high international mobility of financial capital implies

Box 30.1 **The globalization of financial markets**

Technological innovations in communication and financial liberalization have led to a globalization of the financial services industry over the past few decades. Computers, satellite communication systems, reliable telephones with direct worldwide dialling, electronic mail, and fax machines have put people in instantaneous contact anywhere in the world.

As a result of these new technologies, borrowers and lenders can learn about market conditions anywhere in the world and then move their funds instantly in search of the best loan rates. Large firms need transaction balances only while banks in their area are open. Once banks close for the day in each area, the firms will not need these balances until the following day's reopening. Thus, the funds can be moved to another market, where they are used until it closes, and then moved to yet another market. Funds are thus free to move from, say, London to New York to Tokyo and back to London on a daily rotation. This is a degree of global sophistication that was inconceivable before the advent of the computer, when international communication was much slower and costlier than it is now. To facilitate the movement in and out of various national currencies, increasing amounts of bank deposits are denominated in foreign rather than domestic currencies.

One of the first developments in this movement towards globalization was the growth of the foreign currency markets in Europe in the 1960s. At first the main currency involved was the US dollar. (The market for dollar-denominated bank deposits and loans outside the United States was known as the Eurodollar market—not to be confused with the foreign exchange market in which the euro exchanges for the dollar today.) The progressive world-wide lifting of domestic interest rate ceilings and other capital market restrictions that occurred in the 1980s led to a further globalization of financial markets. Particularly important was the abolition of

exchange controls in country after country. The United Kingdom abolished its exchange controls in 1979, Japan did so in 1980, France and Italy in 1989, Spain in 1991, Portugal and Ireland in 1992, and Greece in 1994. Once such restrictions were abolished, the wholesale money markets integrated with the international money markets very quickly. This is because sophisticated borrowers and lenders dealing with large amounts of money have an incentive to shop around for the best terms.

The increasing sophistication of information transfer has also led to a breakdown of the high degree of specialization that had characterized financial markets in earlier decades. When information was difficult to obtain and analyse, an efficient division of labour called for a host of specialist institutions, each with expertise in a narrow range of transactions. New developments in communications technology created economies of scale that led to the integration of various financial operations within one firm. For example, in many countries banks have moved into the markets where securities are traded, while many security-trading firms have begun to offer a range of banking services. As the scale of such integrated firms increases, they find it easier to extend their operations geographically as well as functionally. The introduction of the euro in 1999 added further impetus to globalization as it increased the integration of EU financial markets and created a currency that has become an important international instrument.

The heavy government intervention in domestic capital markets and government control over international capital flows that characterized the 1950s and 1960s is no longer possible. International markets are just too sophisticated. Globalization is here to stay, and, by removing domestic restrictions and exchange controls, governments in advanced countries were only bowing to the inevitable.

---

that money markets in one country are influenced by what happens in the rest of the world's financial markets. Third, the exchange rate regime matters for the conduct of monetary policy because it affects the possibilities for *arbitrage* between domestic and overseas financial markets (and therefore the link between domestic and overseas interest rates). **Arbitrage** involves buying where a price is low and selling where it is high, in order to make profit. The process of arbitrage tends to drive prices together in different locations.

We need to expand a little on each of these three factors before we proceed to an explicit analysis of the macro model in which capital flows are included and explicit attention is paid to the trade balance.

Net exports

Our macro model, from Chapter 24 onwards, included net exports, *NX*. The first thing we learned about the *NX* function was that it is negatively sloped. This means that net exports fall as GDP rises—because induced imports rise while autonomous exports are constant.

We also discovered that the net export function will shift if there is an exogenous (autonomous) change in export demand, and if there is a change in the domestic price level relative to foreign prices (caused either by an exchange rate change with a given price level, or a price level change with a given exchange rate). An autonomous rise in exports increases net exports (shifts the *NX* function upwards for each level of GDP—see Figures 24.2 and 24.3 on pages 431–2). A rise in domestic relative prices reduces net exports (shifts the *NX* function down and changes its slope).

When we studied how fiscal and monetary policy can be used to speed up the adjustment of GDP back to equilibrium (see pages 507–9), we ignored any repercussions that might be induced by changes in the balance of trade. We can no longer do so. We now analyse the impacts of monetary and fiscal policies taking explicit account of the forces that are put in play by the change in the trade balance as GDP changes. The nature of these effects is influenced by the degree of mobility of financial capital and by the exchange rate regime. We will focus on the case of highly mobile financial capital, because this conforms most closely to the modern world.

Mobile capital

Recall that, when we talk about capital flows in the context of the balance of payments, we are *not* talking about imports and exports of capital goods, such as machine tools and heavy equipment. Rather, we are talking about trade in assets and liabilities, such as shares and bonds, or lending by banks in one country to customers in another.

Capital flows matter for two reasons. First, as we saw in Chapter 29, net capital flows must equal (with opposite sign) the current account balance. Since this relationship is true by definition, it must always hold. It is important to realize, however, that changes affecting capital flows have implications for net exports (possibly via exchange rate changes), just as shifts affecting net exports have implications for the capital account. We will be more specific about these linkages below.

The second reason why capital flows matter for the macro model is that they influence the domestic interest rate. If everyone is free to borrow and lend both domestically and internationally, they will borrow where the interest rate is lowest and lend where it is highest. Mobile capital tends to drive the domestic interest rate towards the level of interest rates in world markets. In effect, the domestic economy is close to a price-taker in world financial markets.

We will examine how capital mobility affects our model below. The key point to notice now is that, in an open economy with mobile financial capital, we cannot analyse the determination of the domestic interest rate using domestic demand and supply forces alone. Changes in the domestic interest rate brought about by domestic shocks and policy responses will generate reactions through international capital flows and net exports that will inevitably complicate the picture.

It may seem that what we are saying here conflicts with the fact that domestic monetary authorities set interest rates. How can they also be set in world financial markets? These statements are not inconsistent. Monetary authorities set a specific nominal interest rate for short-term borrowing in money markets, but, as we shall see below, their freedom of manoeuvre depends on the exchange regime in which they operate. With a pegged exchange rate, they have no choice in the interest rate they set. Under floating exchange rates they have more discretion, but world market forces also matter.

In our model developed above, we have only one interest rate. However, in the real world there are many interest rates for loans of different type and duration. Monetary authorities set short-term *nominal* rates, but world markets set longer-term *real* rates.

We continue to assume a simple financial structure in our model, but this need not stop us making statements about financial forces in the real world, which is more complicated.

The exchange rate regime

The exchange rate regime matters because it determines which variables are free to adjust. Fixing the exchange rate ties down other variables as well as the exchange rate. Fixed exchange rates tie together the value of domestic and foreign money, which implies that the domestic price level cannot deviate from the foreign price level in the long run.

Fixed exchange rates, with mobile capital, also tie domestic and foreign interest rates together because there is no exchange rate uncertainty. In such circumstances the domestic monetary authorities have no discretion in setting the domestic interest rates. The money supply is endogenously determined by demand, at whatever interest rate is dictated by world money markets. This explains why the UK authorities had no discretion to lower interest rates (as would have been dictated by internal considerations alone) during October 1990–September 1992, when the UK was a member of the ERM. It is also relevant to understanding the behaviour of the economies of the twelve members of the euro zone after January 1999. For these countries there is only one interest rate, set by the European Central Bank, so monetary policy is the same for all.

We shall see that in general, the monetary authorities of nations with independent currencies can fix any one (but only one) of the interest rate, the exchange rate, and the money supply. Once they choose one of these, the other two become endogenous. Fixing the exchange rate is one possible monetary policy, but, having done this, the authorities cannot also control either the interest rate or the money supply. Most major countries (outside the euro zone) set short-term interest rates and let the money supply and the exchange rate adjust.

Under floating exchange rates, much of the adjustment to shocks comes through exchange rate changes and the resulting effect on the relative prices of domestic and foreign goods (and assets). In contrast, under fixed exchange rates much more of the adjustment to shocks is worked out via aggregate demand, money stock, and output changes at given relative prices. These differences will become clearer as we work through specific examples below.

We now turn to a discussion of how the macro model is modified by the inclusion of capital flows, and how the presence of capital flows alters the impact of monetary and fiscal policies.

Macro policy in a world with perfect capital mobility

As we have seen, financial flows in the balance of payments accounts include net cross-border sales of a wide variety of domestic and foreign assets—shares and bonds, etc. To keep things as simple as possible, we assume that there are just two types of asset: domestic bonds and foreign bonds. Domestic bonds are denominated in pounds sterling and foreign bonds are denominated in US dollars. (Which foreign currency we select is not critical; in our model it represents the rest of the world.)

Capital flows into the home economy when asset-holders switch from foreign bonds to domestic bonds. Capital flows out of the home economy when asset-holders switch from domestic bonds to foreign bonds. The process of switching involves sales of one currency for the other, so it creates a demand or supply of foreign exchange in the foreign exchange market.

An important assumption we make throughout is that net exports (the goods and services balance) and the current account of the balance of payments are identical. In effect, this means that we are ignoring the net income and transfers components of the current account.[1] This is a reasonable assumption for the United Kingdom in 2001; as Table 29.1 on page 523 shows, the balance of these was around 0.2 per cent of GDP in that year. Even if this item were not so small, it could be ignored for analytical purposes, because it does not vary much in response to short-run changes in exchange rates or GDP.

In order to incorporate capital flows into the macro model, we need to use the *IS* and *LM* curves discussed on pages 515–21, so it is worth reviewing the derivation of those curves. Recall that the *IS* and *LM* curves are just a convenient way of showing how the monetary sector interacts with the determinants of aggregate spending to determine the position of the aggregate demand curve.

The macro model with capital flows

Two relationships must be kept in mind when incorporating capital flows into our model. First, since net capital flows must be of equal size and opposite sign to the current account balance of payments surplus or deficit, an actual capital inflow implies a current account deficit of equal size. Second, the foreign demand for domestic bonds depends upon the differential in interest rates between domestic and foreign bonds.

We need to make some assumption about how sensitive to this interest differential demand for domestic bonds will be. The analysis of Chapter 28 implicitly assumed immobile financial capital, so that there would be no switching between domestic and foreign bonds at any feasible interest rate. Now we make the opposite assumption that foreign demand for domestic bonds is perfectly elastic with respect to the interest differential. In effect, we are assuming that domestic and foreign bonds are perfect substitutes.[2] This is only one of several possible assumptions, but it is closer to the realities of the modern world of globalized finance and highly mobile international capital than the assumption of perfect immobility. Hence it is a reasonable simplifying assumption to make in the UK context, and also for most other major countries, though it will be inappropriate for economies that still have official exchange controls affecting capital flows.

Perfect substitutability between domestic bonds and foreign bonds is called perfect capital mobility. Its implications are illustrated in Figure 30.1, which shows the *IS/LM* diagram explained in the appendix to Chapter 28, with the addition of a horizontal line labelled *BB*. Points on the *BB* line represent combinations of the interest rate and GDP for which there is equality between the current account balance of payments and capital flows. It joins short-run balance of payments equilibrium points. Its horizontal slope reflects the assumption that capital is perfectly mobile. If the return on domestic bonds were slightly higher than that on foreign bonds, there would be an immediate huge demand for them. This would drive up the price of domestic bonds and drive down their yield. Similarly, if domestic bonds had a yield below foreign bonds, holders would sell them to buy foreign bonds. This would drive their price down and their yield up. The result is that the domestic interest rate must equal the world interest rate i^*.[3] The intuition is that any two commodities that are perfect substitutes must have a common price (because they are, in effect, one commodity).

It is important to notice that the *BB* curve does not represent points for which the current account balance is zero. Indeed, for a given net export function, the current account balance deteriorates as we move to the right (GDP increases). If this involves a deficit, however, borrowing from abroad at the going world rate of interest can finance this. Thus, any point on *BB* for which there is a current

---

[1] This assumption is equivalent to assuming that GNI is equal to GDP.

[2] Since corporate bonds vary in riskiness, at best there will be perfect substitutability only between the bonds issued by governments of major industrial countries, as these have virtually no default risk.

[3] If capital flows were imperfect, the *BB* line would be positively sloped because net exports decrease as GDP increases, and the higher capital flows required to finance an increasing current account deficit could be attracted only at increasing interest rates.

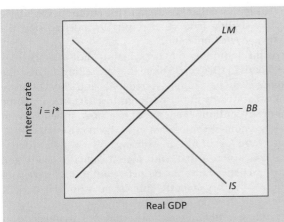

Figure 30.1 The macroeconomic implications of perfect capital mobility

With perfect capital mobility, the domestic interest rate must be equal to the foreign interest rate in equilibrium. The *BB* line shows the combinations of interest rates and GDP for which a current account surplus (deficit) equals the associated capital outflow (inflow). The *BB* line is drawn horizontally at the point where the domestic interest rate is equal to the foreign rate *i**. The shape of *BB* means that any size of current account deficit can be financed by borrowing at the going interest rate on world capital markets.

account imbalance will also be associated with an equal and opposite capital account imbalance. The horizontal shape of *BB* reflects the perfectly elastic supply curve of capital, as discussed above.

How can we be sure that the *BB* line cuts the *IS* and *LM* curves at their intersection? The answer is that initially it may not do so; but if it does not, there will be endogenous adjustments of exchange rates and/or the money supply. These will shift either the *IS* or the *LM* curve (or both) until all three have a common intersection. We will shortly be discussing cases where policy changes create such non-intersections, and we will then see in detail how such adjustment works. The exact process depends upon the exchange rate regime in operation as well as the monetary policy regime.

The implication that domestic and foreign interest rates are equal requires further comment. Recall that domestic and foreign bonds are denominated in different currencies. When exchange rates are fixed (and expected to remain fixed), this causes no complications. The comparative yield is given by the interest differential. Perfect capital mobility does indeed require exact equality of domestic and foreign interest rates—as it would also do for risk-free bonds within the euro zone.

However, under floating exchange rates, where exchange rates are expected to change, the position is more complicated. Here there can be a differential in nominal interest rates that will be equal to the expected rate of change of the

exchange rate. This effect is associated with exchange rate overshooting, and was discussed in Chapter 29 and illustrated in Figure 29.5 on page 537. Suppose, for example, that holders of bonds expect sterling to depreciate against the US dollar by 5 per cent over the next year. If the yield on US bonds is 10 per cent per year, they will need a yield of about 15 per cent per year on sterling bonds to compensate for the expected currency depreciation. In this case the expected returns would be equal, but the nominal interest rates would not.[4]

This means that, when we discuss floating exchange rates, points on the horizontal *BB* line represent the full equilibrium, when there are no further expectations of exchange rate changes—but the economy can deviate from this line during the adjustment process. With fixed exchange rates, on the other hand, the economy must be on it all the time.

Perfect capital mobility means that with fixed exchange rates the domestic interest rate must always equal the foreign interest rate. With floating exchange rates any interest differential must equal the expected exchange rate change. This will be zero in full equilibrium.

The explicit addition of capital flows to our model introduces a new adjustment mechanism that reconciles differences in the desired trade surplus and desired net capital flows via either official reserve changes (under fixed exchange rates) or exchange rate changes (under floating rates). We will explain this using specific examples.

Policy changes with fixed exchange rates

Now we can trace through the effects of monetary and fiscal policy changes in a model that allows for perfect capital mobility. Of particular interest will be the new predictions that follow from the addition of capital flows to the model.

To make it easier to understand how the adjustment mechanism works with capital flows included, initially we consider the effects of policy changes starting from a position of full equilibrium, where $Y = Y^*$. Of course, policy changes would normally be made to correct a disequilibrium that had been caused by some exogenous shock. If we start our analysis from disequilibrium, however, there can be many different reasons for disequilibrium (that is, shocks from many different sources), and the effect of policy changes may depend upon what has caused the

---

[4] The exact expression that must hold for expected yields on the two bonds denominated in different currencies to be equal is: $(1 + i) = (1 + i^*)(e_t/e_{t+1})$, where i is the yield on UK bonds (expressed as a decimal, so 10 per cent is 0.1), i^* is the yield on foreign bonds, e_t is the exchange rate ($ per £) at the beginning of the holding period, and e_{t+1} is the exchange rate expected to obtain at the end of the holding period.

deviation of Y from Y^*. When we start at Y^*, there should be no surprise to find that eventually we return to Y^*. What matters is to understand how the adjustment mechanism of the economy works when perfect capital mobility is assumed, and how the exchange rate regime affects this. We will discuss how the result might change if we start with disequilibrium later. We first discuss a fixed exchange rate regime.

Monetary policy

Starting with an economy in full equilibrium, we assume that the monetary authorities relax the monetary policy stance by reducing the domestic interest rate. The analysis, which is shown in Figure 30.2, is simple under a fixed exchange rate regime.

The policy change, if it could be made to stick, would shift the LM curve to the right (because a lower interest rate would lead to a higher money stock, as discussed in Chapter 28), which in turn would shift the AD curve to the right. However, we do not bother to translate this shift into an aggregate demand shift, because it will have to be reversed immediately. As soon as domestic interest rates dip slightly below world rates, there will be a massive sale of domestic bonds. This will create an excess supply of sterling in the foreign exchange market (because holders are selling sterling bonds and converting the proceeds into

dollars to buy dollar bonds), and the authorities will have to buy sterling (and sell reserves) in order to stop the exchange rate from falling.

As the authorities buy back sterling, just as when they sell bonds in Chapter 28 (here they are selling dollars), the domestic money supply is reduced, and the LM curve shifts back to its initial position. In effect, the domestic monetary authorities are forced to abandon their attempt to lower domestic interest rates by the massive capital outflows (and loss of foreign exchange reserves) that follow. The conclusion is that, with perfect capital mobility and fixed exchange rates, the monetary authorities have control over neither domestic interest rates nor the stock of money. If they do not set the domestic interest rates at the ruling world interest rate, they are swamped with massive inflows or outflows of financial capital (bond sales or purchases). Thus, perfect capital mobility means that it is impossible to use monetary policy to influence real economic activity under fixed exchange rates. For exactly the same reasons, there cannot be independent monetary policies in the member states of the euro zone. The ECB can change the interest rate for all member countries, but no single country can change its own interest rate. (Indeed, there is only one interest rate for all member countries.)

Monetary policy under fixed exchange rates and perfect capital mobility cannot exert any independent influence over real economic activity.

Fiscal policy

The analysis of what happens when fiscal policy changes is more complicated than in the case of a monetary policy change. It is also very different from events in the absence of capital flows. The course of events is illustrated in Figure 30.3.

Again, we start with the economy in full equilibrium. We need also to clarify what the monetary authorities are doing. As we explained above, the monetary authorities cannot set *both* the domestic interest rate *and* the exchange rate. Since we are studying the fixed exchange rate case here, we must temporarily drop the assumption that the monetary authorities are fixing the domestic interest rate. Rather, the monetary policy is pegging the exchange rate, and the interest rate is determined by world interest rates.

The assumed fiscal policy change is an increase in government spending. The initial effect of this increase is to shift the IS curve to the right. With a given initial nominal money stock (given LM curve), this will put upward pressure on domestic interest rates. However, even the smallest rise in domestic interest rates generates a capital inflow (foreign demand for domestic bonds) and creates excess demand for sterling in the foreign exchange markets. To stop the exchange rate rising, the monetary authorities have to sell sterling and buy foreign currency. These sales

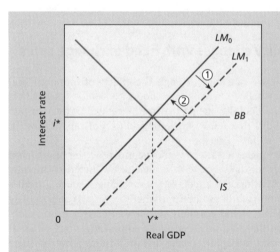

Figure 30.2 Monetary policy with fixed exchange rates and perfect capital mobility

Monetary policy is powerless to influence economic activity under fixed exchange rates and perfect capital mobility. An attempted cut in domestic interest rates increases the money supply and shifts the LM curve to the right from LM_0 to LM_1. However, the smallest fall in domestic interest rates causes a massive desired capital outflow. This puts downward pressure on the exchange rate. The monetary authorities are forced to buy sterling immediately in order to stop the exchange rate falling, and the LM curve shifts back to its original position, LM_0.

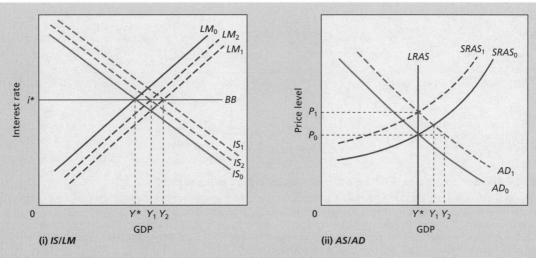

Figure 30.3 Fiscal policy with fixed exchange rates and perfect capital mobility

Starting from full equilibrium, an increase in government spending creates a significant stimulus to real activity in the short run, but in the long run it leads to a higher price level and a current account deficit. The increase in government spending shifts the *IS* curve from IS_0 to IS_1 in part (i). With a given money supply, this puts upward pressure on domestic interest rates. The slightest rise in domestic interest rates causes a massive capital inflow, which puts upward pressure on the exchange rate. To stop the exchange rate rising, the monetary authorities sell sterling in the foreign exchange market. This increases the money supply and shifts the *LM* curve to the right, from LM_0 to LM_1. The combined effect of the *IS* and *LM* curves shifting is that *AD* shifts right, from AD_0 to AD_1, as shown in part (ii).

The increase in aggregate demand causes GDP to increase from Y^* to Y_1 in the short run, and there is a small initial increase in the price level. (This price level rise shifts the *IS* and *LM* curves slightly leftward to IS_2 and LM_2 so that they intersect at Y_1 rather than Y_2.) Net exports become negative. In the long run inflationary pressure causes the price level to rise to P_1 as the *SRAS* curve shifts up to $SRAS_1$ and GDP returns to Y^*. However, the sustained rise in the price level (for given foreign prices) causes a permanent trade deficit, which is equal to the budget deficit. At price level P_1 the real money supply has fallen, so the *LM* curve shifts back to LM_0. The higher price of domestic goods causes net exports to shift downwards, so *IS* also shifts back to its original position, IS_0.

of sterling increase the supply of money and shift the *LM* curve to the right.

Thus, the initial rightward shift of the *IS* curve has been reinforced by a rightward shift of the *LM* curve. The *AD* curve shifts to the right as a result of each of these shifts. The combined effect is shown in part (ii) of the figure. This is a bigger shift of *AD* than would have resulted from a shift in the *IS* curve alone. Indeed, the size of the horizontal shift of *AD* is equal to the full value of the simple (open economy) multiplier, because there is no negative feedback (via higher interest rates) from the monetary sector. This comes about because interest rates cannot rise, so the authorities have to increase the money supply to avoid an exchange rate appreciation.

This is not the end of the story. The increase in aggregate demand shifts the aggregate demand curve to intersect the initial short-run aggregate supply curve at a level of GDP well above its potential level. The resulting inflationary gap causes a short-term boom in the economy, and real GDP rises temporarily above its potential level.

The inflationary gap, once created, puts upward pressure on the domestic price level. Initially this is felt only in output prices. The increase in output prices, combined with

the increase in real GDP, creates a trade deficit. The current account balance deteriorates because (induced) imports increase with domestic income. The price level rise reinforces this increase because (with a fixed exchange rate and given foreign prices) domestic goods become more expensive relative to foreign goods. Thus, there is a change in the import propensity and a fall in net exports. Indeed, it is this price level rise that moves the economy back up the *AD* curve and reduces the impact on GDP, compared with the full impact of the simple multiplier (as measured by the horizontal shift in *AD*).

In the longer term, inflationary forces pass through to input prices, and the short-run aggregate supply curve shifts up to the left. This raises the price level further, as the economy moves back up the *AD* curve and GDP returns to its potential level. The higher price level reduces the real money supply, and so the *LM* curve shifts back leftwards to its initial position. It also further increases the trade deficit, and this downward shift in net exports also shifts the *IS* curve back leftwards to its original position.

Thus, instead of crowding out investment (as would happen in the absence of capital flows), the increase in government spending has led to a trade deficit of equal value.

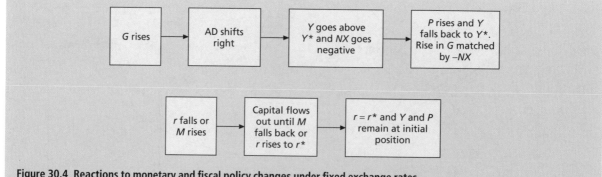

Figure 30.4 Reactions to monetary and fiscal policy changes under fixed exchange rates

Monetary policy is powerless under fixed exchange rates but fiscal policy is not. Any change in monetary policy generates capital flow and a change in reserves that force the monetary authorities to reverse their actions. A fiscal policy change shifts the *IS* and *AD* curves to the right and takes GDP above potential. The extra spending in the economy makes domestic spending greater than domestic output so net exports become negative. The excess of output over potential starts to put upward pressure on domestic prices. As prices rise, *Y* falls back to *Y**, and at the new equilibrium *Y* is equal to *Y**, the price level is higher, and the increase in *G* is just equal to the (negative) increase in net exports.

(Real GDP returns to its original level, but real national spending has risen by the amount of extra government spending. The excess of national spending over national output is equal to the trade deficit.)

An increase in government spending (starting at full equilibrium), with fixed exchange rates and perfect capital mobility, creates a short-run economic boom, but the long-run effect is an increase in the domestic price level and a trade deficit.

This trade deficit will be equal to the government budget deficit if the initial position was one of budget balance and trade balance. Notice also that the mechanism that brought about the trade deficit was a rise in domestic prices (relative to foreign prices). This is equivalent to a rise in the real exchange rate, even though the nominal exchange rate is fixed. However, in this case there has been no crowding out of investment because fiscal policy is powerless to influence interest rates. In effect, domestic investment can be financed at the going world interest rate. The trade deficit is matched by a capital inflow (foreign purchases of domestic bonds) of equal size.

This is the end of the story in our model, but it cannot be the end of the story in reality. We have an equilibrium in which there is a current account deficit on the balance of payments and, therefore, continuing capital inflows. The domestic economy is borrowing from the rest of the world to finance the excess of spending over output.

If this borrowing finances current consumption (government consumption in this case), the wealth of the economy will be falling (relative to the initial trend position), and this cannot go on for ever. At some point the wealth effects will lead to either a shift in domestic spending (downward) or a reversal of government policy. (The

government cannot build up infinite debt, and any financing problems may cause reserve losses.) The modelling of such wealth effects is beyond the scope of this book. Readers should merely note that some further adjustment must happen.

However, if the borrowing finances real investment (or if an equivalent amount of real investment takes place anyway), the story could be quite different. If the return on real investment were greater than the interest rate on foreign borrowing, this economy would be increasing its wealth over time. So long as investment returns continued to exceed interest costs, this position could be sustained and potential GDP would be growing over time. Therefore, one cannot assume that a current account balance of payments deficit is always undesirable. This reinforces the point first stated in Chapter 29.

A summary of the main reactions to monetary and fiscal policy under fixed rates is shown in Figure 30.4.

Policy changes with floating exchange rates

We now turn to the analysis of policy changes under a regime of floating exchange rates. This is the current regime in the United Kingdom, as it is for most major countries (where the euro zone is counted as one country), so this analysis is the one that is appropriate for analysing the effects of macroeconomic policy in the major economies today. It represents the culmination of all our efforts to build a macroeconomic model. We return to a framework in which the monetary authorities set the interest rate (as the exchange rate is set by market forces in a floating exchange rate regime).

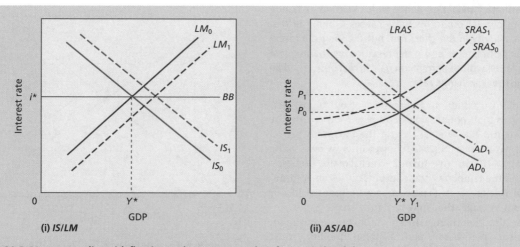

Figure 30.5 Monetary policy with floating exchange rates and perfect capital mobility

Starting at full equilibrium, a monetary loosening causes an output boom in the short run but in the long run causes only higher prices and currency depreciation. The LM curve shifts to the right. Any fall in the domestic interest rate causes the exchange rate to depreciate to a point from which it is expected to appreciate. This involves overshooting and a fall in the real exchange rate. This fall in the real exchange rate shifts the net export function upwards, so, as part (i) shows, there is a shift in the IS curve from IS_0 to IS_1 accompanying the initial shift in the LM curve from LM_0 to LM_1. The combined effect of these two shifts on aggregate demand is shown in part (ii) as the shift from AD_0 to AD_1.

The increase in aggregate demand creates an inflationary gap. GDP increases from Y^* to Y_1 in the short run, and the price level starts to rise to the level indicated by the intersection of AD_1 and $SRAS_0$. Eventually inflationary pressure works through to input prices, and the short-run aggregate supply curve shifts upwards to $SRAS_1$. The price level rises to P_1, and GDP falls back to Y^*. The LM curve shifts back to LM_0 as the rise in price level reduces the real money supply. The IS curve shifts back to IS_0 as higher domestic prices raise the relative price of domestic goods and the net export function shifts downwards. The long-run outcome is an increase in prices but the same real GDP.

Monetary policy

Again, we start with a relaxation of domestic monetary policy in the form of a reduction in the interest rate initiated by the domestic monetary authorities from a position of full equilibrium, as illustrated in Figure 30.5. This shifts the LM curve downward to the right (because the authorities buy bonds and increase the money stock in order to lower the market interest rate).

The fall in domestic interest rates, with perfect capital mobility, would normally cause a massive capital outflow. However, since the exchange rate is floating, the emergence of an excess supply of sterling causes an immediate drop in the exchange rate. It drops to the point where it is expected to appreciate at a rate sufficient to compensate for the lower domestic interest rate; in other words, it overshoots its long-run equilibrium in a downward direction. We discussed this notion of overshooting in Chapter 29, pages 535–8.

The fall in the nominal exchange rate also represents a fall in the real exchange rate, because the domestic price level does not change quickly, while the exchange rate has fallen instantaneously. So the relative price of domestic goods has fallen. This leads to an upward shift in the net export function, which causes a shift of the IS curve to the right. The combined effect of the rightward shifts of the LM and IS curves causes a rightward shift in the AD curve.

The increase in aggregate demand takes GDP beyond its potential level and creates an inflationary gap. In the short run the economy experiences a boom in output and a small increase in the domestic price level. This increase in prices reduces the real money supply slightly and also offsets a little the upward shift in net exports; so both the IS and LM curves shift back a fraction relative to their new positions. However, the full adjustment takes place in the longer term, when inflationary pressure works through into input costs and the short-run aggregate supply curve shifts upwards.

As the price level rises to its long-run equilibrium, the real money supply returns to its original level, so the LM curve shifts back to its initial position, reversing the initial interest rate fall. Also, the real exchange rate returns to its initial position (the price level rises in proportion to the long-run currency depreciation), so net exports shift back to where they started. Notice, however, that during the adjustment period the current account has been in surplus because of the lower real exchange rate (and therefore there have been capital outflows), and so there has been an accumulation of net foreign assets (or a rundown of foreign liabilities). This accumulation has occurred because national spending has been less than national output during the adjustment process (i.e. there has been a trade surplus). The current account is back in balance at the long-run equilibrium.

An expansionary monetary policy under floating exchange rates with perfect capital mobility causes a boom in real economic activity in the short run, but the long-run effect is a higher price level and a depreciation of the nominal exchange rate, with no permanent gain in real output and an unchanged real exchange rate.

Although we assume in the context of our model that GDP returns to its potential level, in practice there may be some long-run real effects. During the transition period national wealth has increased. Lower interest rates cause a temporary rise in investment, which creates domestic assets, and the temporary trade surplus causes an accumulation of foreign assets. These effects are ignored in our model, but in reality they may be significant.

Notice also the change in the monetary adjustment mechanism when there is perfect capital mobility. In the absence of capital flows the monetary expansion creates a desired current account deficit, whereas in the presence of capital flows it creates an exchange rate depreciation, which results in an actual current account surplus and a capital outflow. In the long run the outcome is the same (a higher price level and proportional depreciation of the currency with the same real GDP), but external payments adjustment during the transition to full equilibrium is quite different.

Fiscal policy

The case of a fiscal policy expansion under floating exchange rates with perfect capital mobility is illustrated in Figure 30.6. Again, we take as our policy change an increase in government spending at full equilibrium.

The increase in government spending shifts the *IS* curve to the right. What happens next depends on what the monetary authorities do. We examine two cases. In the first the authorities adjust the domestic interest rate upwards in order to maintain a constant money stock; and in the second the authorities hold the domestic interest rate fixed by buying bonds and increasing the money stock.

Fixed money stock With a given money supply (fixed *LM* curve), a rightward shift of the *IS* curve, resulting from the expansionary fiscal policy, puts upward pressure on domestic interest rates. Any rise in domestic interest rates creates massive desired capital inflows and thereby puts upward pressure on the exchange rate. The exchange rate immediately appreciates to a point from which it can be expected to depreciate at a rate equal to the interest differential.

The exchange rate appreciation, for a given initial price level, also appreciates the real exchange rate, which means that domestic goods become more expensive than foreign goods. This rise in the relative price of domestic goods shifts the net export function downwards, and therefore also shifts the *IS* curve back towards its original position. A

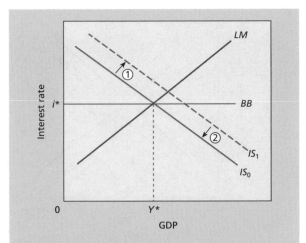

Figure 30.6 Fiscal policy with floating exchange rates and perfect capital mobility

Starting at full equilibrium, a fiscal expansion leads to a currency appreciation which crowds out an equivalent volume of net exports, causing a current account deficit but little or no stimulus to GDP. The initial increase in government spending shifts the *IS* curve to the right from *IS₀* to *IS₁*. But the resulting appreciation of the exchange rate (real and nominal) shifts the net export function downwards, which shifts the *IS* curve back to the left.

current account balance of payments deficit results, which is matched by net capital inflows.

There is ambiguity about the precise course of aggregate demand in the short run. The increase in government spending shifts *AD* to the right, but the downward shift in net exports shifts it back to the left. On balance, the likely outcome is that it will remain roughly at its initial position. The factors affecting the adjustment of net exports to an exchange rate change are discussed in Box 30.2. In any event the effect on real GDP, even in the short run, may well be negligible.

The long-run outcome is that there is a trade deficit that matches the government budget deficit. There is also a permanent increase in the real exchange rate, brought about by a sustained appreciation of the nominal exchange rate, though less than the appreciation achieved during the overshooting phase. There is a significant difference between short-run adjustment to a fiscal policy expansion under floating exchange rates with perfect capital mobility and the case with no capital flows. With no capital flows the increase in *G* creates an inflationary gap and a currency depreciation, the domestic price level rises, and interest rates rise, thereby crowding out investment. With capital flows the same increase in the relative price of domestic output is brought about by exchange rate appreciation, but there is no interest rate rise, and no sustained crowding-out of investment. There is, however, a trade deficit that matches the budget deficit.

Box 30.2 The J-curve

In this chapter we consider what happens when there is a change in monetary or fiscal policy under fixed or floating exchange rates. We do not ask what happens under a fixed exchange rate regime if there is a discrete devaluation. Under such a devaluation there is a sudden fall in the exchange rate at which the currency is pegged.

Devaluations usually occur when a persistent current account deficit is causing a serious drain on official reserves. Their purpose is to reduce the deficit and thereby reduce outflows of official international reserves. However, the effect on the current account is often not immediately positive. A common pattern is for the current account first to deteriorate further but later to improve. This pattern is known as the J-curve because of the shape of the curve the current account traces over time. The figure plots the path of the current account over time, starting in deficit. Devaluation at time t_0 initially makes the deficit worse, but eventually it leads to a surplus after a lag of perhaps two years.

The reason for the initial deterioration in the current account is that volumes of imports and exports take time to adjust to the new relative prices. Devaluation makes domestic goods cheaper than foreign goods, and if volumes did not change at all the domestic currency value of exports would stay the same but the domestic currency value of imports would rise (because their price has gone up in domestic currency terms).

It is only when the volumes of imports and exports adjust more than in proportion to the change in relative goods prices that the current account of the balance of payments improves. After the 1967 devaluation of sterling, it took between eighteen months and two years for the current account to move into surplus.

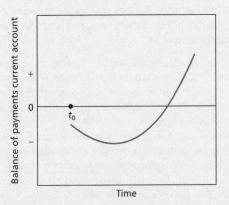

The J-curve is also applicable to a world of floating exchange rates after a sudden sustained exchange rate change. It helps us to understand that it takes many months, if not years, for the trade account fully to adjust to such exchange rate changes. Thus, when the UK left the ERM in September 1992 its currency devalued by about 20 per cent against the US dollar, and the effects of this took several years to work through. When exchange rates change in small steps, the economic adjustments are still there, but they are harder to detect. Once the exchange rate is endogenous, of course, it becomes virtually impossible to determine the direction of causation—the exchange rate and the balance of payment are jointly determined by many other factors.

Again, this cannot be the end of the story, because there is ongoing borrowing by the government and increasing indebtedness to foreigners. Thus, wealth effects similar to those we discussed in the context of fiscal policy arise under fixed exchange rates. The big difference, however, is that under floating exchange rates a fiscal expansion, holding M constant, creates a minimal stimulus to real GDP, whereas under fixed rates a fiscal expansion leads to a short-run boom.

An expansionary fiscal policy, under floating exchange rates, has little impact on real GDP in the short run when the money stock is fixed; rather, it causes an exchange rate appreciation and a trade deficit. In the long run there is a permanent appreciation of the real exchange rate, and the government budget deficit is equal to the trade deficit.

Fixed interest rate The response to a fiscal policy change is somewhat different if the monetary authorities maintain a fixed interest rate, rather than raising rates in order to keep the money supply constant. Indeed, the outcome is initially similar to that illustrated in Figure 30.5. The fiscal policy expansion shifts the IS curve to the right, and the money supply increase that results from the authorities' attempts to keep the interest rate from rising shifts the LM curve to the right. Thus, the AD curve shifts to the right and GDP goes from Y^* to Y_1, as shown in Figure 30.5(ii). This creates an inflationary gap, and wage rises eventually shift the SRAS curve to the left, returning the economy to equilibrium at the original level of GDP but with a higher price level.

This is different from the case where the money stock is fixed because the fiscal expansion has given a temporary stimulus to real output. The increase in aggregate spending coming from higher government consumption does not crowd out net exports via a rapid rise in the real exchange rate. Rather, an expansion of the money stock acts to keep the real exchange rate down. Thus, the money stock expansion created by the monetary authorities reinforces the expansionary effect of fiscal policy in the short run. However, this expansion of the money stock must eventually lead to a higher price level, and this rise in the price level will eventually crowd out net exports. Investment is not crowded out because interest rates do not change. But something has to be crowded out once the level of GDP returns to its potential level, Y^*: because G is bigger, some other component of $C + I + G + NX$ must be smaller. Thus, the economy returns to equilibrium with a current account deficit. Borrowing from abroad will finance this deficit.

A fiscal policy expansion does have a short-run expansionary effect on the economy if the monetary authorities increase the money supply to accommodate the increase in GDP at a constant interest rate. But net exports are crowded out in the long run by a higher domestic price level which raises the real exchange rate.

Again, this cannot be the end of the story, as the current account deficit will lead to declining national wealth. This decline in wealth will eventually lead to a fall in spending which will correct the imbalance in external payments; however, this is where our analysis stops.

Let us now summarize what we have learned about the adjustment to monetary and fiscal policy changes in the presence of perfect capital mobility, assuming that we start in full equilibrium. We will then see whether starting in disequilibrium makes any difference.

1. *Under fixed exchange rates* monetary policy is powerless to influence real economic activity. The money supply is demand-determined, and the authorities have no discretion over interest rates. A fiscal policy expansion under fixed exchange rates causes a short-run boom in real activity, but this leads to inflation. The long-run effect is a permanent rise in the domestic price level and the real exchange rate, a budget deficit, and a trade deficit financed by capital inflows.

2. *Under floating exchange rates* an expansionary monetary policy creates an inflationary boom in real activity in the short run; in the long run the price level rises in proportion to the money stock increase, and the nominal exchange rate depreciates in the same proportion. A fiscal policy expansion under floating exchange rates creates little or no increase in real GDP if the money stock is held fixed, even in the short run. In the long run there is a sustained real and nominal exchange rate appreciation, and the government budget deficit is matched by a trade deficit and capital account surplus. In contrast, if the monetary authorities maintain a fixed interest rate, and therefore increase the money stock to accompany the fiscal policy expansion, there will be a short-term stimulus to real GDP. In the long run the price level will rise and net exports will be crowded out, via a real exchange rate rise as before.

A summary of these main channels of causation for floating rates is shown in diagrammatic form in Figure 30.7.

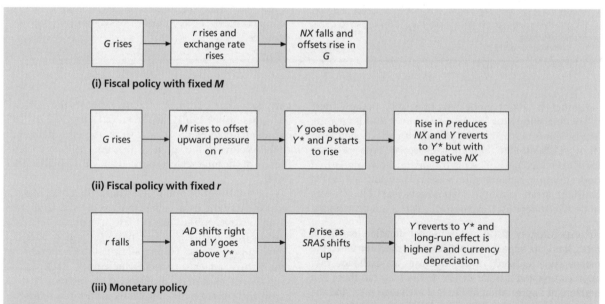

(i) Fiscal policy with fixed M

(ii) Fiscal policy with fixed r

(iii) Monetary policy

Figure 30.7 Reactions to monetary and fiscal policy changes under floating exchange rates

With floating rates monetary policy is more powerful than fiscal policy, though the effects of the latter depend on what monetary policy is followed. If the monetary authorities are fixing the money stock, as in case (i), a rise in G leads to a rise in the domestic interest rate and an appreciation of the currency. This leads to a fall in net exports that offsets the increase in G, so the government spending expansion just crowds out net exports with minimal impact on Y. If the monetary authorities are setting the interest rate, as in case (ii), and hold it constant in the face of an increase in G, then the money stock will rise (to offset upward pressure on r, and this stops the exchange rate rising) and the rightward shift in AD will take Y above Y*. Prices will then tend to rise and net exports will be crowded out. Ultimately Y will equal Y*, P will be higher, and the increase in G will be offset by a fall in NX.

A monetary expansion is implemented by lowering r, as in case (iii). This shifts the LM and AD curves to the right. The lower r permits an increase in M and stimulates an increase in I. This extra spending takes Y above Y* and upward pressure on prices results. As prices rise, the SRAS curve shifts leftwards and the currency depreciates. In equilibrium there is no gain in real output, a higher price level, and a depreciated currency.

Policy changes to correct disequilibrium

We now need to check if our conclusions are specific to the case in which the economy is initially in equilibrium. In reality, policy-makers use monetary and fiscal policies as tools for returning the economy to equilibrium, not for moving it away. There are many possible examples, but we can get a feel for the significance of the equilibrium assumption by studying a few illustrative cases in depth. We will look closely only at flexible exchange rates, as that is the current situation for most major economies, and we will consider only the response to a negative aggregate demand shock. However, the fixed exchange rate case is easy to summarize, and we will now do that before proceeding.

Let us suppose that the economy is in a situation where Y is less than Y^*, and that this has come about because of an autonomous fall in domestic investment. Under a fixed exchange rate regime with perfect capital mobility, monetary policy can do nothing to change this situation. The monetary authorities cannot lower interest rates (because of the horizontal BB curve), nor can they increase the money supply. Hence the conclusion about the impotence of monetary policy under fixed exchange rates is robust, even when we start in disequilibrium. This result carries over to the individual economies of those EU countries that are members of the euro zone. Essentially the national monetary authorities have no power to affect monetary conditions in their own country. Only the ECB can change the monetary stance (for all twelve member countries at once).

Fiscal policy, however, can have a beneficial effect. The fall in investment shifts the IS and AD curves to the left. An increase in government spending shifts these two curves back to their initial position without any of the longer-term harmful effects that arise when G is increased starting from full equilibrium.[5] There is no real exchange rate appreciation or crowding-out of the balance of payments, though there is a budget deficit. Certainly, government spending has replaced investment spending in equilibrium GDP, but this is not a crowding-out since the causation is reversed—G is filling the gap left by an autonomous fall in I. Crowding-out involves higher G causing lower I through higher interest rates.

Now let the initial negative demand shock be an exogenous fall in export demand, rather than an autonomous fall in investment. The offsetting increase in G and the accompanying budget deficit will be matched by a current account balance of payments deficit in equilibrium. But again this is not crowding-out, because of the reversed causality. Also the increase in G will improve the outcome only if it is timed correctly. This point also arises under a floating exchange rate, so let us now look more closely at policy responses to a negative demand shock under floating exchange rates.

Monetary policy

Let us suppose, again, that a negative demand shock results from an autonomous fall in investment with a given initial money stock. The situation created by this investment fall is illustrated in Figure 30.8. The fall in investment shifts the IS curve to the left. This is associated with a shift to the left of the AD curve. The leftward shift of AD leads to a small fall in the price level, given an upward-sloping $SRAS$ curve; so with a constant nominal money stock the LM curve shifts slightly to the right, because the real money stock has risen. Hence the effect of the fall in investment is to lower GDP from Y^* to Y_1 in the figure.[6]

With the economy at Y_1, if the monetary authorities permit interest rates to fall in order to keep the nominal money stock fixed, desired capital outflows will cause the exchange rate to depreciate. It will fall to the point where it is expected to appreciate at just the right rate to compensate for the lower domestic interest rate. The currency depreciation, combined with the lower price level, means that domestic goods have fallen in price relative to foreign goods. There has been a real exchange rate depreciation. This causes an upward shift in the net export function and an associated current account balance of payments surplus.

The upward shift in the net export function shifts the IS curve back to the right, and this could be sufficient to return the economy to equilibrium at Y^*. However, it is possible that the initial recessionary gap may also cause the $SRAS$ curve to shift to the right, via a reduction in money wage rates. Both of these responses, however, take some time, so the monetary authorities could, in principle, speed up the return to Y^* by increasing the nominal money supply, which would shift the LM curve to the right.

The advisability of such a monetary response depends upon the authorities being able to achieve their effects quickly. Some economists believe that monetary policy works with 'long and variable lags'. If the effects of this monetary stimulus are not felt until GDP has already returned to a level close to potential, then, rather than help end the recession, it could cause the economy to overshoot into an inflationary boom. In any event, the monetary stimulus would have to be reversed at some stage if inflation is to be avoided in the longer term.

Monetary policy can be used in the short term to offset the recessionary effects of a negative demand shock, but

---

[5] Notice, however, that the Stability and Growth Pact imposes some restrictions on the size of budget deficits for EU member countries. These are discussed in Chapter 35.

[6] The initial fall in GDP would be much greater if the monetary authorities were pegging the interest rate rather than the nominal money stock. In that case GDP would initially fall to Y_2 in the figure. The authorities would have to abandon this pegged interest rate policy in order to use monetary policy to stimulate the economy, so we revert to the assumption of an initially fixed nominal money supply.

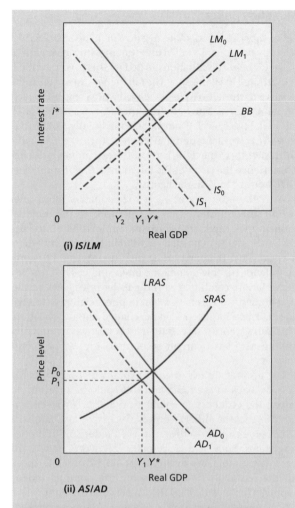

Figure 30.8 Macro policies to correct a disequilibrium

Monetary and fiscal policy can help the economy recover from a negative demand shock, so long as they are appropriately timed. The negative demand shock is assumed to be an autonomous fall in investment. The economy is initially in full equilibrium at Y^*. The fall in investment shifts the *IS* curve from IS_0 to IS_1 in part (i), and it shifts the *AD* curve from AD_0 to AD_1 in part (ii). The resulting fall in the price level from P_0 to P_1 increases the real money supply (assuming that the authorities adjust interest rates to hold the money stock constant), which shifts the *LM* curve to LM_1. The economy thus goes to GDP level Y_1, where there is a recessionary gap.

In the absence of policy changes, the automatic adjustment mechanism will eventually bring GDP back to Y^*. Monetary policy can speed up this adjustment process by lowering domestic interest rates and causing currency depreciation. Fiscal policy can shift the *IS* and *AD* curves back to their original positions.

whether this can be done with enough accuracy to improve on the automatic adjustment mechanisms is controversial.

Monetary policy affects the real economy via effects of the exchange rate on net exports, and via effects of interest

rate changes on investment, but timing this response correctly is difficult. See the appendix to this chapter for an outline of how the UK monetary authorities perceive that monetary policy works.

Fiscal policy

Now let us consider the possibilities of a fiscal reaction to the same negative demand shock that is illustrated in Figure 30.8. As a result of the fall in investment, GDP has fallen from Y^* to Y_1, assuming that the authorities have adjusted interest rates downward to maintain a constant money stock.

An appropriate increase in government spending would shift the *IS* and *AD* curves back to their initial positions and thereby restore GDP to Y^*. If this could be timed exactly to coincide with the fall in investment, there would be no need for a fall in interest rates and no exchange rate depreciation, and so there would be no shift in the net export function. The only change at full equilibrium would be lower investment and a budget deficit (assuming that the budget was in balance before the increase in government spending).[7] However, as with monetary policy, there is the problem of getting the timing right. If the increase in government spending takes effect after the automatic adjustment process does its job, then the increased spending could create an inflationary gap (as happens when G is increased with the economy starting at Y^* as above).

There is, however, an important difference between fiscal and monetary stabilization in response to this same negative demand shock. Monetary stabilization policy speeds up the automatic response mechanism by lowering the interest rate and exchange rate further than they would otherwise go. If monetary policy is timed accurately, the long-run outcome is the same as if automatic stabilizing forces did the work. Monetary policy just helps to get the economy to full equilibrium more quickly.

By contrast, fiscal policy cuts out the automatic adjustment mechanism and leads to a different composition of final demand in equilibrium. The increased budget deficit crowds out an equivalent volume of net exports, relative to what would have happened if the automatic adjustment had been left alone. This is because the fiscal stimulus stops the fall in the nominal and real exchange rate that would otherwise have shifted the net export function upwards.

In the case of an initial fall in investment, the automatic adjustment mechanism creates a current account balance of payments surplus at full equilibrium. A fiscal stimulus replaces this with a budget deficit (and a current account balance at full equilibrium). If the initial negative demand shock had been caused by a fall in net exports, the

---

[7] If the negative demand shock had been caused by an exogenous fall in net exports, rather than by investment, the net effect would be a sustained budget deficit and a balance of payments deficit in full equilibrium.

automatic adjustment mechanism would have restored the current account balance at full equilibrium. But an offsetting fiscal stimulus would mean that there was both a current account deficit and a budget deficit at full employment.

In short, when the economy starts at less than potential GDP and has a flexible exchange rate, both monetary and fiscal policies can speed up the adjustment of GDP back to its potential level. However, whether actual fiscal and monetary policies improve on the automatic adjustment mechanism in practice depends crucially on timing. If the impact of policy is felt too late, it will push the recovery of GDP beyond potential GDP and into an inflationary boom, even though it was conceived as a response to an earlier recessionary gap.

Some implications

Some of you may have found the material in this chapter hard going, on first reading. However, the effort is worthwhile because we have now reached a very advanced level of understanding of a coherent model of the macroeconomy. In the following chapters we will discuss a number of important policy issues. Before doing so, it is worth drawing together some of the implications of what we have already learned.

The transmission of monetary policy

When we first introduced a monetary sector into our macro model in Chapter 28, we discussed the way in which changes in monetary policy are transmitted to the real economy via changes in domestic interest rates.

The transmission mechanism was set out as follows. The monetary authorities decide to stimulate the economy by lowering the interest rate. In order to lower the interest rate they buy bonds, and this leads to an increase in the money supply. The lower interest rate increases investment, which, via the multiplier, increases desired aggregate spending. This increase in desired aggregate spending means that there is an increase in aggregate demand. The increase in aggregate demand then leads to an increase in real GDP and a rise in the price level. As the price level rises further, in response to inflationary pressure, the real money stock falls and GDP returns to its potential level at a higher price level.

By now we have learned that the transmission of monetary policy does not work quite like this in most forms of open economy. With fixed exchange rates, monetary policy is powerless to influence the real economy, because excess supply of the home currency in the foreign exchange market will rapidly force a policy reversal. This happens especially quickly in the modern world of highly mobile financial capital.

Under floating exchange rates with perfect capital mobility, monetary policy is able to stimulate real activity in the short run. It does so largely because an expansionary monetary policy depreciates the real exchange rate, which stimulates net exports. Deliberate use of monetary policy can be helpful in speeding the adjustment to a negative demand shock. In our model nominal interest rates fall temporarily and this stimulates investment. However, in practice the effect on investment may be small. Hence it is likely that the principal link in the transmission mechanism from the monetary sector to real activity in an open economy, with floating exchange rates, is through the exchange rate to net exports.

The MPC's views of the transmission mechanism, set out in the appendix to this chapter, are entirely consistent with what we have said, though they include some other channels. There are, for example, some direct effects of interest rates on consumption, there are wealth effects via asset prices, and there are effects via expectations and confidence. Textbook models are intended to illustrate the main channels while making some simplifying assumptions for the sake of clarity. The real-world policy-makers need to take on board the full reality of what they are doing. If you have understood our exposition so far, you should have no difficulty in following what a real-world monetary authority thinks it is doing when it changes interest rates.

The efficacy of fiscal policy

We have found that fiscal policy is a very powerful tool for stimulating real activity in the short run in an economy with fixed exchange rates and mobile international capital. In that case, the monetary authorities are forced by capital inflows to reinforce the fiscal expansion with an increase in the money supply.

Under floating exchange rates with mobile capital and a fixed money supply, however, the expansionary fiscal policy creates a currency appreciation, which neutralizes the stimulation to real activity. A fiscal stimulus would give a temporary boost to the real economy where the monetary authorities peg the interest rate—and thus would create an accommodatory rise in the money stock. The long-run effect of a fiscal expansion with no capital flows is to crowd out investment. But with mobile capital a fiscal expansion crowds out net exports via an appreciation of the real exchange rate.

There is a potential role for fiscal policy in offsetting the negative demand shocks that cause recessionary gaps. In such cases, at best, fiscal adjustment would replace the automatic adjustment mechanism of the economy and would lead to a deterioration of the budget balance in equilibrium. However, there may be situations in which this is preferable to waiting for recovery.

In general, the role of fiscal policy in influencing macroeconomic activity is much more limited in a world of floating exchange rates and mobile international capital than it is under a fixed exchange rate regime, or in the world of restricted capital flows.

Global transmission of cycles

Small countries may be price-takers in globalized financial markets, so that they have only limited freedom to influence domestic nominal interest rates, and even less freedom to influence domestic real interest rates. But this does not mean that the world interest rates will not move. Rather, it means that interest rates will tend to move up and down together as the demand and supply of savings and loans moves up and down at the world level.

World interest rate movements will be transmitted to real activity through our original transmission mechanism. Correlation of interest rate movements around the world also causes correlation of the cycles in real activity. Chart (i) in Box 30.3 shows the growth rate of world GDP since 1970. Also shown, in the two parts of chart (ii), are the GDP gaps over the most recent economic cycle for several of the major economies. Clearly, there is a very high level of correlation of the cycles about trend GDP in most of the industrial countries of the world. This suggests that one

---

Box 30.3 International policy co-ordination?

The analyses of macroeconomic policy in this chapter have taken place in the context of a single economy. However, openness to foreign trade and the globalization of financial markets have caused all major countries in the world to be influenced at least as much by global economic forces as by local conditions. No country has been able to insulate itself from the effects of a world-wide recession, of which there have been three since 1970 (1974–5, 1980–2, and 1990–2). Chart (i) shows the growth rate of GDP for the world, illustrating the three periods of slowdown.

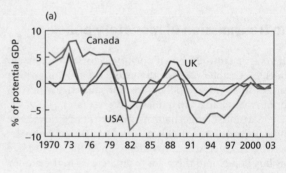
(a)

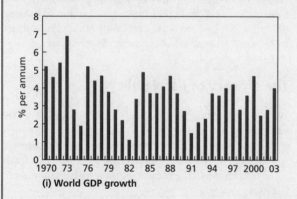
(i) World GDP growth

The two parts of chart (ii) show the GDP gaps of the G7 countries since 1982; that is, the difference between actual and potential GDP. Clearly, the cycles in all these countries are closely related, though the USA, the UK, and Canada peaked earlier and started to recover earlier than Germany, France, Italy, and Japan.

Open economies are ultimately constrained by world aggregate demand and appear unable significantly to offset swings in world demand by local monetary or fiscal policy changes. No one country acting alone (except perhaps the United States, or the EU countries acting together) can influence world aggregate demand substantially. So perhaps the only possibility of stabilizing world aggregate demand is for countries to co-ordinate their macroeconomic policies.

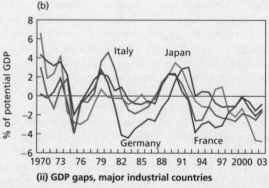
(b)

(ii) GDP gaps, major industrial countries

However, the realities of the politics of policy formation create formidable obstacles to co-ordinated action. There are already decision lags and implementation lags in the policy formation process in each country. These would be magnified if policy were to be determined at the supranational level. Realistically, explicit co-ordination of macroeconomic policies is not going to happen in the foreseeable future. This may mean that the global business cycle is a phenomenon that countries will have to continue to live with.

country acting alone cannot do much to stabilize its economic cycle, as it will still be subject to fluctuations in world demand (and supply). The world cycle may only be controllable, if at all, by co-ordinated stabilization policy among groups of countries, or at the world level.

This argument should not be taken to mean that domestic macro policies do not matter. Rather, the point is that they are not the only things that matter. External influences are much more important today than they were, say, in the 1950s. But there are many things that domestic policy-makers can do that affect the performance of their home economy for better or worse. Despite the clear existence of a global business cycle, there have been widely differing experiences with regard to inflation and unemployment among economies more or less equally exposed to external forces. It is to the causes and cures of inflation and unemployment that we turn in Chapters 31 and 32.

SUMMARY

Why does openness matter?

■ Openness of the economy matters because trade and capital flows influence real activity, international financial markets influence domestic money markets, and the exchange rate regime determines which monetary instruments are available to the authorities.

Macro policy in a world with perfect capital mobility

■ Perfect capital mobility can be represented by a horizontal *BB* line in the *IS/LM* diagram.

■ Under fixed exchange rates and perfect capital mobility, an expansionary monetary policy is rapidly reversed through losses of foreign exchange reserves. It has no real impact.

■ Starting from equilibrium GDP, an increase in government spending, under fixed exchange rates and perfect capital mobility, creates an inflationary gap and a significant stimulus to real GDP in the short run. In the long run there is a rise in the relative price of domestic goods, a budget deficit, and a trade deficit.

■ Starting from equilibrium, a monetary policy expansion, under floating exchange rates and perfect capital mobility, leads to a currency depreciation and creates an inflationary gap. In the long run the price level rises in proportion to the money supply increase and the exchange rate depreciates in the same proportion.

■ Starting from equilibrium, an increase in government spending, with floating exchange rates and perfect capital mobility, creates little or no stimulus to real GDP if the money stock is held constant; but it does create a temporary stimulus if the interest rate is held constant. In the long run in both cases it leads to a real exchange rate appreciation and a trade deficit. The budget deficit and the trade deficit are of equal size.

■ Starting with a recessionary gap, both monetary and fiscal policies can speed up the return to potential GDP if they are timed correctly. Fiscal policy can be used to increase final demand, while monetary policy can lower interest rates and/or the exchange rate.

Some implications

■ The transmission mechanism of monetary policy and the efficacy of fiscal policy are both affected by openness and capital mobility.

■ Financial and spending linkages between economies mean that business cycles are a global phenomenon, and cycles in one country are often closely related to cycles in other important economies.

TOPICS FOR REVIEW

■ Monetary policy

■ Fiscal policy

■ Fixed exchange rates

■ Floating exchange rates

■ Capital mobility

■ Overshooting

■ Crowding-out

DISCUSSION QUESTIONS

1 If UK annual interest rates are currently 4 per cent and those in the USA are 2 per cent, while the sterling-dollar exchange rate is $1.5 per £, in which direction does the market expect the sterling–dollar rate to move in one year's time? What would the answer be if UK interest rates were 4 per cent and US rates were 10 per cent?

2 Using the initial position in question 1 and an interest rate in the euro area of 6 per cent and an initial exchange rate between dollar and euro of $1.0 per euro, what is the market's expectation of the direction of change in the exchange rate between the euro and sterling in one year's time?

3 Explain how monetary and fiscal policies influence GDP and the price level under fixed exchange rates with perfect capital mobility.

4 Explain how monetary and fiscal policies influence GDP and the price level under floating exchange rates with perfect capital mobility.

5 Has the globalization of financial markets diminished the power of the monetary authorities to influence their own economy?

6 What macroeconomic policy options are available for a single member of the euro zone?

7 Should macro policy be co-ordinated between major countries?

Appendix The transmission mechanism of monetary policy

The Monetary Policy Committee, Bank of England

This report has been prepared by Bank of England staff under the guidance of the Monetary Policy Committee in response to suggestions by the Treasury Committee of the House of Commons and the House of Lords Select Committee on the Monetary Policy Committee of the Bank of England.

The Monetary Policy Committee (in April 1999):
Eddie George, Governor
Mervyn King, Deputy Governor responsible for monetary stability
David Clementi, Deputy Governor responsible for financial stability
Alan Budd
Willem Buiter
Charles Goodhart
DeAnne Julius
Ian Plenderleith
John Vickers

This report is also available on the Bank's web site: www.bankofengland.co.uk

Introduction and summary

The Monetary Policy Committee (MPC) sets the short-term interest rate at which the Bank of England deals with the money markets. Decisions about that official interest rate affect economic activity and inflation through several channels, which are known collectively as the 'transmission mechanism' of monetary policy.

The purpose of this paper is to describe the MPC's view of the transmission mechanism. The key links in that mechanism are illustrated in Chart 1.

First, official interest rate decisions affect market interest rates (such as mortgage rates and bank deposit rates), to varying degrees. At the same time, policy actions and announcements affect expectations about the future course of the economy and the confidence with which these expectations are held, as well as affecting asset prices and the exchange rate.

Second, these changes in turn affect the spending, saving and investment behaviour of individuals and firms in the economy. For example, other things being equal, higher interest rates tend to encourage saving rather than spending, and a higher value of sterling in foreign exchange markets, which makes foreign goods less expensive relative to goods produced at home. So changes in the official interest rate affect the demand for goods and services produced in the United Kingdom.

Third, the level of demand relative to domestic supply capacity —in the labour market and elsewhere—is a key influence on domestic inflationary pressure. For example, if demand for labour exceeds the supply available, there will tend to be upward pressure on wage increases, which some firms may be able to pass through into higher prices charged to consumers.

Fourth, exchange rate movements have a direct effect, though often delayed, on the domestic prices of imported goods and services, and an indirect effect on the prices of those goods and services that compete with imports or use imported inputs, and hence on the component of overall inflation that is imported.

Part I of this paper describes in more detail these and other links from official interest rate decisions to economic activity and inflation. It discusses important aspects that have been glossed over in the summary account above—such as the distinction between real and nominal interest rates, the role of expectations, and the interlinking of many of the effects mentioned. There is also a discussion of the role of monetary aggregates in the transmission mechanism.

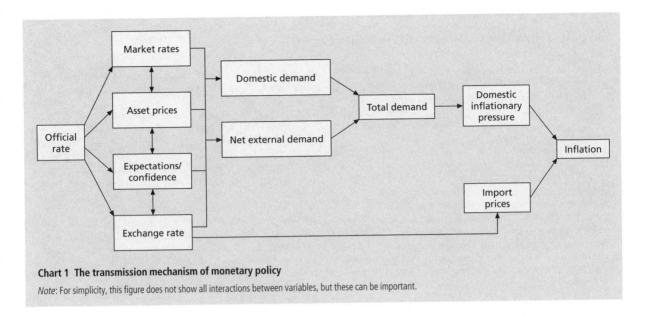

Chart 1 The transmission mechanism of monetary policy

Note: For simplicity, this figure does not show all interactions between variables, but these can be important.

Part II provides some broad quantification of the effects of official interest rate changes under particular assumptions. There is inevitably great uncertainty about both the timing and size of these effects. As to timing, in the Bank's macroeconometric model (used to generate the simulations shown at the end of this paper), official interest rate decisions have their fullest effect on output with a lag of around one year, and their fullest effect on inflation with a lag of around two years. As to size, depending on the circumstances, the same model suggests that temporarily raising rates relative to a base case by 1 percentage point for one year might be expected to lower output by something of the order of 0.2 per cent to 0.35 per cent after about a year, and to reduce inflation by around 0.2 percentage points to 0.4 percentage points a year or so after that, all relative to the base case.

I Links in the chain

Monetary policy works largely via its influence on aggregate demand in the economy. It has little direct effect on the trend path of supply capacity. Rather, in the long run, monetary policy determines the nominal or money values of goods and services —that is, the general price level. An equivalent way of making the same point is to say that in the long run, monetary policy in essence determines the value of money—movements in the general price level indicate how much the purchasing power of money has changed over time. Inflation, in this sense, is a monetary phenomenon.

However, monetary policy changes do have an effect on real activity in the short to medium term. And though monetary policy is the dominant determinant of the price level in the long run, there are many other potential influences on price-level movements at shorter horizons. There are several links in the chain of causation running from monetary policy changes to their ultimate effects on the economy.

From a change in the official rate to other financial and asset markets

A central bank derives the power to determine a specific interest rate in the wholesale money markets from the fact that it is the monopoly supplier of 'high-powered' money, which is also known as 'base money'.[1] The operating procedure of the Bank of England is similar to that of many other central banks, though instiutional details differ slightly from country to country. The key point is that the Bank chooses the price at which it will lend high-powered money to private sector institutions. In the United Kingdom, the Bank lends predominantly through gilt sale and repurchase agreements (repo) at the two-week maturity. This repo rate is the 'official rate' mentioned above. The box opposite outlines how the Bank implements an official rate decision in the money markets.

The quantitative effect of a change in the official rate on other interest rates, and on financial markets in general, will depend on the extent to which the policy change was anticipated and how the change affects expectations of future policy. We assume here for simplicity that changes in the official rate are not expected to be reversed quickly, and that no further future changes are anticipated as a result of the change. This is a reasonable assumption for purposes of illustration, but it should be borne in mind that some of the effects described may occur when market expectations about policy change, rather than when the official rate itself changes.

Short-term interest rates A change in the official rate is immediately transmitted to other short-term sterling wholesale money-market rates, both to money-market instruments of different maturity (such as rates on repo contracts of maturities other than two weeks) and to other short-term rates, such as

[1] The monetary base, M0, consists of notes and coin plus bankers' deposits at the Bank of England.

Box 30A How the Bank sets interest rates

The Bank implements monetary policy by lending to the money market at the official repo rate chosen by the MPC. The Bank's dealing rate changes only when the MPC decides that it should. Arbitrage between markets ensures that the MPC's decisions are reflected across the spectrum of short-term sterling markets.

The Bank holds on its balance sheet assets acquired from its counterparties in its money-market operations. These are mostly private sector obligations; they are short-term, and a proportion of them matures every business day. This means that at the start of each day, the private sector is due to pay money to the Bank to redeem these obligations. However, in order to do so, the Bank's counterparties typically have to borrow additional funds from the Bank. This gives the Bank the opportunity to provide the necessary finance once more, at its official repo rate. The fact that this 'stock of refinancing' is turning over regularly is the main factor creating the demand for base money (the 'shortage') in the market each day.

The panel below shows the announcements that the Bank's dealers made to the market on 8 April, a day on which rates were changed. At 9.45 am, the Bank announced the estimated size of that day's shortage and the main factors behind it. At 12 noon, it published the outcome of the MPC meeting, and market rates adjusted immediately. The first round of operations was not conducted until 12.15 pm, but the knowledge that the dealing rate would be 5.25 per cent, down from 5.5 per cent, moved market rates ahead of that. The bulk of

the day's shortage was financed at 12.15 pm, and the (downwardly revised) remainder in a further round of operations at 2.30 pm.

In its open market operations, the Bank deals with a small group of counterparties who are active in the money market: banks, securities dealers and building societies are eligible to take on this role. Finance is provided primarily in the form of repo, which is short for 'sale and repurchase agreement'. Counterparties sell assets to the Bank with an agreement to buy them back in about a fortnight's time, and the repo rate is the (annualized) rate of interest implied by the difference between the sale and repurchase price in these transactions. The assets eligible for repo are gilts and sterling Treasury bills, UK government foreign-currency debt, eligible bank and local authority bills, and certain sterling bonds issued by supranational organizations and by governments in the European Economic Area. The Bank also buys outright Treasury bills and other eligible bills.

On non-MPC days, the first round of operations is held at 9.45 am rather than 12 pm. The timetable is otherwise the same. If the remaining shortage is not entirely relieved at 2.30 pm, the Bank holds a round of overnight operations at 3.30 pm. If the system is still short at 4.20 pm, the Bank deals directly with the settlement banks, whose accounts at the Bank of England need to be in credit at the end of the day. But on 8 April, no operations were needed at 3.30 pm or 4.20 pm.

Bank of England messages to money markets via screen services on 8 April 1999

9.45 am	Initial liquidity forecast Stg 1150 mn shortage
	Principal factors in the forecast
	Treasury bills and maturing outright purchases −596
	Maturing bill/gilt repo −216
	Bank/Exchequer transactions −180
	Rise in note circulation −105
	Maturing settlement bank late repo facility −39
	Bankers' balances below target −20
12.00 pm	BANK OF ENGLAND REDUCES INTEREST RATES BY 0.25% TO 5.25%
	The Bank of England's Monetary Policy Committee today voted to reduce the Bank's repo rate by 0.25% to 5.25%.
	The minutes of the meeting will be published at 9.30 am on Wednesday 21 April.
12.15 pm	Liquidity forecast revision—Stg 1100 mn
	A round of fixed-rate operations is invited. The Bank's repo rate is 5.25%. The operations will comprise repos to 22 and 23 April and outright offers of bills maturing on or before 23 April.
12.24 pm	Total amount allotted—Stg 900 mn
	of which—outright Stg 57 mn, repo Stg 843 mn
2.30 pm	Liquidity forecast revision—Stg 1000 mn. Residual shortage—Stg 100 mn
	A round of fixed-rate operations is invited. The Bank's repo rate is 5.25%. The operations will comprise repos to 22 and 23 April and outright offers of bills maturing on or before 23 April.
2.35 pm	Total amount allotted—Stg 100 mn
	of which—outright Stg 16 mn, repo Stg 84 mn
3.30 pm	No residual shortage
	No further operations invited
4.20 pm	No liquidity forecast revision
	No residual shortage
	The settlement bank late repo facility will not operate today

interbank deposits. But these rates may not always move by the exact amount of the official rate change. Soon after the official rate change (typically the same day), banks adjust their standard lending rates (base rates), usually by the exact amount of the policy change. This quickly affects the interest rates that banks charge their customers for variable-rate loans, including overdrafts. Rates on standard variable-rate mortgages may also be changed, though this is not automatic and may be delayed. Rates offered to savers also change, in order to preserve the margin between deposit and loan rates. This margin can vary over time, according to, for example, changing competitive conditions in the markets involved, but it does not normally change in response to policy changes alone.

Long-term interest rates Though a change in the official rate unambiguously moves other short-term rates in the same direction (even if some are slow to adjust), the impact on longer-term interest rates can go either way. This is because long-term interest rates are influenced by an average of current and expected future short-term rates, so the outcome depends upon the direction and extent of the impact of the official rate change on expectations of the future path of interest rates. A rise in the official rate could, for example, generate an expectation of lower future interest rates, in which case long rates might fall in response to an official rate rise. The actual effect on long rates of an official rate change will partly depend on the impact of the policy change on inflation expectations. The role of inflation expectations is discussed more fully below.

Asset prices Changes in the official rate also affect the market value of securities, such as bonds and equities. The price of bonds is inversely related to the long-term interest rate, so a rise in long-term interest rates lowers bond prices, and *vice versa* for a fall in long rates. If other things are equal (especially inflation expectations), higher interest rates also lower other securities prices, such as equities. This is because expected future returns are discounted by a larger factor, so the present value of any given future income stream falls. Other things may not be equal—for example, policy changes may have indirect effects on expectations or confidence—but these are considered separately below. The effect on prices of physical assets, such as housing, is discussed later.

The exchange rate Policy-induced changes in interest rates can also affect the exchange rate. The exchange rate is the relative price of domestic and foreign money, so it depends on both domestic and foreign monetary conditions. The precise impact on exchange rates of an official rate change is uncertain, as it will depend on expectations about domestic and foreign interest rates and inflation, which may themselves be affected by a policy change. However, other things being equal, an unexpected rise in the official rate will probably lead to an immediate appreciation of the domestic currency in foreign exchange markets, and *vice versa* for a similar rate fall. The exchange rate appreciation follows from the fact that higher domestic interest rates, relative to interest rates on equivalent foreign-currency assets, make sterling assets more attractive to international investors. The exchange rate should move to a level where investors expect a future depreciation just large enough to make them indifferent between holding sterling and foreign-currency assets. (At this point, the corresponding interest differential at any maturity is approximately equal to the expected rate of change of the exchange rate up to the same time-horizon.)

Exchange rate changes lead to changes in the relative prices of domestic and foreign goods and services, at least for a while, though some of these price changes may take many months to work their way through to the domestic economy, and even longer to affect the pattern of spending.

Expectations and confidence Official rate changes can influence expectations about the future course of real activity in the economy, and the confidence with which those expectations are held (in addition to the inflation expectations already mentioned). Such changes in perception will affect participants in financial markets, and they may also affect other parts of the economy via, for example, changes in expected future labour income, unemployment, sales and profits. The direction in which such effects work is hard to predict, and can vary from time to time. A rate rise could, for example, be interpreted as indicating that the MPC believes that the economy is likely to be growing faster than previously thought, giving a boost to expectations of future growth and confidence in general. However, it is also possible that a rate rise would be interpreted as signalling that the MPC perceives the need to slow the growth in the economy in order to hit the inflation target, and this could dent expectations of future growth and lower confidence.

The possibility of such effects contributes to the uncertainty of the impact of any policy change, and increases the importance of having a credible and transparent monetary policy regime. We return to these issues below.

In summary, though monetary policy-makers have direct control over only a specific short-term interest rate, changes in the official rate affect market interest rates, asset prices, and the exchange rate. The response of all these will vary considerably from time to time, as the external environment, policy regime and market sentiment are not constant. However, monetary policy changes (relative to interest rate expectations) normally affect financial markets as described above.

From financial markets to spending behaviour

We now consider how the spending decisions of individuals and firms respond to the changes in interest rates, asset prices and the exchange rate just discussed. Here, we focus on the immediate effects of a monetary policy change. Those resulting from subsequent changes in aggregate income, employment and inflation are considered below. Since the effects of policy changes on expectations and confidence are ambiguous, we proceed on the basis of a given level of expectations about the future course of real activity and inflation, and a given degree of confidence with which those expectations are held. We also assume an unchanged fiscal policy stance by the government in response to the change in monetary policy.

Individuals Individuals are affected by a monetary policy change in several ways. There are three direct effects. First, they face new rates of interest on their savings and debts. So the disposable incomes of savers and borrowers alter, as does the incentive to save rather than consume now. Second, the value of individuals' financial wealth changes as a result of changes in asset prices. Third, any exchange rate adjustment changes the relative prices of goods and services priced in domestic and foreign currency. Of these three effects, the one felt most acutely and directly by a significant number of individuals is that working through the interest rate charged on personal debt, especially mortgages, and the interest rate paid on their savings. We focus first on those with significant debts, and return to those with net savings below.

Loans secured on houses make up about 80 per cent of personal debt, and most mortgages in the United Kingdom are still floating-rate. Any rise in the mortgage rate reduces the remaining disposable income of those affected and so, for any given gross income, reduces the flow of funds available to spend on goods and services. Higher interest rates on unsecured loans have a similar effect. Previous spending levels cannot be sustained without incurring further debts (or running down savings), so a fall in consumer spending is likely to follow. Those with fixed-rate mortgages will not face higher payments until their fixed term expires, but all new borrowers taking out such loans will be affected by rate changes from the start of their loan (though the fixed interest rate will be linked to interest rates of the relevant term, rather than short rates).

Wealth effects will also be likely to work in the same direction. Higher interest rates (current and expected) tend to reduce asset values, and lower wealth leads to lower spending. Securities prices were mentioned above; another important personal asset is houses. Higher interest rates generally increase the cost of financing house purchase, and so reduce demand. A fall in demand will lower the rate of increase of house prices, and sometimes house prices may even fall. Houses are a major component of (gross) personal wealth. Changes in the value of housing wealth affect consumer spending in the same direction as changes in financial wealth, but not necessarily by the same amount. Part of this effect comes from the fact that individuals may feel poorer when the market value of their house falls, and another part results from the fact that houses are used as collateral for loans, so lower net worth in housing makes it harder to borrow. As an example of this, the house-price boom of the late 1980s was linked to rapid consumption growth, and declining house prices in the early 1990s exerted a major restraint on consumer spending.

Some individuals have neither mortgage debt nor significant financial and housing wealth. They may, however, have credit card debts or bank loans. Monetary policy affects interest rates charged on these, and higher rates will tend to discourage borrowing to finance consumption. Even for those with no debts, higher interest rates may make returns on savings products more attractive, encouraging some individuals to save more—and so to spend less. In essence, higher interest rates (for given inflation expectations) encourage the postponement of consumption, by increasing the amount of future consumption that can be achieved by sacrificing a given amount of consumption today. Future consumption is substituted for current consumption.

Another influence on consumer spending arises from the effects of an official rate change on consumer confidence and expectations of future employment and earnings prospects. Such effects vary with the circumstances of the time, but where a policy change is expected to stimulate economic activity, this is likely to increase confidence and expectations of future employment and earnings growth, leading to higher spending. The reverse will follow a policy change expected to slow the growth of activity.

So far, the effects mentioned all normally work in the same direction, so that higher interest rates, other things being equal, lead to a reduction in consumer spending, and lower interest rates tend to encourage it. However, this is not true for all individuals. For example, a person living off income from savings deposits, or someone about to purchase an annuity, would receive a larger money income if interest rates were higher than if they were lower. This higher income could sustain a higher level of spending than would otherwise be possible. So interest rate rises (falls) have redistributional effects—net borrowers are made worse (better) off and net savers are made better (worse) off. And to complicate matters further, the spending of these different groups may respond differently to their respective changes in disposable income.

However, the MPC sets one interest rate for the economy as a whole, and can only take account of the impact of official rate changes on the aggregate of individuals in the economy. From this perspective, the overall impact of the effects mentioned above on consumers appears to be that higher interest rates tend to reduce total current consumption spending, and lower interest rates tend to increase it.

Exchange rate changes can also affect the level of spending by individuals. This could happen, for example, if significant levels of wealth (or debt) were denominated in foreign currency, so that an exchange rate change caused a change in net wealth —though this is probably not an important factor for most individuals in the United Kingdom. But there will be effects on the composition of spending, even if there are none on its level. An exchange rate rise makes imported goods and services relatively cheaper than before. This affects the competitiveness of domestic producers of exports and of import-competing goods, and it also affects service industries such as tourism, as foreign holidays become relatively cheaper. Such a change in relative prices is likely to encourage a switch of spending away from home-produced goods and services towards those produced overseas. Of course, official rate changes are not the only influence on exchange rates—the appreciation of sterling in 1996, for example, appears to have been driven to a significant extent by other factors.

In summary, a rise in the official interest rate, other things (notably expectations and confidence) being equal, leads to a reduction in spending by consumers overall and, via an exchange rate rise, to a shift of spending away from home-produced towards foreign-produced goods and services. A reduction in the official rate has the opposite effect. The size—and even the direction—of these effects could be altered by changes in expectations and confidence brought about by a policy change, and these influences vary with the particular circumstances.

Firms The other main group of private sector agents in the economy is firms. They combine capital, labour and purchased inputs in some production process in order to make and sell goods or services for profit. Firms are affected by the changes in market interest rates, asset prices and the exchange rate that may follow a monetary policy change. However, the importance of the impact will vary depending on the nature of the business, the size of the firm and its sources of finance. Again, we focus first on the direct effects of a monetary policy change, holding all other influences constant, and discuss indirect effects working through aggregate demand later (though these indirect effects may be more important).

An increase in the official interest rate will have a direct effect on all firms that rely on bank borrowing or on loans of any kind linked to short-term money-market interest rates. A rise in interest rates increases borrowing costs (and *vice versa* for a fall). The rise in interest costs reduces the profits of such firms and increases the return that firms will require from new investment projects, making it less likely that they will start them. Interest costs affect the cost of holding inventories, which are often financed by bank loans. Higher interest costs also make it less likely that the affected firms will hire more staff, and more likely that they will reduce employment or hours worked. In contrast, when interest rates are falling, it is cheaper for firms to finance investment in new plant and equipment, and more likely that they will expand their labour force.

Of course, not all firms are adversely affected by interest rate rises. Cash-rich firms will receive a higher income from funds deposited with banks or placed in the money markets, thus improving their cash flow. This improved cash flow could help them to invest in more capacity or increase employment, but it is also possible that it will encourage them to shift resources into financial assets, or to pay higher dividends to shareholders.

Some firms may be less affected by the direct impact of short-term interest rate changes. This could be either because they have minimal short-term borrowing and/or liquid assets, or because their short-term liquid assets and liabilities are roughly matched, so that changes in the level or short rates leave their cash flow largely unaffected. Even here, however, they may be affected by the impact of policy on long-term interest rates whenever they use capital markets in order to fund long-term investments.

The cost of capital is an important determinant of investment for all firms. We have mentioned that monetary policy changes have only indirect effects on interest rates on long-term bonds. The effects on the costs of equity finance are also indirect and hard to predict. This means that there is no simple link from official rate changes to the cost of capital. This is particularly true for large and multinational firms with access to international capital markets, whose financing costs may therefore be little affected by changes in domestic short-term interest rates.

Changes in asset prices also affect firms' behaviour in other ways. Bank loans to firms (especially small firms) are often secured on assets, so a fall in asset prices can make it harder for them to borrow, since low asset prices reduce the net worth of the firm. This is sometimes called a 'financial accelerator' effect. Equity finance for listed companies is also generally easier to raise when interest rates are low and asset valuations are high, so that firms' balance sheets are healthy.

Exchange rate changes also have an important impact on many firms, though official rate changes explain only a small proportion of exchange rate variation. A firm producing in the United Kingdom, for example, would have many of its costs fixed (at least temporarily) in sterling terms, but might face competition from firms whose costs were fixed in other currencies. An appreciation of sterling in the foreign exchange market would then worsen the competitive position of the UK-based firm for some time, generating lower profit margins or lower sales, or both. This effect is likely to be felt acutely by many manufacturing firms, because they tend to be most exposed to foreign competition. Producers of exports and import-competing goods would certainly both be affected. However, significant parts of other sectors, such as agriculture, may also feel the effects of such changes in the exchange rate, as would parts of the service sector, such as hotels, restaurants, shops and theatres

reliant on the tourist trade, financial and business services, and consultancy.

The impact of monetary policy changes on firms' expectations about the future course of the economy and the confidence with which these expectations are held affects business investment decisions. Once made, investments in fixed capital are difficult, or impossible, to reverse, so projections of future demand and risk assessments are an important input into investment appraisals. A fall (rise) in the expected future path of demand will tend to lead to a fall (rise) in spending on capital projects. The confidence with which expectations are held is also important, as greater uncertainty about the future is likely to encourage at least postponement of investment spending until prospects seem clearer. Again, it is hard to predict the effect of any official rate change on firms' expectations and confidence, but there can be little doubt that such effects are a potentially important influence on business investment.

In summary, many firms depend on sterling bank finance or short-term money-market borrowing, and they are sensitive to the direct effects of interest rates changes. Higher interest rates worsen the financial position of firms dependent on such short-term borrowing (other things being equal) and lower rates improve their financial position. Changes in firms' financial position in turn may lead to changes in their investment and employment plans. More generally, by altering required rates of return, higher interest rates encourage postponement of investment spending and reduced inventories, whereas lower rates encourage an expansion of activity. Policy changes also alter expectations about the future course of the economy and the confidence with which those expectations are held, thereby affecting investment spending, in addition to the direct effect of changes in interest rates, asset prices, and the exchange rate.

From changes in spending behaviour to GDP and inflation

All of the changes in individuals' and firms' behaviour discussed above, when added up across the whole economy, generate changes in aggregate spending. Total domestic expenditure in the economy is equal by definition to the sum of private consumption expenditure, government consumption expenditure and investment spending. Total domestic expenditure plus the balance of trade in goods and services (net exports) reflects aggregate demand in the economy, and is equal to gross domestic product at market prices (GDP).

Second-round effects We have set out above how a change in the official interest rate affects the spending behaviour of individuals and firms. The resulting change in spending in aggregate will then have further effects on other agents, even if these agents were unaffected by the direct financial effects of the monetary policy change. So a firm that was not affected directly by changes in interest rates, securities prices or the exchange rate could nonetheless be affected by changes in consumer spending or by other firms' demand for produced inputs—a steel-maker, for example, would be affected by changes in demand from a car manufacturer. Moreover, the fact that these indirect effects can be anticipated by others means that there can be a large impact on expectations and confidence. So any induced change in aggregate spending is likely to affect most parts of the private sector producing for the home market, and these effects in turn can create further effects on their suppliers. Indeed, it is in the nature of business cycles that in upturns many sectors of the economy expand together and there is a general rise in confidence, which further feeds into spending. In downturns, many suffer a similar slowdown and confidence is generally low, reinforcing the cautious attitude to spending. This means that the individuals and firms most directly affected by changes in the official rate are not necessarily those most affected by its full repercussions.

Time-lags Any change in the official rate takes time to have its full impact on the economy. It was stated above that a monetary policy change affects other wholesale money-market interest rates and sterling financial asset prices very quickly, but the impact on some retail interest rates may be much slower. In some cases, it may be several months before higher official rates affect the payments made by some mortgage-holders (or received by savings deposit-holders). It may be even longer before changes in their mortgage payments (or income from savings) lead to changes in their spending in the shops. Changes in consumer spending not fully anticipated by firms affect retailers' inventories, and this then leads to changes in orders from distributors. Changes in distributors' orders then affect producers' inventories, and when these become unusually large or small, production changes follow, which in turn lead to employment and earnings changes. These then feed into further consumer spending changes. All this takes time.

The empirical evidence is that on average it takes up to about one year in this and other industrial economies for the response to a monetary policy change to have its peak effect on demand and production, and that it takes up to a further year for these activity changes to have their fullest impact on the inflation rate. However, there is a great deal of variation and uncertainty around these average time-lags. In particular, the precise effect will depend on many other factors such as the state of business and consumer confidence and how this responds to the policy change, the stage of the business cycle, events in the world economy, and expectations about future inflation. These other influences are beyond the direct control of the monetary authorities, but combine with slow adjustments to ensure that the impact of monetary policy is subject to long, variable and uncertain lags. This slow adjustment involves both delays in changing real spending decisions, as discussed above, and delays in adjusting wages and prices, to which we turn next. A quantitative estimate of the lags derived from the Bank's macroeconometric model appears below.

GDP and inflation In the long run, real GDP grows as a result of supply-side factors in the economy, such as technical progress, capital accumulation, and the size and quality of the labour force. Some government policies may be able to influence these supply-side factors, but monetary policy generally cannot do so directly, at least not to raise trend growth in the economy. There is always some level of national output at which firms in the economy would be working at their normal-capacity output, and would be under no pressure to change output or product prices faster than at the expected rate of inflation. This is called the 'potential' level of GDP. When actual GDP is at potential, production levels are such as to impart no upward or downward pressures on output price inflation in goods markets, and employment levels are such that there is no upward pressure on

unit cost growth from earnings growth in labour markets. There is a broad balance between the demand for, and supply of, domestic output.

The difference between actual GDP and potential GDP is known as the 'output gap'. When there is a positive output gap, a high level of aggregate demand has taken actual output to a level above its sustainable level, and firms are working above their normal-capacity levels. Excess demand may partly be reflected in a balance of payments deficit on the current account, but it is also likely to increase domestic inflationary pressures. For some firms, unit cost growth will rise, as they are working above their most efficient output level. Some firms may also feel the need to attract more employees, and/or increase hours worked by existing employees, to support their extra production. This extra demand for labour and improved employment prospects will be associated with upward pressure on money wage growth and price inflation. Some firms may also take the opportunity of periods of high demand to raise their profit margins, and so to increase their prices more than in proportion to increases in unit costs. When there is a negative output gap, the reverse is generally true. So booms in the economy that take the level of output significantly above its potential level are usually followed by a pick-up of inflation, and recessions that take the level of output below its potential are generally associated with a reduction in inflationary pressure.

The output gap cannot be measured with much precision. For example, changes in the pattern of labour supply and industrial structure, and labour market reforms, mean that the point at which producers reach capacity is uncertain and subject to change. There are many heterogeneous sectors in the economy, and different industries start to hit bottlenecks at different stages of an upturn and are likely to lay off workers at different stages of a downturn. No two business cycles are exactly alike, so some industries expand more in one cycle than another. And the (trend) rate of growth of productivity can vary over time. The latter is particularly hard to measure except long after the event. So the concept of an output gap—even if it could be estimated with any precision—is not one that has a unique numerical link to inflationary pressure. Rather, it is helpful in indicating that in order to keep inflation under control, there is some level of aggregate activity at which aggregate demand and aggregate supply are broadly in balance. This is its potential level.

Holding real GDP at its potential level would in theory (in the absence of external shocks) be sufficient to maintain the inflation rate at its target level only if this were the inflation rate expected to occur by the agents in the economy. The absence of an output gap is consistent with any constant inflation rate that is expected. This is because holding aggregate demand at a level consistent with potential output only delivers the rate of inflation that agents expect—as it is these expectations that are reflected in wage settlements and are in turn passed on in some product prices. So holding output at its potential level, if maintained, could in theory be consistent with a high and stable inflation rate, as well as a low and stable one. The level at which inflation ultimately stabilises is determined by the monetary policy actions of the central bank and the credibility of the inflation target. In the shorter run, the level of inflation when output is at potential will depend on the level of inflation expectations, and other factors that impart inertia to the inflation rate.

Inflation expectations and real interest rates In discussing the impact of monetary policy changes on individuals and firms, one of the important variables that we explicitly held constant was the expected rate of inflation. Inflation expectations matter in two important areas. First, they influence the level of real interest rates and so determine the impact of any specific nominal interest rate. Second, they influence price and money wage-setting and so feed through into actual inflation in subsequent periods. We discuss each of these in turn.

The real interest rate is approximately equal to the nominal interest rate minus the expected inflation rate. The real interest rate matters because rational agents who are not credit-constrained will typically base their investment and saving decisions on real rather than nominal interest rates. This is because they are making comparisons between what they consume today and what they hope to consume in the future. For credit-constrained individuals, who cannot borrow as much today as they would like to finance activities today, nominal interest rates also matter, as they affect their cash flow.

It is only by considering the level of real interest rates that it is possible, even in principle, to assess whether any given nominal interest rate represents a relatively tight or loose monetary policy stance. For example, if expected inflation were 10 per cent, then a nominal interest rate of 10 per cent would represent a real interest rate of zero, whereas if expected inflation were 3 per cent, a nominal interest rate of 10 per cent would imply a real interest rate of 7 per cent. So for given inflation expectations, changes in nominal and real interest rates are equivalent; but if inflation expectations are changing, the distinction becomes important. Moreover, these calculations should be done on an after-tax basis so that the interaction between inflation and the tax burden is taken into account, but such complications are not considered further here.

Money wage increases in excess of the rate of growth of labour productivity reflect the combined effect of a positive expected rate of inflation and a (positive or negative) component resulting from pressure of demand in labour markets. Wage increases that do not exceed productivity growth do not increase unit labour costs of production, and so are unlikely to be passed on in the prices charged by firms for their outputs. However, wage increases reflecting inflation expectations or demand pressures do raise unit labour costs, and firms may attempt to pass them on in their prices. So even if there is no excess demand for labour, unit costs will tend to increase by the expected rate of inflation simply because workers and firms bargain about real wages. This increase in unit costs—to a greater or lesser extent—will be passed on in goods prices. It is for this reason that, when GDP is at its potential level and there is no significant excess demand or supply of labour, the coincidence of actual and potential GDP delivers the inflation rate that was expected. This will only equal the inflation target once the target is credible (and so is expected to be hit).

Imported inflation So far, this paper has set out how changes in the official rate lead to changes in the demand for domestic output, and how the balance of domestic demand relative to potential supply determines the degree of inflationary pressure. In doing so, it considered the impact of exchange rate changes on net exports, via the effects of changes in the competitive position of domestic firms *vis à vis* overseas firms on the relative demand for domestic-produced goods and services. There is also a more direct effect of exchange rate changes on domestic inflation. This arises because exchange rate changes affect the sterling prices of imported goods, which are important determinants of many firms' costs and of the retail prices of many goods and services. An appreciation of sterling lowers the sterling price of imported goods, and a depreciation raises it. The effects may take many months to work their way fully through the pricing chain. The link between the exchange rate and domestic prices is not uni-directional—for example, an exchange rate change resulting from a change in foreign monetary policy will lead to domestic price changes, and domestic price rises caused by, say, a domestic demand increase will have exchange rate implications. Indeed, both the exchange rate and the domestic price level are related indicators of the same thing—the value of domestic money. The exchange rate is the value of domestic money against other currencies, and the price level measures the value of domestic money in terms of a basket of goods and services.

The role of money

So far, we have discussed how monetary policy changes affect output and inflation, with barely a mention of the quantity of money. (The entire discussion has been about the price of borrowing or lending money, ie the interest rate.) This may seem to be at variance with the well known dictum that 'inflation is always and everywhere a monetary phenomenon'. It is also rather different from the expositions found in many textbooks that explain the transmission mechanism as working through policy-induced changes in the money supply, which then create excess demand or supply of money that in turn leads, via changes in short-term interest rates, to spending and price-level changes.

The money supply does play an important role in the transmission mechanism but it is not, under the United Kingdom's monetary arrangements, a policy instrument. It could be a target of policy, but it need not be so. In the United Kingdom it is not, as we have an inflation target, and so monetary aggregates are indicators only. However, for each path of the official rate given by the decisions of the MPC, there is an implied path for the monetary aggregates. And in some circumstances monetary aggregates might be a better indicator than interest rates of the stance of monetary policy. In the long run, there is a positive relationship between each monetary aggregate and the general level of prices. Sustained increases in prices cannot occur without accompanying increases in the monetary aggregates. It is in this sense that money is the nominal anchor of the system. In the current policy framework, where the official interest rate is the policy instrument, both the money stock and inflation are jointly caused by other variables.

Monetary adjustment normally fits into the transmission mechanism in the following way. Suppose that monetary policy has been relaxed by the implementation of a cut in the official interest rate. Commercial banks correspondingly reduce the interest rates they charge on their loans. This is likely to lead to an increased demand for loans (partly to finance the extra spending discussed above), and an increased extension of loans by banks creates new bank deposits that will be measured as an increase in the broad money supply (M4). So the change in spending by individuals and firms that results from a monetary policy change will also be accompanied by a change in both bank lending and bank deposits. Increases in retail sales are also likely to be associated with an increased demand for notes and coin in circulation. Data on monetary aggregates—lending, deposits, and cash—are helpful in the formation of monetary policy, as they provide corroborative, or sometimes leading, indicators of the course of spending behaviour, and they are available in advance of much of the national accounts data.

In the long run, monetary and credit aggregates must be willingly held by agents in the economy. Monetary growth persistently in excess of that warranted by growth in the real economy will inevitably be the reflection of an interest rate policy that is inconsistent with stable inflation. So control of inflation always ultimately implies control of the monetary growth rate. However, the relationship between the monetary aggregates and nominal GDP in the United Kingdom appears to be insufficiently stable (partly owing to financial innovation) for the monetary aggregates to provide a robust indicator of likely future inflation developments in the near term. It is for this reason that an inflation-targeting regime is thought to be superior to one of monetary targeting when the intention is to control inflation itself. In other words, money matters, but not in such a precise way as to provide a reliable quantitative guide for monetary policy in the short to medium term.

Another reason why monetary policy-makers need to monitor developments in monetary aggregates and bank lending closely is that shocks to spending can have their origin in the banking system. From time to time, there may be effects running from the banking sector to spending behaviour that are not directly caused by changes in interest rates.[2] There could, for example, be a fall in bank lending caused by losses of capital on bad loans or by a tightening of the regulatory environment. Negative shocks of this kind are sometimes referred to as a 'credit crunch'. Positive shocks (such as followed from the removal of the 'Corset' and consumer-credit controls in the early 1980s) may by contrast induce a credit boom that has inflationary consequences. The potential existence of shocks originating in the monetary system complicates the task of monetary policy-makers, as it makes it much more difficult to judge the quantitative effects of monetary policy on the economy in any specific period. But this is only one of many uncertainties affecting this assessment.

II The impact of a policy change on GDP and inflation: orders of magnitude

We now illustrate the broad orders of magnitude involved when changes in monetary policy affect GDP and the inflation rate. Two major caveats are necessary at this point. First, we have talked above as if monetary policy changes were causing a perturbation in the economy relative to some equilibrium state. For the purposes of exposition, this is how the impact of a change in monetary policy is illustrated below. But in reality, the economy is continually being affected by a variety of disturbances, and the aim of monetary policy is to return the economy to some equilibrium, rather than to disturb it. Disentangling the effects of monetary policy from those of the initial shocks is often very difficult. Second, at many points above we have talked about the effect of a policy change 'other things being equal'. Other things are rarely equal between episodes of policy tightening or loosening. The actual outcome of any policy change will depend on

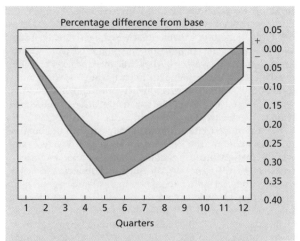

Chart 2 Effect on real GDP, relative to base, of 100 basis point increase in the official rate maintained for one year

Note: The shaded area represents the range between the paths of two specific simulations, as explained in the text.

factors such as the extent to which it was anticipated, business and consumer confidence at home and abroad, the path of fiscal policy, the state of the world economy, and the credibility of the monetary policy regime itself.

In order to give some broad idea of the size and time-path of the responses involved, we illustrate a simulation range using the Bank's macroeconometric model (see Charts 2 and 3). There is no sense in which this represents a forecast of what would happen in any real situation (as this would require, among other things, forecasts of many exogenous variables, such as world trade, which are here held at their base level). Nor is there any probability assigned to the outcome being within this range. Rather, this band is constructed from two alternative simulations, making different assumptions about monetary and fiscal policy reaction functions. Other simulations could give paths outside this range.[3] The upper limit of the bands in both the charts is derived from a simulation that assumes a price-level targeting rule for monetary policy, with government consumption spending fixed in money terms. The lower limit assumes a monetary policy rule that feeds back from both the output gap and deviations of inflation from target, with government consumption fixed as a proportion of GDP.

Charts 2 and 3 show the response of real GDP and inflation (relative to a base projection) to an unexpected 1 percentage point rise in the official rate that lasts for one year. In both the

[2] This is sometimes referred to as the 'bank lending channel'. Another aspect of what is more generally called the 'credit channel' is the financial accelerator effect, which was mentioned above in the context of the effect of firms' asset values on their ability to borrow. The financial accelerator effect is a normal part of the monetary transmission mechanism, but the bank lending channel is not.

[3] More details and an additional simulation that falls within the band, plus the full model-listing used to generate these charts, are reported in Chapter 2 of *Economic Models at the Bank of England*, Bank of England, April 1999.

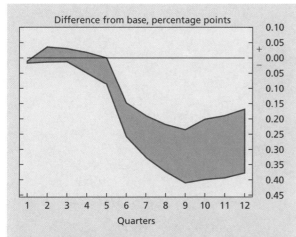

Difference from base, percentage points

Chart 3 Effect on inflation rate, relative to base, of 100 basis point increase in the official rate maintained for one year

Note: The shaded area represents the range between the paths of two specific simulations, as explained in the text.

smoothly to base, as a result both of the effects of the equilibrating forces within the model and of the reversal of policy.

The course of inflation, in contrast, is little changed during the first year under either of the simulations reported. But in the second year, inflation falls sharply, and the maximum effect is felt after about nine quarters. In one case, the fall is about 0.2 percentage points at its largest, and in the other, it is around 0.4 percentage points. In both cases, the impact on inflation then starts to diminish, but it has not returned to base three years after the initial policy change, even though policy was reversed after one year. It should be stressed that this simulation is only illustrative, and the explicit assumption that the hypothetical policy change is reversed after one year means that this chart cannot be used to infer how much interest rates would need to be changed on a sustained basis to achieve any given reduction in inflation. The key point to note is that monetary policy changes affect output and inflation with lags.

A final issue that needs clarification is whether the response of the economy to official rate changes is symmetric. The Bank's macroeconometric model used to generate the simulations discussed above is approximately linear, so rises and falls in the official rate of equal size would have effects of similar magnitude but opposite sign. But for some changes in official interest rates, where expectations and confidence effects are particularly important, the quantitative impact and the lags involved may exhibit considerable variation. This is as true for moves at different times in the same direction as it is for moves in the opposite direction.

upper and lower example of Chart 2, real GDP starts to fall quite quickly after the initial policy change. It reaches a maximum fall of between 0.2 per cent and 0.35 per cent of GDP after around five quarters. From the fifth quarter onwards, GDP returns

PART SEVEN

GLOBAL ECONOMIC ISSUES

Chapter 31

INFLATION

Policies to avoid inflation and unemployment, and to encourage growth, are the big macroeconomic issues of our time. We discussed growth in Chapter 22. In this chapter we focus on inflation, while the following chapter concentrates on unemployment. Is inflation a thing of the past? How are today's policies influenced by the desire to prevent its return? Is there a trade of between inflation and unemployment? Are the causes of sustained inflations different from those of one-off price level changes? These are some of the questions we address in this chapter. In particular, you will learn that:

• Inflation and unemployment are closely related, at least in the short term.

• Attempts to reduce unemployment have often been accompanied by a rise in inflation, and attempts to reduce inflation have usually led to episodes of increased unemployment, which although temporary are often severe.

• Macroeconomic policy-makers must walk a tightrope with inflation on one side and unemployment on the other.

• Inflation is related to the output gap and to expected inflation.

• Inflation is currently under control in most countries, but this could change if policy-makers are change their priorities.

• Inflation is generally considered to be undesirable, especially when it is unexpected, because it distorts the signals that are provided by the price system; it creates arbitrary redistribution from debtors to creditors; it creates incentives for speculative as opposed to productive investment activity; and is usually costly to eliminate.

• Unemployment is generally considered to be undesirable because it disrupts lives and is associated with a loss of real output that cannot be recovered.

The recent history of inflation and unemployment in the United Kingdom is set out in Figure 31.1(i). In the 1950s and 1960s both were low. Inflation averaged about 3.5 per cent and unemployment was always below 750,000, averaging about 1.5 per cent of the workforce. However, this picture changed dramatically in the 1970s. Inflation rose to over 25 per cent in 1975 (the highest peace-time inflation rate in the United Kingdom for at least 300 years) and unemployment fluctuated about a rising trend, reaching 1.5 million in 1977 and over 3 million by 1983. Inflation fell to under 5 per cent by the mid-1980s, but it rose again to around 10 per cent as a result of the late-1980s boom. This boom also brought unemployment down to around 1.5 million but it rose again to around 3 million in the recession of the early 1990s. Over the same period, inflation fell to around 2 per cent. The negative relationship between inflation and unemployment, at least from the end of the 1970s to the late 1990s, is evident from the figure. However, in the late 1990s and first three years of the twenty-first century inflation and unemployment were both low:[1] inflation was typically below the 2.5 per cent target that the government had set for it, and unemployment fell to levels not seen since the 1970s.

Figure 31.1(ii) shows average inflation in developing and advanced economies since 1970. Inflation rose worldwide in the early 1970s. It fluctuated at a historically high level through the 1970s and fell sharply in the advanced economies in the 1980s; but the fall in developing economies came only in the early 1990s. The IMF projects that inflation will remain low through to the middle years of the 2000s. We want to understand the forces that caused inflation in the 1970s and 1980s so that we can understand the current policies that are designed to prevent the mistakes of the past from being repeated. Inflation may finally be under control around the world, but it could easily return.

We start by using our macroeconomic model to investigate the causes of inflation. We then set out a theoretical framework for analysing the trade-off between inflation and unemployment. Finally, we discuss the implications of our analysis for counter-inflationary policy-making.

---

[1] There have been some changes in the way unemployment is measured that are discussed in the next chapter.

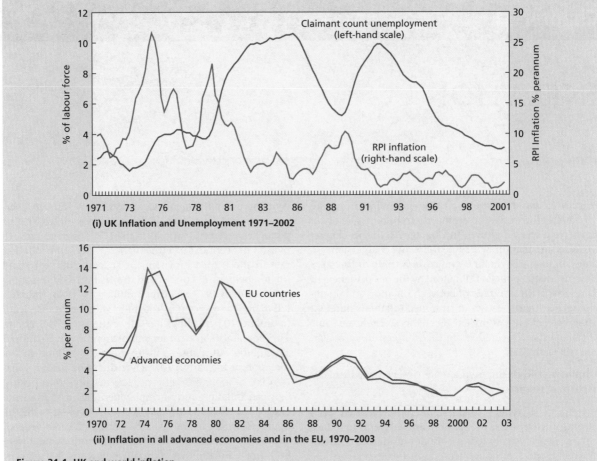

Figure 31.1 UK and world inflation

Much of the world has had similar inflation experience. Part (i) shows that UK inflation was high in the 1970s and unemployment was high in the 1980s. Part (ii) shows that inflation was a worldwide problem in the 1970s, but by the late 1990s it was low in both advanced and EU countries. Data for 2002 and 2003 are IMF staff projections.

Sources: part (i): ONS, *Economic Trends*; part (ii): IMF, *World Economic Outlook*, September 2002.

Inflation in the macro model

Although any increase in the price level is usually called an inflation, we need to distinguish between the forces that cause a once-and-for-all increase in the price level and those that cause a continuing, or sustained, increase. Any event that tends to drive the price level upwards is called an *inflationary shock*. To examine such shocks, we begin with an economy in long-run macroeconomic equilibrium operating under a flexible exchange rate regime. The price level is stable, and GDP is at its potential level. We then study the economy as different types of inflationary shock buffet it.

Supply shocks

Suppose there is a negative supply shock that shifts the *SRAS* curve upwards. This might be caused by a rise in the costs of imported raw materials or by a rise in domestic wage costs per unit of output, such as from the introduction of a high minimum wage. With a given *AD* curve, the impact effect is for output to fall and the price level to rise. That is, GDP falls while inflation picks up. What happens next depends on how the monetary authorities react. The authorities now have two alternatives.

First, they can lower the interest rate sufficiently to shift the *AD* curve rightwards, so that it intersects the new *SRAS* curve at potential GDP. To achieve this, they must buy bonds and supply money in return. This injects new money into the system, thereby shifting *AD* rightwards. The supply shock is then said to be 'accommodated' by an increase in the money supply. This is a case of monetary **accommodation**.

Second, the authorities can adopt an interest rate policy that keeps the money supply constant and the *AD* curve in its initial position.[2] We then say that the supply shock is 'not accommodated' by an increase in the money supply. This is the case of *no monetary accommodation*.

What happens also depends on whether the supply shock is an isolated event or one of a series of continued shocks. We take these two cases in turn.

Isolated supply shocks

Suppose that the leftward shift in the *SRAS* curve is an isolated event. It might, for example, be caused by a once-and-for-all increase in the cost of imported raw materials.

No monetary accommodation The leftward shift in the *SRAS* curve causes the price level to rise and pushes GDP below its potential level, opening up a recessionary gap. As a result of this recessionary gap, market pressures tend to cause wages and other factor costs to fall relative to productivity. When this happens, the *SRAS* curve shifts downward, causing a return of GDP to its potential level, and a fall in the price level. The period of inflation accompanying the original supply shock is followed by a period of deflation, which continues until long-run equilibrium is re-established. This sequence is illustrated in Figure 31.2. Since money wages tend to react only sluggishly to excess supply in the labour market, unit costs of production fall only slowly, so the recovery to full equilibrium at Y^* may take a long time.

Monetary accommodation Now suppose that the monetary authorities react by loosening their monetary stance, buying bonds and generating an increase in the money supply. This shifts the *AD* curve to the right, causing both the price level and output to rise. (Part of this adjustment may come from currency depreciation, causing an upward shift of the net export function.) When the recessionary gap is eliminated, the price level, rather than falling back to its original value, will have risen further. These effects are also shown in Figure 31.2.

The monetary authorities might decide to accommodate the supply shock because relying on cost deflation to restore activity to its potential level forces the economy to suffer an extended slump.

Monetary accommodation can return the economy to potential GDP relatively quickly, but at the cost of a once-and-for-all increase in the price level.

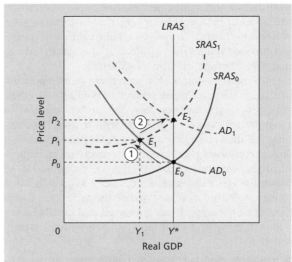

Figure 31.2 A single supply shock
The final effect of a single supply shock depends on whether or not it is accommodated by monetary expansion. A supply shock causes the SRAS curve to shift leftward from $SRAS_0$ to $SRAS_1$, as shown by arrow 1. Short-run equilibrium is established at E_1. If there is no monetary accommodation, the unemployment will exert a downward pressure on wage costs, causing the SRAS curve to shift slowly back to the right to $SRAS_0$. Prices will fall, and output will rise, until the original equilibrium is restored at E_0. If there is monetary accommodation, the AD curve shifts from AD_0 to AD_1, as shown by arrow 2. This re-establishes full-employment equilibrium at E_2, but with a higher price level, P_2.

Repeated supply shocks

As an example of a repeated supply shock, assume that powerful unions are able to raise money wages faster than productivity is increasing, even in the face of a significant excess supply of labour. Firms then pass these higher wages on in the form of higher prices. This type of supply shock causes what is called a wage-cost push inflation—an increase in the price level due to increases in money wages that are not associated with an excess demand for labour.

No monetary accommodation Suppose the monetary authorities do not accommodate these supply shocks. The initial effect of the leftward shift in the *SRAS* curve is to open up a recessionary gap, as shown in Figure 31.2. If unions continue to negotiate increases in wages, subjecting the economy to further supply shocks, prices continue to rise

---

[2] Whether this requires higher, constant (or even lower) interest rates depends on what happens to demand for money. Output has fallen, lowering money demand; but prices have risen, raising money demand. If there is a net increase in money demand following the supply shock, interest rates will have to rise to maintain a constant money supply. If money demand is unchanged, constant interest rates will be consistent with a constant money stock.

while output and employment continue to fall. Eventually the trade-off between higher wages and unemployment will become obvious to everyone. Long before everyone is unemployed, unions will cease forcing up wages in order to maintain jobs for those who are still employed.

Once the wage-cost push ceases, there are two possibilities. First, the unions may succeed in holding on to their high real wages, but not push for further increases of money wages in excess of productivity increases. The economy will then come to rest with a stable price level and a large recessionary gap. Second, the persistent unemployment may eventually erode the power of the unions, so that real wages and hence unit costs begin to fall, because money wages rise more slowly than productivity is rising. In this case the supply shock is reversed, and the *SRAS* curve will shift downward until full employment is eventually restored.

A non-accommodated wage-cost push tends to be self-limiting because the rising unemployment that it causes tends to restrain further wage increases.

Monetary accommodation Now suppose that the monetary authorities accommodate the shock by relaxing their monetary policy stance, lowering interest rates relative to where they would otherwise be by buying bonds and increasing the money supply. This shifts the *AD* curve to the right, as shown in Figure 31.2. In the new full-employment equilibrium, where GDP is at its potential level, both money wages and prices have risen. The rise in wages has been offset by a rise in prices. Workers are no better off than they were originally, although those who remained in jobs were temporarily better off in the transition period when wages had risen (taking equilibrium to E_1 in Figure 31.2) but before the price level had risen enough to restore full employment (taking equilibrium to E_2).

The stage is now set for the unions to try again. If they succeed in negotiating further increases in money wages, they hit the economy with another supply shock. If the monetary authorities again accommodate the shock, full employment is maintained, but at the cost of a further round of inflation. If this process goes on repeatedly, it can give rise to a continual wage-cost push inflation as shown in Figure 31.3. The wage-cost push tends to cause a stagflation, with rising prices and falling output. Monetary accommodation tends to reinforce the rise in prices and to offset the fall in output. It will also be associated with repeated currency depreciation.

There are two requirements for continuing wage-cost push inflation. First, powerful groups, such as industrial unions or government employees, must press for, and employers must grant, increases in money wages in excess of productivity growth, even in the absence of excess demand for labour and goods. Second, the monetary authorities must accommodate the resulting inflation by loosening their monetary stance, in order to prevent the rising unem-

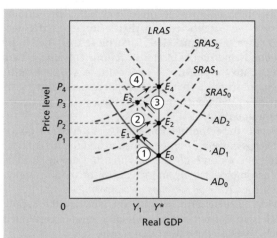

Figure 31.3 Monetary accommodation of a repeated supply shock

Monetary accommodation of a repeated supply shock causes a continuous inflation in the absence of excess demand. The initial equilibrium is at E_0. A supply shock then takes equilibrium to E_1, just as in Figure 30.2. This is the stagflation phase of rising prices and falling output; it is indicated by arrow 1. If the monetary authorities then accommodate the supply shock, the *AD* curve shifts to AD_1, taking equilibrium to E_2. This is the expansionary phase of rising prices and rising output (arrow 2). A second supply shock takes equilibrium to E_3 (arrow 3), and a second round of monetary accommodation takes it to E_4 (arrow 4). As long as the supply shocks and the monetary accommodation continue, the inflation continues.

ployment that would otherwise occur. The process set up by this sequence of wage-cost push and monetary accommodation is often called a wage–price spiral.

Is monetary accommodation desirable? Once started, a wage–price spiral can be halted only if the monetary authorities stop accommodating the supply shocks that are causing the inflation. The longer they wait to do so, the more entrenched will become the expectations of continuing inflation. These entrenched expectations may cause wages to continue to rise after accommodation has ceased. Because employers expect prices to rise, they go on granting wage increases. If expectations are firmly enough entrenched, the wage push can continue for quite some time, in spite of the downward pressure caused by the rising unemployment associated with the growing recessionary gap.

Evidence suggests that, when politicians run monetary policy, they typically accommodate supply shocks to avoid the short-term unpopularity that is generated by rising unemployment. For this reason many economists have recommended that central banks be given the clear objective of maintaining a stable price level and then be insulated from further political direction. This is what has been done in the United Kingdom since May 1997.[3] Although the Bank of England's Monetary Policy Committee may elect to accommodate some isolated supply shocks, the Bank's independence makes it unlikely that persistent wage–price spirals will be permitted to develop through continued monetary accommodation. The same applies in the euro zone, where the European Central Bank (ECB) has been given the goal of achieving price stability and has been insulated from short-term political pressures.

Accommodating a negative supply shock risks setting off a wage–price spiral, but accommodating the first-round effects of shocks may limit the output and employment losses that are otherwise inevitable.

This may not seem like a big issue in the early twenty-first century, but it certainly was important in the 1970s and 1980s, and may be again in the future. Notice also that wage shocks are not the only type of possible supply shock. The energy price rises of 1973 and 1979 (oil shocks) were very important, and their effects can be analysed just as above. Equally, a price rise in any imported material would have a similar effect. Exchange rate depreciations contribute to input price shocks because the price of imported materials rises, but exchange rate changes have demand dimensions as well, as they shift the net export function.

Demand shocks

Now suppose that an initial equilibrium is disturbed by a rightward shift in the aggregate demand curve, a shift that could have been caused by either an increase in some category of autonomous spending or a relaxation of monetary policy. This causes the price level and output to rise. If the monetary authorities react to the increase in the demand for money that accompanies an increase in autonomous spending by permitting the money supply to rise, they are said to be **validating** the shock. (Notice that this terminology distinguishes between the response to a supply shock, which is described as 'accommodating' the shock, and the response to a demand shock, which is described as 'validating' the shock.)

No monetary validation This is the standard case of a once-and-for-all increase in aggregate demand, such as shown in Figure 28.6 on page 507. Because the initial AD shock takes output above the full-employment level, an inflationary gap opens up. The pressure of excess demand soon causes wages to rise faster than productivity, shifting the $SRAS$ curve upwards. As output and prices are higher, money demand increases. In order to hold the money supply constant in the face of a higher money demand, the monetary authorities will have to sell bonds and raise interest rates, thus choking off the excess demand for money. As long as the authorities follow an interest rate policy that holds the

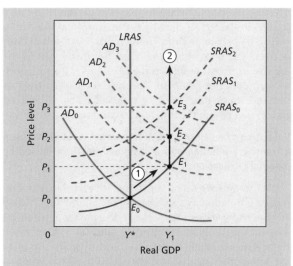

Figure 31.4 A validated demand-shock inflation

Monetary validation will cause the AD curve to shift, offsetting the leftward shift in the $SRAS$ curve and maintaining an inflationary gap in spite of the ever-rising price level. An initial demand shock shifts equilibrium from E_0 to E_1 (along the path indicated by arrow 1), taking GDP to Y_1 and the price level to P_1. The resulting inflationary gap then causes the $SRAS$ curve to shift to the left. This time, however, the money supply increases, shifting the AD curve to the right. By the time the aggregate supply curve has reached $SRAS_1$, the aggregate demand curve has reached AD_2, taking equilibrium to E_2. GDP remains constant at Y_1, while the price level rises to P_2.

The persistent inflationary gap continues to push the $SRAS$ curve to the left, while the continued monetary validation continues to push the AD curve to the right. By the time aggregate supply reaches $SRAS_2$, aggregate demand has reached AD_3. The price level has risen still further to P_3, but the inflationary gap remains unchanged at $Y_1 - Y^*$. As long as this monetary validation continues, the economy moves along the vertical path of arrow 2.

money supply constant, the rise in the price level moves the economy upwards along its fixed AD curve. The rise in the price level thus eventually eliminates the inflationary gap. In this case the initial period of inflation is followed by further inflation, which continues until the new long-run equilibrium is reached. The potential level of GDP and a stable price level are then restored.

Monetary validation Next suppose that, once the initial demand shock has created an inflationary gap, the monetary authorities frustrate the forces that would return GDP to its potential level by relaxing monetary policy, thereby permitting the nominal money supply to rise when output starts to fall. This is the case illustrated in Figure 31.4. Two forces are now brought into play. Spurred by the

---
[3] The framework for setting and implementing monetary policy in the Bank of England and the ECB is discussed in Chapter 28.

inflationary gap, the wage increases cause the *SRAS* curve to shift to the left. Fuelled by the expansionary monetary policy, the *AD* curve shifts to the right. As a result of both of these shifts, the price level rises. But if the shift in the *AD* curve offsets the shift in the *SRAS* curve, the inflationary gap does not diminish. The validation of an isolated demand shock thus creates a series of repeated demand shocks that permit the inflation to continue.

Validation of a demand shock turns what would have been a transitory inflation into a sustained inflation fuelled by monetary expansion.

We can now see why a rise in the price level may not remove an inflationary gap. Because the money supply may expand endogenously to meet any demand for it, when the monetary authorities are pegging nominal interest rates, there is no automatic adjustment mechanism to eliminate the inflationary gap. As the price level rises, the nominal money supply rises sufficiently to keep the real money supply constant, and the inflationary gap is not reduced. This sequence requires either that the monetary authorities do not pick up the warnings of impending inflation coming from the rising money supply figures, or that they decide on an inflationary policy.

Although there is controversy over how much control the monetary authorities can have over the money supply, few economists doubt that a determined enough anti-inflationary policy can stop the nominal money supply from expanding as fast as prices are rising. Most monetary authorities have pursued such a policy at one time or another over the past few decades, thereby ending an inflation in their own country. Thus, in the world in which we live, inflations cannot go on indefinitely unless they are validated by policy decisions taken by the monetary authorities. Notice also that the Taylor Rule (explained in Box 28.4 on page 508) has monetary authorities reacting to deviations of inflation from its target rate and to deviations of GDP from its potential level. Thus, in a world of inflation targeting, central banks are unlikely to validate any inflation that occurs because of a temporary shock. The authorities will raise interest rates both when inflation goes above target and when actual GDP exceeds potential GDP.

Figure 31.5 summarizes all the cases of supply and demand shock with or without accommodation or validation.

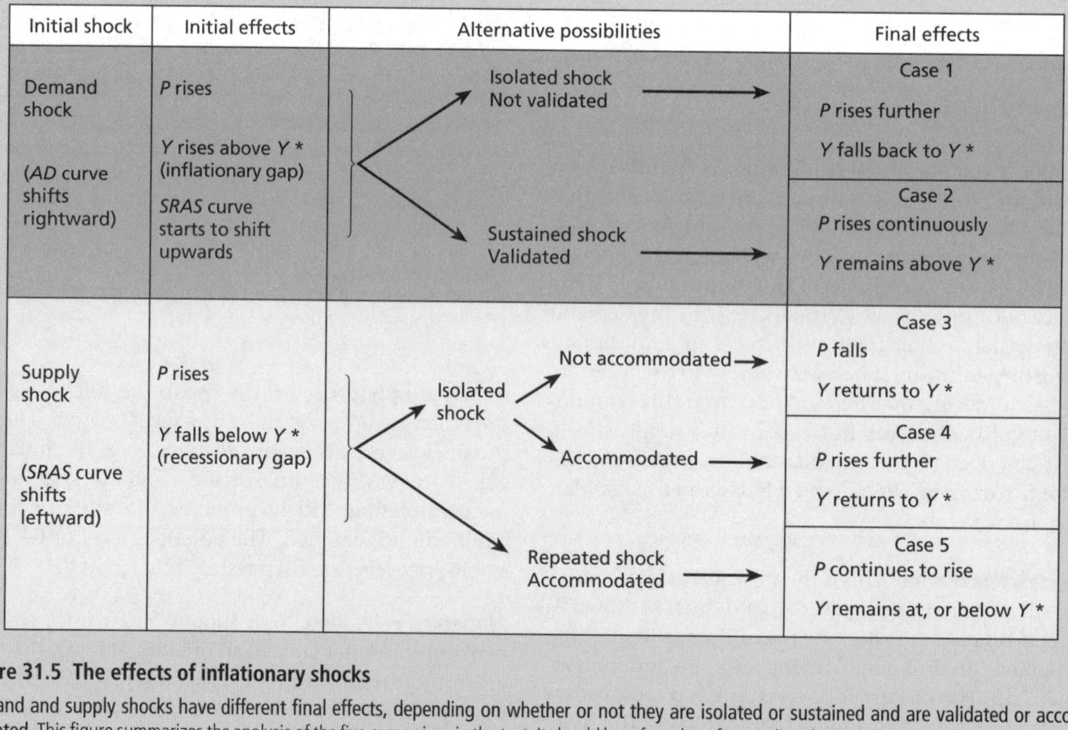

Initial shock	Initial effects	Alternative possibilities		Final effects
Demand shock (*AD* curve shifts rightward)	*P* rises *Y* rises above *Y* * (inflationary gap) *SRAS* curve starts to shift upwards	Isolated shock Not validated ⟶		**Case 1** *P* rises further *Y* falls back to *Y* *
		Sustained shock Validated ⟶		**Case 2** *P* rises continuously *Y* remains above *Y* *
Supply shock (*SRAS* curve shifts leftward)	*P* rises *Y* falls below *Y* * (recessionary gap)	Isolated shock	Not accommodated ⟶	**Case 3** *P* falls *Y* returns to *Y* *
			Accommodated ⟶	**Case 4** *P* rises further *Y* returns to *Y* *
		Repeated shock Accommodated ⟶		**Case 5** *P* continues to rise *Y* remains at, or below *Y* *

Figure 31.5 The effects of inflationary shocks

Demand and supply shocks have different final effects, depending on whether or not they are isolated or sustained and are validated or accommodated. This figure summarizes the analysis of the five cases given in the text. It should be referred to after reading the text discussion of each of the cases. All comparisons assume that GDP starts at its potential level and that initially the price level is stable.

The initial effects of a demand shock are to raise GDP and the price level. If the shock is isolated, the price level continues to rise until GDP falls back to its potential level (case 1). If the shock is sustained and validated (validation turns an isolated shock into a sustained shock), the price level continues to rise while GDP stays above its potential level (case 2).

The initial effects of a supply shock are to raise the price level but to reduce GDP. Once the shock is over, GDP will return to its potential level, with a lowered price level if there is no accommodation (case 3), and with a higher price level if there is accommodation (case 4). If the shock is sustained and accommodated, the price level can continue to rise, with or without a persistent recessionary gap (case 5).

Inflation as a monetary phenomenon

Economists have debated the extent to which inflation is a monetary phenomenon. Does it have purely monetary causes—e.g. increases in the supply of money? Does it have purely monetary consequences—say, when only the price level is affected? The US economist Milton Friedman made the famous remark: 'Inflation is everywhere and always a monetary phenomenon.' This could be a mere tautology, since inflation is by definition a fall in the purchasing power of money. However, avoiding semantics, let us summarize what we have already learned about the causes of inflation.

1. Many forces can cause the price level to rise. On the demand side, anything that shifts the *AD* curve to the right will have this result—*ceteris paribus*, increases in desired spending on exports, government spending, investment, and consumption, as well as a relaxation of monetary policy or decreases in money demand. On the supply side, anything that increases unit costs of production will shift the *SRAS* curve to the left and cause the price level to rise.

2. Such inflation can continue for some time without any increases in the money supply.

3. The rise in prices must eventually come to a halt, unless monetary expansion occurs.

Points 1 and 2 indicate that a temporary burst of inflation may or may not be a monetary phenomenon; it need not have monetary causes, and it need not be accompanied by monetary expansion. Point 3 implies that a sustained inflation must be a monetary phenomenon. If a rise in prices is to continue, it must be accompanied by continuing increases in the money supply (or decreases in money demand). This is true regardless of the cause that set the rise in prices in motion. What happens when monetary validation gets out of hand is discussed in Box 31.1.

Now let us summarize what we have learned about the consequences of an inflation, assuming that the economy begins from a situation of full employment and a stable price level.

1. In the short run a demand-shock inflation tends to be accompanied by an increase in GDP.

2. In the short run a supply-shock inflation tends to be accompanied by a decrease in GDP.

3. When all adjustments have been fully made, so that the relevant supply-side curve is the *LRAS* curve, shifts in either the *AD* or *SRAS* curve will leave GDP unchanged and will affect only the price level.

Points 1 and 2 are saying that inflation is not, in the short run, a purely monetary phenomenon; it has real consequences for output and employment. Point 3 states that, from the point of view of long-run equilibrium, inflation is a purely monetary phenomenon.

We have now established three important conclusions:

1. Without monetary accommodation, supply shocks cause temporary bursts of inflation accompanied by recessionary gaps. The gaps are removed if, and when, unit costs of production fall, restoring equilibrium at potential GDP and at the initial price level.

2. Without monetary validation, demand shocks cause temporary bursts of inflation accompanied by inflationary gaps. The gaps are removed as wages rise, returning GDP to its potential level, but at a higher price level.

3. With an appropriate response from the monetary authorities, an inflation initiated by either supply or demand shocks can continue indefinitely; an ever-increasing money supply is necessary for an ever-continuing inflation.

Fortunately, the lessons from the inflation episodes of the 1970s and 1980s have been learned by policy-makers, and in many countries central banks have been told that their job is to maintain low inflation. So sustained periods of rapid inflation are much less likely to occur in the near future. Politicians learned these lessons the hard way, rather than by reading textbooks such as this.

The Phillips curve

Up to now it has been enough to say that an inflationary gap implies excess demand for labour, low unemployment, pressure on wages to rise faster than productivity, and hence an upward-shifting *SRAS* curve. But now we need to look in more detail at the influence of wages on inflation. To do this, we make use of a famous relation called the Phillips curve, which helps us understand how fast the *SRAS* curve shifts. We first present the Phillips curve in its original form and then transform it into a form more applicable to the *AD–AS* model. Since the original curve uses unemployment rather than GDP as its indicator of excess demand in labour markets, we must first show the relation between the two.

The NAIRU When current GDP is at its potential level, unemployment is not zero, even though we sometimes refer to this situation as 'full employment'. Instead, there may be a substantial amount of *frictional unemployment*, caused by the movement of people among jobs, and *structural unemployment*, caused by a mismatch between the

Box 31.1 **Hyperinflation**

Monetary validation of ongoing inflation sometimes gets out of hand. In extreme cases it leads to hyperinflation, in which inflation is so rapid that money ceases to be useful as a medium of exchange and a store of value. However, inflation rates of 50, 100, and even 200 per cent or more per year have occurred year after year in some countries and have proven to be manageable as people adjust their contracts in real terms. Although there are strains and side-effects, the evidence shows such situations to be possible without causing money to become useless.

Does this mean that there is no reason to fear that rapid inflation will turn into a hyperinflation that will destroy the value of money completely? The historical record is not entirely reassuring. There have been a number of cases in which prices began to rise at an ever-accelerating rate until a nation's money ceased to be a satisfactory store of value, even for the short period between receipt and spending, and hence ceased also to be useful as a medium of exchange.

The index of wholesale prices in Germany before and after the First World War is given in the table. The index shows that a product purchased with one 100 mark note in July 1923 would have required ten million 100 mark notes for its purchase only four months later! Although Germany had experienced substantial inflation during the war, averaging more than 30 per cent per year, the immediate postwar years of 1920 and 1921 gave no sign of an explosive inflation; indeed, during 1920 price stability was experienced. In 1922 and 1923, however, the price level exploded. On 15 November 1923 the mark was officially repudiated, its value wholly destroyed. How could this happen?

German wholesale price index (1913 = 1)

January 1913	1
January 1920	13
January 1921	14
January 1922	37
July 1922	101
January 1923	2,785
July 1923	74,800
August 1923	944,000
September 1923	23,900,000
October 1923	7,096,000,000
November 1923	750,000,000,000

When inflation becomes so rapid that people lose confidence in the purchasing power of their currency, they rush to spend it. People who have goods become increasingly reluctant to accept the rapidly depreciating money in exchange. The rush to spend money accelerates the increase in prices until people finally become unwilling to accept money on any terms. What was once money ceases to be money.

The price system can then be restored only by repudiation of the old monetary unit and its replacement by a new unit. This destroys the value of monetary savings and of all contracts specified in terms of the old monetary unit.

There are about a dozen documented hyperinflations in world history, among them the collapses of the continental* during the American War of Independence, the rouble during the Russian Revolution, the drachma during and after the German occupation of Greece in the Second World War, the pengo in Hungary during 1945–6, and the Chinese national currency during 1946–8. Every one of these hyperinflations was accompanied by great increases in the money supply; new money was printed to give governments the purchasing power that they could not or would not obtain by taxation. Further, each one occurred in the midst of a major political upheaval in which grave doubts existed about the stability and the future of the government itself.

Is hyperinflation likely in the absence of civil war, revolution, or collapse of the government? Most economists think not. Further, it is clear that high inflation rates over a period of time do not mean the inevitable or even the likely onset of hyperinflation.

However, do not assume that hyperinflation is a curiosity only to be found in the history books. The following is an extract from a newspaper report on events in Serbia in 1993 and 1994:

Worried that Serbian cities might starve during the winter, the government announced [in July 1993] that it would buy a million tons of the wheat harvest from private farmers at guaranteed prices. . . . The entire country, now highly attuned to living with an unstable currency, realised what this would mean. The government could only pay by printing a lot more money, which the peasants would switch into marks the moment they were paid. It would, in short, kill the currency.

Sure enough, three times during July, the dinar/mark exchange rate lurched downwards. Then it spun out of control.

The exponential growth of inflation during these months still astonishes even the Yugoslav economists who had seen it coming. Between July and the end of the year it went from 500 per cent to 2,000 per cent a month, to 20,000 per cent, then 500,000 per cent and onwards. By January, prices were rising faster than 100 per cent an hour.

At the final assessment before the recovery plan was put into effect on January 24th [1994], the monthly inflation rate had reached a mind-blowing 302 million per cent. Compare that with the inflation rate in Germany, which at its height in 1923 reached only 332 per cent per month, while inflation in Latin American countries during the 1980s never went beyond 300 per cent per year.

(*Independent on Sunday*, 9 October 1994, p. 9)

* This is the name given to the notes issued by the American Continental Congress at that time.

characteristics of the demand for labour and the characteristics of its supply. The amount of frictional and structural unemployment that exists when GDP is at its potential level is called the **NAIRU**, or the **natural rate of unemployment** (U^*).[4] We use the term NAIRU rather than natural rate because the latter term may give the erroneous impression that nothing can be done to reduce unemployment below a rate that is 'natural'.

It follows from the definition of the NAIRU that, when GDP exceeds potential GDP ($Y > Y^*$), unemployment will be less than the NAIRU ($U < U^*$); and when GDP is less than potential GDP ($Y < Y^*$), unemployment will exceed the NAIRU ($U > U^*$).[5]

We can now use the NAIRU terminology to restate our earlier assumptions about the pressure that is put on wage rates, and through them on the *SRAS* curve, by inflationary and recessionary gaps.

When the unemployment rate is below the NAIRU, demand forces put pressure on wages to rise faster than productivity. When the unemployment rate is above the NAIRU, demand forces put pressure on wages to rise more slowly than productivity, or even to fall. When unemployment is at the NAIRU, demand forces exert neither upward nor downward pressure on wages relative to productivity.

The theory of the Phillips curve

In the 1950s Professor A. W. Phillips (1914–75) was doing research on stabilization policy at the London School of Economics. He was interested in the question of the speed with which input prices responded to excess demand and excess supply. To study this question, he looked at the rate of change of money wage rates in the United Kingdom over a period of 100 years. By relating these wage changes to the level of unemployment, he discovered a remarkable relationship that came to be known as the 'Phillips curve'. This was an empirical relationship which later theoretical work tried to explain. We will incorporate the key elements of Phillips curve theory into the context of our macro model.

The **Phillips curve** relates the percentage rate of change of money wage rates (measured at an annual rate) to the level of unemployment (measured as the percentage of the labour force unemployed). Unemployment is plotted on the horizontal axis, and wage changes on the vertical axis. Thus, any point on the curve relates a particular level of unemployment to a particular rate of increase of money wages. At the outset we assume that the price level is expected to remain relatively stable. Later, we consider what happens to the curve when people expect a significant rate of inflation to persist.

So far in this book we have dealt with the levels of variables. The Phillips curve relates the amount of unemployment to the rate of change of money wages. Letting ΔW

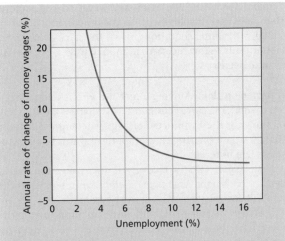

Figure 31.6 A Phillips curve

The Phillips curve relates the level of unemployment to the rate of change of money wage rates. The figure shows a numerical example of a Phillips curve. According to the example, an increase in unemployment by four percentage points, from 8 to 12 per cent, will lower wage inflation from 3 to 2 per cent, while a reduction in unemployment by four percentage points, from 8 to 4 per cent, will raise wage inflation from 3 to 14 per cent.

stand for the change in money wage rates from one year to the next, and W for the level of wage rates in the first year, the equation of the Phillips curve is

$$(\Delta W/W) = f(U), \tag{1}$$

where f stands for a functional relation.

A numerical example of a Phillips curve is shown in Figure 31.6. The numbers on the figure are hypothetical. (The original curve became negative at high rates of unemployment.) We will see that, appropriately interpreted, the Phillips curve can handle all of the causes of inflation. For the moment we will concentrate on the influence of demand forces.

The shape of the Phillips curve

A negative slope Note first that the Phillips curve has a negative slope, showing that the lower is the level of unemployment, the higher is the rate of change of money wages. This should not surprise us. Low rates of unemployment are associated with boom conditions, when excess

[4] 'NAIRU' is an acronym for non-accelerating-inflation rate of unemployment. The reason for this name will become apparent later in the chapter. We talk about the natural rate of unemployment and the NAIRU as if they were the same concept: in reality, they are different except when the economy is in full equilibrium.

[5] In more complex models it is possible that the correspondence between the NAIRU and Y^* may not hold, but for simplicity we assume here that it does hold.

demand for labour causes money wages to rise rapidly. High rates of unemployment, on the other hand, are associated with slump conditions, when the slack demand for labour leads to low increases in money wages, or possibly even to decreases.

A flattening slope Moving along the Phillips curve from left to right, the curve gets flatter. This shape is another way of showing the asymmetry of aggregate supply, namely that input prices change more rapidly upwards than downwards. Let us recall why.

First, assume that a recovery is increasing the excess demand for labour. As a boom develops, the unemployment rate will decrease towards, but will never reach, zero. (There will always be some frictional and structural unemployment.) At the same time, the growing excess demand for labour will be bidding up wage rates more and more rapidly. This behaviour causes the Phillips curve to get very steep and to lie far above the horizontal axis at its left-hand end. The further the curve is above the axis, the faster wages are rising.

The steepness of the curve in the range of low unemployment shows that wage inflation is very responsive to changes in unemployment in that range.

Second, consider the onset of a recession that raises unemployment. This recession restrains wage increases. As a result, the Phillips curve comes closer and closer to the horizontal axis, indicating less and less upward pressure on wages the higher the level of unemployment. If the curve fell below the axis, then money wages would actually be falling over some range of high unemployment. We do not show this case in the figure but instead assume that, as unemployment gets very high, the rate of increase in money wages approaches zero but never becomes negative.

The flatness of the Phillips curve in the range of high unemployment shows that the rate of wage inflation is relatively unresponsive to changes in unemployment over that range.

The Phillips curve and the *SRAS* curve

To see what is happening to unit costs of production, we need to relate the increase in wage rates to the increase in labour productivity. For simplicity, in the rest of the discussion we will assume that labour is the only variable factor used by firms. This allows us to associate the labour costs of each unit of output with total variable costs per unit of output. (We could equally well have assumed that all input prices change at the same rate as does the price of labour.)

What happens to unit costs of production now depends only on the differences between what labour costs the firm and what labour produces for the firm. To illustrate what is involved, we repeat in part (i) of Figure 31.7 the Phillips curve from Figure 31.6. We then add to it a horizontal line labelled *g*, for growth in output per unit of labour input, which shows the rate at which labour productivity is growing year by year. In the hypothetical example of the figure, we have assumed that productivity is rising at 3 per cent per year. The intersection of the Phillips curve and the productivity line at the point *x* now divides the graph into an inflationary and a deflationary range described in the numbered points below. Given the assumptions about wage behaviour made earlier, point *x* must occur at the NAIRU (labelled U^*)—which corresponds to a level of output equal to potential GDP, Y^*.

1. At unemployment rates less than at the intersection point, wages are rising faster than productivity and thus unit costs of production (input costs per unit of output) are rising. If unit costs are rising, the *SRAS* curve must be shifting upwards.

2. At unemployment rates greater than at the intersection point, money wage rates are rising more slowly than productivity is rising. Thus, unit costs are falling. If unit costs are falling, the *SRAS* curve must be shifting downwards.

Notice that, although we have drawn the Phillips curve to show complete downward inflexibility of money wages, this does not imply complete downward inflexibility of unit costs. As long as money wages rise less than productivity rises, unit costs of production will be falling, and the *SRAS* curve will be shifting downwards. Complete downward inflexibility of unit costs—and thus the total absence of the equilibrating mechanism that comes from downward shifts in the *SRAS* curve—requires more than the downward inflexibility of money wages: it requires that money wages never rise by less than the increase in productivity.

We will now derive from the Phillips curve a new curve that expresses the verbal argument just given.

Part (ii) of Figure 31.7 shows a new curve that relates the rate of unemployment to the change in unit costs, rather than to the change in money wage rates. The new curve still has unemployment on the horizontal axis, but now it is plotted against the rate of increase in unit costs on the vertical axis. Since this is merely the rate of increase in money wage rates minus the rate of increase of productivity, the new diagram is the same as part (i) of the figure, except that the origin on the vertical axis has been shifted by the rate of productivity growth.

The new curve tells us the rate at which unit costs of production are changing—and thus the rate at which the *SRAS* curve is shifting upwards or downwards—at each level of unemployment.

So far we have followed Phillips in plotting unemployment on the horizontal axis. The *SRAS* curve, however, plots GDP on its horizontal axis. To get a curve that relates

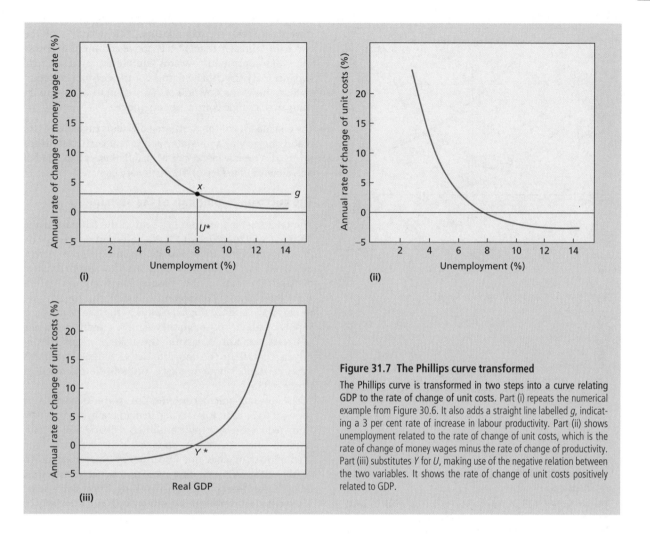

Figure 31.7 The Phillips curve transformed

The Phillips curve is transformed in two steps into a curve relating GDP to the rate of change of unit costs. Part (i) repeats the numerical example from Figure 30.6. It also adds a straight line labelled *g*, indicating a 3 per cent rate of increase in labour productivity. Part (ii) shows unemployment related to the rate of change of unit costs, which is the rate of change of money wages minus the rate of change of productivity. Part (iii) substitutes *Y* for *U*, making use of the negative relation between the two variables. It shows the rate of change of unit costs positively related to GDP.

the change in unit costs of production to the level of GDP, we note that unemployment is negatively related to the level of GDP. As GDP rises, unemployment tends to fall. To make the relation precise, we assume that the labour force remains constant. Now any short-run increase in GDP, which means that more labour is employed, must mean that less labour is unemployed. In this case any increase in GDP must mean a decrease in unemployment.

We can now transform the curve in part (ii) of Figure 31.7, which plots changes in unit costs of production against the unemployment rate, into a new relationship, shown in part (iii) of the figure. This curve shows the same rate of change in unit costs of production, but plots it against the level of GDP. Since GDP and unemployment vary negatively with each other, the curve in part (iii) of the figure has the opposite slope to the curve in part (ii) of the same figure.[6] We call this new curve the transformed Phillips curve.

Shifts in the *SRAS* curve explained

Figure 31.8(i) shows the familiar aggregate demand/aggregate supply diagram. Part (ii) shows the transformed Phillips curve (*PC*), relating the rate of change of unit costs to GDP. Both parts have GDP on their horizontal axes, and by lining these up we can compare one with the other. The *AD* and *SRAS* curves in part (i) determine the short-run levels of prices and GDP. Given the GDP so determined, the transformed Phillips curve tells us the rate at which the *SRAS* curve is shifting. Since from now on we will always be working with this transformed curve, we will just call it a

[6] We started with the relation $\Delta W/W = f(U)$, which is the original Phillips curve. We then subtracted productivity growth, *g*, to get a unit-cost-increase curve: $\Delta c/c = f(U) - g$. Then we substituted a relation between unemployment and national income, $U = u(Y)$, to get a curve relating the rate of increase in unit costs to the level of unemployment: $\Delta c/c = f(u(Y))$.

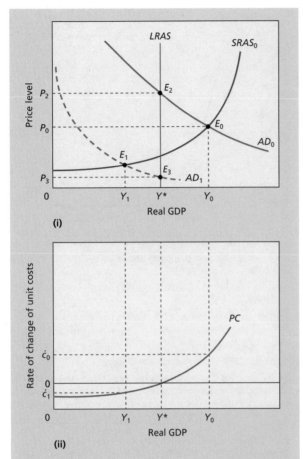

(i)

(ii)

Figure 31.8 The Phillips curve and the AS–AD relationship

The transformed Phillips curve shows the speed with which the SRAS curve is shifting upwards. When the curves are AD_0 and $SRAS_0$ in part (i), they intersect at E_0 to produce equilibrium GDP of Y_0. Part (ii) shows that when GDP is Y_0 the rate of change of unit costs, and hence the rate of increase in the SRAS curve, is $\dot{c}_0$ per cent per year. Thus, equilibrium GDP is moving rapidly towards Y^* as the point of macroeconomic equilibrium moves up the fixed AD curve towards the long-run equilibrium at E_2.

When the curves are AD_1 and $SRAS_0$ in part (i), equilibrium is at E_1, with GDP Y_1. Part (ii) shows that when GDP is Y_1, unit costs, and hence the SRAS curve, will be shifting downwards at the rate of $\dot{c}_1$ per cent per year. Thus, equilibrium GDP is moving slowly along AD_1 towards a long-run equilibrium at E_3. Each long-run equilibrium has the same level of GDP but a different price level.

Phillips curve. (Notice that, to emphasize that we are dealing with rates of change, we place a dot over the variable to indicate its annual percentage rate of change—in this case the symbol is $\dot{c}$.)

The long-run equilibrium of the economy is at potential GDP. All that the curve in part (ii) tells us is how fast the SRAS curve in part (i) is shifting, moving the economy towards its long-run equilibrium. The steepness of the curve for Y greater than Y* (i.e. above equilibrium) shows the rapid adjustment towards equilibrium after a single expansionary shock. The flatness of the curve below equilibrium shows the slowness of adjustment towards equilibrium after a single contractionary shock.

The nonlinearity of the transformed Phillips curve expresses the asymmetry of aggregate supply: that costs, and hence prices, rise rapidly in the face of an inflationary gap, but fall only slowly in the face of a recessionary gap.

The micro underpinnings of the asymmetry

The micro behaviour that lies behind the flat part of the Phillips curve to the left of Y* is explained in two parts. The first concerns the theory of short-run oligopoly pricing described in Chapter 12—firms tend to absorb cyclical demand fluctuations by varying their outputs rather than their prices. The second concerns the theory that money wage rates do not fall rapidly in the face of an excess supply of labour, although they can rise rapidly in the face of excess demand for labour. This issue of wage inflexibility is central to the modern New Keynesian attempts to understand labour markets, and will be discussed in Chapter 32.

The overall microeconomics of wage behaviour is thought to be as follows. When demand falls, oligopolistic firms reduce their outputs and their demands for labour, holding their mark-ups approximately constant. The unemployment does not force money wage rates down significantly, so firms' unit costs, and hence their prices, fall no faster than productivity is rising. There will also be some downward pressure on money wages (particularly in non-unionized markets) and on prices in more competitive markets, and the result will be a slow downward drift of the price level. When demand rises above potential output, firms try to expand output by hiring more labour, and the labour shortages that develop cause wages to rise. As costs rise, firms pass these on in higher prices. This is a continuing process, which goes on as long as excess demand holds GDP above its potential level.

Expectational forces

We must now drop our assumption that people expect the price level to remain relatively stable in order to consider the effect of expectations of inflation. Suppose, for example, that both employers and employees expect a 4 per cent inflation rate next year. Unions will start negotiations from a base of a 4 per cent increase in money wages, which would hold their real wages constant. Firms also may be inclined to begin bargaining by conceding at least a 4 per cent increase in money wages, since they expect that the prices at which they sell their products will rise by 4 per cent. Starting from that base, unions will attempt to obtain some desired increase in their real wages. At this point such factors as profits, productivity, and bargaining power become important.

The general expectation of an x per cent inflation creates pressures for wages to rise by x per cent more than productivity, and hence for the SRAS curve to shift upwards by x per cent.

The key point is that the SRAS curve can be shifting upwards even if there is no inflationary gap. As long as people *expect* prices to rise, their behaviour will push money wages and unit costs up. This brings about the rise in prices that was expected. This is an example of the phenomenon of self-fulfilling expectations—if everyone thinks that event X is going to occur, their actions in anticipation of X may make X occur.

Expectations formation

We have already discussed expectations in Chapter 29, in the context of exchange rate determination. Expectations are also important in investment behaviour, since firms invest in the expectation of increasing future profits. Here we consider the importance of inflation expectations in the context of the Phillips curve.

Backward-looking theories Keynesian theories of expectations assume that expectations are slow to change. The theory of *extrapolative expectations* says that expectations depend on extrapolations of past behaviour and respond only slowly to what is currently happening to costs. In one simple form of the theory, the expected future inflation rate is merely a moving average of past actual rates. The rationale is that, unless a deviation from past trends persists, firms and workers will dismiss the deviation as transitory. They will not let it influence their wage- and price-setting behaviour.

The theory of *adaptive expectations* states that the expectation of future inflation rates adjusts to the error in predicting the current rate. Thus, if you thought the current rate was going to be 6 per cent and it turned out to be 10 per cent, you might revise your estimate of the next period's inflation rate upwards by, say, half of your error, making the new expectation 8 per cent.

These two theories make expectations about future inflation depend on past actual rates. In an obvious sense such expectations are backward-looking, since the expectation can be calculated using data on what has happened already.

Forward-looking theories **Rational expectations** are forward-looking. The rational expectations hypothesis assumes that people do not continue to make persistent, systematic errors in forming their expectations. Thus, if the economic system about which they are forming expectations remains stable, their expectations will be correct *on average*. Any individual's expectations at any time about next year's price level can thus be thought of as the actual price level that will occur next year plus a random error term which has a mean of zero.

Rational expectations have the effect of speeding up the adjustment of expectations. Instead of being based on past inflation rates, expected inflation is based on an informed forecast of the outcome of existing (and expected) policies.

Backward-looking expectations are overly naïve. People do look ahead to the future and assess future possibilities rather than just blindly reacting to what has gone before. Yet the assumption of unbiased forward-looking expectations requires that workers and firms have a degree of understanding of inflation forecasting that few economists would claim to have. It is possible that in reality wage-setting is a mixture of rational, forward-looking behaviour and expectations based on the experience of the recent past. Depending on the circumstances, expectations will sometimes tend to rely more on past experience, and at other times to rely more on present events whose effects are expected to influence the future.

Of course, people will not make the error of consistently underpredicting (or overpredicting) the inflation rate for decades, but it can happen for several years, whenever people do not fully understand the causes of current inflation. Every past period of inflation has led to intense debate among economists about its causes, cures, and probable future course. If professionals are uncertain, it would be surprising if wage- and price-setters got these matters right even on average. None the less, economists can use assumptions such as rational expectations in their models and then test the predictions to see if they are consistent with the data.

The belief that expectations are at least to some extent rational is one of the reasons that politicians around the world have sought to establish *credible* regimes for the control of inflation. Independent central banks with clearly defined low-inflation objectives have been put in place not just to control inflation directly, but also to *make people believe that inflation really will be kept under control*. Once people believe that inflation will be low, it is very much easier (in terms of output and employment costs) for policy-makers to keep it low.

Random shocks

Forces other than excess demand and expectations of inflation also affect wage changes. These forces can be positive, pushing wages higher than they would otherwise go, or negative, pushing wages lower than they would otherwise go. One such shock occurs when an exceptionally strong union, or an exceptionally weak management, comes to the bargaining table and produces a wage increase that is a percentage point or two higher than would have occurred under more typical bargaining conditions.

One simple approach is to assume that there are many sources of shock, and that they are independent of one another. This means that, overall, they exert a random influence on wages—sometimes speeding wage changes up a bit, sometimes slowing them down a bit, but having a net effect that more or less cancels out when taken over several years. Over the long term they may be regarded as random events and are referred to as random shocks.

Random shocks may have a large positive or negative effect in any one year. Over the period of a sustained inflation, however, positive shocks in some years will tend to be offset by negative shocks in other years, so that overall they contribute little to the long-term trend of the price level.

The overall effect on wages

The overall change in wage costs is a result of the three basic forces just studied. We may express this as follows:

$$\begin{array}{l}\text{Percentage}\\ \text{increase}\\ \text{in unit}\\ \text{wage costs}\end{array} = \text{demand} + \text{expectational} + \text{shock.} \quad (2)\\ \text{effect}\text{effect}\text{effect}$$

The expectations-augmented Phillips curve

We can now add the forces of expectations and random shocks to the Phillips curve determining the behaviour of unit labour costs. The Phillips curve in Figure 31.7 shows the effects only of demand pressures. It will predict actual inflation only if the expected inflation rate is zero and there are no random shocks.

The relationship shown in equation (2) above defines a whole set of Phillips curves. Each curve is drawn for zero shocks and a given expected rate of inflation, which enters as an additive constant. At Y^* there are no demand pressures on wages, so the height of the Phillips curve above the axis at that point is determined by the expected rate of inflation. The whole Phillips curve then shows how much the rate of change of unit costs varies from the expected inflation rate as a result of excess demand or excess supply in the labour market. Any particular Phillips curve drawn for a given expected rate of inflation is called a **short-run Phillips curve** (*SRPC*) or an **expectations-augmented Phillips curve**.

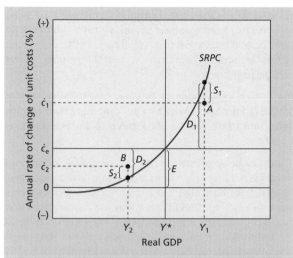

Figure 31.9 The components of cost inflation illustrated

The rate of cost inflation can be separated into three components: expectational inflation, demand inflation, and shock inflation. The Phillips curve is drawn for a given expected rate of inflation and hence is labelled a short-run Phillips curve. The given expected inflation rate, $\dot{c}_e$, is shown by the height of the horizontal solid blue line. Point A indicates a GDP of Y_1 combined with a rate of cost inflation of $\dot{c}_1$. This rate is composed of a rate to match expected inflation, shown by the bracket E; a positive demand component, shown by the bracket D_1 (determined by the shape of $SRPC$); and a negative shock component, shown by the bracket S_1. Point B indicates a GDP of Y_2 combined with a rate of cost inflation of $\dot{c}_2$. This rate is composed of a rate to match expected inflation, once again shown by the bracket E; the demand component, shown by the bracket D_2, which is now negative (since income Y_2 is less than Y^*); and a positive shock component, shown by the bracket S_2.

Figure 31.9 gives an example of one short-run curve and uses it to illustrate the relationships shown in equation (2). It shows unit costs rising as a result of increases in wage costs brought about by demand pressures (shown by the Phillips curve), expectations of inflation (which determine the height of the Phillips curve above the axis at Y^*), and random shocks (which are shown as deviations from the Phillips curve).

The long-run Phillips curve

Is there any level of GDP in this model that is compatible with a constant rate of inflation? The answer is yes: potential GDP. When GDP is at Y^*, the demand component of inflation is zero, as shown in Figure 31.8. This means that actual inflation equals expected inflation. There are no surprises. No one's plans are upset, so no one has any incentive to alter plans as a result of what actually happens to inflation.

Provided the inflation rate is fully validated, any rate of inflation can persist indefinitely as long as GDP is held at its potential level.[7]

We now define the **long-run Phillips curve (*LRPC*)** as the relationship between GDP and stable rates of inflation that neither accelerate nor decelerate. This occurs when the expected and actual inflation rates are equal. On the theory just described, the long-run Phillips curve is vertical, because only at Y^* can the expected and actual rates of inflation be equal. The long-run Phillips curve is shown in Figure 31.10.

Points on the *LRPC* are consistent with any stable rate of inflation. This could be zero, but it could also be some large positive number. Of course, to remain at a stable high rate, the inflation would have to be validated by the monetary authority permitting the money stock to rise. If the inflation rate were not validated the real money stock would fall, shifting *AD* to the left and eventually causing Y to be below Y^* and for deflationary pressure to rise.

The long-run Phillips curve is vertical at Y^*; only Y^* is compatible with a stable rate of inflation; and any stable rate is, if fully accommodated, compatible with Y^*.

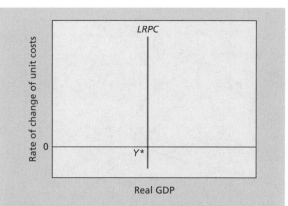

Figure 31.10 The vertical long-run Phillips curve

When actual inflation equals expected inflation, there is no trade-off between inflation and unemployment. In long-term equilibrium the actual rate of inflation must remain equal to the expected rate (otherwise expectations would be revised). This can occur only at potential GDP Y^*, that is, along the *LRPC*. At Y^* there is no demand pressure on the price level; hence the only influence on actual inflation is expected inflation. Any stable rate of inflation (provided it is accommodated by the appropriate rate of monetary expansion) is compatible with Y^* and its associated NAIRU.

The Lucas aggregate supply function

A concept that is closely related to the expectation augmented Phillips curve under rational expectations is the Lucas aggregate supply curve. This is associated with the New Classical Approach to macroeconomics that was popular in the 1970s. The key element in the New Classical approach is a particular specification of the aggregate supply function that was formulated by US economist Robert Lucas (the 1995 Nobel Laureate in economics).

In Chapter 25, where we first set out the *SRAS* curve, we assumed that in the short run output prices are variable (they can respond to changes in demand in the current period) while input prices (we will concentrate here on wages) are fixed. In the long run, if output prices rise, wages get negotiated upwards to catch up with prices. This is what makes the *LRAS* curve vertical.

In the Lucas approach wages are not just given on the basis of last period's equilibrium; rather, they are set at the beginning of the current period at the market-clearing level for *given expectations of what output prices in the current period will be*. In other words, they are set on the basis of forward-looking expectations of what the market outcome will be.

This may seem like a harmless modification of our original assumption, but it turns out to have fundamental implications. Figure 31.11 illustrates the implications for aggregate supply behaviour. The key point is that any shift in aggregate demand that is expected at the time wages are set, such as an announced (or anticipated) increase in the money supply, will cause the *SRAS* curve to shift up immediately. The economy will therefore experience an immediate increase in the price level and no increase in GDP. Only an *unexpected* increase in *AD* will lead to an increase in GDP in the short run. Lucas assumed that this shock to *AD* would be an unexpected increase in the money supply.

In the New Classical approach, cycles in real economic activity are triggered by unexpected increases in the money supply.

New Classical economists assume that the actors in the private sector of the economy have *rational expectations*. This assumes that agents form expectations based upon

[7] We now see why the level of unemployment associated with potential GDP is called the non-accelerating-inflation rate of unemployment (NAIRU). At any lower level of unemployment GDP exceeds potential GDP and the inflation rate will tend to rise. At any higher level of unemployment GDP is below potential GDP and inflation will tend to fall. (Money wage increases are lower than the rate of productivity growth.)

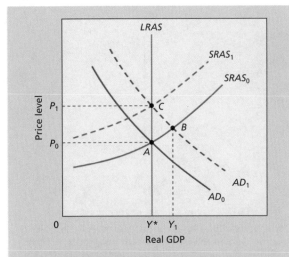

Figure 31.11 The Lucas aggregate supply curve

In the new classical approach a given *SRAS* curve applies only to unexpected shifts in *AD*. Suppose there is a shift in aggregate demand from AD_0 to AD_1. If the shift is unexpected, the economy will move from the initial position at point *A* to point *B*, at the intersection of $SRAS_0$ and AD_1. However, if the shift in *AD* is expected, agents will negotiate higher wages immediately on the basis of this expectation, and the *SRAS* curve will shift up to $SRAS_1$. The price level will go straight from P_0 to P_1, and the economy will move from *A* to *C*, with no increase in GDP.

Policy ineffectiveness follows from the same analysis. Any predictable change in monetary or fiscal policy causing a change in aggregate demand, such as the shift in *AD* from AD_0 to AD_1, will lead to an immediate rise in prices from P_0 to P_1 and will have no effect on real GDP. An unexpected policy change of the same magnitude, however, would take the economy from point *A* to point *B* in the short run, and to *C* only in the long run.

all available information about the future at the time they take the decision. So agents make only random errors in forecasting the future course of economic variables. This means that the expectational errors that trigger cycles cannot be systematic. (If they were systematic, agents could learn from the pattern of mistakes and improve their forecasts.) It would be tempting to conclude from this that deviations from potential output must, therefore, be random—which is clearly contradicted by evidence. However, to avoid this erroneous implication, Lucas added a lagged adjustment process to his model. This means that any random shock can cause a slow adjustment process within the economy that has some persistence.

Policy invariance

A perhaps surprising implication of the New Classical approach is that changes in monetary or fiscal policy, which may be intended to influence economic activity by shifting the *AD* curve, will have real effects only if they are unexpected. For example, a stimulus to demand involving an announced reduction in interest rates (and consequent

increase in the money supply) will create expectations of rising prices. These expectations will influence wage-setting, so the *SRAS* curve will shift up immediately and prices will rise straight away with no temporary increase in output. This outcome is illustrated in Figure 31.11 by the fact that an anticipated interest rate reduction shifts the *AD* curve to the right and the *SRAS* curve to the left, the net effect being that the economy moves straight up the *LRAS* curve, the price level rising but real GDP remaining unchanged.

According to the New Classical approach, only unanticipated policy changes lead to changes in real national income. Systematic policy changes will be predictable and will have no real effects.

Most economists do not accept the proposition that only unexpected policy changes will have real effects. One reason is that there is so much inertia in price- and wage-setting behaviour that very few contracts can be renegotiated as soon as a policy change is announced. Hence the policy-makers certainly have some leverage over real activity, even when making policy changes that are predictable.

A second reason is that the massive complexity of the economy makes it impossible for individual agents to know how some shock will affect all the relevant prices and quantities that matter to them over any specified period of time. The idea of everyone knowing the exact nature of some policy disturbance and solving the equations of the economy to determine the exact outcome, and of their acting to anticipate these outcomes, is far-fetched. After all, the great virtue of the price system is that it co-ordinates activity without the need for anyone to have knowledge of all the prices and quantities that exist. However, the New Classical presumption that private agents have expectations of what policy-makers are going to do, and that this influences private behaviour, is important. Without assuming omniscience, but just reasonable approximate expectations, private anticipation of government action can affect the outcome of policies. This realization has had a fundamental impact on macroeconomic policy analysis. In our model above the government is exogenous to the model. However, in the New Classical framework the government and the private sector interact by trying to guess what the other is going to do. The conduct of policy becomes more like a 'game', where strategy and perception of the other players matter.

This change in perception of policy as interactive rather than exogenous has two important implications. The first follows below and the second, known as the Lucas Critique is explained in Box 31.2.

Policy credibility

If private agents are watching the government (and the monetary authorities, where these are different) and trying to form expectations of its future behaviour, not only does

Box 31.2 The Lucas Critique

The assumption that private agents form expectations of government behaviour has important implications for how economic models can be used to predict the effects of changes in policy.

A great deal of effort over the last thirty years has gone into building empirical econometric macroeconomic models of the economy for forecasting purposes (such as the National Institute model and the Bank of England model). Lucas pointed out that such models contain estimates of key behavioural parameters that were derived from past data. These data were collected under particular policy regimes.

Any attempt to use such a model to predict the consequences of significant policy changes may be erroneous. This is because the behaviour of private agents may change when the behaviour of policy-makers changes, as they are interdependent in some areas.

One example is the failure of the government to understand (and of the forecasters to forecast) the buildup of inflationary pressures in the UK economy in the late 1980s, following the financial innovations of the mid-1980s. Another is the difficulty of forecasting behaviour of agents in the EU following the introduction in January 1999 of the new single currency, the euro.

The Lucas critique suggests that there will be shifts in many private sector behaviour functions when there are significant changes in the policy regime. Hence the effects of such regime changes will be impossible to forecast accurately using traditional macro models.

---

it matter what the government does, but it also matters what agents think it will do in future. This means that a government needs more than just the correct current policies. It also needs to establish **credibility** that it will follow the correct policies in future.

Suppose, for example, that a government enters office with a commitment to control inflation. It introduces tight monetary and fiscal policies, which in due course succeed in bringing down inflation. Now, however, there is an election approaching, and the government would like to increase real GDP to improve its chances of re-election. It may be tempted to break its original commitment to anti-inflationary policies.[8] However, private agents know that this incentive exists, so it matters to the outcome whether or not the private agents anticipate that the government will break its word. In other words, the government's credibility actually affects private behaviour. Of course, once the government has broken its commitments, it will be very hard for it to establish credibility again—at least without a change in personnel.

Recognition of the importance of credibility has been behind the ceding of power to set interest rates to independent central banks. The banks have an incentive to behave transparently and with high credibility as this influences inflation expectations and makes actual inflation much easier to control.

Is inflation dead?

In Figure 31.1 on page 572 we saw that inflation is projected to stay low in the advanced economies at least for the first few years of the twenty-first century. One should not conclude from this that inflation no longer matters. On the contrary, the correct conclusion is that high inflation is so disruptive to a modern economy—and the costs of eliminating it, once it is entrenched, are so great—that it is important that the lessons of the recent past be learned and remembered by future generations, so that similar mistakes are not repeated.

It is not an accident that central banks around the world, from New Zealand to the United Kingdom, and within the euro zone, have been given the power to determine monetary policy independently of elected politicians. This is to avoid the inflationary bias created when politicians are tempted to generate pre-election booms in order to aid their re-election. This problem, as noted above, is known as time-inconsistency, since it is in the self-interest of politicians to promise low inflation, but then also to break their promise at a later date, once inflation expectations are low. This means that leaving the control of inflation to elected politicians can bring into question the credibility of counterinflationary credentials. A central bank with, at least, instrument independence can solve this problem. It is in the interest of the appointed central bankers to deliver on the imposed objective of price stability. Central bankers who do not stand for re-election have less problem in establishing a highly credible low-inflation regime.

---

[8] US economists F. Kydland and E Prescott labelled the fact that it may now be rational for the government to renege on its commitments *time inconsistency*.

This regime change is an important component in the explanation of why inflation has fallen and why it is expected to stay low. However, the underlying cause has been both a public determination to support anti-inflation policies and a realization by the politicians themselves that inflation does not deliver prosperity. This determination is shown by the fact that, even in countries such as the United States and Canada, where the ultimate determination of monetary policy remains with the government, inflation rates have been held at low levels. Economists have played an important role in the debate about the causes of and cures for inflation, and it was economic analysis that underpinned the case for independent central banks.

While inflation has generally been conquered today, there is no guarantee that it will stay low for ever. After all, it was low throughout the 1950s and 1960s, yet the 1970s followed. Only sound monetary policies can deliver continued low inflation. Monetary policy is made by human beings, as are the institutions within which monetary policies are formulated. Thus, it is important that economists continue to study, and to increase their understanding of, inflation, so that future generations can learn by our mistakes rather than from their own.

The efforts of the 1980s and 1990s to bring down inflation have not been costless. Many millions of workers have spent time in unemployment, and many owners of businesses have seen their business go bust, in the recessions that followed episodes of sharp monetary tightening. Indeed, in the late 1990s unemployment across Europe was at very high levels by historical standards, and one of the proximate causes was the tight monetary and fiscal policies of the earlier 1990s. The issue then is not just how to control inflation, but how to control inflation *and* maintain a high level of employment and economic activity. It is to the issue of employment and unemployment that we now turn.

SUMMARY

Inflation in the macro model

■ A shift in the *SRAS* curve is called a supply shock, while a shift in the *AD* curve is called a demand shock.

■ A single leftward shift in the *SRAS* curve causes a rise in the price level and a fall in GDP. Full employment can be restored either by a fall in unit wage costs, which shifts the *SRAS* curve to the right, or by a monetary expansion, which shifts the *AD* curve to the right.

■ Repeated supply shocks in terms of leftward shifts of the *SRAS* curve carry their own restraining force in terms of ever-rising unemployment if they are not accommodated by monetary expansion. If accommodated, they can give rise to a sustained supply-side inflation.

■ An isolated expansionary demand shock leads to a temporary rise in GDP and a rise in the price level. If it is not validated, output will fall while the price level rises as GDP returns to its potential level.

■ Sustained demand shocks that are validated by monetary expansion lead to sustained inflation with GDP remaining above potential.

The Phillips curve

■ The original Phillips curve relates wage inflation to the level of unemployment; suitably transformed, it relates unit cost inflation to GDP. It thus determines the rate at which the *SRAS* curve is shifting.

■ Unit cost inflation depends on the state of demand—being positive when $Y > Y^*$ and negative when $Y < Y^*$—and on expectations of inflation and random shocks. The expectations-augmented Phillips curve relates GDP to unit cost inflation and is displaced from the point of zero demand inflation at $Y = Y^*$ by the amount of expectational inflation.

■ A sustained inflation at a constant rate is possible only when $Y = Y^*$ and the monetary authorities accommodate the inflation. Expected inflation is then equal to actual inflation.

The Lucas aggregate supply function

■ With the Lucas aggregate supply curve only unexpected shifts in aggregate demand will have real effects, but this result is not generally accepted to apply to today's economies with their short-term rigidities and long adjustment lags.

■ Policy credibility is important once it is perceived that private agents' behaviour is influenced by their expectations of the government's future policy actions.

Is inflation dead?

■ The establishment of a low-inflation environment at the end of the 1990s was aided by the institutional changes that put monetary policy in the hands of central banks with independent control over the monetary policy instruments (as discussed in Chapter 28).

TOPICS FOR REVIEW

- Causes and consequences of demand and supply shocks
- Once-and-for-all and sustained inflations
- Wage inflation, productivity growth, and unit costs
- The NAIRU
- Original, transformed, and expectations-augmented Phillips curves
- Causes of sustained inflations
- Lucas aggregate supply curve
- Time inconsistency
- Credibility of independent central banks

DISCUSSION QUESTIONS

1 'Inflation is always and everywhere a monetary phenomenon.' Does this mean that changes in the money stock always cause changes in inflation and that controlling the money stock is the only way to control inflation?

2 What is the relationship between the short-run Phillips curve and the *SRAS* curve?

3 What is the relationship between the long-run Phillips curve and the *LRAS* curve?

4 Starting from equilibrium, explain what happens to inflation when there is a one-off rise in the price of oil but the monetary authorities do not accommodate the shock.

5 Repeat question 4, but now assume that the monetary authorities relax monetary policy in an attempt to avoid any short-run output loss from the supply shock.

6 Using the Phillips curve framework, outline how inflation and unemployment respond (starting from zero inflation and at the NAIRU) to a positive exogenous shock to aggregate demand. Make clear what you are assuming about the monetary policy response.

7 Repeat question 6 but now assume that there has been an exogenous negative supply shock.

8 What factors lay behind the high inflation of the 1970s, and what changed by the 1990s to bring about the apparent elimination of inflation?

Chapter 32

EMPLOYMENT AND UNEMPLOYMENT

Can the economy create jobs for all who want to work? Is mass unemployment a thing of the past? Will technology destroy jobs? These are some of the issues we address in this chapter. In particular, you will learn that:

- Prospects for unemployment to remain low are better in the early 2000s than they appeared in the 1980s and early 1990s.

- Unemployment can be thought of as made up of cyclical, frictional, and structural unemployment. The latter two make up equilibrium unemployment.

- Nominal wage rigidities help explain why demand cycles cause cycles in unemployment.

- Equilibrium unemployment arises from frictions in the economy, from structural changes in the nature of economic activity, and from the benefit system.

- Aggregate demand management can reduce cyclical unemployment

- Lower benefits, active manpower policies, and reformed wage bargaining institutions can reduce equilibrium unemployment.

- It is neither possible nor desirable to reduce unemployment to zero.

In the previous chapter we learned that inflation was a major problem in the 1970s and 1980s but that it had largely been brought under control by the late 1990s and remained low in the early 2000s. Part of the price paid for bringing inflation down was higher unemployment, though the high unemployment levels often associated with lowering inflation are usually temporary. Indeed, unemployment too has fallen in several countries, such as the United States and the United Kingdom, where in the second half of the 1990s and into the 2000s it fell to levels not seen since the 1970s. But unemployment remained a problem in many economies, especially within the European Union. As the OECD put it,

Unemployment is probably the most widely feared phenomenon of our times. It touches all parts of society. There are 35 million people unemployed in OECD countries (about 8.5 per cent of the labour force). Perhaps another 15 million have either given up looking for work or unwillingly accepted a part-time job. As many as a third of young workers in some OECD countries have no job.

Economic growth will play a part in reducing unemployment. But beyond the cyclical component of unemployment is a structural element that persists even into recovery. This is harder to reduce and is even more troubling.

Structural unemployment grows from the gap between the pressure on the economies to adapt to change and their ability to do so. Adaptation is fundamental to progress in a world of new technologies, globalisation and intense national and international competition.[1]

The Keynesian revolution, which established the branch of economics we now call macroeconomics, was stimulated by the need to explain and then solve the high unemployment problems of the 1930s. The proposed solution focused on the use of countercyclical aggregate demand policies to cure unemployment. But the simple message that stimulating demand can cure unemployment is no longer accepted in its original form. This is because these policies did not distinguish between unemployment that arises when the economy is below potential output and the unemployment that would exist even when the economy were in equilibrium at the potential level of GDP, and focused mainly on the former, which is called *cyclical* unemployment. We now know that the latter type of unemployment, called *equilibrium* unemployment, is also important. Hence we need explanations of both cyclical and equilibrium unemployment.

In this chapter we first introduce some definitions and measurement issues relating to unemployment. Next we set out some of the main facts. We then study cyclical unemployment. Finally, we discuss equilibrium unemployment and the NAIRU[2] in much more detail. In particular, we ask why equilibrium unemployment exists and why it changes. Then we discuss whether government policy can do anything to reduce the NAIRU.

---

[1] *Jobs Study*, OECD, Paris, 1994.
[2] The non-accelerating-inflation rate of unemployment (NAIRU) was explained in Chapter 31.

Employment and unemployment characteristics

Measurement and definitions

For purposes of study, the unemployed can be classified in various ways. They can be grouped by personal characteristics, such as age, sex, degree of skill or education, and ethnic group. They can also be classified by geographical location, by occupation, by the duration of their unemployment, or by the reasons for their unemployment. In this chapter we are concerned with explanations of unemployment. Although it is not always possible to say why a particular person does not have a job, it is usually possible to test hypotheses about the causes of differences in aggregate unemployment, both over time for one country and between countries at the same point in time.

The recorded figures for unemployment may significantly understate or overstate the numbers who are actually willing to work at the existing set of wage rates. Overstatement arises because measured unemployment includes people who are not interested in work but who say they are in order to collect unemployment benefits. Understatement arises because of the voluntary withdrawal from the labour force of people who would like to work but have ceased to believe that suitable jobs are available. Although these people may not be measured in the unemployment figures, they are unemployed in the sense that they would accept a job if one were available at the going wage rate. People in this category are referred to as *discouraged workers*. They have voluntarily withdrawn from the labour force, not because they do not want to work, but because they believe that they cannot find a job given current labour market conditions.

The ways in which unemployment is measured have changed many times over the years. UK figures used to include only those people actively looking for work and registering for benefits. This is referred to as the *claimant count*. The claimant count is still published, but it is more common to use a measure of unemployment based upon a survey of the labour force. These two measures of unemployment are explained in Box 32.1.

There are three main types of unemployment that we will refer to in this chapter. **Cyclical** or **demand-deficient unemployment** occurs when aggregate desired expenditures in the economy are insufficient to purchase the output that would be supplied when the economy is at potential GDP. An alternative definition, which focuses on the labour market rather than the goods market, is that this is unemployment in excess of the NAIRU.

Frictional unemployment is unemployment that arises as part of the normal turnover of labour. For example, in a market economy firms and products are continually changing and workers are moving from one job to another, or from work to training and from training to work. In the course of this dynamic movement, there will always be some workers who are between jobs and classified as unemployed.

Structural unemployment occurs when there is a mismatch between the characteristics and skills of the people looking for work and those characteristics and skills desired by potential employers. Jobs may exist in London while the workers available are in Liverpool, or there may be plenty of opportunities for computer programmers while there are many social workers looking for jobs.

Frictional and structural unemployment make up **equilibrium unemployment**, which is defined as the unemployment that exists when GDP is at its potential level, and hence when there is neither a recessionary nor an inflationary gap. In what follows we assume that equilibrium unemployment and the NAIRU are the same.

UK experience

Figure 32.1 shows UK unemployment since 1885.[3] There was highly cyclical unemployment before the First World War, very high unemployment in the interwar period, and then very low and stable unemployment from the Second World War until the 1970s. There was a rising trend in UK unemployment in successive cycles, through the 1970s and into the 1980s. But there was a steady fall in the 1990s and early 2000s. A perspective over the last century or so suggests that there is no long-term upward or downward trend. Rather, there is a high degree of persistence. Once unemployment is high it tends to stay high; once low it tends to stay low. In the interwar period unemployment was consistently high, but in the 1950s and 1960s it was consistently low. In the 1980s and early 1990s it was high, but not as high as in the 1930s.

Unemployment varies much more between business cycles than within business cycles. For example, in the 1920s and 1930s unemployment cycled about a high average level, but in the 1950s it cycled about a low level. Also, compare the low average unemployment levels of the 1960s and early 1970s with the high levels of the 1980s. This evidence suggests that there are long-term changes in social institutions affecting employment and unemployment, and perhaps that big shocks to the economic system—a major war being the obvious example—have long-lasting effects.

---

[3] There have been many changes in definition over the years. Data since the 1950s is based on the claimant count, which has been affected by changes in the nature of benefits as these influence who can register.

Box 32.1 **How is unemployment measured?**

Figure 32.1 shows data for the percentage of the workforce unemployed in the United Kingdom from 1885 to 2001. This figure uses a measure of unemployment known as the *claimant count*. The claimant count gives us the longest available data series on UK unemployment, but it has been replaced as the standard measure of unemployment by a different series. This alternative measure is an international standard defined by the United Nations International Labour Office, and hence it is known as *ILO unemployment*. The European Union and the OECD have adopted the ILO unemployment definition. So what is the difference between the claimant count and ILO unemployment?

The claimant count

The UK claimant count covers all those people claiming unemployment-related benefits at Employment Service offices. In 2002 the relevant benefits that could be claimed were the Jobseeker's Allowance and National Insurance credits. Percentage unemployment is then expressed using the numbers of claimants as a percentage of 'workforce jobs' plus claimant unemployment. *Workforce jobs* is a measure of the number of full-time and part-time jobs in the economy.

One big advantage of the claimant count is that it is an accurate measure of *all* those claiming benefits. It gives a correct picture of who is registered for benefits at both national and local level, and it is timely in that it does not take long to produce an unemployment figure. But there are several disadvantages. First, as the benefits system changes, so the numbers able to claim benefits change. Second, it does not measure anyone who is unemployed but does not bother to claim benefit. Third, the measure of workforce jobs overestimates the numbers in work because it counts twice anyone with two jobs, so the *percentage* of persons unemployed is underestimated.

ILO unemployment

Under the ILO approach, all people aged 16 and over are classified into one of three states: in employment, ILO unemployed, or economically inactive. ILO unemployed are those who either

- are out of work, want a job, have actively sought work in the last four weeks, and are available to start work in the next two weeks, or

- are out of work, have found a job, and are waiting to start it in the next two weeks.

Anyone who carries out at least one hour's paid work in a week, is on a government-supported training scheme, does unpaid work for a family business, or is away temporarily from a job (such as on vacation) is counted as being in employment. Those who are out of work but do not meet the criteria for ILO unemployment are defined as economically inactive. The unemployment percentage expresses numbers of ILO unemployed as a percentage of the total numbers of economically active.

ILO unemployment is measured by means of a monthly survey, which in the United Kingdom is called the Labour Force Survey (LFS), and hence ILO unemployment is sometimes also referred to as *LFS unemployment*. About 40,000 individuals are interviewed each month, and the unemployment figure announced is the average of data for the previous three months.

The advantage of the ILO measure of unemployment is that it is comprehensive—it measures those who say they are unemployed and not just those claiming benefits. The disadvantages are that it is based on a survey and so is subject to sampling error; it takes time to produce; it lumps together as 'employed' anyone who takes even one hour's paid work with those who work much longer hours; and, because of the small numbers involved, it is not accurate at the local level.

In the first quarter of 2002 UK unemployment by the ILO definition was 1.538 million, while the claimant count was 0.948 million. The unemployment percentage was 5.1 by the ILO definition and 3.1 by the claimant count definition. These are by no means insignificant differences; missing out half a million people who are looking for work from the unemployment measure is not a trivial matter. In the same period the ILO unemployment percentage was 5.6 in the United States, 8.1 in Germany, and 8.8 in France.

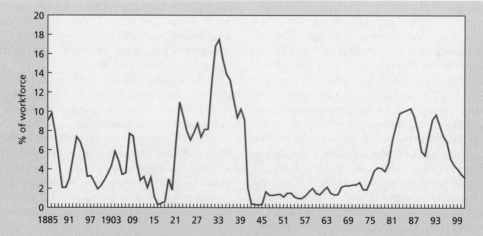

Figure 32.1 UK unemployment 1885–2001

UK unemployment has varied greatly over the past century or so. Unemployment was high in the interwar period and in the 1980s, but it was low in the 1950s and 1960s.

The trend of total employment in the United Kingdom has been slowly rising over the postwar period. The numbers in employment in 2001 were about 17 per cent higher than in 1960, over four decades earlier. This slow growth is explained partly by low rate of population growth. However, there have also been some big structural changes in the pattern of employment. There were, for example, big shifts between sectors, such as a decline in manufacturing employment and a rise in services. There have also been changes in the composition of the labour force, with declining male employment being offset by increased female participation rates.

International comparisons

Unemployment has not been a uniquely UK problem. Hence international comparisons are instructive.

There has been a dramatic contrast over the past three decades between employment growth in the United States and employment growth in Europe. Total employment grew by only about 10 per cent in EU countries between 1970 and 2000, whereas in the USA it grew by over 60 per cent in the same period. This is shown in part (ii) of Figure 32.2.

In part this reflects slow population growth in Europe, compared with high levels of immigration into the United States. However, Europe also experienced much higher levels of unemployment than the USA throughout this period, as shown in Figure 32.2(i). Both had consistently higher unemployment than did Japan, at least until the end of 1990s when Japanese unemployment rose sharply.[4]

Unemployment varies among countries, even within the European Union. In 2002, for example, unemployment in EU member states varied from a low of 2.5 per cent in the Netherlands to a high of 11.4 per cent in Spain. Figure 32.3 shows that unemployment in France, Germany, and Italy rose up to 1999; it fell slightly after that but remained high until at least 2002. In Ireland, the Netherlands, Denmark, and the United Kingdom unemployment fell steadily after 1994, but appeared to have stopped falling in 2001.

It is dangerous to make comparisons when countries may be at different stages of the business cycle and may use different definitions of unemployment. However, there is one broad generalization that will be helpful in understanding the causes of equilibrium unemployment. Unemployment is the result of the balance of two continuous flows: the flow of potential workers into unemployment (leaving employment but seeking work, or joining the labour force but not finding employment) and the flow of workers out of unemployment (finding jobs, or withdrawing from the labour force).

In EU countries the flow into unemployment is quite small and does not change much over time. However, the outflow is also small, so very high proportions of workers who are unemployed have been unemployed for a long

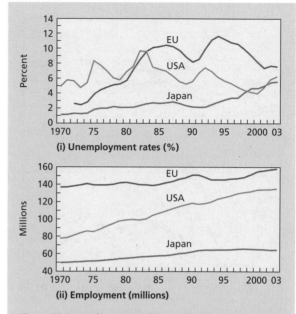

Figure 32.2 Employment and unemployment in the EU, the USA, and Japan, 1970–2002

The behaviour of employment and unemployment has varied considerably within the industrialized world.

Part (i) shows that unemployment was high in the EU in the 1980s and 1990s, but it fell in the USA and remained low in Japan. The chart is based on national definitions.

Part (ii) shows that the US economy created over 50 million jobs between 1970 and 2002 whereas the EU created only about 10 million. Data for 2002 and 2003 are IMF staff projections.

Source: IMF, *World Economic Outlook*, September 2002.

time. For example, in Belgium, Ireland, and Italy around 60 per cent of the unemployed (at the peak of the unemployment upturn in the 1990s) had been unemployed for more than twelve months, defined as long-term unemployment. The comparable figures for Germany, France, and the United Kingdom were all around 35 per cent. This contrasts with Canada and the United States, where only just over 10 per cent had been unemployed for more than twelve months. In the United States, in particular, flows into unemployment are high but flows out are just as high, so the level of long-term unemployment is low.

This may give an important clue as to the reasons for the higher persistence of unemployment in the European Union. Skills and human capital deteriorate during periods out of employment, so the long-term unemployed are perceived (rightly or wrongly) as being less employable than those who have recently been in work.

---

[4] Japanese unemployment measures differ from European ones and are generally considered to underestimate the true level of unemployment.

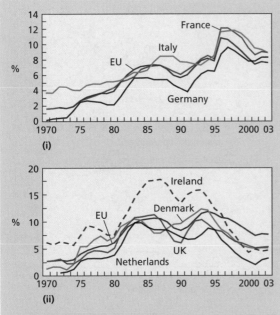
(i)

(ii)

Figure 32.3 Unemployment rates in specific EU countries, 1970–2002

Unemployment reached peaks in the EU and in Germany, France, and Italy in 1999. In the UK, the Netherlands, Denmark, and Ireland, however, unemployment has declined since 1994. The charts are based on national definitions of unemployment, and data for 2002 and 2003 are IMF staff projections.

Source: IMF, *World Economic Outlook*, September 2002.

A common pattern across countries is that low-skilled workers are four or five times more likely to be unemployed than skilled or professional workers. About 75 per cent of unemployed men are manual workers. This suggests that it is the unemployment of unskilled manual workers that should be the main focus of study.

Older workers are less likely to be unemployed than young workers are. Youth unemployment is universally higher than adult unemployment. Extreme cases at the height of the recession in the early 1990s included Spain with 43 per cent youth unemployment and Italy with 30 per cent. The UK figure was 17 per cent at the same time, when the overall unemployment rate was around 10 per cent.

In most EU countries female unemployment is greater than male unemployment. The United Kingdom is the exception, with 4.4 per cent female unemployment compared with around 5.8 per cent for males in the first quarter of 2002 (although a high proportion of female employment is part-time[5]).

Another universal feature of unemployment is that movement into the ranks of the unemployed is predominantly the result of redundancy rather than voluntary job

leaving. This may seem obvious, but it is important from an economic theory perspective, because some economists have attempted to explain unemployment as a voluntary choice made by workers. There is certainly some element of choice involved in deciding whether or not to accept a job offer once one has been located, but that is very different from having chosen to be unemployed in the first place. Hence most economists believe that the majority of those who are recorded as unemployed are involuntarily unemployed. Someone is **involuntarily unemployed** if she would accept an offer of work in a job for which she was trained, at the going wage rate, if such an offer could be found.

Consequences of unemployment

Involuntary unemployment is regarded by most people as a social 'bad' just as much as output is regarded a social 'good'. The harm caused by involuntary unemployment is measured in terms of the output lost to the whole economy and the harm done to the individuals who are affected.

Lost output

Every involuntarily unemployed person is someone willing and able to work but unable to find a job. Unemployed workers are valuable resources whose potential output is wasted. The material counterpart of unemployment is the recessionary gap—potential GDP that is not produced. The cumulative loss of UK output in the seven years 1991–7 was £55 billion (at 1990 prices);[6] this is nearly £1,000 for every member of the population, or about £2,000 for each member of the labour force. In a world of scarcity with many unsatisfied wants, this loss is serious. It represents goods and services that could have been produced but are gone for ever. From 1997 until 2002 UK output was very close to potential, so there were no further losses over this period.

Personal costs

The social welfare system, designed to alleviate the short-term economic consequences of unemployment, was

---

[5] A survey of females in part-time jobs found that 80 per cent did not want full-time employment, 10 per cent could not find a full-time job, and most of the rest were studying part-time. Among the much smaller group of males in part-time jobs, 30 per cent would have preferred a full-time job (CSO, *Social Trends*, 1994, Table 4.13). Note also that data here for male and female unemployment relate to the ILO measure of unemployment.

[6] This figure is calculated using the IMF estimates of actual and potential GDP shown in Figure 22.1 on page 389. The loss is just the sum of the gaps between actual and potential output in each of these seven years.

extended in the postwar period. Being unemployed in the United Kingdom, even for some substantial period of time, is no longer quite the personal disaster that it once was. But the longer-term effects of high unemployment rates for the disillusioned, who have given up trying to make it within the system and who contribute to social unrest, should be a matter of serious concern to the haves as well as the have-nots. As UK economists Richard Layard, Stephen Nickell, and Richard Jackman put it:

Unemployment matters. It generally reduces output and aggregate income. It increases inequality, since the unemployed lose more than the employed. It erodes human capital. And, finally, it involves psychic costs. People need to be needed. Though unemployment increases leisure, the value of this is largely offset by the pain of rejection.[7]

Next we study the causes of cyclical and structural unemployment.

Cyclical unemployment

Cyclical unemployment, or demand-deficient unemployment, occurs whenever total demand is insufficient to purchase all of the economy's potential output, causing a recessionary gap in which actual output is less than potential output. Cyclical unemployment can be measured as the number of people who would be employed if the economy were at potential GDP minus the number of persons currently employed. When cyclical unemployment is zero, all existing unemployment is either structural or frictional, and the rate of unemployment is the NAIRU. Notice that cyclical unemployment can be less than zero, because GDP can be above potential GDP, at least temporarily.

Macroeconomic theory has traditionally sought to explain only cyclical unemployment.

Equilibrium unemployment was once presumed to be outside the scope of macroeconomics. However, we will see below that it is unwise to try to establish a simple dichotomy between cyclical unemployment (as being due to macro causes) and equilibrium unemployment (as being due to micro causes). Both micro and macro factors contribute to cyclical unemployment and to equilibrium unemployment. (The microeconomics of labour markets is discussed in Chapter 16.) Indeed, we will find that a strong case can be made for the view that high cyclical unemployment raises the level of equilibrium unemployment for some time. Hence we must caution against the presumption that cyclical unemployment and equilibrium unemployment have different causes—or, indeed, that they are unrelated. However, it is useful to analyse cyclical unemployment separately, because this is the component of unemployment that can be reduced by monetary and fiscal policies, via their effect in shifting aggregate demand.

Fluctuations in GDP are not sufficient to create fluctuations in involuntary unemployment. Something else is needed. Suppose, for example, that aggregate demand is fluctuating, causing GDP to fluctuate around its potential level. This fluctuation will cause the demand for labour to fluctuate as well, rising in booms and falling in slumps. If the labour market had fully flexible wage rates, then wages would fluctuate to keep quantity demanded equal to quantity supplied. We would observe cyclical fluctuations in employment (and therefore also in voluntary unemployment) and in the wage rate, but no changes in involuntary unemployment. Employment and wages would vary procyclically (i.e. rising in booms and falling in slumps), but there would be no significant amounts of involuntary unemployment. Such behaviour is shown for a typical labour market in Figure 32.4.

The hypothetical situation we have just described is not what we actually observe. Instead we see cyclical fluctuations not only in employment, but also in involuntary unemployment. Furthermore, the changes in wage rates that do occur are insufficient to equate demand and supply, as is shown in Figure 32.5. Unemployment exceeds the NAIRU in slumps and is below it in booms. Although wages do tend to vary procyclically over the cycle, the fluctuations are not sufficient to remove all cyclical variations in unemployment. Why is this so?

Two types of explanation have been advanced over the years. The line that we consider first is associated with the New Classical school, discussed further in the appendix to this chapter. Their explanation assumes that labour markets are always in equilibrium, in the sense that quantity demanded is continually equated with quantity supplied. While the New Classical approach is hard to accept as a description of the causes of unemployment, for reasons already mentioned (such as the assumption of no involuntary lay-offs), the New Classical school set down a challenge which was met by what is called the New Keynesian agenda. Also, it is worth noting that the predictions of New Classical and New Keynesian models, while based on very different assumptions, are difficult to distinguish empirically.

---

[7] *The Unemployment Crisis* (Oxford: OUP, 1994).

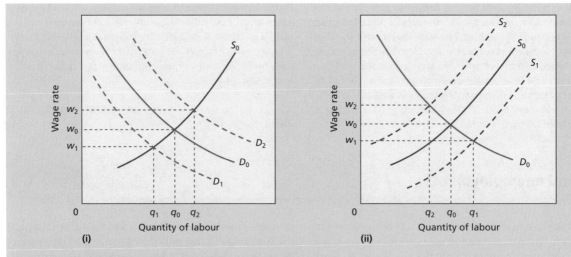

Figure 32.4 Employment and wages in a single competitive labour market

In a perfectly competitive labour market, wages and employment fluctuate in the same direction when demand fluctuates and in opposite directions when supply fluctuates; in both cases there is no involuntary unemployment. The figure shows a single perfectly competitive market for one type of labour. In part (i) the demand curves D_1, D_2, and D_0 are the demands for this market when there is a slump, a boom, and when aggregate GDP is at its potential level. As demand rises from D_1 to D_0 to D_2, wages rise from w_1 to w_0 to w_2 and employment rises from q_1 to q_0 to q_2. At no time, however, is there any involuntary unemployment.

In part (ii) the supply of labour fluctuates from S_1 to S_0 to S_2, and wages fluctuate from w_1 to w_0 to w_2. In this case wages fall when employment rises and vice versa, but again there is no involuntary unemployment.

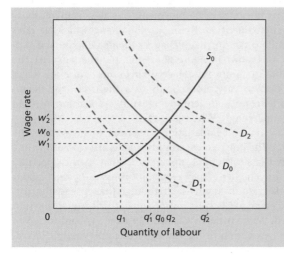

Figure 32.5 Unemployment in a single labour market with sticky wages

When the wage rate does not change enough to equate quantity demanded and quantity supplied at all times, there will be unemployment in slumps and labour shortages in booms in each individual labour market. When demand is at its normal level, D_0, the market is cleared with wage rate w_0, employment is q_0, and there is no unemployment. In a recession demand falls to D_1, but the wage falls only to w_1'. As a result, q_1 labour is demanded, but q_1' is supplied. Employment is determined by the quantity demanded at q_1; the remainder of the supply for which there is no demand, q_1q_1', is unemployed. In a boom demand rises to D_2, but the wage rate rises only to w_2'. As a result the quantity demanded is q_2', whereas only q_2 is supplied. Employment rises to q_2, that is, the amount supplied; the rest of the demand cannot be satisfied, making an excess demand for labour of q_2q_2'.

The New Classical approach

The major characteristic of the New Classical approach is that agents continuously optimize and markets continuously clear; hence there can be no involuntary unemployment. Advocates of this approach then seek to explain unemployment as the outcome of voluntary decisions made by rational people who are choosing to do what they do, including spending some time out of employment. Notice the contrast with traditional Keynesian (and early monetarist) macroeconomics. Theories in this class assume that unemployment is a sign of market failure, associated with non-market-clearing prices and/or wages, and that a high proportion of unemployment is involuntary.

One New Classical explanation of cyclical fluctuations in employment assumes that they are caused by fluctuations in the willingness of people to supply their labour, as shown in part (ii) of Figure 32.4. If the supply curve of labour fluctuates cyclically, this will lead to cyclical variations in employment. This explanation of cyclical behaviour in the labour market has two problems. First, the wage will tend to rise in slumps and fall in booms, which is not what we observe. Second, there will still be no systematic cyclical *involuntary unemployment*, since labour markets always clear, leaving everyone who wishes to work actually working. Supply-induced fluctuations in employment form part of the basis of what is called real business cycle theory, which is discussed in the appendix to this chapter. However, the real supply shocks that trigger 'real' business cycles cause changes in the NAIRU, so at best this explains variations in equilibrium but not cyclical unemployment.[8]

A second line of New Classical explanation lies in errors on the part of workers and employers in predicting the course of the price level over the business cycle. To understand the argument, start by assuming that each of the economy's markets is in equilibrium, that there is full employment, that prices are stable, and that the actual and the expected rates of inflation are zero. Now suppose that the government relaxes monetary policy to permit the money supply to increase unexpectedly by 5 per cent in such a way that inflation expectations are unaffected. People find themselves with unwanted money balances, which they seek to spend. For simplicity, assume that the increased money supply leads to an increase in desired expenditure on *all* commodities. The demand for each commodity shifts to the right, and all prices, being competitively determined, rise. Individual decision-makers see their selling prices go up and mistakenly interpret the increase as a rise in their own relative price. This is because they expect the overall inflation rate to be zero. Firms will produce more, and workers will work more, because both groups think they are getting an increased *relative* price for what they sell. Thus, total output and employment rise.

When both groups eventually realize that their own relative prices are in fact unchanged, output and employment fall back to their initial levels. The extra output and employment occur only while people are being fooled. When they realize that *all* prices have risen by 5 per cent, they revert to their initial behaviour. The only difference is that now the price level has risen by 5 per cent, leaving relative prices unchanged.

A similar argument shows that an unanticipated monetary contraction would cause output to fall below its full-employment level.

All New Classical explanations assume that labour markets clear, and then look for reasons why employment fluctuates. They all imply, therefore, that people who are not working have voluntarily withdrawn from the labour market, either because this is their optimal decision or because they have misinterpreted market signals.

The New Keynesian agenda

Many economists find New Classical explanations implausible. They believe that people correctly read market signals but react in ways that do not cause markets to be in equilibrium at all times. These economists believe that many who are recorded as unemployed are involuntarily unemployed.

However, the New Classical approach has attractions. It assumes rational agents who are always optimizing. In other words, it has rigorous micro foundations which are attractive to economists trained to analyse the utility-maximizing behaviour of agents interacting in clearing markets. Economists so trained are uncomfortable with the early Keynesian assumptions of arbitrary price and wage stickiness (in the face of sustained excess supply) and markets that do not clear. Those who are unhappy to assume no involuntary unemployment therefore seek to explain why there could be a labour market *equilibrium* in which there is an excess supply of labour at the going wage. We refer to this as the New Keynesian 'agenda' rather than 'theory', because there are many different theories encompassed by it and it is ongoing.[9]

Most attempts to explain involuntary unemployment examine the forces that determine wage-setting and hiring decisions in realistic labour market institutions. They look for reasons (consistent with optimizing behaviour by participants) why wages do not respond quickly to shifts in supply and demand in the labour market.[10] So quantity supplied and quantity demanded may *not* be equated for extended periods of time. Labour markets will then display unemployment during recessions and excess demand during booms. This is shown for one typical labour market in Figure 32.5.

These theories start with the everyday observation that wage rates do not change every time demand or supply shifts. When unemployed workers are looking for jobs, they do not knock on employers' doors and offer to work at lower wages than are being paid to current workers. Instead, they answer job advertisements and hope to get the jobs offered, but often are disappointed. Similarly, employers,

---

[8] The distinction here is semantic if the NAIRU is cyclical. We do not pursue the argument further because, although supply shocks are undoubtedly important, the assumption of continuous market-clearing seems unnecessarily restrictive and implausible.

[9] Many economists working in this area might not accept the label 'Keynesian'. Indeed, some of the new approaches explain why real wages may be held 'too high' to generate employment for all those seeking work at the going wage. This used to be called 'Classical' unemployment. 'Keynesian' used to be reserved for demand-deficient unemployment. Thus, much of the new work makes these old taxonomies irrelevant.

[10] We discuss some reasons why employers may not change wage rates in response to demand and supply in Chapter 16. One argument is that efficiency wages are used to provide incentives for existing workers. This and other explanations are further discussed below.

seeing an excess of applicants for the few jobs that are available, do not go to their current workers and reduce their wages until there is no one who is looking for a job.[11]

In discussing New Keynesian approaches, it is helpful to divide them into two groups. The first seeks to explain nominal wage and price rigidities that slow the adjustment towards full equilibrium. The second focuses on real wage rigidities that are not eliminated over time, but continue in full equilibrium. We will associate the former approaches with long-term relationships and menu costs; the latter we will consider in the context of efficiency wages and union bargaining models. Chapter 16 also discusses labour markets and covers some of the same issues in more detail.

Long-term relationships

One set of theories explains the familiar observation that money wages do not adjust to clear labour markets as resulting from the advantages to both workers and employers of relatively long-term, stable employment relationships. Workers want job security in the face of fluctuating demand; employers want workers who understand the firm's organization, production, and marketing plans. Under these circumstances both parties care about things in addition to the wage rate, and wages become somewhat less sensitive to fluctuations in current economic conditions. Wages are in effect regular payments to workers over an extended employment relationship, rather than a device for fine-tuning the current supplies and demands for labour. Given this situation, the tendency is for employers to 'smooth out' the income of employees by paying a steady money wage and letting profits and employment fluctuate to absorb the effects of temporary increases and decreases in demand for the firm's product.

A number of labour market institutions work to achieve these results. Employment contracts provide for a schedule of money wages over a period of several years. Fringe benefits, such as membership of the company pension scheme, a company car, and perhaps private health insurance, tend to bind workers to their employers. A worker's pay tends to rise with years of service, despite the known fact that the output attributable to workers rises rapidly as they gain experience, reaches a peak, and then falls off as they age. Under gradually rising wages, workers who spend a long time in the same firm tend to get less than the value of their marginal product when they are young and more than the value of their marginal product as they near retirement. But over the long haul they are paid, on average, the value of their marginal product, just as microeconomic theory predicts. Such features help to bind the employee to the company, whereas redundancy pay, related to years of service, tends to bind the employer to the long-term worker, who would cost the firm more to dismiss.

In labour markets characterized by long-term relationships, the wage rate does not fluctuate to clear the market.

Wages are written over what has been called the long-term 'economic climate' rather than the short-term 'economic weather'. Optimizing firms in such an environment will adjust employment rather than wages during the cycle. However, employees might prefer to accept a lower wage than be laid off. So it remains unclear why sticky wages are optimal for both workers and firms.

Menu costs and wage contracts

A typical large manufacturing firm sells differentiated products numbered in the thousands and employs hundreds of different types of labour. Changing prices and wages in response to every minor fluctuation in demand is a costly and time-consuming activity. Firms find it optimal to keep their price lists (*menus*) constant for significant periods of time. Since all manufacturing firms are operating in imperfectly competitive markets, they have some discretion over price. Hence it may be optimal for firms to react to small changes in demand by holding prices constant and responding with changes in output and employment. If many firms are behaving this way, output and employment will respond to changes in aggregate demand.

The UK evidence is consistent with the existence of sluggish price adjustment by manufacturers. This, of course, is where Keynesian economics came in (with an assumption of price stickiness). The New Keynesian literature attempts to model it as an optimal response to adjustment costs and adverse customer reactions.

Money wages tend to be inflexible in the short term because wage rates are generally set on an annual basis. In some other countries they are set for longer periods—three years is not uncommon with union contracts in North America. Such short-term inflexibility of wages, particularly in the face of negative supply shocks such as the oil price shocks of the 1970s, will lead to increases in unemployment.

We now turn to a discussion of the New Keynesian approaches that focus on real rigidities in labour markets.

Efficiency wages

The idea of the *efficiency wage* forms the core of a strand of thinking about why it may be optimal for firms to set wages permanently above the level that would clear the labour market. Efficiency wage theory applies to hiring, to productivity on the job, and to worker turnover.

Workers are not homogeneous. There are good workers and bad workers, but there is *asymmetrical information*: firms do not know the characteristics of a specific worker until after they have sunk costs into hiring and training

---

[11] This observation concerns cyclical variations in the demand for labour. It does not conflict with the different observation that when firms get into long-term competitive trouble workers sometimes renegotiate contracts and agree to wage cuts in order to save the firm, and their jobs.

him. Good workers know who they are and are likely to have a higher reservation wage (the wage at which they are prepared to work) than bad workers. By lowering the wage they offer, firms will significantly lower the average ability of the workers who apply to them for jobs, and so they could find that paying lower wages makes them worse off. This is known as *adverse selection*. It is a concept we have already met in the context of insurance (see pages 221–3), but it is also an essential feature of labour markets.

In labour markets with informational asymmetries, where unobserved characteristics of job applicants are correlated with the reservation wage, it may not be optimal for firms to pay the market-clearing wage.

Once in employment, workers are likely to give greater effort if they feel they are being well rewarded and the costs of losing their job are high. If wages are so low that workers are just indifferent between staying and losing their jobs, they are likely to please themselves how hard they work and they will not be afraid of getting the sack. Employers have a problem of monitoring and enforcing efficient work practices—this is another case of the principal–agent problem discussed on page 238. Paying a high wage reduces the problem, both because workers will expect to be much worse off if they lose their current job, and because there will be a queue of good-quality workers prepared to work for the higher wage. The high wage improves efficiency—hence the term *efficiency wages*.

Another way in which higher wages may improve productivity is through the direct effects on worker nutrition and general health. In improving the physical well-being of the worker, the marginal productivity of workers may be increased. This is a very important effect in developing countries, but it may also apply in some sectors of developed economies. However, an effect that clearly does apply in developed countries is that workers who are paid well above their best alternative wage have an incentive to invest in self-education and skill acquisition in order to secure their continued employment prospects.

Finally, firms for which high quit rates are costly will be reluctant to lower the wages of existing workers, even in the face of an excess supply of labour. It is possible for firms to pay lower wages to new workers, but tiered wage structures, in which several people doing the same job get different rates of pay, often cause morale problems. This does not prevent firms from paying experienced workers more than inexperienced ones. But it does restrain firms from responding to job queues by offering new workers a lower lifetime earnings profile than that enjoyed by existing workers.

Efficiency wage theory implies that firms may find it advantageous to pay high enough wages so that working is a clearly superior alternative to being laid off. This will improve the quality of workers' output without firms having to spend heavily to monitor workers' performance.

Efficiency wage theory helps us to understand much about labour markets. It also explains why firms may wish to pay wages above market-clearing levels. This helps to explain why involuntary unemployment can persist in equilibrium when GDP is at its potential level.

Union bargaining

The final theoretical approach to be considered under the New Keynesian agenda assumes that those already in employment ('insiders') have more say in wage bargaining than those out of work ('outsiders'). Typically, a union negotiates the wage rate with firms. The union will generally represent the interests of its members, the bulk of whom will be in employment. It will not necessarily reflect the interests of those excluded from employment.

It is easy to see that insiders will wish to bid up wages even though to do so will harm the employment prospects of outsiders. Hence this framework can generate an outcome to the bargaining process between firms and unions in which the wage is set higher than the market-clearing level, just as with the efficiency wage.

Again, these models help explain the existence of involuntary unemployment even when GDP is at its potential level. However, they do add one important new insight into the causes of international differences in unemployment.

In some countries unions bargain at the level of the firm; in others they bargain at the level of the whole industry or the whole economy. Where bargaining is decentralized, the union can push for higher wages for the insiders without worrying about effects on the rest of the economy or on outsiders. However, where bargaining is centralized, the effects on the rest of the economy become internalized into the bargaining process, because union negotiators are bargaining on behalf of all workers (and potential workers), rather than just those in one firm.

The prediction is that decentralized bargaining with strong unions will lead to higher than market-clearing wages, and outsiders being excluded from jobs, whereas centralized bargaining will produce an outcome closer to the market-clearing outcome (because outsider concerns are voiced), so unemployment will be low.

The third alternative to centralized and decentralized union bargaining is no union bargaining at all because unionization is low and unions are weak. This too will produce an outcome close to the free-market rate, even in the absence of efficiency wage considerations. This analysis may explain why unemployment is relatively high in EU countries, where unions are strong but bargaining is decentralized, but lower in Scandinavia, where unions are also strong but bargaining is centralized, and the United States, where unions are weak.

The basic message of New Keynesian theories of unemployment is that labour markets cannot be relied upon to

eliminate involuntary unemployment by equating current demand for labour with current supply.

The New Keynesian theories have concentrated on explaining why wages do not fluctuate to clear labour markets instantaneously. This helps to explain the existence of involuntary cyclical unemployment in the face of fluctuations in aggregate demand. These demand fluctuations are, however, still a necessary part of the explanation of cyclical fluctuations. They leave the emphasis of anticyclical policy on demand-side measures whenever the automatic adjustment mechanism does not work fast enough. To the extent that the theories explain why wages do not clear labour markets even in the long term, they help to explain high *equilibrium unemployment*. It is to this that we now turn.

Equilibrium unemployment: the NAIRU

Equilibrium unemployment, or the NAIRU, is composed of *frictional* and *structural* unemployment.

Frictional unemployment Frictional unemployment results from the normal turnover of labour. An important source of frictional unemployment is young people who enter the labour force looking for jobs. Another source is people who are in the process of changing their jobs and are caught between one job and the next. Some may quit because they are dissatisfied with the type of work or their working conditions; others may be sacked. Whatever the reason, they must search for new jobs and this takes time. People who are unemployed while searching for jobs are said to be frictionally unemployed or, alternatively, in 'search unemployment'.

The normal turnover of labour would cause some frictional unemployment to persist, even if the economy were at potential GDP and the structure of jobs in terms of skills, industries, occupations, and location were unchanging.

Structural unemployment Structural adjustments can cause unemployment. When the pattern of demand for goods changes, the pattern of the demand for labour changes. Until labour adjusts fully, there is structural unemployment. This may be defined as unemployment caused by a mismatch between the structure of the labour force—in terms of skills, occupations, industries, or geographical locations—and the structure of the demand for labour.

Endogenous change

Changes that accompany economic growth shift the structure of the demand for labour. One of the more dramatic recent structural changes has been in the organization of the firm. Large firms used to be organized much like an army, with a pyramid command structure. Most key strategic decisions were made near the top, with lesser ones concerning implementation made at lower levels. This structure required an array of middle-level managers, who passed information upward to the top level and downward to the production level, and who made various secondary decisions themselves. Recent changes associated with the IT revolution have led to a much looser organization with much more local autonomy among the subsections of the firm. As a result, large numbers of middle managers have been made redundant. They find themselves on the labour market at middle age and with many of their skills rendered obsolete.

Another key structural change in the UK (and in many other economies) has been the decline in manufacturing and the rise in service employment. Employment in manufacturing has been declining since the late 1950s, but the UK real exchange rate appreciation of the late 1970s and early 1980s (partly associated with another structural change —the emergence of North Sea oil production) accelerated this adjustment in the UK. Many factories closed in the early 1980s or were replaced by capital-intensive rather than labour-intensive plant. Although the total of available jobs has not changed much, it has not always been easy for a newly unemployed factory worker to find employment in the expanding service sector, particularly when many of the new jobs require new skills.

Increases in international competition can have effects similar to those of economic growth and change. As the geographical distribution of world production changes, so does the composition of production and of labour demand in any one country. Labour adapts to such shifts by changing jobs, skills, and locations, but until the transition is complete, structural unemployment remains.

Structural unemployment increases if there is either an increase in the speed at which the structure of the demand for labour is changing or a decrease in the speed at which labour is adapting to these changes.

Policy influences

Government policies can influence the speed with which labour markets adapt to change. Some countries have adopted policies that discourage movement among regions, industries, and occupations. These policies tend to raise structural unemployment, though state subsidies may disguise it for a while. The EU Common Agricultural Policy (CAP), for example, is intended (partly) to resist the decline of incomes and employment in agriculture, even though employment in agriculture has been declining in Europe since the late eighteenth century. Other countries, such as Sweden, have done the reverse and have encouraged workers to adapt to change. Partly for this reason, Sweden's unemployment rates were well below the European average during the 1980s.

Policies that discourage firms from replacing labour with machines may protect employment over the short term. However, if such policies lead to the decline of an industry because it cannot compete effectively with innovative foreign competitors, serious structural unemployment can result in the long run.

High minimum-wage laws may cause structural unemployment by pricing low-skilled labour out of the market. As explained in Chapter 16, minimum-wage laws have two effects when they are imposed on competitive markets: they reduce employment of the unskilled, and they raise the wages of the unskilled who retain their jobs.

Why does the NAIRU change?

We have noted that structural unemployment can increase because the pace of change accelerates or the pace of adjustment to change slows down. An increase in the rate of growth, for example, usually speeds up the rate at which the structure of the demand for labour is changing. The adaptation of labour to the changing structure of demand may be slowed by such diverse factors as a decline in educational achievement and regulations which make it harder for workers in a given occupation to take new jobs in other areas or occupations. Any of these changes will cause the NAIRU to rise. Changes in the opposite direction will cause the NAIRU to fall.

Demographic changes

Because people usually try several jobs before settling into one for a longer period of time, young or inexperienced workers have higher unemployment rates than experienced workers. The proportion of inexperienced workers in the labour force rose significantly as the postwar baby boom generation entered the labour force in the late 1960s and 1970s, along with an unprecedented number of women who elected to work outside the home. In the 1980s youth unemployment became an even bigger problem, because school-leavers found it hard to get a foothold on the career ladder when unemployment was rising and even experienced workers were being laid off.

Even if youth unemployment should fall in future, many observers worry about the long-term consequences for some individuals. Learning through on-the-job experience is a critical part of developing marketable labour skills, and those who suffered prolonged unemployment during their teens and twenties have been denied that experience early in their working careers. These workers may have little option later in life but to take temporary jobs at low pay and with little future job security, or to drop out of the labour force entirely.

The significant increase in female participation rates, and the related increase in the number of households with more than one income-earner, has also affected the NAIRU. When both husband and wife work, it is possible for one to support both while the other looks for 'a really good job' rather than accepting the first job offer that comes along, or spends time in retraining. This can increase recorded unemployment while not inflicting excessive hardship on those involved.

Hysteresis

Recent models of unemployment show that the size of the NAIRU can be influenced by the *size* of the actual current rate of unemployment. Such models get their name from the Greek word **hysteresis**, meaning 'coming late'.[12] In economics it means that the current equilibrium is not independent of what has gone before—it is path-dependent. This means that the NAIRU will be higher after periods of high unemployment than after periods of low unemployment. If this is correct, we have to distinguish between the short-run NAIRU and the long-run **natural rate**. The latter is the true long-run equilibrium towards which the short-run NAIRU will adjust slowly over time.

One mechanism that can lead to hysteresis in labour markets has already been noted. It arises from the importance of experience and on-the-job training. Suppose, for example, that a period of recession causes a significant group of new entrants to the labour force to have unusual difficulty in obtaining their first jobs. As a result, the unlucky group will be slow to acquire the important skills that workers generally learn in their first jobs. When demand increases again, this group of workers will be at a disadvantage relative to workers with normal histories of job experience, and the unlucky group may have unemployment rates that will be higher than average. Thus, the NAIRU will be higher than it would have been had there been no recession.

Another force that can cause such effects is insider–outsider segregation in a heavily unionized labour force with decentralized bargaining, discussed above. In times of high unemployment, people who are currently employed

---

[12] It was first used in electronics to relate to effects coming after their causes, i.e. lagged effects.

(insiders) may use their bargaining power to ensure that their own status is maintained and to prevent new entrants to the labour force (outsiders) from competing effectively. In an insider–outsider model of this type a period of prolonged high unemployment—whatever its initial cause—will tend to become 'locked in'. If outsiders are denied access to the labour market, their unemployment will fail to exert downward pressure on wages, and the NAIRU will tend to rise.

Hysteresis is part of the explanation of the high levels of persistent unemployment in many EU countries, including the United Kingdom.

Increasing structural change

The amount of industrial restructuring, both locally and internationally, increased in the 1980s and 1990s and appears to be continuing in the 2000s. In part, this is the result of the increasing integration of the UK economy with the European Union and the rest of the world, and the globalization of world markets. Most observers feel that this integration has been beneficial overall. One less fortunate consequence, however, is that labour markets are increasingly affected by changes in demand and supply conditions anywhere in the world.

The following numerous structural changes have created a continuing need for rapid adjustments:

* the collapse of communism and the conversion of the countries of Eastern Europe to market economies;
* increases in the supply of agricultural products owing to the green revolution in less developed countries and heavy agricultural subsidization in the European Union;
* enormous OPEC-induced increases in the price of oil in the 1970s and early 1980s, followed by almost equally precipitous declines in the mid-1980s that carried through into the 1990s;
* the emergence of several Asian countries as industrial economies, of which China will, in the long run, be the most important;
* the communications revolution, leading to the decentralization of industry, with components produced in various countries and assembled in others;
* robotization, which has increased industrial productivity and reduced the demand for assembly-line workers;
* the growth of knowledge-intensive industries, which require highly educated and geographically mobile workforces;
* the globalization of competition, with fewer and fewer domestic markets that are sheltered by artificial barriers;
* changes in the organization of firms;
* the privatization of large sections of formerly state-owned industries;
* the decline of employment in manufacturing;
* the enormous growth in service employment.

Although evidence is difficult to obtain, some observers argue that the increasing pace and the changing nature of technological change since the mid-1970s have contributed to an increase in the level of structural unemployment.

Mismatch Structural change that creates unemployed workers with the wrong characteristics (skills, experience, location) for the available jobs is known as *mismatch*. As we saw above, the biggest mismatch is likely to be that modern industry requires skilled and flexible workers while the majority of the unemployed are unskilled. Intuitively, this makes sense—a metal-worker made redundant in Sheffield in 1980 is unlikely to have found work (quickly) as an advertising executive, even if vacancies existed.

Researchers studying UK unemployment have found mismatch to be important in increasing the NAIRU, but mismatch does not appear to have increased markedly since the early 1970s. Thus, it explains the rise in the NAIRU between the 1960s and 1970s but not subsequent rises—though further studies may produce different evidence.

Unemployment benefits

Workers who lose their jobs receive unemployment benefit. The size of the benefits paid, relative to pay levels in work, is known as the **replacement ratio**. A high replacement ratio raises the NAIRU. It affects the willingness of the unemployed to accept job offers, and it affects the intensity with which they search for work.

Changes in the replacement ratio do have significant statistical effects on the NAIRU, but the authors of *The Unemployment Crisis*[13] found that it explains only 0.8 percentage points of the 6.2 percentage point rise in equilibrium unemployment between the 1960s and 1980s.

However, differences in benefit systems between countries do seem to play a very important role in explaining international differences in unemployment. It is not just the replacement ratio faced by a newly unemployed worker that matters; also important is the duration for which that benefit is provided (if it is for a short period, the worker has an incentive to find work very quickly) and the degree to which the benefit is conditional on job-seeking activity. Countries with only temporary benefits and both the incentive and assistance with finding work tend to have lower equilibrium unemployment rates.

---

[13] See fn. 7 above.

Other effects

Two other factors are often reported to have at least a temporary effect on the NAIRU. The first is the tax wedge. This is the difference between what an employer has to pay to hire a worker and what the worker receives in take-home pay. Increasing the tax wedge for a given quantity of labour demanded reduces take-home pay. This is likely to increase wage-bargaining pressure as a result of workers' reluctance to accept lower real wages. In effect, this shifts up the short-run Phillips curve, thereby worsening the inflation–unemployment trade-off in the short run. However, this has no long-run effect on the NAIRU, as the tax wedge cannot keep increasing.

The second factor is associated with a terms-of-trade loss, or real exchange rate depreciation. This is argued to have a similar effect; because it raises import prices, it also reduces real wages. Real-wage resistance shifts the short-run Phillips curve upwards and we get the same result as in the previous paragraph.

Explaining unemployment

By combining the analysis of demand and supply shocks and the Phillips curve of Chapter 31 with what we have learned about labour markets above, we can now produce an explanation for the unemployment experience which we summarized at the beginning of this chapter. This explanation is broadly that set out by Layard, Nickell, and Jackman in *The Unemployment Crisis*, mentioned above.

Supply shocks

Most countries were subjected to two major supply shocks associated with the oil price rises of 1973 and 1979. Countries with more centralized wage bargaining suffered less unemployment than others, because wage negotiators were more prepared to accept cuts in real wages. The shock was complicated in the United Kingdom by structural adjustment resulting from the emergence of an oil-producing sector. The pace of technological and organizational change has speeded up and affected unemployment most in those countries with inflexible labour market institutions and regulations.

Demand shocks

Governments reacted to high inflation in the 1970s with tight monetary and fiscal policies. Slow downward adjustment of inflation expectations, combined with negative demand shocks, created recessionary gaps and rising unemployment. The short-run impact of these demand shocks on unemployment was less, the more flexible were wage contracts.

Persistence

Unemployment became persistent in those countries with open-ended unemployment benefits and, once in place, was sustained by hysteresis effects. Countries that did least to get the long-term unemployed back to work suffered most in terms of rising equilibrium unemployment rates.

Reducing unemployment

Other things being equal, all governments would like to reduce unemployment. The questions are 'Can it be done?' and 'If so, at what cost?' Some commonly aired 'solutions' which will almost certainly not help are discussed in Box 32.2.

In this section we review the policies that governments could use to help lower unemployment once it is high. The simple solution, in view of what we have learned about persistence, is: don't start from here! That is to say, governments should not wait for high unemployment to get established before they worry about it. It may be easier to prevent it from getting high than to bring it down once it is entrenched. This is so whatever the size of the NAIRU. And it suggests that the authorities should act quickly to accommodate the effects of a negative shock to aggregate supply before they generate high unemployment.

With GDP close to its potential level, however, an increase in aggregate demand intended to reduce equilibrium unemployment would rapidly lead to a rise in inflation. By definition, inflation will start to accelerate once unemployment falls below the NAIRU.

This means that the most that demand management can do about equilibrium unemployment is to try to make sure that it does not rise as a result of hysteresis effects associated with major deflations. Unfortunately, it was attempts to eliminate inflation rapidly by restrictive aggregate demand policies that contributed to high unemployment in the first place.

Once inflation is low and the unemployment level is close to the NAIRU, aggregate demand policy should be neutral; that is, it should aim to maintain GDP at its potential level.

Reducing persistence

The reduction of persistence and hysteresis effects is a major challenge. It probably requires both a reform of the

Box 32.2 **False trails: what won't cure unemployment**

The existence of high unemployment prompts many well-meaning but ill-considered suggestions for solving the problem. The most common error made when thinking about unemployment is to assume that there is a fixed number of jobs available to be shared out. This leads to proposals for compulsory job sharing and enforced early retirement to divide existing jobs among available workers, proposals to halt new technology 'destroying' jobs, and protectionism to stop 'our jobs' being taken by low-wage foreigners.

The following arguments have been made against these false assumptions.*

Job sharing

Enforced job sharing and involuntary early retirement reduce potential GDP because they prevent those who are willing and able to work productively from doing so. It makes the individuals so restricted worse off, and it makes society as a whole worse off. Indeed, it is a form of forced unemployment. As the OECD *Jobs Study* puts it (p. 27),

Legislated, across-the-board, work-sharing addresses the unemployment problem not by increasing the number of jobs through more economic activity, but through rationing gainful work. Enforced work-sharing has never succeeded in cutting unemployment significantly, not least because of workers' resistance to reduced income.

This is not to say that flexible working practices, which enable part-time working for those who would otherwise be unable to work, are a bad thing: on the contrary, the key is that each individual should be able to maximize her productive activity in the manner most suited to her needs and commitments. Anything that limits the opportunity to work is harmful.

Technology

In 1811 Nottinghamshire frameworkers (led by the probably mythical Ned Ludd) smashed new machinery. This was because they thought that the new technology of the industrial revolution was doing them out of a livelihood, as indeed was true for those not prepared to learn new skills. Before that time real wages were constant, possibly for centuries. Since that time real wages have multiplied at least ten-fold even for manual workers, and job opportunities have multiplied in incalculable ways. To quote the OECD study again (p. 29),

History has shown that when technological progress accelerates, so do growth, living standards and employment. Technological progress would lead to high unemployment only in a world of saturated wants or perpetual restriction of demand, conditions that have not occurred in the past, and seem unlikely in the foreseeable future. Furthermore, worries about a new era of 'jobless growth' appear unfounded: the current upswing in the United States and a number of other countries has brought job growth in its train, and broadly in line with past relationships between growth and employment.

Protectionism

It is an erroneous but widely held view in Europe that competition from low-wage countries, especially in Asia, is responsible for much of the current unemployment. This is an argument that the OECD economists are able to dismiss (p. 28):

The weight of low-wage countries' exports in the overall expenditure of OECD countries on goods and services is only about 1.5 per cent. The number of markets which they contest is greater, and their effect on the intensity of competition is increasing. But the judgement on present evidence is that the overall impact both of imports from these countries and their contestation of OECD markets is too small to account for a significant part of either current unemployment or falling relative wages of the low-skilled. On the other hand, these countries represent a large and growing potential market for OECD exports of goods and services, and hence represent an important source of current and future growth and employment.

On the case for using protectionism to 'keep jobs at home', the OECD has no doubts (p. 29):

Protectionism reduces overall economic welfare; increases costs to consumers, often hurting most those with lowest incomes; penalises successful enterprise; harms exports; encourages tariff factories; harms developing countries' trade; and increases the pressures for international migration. It encourages domestic monopolies, while cutting the economy off from mainstream developments in the world outside. Producers, dependent on protection for their survival, ultimately become prepared to spend large sums to preserve its continuance. Lobbying, and even bribery and corruption, become more widespread.

* These are based on the OECD *Job Study*, 1994.

benefits system and active policies to ensure that those in danger of long-term unemployment get work experience and training. The feature of the benefits system that seems to be most harmful (in the sense of creating long-term unemployment) is an indefinite period of benefits payments. This reduces the incentive of the recently unemployed to seek work urgently. Some commentators advocate compulsory public sector work for the unemployed after some period of time; others advocate state subsidies towards private sector employment as a way of getting people back into the labour market. The general point however is that,

whatever the policies are, they have to be targeted on the unemployed directly, rather than in the form of general reflation.

Another aspect of persistence is mismatch. Policies to reduce this must involve making it easier for workers to change occupations by assistance for retraining and relocation. It could be argued that it is the responsibility of individuals or firms to finance retraining. However, individuals may be financially constrained, and firms may feel that it is not worth training a worker who may go elsewhere. The state funds education for the young, so there is no reason, in principle, why those needing retraining should be treated differently.

Labour market reform

A third class of policies that may help to reduce unemployment involves labour market reforms, especially the structure of wage bargaining. We have seen that insiders may hold wage rates high, to the detriment of outsiders. We have also seen that centralized wage bargaining may generate lower unemployment than decentralized bargaining. However, union structures have evolved over decades, and it is no easy matter in a free society to scrap the lot and start again.

Conclusion

Unemployment is a major problem of our time. We have been able to understand, with a combination of the tools provided by the macro model and our new understanding of labour markets, how unemployment came about and why it is characterized by persistence. We have also learned why the traditional macroeconomic approach to reducing unemployment is no longer adequate. The bad news is that reducing equilibrium unemployment is likely to be a slow process. The good news is that persistence does not mean permanence. Normal economic change and new economic policies can make progress against persistence, which need not be accepted as inevitable.

SUMMARY

Employment and unemployment characteristics

- Employment has grown little in Europe in the last three decades, and unemployment appeared to have an upward trend in the 1970s and 1980s. However, unemployment is untrended in the long run, and there were signs that the prospects for reducing unemployment might be improving at the end of the 1990s and in the early 2000s.

- It is useful to distinguish among several kinds of unemployment: (a) cyclical unemployment, which is caused by too low a level of aggregate demand; (b) frictional unemployment, which is caused by the length of time it takes to find a first job and to move from job to job as a result of normal labour turnover; and (c) structural unemployment, which is caused by the need to reallocate resources among occupations, regions, and industries as the structure of demands and supplies changes. Together frictional unemployment and structural unemployment make up equilibrium unemployment, the NAIRU, which is then expressed as a percentage of the total labour force.

Cyclical unemployment

- New Classical theories look to explanations that allow the labour market to be cleared continuously. Such theories can explain cyclical variations in employment but do not explain involuntary unemployment, that is, the unemployment of workers who would like to work at the going wage rates but for whom jobs are not available.

- Recent New Keynesian theories have focused on the long-term nature of employer–worker relationships and on the possibility that it is efficient for employers to pay wages that are above the level that would clear the labour market. These explain why wages may be rigid enough for demand fluctuations to produce cyclical fluctuations in unemployment.

Equilibrium unemployment: the NAIRU

- The NAIRU will always be positive because it takes time for labour to move between jobs, both in normal turnover and in response to changes in the structure of the demand for labour. Government policies can also influence the NAIRU.

- Changes in the NAIRU can result from demographic changes, hysteresis effects, structural change in the economy, or changes in the unemployment benefit system.

Reducing unemployment

- Cyclical unemployment can be reduced by aggregate demand policies.

- Equilibrium unemployment can be reduced by lowering benefits (level and duration), imposing active manpower policies, and reforming wage-bargaining institutions.

- In a growing, changing economy populated by people who wish to change jobs for many reasons, it is neither possible nor desirable to reduce unemployment to zero. Most important is the avoidance of the buildup of long-term unemployment.

TOPICS FOR REVIEW

- Cyclical unemployment
- Frictional unemployment
- Structural unemployment
- Efficiency wages

- Hysteresis
- Persistence
- Determinants of the size of the NAIRU
- Policies to reduce unemployment

DISCUSSION QUESTIONS

1 Explain the differences between cyclical, frictional, and structural unemployment.

2 Why does it matter whether unemployment is voluntary or involuntary?

3 Why does the issue of whether or not wage rates are sticky enter into the question of what determines unemployment?

4 How do efficiency wage theories explain why firms are unwilling to adjust wages in response to an excess supply of labour?

5 Outline potential policy solutions to (*a*) cyclical and (*b*) structural unemployment.

6 What are the main determinants of the NAIRU?

7 What is the difference between claimant count and LFS unemployment?

Appendix Cyclical controversies

Many of the different schools of thought in economics have had their own approach to explaining unemployment and business cycles; indeed, attempts to document and explain the cycle in economic activity predate modern macroeconomics. We concentrate here on the views of the major schools of thought that have existed within macroeconomics over the last half century or so.

The monetarist approach

Monetarists believe that the economy is inherently stable because private sector expenditure functions are relatively stable and price adjustment will bring the economy back to potential output. In addition, they believe that shifts in the aggregate demand curve are due mainly to policy-induced changes in the money supply.

The view that business cycles have mainly monetary causes originally relied partly on the evidence advanced by Milton Friedman and Anna Schwartz in their classic study *A Monetary History of the United States, 1867–1960* (1963). The authors purported to have established a strong correlation between changes in the money supply and changes in economic activity. Major recessions have been associated with absolute declines in the money supply and minor recessions with the slowing of the rate of increase in the money supply below its long-term trend.

More recent work has shown that the Friedman–Schwartz relations are not as close, even in the United States, as these authors tried to show. Attempts to establish a similar close relation for the United Kingdom have not been successful. None the less, there is a broad—if loose—association between changes in the money supply and changes in money GDP. The sustained increases in the price level that result from a major inflation are invariably accompanied by a sustained increase in the money stock.

The rough correlation between changes in the money supply and changes in the level of economic activity is accepted by many economists. But there is controversy over how this correlation is to be interpreted. Do changes in money supply cause changes in the level of aggregate demand, and hence of business activity, or vice versa?

Friedman and Schwartz maintained that changes in the money supply cause changes in business activity. They argued, for example, that the severity of the Great Depression was due to a major contraction in the money supply, which shifted the aggregate demand curve far to the left.

According to monetarists, fluctuations in the money supply cause fluctuations in GDP.

This led the monetarists to advocate a policy of stabilizing the growth of the money supply. In their view this would avoid policy-induced instability of the aggregate demand curve.

The Keynesian approach

The traditional Keynesian explanation of cyclical fluctuations in the economy has two parts. First, it emphasizes variations in investment as a cause of business cycles and stresses the non-monetary causes of such variations, such as expectations or, as Keynes put it, 'animal spirits'.

Keynesians reject what they regard as the extreme monetarist view that only money matters in explaining cyclical fluctuations. Many Keynesians believe that both monetary and non-monetary forces are important in explaining cycles. Although they accept serious monetary mismanagement as one potential source of economic fluctuations, they do not believe that it is the only, or even the major, source of such fluctuations. Thus, they deny the monetary interpretation of business cycle history given by Friedman and Schwartz. They believe that most fluctuations in the aggregate demand curve are due to variations in the desire to spend on the part of the private sector and are not induced by government policy.

Keynesians also believe that the economy lacks strong natural corrective mechanisms that will always force it easily and quickly back to full employment. They believe that, while the price level rises fairly quickly to eliminate *inflationary* gaps, prices and wages fall only slowly in response to *recessionary* gaps. As a result, Keynesians believe that recessionary gaps can sometimes persist for long periods of time unless they are eliminated by an active stabilization policy.

The second part of the Keynesian view on cyclical fluctuations concerns the alleged correlation between changes in the money supply and changes in the level of economic activity. In so far as this correlation exists, the Keynesian explanation reverses the causality suggested by the monetarists. Keynesians argue that changes in the level of economic activity often cause changes in the money supply.

Certainly, Keynesians are on strong ground when the monetary authorities are setting interest rates (or when there is a fixed exchange rate regime, as we saw in Chapter 30) as the money stock is endogenously determined by demand under this regime. For a given interest rate, changes in GDP will cause changes in the money stock, rather than vice versa.

According to Keynesians, fluctuations in GDP are often caused by fluctuations in autonomous expenditures. Further, they believe that fluctuations in GDP usually cause fluctuations in the money supply.

Nevertheless, most Keynesians also agree that deliberate changes in monetary policy can cause GDP to change, via induced changes in aggregate demand. However, notice that the monetarist approach makes the monetary authorities the main cause of cycles—hence the recommendation that they should be constrained to follow a rigid policy rule. For many Keynesians it is fluctuations in private sector investment behaviour (and perhaps exports) that matter, and the authorities are the 'good guys' who can offset this privately generated instability. It is for this reason that Keynesians are often interventionist and monetarists are usually non-interventionist.

A shift of emphasis within the Keynesian school has come out of the New Keynesian research agenda (discussed in this chapter). Early Keynesians focused mainly on the use of aggregate demand (especially fiscal) policies to stabilize the cycle; New Keynesians hope to see GDP kept close to its potential level by whatever means possible, but place more stress on supply-side (labour market) policies to eliminate persistent (equilibrium) unemployment than did their Keynesian predecessors.

The New Classical approach

The New Classical approach to explaining business cycles has something in common with the monetarists, in that the shock that sets off the cycle is a change in the money supply. However, the New Classical story is quite different from traditional (monetarist or Keynesian) business cycle theory, because the New Classical school wanted a model in which markets were always in equilibrium. An alternative approach to modelling business cycles in 'equilibrium' models, which does not rely on monetary shocks, is discussed below.

New Classical economists assume that the actors in the private sector of the economy have **rational expectations**. This assumes that agents form expectations based upon all available information about the future at the time they take the decision. So agents make only random errors in forecasting the future course of economic variables. This means that the expectational errors that trigger cycles cannot be systematic. (If they were systematic, agents could learn from the pattern of mistakes and improve their forecasts.)

A perhaps surprising implication of the New Classical approach is that changes in monetary or fiscal policy, which may be intended to influence economic activity by shifting the *AD* curve, will have real effects only if they are unexpected. For example, a stimulus to demand involving an announced reduction in interest rates (and consequent increase in the money supply) will create expectations of rising prices. These expectations will influence wage-setting, so the *SRAS* curve will shift up immediately and prices will rise straight away with no temporary increase in output. (See the discussion of the Lucas aggregate supply curve on page 585).

According to the New Classical approach, only unanticipated policy changes lead to changes in real national income. Systematic policy changes will be predictable and will have no real effects.

Most economists do not accept the proposition that only unexpected policy changes will have real effects. One reason is that there is so much inertia in price- and wage-setting behaviour that very few contracts can be renegotiated as soon as a policy change is announced. Hence the policy-makers certainly have some leverage over real activity, even when making policy changes that are predictable.

A second reason is that the massive complexity of the economy makes it impossible for individual agents to know how some shock will affect all the relevant prices and quantities that matter to them over any specified period of time. The idea of everyone knowing the exact nature of some policy disturbance and solving the equations of the economy to determine the exact outcome, and of their acting to anticipate these outcomes, is far-fetched. After all, the great virtue of the price system is that it co-ordinates activity without the need for anyone to have knowledge of all the prices and quantities that exist.

However, the New Classical presumption that private agents have expectations of what policy-makers are going to do, and that this influences private behaviour, is important. Without assuming omniscience, just reasonable approximate expectations, private anticipation of government action can affect the outcome of policies. This realization has had a fundamental impact on macroeconomic policy analysis. In both Keynesian and monetarist models the government was exogenous to the model. However, in the New Classical framework the government and the private sector interact by trying to guess what the other is going to do. The conduct of policy becomes more like a 'game', where strategy and perception of the other players matter.

This change in perception of policy as interactive rather than exogenous has two important implications.

Policy credibility If private agents are watching the government (and the monetary authorities, where these are different) and trying to form expectations of its future behaviour, not only does it matter what the government does, but it also matters what agents think it will do in future. This means that a government needs more than just the correct current policies. It also needs to establish **credibility** that it will follow the correct policies in future.

Suppose, for example, that a government enters office with a commitment to control inflation. It introduces tight monetary and fiscal policies, which in due course succeed in bringing down inflation. Now, however, there is an election approaching, and the government would like to increase real GDP to improve its chances of re-election. It may be tempted to break its original commitment to anti-inflationary policies. However, private agents know that this incentive exists, so it matters to the outcome whether or not the private agents anticipate the government's breaking its word. In other words, the government's credibility actually affects private behaviour. Of course, once the government has broken its commitments, it will be very hard for it to establish credibility again—at least without a change in personnel.

The New Classical approach to business cycles clearly supports a non-interventionist approach to macroeconomic policy. Governments can initiate shocks, but systematic attempts to stabilize cycles will be frustrated by their very predictability.

Real business cycles

Another group has taken up the task of explaining business cycles in the context of equilibrium models of the economy. Real business cycle (RBC) research has evolved from the New Classical attempt to explain cyclical fluctuations in the context of models in which equilibrium prevails at all times. In this sense

the models can be seen as an extension of the New Classical approach.

The view of the business cycle found in RBC models is that fluctuations in national income are caused by fluctuations in the vertical *LRAS* curve arising from *technology shocks*. In contrast, the previous three approaches to fluctuations were based on fluctuations in the *AD* curve.

The explanation of cyclical fluctuations that arises in RBC models is based on the role of supply (productivity) shocks originating from sources such as oil price changes, technical progress, and changes in tastes.

In this view output is always equal to potential GDP, but it is potential GDP itself that fluctuates.

Because the approach gives no role to aggregate demand in influencing business cycles, it provides no role for stabilization operating through monetary and fiscal policies. Indeed, the models used by this school to date predict that the use of such demand management policies can be harmful.

The basis for this prediction is the proposition in RBC models that cycles represent *efficient* responses to the shocks that are hitting the economy. Policy-makers may mistakenly interpret cyclical fluctuations as deviations from full-employment equilibrium that are caused by fluctuations in aggregate demand. The policy-makers may try to stabilize output and thereby distort the maximizing decisions made by households and firms. In turn, this distortion will cause the responses to the real shocks (as opposed to nominal, monetary shocks) to be inefficient.

Although only a minority of economists espouse these models as complete or even reasonable descriptions of the business cycle, and thus only a minority take seriously the strict implications for policy, many accept the view that real disturbances can play an important role in business cycles. It is, of course, highly controversial to argue that whatever the cycles in the economy, they are an optimal response to shocks, upon which no policy actions can improve. Indeed, if this were the case, macroeconomics as a subject would have no purpose—invented as it was to help policy-makers cure recessions and alleviate unemployment—and the unemployed will have been voluntarily idle, either because they have preferred leisure to work at correctly perceived real wage rates, or because, in contradiction of rational expectations, they have been systematically underpredicting the real wage rate for many years in succession.

Chapter 33

INTERNATIONAL TRADE

Do imports of goods made with cheap foreign labour destroy jobs at home? Is globalization making the rich richer and the poor poorer? Should our government subsidize domestic industries to help them compete internationally? These are some of the questions we address in this and the subsequent chapter. In this chapter we focus on trade issues affecting all major economies, and in the following chapter we look at specific issues affecting developing and transition economies. In particular, you will learn in this chapter that:

• Gains from trade result from comparative advantage, which arises whenever there are differences in opportunity costs of production.

• Terms of trade determine how the gains from trade are distributed.

• Free trade tends to maximize world income.

• Protectionism may make one country better off, but the world as a whole tends to be made worse off by protection.

• The World Trade Organization polices world trade rules and the commercial policies of member governments.

• Regional free-trade areas and common markets bring efficiency gains through trade creation and efficiency losses through trade diversion.

Sales and purchases of goods and services that take place across international boundaries are *international trade*. For example, the British buy BMWs made in Germany, Germans take holidays in Italy, Italians buy spices from Tanzania, Belgians import oil from Kuwait, Egyptians buy Japanese cameras, and the Japanese depend heavily on American soybeans as a source of food.

There is substantial evidence to show that international trade and economic growth are positively linked. In this chapter we explain why trade increases output and incomes. We then ask why, if trade is generally beneficial, governments have often attempted to restrict the freedom to trade. Finally, we discuss some of the institutional arrangements that affect world trade.

Sources of the gains from trade

An economy that engages in international trade is an **open economy**. One that does not is a **closed economy**. A situation in which a country conducts no foreign trade is called **autarky**. The advantages realized as a result of trade are called the **gains from trade**. Although politicians often regard foreign trade as being different from domestic trade, economists from Adam Smith on have argued that the causes and consequences of international trade are simply an extension of the principles governing domestic trade. What are the benefits to be derived from trade among individuals, among groups, among regions, or among countries?

Interpersonal, interregional, and international trade

Let us start by thinking about trade between individuals. Without trade, each person would have to be self-sufficient; each would have to produce all the food, clothing, shelter, medical services, entertainment, and luxuries that she needed or wished to consume. A world of individual self-sufficiency would be a world with extremely low living standards.

Trade between individuals allows people to specialize in those activities they can do relatively well and to buy from others the goods and services they themselves cannot easily produce. A good doctor who is a bad carpenter can provide medical services not only for his own family, but also for an excellent carpenter who lacks the training or the ability to practise medicine. Thus, trade and specialization are intimately connected. Without trade, everyone must be self-sufficient. With trade, everyone can specialize in what they do well and satisfy other needs by trading.

The same principles apply to regions. Without interregional trade, each region would be forced to be self-sufficient. With trade, each region can specialize in producing those goods or services for which it has some natural or acquired advantage. Plains regions can specialize in growing grain, mountain regions can specialize in mining and forest products, and regions with abundant manpower can specialize in manufacturing. Cool regions can produce dairy products and wool along with crops that thrive in temperate climates, and hot regions can grow such tropical crops as rice, cotton, bananas, sugar, and coffee. Places with lots of sunshine and sandy beaches can specialize in the tourist trade. The living standards of the inhabitants of all regions will be higher when each region specializes in products in which it has some natural or acquired advantage and obtains other products by trade than when all regions seek to be self-sufficient.

The same principle also applies to nations. Nations, like regions or persons, can gain from specialization. Almost all countries produce more of some goods than their residents wish to consume. At the same time, they consume more than they produce of some other goods.

International trade is necessary to achieve the gains that international specialization makes possible. Trade allows each individual, region, or nation to concentrate on producing those goods and services that it produces relatively efficiently while trading to obtain goods and services that it would produce less efficiently than others.

Specialization and trade go hand in hand, because there is no motivation to achieve the gains from specialization without being able to trade the goods produced for the different goods desired. The term 'gains from trade' encompasses the results of both. This was first discussed in Chapter 1, and it would be worth rereading now pages 1–10 and Box 1.3.

There are two main sources of gains from trade. The first is differences between regions of the world in climate and resource endowment, which lead to advantages in producing certain goods and disadvantages in producing others. These gains occur even though each country's costs of production are unchanged by the existence of trade. The second source is the reduction in each country's costs of production resulting from the greater production that specialization brings.

The gains from specialization with given costs

In order to focus on differences in countries' conditions of production, suppose that each country's average costs of production are constant. We will use an example below involving only two countries and two products, but the general principles apply as well to the real-world case of many countries and many products.

Absolute advantage

Box 1.3 on page 9 showed the simple case of absolute advantage. One region is said to have an **absolute advantage** over another in the production of good X when an equal quantity of resources can produce more X in the first region than in the second. If we rename the individuals in the box as countries, we see what is obvious. Total production can be increased if each country specializes in producing the product for which it has an absolute advantage.

These gains from specialization make possible the gains from trade. If consumers in both countries are to get the goods they desire in the required proportions, each must export some of the commodity in which it specializes and import commodities in which other countries are specialized.

Comparative advantage

When each country has an absolute advantage over others in a product, the gains from trade are obvious. But what if one country can produce all commodities more efficiently than other countries? In essence, this was the question English economist David Ricardo (1772–1823) posed 200 years ago. His answer underlies the *theory of comparative advantage* and is still accepted by economists today as a valid statement of the potential gains from trade.

The gains from specialization and trade depend on the pattern of comparative, not absolute, advantage. Although this point was illustrated in Box 1.3, it is important enough to justify another example. Let us assume that there are two countries, the United States and the European Union. Both countries produce the same two goods, wheat and cloth, but the opportunity costs of producing these two products differ between them. Recall from Chapter 1 that the *opportunity cost* in production is given by the slope of the production-possibility frontier, and it tells us how much of one good we have to give up in order to produce one more unit of the other. For the moment we assume that this opportunity cost is constant in each country at all combinations of outputs.

For the purposes of our example, we assume that the opportunity cost of producing 1 kilogram of wheat is 0.60 metre of cloth in the United States, while in the European Union it is 2 metres of cloth. These data are summarized in

Table 33.1 **Opportunity cost of wheat and cloth in the USA and the EU**

	Wheat (kg)	Cloth (metres)
USA	0.60 m cloth	1.67 kg wheat
EU	2.00 m cloth	0.50 kg wheat

Comparative advantages reflect opportunity costs that differ between countries. Column (1) expresses opportunity cost per kilogram of wheat. Column (2) expresses the same information in terms of metres of cloth. The USA has a comparative advantage in wheat production, the EU in cloth.

Table 33.1. The second column of this table gives the same information again but expressed as the opportunity cost of 1 metre of cloth (so the numbers there are the reciprocals of the numbers in the first column).

The sacrifice of cloth involved in producing wheat is much lower in the United States than it is in the European Union. World wheat production can be increased if the USA rather than the EU produces it. Looking at cloth production, we can see that the loss of wheat involved in producing one unit of cloth is lower in the EU than in the USA. World cloth production can be increased if the EU rather than the USA produces it. The gains from a US shift towards wheat production and an EU shift towards cloth production are shown in Table 33.2.

The gains from trade arise from differing opportunity costs in the two countries.

The slope of the production-possibility boundary indicates the opportunity costs, and the existence of different

Table 33.2 **Gains from specialization with differing opportunity costs**

	Changes from each producing one more unit of the product in which it has the lower opportunity cost	
	Wheat (kg)	Cloth (metres)
USA	+1.0	−0.6
EU	−0.5	+1.0
Total	+0.5	+0.4

Whenever opportunity costs differ between countries, specialization can increase the production of both products. These calculations show that there are gains from specialization given the opportunity costs of Table 33.1. To produce one more kilogram of wheat, the USA must sacrifice 0.6 m of cloth. To produce one more metre of cloth, the EU must sacrifice 0.5 kg of wheat. Making both changes raises world production of both wheat and cloth.

opportunity costs implies comparative advantages and disadvantages that can lead to gains from trade. Figure 33.1 illustrates how two countries can both gain from trade when they have different opportunity costs in production and the opportunity costs are independent of the level of production. An alternative diagrammatic illustration of the gains from trade appears in Box 33.1, where the production-possibility frontier is concave (which means that opportunity cost varies with the composition of output).

The conclusions about the gains from trade arising from international differences in opportunity costs can be summarized as follows.

1. Country A has a *comparative advantage* over country B in producing a product when the opportunity cost (in terms of some other product) of production in country A is lower. This implies, however, that it has a comparative disadvantage in the other product.

2. Opportunity costs depend on the relative costs of producing two products, not on absolute costs.

3. When opportunity costs are the same in all countries, there is no comparative advantage and there is no possibility of gains from specialization and trade.

4. When opportunity costs differ in any two countries, and both countries are producing both products, it is always possible to increase production of both products by a suitable reallocation of resources within each country.

Gains from specialization with variable costs

So far, apart from in Box 33.1, we have assumed that unit costs are the same whatever the scale of output, and we have seen that there are gains from specialization and trade as long as there are interregional differences in opportunity costs. If costs vary with the level of output, or as experience is acquired via specialization, *additional* sources of gain are possible.

Scale and imperfect competition

Real production costs, measured in terms of resources used, often fall as the scale of output increases. The larger the scale of operations, the more efficiently large-scale machinery can be used and the more efficient the division of labour that is possible. Smaller countries such as Switzerland, Belgium, and Israel, whose domestic markets are not large enough to exploit economies of scale, would find it prohibitively expensive to become self-sufficient by producing a little bit of everything at very great cost.

Trade allows smaller countries to specialize and produce a few products at high enough levels of output to reap the available economies of scale.

Box 33.1 **The gains from trade with varying opportunity costs**

International trade leads to an expansion of the set of goods that can be consumed in the economy in two ways: by allowing the bundle of goods consumed to differ from the bundle produced, and by permitting a profitable change in the pattern of production. Without international trade, the bundle of goods produced is the bundle consumed. With international trade, the consumption and production bundles can be altered independently to reflect the relative values placed on goods by international markets.

The graphical demonstration of the gains from trade proceeds in two stages.

Stage 1: fixed production

In each part of the figure the red curve is the economy's production-possibility boundary. If there is no international trade, the economy must consume the same bundle of goods that it produces. Thus, the production-possibility boundary is also the consumption-possibility boundary. (In contrast to Figure 33.1, opportunity cost here varies along the boundary.) Suppose the economy produces, and consumes, at point a, with x_1 of good X and y_1 of good Y, as in part (i) of the figure.

Next, suppose that, with production point a, good Y can be exchanged for good X internationally. The consumption possibilities are now shown by the line tt drawn through point a. The slope of tt indicates the quantity of Y that exchanges for a unit of X on the international market.

Although production is fixed at a, consumption can now be anywhere on the line tt. For example, the consumption point could be at b. This could be achieved by exporting $y_1 - y_2$ units of Y and importing $x_2 - x_1$ units of X.

Since point b (and all others on line tt to the right of a) lies outside the production-possibility boundary, there are potential gains from trade. Consumers are no longer limited by their country's production possibilities. Let us suppose they prefer point b to point a. They have achieved a gain from trade by being allowed to exchange some of their production of good Y for some quantity of good X and thus to consume more of good X than is produced at home.

Stage 2: variable production

There is a further opportunity for the expansion of the country's consumption possibilities: with trade, the production bundle may be profitably altered in response to international prices. The country may produce the bundle of goods that is most valuable in world markets. This is represented by the bundle d in part (ii). The consumption-possibility set is shifted to the line $t't'$ by changing production from a to d and thereby increasing the country's degree of specialization in good Y. For every point on the original consumption-possibility set, tt, there are points on the new set, $t't'$, which allow more consumption of both goods; compare points b and f, for example. Notice also that, except at the zero-trade point, d, the new consumption-possibility set lies everywhere above the production-possibility curve.

The benefits of moving from a no-trade position such as a to a trading position such as b or f are the gains from trade to the country. When the production of good Y is increased and the production of good X decreased, the country is able to move to a point such as f by producing more of good Y, in which the country has a comparative advantage, and trading the additional production for good X.

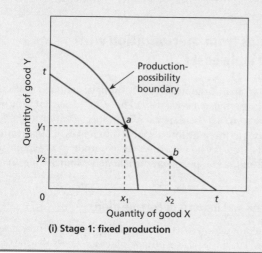

(i) Stage 1: fixed production

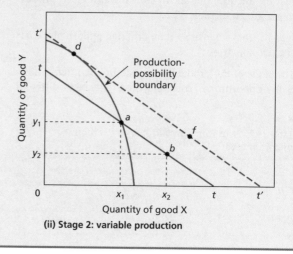

(ii) Stage 2: variable production

One of the important lessons learned from patterns of world trade since the Second World War results from imperfect competition and product differentiation. Virtually all of today's manufactured consumer goods are produced in multiple differentiated product lines. In some industries many firms produce this range; in others only a few firms produce the entire product range. In both cases firms are not price-takers, and they do not exhaust all available

economies of scale, as a perfectly competitive firm would do. This means that an increase in the size of the market, even in an economy as large as the USA or the EU, may allow the exploitation of some previously unexploited scale economies in individual product lines.

These possibilities were first dramatically illustrated when the European Common Market (now called the European Union, the EU) was set up in the late 1950s.

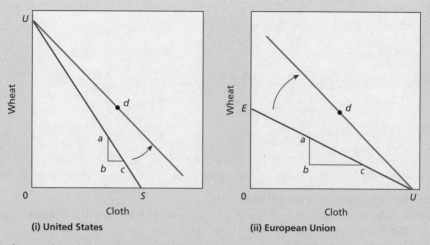

Figure 33.1 Gains from trade with constant opportunity costs

International trade leads to specialization in production and increased consumption possibilities. The blue lines in parts (i) and (ii) represent the production-possibility boundary for the USA and the EU, respectively. In the absence of any international trade, these also represent each country's consumption possibilities.

The difference in the slopes of the production-possibility boundaries reflects differences in comparative advantage, as shown in Table 33.1. In each part the opportunity cost of increasing production of wheat by the same amount (measured by the distance ba) is the amount by which the production of cloth must be reduced (measured by the distance bc). The relatively steep production-possibility boundary for the USA thus indicates that the opportunity cost of producing wheat in the USA is less than that in the EU.

If trade is possible at some terms of trade between the two countries' opportunity costs of production, each country will specialize in the production of the good in which it has a comparative advantage. In each part of the figure production occurs at U; the USA produces only wheat, and the EU produces only cloth.

Consumption possibilities are given by the red line that passes through U and has a slope equal to the terms of trade. Consumption possibilities are increased in both countries; consumption may occur at some point such as d that involves a combination of wheat and cloth that was not obtainable in the absence of trade.

Economists had expected that specialization would occur according to the classical theory of comparative advantage, with one country specializing in cars, another in refrigerators, another in fashion clothes, another in shoes, and so on. This is not the way it worked out. Instead, much of the vast growth of trade was in intra-industry trade. Today one can buy French, English, Italian, and German fashion goods, cars, shoes, appliances, and a host of other goods in the shops of London, Paris, Bonn, and Rome. Ships loaded with Swedish furniture bound for London pass ships loaded with English furniture bound for Stockholm; and so on.

What free European trade did was to allow a proliferation of differentiated products, with different countries each specializing in differentiated sub-product lines. Consumers have shown by their spending patterns that they value this enormous increase in the range of choice between differentiated products. As Asian countries have expanded into European and American markets with textiles, cars, and electronic goods, European and American manufacturers have increasingly specialized their production, and they now export textiles, cars, and electronic equipment to Japan even while importing similar but differentiated products from Japan.

Learning by doing

The discussion so far has assumed that costs vary only with the level of output. They may also vary with the experience accumulated in producing a good over time.

Some economists place great importance on a factor that we now call *learning by doing*. They argue that, as countries gain experience in particular tasks, workers and managers become more efficient in performing them. As people acquire expertise, costs tend to fall. There is substantial evidence that such learning by doing does occur.

The distinction between this phenomenon and the gains from economies of scale is illustrated in Figure 33.2. This is one more example of the difference between a movement along a curve and a shift of the curve.

Recognition of the opportunities for learning by doing leads to an important implication: policy-makers need not accept *current* comparative advantages as given. Through

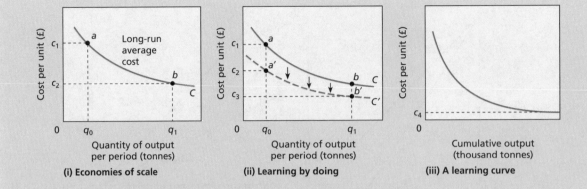

Figure 33.2 Gains from specialization with variable costs

Specialization may lead to gains from trade by permitting economies of larger-scale output, by leading to downward shifts of cost curves, or both. A country can produce output q_0 at an average cost per unit of c_1 and can export the quantity $q_1 - q_0$ if it produces q_1. This may lead to cost savings in two ways. (i) The increased level of production of q_1 compared with q_0 permits it to *move along* its cost curve, C, from a to b, thus reducing costs per unit to c_2. This is an economy of scale. (ii) As workers and managements learn, they may increase productivity and shift the cost curve from C to C'. This is learning by doing. The downward *shift*, shown by the arrows, lowers the cost of producing every unit of output. At output q_1 costs per unit fall to c_3. The movement from a to b' incorporates both economies of scale and learning by doing.

Part (iii) shows a learning curve. This shows the relation between the costs of producing a given output per period and the total output over the whole time during which production has taken place. When all learning possibilities have been exploited, costs reach a minimum level, shown by c_4 in the figure.

such means as training and tax incentives, they can seek to develop new comparative advantages. Moreover, countries cannot complacently assume that their existing comparative advantages will persist. Misguided tax incentives and subsidies, or policies that discourage risk-taking, can lead to the rapid erosion of a country's comparative advantage in particular products. So, too, can developments in other countries.

The terms of trade

So far we have seen that world production can be increased when countries specialize in the production of the goods and services in which they have a comparative advantage, and then trade with one another. We now ask how these gains from specialization and trade will be shared between countries. The division of the gain depends on the **terms of trade**, which measure the quantity of imported goods that can be obtained per unit of goods exported.

A rise in the price of imported goods, with the price of exports unchanged, indicates a fall in the terms of trade; it will now take more exports to buy the same quantity of imports. Similarly, a rise in the price of exported goods, with the price of imports unchanged, indicates a rise in terms of trade; it will now take fewer exports to buy the same quantity of imports. Thus, the ratio of these prices measures the amount of imports that can be obtained per unit of goods exported.

Because actual international trade involves many countries and many products, a country's terms of trade are computed as an index number:

$$\text{Terms of trade} = \frac{\text{Index of export prices}}{\text{Index of import prices}} \times 100.$$

A rise in the index is referred to as a *favourable* change in a country's terms of trade. A favourable change means that more can be imported per unit of goods exported than previously. For example, if the export price index rises from 100 to 120 while the import price index rises from 100 to 110, the terms of trade index rises from 100 to 109. At the new terms of trade, a unit of exports will buy 9 per cent more imports than at the old terms.

A decrease in the index of the terms of trade, called an *unfavourable* change, means that the country can import less in return for any given amount of exports or, equivalently, that it must export more to pay for any given amount of imports. For example, the sharp rise in oil prices in the 1970s led to large unfavourable shifts in the terms of trade of oil-importing countries. When oil prices fell sharply in the mid-1980s, the terms of trade of oil-importing countries changed favourably. The converse was true for oil-exporting countries.

There are two other concepts closely related to the terms of trade that we have come across before, especially in Chapter 29. These are the *real exchange rate* and *competitiveness*. They too are indexes of the relative prices of domestic and foreign goods. However, both competitiveness and the real exchange rate normally relate to the prices of domestic production relative to foreign production, while terms of trade apply just to the subset of outputs that are imported and exported.

Notice, however, an interesting ambiguity in terminology. We have said above that an improvement in the terms of trade is 'favourable'; but a rise in domestic prices relative to foreign prices could also be described as a *loss of competitiveness*. This would normally be considered 'unfavourable'. Clearly, the same event cannot switch from good to bad just because of what we call it. The reality is that whether a relative rise in domestic prices is good or bad depends upon why it came about. If the prices of the things we produce and sell in world markets rise because they are in high demand, then this is a good thing and we are better off for it (even though it could be described as a loss of competitiveness). However, if our prices rise because of inefficiency or higher wage bills *for a given level of world demand for our output*, then we will lose sales to foreign competitors and we will be worse off.

We now turn to a discussion of the arguments for and against government intervention in international trade.

The theory of commercial policy

Government policy towards international trade is known as **commercial policy**. Complete freedom from interference with trade is known as a **free trade** policy. Any departure from free trade designed to give some protection to domestic industries from foreign competition is called **protectionism**.

Today debates over commercial policy are as heated as they were 200 years ago when the theory of the gains from trade that we presented above was still being worked out. Should a country permit the free flow of international trade, or should it seek to protect its local producers from foreign competition? Such protection may be achieved either by **tariffs**, which are taxes designed to raise the price of foreign goods, or by **non-tariff barriers**, which are devices other than tariffs that are designed to reduce the flow of imports. Examples of the latter include quotas and customs procedures deliberately made more cumbersome than is necessary.

The case for free trade

The case for free trade is based on the analysis presented above. We saw that, *for any given set of costs* whenever opportunity costs differ among countries, specialization and trade will raise world living standards. Free trade allows all countries to specialize in producing products in which they have a comparative advantage.

Free trade allows the maximization of world production, thus making it possible for each consumer in the world to consume more goods than she could without free trade.

This does not necessarily mean that everyone will be better off with free trade than without it. Protectionism could allow some people to obtain a larger share of a smaller world output so that they would benefit even though the average person would lose. If we ask whether it is possible for free trade to improve everyone's living standards, the answer is 'yes'. But if we ask whether free trade does in fact always do so, the answer is 'not necessarily'.

There is abundant evidence that significant differences in opportunity costs exist and that large gains are realized from international trade because of these differences. What needs explanation is the fact that trade is not wholly free. Why do tariffs and non-tariff barriers to trade continue to exist two centuries after Adam Smith and David Ricardo stated the case for free trade? Is there a valid case for protectionism?

The case for protectionism

Two kinds of argument for protection are commonly offered. The first concerns national objectives other than total income; the second concerns the desire to increase one country's national income, possibly at the expense of world national income.

Objectives other than maximizing national income as reasons for protectionism

It is possible to accept the proposition that national income is higher with free trade, and yet rationally to oppose free trade, because of a concern with policy objectives other than maximizing income.

Non-economic advantages of diversification Comparative advantage might dictate that a country should specialize in producing a narrow range of products. The government might decide, however, that there are distinct social advantages in encouraging a more diverse economy. Citizens would be given a wider range of occupations, and the social and psychological advantages of diversification would more than compensate for a reduction in living standards to, say, 5 per cent below what they could be with complete specialization of production according to comparative advantage.

Risks of specialization   For a very small country, specializing in the production of only a few products—though dictated by comparative advantage—may involve risks that the country does not wish to take. One such risk is that technological advances may render its major product obsolete. Everyone understands this risk, but there is debate over what governments can do about it. The pro-tariff argument is that the government can encourage a more diversified economy by protecting industries that otherwise could not compete. Opponents argue that governments, being naturally influenced by political motives, are in the final analysis poor judges of which industries can be protected in order to produce diversification at a reasonable cost.

National defence   Another non-economic reason for protectionism concerns national defence. It used to be argued, for example, that the United Kingdom needed an experienced merchant navy in case of war, and that this industry should be fostered by protectionist policies even though it was less efficient than the foreign competition. The same argument is sometimes made for the aircraft industry. Agriculture has also been protected for strategic reasons in the past—we would need to feed ourselves if trade were disrupted by war.

Protection of specific groups   Although free trade will maximize per capita GDP over the whole economy, some specific groups may have higher incomes under protection than under free trade. An obvious example is a firm or industry that is given monopoly power when tariffs are used to restrict foreign competition. If a small group of firms, and possibly their employees, find their incomes increased by, say, 25 per cent when they get tariff protection, they may not be concerned that everyone else's incomes fall by, say, 2 per cent. They get a much larger share of a slightly smaller total income and end up better off. If they gain from the tariff, they will lose from free trade.

Tariffs tend to raise the relative income of a group of people who are in short supply domestically and to lower the relative income of a group of people who are in plentiful supply domestically. Free trade does the opposite.

Conclusion   Other things being equal, most people prefer more income to less. Economists cannot say that it is irrational for a society to sacrifice some income in order to achieve other goals. Economists can, however, do three things when faced with such reasons for adopting protectionist measures. First, they can ask if the proposed measures really do achieve the ends suggested. Second, they can calculate the cost of the measures in terms of lowered living standards. Third, they can see if there are alternative means of achieving the stated goals at lower cost in terms of lost output.

Maximizing national income as a reason for protectionism

Next, we consider five important arguments for the use of tariffs when the objective is to make national income as large as possible.

To protect infant industries   The oldest valid argument for protectionism as a means of raising living standards concerns economies of scale. It is usually called the **infant industry argument**.

It comes in a static and dynamic form. The static form assumes that world technology is given and constant. If an industry has large economies of scale, costs will be high when the industry is small, but will fall as the industry grows. In such industries the country first in the field has a tremendous advantage. A newly developing country may find that in the early stages of development its industries are unable to compete with established foreign rivals. A trade restriction may protect these industries from foreign competition while they grow up. When they are large enough, they will be able to produce as cheaply as foreign rivals and thus will be able to compete without protection.

The dynamic form of the argument emphasizes that technology is constantly changing endogenously and that those countries who are at the frontier of technological advance have an enormous advantage of experience and acquired ability in inventing and innovating over those who seek to industrialize later on. To develop these abilities, so goes the argument, a country needs to protect its domestic industries during the early stages of development. The object is not to move along a given falling long-run cost curve, but rather to develop industries that will have cost curves that fall over time as fast as the similar cost curves are falling in the advanced countries because of invention and innovation. To prevent the new industries from becoming stagnant under the protection that shields them from foreign competition, protection must, so goes the argument, be contingent on achieving success in foreign markets within a stated period of time. Once they have developed the skills needed to hold their own in the intense international competition associated with new technologies, the protection can be removed. The advocates of this argument for early protection point out that virtually all the economically advanced countries developed their early industries under tariff protection. This was true of

Germany and France (and to some extent also of the early English industries in the Industrial Revolution, which were helped by the prohibition of imports of Indian cotton goods), the United States, Canada, Australia and New Zealand, as well as the most successful of the Asian economies, such as Taiwan, South Korea, and Singapore. Those who support such polices argue that the assumption of fixed technology that is implicit in the major arguments for completely free trade is very misleading in a world in which most competition is in terms of the technological change. They also point out that the argument does not deny the importance of trade: it just holds that, to take part in globalized trade as a fully developed country, early protection may be needed—for reasons found both in the theory of endogenous technological change and in the evidence of what most developed countries actually did in the early stages of their development.

To encourage learning by doing
The dynamic version of the infant industry argument is supported by the argument based on learning by doing. Skills and other things that help to create comparative advantages are not fixed for ever; they can be learned by producing the new products if enough time is allowed for the learning to take place. Learning by doing thus suggests that the pattern of comparative advantage can be changed. If a country learns enough through producing products in which it currently is at a comparative disadvantage, it may gain in the long run by specializing in those products, and could develop a comparative advantage as the learning process lowers their costs.

The successes of such newly industrializing countries (NICs) as Brazil, Hong Kong, South Korea, Singapore, and Taiwan seem to many observers to be based on acquired skills and government policies that created favourable business conditions. For example, nothing in Singapore or Taiwan in 1960, in terms of natural resources, capital, or skills, suggested that these countries would become major producers of state-of-the-art electronic products well before the end of the twentieth century. This type of experience provides evidence that comparative advantages can change, and that they can be developed by suitable government policies.

Protecting a domestic industry from foreign competition may give its management time to learn to be efficient, and its labour force time to acquire the needed skills.

If this is so, it may pay in the very long run to protect the industry from foreign competition while a dynamic comparative advantage is being developed.

Some countries have succeeded in developing strong comparative advantages in targeted industries, but others have failed. One reason such policies sometimes fail is that protecting local industries from foreign competition may make the industries unadaptive and complacent. Another

reason is the difficulty of identifying the industries that will be able to succeed in the long run. All too often the protected infant grows up to be a weakling requiring permanent tariff protection for its continued existence; or else the rate of learning is slower than for similar industries in countries that do not provide protection from the chill winds of international competition. In these instances the anticipated comparative advantage never materializes.

To create or to exploit a strategic trade advantage
An important recent argument for tariffs or other trade restrictions is the need to create a strategic advantage in producing or marketing some new product that is expected to generate profits. To the extent that all lines of production earn normal profits, there is no reason to produce goods other than ones for which a country has a comparative advantage. Some goods, however, are produced in industries containing a few large firms, where large-scale economies provide a natural barrier to further entry. Firms in these industries can earn extra-high profits over long periods of time. Where such industries are already well established, there is little chance that a new firm will replace one of the existing giants.

The situation is, however, more fluid with new products. The first firm to develop and market a new product successfully may earn a substantial pure profit over all of its opportunity costs and become one of the few established firms in the industry. If protection of the domestic market can increase the chance that one of the protected domestic firms will become one of the established firms in the international market, the protection may pay off.

Many of today's high-tech industries have declining average total cost curves because of their large fixed costs of product development. For a new generation of civilian aircraft, silicon chips, computers, software, and pharmaceuticals, a very high proportion of each producer's total costs goes to product development. These are fixed costs of entering the market, and they must be incurred before a single unit of output can be sold. In such industries there may be room for only a few firms.

The production of full-sized commercial jet aeroplanes provides an example of an industry that possesses many of these characteristics. The development costs of a new generation of jet aircraft have risen with each new generation. If the aircraft manufacturers are to recover these costs, each of them must have a large volume of sales. Thus, the number of firms that the market can support has diminished steadily, until today there is room in the world aircraft industry for only two or three firms producing a full range of commercial jets.

The characteristics just described are sometimes used to provide arguments for subsidizing the development of such industries and/or protecting their home markets with a tariff. Suppose, for example, that there is room in the aircraft industry for only three major producers of the next round of passenger jets. If a government assists a domestic firm, this firm may become one of the three that succeed, and the profits that are subsequently earned may more than repay the cost of the subsidy. Furthermore, another country's firm, which was not subsidized, may have been just as good as the three that succeeded; without the subsidy, however, this firm may lose out in the battle to establish itself as one of the three surviving firms in the market.

This example is not unlike the story of the European Airbus. The European producers received many direct subsidies (and they charge that their main competitor, the Boeing 767, received many indirect ones). Whatever the merits of the argument, several things are clear: the civilian jet aircraft industry remains profitable; there is room for only two or three major producers; and one of these would not have been the European consortium if it had not been for substantial government assistance.

Generalizing from this and similar cases, some economists advocate that their governments should adopt *strategic trade policies* more broadly than they now do. This means, for high-tech industries, government protection of the home market and government subsidization (either openly or by more subtle back-door methods) of the product development stage. These economists say that if the country does not follow their advice it will lose out in industry after industry to the more aggressive Japanese and North American competition—a competition that is adept at combining private innovative activity with government assistance.

Opponents argue that, once all countries try to be strategic, they will all waste vast sums trying to break into industries in which there is no room for most of them. Advocates of strategic trade policy reply that a country cannot afford to stand by while others play the strategic game.

Advocates also argue that there are key industries that have major 'spillovers' into the rest of the economy. If a country wants to have a high living standard, it must, they argue, compete with the best. If a country lets all of its key industries migrate to other countries, many of the others will follow. The country then risks being reduced to the status of a less developed nation.

Opponents argue that strategic trade policy is just the modern version of mercantilism, a policy of trying to enrich oneself at the expense of one's neighbours rather than looking for mutually beneficial gains from trade. They point to the rising world prosperity of the entire period following the Second World War, which has been built largely on a rising volume of relatively free international trade. There are real doubts that such prosperity could be maintained if the volume of trade were to shrink steadily because of growing trade barriers.

To protect against 'unfair' actions by foreign firms and governments Tariffs may be used to prevent foreign industries from gaining an advantage over domestic industries by use of predatory practices that will harm domestic industries and hence lower national income. Two common practices are subsidies paid by foreign governments to their exporters, and price discrimination by foreign firms, which is called *dumping* when it is done across international borders. These practices are typically countered by levying tariffs called countervailing and anti-dumping duties.

To alter the terms of trade Trade restrictions can be used to turn the terms of trade in favour of countries that produce, and export, a large fraction of the world's supply of some product. They can also be used to turn the terms of trade in favour of countries that constitute a large fraction of the world demand for some product that they import.

When the OPEC countries restricted their output of oil in the 1970s, they were able to drive up the price of oil relative to the prices of other traded goods. This turned the terms of trade in their favour; for every barrel of oil exported, they were able to obtain a larger quantity of imports. When the output of oil grew greatly in the mid-1980s, the relative price of oil fell dramatically, and the terms of trade turned unfavourably for the oil-exploring companies. These are illustrations of how changes in the quantities of exports can affect the terms of trade.

Now consider a country that provides a large fraction of the total demand for some product that it imports. By restricting its demand for that product through tariffs, it can force the price of that product down. This turns the terms of trade in its favour because it can now get more units of imports per unit of exports.

Both of these techniques lower world output. They can, however, make it possible for a small group of countries to gain, by deriving a sufficiently larger share of the smaller world output. However, if foreign countries retaliate by raising their tariffs, the ensuing tariff war can easily leave every country with a lowered income.

Conclusion In today's world a country's products must stand up to international competition if they are to survive. Over time this requires that they hold their own in competition for successful innovations. Protection, by conferring a national monopoly, reduces the incentive for industries to fight to hold their own internationally. If any one country adopts high tariffs unilaterally, its domestic industries will become less competitive. Secure in its home market because of the tariff wall, the protected industries are likely to become less and less competitive in the international market. As the gap between domestic and foreign industries widens, any tariff wall will provide less and less protection. Eventually, the domestic industries will succumb to the foreign competition.

Although restrictive policies have sometimes been pursued following a rational assessment of the approximate cost, it is hard to avoid the conclusion that, more often than not, such policies are often pursued for political objectives, or on fallacious economic grounds, with little appreciation of the actual costs involved.

Some recent criticisms of the global trading system are discussed in Box 33.2.

Methods of protection

We have now studied some of the many reasons why governments may wish to provide some protection for some of their domestic industries. The next task is to see how they do it. What are the tools that provide protection?

  ### Box 33.2 Anti-capitalism, anti-globalization and fair trade

In recent years there have been many demonstrations against the World Trade Organization (WTO), the International Monetary Fund (IMF), and the World Bank. These have been labelled as 'anti-capitalist' or 'anti-globalization' demonstrations. Some of the arguments made by the protesters are difficult to disagree with (like the desirability of reducing poverty in the poorest countries), but others are plain wrong. Virtually all economists, for example, would agree that globalization in the form of greater international trade in goods and services is both wealth and welfare-increasing, and that closing down international trade would make the world a very much poorer place for all.

There have long been debates about free trade and there have certainly been times when there have been doubts about whether capitalism is the best system. The collapse of communism helped to squash the latter doubts, but the case for a free and open trading system has come under renewed threat in recent years from a number of apparently rational sources. (Specific criticisms of the IMF and its handling of financial crises in developing countries are discussed in Box 34.5 on page 645.)

Professor Jagdish Bhagwati of Columbia University identifies four different new critiques that question the benefits of an open trading system:

• 'Demands' for 'fair trade' that either mask protectionism or degenerate into it, in both cases charging that free trade lacks fairness and that fair trade restores it.

• Concerns that free trade harms the environment.

• Charges that free trade (and its chief institution, the WTO) is incompatible with the advancement of social and moral agendas.

• Fears that free trade hurts the real wages of workers and that rich countries trading with poor countries create poor in rich countries, and in poor countries that free trade accentuates poverty.*

Let us look at each of these issues in turn.

Fair trade

'Fair' trade seems hard to object to, as who could possibly support 'unfair' trade? One common form of this argument is similar to what used to be called 'the sweated labour fallacy'. This says that we should restrict imports from countries that have lower labour or environmental standards (in extreme cases they may use child labour) as this is not fair competition with domestic suppliers. To restrict such trade would of course hurt the poor country, whose best chance of reducing poverty and increasing labour standards is to export to rich countries. So this is just an excuse for protectionism and for restricting the benefits that flow from comparative advantage. This is the version of fair trade that Bhagwati criticizes above.

There are two different forms of the fair trade argument that are less problematic. The first is that industrial countries have pressured some

developing countries to open their markets to the products of the richer countries while at the same time imposing restrictions on developing country exports into rich country markets. This is a case of uneven bargaining power, and the poorer countries clearly have a good case. The case for free trade has to apply to all, and not in one direction only. The second argument for fair trade applies to products like bananas and coffee, where some charitable groups argue that industrial countries' monopsony power has depressed the prices of such commodities. They aim to counter these poverty-inducing low prices by offering a 'fair trade' product at a higher price, the revenues from which go to the poor country producers. Rich country consumers are free to buy these 'fair trade' products, as they are sold alongside comparable but cheaper products in supermarkets. This form of fair trade allows people who so wish to direct charitable giving to specific producers, and there is nothing in economics to say that they should not do this. The only doubt is whether this will catch on in a big enough way to solve the underlying problem. Counteracting monopsony power in commodity markets is likely to require a stronger intervention from governments if this is the true nature of the problem. Notice, however, that our discussion of coffee prices on pages 77–9 points out that the main problem in coffee markets is over-production.

Trade and the environment

The environment is important for all of us and perhaps especially for our children and grandchildren. Economic analysis clearly shows that free markets may not adequately protect the environment and that government intervention is necessary to deliver the social optimum resource use (see pages xxx–x above). This applies to many common property resources like fisheries and rain forests. It also applies to pollution issues like greenhouse gases and acid rain.

However, it makes no sense to address environmental problems by closing down world trade. Environmental issues should be handled directly with suitable policies to solve the problem in hand. World trade *per se* is not the cause of environmental problems. Indeed, the higher standards of living that world trade provides can be helpful in providing the extra output that takes living standards sufficiently above subsistence so that quality of life is also in high demand.

Social and moral agendas

Some politicians have sought to include a 'social clause' in the WTO rules. This would permit use of trade sanctions against countries whose labour laws or social conventions we did not like. This is presented as a moral crusade to help poor people, but as Bhagwati points out, 'These demands are widely seen as protectionism hiding behind a moral mask.' And it is a mistake to bundle together two issues that should be dealt with by separate

* J. Bhagwati, *Free Trade Today*, (Princeton University Press, 2002), p. 50.

Box 33.2 (Cont'd)

processes and institutions: 'By trying to kill these two birds [i.e. social agendas and freer trade] with one stone [i.e. trade treaties and institutions], you are likely to miss both.' Rather, he argues, it is important to pursue these different goals in international agencies suited to the specific agendas for which they were set up: 'the WTO for trade liberalization, the International Labour Organization for labour standards, the UN Environment Program for environmental issues, UNICEF for children's rights, UNESCO for cultural preservation, and so on'.

Trade is bad for wages

There are two elements to this argument depending on whether we are talking about workers in rich or poor countries. In rich countries, it is certainly true that some specific workers may be hurt if their employer loses business to cheaper imports from abroad. However, the overwhelming weight of evidence is that the growth of real GDP that is supported by growth in international trade during the past three decades or so has been associated with rising real wages for most classes of worker in the rich countries. Some have tried to argue that trade has hurt unskilled workers in

the rich countries, but the case remains unproven, as it is difficult to disentangle the effects of trade from changes in technology that have been occurring at the same time.

For the workers in poor countries, here is Bhagwati again:

Speaking at least for India, I would say that autarky helped produce a slow average growth rate of 3.5 per cent annually for over a quarter of a century until early 1980s. During this period, it was virtually impossible to pull people up into gainful employment, and out of poverty, in a significant way. With the 1980s, the increasing pace of outward-oriented reforms has been associated with growth rates closer to 6–6.5 per cent annually; and after much controversy, there is a fair degree of consensus that poverty has been dented. Contradicting the anti-free-trade rhetoric that flows ceaselessly from the street theater and even from certain international agencies, the facts show that a shift out of autarky into closer integration into the world economy is producing better, not worse, results for poverty reduction.

The two main types of protectionist policy are illustrated in Figure 33.3. Both cause the price of the imported good to rise and its quantity to fall. They differ, however, in how they achieve these results. The caption to the figure analyses these two types of policy.

Policies that directly raise prices

The first type of protectionist policy directly raises the *price* of the imported product. A tariff, also often called an *import duty*, is the most common policy of this type. Other such policies include any rules or regulations that fulfil three conditions: they are costly to comply with; they do not apply to competing, domestically produced products; and they are more than is required to meet any purpose other than restricting trade.

As shown in part (ii) of Figure 33.3, tariffs affect both foreign and domestic producers, as well as domestic consumers. The initial effect is to raise the domestic price of the imported product above its world price by the amount of the tariff. Imports fall, and as a result foreign producers sell less and so must transfer resources to other lines of production. The price received on domestically produced units rises, as does the quantity produced domestically. On both counts domestic producers earn more. However, the cost of producing the extra output at home exceeds the price at which it could be purchased on the world market. Thus, the benefit to domestic producers comes at the expense of domestic consumers. Indeed, domestic consumers lose on two counts: first, they consume less of the product because its price rises; and second, they pay a higher price for the amount that they do consume. This extra spending ends

up in two places: the extra that is paid on all units produced at home goes to domestic producers (partly in the resource costs of extra production and partly in profit), and the extra that is paid on units still imported goes to the government as tariff revenue.

Policies that directly lower quantities

The second type of protectionist policy directly restricts the quantity of an imported product. Any implicit or explicit restriction on trade that does not involve a tariff is known as a **non-tariff barrier**. These can take various subtle forms, including quality standards that are complicated to interpret or customs forms that take weeks to get approved. But many non-tariff barriers are more obvious and easy to understand. A common example is the **import quota**, by which the importing country sets a maximum on the quantity of some product that may be imported each year. Increasingly popular in the recent past, however, has been the **voluntary export restriction** (VER), an agreement by an exporting country to limit the amount of a good that it sells to the importing country.

The European Union and the United States have used VERs extensively, and the European Union also makes frequent use of import quotas. Japan has been pressured into negotiating several VERs with the European Union and the United States in order to limit sales of some of the Japanese goods that have had the most success in international competition. For example, in 1983 the United States and Canada negotiated VERs whereby the Japanese government agreed to restrict total sales of Japanese cars to these two countries for three years. When the agreements ran out

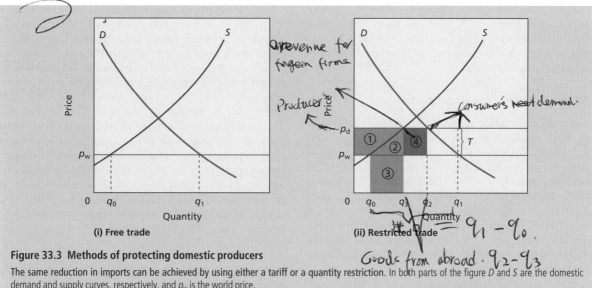

Figure 33.3 Methods of protecting domestic producers

The same reduction in imports can be achieved by using either a tariff or a quantity restriction. In both parts of the figure D and S are the domestic demand and supply curves, respectively, and p_w is the world price.

Part (i) of the figure shows the situation under free trade. Domestic consumption is q_1, domestic production is q_0, and imports are $q_0 - q_1$.

Part (ii) shows what happens when protectionist policies restrict imports to the amount $q_2 - q_3$. When this is done by levying a tariff of T per unit, the price in the domestic market rises by the full amount of the tariff to p_d. Consumers reduce consumption from q_1 to q_2 and pay an extra amount, shown by areas 1, 2, and 4, for the q_2 that they now purchase. Domestic production rises from q_0 to q_3. Since domestic producers receive the domestic price, their receipts rise by areas 1, 2, and 3. Area 3 is revenue that was earned by foreign producers under free trade, while areas 1 and 2 are paid by domestic consumers because of the higher prices they now face. Foreign suppliers of the imported good continue to receive the world price, so the government receives as tariff revenue the extra amount paid by consumers for the $q_3 - q_2$ units that are still imported (shown by area 4).

When the same result is accomplished by a quantity restriction, the government—through either a quota or a *voluntary export agreement (VER)*—reduces imports to $q_2 - q_3$. This drives the domestic market price up to p_d and has the same effect on domestic producers and consumers as the tariff. Since the government has merely restricted the quantity of imports, both foreign and domestic suppliers get the higher price in the domestic market. Thus, foreign suppliers now receive the extra amount paid by domestic consumers (represented by area 4) for the units that are still imported.

in 1986, the Japanese continued to restrain their car sales by unilateral voluntary action.

Fallacious trade-policy arguments

We saw above that there are potential gains from trade and specialization. We have also seen that there are some valid arguments for a moderate degree of protectionism for one specific country. There are also many claims that do not advance the debate. Fallacious arguments are heard on both sides, and they colour much of the popular discussion. These arguments have been around for a long time, but their survival does not make them true. We examine them now to see where their fallacies lie.

Fallacious arguments for free trade

Free trade always benefits all countries This is not necessarily so. We saw above that a small group of countries may gain by restricting trade in order to get a sufficiently favourable shift in their terms of trade. Such countries would lose if they gave up these tariffs and adopted free trade unilaterally.

Infant industries never abandon their tariff protection It is argued that granting protection to infant industries is a mistake because these industries seldom admit to growing up, and will cling to their protection even when fully grown. But infant industry tariffs are a mistake only if these industries never grow up. In this case permanent tariff protection would be required to protect a weak industry never able to compete on an equal footing in the international market. But if the industries do grow up and achieve the expected scale and learning economies, the real costs of production are reduced and resources are freed for other uses. Whether or not the trade barriers remain, a cost saving has been effected by the scale economies.

Free trade maximizes world income under real-world conditions Free trade can be shown to maximize world income when technology and comparative costs are given. But if technology is changing endogenously, as a result of conscious decisions taken by firms and other agents of change, it cannot be proved that completely free markets will maximize income over time. It is possible that some types of government interventions, or market imperfections, will produce more technological change than completely free and fully competitive markets.

Fallacious arguments for protectionism

To prevent exploitation According to the exploitation theory, trade can never be mutually advantageous: one trading partner must always reap a gain at the other's expense. Thus, the weaker trading partner must protect itself by restricting its trade with the stronger partner. By showing that both parties can gain from trade, the principle of comparative advantage refutes the exploitation doctrine of trade. When opportunity–cost ratios differ in two countries, specialization and the accompanying trade make it possible to produce more of all products. This makes it possible for both parties to consume more as a result of trade than they could get in its absence.

To protect against low-wage foreign labour Surely, this argument says, in industrialized nations the products of low-wage countries will drive domestic products from the market, and the high domestic standard of living will be dragged down to that of its poorer trading partners. Arguments of this sort have swayed many voters through the years.

As a prelude to considering them, stop and think what the argument would imply if taken out of the international context and put into a local one, where the same principles govern the gains from trade. Is it really impossible for a rich person to gain from trading with a poor person? Would the CEO of a high street retail chain be better off if she did all her own typing, gardening, and cooking? No one believes that a rich (and busy) person cannot gain from trading with those who are less rich (and less busy).

Why then must a rich group of people lose from trading with a poor group? 'Well,' some may say, 'the poor group will price their goods too cheaply.' Does anyone believe that consumers lose from buying in supermarkets just because the prices are lower there than at the old-fashioned corner shop? Consumers gain when they can buy the same goods at a lower price. If the Koreans pay low wages and sell their goods cheaply, Korean labour may suffer, but the EU will gain by obtaining imports at a low cost in terms of the goods that must be exported in return. The cheaper our imports are, the better off we are in terms of the goods and services available for domestic consumption.

Stated in more formal terms, the gains from trade depend on comparative, not absolute, advantages. World production is higher when any two areas, say the EU and Japan, specialize in the production of the goods for which they have a comparative advantage than when they both try to be self-sufficient.

Might it not be possible, however, that Japan will undersell the EU in all lines of production, and thus appropriate all—or more than all—of the gains for itself, leaving the EU no better off, or even worse off, than if it had no trade with Japan? The answer is no. The reason for this depends on the behaviour of exchange rates, which were discussed in Chapter 29. As we saw in that chapter, equality of demand and supply in foreign exchange markets ensures that trade flows in both directions. The reason a country cannot import for long without exporting may also be stated intuitively as follows. Imports can be obtained only by spending the currency of the country that produces the imports. Claims to this currency can be obtained only by exporting goods and services, or by borrowing. Thus, lending and borrowing aside, imports must equal exports. All trade must be in two directions; we can buy only if we can also sell.

In the long run trade cannot hurt a country by causing it to import without exporting.

Trade, then, always provides scope for international specialization, with each country producing and exporting those goods for which it has a comparative advantage and importing those goods for which it does not.

Exports raise living standards; imports lower them Exports create domestic income and employment; imports create income and employment for foreigners. Thus, other things being equal, exports tend to increase our total national income and imports, to reduce it. Surely, then, it is desirable to encourage exports by subsidizing them and to discourage imports by taxing them.

This is an appealing argument, but it is incorrect. Exports raise national income by adding to the value of domestic output, but they do not add to the value of domestic consumption. In fact, exports are goods produced at home and consumed abroad, while imports are goods produced abroad and consumed at home. The standard of living in a country depends on the goods and services available for consumption, not on what is produced.

The living standards of a country depend on the goods and services consumed in that country. The importance of exports is that they permit other goods to be imported. This two-way international exchange is valuable because more goods can be imported than could be obtained if the same goods were produced at home.

To create domestic jobs and reduce unemployment It is sometimes said that an economy with substantial unemployment, such as the EU in the 1990s, provides an exception to the case for freer trade. Suppose that tariffs or import quotas cut the imports of Japanese cars, Korean textiles, US computers, and Polish vodka. Surely, the argument maintains, this will create more employment in local industries producing similar products. The answer is that it will—initially. But the Japanese, Koreans, Americans, and Poles can buy from the EU only if they earn euros by selling things to (or by borrowing euros from) the EU. The decline in their sales of cars, textiles, computers, and vodka will decrease their purchases of Spanish vegetables, French fruit, and wine, and holidays in Greece. Jobs will be lost in EU export industries, and gained in those industries that formerly faced competition from imports. The likely long-term effect is that overall employment will not be increased, but merely redistributed among industries. In the process, living standards will be reduced because employment expands in inefficient import-competing industries and contracts in efficient exporting industries.

Industries and unions that compete with imports often favour protectionism, while those with large exports usually favour more trade. Protection is an ineffective means to reduce unemployment.

Global commercial policy

We now discuss supranational influences on commercial policy in the world today. We start with the many international agreements that govern current commercial policies and then look in a little more detail at the European Union.

Before 1947 any country was free to impose any tariffs on its imports. However, when one country increased its tariffs, the action often triggered retaliatory actions by its trading partners. The Great Depression of the 1930s saw a high-water mark of world protectionism, as each country sought to raise its employment by raising its tariffs. The end result was lowered efficiency, less trade—but no increase in employment. Since that time much effort has been devoted to reducing tariff barriers, on both a multilateral and a regional basis.

The GATT and the WTO

One of the most notable achievements of the postwar era was the creation of the General Agreement on Tariffs and Trade (GATT). The principle of the GATT is that each member country agrees not to make unilateral tariff increases. This prevents the outbreak of tariff wars in which countries raise tariffs to protect particular domestic industries and to retaliate against other countries' tariff increases. Such wars usually harm all countries, as mutually beneficial trade shrinks under the impact of escalating tariff barriers.

There have been eight 'rounds' of global trade talks since 1948. The three most recently completed rounds of GATT agreements—the Kennedy round (completed 1967), the Tokyo round (completed 1979), and the Uruguay round (completed 1993)—have each agreed to reduce world tariffs substantially, the first two by about one-third each, and the last by about 40 per cent.

The Uruguay round created a new body, the World Trade Organization (WTO), which superseded the GATT in 1995. It also created a new legal structure for multilateral trading. Under this new structure all members have equal mutual rights and obligations. Until the WTO was formed, developing countries who were in the GATT enjoyed all the GATT rights but were exempt from most of its obligations to liberalize trade—obligations that applied only to the developed countries. Such special treatments were phased out over seven years up to 2002. There is also a new dispute-settlement mechanism with much more power to enforce rulings over non-tariff barriers than existed in the past. In its first three years the WTO dealt with 132 complaints; while the GATT only heard 300 in forty-seven years!

In 1997, three strands of negotiation that had been left incomplete in the Uruguay round were completed, involving agreements to lower trade barriers in telecommunications, financial services, and information technology. These agreements were important because they greatly increase the amount of trade covered by WTO rules and dispute-settlement procedures; also, they may lead to larger trade volume gains than the entire Uruguay round, and they complete most of the unfinished business from Uruguay, clearing the way for a new global trade round.

By January 2002 the WTO had 144 member countries including China, with a further thirty including Russia hoping to join.[1] It is thus growing into a truly global forum for the regulation of government involvement in world trade. Figure 33.4 shows that world trade has grown faster than world GDP since 1950. Indeed, while real GDP has grown seven-fold, world export volumes have grown twenty-one fold. It is hard to believe that this could have occurred without the liberalization of international trade brought about through successive rounds of tariff negotiation.

Types of regional agreement

Regional agreements seek to liberalize trade over a much smaller set of countries than the WTO membership. Three

---

[1] The latest information about the WTO can be found on the internet at www.wto.org.

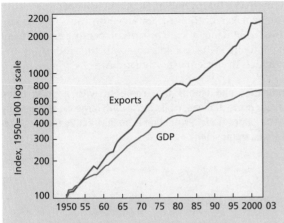

Figure 33.4 World real GDP and export volume, 1950–2003 (index: 1950 = 100)

Trade has grown more than GDP in the postwar period. Since 1950 world real GDP has increased six-fold while the volume of world trade has risen twenty-fold. Data for 2002 and 2003 are IMF staff projections. *Source: The Economist,* 28 Sept.–4 Oct. 2002, and IMF, *World Economic Outlook,* Sept. 2002.

standard forms of regional trade-liberalizing agreement are free-trade areas, customs unions, and common markets.

Free-trade area (FTA) This is the least comprehensive of the three. It allows for tariff-free trade among the member countries, but it leaves each member able to impose its own trade restrictions on imports from other countries. As a result, members must maintain customs points at their common borders to make sure that imports into the free-trade area do not all enter through the member that is levying the lowest tariff on each item. They must also agree on rules of origin to establish when a good is made in a member country, and hence is able to pass duty-free across its borders, and when it is imported from outside the free-trade area, and hence is liable to pay duties when it crosses borders within the free-trade area.

Customs union This is a free-trade area *plus* an agreement to establish common barriers to trade with the rest of the world. Because they have a common tariff against the outside world, the members need neither customs controls on goods moving among themselves nor rules of origin.

Common market A common market is a customs union that also has free movement of labour and capital among its members.

Trade creation and trade diversion

A major effect of regional trade liberalization is on resource reallocation. Economic theory divides these effects into two categories.

Trade creation This occurs when producers in one member country find that they can undersell producers in another member country because the latter lose their tariff protection. For example, when the North American Free Trade Agreement (NAFTA) came into force, some Mexican firms found that they could undersell their US competitors in some product lines, while some US firms found that they could undersell their Mexican competitors in others, once tariffs were eliminated. As a result, specialization occurred and new international trade developed.

Trade diversion This occurs when exporters in one member country replace foreign exporters as suppliers to another member country as a result of preferential tariff treatment. For example, US trade diversion occurs when Mexican firms find that they can undersell competitors from the rest of the world in the US market, not because they are the cheapest source of supply, but because their tariff-free prices are lower than the tariff-burdened prices of imports from other countries. This effect is a gain to Mexican firms but a cost to the United States—which now has to export more goods for any given amount of imports than before the trade diversion occurred.

From the global perspective, trade diversion represents an inefficient use of resources.

From the narrower national points of view of Mexico and the United States, however, trade diversion brings some gain as well as some loss. In so far as there is a shared desire to increase domestic manufacturing production, trade diversion brings mutual benefit to both countries. It gives producers within the two countries an advantage over producers in the rest of the world, which has the effect of increasing the total amount of production and trade that occurs among the member countries while reducing what comes in from third countries.

EFTA, NAFTA, and other FTAs

The first important free-trade area in the modern era was the European Free Trade Association (EFTA). It was formed in 1960 by a group of European countries that were unwilling to join the European Economic Community, as the EU was then called, because of its all-embracing character. Not wanting to be left out of the gains from trade, they formed an association whose sole purpose was tariff removal. First, they removed all tariffs on trade among themselves. Then each country signed a free-trade-area agreement with the EEC. This made the EEC–EFTA market the largest tariff-free market in the world (over 300 million people). Three of the EFTA countries switched to full membership of the EU in 1995.

In 1988 a sweeping agreement was signed between Canada and the United States, instituting free trade on all goods and most non-government services, and covering what is the world's largest flow of international trade between any two countries. In 1993 this agreement was extended into the North American Free Trade Agreement (NAFTA) by renegotiation of the Canada–USA agreement to include Mexico. Australia and New Zealand have also entered into an association that removes restrictions on trade in goods and services between their two countries, and a group of countries in Southeast Asia have formed the ASEAN trade group.

The countries of Latin America have been experimenting with free-trade areas for many decades. Most earlier attempts failed, but in the last few years a more durable free-trade area has been formed, known as Mercosur. In 1994 an initiative was started to put in place a free-trade area for the whole of the Americas. Negotiations began in 1998 and are scheduled to be concluded by January 2005 for implementation by December 2005. If the countries go through with this as promised, it would in effect be based upon a merger of NAFTA and Mercosur. The new free trade area is to be called the Free Trade Area of the Americas (FTAA).[2]

Common markets: the European Union

By far the most successful common market, which is now referred to as a single market, is the European Union. Its origins go back to the period immediately following the end of the Second World War in 1945. After the war there was a strong belief throughout Europe that the way to avoid future military conflict was to create a high level of economic integration between the existing nation-states. Later the motivation switched to creating a powerful economic bloc that could be competitive with Japan and the USA.

In 1952, as a first step towards economic union, France, Belgium, West Germany, Italy, Luxembourg, and Holland formed the European Coal and Steel Community. This removed trade restrictions on coal, steel, and iron ore among these six countries. In 1957 the same six countries signed the Treaty of Rome. This created the European Economic Community (EEC), which later became the European Community (EC), and after 1993 the European Union (EU). In 1973 the United Kingdom, Denmark, and Ireland joined, and they were followed in 1981 by Greece and in 1986 by Spain and Portugal. Austria, Sweden, and Finland entered in 1995. Several other countries, including Poland, Hungary, the Czech Republic, and Cyprus, are currently negotiating to join.

In the first two decades of its existence, the main economic achievements of the EEC were the elimination of internal tariff barriers and the establishment of common external tariffs (in other words, the establishment of a customs union), and the establishment of the Common Agricultural Policy, which, for better or for worse, guarantees farm prices by means of intervention and an import levy (see Chapter 5). There were other significant EEC policies, such as regional aid and competition policies, but they did not have great economic impacts early on.

By the mid-1980s it was clear that the intended 'Common Market' had not been achieved. There remained many non-tariff barriers to trade and to the mobility of labour. These included quality standards, licensing requirements, and a lack of recognition of qualifications. In financial services there were explicit exchange controls and other regulatory restrictions on cross-border trade. In response, a new push to turn the customs union into a genuine common market began in 1985.

The Single Market Programme

The Single Market Act was signed in 1986. Its intention was to remove all remaining barriers to the creation of a fully integrated single market by the end of 1992. The Single Market Act did not in itself create the single market. Rather, it was a statement (or treaty) of intent which instituted a simplified administrative procedure whereby most of the single market legislation needed only 'weighted majority' support, rather than unanimity. The single market itself was to be created by a large number of Directives, which are drafted by the European Commission, the EU's civil service. These become Community law after they have been 'adopted' by the European Council (a committee of the heads of state or other ministers of member states). They then have to be ratified in the law of each member state. Once in force, they have precedence over the domestic laws of member states if there is a conflict.

Eliminating non-tariff barriers has been approached on a product-by-product basis. Only in this way could minimum quality standards be created which would permit cross-border trade without the threat of quality checks as a prerequisite to entry (a problem that plagues some branches of Canada–USA trade). This has required a complicated set of negotiations on quality standards relating to everything from condoms to sausages and from toys to telecommunications. There is even a quality standard for the bacterial content of aqueous toys—transparent plastic souvenirs containing, perhaps, a model of Big Ben or the Eiffel Tower, which, when shaken, create a snow scene.

All countries have such safety or quality standards for their products, and what has been taking place is the harmonization of these standards, which is something that Canada and the United States have been trying to do since their Agreement was put into force in 1989.

The Single Market Programme is an ongoing process, not a discrete jump. Some of the intended measures have been implemented, but many are still in the pipeline. The process will continue well into the early decades of this century.

---

[2] See www.ftaa-alca.org.

Many important steps were achieved by the end of 1992, including the removal of some border checks. (At UK ports and airports, this means a 'blue' channel through which EU citizens are permitted to carry as many goods as they like, if bought in other EU countries, so long as they are for personal use.) But the process of increasing economic integration continues today.

The single market in financial services

Perhaps the most significant achievements of the Single Market Programme to date have been in the area of trade in financial services. Although the Treaty of Rome called for free movement of capital as well as goods, this was ignored until the mid-1980s. Most member countries had exchange controls on capital movements until recently. These controls prohibited residents of each country from investing in any other country. The Capital Liberalization Directive required all member states to abolish exchange controls by June 1990. Some member states, such as the UK and Germany, had already abolished controls. France and Italy, which had not, were forced to do so by the Directive. Spain, Portugal, Ireland, and Greece were given longer to comply. All except Greece fully abolished their controls by the end of 1992, and Greece abolished most of its controls by 1994.

Once exchange controls were abolished, it could be argued that nothing else had to be done to create a single market in financial services. Certainly wholesale financial markets rapidly integrated with the global financial system, once they were free to do so. Indeed, this is one of the key elements of globalization, which was discussed in Box 30.1 on page 542.

However, agreement was still needed on how to facilitate greater cross-border competition in retail financial markets. Each country in isolation had already created a domestic regulatory regime designed, in part, to protect the consumer. How was the EU to encourage competition but maintain a sensible regime of consumer protection? Financial services are particularly prone to fraud, because the profit margin for a crook is 100 per cent—even a used car salesman has to show you a car, but the seller of an investment product offers only future promises!

The European Union adopted a pragmatic approach based upon the assumption of existing regulators' competence. Firms in each sector were to be authorized as 'fit and proper' by their home country regulator, and they would then be presumed to be fit and proper to trade in any member state. In effect, the home country gave a driving licence which then permitted an authorized company to 'drive' anywhere in the Union. This mutual recognition of regulators has been wrongly interpreted as permitting financial services firms to trade anywhere in the European Union on the basis of their home country's rules. A moment's thought will tell you why this has to be wrong.

Imagine, for example, British drivers being permitted to drive on the left in France just because that is the law in Britain. It is just as disastrous to have banks in any one location trading under fifteen different legal structures.

The single market in financial services is built on a dual set of principles: home country authorization, and host country conduct of business rules. This means that a firm can be authorized to trade throughout the Union by the home regulator, but the trade itself must obey the local laws in the country concerned.

Allowing home countries to regulate entry and host countries to regulate performance is a simple application of the principle of *national treatment* that was developed in the context of the Uruguay round. It means that foreign firms get treated just the same as local firms.

The Cecchini Report of 1989 estimated that the completion of the Single Market Programme could increase the GDP of the European Union by up to 6 per cent. However, a well-known American economist, Richard Baldwin, challenged that figure, suggesting that the gains could be at least twice as large (owing to economies of scale external to firms). And this would be the gain in just one year; similar gains would continue to flow in future years. Thus, while politically tortuous, the process of reducing trade barriers, even within groups of countries, is capable of creating considerable gains in economic efficiency.

The Maastricht Treaty

The Maastricht Treaty, signed in 1992, pushed the process of EU integration further. It included an agreement creating the common currency, the euro, that came into being in January 1999. The introduction of the single currency has been a major move towards further integration of the economies of the European Union (at least for the members of the euro zone), as it has made the price system much more transparent and eliminated exchange rate risk. The full effects of the single currency are still in the process of making themselves felt in the economies of the euro zone.

The Maastricht Treaty also contained a Social Chapter, covering harmonization of policies with respect to labour markets and other social areas. The United Kingdom opted out of this Chapter initially, but opted back in 1997.

The future of the multilateral trading system

At the end of the Second World War the United States took the lead in forming the GATT and in pressing for reductions in world tariffs through successive rounds of negotiations. Largely as a result of this US initiative, the world's tariff barriers have been greatly reduced, while the volume of world trade has risen steadily (see Figure 33.4 on page 624).

The next few years will be critical for the future of the multilateral trading system, which has served the world so well since the end of the Second World War. The dangers are, first, a growth of regional trading blocs that will trade more with their own member countries and less with others, and, second, the growth of state-managed trade.

The 1920s and 1930s provide a cautionary tale. Arguments for restricting trade always have a superficial appeal and sometimes have real short-term payoffs. In the long term, however, a major world-wide escalation of tariffs would lower efficiency and incomes and restrict global trade, while doing nothing to raise employment. Both economic theory and the evidence of history support this proposition. Although most agree that pressure should be put on countries that restrict trade, the above analysis suggests that these pressures are best applied using the multilateral institution, the WTO. Unilateral imposition of restrictions in response to the perceived restrictions in other countries can all too easily degenerate into a round of mutually escalating trade barriers.

In the first few years of this century, the United States has been more protectionist than at any other time during the last half of the previous century. New heavy anti-dumping duties on steel and softwood lumber and big new protec-tionist measures for its agricultural industry, already the most efficient producers in world, are causing worrying ripples internationally. If the USA abandons the position it established over the last sixty years as the leader of the movement for trade liberalization, there is no obvious successor.

The European Union, although it has achieved something close to free trade within the Union, has been equivocal on free trade with the rest of the world. Anti-dumping duties, voluntary export agreements, and other non-tariff barriers have been used with effect against successful importers—particularly the Japanese. Although these measures may bring short-term gains, both economic theory and historical experience suggest that they will bring losses in the long term. Protectionism reduces incomes because low-priced goods are excluded to the detriment of current consumers, particularly those with lower incomes. It also reduces employment because restrictions on imports are sooner or later balanced by restrictions on exports as other countries retaliate. And it inhibits the technological dynamism that is the source of long-term growth, by shielding domestic producers from the need that free international competition forces on them: to keep up with all foreign competitors.

SUMMARY

Sources of the gains from trade

- Potential gains from trade exist when one country, region, firm, or individual has a comparative advantage in the production of some good or service.

- Comparative advantage occurs whenever countries have different opportunity costs of producing particular goods. World production of all products can be increased if each country transfers resources into the production of the products in which it has a comparative advantage, which means those in which it has the lower opportunity cost.

- The most important proposition in the theory of the gains from trade is that trade allows all countries to obtain the goods in which they do not have a comparative advantage at a lower opportunity cost than they would face if they were to produce all products for themselves; this allows all countries to have more of all products than they could have if they tried to be self-sufficient.

- As well as gaining the advantages of specialization arising from comparative advantage, a nation that engages in trade and specialization may realize the benefits of economies of large-scale production and of learning by doing.

- Classical theory regarded comparative advantage as being determined largely by natural resource endowments, and thus as difficult to change. Economists now believe that some comparative advantages are acquired and thus can be changed. A country may, in this view, influence its role in world production and trade. Successful intervention leads to a country acquiring a comparative advantage; unsuccessful intervention fails to develop such an advantage.

The terms of trade

- The 'terms of trade' refers to the ratio of the prices of goods exported to those imported, which determines the quantity of imports that can be obtained per unit of exports. The terms of trade determine how the gains from trade are shared. A favourable change in the terms of trade—that is, a rise in export prices relative to import prices—means that a country can acquire more imports per unit of exports.

The theory of commercial policy

- Protection can be a means to ends other than maximizing world living standards. It is also sometimes justified on the grounds that it may lead to higher living standards for the protectionist country than would a policy of free trade. Such a result might come about by developing a dynamic comparative advantage allowing inexperienced or uneconomically small industries to become efficient enough to compete with foreign industries. A recent argument for protection is that, by operating a strategic trade policy, a country can attract firms in oligopolistic industries that, because of scale economies, can earn large profits even in equilibrium.

■ Domestic industries may be protected from foreign competition by tariffs, which affect the prices of imports, or by non-tariff barriers, which affect the quantities of imports.

■ Some fallacious free-trade arguments are that (a) because free trade maximizes world income, it will maximize the income of every individual country; and (b) because infant industries seldom admit to growing up and thus try to retain their protection indefinitely, the whole country necessarily loses by protecting its infant industries.

■ Some fallacious protectionist arguments are that (a) mutually advantageous trade is impossible because one trader's gain

must always be the other's loss; (b) our high-paid workers must be protected against the competition from low-paid foreign workers; and (c) imports are to be discouraged because they lower national income and cause unemployment.

Global commercial policy

■ The World Trade Organization (WTO) has taken over from the General Agreement on Tariffs and Trade (GATT) the role of policing world trade rules relating to government commercial policies and providing a forum for further international co-operation in evolving the global trade regime.

■ Regional trade-liberalizing agreements such as free-trade areas and common markets bring efficiency gains through trade creation and efficiency losses through trade diversion. The North American Free Trade Agreement (NAFTA) is the world's largest and most successful free-trade area, while the European Union is the world's largest and most successful common market (now called a single market).

TOPICS FOR REVIEW

■ Comparative advantage

■ Gains from trade

■ Terms of trade

■ Free trade and protectionism

■ Tariff and non-tariff barriers to trade

■ General Agreement on Tariffs and Trade (GATT)

■ World Trade Organization (WTO)

■ Common markets, customs unions, and free-trade associations

■ North American Free Trade Agreement (NAFTA)

■ European Union (EU)

DISCUSSION QUESTIONS

1 It is quite common for governments from time to time to encourage their citizens to buy home-produced goods in preference to foreign-produced goods. (For example, in the United Kingdom a 'buy British' policy has been encouraged in the past.) In what ways if any could such encouragement be good for the domestic economy?

2 Outline the arguments for and against free trade.

3 Compare and contrast tariffs and quotas as methods of restricting trade.

4 Why does trading with countries where workers have lower real incomes *not* make us worse off?

5 Why might openness to foreign competition be good for economic growth?

6 What are some of the arguments used by recent protesters against globalization? Critically evaluate these claims.

Chapter 34

ECONOMICS OF DEVELOPING AND TRANSITION COUNTRIES

Why are some countries getting poorer while much of the world is getting richer? How well are the former communist countries succeeding in their transition to market economies? Are the policies of the IMF and the World Bank helping to make countries grow or are they part of the problem? These are some of the important questions we address in this chapter. In particular, you will learn that:

• Around a quarter of the world's population still lives at bare subsistence levels and more than three-quarters live on an income that is below 20 per cent of per capita income in the United States.

• Some poorer countries have managed to grow rapidly, but the gap between richest and poorest is large and is not decreasing.

• An older design for development recommended a heavily protected economy and substantial government direction of the economy.

• More recent views recommend openness, a market economy and private sector production.

• Governments are needed to provide public services such as health and education, law and order, and infrastructure such as roads.

• The Washington Consensus has guided policies of the IMF and World Bank towards developing countries, but this has been much criticized recently.

The main issue facing poor countries is how to generate growth of incomes so that the living standards of the population can be improved. The problem is thus to raise the trend rate of growth. Economic growth is a topic that we addressed in Chapter 21. Traditionally, in economics the growth of high-income countries has been treated as a separate subject from the growth of lower-income countries, and the latter subject is often not included in introductory courses. For this reason, this chapter has been made self-contained so that it can be skipped if desired.

We include this material here for three main reasons. First, the gap between rich and poor in the world is one of the big issues of our time. It is an issue that all responsible citizens should think about and it is important that the public debate is as well informed as possible. It would be inexcusable for anyone training in economics to be unaware of one of the biggest challenge that the world economy faces. Second, the deeper understanding that economists are developing of the role that technological change plays in economic growth is blurring the traditional distinction between the forces that cause growth in high-income and in lower-income countries. Third, the growth successes of Japan in the mid-twentieth century and of several Southeast Asian countries later in the century has blurred what earlier seemed to be a clear distinction between the high-income, largely industrialized, countries and all the rest. We now see what looks more like a continuous gradation from the very-highest-income countries, which include the USA, most countries of the EU, and Japan, through South Korea, Hong Kong, Singapore, Taiwan, some of the lower-income countries of the EU (among others), and some of the higher-income countries of Latin America at the upper–middle end of the scale, through countries such as Indonesia and Malaysia a little further down, followed by a rapidly growing China and India, to yet others, particularly many of the countries of sub-Saharan Africa, with incomes that are not only very low, but also static.

For these and other reasons, it no longer seems reasonable to assume that the forces that govern growth in rich countries are fundamentally different from the forces that govern growth in middle- and lower-rank countries.

From the outset, development economics has had a micro component, concentrating on social and economic structures as influences on growth. However, it should not be forgotten that macro influences of aggregate saving and investment and cyclical factors are important, especially when crises throw the economy off course. But the big issue is how to raise trend growth. In this regard, those economists who study technological change in high-income countries have come to place increasing emphasis on the microeconomic aspects of social and economic structure that encourage the innovation and diffusion of new technologies in the countries that they study. (See for example Box 34.6, on page 646.)

Probably the most important boundary that divides countries for which different explanations of growth are required is between those that have very low and static incomes and all the rest. A country that has shown no significant economic growth for decades (or even for centuries) probably has economic and social structures, as well as fundamental direction to its economic policies, that are basically unfavourable to growth. If the people of that country wish to grow, they must contemplate fundamental structural changes, as well as major reversals in their economic policies. All the other countries, in which growth is occurring (although sometimes at a rate that is regarded as too low), face many common problems, whether they are low-, middle-, or high-income countries. The relative importance of individual forces may vary, but overall these countries face problems that have a significant degree of similarity. Of course, their underlying social and economic structures do affect their growth rates; but since they are currently growing, they do not face the same urgent need to consider major alterations of these structures as do the non-growing countries.

The uneven pattern of development

In the civilized and comfortable urban life of today's developed countries, most people have lost sight of the fact that a short time ago—very short, in terms of the lifespan of the Earth—people were nomadic food-gatherers, existing as best they could from what nature threw their way. It has been only about 10,000 years since the Neolithic Agricultural Revolution, when people changed from food-gatherers to food-producers. Throughout most of subsequent human history, civilizations have been based on a comfortable life for a privileged minority and unremitting toil for the vast majority. It has been only within the last two centuries that ordinary people have become able to expect leisure and high consumption standards—and then only in the world's economically developed countries. Over 6 billion people are alive today, but the wealthy parts of the world—where people work no more than 40 or 50 hours per week, enjoy substantial leisure, and have a level of consumption at least *half* that attained by the United States (the country with the highest per capita GNI[1])—contain no more than 15 per cent of the world's population. Many of the rest struggle for subsistence, existing on a level at or below that endured by peasants in ancient Egypt or Babylon.

The richest countries with the highest per capita incomes are referred to by the United Nations as **developed countries**. These include the United States, Canada, most of the countries of Western Europe, South Africa, Australia, New Zealand, Japan, and a few others. The poorer countries are referred to by the UN as the **developing countries**[2] and include a diverse set of nations. Some, such as Vietnam and China, have grown very rapidly in the 1990s, while others, such as Burundi and Djibouti, experienced negative growth rates of per capita real income. Between these two is another group of nations, variously called newly industrialized economies (NIEs) or **newly industrialized countries (NICs)**; they include South Korea, Singapore, Taiwan, Brazil, and Hong Kong. These countries have grown rapidly and typically have per capita incomes that have risen above 50 per cent of those found in the developed nations. Several other countries in Southeast Asia are close behind the NICs, including Malaysia and Thailand. A new group of developing countries has been given a collective label since about 1990. These are the countries of the former Soviet bloc that used to have centrally planned economies but are now trying to build market economies. These are known as **transition economies**. Examples are Poland, Hungary, the Czech Republic, and Russia.

Data on per capita incomes throughout the world are summarized in Table 34.1.[3] The data reflect enormous real differences in living standards that no statistical inaccuracies can hide. The **development gap**—the discrepancy between the standards of living in countries at either end of the distribution—is real and large.[4]

---

[1] Some small countries, such as Luxembourg, have higher per capita incomes, but these are not broad-based economies and have very small populations.

[2] The terminology of development is often confusing. 'Underdeveloped', 'less developed', and 'developing' do not mean the same thing in ordinary English, yet each has been used to describe the same phenomenon. For the most part, we will use the term 'developing', which is the term currently used by the United Nations to describe the lower-income countries. Some of these countries are making progress in raising their living standards; that is, they are developing in the ordinary sense of that word. Others are not.

[3] There are many problems when we compare incomes across countries. For example, home-grown food is vitally important to living standards in developing countries, but it is excluded, or at best imperfectly included, in the national income statistics of most countries. In Norway significant amounts of income go to heating houses during cold winters. Such heating is not necessary in countries that have warm climates.

[4] You will find large differences in international comparisons depending on the exchange rates that are used to convert incomes valued in domestic currencies to a common currency unit. Use of rates based on the relative purchasing powers of national currencies (called purchasing power parity rates and described in Chapter 29) is more satisfactory, while use of current rates causes international standings to vary substantially from one year to the next.

Table 34.1 Income and population differences among groups of countries, 2002

Income groups by GNI per capita	Number of countries (1)	GNI (US$ m) (2)	Population (m) (3)	GNI per capita (US$) (4)	% of world population (5)	% of world GNI (6)
Low ($785 or less)	63	917	2,460	410	41	3.2
Lower-middle ($786–$3,115)	54	2,324	2,048	1,130	34	7.4
Upper-middle ($3,116–$9,635)	38	3,001	647	4,640	11	9.6
High ($9,636 or more)	52	24,994	903	27,680	15	79.8
World	207	31,315	6,057	5,170	100	100

The unequal distribution of world income is shown in columns (5) and (6). The poorest 41 per cent of the world's population earn only 3.2 per cent of the world income; the richest 15 per cent earn 80 per cent of world income.

Source: World Bank, *World Atlas 2002* (Washington, DC).

The 2003 *World Development Report* from the World Bank points out that much has been achieved in poverty reduction but much more remains to be done:

There has been a significant drop in the percentage of people living in extreme poverty (that is living on less than $1 per day). Even the absolute number of very poor people declined between 1980 and 1998 by at least 200 million, to almost 1.2 billion. The decrease was primarily due to the decline in the number of very poor people in China as a result of its strong growth from 1980 onward. Since 1993, there have also been encouraging signs of renewed poverty reduction in India. Sub-Saharan Africa, by contrast, has seen its number of very poor people increase steadily. . . . Development strategies will need to do better in eliminating abject poverty. The estimated 1 billion very poor people is of the same order of magnitude as the independently generated figures on the number of people who are undernourished and underweight.

The average income in the richest 20 countries is now 37 times that in the poorest 20. This ratio has doubled in the past 40 years, mainly because of lack of growth in the poorest countries. (World Bank, *World Development Report*, 2003, p. 2)

The consequences of very low income levels can be severe. In a rich country such as the United Kingdom, variations in rainfall are reflected in farm output and farm income. In very poor countries variations in rainfall are often reflected in the death rate. In these countries many people live so close to a subsistence level that even slight fluctuations in the food supply can bring death by starvation to large numbers. Other, less dramatic, characteristics of poverty include inadequate diet, poor health, short life-expectancy, and illiteracy.

For these reasons, reformers in very-low-income countries feel a sense of urgency not felt by their counterparts in higher-income countries. Yet as Table 34.2 shows, some of

Table 34.2 The relationship between the level and the rate of growth of per capita income, 1990–2000

Growth of GNI per capita 1990–2000 (%)	Number of countries	GNI, 2000 (US$ bn)	Population, 2000 (m)	GNI per capita, 2000 (US$)
Less than 0	53	943	752	1,250
0–0.9	17	496	166	2,980
1.0–1.9	41	12,578	1,122	11,210
2.0–2.9	31	13,550	975	13,890
3.0 or more	36	3,618	2,933	1,230
No data	29	129	108	1,190

Some of the very poorest countries spend much of their increase in income on a rising population. The gap in income between rich and many of the very poor countries is not closing; however, some countries with low per capita GNI were among the faster growing in this period. Notice that there are no consistent growth data for 29 of the poorest countries.

Source: World Bank, *World Bank Atlas, 2002*.

the poorest countries in the world are among those with very low or negative growth rates of per capita GNI. As a result,

The development gap has been widening for the very poorest countries.

As we will see, this is a problem of both output and population. It is also an international political problem. What are the causes of underdevelopment, and how may they be overcome?

Restraints on economic development

Per capita income grows when aggregate national income grows faster than population. Many forces can impede such growth. Here we study a list of possible restraints that starts with natural resources and ends with infrastructure. These can apply to countries at all income levels, but they tend to be most severe in the poorest countries. Box 34.1 presents a recent assessment by the World Bank on the drivers of economic growth in developing countries.

Inadequate natural resources

A country's supply of natural resources is important. A country with infertile land and inadequate supplies of natural resources will find growth in income more difficult to achieve than one that is richly endowed with such resources.

How these resources are managed also matters. When farmland is divided into many small parcels, it may be

---

 ## Box 34.1 What drives economic growth?

The following is an excerpt from the 2000/01 *World Development Report* from the World Bank.

Wide divergences in growth reflect the outcome of interactions among countries' initial conditions, their institutions, their policy choices, the external shocks they receive, and no small measure of good luck.

There is evidence that growth depends on education and life expectancy, particularly at lower incomes. For example, it has been shown that female literacy and girls' education are good for overall economic growth. There is also some evidence that rapid population growth is negatively associated with per capita GDP growth and that changing age structure of population can also affect growth.

Some economic policies—such as openness to international trade, sound monetary and fiscal polices (reflecting moderate budget deficits and the absence of high inflation), a well-developed financial system, and a moderately sized government—are also strongly conducive to economic growth. Aid can boost growth if such policies are in place, but not if they are absent. Both domestic and external shocks matter as well. Not surprisingly, wars, civil unrest, and natural disasters all lower growth rates. Less dramatically, so do macroeconomic volatility, adverse terms of trade shocks, and slower growth among trading partners. Poorly sequenced and badly implemented reforms can lead to sudden reversals in capital flows or other macroeconomic disruptions, also slowing growth. These collapses in growth can be particularly devastating for poor people, who have weaker support mechanisms and generally lead a more precarious life than the better-off.

Institutional factors are also important for growth. For example, there is evidence that strong rule of law and the absence of corruption contribute to growth—by providing a fair, rule-based environment in which firms can invest and grow. Strong institutions can also have powerful indirect benefits. For example, adjusting to

adverse shocks often requires painful but necessary changes in domestic economic policies. In countries where conflicts between competing interests are pronounced, and the institutions to resolve these conflicts are weak, recovery from shocks is often slower than it is where these institutions are strong.

Similarly, there is growing evidence that ethnic fragmentation has adverse effects on growth. Ethnically fragmented countries and regions within countries tend to provide fewer—and poorer quality—public goods, especially education. Such areas are also more prone to violent ethnic conflict. Institutions that guarantee minority rights and provide opportunities to resolve conflicts have been shown to offset the side effects of polarized societies.

On average, initially poor countries have grown more slowly than rich countries, so that the gap between rich and poor countries has widened. However, there is strong evidence that, controlling for some of the factors mentioned above, growth is faster in countries that are initially poor. This relationship may not be linear, with higher growth kicking in only after countries reach a threshold level of income. This raises the possibility of poverty traps at very low levels of development. . . .

What determines the sustainability of growth? In addition to the factors mentioned above, a further important consideration is whether or not growth is accompanied by environmental degradation, which can in turn undermine growth. Environmental degradation can exact a heavy toll on the economy through poor health and reduced agricultural productivity. . . . In the long run especially, attending to the quality of the environment and the efficiency of resource use is likely to boost investment, accumulation, and growth. Rapid growth and environmental protection can go together—because new additions to industrial capacity can take advantage of cleaner technologies and accelerate the replacement of high-pollution technologies. (World Bank, *World Development Report, 2000/2001*, pp. 49–52) much more difficult to achieve the advantages of modern agriculture than when the land is available in huge tracts for large-scale farming. Fragmented land-holdings may result from a dowry or inheritance system, or they may be politically imposed. One of the popular policies following the Mexican revolution early in the twentieth century was the redistribution of land from large landowners to ordinary peasants. Today, however, the fragmented land-ownership prevents Mexican agriculture from producing many products at costs low enough to compete in international markets. Since it has joined the North American Free Trade Association (NAFTA), the Mexican government can no longer choose to continue to protect a large agricultural sector whose inefficiency has been increasing relative to competing suppliers. Market forces will lead to much larger land-holdings. Although average incomes will rise as a result, many smallholders will suffer in the transition.

Although abundant supplies of natural resources can assist growth, they are neither sufficient to ensure growth nor necessary for it. Some countries with large supplies of natural resources have poor growth performances because their economic structure or political system inhibits growth; prime examples are Russia, Ukraine, and Argentina up until the 1990s. In contrast, other countries have enjoyed rapid rates of economic growth based on human capital and entrepreneurial ability in spite of a dearth of natural resources; prime examples are Japan over the last 100 years, and Singapore, Hong Kong, Israel, and Taiwan in the last 40 years.

Inefficiently used natural resources

Three kinds of economic inefficiency need to be distinguished. *Allocative inefficiency* occurs when resources are used to make an inefficient combination of goods. There are too many of some goods and too few of others. This means that the economy is at the 'wrong' point on its production-possibility boundary. If resources are reallocated to produce fewer of some and more of other types of good, some people can be made better off while no one need be made worse off.

Productive inefficiency occurs when inputs are used in inefficient combinations. Given the prices of capital and labour, some production processes use too much capital relative to labour, while others use too little. This means that the economy is inside its production-possibility boundary (as illustrated in Figure 1.1 on page 5). If input combinations are altered, more of all goods can be produced. Monopolistic market structures, as well as taxes, tariffs, and subsidies, are important sources of the distortions that lead to both allocative and productive inefficiencies.

A third kind of inefficiency, called *X*-**inefficiency**, occurs either when firms do not seek to maximize their profits or when owners of resources do not seek to maximize their material welfare. *X*-inefficiency also puts the economy inside its production-possibility boundary.

Professor Harvey Leibenstein of the University of California, the economist who developed the concept, has studied *X*-inefficiency in developing countries. He cites psychological evidence to show that non-maximizing behaviour is typical of situations in which the pressure that has been placed on decision-makers is either very low or very high. If the customary living standard can be obtained with little effort, according to this evidence, people are likely to follow customary behaviour and spend little time trying to make optimal decisions. When pressure builds up, so that making a reasonable income becomes more difficult, optimizing behaviour becomes more common. Under extreme pressure, however, such as very low living standards or a rapidly deteriorating environment, people become disoriented and once again do not adopt optimizing behaviour.

X-**inefficiency may be typical of industries, and whole economies, where customary behaviour leads to acceptable living standards or where the challenges become overwhelming.**[5]

Inefficient agriculture

A developing country whose labour force is devoted mainly to agriculture has little choice but to accept this basic allocation of resources. It can build up its manufacturing and service sectors, and if its efforts are successful the proportion of the population devoted to urban pursuits will rise. But the change will come slowly, leaving a large portion of the country's resources in rural pursuits for a long time to come.

It follows that policies to help the agricultural sector raise productivity are an important part of the development strategy in any agriculture-based poor country. These policies can fill the dual purposes of raising the incomes of rural workers and reducing the cost of food for urban workers.

A developing country's government may choose to devote a major portion of its resources to stimulating agricultural production, for example by mechanizing farms, irrigating land, using new seeds and fertilizers, and promoting agricultural R&D. If successful, the country will stave off starvation for its current population, and it may even develop an excess over current needs and so have foodstuffs available for export. A food surplus can thereby earn foreign exchange to buy needed imports.

In the last three decades India, Pakistan, Taiwan, and other Asian countries have achieved dramatic increases in

---

[5] Although such behaviour is no doubt often found in some developing economies, it is also sometimes found in advanced countries. For example, studies of monopolies have often indicated a preference on the part of their managers and workers for the 'quiet life' rather than an active search for profit- and income-maximizing forms of behaviour.

food production by the application of new technology and the use of new seed in agricultural production. This has been labelled the *green revolution*.

The gains from this strategy, while large at first, are subject to diminishing returns. Further gains in agricultural production have an ever higher opportunity cost, measured in terms of the resources needed to irrigate land and to mechanize production. Critics of reliance on agricultural output argue that newly developing economies must start at once to develop other bases for economic growth.

Many developing countries (as well as many developed ones) suffer from misguided government intervention in the agriculture sector. In India, for example, the government has encouraged crops such as oilseeds and sugar cane, in which India has a comparative disadvantage, and discouraged crops such as rice, wheat, and cotton, in which India has a strong comparative advantage. It has subsidized food prices, thus giving large benefits to the urban population. About 8 per cent of all Indian government spending is on subsidies that go to fertilizers, to farmers' debt payments, and to urban food consumption.

Rapid population growth

Population growth is one of the central problems of economic development. For example, in the decade 1990–2000 Cameroon, Kenya, and Zambia had growth rates of population of 2.7, 2.4, and 2.6 per cent per year alongside GDP growth rates of 1.7, 2.1, and 0.5 per cent, respectively. Hence they experienced *negative* rates of growth of GDP *per capita* (of −1.0, −0.3, and −2.1 per cent per year). Many less developed countries have rates of population growth that are nearly as large as their rates of growth of GDP. As a result, their standards of living are barely higher than they were 100 years ago. They have made appreciable gains in aggregate income, but most of the gains have been literally eaten up by the increasing population. The fact that fifty three countries had negative growth rates of GDP per head during the 1990–2000 period is shown in Table 34.2 on page 631, and many of these countries were already among the poorest in the world.

The Reverend Thomas Malthus perceived the critical importance of population growth to living standards early in the nineteenth century. He asserted two relationships about rates of increase. First, food production tends to increase in an arithmetic progression (e.g. 100, 103, 106, 109, 112, where the increments in this example are 3 *units* per period). Second, population tends to increase in a geometric progression (e.g., 100, 103, 106.09, 109.27, 112.55, where the increase in this example is 3 *per cent* per period). As a result of these relationships Malthus argued that population growth will always tend to outrun the growth in food supply. The difference in the above example may not seem like much after only five periods. But after twenty

periods the arithmetic increase in food supply has increased it to 160 while the geometric increase in the population has increased it to 181.

Malthus's prediction gave economics the name of 'the dismal science'. In some poor areas of the world the predictions seem all too accurate, even today. There, agricultural methods are fairly traditional, so that food production increases only slowly while population tends to increase at more rapid rates. The result is subsistence living, with population held in check by low life-expectancies and periodic famines.

Fortunately, over most of the world Malthus's predictions have been proved false. Two reasons are paramount. First, Malthus underestimated the importance of technological change, which has increased productivity in agriculture at a *geometric* rather than an arithmetic rate, and a rate far higher than the rate at which the demand for food has been growing in most advanced countries. Second, he underestimated the extent of voluntary restrictions of population growth. As a result, population has grown more slowly than has the production of food (and most other things) in developed countries. For them living standards have been rising rather than falling.

For the more advanced industrialized countries, Malthusian pressures are not a problem today. However, for many poor countries, where people subsist on what they grow for themselves, the tendency for the growth in population to outstrip the growth in the food supply makes Malthusian pressures a current threat.

Figure 34.1 illustrates actual and projected world population. By now the population problem is almost completely limited to the low-income countries. About 97 per cent of the expected growth in the world's population between now and 2050 will be in the developing countries of Africa, Asia, and Latin America.

Inadequate human resources

Numbers of people matter, and so do their training and experience. A well-developed entrepreneurial class motivated and trained to organize resources for efficient production is often missing in poor countries. The reason may be that managerial positions are awarded on the basis of family status or political patronage (leading to X-inefficiency). It may be the presence of economic or cultural attitudes that do not favour acquisition of wealth by organizing productive activities; or it may simply be the absence of the quantity or quality of education or training that is required.

In today's world much production is knowledge-intensive. This puts a premium on a well-educated workforce. The abilities to read, do basic calculations, operate electronic equipment, and follow relatively complex instructions are important requirements for much modern labour. Failure

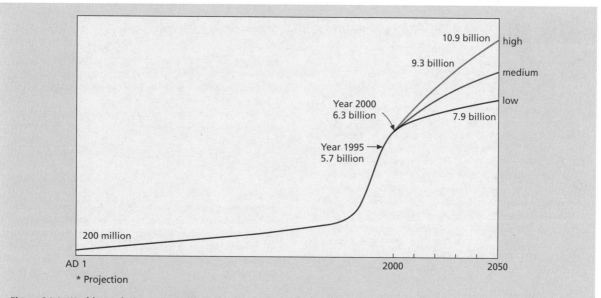

Figure 34.1 World population AD 1-2050

World population reached 6 billion in 1999. For 2050, UN demographers cite three population projections—a 'low' of 7.9 billion; a 'medium' of 9.3 billion and a 'high' of 10.9 billion—each variant based on slightly different assumptions about future birth rates. The annual rate of world population growth peaked at about 2 per cent in the early 1960s. Since then it has gradually slowed to 1.3 per cent. The population of industrialized countries has nearly stabilized. But in developing countries the population is still growing. All of the projected population growth between now and 2050 will occur in developing countries, by which time today's developing countries will account for over 85 per cent of world population.

Source: United Nations Population Fund.

to create such essential labour skills can be an important cause of lack of growth.

Poor health is another source of inadequate human resources. When the labour force is healthy, less time is lost and more effective effort is expended. Box 34.2 discusses one of the major health-related problems affecting economic development, the spread of HIV/Aids. At the time of writing this is having a major impact in sub-Saharan Africa, but it is also projected to be a serious problem in India, China, Russia, and Nigeria.

Cultural barriers

Traditions and habitual ways of doing business vary, and not all are equally conducive to high productivity. Often in developing countries cultural forces are a source of X-inefficiency. Sometimes personal considerations of family, past favours, or traditional friendship or enmity are more important than market incentives in motivating behaviour. One may find a firm that is too small struggling to survive against a larger rival, and learn that the owner prefers to remain small because expansion would require use of non-family capital or leadership. To avoid paying too harsh a competitive price for built-in inefficiency, the firm's owners may then attempt to influence the govern-

ment to prevent larger firms from being formed, or try to secure restrictions on the sale of output—and they may well succeed. Such behaviour will inhibit economic growth.

In a society in which people believe that it is more important who your father is than what you do, it may take a generation to persuade employers to change their attitudes, and another generation to persuade workers that times have changed. It is more difficult for the workforce to change its characteristics and to adapt to the requirements of growth in a traditional society, in which children are expected to follow their parents' occupations, than in a society in which upward mobility is itself a goal.

There has been a lively debate about the importance of differing cultural attitudes. Some analysts believe that traditional considerations dominate peasant societies to the exclusion of economic responses; others suggest that any resulting inefficiency may be relatively small. A country that wants development must accept some alteration in its traditional ways of doing things. However, a trade-off between speed of development and amount of social upheaval can be made. Many critics argue that development plans, particularly when imposed by economists from advanced countries, pay too little attention to local cultural and religious values. An even more unfavourable possibility is that the social upheaval will occur without

Box 34.2 The impact of HIV/AIDS on economic development

The following is an extract from a fact sheet prepared by UNAIDS* that summarizes the scale and impact of HIV/AIDS.

More than 60 million people have been infected with HIV since the epidemic began two decades ago. In 2001, it claimed an estimated 3 million lives. In the 45 most affected countries, it is projected that, between 2000 and 2020, 68 million people will die prematurely as a result of AIDS. The projected toll is greatest in sub-Saharan Africa where 55 million additional deaths can be expected.

In many countries, AIDS is erasing decades of progress in life expectancy. The average life expectancy in sub-Saharan Africa is currently 47 years. Without AIDS, it would have been 62 years. . . . Children and young people are especially hard-hit by the epidemic. The under-five mortality rates of seven countries in sub-Saharan Africa have increased 20–40 per cent due to HIV/AIDS. The number of excess AIDS-related deaths among South Africans aged 15–34 is projected to peak in 2010–2015, with an estimated 17 times as many deaths as there would have been in the absence of AIDS.

AIDS pushes people deeper into poverty as households lose their breadwinners, livelihoods are compromised and savings are consumed by the cost of health care and funerals. Research shows that, in two-thirds of Zambian families where the father died, monthly disposable income fell by more than 80 per cent. . . . The loss of assets and productive workers severely affects households' capacities to produce and purchase food.

In all affected countries, the HIV/AIDS epidemic is putting the health sector under more strain. . . . The epidemic is reducing the overall quality of care provided. . . . At the same time, the demand for health services is expanding and more health-care personnel are being affected by HIV/AIDS.

A decline in school enrolment is one of the most visible effects of the epidemic. According to the World Bank, the number of primary school pupils in 2010 will shrink by 24 per cent in Zimbabwe, 14 per cent in Kenya and 12 per cent in Uganda.

The vast majority of people living with HIV/AIDS worldwide are in the prime of their working lives. By 2005, Zimbabwe will have lost 19 per cent of its workforce to AIDS, Botswana 17 per cent, South Africa 11 per cent, Tanzania 9 per cent and Côte d'Ivoire 8 per cent.

AIDS weakens economic activity by squeezing productivity, adding costs, diverting productive resources, and depleting skills. The epidemic hits productivity mainly through increased absenteeism, organizational disruption, and the loss of skills and 'organizational memory'. Loss of know-how tends to be the most often cited cost factor on the shop floor. Thus, even in high unemployment areas (with an apparently 'bottomless' pool of unskilled or semi-skilled labour), the drain in visible and invisible skills and knowledge end up being considerable.

AIDS has a profound impact on growth, income and poverty. For those countries with national HIV/AIDS prevalence rates of 20 per cent or more, GDP growth has been estimated to drop by an average of 2.6 percentage points annually. . . . Studies have forecast that, by 2015, the economies of Botswana and Swaziland would grow by 2.5 and 1.1 percentage points less, respectively, than they would have in the absence of the epidemic.

* UNAIDS, Fact Sheet 2002, *The impact of HIV/AIDS*, 2 July 2002. See: www.unaids.org for this and more recent information.

---

achieving even the expected benefits of a rising GDP. If the development policy does not take local values into account, the local population may not respond as predicted by Western economic theories. In this case the results of the development effort may be disappointingly small.

Inadequate financial institutions

The lack of an adequate, trustworthy, and trusted system of financial institutions is often a restraint on development. Investment plays a key role in growth, and an important source of funds for investment is the savings of households and firms. When banks and other financial institutions do not function effectively, the link between private saving and investment may be broken, making it difficult to raise funds for investment.

Many people in poor countries do not trust banks—sometimes with good reason, but often without. Either they do not maintain deposits, or else they panic periodically, withdrawing their balances and seeking security for their money under mattresses, in gold, or in real estate.

When banks cannot count on their deposits being left in the banking system, they cannot engage in the kind of long-term loans that are needed to finance investments. When this happens, savings do not become available for investment in productive capacity.

More importantly, a poorly functioning banking system, often one that is nationalized or dominated by a strong government-supported union, can seriously slow growth. India was still in this situation at the start of the present century; although governments have introduced many market-oriented reforms over the last decade, they have so far been unwilling to take on the unions that dominate India's large, inefficient banking system.

Inadequate domestic savings

Although modern development strategies in many instances seek an infusion of foreign capital imported by transnational corporations (TNCs), the rise of domestically owned firms, which will reap some of the externalities created by foreign technology, is one key to sustained development. And a supply of domestic savings is needed to finance the growth of domestic firms.

If more domestic capital is to be created by a country's own efforts, resources must be diverted from the production of goods for current consumption. This means a cut in present living standards. If living standards are already at or near subsistence level, such a diversion will be difficult. At best it will be possible to reallocate only a small proportion of resources to the production of capital goods.

Such a situation is often described as the *vicious circle of poverty*. Because a country has little capital per head, it is poor. Because it is poor, it can devote few resources to creating new capital rather than to producing goods for consumption. Because little new capital can be produced, capital per head remains low, and the country remains poor.

The vicious circle can be made to seem an absolute constraint on growth rates. Of course, it is not; if it were, we would all still be at the level of the early agricultural civilizations. The grain of truth in the vicious-circle argument is that some surplus must be available somewhere in the society to allow saving and investment. In a poor society with an even distribution of income, in which nearly everyone is at the subsistence level, saving may be very difficult. But this is not the common experience. Usually there is at least a small middle class that can save and invest if opportunities for the profitable use of funds arise. Also, in most poor societies today the average household is above the physical subsistence level. Even the poorest households will find that they can sacrifice some present living standards for a future gain. For example, presented with a profitable opportunity, villagers in Ghana planted cocoa plants at the start of the twentieth century, even though there was a seven-year growing period before any return could be expected.

Where social attitudes do not sanction the sacrifice of current living standards in order to generate a large volume of domestic saving, a government can impose compulsory saving, or seek to increase the national savings rate through fiscal and monetary policies. Unfortunately, even where the governments of developing countries have succeeded in raising their national savings rate, a large proportion of the savings was wasted in inefficient state-owned enterprises that could never become profitable. If the funds had been invested in the much-needed infrastructure that only a government can create, then government intervention might have been effective in encouraging development.

An important consideration is that in less developed countries one resource that is often *not* scarce is labour. Profitable home or village investment that requires mainly labour inputs may be made with relatively little sacrifice in current living standards. Unfortunately, this kind of investment frequently does not appeal to local governments, which are too often mesmerized by large and symbolic investments, such as dams, nuclear power stations, and steel mills.

Inadequate infrastructure

Key services such as transportation and a communications network, called **infrastructure**, are necessary for efficient commerce. Roads, bridges, railways, and harbours are needed to transport people, materials, and finished goods. Phone and postal services, a safe water supply, and sanitation are essential to economic development.

The absence, for whatever reason, of a dependable infrastructure can impose severe barriers to economic development.

Many governments feel that money spent on a new steel mill shows more impressive results than money spent on such infrastructure investments as automating the telephone system. Yet private, growth-creating, entrepreneurial activity will be discouraged more by the absence of good communications than by the lack of domestically produced steel.

Development policies

The past twenty-five or so years have seen a remarkable change in the views of appropriate policies for industrial development. The views that dominated development policies during the period from 1945 to the early 1980s have given way to a new set of views that reflect the experience of the earlier period.

The older view

The dominant views on appropriate development strategies from 1945 to the early 1980s were inward-looking and interventionist.

They were inward-looking in the sense that local industries were fostered primarily to replace imports. These local industries were usually protected with high tariffs, typically well over 100 per cent, and supported by large subsidies and favourable tax treatment. The exchange rate was almost always pegged, usually at an overvalued rate. As we saw in Chapter 29, fixing the exchange rate above its free-market level raises the prices of exports and lowers the prices of imports, which leads to an excess demand for foreign exchange. The argument for keeping export prices high was that foreign demand for traditional exports was inelastic. As we saw in Chapter 4, raising the prices of goods with inelastic demands raises the amount received by their sellers. The excess demand for foreign exchange caused by the overvaluation of the currency led to a host of import restrictions and exchange controls, such as import licences and quotas issued by government officials.

Many governments were hostile to foreign investment and made it difficult for multinational firms to locate in their countries. For example, many had local ownership rules, requiring that any foreign firm wanting to invest in the region must set up a subsidiary in which local residents would own at least half of the shares. Much new investment was undertaken by government-owned industries, while subsidization of privately owned local industries was often heavy and indiscriminate. Industrial activity was often controlled, with a licence being required to set up a firm or to purchase supplies of scarce commodities. Much investment was financed by local savings, sometimes voluntarily and sometimes enforced by the government. One method of enforcement was for a state marketing board to be empowered to buy all the outputs of traditional export industries at very low prices, sell them abroad at high prices, and use the profits so generated to finance government-owned industries. Often, as with cocoa in Ghana, the prices paid to farmers were too low to encourage them to be efficient, and government funds were wasted on grandiose but ultimately unprofitable projects.

The focus of commercial policy was on *import substitution*. Strictly, 'import substitution' refers to the attempt to build local industries behind protectionist walls to replace imports. Often, however, the term is used to refer to the set of related measures just described.

These interventionist measures gave great power to government officials, and not surprisingly corruption was rife. Bribes were needed to obtain many things, including state subsidies, licences, and quotas. As a result many resources were allocated to those who had the most political power and were willing to pay the highest bribes, rather than to those who could use the resources most efficiently.

Heavy subsidization of private firms and state investment in public firms required much money, and the tax structures of many poor countries could not provide sufficient funds. As a result, *inflationary finance* was often used.[6] Persistent inflation was a major problem in many of these countries. It was almost always in the two-digit range, and quite often soared to figures of several hundred per cent per year.

Most of the economies in which these policies were employed fell short of full central planning and full state ownership of resources. As a result there was still some private initiative and some profit-seeking through normal market means. But the overall policy thrust was interventionist and inward-looking.

The rise of the new view

During the 1980s four important events contributed to a reappraisal of this development model. First, the developing countries that had followed these policies most faithfully had some of the poorest growth records. Second, the GDP growth rates of the more industrialized countries of Eastern Europe and the Soviet Union that had followed interventionist, non-market approaches to their own growth were visibly falling behind those of the market-based economies. Third, Taiwan, Singapore, South Korea, and Hong Kong, which had departed from the accepted model by adopting more market-based policies, were prospering and growing rapidly. Fourth, the globalization of the world's economy led to an understanding that countries could no longer play a full part in world economic growth without a substantial presence of multinational corporations within their boundaries. Given the size of developing countries, this mainly meant the presence of foreign-owned multinationals. We discuss each of these four events in more detail in the next four sections.

The experience of the developing countries

Highly interventionist economies fared poorly in the 1950s, 1960s, and 1970s. Economies as varied as Argentina, Myanmar, Tanzania, Ethiopia, and Ghana were all interventionist and all grew slowly, if at all. In Ethiopia the emperor was overthrown, and the new government adopted rigid Soviet-style policies. Attempts to collectivize agriculture led, as they had fifty years earlier in the Soviet Union, to widespread famine. Some countries, such as Ghana and Nigeria, started from relatively strong economic positions when they first gained their independence, only to see their GDPs and living standards shrink. Other countries, such as India and Kenya, sought a middle way between capitalism and communism. They fared better than their more highly interventionist neighbours, but their development was still disappointingly slow.

The experience of the transition economies

Underdevelopment is as old as civilization. Concern with it as a remediable condition, however, became a compelling policy issue only within the twentieth century. One incentive behind this new attention to development was the apparent success of planned programmes of 'crash' development, of which the Soviet experience has been the most remarkable, and the Chinese the most recent. Not surprisingly, therefore, the early successes of the growth policies of many communist countries provided role models for many of the early development policies of the poorer countries. Their governments sought to copy the planning techniques that appeared to underlie these earlier successes.

In recent decades, however, the more developed communist countries began to discover the limitations of their

---

[6] Under inflationary finance, the government sells newly created bonds to the central bank, which pays for them with newly created money. The large increase in money supply creates rapid inflation, as we saw in Box 31.1 on page 578.

Table 34.3 **Growth in transition economies**

Country	Ave. % GDP growth, 1990–2001	GDP per head growth, 2000–01	Annual ave. inflation (GDP deflator), 1990–2001
Belarus	−0.8	4.4	318.1
China	10.2	6.5	6.2
Czech republic	1.1	3.6	10.6
Georgia	−5.6	4.6	279.0
Hungary	1.9	4.0	18.3
Lithuania	−2.3	4.3	63.3
Poland	4.5	1.2	21.4
Russia	−3.7	5.5	139.6
Ukraine	−7.9	10.0	220.9

Transition economies fall into two main groups. All experienced negative GDP growth in the first year or two of transition. One group, including Poland, Hungary and the Czech Republic, managed to achieve positive real growth for the rest of the 1990s with moderate inflation. The other group, including Georgia, Russia, and Ukraine, had negative GDP growth for most of the 1990s, accompanied by very rapid inflation, but all were exhibiting real growth in the first few years of this century. China, however, exhibited the best growth performance and lowest inflation, in part by not attempting to make the transition too rapidly.

Source: World Bank, *World Development Report 2003*.

planning techniques. Highly planned government intervention seems most successful in providing infrastructure and developing basic industries such as electric power and steel—where these are needed, and where the technology could be copied from more market-oriented economies. It is now seen to be much less successful in providing the entrepreneurial activity, risk-taking, and adaptability to change that are key ingredients to *sustained* economic growth and technological change.

The discrediting of the Soviet approach to development was given added emphasis when the countries of Eastern Europe and the former Soviet Union abandoned their system *en masse* and took the difficult path of rapidly introducing market economies. As Table 34.3 shows, some of the transition countries, e.g. Poland, Hungary and the Czech Republic, managed to turn in positive growth performances in the 1990s, but for many others (e.g. Russia, Ukraine, and Georgia) the 1990s were a time of rapidly declining real GDP and very high inflation. The reasons for the poor performance of these latter countries during their first decade of transition to market economies will take many years to determine, but a likely explanation is that they tried to move too fast to private ownership and market mechanisms before proper institutions to manage the new structure were put in place. Privatization, for example, created incentives for recipients of firms to asset-strip rather than invest in improvements and plan for the future. Whatever the explanation, however, the growth prospects of even the worst performing transition economies of the 1990s seemed to have improved substantially by the early 2000s. Negative growth rates had been turned around and virtually all transition economies were exhibiting positive growth. Box 34.3 outlines the problems

of making a transition from a centrally planned to a market economy.

Although China, the last major centrally planned economy to hold out (apart from Cuba and North Korea), has been posting impressive growth figures, two very 'non-communist' reasons are important in explaining this performance. First, over 90 per cent of the population is engaged in basically free-market agriculture—because that sector has long been free of the central planning apparatus that so hampered agriculture in the former Soviet Union. Second, while the state-controlled industries suffer increasing inefficiencies and absorb ever-larger proportions of the state budget in subsidies, a major investment boom has gone on in China's southeast coastal provinces. Here foreign investment, largely from Japan and the Asian NIEs, has introduced a rapidly growing, and highly efficient, industrialized market sector. Indeed, those who criticize the 'big bang' approach to transition that was adopted by many of the former Soviet bloc (and recommended to them by many Western advisers) point to China as an example of how to manage transition successfully, i.e. by a gradual process of adaptation, which avoids the massive output and infrastructure losses that occurred in those economies that tried to move too fast. None the less, the Chinese economy faces many current challenges that will have to be surmounted by effective policies over the next decade. These include a weak financial system with large amounts of unproductive loans made to the inefficient state owned industries; rising unemployment, as people flood from the farms to the cities in search of higher wages; and the absence of an urban social safety net, which was formerly provided by families in the country and the state industries in the towns, and which has not been replaced

Box 34.3 Transition economies: from plan to market

Between 1917 and 1950, countries containing one-third of the world's population seceded from the market economy and launched an experiment in constructing an alternative economic system. First in the former Russian Empire and Mongolia, then, after World War II, in Central and Eastern Europe and the Baltic States, and subsequently in China, northern Korea, and Vietnam (with offshoots and imitators elsewhere), a massive effort was made to centralize control of production and allocate resources through state planning. This vast experiment transformed the political and the economic map of the world and set the course of much of the twentieth century. Now its failure has set in motion just as radical a transformation, as these same countries change course, seeking to rebuild markets and reintegrate themselves into the world economy. . . .

The long-term goal of transition is the same as that of economic reforms elsewhere: to build a thriving market economy capable of delivering long-term growth in living standards. What distinguishes transition from reforms in other countries is the systemic change involved: reform must penetrate to the fundamental rules of the game, to the institutions that shape behavior and guide organizations. This makes it a profound social transition as well as an economic one. Similar changes have been needed in many other countries, and the transition experience is therefore of interest to them as well. But most of their reform programs pale in comparison to the scale and intensity of the transition from plan to market. . . .

The economic challenge of transition is daunting in itself. Planned economies were autarkic . . . none traded extensively with the world at large. Decades of bureaucratic allocation created serious distortions, with some sectors (particularly heavy industry) massively overbuilt and others (light industry and services) severely repressed; perhaps as much as a quarter of the Soviet economy served the military alone. Relative prices diverged greatly from market patterns, and this meant massive explicit or implicit subsidies among sectors. Energy, housing, public transport, and staple foods were extraordinarily cheap, whereas consumer manufactures, if available at all, were often shoddy. Pervasive shortages allowed firms to operate in sellers' markets and reduced incentives to improve quality. With near-complete state ownership, enterprises lacked the defined property rights that spur work effort and profitmaking in market economies. Firms had little reason to use inputs efficiently and strong incentives to hoard both labor and raw materials. Many firms added negative value; at world prices

the costs of their inputs would have exceeded the value of their output. The combination of dominant heavy industry, low energy prices, and wasteful use of inputs caused energy intensity to rise to several times its level in market economies and had harsh environmental impacts.

Transition must therefore unleash a complex process of creation, adaptation, and destruction. Queuing gives way to markets. The shortage economy gives way to an economy of vast choice, with repressed sectors and activities growing rapidly and overbuilt sectors contracting or adjusting. Property rights are formally established and distributed, and large amounts of wealth cease to be state owned and controlled. Old institutions and organizations evolve, or are replaced, requiring new skills and attitudes. And the relationship between citizens and the state changes fundamentally, with greater freedom of choice but also much greater economic risk. True, changes of a similar nature may be needed in many countries around the world. But in the transition economies the magnitudes are exponentially greater. For example, transition economies have privatized more than 30,000 large and medium-size enterprises in five years. In eleven years between 1980 and 1991 the rest of the world privatized fewer than 7,000. Countries will have completed their transition only when their problems and further reforms come to resemble those of long-established market economies at similar levels of income. (World Bank, *From Plan to Market, World Development Report 1996*, New York: Oxford University Press for the World Bank, June 1996)

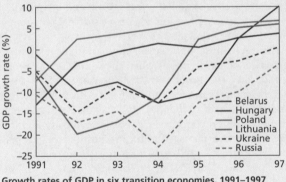

Growth rates of GDP in six transition economies, 1991–1997

by the welfare measures typically found in industrialized countries.

The experience of the NIEs

South Korea, Taiwan, Hong Kong, and Singapore are often called Asian Tigers. All of these have turned themselves from poor countries into relatively high-income, industrialized countries in the course of less than forty years.

During the early stages of their development, their governments used import restrictions to build up local industries and to develop labour forces with the requisite skills and experiences. In the 1950s and early 1960s, however, each of the four abandoned many of the interventionist aspects of the older development model. They created market-oriented economies with less direct government intervention than other developing economies that stuck with the accepted development model.

South Korea and Singapore did not adopt a *laissez-faire* stance. Instead, both followed quite strong policies that targeted specific areas for development and encouraged those areas with economic incentives. In contrast, Hong Kong had a much more *laissez-faire* attitude towards the direction of industrial development. Taiwan was somewhere between these extremes. In contrast to South Korea, it relied on small entrepreneurial firms rather than massive conglomerates; in contrast to Hong Kong, it assisted many infant industries. For example, the government initially developed the electronics sector through state-owned firms, which it transferred to private owners after they had become established.

After local industries had been established, all four of these countries adopted outward-looking, market-based, export-oriented policies. This tested the success of various policies to encourage specific industries by their ability to compete in the international marketplace. With industries designed to serve a sheltered home market, it is all too easy to shelter inefficiency more or less indefinitely. With export-oriented policies *not based on subsidies*, the success of targeted firms and industries is tested in international markets, and unprofitable firms fail.

Each country has experienced great successes and some failures of policy. Taiwan was typical in demonstrating the value of the new market-oriented approach when, in the period 1956–60, it abandoned most of the apparatus of the older development model and moved to market-oriented policies. Before long its growth rate increased, and it started on a path that has taken it from a per capita GDP of about 10 per cent of that of the United States in 1955 to one of over 50 per cent in the late 1990s. Today Taiwan has become a major foreign investor as its less skill-intensive industries migrate to mainland China and other locations in Southeast Asia. In Taiwan real wages have risen, making low-skill-intensive manufacturing uneconomic. Two responses have been apparent. First, local industries have moved to higher-value-added lines of production which can support higher wages and hence higher living standards for the workers. Second, Taiwanese firms have transferred much of their low-skilled production to China and thus have been major contributors to Chinese economic growth.

Not far behind the NIEs is a second generation of Asian and Latin American countries that have also adopted more market-oriented policies and have seen substantial growth follow; Thailand, the Philippines, Mexico, Chile, and Argentina are examples. Even Vietnam and Laos are liberalizing their economies as communist governments come to accept that a market economy is a necessary condition for sustained economic growth.

A setback in the success story of rapid growth by the NIEs of Southeast Asia occurred in and after the summer of 1997 with a major financial crisis. This affected all the countries in the region to some degree, but it was especially serious in Thailand, South Korea, and Indonesia. We discuss the events surrounding this crisis more fully in Chapter 35. There have also been discouraging setbacks in the two major South American countries of Brazil and Argentina.

Globalization of trade and investment by transnationals

At the heart of globalization lie the rapid reduction in transportation costs and the revolution in information technology that have characterized the last two decades. One consequence has been that the internal organization of firms, whether multinational or not, is changing to become less hierarchical and rigid, and more decentralized and fluid. Another consequence is that the strategies of transnational corporations (TNCs), which span national borders in their organizational structures, are driving globalization and much of economic development. Because most trade, and much investment, is undertaken by TNCs, no country can develop into an integrated part of the world economy without a substantial presence of TNCs within its borders. This is now recognized, and most aspiring developing countries generally put out a welcome mat for TNCs. A few countries, such as India, still put obstacles in the way of foreign investment; but even in these cases the attitudes are softening, so that foreign investment is increasingly tolerated, and even encouraged. Unfortunately, the new Indian government that took power after the 1998 elections re-adopted many of the long-discredited inward-looking policies, including higher tariffs and heavier restrictions on foreign investment.

In industries that sell undifferentiated products such as steel and paper, and in industries with substantial scale economies such as aircraft, production tends to be concentrated in the home country while the output is exported. In contrast, foreign direct investment (FDI) tends to be high in industries selling differentiated products not subject to major scale economies, which includes many consumer goods. The FDI allows the local market to be served with suitable product variations and often creates multidirectional trade in different varieties of the same basic product, much of which is intra-firm trade.

TNCs increasingly operate in high-tech sectors, in complex manufacturing, and in services. TNCs that produce in these sectors tend to concentrate in countries where the productivity of capital is high, the business environment is favourable, and other investors are present. This FDI is often undertaken by domestic firms that have built up some advantage in the local market, such as patents and know-how, that gives them advantages when they move into foreign markets.

Although some countries, such as Japan and Taiwan, did industrialize without major infusions of FDI, they did so before the globalization of the world's economy. It is doubtful that many (or any) of today's poor countries

Box 34.4 **The importance of foreign direct investment**

Foreign direct investment (FDI) provides a major source of capital which brings with it up-to-date technology. It would be difficult to generate this capital through domestic savings, and even if it were not, it would still be difficult to import the necessary technology from abroad, since the transfer of technology to firms with no previous experience of using it is difficult, risky, and expensive.

Over a long period of time FDI creates many externalities in the form of benefits available to the whole economy which the TNCs cannot appropriate as part of their own income. These include transfers of general knowledge and of specific technologies in production and distribution, industrial upgrading, work experience for the labour force, the introduction of modern management and accounting methods, the establishment of finance-related and trading networks, and the upgrading of telecommunications services. FDI in services affects the host country's competitiveness by raising the productivity of capital and enabling the host country to attract new capital on favourable terms. It also creates services that can be used as strategic inputs in the traditional export sector to expand the volume of trade and to upgrade production through product and process innovation.

By altering a country's comparative advantages and improving its competitiveness through technology transfer and the effects of myriad externalities, foreign as well as domestic investment can alter a country's volume and pattern of trade in many income-enhancing directions.

could achieve sustained, rapid growth paths without a substantial amount of FDI brought in by foreign-owned transnationals. Without such FDI, both the transfer of technology and foreign networking would be difficult to achieve.

Developing countries have gradually come to accept the advantages in dropping their traditional hostility to foreign direct investment. First, FDI often provides somewhat higher-paying jobs than might otherwise be available to local inhabitants. Second, it provides investment that does not have to be financed by local savings. Third, it links the local economy into the world economy in ways that would be hard to accomplish by new firms of a purely local origin. Fourth, it provides training in worker and management skills that come from working with large firms linked into the global market. Fifth, it can provide advanced technology that is not easily transferred outside of the firms that are already familiar with its use.

Today most developing countries encourage foreign TNCs to locate within their borders. Where governments used to worry that their countries had too much FDI, they now worry that there may be too little.

Box 34.4 discusses the place of foreign investment in development.

Elements of the new view

As a result of the above experiences, a new consensus on development policy emerged towards the end of the last century. The revised model calls for a more *outward-looking, international-trade-oriented, market-incentive-based route to development*. It calls for accepting market prices as an instrument for the allocation of resources. This means abandoning both the heavy subsidization and the pervasive regulations that characterized the older approach.

One of the most important parts of this new consensus is an acceptance of the beneficial role played by competition (in its broadest sense) as a defender of the public interest and as a stimulus to growth-creating innovation. The other side of the coin is a recognition of the harmful role played by monopolies (in the broadest sense), whether of private firms, closed-shop union agreements, communications media, government institutions, or government-owned industries.

Another important part of the consensus is that it is more efficient to locate economic activities in the private than in the public sector (unless there are compelling reasons for doing otherwise, as there may be with a range of 'social services' such as medical and hospital care). A number of reasons lie behind this presumption, including the incentives for efficiency when managers are responsible to owners who are risking their own wealth; the constraint provided by the need to be profitable, which acts as a rapid cut-off device when failure is evident; and the corrective for inefficiency provided by the possibility of a hostile takeover.

A view about the appropriate role of government is another part of the new consensus. Two basic classes of activity are important. First, the government needs to provide a framework for the market economy, which is given by such things as well-defined property rights secure from arbitrary confiscation; security and enforcement of contracts; law and order; a sound money; ensuring the basic rights of the individual to locate, sell, and invest where and how he decides; and the provision of infrastructure.

Second, state activity is needed to resolve conflicts of interest, to handle market failures, and to redistribute income in line with currently accepted ideas of social justice. Redistributive policies cannot be judged in isolation (nor can growth policies). Instead, they must be constantly scrutinized for their impacts on growth; where these are significant, trade-offs need to be consciously made.

The Washington Consensus

What is called the Washington Consensus describes the conditions that, according to the newer views, are necessary for a poorer country to get itself on a path of sustained development. These views are accepted by a number of international agencies, including the World Bank, the IMF, and several UN organizations. The main elements are as follows.

1. Sound fiscal policies are required. Large budget deficits financed by bonds sold to the central bank can lead to rapid inflation and financial instability. For example, Brazil ended an excellent growth performance largely as a result of unsound macro policies, though it later set up a new monetary policy regime that had considerable success in bringing inflation down.

2. The tax base should be broad, and marginal rates should be moderate.

3. Markets should be allowed to determine prices and the allocation of resources. Policies designed to affect resource allocation should work through price incentives rather than through either central planning or price-distorting interventions. Market forces should determine exchange rates. Trade liberalization is desirable; in particular, import licensing, with its potential for corruption, should be avoided.

4. The desirability of free trade is, however, subject to the qualification of the infant industry argument discussed in Chapter 33 above. This allows targeted protection for specific industries and a moderate general tariff of, say, 10–20 per cent to provide a bias towards widening the industrial base of a less developed country. Such protection should be for a specified period that is not easily extended.

5. In today's world, however, measures to insulate the home market by domestic protection should be held to the minimum possible level consistent with developing strategic clusters of new industries. Industrial development should rely to an important extent on local firms and on attracting FDI and subjecting it to a minimum of local restrictions that discriminate between local and foreign firms. (Of course, restrictions will be required for such things as environmental policies, but these should apply to all firms, whether foreign-owned or locally owned.)

6. An export orientation provides a powerful impetus to the development of national capabilities (as long as exports do not rely on permanent subsidies). It provides competitive incentives for the building of skills and technologies geared to world markets; it permits the realization of scale economies; it furnishes the foreign exchange required for needed imports of capital; and it provides access to valuable information flows from buyers and competitors in advanced countries.

7. Education, health (especially for the disadvantaged), and infrastructure investment are desirable forms of public expenditure. Creating the appropriate factors of production is critical to creating comparative advantages in products that can be exported. This means general education, trade schools, and other appropriate institutions for formal education as well as assistance to increase on-the-job training within firms. Because future demands are hard to predict and subject to rapid change, a balance must be struck between training for specific skills and training to develop generalized, and adaptive, abilities.

8. Finally, emphasis needs to be placed on the reduction of poverty, for at least two reasons. First, poverty can exert powerful anti-growth effects. People living in poverty will not develop the skills to provide an attractive labour force, and they may not even respond to incentives when these are provided; malnutrition in early childhood can affect a person's capacities for life. Second, although economic growth tends to reduce the incidence of poverty, it does not eliminate it. Commonly accepted views of equity call for some of the benefits of growth to be made available to those who do not gain from it through the normal operations of the market. Self-interest calls for avoiding growing inequality in the distribution of income as those who benefit from growth (including employed workers) enjoy rising incomes, while major groups are untouched by the growth process and suffer static or declining incomes.

Debate beyond the Washington Consensus

The basic Washington Consensus on outward-looking, market-oriented, fiscally sound economic policies provides what many people believe are necessary conditions for a country to achieve a sustained growth path in today's world—which in most cases will require that it is able to attract quite a large volume of FDI. None the less, there are two current debates about the applicability of this consensus. Does it describe a sufficient set of policies or only just a necessary set, and can it be interpreted in too extreme a fashion?

Sufficient or just necessary?

There has been substantial debate about one crucial issue: are the conditions of the Washington Consensus *sufficient* to encourage the kinds and volumes of both domestic and foreign investments needed to develop dynamic comparative advantages in higher-value-added industries, or are they merely *necessary*?

Some observers believe that they are sufficient. In their view all a country needs to do is to meet these conditions; then domestic savings will finance domestic investments, FDI will flow in, and a sustained growth path will be established. Other economists worry that many countries may have only limited ability to attract FDI, to benefit from it, and to create sufficient domestic investment, even after fulfilling the necessary conditions of the Washington Consensus. The latter set of economists point to the experience of some African countries in which TNCs operated extractive industries which despoiled the countryside and left little permanent benefit behind them; the corporations merely extracted the available resources and then left. Others point out that there is a major difference between purely extractive enterprises and manufacturing enterprises, the latter having more potential spillovers to the local economy than the former.

Such policies relate, in British economist John Dunning's words, to the 'interface between the global strategies of TNCs designed to advance corporate profitability and growth, and the strategies of national governments intended to promote the economic and social welfare of their citizens'.

Policies that go beyond the Washington Consensus are directed at *the interactions between governments and the private sector*, particularly as represented by TNCs.

Overly extreme application

A recent debate relating to the Washington Consensus has centred on the handling of crises by the IMF. Some argue that the policy changes required by the IMF in exchange for financial support tend to make the countries' problems worse. The basic argument is that the policies are applied to all countries, without recognition of individual circumstances that may temper their applicability, especially in the short run. For example, privatizing government-owned industries may make matters worse if the new owners merely sell the firm's assets abroad and leave its former employees without jobs where alternative employment does not exist. A summary of the criticisms and a response by the IMF Chief Economist is presented in Box 34.5.

Implications of modern growth theory

The key insight of the new growth theory is that *endogenous* technological innovation is the mainspring of economic growth. Things emphasized by economists for centuries, such as aggregate savings and investment, are still essential, but technological change is now seen to lie at the core of the growth process.

Technological change is a costly process, one that is undertaken mainly by firms in pursuit of profit and that responds to economic incentives. Research and development are in their nature highly risky and highly uncertain activities. The technological path followed by firms and industries is evolutionary in the sense that it develops as experiments and errors are made.

For developing countries one of the most important of the many new insights stemming from research into the growth process is that adopting someone else's technology is not a simple, costless task. Substantial R&D capacity is needed to adapt other people's technology to one's own purposes, and to learn how to use it. For one thing, much of the knowledge required to use a technology is tacit; it can be obtained only from learning by doing and learning by using. This creates difficulties in imitating the knowledge, as well as uncertainty regarding which modifications will work in any new situation. This is true even when technology moves from one firm to another in the same industry and the same country. It follows that not all knowledge is freely tradable. Neither a firm nor a government can go out and buy it ready to use. Acquiring *working* technological knowledge requires both investment (sometimes in large, indivisible lumps) and the experience that allows workers and management slowly to acquire the needed tacit knowledge. Box 34.6 discusses the diffusion process.

Usable new knowledge comes to a less developed country through a slow, costly diffusion process.

What may be needed

Some economists argue for active government policies that go beyond the Washington Consensus. Such policies work by developing the externalities that come from initial investment in the local economy, and that give benefits not captured by the firms that help to confer them. The policies also take account of the fact that technology is not bought in competitive markets and imported 'ready to go'. The recommended policies would thus do more than just attract FDI and create favourable market conditions. They would be designed to encourage the diffusion of technological capacities into the local economy so that all parts of the economy could benefit and grow. This requires the kind of public assistance that was provided in varying degrees by the governments of the Asian Tigers.

Experience suggests, however, that the appropriate set of policies is usually highly country-specific. What works well in one environment may fail in another. Many local details need to be assessed before appropriate policies can be designed for one country. These depend, among many other things, on location, size of economy, existing natural and human resources, infrastructure, social and cultural attitudes, and development stage.

Protection of the domestic market Policies that protect the domestic market for local firms can be useful at the early stages of development. Virtually every country that has moved to a sustained growth path in the past, including the United States, Canada, Japan, and all of the NIEs, has done so using import substitution in its early stages of industrialization. A protected home market provides a possible solution to the problem of coping with the enormous externalities involved in building up an infrastructure of physical and human capital as well as the required tacit knowledge and abilities. Even if not all the specific infants

Box 34.5 **The IMF and its critics**

In his book *Globalization and its Discontents*, 2001 Nobel Laureate Professor Joseph Stiglitz argued that

[the] IMF has made mistakes in all areas it has been involved in: development, crisis management, and in countries making the transition from communism to capitalism. Structural adjustment programs did not bring sustained growth even to those, like Bolivia, that adhered to its strictures; in many countries, excessive austerity stifled growth; successful economic programs require extreme care in sequencing—the order in which reforms occur—and pacing . . . mistakes in sequencing and pacing led to rising unemployment and increased poverty. After the 1997 Asian crisis, IMF policies exacerbated the crises in Indonesia and Thailand. . . . The collapse of Argentina in 2001 is one of the most recent of a series of failures over the past few years. . . . the result for many people has been poverty and for many countries social and political chaos. (London: Allen Lane/Penguin Press, 2002, p. 18)

In a reply to criticism of this kind, Kenneth Rogoff, the chief economist at the IMF, has written:

Many people view the International Monetary Fund as an agent of austerity. Indeed, the popularity of this view is surely one reason why left-leaning anti-Fund polemics sometimes sell well in bookshops, even while right-leaning critics call for the IMF to stop interfering with the natural selection process of market forces.

While the 'IMF promotes austerity' view has emotional appeal, in reality the opposite is true—and many Fund-supported programmes allow for sizeable budget deficits. Distressed emerging-market debtors come to the IMF precisely because its financial assistance, combined with the policies it supports, generally alleviates austerity rather than intensifying it.

Emerging-market debtors typically come to the IMF only when their finances are under extreme duress—usually through imprudence and bad luck—and other creditors have turned their backs. These countries would otherwise have no choice but to tighten their belts, cutting domestic spending relative to output through a mix of tax increases, expenditure cuts and higher interest rates. An IMF loan typically loosens the belt, both directly via added funds and indirectly by helping to stabilise markets. Saying the IMF causes austerity is like saying doctors cause plagues because you often find them around sick people.

There are some who think misguided IMF policies more than cancel out any good its limited resources bring. These critics say that if only the IMF understood its main task to be fighting recessions, it would be prescribing counter-cyclical policies for crisis countries, not restrictive policies. They claim that what creditors really want to see is growth. Ergo, the best way to defend a currency is by cutting interest rates to expand the economy. Similarly, if a country wants to calm creditors, it should be borrowing more money, not less. They think the resulting growth would alow the country to carry proportionately more debt. Were this true, crisis countries could have their cake and eat it. Indeed, why not just keep stuffing themselves?

Sadly, the clear weight of logic and evidence suggests the opposite. Surely, if it were feasible to fend off a crisis by simply borrowing more money and lowering interest rates, policy makers whose ears are close to markets would have figured it out by now.

Now, there is a real risk in any IMF programme that interest rates might be raised too sharply and the path of fiscal policy set too tight. If so, either the recession will be steeper than it has to be or, perhaps worse, the programme will be politically unsustainable and creditors will keep racing for the doors. Indeed, as the Asian crisis of 1997–98 evolved and it became clear that the economic downturn was worse than initially thought (not only by the IMF but also by just about everyone), the IMF changed its advice to allow fiscal policies to be less restrictive.

On the other hand, if the programme does not embody sufficiently ambitious targets, it will collapse for lack of credibility. In some of the 1990s crisis countries, for example, policies were relaxed prematurely, throwing programmes off course and postponing recovery. Given the delicate balancing act involved in re-establishing credibility after a crisis, it is no surprise that even the best-crafted IMF programme seems too loose to some and too tight to others.

One way the IMF could make its programmes systematically more expansionary is by extending the repayment horizon for its loans, now typically only a few years. Indeed, many purveyors of the austerity view seem to believe that all IMF loans should be for 40 years or more, the price supposedly being paid by rich countries that ought to be giving more aid through other channels anyway. But who would the real losers be? The IMF does not run for profit; it does not pay dividends to private shareholders. Instead, it continually recycles the money repaid by one developing country to help others. If IMF money were recycled only every 40 years instead of every three or four, the Fund's limited resources would quickly be tied up. And who would be around to help countries engulfed in the next emerging market financial crisis?

The IMF is not perfect and it has made mistakes. We need to find ways to improve the trade-off that crisis countries face in the short term between restoring credibility and restoring growth. But the naïve view that the IMF goes around advocating austerity where none is called for denies policy trade-offs that are real—and confuses correlation with causation. (*Financial Times*, 27 September 2002, p. 21)

---

that are protected by the import substitution policy grow into self-sufficient adults, the externalities may still be created and become available for a second generation of more profitable firms.

Protection of the home market from international competition can, however, pose serious problems unless it is selective and temporary. Investment may occur mainly in areas where comparative advantage never develops. High costs of protected industries may create a lack of competitiveness of other domestic industries whose inputs are the outputs of the protected industries. Potential comparative advantages may not be exploited because of the distorting

Box 34.6 The importance of diffusion

In the past, one reason for making a clear distinction between the economics of developed and developing countries arose from the belief that advanced countries grew by innovating in new technologies while poorer countries grew by copying technologies from the advanced countries—that is, from the diffusion of technologies that had been fully developed in the advanced countries. If this were so, then the economics of growth in advanced countries would be the economics of innovation, while the economics of growth in poorer countries would be the economics of diffusion. This view was in line with early theories of technological change, which assumed that a new technology was invented and put in place in fully developed form by some innovator and that its use then diffused in more or less unchanged form to other firms, industries, and countries.

Modern research into invention, diffusion, and innovation has shown that this clear line does not exist in reality. A new technology almost always comes into existence in rudimentary form with few uses and high operating costs. As the technology is used, it is developed continually, and its costs of operation fall while the quality of its performance and the range of its application rise.

For example, electronic computers were first developed for military applications during the early 1940s. By modern standards these early computers were extremely limited in what they could do and were both slow and costly in doing it. When the first commercial applications were developed at the end of the Second World War, the world demand was thought to be for about twelve computers! The efficiency of computers was increased slowly over the decades, and it made a quantum leap when transistors were substituted for vacuum tubes as the switching device. At the same time, the costs were lowered and the range of applications was increased as computers became more varied and more flexible. These were not small improvements, but orders-of-magnitude changes occurring every few years. Today the product that was a technological curiosity fifty years ago is revolutionizing all of production, distribution, design, and just about every other economic activity.

A similar story can be told about the aeroplane. Its modern story began in 1903 with the first heavier-than-air flight (covering less than 100 yards). The aeroplane became really successful commercially in 1936 with the introduction of the DC3. It improved through slow design changes and discontinuous innovations, such as the replacement of piston engines with jets, until by the 1970s it had become the dominant method of transporting people over long distances.

So the diffusion of technologies is not just a flow that goes from advanced to less advanced nations. Diffusion is a key part of technological change in advanced as well as developing nations, and it follows similar patterns in each.

In any one high-income nation most of the technological advances that come into use have been originally developed in other nations. Indeed, a small subset of the advanced nations does most of the development of fundamental new technologies, which then diffuse to other high-income countries, being adapted and improved in the process.

It is true that a country just beginning to move from a subsistence to a market economy can grow quickly by adopting technologies developed elsewhere (and adapting them to local conditions), but it is not true that the world's growth problems can be understood simply in terms of the conditions needed to invent technologies in rich countries and those needed to copy them in poor countries. Since many of the processes that govern the flow of technology and capital between rich and poor countries also govern the flows among rich countries (and among sectors in each rich country), it is clear that many problems will be similar in the two groups of countries. Of course, institutional arrangements will affect the diffusion and improvement of both major and minor innovations in developing countries. But they also do so in developed countries, where forces such as competition policy, industrial concentration, national attitudes to risk-taking, support of R&D, and the organization of university research are thought to influence the development and diffusion of new technologies.

---

effects of existing tariffs, and, as always, consumers bear much of the cost through high prices of protected outputs.

Innovation policies Other methods of building an industrial and R&D capacity include the much-needed public investment in infrastructure and human capital and many other things, such as the provision of adequate financial schemes to favour investment in physical and intangible assets; procurement and tax incentives; provision of technical and marketing information; consulting services for assisting firms in industrial restructuring and in the adoption of new technologies and organizational techniques; support services in design, quality assurance, and standards; schemes for training and retraining personnel; and facilities for start-up companies.

Those who advocate such a policy package stress the importance of having the above incentives operate as a part of a more general innovation and competition policy in order to encourage technological transfer to the local economy. Linkages among firms, and between firms and universities and research institutions, both within the country and in the rest of the world, are also important.

Policies that encourage the development of small and medium-sized enterprises are important to any development strategy. These tend to be locally owned and to be the vehicle by which know-how and best practices are transferred from TNCs to the local economy. They are also in the sector most vulnerable to excessive red tape, rules and regulations, profit taxes, and other interference that raises the cost of doing business.

A cautionary note There is no doubt that the governments of many poor countries have been highly interventionist—and some still are. Thus, a good first strategy is often to diminish the government's place in the economy. There is no point adopting a new, relatively rational, technology promotion strategy if existing government interventions are irrational and heavy. What is needed is to clear away unproductive interventions first. This does not however imply that, if a government were starting from scratch, the best objective would be to minimize its place in the economy.

Whatever methods are chosen, selective intervention is a delicate instrument, highly dangerous when used by inept hands; even when it is used by practised hands, much damage can be done.

Even those who advocate intervention accept that it needs to be carefully tailored to get specific results and to reduce the opportunities for small groups to gain at the expense of others. They also agree that as a rule most assistance should be terminated after a specified period. Others feel that the risks are too great and would not take government policy beyond the Washington Consensus.

Liberalization of capital flows

Another controversy has surrounded the issue of controls on capital flows in developing countries. The view associated with the Washington Consensus is that countries are better off eliminating all exchange controls and permitting free flow of financial capital. This encourages an integration of domestic and international financial markets and gives access of domestic firms to world capital markets.

The critics point out, however, that many of the major industrial countries preserved restrictions on capital flows until very recently, so it is unreasonable to impose unrestricted capital flows on countries that have less sophisticated financial markets. Virtually all of the financial crises in developing countries in the past decade were associated with a sudden reversal of capital flows. During the Asian crisis of 1997 Malaysia was widely criticized for introducing capital controls, but the result of this was that the impact of the crisis on Malaysia was much less than on many other countries. Hence it is argued that countries should not rush to liberalize their international capital transactions until their domestic economies and financial systems can sustain a free flow of financial capital.

Next steps

The UN summit of 2002 reiterated the world development goals established in the 1990s. The targets set for 2015 (or earlier where stated) are:

- Reduce by half the proportion of people living in extreme poverty (less that $1 per day).
- Ensure universal primary education.
- Eliminate gender disparity in primary and secondary education (by 2005).
- Reduce infant and child mortality by two-thirds.
- Reduce maternal mortality by three-quarters.
- Ensure universal access to reproductive health services.
- Implement national strategies for sustainable development in every country by 2005, so as to reverse the loss of environmental resources by 2015.

SUMMARY

The uneven pattern of development

■ About one-quarter of the world's population still exists at a level of bare subsistence, and over 80 per cent live in countries with income per head that is less than 20 per cent of income per head in the USA. Although some poorer societies have grown rapidly, the gap between the very richest and the very poorest remains large and is not decreasing.

Restraints on economic development

■ Impediments to economic development include excessive population growth; resource limitations; inefficient use of resources, particularly those that are related to X-inefficiency; inadequate infrastructure; excessive government intervention; and institutional and cultural patterns that make economic growth difficult.

Development policies

■ The older model for development policies included (a) heavy tariff barriers and a hostility to foreign direct investment to protect the home market for local firms; (b) many government controls over, and subsidization of, local activities; and (c) exchange rates pegged at overly high values with imports regulated by licences.

■ During the 1980s many governments became sceptical of this model after observing (a) the poor growth performances both of the planned economies and of those developing countries that adhered closely to this model; (b) the good performances of those that did not follow the model; and (c) the globalization of the world economy, which made transnational corporations and foreign direct investment increasingly important. Today no developing country can play a part in the global trading system without some significant presence of TNCs within its borders.

■ The newer view holds that (a) heavy indiscriminate protection of home markets should be avoided; (b) protection that does exist should be targeted to sectors that have a real chance of creating comparative advantage, and should be for only a moderate period of time so that market tests of success and failure can be allowed to operate; (c) competition is an important spur to efficiency and innovation; (d) quantitative controls should be avoided and exchange rates set at a market-clearing value; and (e) production of most goods and services should be in the private sector, except where there are strong reasons for preferring the public sector, as might be the case in, say, medical and health services.

■ Part of this new view is given in the Washington Consensus, which calls for (a) sound fiscal and monetary policies; (b) broadly based taxes, levied at moderate rates; (c) market determination of prices and quantities; (d) discriminating use of infant industry protection for moderate time-periods; (e) an acceptance of FDI and the presence of TNCs; (f) active government provision of education, health care, and infrastructure; and (g) anti-poverty programmes to help in human resource development and to aid those who are left behind by the growth process.

■ An active debate turns on whether the conditions of the Washington Consensus are sufficient, or just necessary, to establish a country on a sustained growth path. Those who regard them as sufficient feel that, once unleashed, natural market forces will create sustained growth. Those who regard the conditions of the Washington Consensus as just necessary point to substantial externalities and pervasive market failures in the diffusion of technological knowledge from advanced to less advanced nations. They argue that foreign firms will not invest enough because they cannot capture in their profits many of the benefits they confer on the local economy (externalities), and that much of the technological know-how will not diffuse to local firms because such knowledge is not easy to transfer (market failure). These economists call for active government innovation policies to augment investment and to assist in the transfer of technological know-how and practice to the local economy.

TOPICS FOR REVIEW

■ Barriers to development
■ The vicious circle of poverty
■ NIEs

■ TNCs and FDI
■ The Washington Consensus
■ Externalities and market failures in the diffusion of technology

DISCUSSION QUESTIONS

1 Outline the factors that contribute to holding back the growth of some countries even though they are abundant in natural resources.

2 Discuss some of the reasons for the success of countries like Singapore and Taiwan, which have grown rapidly in the last few decades despite a limited endowment of natural resources.

3 Why is foreign investment important in the development process?

4 Is growth in the developing world good or bad for the developed economies, and vice versa?

5 Critically assess the policies proposed under the Washington Consensus.

Chapter 35

GLOBAL MACROECONOMICS IN ACTION

In this final chapter you will find that macroeconomic analysis can help you to understand some events and policy issues that were current in the early 2000s. Many of these issues will continue to be important in years to come, and others are sure to emerge. The point to note is that our analytical tools help us to understand a wide range of economic phenomena *in all parts of the world*. There is no such thing as British economics or American economics. There is just economics, and it helps us to understand events anywhere. Of course, institutions and cultures differ around the world, and a well trained economist needs to be able to incorporate these local differences into his or her analysis in order to derive correct conclusions. In particular, we focus on the following applications:

• In Japan the macro policy options were heavily constrained in the late 1990s and early 2000s by the fact that the economy was in recession but interest rates were already close to zero and so could not be set any lower.

• In Europe the creation of the single currency, the euro, in 1999 has created a whole new set of macro policy problems for the first decades of this century—problems that have not been experienced in recent history in quite this form. Twelve countries suddenly became subject to a 'one-size-fits-all' monetary policy regime, and at the same time constraints were imposed on fiscal deficits. In such circumstances can there be any stabilization policy at all?

• The financial crisis in Southeast Asia that broke out in late 1997 and continued for several years in some countries illustrates the interaction of domestic economic management with the global capital markets. It also provides lessons for all economies in the modern world of internationally mobile finance.

• Countries of South America have had periodic crises over the last three decades. We focus especially on the crisis in Argentina in 2002, which was triggered by lack of co-ordination between monetary and fiscal policies and an attempt to peg the domestic currency rigidly to the US dollar.

• The US stockmarket boom in the late 1990s and bust in the early 2000s, which created big swings in asset prices and personal wealth, gave rise to a debate about what role asset prices should play in macro policy. A similar issue has arisen in the UK: should house prices affect monetary policy, or is it only the prices of currently produced goods and services that matter?

• Finally, we discuss some world-wide phenomena that are important for all countries. These include the trend to lower world-wide inflation that was evident in the early 2000s; the implications for world real interest rates of fiscal consolidation, that is, reduction or elimination of government budget deficits, in most of the major countries of the world; and the effects of globalization on the world business cycle.

Japan in the early 2000s: the liquidity trap revived?

Japan has been one of the most successful economies of the post-Second World War period. It experienced spectacular growth rates of real GDP in the 1950s and 1960s averaging nearly 10 per cent. This rapid growth moderated somewhat in the 1970s, but in the ten-year period 1979–88 Japan still had the highest average growth rate of all the major industrial countries at 3.8 per cent, compared with an average for the seven major industrial countries (the G7) of 2.9 per cent. In the next ten years, 1989–98, however, Japanese economic growth at 2.4 per cent had fallen very close to the G7 average of 2.2 per cent. Then in 1998–2002 Japan had the *lowest* rate of economic growth of all the major economies.

The general prospects for the Japanese economy in the medium term appeared quite good—by 2000 Japan had

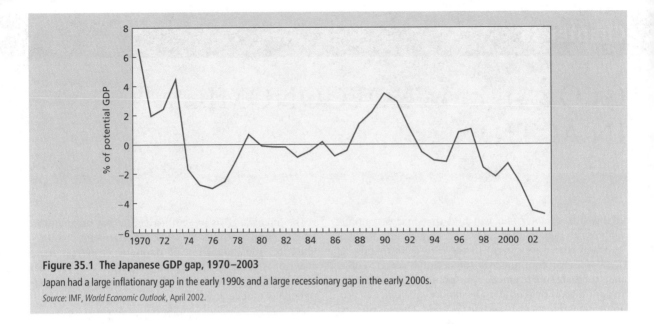

Figure 35.1 The Japanese GDP gap, 1970–2003

Japan had a large inflationary gap in the early 1990s and a large recessionary gap in the early 2000s.

Source: IMF, *World Economic Outlook*, April 2002.

attained a level of real GDP per capita that was about 85 per cent of the US level, and it could expect to continue growing on average at rates no lower than those experienced by other mature economies, around 2.5 per cent—or better, given Japan's high saving rate. The problem for Japan was mainly a cyclical one, compounded by problems in the financial system, associated partly with adjustments to the new slower growth environment.

We look first at the course of the Japanese economy in terms of its actual and projected output gap. We then consider some of the main elements of the 'shocks' that brought the problem about. Finally, we consider the difficulties faced by policy-makers in trying to rectify the situation.

The output gap

Figure 35.1 shows IMF data for the GDP gap for Japan from 1970 to 2003, with the 2002 and 2003 figures being forecasts. The facts are clear. Japan's GDP was slightly above potential 1996 and 1997. It fell below potential in 1998 and remained there through until 2001 and was projected by the IMF to fall further below potential in 2002 and 2003.

This created a serious economic crisis for a country that had experienced fast growth and high employment levels for the previous four decades. In May 2002 unemployment reached 5.4 per cent, the highest level since the Second World War, and seemed to be heading higher still. This may not seem like a high unemployment rate by the standards of other countries, but disguised unemployment is thought to be high in Japan, so that its figures are difficult

to compare with those of other countries, and the real level of unemployment was probably much higher.

Where did the crisis come from?

Asset prices

The problems of the Japanese economy in the second half of the 1990s and early 2000s were to an important extent a product of the extreme success of the Japanese economy in the previous four decades. Rapid real growth became the norm, and expectations of continued rapid growth got built into market prices. In 1991 the Japanese stock market index peaked at around 38,000, but by August 1998 it stood at around 15,000 and in October 2002 it was around 8,500—less than a quarter of its peak value. This collapse of share prices was mirrored in property prices, which also fell dramatically in the second half of the 1990s and early 2000s.

Assets prices are an important influence on spending decisions. We discussed in Chapter 23 the importance of wealth effects on consumer spending and we discuss below the impact of stock prices in the United States. As wealth rose in the 1980s Japanese consumers felt very well off, and they increased their spending on both consumer goods and property. However, the collapse of wealth had the reverse effect, causing them to cut their spending and feel increasingly cautious about the future.

Asset prices are also very important in spending decisions of companies and lending decisions by banks. Companies with a high stock market value find it easier to raise more

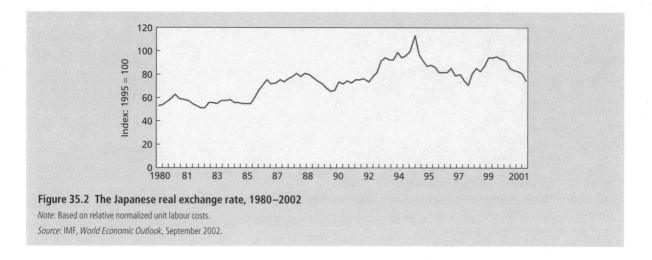

Figure 35.2 The Japanese real exchange rate, 1980–2002

Note: Based on relative normalized unit labour costs.

Source: IMF, *World Economic Outlook*, September 2002.

capital, and banks are happy to lend on the basis of high property values or share holdings. Banks in Japan also hold shares in companies directly, so a fall in share values affects the capital of the banks, and thereby their ability to make further loans.

Thus, falling assets prices and falling spending and loss of confidence create a process that can spiral downwards for some time. Some elements of this downward spiral are evident in any recession. However, in Japan in the late 1990s the situation was worse than a normal cyclical recession because of the abnormally large falls in asset prices. This experience was labelled by American economist Irving Fisher (1867–1947) as a situation of **debt deflation**.

The process of debt deflation will not go on for ever, but it may take the economy into a very deep recession before it is reversed. At some stage, however, goods and asset prices fall to a level so low that they appear cheap. Consumers start spending again, and firms want to invest. Once confidence returns, the interaction of the multiplier and the accelerator (see Box 28.3 on page 506) help to run any initial increase in spending into an upturn as the spiral starts in an upward direction. In an open economy like Japan, this process can be reinforced by swings in the exchange rate.

The exchange rate

One further important element of the Japanese situation is the path of the Japanese real exchange rate. As Figure 35.2 shows, the real exchange rate for Japan rose steadily from the early 1980s up to the mid-1990s. This meant that Japanese goods became expensive relative to competitors' goods. This made it difficult for Japanese producers to compete in world markets, so they increasingly produced overseas and sourced their inputs in other countries.

In effect, the high real exchange rate added to the deflationary forces in the domestic economy, as domestic firms switched their investments overseas and net exports were lower than they otherwise would have been.

In Chapter 29 we discussed the concept of purchasing power parity (PPP). We argued that PPP was likely to hold approximately in the long run, because in a global economy one country's prices cannot diverge increasingly from prices elsewhere in the world. For a long time it seemed that this prediction did not apply to Japan, as the Japanese real exchange rate appreciated steadily through the 1980s and early 1990s. However, it now seems likely that Japan will not prove to be an exception once recent years are taken into account. Since 1995 the Japanese real and nominal exchange rates have fallen back sharply from their peak. In 1995 the nominal exchange rate of the yen reached a peak against the US dollar of about ¥85 per dollar. In 2002 it had settled at around ¥120 per dollar.

Policy responses

Given the overall scenario of an economy exhibiting a large negative GDP gap, what could the Japanese authorities do to help improve the situation? The main policy tools at their disposal are the monetary and fiscal policy instruments that we have discussed extensively in our analysis of macroeconomics.

Monetary policy

A standard monetary policy intervention involves the authorities changing the interest rate at which they will lend to the money markets. In Japan this is the official discount rate. For an economy in recession, a monetary policy reaction that was intended to stimulate the economy would involve lowering the interest rate.

Figure 35.3 shows that the Japanese monetary authorities did indeed lower their interest rate steadily from 1991.

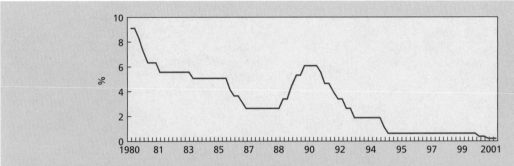

Figure 35.3 The Japanese official discount rate, 1991–2002

The Japanese official discount rate was 0.5 per cent from the end of 1995 to the end of 2000. It was then lowered to 0.25 per cent for two quarters and from mid-2001 was at 0.1 per cent.

Source: IMF, *World Economic Outlook*, April 2002.

This was almost certainly an attempt to moderate the rise in the real exchange rate, rather than to stimulate output directly, as at that time the Japanese economy was above potential GDP. However, in the late 1990s and early 2000s, when the economy was running well below potential, there was no room to lower interest rates further. At this stage the problem became a somewhat unusual one. *When interest rates have already been pushed down as low as they can go, what can the monetary authorities do in order to stimulate aggregate demand?* The answer is: not much, with monetary policy tools.

This problem was encountered during the recession of the early 1930s, and it was extensively discussed in debates associated with the Keynesian revolution. The problem was known as the **liquidity trap**. It arises when interest rates are so low that nothing more can be done to stimulate spending via even lower rates. If investors cannot be encouraged to invest when interest rates are close to zero, it is not clear what else the monetary authorities can do to increase aggregate demand.

Even if the government were simply to print more money and give it to people,[1] in a liquidity trap this does not necessarily increase spending, as people may simply save the money (owing to lack of confidence in the future). Keynes described this powerlessness of monetary policy in a liquidity trap as like trying to move an object by 'pushing on a string'.

In the postwar period most economists in the major economies had dismissed the liquidity trap as a phenomenon that was possible in theory but did not arise in practice. Clearly this is a rare occurrence, but it does help to explain the problems of Japan in the late 1990s and early 2000s.

Fiscal policy

When monetary policy becomes powerless, fiscal policy is an alternative. Cuts in taxes and increases in spending by the government can create public demand where private demand is lacking.

In the 1980s Japanese fiscal policy was generally designed to reduce aggregate demand, but from 1992 to 1996 it was stimulatory. In 1997 fiscal policy was tightened sharply, but by late 1997, when the Asian crisis broke out (see below), it became clear that Japan was heading into a major slowdown. In April 1998 the Japanese government announced a package of fiscal stimuli in addition to some financial support for weak financial institutions. The net effect of the fiscal package was claimed to be a boost to demand by about 2–3 per cent of GDP, though some commentators thought that the effect would be less, and the net effect did little more than reverse the tightening of the previous year. In any event, the fiscal stimulus was insufficient to keep Japan from recession. The budget deficit rose to 8 per cent of GDP in 2002, but much of this was the product of lower tax revenues as output growth slowed. By 2002 government debt had reached 140 per cent of GDP, well above what is generally considered prudent. So there seems to be limited scope for further fiscal stimulus.

The Japanese economy exhibited a severe recessionary gap in the late 1990s and early 2000s. Monetary policy actions were constrained by the fact that interest rates could go no lower, and the fiscal authorities were unable or unwilling to introduce a major fiscal stimulus. Hence Japan seemed likely to rely on the automatic adjustment mechanisms to return it to potential output, but this seems likely to leave the Japanese economy well below potential up to at least the mid-2000s.

---

[1] In practice, the monetary authorities would not usually literally print money and spend it; rather, as we explained in Chapters 27 and 28, they would buy long-term government debt with high-powered money. This increases the liquidity of both the public and the banks, with possible positive effects on spending.

Structural reforms

Monetary and fiscal policies are the main macro stabilization tools available, but many observers believe that some structural reforms in the Japanese economy could also be helpful, at least in the medium term. There are three main areas in which structural reforms have been suggested. First, the Japanese banking system needed reform because too many banks had too many outstanding bad loans and low-valued assets, which put them in a weak position to finance new investment. This position was compounded by the complicated links between banks and industrial conglomerates, which made it hard to assess the performance of banks independently of the corporations to which they were linked. Restructuring of banks would be politically difficult but beneficial to economic performance in the long run.

The second area of proposed structural reform is agriculture. The OECD has estimated that producer subsidies to agriculture in Japan amount to about 70 per cent of the value of agricultural production. These subsidies include direct subsidies, cheap loans, and guaranteed prices. They benefit about 2 per cent of the population who work on the land at the expense of the remaining 98 per cent of the population. Consumers would gain substantially from cheaper food prices if subsidies and protection were removed. Increases in food imports would also reduce the current account surplus and lower the exchange rate, thereby giving a stimulus to domestic industry.

The third area in which structural reform could help the Japanese economy is in distribution. Japan has a highly restricted and inefficient system of wholesale and retail distribution. If the authorities were to permit free entry of new firms into the distribution sector, this would lower consumer prices and stimulate domestic demand, improving the prospects for a return to more rapid GDP growth.

Of course, structural reforms need time to take effect, and they generate losers as well as winners. The net gains they can bring are often not evident for many years or even decades. However, postponement can do little but add to inefficiencies in an already struggling economy.

Stabilization policy in the euro zone

In January 1999 twelve EU member states embarked upon a monetary experiment. They established a single common currency for all their countries, the euro, with a single common monetary authority, the European Central Bank.[2] We have discussed the monetary operations of the ECB in Chapter 28. Here we consider how monetary and fiscal policies can be used for stabilization of the euro zone economies under the new regime.

Monetary policy

As mentioned in Chapter 28, monetary policy is targeted on achieving price stability in the euro zone as a whole. Price stability is defined as inflation of 2 per cent or less in the harmonized index of consumer prices (HICP) for the euro zone as a whole, and there is a reference value for the growth rate of euro area M3 of 4.5 per cent.[3] The ECB aims to tighten monetary policy by raising interest rates when, according to their judgement, there is inflationary pressure, and it aims to relax monetary policy by lowering interest rates when there is deflationary pressure.

In effect, the ECB tries to assess whether there is an inflationary gap or a deflationary gap for *the euro zone as a whole*, and it responds by either tightening or loosening monetary policy. In this way it performs the same exercise that the member country monetary authorities individually (under floating exchange rate regimes) were performing, but now it does it as if the euro zone were one country. Thus, monetary policy is an important tool for controlling aggregate demand across the whole euro zone, but it is powerless to affect the relative aggregate demands among member states. In the same way, the UK Monetary Policy Committee sets interest rates for the whole of the United Kingdom but is unable to exert any differential influence over monetary conditions between Yorkshire and Scotland.

Such monetary policy may be effective if the countries of the euro zone are hit by common shocks and move more or less together. However, monetary policy will be powerless to help correct the imbalance if one member country is in recession while other member countries are booming.

Monetary policy in the euro zone has to be aimed at the behaviour of euro zone aggregates and to ignore individual country differences.

This may not be as bad as it seems, because it may be better than the situation that ruled under ERM, where monetary policy was in effect set by Germany largely with German conditions in mind. However, it does mean that some other method is needed to cope with shocks to one

---

[2] Strictly, it is the European System of Central Banks (ESCB), which is made up of the central banks of each euro zone member plus the ECB; however, monetary policy is made by the ECB.

[3] The reference value is not a target, but rather a statement that growth higher than this for long periods will be considered problematic.

country that do not affect others. Here one might think that fiscal policy could be used to fill the gap; however, severe restrictions have been placed on fiscal policy discretion as well.

Fiscal policy: the Stability and Growth Pact

The Maastricht Treaty of 1992 required potential members of the euro zone to get their budget deficits below 3 per cent of GDP in order to qualify for membership. Subsequently an agreement was reached, known as the Stability and Growth Pact, that extended indefinitely the commitment to keep deficits below 3 per cent.

Countries are allowed to breach the 3 per cent limit 'in exceptional and temporary circumstances'. A government deficit greater than 3 per cent of GDP is considered 'exceptional and temporary' if it results from an unusual event outside the control of the member state in question or from a severe economic downturn, provided also that, once the temporary cause has passed, EU Commission projections for the following year forecast the deficit to fall back to 3 per cent or less. A decline in GDP of 2 per cent or more in one year will as a rule be regarded as a severe downturn.

Countries that are identified as having excessive deficits can be subject to financial penalties, though they have a further year in which to remove the excess deficit after being warned. Sanctions have not so far been imposed on any country, but there is a possibility that fines may be imposed.

IMF staff have calculated that an average EU country that had a fiscal balance when its GDP was at its potential level would tend to reach a 3 per cent deficit with a GDP gap of around 5 per cent of GDP. (Recall that tax revenues fall as GDP falls and some government expenditures, like unemployment benefit, rise.) This means that automatic stabilizers could accommodate a fluctuation of up to 5 per cent of GDP around trend while meeting the limits of the Stability and Growth Pact, and this is well within the normal range of business cycle fluctuations.

Thus, so long as member states have a fiscal balance when the economy is at potential GDP—a situation referred to as one of *structural balance*—budget deficits will be able to rise during recessions and fall during booms without breaching the 3 per cent limit. However, problems will be caused if member states change their fiscal stance, and it remains to be seen whether any member will really end up being fined or whether some political fudge will be resorted to. It would be ironic if the outcome were to increase political tensions when the aim of the single currency is to enhance the integration of EU member states.

It is tempting to conclude that the Stability and Growth Pact will leave member states with very severe restrictions on their fiscal freedom. However, the restrictions under the new regime may actually be less severe than in the recent past, when governments have been trying to eliminate high budget deficits in order to meet the Maastricht criteria. As an IMF assessment put it,

In any event, concerns about the potentially constraining effects on countries' abilities to pursue countercyclical fiscal policies need to be put into the perspective of the constraints imposed by large deficits in most EU countries over much of the past twenty-five years. From this viewpoint, the increased discipline involved in adhering to the pact may well permit a greater stabilizing role for fiscal policy than has been possible in most of these countries in many years. At the same time, the achievement of a high degree of price stability, together with the focus of the European System of Central banks on conditions throughout the euro area (in contrast to the dominant influence of German economic conditions on monetary policy in countries participating in the exchange rate mechanism (ERM)), should allow monetary policy to play a greater stabilizing role than in the past for the euro area as a whole.[4]

The single currency in Europe poses new challenges for monetary and fiscal policies. Monetary policy is 'one-size-fits-all', and the Stability and Growth Pact restrains fiscal policy. It remains to be seen whether the outcome will be better or worse than under the previous regime.

One reason why policy may be better in future than it has been in the past is that policy-makers have often made mistakes. It would be an error to compare regimes on the assumption that policy changes in the past have always been stabilizing. In practice, mistimed policy interventions have often made the business cycle worse. Hence the merging of monetary policy under the aegis of one authority and the restraints on budget deficits may improve the policy outcome *simply by making it harder for governments to get it wrong.* As US Nobel laureate Robert Solow once said, 'If you don't know what you're doing, don't do much of it!'

At the time of writing, however, it seems unlikely that the existing combination of monetary and fiscal restraints can remain unchanged. Here are two recent newspaper commentaries. The first compares the problems in Germany with those in Japan (discussed above), and the second points out that the fiscal restrictions are affecting other countries as well as Germany.

Both Japan and Germany have lost control over real short-term interest rates. For Japan, this is because nominal short rates have reached the lower limit of zero and inflation is stuck in negative territory. For Germany, the European Central Bank has to set interest rates to achieve price stability across all euro zone countries. Though the cause is different, the effect is the same: interest rates are too high for both Germany and Japan. . . . Both Germany and Japan also suffer from high real effective exchange rates. Japan's persistently high current account surplus prevents a meaningful decline in the yen's exchange rate. Meanwhile, Germany's exchange rate has been irrevocably fixed against its

---

[4] IMF, *World Economic Outlook*, October 1997, p. 59.

main trading partners within the euro zone . . . so the two countries suffer from inappropriately tight monetary conditions. Both countries are also unable aggressively to stimulate the economy via a loosening of the fiscal stance. Japan cannot afford to do so because the size of its deficit is already high. In the face of zero nominal growth and an already high debt to GDP ratio, Japan is under pressure to reduce its deficit. Germany's flexibility is cramped by the euro zone's growth and stability pact, which requires Germany to prevent its high fiscal deficit from rising further. (David Barker, *Financial Times*, 18 September 2002, p. 19)

Europe is coming under increasing pressure to reform its controversial rules on tax and spending, amid growing signs that four of its largest economies will breach tough Brussels standards this year. France, Germany, Italy, and Portugal are all running perilously close to the 3 per cent ceiling on government deficits laid down in Europe's Stability and Growth Pact. Analysts believe that the global slowdown will provide the biggest test yet for the contentious economic agreement, and could be the catalyst for fundamental reform. (Lea Paterson, *The Times*, 10 September 2002, p. 29)

The Asian crisis

In the summer of 1997, a major financial crisis broke out affecting several countries in Southeast Asia. This crisis was largely unforeseen, as many of the countries involved appeared to have rapidly growing economies and governments with sound fiscal positions. However, crisis there was, and at the time of writing (mid-2002) its aftermath was still affecting some of the countries involved.

We first examine the nature of financial crises. We then look at the events, before drawing some conclusions about the problems revealed.

Financial crises

There are four general types of economic or financial crisis, and any actual crisis situation may have elements of one, some, or all of these. We consider each in turn.

Currency crisis A currency crisis shows up when there is a speculative attack on the exchange rate, resulting in a devaluation of a pegged currency or sharp depreciation of a floating currency. (See Chapter 29 for an analysis of currency pegging.) When a currency crisis occurs the domestic monetary authorities usually lose large amounts of their international reserves and/or raise interest rates very sharply in order to try to discourage capital outflows.

Banking crisis A banking crisis may arise because depositors lose confidence in the solvency of banks and attempt to withdraw their deposits, thereby causing a run on the banks. Alternatively, it may occur because banks make so many bad loans and investments that they become insolvent without any depositors' panic. In either case, banks are forced to close or seek financial support from their government. Failure of one small bank might not produce a crisis, but failure of a bank that has a large share of deposits would, as would failure of a number of banks at the same time.

Systemic financial crisis The third type of financial crisis involves a severe disruption in domestic financial markets, hampering the working of the real economy. Such a crisis is harmful to real activity because it disrupts the payments system and leads to a breakdown of all those markets that channel funds from savers to borrowers. Banking and currency crises may be components of a systemic financial crisis, but this is something bigger than either of these two, involving equity and bond markets as well as money market institutions.

Foreign debt crisis The final type of crisis arises when one or more countries find that they are unable to keep up the interest payments on their foreign debt. This situation may trigger loss of confidence in the economy or the government, and so could bring about a currency and banking crisis. It also frequently involves application to the IMF for financial assistance (which could happen in response to any of the other types of crisis, especially a currency crisis). When granting a loan, the IMF typically imposes some *conditionality*, or special terms, which often involves monetary and fiscal policy tightening. There will also usually be some negotiation between debtors and creditors in order to reschedule the debt, that is, turn unpaid interest into a further loan. As the IMF reports,

Crises of all types have often had common origins: the buildup of unsustainable economic imbalances and misalignments in asset prices or exchange rates, often in a context of financial sector distortions and structural rigidities. A crisis may be triggered by a sudden loss of confidence in the currency or banking system, prompted by such developments as a sudden correction in asset prices, or by disruption to credit or external financing flows that expose underlying economic and financial weaknesses. Crises may involve sharp declines in assets, and failures of financial institutions and non-financial corporations. Of course, not all corrections of imbalances involve a crisis. Whether they do or not depends, apart from the magnitude of the imbalances themselves, on the credibility of policies to correct the imbalances and achieve a 'soft landing' and on the robustness of the country's financial system. These factors together determine the economy's vulnerability to crises. Crises may then be considered to be the consequence of financial or economic disturbances when economies suffer from a high degree of vulnerability.[5]

There have been many financial crises in recent history. There was a currency crisis in Europe in September 1992 when the United Kingdom and Italy were forced to leave the ERM. There was another in the summer of 1993 when the remaining ERM members adopted wide fluctuation bands in order to accommodate exchange rate changes without destroying the principles of the exchange rate mechanism.

The most famous banking crisis of all time happened in the United States in the early 1930s, when over 10,000 banks went bust. More recent examples include a crisis in Sweden in 1993, the secondary banking crisis in Britain in 1974, and the collapse of many savings and loans institutions (equivalent to UK building societies) in the United States in the 1980s.

Systemic financial crises have, fortunately, been less frequent, but they have arisen when there has been political breakdown, often associated with war or revolution. A recent example occurred in Serbia in 1993, where the breakdown of the financial system was accompanied by hyperinflation (see Box 31.1 on page 578).

Foreign debt crises have been all too frequent in the last two decades. A major crisis affecting many countries in Latin America, including Mexico, Brazil, and Argentina, broke out in 1982. This crisis was so severe that it threatened the survival of many major US and UK banks that had lent large amounts of money to these countries. Mexico had a further severe debt crisis in 1994. The crisis in Argentina in 2001–2 is discussed below.

Events in Southeast Asia 1997–1998

The Asian crisis that broke out in the summer of 1997 had elements of a currency crisis, a banking crisis, and a foreign debt crisis, though the currency and banking crises were the dominant elements. The worst effects of the crisis were felt by five countries: Korea, Thailand, Malaysia, the Philippines, and Indonesia. Indonesia was affected worst of all, as the economic effects led to political turbulence that brought down President Suharto in May 1998, and the new government had trouble restoring confidence. While the situation was slightly different in each country, we concentrate on the common factors.

The currency crisis

The background to the crisis in this region, as in Japan, was a sustained period of high real growth. Collectively these economies, together with some others such as Singapore, Taiwan, and Hong Kong, were called the 'Asian Tigers', and

through the early 1990s they were the success story of the world economy. In the 1980s their average real growth rate was 7.7 per cent, and in the 1990s it was still over 6 per cent.

Because this region was growing quickly at a time when many of the industrial countries were stagnating, or growing only slowly, financial capital was attracted for investment in these so-called emerging markets. Most of the countries involved pegged their exchange rates to the dollar, and the substantial inflows of capital during the first half of the 1990s meant that the monetary authorities were able to build up healthy reserves of foreign exchange. This increased both the confidence of foreign investors and the belief of domestic borrowers that they did not face any exchange rate risk on dollar debts.

Thailand was the first country to feel the buildup of a currency crisis. There had already been concerns in 1996 about the sustainability of the dollar peg, and in early 1997 there was renewed pressure on the currency. Also there had been falls in equity prices from 1996 and a collapse of property prices. This was made worse by a growing current account deficit on the balance of payments and concerns that the short-term external debt was becoming excessive.

Capital flowed out of Thailand in increasing volume, and on 2 July 1997 the Thai authorities abandoned the exchange rate peg to the dollar. The value of the baht (the Thai currency) fell initially by 10 per cent, but then continued to fall as concerns built up about the political situation and policy-makers delayed taking corrective action. The stability of major financial institutions came into question as elements of a banking crisis started to take over.

The currency crisis in Thailand and the resulting collapse in the exchange rate turned the focus on to neighbouring countries. Speculative pressure forced the Philippines, Malaysia, and Indonesia to follow Thailand in floating their currencies, and all floated downwards by substantial amounts, as shown in Figure 35.4(ii) for Korea, Thailand, and Indonesia. Last of the five most affected countries to be hit by a currency crisis was Korea, but its exchange rate fall, when it came, was as severe as all but Indonesia's. At the worst point the value of these five currencies had fallen by amounts ranging from around 40 per cent (for Malaysia and the Philippines) to over 80 per cent (for Indonesia).

Currency devaluations of such large size have one good effect—they lower domestic output prices relative to foreign goods and so boost net exports. However, they have several bad effects that tend to dominate in the short run. First, prices of imported materials rise, and this boosts domestic inflation—this effect alone led to riots in Indonesia as petrol and food prices rose very sharply. Second, the domestic value of foreign currency debts rises sharply, putting the viability of companies and financial institutions at risk. Third, domestic authorities tend to raise interest rates and taxes, both to defend the currency and to

[5] IMF, *World Economic Outlook*, May 1998, p. 75.

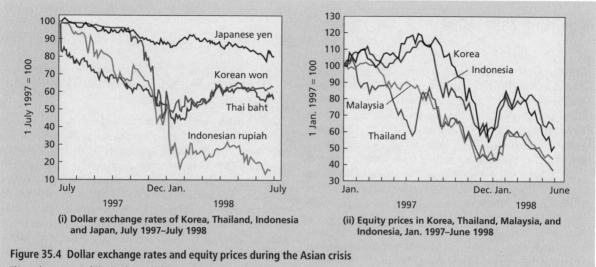

(i) Dollar exchange rates of Korea, Thailand, Indonesia and Japan, July 1997–July 1998

(ii) Equity prices in Korea, Thailand, Malaysia, and Indonesia, Jan. 1997–June 1998

Figure 35.4 Dollar exchange rates and equity prices during the Asian crisis

The exchange rate of Thailand was the first to fall, in July 1997. The Korean collapse started in October 1997. Equity prices also fell in late 1997, recovering temporarily in early 1998, but falling again in April–May 1998.

Sources: part (i): *Financial Times*, 1 July 1998, p. 23; part (ii): Thomson Datastream.

avoid further capital flight. This puts severe financial pressure on all those who have borrowed money at floating interest rates, since their repayments rise sharply. Fourth, the resulting financial squeeze forces investors to sell assets and causes profits to fall. This in turn leads to a collapse of equity and property prices. Domestic economic activity slows sharply as both consumer spending and investment spending are severely curtailed.

The banking crisis

The currency crisis soon also developed into a banking crisis, as a result of which many banks were forced to close or to be restructured. There were three main components to the banking crisis in Asia in 1997–8.

First, the countries involved had experienced many years of high growth. It is easy to make good loans in such periods because profits are generally rising, as are equity prices and property prices. Loan defaults form a very small percentage of loans made, and so bankers tend to get overconfident about the ability of borrowers to repay their loans. This is especially true of young bankers, who have never known anything other than boom conditions. So as time goes by they start to make loans that are increasingly risky. Indeed, even safe loans in good times will turn out to be bad loans once a major downturn occurs. The profusion of unsound loans tends to be reinforced by asset price bubbles in which speculators borrow money to buy assets, which in turn drives asset prices up further and feeds even more speculative buying. Widespread bankruptcies result when the asset price bubble bursts.

The second element behind the banking crisis was the false assumption by many banks that the currency would remain pegged to the US dollar. This encouraged them to borrow in dollars in order to make domestic currency loans. As US dollar interest rates were low relative to domestic interest rates, this was a highly profitable strategy for a while. However, once the exchange rate peg was broken, the true level of foreign exchange rate risk was revealed, as the domestic value of interest payments denominated in US dollars rose, making many banks insolvent in the process.

Finally, the rapid growth in these countries had disguised the facts that many banks were badly run and that the system of banking regulation was inadequate. The 1982 debt crisis had already led to the introduction of a new global bank regulatory regime from 1992. However, the crisis revealed inadequate application of these new prudential regulations in some of the countries of Southeast Asia. This served to make worse a crisis that would have brought down some banking institutions even under an adequate regulatory regime.

The currency and banking crises in Asia caused major disruption to the economies involved, imposing bankruptcy and financial hardship on millions of people.

As in the case of Japan, discussed above, there were also other structural problems in the economies involved. Many of these resulted from government intervention which led to inefficiencies and lack of international competitiveness in various sectors. However, the detail is different in each country, and a detailed examination of these issues is beyond our scope.

Argentina 2001–2002

In 1989 Argentina had an annual inflation rate of 3080 per cent and in 1990 its inflation was still 2314 per cent. This was caused by big fiscal deficits and rapidly expanding money supply (in part, printing money to finance the deficit). In 1991 the government decided that inflation had to be brought under control and it pegged its currency rigidly to the US dollar by setting up a currency board. Currency boards maintain convertibility of a currency by ensuring that domestic currency issuance is only such as can be converted into the international reserve currency that is held by the board. In effect, they limit the issuance of domestic currency. This policy was remarkably successful in bringing down inflation. In 1991 inflation was down to 170 per cent and by 1994 it was in single figures and stayed very close to zero throughout the rest of the decade (see Figure 35.5).

At the same time, real economic growth, which had been erratic throughout the 1970s and 1980s, improved noticeably in the 1990s. Apart from 1995 (when there was a spillover from the 1994 Mexican debt crisis), Argentina experienced strong positive growth in every year from 1991 to 1998 (see Figure 35.6). Low inflation and high growth after years of economic instability seemed like good news at last for Argentina.

Unfortunately it did not last. Real GDP was projected to fall by over 15 per cent in 2002[6] and inflation was projected to be up to around 30 per cent in 2002, rising to nearly 50 per cent in 2003. So what went wrong?

According to Anne Kreuger, deputy managing director of the IMF, 'Two factors came together in a destructive cocktail: weak fiscal policy and mounting overvaluation.' The weak fiscal policy led to a growing debt burden, which eventually became unsustainable:

The protracted weakness of the public finances soon made its impact felt on Argentina's consolidated public debt burden, which rose from less than 33 per cent of GDP in early 1990s to more than 41 per cent in 1998 . . . and much of the debt had to be serviced in foreign currency, which was made more difficult by Argentina's low export-to-GDP ratio. . . . In addition, the fixed exchange rate regime under the convertibility plan further reduced the degrees of freedom for fiscal deficits and debt. External debt had already climbed to 50 per cent of GDP in 2000, but of course markets feared that, in the absence of fiscal and other policies strong enough to support the convertibility plan, the currency board would collapse, the exchange rate would plummet, and the debt plan would balloon. These fears were duly realized and by the end of 2001 the debt–GDP ratio stood at 130 per cent.[7]

The other problem for Argentina was having its peso tied to the US dollar at a time when the dollar was strong, making the Argentine real exchange rate very high relative to those of its competitors. This became even worse in 1999 when Brazil devalued its currency. GDP growth was negative in Argentina for four years in a row over 1999–2002, with 2002 being worst of all. By early 2002 the

---

[6] IMF *World Economic Outlook*, September 2002.
[7] Speech at the NBER, 17 July 2002; available on www.imf.org/external/np/speeches/2002/071702.htm.

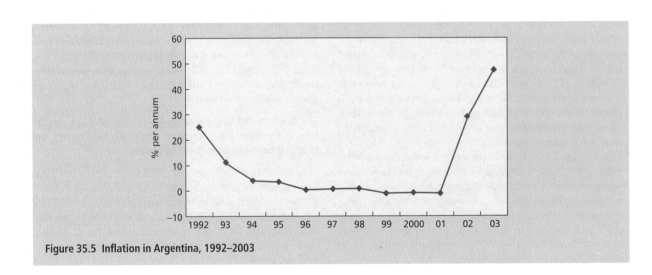

Figure 35.5 Inflation in Argentina, 1992–2003

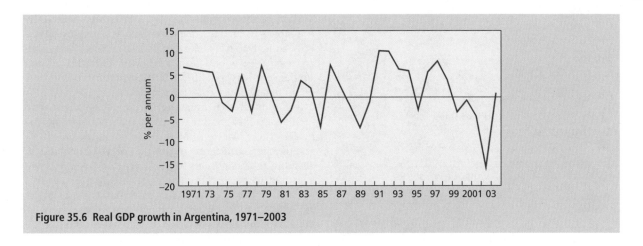

Figure 35.6 Real GDP growth in Argentina, 1971–2003

currency board had collapsed and the peso was floated, falling substantially in value against the dollar. This in turn led to a substantial burst of inflation (see Figure 35.5 on page 658).

Argentina clearly needs a new and credible monetary regime to get its inflation back under control, and it also need a fiscal policy regime that adds credibility to the monetary regime rather than undermining it. However,

that monetary regime in itself needs to avoid the chronic currency overvaluation that resulted from rigid pegging to the US dollar. The peg helped control inflation but only for a time. A tight monetary regime on its own is not sustainable if other policies are not consistent with this, and necessary adjustment can take place in other ways. There is little explanation of what caused the inflation other than the oblique reference by Kruger.

Asset price bubbles

Monetary policy-makers in the Bank of England and the ECB (and some other central banks) are charged with keeping prices under control. However, the targets that are used for this purpose are based upon consumer prices, that is, prices of currently produced retail goods and services. In recent years consumer price inflation has generally been under control, and in this respect monetary policy has been very successful. However, other prices—notably asset prices—have been very volatile, and the boom-and-bust in these prices has been associated with considerable disruption to the economy as a whole. The question then arises: should monetary policy-makers try to influence asset prices as well as consumer prices? Notice that asset prices are partly the prices of assets, such as houses and factories produced in the past, and partly prices of securities, such as company shares, the values of which are determined by profit stream expected in the future.

The conventional view until recently has been that monetary policy should stick to targeting retail price inflation, i.e. the prices of currently produced goods and services. If it succeeds in controlling that, then it cannot achieve much more. Indeed, if retail prices are stable, it is argued that

asset prices too will tend to stabilize in time. Some go further and argue that because asset prices are so volatile any attempt to target them would make monetary policy too unstable, inducing policy cycles which would cause unnecessary volatility in real activity.

The counter-argument to this is that, if bubbles in asset prices are ignored, they can cause significant disruption to real activity, which might have been avoided by timely policy interventions. Stock market bubbles in Japan and the United States in recent decades have been associated with major boom-and-bust cycles in their respective economies. Figure 35.7 traces share prices in Japan for 1981–92 and US share prices for 1991–2002. The boom-and-bust patterns are remarkably similar. We have outlined above the severe problems experienced by Japan subsequent to this boom-and-bust cycle. It is too early to say if the United States will suffer similar problems, but clearly the US economy has suffered a slowdown associated with the stock market collapse. Cause and effect are hard to disentangle, but it is certainly possible that the downturn in 2001–2 would have been less severe if the stock market boom-and-bust had been more moderate.

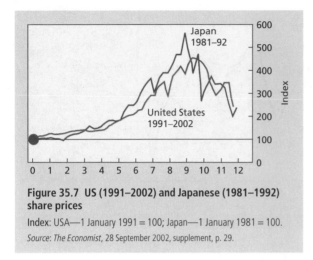

Figure 35.7 US (1991–2002) and Japanese (1981–1992) share prices

Index: USA—1 January 1991 = 100; Japan—1 January 1981 = 100.

Source: The Economist, 28 September 2002, supplement, p. 29.

Many countries including the UK have been affected by the same sort of stock market bubble as happened in the USA, though to a lesser extent. However, the UK has seen an asset price bubble associated with house prices, and similar concerns about the influence that this should have on monetary policy have been raised.

It is unlikely that inflation targets will be changed to include asset prices. But it is likely that monetary policy-makers themselves will be very careful in future in assessing the significance of asset price volatility and in deciding whether there is anything that policy should be doing to avoid the bubble over-inflating or possibly to help deflate it gently. This means that assets prices are unlikely to be included explicitly in inflation targets, but that monetary policy-makers will take account of the information imparted by asset prices in making their policy decisions.

Economics of the global village

We conclude our study of macroeconomics by returning our attention to the main industrial countries and pointing out that they are all subject to some common trends. This is indicative of an increasing interdependence, both through the increased integration of economies and through the commonality of ideas. The three important phenomena are the apparent conquest of inflation, the acceptance of fiscal consolidation as a policy goal, and the submergence of country-specific cycles under the world business cycle.

The death of inflation?

Figure 35.8 shows the path of inflation in many of the developed countries of the world. Inflation was generally low in the 1950s and 1960s, but it rose almost everywhere in the 1970s. By the mid-1990s, however, with remarkable uniformity, inflation had fallen to very low levels, typically in the range of 1–3 per cent. The obvious question to ask is: Has rapid inflation gone for good, or could it return sometime soon?

The answer to this important question is that inflation certainly *could* return, but that many hope that the makers of monetary policy have learned lessons from the mistakes of the 1970s so that they will be able to keep inflation under control in future. Two important developments in this respect are that in many countries central banks have been given an explicit target of price stability or low inflation and a degree of independence from elected politicians. The new institutional structures in the United Kingdom and the euro zone were set out in Chapter 28.

One important lesson that was learned by most countries in the 1970s and 1980s is that higher inflation does not generate higher output growth. On the contrary, it became clear that, once inflation is established, the cost of eliminating it is measured in large amounts of lost output. Most agree that long-term economic growth is a desirable goal, and it is now widely accepted that an environment of low and stable inflation is most conducive to growth.

This conclusion seems almost a cliché today, but it would not have been widely accepted a few years ago. The change is an illustration of how the study of economics advances our understanding of the world in which we live, and ultimately influences the policies of even non-economists. It is therefore worth spelling out how perceptions of the nature of the problem have evolved since the Second World War.

Early Keynesian macroeconomics focused almost exclusively on the problem of unemployment. This was because the high unemployment of the early 1930s was fresh in everyone's thoughts. The cure for unemployment was for the monetary and fiscal authorities to maintain a high level of aggregate demand. However, even in the early postwar years some economists warned of the possibility of endemic cost–push inflation, as a result of running the economy at a high level of demand. They worried that strong labour unions would force up wages even in the absence of a significant inflationary gap; that oligopolistic industries would pass these wage increases on as increased prices; and that the government's commitment to full employment would lead the monetary authorities to accommodate supply-side inflation.

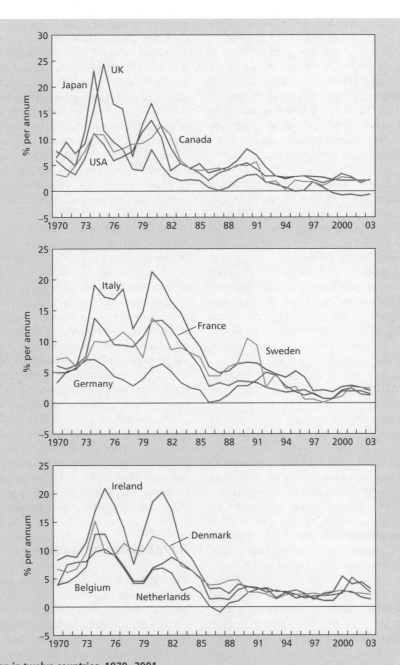

Figure 35.8 Inflation in twelve countries, 1970–2001

Inflation rose in all countries in the 1970s but had fallen universally by the mid-1990s. Data for 2002 and 2003 are IMF projections.

Source: IMF, *World Economic Outlook*, April 2002.

As a solution to this problem, some recommended *incomes policies*, which involved government control of wage increases and in some cases price increases. Attempts at incomes policies always failed in their goal of controlling inflation, though they were tried repeatedly in several countries, including the UK, in the 1960s and 1970s. But the very high inflation rates of the 1970s convinced many people that this approach was wrong.

By the early 1980s several things started to change. Governments around the world came to worry more and more about inflation, and abandoned their commitment to full employment at any price. In the United Kingdom Prime Minister Margaret Thatcher committed herself to controlling inflation via strict monetary and fiscal policies. She also made a direct attack on the power of trade unions —most notably by refusing to give in to the coalminers in 1984—and she sold off the major state-owned industries so that the government became a less significant employer. In the private sector, technological change led to fewer oligopolies and produced more small firms in highly competitive industries.

The inflation of the late 1970s–early 1980s was broken at substantial cost in terms of unemployment. In retrospect, this high unemployment can be seen as the cost of gaining a new reputation for being willing to impose major sacrifices to eliminate inflation. All of these things combined to produce a more flexible private sector, and a public sector concerned more about stable prices and fiscal rectitude than about unemployment. Ironically, this new approach of low inflation and fiscal conservatism may produce better prospects for high employment and real growth than the old policy of full employment at any price.

Fiscal consolidation

The control of inflation can be thought of as the product of a greater understanding of what causes inflation and how to control it. Inflation is a fall in the value of money, so low inflation is inevitably the product of monetary policy that either causes such a fall directly or accommodates it when it is initiated by non-monetary causes. Fiscal policy is the other major instrument for controlling aggregate demand; this has been discussed extensively from Chapter 24 onwards. **Fiscal consolidation** refers to the process of governments reducing their budget deficits, and in many cases adopting rules to limit future deficits.

Attitudes to fiscal policy have changed in the last decade or so just as radically as have attitudes to monetary policy. In the 1970s many governments ran substantial fiscal deficits and some built up substantial levels of debt. Again, it was discovered that these fiscal deficits were not good for the healthy growth of the economy. High government borrowing crowds out private investment, and high debt interest payments restrict the ability of the government to spend on education, health, and infrastructure investments. Government subsidies to inefficient industries do not make them efficient: rather, they allocate resources to areas where their return is low.

In Europe many governments were forced by the Maastricht Treaty to change their attitude to deficits and debt. The Stability and Growth Pact seems likely to keep up pressure on all EU members to preserve fiscal positions close to structural balance for the indefinite future (as discussed above). Moreover, Europe is not the only area of the world in which fiscal consolidation is the order of the day. The United States was heading for a budget surplus in 1999 after two decades of severe fiscal deficits (though in 2002 it looked as though it was heading for a growing fiscal deficit). Canada had a fiscal crisis in the early 1990s as its debt mushroomed. Fiscal tightening was instituted, and a large budget surplus was achieved in 1998. New Zealand offers a similar story, and a budget that is balanced on average over the cycle became the goal. Many of these budget surpluses disappeared in the slowdown of the early 2000s, but the intention of running conservative fiscal policies remains.

The impact of fiscal consolidation around the world is yet to be fully felt, but it could be beneficial to growth. In the short term, fiscal cutbacks involve a fall in aggregate demand. The high unemployment in parts of the EU is evidence of this short-run cost, as well as of the structural rigidities that prolong the period of adjustment. However, there is a longer-term benefit when the reduction in government borrowing reduces the high taxes that must be levied in order to meet the interest payments on outstanding government debt. Governments borrow less, and hence more of the world's savings is left to finance private investment expenditure. Investment gets 'crowded in' rather than 'crowded out', and real interest rates fall.

The extent of these beneficial effects is uncertain, though some economic models predict that they will be substantial. However, what is not uncertain is that semi-permanent structural fiscal deficits are a thing of the past. It seems unlikely that this big structural change will fail to have major effects on the world economy. Only time will tell if higher growth is one of them.

A global business cycle?

Throughout this book we have repeatedly mentioned the important trend towards globalization. An important aspect of globalization is that goods markets and financial markets around the world are increasingly integrated. One implication of this trend is that the business cycle around the world has become an increasingly shared phenomenon. Throughout our discussion of macroeconomics, we have often talked as if a single country is the relevant entity for analysis. In reality, the world economy is sufficiently integrated that only the largest countries can influence this global cycle by their own actions.

The trend towards the integration of goods and financial market is not the whole story, however. Manufacturing has declined relative to services in most economies, and many services are not traded internationally, so there remain many sectors that are not so integrated in the world economy and some of those sectors are growing in

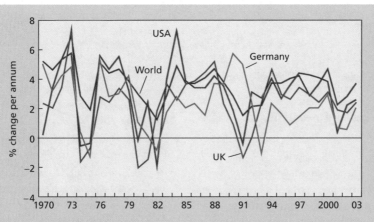

Figure 35.9 The growth rate of real GDP, 1970–2003

Growth rates in many countries follow similar cycles. Most major countries had a recession in 1974–5, 1980–2, and 1990–2. The figure shows growth rates of real GDP for USA, Germany, the UK, and the average of the world. Data for 2002 and 2003 are IMF projections.

Source: IMF, *World Economic Outlook*, September 2002.

importance. None the less, the greater sensitivity of those sectors that are internationally exposed seems to be an important channel between economies.

Figure 35.9 shows the growth rates of real GDP for three countries plus the weighted average for the world. It is clear that there is a common pattern to the cycle. There was a general recession in 1974–5, 1980–2, and 1990–2 and a general period of slower growth in 2001–2. This is not just coincidence. All economies were affected by the oil price rises of 1973 and 1979, and all were affected by the slowdown in world demand in the early 1990s and the US slowdown in 2001–2. It should not be surprising that economies that are substantially open to trade should be affected by supply shocks and demand shocks originating in the world economy.

The surprising feature is that most of the economies involved have looked for domestic explanations and policy remedies for their own cycle. But if all these countries have imported their cycles from the world economy, there may be very little that domestic monetary and fiscal policies can do to stabilize specific economies. Rather, only policies at the supranational level, or co-ordinated policies among a group of countries acting together, could be expected to carry sufficient weight to influence the world cycle.

Indeed, one interpretation of the incentives for the creation of the European Central Bank and the common monetary policy for twelve European countries is that acting alone, they were at the mercy of world market forces, but acting together, they may have some influence over their economic environment.

Conclusion

Macroeconomics deals with many of the most interesting and important issues facing the world economy. The macroeconomic theory we have developed in this book is relevant to all economies; indeed, the only truly self-sufficient macroeconomy is the world economy itself. Each nation-state within the world economy has some things that it can influence for itself, but it has many others, including the markets for its imports and exports and for

financial capital, that are world markets. Hence we cannot understand the macroeconomics of any single country by studying events in that country alone. But we can use the tools of macroeconomics that we have developed above to understand both the behaviour of the economy in which we live and the behaviour of the other economies that affect us.

SUMMARY

- Macroeconomics can be applied to economies throughout the world, and to the world economy itself.

Japan in the early 2000s: the liquidity trap revived?

- The Japanese economy suffered because its high growth rate and appreciating real exchange rate were unsustainable.

- At the end of the 1990s there was a major recession, and the monetary authorities were unable to lower interest rates because they were already close to zero.

- The fiscal authorities were reluctant to incur too great a deficit, and the politicians were slow to address structural problems in the economy.

Stabilization policy in the euro zone

- The creation of a single currency means that monetary policy will have to be targeted on the behaviour of the euro zone in general and so cannot influence demand conditions in any one country.

- Fiscal policy is constrained by the Stability and Growth Pact, which punishes member states for excessive deficits.

The Asian crisis

- Financial crises can be of four types: a currency crisis, a banking crisis, a foreign debt crisis, or a systemic financial crisis.

- The 1997–8 crisis in Asia was both a banking crisis and a currency crisis, with some elements of a foreign debt crisis.

Argentina 2001/2

- Argentina eliminated very high inflation in the 1990s by pegging its currency to the dollar.

- The combination of fiscal deficits, accumulating debt, and an overvalued curency led to the abandonment of pegging in early 2002 and the crisis is expected to generate a return to high inflation and (in 2002) a substantial fall in real GDP.

Asset price bubbles

- Asset prices play an important role in business cycles but they are not targeted by monetary policy-makers. Some argue that the authorities should attempt to avoid bubbles in asset prices and this would help stabilize the economy.

Economics of the global village

- Inflation has been brought under control in most countries around the world.

- Many governments have chosen to reduce, or even eliminate, their budget deficits.

- Most economies are greatly affected by the global business cycle, and there is very little that any one country can do to influence it.

TOPICS FOR REVIEW

- The liquidity trap
- Monetary policy in the euro zone
- The Stability and Growth Pact
- Supply shocks

- Financial crises
- Death of inflation
- Fiscal consolidation
- Global business cycles

DISCUSSION QUESTIONS

1 Collect the most recent information available on the Japanese economy from sources such as the IMF's *World Economic Outlook* and *The Economist* and assess how the Japanese economy has evolved since late 2002 (when this book was written). Have there been any policy changes, and has the Japanese GDP gap been eliminated?

2 Outline the policy targets that have been established by the European Central Bank. Does the ECB have an inflation or a

money supply target? Assess the extent to which the ECB has been successful in hitting this target.

3 Assess the extent to which the Asian crisis of 1997–8 is still affecting the economies of Thailand, Korea, Indonesia, and Malaysia. Was this just a temporary setback, or did it change the growth prospects of these countries for many years?

4 Is the world inflation environment still as benign as it was in 2002? Examine data for inflation in the major industrial countries. What is happening to commodity prices? Would it still

be true to say that inflation is dead? If so what conditions contribute to the continuance of low inflation rates?

5 Is there a global business cycle, or are major countries at different stages of the cycle? Collect data on the growth rates of GDP in the USA, Germany, Canada, and France. Do these countries have similar cycles? Explain what you have found.

6 Is it still true (or was it recently true) that there is fiscal retrenchment in the UK, the USA, Japan, France, and Germany? What has happened to the fiscal deficits in USA, Japan, France, Germany and UK since 2002?

GLOSSARY

absolute advantage The advantage that one region is said to have over another in the production of some commodity when an equal quantity of resources can produce more of that commodity in the first region than in the second. Compare *comparative advantage*.

absolute price The price of a good or a service expressed in monetary units. Also called a money price.

accelerator theory of investment The theory that the level of investment depends on the rate of change of output.

accommodation Said to occur when the monetary authorities increase the money supply in response to a negative *aggregate supply shock*. Accommodation has the effect of offsetting the downward impact of the shock on real GDP at the cost of a permanently higher price level.

actual GDP The level of GDP actually produced over a given period.

AD curve See *aggregate demand curve*.

ad valorem tax A tax levied as a percentage of the value of some transaction.

adaptive expectations The expectation of the future value of a variable formed on the basis of an adjustment which is some proportion of the error in expectations made last period. The error is the difference between what was expected last period and what actually happened.

administered price A price that is set by the decisions of individual firms rather than by impersonal market forces.

adverse selection The tendency for people most at risk to insure, while people least at risk do not, so that the insurers get an unrepresentative sample of clients within any one fee category.

agents All decision-makers, including consumers, workers, firms, and government bodies.

aggregate demand (AD) The total desired purchases of all the nation's buyers of final output.

aggregate demand curve A curve that plots all combinations of the price level and national income that yield equilibrium in the goods and the asset markets—i.e. that yield *IS–LM* equilibrium.

aggregate demand shock A shift in the *aggregate demand curve* resulting from an autonomous change in exogenous expenditures or the money supply (or equivalently, a policy-induced change in interest rates).

aggregate (desired) expenditure (AE) The total volume of purchases of currently produced goods and services that all spending units in the economy wish to make.

aggregate production function The technical relation which expresses the maximum national output that can be produced with each possible combination of capital, labour, and other resource inputs. See also *production function*.

aggregate spending See *aggregate expenditure*.

aggregate supply (AS) The total desired output of all the nation's producers.

aggregate supply curve A curve relating the economy's producers' total desired output, Y, to the price level, P.

aggregate supply shock A shift in the *aggregate supply curve* resulting from an exogenous change in input prices or from technical change (exogenous or endogenous). One example is the oil price shocks of the 1970s.

allocative efficiency Resources cannot be reallocated to produce a different bundle of goods which will then allow someone to be made better off while no one is made worse off.

allocative inefficiency Resources can be reallocated to produce a different bundle of goods which will then allow someone to be made better off while no one is made worse off.

appreciation When a change in the free-market exchange rate raises the value of one currency relative to others.

arbitrage Trading activity based on buying where a product is cheap and selling where it has a higher price (from the French word 'arbitrer': to referee or arbitrate). Arbitrage activity helps to bring prices closer in different segments of the market.

arc elasticity A measure of the average responsiveness of quantity to price over an interval of the demand curve: $(\Delta q/q)\times(p/\Delta p)$. See also *point elasticity*.

asymmetric information A situation in which some economic agents have more information than others and this affects the outcome of a bargain between them.

auction prices Prices that are set by the continuous bidding of buyers, and often against each other.

autarky Situation existing when a country does no foreign trade.

automatic fiscal stabilizers Stabilizers that arise because the value of some tax revenues and benefits changes with the level of economic activity. For example, income tax revenue rises as personal incomes rise, corporation tax revenue increases with company profits, and unemployment benefit falls as employment increases.

autonomous expenditures Expenditures that are determined outside the domestic economy or are independent of the current level of GDP.

autonomous variable See *exogenous variable*.

average fixed costs (AFC) *Total fixed costs* divided by the number of units produced.

average product (AP) Total output divided by the number of units of the *variable factor* used in its production.

average propensity to consume (APC) Total consumption expenditure divided by total national income, C/Y.

average propensity to import Total imports divided by total national income (or expenditure), IM/Y.

average propensity to save (APS) Total saving divided by total national income, S/Y. Also known as the savings ratio.

average propensity to tax Total tax revenue divided by total national income, T/Y.

average revenue (AR) *Total revenue* divided by the number of units sold.

average total cost (ATC) The total cost of producing any given output divided by the number of units produced, i.e. the cost per unit.

average variable cost (AVC) *Total variable cost* divided by the number of units produced. Also called unit cost.

balance of payments accounts A summary record of a country's transactions involving payment or receipts of foreign exchange.

balance of trade The difference between imports and exports.

balanced budget A situation in which current revenue is exactly equal to current expenditure.

balanced budget multiplier Measures the change in GDP divided by the balanced budget change in government expenditure that brought it about.

balanced growth Occurs when most major sectors of the economy grow together at similar rates.

barriers to entry Anything that prevents new firms from entering an industry that is earning profits.

barter The trading of goods directly for other goods.

base period A time-period chosen for comparison purposes in order to express or compute index numbers. Values in all other periods are expressed as percentages of the base-period value.

base rate The interest rate quoted by UK banks as the reference rate for much of their loan business. For example, a company may be given a loan at 'base plus 2%'. The base rate changes periodically when the monetary authorities signal that they wish money market rates in general to change. The equivalent term used by US banks is prime rate.

base year A *base period* that is a year.

basic prices Used in national accounts to refer to prices received by producers that exclude taxes on products, as in 'gross value added at basic prices'.

BB line The locus of levels of the interest rate and real GDP for which the desired current account balance of payments surplus (deficit) just equals the desired capital account deficit (surplus).

beta The relationship between the price of a share and the share market in general. A beta of 1 implies a perfect correlation between the share in question and the market.

bill A tradable security, usually with an initial maturity of up to six months, which pays no explicit interest and so trades at a discount to its maturity value.

black market A market in which goods are sold at prices that violate some legally imposed pricing restriction.

bond In economic theory, any evidence of a debt carrying a legal obligation to pay interest and repay the principal at some stated future time. This concept covers many different debt instruments that are found in practice.

boom Period of high output and high employment. See also *slump*.

break-even price The price at which a firm is just able to cover all of its costs, including the opportunity cost of capital. See also *shutdown price*.

budget balance See *balanced budget*.

budget deficit The shortfall of current revenue below current expenditure, usually with reference to the government.

budget line Shows all those combinations of commodities that are just obtainable given a household's income and the prices of all commodities.

budget surplus The excess of current revenue over current expenditure, usually with reference to the government.

built-in stabilizer Anything that reduces the economy's cyclical fluctuations and that is activated without a conscious government decision. See also *automatic fiscal stabilizers*.

business cycles Fluctuations in the general level of activity in an economy that affect many sectors at roughly the same time, though not necessarily to the same extent. In recent times, the period from the peak of one cycle to the peak of the next has varied in the range of five to ten years. Used to be known as trade cycles.

buyout When a group of investors buys up a controlling interest in a firm.

capacity The output that corresponds to the minimum short-run *average total cost*.

capital All those man-made aids to further production, such as tools, machinery, and factories, which are used up in the process of making other goods and services rather than being consumed for their own sake.

capital and financial account Part of the balance of payments accounts that records international transactions in assets and liabilities.

capital consumption allowance An estimate of the amount by which the capital stock is depleted through wear and tear. Also called *depreciation*.

capital inflow Arises when overseas residents buy assets in the domestic economy or domestic residents sell foreign assets.

capital–labour ratio The ratio of the amount of capital to the amount of labour used in production.

capital outflow Arises when overseas residents sell assets in the domestic economy or domestic residents buy foreign assets.

capital stock The total quantity of physical capital in existence.

capital widening Increasing the quantity of capital without changing the proportions in which the factors of production are used.

cartel A group of firms that agree to act as if they were a single seller.

cash base See *high-powered money* and *M0*.

central authorities See *government*.

central bank A bank that acts as banker to the commercial banking system and often to the government as well. In the modern world it is usually a government-owned institution that is the sole money-issuing authority and has a key role in the setting and implementation of *monetary policy*.

centrally planned economy See *command economy*.

ceteris paribus 'Other things being equal', commonly used to describe a situation in which all but one of the *independent variables* are held constant in order to study the effect that a change in the remaining independent variable has on the variables of interest.

change in demand A shift in the whole demand curve, i.e. a change in the amount that will be bought at each price.

change in the quantity demanded An increase or decrease in the specific quantity bought at a specified price, represented by a movement along a demand curve.

circular flow of income The flow of expenditures on output and factor services passing between domestic (as opposed to foreign) firms and domestic households.

classical dichotomy Concept in *classical economics* that monetary forces could influence the general price level but had no effect on real activity. Related to the concept of *neutrality of money*.

classical economics Usually refers to the body of thought on economics which had built up in the hundred years or so before the 1930s; often associated (probably incorrectly) with the notion that government policy cannot influence the level of economic activity. Contrasted with *Keynesian economics*, which attempted to break down the *classical dichotomy*.

closed economy An economy that does not engage in international trade (*autarky*).

closed shop A firm in which only union members can be employed. Closed shops may be either 'pre-entry', where the worker must be a member of the union before being employed, or 'post-entry', where the worker must join the union on becoming employed.

Coase theorem The proposition that if those creating an externality and those affected by it can bargain together with zero transactions costs, the externality will be *internalized* independently of whether it is the creators of or the sufferers from the externality who have the property rights.

collective consumption goods See *public goods*.

command economy An economy in which the decisions of the central authorities (as distinct from households and firms) exert the major influence over the allocation of resources and the distribution of income. Also called a centrally planned economy.

commercial policy The government's policy towards international trade, investment, and related matters.

commodities A term that usually refers to basic goods, such as wheat and iron ore, which are produced by the primary sector of the economy. Sometimes also used by economists to refer to all goods and services.

common market An agreement among a group of countries to have free trade among themselves, a common set of barriers to trade with other countries, and free movement of labour and capital among themselves.

common property resource A resource that is owned by no one and may be used by anyone.

comparative advantage The ability of one nation (or region or individual) to produce a commodity at a lower opportunity cost in terms of other products forgone than another nation (or region or individual). Compare *absolute advantage*.

comparative statics Short for 'comparative-static equilibrium analysis'; studying the effect of a change in some variable by comparing the positions of static equilibrium before and after the change.

compensating variation The amount of income that has to be taken away from a consumer following a price fall in one good in order to return the consumer to the original indifference curve and thus leave her feeling equally well off.

competition policy Policy designed to prohibit the acquisition and exercise of monopoly power by business firms.

complements Two goods for which the quantity demanded of one is negatively related to the price of the other.

concentration ratio The fraction of total market sales (or some other measure of market occupancy) accounted for by a specific number of the industry's largest firms, four-firm and eight-firm concentration ratios being the most frequently used.

constant returns Situation existing when a firm's output increases at the same rate as all its inputs increase.

consumer An agent who consumes goods or services.

consumers' surplus The difference between the total value consumers place on all units consumed of a commodity and the payment they must make to purchase that amount of the commodity.

consumption The act of using goods and services to satisfy wants.

consumption expenditure The amount that individuals spend on purchasing goods and services for consumption.

consumption function The relationship between personal planned consumption expenditure and the variables that affect it, such as *disposable income* and wealth.

contestable market A market is perfectly contestable if there are no *sunk costs* of entry or exit, so that potential entry may hold the profits of existing firms to low levels—zero in the case of perfect contestability.

co-operative solution A situation in which existing firms co-operate to maximize their joint profits.

cost minimization An implication of profit maximization that the firm will choose the method that produces any specific output at the lowest attainable cost.

creative destruction Schumpeter's theory that high profits and wages earned by monopolistic or oligopolistic firms and unions are the spur for others to invent cheaper or better substitute products and techniques that allow their suppliers to gain some of these profits.

credibility The extent to which actors in the private sector of the economy believe that the government will carry out the policy it promises in the future. It is important in policy analysis in macro models which assume *rational expectations*, since expectations of future policy action influence current behaviour.

cross-elasticity of demand The responsiveness of demand for one commodity to changes in the price of another, defined as the percentage change in quantity demanded of one commodity divided by the percentage change in the price of another commodity.

cross-sectional data A number of observations on the same variable, such as individuals' savings or the price of eggs, all taken at the same time but in different places or for different agents.

current account Account recording all international transactions related to goods and services.

customs union A group of countries that agree to have free trade among themselves and a common set of barriers against imports from the rest of the world.

cyclical unemployment See *demand-deficient unemployment.*

debt Anything that is owed by one agent to another. In the context of corporate finance it is bonds or bank loans, but not equity.

debt deflation A fall in aggregate demand that is associated with falling asset values, causing a negative wealth effect on consumption. It could also involve a decline in investment as investors wait for asset values to stop falling.

debt instruments Any written documents that record the terms of a debt, often providing legal proof of the conditions under which interest will be paid and the principal repaid.

decision lag The time it takes to assess a situation and decide what corrective action should be taken.

decreasing returns to scale A situation in which output increases less than proportionately to inputs as the scale of production increases.

deflation A decrease in the general price level.

degree of risk A measurement of the amount of risk associated with some action such as lending money or innovating. When the nature of the risk is known, the degree can be measured by the variance of the probability distribution describing the possible outcomes.

demand The entire relationship between the quantity of a commodity that buyers wish to purchase per period of time and the price of that commodity, other things being equal.

demand curve A graphical relation showing the quantity of some commodity that households would like to buy at each possible price.

demand-deficient unemployment Unemployment that occurs because aggregate desired expenditure is insufficient to purchase all of the output of a fully employed labour force. Also called cyclical unemployment.

demand for money The amount of wealth agents in the economy wish to hold in the form of money balances.

demand for money function The relation between the quantity of money demanded and its principle determinants such as income, wealth, and interest rates.

demand function A functional relation between quantity demanded and all of the variables that influence it.

demand management Policies that seek to shift the aggregate demand curve by shifting either the *IS* curve (fiscal policy) or the *LM* curve (monetary policy).

demand schedule A numerical tabulation showing the quantities that are demanded at selected prices.

demand shock In macroeconomics it is a change of an exogenous variable that causes the AD curve to shift.

dependent variable The variable that is determined by the *independent variables*; e.g. in the consumption function consumption is the dependent variable.

depreciation (1) The loss in value of an asset over a period of time owing to physical wear and tear and obsolescence. (2) A fall in the free-market value of domestic currency in terms of foreign currencies. See also *capital consumption allowance.*

depression A prolonged period of very low economic activity with very high unemployment and high excess capacity.

derived demand The demand for a factor of production that results from the demand for the products it is used to make.

developed countries Usually refers to the rich industrial countries of North America, Western Europe, Japan, and Australasia.

developing countries See *less developed countries.*

development gap The gap between *less developed countries* and *developed countries.*

differentiated product A product that is produced in several distinct varieties, or brands, all of which are sufficiently similar to distinguish them, as a group, from other products (e.g. cars).

diminishing marginal rate of substitution The hypothesis that the less of one commodity is presently being consumed, the less willing will the consumer be to give up a unit of that commodity to obtain an additional unit of a second commodity; its geometrical expression is the decreasing absolute slope of an indifference curve as one moves along it to the right.

direct investment See *foreign direct investment.*

direct taxes Taxes levied on persons that can vary with the status of the taxpayer, e.g. income tax.

discount rate The difference between the current price of a bill and its maturity value expressed as an annualized interest rate.

discouraged worker Someone of working age who has withdrawn permanently from the labour force because of the poor prospects of employment.

diseconomies of scale See *decreasing returns to scale.*

disembodied technical change Technical change that is the result of changes in the organization of production that are not embodied in specific capital goods, e.g. improved management techniques.

disequilibrium A state of imbalance between opposing forces so that there is a tendency to change, as when quantity demanded does not equal quantity supplied at the prevailing price.

disposable income The after-tax income that individuals have at their disposal to spend or to save.

distortions Anything that creates a deviation from some optimality conditions, and thereby induces some inefficiency.

distribution of income The division of total national income among various groups. See also *functional* and *size distribution of income.*

distribution theory The theory of what determines the way in which the nation's total income is divided among various groups. See also *functional* and *size distribution of income.*

dividends Profits that are paid out to shareholders.

division of labour The breaking-up of a production process into a series of repetitive tasks, each done by a different worker.

double counting In national income accounting, adding up the total outputs of all the sectors in the economy so that the value of intermediate goods is counted both in the sector that produces them and every time they are purchased as an input by another sector.

dominant strategy A strategy that offers the best choices for one player independent of what the other players do.

dumping When a commodity is sold in a foreign country at prices below its domestic sale price for reasons not related to costs.

duopoly An industry containing exactly two firms.

economic growth The positive trend in the nation's total real output or GDP over the long term.

economic models A term used in several related ways: sometimes as a synonym for theory, sometimes for a specific quantification of a general theory, sometimes for the application of a general theory to a specific context, and sometimes for an abstraction designed to illustrate some point but not meant as a full theory on its own.

economic profits The difference between the revenues received from the sale of output and the full opportunity cost of the inputs used to make the output. The cost includes the *opportunity cost* of the owners' capital. Also called pure profits or simply *profits*.

economic rent Any excess that a factor is paid above what is needed to keep it in its present use.

economies of scale See *increasing returns to scale*.

economies of scope Economies achieved by a multi-product firm owing to its overall size not its amount of production of any one product; typically associated with large-scale distribution, advertising, and purchasing and lower cost of borrowing money.

economy Any specified collection of interrelated marketed and non-marketed productive activities.

effective exchange rate An index number of the value of a nation's currency relative to a weighted basket of other currencies. Whereas an *exchange rate* measures the rate of exchange of a currency for one other currency, changes in the effective exchange rate indicate movements in a single currency's value against other currencies in general.

efficiency wage A wage rate above the market-clearing level which enables employers to attract and keep the best workers as well as providing employees with an incentive to perform well and avoid being sacked.

elastic The percentage change in quantity is greater than the percentage change in price (elasticity is greater than 1).

elasticity of demand See *price elasticity of demand*.

elasticity of supply See *price elasticity of supply*.

embodied technical change A technical change that is the result of changes in the form of particular capital goods.

endogenous variable A variable that is explained within a theory. Also called an induced variable.

entrepreneur One who innovates, i.e. one who takes risks by introducing both new products and new ways of making old products.

entrepreneurship The skill required to be an *entrepreneur*.

entry barrier Any natural barrier to the entry of new firms into an industry, such as a large *minimum efficient scale* for firms, or any firm-created barrier, such as a patent.

envelope Any curve that encloses, by being tangent to, a series of other curves. In particular, the envelope cost curve is the *LRAC* curve, which encloses the *SRAC* curves by being tangent to each without cutting any of them.

equation of exchange $MV = PT$, where M is the money stock, V is the velocity of circulation, P is the average price of trans-

actions, and T is the number of transactions. As usually defined, it is an identity which says that the value of money spent is equal to the value of goods and services sold. However, with additional assumptions it provides a basis for the *quantity theory of money*.

equilibrium A state of balance between opposing forces so that there is no tendency to change.

equilibrium differentials Differentials in the prices of factors that persist in equilibrium without generating forces to eliminate them.

equilibrium employment (unemployment) The level of employment (unemployment) achieved when GDP is at its potential level. Traditionally referred to as full employment. Equilibrium unemployment (*frictional* plus *structural*) is total unemployment minus *demand-deficient unemployment*.

equilibrium price The price at which quantity demanded equals quantity supplied.

equilibrium quantity The amount that is bought and sold at the *equilibrium price*.

equities Certificates indicating part ownership of a joint-stock company.

equivalent variation The change in income that leaves a consumer just as well off as some specific change in the price of a good.

excess capacity theorem The prediction that each firm in a monopolistically competitive industry is producing below its minimum efficient scale and hence at an average cost that is higher than it could achieve by producing its capacity output.

excess demand The amount by which quantity demanded exceeds quantity supplied at some price; negative *excess supply*.

excess supply The amount by which quantity supplied exceeds quantity demanded at some price; negative *excess demand*.

exchange rate The rate at which two national currencies exchange for each other. Often expressed as the amount of domestic currency needed to buy one unit of foreign currency.

excludable The owner of an excludable good can prevent others from consuming it or its services.

execution lag The time it takes to initiate corrective policies and for their full influence to be felt.

exhaustible resource See *non-renewable resource*.

exhaustive expenditures Government purchases of currently produced goods and services. Also called government direct expenditures.

exogenous variable A variable that influences other variables within a theory but is itself determined by factors outside the theory. Also called an autonomous variable.

expectations-augmented Phillips curve See *short-run Phillips curve*.

expected value The most likely outcome of some procedure that is repeated over and over again; the mean of the probability distribution expressing the possible outcomes.

explicit collusion When firms explicitly agree to co-operate rather than compete. See also *tacit collusion*.

extensive form game Players make moves in some order over time.

external economies Economies of scale that arise from sources outside the firm.

externalities Costs or benefits of a transaction that fall on people not involved in that transaction.

extrapolative expectations Expectation formation based on the assumption that a past trend will continue into the future. The simplest form of extrapolation would be to assume that next period's value of a variable will be the same as this period's.

factor markets Markets where factor services are bought and sold.

factor price theory The theory of the determination of the prices of factors of production.

factors of production Resources used to produce goods and services; frequently divided into the basic categories of land, labour, and capital. Sometimes entrepreneurship is distinguished as a fourth factor; sometimes it is included in the category of labour.

fiat money Inconvertible paper money that is issued by government order (or fiat).

final demand Demand for the *final goods and services* produced in the economy.

final goods and services The outputs of the economy after eliminating all *double counting*, i.e. excluding all intermediate goods.

financial capital The funds used to finance a firm, including both equity capital and debt. Also called money capital.

financial innovation Occurs when new products are introduced into the financial system, or when existing suppliers behave in new ways. Changes are often a complex interaction of regulatory changes, changing technology, and competitive pressures.

financial intermediaries Financial institutions that stand between those who deposit money and those who borrow it.

fine-tuning The attempt to maintain national income at, or near, its full-employment level by means of frequent changes in fiscal and/or monetary policy. Compare *gross-tuning*.

firm The unit that employs factors of production to produce commodities that it sells to other firms, to households, or to the government.

fiscal consolidation A situation in which governments that have been running substantial budget deficits decide to aim for a sustainable budgetary position, usually by getting their expenditure under control.

fiscal policy Attempts to influence the aggregate demand curve by altering government expenditures and/or taxes, thus shifting the *IS* curve.

fixed capital formation See *fixed investment*.

fixed cost A cost that does not change with output. Also called overhead cost, unavoidable cost, or indirect cost.

fixed exchange rate An exchange rate that is held within a narrow band around some pre-announced par value by intervention of the country's central bank in the foreign exchange market.

fixed factors Inputs whose available amount is fixed in the short run.

fixed investment Investment in plant and equipment.

fixed prices See *administered prices*.

flexible prices See *auction prices*.

floating exchange rate An exchange rate that is left free to be determined on the foreign exchange market by the forces of demand and supply.

flow variable See *stock variable*.

foreign direct investment (FDI) Non-resident investment in the form of a takeover or capital investment in a domestic branch, plant, or subsidiary corporation in which the investor has voting control. See also *portfolio investment*.

foreign exchange Foreign currencies and claims to them in such forms as bank deposits, cheques, and promissory notes payable in the currency.

foreign exchange market The market where foreign exchange is traded—at a price that is expressed by the *exchange rate*.

45° line Used in macroeconomics to indicate points where expenditures and output are equal, so that what firms produce is just equal to what agents wish to buy.

free-market economy An economy in which the decisions of individuals and firms (as distinct from the central authorities) exert the major influence over the allocation of resources.

free-rider problem The problem that arises because people have a self-interest in not revealing the strength of their own preferences for a *public good* in the hope that others will pay for it.

free trade An absence of any form of government interference with the free flow of international trade.

free-trade area An agreement between two or more countries to abolish tariffs on all, or most, of the trade among themselves, while each remains free to set its own tariffs against other countries.

frictional unemployment Unemployment that is associated with the normal turnover of labour.

function Loosely, an expression of a relationship between two or more variables. Precisely, Y is a function of the variables $X_1, \ldots, X_n$ if for every set of values of the variables $X_1, \ldots, X_n$ there is associated a unique value of the variable Y. Also referred to as a *functional relation*.

functional distribution of income The distribution of income among major factors of production.

functional relation A mathematical relation between two or more variables such that for every value of the independent variables there is one and only one associated value of the dependent variable.

gains from trade Advantages realized as a result of specialization made possible by trade.

game theory The study of the strategic choices between firms, applicable when the outcome for one firm depends on the behaviour of the others.

GDP See *gross domestic product*.

GDP gap See *output gap*.

general price level Average level of the prices of all goods and services produced in the economy. Usually just called the price level.

Giffen good A good with a positively sloped demand curve.

gilt-edged securities UK government bonds; so called because they are considered to carry lower risk than private sector debt.

given period Any particular period that is being compared with a *base period* by an index number.

globalization The increased worldwide interdependence of most economies. Integrated financial markets, the sourcing of the production of components throughout the world, the growing importance of transnational firms, and the linking of many service activities through the new information and communications technologies are some of its many manifestations.

GNI See *gross national income*.

GNP See *gross national product*.

gold standard Currency standard whereby a country's money is convertible into gold.

Goodhart's law The view that many statistical relations (particularly those established by monetarists) cannot be used for policy purposes because they do not depend on causal relations and are, therefore, unstable.

goods Tangible production, such as cars or shoes. Sometimes all goods and services are loosely referred to as goods.

goods markets Markets where goods and services are bought and sold.

government In economics, all public agencies, government bodies, and other organizations belonging to, or owing their existence to, the government; sometimes (more accurately) called the central authorities.

government direct expenditures See *exhaustive expenditures*.

government failure Where government intervention imposes costs that would not have been accrued if it had acted efficiently.

Gresham's law Bad money (i.e. money whose intrinsic value is less than its face value) drives good money (i.e. money whose intrinsic value exceeds its face value) out of circulation.

gross capital formation See *gross investment*.

gross domestic product (GDP) The value of total output actually produced in the whole economy over some period, usually a year (although quarterly data are also available).

gross investment The total value of all investment goods produced in the economy during a stated period of time.

gross national income (GNI) A measure of what a nation earns from all its economic activity anywhere in the world. It differs from *gross domestic product*, which measures only what is produced in the domestic economy (some of which may generate income for non-residents). Used to be known as *gross national product*.

gross national product (GNP) A national accounts concept equivalent to *gross national income* used prior to 1998. It measures income earned by domestic residents in return for contributions to current production, whether production is located at home or abroad, and is equal to GDP plus net property income from abroad.

gross return on capital The market value of output minus all non-capital costs; the gross return is made up of depreciation, the pure return on capital, any risk premium, and the residual, which is *pure profit*.

gross-tuning Use of monetary and fiscal policies to attempt to correct only large deviations from potential national income. It is contrasted with *fine-tuning*, which aims to adjust aggregate demand frequently in order to keep national income close to its potential level at all times.

high-powered money The monetary magnitude that is under the direct control of the central bank. In the UK, it is composed of cash in the hands of the public, bank reserves of currency, and clearing balances held by the commercial banks with the Bank of England. Measured by M0.

hog cycles A term used to characterize cycles of over- and under-production because of time-lags in the production process. For example, high prices for pork today lead many farmers to start breeding pigs; when the pigs mature there will be an increased supply of pork, which will drive down its price; so fewer farmers will breed pigs and the price will later rise again, starting the cycle over again.

homogeneous product A product is homogeneous when, as far as purchasers are concerned, every unit is identical to every other unit.

horizontal equity Treating similar groups equitably, which usually means treating them similarly. Compare *vertical equity*.

household All the people who live under one roof and who take, or are subject to others taking for them, joint financial decisions.

human capital The capitalized value of productive investments in persons. Usually refers to value derived from expenditures on education, training, and health improvements.

hyperinflation Episodes of very rapid inflation.

hysteresis The lagging of effects behind their causes. In economics the term has come to relate to persistence or irreversibility of effects. An example is the difficulty of returning the long-term unemployed to work because their skills have deteriorated. It also implies path-dependency, which means that the ultimate equilibrium is not independent of how the economy gets there (i.e. it is not unique).

identification problem The problem of how to estimate both demand and supply curves from observed market data on prices and quantities actually traded.

import quota A maximum amount of some product that may be imported each year.

imputed costs The costs of using factors of production already owned by the firm, measured by the earnings they could have received in their best alternative employment.

incentives Motivational influences that drive the behaviour of economic agents. Consumers make choices to increase their satisfaction or utility, while firms respond to choices that increase their profit.

incidence In tax theory, where the burden of a tax finally falls.

income–consumption line On an indifference-curve diagram, a line showing how consumption bundles change as income changes, with prices held constant.

income effect The effect on quantity demanded of a change in real income, relative prices held constant.

income-elastic The percentage change in quantity demanded exceeds the percentage change in income.

income elasticity of demand The responsiveness of quantity demanded to a change in income as measured by the percentage change in quantity divided by the percentage change in income.

income-inelastic The percentage change in quantity demanded is smaller than the percentage change in income.

increasing returns to scale A situation in which output increases more than in proportion to inputs as the scale of a firm's production increases. A firm in this situation, with fixed factor prices, is a decreasing-cost firm.

incremental ratio When Y is a function of X, the incremental ratio is the change in Y divided by the change in X that brought it about, $\Delta Y/\Delta X$. The limit of this ratio as ΔX approaches 0 is the derivative of Y with respect to X, dY/dX.

independent variable A variable that can take on any value in some specified range; it determines the value of the dependent variable.

index number An observation in a given time-period expressed as a ratio to the observation in a *base period* and then multiplied by 100.

index of retail prices See *retail price index*.

indexation When a contract, for wages, pensions, or repayment of debt, is specified in real terms. Any specified money payment would be increased to compensate for actual inflation. More generally, the term applies to any contingent contract tied to an index number.

indicators Variables that policymakers monitor for the information they yield about the state of the economy.

indifference curve A curve showing all combinations of commodities that yield equal satisfaction to the consumer.

indifference map A set of indifference curves in which curves further away from the origin indicate higher levels of satisfaction than curves closer to the origin.

indirect tax A tax levied on a transaction that is paid by an individual by virtue of his or her association with that activity and does not vary with the circumstances of the individual who pays it, e.g. VAT on a restaurant meal.

induced Anything that is determined from within a theory. The opposite of autonomous or exogenous; also called endogenous.

induced expenditure Any expenditure flow that is related to national income (or to any other variable explained by the theory).

induced variable See *endogenous variable*.

industrial union A single union representing all workers in a given industry, whatever their trade.

industry A group of firms that sell a well-defined product or closely related set of products.

inelastic The percentage change in quantity is less than the percentage change in price (elasticity is less than 1).

infant industry argument The argument that new domestic industries with potential economies of scale need to be protected from competition from established low-cost foreign producers so that they can grow large enough to achieve costs as low as those of foreign producers.

inferior good A commodity with a negative *income elasticity*; demand for it diminishes when income increases.

inflation A positive rate of growth of the general price level.

inflationary gap A negative output gap, i.e. actual GDP exceeds *potential output* (GDP).

inflationary shock Any autonomous shift in aggregate demand or aggregate supply which causes the price level to rise.

information lag The time between an event happening and policymakers learning about it. For example, national accounts data for a quarter do not arrive until six weeks or so after the quarter ends and are then revised several times subsequently.

infrastructure The basic facilities (especially transportation and communications systems) on which the commerce of a community depends.

injections Exogenous expenditure flows into the home economy. The main injections in the macro model are government spending, exports, and investment.

innovation The introduction of something new, either a new product or a new way of making an old product. See also *entrepreneur*.

innovators Those who innovate. Also called *entrepreneurs*.

inputs The materials and factor services used in the process of production.

insider–outsider model An analysis of labour markets which gives more influence over market outcomes to those in employment (usually via trade union representation) than to the unemployed.

instruments The variables that policymakers can control directly. (In econometrics instruments are proxy variables used in regression equations because of their desirable statistical properties—usually independence from the equation error.)

interest The amount paid each year on a loan, usually expressed as a percentage (e.g. 5%) or as a ratio (e.g. 0.05) of the principal of the loan.

intermediate goods and services All goods and services used as inputs into a further stage of production.

internal economies Economies of scale that arise from sources within the firm.

internal labour market The market inside the firm in which employees compete against each other, particularly for promotion.

internalize an externality To do something that makes an *externality* enter into the firm's own calculations of its private costs and benefits.

inventories Goods and materials that are held during the production or distribution process. See also *stocks*.

investment The act of producing or purchasing goods that are not for immediate consumption.

investment demand function A negative relationship between the quantity of investment per period and the interest rate, holding other things constant. Used to be more commonly called the marginal efficiency of investment.

investment expenditure Expenditure on capital goods.

investment goods Goods produced not for present consumption, i.e. capital goods, inventories, and residential housing.

invisibles Services, especially in the context of the balance of payments accounts, that we cannot see crossing the frontier, such as insurance, freight haulage, and tourist expenditures.

involuntary unemployment Unemployment that occurs when a person is willing to accept a job at the going wage rate but cannot find such a job.

IS curve The locus of combinations of the interest rate and the level of real GDP for which desired aggregate expenditure equals actual national output. So called because, in a closed economy with no government, it also reflects the combinations of the interest rate and national income for which investment equals saving, $I = S$. In general it reflects points for which *injections* equal *withdrawals*.

IS/LM model A diagrammatic representation of a model of aggregate demand determination based upon the locus of equilibrium points in the aggregate expenditure sector (*IS*) and the monetary sector (*LM*). It is incomplete as a model of GDP determination because it does not include an aggregate supply curve.

isocost line A line showing all combinations of inputs that have the same total cost to the firm.

isoquant A curve showing all technologically efficient factor combinations for producing a given level of output.

isoquant map A series of *isoquants* from the same production function, each isoquant relating to a specific level of output.

J-curve Pattern usually followed by the *balance of trade* after a devaluation of the domestic currency. Initially the trade balance deteriorates, and then, after a lag, it improves.

joint-stock company A firm regarded in law as having an identity of its own. Its owners, who are its shareholders, are not personally responsible for anything that is done in the name of the firm. Called a corporation in North America.

Keynesian economics Economic theories based on *AE, IS, LM, AD,* and *AS* curves and assuming enough short-run price inflexibility that *AD* and *AS* shocks cause substantial deviations of real GDP from its potential level.

Keynesian revolution Adoption of the idea that government could use monetary and fiscal policy to control aggregate demand and thereby influence the level of GDP. For a while it was believed that Keynesian economics had found ways in which policymakers could smooth business cycles and eliminate unemployment.

Kondratieff cycles Long cycles in economic activity of around fifty years' duration. Sometimes referred to as long waves.

labour All productive human resources, mental and physical, both inherited and acquired.

labour force See *working population*.

labour force participation rate The percentage of the population of working age that is actually in the labour force (i.e. either working or seeking work).

labour productivity Total output divided by the labour used in producing it, i.e. output per unit of labour.

Laffer curve A curve relating total tax revenue to the tax rate.

land All free gifts of nature, such as land, forests, minerals, etc. Sometimes called natural resources.

law of demand A lower price increases the quantity demanded and vice versa, that is, demand curves have a negative slope.

law of diminishing returns Law stating that if increasing quantities of a variable input are applied to a given quantity of a fixed input, the *marginal product*, and the *average product*, of the variable input will eventually decrease.

law of price adjustment If there is an excess demand price will rise, if there is an excess supply price will fall.

leakages See *withdrawals*.

learning by doing The increase in output per worker that often results as workers learn on the job through repeatedly performing the same tasks. It causes a downward shift in the average variable cost curve.

legal tender Currency that is recognized in law as the acceptable medium for payment of debts. Bank of England notes became legal tender in England and Wales in 1833. Euro notes issued by the European Central Bank are expected to become legal tender for members of the euro zone in 2002.

less developed countries (LDCs) The lower-income countries of the world, most of which are in Asia, Africa, and South and Central America. Also called underdeveloped countries and developing countries.

life-cycle theory A theory that relates a household's actual consumption to its expected lifetime income.

limited partnership A form of business organization in which the firm has two classes of owner: general partners, who take part in managing the firm and who are personally liable for all of the firm's actions and debts, and limited partners, who take no part in the management of the firm and who risk only the money that they have invested.

liquidity The ease with which an asset can be converted into money. Sometimes refers to money itself—*liquidity preference* used to be widely used in economics as an expression meaning demand for money.

liquidity preference The demand to hold wealth as money rather than as interest-earning assets. Also called the *demand for money*.

liquidity trap A situation that may arise when interest rates are so low that further reductions are either not possible or do not stimulate spending. In such situations the monetary authorities cannot stimulate aggregate demand by interest rate changes alone.

LM curve The locus of combinations of the interest rate and real GDP for which money demand equals money supply. So called because it represents the points where *liquidity preference* equals the money supply.

logarithmic scale A scale on which equal proportional changes are shown as equal distances (e.g. 1 cm may always represent doubling of a variable, whether from 3 to 6 or 50 to 100). Also called log scale or ratio scale.

long run A period of time in which all inputs may be varied but the basic technology of production is unchanged.

long-run aggregate supply (LRAS) curve A curve that relates the price level to equilibrium real GDP, after all input costs, including wage rates, have been fully adjusted to eliminate any excess demand or supply.

long-run average cost (LRAC) curve Curve showing the least-cost method of producing each level of output when all inputs can be varied. Also sometimes called the long-run average total cost curve.

long-run industry supply (LRS) curve Curve showing the relation between equilibrium price and the output that the firms in an industry will be willing to supply after all desired entry or exit has occurred.

long-run Phillips curve (LRPC) Curve showing the relation between unemployment and stable rates of inflation that neither accelerate nor decelerate (and therefore for which actual and expected inflation are equal). Usually thought to be vertical at the *natural rate of unemployment* or *NAIRU*.

long wave See *Kondratieff cycles*.

Lorenz curve A curve showing the extent of departure from equality of income distribution. It graphs the proportion of total income earned by all people up to each stated point in the income distribution, such as the proportion earned by the bottom quarter, the bottom half, and the bottom three-quarters.

Lucas aggregate supply curve An aggregate supply curve which is positively sloped for unexpected increases in the price level but vertical for anticipated increases in the price level. Also known as the 'surprise' aggregate supply curve.

Lucas critique The proposition that forecasts and simulations using empirical macro models will be inaccurate when used to predict the effects of changes in policy. This is because the behaviour of agents will be different under different policy regimes.

M0 Currency held by the non-bank public plus bankers' deposits with the central bank. Also known as the monetary base, the cash base, or *high-powered money*.

M1 A measure of the money stock which includes currency plus current account bank deposits. This measure is no longer reported by the Bank of England.

M2 Currency held by the public plus retail current and savings accounts in banks and building societies. Also known as 'retail M4'.

M3 Measure of broad money no longer used by the UK authorities. It was equal to M1 plus all savings deposits in banks. A harmonized measure of M3, **M3H**, is in use in the euro area as a monetary indicator; however, this has a different definition, as it is equal to M4 plus foreign currency and some other deposits.

M4 Currency in circulation plus all sterling deposits in banks and building societies.

macroeconomic policy Any measure directed at influencing such macroeconomic variables as the overall levels of employment, unemployment, GDP, and prices.

macroeconomics The study of the determination of economic aggregates and averages, such as total output, total employment, the general price level, and the rate of economic growth.

marginal cost (MC) The increase in total cost resulting from raising the rate of production by one unit.

marginal cost pricing A policy of setting the price of a product equal to its marginal cost.

marginal efficiency of capital The rate at which the value of the stream of output of a marginal unit of capital must be discounted to make it equal to £1.

marginal efficiency of capital schedule A schedule that relates the marginal efficiency of each additional £1 worth of capital to the size of the capital stock.

marginal efficiency of investment The relation between desired investment and the rate of interest, assuming all other things are equal.

marginal physical product (MPP) See *marginal product*.

marginal product (MP) The change in total product resulting from using one more (or less) unit of the variable factor. Also called marginal physical product. Mathematically, the partial derivative of total product with respect to the variable factor.

marginal productivity theory The demand half of the *neoclassical theory of income distribution*, in which the demand for any variable factor is determined by the value of that factor's *marginal revenue product*.

marginal propensity not to spend The proportion of any new increment of income that is not passed on in spending, and instead leaks out of (i.e. is withdrawn from) the circular flow of income. Also called the marginal propensity to withdraw and the marginal propensity to leak.

marginal propensity to consume (MPC) The proportion of any new increment of income that is spent on consumption, $\Delta C / \Delta Y$.

marginal propensity to import The proportion of any new increment of income that is spent on imports, $\Delta M / \Delta Y$.

marginal propensity to leak See *marginal propensity not to spend*.

marginal propensity to save (MPS) The proportion of any new increment of income that is saved, $\Delta S / \Delta Y$.

marginal propensity to spend The ratio of any increment of induced expenditure to the increment in income that brought it about.

marginal propensity to tax The proportion of any increment in income that is taxed away by the government, $\Delta T / \Delta Y$.

marginal propensity to withdraw See *marginal propensity not to spend*.

marginal rate of substitution (MRS) The rate at which one factor is substituted for another with output held constant. Graphically, the slope of the *isoquant*.

marginal rate of transformation The slope of the *production-possibility boundary*, indicating the rate of substitution of production of one good for that of another.

marginal revenue The change in total revenue resulting from a unit change in the sales per period of time. Mathematically, the derivative of total revenue with respect to quantity sold.

marginal revenue product (MRP) The addition to a firm's revenue resulting from the sale of the output produced by an additional unit of the variable factor.

marginal utility The change in satisfaction resulting from consuming one unit more or one unit less of a commodity.

market An area over which buyers and sellers negotiate the exchange of a well-defined commodity.

market economy A society in which people specialize in productive activities and meet most of their material wants through exchanges voluntarily agreed upon by the contracting parties.

market failure Any market performance that is less than the most efficient possible (the optimal) performance.

market for corporate control Where potential buyers and sellers (both willing and unwilling) bargain about transferring ownership of firms.

market prices In national accounts refers to the fact that expenditures are measured in the prices actually paid by consumers and so include taxes on products. See also *basic prices*.

market sector That portion of an economy in which producers must cover their costs by selling their output to consumers.

market structure The characteristics of a market that influence the behaviour and performance of firms that sell in the market. The four main market structures are *perfect competition, monopolistic competition, oligopoly*, and *monopoly*.

maturity The length of time until the redemption date of a security such as a bond.

medium of exchange A commodity or token which is widely accepted in payment for goods and services.

menu costs Costs associated with changing prices, such as the costs of reprinting catalogues or menus. These costs make it rational for producers to keep output prices fixed until input prices have changed significantly, or to respond only periodically.

mercantilism The doctrine that the gains from trade are a function of the balance of trade, in contrast with the classical theory, in which the gains from trade are a function of the volume of trade.

merchandise account The part of the balance of payments accounts relating to trade in goods.

merchandise trade Trade in physical products. Same as *visible trade*.

merger The uniting of two or more formerly independent firms.

merit goods Goods which the government decides have sufficient merit that more should be produced and consumed than people would choose to purchase if left to themselves.

microeconomics The study of the allocation of resources and the distribution of income as they are affected by the working of the price system and by the policies of the central authorities.

minimum efficient scale (MES) The smallest level of output at which long-run average cost is at a minimum; the smallest output required to achieve all economies of scale in production.

mismatch See *structural unemployment*.

mixed economy An economy in which some decisions about the allocation of resources are made by firms and households and some by the government.

monetarism The doctrine that monetary magnitudes exert powerful influences in the economy and that control of these magnitudes is a potent means of affecting the economy's macroeconomic behaviour.

monetary base See *high-powered money* and *M0*.

monetary equilibrium A situation in which there is no excess demand for or supply of money.

monetary policy Policy of trying to control aggregate demand (and ultimately inflation) via the setting of short-term interest rates.

monetary transmission mechanism The mechanism that turns a monetary shock into a real expenditure shock and thus links the monetary and the real sides of the economy.

money Any generally accepted medium of exchange, i.e. anything that will be accepted in exchange for goods and services.

money demand function The function that determines the demand to hold money balances.

money income Income measured in terms of some monetary unit. See also *real income*.

money multiplier The ratio of the money stock to the monetary base (*high-powered money*).

money price See *absolute price*.

money rate of interest The rate of interest as measured in monetary units.

money stock See *supply of money*.

money supply See *supply of money*.

monopolist A single seller in any market.

monopolistic competition A market structure in which there are many sellers and freedom of entry but in which each firm sells a differentiated version of some generic product and, as a result, faces a negatively sloped demand curve for its own product.

monopoly A market structure in which the industry contains only one firm.

monopsonist A single purchaser in any market.

moral hazard Any change in behaviour resulting from the fact that a contract has been agreed. One example is drivers who drive more recklessly because they have accident insurance; another is employees who do not work hard because employers cannot monitor their performance effectively.

multinational enterprises (MNEs) See *transnational corporations*.

multiplier The ratio of the change in GDP to the change in autonomous expenditure that brought it about.

multiplier–accelerator theory An element of business-cycle dynamics caused by the interaction of the multiplier and the accelerator, which can make the economy follow a cyclical path in response to a one-off exogenous shock.

NAIRU The amount of unemployment (all of it *frictional* or *structural*) that exists when GDP is at its potential level and that, if maintained, will result in a stable rate of inflation. The acronym stands for 'non-accelerating-inflation rate of unemployment'. In the long run the NAIRU is equivalent to the *natural rate of unemployment*.

Nash equilibrium In the case of firms, an equilibrium that results when each firm in an industry is currently doing the best that it can, given the current behaviour of all other firms.

Nash theorem Every game with a finite number of players and a finite number of strategies will have at least one Nash equilibrium (so long as some random element to strategies is possible).

national debt The debt of the central government.

national income In general, the value of the nation's total output, and the value of the income generated by the production of that output. Measured in practice by *gross national income* and assumed in most of this book to be equivalent to GDP.

national product A generic term for the nation's total output, which might be measured more specifically by GDP. See *gross national product*.

natural monopoly An industry whose market demand is insufficient to allow more than one firm to cover costs at any positive level of output.

natural rate of unemployment The level of unemployment in a competitive economy that corresponds to potential GDP in long-run equilibrium and that is associated with stable inflation. For most purposes it is equivalent to the *NAIRU*, but the latter may differ when the economy is adjusting slowly back to full equilibrium following some large shock.

natural scale A scale on which equal absolute amounts are represented by equal distances. Compare *logarithmic scale*.

negatively related Refers to the relationship where an increase in one variable is associated with a decrease in the other.

neoclassical theory In general, a theory based on the maximizing choices of well-informed agents pursuing their own self-interest. In **distribution** it is a theory that factor incomes are determined by demand and supply, where demand depends on the value of the factor's marginal product and supply depends on the maximizing decisions of those who own the factors.

net exports Total exports minus total imports ($X - IM$).

net investment Gross investment minus replacement investment, which is new capital that represents net additions to the capital stock.

net present value The difference between the present value of revenues and the present value of costs.

net taxes Total tax receipts net of *transfer payments*.

neutrality of money Hypothesis that the level of real national income is independent of the level of the money stock.

New Classical theory A theory that assumes that the economy behaves as if it were perfectly competitive with all markets always clearing; where deviations from full employment can occur only if people make mistakes and where, given rational expectations, these mistakes will not be systematic.

New Keynesian economics Recent research agenda which has focused on explaining why prices do not adjust to clear markets, especially the labour market. It differs from the traditional Keynesian approach in its concern for *equilibrium unemployment* as well as *demand-deficient unemployment*.

newly industrialized countries (NICs) Formerly *less developed countries* that have become major industrial exporters in recent times. Sometimes called newly industrialized economies (NIEs).

nominal interest rate Actual interest rate in money terms. It is contrasted with the real interest rate, which is the nominal interest rate minus the inflation rate (or expected inflation rate).

nominal money supply The money supply measured in monetary units.

nominal national product Total output valued at current prices and usually measured by 'money GDP'.

non-cooperative equilibrium The equilibrium reached when firms calculate their own best policy without considering competitors' reactions and without explicit collusion.

non-excludable A good or service is non-excludable if its owners cannot dictate who will consume it.

non-market sector That portion of an economy in which producers must cover their costs from some source other than sales revenue.

non-renewable (or exhaustible) resource Any productive resource that exists as a fixed stock that cannot be replaced once it is used, such as natural petroleum.

non-rivalrous A good or a service is non-rivalrous if a given unit of it can be consumed by everyone. Thus one person's consumption of it does not reduce the ability of another person to consume it, as with knowledge, national defence, police protection, and navigational aids.

non-strategic behaviour Behaviour which does not take account of the reactions of others, as when a firm acts in perfect or monopolistic competition.

non-tariff barriers Devices other than tariffs that are designed to reduce the flow of imports.

non-tradables Goods and services that are produced and sold domestically but do not enter into international trade.

normal good A commodity whose demand increases when income increases. Compare *inferior good*.

normal form game Players make choices based on expected pay-offs simultaneously.

normative Things that concern what ought to be and thus depend on value judgements. Compare *positive*.

oligopoly An industry that contains only a few firms.

open economy An economy that engages in international trade.

open-market operations Sales or purchases of securities by the central bank aimed at influencing monetary conditions.

open shop A place of employment in which a union represents its members but does not have bargaining jurisdiction for all workers, and where membership of the union is not a condition of getting or keeping a job.

opportunity cost Measurement of cost by reference to the alternatives forgone.

optimum output See *profit-maximizing output*.

ordinary partnership An enterprise composed of a group of individuals who are all jointly liable for the debts and other obligations of that enterprise.

output The goods and services that result from the process of production.

output gap The difference between potential output and actual output ($Y^* - Y$); positive output gaps are called *recessionary gaps*; negative output gaps are called *inflationary gaps*.

overshooting Occurs when the impact effect of a shock takes a variable beyond its ultimate equilibrium level. Most widely applied to the exchange rate. A characteristic of a wide class of exchange rate models under rational expectations is that when monetary policy is, say, tightened, the exchange rate initially appreciates to a point from which it will depreciate towards its long-run equilibrium level.

Pareto optimality A situation in which it is impossible to reallocate production activities to produce more of one good without producing less of some other good, and in which it is impossible to reallocate consumption activities to make at least one person better off without making anyone worse off. Also called Pareto efficiency.

partnership An enterprise with two or more joint owners, each of whom is personally responsible for all of the partnership's debts.

paternalism The belief that the individual is not the best judge of his or her own self-interest; i.e. the belief that someone else knows better.

path-dependence Non-uniqueness of equilibrium resulting from the possibility that what happens in one period affects the stock of physical and human capital for a long time subsequently. Sometimes referred to as *hysteresis*.

per capita economic growth The growth of per capita GDP or GNI (GDP or GNI divided by the population).

per-unit tax See *specific tax*.

perfect competition A market structure in which all firms in an industry are price-takers and in which there is freedom of entry into, and exit from, the industry.

permanent income The maximum amount that a person can consume per year into the indefinite future without reducing his or her wealth.

permanent income theory A theory that relates actual consumption to *permanent income*.

perpetuity A bond that pays a fixed sum of money each year for ever and has no redemption date. Sometimes called a con-sol.

personal disposable income (PDI) The gross income of the personal sector less all direct taxes and national insurance contributions.

personal income Income earned by or paid to individuals, before deducting personal income taxes.

Phillips curve Relates the percentage rate of change of money wages (measured at an annual rate) to the level of unemployment (measured as the percentage of the *working population* unemployed).

point elasticity Uses the derivative at a point on the demand curve $(dq/dp)×(p/q)$. See also *arc elasticity*.

political business cycles Cycles in the economy resulting from the political goals of incumbent (or potentially incumbent) politicians. The simplest form is the deliberate pre-election boom, though modern theories are more subtle.

poll tax A tax which takes the same lump sum from everyone.

portfolio investment Investment in bonds and other debt instruments that do not imply ownership, or in minority holdings of shares that do not establish legal control.

positive Refers to statements concerning what is, was, or will be; they assert alleged facts about the universe in which we live. Compare *normative*.

positively related Refers to the relationship where an increase in one variable is associated with an increase in another.

potential output (GDP), Y^* The level of output at which there is a balance between inflationary and deflationary forces. It is also the level of output at which there is no *demand-deficient unemployment* (the economy is at the *NAIRU*) and the existing capital stock is being run at its normal rate of utilization.

precautionary balances The amount of money people wish to hold because of uncertainty about the exact timing of receipts and payments.

present value The value now of a sum to be received in the future. Also called discounted present value.

price–consumption line A line on an indifference curve diagram showing how consumption changes as the price of one commodity changes, *ceteris paribus*.

price control Anything that influences prices by law rather than by market forces.

price discrimination Situation arising when firms sell different units of their output at different prices for reasons not associated with differences in costs.

price elasticity of demand The percentage change in quantity demanded divided by the percentage change in price that brought it about. Often called elasticity of demand.

price elasticity of supply The percentage change in quantity supplied divided by the percentage change in price that brought it about. Often called elasticity of supply.

price index A statistical measure of the average percentage change in some group of prices relative to some base period.

price level See *general price level*.

price-makers Firms that administer their prices. See *administered price*.

price system An economic system in which market-determined prices play a key role in determining the allocation of resources and the distribution of the national product.

price-taker A firm that can alter its rate of production and sales within any feasible range without having any effect on the price of its products.

principal (1) The amount of a loan, or (2) the unit that employs agents to work on its behalf.

principal–agent problem The problem of resource allocation that arises because contracts that will induce agents to act in their principals' best interests are often impossible to write or too costly to monitor.

principle of substitution Methods of production reflect the relative prices of inputs, with relatively more of the cheaper input and relatively less of the more expensive input being used.

prisoner's dilemma A term in game theory for a game in which the *Nash equilibrium* leaves both players less well off than if they co-operated with each other.

private benefits The benefits of some activity that accrue to the parties in that activity.

private consumption expenditure Spending for which the consumption of the goods bought is done by private individuals (even where payment may have been made by the government, such as on health services).

private cost The value of the best alternative use of the resources used in production as valued by the producer.

private sector That portion of an economy in which the organizations that produce goods and services are owned and operated by private units such as households and firms. Compare *public sector*.

pro-cyclical Positively correlated with the business cycle.

producer Any unit that makes goods or services.

producers' surplus Total revenue minus total variable cost; the market value that the firm creates by producing goods, net of the value of the resources currently used to create these goods.

production The act of making goods and services.

production function A mathematical relation showing the maximum output that can be produced by each and every combination of inputs.

production-possibility boundary A curve that shows the alternative combinations of commodities that can just be attained if all available productive resources are used; it is the boundary between attainable and unattainable output combinations.

productive efficiency Production of any output at the lowest attainable cost for that level of output; it is impossible to re-allocate resources and produce more of one output without simultaneously producing less of some other output.

productivity Output per unit of input employed.

products A general term referring to all goods and services. Sometimes also referred to as *commodities*.

profit (1) In ordinary usage, the difference between the value of outputs and the value of inputs. (2) In microeconomics, the difference between revenues received from the sale of goods and the value of inputs, which includes the opportunity cost of capital. Also called *pure profit* or *economic profit*. (3) In macro-economics it is a component of factor incomes (and thus income-based measures of national product) and is measured as trading surpluses plus a component of mixed incomes.

profit-maximizing output The level of output that maximizes a firm's profits. Sometimes also called the optimum output.

progressive tax A tax that takes a larger percentage of people's income the larger their income is. Compare *regressive tax*.

progressivity The general term for the relation between income and the percentage of income paid in taxes.

proportional tax A tax that takes the same percentage of people's income whatever the level of their income.

protectionism Any departure from free trade designed to give some protection to domestic industries from foreign competition.

public corporation A body set up to run a nationalized industry. It is owned by the state but is usually under the direction of a more or less independent, state-appointed board.

public goods Goods and services which, once produced, can be consumed by everyone in the society. Also called collective consumption goods.

public sector That portion of an economy in which production is owned and operated by the government or by bodies created by it, such as nationalized industries. Compare *private sector*.

purchasing power parity (PPP) exchange rate The exchange rate between two currencies that equates their purchasing powers and hence adjusts for relative inflation rates.

purchasing power parity theory The theory that the equilibrium exchange rate between two national currencies will be the one that equates their purchasing powers.

pure market economy An economy in which all decisions, without exception, are made by individuals and firms acting through unhindered markets.

pure profit Any excess of a firm's revenue over all opportunity costs including those of capital. Also called economic profit.

pure rate of interest See *pure return on capital*.

pure return on capital The amount that capital can earn in a risk-less investment. Also called the pure rate of interest.

quantity actually bought and sold The amount of a commodity that consumers and firms actually succeed in purchasing and selling.

quantity actually purchased See *quantity actually bought and sold*.

quantity demanded The amount of a commodity that house-holds wish to purchase in some time-period.

quantity supplied The amount of a commodity that firms offer for sale in some time-period.

quantity theory of money Theory predicting that the price level and the quantity of money vary in exact proportion to each other—i.e. changing M by X% changes P by X%.

ratio scale See *logarithmic scale*.

rational expectations The theory that people understand how the economy works and learn quickly from their mistakes, so that, while random errors may be made, systematic and per-sistent errors are not made.

rational ignorance This occurs when agents have no incentive to inform themselves about some government action because the costs of so doing greatly exceed the potential benefits of any action the agent could take as a result of having the correct information.

reaction curve The optimal choices that will be made by one firm in the light of each possible choice made by a rival firm. Could refer to the price reaction or the output reaction, but usually relates to output.

real business cycles An approach to the explanation of business cycles which uses dynamic equilibrium market-clearing models and relies on productivity shocks as a trigger. In such models all cycles are an optimal response to the real shock and there are no deviations from potential output: rather, it is the full equilibrium that fluctuates over time.

real capital Physical assets that include factories, machinery, and stocks of material and finished goods. Also called physical capital.

real exchange rate An index of the relative prices of domestic and foreign goods.

real income The purchasing power of *money income*, measured by deflating nominal income by an index of the price level.

real money supply The money supply measured in purchasing power units, measured as the nominal money supply divided by a price index.

real national product Total output valued at base-year prices, measured for example by GDP at 1999 prices.

real product wage The proportion of the sale value of each unit that is accounted for by labour costs (including the pre-tax nominal wage rate, benefits, and the firm's national insurance contributions).

real rate of interest The money rate of interest minus the inflation rate (or expected inflation rate), which expresses the real return on a loan.

real wage The money wage deflated by a price index to measure the wage's purchasing power.

reallocation of resources Some change in the uses to which the economy's resources are put.

recession A sustained drop in the level of economic activity.

recessionary gap A positive output gap, when actual national income falls short of potential national income.

redemption date The time at which the principal of a loan is to be repaid.

regressive tax A tax that takes a smaller percentage of people's incomes the larger their income is. Compare *progressive tax*.

relative price Any price expressed as a ratio of another price.

renewable resources Productive resources that can be replaced as they are used up, as with *real capital* or forests; distinguished from *non-renewable resources*, which are available in a fixed stock that can be depleted but not replaced, as with natural oil and coal.

replacement investment Investment which replaces capital as it wears out but does not increase the capital stock.

replacement ratio Benefits received by those out of work as a proportion of the wage of those in employment.

repo Short for a 'sale and repurchase agreement' whereby a firm sells a security (such as a gilt) to a bank and agrees to buy it back at some future time. The difference in price between sale and repurchase reflects the ruling rate of interest. The deal is a loan (usually short term) secured on the security involved. Central banks typically set the rate of interest in repo transactions for a specific term. In the UK the Bank of England sets the two-week repo rate.

reservation price The price below which some action will not be taken, such as selling a commodity or accepting a job.

resource allocation The allocation of the economy's scarce resources among alternative uses.

retail price index (RPI) An index of the general price level based on the consumption pattern of typical consumers.

reverse repo Similar to a *repo*, but here the bank sells the security to the firm and agrees to buy it back at some future date.

risk-averse Describes people who wish to avoid risks and so will only play games that are sufficiently biased in their favour to overcome their aversion to risk; they will be unwilling to play mathematically fair games, let alone games that are biased against them.

risk-loving Describes people who are willing to play some games that are biased against them, the extent of the love of risk being measured by the degree of bias that they are willing to accept.

risk-neutral Describes people who are indifferent about playing a mathematically fair game and so are willing to play games that are biased in their favour but not games that are biased against them.

risk premium The return on capital necessary to compensate owners of capital for the risk of loss of their capital.

rivalrous A good or service is rivalrous if, when one person consumes a unit of it, no other person can also consume that unit, as with all ordinary goods and services such as apples or haircuts.

saving Income received by individuals that they do not spend through *consumption expenditure*.

savings ratio See *average propensity to save*.

scatter diagram Plots a series of observations each made on two variables, e.g. the price and quantity of eggs sold in twenty different cities.

seigniorage The revenue that accrues to the issuer of money.

self-employed Those people who work for themselves.

sellers' preferences Allocation of a commodity that is in excess demand by the decisions of sellers.

services Intangible production that does not produce a physical product, such as haircuts and medical services.

shares See *equities*.

shifting The passing of tax incidence from the person who initially pays it to someone else.

short run The period of time over which the inputs of some factors cannot be varied.

short-run aggregate supply (*SRAS*) curve The total amount that will be produced and offered for sale at each price level on the assumption that all input prices are fixed.

short-run equilibrium Generally, equilibrium subject to fixed factors or other things that cannot change over the time-period being considered.

short-run Phillips curve Any particular Phillips curve drawn for a given expected rate of inflation.

short-run supply curve A curve showing the relation of quantity supplied to price when one or more factor is fixed; under perfect competition it is the horizontal sum of marginal cost curves (above the level of average variable costs) of all firms in an industry.

shutdown price The price that is equal to a firm's average variable costs, below which it will produce no output. See also *break-even price*.

simple multiplier Usually applies to the value of the *multiplier* in the aggregate expenditure system before any account is taken of the feedback from the monetary sector and from aggregate supply.

single proprietorship An enterprise with one owner who is personally responsible for everything that is done. More commonly called a *sole trader*.

size distribution of income A classification of income according to the amount of income received by each individual irrespective of the sources of that income.

slump A period of low output and low employment. See also *boom*.

small open economy (SOE) An economy that is a price-taker for both its imports and its exports. It must buy and sell at the world price, irrespective of the quantities that it buys and sells.

social benefits The value of an activity to the whole society, which includes the internal effects on those who are involved in deciding on it and the external effects on those who are not involved in the activity.

social cost The value of the best alternative use of resources that are available to the whole society.

sole trader A non-incorporated business operated by a single owner. Modern UK terminology for a *single proprietorship*.

specialization of labour The organization of production so that individual workers specialize in the production of particular goods or services (and satisfy their wants by trading) rather than producing everything they consume (and satisfying their wants by being self-sufficient).

specific tax A tax expressed as so much per unit, independent of its price. Also called a per-unit tax.

speculation Taking a financial position that will yield profits if prices move in a particular direction in future but will yield losses if they move the other way.

speculative balances Monetary assets held for their expected rate of return rather than for transactions purposes.

speculative motive The motive that leads agents to hold money in response to the risks inherent in fluctuating bond prices. More generally, it refers to the asset motive, as opposed to the transactions motive, for holding money.

spread The difference between the prices or interest rates on specific assets or loans, such as the spread between deposit and loan rates offered by banks.

SRAS curve See *short-run aggregate supply curve*.

stabilization policy The attempt to reduce fluctuations in GDP, employment, and the price level by use of *monetary* and *fiscal policies*.

stagflation The simultaneous occurrence of a recession (with its accompanying high unemployment) and inflation.

stock See *equities*.

stock variable A variable that does not have a time dimension. It is contrasted with a flow variable, which does.

stockbuilding The process of building *stocks* or inventories.

stocks Accumulation of inputs and outputs held by firms to facilitate a smooth flow of production in spite of variations in delivery of inputs and sales of outputs. Now called inventories in national accounts.

strategic Behaviour that takes into account the reactions of others to one's own actions, as when an oligopolistic firm makes decisions that take account of its competitors' reactions.

strategic form game See *normal form game*.

structural unemployment Unemployment that exists because of a mismatch between the characteristics of the unemployed and the characteristics of the available jobs in terms of region, occupation, or industry.

substitutes Two goods are substitutes if the quantity demanded of one is positively related to the price of the other.

substitution effect The change in quantity demanded of a good resulting from a change in the commodity's relative price, eliminating the effect of the price change on real income.

sunk costs of entry Those costs that must be incurred for a firm to enter a market and that cannot be recouped when the firm leaves.

supergame A game that is repeated an infinite number of times.

supply The whole relation between the quantity supplied of some commodity and its own price.

supply curve The graphical representation of the relation between the quantity of some commodity that producers wish to make and sell per period of time and the price of that commodity, *ceteris paribus*.

supply function A mathematical relation between the quantity supplied and all the variables that influence it.

supply of effort The total number of hours people in the labour force are willing to work. Also called supply of labour.

supply of labour See *supply of effort*.

supply of money The total amount of money available in the entire economy. Also called the money supply or the money stock.

supply schedule A numerical tabulation showing the quantity supplied at a number of alternative prices.

supply shocks A shift in any aggregate supply curve caused by an exogenous change in input prices or technology.

supply-side policies Policies that seek to shift either the short-run or the long-run aggregate supply curve.

surprise aggregate supply curve See *Lucas aggregate supply curve*.

tacit collusion Occurs when firms arrive at the co-operative solution (which maximizes their joint profit) even though they may not have formed an explicit agreement to co-operate.

takeover When one firm buys another firm.

targets The variables in the economy which policymakers wish to influence. Typical policy targets might be inflation, unemployment, and real growth.

tariffs Taxes on imported goods.

term The amount of time between a bond's issue date and its redemption date.

terms of trade The ratio of the average price of a country's exports to the average price of its imports.

theory of games The study of rational decision-making in situations in which each player must anticipate the reactions of competitors to the moves that he or she makes. It can be applied to analysis of the strategic interaction of firms in oligopolistic markets.

third-party effects See *externalities*.

time-inconsistency Problem that arises in rational-expectations models when policymakers have an incentive to abandon their commitments at a later time. The existence of this incentive is generally understood by private sector agents, and it may influence their current behaviour.

time-series data Data on some variable taken at different, usually regularly spaced points in time, such as consumer spending in each quarter for the last ten years.

total cost (TC) The total of all costs of producing a firm's output, usually divided into *fixed* and *variable costs*.

total final expenditure The total expenditure required to purchase all the goods and services that are produced domestically when these are valued at market prices.

total fixed costs The total of a firm's costs that do not vary in the short run.

total product (TP) Total amount produced by a firm during some time-period.

total revenue (TR) The total amount of money that the firm receives from the sale of its output over some period of time.

total utility The total satisfaction derived from consuming some amount of a commodity.

total variable costs The total of those of the firm's costs that do vary in the short run.

tradables Goods and services that enter into international trade.

trade account The part of the balance of payments accounts relating to trade in goods.

trade creation Trade between the members of a customs union or free-trade area where previously protected industries served their own home markets.

trade cycles See *business cycles*.

trade diversion The diversion of the source of a member country's imports from other countries to union members as a result of the preferential removal of tariffs following the formation of a customs union or a free-trade area.

trade or craft union A union covering workers with a common set of skills, no matter where, or for whom, they work.

trade-weighted exchange rate The average of the exchange rates between a particular country's currency and those of each of its major trading partners, with each rate being weighted by the amount of trade with the country in question. Also called the *effective exchange rate*.

traditional economic system One in which behaviour is based primarily on tradition, custom, and habit.

transaction costs Costs involved in making a trade in addition to the price of the product itself, such as the time involved or the cost of transport.

transactions balances Holdings of money intended to be used for buying goods or services at some unknown future time.

transactions demand for money The amount of money that people wish to hold in order to finance their transactions.

transfer earnings The amount that a factor must earn in its present use to prevent it from moving (i.e. transferring) to another use.

transfer payments Payments not made in return for any contribution to current output, such as unemployment benefits.

transition economies Countries that abandoned central planning and have been making the transition to market economies, such as the countries of Eastern Europe and the former Soviet Union.

transmission mechanism See *monetary transmission mechanism*.

transnational corporations (TNCs) Firms that have operations in more than one country. Also called transnationals or multinational enterprises (MNEs).

underdeveloped countries See *less developed countries*.

unit cost See *average variable cost*.

unit elasticity An elasticity with a numerical measure of 1, indicating that the percentage change in quantity is equal to the percentage change in price (so that total expenditure remains constant).

utility See *marginal utility* and *total utility*.

utils An imaginary measure of utility used in the exposition of marginal utility theory, which assumes that utility is cardinally measurable.

validation When the authorities sustain an ongoing inflation by increasing the money supply.

value added The value of a firm's output minus the value of the inputs that it purchases from other firms.

value added tax (VAT) Tax charged as a proportion of a firm's value added.

value of money See *purchasing power of money*.

variable Any well-defined item, such as the price of a commodity or its quantity, that can take on various specific values.

variable cost A cost that varies directly with changes in output. Also called direct cost or avoidable cost.

variable factors Inputs whose amount can be varied in the short run.

velocity of circulation The number of times an average unit of money is used in transactions within a specific period. Defined as the ratio of nominal GDP to the money stock.

vertical equity Equitable treatment of people in different income brackets. Compare *horizontal equity*.

very long run A period of time over which the technological possibilities open to a firm are subject to change.

visible account The part of the balance of payments accounts relating to trade in goods.

visible trade Trade in physical products. Same as merchandise trade.

visibles Goods, i.e. things such as cars, aluminium, coffee, and iron ore, that we can see when they cross international borders.

voluntary export restriction (VER) Restriction whereby an exporting country agrees to limit the amount it sells to a second country.

voluntary unemployment Unemployment that occurs when there is a job available but the unemployed person is not willing to accept it at the existing wage rate.

winner's curse The possibility that the agent who wins the bidding on a contested takeover may pay more than the target firm is really worth because the winner is the one with the highest valuation of all bidders.

withdrawals Spending that leaves the economy and does not create further incomes for domestic residents. Import spending, for example, creates incomes overseas. Also called leakages.

working population The total of the employed, the self-employed, and the unemployed, i.e. those who have a job plus those who are looking for work.

X-inefficiency Failure to use resources efficiently within the firm so that firms are producing above their relevant cost curves and the economy is inside its production-possibility boundary.

yield curve A line on a graph plotting the yield on securities against the term to maturity.

INDEX

Headwords in **green** refer to subjects defined in the Glossary.